COMMUNITY PLANNING

A Casebook on Law and Administration

COMMUNITY PLANNING

A Casebook on Law and Administration

Edited by

J. B. MILNER

Professor, Faculty of Law
University of Toronto

UNIVERSITY OF TORONTO PRESS

Printed in Canada
Reprinted in 2018
ISBN 978-1-4875-7886-2 (paper)

TO BRIDGE

For the sure and true interpretation of all statutes in general (be they penal or beneficial, restrictive or enlarging of the common law) four things are to be discerned and considered:

1st. What was the common law before the making of the Act.

2nd. What was the mischief and defect for which the common law did not provide.

3rd. What remedy the Parliament hath resolved and appointed to cure the disease of the commonwealth.

And, 4th. The true reason of the remedy; and then the office of all the Judges is always to make such construction as shall suppress the mischief, and advance the remedy, and to suppress subtle inventions and evasions for continuance of the mischief, and *pro privato commodo*, and to add force and life to the cure and remedy, according to the true intent of the makers of the Act, *pro bono publico*.

CHIEF BARON SIR ROGER MANWOOD
and the other Barons of the Exchequer
in *Heydon's Case*, 1584

INTRODUCTION

It is not the purpose of this book to make planners out of lawyers or lawyers out of planners. Each has his job to do and the community will be just as well off if each keeps to his own. But it is the purpose of this book to bring together materials that may help the lawyer and the planner talk together with a greater understanding of each other's problems and points of view. The materials are presented in an attempt to show the law student what the professional planner hopes to do; and to show the planner how the law (and the lawyer) expects him to do it.

It is not a text book and it does not present a narrative account of the present state of the law of any jurisdiction. It is a casebook. It contains collections of facts or events, some hypothetical, but most of them historical, that raise serious conflicts of interest and require settlement by some device, either the dictate of some private individual or group, or the exercise of a more orderly "legal" procedure. The fact situations are usually reported cases of legal action of some sort, and the report usually contains somebody's idea of the appropriate solution. Sometimes the idea is stated by itself. This is most obvious in the excerpts of legislation reproduced from various jurisdictions. Sometimes the idea is stated in an article or book written by some author claiming, or recognized as having, competence in his field. The editor asks you to take nothing in here for granted. Ridiculous, and often pompous, propositions by planners or by lawyers have been included—as objects for *critical* examination. The book can only be used effectively by a reader who, in Bacon's words, will chew and digest it.

For the most part the book will probably be used in law school and planning school classrooms. There, it is to be hoped, it will provide a basis for discussion of great issues. This discussion can only take place if the materials are chewed and digested *before* the student enters the classroom. After he enters, he must continue to question. Although some aspects of planning law, such as the law of nuisance and restrictive covenants, *may* be regarded as more or less settled, the statutory aspects at least are in a state of flux. Amendments appear almost every year to the planning legislation of the more rapidly urbanizing jurisdictions of Canada. No single province can regard its present legislation as wholly satisfactory, and almost every year new experience is providing a testing ground for old ideas and promoting new ones.

Although the subject of community planning is as nearly universal as is man's desire to live in communities, the materials presented here have a distinctly Canadian emphasis. This is not dictated by any spirit of chauvinism. Indeed the materials are mildly comparative, and some English and some American cases, statutes and general writings have been included. The reader is reminded, however, that excellent sources of American materials are available, in casebook form: the most recent and complete being Haar, *Land Use Planning* (1959). While no English casebook has yet been published, the literature is extensive, both legal and planning, and frequent references have been made to it in the notes on bibliography. On the other hand, there are almost no easy sources of Canadian materials. Yet the Canadian materials are valuable not only because they deal with situations with which the Canadian student can often get direct experience, but because the Canadian situations and the materials describing them are primitive and expose their problems more readily for critical examination. Even five years after the temporary edition this collection can only be described as experimental. If some of the materials, especially those on planning, seem rather vague, they do no more than reflect the uncertainty that is almost inevitable in a subject with such wide scope as planning. Nevertheless we can hope for more refinement as study in Canada begins to show results in better writing.

The materials deal, generally, with the interference by the state in the private use of land. Since our built-in self-operating propaganda machine has convinced most people in the "western democracies" at least that private property is the basis of our great prosperity, students are recommended to read Schlatter, *Private Property: The History of An Idea*, to get a better perspective. The materials here do not attempt so much to justify either private property or its interference by the state as to expose more clearly *how* the interference takes place and to ask whether that interference is fair and effective.

The materials, then, emphasize *procedures*. More experienced students will realize that legal procedures are sometimes ignored altogether and sometimes follow informal procedures, for the sake of appearances. To *some* extent this reliance on informal procedures is not only inevitable but also desirable. The informal procedures are frequently more effective. As one town planner put it to the editor recently, "That is how things really get done." In *some* cases, however, the supposed benefits may be bought at a very high price in terms of social order and the underlying question to be considered in the chewing and digesting of these materials may be put in these terms: When and to what extent are informal procedures to be preferred to the best legal procedures? This means that informal procedures, which are, almost by definition, not put in writing anywhere, must be compared with existing, *and possible*, formal, or legal procedures.

It may be that informal procedures are preferred because existing legal procedures are ineffective, costly, slow, or perhaps not fully understood. Or, they may be preferred because someone gets an advantage he should not have. The student will have to investigate informal procedures by his own inquiry and share his experience with his fellow students if class discussion in this area is to be enriched by "facts". The value of informal procedures is well illustrated in Col. T. E. Lawrence's advice to Ernest Thurtle, back in 1929. He said, "Your attempt to abolish Church Parade was good. To achieve it you must proceed administratively. The House publicity renders such reforms impossible. Lobby the Archbishop of Canterbury. Persuade him to suggest it to the P.M. See that the change is put on the grounds of true religion. Persuade the P.M. to whisper it to the S. of S. for War. Then ask your question . . . and the S. of S. with a pleased smirk, says, 'The matter has been the subject of ripe consideration in my department, and I am glad to say that the Chaplain General has worked out a scheme (for putting into force immediately) which will meet the changed conditions of our time, in the matter of religious observance.' Always get it settled before you speak to more than two ears at once." Just how proper such a political tactic is for either the lawyer or the planner is a matter of some difference of opinion. There are involved some nice questions of the roles of administrators and politicians, advisers and deciders. If the planner in municipal employment thinks his idea of the "right" course of action is that important, should he engage secretly in action traditionally thought of as "political" to ensure the adoption of his idea? Or should he confine his advice to his superiors? Or should he enter the political arena publicly? Is the Canadian notion that civil servants should keep out of politics an outdated one? Are these questions solely the concern of the professional planner in determining his professional responsibility, or are they of some concern to the lawyer involved in planning practice as well? Has the planning consultant in private practice a different responsibility? How do you distinguish between the development of policy in the political world and in the legal and administrative world? Is the distinction a necessary one? A useful or valuable one? How important are law and order? What is *law*?

On the legal side, the materials emphasize procedure. On the planning side, they emphasize the shape of the future city. Opinions about the traditional city range widely. Nowhere have they been put more succinctly than by two poets (not, surprisingly, sociologists): Wordsworth, speaking of London in 1802 said, "Earth has not anything to show more fair," and Shelley, speaking of the same(?) city in 1817, said, "Hell is a city much like London." In the succeeding century and a half, London has grown many times its size in the early nineteenth century, the motor car is there to stay, and now is typical of contemporary communities spread out for miles in every direction. The modern city, or metropolis (mother city), is upon us, and the question, as Mr. Hans Blumenfeld puts it, "is not *if* we want it to be, but *how* we want it to be."

It proved to be impossible to include the 1963 amendments to the various provincial Acts but where statutes have been reproduced they include amendments up to the end of the 1962 sessions. In Alberta there is a new general Act to which some reference has been made from the preceding Bill. All 1963 and succeeding amendments should be read along with these materials.

ACKNOWLEDGEMENTS

I am glad to acknowledge the kind permission generously given by the following authors and publishers to reproduce copyright material: The Incorporated Council of Law Reporting for England and Wales for material from *The Law Reports*; Butterworth & Co. (Publishers) Ltd., for material from *The All England Law Reports*; the American Institute of Planners for the 1955 report of the Committee on Professional Services (which is not an official document of the Institute); the Canadian Federation of Mayors and Municipalities for material from its submission to the Royal Commission on taxation; the National House Builders Association for material from its submission to the same Commission; the Ontario Department of Municipal Affairs for the selections from *Ontario Planning*; The Town Planning Institute of Canada for material from its submission to the R.A.I.C. Inquiry into the residential environment; Mr. J. M. Bennett, Q.C., for his talk on shopping centres; Mr. Hans Blumenfeld for his talk on "The Form of the Metropolis" and as well to the editor of *Queen's Quarterly* for part of Mr. Blumenfeld's "Transportation in the Modern Metropolis" where it first appeared; Mr. G. Sutton Brown and the editor of *Community Planning Review* for part of "Planning Administration"; Professor Gerald Carrothers for part of *Planning in Manitoba*; Mr. D. H. Clark and Mr. H. Bronson Cowan and the Canadian Tax Foundation for part of their contribution to the panel on "Site Valuation as a Base for Local Taxation"; Professor K. Grant Crawford for material from *Canadian Municipal Government*; Mr. Lorne R. Cumming, Q.C., for part of "Is Zoning Wagging the

Dog"; Holt, Rinehart and Winston, Inc. for material from the late Professor John Dewey's *Human Nature and Conduct*, Professor Allison Dunham and Professor Friedrich von Hayek and the University of Chicago Press as original publisher for their book reviews of Haar, *Land Planning Law in a Free Society* in *The University of Chicago Law Review*; Professor Dunham and the editor of *The Journal of Law and Economics* for part of "City Planning: An Analysis of the Content of the Master Plan"; Professor O. J. Firestone and the Central Mortgage and Housing Corporation for part of *Residential Real Estate in Canada*; Professor Lon Fuller and the Association of American Law Schools for material from the *Journal of Legal Education*, Vol. 6, No. 4 (Summer, 1954), copyright by the Association, and the Harvard Law Review Association for parts of "Freedom—A Suggested Analysis" (1955) and "Positivism and Fidelity to Law—A Reply to Professor Hart" (1958) copyright of both articles being the Association's, and the *Journal of Philosophy* for the lines from "Human Purpose and Natural Law" (1956); Ernest Benn Limited for the short passage from the late Professor Sir Patrick Geddes', *Cities in Evolution*, Professor Charles M. Haar and the *A.I.P. Journal* for part of "The Content of the General Plan" (1955); Mr. Henry T. Hough and the University of Liverpool Press for part of "The Liverpool Corporate Estate" and Mr. Lewis Mumford and the same Press for part of "Planning for the Phases of Life", both articles having first appeared in *The Town Planning Review*; Mr. J. S. L. King for part of "Leasebuy—A Marketing Method For Residential Land"; The University of North Carolina Press for the short passage from Lady Barbara Wootton's *Freedom Under Planning*; Miss Mary Rawson and the Urban Land Institute for part of Research Monograph 4, *Property Taxation and Urban Development*, copyright in the Institute; Professor Lloyd Rodwin and the Harvard University Press for material from *The British New Towns Policy*: *Problems and Implications,* Cambridge, Mass.: Harvard University Press, copyright, 1956, by the President and Fellows of Harvard College; the Russell Sage Foundation, as original publisher, for parts of the late Mr. Edward Bassett's *The Master Plan*; Dr. Thomas Sharp, the Architectural Press and the Oxford City Council for the summary of recommendations from *Oxford Replanned*; Mr. Clarence S. Stein and the Reinhold Publishing Corporation for part of *Toward New Towns for America*, copyright Reinhold Publishing Corporation; Professor Hans Zeisel and the editor of the *Cornell Law Quarterly* for part of "The Uniqueness of Survey Evidence," copyright Cornell University. I have tried faithfully to obtain all necessary permission to use copyright material but if any such material has been used improperly by oversight I hope the error will be brought to my attention so that suitable acknowledgement can be made in a later revision.

I also thank my wife for her invaluable assistance in checking proof, an endless task, Miss Carole Harris for her patience in helping to prepare the manuscript, and Miss Jean Houston of the University of Toronto Press for editorial help. Over several years I have, I hope, benefited from discussion with my colleagues in other law schools and in the Division of Town and Regional Planning of the University of Toronto School of Architecture, but the errors of omission and commission remain entirely my own.

J. B. MILNER

Faculty of Law
University of Toronto, 1963

CONTENTS

TABLE OF CASES

The cases the names of which are italicized are reproduced or noted. At least one citation is shown here of cases mentioned in judgments reproduced or referred to in text passages.

COMMUNITY PLANNING

A Casebook on Law and Administration

CHAPTER 1

NUISANCE

The maxim, Sic utere tuo ut alienum non laedas, is mere verbiage.
ERLE J., *Bonomi* v. *Backhouse* (1858)

1. THE COMMON LAW AND EQUITY

The materials in this chapter show the attitude of the common law courts to the complaints of land owners about "incompatible" land uses. The law of nuisance is sometimes described as the earliest attempt at town planning law in England. It might be more accurate to describe nuisance as the earliest attempt at land use control, but there is, in truth, very little of either planning or controlling, in the sense of regulating, to be found in the law of nuisance. It is chiefly the settlement of disputes between individual land owners arising out of the asserted use of his land by one owner in such a manner that it annoys or harms an adjoining owner. Presumably before they resorted to litigation the owners tried to negotiate a settlement, and failing that, they asked the court to settle it for them. In the unreported instances of successful negotiation there was an earlier form of land use control, by negotiation, or contract. As the cases multiplied the doctrine of *stare decisis* gave rise to precedents of principle from which, hopefully, a land owner could predict whether his intended use of his land would involve him in liability to his neighbour or not. Unfortunately prediction is not as easy and reliable as one might like, partly because the rational bases of the precedents are not clearly settled even after several centuries.

The law of nuisance is variously dealt with under the categories of tort and property law. The tort concepts deal with the "wrongfulness" of the conduct of the person committing the nuisance, and the cases raise questions of "absolute" liability as opposed to liability for not using reasonable care, and the effect of "malicious" acts. The property lawyer, on the other hand, thinks in terms of the scope of the possessory interest. He can even explain the nuisance of industrial noise as a trespass on the plaintiff's land! In these first two chapters, the primary concern is for neither of the conceptual approaches, but rather, the purpose is to illustrate some of the judgments of "incompatible" land use made by the judiciary. The cases do not, of course, present a full picture, and stress has been laid on uses of land affecting personal comfort and enjoyment of land, and the "esthetic interest," as it might be called. For the planners who may use this book, this chapter is of special interest because it illustrates the judicial process, one of the basic processes of the law that is available for controlling land use and facilitating planning. The essential question is, for what purpose is the judicial process best adapted? The special contribution of the lawyer is his knowledge of and experience with the basic processes of law: contract, adjudication and legislation, and his ability to advise which one, or which combination, is best adapted to solve a particular problem.

THE JUDICIAL PROCESS. Adjudication is the procedure by which two disputants solve their dispute by consulting a third person, preferably a person on whom they have agreed, who impartially listens to the evidence and arguments of each, and then decides in favour of one or the other on the basis of the argument made, or on any other idea he may have, but which he discusses with them before settling upon it. Obviously, then, the procedure in our courts is not adjudication in this ideal sense. It differs in three major respects. The resort to the court is not necessarily voluntary by both parties. The selection of the judge is made largely by the state, although at times the parties may attempt to choose one judge rather than another, when this is possible on the court calendar. And the judge does not decide the case only on the arguments advanced by the parties, because he recognizes the authority of the past judgments of higher courts in similar cases, and he may consider how his own decision will affect future cases, about which he really knows nothing. This procedure, almost adjudication, may be called the *judicial process*. In reading the cases that follow, if you are a planning student you should keep in mind some elementary questions that may increase your understanding of the process and at the same time make you more critical of it.

It is often said that "each man knows his own case". Is this true? Or should it be said that if a man doesn't know his own case it is his own fault? Is this more nearly "true"? One of the chief characteristics of the judicial process is the impartiality of the judge. He knows nothing of either party's case at the start. There is, therefore, a grave burden of communication on each party. In the judicial process, this burden is discharged by the *adversary process*, which involves calling witnesses for each side and subjecting them to cross-examination by the other side. Cross-examination is believed by many lawyers to be the best way of exposing and perhaps avoiding the risks of poor *perception* or observation by the witness, poor *memory*, incomplete *narration*, or telling of what he experienced, and possible *insincerity*. Hence the reluctance of lawyers to accept hearsay evidence, that is, evidence of someone's experience reported second hand to the court. Since the actual observer isn't present, he cannot be questioned to expose or avoid the risks just described. The risks are therefore sometimes called the "hearsay dangers". The theory of the adversary process is that by its means the whole truth will emerge since each side will push its own case to the full and criticize the other. Do you think this faith in the process is justified? Consider the poet Coleridge's comment in 1831: "It is of the utmost importance in the administration of justice that knowledge and intellectual power should be as far as possible equalized between the crown and the prisoner, or plaintiff and defendant." Coleridge thought this was done by having a well trained legal profession. Does the judicial process adequately protect the public interest? Who represents the public interest? What is the public interest? How can it be represented?

It might be thought that the judge himself, as a public officer, represents the public interest. Could he effectively represent the public interest and also retain impartiality between himself and the parties? Some idea of the attitude of some Canadian lawyers on this question may be seen from litigation over the propriety of a judge leaving the court room to take a first hand look at the scene of an accident responsibility for which is being contested in his court. The Ontario Court of Appeal appears to think that it is improper for a trial judge so to involve himself. If he does, he becomes a witness and ceases to be impartial. For a contrary view, see a note in (1953), 31 *Canadian Bar Review* 305. Must a witness always be partial? Could a court properly call a witness?

On the judicial process generally, see Cardozo, *The Nature of the Judicial Process* (1921), a reflective piece of writing by an American judge whose ability to "distinguish" precedent led to such a complexity of cases that New York lawyers sometimes called them the "Cardozo mosaic."

QUESTIONS. Is the adjudicative process (and the judicial process) better adapted to the settlement of disputes arising out of past events, the legislative process (private, or contractual, and public) better for the settlement of conflicts about future arrangements? Is this dichotomy between past and future a valid one in this context?

OMYCHUND *v.* BARKER. 1744. 1 Atk. 21; 26 E.R. 15, 22–3 (England. Chancery). WILLIAM MURRAY, Solicitor General, in argument: "All occasions do not arise at once . . . a statute very seldom can take in all cases, therefore the common law, *that works itself pure* by rules drawn from the fountain of justice, is for this reason superior to an act of parliament."

THE QUEST FOR JUSTICE. The passage of Lord Mansfield (Mr. William Murray as he then was) is perhaps more typical of the Eighteenth Century than the Twentieth, for a lawyer could speak seriously and not cynically of *justice*, a word which many lawyers today regard as a meaningless symbol of idealist woolly thinking. Nevertheless most judges probably have some conscience about their task, and it may not be unrealistic to describe the objective of the judges, the lawyers and the legislators, generally, as the quest for justice. In his delightful imaginary case, "The Case of the Contract Signed on Book Day," in *The Problems of Jurisprudence*, Professor Fuller puts these words into the mouth of Mr. Justice Foster, his exponent of "natural law" theories: "If you ask a scientist the true meaning of science he will tell you that it lies, not in the dead acquisitions of today, but in a method of revising and enriching those acquisitions. If you ask what that method is, you will be told that it cannot be defined with exactitude since it must always be adjusted to the task at hand, and no one can predict what tasks science will set itself tomorrow. We can say no more and no less of justice.

"If I were asked to define what I mean by justice as I understand it today, I should say that it is an ordering of men's relations to one another within a group in such a way that the following ends will be advanced: 1) The members of the group are enabled to satisfy their common and separate wants with a minimum of conflict and waste. 2) Goods, burdens and functions are distributed so that each man is treated in a way that bears a rational relationship to his needs, capacities and services. 3) The individual is protected against the interference of others (whether acting corporately or not) where that interference is not justified by the ends just described and would restrict the freedom of the individual to develop himself in the directions to which he is prompted by his own nature.

"This is vague, and necessarily so. It can gain meaning only within a context of institutions and other limiting conditions. The quest for justice must always be conducted with some sense of the proportion of means to end; it may be better to do without roast pig for a while than to burn down the house in order to have it at once. The problems of justice faced by each society are to some degree peculiar to that society."

LLANDUDNO URBAN DISTRICT COUNCIL *v.* WOODS
England (Wales). Chancery Division. [1899] 2 Ch. 705

COZENS-HARDY J.: In this action the plaintiffs claim an injunction to restrain the defendant, who is a clergyman of the Church of England, from delivering addresses, lectures, or sermons upon the foreshore at Llandudno, which has been leased by the Crown to the plaintiffs for a term which will expire in 1901. . . . In June, 1898, [the defendant] applied civilly to the plaintiffs for permission to hold religious services on the shore. In reply he received the following answer:

"Dear Sir,

Your application for permission to hold religious services on the beach was submitted to my council this afternoon, when I was requested to express regret that they cannot accede thereto, inasmuch as they have granted a similar privilege to the organization which has been in the habit of visiting Llandudno in past years and purposes to come again this season.

Yours truly, (signed) Alfred Conolly."

I may observe that the organization referred to in this letter is not antagonistic to the defendant, and that there is ample space on the extensive shore for more than one service. The defendant has since held services on the shore until he was restrained by an interlocutory injunction. The evidence satisfies me that there was no breach of the peace, no disorder worth mentioning, and no inconvenience, except of the most trivial kind, to any of the public resorting to the shore. . . . [Cozens-Hardy J. then held that the plaintiffs, as lessees of the Crown, were entitled to possession of the foreshore.]

The plaintiffs have, therefore, prima facie a right to treat every bather, every nursemaid with a perambulator, every boy riding a donkey, and every preacher, on the shore at Llandudno as a trespasser. In the present case there is no evidence from which I can find the existence of a legal usage or custom entitling the defendant to deliver sermons or addresses on the shore at Llandudno. The defendant seems to imagine that his position as a clergyman of the Established Church, bound to preach the Gospel both in season and out of season, gives him some special and peculiar rights. It is needless for me to say that this contention cannot for one moment be maintained. I must treat the defendant precisely as I should treat a Roman Catholic priest, a Methodist preacher, or a Salvation Army captain. This court has nothing to do with the truth or falsehood of the doctrines which the defendant has preached. I feel bound to say that I consider this action wholly unnecessary, and one which ought not to have been brought. It is no part of the duty of the council, as lessees from the Crown for an unexpired term of two years, to prevent a harmless user of the shore. There are persons who derive satisfaction from listening to the addresses of the defendant, and the defendant derives satisfaction from delivering these addresses. I cannot conceive why they should be deprived of this innocent pleasure. Nobody is obliged to listen. Nobody is molested. This action is an attempt to assert rights which the Crown would never have thought of putting forward, and which are in no way necessary for the peace and good order of the town of Llandudno. Charges have been made against the defendant in the pleadings and in the evidence for which there is no justification. I cannot refuse to make a declaration that the defendant is not entitled, without the consent of the plaintiffs, to hold meetings or deliver addresses, lectures, or sermons on any part of the foreshore in lease from the Crown. But I decline to go further. I decline to grant an injunction. That is a formidable legal weapon which ought to be reserved for less trivial occasions. And I make no order as to costs.

NOTE. In argument in the *Woods* case Eve Q.C. for the plaintiffs, had said: "We do not attack the defendant's motives, but his acts are not a reasonable user of the foreshore, and the forcible language he employs at his meetings is calculated to lead to a breach of the peace. His acts are a trespass and an interference with the reasonable use of the foreshore by the majority of the public."

The defendant argued his own case and is reported to have denied that his language was intemperate or that his meetings caused any real obstruction. The parties who objected to his services could have stayed away.

APPLEBY *v.* ERIE TOBACCO CO.

Ontario. Divisional Court. 1910. 22 O.L.R. 533

The plaintiff, a merchant in Windsor, complained of noxious odours coming from the defendants' tobacco factory and interfering with the plaintiff's enjoyment of his premises in the vicinity of the factory. The plaintiff claimed an injunction in respect of these odours and other matters. At the trial the claim for an injunction was dismissed but a reference granted to assess damages. Plaintiff appealed.

MIDDLETON J. delivered the judgment of the Court: . . . The odour from the tobacco arises chiefly from the processing of steaming, steeping, and stewing which it undergoes, and the boiling of sugar, licorice, and other ingredients with which it is mixed before it is reduced to "plug tobacco" ready for the market. These odours cannot be prevented if the manufacture is to go on, and, upon the evidence, the defendants appear to be doing their best to prevent injury to their neighbours.

Many witnesses were called for the plaintiff who describe the odour as a "most sickening smell" a "very bad smell," "very, very offensive," and "very nauseating." Some say that it produces vertigo and dizziness, others nausea and headache. Some do not find any evil result beyond that incident to the disagreeable nature of the odour. The defendants produce a number of witnesses, many of whom say that the odour is "not unhealthy"; others say that it "does not affect" them; and one enthusiastic lover of the weed describes it as "just splendid."

Upon the whole evidence, there can be no doubt that there is a strong odour that to many, if not most, is extremely disagreeable.

In *Fleming* v. *Hislop* (1886) the standard set by Knight Bruce V.C. in *Walter* v. *Selfe* (1851) is accepted by the Lords. In the older case the defendant was a brickmaker. The smoke was complained of. The Vice-Chancellor says: "Ought this inconvenience to be considered in fact as more than fanciful, more than one of mere delicacy or fastidiousness, as an inconvenience materially interfering with the ordinary comfort physically of human existence, not merely according to the elegant or dainty modes and habits of living, but merely according to plain and sober and simple notions among the English people? . . . As far as the human frame in an average state of health at least is concerned, mere insalubrity, mere unwholesomeness, may possibly . . . be out of the case . . . A smell may be sickening though not in a medical sense . . . A man's body may be in a state of chronic discomfort, still retaining its health . . . The defendant's intended proceedings will, if prosecuted, abridge and diminish seriously and materially the ordinary comfort of existence to the occupier and inmates of the plaintiffs' house."

In *Fleming* v. *Hislop* the Earl of Selborne states his view of the law thus: "What causes material discomfort and annoyance for the ordinary purposes of life to a man's house or to his property, is to be restrained . . . although the evidence does not go to the length of proving that health is in danger." Lord Halsbury states what is substantially the same thing. "What makes life less comfortable and causes sensible discomfort and annoyance is a proper subject of injunction."

Now, it is to be borne in mind that an arbitrary standard cannot be set up which is applicable to all localities. There is a local standard applicable in each particular district, but, though the local standard may be higher in some districts than in others, yet the question in each case ultimately reduces itself to the fact of nuisance or no nuisance, having regard to all the surrounding circumstances. This is shown by the often quoted passage in Lord Halsbury's judgment in *Colls* v. *Home and Colonial Stores, Limited* (1904): "A dweller in towns cannot expect to have as pure air, as free from smoke, smell and noises as if he lived in the country, and distant from other dwellings, and yet an excess of smoke, smell and noise may give a cause of action, but in each of such cases it becomes a question of degree, and the question is in each case whether it is a nuisance which will give a right of action."

In *Rushmer* v. *Polsue and Alfieri Limited* (1907), this principle is applied to the case of a printing office established in a neighbourhood devoted to printing, next door to the plaintiff's residence, and which rendered sleep impossible. Cozens-Hardy L.J. [1906] 1 Ch. at p. 250, sums up the situation in a way that commended itself to the Lords. It was, he says, contended "that a person living in a district specially devoted to a particular trade cannot complain of any nuisance by noise caused by the carrying on of any branch of that trade without carelessness and in a reasonable manner. I cannot assent to this argument. A resident in such a neighbourhood must put up with a certain amount of noise. The standard of comfort differs according to the situation of the property and the class of people who inhabit it. . . . But whatever the standard of comfort in a particular district may be, I think the addition of a fresh noise caused by the defendant's works may be so substantial as to cause a legal nuisance. It does not follow that because I live, say, in the manufacturing part of Sheffield, I cannot complain if a steam-hammer is introduced next door, and so worked as to render sleep at night almost impossible, although previous to its introduction my house was a reasonably comfortable abode, having regard to the local standard; and it would be no answer to say that the steam hammer is of the most modern approved pattern and is reasonably worked. In short . . . it is no answer to say that the neighbourhood is noisy, and that the defendant's machinery is of first-class character." . . .

It is plain, in this case, that the defendants' manufactory does constitute a nuisance. The odours do cause material discomfort and annoyance and render the plaintiff's premises less fit for the ordinary purposes of life, even making all possible allowances for the local standard of the neighbourhood.

The remaining question is: must an injunction follow? . . . The working rule, stated by A. L. Smith L.J., in *Shelfer* v. *City of London Electric Lighting Co.*, (1895) as defining the cases in which damages may be given in lieu of an injunction, shows that here an injunction is the proper remedy. No one should be called upon to submit to the inconvenience and annoyance arising from a noxious and sickening odour for a "small money payment," and the inconvenience and annoyance cannot be adequately "estimated in money." The cases in which damages can be substituted for an injunction sought to abate a nuisance of the first class must be exceedingly rare.

The injunction should, therefore, go, restraining the defendants from so operating their works as to cause a nuisance to the plaintiff by reason of the offensive odours arising from the manufacture of tobacco: the operation of this injunction to be stayed for six months to allow the defendants to abate the nuisance if they can do so, or to make arrangements for the removal of that part of the business causing the odour.

STREETT *v.* MARSHALL

Missouri. Supreme Court in Banc. 1927. 291 S.W. 494

RAGLAND J.: This is an action to perpetually enjoin the defendants from using their premises, known as 5297 Washington Boulevard, in the city of St. Louis, as a "funeral home."...

A lot 50 feet in width adjoining the east line of Union Boulevard, fronting south on Washington Boulevard and extending back north to the alley just described, is the locus in quo. On this lot there is a three-storey brick structure. It was built for a family residence, and was occupied as such for many years, and until acquired by defendants a short time before the commencement of this action.

Washington Boulevard is 70 feet in width. Its length between Lake Avenue and Union Boulevard is approximately 1,000 feet. On both sides of this portion of the street are residences which are located on lots having a frontage of from 40 to 141 feet, and which cost originally from $15,000 to $20,000. All of these houses, except the one which is the subject of this controversy, are occupied by their owners as family residences. These houses when built were in a "restricted" district. Shortly after the restrictions expired, on September 21, 1923, the defendants, who had been engaged in the undertaking business in St. Louis for a number of years, bought the property heretofore described, and announced that they would conduct a "funeral home" there.

The residence which the defendants have converted into a "funeral home" fronts on Washington Boulevard, and it has a large porch extending across the entire front. After the defendants purchased the property, they constructed a small porch on the Union Boulevard side of the house, toward the rear, and replaced two windows with doors. From this side porch defendants' business office can be entered through one of the doors, and one of the three parlors on the first floor can be entered through the other. Aside from the alterations just described the external appearance of the building has not been changed. On the inside, however, the entire lower floor has been suitably arranged, furnished, and draped for the uses required by defendants' business. Defendants themselves, who are husband and wife, occupy the second floor as living quarters. They house in a garage in the rear a white ambulance, which they use in conveying dead bodies from one place to another as occasion requires; and during the day, when the ambulance is not in use, they permit it to stand near the premises on Union Boulevard. They keep in the house embalming fluids, a cooling board and pedestals, catafalques, and certain other funeral paraphernalia....

On the trial defendants testified that it was not their purpose to do any embalming at their premises at 5297 Washington Boulevard; that they would bring there only bodies which had been previously embalmed; and that dead bodies, when properly embalmed, do not give off odours.

The plaintiffs, twenty-four in number, are the several owners and occupants of homes located on both sides of Washington Boulevard, between Lake Avenue and Union Boulevard, and at distances from defendants' "funeral home" which range from 15 feet to 500 feet. In describing the way in which he was affected personally by the proximity of his home to the "funeral home," with its constant reminders of death, one of them said:

"I don't say that it has affected my health, but I am not very cheerful about going by there or any other undertaking establishment. I don't like to see the dead; and I don't like to be in the presence of the dead."

Another said that he experienced—

"only a feeling of uneasiness or a feeling of depression—that sort of a feeling one has when he comes close to death or an operation—a feeling that you would not seek, and would try to keep away from, and try to keep out of your mind."

They all said that the maintenance and operation of the "funeral home" in their midst brought sadness and depression to them and the members of their families, and that such depression, in certain designated individual cases, had been accompanied with extreme nervousness. None, however, was able to say that his or her health had been directly affected. Plaintiffs also called a number of physicians who testified, in substance, that such an undertaking establishment as that conducted by defendants would have a decidedly depressing effect upon the nervous system of persons of nervous temperament, particularly women and children, who lived in its immediate vicinity and that such depression would be deleterious to health. We quote briefly from two of them:

Dr. Lister Tuholske: "I am saying that a constant reminder that people are dying every day or every few days, to people of a nervous temperament, has a depressing effect. Q. Would such a depressing effect be deleterious or beneficial to the health of a person? A. It would be deleterious."

Dr. Floyd Stewart: "That (the effect on persons living near defendants' funeral home) would depend entirely upon the person's ability to withstand the conditions that confront them. Some persons are more sensitive than others, and those very sensitive persons like women and children, it would have a very depressing effect upon, while some hardboiled men it would have little or none upon, but 90 per cent. of the people would be very much depressed."

Plaintiffs further offered an abundance of expert testimony, practically uncontradicted, tending to show that the continuance of the "funeral home" would depreciate the values of their property from 40 to 50 per cent.

Defendants' evidence tended to show that an undertaking establishment and its activities do not in any respect affect adversely the health of the average, normal individual who lives near it; that no sickly zones surround undertaking shops; that from time immemorial men and women have lived within their immediate environment, and lived in the vigor of health, even joyously, until the full measure of life's span had been accomplished. Nor did defendants' experts agree with those who testified for plaintiffs. One of them was of the opinion that the living observer of a passing funeral would, or might, be buoyed up by the thought that another, and not he, was on the way to the cemetery. Another was of the opinion that a person suffering from nervousness or depression might be benefited by being stationed at some point of vantage where he could view passing funeral processions.

The evidence on the part of defendants further disclosed that in the same block in which their "funeral home" is located there are two other undertaking establishments, on Delmar Avenue, and that there is third one across the street on Delmar.

The trial court held in effect that defendants' "funeral home," because of its location in a strictly residential district, constituted a nuisance, and enjoined its further maintenance at that place . . .

In view of these principles, appellants argue that an undertaking establishment where only bodies which have been embalmed are received, thus eliminating all question of communicating disease or fouling the air with noxious offensive odours and gases, cannot be held to be a nuisance, although conducted in an exclusively residential neighbourhood. In other words, in order for such an establishment to constitute a nuisance, its character must be such as to directly affect the health or grossly offend the physical senses. This position is without support in the decided cases. While it is true that in many, if not all of them, the charge was made that the establishment complained of would communicate contagion, and would emit noxious gases and offensive smells, such charge was almost universally found to be without substantial support in the evidence. A careful reading of the cases will disclose that what has been stressed, and in the last analysis made the basis of injunctive relief, is this: Constant reminders of death, such as an undertaking establishment and the activities connected with it give rise to, impair in a substantial way the comfort, repose, and enjoyment of the homes which are subjected to them. . . .

[The opinion has been drastically curtailed. The court concurred in affirming the trial judge's decision.]

QUESTIONS. Are the three other "funeral homes" located on Delmar Avenue now in jeopardy? Where should a "funeral home" be located?

ROCKENBACH *v.* APOSTLE. 1951. 47 N.W. 2d 636 (Michigan. Supreme Court). An action to enjoin the defendants from establishing on lots 7 and 8 on block 94 in the city of Muskegon Heights a funeral home and a parking lot. An injunction was granted. Blocks 94 and 95 (across Peck street) were zoned class "B" residential, which permitted the operation of a funeral home upon consent of a five-sevenths vote of the city council and if certain off street parking were provided. Defendants had the consent and intended to provide the parking. Block 94 contained twelve lots, nine in use for residences, four of which had apartments and two had rooms to let for tourists; three lots were vacant. One house was used for a watch repair business, another for physiotherapy baths. In block 95 there was a grocery shop in a building at the rear, and parking was permitted on an adjoining lot. Both courts held that "the district is a strictly residential district." The plaintiffs were neighbours who claimed, among other things, that the presence of a funeral home is a constant reminder of death and has a depressing effect on the adjoining landowners. The trial judge rejected the contention that there would be depreciation of property values and that there would be undesirable odours and danger of disease. But he accepted the claim that the residents would be depressed by the home. He was upheld on appeal. The zoning ordinance did not help the defendants. BOYLES J.: "The weight of authority is to the effect that an ordinance which allows the establishment or maintenance of a funeral home or undertaking establishment in a district zoned either for residential or commercial purposes is permissive only, and not controlling as to whether such undertaking establishment would constitute a nuisance which might be enjoined by an equity court. However, proof of the existence of such a zoning ordinance is admissible as evidence of the character of the district, and bearing on the question of nuisance. A nuisance will not be upheld solely on the ground that that it has been permitted by municipal ordinance."

MACIEVICH *v.* ANDERSON
Manitoba. Court of Appeal. [1952] 4 D.L.R. 50

ADAMSON J. A. delivered the judgment of the Court: The defendant established a dog hospital on a city lot adjoining a duplex owned by the plaintiffs. The plaintiffs occupy one of the apartments and the other is rented to and occupied by a Mrs. McGill. It was held that the odours from the hospital and from dog-runs outside, and the barking and whining of dogs, constituted a nuisance. An injunction was granted restraining the defendants from carrying on, in, or upon their premises "an animal hospital so as to occasion a nuisance to the plaintiffs, as the owners and occupiers or to other occupiers of the plaintiffs' premises." A reference was also ordered to ascertain and assess the damages suffered by the plaintiffs due to the nuisance. The late Mr. Justice Kelly heard the reference and assessed the damages at the same time as he heard a motion to commit the defendants on the ground that the injunction was and is not obeyed ([1952] 3 D.L.R. 204).

Mr. Justice Kelly granted the plaintiffs $750 damages as compensation for annoyance and discomfort suffered by them to the date of the injunction. He also held that the plaintiffs were not entitled to damages for depreciation of the value of their property and fixed the costs of the reference as to damages at $100 and disbursements. The plaintiffs appeal against the amount allowed for damages, against the denial of damages for depreciation in value of the property, and against the costs allowed.

This Court should not interfere with the assessment of damages or costs by a trial Judge unless such assessment is manifestly wrong. In the present case I am unable to hold that either the damages or costs allowed are inadequate.

The plaintiffs' submission is that the location of the animal hospital next door to the duplex has depreciated the value of their property. If the hospital is carried on in such a way as not to constitute a nuisance, there can be no damage to the property, and that is what the injunction requires. For example: if only five or six dogs were kept at the hospital it might be so conducted as not to constitute a nuisance. On the other hand, it is difficult to conceive, say, a dozen dogs being kept so as not to constitute a nuisance. It would be inconsistent to give the plaintiffs damages for depreciation in the value of their property as well as a permanent injunction restraining the defendants from doing the very thing which caused the depreciation. Damages and injunction are substitutive: *Turtle* v. *Toronto* (1924). I therefore think the trial Judge was right in refusing damages for depreciation in the value of the property.

The appeal against the assessment of damages and costs should be dismissed with costs.

On the motion to commit for breach of the injunction the learned trial Judge found that "no nuisance exists or did exist during the period in question, in so far as the hospital building is concerned, either from offensive odours, the barking of dogs or otherwise" (p. 210). He found also that as "the noise from the barking of dogs in the runway has been greatly diminished and almost eliminated by reason of the subsequent action of the defendants, I must find that there is not a substantial interference with the comfortable use and enjoyment of the plaintiffs' property on that account" (p. 211). The only breach of the injunction which the learned Judge found was "that the defendants are and were at all material times in breach of the injunction with relation to offensive odours from the disposition of garbage and refuse." For this breach no penalty was imposed but the defendants were ordered to pay $75 costs.

The plaintiffs say that the odour and noise from the building has been somewhat lessened but that the smell and noise of barking and whining dogs continues—especially from the dog-runs. This the defendants deny.

There is no doubt or dispute as to certain important facts. There is a distance of 10 or 12 ft. between the hospital and the plaintiffs' duplex. The yard in which the dogs are exercised adjoins the plaintiffs' garden, which, prior to the establishment of the hospital, the plaintiffs and their tenant used and enjoyed. The male defendant says that the hospital has been air-conditioned, the windows sealed, and the doors kept shut. He says, too, that the capacity of the hospital has been reduced from 135 dogs to 75 dogs. The defendants have another establishment where dogs are boarded, which dogs are first delivered to the hospital and then transferred to the boarding kennels. While the capacity of the hospital is 75 dogs, there were 35 kept at the time the motion was made.

There are separate dog-runs in the yard and only one dog is put in each run. They are put out for five or ten minutes—six at a time, four times a day—in the morning after 6 a.m., at noon, at 4 p.m., and again in the evening from 8 to 10 p.m. I am quite unable to see how that number of dogs can be run adjacent to a residence without creating a nuisance. Offensive odours are bound to come from them, no matter how carefully the premises may be cleaned, and with so many dogs there is certain to be barking. During these four periods the doors of the hospital are opened and closed frequently, discharging noise and odours. The hospital is open all night. It does not appear how many dogs are transferred through the hospital to the boarding kennels.

I am unable to believe that such a number of dogs can be handled in this way, adjoining a residence and garden, without creating a nuisance, and I think that by so doing there has been a substantial and serious breach of the injunction. The learned trial Judge, who held otherwise, speaking of the "individual enclosed pens," said, "This means that the dogs are not so apt to bark" and "that the noise from the barking of dogs in the runways has been greatly diminished and almost eliminated." I think he was overly optimistic when he found that that number of ailing dogs, away from their homes, can be exercised without odour and noise. To me it is clear that more than three or four dogs—six at the most—housed on a small lot next door to a residence, and exercised four times a day under the windows of the residence and adjacent to the garden of the residence, will create a substantial and serious nuisance.

Damage for depreciation in value of the property having been disallowed, the injunction should be obeyed so that there is in fact no depreciation. . . .

QUESTIONS. Does it follow that because there is no nuisance there is no depreciation? Is a church ever a nuisance? Is residential land next to a church as marketable as more remote land?

KREBS *v*. HERMAN. 1931. 6 P. 2d. 907. An action to restrain the operation of a kennel of forty to ninety dogs in a semi-residential area on the ground that the loud barking constituted a nuisance. The court said: "The trial judge in his opinion said 'The barking of a dog ought not to disturb an ordinary person. That is a common sound heard in every community. To some ears the barking of a dog, especially on the person's own premises, is a sound that is pleasing, and one which tends to make him feel secure.' Counsel for the defendants in his brief in discussing this subject, refers to the eulogy of the late Senator Vest of Missouri upon a dog. The Senator, however, was speaking only of one dog and not of a collection of forty to ninety dogs, under his window in the night time while he was unsuccessfully trying to sleep and get repose of body and mind. If the Senator had been in his home, trying to obtain sleep and the chorus of forty to ninety dogs had been continuously howling and yelping under his window, we might conjecture, although we do not attempt to state, the blistering language which he probably would have employed because of his inability to sleep."

McBEAN *v.* WYLLIE

Manitoba. King's Bench. 1905. 14 Man. R. 135

The plaintiff who owned and resided in a dwelling house, the grounds attached to which adjoin the westerly limit of the right of way of the Winnipeg Transfer Railway Company, brought this action to restrain the completion by defendant of a large warehouse, partially erected on such right of way, in front of and distant about ten feet easterly from the easterly limit of plaintiff's grounds.

The plaintiff claimed: . . . That it shut off plaintiff's view of the Red River and injured the value of her property. . . . That its erection created a nuisance.

RICHARDS J.: . . . The fact of the warehouse cutting off a view of the river cannot in itself be actionable. The plaintiff, having bought her property with knowledge that it adjoined a railway line, had reason to expect that warehouses might be built on the right of way. . . .

The evidence of nuisance is very meagre. Some smells have been noticed near the warehouse. Passers-by have used as a latrine the sloping ground between its westerly side and plaintiff's grounds. Defendant is not shown to be the lessee or owner of that intervening ground. It is difficult to see how the removal of his warehouse would abate the nuisance. It was suggested that tramps would get under the warehouse floor from the outside. But the evidence showed defendant's intention to board the outside of the building down to the ground, which would keep trespassers out.

The suggestion that defendant meant to store in the building calcium carbide is not proved. The evidence is that defendant's intention is to exclude carbide from it.

It is suggested that cement which is intended to be stored in the building might be handled so carelessly as to scatter some of it on plaintiff's ground. It is impossible to presume in advance that defendant will be guilty of such negligence.

The questions of the class of lumber used and the strength of the foundation do not affect plaintiff.

I find, therefore, that the claim that the building or its use will create a nuisance is not proved. . . .

If, in the use of the warehouse hereafter, defendant should be guilty of creating a nuisance, the plaintiff may have a remedy by injunction. But I cannot presuppose such a state of affairs. [The action was dismissed.]

QUESTIONS. How could you acquire a right to a view? Consider below the related questions of the right to light and to air. Suppose a house has been standing on a property line for forty years. Could the adjoining owner build on his (the same) property line? If not, how far back from the line would he have to go? How does the owner of a building on a line maintain the building without trespassing on the adjoining property for support for a ladder?

THE LIMITATIONS ACT
Ontario. Revised Statutes. 1960. Chapter 214

33. No person shall acquire a right by prescription to the access and use of light or to the access and use of air to or for any dwelling-house, workshop or other building, but this section does not apply to any such right acquired by twenty years use before the 5th day of March, 1880.

OAKLEY *v.* WEBB
Ontario. Appellate Division. 1916. 38 O.L.R. 151

HODGINS J. A. read the judgment of the Court: Appeal by the plaintiff from the judgment of Britton J., dismissing an action to restrain the defendant from carrying on his business as a stone-cutter and sawyer so as to interfere with the health and comfort of the appellant and his family.

The appellant bought, fifteen years ago, on the north side of Summerhill Avenue, and built on the lot a frame house, which he rented but never lived in. In 1913, he built his present residence on the east side of the lot, a solid pressed brick home, costing $4,500, with nine rooms and a sun parlour on top of the kitchen, which forms the north end of the house. This house was rented for ten months after it was finished, but the appellant has lived in it since July, 1914. His lot has 50 feet front by a depth to the railway right of way of 115-130 feet.

The respondent bought the adjoining hundred feet to the east in 1913, just after the appellant began to build, and put on it, in the spring of 1914: (1) an office building in the south-west corner on the street line; (2) a lean-to for chiselling stone and using the compressor, 14 feet by 60, on the western boundary, north of the office and close to the back part of the house; (3) north of the lean-to, a shed in which the air-compressor is placed; (4) on the north-east part of the lot, a brick building called the machine-shop with tin roof and wooden front, in which machines are working.

The work in numbers 2, 3, and 4 is complained of, as also the chopping of stone in the yard. The trouble is said to be noise and dust; the noise being caused by the air-compressors and the planer and saws in the machine-shop. The saw is working more constantly than the planer. It is a gang-saw, in which the respondent has had from one to six saws cutting.

In the lean-to there is chopping and planing of stone done, producing noise from the hammers and chisels and compressed air.

The action was begun in May, 1915. The operations of the respondent begin generally at 8 a.m., and are over for the day at 4.45 p.m. Both parties have lots in a block fronting on Summerhill Avenue and backing on the

Canadian Pacific Railway track. The block extends from Maclennan Avenue, where it is a mere point, eastward, widening as it goes till lot 11 is reached, where the depth is 225 feet. The whole of it is excepted from by-law 5977 of the City of Toronto, passed on the 18th March, 1912, which makes the lands south and east of it a residential district.

Not far from the appellant's house, about a hundred or a hundred and fifty feet, Nelson, the sanitary excavator and house-mover, has a yard where he keeps his horses and waggons, and from which, when there was rain, a smell emanated—the appellant says from the manure-pit and not from the waggons and barrels. Nelson also has a lumber-yard there, filled with big, heavy lumber used in moving buildings. The Canadian Pacific Railway line runs just at the rear of the appellant's property. Across Summerhill Avenue the houses are so built that their backs are towards the street except east of Nelson's property. There is a small grocery store to the west, in a private house, with a display window.

The right of the respondent to carry on his business is a legal right; so is that of the appellant and his family to enjoy their life in reasonable comfort. To enjoin the respondent it is necessary to shew that in the exercise of his right he wrongfully invades that of the appellant; in other words, that his business is so carried on as to amount to a nuisance, and so is an unlawful invasion of the competing right of the appellant.

The character of the neighbourhood is an important element in determining the standard of comfort which may be insisted upon. This strip along the railway right of way has been excluded by the municipal authorities from the adjoining residential area. It offers facilities for sidings, and is perhaps the only spot within a large area where shops may be put. It includes a somewhat unpleasant and unsightly storage-yard within its boundaries. Those who settled there must and do accept the railway noise and smoke as part of the conditions of their residence; and the indifference of all who live near by to the discomforts caused by the operation of freight and passenger trains is significant of the dulling effects of constant familiarity with the clatter and smuts regularly distributed by those agencies. Levy, one of the appellant's witnesses, says that the block is a business block.

Apart from the evidence of the appellant and his daughter, no one was called by him who spent the days at home, except Burns, who testifies to hearing noise—what he calls excruciating. He says that he does not hear it much when the windows are closed. His testimony is the more notable because he lived in his house for six months while the respondent's operations were in full swing, and then exercised his option to buy it, paying therefor $12,000. Mrs. Mack and her mother, called for the respondent, lived near from January, 1914, to May, 1915, and say they could not hear the noise in their home nor in the yard behind. The other witnesses for the appellant leave their homes in the morning, and so are not able to speak of the effects of the noise except for an hour or so in the morning. The appellant's daughter is the only one affected in health, and her complaint is that the noise gets on her nerves on account of its continuousness.

The respondent's witnesses, except Mrs. Mack, afford examples of those who, like all the local residents in regard to railway noises, have become insensible to the noise produced by the sawing and chipping, from being accustomed to it or from not listening for it.

The respondent says his machinery operated from April, 1914, until December, 1914, without any objection as to noise etc., but that when he started building his office, which is out on the street line, objection was made to its location, and that the only comment made by any one before the action was begun was a casual remark of the appellant's that the saw made quite a noise. The respondent admits that if persons were looking for noises and listening for them the noise of his machines might be heard 200 feet away, but says that ordinarily they would not be noticed, though they could be heard on the street.

I think the rule stated by Middleton J., in *Appleby* v. *Erie Tobacco Co.* (1910), and adopted by Sutherland J., in *Beamish* v. *Glenn* (1915), as correct, is the proper test to be applied in this case. It is that "an arbitrary standard cannot be set up which is applicable to all localities. There is a local standard applicable in each particular district, but, though the local standard may be higher in some districts than in others, yet the question in each case ultimately reduces itself to the fact of nuisance or no nuisance, having regard to all the surrounding circumstances."

In dealing with the local standard or surrounding circumstances, Lord Selborne L.C., in *Ball* v. *Ray* (1873), insisted that the Court must consider whether the defendant was using his property reasonably or not, e.g., whether in case of a building it was being used for purposes for which the building was not constructed . . .

The uncertainty of the test makes the question of nuisance or no nuisance a question of fact, and it is so stated by the House of Lords in *Polsue & Alfieri Limited* v. *Rushmer* (1907). In *Gaunt* v. *Fynney* (1872), Lord Selborne L.C., in speaking of nuisances by noise, says: "Such things, to offend against the law, must be done in a manner which, beyond fair controversy, ought to be regarded as excessive and unreasonable."

In view of these and other cases, and after perusing the whole of the evidence, while I think there was evidence from which the learned trial Judge might have arrived at a different result, I am not sufficiently certain that he came to a wrong conclusion to enable me to assent to a reversal of his finding. He had to consider not only the evidence as to the noise but also the character of the neighbourhood, the reasonable use of the respondent's property, and the weight of testimony offered.

The appeal will have to be dismissed with costs.

2. Public Nuisances

McKNIGHT *v.* TORONTO

Ontario. Common Pleas Division. 1883. 3 O.R. 284

By-law 1231 of the city of Toronto provided in section 2 that "No person shall keep, nor shall there be kept within the city of Toronto, any pigs or swine, or any piggery." Section 3 (2) provided that "No cow shall be kept in any stable, byre, yard, or other enclosure (pasture lands and paddocks excepted), situate at a less distance than forty feet from the nearest dwelling-house, and where two cows are kept the stable or byre shall not be situated at a less distance than eighty feet from the nearest dwelling house." The by-law was passed under R.S.O. 1877, c. 174, s. 466 (17) as amended by S.O., 1881, c. 24, s. 12, which authorized by-laws "For preventing or regulating the erection or continuance of slaughter houses, gas works, tanneries, distilleries, or other manufactories or trades which may prove to be nuisances, including the keeping of cattle and pigs or swine, and cattle, or cow byres and piggeries." The plaintiff obtained an order *nisi* to show cause why By-law 1231 should not be quashed.

WILSON C.J.: The municipal enactments are made as well for preventing and abating public nuisances, as for preventing or regulating such acts, erections, and kinds of buildings as in their nature are or are likely to be nuisances; for instance, common begging in the streets, ringing of bells, or making unusual noises in public places, the firing of guns and the like may be prevented, and some of them may also be regulated. The construction of privy vaults may not only be regulated but prevented, and yet their construction may be proper and necessary. Their construction should not therefore be prevented unless they are likely to be a nuisance.

So also the power of prevention should not be exercised against the erection or continuance of gas works, slaughter houses, &c., &c., or other manufactories or trades, unless they are or are likely to prove nuisances, and so the statute expressly in the 17th sub-section declares. Now, in that subsection "the keeping of cattle and pigs or swine, and cattle or cow byres and piggeries," is placed upon the same footing as the erection or continuance of gas works, &c., &c.; that is, they are only to be prevented or regulated in case they "may prove to be nuisances."

If slaughter houses are only to be prevented or regulated if they "may prove to be nuisances," the keeping of cattle, &c., should be subject to the latter qualification, and I think that is so.

It must depend very much upon the site where these erections are, or where these factories or trades are carried on, or where the cattle or pigs are kept, or are to be kept, whether they will prove to be nuisances or not. That which would be a manifest nuisance in a crowded thoroughfare, as, for instance, a slaughter house or tannery, on account of the offensive smell &c., proceeding from it; or a large factory which was carried on with much noise, or which required vans and other conveyances to be constantly standing at its doors on the street, or constantly crossing the crowded sidewalks, or where there was a very frequent deposit of goods on the sidewalks which seriously impeded their usefulness or safety for foot passengers, might not be a nuisance if carried on in a isolated situation or in a sparsely peopled or little frequented part of a city or town, but would be an intolerable nuisance if carried on in a densely peopled or crowded thoroughfare. There are parts of the very extensive area forming the city in which a slaughter house, or tannery, or the keeping of cattle, would not be a nuisance.

It is notorious that cattle are kept in very large numbers in this city in extensive sheds erected for the purpose, but whether they have proved to be a nuisance or not those who reside in that locality, or who have to pass within half a mile of it, will be able to say.

Now, these sheds are maintained and are permitted by the city authorities on the assumption that they are not a nuisance. A general prohibition, therefore, against the keeping of pigs within the city, although the keeping of them is not pretended to be a nuisance, cannot be maintained. There are parts of the city in which pigs might be kept—not, of course, in any numbers, but to a certain number—which are situated at a considerable distance from any dwelling house or thoroughfare, and where the keeping of them could not possibly be a nuisance, and yet this section is a total prohibition, nuisance or no nuisance. The second section of the by-law must, therefore, be quashed.

The third section is not prohibitive, but regulative. Cows are not, in their nature, so offensive as swine, and there is almost a necessity they should be kept within the limits of the city. The section is framed upon that assumption. The regulation is, that a single cow shall not be kept in any stable, byre, yard, or other enclosure (pasture lands and paddocks excepted) situated within a distance of forty feet from the nearest dwelling house, and if two cows are kept the stable, &c., shall not be at a less distance than eighty feet from the nearest dwelling house. The keeping of cows near to a dwelling house may be a nuisance, and there is the power to provide against such buildings, trade, or business which may prove to be a nuisance. It is not necessary the by-law should have declared the keeping of cows within these distances from dwelling houses was or would be, or might be a nuisance, or in the words of the statute was such an act as "may prove to be a nuisance," although it might, perhaps, have been neater draftsmanship to have done so.

The fact that the by-law passed under the sections of the statute relating to nuisances specifies those distances as the nearest limit under which byres &c. shall be placed or kept with regard to dwelling houses, is in effect a sufficient declaration that if they are placed or kept at a less distance they may prove to be nuisances. The distances specified must be such that this Court can say whether they are reasonable or not, or whether they are not in effect prohibitive.

It would not be reasonable to say that no cow shall be kept in the city within a quarter of a mile of any dwelling house or public thoroughfare, nor perhaps within the eighth of a mile, or 660 feet, nor perhaps within a less distance than that; and probably the by-law might be quashed on that ground, if the Court were satisfied the keeping of a cow at such a distance from a dwelling house or other place could not prove to be a nuisance.

But this by-law is not open to that objection, for the distance of forty feet and eighty feet are most reasonable distances, and within which, in the exercise of our ordinary experience, judgment, and knowledge, the Courts can say the keeping of a cow or cows may prove to be a nuisance. The second sub-section of the third section of the by-law cannot be quashed upon that ground.

But, it was contended, this by-law is so generally expressed that it restricted the owner of the cows from keeping them within such distances of his own dwelling house, and that such keeping could not be a nuisance. The by-law is so expressed, but I am not disposed to set it aside on that ground, at the instance of any one whose case is not within the terms of that objection, and who is not proceeded against expressly in respect of it.

I am not, however, certain the by-law is objectionable for that cause. The owner may not personally find the keeping of cows within forty feet of his dwelling house to be a nuisance, but others who have the right to go to the house, as the assessor, the tax collector, perhaps the sheriff or bailiff, or the postman, might find it so.

However that may be, I shall not set aside this section of the by-law, because I am not sure it is an objection, for the reasons just stated; and because the by-law is framed upon the assumption that the cases provided for are or may be nuisances, and an owner having his dwelling house within the prescribed distance may be said not to be within the terms of the by-law; and because also the applicant does not pretend his case is within the terms of this objection, and I do not think he is entitled to the benefit of a not very obvious objection, if it be one.

I shall, therefore, make the order quashing the second section of the by-law, and discharge the residue of the order to shew cause, giving to each party the costs of that portion of the order on which each of them has respectively succeeded.

PILLOW *v*. RECORDER'S COURT OF THE CITY OF MONTREAL. 1885. 1 Montreal L.R. 401 (Quebec. Queen's Bench). The appellants, manufacturers of iron bolts, were prosecuted before the Recorder's Court for "that the chimney of their manufactory in Montreal did send forth smoke in such a quantity as to be a nuisance, the said nuisance being then and there hurtful to public health and safety, and did then and there neglect to abate the said nuisance, contrary to the by-law of the City Council." The words of the charge substantially follow the by-law, which was enacted pursuant to an 1879 Act (S.Q. 1874, c. 53) in virtually the same language: "any chimney (not being the chimney of a private dwelling house) sending forth smoke in such quantity as to be a nuisance—shall be deemed to be nuisances (a nuisance)..." This was a hearing on an application for prohibition contesting the jurisdiction of the Recorder's court. RAMSAY J.: "At the argument it was contended that the Act and the By-law were illegal, the legislature of Quebec not having authority to deal with a common nuisance as it was part of the criminal law. There is no difference of opinion possible on the subject that criminal law is not within the powers of the local parliaments; but what is interference with the local law becomes a more delicate question. The appellants seemed to think that the use of words commonly employed in the criminal law determined the question. I am inclined to think this demands a distinction. If by the words it is attempted to give jurisdiction to punish that which is already part of the criminal law the Act would be *ultra vires*. But if the terms of the criminal law were used to characterize an offence within the jurisdiction of the local legislature it would be otherwise. For instance, if a local law declared it to be 'a common nuisance' not to clear the snow away from the foot-path, the law would not by that be *ultra vires*. The power depends on the thing done, not in the words used to set it forth. Of course, the same thing might be made a crime by a Dominion law, and then, probably the local law would cease to be operative. But that is not the question here. The law says that a particular thing shall be a nuisance, and that it shall be deemed to be hurtful to public health and safety; that is not giving jurisdiction to punish a thing which the law now declares to be a common nuisance. That the By-law follows the terms of the law seems to be admitted, and no point is made that it does not. I am therefore of opinion that the Recorder had jurisdiction, and that the Prohibition should be set aside. It is of course possible that the evidence might disclose a criminal offence, and in such it would be the duty of the Recorder to commit the offender for trial ... It seems to me that the difficulty in reconciling conflicting powers does not arise when dealing with criminal law, which, by its nature, is absolute. The line of demarcation of the criminal law appears to me to suffer no interference. The matter must be either criminal or civil, and the local legislature can no more deal with an indictable misdemeanor than with a felony. I am to confirm."

REX *v*. CAPILANO TIMBER CO.

British Columbia. Magistrate's Court. 1949. 96 C.C.C. 141

OSCAR ORR, K.C. D.P.M. (oral):—In this case I have to find the defendant guilty. There is no serious conflict of evidence in this case....

This company was charged that it "unlawfully did allow to be emitted from a fuel burning equipment solid matter which was a nuisance to persons not being therein engaged", from s. 10 of By-law 3050, the *Smoke and Solid Matter By-law,* of the City of Vancouver, which section reads as follows: "No person shall cause, suffer or allow to be emitted from any fuel burning equipment, engine, vehicle, premises, open fire or chimney, any smoke, gases, fumes or solid matter that are a detriment to the property of others, or that are a nuisance to any person not being therein or thereupon engaged." At first I thought the charge here might be for an act indictable under the Criminal Code and beyond the power of the by-law, but I do not now so believe. By this, I refer to criminal and non-criminal common nuisances set out in Code ss. 221, 222, and 223 [am. 1936, c. 29, s. 6].

A reference to 8 C.E.D. (Ont.) shows there is a local standard applicable to each district, but though higher in some and lower in others the question in each case reduces itself to one of nuisance or no nuisance having regard to all the surrounding circumstances. . . .

In the case at bar the defendant's operation has been carried on in the locality for upwards of 50 years, perhaps longer. The mill or burner site is zoned for heavy industry. The residential area affected, whether included in this zone or not appears to be, as shown in the photograph of the area, ex. 1, a well-kept residential district. . . .

The maxim *de minimis non* runs through all those cases and trifling inconveniences are not to be considered. I have kept this in mind. I have also kept in mind the fact that the defendant has spent large sums in alteration or installation and has procured competent engineering advice for the purpose of preventing infractions of this law and still be able to burn waste. Although not directly stated, the evidence leaves the inference that no further remedial action can be taken.

I have considered this case from the point of view of a civil case to determine whether or not a nuisance has been caused within the meaning of the by-law because the by-law uses the term nuisance. Now while there is no doubt in my mind that there is solid matter in the air other than that from the defendant's combustion apparatus, I must find that the defendant has permitted the emission of solid particles from his fuel consuming device to an extent sufficient to cause a nuisance as charged.

In this case I have gone into the facts as fully as I can. Now this is a limited company and the maximum fine is $100. This is a first offence and it is quite obvious they have used every—I won't say every but a good many efforts to abate this nuisance and it has not been successful. I don't see any reason for imposing any more than I imposed in the other case, $25 and in default distress.

[The Criminal Code sections are now section 165:

(1) Every one who commits a common nuisance and thereby

(a) endangers the lives, safety or health of the public, or

(b) causes physical injury to any person,

is guilty of an indictable offence and is liable to imprisonment for two years.

(2) For the purpose of this section, every one commits a common nuisance who does an unlawful act or fails to discharge a legal duty and thereby

(a) endangers the lives, safety, health, property or comfort of the public, or

(b) obstructs the public in the exercise or enjoyment of any right that is common to all the subjects of Her Majesty in Canada.]

REGINA EX REL. COLLINS *v*. PUGLIESE. 1953. 107 C.C.C. 38 (Ontario. Magistrate's Court). The Village of Crystal Beach enacted By-law 845 which provided that "No person shall sell . . . fireworks of any kind within the limits of the Village . . ." The accused was charged with the unlawful sale of fireworks and admitted the sale but contested the validity of the By-law. Held, for the accused. ROBERTS Magistrate: "The only other question remaining to be determined is whether or not the by-law can be sustained under s. 338 (1) (para. 113) of the *Municipal Act,* which provides that by-laws may be passed by the councils of local municipalities 'For prohibiting and abating public nuisances'. The best definition of a public nuisance which I have been able to find is 'an act or omission which obstructs or causes inconvenience or damage to the public in the exercise of rights common to all Her Majesty's Subjects': Stephen's *General View of the Criminal Law of England,* 2nd ed., p. 105; Salmond, *Law of Torts,* 11th ed., p. 247. In the present case it is submitted by Mr. Brooks [one of counsel] that the sale of fireworks creates or contributes to a public nuisance and that the by-law is to prevent that nuisance. It is the setting-off or firing of the fireworks, not the sale of the fireworks, that undoubtedly creates the conditions which it has been stated in evidence exist in Crystal Beach during the summer months. It is a matter of conjecture whether the prohibition of the sale of fireworks within the village would prevent or even abate the nuisance which it is said exists. In my opinion, the by-law cannot be sustained under s. 388 (1) (para. 113), since it cannot be said that the sale of fireworks creates any public nuisance."

THE MUNICIPAL ACT

Ontario. Revised Statutes. 1960. Chapter 249

379. (1) By-laws may be passed by the councils of local municipalities:

110. For prohibiting or regulating the erection or continuance of gas works, tanneries or distilleries or other manufactories or trades that, in the opinion of the council, may prove to be or may cause nuisances.

111. For regulating manufactures and trades that in the opinion of the council may prove to be or may cause nuisances.

112. For prohibiting or regulating and inspecting the use of any land or structures within the municipality or any defined area or areas thereof for dumping or disposing of garbage, refuse, or domestic or industrial waste of any kind.

(a) A by-law under this paragraph,

(i) may establish a schedule of fees chargeable upon inspection of such regulated land or structures,

(ii) may require the owners, lessees or occupants of such land or structures, at the expense of the owners, lessees or occupants, to cease using such land or structures for such purposes, or to cover over any garbage, refuse, or domestic or industrial waste in any prescribed manner, whether or not such land or structures were so used before the passing of the by-law,

(iii) may define industrial or domestic waste.

113. For prohibiting or regulating and inspecting the use of any land or structures for storing used motor vehicles for the purpose of wrecking or dismantling them or salvaging parts thereof for sale or other disposal.

114. For prohibiting or regulating the ringing of bells, the blowing of

horns, shouting and unusual noises, or noises calculated to disturb the inhabitants.

116. For prohibiting and abating public nuisances.

118. For prohibiting the carrying on or operation of a pit or quarry in any area in which the use of land is restricted to residential or commercial use by a by-law passed, or an official plan adopted, before the 1st day of January, 1959, provided no by-law passed under this paragraph shall come into force until approved by the Municipal Board or shall apply to a pit or quarry made or established before the 1st day of January, 1959, except to prohibit the enlargement or extension of any such pit or quarry beyond the limits of the land owned and used in connection therewith on the 1st day of January, 1959.

119. For regulating the operation of pits and quarries within the municipality and for requiring the owners of pits and quarries that are located within 300 feet of a road and that have not been in operation for a period of twelve consecutive months to level and grade the floor and sides thereof and the area within 300 feet of their edge or rim so that they will not be dangerous or unsightly to the public.

120. For regulating the location, erection and use of stables, garages, barns, outhouses and manure pits.

125. For prohibiting and regulating the discharge of any gaseous, liquid or solid matter into land drainage works, private branch drains and connections to any sewer, sewer system or sewage works for the carrying away of domestic sewage or industrial wastes or both, whether connected to a treatment works or not.

3. Pollution of Natural Resources

RUSSELL TRANSPORT LTD. *v.* ONTARIO MALLEABLE IRON CO. LTD.

Ontario High Court. [1952] 4 D.L.R. 719

The defendant had been carrying on the business of a foundry at its present site in the City of Oshawa, Ontario, since 1907. The plaintiff bought land in the vicinity in 1949 which it used, in connection with its business of transporting new motor vehicles by truck, as a marshalling-yard for vehicles to be transported. In 1951 complaints were received that the finish on motor cars transported by it was contaminated and damaged and the cause was traced to particles of iron, manganese sulphide and other materials incident to foundry operation. Faced with a demand by its customers that motor vehicles must be removed from its marshalling yard, the plaintiff brought action for nuisance to recover damages and for an injunction.

McRuer C. J.H.C. [after a lengthy examination of the scientific evidence dealing with the nature and effect of tests made to establish the source of the damage to the vehicles on plaintiffs' land]: The irresistible conclusion on the evidence is, and I so find, that the defendant emits from its plant particles of iron and iron oxide together with other matters which settle on the plaintiffs' lands, rendering the plaintiffs' property unfit for the purpose for which it was purchased and developed. The plaintiffs have therefore suffered and will continue to suffer material and substantial damage to their property unless the emission of injurious substances is abated....

Salmond on Torts, 10th ed., pp. 228–31, summarizes in a comprehensive manner "Ineffectual Defences" as follows:

1. It is no defence that the plaintiffs themselves came to the nuisance.
2. It is no defence that the nuisance, although injurious to the plaintiffs, is beneficial to the public at large.
3. It is no defence that the place from which the nuisance proceeds is a suitable one for carrying on the operation complained of, and that no other place is available in which less mischief would result.
4. It is no defence that all possible care and skill are being used to prevent the operation complained of from amounting to a nuisance. Nuisance is not a branch of the law of negligence.
5. It is no defence that the act of the defendant would not amount to a nuisance unless other persons acting independently of him did the same thing at the same time.
6. He who causes a nuisance cannot avail himself of the defence that he is merely making a reasonable use of his own property. No use of property is reasonable which causes substantial discomfort to others or is a source of damage to their property.

In opening his argument, Mr. Sedgwick stated that the principal defences relied on by the defendant were a reasonable use of its land, and prescriptive right.

It is argued that the plaintiffs established their marshalling-yard in an industrial area unsuitable for a business of that character. In the first place, the facts do not support this contention even if there were a sound basis of law for it . . . It was not until the business had been carried on for nearly 2 years that either the plaintiffs or the defendant became aware of the nuisance . . .

Any argument based on the fact that the nuisance may have existed before the plaintiffs purchased their property is completely answered by the statement of Lord Halsbury in *Fleming* v. *Hislop* (1886), where he said: "If the Lord Justice Clerk means to convey that there was anything in the law which diminished the right of a man to complain of a nuisance because the nuisance existed before he went to it, I venture to think that neither in the law of England nor in that of Scotland is there any foundation for any such contention. It is clear that whether the man went to the nuisance or the nuisance came to the man, the rights are the same, and I think that the law of England has been settled, certainly for more than 200 years, by a judgment of Lord Chief Justice Hide."

The last proposition that I have quoted from Salmond requires some qualification, but only a very limited one. Counsel bases his whole argument on the defence of reasonable use of the defendant's lands on a passage from the judgment of Thesiger L.J., in *Sturges* v. *Bridgman* (1879), where the learned Lord Justice, in dealing with two hypothetical cases said: "As regards the first, it may be answered that whether anything is a nuisance or not is a question to be determined, not merely by an abstract consideration of the thing itself but in reference to its circumstances; what would be a nuisance in Belgrave Square would not necessarily be so in Bermondsey; and, where a locality is devoted to a particular trade or manufacture carried on by the traders or manufacturers in a particular and established manner not constituting a public nuisance, Judges and juries would be justified in finding, and may be trusted to find, that the trade or manufacture so carried on in that locality is not a private or actionable wrong."

This statement of the law has been applied with caution in some cases arising out of an alleged nuisance producing sensible personal discomfort, but it is not to be broadly applied nor is it to be isolated from the general body of law on the subject. It was an expression used in a case arising out of noise and vibration.

The judgment of the Lord Chancellor in *St. Helen's Smelting Co.* v. *Tipping* (1865), is the classic authority in all cases similar to the one before me:

"My Lords, in matters of this description, it appears to me that it is a very desirable thing to mark the difference between an action brought for a nuisance upon the ground that the alleged nuisance produces material injury to the property, and an action brought for a nuisance on the ground that the thing alleged to be a nuisance is productive of sensible personal discomfort. With regard to the latter, namely, the personal inconvenience and interference with one's enjoyment, one's quiet, one's personal freedom, anything that discomposes or injuriously affects the senses or the nerves, whether that may or may not be denominated a nuisance, must undoubtedly depend greatly on the circumstances of the place where the thing complained of actually occurs. If a man lives in a town, it is necessary that he should subject himself to the consequences of those operations of trade which may be carried on in his immediate locality, which are actually necessary for trade and commerce and also for the enjoyment of property, and for the benefit of the inhabitants of the town and of the public at large. If a man lives on a street where there are numerous shops, and a shop is opened next door to him, which is carried on in a fair and reasonable way, he has no ground for complaint, because to himself individually there may arise much discomfort from the trade carried on in that shop. But when an occupation is carried on by one person in the neighbourhood of another, and the result of that trade, or occupation, or business, is a material injury to property, then there unquestionably arises a very different consideration. I think, my Lords, that in a case of that description, the submission which is required from persons living in society to that amount of discomfort which may be necessary for the legitimate and free exercise of the trade of their neighbours, would not apply to circumstances the immediate result of which is sensible injury to the value of the property."...

Even if on any argument a doctrine of reasonable use of the defendant's lands could be expanded to cover a case where there is substantial and material injury to the plaintiffs' property I do not think it could be applied to this case. "Reasonable" as used in the law of nuisance must be distinguished from its use elsewhere in the law of tort and especially as it is used in negligence actions. "In negligence, assuming that the duty to take care has been established, the vital question is, 'did the defendant take reasonable care?' But in nuisance the defendant is not necessarily quit of liability even if he has taken reasonable care. It is true that the result of a long chain of decisions is that unreasonableness is a main ingredient of liability for nuisance. But here 'reasonable' means something more than merely 'taking proper care'. It signifies what is legally right between the parties, taking into account all the circumstances of the case, and some of these circumstances are often such as a man on the Clapham omnibus could not fully appreciate": *Winfield on Torts,* 5th ed., p. 448. "At common law, if I am sued for a nuisance, and the nuisance is proved, it is not defence on my part to say, and to prove, that I have taken all reasonable care to prevent it": per Lindley L.J., in *Rapier* v. *London Tramways Co.* (1893), 599–600. This is not to be interpreted to mean that taking care is never relevant to liability for nuisance. In some cases if the defendant has conducted his trade or business as a reasonable man would have done, he has gone some way toward making out a defence, but only some of the way: *Stockport Waterworks Co.* v. *Potter* (1861).

On the other hand, if the defendant has taken no reasonable precautions to protect his neighbour from injury by reason of operations on his own property the defence of reasonable user is of little avail.

The evidence shows that in so far as the emissions from the cupola are responsible for the injury to the plaintiffs, and I think they are in large measure responsible for the injury complained of, the defendant has adopted no method of modern smoke or fume control. . . . The defendant has considered the installation of a fume control system in the cupola but has refrained from doing anything pending the outcome of this action. . . .

To give effect to the defence of reasonable user of the defendant's lands in this case would be to expand the doctrine of law involved in this defence far beyond any authority in British jurisprudence.

Mr. Sedgwick sought to bring the plaintiffs' business within that class of case referred to as an exceptionally delicate trade.

In *Robinson* v. *Kilvert* (1889), Lopes L.J., said: "A man who carries on an exceptionally delicate trade cannot complain because it is injured by his neighbour doing something lawful on his property, if it is something which would not injure anything but an exceptionally delicate trade."

This statement is to be taken in the light of what was said in *Cooke* v. *Forbes* (1867), referred to by the learned Lord Justice and Lindley L.J., in the same case. In the *Cooke* v. *Forbes* case Sir W. Page Wood V.C., said: "Consequently, it appears to me quite plain that a person has a right to carry on upon his own property a manufacturing process in which he uses chloride of tin, or any sort of metallic dye, and that his neighbour is not at liberty to pour in gas which will interfere with his manufacture. If it can be traced to the neighbour, then, I apprehend, clearly he will have a right to come here and ask for relief."

In *McKinnon Industries Ltd.* v. *Walker* (1951), Lord Simonds dealt with the argument that the injunction granted at the trial should be modified so as in some way to exclude from its operation damage to orchids. The ground of this contention was that growing orchids is from the horticultural point of view, a particularly difficult and delicate operation. The learned law Lord disposed of this argument in these words . . . "there is no reason to treat damage to orchids differently from damage to any other flower, plant or shrub when the wrongdoer admits, as the appellant Company has here admitted, that it has violated the respondent's legal right by damaging his orchids."

Although in this case there is no admission that the defendant has violated the plaintiffs' legal right by damaging the motor vehicles stored on their property, I find as a fact that it has done so, and I cannot find that the storing of automobiles in the open air on the lots in question is a particularly delicate trade or operation. The finish of an automobile is designed to resist reasonable atmospheric contamination and it would be manifestly unjust to hold that property owners in the vicinity of the defendant's plant have no legal right to have their automobiles protected from the emissions from the defendant's foundry simply because they do not keep them under cover.

The defence of prescriptive right remains to be dealt with. The defendant pleads that it and its predecessors in title have for a period of 40 years and more before the commencement of the action enjoyed as of right and without interruption the right to do those things which the plaintiffs claim gives them a right of action and their claim is, therefore, barred by the *Limitations Act*, R.S.O. 1950, c. 207, ss. 34 and 35. . . .

In asserting the defence of prescription, the onus rests on the defendant. . . . The defendant must not only show that it had exercised the right to deposit the substances herein complained of on the plaintiffs' lands, for the prescribed period, but that the exercise of the right amounted to a nuisance actionable at the instance of the plaintiffs and their predecessors in title for the full period of 20 years: *Sturges* v. *Bridgman; Danforth Glebe Estates Ltd.* v. *W. Harris & Co.* (1919).

The latter case was a case arising out of the emission of offensive odours from the defendant's plant. After referring to *Sturges* v. *Bridgman,* Riddell J., said: "So long as the adjoining land remained wholly vacant, and no attempt was made to sell it, and no other damage could be shown, the time did not begin to run. Nothing of the kind was shown to have taken place 20 years before this action." . . .

Even if on any view of the evidence it could be considered that iron oxide and iron particles were being emitted from the defendant's plant for a period of 20 years next preceding the issue of the writ in this action, to the same extent and in the same manner as they are now being emitted, I think the defence of prescriptive right would still fail. In order to obtain a prescriptive right, the enjoyment of the right must not be secret and the servient owner must have either actual or constructive knowledge of it.

The evidence clearly shows that neither the plaintiffs nor the defendant's officers had any knowledge that any injurious particles were being deposited on the plaintiffs' lands as emissions from the defendant's plant until late in the autumn of 1951. *Sturges* v. *Bridgman* has always been recognized as the leading authority for the proposition stated therein: "The laws governing the acquisition of easements by user stands thus: Consent or acquiescence of the owner of the servient tenement lies at the root of prescription, and of the fiction of a lost grant and hence the acts or user, which go to the proof of either the one or the other, must be, in the language of the civil law, *nec vi nec clam nec precario;* for a man cannot, as a general rule, be said to consent to or acquiesce in the acquisition by his neighbour of an easement through an enjoyment of which he has no knowledge, actual or constructive, or which he contests and endeavours to interrupt, or which he temporarily licenses. It is a mere extension of the same notion, or rather it is a principle into which by strict analysis it may be resolved, to hold, that an enjoyment which a man cannot prevent raises no presumption of consent or acquiesence."

In that case a confectioner had for more than 20 years used a pestle and mortar in his back premises, which abutted on the garden of a physician, and the noise and vibration were not felt as a nuisance and were not complained of, but in 1873 the physician erected a consulting-room at the end of his garden and then the noise and vibration became a nuisance to him. It was held that there being no right of action against the defendant until the plaintiff had built the consulting room, the time for prescription did not commence to run until the offensive trade became actionable.

The history of the plaintiffs' property . . . shows that for more than 20 years prior to the commencement of the action it was low-lying vacant land, formerly the site of a disused foundry. . . . Applying the principle followed in *Sturges* v. *Bridgman* and *Danforth Glebe Estates Ltd.* v. *Harris & Co.,* I do not think it can be said that the evidence would warrant me in finding that for the whole period of 20 years prior to 1952 the plaintiffs or their predecessors in title could have maintained an action against the defendant for nuisance. . . .

The form of the relief is one that has given me considerable concern. . . . In a case of this character, in considering the plaintiffs' damages the diminution of the value of the plaintiffs' property cannot be taken into consideration in assessing the damages as the continuation of the nuisance gives rise to a new cause of action from day to day. . . . It is, therefore, clear that a judgment for damages only would not afford the plaintiffs adequate relief. . . .

Judgment will therefore go for an injunction that the defendant, its servants and agents, be restrained from discharging or allowing to be discharged from its works in the pleadings mentioned any substance, gas or matter in such a manner or to such an extent as to occasion damage to the plaintiffs' property or the buildings thereon and/or motor vehicles or vehicles of like character that may be thereon; provided, however, that the operation of the injunction will be suspended until January 1, 1953.

There will be a reference to the County Judge of the County of Ontario to fix the amount of damages that the respective plaintiffs have suffered and will suffer until the injunction becomes effective. . . .

THE AIR POLLUTION CONTROL ACT

Ontario. Revised Statutes. 1960. Chapter 12

1. (1) In this Act,

(*a*) "air contaminant" means a solid, liquid or gas or combination of any of them in the outdoor atmosphere that contributes to air pollution;

(*b*) "air pollution" means the presence in the outdoor atmosphere of an air contaminant in quantities that may cause discomfort to or endanger the health or safety of persons, or that may cause injury or damage to property or to plant or animal life;

(2) The density of an air contaminant that is approximately black shall be determined by means of a chart commonly known as the Ringelmann Chart, a Micro-Ringelmann Chart, or by a comparable chart having black dots or lines upon a white ground, or by a glass comparator, so as to produce:

No. 1 density—approximately 20% black with approximately 80% of the ground white.

No. 2 density — approximately 40% black with approximately 60% of the ground white.

No. 3 density — approximately 60% black with approximately 40% of the ground white.

No. 4 density — approximately 80% black with approximately 20% of the ground white.

No. 5 density — approximately 100% black.

(3) The density of an air contaminant to which subsection 2 does not apply shall be determined by its opacity by means of visual inspection thereof and shall be related to the density of an air contaminant under subsection 2 that has approximately the same degree of opacity.

3. (1) The council of any municipality may pass by-laws for prohibiting or regulating the emission from any source of air contaminants or any type or class thereof.

(2) Without limiting the generality of subsection 1, the council of any municipality may pass by-laws, . . .

(*h*) for requiring that plans and specifications for the erection, construction, reconstruction, installation, alteration or repair of any equipment apparatus, device, mechanism or structure from which an air contaminant may be emitted and such information as a municipal officer may require with respect thereto be filed with a municipal officer, and for requiring approval of such plans and specifications by a municipal officer and that without such approval no such erection, construction, reconstruction, installation, alteration or repair shall be commenced, and for requiring that the work so approved be commenced and proceeded with within one year from the date of such approval and that otherwise such approval shall be void, and for inspecting the work when completed and for issuing a certificate that the work complies with the plans and specifications filed and with the by-law, and for providing that without such certificate no such equipment, apparatus, device, mechanism or structure shall be operated or used, and for charging fees for such approval of plans and specifications, and for such certificates;

(*i*) for appointing one or more municipal officers to administer and enforce any air pollution control by-law and for authorizing any such officer to enter in or upon any premises at any reasonable time and make such examinations, tests and inquiries as he deems necessary or advisable for the purposes of the by-law, and for requiring any owner or occupant of premises, his employees and agents to furnish all means in his or their power that may be required by the officer under this clause, and for authorizing any such officer to require such installations of or alterations in any equipment, apparatus, device, mechanism or structure or such changes in the manner of operating them as may be necessary to prevent or lessen the emission of an air contaminant within such time as he requires;

(*j*) for authorizing a municipal officer to permit deviations from the requirements of any air pollution control by-law;

(*k*) for imposing fines recoverable under *The Summary Convictions Act*, for a first offence, of not more than $100, and for a second or subsequent offence, of not more than $300, upon every person who contravenes or fails to comply with any by-law passed under this section or any order of a municipal officer, and for providing that each day that a person contravenes or fails to comply with any such by-law or order constitutes a separate offence.

(3) A proposed by-law under subsection 1 or 2 shall be submitted to the Minister for his review and advice and shall not be passed until thirty days have elapsed after it has been so submitted.

(4) Subsection 1, with respect to products of combustion, and clauses *a, b, c, d, g* and *h* of subsection 2 do not apply to heating equipment used or intended to be used for the heating of a one-, two- or three-family dwelling or for the heating of less than 35,000 cubic feet of space in a commercial establishment.

(5) Clause *h* of subsection 2 does not apply to internal combustion engines or to routine maintenance work, minor alterations or emergency repairs that do not increase the emission of air contaminants.

(6) No by-law passed under subsection 1 or 2 applies to products of combustion until ninety days after it or a synopsis of it has been published in a newspaper having general circulation in the municipality.

(7) No by-law passed under subsection 1 or 2 applies to air con-

taminants, other than products of combustion, until two years after it or a synopsis of it has been published in a newspaper having general circulation in the municipality.

(9) No by-law passed or regulation made under this Act applies to sulphur fumes arising from the operations designated in *The Damage by Fumes Arbitration Act*.

4. (1) Where a municipality passes an air pollution control by-law and appoints a municipal officer with power to exercise the powers mentioned in clause *i* of subsection 2 of section 3, the council shall by by-law establish an appeal board composed of not fewer than three and not more than five members, a majority of whom shall not be members of a municipal council, to hear and determine appeals from orders of municipal officers and provide for such appeals, prescribe the time within which such appeals may be made and the procedure on such appeals.

(2) Any person who deems himself aggrieved by a decision of an appeal board may appeal to a judge of the county or district court of the county or district in which the municipality is situate within thirty days after the receipt of a copy of the decision by the owner or occupant of the premises with respect to which the decision was made and such appeal shall be a hearing *de novo* and the judge may allow or dismiss the appeal or vary the decision of the appeal board and the decision of the judge is final and not subject to any further appeal.

8. Where a person complains that it is not technically feasible to comply with an order of a municipal or provincial officer or with a decision of an appeal board within the time required by the order or decision, he may appeal to the Minister who may reject the appeal or extend the time for compliance with such order or decision.

THE DAMAGE BY FUMES ARBITRATION ACT

Ontario. Revised Statutes. 1960. Chapter 86

1. The Lieutenant Governor in Council may appoint an arbitrator for the purposes of this Act and may limit his jurisdiction either territorially or as to subject matter and may extend such limited jurisdiction or diminish it from time to time.

2. (1) Where damage is occasioned directly or indirectly to crops, trees or other vegetation by sulphur fumes arising from the smelting or roasting of nickel-copper ore or iron ore or from the treatment of sulphides for the production of sulphur or sulphuric acid for commercial purposes, such damage may, subject to section 3, be determined by the arbitrator who has exclusive jurisdiction to determine the amount of such damage and to make an award.

(2) The remedies provided in this Act are in lieu of all remedies whether in law or in equity to which any person would be entitled but for the passing of this Act and no action shall be taken by way of injunction or otherwise.

[Sections 3 to 7 have been omitted.]

GILES *v.* WALKER

England. Queen's Bench Division. 1890. 24 Q.B.D. 656

The defendant, a farmer, occupied land which had originally been forest land, but which had some years prior to 1883, when the defendant's occupation of it commenced, been brought into cultivation by the then occupier. The forest land prior to cultivation did not bear thistles; but immediately upon its being cultivated thistles sprang up all over it. The defendant neglected to mow the thistles periodically so as to prevent them from seeding, and in the years 1887 and 1888 there were thousands of thistles on his land in full seed. The consequence was that the thistle seeds were blown by the wind in large quantities on to the adjoining land of the plaintiff, where they took root and did damage. The plaintiff sued the defendant for such damage in the Leicester County Court. The judge left to the jury the question whether the defendant in not cutting the thistles had been guilty of negligence. The jury found that he was negligent, and judgment was accordingly entered for the plaintiff. The defendant appealed.

R. Bray, for the plantiff. If the defendant's predecessor had left the land in its original condition as forest land the thistles would never have grown. By bringing it into cultivation and so disturbing the natural condition of things, he caused the thistles to grow, thereby creating a nuisance on the land just as much as if he had intentionally grown them. The defendant, by entering into occupation of the land with the nuisance on it, was under a duty to prevent damage from thereby accruing to his neighbour. The case resembles that of *Crowhurst* v. *Amersham Burial Board* where the defendants were held responsible for allowing the branches of their yew trees to grow over their boundary, whereby a horse of the plaintiff, being placed at pasture in the adjoining field, ate some of the yew twigs and died.

LORD COLERIDGE, C.J. I never heard of such an action as this. There can be no duty as between adjoining occupiers to cut the thistles, which are the natural growth of the soil. The appeal must be allowed.

[Lord Esher agreed.]

THE WEED CONTROL ACT
Ontario. Revised Statutes. 1960. Chapter 427

3. (1) Every person in possession of land shall destroy all noxious weeds thereon as often in every year as is necessary to prevent the ripening of their seeds.

(2) Where land abuts a river, stream or lake or other natural body of water, the person in possession of the land shall destroy all noxious weeds as required under subsection 1 that are growing between the limit of his land and the low water mark of that body of water.

5. (1) The council of every county, city and separated town and of every municipality in a territorial district shall pass by-laws appointing one or more persons as county weed inspectors, municipal weed inspectors or local weed inspectors, as the case may be, to enforce this Act in the area within its jurisdiction and fixing their remuneration or other compensation.

(4) If in the opinion of the Minister any inspector is incompetent or fails to carry out his duties, the Minister, after a hearing giving the inspector and the council that appointed him an opportunity to make representations in that regard, may annul the appointment of the inspector.

(5) If in the opinion of the Minister a council has wrongfully revoked the appointment of an inspector appointed under subsection 1, the Minister, after giving the council and the inspector an opportunity to make representations in that regard, may, in writing addressed to the council concerned, require the council to reinstate the appointment for the remainder of the year.

10. (1) Where an inspector finds noxious weeds or weed seeds on land in the area within his jurisdiction, he may order the person in possession of the land to destroy the noxious weeds or weed seeds within such period of time as is necessary to prevent the weed seeds from ripening.

15. No person shall deposit or permit to be deposited any noxious weeds or weed seeds in any place where the weeds or weed seeds might grow or spread.

19. Every person who contravenes any of the provisions of this Act or of the regulations, or of any order made under this Act, is guilty of an offence and on summary conviction is liable for a first offence to a fine of not more than $25 and for a second or subsequent offence to a fine of not less than $25 and not more than $100.

ROSE *v*. SOCONY-VACUUM CORPORATION
Rhode Island. Supreme Court. 1934. 173 A. 627

MURDOCK J.: These cases, described in the writs as trespass on the case for causing a nuisance, were heard together for the reason that the same questions of law are involved in each case. They are here on plaintiffs' exceptions to a ruling of the superior court sustaining demurrers to the declarations which are summarized in plaintiffs' brief as follows:

"The plaintiff (Manuel Rose) for thirty years prior to and in June, 1930, owned a farm in East Providence, bounding southerly on the state highway known as the Wampanoag Trail, comprising fifty-seven acres with a dwelling house, large barn and other out buildings thereon, and occupied by him and his family. On the farm was a well of pure water used for drinking purposes, and on the westerly part of the farm was a stream in part fed by percolations of water in and under the land of the defendant and said highway and into said stream. On the farm was a large piggery and a hennery, the hens supplied by water from the well, and the pigs supplied by water of the stream. On the southerly side of and bounding northerly on said highway and opposite said farm the defendant had a large tract of land at a higher elevation than the farm.

"Years before 1930, the defendant acquired said tract of land and built upon it a large oil refinery and a large number of tanks for storing petroleum, gasoline and other petroleum products, and operated the same and from time to time suffered and permitted to be discharged on its land and into settling basins, bodies of water and natural water ponds and ways thereon large quantities of petroleum, gasoline, petroleum products and waste substances from its refinery and tanks with the result that large parts of its said land, basins, bodies of water and natural water ponds and ways became impregnated, and polluted by the same, and that it was the duty of the defendant to confine to its said land said polluting matters and substances and said waters in their polluted condition and not suffer or permit the same to be discharged or escape from its land to, in, under and on any adjoining or neighbouring land, and thereby create a nuisance thereon to its injury, but the defendant, disregarding its duty wrongfully and injuriously suffered and permitted large quantities of said polluting matters and substances and said waters in their polluted condition to escape from time to time from its land by means of percolations thereof in, under and through its land to, in, under and through said highway and to, in, under, on and through said farm and parts thereof and to and into said well and said stream, with the direct result that in said June, 1930, said well became polluted by the same and especially by gasoline and rendered unfit as drinking water for use by man or beast, and also said stream theretofore fit for use then became polluted and unfit for use by man or beast with the direct result that the plaintiff in June, 1930, and until the present time was deprived of the use of said well and stream and obliged since to obtain water from other sources off his farm for the supply of his house for drinking and domestic uses and watering his hens and for watering his hogs and pigs and other uses for which the stream was available.

"Further the declaration sets forth that because of the pollution of the stream 136 of his hogs and pigs died from drinking the waters, including 75 breeding sows, and because of the pollution of the well about 700 of his hens died from drinking the well waters, and that because of a lack of a wholesome water supply the plaintiff has been deprived of raising on his farm as large a number of pigs and hens as theretofore and his business in raising and selling the same interfered with and greatly reduced in amount to his monetary damage and loss. The declaration concludes with a general allegation as to other damages from said nuisance caused by the defendant."

The declarations allege no negligent act, and recovery is sought principally on the ground that the acts set forth in the declarations have resulted in a nuisance for which defendant is liable even though not negligent. The assertion that the acts of the defendant complained of have resulted in a nuisance is petitio principii.

There is no wholly satisfactory definition of what constitutes a nuisance, but it is generally agreed that a nuisance has its origin in the invasion of a legal right. In *Cooley on Torts*, vol. 3 (4th Ed.) § 398, it is said that "An actionable nuisance may, therefore, be said to be anything wrongfully done or permitted which injures or annoys another in the enjoyment of his legal rights," and in *Joyce on Nuisances*, § 29, that "a nuisance does not necessarily exist even though one may by the use of his property cause an injury or damage to another." The plaintiffs must therefore go further to establish liability than the mere assertion that a nuisance exists on their land by reason of the acts of the defendant.

The plaintiffs' cases rest on the proposition that they have a cause of action from the fact that contaminating and deleterious substances have escaped from the land of the defendant through the medium of percolating waters to their land. The plaintiffs rely on the much-discussed case of *Rylands* v. *Fletcher,* where the following rule laid down by Mr. Justice Blackburn in *Fletcher* v. *Rylands*, was approved: "We think that the true rule of law is, that the person who, for his own purposes, brings on his land and collects and keeps there anything likely to do mischief if it escapes, must keep it in at his peril, and if he does not do so, is prima facie answerable for all the damage which is the natural consequence of its escape. He can excuse himself by shewing that the escape was owing to the plaintiff's default; or, perhaps that it was the consequence of vis major, or the act of God; but as nothing of this sort exists here, it is unnecessary to inquire what excuse would be sufficient. The general rule, as above stated, seems on principle just . . . and it seems but reasonable and just that the neighbour who has brought something on his own property (which was not naturally there), harmless to others so long as it is confined to his own property, but which he knows will be mischievous if it gets on his neighbour's, should be obliged to make good the damage which ensues if he does not succeed in confining it to his own property." This rule is a radical departure from the commonly accepted doctrine of the law of torts that liability is predicated on fault. It has not found general acceptance in this country, and in England it has been greatly modified by later decisions. . . .

A profound criticism of the rule is found in the opinion of Mr. Justice Doe in *Brown* v. *Collins*, where it is said: "Everything that a man can bring on his land is capable of escaping,—against his will, and without his fault, with or without assistance, in some form, solid, liquid, or gaseous, changed or unchanged by the transforming processes of nature or art,—and of doing damage after its escape. Moreover, if there is a legal principle that makes a man liable for the natural consequences of the escape of things which he brings on his land, the application of such a principle cannot be limited to those things; it must be applied to all his acts that disturb the original order of creation; or, at least, to all things which he undertakes to possess or control anywhere, and which were not used and enjoyed in what is called the natural or primitive condition of mankind, whatever that may have been. This is going back a long way for a standard of legal rights, and adopting an arbitrary test of responsibility that confounds all degrees of danger, pays no heed to the essential elements of actual fault, puts a clog upon natural and reasonably necessary uses of matter, and tends to embarrass and obstruct much of the work which it seems to be man's duty carefully to do." *Losee* v. *Buchanan,* Burdick, *Law of Torts* (4th Ed.) § 12: "The rule in *Rylands* v. *Fletcher,* even with the recognized limitations, finds no favor even in England, and American courts have generally refused to follow it." See, also, Bohlen, *Studies in the Law of Torts*, p. 421.

We think, therefore, that reason and the great weight of authority in this country sustain us in refusing to adopt the rule of absolute liability as stated in *Rylands* v. *Fletcher, supra.*

The plaintiffs lean heavily on the maxim sic utere tuo ut alienum non laedas. This maxim, so often cited as the governing principle of decisions, affords little, if any, aid in the determination of the rights of parties in litigation. If it be taken to mean any injury to another by the use of one's own, it is not true, and, if it means legal injury, it is simply a restatement of what has already been determined. "The maxim, sic utere tuo ut alienum non laedas, is mere verbiage. A party may damage the property of another where the law permits; and he may not where the law prohibits: so that the maxim can never be applied till the law is ascertained; and, when it is, the maxim is superfluous." Erle, J., in *Bonomi* v. *Backhouse.* The maxim is undoubtedly a sound moral precept expressing an ideal never fully attained in the social state.

We must therefore look for some fault on the part of the defendant. It is well-settled law that one who accumulates filth or other deleterious matter on his land must confine it there and not allow it to spread over the surface of his land to the surface of the land of another. "Where one has filth deposited on his premises, he whose dirt it is must keep it that it may not trespass." *Tenant* v. *Goldwin.* And this rule will apply where the objectional matter permeates the soil superficially and by the action of the elements reaches the soil of another. Liability in this class of cases sounds in trespass.

The owner of land bounding on a surface stream may not pollute the same to the impairment of the use and enjoyment of the stream by other riparian owners; and this rule applies to subterranean streams following a known or readily ascertainable and well defined course. 27 R.C.L. p. 1170. Liability for the pollution of a surface stream or subterranean stream following a well-defined course is predicated on the invasion of a correlative right of the injured party in such waters. This leads to an inquiry into the nature and extent of the right of a landowner in the waters beneath the soil which pass from his land, not in a well-defined stream, but by percolation or seepage.

The leading case on this question is *Acton* v. *Blundell,* decided in 1843. In that case it was held that the right to the waters in the soil was not governed by the rule applicable to surface streams. The court at page 351 said: "But the difference between the two cases with respect to the consequences, if the same law is to be applied to both, is still more apparent. In the case of the running stream, the owner of the soil merely transmits the water over its surface; he receives as much from his higher neighbour as he sends down to his neighbour below: he is neither better nor worse: the level of the water remains the same . . . and we think the present case, for the reasons above given, is not to be governed by the law which applies to rivers and flowing streams, but that it rather falls within that principle, which gives to the owner of the soil all that lies beneath his surface; that the land immediately below his property, whether it is solid rock, or porous ground, or venous earth, or part soil, part water; that the person who owns the surface may dig therein, and apply all that is there found to his own purposes at his free will and pleasure; and that if, in the exercise of such right, he intercepts or drains off the water collected from underground springs in his neighbour's well, this inconvenience to his neighbour falls within the description of damnum absque injuria, which cannot become the ground of an action."

In England this right to underground waters has been held to be absolute, and the motive of the owner in appropriating or diverting the same is immaterial. *Mayor of Bradford* v. *Pickles* (1895). In this country the authorities are in conflict as to the nature of the right in underground waters. Some jurisdictions follow the English rule and others modify the rule to the extent that the owner of land may not through malice or negligence deprive the adjoining owner of percolating waters. To this extent in the latter jurisdictions the right is not absolute but relative. . . .

In this state the right to subterranean waters appears to be relative to the extent that they may not be purposely or negligently diverted. . . .

While the defendant could appropriate to its own use the percolating waters under its soil, providing that in so doing it was not actuated by an improper motive and was not negligent, can it, by the use to which it puts its land, deprive the plaintiffs of such waters by rendering them unfit for plaintiffs' use by contamination? Authorities, few in number, which bear directly on this question, are in conflict. . . . The rationale of these opinions is that the courses of subterranean waters are as a rule indefinite and obscure, and therefore the rights relating to them cannot well be defined as in the case of surface streams. To give to others a right in such waters may subject a landowner to liability for consequences, arising from a legitimate use of his land, which he did not intend and which he could not foresee. . . .

Kinnaird v. *Standard Oil Co.,* supports plaintiffs' view of the law. The opinion discusses the above cases holding to the contrary and refuses to follow them; it recognizes the right of the landowner to appropriate to his own use the percolating waters under his soil, but holds him liable if he contaminates them. . . .

A query arises as to whether the divergence of views expressed in these cases is not due to the influence of the predominating economic interests of the jurisdictions to which these apply; in other words, whether these opinions do not rest on public policy rather than legal theory. On the question of public policy as a ground of judicial decision, see an article by Mr. Justice Holmes in 8 *Harvard Law Review,* 1.

It will be observed that in jurisdictions holding that, even though there is no negligence, there is liability for the pollution of subterranean waters, the predominating economic interest is agricultural.

Defendant's refinery is located at the head of Narragansett Bay, a natural waterway for commerce. This plant is situated in the heart of a region highly developed industrially. Here it prepares for use and distributes a product which has become one of the prime necessities of modern life. It is an unavoidable incident of the growth of population and its segregation in restricted areas that individual rights recognized in a sparsely settled state have to be surrendered for the benefit of the community as it develops and expands. If, in the process of refining petroleum, injury is occasioned to those in the vicinity, not through negligence or lack of skill or the invasion of a recognized legal right, but by the contamination of percolating waters whose courses are not known, we think that public policy justifies a determination that such harm is *damnum absque injuria.*

The plaintiff's exceptions in each case are overruled, and each case is remitted to the superior court for further proceedings.

K.V.P. CO. LTD. *v.* McKIE

Ontario. Supreme Court of Canada. [1949] 4 D.L.R. 497

KERWIN J. delivered the judgment of the court: The K.V.P. Co. Ltd. appeals from five judgments of the Court of Appeal for Ontario affirming, with a variation, the judgments of the Chief Justice of the High Court granting the plaintiffs in each action damages for the pollution of the Spanish River, and an injunction.

The respondents (plaintiffs) are owners of lands on the Spanish River, which flows into Lake Huron, and the appellant operates a pulp and paper mill higher up the river. While the respondents' lands are not particularly suitable for agriculture, some are farmed and are used to grow vegetables. The respondent in one action has a summer residence on his property; another has a grant of a water lot on the river so that in his case the injunction applies to the water flowing over his lands; and the lands of the others have cabins erected on them which, together with the house in some cases, are used for roomers and boarders in the tourist industry.

The trial Judge found that the appellant had polluted the waters of the river and awarded the respondents damages of $450, $1,250, $300, $2,100, $1,000 and $500. The Court of Appeal agreed with these findings and the appellant does not now attack them. The sole point argued before us was as to the injunction.

The suggestion that there should be a new trial upon any terms that the Court might see fit to impose, limited to the issue as to whether an injunction should be granted, cannot be entertained as it is not shown in any way that new evidence has been found which could not have been discovered by the appellant by the exercise of reasonable diligence and that, if adduced, it would be practically conclusive. . . . It was then argued that by s. 30 of the *Lakes and Rivers Improvement Act,* R.S.O. 1937, c. 45, as amended by s. 6 of 1949 c. 48, this Court is empowered to refuse to grant an injunction against the owner or occupier of a mill under certain named conditions, or to grant an injunction to take effect after such lapse of time or upon such terms and conditions or subject to such limitations or restrictions as may be deemed proper, or, in lieu of granting an injunction, to direct that the owner or occupant of the mill take such measures or perform such acts to prevent, avoid, lessen or diminish the injury, damage or interference complained of as may be deemed proper. Other provisions are made as to damages already suffered and as to subsequent damages. Reliance is placed upon s. 6 (2) by which it is provided that s. 6 (1), re-enacting s. 30 of the original Act, shall apply to every action or proceeding in which an injunction is claimed in respect of any of the matters mentioned including every pending action and proceeding and including every action or proceeding in which an injunction has been granted and in which any appeal is "pending." The amended Act came into force on the day it received the Royal Assent, April 1, 1949, and while the Judgment of the Court of Appeal was given November 22, 1948, it is contended that the appeal to this Court is "pending" within the meaning of the enactment.

It has been decided in *Boulevard Heights* v. *Veilleux* (1915), that since s. 46 of the *Supreme Court Act* [now R.S.C. 1952, c. 259] provides that this Court may dismiss an appeal or give the judgment which the Court whose decision is appealed should have given, and since a provincial Legislature may not extend the jurisdiction of this Court as conferred by Parliament, such a provision as the one here in question would not, even if it purported so to do, enable this Court to give a judgment that was impossible in law at the time of the decision of the Court of Appeal. The 1949 Act is not an enactment declaratory of what the law was deemed to be. Mr. Cartwright sought to overcome this difficulty by pointing to the amendment to the *Supreme Court Act* in 1928 (c. 9, s. 3) by which the following proviso was added to s. 68: "Provided that the Court may, in its discretion, on special grounds, and by special leave, receive further evidence upon any question of fact, such evidence to be taken in the manner authorized by this Act, either by oral examination in Court, by affidavit, or by deposition, as the Court may direct."

It is apparent that this refers only to further evidence upon any question of fact, and the decision in the *Boulevard Heights* case therefore applies. Leave was asked to file an affidavit of Ralph A. Hayward under this proviso but leave has never yet been given thereunder and the circumstances are not such as to warrant making an order on this occasion.

It was next contended that on the evidence in the record and even without the 1949 amendment to the *Lakes and Rivers Improvement Act,* this Court should, in the circumstances, decline to grant an injunction and should confine the respondents to damages. The damages are those assessed by the trial Judge and those to be fixed by the Local Master at Sudbury upon a reference directed to him to ascertain the damages sustained by the respondents from the date of trial "to the date that the injunction becomes effective," which date was fixed as the expiration of 6 months from the date of the trial judgment, April 15, 1948. Following the notice of appeal from the judgment of the Court of Appeal to this Court, the appellant obtained an order staying the operation of the injunction until the final determination of the appeal.

The rights of riparian owners have always been zealously guarded by the Courts. It is unnecessary to discuss all the decisions referred to by Mr. Cartwright and it suffices to quote the remarks of Lord Sumner, speaking on behalf of the Judicial Committee, in *Stollmeyer* v. *Petroleum Dev. Co.* (1918): "The grant of an injunction is the proper remedy for a violation of right according to a current of authority, which is of many years' standing and is practically unbroken. . . ."

Section 17 of the *Ontario Judicature Act* provides: "Where the Court has jurisdiction to entertain an application for an injunction against a breach of a covenant, contract or agreement or against the commission or continuance of a wrongful act, or for the specific performance of a covenant, contract or agreement, the Court may award damages to the party injured either in addition to or in substitution for such injunction or specific performance, and such damages may be ascertained in such manner as the Court may direct, or the Court may grant such other relief as may be deemed just."

Under the precursor of this section, Lord Cairns' Act, (1858), the House of Lords decided in *Leeds Industrial Co-operative Soc.* v. *Slack* (1924), that jurisdiction was thereby conferred to award damages in lieu of an injunction in the case of a threatened injury, but Viscount Finlay, with whom Lord Birkenhead expressly agreed, and of whose judgment Lord Dunedin stated that "he has exactly expressed my views", pointed out at p. 860 that the Courts have on more than one occasion expressed their determination to prevent any abuse of the Act by legalizing the commission of torts by any defendant who was able and willing to pay damages.

Pollution has been shown to exist, damages would not be a complete and adequate remedy, and the Court's discretion should not be exercised against the "current of authority, which is of many years' standing."

An injunction should, therefore, go but it is argued that this Court should adopt the course followed by the Judicial Committee in the *Stollmeyer* case, referred to above. Before considering that case attention should be directed to the decision of the Judicial Committee immediately preceding in the case of *Stollmeyer* v. *Trinidad Lake Petroleum Co. Ltd.* (1918). There it was held that an owner of land upon a stream flowing in a permanent defined channel, although fed exclusively by rain water running off the surface of the land in certain seasons, was entitled to have the natural flow of the water without sensible diminution or increase (subject to the lawful rights of upper riparian owners) and without sensible alteration in its character or quality. A stream of the above description flowed through lands, the whole of which belonged to the respondents with the exception of a plot situated at its mouth, which belonged to the appellants. The latter's land was unsuitable for agriculture and it was not used for any purpose. The respondents carried on upon their land the business of boring for oil, which was the sole industry of the locality, and diverted part of the water of the stream in order to supply water to other property, thereby sensibly diminishing the flow past appellants' land. They also, without negligence, caused a sensible pollution of the water by oil and salt. The appellants had suffered no pecuniary damage and the Trinidad Courts dismissed an action for damages and an injunction. The Judicial Committee decided that the appellant had suffered an *injuria* and was entitled to an injunction. The Judicial Committee made certain declarations as to the use of the water by the respondents and as to the pollution of the River Vessigny and then gave leave to the appellants to apply for an injunction to the Court of first instance after a period of 2 years. In that case it will be noted that (1) the lands of the appellants were unsuited for agriculture; (2) the lands were not being used for anything; (3) the appellants had suffered no damage; (4) the Courts below had refused the injunction.

When we come to the subsequent case, we find that the respondent and the appellant were respectively upper and lower riparian owners upon the banks of a river in Trinidad and carried on upon their respective lands the business of boring for oil. The trial Judge found that the respondents had polluted the water for both oil and salt, and awarded the appellant $50 damages, but refused to grant an injunction. An appeal to the Full Court against the refusal to grant an injunction was dismissed upon an equal division of opinion between the two members of the Court. The Judicial Committee reversed that decision and it was in the course of delivering the judgment of their Lordships that Lord Sumner used the language quoted above. At the conclusion he pointed out that the loss to the respondents would be out of all proportion to the appellant's gain and that, the respondents undertaking to pay from time to time such pecuniary damages as their work may be found to have caused to the appellant on inquiry before the Court of first instance, the operation of the injunction should be suspended for 2 years to give an ample opportunity to the respondents to carry out any works necessary to remove the causes of complaint with liberty to apply to the Court of first instance for a further suspension if special grounds could be shown.

The writs in the actions before us were issued in May and June, 1947, complaining of damages since May 1, 1946. The actions were tried in December, 1947, and judgment was given by the Chief Justice of the High Court on April 15, 1948. The judgment of the Court of Appeal was given November 22, 1948, and the appeals before us were argued on June 13th and 14th, 1949. The lands of the respondents are being used; considerable damages have been awarded, and the appellant has had before it the fact of the injunction since April 15, 1948. The two cases decided by the Judicial Committee are quite distinguishable but, under all the circumstances, we have concluded that the operation of the injunction should be stayed for a period of 6 months.

Subject to this variation, the appeal and the appellant's motion to introduce new evidence should be dismissed with costs. Notice of a motion had been given by the respondents for leave to file an affidavit of Maurice Adelman, but the matter was not mentioned at the argument, and that motion should, therefore, be dismissed without costs.

[A petition for special leave to appeal to the Privy Council was dismissed with costs on January 12, 1950.]

BLACK *v.* CANADIAN COPPER CO. (1917), 12 O.W.N. 243 (Ontario, High Court). An action for an injunction to restrain excessive smoke from copper smelters in Sudbury, Ontario. MIDDLETON J.: "Mines cannot be operated without the production of smoke from the roast-yards and smelters, which smoke contains very large quantities of sulphur dioxide. There are circumstances in which it is impossible for the individual so to assert his individual rights as to inflict a substantial injury upon the whole community. If the mines should be prevented from operating, the community could not exist at all. Once close the mines, and the mining community would be at an end, and farming would not long continue. Any capable farmer would find farms easier to operate and nearer general markets, if the local market ceased. The consideration of this situation induced the plaintiffs' counsel to abandon the claims for injunctions. The court ought not to destroy the mining industry—nickel is of great value to the world—even if a few farms are damaged or destroyed: but in all such cases compensation, liberally estimated, ought to be awarded. The Court has now, by statute, discretion to refuse an injunction and award damages in lieu thereof."

JUDICATURE ACT

New Brunswick. Revised Statutes. 1952. Chapter 120

35. . . . but without leave of the Attorney-General no injunction shall be applied for which, if granted, would delay or prevent the construction or operation of any manufacturing or industrial plant on the ground that the discharge from such plan is injurious to some other interest.

[Introduced by S.N.B., 1929, c. 39, s. 2.]

THE KVP COMPANY LIMITED ACT 1950

Ontario. Statutes. 1950. Chapter 33

1. (1) Whether or not its operation is now stayed, every injunction heretofore granted against The KVP Company Limited, herein called "the Company" restraining the Company from polluting the waters of the Spanish River, is dissolved.

(2) The dissolution of any such injunction shall not prejudice the right of any person to damages heretofore awarded in the action in which any such injunction was granted and shall not prejudice the right of any person to damages suffered from the date of the trial in which any such injunction was granted to the date when the injunction would have, but for this Act, become effective.

2. Nothing in this Act shall prejudice the right of any person to bring any action against the Company arising from the pollution of the waters of the Spanish River.

3. (1) In lieu of bringing an action against the Company, any person who claims that he has suffered or is suffering damage caused by the pollution of the waters of the Spanish River by the Company may, by notice in writing to the Company, require the Company to submit the matter to arbitration on such terms as may be agreed upon.

(2) Upon receipt of a notice under subsection 1, the Company and the claimant shall forthwith negotiate the terms of the submission and proceed therewith in accordance with its terms.

(3) If the claimant and the Company are unable to agree as to the terms of the submission, any term in dispute may at any time be referred by either party to the judge of the district court of the district in which the damage claimed occurred, and the judge shall, after hearing both parties, determine any such term and his determination shall be final and shall be acted upon by the parties.

4. (1) The Research Council of Ontario shall endeavour to develop methods that, if applied by the Company, would abate or lessen the pollution of the waters of the Spanish River by the Company.

(2) The cost of carrying out its duties under subsection 1 shall be deemed to be a debt due by the Company to the Research Council of Ontario.

5. This Act shall come into force on the day it receives the Royal Assent.

NOTE. The Royal Assent was given on April 30, 1950. In March, 1950 the Minister of Lands and Forests requested the Research Council of Ontario (now absorbed by the Ontario Research Foundation) to study the conditions of the Spanish River in the vicinity of Espanola as a basis for developing methods of remedying any contaminating causes found. The Council's report was tabled by the Minister in the Legislature on March 31, 1952. It has been published as Research Report No. 25 of the Division of Research of the Ontario Department of Lands and Forests under the title *Pollution of the Spanish River*.

MILLER *v.* SCHOENE

Virginia. United States Supreme Court. 1927. 276 U.S. 272

STONE J. delivered the opinion of the Court: Acting under the *Cedar Rust Act* of Virginia, Va. Acts 1914, c. 36, as amended by Va. Acts 1921, c. 260, now embodied in Va. Code (1924) as sections 885 to 893, defendant in error, the state entomologist, ordered the plaintiffs in error to cut down a large number of ornamental red cedar trees growing on their property, as a means of preventing the communication of a rust or plant disease with which they were infected to the apple orchards in the vicinity. The plaintiffs in error appealed from the order to the Circuit Court of Shenandoah county which, after a hearing and a consideration of evidence, affirmed the order and allowed to plaintiffs in error $100 to cover the expense of removal of the cedars. Neither the judgment of the court nor the statute as interpreted allows compensation for the value of the standing cedars or the decrease in the market value of the realty caused by their destruction, whether considered as ornamental trees or otherwise. But they save to plaintiffs in error the privilege of using the trees when felled. On appeal the Supreme Court of Appeals of Virginia affirmed the judgment. *Miller* v. *State Entomologist.* Both in the Circuit Court and the Supreme Court of Appeals plaintiffs in error challenged the constitutionality of the statute under the due process clause of the Fourteenth Amendment and the case is properly here on writ of error. . . .

The Virginia statute presents a comprehensive scheme for the condemnation and destruction of red cedar trees infected by cedar rust. By section 1 it is declared to be unlawful for any person to "own, plant or keep alive and standing" on his premises any red cedar tree which is or may be the source or "host plant" of the communicable plant disease known as cedar rust, and any such tree growing within a certain radius of any apple orchard is declared to be a public nuisance, subject to destruction. Section 2 makes it the duty of the state entomologist, "upon the request in writing of ten or more reputable free-holders of any county or magisterial district, to make a preliminary investigation of the locality . . . to ascertain if any cedar tree or trees . . . are the source of harbor or constitute the host plant for the said disease . . . and constitute a menace to the health of any apple orchard in said locality, and that said cedar tree or trees exist within a radius of two miles of an apple orchard in said locality." If affirmative findings are so made, he is required to direct the owner in writing to destroy the trees and, in his notice, to furnish a statement of the "fact found to exist whereby it is deemed necessary or proper to destroy" the trees and to call attention to the law under which it is proposed to destroy them. Section 5 authorizes the state entomologist to destroy the trees if the owner, after being notified, fails to do so. Section 7 furnishes a mode of appealing from the order of the entomologist to the circuit court of the county, which is authorized to "hear the objections" and "pass upon all questions involved," the procedure followed in the present case.

As shown by the evidence and as recognized in other cases involving the validity of this statute . . . cedar rust is an infectious plant disease in the form of a fungoid organism which is destructive of the fruit and foliage of the apple but without effect on the value of the cedar. Its life cycle has two phases, which are passed alternately as a growth on red cedar and on apple trees. It is communicated by spores from one to the other over a radius of at least two miles. It appears not to be communicable between trees of the same species but only from one species to the other, and other plants seem not to be appreciably affected by it. The only practicable method of controlling the disease and protecting apple trees from its ravages is the destruction of all red cedar trees, subject to the infection, located within two miles of apple orchards.

The red cedar, aside from its ornagmental use, has occasional use and value as lumber. It is indigenous to Virginia, is not cultivated or dealt in commercially on any substantial scale, and its value throughout the state is shown to be small as compared with that of the apple orchards of the state. Apple growing is one of the principal agricultural pursuits in Virginia. The apple is used there and exported in large quantities. Many millions of dollars are invested in the orchards, which furnish employment for a large portion of the population and have induced the development of attendant railroad and cold storage facilities.

On the evidence, we may accept the conclusion of the Supreme Court of Appeals that the state was under the necessity of making a choice between the preservation of one class of property and that of the other, wherever both existed in dangerous proximity. It would have been none the less a choice if, instead of enacting the present statute, the state, by doing nothing, had permitted serious injury to the apple orchards within its borders to go on unchecked. When forced to such a choice, the state does not exceed its constitutional powers by deciding upon the destruction of one class of property in order to save another which, in the judgment of the legislature is of greater value to the public. It will not do to say that the case is merely one of a conflict of two private interests and that the misfortune of apple growers may not be shifted to cedar owners by ordering the destruction of their property; for it is obvious that there may be, and that here there is, a preponderant public concern in the preservation of the one interest over the other. And where the public interest is involved preferment of that interest over the property interest of the individual, to the extent even of its destruction, is one of the distinguishing characteristics of every exercise of the police power which affects property.

We need not weigh with nicety the question whether the infected cedars constitute a nuisance according to the common law; or whether they may be so declared by statute. . . . For where, as here, the choice is unavoidable, we cannot say that its exercise, controlled by considerations of social policy which are not unreasonable, involves any denial of due process. . . .

The statute is not, as plaintiffs in error argue, subject to the vice which invalidated the ordinance considered by this Court in *Eubank* v. *Richmond.* That ordinance directed the committee on streets of the city of Richmond to establish a building line, not less than five nor more than thirty feet from the street line whenever requested to do so by the owners of two-thirds of the property abutting on the street in question. No property owner might build beyond the line so established. Of this the Court said (p. 143). "It (the ordinance) leaves no discretion in the committee on streets as to whether the street (building, semble) line shall not be established in a given case. The action of the committee is determined by two-thirds of the property owners. In other words, part of the property owners fronting on the block determine the extent of use that other owners shall make of their lots, and against the restriction they are impotent."

The function of the property owners there is in no way comparable to that of the "ten or more reputable freeholders" in the Cedar Rust Act. They do not determine the action of the state entomologist. They merely request him to conduct an investigation. In him is vested the discretion to decide, after investigation, whether or not conditions are such that the other provisions of the statute shall be brought into action; and his determination is subject to judicial review. The property of plaintiffs in error is not subjected to the possibly arbitrary and irresponsible action of a group of private citizens.

The objection of plaintiffs in error to the vagueness of the statute is without weight. The state court has held it to be applicable and that is enough when, by the statute, no penalty can be incurred or disadvantage suffered in advance of the judicial ascertainment of its applicability.

NOTE. The Fourteenth Amendment of the Constitution of the United States was adopted in 1868 and provides in part, in Section 1: ". . . nor shall any State deprive any person of life, liberty or property, without due process of law; nor deny to any person within its jurisdiction the equal protection of the laws." What is meant by "due process of law" is a matter to be determined, in the last analysis, by the United States Supreme Court. Here it is inquiring whether the use of the legislative process of law has been "due." Compare the Fifth Amendment (the first ten amendments, sometimes called the Bill of Rights, were adopted between 1789-1791), applicable to federal matters as well: "nor shall any person . . . be deprived of life, liberty or property, without due process of law. . . ."

QUESTION. What is the meaning of the phrase "the police power"?

STEPHENS *v.* VILLAGE OF RICHMOND HILL
Ontario. Court of Appeal. 1956. 1 D.L.R. (2d) 569

LAIDLAW J.A. delivered the judgment of the Court: This is an appeal by the defendant from a judgment pronounced by Stewart J. on August 10, 1955, [1955] 4 D.L.R. 572, whereby the defendant was "perpetually restrained from discharging or permitting to be discharged effluent or storm overflow from its sewerage system into the waters of a branch of the Don River and from polluting the said waters in any manner and from causing the said waters to be less than otherwise they would be where the plaintiff's land borders upon the said river." It was ordered that the injunction "shall not take effect until the 1st of September, 1956 and on and after the said 1st day of September, 1956 shall have full force and effect." The Court further ordered that the plaintiff recover from the defendant the sum of $500 together with the costs of the action.

In 1941 the respondent became the owner of parts of Lots 42 and 43, containing 60 acres more or less, in Concession 1 in the Township of Markham. The parcel is bounded on the west by Yonge St., on the south by Observatory Lane, on the east by the right-of-way of the Canadian National Railway Company, and on the north by Hunt Lane. It is situate about 3,000 ft. south of Markham St. which runs in an easterly and westerly direction in the Village of Richmond Hill, and which at times material in this case was the south limit of the municipality.

A branch of the Don River (sometimes hereinafter called "the stream") has its source from springs in a cedar bush in the Township of Markham on the east side of Yonge St. and about three miles north of Markham St. The stream flows in a southerly direction through the township and, according to a plan filed at trial by the defendant as ex. 26, no part of the stream in the vicinity of Markham St. and for more than 1,000 ft. to the north of that street was within the limits of the Village of Richmond Hill. That part of the stream is a short distance east of the east boundary of the municipality as that boundary was located prior to January 1, 1953. The stream continues to flow in the Township of Markham in a southerly direction from Markham St., produced easterly, to Hunt Lane, thence through the middle of the respondent's lands to Observatory Lane, and continues thereafter in a southerly direction.

In November, 1950, the Village of Richmond Hill received from the Department of Health of the Province of Ontario a preliminary certificate of approval for the construction of a sewerage project. Under date of July 30, 1951, the Department of Health issued a final certificate of approval. That certificate shows that the Village of Richmond Hill submitted to the Department of Health "plans, specifications and an application for the approval for the construction of a sewerage system consisting of sanitary sewers" on streets listed in the certificate, and including Markham Road "from 250′ E. of Church Street to East Village Limits." The certificate further shows that the Department of Health "inquired into and reported upon the work to be undertaken as to whether the same is calculated to meet the sanitary requirements of the inhabitants affected thereby and as to whether such works are likely to prove prejudicial to the health of the inhabitants of the municipality or of any other municipality liable to be affected thereby." On the same day (July 30, 1951) the municipal council of the village read a first second and third time, and finally passed, By-law 596A "to authorize the construction and installing of a sanitary sewerage system in the Village of Richmond Hill." That by-law contains a recital that a report of the work to be performed had been presented to the council by engineers engaged for this purpose; that the installing of the sanitary sewerage system had been approved by the Department of Health of the Province of Ontario by certificate dated July 30, 1951, and that the Ontario Municipal Board had approved the passing of all requisite by-laws. It was enacted that the construction work "be undertaken in accordance with the said report of the said engineers" and that: "the work shall be carried on and executed under the superintendence and according to the directions and orders of such engineer."

The work of construction was completed and the system was put into operation in December, 1952. Neither the plans of the system as designed or constructed, nor the report of the engineers, is before the Court. . .

The claim made by the plaintiff (respondent) in the action, commenced on September 28, 1954, as appears from the statement of claim, is, in substance, that the defendant (appellant) has polluted the water in the stream flowing through her lands and that since December, 1952, it has been "foul, noxious, and unfit for use." It was pleaded that: "The plaintiff's riparian rights in the said stream have been destroyed by the defendant's pollution of the said waters and the plaintiff sustained loss and her lands have been lessened in value."

In the statement of defence it was denied expressly that the defendant polluted the water in the stream as alleged by the plaintiff "or that the water is or has been by reason of any act of the Defendant, foul, noxious or unsatisfactory for use or that by any act of the Defendant the Plaintiff has been deprived of use of the water." The defendant pleaded expressly the provisions of the *Public Health Act,* R.S.O. 1950, c. 306, and particularly s. 106, and alleged that "it has a duty to operate the Sewerage Project aforesaid in the manner in which it is now and which it has been operated." By an amendment the defendant pleaded as follows:

"7A. The Defendant says in any event that at all material times it has carried out its statutory powers and duties in a reasonable and proper manner and with due care and skill. If, which is not admitted, any injury or damage has been or is or will be caused to the Plaintiff by the Defendant as alleged, or at all, the Defendant says that such injury or damage could not have been and cannot now or in the future be avoided by the exercise of reasonable care on the part of the Defendant and that the Plaintiff has no cause of action in respect of same. . . ."

There are two main questions for consideration and determination in this case: Has the respondent a prima facie cause of action? If so, has the appellant a defence by reason of statutory authority?

The respondent is a riparian proprietor, and the rights of such a proprietor have been stated with great clarity and authority by Lord Macnaghten in *John Young & Co.* v. *The Bankier Distillery Co.* (1893). Lord Macnaghten said: "A riparian proprietor is entitled to have the water of the stream, on the banks of which his property lies, flow down as it has been accustomed to flow down to his property, subject to the ordinary use of the flowing water by upper proprietors, and to such further use, if any, on their part in connection with their property as may be reasonable under the circumstances. Every riparian proprietor is thus entitled to the water of his stream, in its natural flow, without sensible diminution or increase and without sensible alteration in its character or quality. Any invasion of this right causing actual damage or calculated to found a claim which may ripen into an adverse right entitles the party injured to the intervention of the Court."

The learned trial Judge reviewed and considered the evidence relating to the condition of the stream before and after the sewage disposal system was put into operation. He accepted the evidence adduced on behalf of the respondent that "prior to the installation of a sewage-disposal plant by the defendant corporation, the stream was ever-flowing and sparkling; that it abounded in fish and watercress; that it was used by children for swimming; that it was used for drinking and watering stock; that its bottom was of gravel and the stream always clear [p. 574]." The learned trial Judge then proceeded as follows [p. 575]:

"The witnesses . . . [whose testimony he accepted] say that the stream has increased its flow and is dirty, the banks are overgrown with weeds hitherto unknown, that and dark matter in suspension is found in the water at all times, whereas previously only the spring freshet muddied its otherwise sparkling waters. They say the water and the surrounding area smell of sewage, that toilet-paper and condoms are to be found caught on the vegetation at the side of the stream; that no fish, frogs or waterbugs are now present, as opposed to their former frequent occurrence; that the algae in the water are now grey or yellow instead of their former green state; that the rocks are now slimy whereas before they were bright and sparkling; and that now little, if any, watercress appears."

He discussed at length evidence given by Dr. Norman J. Howard, an expert of great experience and qualification, and he accepted the evidence of that witness "that all samples of water taken north of the plant were clear and unpolluted and, all samples taken south of the plant were grey, smelly, polluted and, except on two occasions, seriously polluted." He agreed with Dr. Howard's conclusion that "the plant is not big enough for the population and that chloridation is inadequate and not properly controlled."

Finally, the learned Judge made these express and clearly-stated findings: I quote [p. 576]: "I therefore find that the stream has, in fact, become polluted since the installation of the sewage-disposal plant; that the operations of the defendant corporation has caused such pollution; that the plaintiff's riparian rights have been seriously interfered with; and that she has suffered damages thereby."

I accept the findings of fact made by the learned trial Judge, excepting only the finding that the respondent has suffered damages, which I shall considered later. . . .

I now proceed to consider the argument on behalf of the appellant that the municipal corporation is protected against liability by reason of the statutory authority under which the sewerage plant was constructeed and put into operation. . . .

[Laidlaw J.A. considered the effect of s. 386 (12) of the *Municipal Act*, R.S.O., 1950, c. 243, and of s. 106 of the *Public Health Act* and concluded that the appellant corporation had no authority under those Acts to construct the sewer. He continued:]

I prefer to not rest my judgment solely on the ground that the appellant had no lawful authority to construct the sewerage project. I shall assume, contrary to my view, that it had such authority, and proceeded to consider first the argument that it constructed, and thereafter operated, the system without negligence, and then the argument that the injury resulting to the respondent from the exercise of its authority was the inevitable consequence of that which was authorized and contemplated.

It was made plain by Evershed M.R. in *Pride of Derby & Derbyshire Angling Ass'n* v. *British Celanese Ltd.* (1953), that as regards sewers and drains it is necessary to keep clearly in mind a possibility of two distinct causes of action, viz.: (1) for nuisance and (2) for negligence. In the instant case there is no allegation of negligence in the statement of claim. The cause of action is clearly for nuisance. Evershed M.R. said at p. 195: "As regards nuisance, the question is whether the thing complained of as a nuisance is expressly or impliedly authorized by the Act of Parliament in accordance with which the works were constructed, or whether (and this is, perhaps, the same thing) the nuisance complained of is the inevitable consequence of that which the Act both authorized and contemplated."

It is plain that neither the designing engineers, nor the responsible officials of the Village of Richmond Hill, nor the Department of Health, contemplated that raw, untreated sewage would be discharged into the stream . . .

But in any event, the Department of Health had no express authority and, in my opinion, had no implied authority to authorize the appellant to pollute the stream flowing through the respondent's land without regard to the rights of the respondent and other riparian proprietors in the Township of Markham.

Counsel for the respondent referred to and relied upon s. 103 (1) of the *Public Health Act,* which I quote as follows:

"103 (1) No garbage, excreta, manure, vegetable or animal matter or filth shall be discharged into or be deposited in any of the lakes, rivers, streams or other waters in Ontario or on the shores or banks thereof, and no industrial or other wastes dangerous or liable to become dangerous to health or to become a nuisance or to impair the safety, palatability or potability of the water supply of any municipality or riparian owner, shall be discharged into or be deposited in any of the lakes, rivers, streams or other waters of Ontario, or on the shores or banks thereof."

It is plain that the Department of Health cannot in any case disregard the express prohibition contained in that section. It has no express authority to authorize the doing of something in direct violation of that section. It cannot be argued successfully that in the absence of power, expressed in the plainest possible terms, either the Department of Health or the Municipal Board could make lawful what the Legislature declared in express terms to be unlawful. The relevant legislation contemplates three things:

1. To empower a municipal corporation to construct a sewerage project;
2. To safeguard the sanitary requirements and the health of the inhabitants of a municipality liable to be affected by the proposed work;
3. To prohibit the approval and the construction of a sewerage project of an urban municipality which continues into or through or is to be situate in an adjoining township municipality, unless and until that municipality and the inhabitants thereof have notice of the proposed works and location thereof and have full opportunity to make their objections before the Municipal Board and seek protection of their rights.

The legislation does not contemplate the creation of a private nuisance. Counsel for the appellant did not suggest that the terms of the Municipal Act are imperative, but conceded in the course of his argument that they are permissive. In such case, Lord Watson said in *Metropolitan Asylum Dist.* v. *Hill* (1881): "I think the fair inference is that the Legislature intended that discretion to be exercised in strict conformity with private rights, and did not intend to confer license to commit nuisance in any place which might be selected for the purpose."

Even if it be assumed (and again I say, contrary to my opinion) that the appellant had lawful authority to construct the sewerage project at a specified place as shown in plans submitted to the Department of Health and approved by the Department, and also that the Department gave approval to the discharge of the effluent and overflow from the sewerage system into the stream, nevertheless, proof of those facts falls far short of proof of lawful authority to produce the nuisance of which the respondent complains in this case. Again, even if it be assumed that the Department of Health, by its approval of plans for the sewerage project, gave lawful authority to the appellant to discharge the effluent and overflow from the sewerage system into the stream, that approval and authority must be regarded as subject expressly to the prohibition against pollution of the stream contained in s. 103 of the *Public Health Act*.

The appellant has failed to show that the nuisance complained of by the respondent was the inevitable consequence of the construction and operation of the sewerage project. How can the Court make a finding that the conditions as described in evidence accepted by the learned trial Judge were inevitable when Mr. W. B. Redfern, one of the designers of the sewerage system, admitted that such a result was not contemplated in the design of the plant, that they expected that raw, untreated sewage would not run into the stream, and that he did not know how to explain the conditions described by Dr. Howard? The onus of proving that the creation of the nuisance was the inevitable result of the construction and operation of the sewerage project rested on the appellant, and that onus has not been discharged: *Metropolitan Asylum Dist.* v. *Hill.*

Finally, the learned trial Judge reached the conclusion from the evidence "that the defendant has not established the inevitability of the damage." I concur with that conclusion.

Counsel for the appellant referred to and relied on the judgment in *Edgington* v. *Swindon Corp.* (1939). That case is distinguishable from the case now before the Court. It did not arise out of the pollution of a stream, and it did not involve consideration of legislation comparable to that contained in ss. 103 and 106 of the *Public Health Act.* The decision depended upon the effect of the provisions in the *Swindon Corporation Act* (1926) and the finding that the defendants "are authorized to do something which the Legislature must have contemplated would result in an interference with private rights." It was on that ground that the action failed and was dismissed.

In the notice of appeal the ground is set forth "that the Injunction granted [should] be set aside on the grounds that the damages awarded are an adequate remedy for the injury suffered by the Plaintiff." That ground of appeal was not pressed before this Court, and I refer to *Pride of Derby & Derbyshire Angling Ass'n* v. *British Celanese Ltd.* (1953), where Evershed M.R. said: "It is, I think, well settled that, if A. proves that his proprietory rights are being wrongfully interfered with by B., and that B. intends to continue his wrong, then A. is prima facie entitled to an injunction, and he will be deprived of that remedy only if special circumstances exist, including the circumstance that damages are an adequate remedy for the wrong that he has suffered.". . .

During the course of argument the terms of the injunction were the subject of some discussion. I was disposed at that time to think that the terms were too broad, but after consideration of the matter, and having in mind particularly my view that the appellant did not have lawful authority to construct the sewerage project, I refrain from making any alteration of the terms as settled by the learned trial Judge.

Counsel for the appellant takes the objection that the respondent failed to prove that any damages were suffered by her by reason of interference with her riparian rights. She did not reside on the parcel of land through which the stream flows, but on land situated opposite that parcel on the west side of Yonge St. At trial, counsel for the plaintiff stated that there was no claim for damages for anything in connection with that property. The land through which the stream flows is occupied by the plaintiff's son and daughter-in-law. Neither of those persons was called as a witness. There was an allegation in the statement of claim that wells on that land were polluted from sewage in the stream. When the attention of the plaintiff was directed to that allegation in the course of cross-examination, she stated that she did not know "what the action says" and she then said: "I am not claiming any damages." Her counsel stated that the condition of the wells could be eliminated "as an element of damage." I am unable to find any evidence upon which the learned trial Judge could find that the plaintiff suffered damages amounting to $500. In my opinion there was no evidence that she suffered any actual damage. I think the judgment in appeal should be amended by striking out the order therein directing the defendant to pay the plaintiff the sum of $500. In place thereof, the claim of the plaintiff for damages should be dismissed. Except as directed in respect of that claim, the appeal should be dismissed.

The principal matter in controversy in the appeal was the right of the respondent to an injunction as granted. On that ground the appeal fails, and I would, therefore, direct that the appellant pay to the respondent the costs of the appeal.

NOTE. The court referred to the respondent's application to the Ontario Municipal Board for approval of a plan of subdivision which was refused "because of . . . the effect of the creek running through the plan of the proposed subdivision, which creek carries open effluent from the disposal plant of the Village of Richmond Hill. . . ." The court did not discuss the evidence rule by virtue of which it received this evidence.

NOTE. In the trial court Stewart J. said, in part (at pp. 578–9): "It has been further argued that, should these claims be granted, the people of Richmond Hill may in effect be deprived of the only readily and economically available method of disposing of their sewage. In fact, Mr. Wilson says that 95% of all muncipalities which have similar sewage-disposal systems may be put to great expense in improving or changing them. It is quite natural and proper that Dr. Berry, Dr. King, Mr. Redfern, and Caverly (a member of the council of Richmond Hill) should insist upon the importance of the welfare of the people at large, but I conceive that it is not for the judiciary to permit the doctrine of utilitarianism to be used as a make-weight in the scales of justice. In civil matters, the function of the Court is to determine rights between parties. It investigates facts by hearing 'evidence' (as tested by long-settled rules) and it investigates the law by consulting precedents. Rights or liabilities so ascertained cannot, in theory, be refused recognition and enforcement, and no judicial tribunal claims the power of refusal: per Masten J.A. in *Re Ashby* (1934), quoting 49 L. Q. Rev., pp. 106–8.

"It is the duty of the state (and of statesmen) to seek the greatest good for the greatest number. To this end, all civilized nations have entrusted much individual independence to their Governments. But be it ever remembered that no one is above the law. Neither those who govern our affairs, their appointed advisers, nor those retained to build great works for society's benefit, may act so as to abrogate the slightest right of the individual, save within the law. It is for Government to protect the general by wise and benevolent enactment. It is for me, or so I think, to interpret the law, determine the rights of the individual and to invoke the remedy required for their enforcement."

METROPOLITAN ASYLUM DISTRICT *v*. HILL. 1881. 6 App. Cas. 193 (England. House of Lords). A statute authorized local boards to erect buildings for the care of the sick, etc. A hospital for the reception of patients suffering from small-pox and other infectious and contagious diseases was erected near the plaintiff's property. It was found at the trial that the hospital was a nuisance and an injunction was granted against its continuance. As a result of a series of appeals, the question of the right in law to maintain the hospital in its existing condition was brought before the House of Lords. LORD SELBORNE L.C.: "The result is: (1) That this [enabling] Act does not necessarily require anything to be done under it which might not be done without causing a nuisance; (2) That as to those things which may or may not be done under it, there is no evidence on the face of the Act that the Legislature supposed it to be impossible for any of them to be done (if they were done at all) somewhere and under some circumstances, without creating a nuisance; and (3) that the Legislature has manifested no intention that any of these optional powers, as to asylums, should be exercised at the expense of, or so as to interfere with, any man's private rights. The only sense in which the Legislature can be properly said to have authorized these things to be done is, that it has enabled the Poor Law Board to order, and the managers to do them, if, and when, and where, they can obtain by free bargain and contract the means of doing so."

THE PUBLIC HEALTH AMENDMENT ACT, 1956
Ontario. Statutes. 1956. Chapter 71

6. (3) Whether or not its operation is now stayed, every injunction heretofore granted against The Corporation of the Village of Richmond Hill restraining the Corporation from discharging effluent or storm overflow from its sewerage system is dissolved and such sewerage system shall be deemed to have been constructed by statutory authority and shall be deemed to have been maintained and operated prior to the coming into force of this section by statutory authority.

(4) Nothing in subsection 2 or 3 affects the right of any person to damages or costs heretofore awarded in the action in which any such injunction was granted or affects the right of any person to claim for compensation or damages for land injuriously affected or for negligence or nuisance arising from the construction, maintenance or operation of any sewerage project whether arising before or after the date of trial of such action.

(5) The Department of Health shall make or cause to be made an inquiry and investigation of the construction and operation of the sewage disposal plant and sewerage system mentioned in subsections 2 and 3 and may modify or alter the terms and conditions previously imposed as to the treatment or disposal of sewage and may impose additional terms and conditions in accordance with the powers and duties of the Department under this Act.

106. (22) Any sewerage project which is to be, is being or has been constructed, maintained or operated with the approval of the Department and in accordance with the terms and conditions imposed in any order, direction, report or regulation of the Department, the Minister or the Board under the authority of this Act, or any predecessor of this Act, when it is being so constructed or is so constructed, maintained or operated, shall be deemed to be under construction, constructed, maintained or operated by statutory authority.

(23) Subsection 22 does not apply to any sewerage project which is to be or is being or has been constructed, maintained or operated in violation of any general or special Act or any official plan under *The Planning Act, 1955* or any municipal by-law.

(24) Nothing in subsection 22 affects the right of any person to claim for compensation or damages for land injuriously affected or for negligence or nuisance arising from the construction, maintenance or operation of any sewerage project.

NOTE. Section 6(3) was proclaimed effective August 31, 1956. Section 6(2) dissolved a similar injunction granted against the City of Woodstock. See *Burgess* v. *City of Woodstock* (1955).

NOTE ON THE ONTARIO WATER RESOURCES COMMISSION. In

1957 the Ontario legislature took an important step in solving problems of pollution in Ontario by the establishment of the Ontario Water Resources Commission. See now *The Ontario Water Resources Commission Act*, R.S.O., 1960, c. 281. At that time the principal consideration was the economic and efficient supply of water to Ontario municipalities, and sewage disposal was a second concern. Since then it has become increasing apparent that sewage disposal is, at least in terms of expense, the more important. In an undated mimeographed statement of "Objectives for Water Quality in the Province of Ontario" adopted by the Commission the general objectives are stated to be:

"All wastes, including sanitary sewage, storm water, and industrial effluents, shall be in such condition when discharged into any receiving waters that they will not create conditions which will adversely affect the use of these waters for the following purposes; source of domestic water supply, navigation, fish and wild life, bathing, recreation, agriculture and other riparian activities.

"In general, adverse conditions are caused by:

(a) Excessive bacterial, physical or chemical contamination.

(b) Unnatural deposits in the stream, interfering with navigation, fish and wild life, bathing, recreation or destruction of aesthetic values.

(c) Toxic substances and materials imparting objectionable tastes and odours to waters used for domestic or industrial purposes.

(d) Floating materials, including oils, grease, garbage, sewage solids, or other refuse.

(e) Discharges causing abnormal temperature, colour or other changes."

These objectives are to be attained by financial assistance to municipalities and by the exercise of various controls. Under the Act the Commission has the supervision of all surface waters and ground waters in Ontario used as a source of water supply. It may hear and report on complaints of pollution and it or any interested person may apply to a judge of the Supreme Court for an order for the removal or abatement of the injury found. A municipality or person who discharges material that may impair the quality of the waters in a water supply, of almost any description is guilty of an offence and liable on summary conviction to a fine of $1,000 or a year in prison or both. Other offences are described as well. The Commission licenses well drillers and may approve proposed private or municipal water works and sewage works which, without the approval, may not be undertaken.

Financial assistance is provided by means of delayed payments by municipalities for water or sewage works constructed and operated by the Commission for the municipality, or municipalities, where two or more of them have applied for the service. The capital cost payments may be delayed, by agreement, for as long as five years, which, among other advantages, allows the municipality time to try to attract added industrial assessment thus providing it with more taxes with which to meet the annual payments to the Commission when they commence.

The principal administrative sanction of the Commission is its power, under section 50, to require an industrial or commercial enterprise to make sewage disposal arrangements satisfactory to the Commission. The Commission may make regulations, subject to the approval of the Lieutenant-Governor in Council, respecting any matters necessary or advisable to carry out effectively the intent and purpose of the Act. No publicity has been given to an application of section 50, if any.

ONTARIO WATER RESOURCES COMMISSION, SIXTH ANNUAL REPORT, 1961

Summary of Significant Activities. The report of each division of the Commission contains a review of the main features included in the year's program. A summary of the more significant of these items will reveal the progress made during the year as well as the scope of the activities carried on.

Certificates for Water and Sewage Works. Since the legislation makes it a requirement that the approval of the Commission be obtained for the installation or extension of all public water and sewage works in the province. These certificates indicate the extent of the work going on in the province, the number of certificates issued along with the estimated expenditures for 1961 showed that the total number of certificates issued reached the figure of 1,603 in comparison with a total of 1,695 during 1960. The expenditures involved in these certificates totalled $107,027,062.42 as compared with a total of $111,037,642.58 for the previous year. While there was some decrease in estimated expenditures in regard to applications approved, the difference was relatively small and might be attributed to the fact that in some of the larger centres, the major works had passed the stage of major activity. It is interesting to note that the expenditures approved by the Commission each year reaches a figure of about $110 to $120 millions. In addition to this there are expenditures for water and sewage works throughout the province which do not require approval of the Commission. When these are added together, it can be seen that the total expenditures would well pass the mark of $10 million per month. These projects continue to go forward at a rapid rate and to provide facilities for the expanding population and for the industrial growth of the province.

The following summary contains the estimated expenditures for these works—

Water Works:	*Estimated Cost*
Extensions to existing systems	$23,264,916.01
Purification of water supplies	3,807,421.86
New systems	1,859,635.67
Total	$28,931,973.56
Sewage Works:	*Estimated Cost*
Extensions to existing systems	$64,319,102.79
Treatment works	10,692,048.00
New systems	3,083,938.07
Total	$78,095,088.86
Grand Total All Works	$107,027,062.42

The details of the certificates issued are included in the report of the Division of Sanitary Engineering.

OWRC Projects. The Commission has been undertaking water and sewage projects for municipalities since 1957. In this program it enters into agreements with municipalities and others to provide water supply works and purification, and trunk sewers and sewage treatment facilities. During the year 1961, 155 certificates were issued for OWRC projects amounting to a total of $19,884,870.77. These figures may be compared with 124 certificates of the previous year for a total expenditure of

$16,068,113.74. The 1961 certificates on these projects included 51 for water works at a total estimated cost of $3,868,015.85 and 104 certificates for sewage works at a total estimated cost of $16,016,854.92. Once again, it was apparent the great volume of the expenditure was concerned with sewage works.

The Construction Program of the OWRC. Agreements between the Commission and municipalities continued to increase at a rapid rate. The facilities of the Commission were made available to municipalities for the design, construction, financing, and operation of works involved in water supply, purification and distribution, trunk sewers, and sewage disposal facilities. At the end of the year, these projects numbered a total of 192 for an estimated expenditure of $78,702,482. This may be compared with 142 projects at the end of 1960 for an estimated expenditure of $55,715,616. Expenditures on sewage works continued to rise more rapidly than those on water works, and at the end of the year, while the number of water works projects was 93 as compared with 99 sewage works, the costs involved were $22,420,307 for water works and $56,282,175 for sewage works. These 192 projects involved agreements with 146 municipalities as compared with 114 municipalities at the end of 1960.

The OWRC projects are listed herewith to indicate those in operation and those under construction, as well as others which are in the development process, chiefly in the preparation of engineering plans and specifications. . . .

The federal legislation of financial assistance to municipalities for certain parts of sewage works had been in effect for over one year as 1961 ended. This was found to be a distinct advantage to municipalities with works which qualified under the requirements of the legislation. Central Mortgage and Housing Corporation was authorized to lend two-thirds of the cost of that part of the sewage works project which qualified and to forgive 25% of this loan, if the work was completed prior to March 1st, 1963. Many municipalities took advantage of this assistance in 1961 and others were advancing their projects to meet the time requirement. This federal assistance program was integrated closely with the program of this Commission, and in OWRC projects the Commission financed that part of sewage works which was not applicable under the federal plan and also all of the expenditures for water projects.

[The federal legislation referred to is *An Act to amend the National Housing Act, 1954*, being chapter 1 of the Statutes of Canada, 1960–61, assented to on December 2, 1960.]

BIBLIOGRAPHY. The problems of pollution are too substantial to be dealt with here. A useful summary appeared in *Civic Administration* for March 1962, part of which was reprinted as *The Civic Administration Handbook of Environmental Pollution Control.* There is a bibliography included. Among the books one outstanding title is Rachel Carson's *The Silent Spring,* a controversial report on pollution, particularly interesting on the subject of agricultural sprays. Critics rather obviously representing agricultural interests or the chemical industries have disagreed strongly with some of Miss Carson's statements. Even more controversial is the problem of pollution by fissionable materials. Interesting questions of control and politics are lying in wait for the next generation of Canadian (and international) lawyers.

CHAPTER 2

THE *MEANING* OF "PLANNING"

The meaning doesn't matter if it's only idle chatter of a transcendental kind.
W. S. GILBERT

ROYAL COMMISSION ON CANADA'S ECONOMIC PROSPECTS, FINAL REPORT (1957)

Housing and Social Capital Needs. . . . One of the most significant forces bearing on future housing and social capital requirements will be urbanization—the burgeoning of cities and towns; the increasing ratio of urban to rural population. This will affect not just the location of need, but its amount and intensity. Rural people, of course, need housing, schools and roads. But their requirements do not as a rule extend to civic squares, day nurseries, sidewalks, curbs, sewage disposal plants, and elevated expressways. Important as it will be to meet the changing requirements of the rural community, by far the larger part of the bill for new housing and social capital will be incurred in areas which, if they are not urban today, are destined to become so.

We may, by laying so much stress on this, appear to labour the obvious. Urbanization, after all, has been going on through most of the history of Canada. It has shown up in nearly every census since Confederation. It has been one of the most outstanding and talked-about developments of the post-war boom.

In a wider sense, however—in the sense which embraces not merely the fact but its full implications—urbanization is not so obvious. Canadians have flocked to the cities, but their institutions, their habits of mind, and especially, perhaps, their mythology, have lagged behind. The jut-jawed outdoorsman, still vivid against a prairie sky, a rocky coastline or a stand of black spruce, still works long hours as a national symbol. To a degree, this is very well: such people exist, and their race will, we profoundly trust, endure, providing a flesh-and-blood link with the pioneer past. But the unromantic fact is that most Canadians today are not like this at all. They live and work in cities and towns; their environment, for most of the year at least, is an urban and largely man-made one. It is of no small importance that they should see themselves and their surroundings for what they are. The spectacle may not in all respects be pleasant to contemplate, but contemplated it must be as the vital first step in moving toward more efficient and more rewarding patterns of urban life.

Our expectations regarding the future urban-rural distribution of Canada's population are summarized in the accompanying table. In brief, we anticipate that the urban population will more than double. By 1980, Canadians living in cities, towns and villages of 1,000 population or more, and in other settlements forming part of large urban areas, will account for almost 80 per cent of the total population, compared with just over 60 per cent in 1951. Close to 50 per cent will be living in enlarged versions of the present 15 census metropolitan areas, and more than half the population will be living in metropolitan and urban areas of over 100,000 population.

Meanwhile, the rural population may increase somewhat in absolute terms, but decline relatively to the total. The rural *farm* population will decline both relatively and absolutely, dropping from roughly 2,800,000 in 1951 to approximately 2,350,000 in 1980. Only about 9 per cent of Canadians in 1980 will be living on farms in rural areas, compared with 20 per cent in 1951.

FORECAST OF URBAN-RURAL DISTRIBUTION OF POPULATION
(assumed net immigration—75,000 per annum)

	1951 (actual)		1980 (forecast)	
	Thousands of persons	Per cent	Thousands of persons	Per cent
15 metropolitan areas	5,190	37	12,000	45
Other urban	3,433	25	9,010	34
Total	8,623	62	21,010	79
Rural non-farms	2,534	18	3,294	12
Rural farms	2,827	20	2,346	9
Total rural	5,361	38	5,640	21
Total population of Canada (excluding Yukon and N.W.T.)	13,984	100	26,650	100

This forecast, which is developed in the separate study prepared for us, *Housing and Social Capital*, rests on two main assumptions: first, that the developments which we foresee in the agricultural industry will be associated with a considerable further net decline in the rural farm population; and second, that the larger metropolitan and urban areas, regarded as a group, will draw to themselves as great a share of net increase in the national population as they have drawn in the recent past. Smaller urban places will grow—indeed, they may grow more rapidly in percentage terms than the metropolises. There will be some new Kitimats, too. But well over half the net increase in Canada's population will accrue to urban areas which already have more than 40,000 people in them.

These assumptions and the conclusions to which they give rise may well be unacceptable to many of our readers. Some may think simply that we are wrong—that we are misreading the trends. Others may think that we perceive the trends well enough, but that when Canadians see where those trends are leading—to a Montreal of perhaps three million people and a Toronto of comparable size—they will recoil in horror, mend their ways, and initiate a process of decentralization.

We have a great deal of sympathy with those who would attempt to limit the size of cities and divert growth away from the larger metropolises into smaller places. Advocates of this course have powerful arguments on their side. When they claim that in the long run, and all things considered, their way would be best and cheapest, we suspect that they may be right. If the full social costs are taken into account, locating a major proportion of a country's industry and population in a few large centres may indeed be uneconomic, as well perhaps as a dangerous thing to do from a defence point of view.

At the same time, we must be realistic. Twenty-five years seems all too short a space in which to accomplish such a giant step forward in human rationality. For some centuries, cities in general have gone on getting bigger, adapting their modes of growth to technological and other change, and defying every sort of anathema, prediction of doom, and plea for common sense. William Cobbett, writing in the early part of the nineteenth century, referred to London, then little if any more populous than Montreal and its suburbs in 1956, as "the Great Wen". What epithet would he coin today? The complex attractions of the metropolis, with its multifarious demands for goods and services, its pool of skilled labour, and its variety of diversions and conditions of life, must never be under-estimated.

Developments in road transport and energy supply have, certainly, gone far to loosen the pattern of industrial, commercial and residential location. They have made decentralization more feasible for many lines of activity and they have brought welcome new industry to many small towns. But one of their major results has been to produce a new kind of big city—the Los Angeles kind. Sprawling, patchy, less a city perhaps than an urban region, this post-Henry-Ford phenomenon is yet a broadly recognizable entity, with many of the old urban problems and some new ones besides.

We conclude therefore that while opportunities to spur on real decentralization should not be missed, Canadians should expect their larger as well as their smaller urban agglomerations to double or more than double in size. This could be a very bad thing; but it need not be nearly as bad as it sounds, provided adequate resources of energy and intelligence are thrown into the task of recognizing, studying and influencing the forces of urban growth.

Aspects of Urbanization. We may, in appearance, have wandered away from our subject. But not in reality. To a large degree, the provision of housing and social capital requirements over the next quarter century will consist of the extension and revamping of the urban environment—that environment in which most Canadians will spend the greater part of their lives.

What sort of places are Canada's larger centres of population? We cannot, quite obviously, attempt to answer this question fully here. History, geography, and patterns of economic development have made each of Canada's bigger cities and urban areas importantly different, one from another. There is probably no single generalization or prescription for betterment that can be applied without qualification to them all. And yet there are features and problems common to many. Perhaps the easiest way of stating what some of these are is to describe, in a crude and oversimplified way, an imaginary but not altogether untypical Canadian metropolis—a place of some size, let us suppose, which has experienced an average share of post-war prosperity and growth.

To begin at the centre, there is the downtown business district, containing most of the larger stores, offices, banks, cinemas and public buildings. Signs of growth are evident: many of the buildings are new and larger than the ones they replaced. This district has expanded, both outward and upward. The daytime population density has increased, and the density of traffic has increased even more, reflecting a greater per capita ownership of motor vehicles. Many of the streets are now one-way, curb parking has been severely restricted or banned altogether, and some off-street parking facilities have been provided. All these developments have helped but they have not been enough to arrest an underlying tendency for the traffic situation to became gradually worse. One effect of this worsening has been to speed up the relative movement of commerce and industry to the suburbs. As a group, the downtown stores are doing a larger volume of business, but it is not as large a share as it used to be of the total business. A number of leading businessmen, together with the mayor, the city planner and others, are becoming seriously concerned over the future of the entire district.

Ringing the centre is a belt which contains some of the oldest and least desirable housing that the area has to offer. Looking back toward the centre, one sees in places a striking contrast of slum and skyscraper. Not all of the structures in the district are housing, and not all of them are in bad condition; indeed, the observer's principal impression is likely to be one of confusion and patchiness. Essentially incompatible land uses—an auto body shop, say, and a multi-family dwelling—huddle unhappily together. The old industrial and warehousing quarter and the coal and railway complex are all too close at hand. The proximity of these and of the downtown "core" makes for heavy flows of the noisiest and most earth-shaking sort of vehicular traffic. Like its structures, the district's people are a varied group: not all, by any means, resemble the conventional picture of slum-dwellers. Some, for example, are recent immigrants who could afford to live better, but who are economizing in order to build up a stake. As a whole, however, the district accounts for much more than an average share of the city's expenditure on social services and policing, as well as on fire protection.

As one moves further outwards, the houses, though still mostly quite old, become larger and less crammed together. Part of this ring is where the Victorian and Edwardian "carriage-trade" used to originate, and even today a measure of spaciousness and dignity remains. Some of the houses continue to be occupied by single families; others, however, have been converted into apartments and offices. Still others have been torn down—not always without protest—to make way for new apartment blocks. Young families have tended to move away to the suburbs, with the result that there are not so many children about as there used to be. Some of the schools actually have capacity to spare.

The next ring (no real Canadian city, of course, is ever this geometrically precise) consists of the erstwhile suburbs of the first four decades of the twentieth century. For the most part, these are now thoroughly built up and "citified", with a good range of municipal services and amenities: paved streets, curbs, sidewalks, street-lights, sewers, watermains, transit service, elementary and secondary schools (including two technical institutes), police and fire stations, parks and a couple of branch libraries. The pattern of streets is mostly a monotonous grid, none too well adapted to the steadily increasing traffic load it has to bear. Some of the wider streets combine the functions of urban arteries, highway connections, and secondary commercial districts. In the morning and evening rush hours, they fail to perform any of these duties satisfactorily.

From here on, the picture becomes much more varied. The density of population and of structures tends to thin out, but the thinning does not occur smoothly or evenly. Wherever there is a good highway, the built-up area ribbons out along it, generating local traffic and greatly reducing the road's capacity as a medium and long-distance artery. There is no regular or well-defined periphery. In some places, sub-division has leapfrogged clear into the open country. The structures are of many types and qualities. There are some semi-rural "Jerryvilles", havens from city taxes and building by-laws, where people have built or are building their own houses, in stages, on minimum budgets. There are streets of one-and-a-half-storey boxes, dating from the early post-war period; there are $30,000 ranch bungalows and split levels on half-acre lots; and there are many other categories of housing, including some apartment blocks. There is industry: long, low, often attractively landscaped plants, freed from the limitations of downtown congestion and land costs, and adapted to modern, mechanized methods of handling and production. There are shopping centres, and there are the usual gauntlets of gas stations, motels and hot-dog stands. All this, sprawled over a vast acreage which was once mainly devoted to market gardening and dairy and chicken farming, and which still is agricultural in spots.

As a whole, the fringe of "Metropolis" amounts to a major manifestation of post-war prosperity and growth. All the more striking, therefore, is the fact that much of it—the outermost part, especially—is decidedly poor in municipal amenities and services. In the 1920's, housing construction tended to follow the extension of at least the basic services: now the reverse seems almost more true. Much of the road and street mileage is rough and unpaved, without curbs or sidewalks. Ditches, as deep in places as a small child is high, are often the only storm sewers. For many householders, water and sanitation is a matter of individual wells and septic tanks, both of varying reliability. One large, outlying development boasts a community well, water-mains, sewers, and a "package" disposal plant. These worked admirably for a time: now, however, as the development grows, the basic water supply is giving cause for concern, while the disposal plant has become overloaded and is contributing to the pollution of a once pleasant stream. Throughout the fringe, schools, though new, are moderately to badly overcrowded. Public and fire protection exists, but is thinly spread. Transit service is reluctantly and sparsely provided, at a financial loss. Curiously enough, in view of the sprawling, land-prodigal nature of the area, there are large residential tracts in which little or no space has been left for parks.

One might think that these shortages were simply a result of the haste with which development had gone forward and that most of them would be corrected before very long. Unfortunately, one cannot be altogether sure of this. Even less can one be sure that when the shortages are made good, the total result will prove to have been an attractive and reasonably economic extension of Metropolis. Already it is becoming obvious that much of the fringe—there are honourable exceptions—has developed quite haphazardly, in such a way as to make the provision of proper municipal services far more difficult and expensive than it really need be. Moreover, for all that the fringe's location and character have been made possible by the automobile, not enough account has been taken of the needs and habits of that vehicle. Many of the street layouts and distributions of land use generate unnecessary vehicle movement or make insufficient separation between through and local traffic. This will become clearer as development continues and traffic increases.

A key fact about Metropolis is that, notwithstanding a large-scale annexation some years ago, more and more of the growth has been occurring outside the boundaries of the city proper. To illustrate some of the significance of this, we may point to "Edgetown", one of the less favourably situated fringe municipalities. In 1945, Edgetown was predominantly rural (and indeed still is nominally organized as a rural municipality). When the first new housing developments appeared, they were welcomed: the municipality's tax revenues were enhanced, and farmers' regrets at losing their land were mitigated by the prices they received for it (although some now fervently wish they had held out longer). As time went on, however, the council became painfully aware that for a municipality, urban housing is far from clear gain. The new residents began to demand good schools and a growing list of expensive services and amenities. When they first moved to what was then almost the country, they probably did not expect to need so much in the way of city-type facilities. But they changed their minds.

Now, with much of the best land already taken up, the municipal fathers are of the opinion that, housing shortage or no, they should have held back residential development and corralled more industry. A good, fat proportion of industrial assessment, yielding more in taxes than it received back directly in services, would have provided extra revenue with which to service the residential areas. "Industriburbia", another fringe municipality next door, acquired just such a proportion and is doing well out of it, an ironic feature of the situation being that not a few of Edgetown's residents settled where they did in order to be close to their jobs in Industriburbia (Metropolis city has a similar complaint).

However, it is too late now: Edgetown finds itself with comparatively high residential taxes, low residual borrowing powers (these are determined by the provincial government, largely on the basis of assessment), and a big backlog of capital works. Developers approaching the council with subdivision proposals get a cooler reception than they did formerly: their plans are only approved on condition that they undertake to provide paved roads, curbs, and sewer and water laterals. In effect, the financing of local improvements has been shifted from municipal debentures to National Housing Act mortgages. The citizens continue to pay, but as homeowners rather than taxpayers.

Some Edgetown residents have begun to inquire into the possibility of annexation to the city. The city authorities are not, on balance, enthusiastic. They would like, certainly, to exert more control over development in the fringe. For some time, they have been unhappy about the way things are going out there. They have been aware of definite adverse repercussions on the city; moreover, they have a suspicion that sooner or later, in one way or another, they will find themselves responsible for servicing much of the present fringe—for, as they put it, "straightening out the mess". But to take on Edgetown, or a large part of it, would be to take on a formidable backlog of capital expenditure and the city has a backlog of its own. The previous annexation has not yet been fully digested; there is still some vacant land within the city limits; two large new residential developments will need servicing. Work has just begun on a major expressway. A slum clearance and urban renewal project in the near-downtown district is being discussed. The city is being pressed to start treating its sewage instead of discharging it raw into the "Metropolis River". The city, therefore, is chary of annexing more territory just at present—particularly territory which, demonstrably, would cost more to service than it yielded in taxes at prevailing city assessments and rates. If the proposed annexation took in a larger area—if, for example, it included Industriburbia, together with "Manybucks Village", which has no industry (heaven forbid!) but which manages to support an excellent school and what its resident consider to be an adequate level of other services—then, perhaps, it would be more worth while—some day. Both Industriburbia and Manybucks would probably fight annexation. The city's case would have to be carefully prepared.

This, then, is Metropolis—fundamentally, an expanding social and economic entity, with numerous ties of interdependence between its principal parts—governmentally, something else again. As a mechanism, or an organism, it has serious defects. With the inestimable benefit of hindsight, one can see many ways in which its post-war expansion could have been better managed.

We are guilty of overdrawing, as well as of oversimplifying. Many large urban centres in Canada have managed to handle their growth problems a great deal better than our imaginary Metropolis. Some cities were fortunate enough to begin the post-war period with overextended boundaries inherited from previous booms, and with large tracts of land acquired through tax defaults. Advantage was taken of this circumstance to exert a close and farsighted control over new development. Nevertheless, many of the problems and situations which we have described will be familiar to numbers of Canadians. Examples of them, or of problems and situations very like them, exist today and can be readily identified. We would ask our readers to consider whether, on the assumption that our forecast of urban growth is broadly correct, the manner in which many Canadian centres have expanded and still are expanding should not be a subject of serious public concern.

Urban growth is a complex thing; it changes character over time and has a way of resisting or eluding most panaceas. We will not undertake to say either what form Canada's larger cities are likely to take by 1980, or what form they should take. Possibly a roughly concentric arrangement of Metropolis plus green belts plus well-planned and semi-self-sufficient satellites should be the ideal. Possibly something else will prove to be more in accord with the social and technological facts of life twenty-five years hence.

It does seem to us, however, that if the expansion of large urban areas is ever to be brought under an adequate degree of rational control, it will have to be done by governments or joint authorities exercising jurisdiction over all or most of their respective areas. Annexation, amalgamation, metropolitan federation as in Toronto—there are various alternatives. The essential is that the big problems, the area problems, be dealt with on an area basis. When numerous individual municipalities attempt to handle such problems without reference to any joint or overriding authority, it is virtually in the nature of things that they should get at cross-purposes with one another. It is also quite likely that when, as a means of resolving the impasse, some large-scale annexation or other form of union is proposed, one or more of the affected municipalities will balk, judging that it has more to lose than to gain. This, however, may only be true from a narrow, short-run point of view. The great majority of the area's citizens, including many residing in the recalcitrant municipality, may be in favour of going ahead. If such is the case, and if the entire matter has received adequate study and publicity, there would seem to be justification for the provincial government concerned to act in the interests of the majority.

It may be that the pattern of urban growth in some parts of Canada will become so extensive as greatly to exceed the scope of even the largest practicable municipalities or municipal federations. Already, there appears to be some need for regional planning bodies with wide geographical purviews than most which have hitherto existed and with responsibilities relating to agriculture and other non-urban interests. As time goes on, these bodies may have to be given additional powers and functions. How this is to be done while maintaining the essentials of local democracy may be one of the knottier problems of the future. [Pages 292–301.]

CARROTHERS, PLANNING IN MANITOBA (1956).

Community Planning Defined. In any discussion of community planning it is important in the light of the prevalent confusion of interpretation, to establish what is meant by the term "planning". That this is particularly desirable is clear. There are few other terms more misused and misunderstood, with the result that there are almost as many meanings attached to the word as there are persons who use it. Unless it is clearly defined for purposes of analysis there is a danger of falling into a confusion of political and philosophical concepts which it is not possible to resolve within the scope of this report.

There is nothing new or alarming in the concept of community planning: the process has been going on ever since earliest man determined to "descend from the trees" and establish permanent residence on the ground in company with others.

In the most basic sense there is an element of planning in the personal life of everyone. When one arises in the morning the sequence of getting dressed is "planned"; breakfast, "planned" before preparation, is eaten in a "planned" fashion; travel to one's place of work must be "planned", as must the day's work itself; recreational activities for the evening are "planned"; and one retires at a "planned" hour, to arise in continuation of this daily "planning". Furthermore, occasional major decisions such as the determination of one's life vocation are the subject of careful "planning" analysis and consideration.

This planning is carried out in order that an individual's physical and mental capacities may be utilized to their best advantage without jeopardizing the well-being of any one of them. The more intelligently it is applied, the more pleasant, satisfactory, and productive will be his existence. At times a conscious choice must be made, by an individual, among different courses of action. The relative advantages of such alternatives as continuing a poker game throughout the night or going to bed to ensure one's well-being the following day must be weighed consciously, or unconsciously, and the consequences of the decision accepted. For this, there must be sufficient "compensation" to justify whatever "cost."

In essence, community planning is as straightforward as this. The community will continue to exist and all the activities with which planning is concerned will go on, whether or not a conscious program is undertaken. The purpose of community planning is to make these activities easier, more useful and more equitable. As in the case of the individual, the more intelligently "community" planning is carried out, the more attractive and productive will be the community.

In the process of community planning it is often necessary to organize certain of the activities of the individuals for the greater benefit of the whole. On occasion, there are a few persons who are prepared to gain real or imagined benefits from activities which are detrimental to the general welfare of the community. Even though this minority is often the most vociferous about the curtailment of individual rights by community planning, the vast majority of the residents of a community benefit by this necessary restriction.

However, there is a real danger in over-simplifying community planning. This is apparent when its ramifications are properly understood. All too often the basic concept of community planning is lost sight of and planning *techniques* are confused with the fundamental *purpose* of the activity. Undoubtedly some of the objectives and some of the elements of planning are relatively simple, but those who would characterize the *total* process as being simple tend to make the mistake of treating these objectives and elements as if they alone were community planning. In reality they are only parts, albeit necessary ones, of the community planning process.

What is Meant by Community Planning. There are two common misconceptions of community planning, which it is important to emphasize at the outset, that do not constitute the activity. In the minds of many people and even of some civic authorities, community planning still means only the creation and the embellishment of a "city beautiful." It is true that public acceptance of the concepts of community planning was given strong support by the "city beautiful" movement of the late nineteenth and early twentieth centuries, but community planning must be a more fundamental and effective function than were activities initiated by that movement. Neither is community planning a "socialistic" subterfuge, designed to make the individual subservient to an all-powerful state. On the contrary, it is intended to make possible the freest choice of individual action, in order to permit the most efficient functioning of our "free enterprise" and democratic systems of social organization.

Having thus established emphatically what community planning is *not,* it is important for the purposes of following discussion to establish, in a positive fashion, what *is* meant by community planning.

Funk and Wagnalls' dictionary defines a plan: "a methodical arrangement of the various means or successive steps believed to be necessary or conducive to the attainment of some object; a formulated scheme for reaching some result." Thus, in a very general sense, community planning can be understood as involving a process for achieving a desired end. In practical terms it is necessary to identify both the "desired end" and the "process."

The fundamental objective of community planning is the conscious achievement of the best possible surroundings for carrying out the various activities of living of the individuals who make up the community. Few would take exception to the objective of community planning expressed in these terms. Agreement is not so easily reached as to exactly what conditions are necessary to make the community the best place possible. Nor is it as easy to establish how to go about accomplishing this end. Thus, while the ultimate objective of community planning is clear, the component short term objectives and processes are another matter. It is because of this duality of content that there is confusion as to the meaning of community planning.

In clarifying the meaning of community planning, two basic aspects may be recognized. The first is concerned with the physical surroundings of the community; the organization of land use, streets, buildings, recreation areas and the like. In this sense community planning seeks to achieve that physical environment that will best promote the economic, social and moral welfare of those persons living in the community. Essential to such an environment are both beauty and utility. The second aspect of community planning emphasizes the social and economic relationships and characteristics of the community; family life, recreational, cultural, political, and other group activities. In this sense, community planning attempts to make possible the accomplishment of such activities with the most convenience and efficiency. Closely related to these basic concepts and, in fact, forming an essential part of them, are the administrative activities through which they are brought into reality—the day-to-day decisions which so often determine the success or failure of community planning.

Obviously, the two fundamental concepts are closely interrelated. Any planning of the physical organization of the community will have little meaning without the social and moral objectives of the second aspect. At the same time, the accomplishment of such physical organization is necessary for these social and moral objectives to be fully effective. One cannot truly exist without the other. A hint of the significance of this interrelationship was given by Winston Churchill when, at the beginning of reconstruction in Britain at the end of the war, he suggested that we first shape our buildings and surroundings and afterwards they shape us. Historically, there has been a tendency to separate these two basic aspects of planning; to carry them on as isolated activities, or to overemphasize one to the detriment of the other. Where community planning has proved to be a truly successful endeavour, there has been a careful balance of the two.

Community planning, then, is not only a matter of physical design, but also involves considerations of the economic and social functions of the community. It is concerned with physical design—the relationship of buildings and the layout of streets and parks,—etc. as interrelated with the economic base of the community, its tax structure, and the provision of community services; with the economic and social ramifications of type and density of land use; and with sociological requirements of such things as education, health and public welfare.

The objectives of the physical aspect of community planning are more readily accomplished and do not impinge to as great an extent on what are generally considered to be individual prerogatives. Therefore this aspect has become more closely identified with the activities of community planning, with the result that techniques and tools of physical planning that have been evolved are more commonly accepted. Thus it is inevitable that any discussion of community planning as it is presently carried on must necessarily emphasize this aspect, but it is important to keep in mind that the other, though less tangible, objectives of economic and social community development must form an integral part of community planning. At times in this report this relationship is necessarily implicit rather than explicitly expressed.

The Planning Process. Whatever emphasis is placed upon the objectives of community planning, in application the activity must consist of a process of synthesis and coordination. The bits and pieces which constitute the mosaic of the community must be fitted together before any overall pattern of objectives can emerge. Although phases of activity can be recognized in the process, there is no clearcut division between them and to think of them as being separable is, again, an over-simplification.

First, before any technical planning activity can take place, it is necessary to identify the broad goals and objectives which it is wished to attain by means of community planning. Then all aspects of the present physical, economic, and social structure of the community, relevant to these goals, need to be inventoried, and past trends and processes which have brought about these conditions analysed. Following from such an analysis, predictions can be made concerning future trends and possibilities. It is then possible to consider various courses of future action and to establish procedures and programs to accomplish the broad objectives originally conceived. This will entail establishing definite short term objectives in order to give meaning to immediate activities. Finally comes the carrying out of such plans by means of administrative activity in the form of specific programs, regulation, and operation. But even when this point in the process is reached, the activity cannot end. By the very nature of a community, planning cannot be a static activity. External and internal forces are continually changing the circumstances and needs of any community. The preparation of plans will not halt that process. As conditions change, emphasis and direction in planning must also change: it is important that new problems be recognized and grappled with before they become serious or even beyond solution. An obvious illustration of such changing forces is contained in the effect which the widespread use of the automobile has had in the past and is still having on our communities. The effect on the processes of planning resulting from this single influence requires no elaboration here. As a consequence, community planning must be a continuous process, forever adapting itself to changing objectives, which result from changing needs and conditions.

True community planning is the result of the intelligent blending of all the various phases just described. No one of them alone can be considered as constituting the overall process. In the failure to recognizc this interdependence can be found the weakness of much community planning activity of the past: too often it has consisted of the preparation of a rigid plan for only the physical development of the community; economic and social conditions have too often been subordinate or ignored; and concern too rarely paid to the actual accomplishment of the plan or to necessary adjustments to suit changing conditions. Such planning is foredoomed to failure.

In very broad terms, then, community planning consists of the synthesis of the following phases:

1. The identification of long term and immediate goals and objectives by means both of legislation establishing community planning and of broad statements of policy;
2. The gathering and analysis of facts and trends concerning the community, relevant to these goals;
3. The preparation of operational plans and programs, with a full measure of citizen participation;
4. The carrying out of such plans by means of administrative activity. During every phase, it is necessary to reconsider, reanalyse, and redesign in order to adjust to continually changing conditions and circumstances . . .

The Orientation of Community Planning. Although sometimes it is necessary to subordinate certain personal interests for the greater general benefit of the community, the fundamental orientation of the community planning is toward the well-being of the individual. Therefore, planning activity should originate with the smallest unit of self-government. Furthermore, because of the flexible and continuing nature of the process, it cannot be separated from the local setting, and individuals charged with carrying out community planning activities need to be thoroughly acquainted with local conditions and problems.

The previous discussion of the planning process would suggest that community planning cannot successfully be carried out by any one person alone. To be successful planning cannot be an isolated activity: it must be truly cooperative and must receive the active support and participation of all persons concerned with local administration. Decisions of the elected council, the operational committees of council, of the executive head, and of municipal employees all have vital bearing on the effectiveness of community planning. In this sense, every local official must be a "planner." But there must also be a planner in a more specific sense.

In most cases the pressure of day-to-day activities gives local officials little time to consider the planning aspects of their immediate responsibilities. Not always is there an inclination to approach such duties in this way, nor is there always natural agreement on planning matters. Within most local governmental organizations there is a need for information and assistance which will enable responsible officials to coordinate their activities and relate them to long term objectives. Thus there is a need for some individual or group of individuals to be charged with the active responsibilities of community planning, who has an understanding of the ramifications of the planning process and who can facilitate the coordination of activities related to community development. But it is important to emphasize that this "planner", whether he be a municipal employee or a professional consultant, cannot alone accomplish community planning. While obviously he must carry out certain technical aspects of the planning process, his most significant responsibility should be to guide, assist, and coordinate activities of others. Consequently, technical planning should be carried out by officials responsible to the community through the elected council, who in turn should receive the additional advice, guidance and counsel of an advisory planning commission as a disinterested citizen group.

An analogy to the role of the professional community planner may be found in the functions of the general medical practitioner. There are many aspects of the human body concerning which the general medical practitioner is not an expert, yet he must be sufficiently competent in all the various specialties in order to diagnose the ailments of the individual. Once the ailment is known, then he has at his call various specialists who can help him deal with the particular difficulty. Also, in the field of preventive medicine, the general practitioner must be able to anticipate the dangers of illnesses and carry out preventive measures.

Similarly, while the community planner cannot be an expert in all aspects of the physical, social and economic life of the community, he must have sufficient awareness and understanding of all the related fields so that he can diagnose "urban ailments" and utilize the proper specialists to perform the necessary operations on the "urban body." Furthermore, he must be able to anticipate problems of community development likely to arise in the future and to make suggestions for preventing them or for reducing to a minimum their detrimental influence.

The role of the citizen in the responsibilities of community planning is a vital one. . . . Community planning can only be successful if it is carried out with the full support and cooperation of the people of the community. As with an individual, the character of the community is successfully moulded only by persons intimately associated with it and having a personal understanding of its strengths and weaknesses. Within the concept of democratic freedom of action, purely external authorities cannot successfully impose this activity: it must receive the wholehearted support of the local citizens of the community.

Nevertheless, in spite of this local bias of community planning, there are aspects of the function which cannot be handled on the local level alone. Many of the problems involved in planning affect other areas or overlap local jurisdictions and must be subject to the combined action of two or more local authorities. Moreover, there are activities carried on at the provincial level, such as highway development, which vitally affect local planning and which need to be coordinated with local activities. In these cases external authorities must actively participate in the planning function. . . .

PARLIAMENTARY DEBATES

United Kingdom. House of Commons. 1943. Volume 393. Col. 403

The Prime Minister (Mr. Churchill): I beg to move, "That a Select Committee be appointed to consider and report upon plans for the rebuilding of the House of Commons and upon such alterations as may be considered desirable while preserving all its essential features."

On the night of 10th May, 1941, with one of the last bombs of the last serious raid, our House of Commons was destroyed by the violence of the enemy, and we have now to consider whether we should build it up again, and how, and when. We shape our buildings and afterwards our buildings shape us. Having dwelt and served for more than 40 years in the late Chamber, and having derived very great pleasure and advantage therefrom, I, naturally, would like to see it restored in all essentials to its old form, convenience and dignity. I believe that will be the opinion of the great majority of its Members. It is certainly the opinion of His Majesty's Government and we propose to support this resolution to the best of our ability.

There are two main characteristics of the House of Commons which will command the approval and the support of reflective and experienced Members. They will, I have no doubt, sound odd to foreign ears. The first is that its shape should be oblong and not semi-circular. Here is a very potent factor in our political life. The semi-circular assembly, which appeals to political theorists, enables every individual or every group to move round the centre, adopting various shades of pink according as the weather changes. I am a convinced supporter of the party system in preference to the group system. I have seen many earnest and ardent Parliaments destroyed by the group system. The party system is much favoured by the oblong form of Chamber. It is easy for an individual to move through those insensible gradations from Left to Right but the act of crossing the Floor is one which requires serious consideration. I am well informed on this matter, for I have accomplished that difficult process not only once but twice. Logic is a poor guide compared with custom. Logic which has created in so many countries semi-circular assemblies which have buildings which give to every Member, not only a seat to sit in but often a desk to write at, with a lid to bang, has proved fatal to Parliamentary Government as we know it here in its home and in the land of its birth.

The second characteristic of the Chamber formed on the lines of the House of Commons is that it should not be big enough to contain all its Members at once without over-crowding and that there should be no question of every Member having a separate seat reserved for him. The reason for this has long been a puzzle to uninstructed outsiders and has frequently excited the curiosity and even the criticism of new Members. Yet it is not so difficult to understand if you look at it from a practical point of view. If the House is big enough to contain all its Members, nine-tenths of its Debates will be conducted in the depressing atmosphere of an almost empty or half-empty Chamber. The essence of good House of Commons speaking is the conversational style, the facility for quick, informal interruptions and interchanges. Harangues from a rostrum would be a bad substitute for the conversational style in which so much of our business is done. But the conversational style requires a fairly small space, and there should be on great occasions a sense of crowd and urgency. There should be a sense of the importance of much that is said and a sense that great matters are being decided, there and then, by the House.

We attach immense importance to the survival of Parliamentary democracy. In this country this is one of our war aims. We wish to see our Parliament a strong, easy, flexible instrument of free Debate. For this purpose a small Chamber and a sense of intimacy are indispensable. It is notable that the Parliaments of the British Commonwealth have to a very large extent reproduced our Parliamentary institutions in their form as well as in their spirit, even to the Chair in which the Speakers of the different Assemblies sit. We do not seek to impose our ideas on others; we make no invidious criticisms of other nations. All the same we hold, none the less, tenaciously to them ourselves. The vitality and the authority of the House of Commons and its hold upon an electorate, based upon universal suffrage, depends to no small extent upon its episodes and great moments, even upon its scenes and rows, which, as everyone will agree, are better conducted at close quarters. Destroy that hold which Parliament has upon the public mind and has preserved through all these changing, turbulent times and the living organism of the House of Commons would be greatly impaired. You may have a machine, but the House of Commons is much more than a machine; it has earned and captured and held through long generations the imagination and respect of the British nation. It is not free from shortcomings; they mark all human institutions. Nevertheless, I submit to what is probably not an unfriendly audience on that subject that our House has proved itself capable of adapting itself to every change which the swift pace of modern life has brought upon us. It has a collective personality which enjoys the regard of the public and which imposes itself upon the conduct not only of individual Members but of parties. It has a code of its own which everyone knows, and it has means of its own of enforcing those manners and habits which have grown up and have been found to be an essential part of our Parliamentary life.

The House of Commons has lifted our affairs above the mechanical sphere into the human sphere. It thrives on criticism, it is perfectly impervious to newspaper abuse or taunts from any quarter, and it is capable of digesting almost anything or almost any body of gentlemen, whatever be the views with which they arrive. There is no situation to which it cannot address itself with vigour and ingenuity. It is the citadel of British liberty; it is the foundation of our laws; its traditions and its privileges are as lively to-day as when it broke the arbitrary power of the Crown and substituted that Constitutional Monarchy under which we have enjoyed so many blessings. In this war the House of Commons has proved itself to be a rock which an Administration, without losing the confidence of the House, has been able to confront the most terrible emergencies. The House has shown itself able to face the possibility of national destruction with classical composure. It can change Governments, and has changed them by heat of passion. It can sustain Governments in long, adverse, disappointing struggles through many dark, grey months and even years until the sun comes out again. I do not know how else this country can be governed other than by the House of Commons playing its part in all its broad freedom in British public life. We have learned—with these so recently confirmed facts around us and before us—not to alter improvidently the physical structures which have enabled so remarkable an organism to carry on its work of banning dictatorships within this island and pursuing and beating into ruin all dictators who have molested us from outside.

MR. TINKER (Leigh): Will the right hon. Gentleman allow me—

THE PRIME MINISTER: I think I might be allowed to proceed. I shall not be very long, and then perhaps my hon. Friend can make his own speech. His Majesty's Government are most anxious and are indeed resolved to ask the House to adhere firmly in principle to the structure and characteristics of the House of Commons we have known, and I do not doubt that that is the wish of the great majority of the Members in this the second longest Parliament of our history. If challenged, we must take issue upon that by the customary Parliamentary method of Debate followed by a Division. The question of Divisions again relates very directly to the structure of the House of Commons. We must look forward to periods when Divisions will be much more frequent than they are now. Many of us have seen 20 or 30 in a single Parliamentary Sitting, and in the Lobbies of the Chamber which Hitler shattered we had facilities and conveniences far exceeding those which we are able to enjoy in this lordly abode. I am, therefore, proposing in the name of His Majesty's Government that we decide to rebuild the House of Commons on its old foundations, which are intact, and in principle within its old dimensions, and that we utilise so far as possible its shattered walls. That is also the most cheap and expeditious method we could pursue to provide ourselves with a habitation.

I now come to some of the more practical issues which are involved. . . .

FULLER, "HUMAN PURPOSE AND NATURAL LAW." 1956. 53 *Journal of Philosophy* 697. "These forms [of social order: contract, adjudication, the majority principle, and the three-strike, four-ball rule] are generally viewed only in their most obvious aspect, that is, as means to the realization of human ends. But they are also themselves ends, in two closely related senses. They are ends in the sense that, although we make them, they help to make us what we are, man's dependence on society being what it is. Any particular economic system not only serves to satisfy antecedent wants, but also generates its own peculiar pattern of human wants. Secondly, any form of social order contains, as it were, its own internal morality. . . ."

DEWEY, HUMAN NATURE AND CONDUCT (1922)

. . . In fact, ends are ends-in-view or aims. They arise out of natural effects or consequences which in the beginning are hit upon, stumbled upon so far as any purpose is concerned. Men *like* some of the consequences and *dislike* others. Henceforth (or till attraction and repulsion alter) attaining or averting similar consequences are aims or ends. These consequences constitute the meaning and value of an activity as it comes under deliberation. Meantime of course imagination is busy. Old consequences are enhanced, recombined, modified in imagination. Invention operates. Actual consequences, that is effects which have happened in the past, become possible future consequences of acts still to be performed. This operation of imaginative thought complicates the relation of ends to activity, but it does not alter the substantial fact: Ends are foreseen consequences which arise in the course of activity and which are employed to give activity added meaning and to direct its further course. They are in no sense ends *of* action. In being ends of *deliberation* they are redirecting pivots in action. . . . [p. 225]

A mariner does not sail towards the stars, but by noting the stars he is aided in conducting his present activity of sailing. A port or harbor is his objective, but only in the sense of *reaching* it not of taking possession of it. The harbor stands in his thought as a significant point at which his activity will need re-direction. Activity will not cease when the port is attained, but merely the *present direction* of activity. The port is as truly the beginning of another mode of activity as it is the termination of the present one. The only reason we ignore this fact is because it is empirically taken for granted. We know without thinking that our "ends" are perforce beginnings. But theories of ends and ideals have converted a theoretical ignoring which is equivalent to practical acknowledgment into an intellectual denial, and have thereby confused and perverted the nature of ends. . . . [pp. 226–7]

Even admitting that lying will save a man's soul, whatever that may mean, it would still be true that lying will have other consequences, namely, the usual consequences that follow from tampering with good faith and that lead lying to be condemned. It is wilful folly to fasten upon some single end or consequences which is liked, and permit the view of that to blot from perception all other undesired and undesirable consequences. It is like supposing that when a finger held close to the eye covers up a distant mountain the finger is really larger than the mountain. Not *the* end —in the singular—justifies the means; for there is no such thing as the single important end. . . . [pp. 228–9]

Politicians, especially if they have to do with the foreign affairs of a nation and are called statesmen, almost uniformly act upon the doctrine that the welfare of their own country justifies any measure irrespective of all the demoralization it works. Captains of industry, great executives in all lines, usually work upon this plan. But they are not the original offenders by any means. Every man works upon it so far as he permits himself to become so absorbed in one aspect of what he is doing that he loses a view of its varied consequences, hypnotizing his attention by consideration of just those consequences which in the abstract are desirable and slurring over other consequences equally real. Every man works upon this principle who becomes over-interested in any cause or project, and who uses its desirability in the abstract to justify himself in employing any means that will assist him in arriving, ignoring all the collateral "ends" of his behavior. It is frequently pointed out that there is a type of executive-man whose conduct seems to be as non-moral as the action of the forces of nature. We all tend to relapse into this non-moral condition whenever we want any one thing intensely. In general, the identification of the end prominent in conscious desire and effort with *the* end is part of the technique of avoiding a reasonable survey of consequences. The survey is avoided because of a subconscious recognition that it would reveal desire in its true worth and thus preclude action to satisfy it—or at all events give us an uneasy conscience in striving to realize it. Thus the doctrine of the isolated, complete or fixed end limits intelligent examination, encourages insincerity, and puts a pseudo-stamp of moral justification upon success at any price.

Moralistic persons are given to escaping this evil by falling into another pit. They deny that consequences have anything at all to do with the morality of acts. Not ends but motives they say justify or condemn acts. The thing to do, accordingly, is to cultivate certain motives or dispositions: benevolence, purity, love of perfection, loyalty. The denial of consequences thus turns out formal, verbal. In reality a consequence is set up at which to aim, only it is a subjective consequence. "Meaning well" is selected as *the* consequence or end to be cultivated at all hazards, an end which is all-justifying and to which everything else is offered up in sacrifice. The result is a sentimental futile complacency rather than the brutal efficiency of the executive. But the root of both evils is the same. One man selects some external consequence, the other man a state of internal feeling, to serve as the end. The doctrine of meaning well as *the* end is if anything the more contemptible of the two, for it shrinks from accepting any responsibility for actual results. It is negative, self-protective and sloppy. It lends itself to complete self-deception. . . . [pp. 229–31]

Ends are, in fact, literally endless, forever coming into existence as new activities occasion new consequences. "Endless ends" is a way of saying that there are no ends—that is no fixed self-enclosed finalities. . . . [p. 232] [The paging is that of the Modern Library edition, 1930.]

WOOTTON, FREEDOM UNDER PLANNING (1945)

. . . In the background of any discussion of the compatibility of economic planning and cultural freedom, there lurks a fundamental philosophic issue. Is it in fact possible to plan for indeterminate cultural ends? The real cultural freedom demands not merely variety, but actual indeterminacy, of cultural ends. Such freedom is not achieved, unless economic planning sets people free to do and say things of their own choosing—things which are not known before-hand to, much less decided by, the planners. That would imply a fundamental difference between the political state and all other forms of association which involve organized action. The political state, where there is real cultural freedom, is no more than a convenient instrument for promoting the joint and several purposes of its members, and has no specific, determinate purpose of its own beyond this. A trade union exists to create better conditions of employment for its members, a church to promote the worship of God, a dramatic society to produce, if not to appreciate, drama; but the state exists—for what? To make it possible for men and women to live their own lievs in their own way. . . . [p. 23]

The problem of planning for freedom thus resolves itself into the problem of determinate planning for indeterminate cultural ends. Stated thus it sounds insoluble. Once again, however, a problem which is theoretically insoluble in the limiting case, turns out to be quite tractable in the concrete form in which it is likely to crop up in practice. We need not despair of the possibility of combining useful planning and cultural freedom, provided that certain conditions are observed.

The first condition is the obvious one that such planning must know where to stop. . . . [p. 26]

As Dr. Mannheim has remarked, it is possible to "co-ordinate the time tables of the different railway lines without controlling the topics of conversation inside the carriages. . . . [p. 27]

The second condition of successful economic planning for indeterminate cultural ends is that the planners should show a nice discrimination in their methods. . . . [p. 32]

GEDDES, CITIES IN EVOLUTION (1915)

. . . Our town plans are thus not merely maps but also symbols, a notation of thought which may concretely aid us towards bettering the towns of the present, and thus preparing for the nobler cities of a not necessarily distant future. It may, again, be said, each of these cities is a logical dream: the city is not so bad as your Inferno, nor is it ever likely to be as good as your Utopia. So far admitted. Every science works with ideal concepts, like the mathematician's zero and infinity, like the geographer's directions—north, south, east and west—and can do nothing without these. True, the mathematician's progress towards infinity never gets him there, nor do the geographer's journeyings, the astronomer's search attain the ultimate poles. Still, without these unattainable directions, these cardinal points, who could move from where he stands, save to sink down into a hole? So far then from losing ourselves . . . these extremes are what enable us to measure and to criticise the city of the present, and to make provision for its betterment, its essential renewal. . . .

[This passage is taken from the 1949 revised edition.]

SHAKESPEARE, AS YOU LIKE IT

JAQUES: All the world's a stage
And all the men and women merely players:
They have their exits and their entrances;
And one man in his time plays many parts,
His acts being seven ages. At first the infant,
Mewling and puking in the nurse's arms.
And then the whining school-boy, with his satchel
And shining morning face, creeping like snail
Unwillingly to school. And then the lover,
Sighing like furnace, with a woeful ballad
Made to his mistress' eyebrow. Then a soldier,
Full of strange oaths and bearded like the pard,
Jealous in honour, sudden and quick in quarrel,
Seeking the bubble reputation
Even in the cannon's mouth. And then the justice,
In fair round belly with good capon lined,
With eyes severe and beard of formal cut,
Full of wise saws and modern instances;
And so he plays his part. The sixth age shifts
Into the lean and slipper'd pantaloon,
With spectacles on nose and pouch on side,
His youthful hose, well saved, a world too wide
For his shrunk shank; and his big manly voice,
Turning again toward childish treble, pipes
And whistles in his sound. Last scene of all,
That ends this strange eventful history,
Is second childishness and mere oblivion,
Sans teeth, sans eyes, sans taste, sans everything.

MUMFORD, "PLANNING FOR THE PHASES OF LIFE"

Liverpool 1949. 20 Town Planning Review 5

Almost a generation ago Dr. Joseph K. Hart, in the Regional Planning number of the *Survey Graphic* (May 1925), pointed out that city planning was mainly conceived in terms of a single phase of life: that of adults without family responsibilities. He noted the significance of the old saying, that the crowd on the boulevards never grows old: namely, that the boulevard, by reason of its purpose and design, draws to it the same age groups, following the same interests, pursuing the same ends.

In spite of that timely reminder, the city planner has not yet come to realize the full nature of his task: the provision of an environment suited to every phase of life and growth, from infancy to senescence. Too much of our recent planning up to now, certainly in the United States, has been concentrated on adult life: indeed, on the adult life of mainly the masculine half of the population, and on only so much of this life as is concerned with business, industry, administration, traffic, transportation. Even in handling adults, the city planner has omitted important areas of activity.

The purpose of this paper is to make a preliminary exploration of the territory Dr. Hart's original question opened up. In its brief compass, it seeks to suggest how a consciousness of the phases of life may perhaps alter the planner's attitude toward both the methods and the ends of planning; and even lead to a reconsideration of the design of certain units, like playgrounds, where administrative convenience has caused us, at least in America, to concentrate upon forms whose outward order reflects mainly their inner sterility. If a consciousness of the human life cycle does nothing else, it may at least serve as a check list of requirements: enabling one to spot the weak places in a seemingly admirable design.

First Phase: Infancy. Let us begin with the newborn infant and inquire what planning does for him, till the time he is ready for school. This is partly, to begin with, a matter of housing from the very hour of birth onward; and whereas in every country, during the last generation, there has been a steady movement to provide for childbirth in hospitals, we now begin to suspect that these are not the best conditions for a normal delivery and for the earliest days of an infant's life. The experience of the Peckham Health Center, and elsewhere, seems to show that there is a balance of advantages, very strong on the psychological side, in favor of home confinement: yet even where housing conditions are as good as they are in a British housing estate of pre-1940 standards, childbirth itself tends to disrupt the household and cause temporary overcrowding.

At this point the planner might well consider if there is not, in terms of planning, an intermediate solution: midway between the expensive heavily equipped hospital, ready for every emergency, and the normal household, capable of handling minor illnesses, but without the space or equipment for handling childbirth. Such a solution would be in the nature of a small nursing home: established as an integral part of a unit of say, 250 to 500 families: attached perhaps to a local medical clinic, which needs so many of the same facilities. Confined in such a place, a mother would have access to her other children, could be visited easily by her husband, and could be looked after by relatives or neighbours, except where special care was required: an important economy. Such a solution would restore the missing human element, an element lost through what Dr. Richardson, the Victorian hygienist, once mordantly described as the 'warehousing of disease.'

I shall return to this matter of scale, simplicity and intimacy when I come to old age.

In planning further for the infant's life the first care must be to give the mother peace and respite from the too constant pressure of household duties: absence of tension in her is one of the conditions for a happy and affectionate relation between the two. At no period can even the most limited household be wholly a self-contained unit: people need their neighbours, in the emergencies of life, certainly, but also in their daily routine; and that need should not be confined, by inept planning, to those dire moments when an air-raid brings people compulsively together in a common shelter, or causes them to queue up for their daily food. Even in housing estates that are laid out at twelve families to the acre—perhaps one should say especially there—there is often a lack of common meeting places for the mothers, where, on a good day, they might come together under a big tree, or a pergola, to sew or gossip, while their infants slept in a pram or their runabout children grubbed around in a play pit. Perhaps the best part of Sir Charles Reilly's plans for village greens was that they provided for such common activities: as the planners of Sunnyside, Long Island, Messrs. Stein and Wright, had done as early as 1924.

There should be something snug, intimate, protective about this order of planning, if it is to correspond to the needs of the very young, who have perhaps not altogether forgotten the environment from which they originally emerged. Little children—perhaps even up to the age of ten—need hiding places and cubby-holes: walls and bushes, if not caves and pits, perform their function in the open. Above all, the little ones, especially those under six, must get the feel of their environment: they need sand, gravel, stones, boards, branches, billets, for their play activities; and to prevent these materials from being put to destructive uses, the most elemental type of playground might well be placed in a shallow, well-drained sand pit, surrounded by a stone or brick wall, around which their mothers could sit: this area, in turn, should be walled off from the rest of the precinct, and reached through a gate whose latch would be well above a child's reach. Such an area might have a great stone or concrete animal in the middle, which children could climb upon: even an abstract shape, such as the sculptor Noguchi has designed for older playgroups, might be used, particularly if it provided little caves, hiding places. Once built, the chief administrative problem arising from such play areas is that of policing them at night against their misappropriation by cats: but a charged wire on the wall would probably handle that difficulty. People who love gardens and haven't too much space for them tend to begrudge a child the freedom he needs in digging and grubbing; so that a collective way of handling the early play of children, solitary though it so often is, would, at the very moment it brought the mothers together and prepared them for other forms of co-operation, also give more liberty to the child.

Second Phase: The School Child. The transition from home to school is a critical one for the child; and we perhaps have minimized too glibly the shock and inner disorder that comes, not only from leaving the protective oversight of the mother, but also from the change of physical scale from the single dwelling to what is often, from the child's point of view, a gigantic complex building: awful in its impersonal immensity. There are places like California, where even in big cities like San Francisco the elementary school has been kept relatively small, and where the unit, in the newer schools, is the classroom with its own play-area, not wholly absorbed into the bigger structure. But perhaps the best way to effect the transition is through a nursery group in the neighborhood unit; and to make this possible, I for one would willingly forego wholly professional care in exchange for the more amateurish part-time treatment by partly trained mothers, working for a nominal reward. Planning cannot, of course, anticipate too many new social arrangements: but it may occasionally suggest them and point to the appropriate social arrangement. There are housing developments in Zurich where, if my memory serves, this has long been done.

With the child's walk to school comes a new problem in planning: that of making his walk an amusing and—in an unconscious way—an educative one. Among the many things that damn the habits of suburban segregation and class zoning we have practised so widely in the United States, not least perhaps is the blank dullness of the walk to school. Fortunately, a child will often pick unsuspected treasures out of a rubbish heap: a puddle, left by a poor drainage system will become a lake, and a branch, twisted off in a storm, will become a war club; but there is nothing like a trim, orderly, defensively respectable suburban environment to discourage a child's imagination—or for that matter an adult's. When I lived on the campus of Stanford University, I had for choice, in my walks to the university, either the sight of the trimly tailored front lawns of the prosperous houses, or the rear service lanes that ran parallel, with their outbuildings and occasional clutter, their unexpected glimpses of carpenter sheds and garden tools, of a motor car being repaired or a heap of plant clippings waiting to be carted away; and more often than not, I would prefer the rear alley, precisely for all these little hints of life, activity, transition, which the placid visual arts of suburbia did their best to suppress or politely disguise. Animation, though at the price of a little disorder, is more exhilarating, even esthetically, than frozen respectability.

For a child to get a true sense of the world that he lives in, he should at least have a glimpse, on his walk to school, either of nature plain, as at Radburn, or of man's work, in the form of workshops, minor industrial operations, markets. The activities that serve a neighborhood's life should not be too severely segregated: they should be at least within a school child's walking distance; and running errands and fetching should be part of his experience of life. This is an injunction perhaps less needed in Europe than in America, where middle class canons of respectability and the reliance on motor cars have effected a fantastic separation of commercial areas from residential areas. But if a quarter or a third mile is the normal radius of play—so that a play field beyond will, till adolescence, not be frequently used, distances of the same order will hold for other activities.

In our efforts to provide space for the formalized play of children in cities, we have forgotten, especially in new communities, the role of spontaneous play. The endeavour to take children off the dangerous street, in crowded urban areas, has made us too easily content with creating equivalent asphalted areas, that lend themselves to a most limited round of activities: slides, swings, or—in America—jungle-gyms, apparatus for danger-free climbing, safe, easily kept up, but from the child's standpoint, often inhibiting. Meanwhile, in the bombed out areas in London, we have discovered a new kind of playground: more to the fancy of children above the age of six: old foundations, opened up cellars, rock and rubble for clambering over, sometimes a pool of undrained water for dabbling in or sailing an impromptu boat.

Such playgrounds have a fascination for the child that never becomes dulled. Growing up in New York, almost half a century ago, I still had the run of open lots, with rocky uneven surfaces, where the boys of my street roasted apples and potatoes; and where we played games impossible on pavement or street. Bushes and parapets may be used to separate such informal play areas, visually, from the rest of the community; but a certain untidy plentitude of facilities—old boards, stones, boxes—may increase their value for play. They are the urban equivalent for the more primeval type of wilderness which so delights the heart of children. Such areas would afford a channel where destructive impulses could innocently run off and lose their force: countered, often in the same area, by the urge to build and construct. Perhaps the only special contribution to such areas would be to design them in depth: grading down some of the hazards, or, by digging and quarrying, creating artful opportunities for adventure.

Third Phase: *Adolescence*. With adolescence, the neighborhood unit no longer is the sole focus of a child's activities. Going to a secondary school, even in a relatively small community, he meets children from other neighborhoods: in the organized games of adolescence, he needs broad playing fields for cricket or baseball, football or soccer: he not merely visits back and forth within the city, but begins to go on hikes and picnics and outings in the surrounding region. At some point in the development of our civilization the idea that has long been brewing in the minds of philosophers and educators, of Fourier and Goethe, of Schreber and William James and Rosenstock-Huessy, the idea of work-armies, will finally become implanted in our educational systems. Just as there is no way of making a parent assume the responsibilities of parenthood, like giving him and her the active care of a child, so there is no way of making citizens like turning some of the care of the community over to the young: in such fields, an hour of practice is worth a week of book-learning.

Now perhaps the best place to begin with the constructive tasks of work armies is the care and upkeep of our common environment. The initiative of the Civilian Conservation Camps, instituted by the Roosevelt administration during the depression, need not be limited to tree planting and fire-protection activities in rural or wilderness areas. Actually, if we are to afford the parks and park-strips and gardens we envisage for the new type of open planning, we shall find the cost of their upkeep prohibitive unless we can make it a service of citizenship: voluntary if possible, compulsory if necessary. Otherwise, the eventual unkemptness of the great public spaces that are being laid out in the new towns of England for example, may cause a swing back to more constricted and petrified open areas, which have some prospects of remaining comely and decent, if not actively pleasant. The planting and gardening and policing of open areas might well be the task of the next generation of adolescents: one of many moral equivalents of war that a peace-minded generation will have to devise.

In some ways, this task would be a preparatory one; for its chief beneficiaries would be the youths themselves, at their next phase of growth: that marked by courtship. The period of late adolescence, when sexual energies run high and direct outlets are relatively few, is a trying and difficult one for both boys and girls. Often it is a period of inner disruption, whose very turmoil should be counterbalanced by the wonder and beauty of the environment. If prolongation of infancy was the first mark of Man's ascent, the prolongation of courtship, with all its rich by-products in art, literature, music and religion, represents a further stage. This elaboration of the erotic impulse also intensified it, adding meaning and emotional color to purely instinctual manifestations. In the open country, lovers have little difficulty in finding places of seclusion that match their mood, but the lack of such walks and retreats in our cities, even in our parks, makes courtship too often either brief or furtive, harassed or embarassed to the point of desperation.

Helen Thomas, the wife of the poet, left a memorable picture in *As It Was* of urban courting, at the end of the last century, in a common that had some of the romantic attributes of concealment, but much of the planning that has been done since, certainly in America, has been conceived as if openness and publicity were the sole qualities to be embodied in design. What lovers need are accessible places where they can easily lose themselves and get away from the visible presence of others. The maze, that favorite device of Baroque planners, certainly served that purpose; and Frederick Law Olmsted, in designing Central Park in New York deliberately made The Ramble, with its irregular topography, a place to get lost in; with the admirable result that it is perhaps the once place well adapted to love making in the whole city of New York. If planners were conscious of the phases of life, they would not be so blank about the need of late adolescence for places of secluded beauty, accentuating and expanding, and yet tempering, their erotic needs; and enriching, with happy visual images, their erotic rewards.

Maturity: *Work Phase*. Along with the increasing division of labor, in modern times, has gone another process: the intensification and segregation of work. Both the farm worker and the manual worker, in an earlier day, worked for longer hours than their modern counterpart; but work itself went on in an environment which had many other aspects and uses, within sight of the family, for example, and often with the cooperation, in different degrees, of all its members. There were no walls, visual or functional, between business, domesticity, education. The age of specialization, concentrating on mechanical efficiency alone, has robbed working life of some of its esthetic and human dimensions. Here as elsewhere in modern cities a deliberate attempt must be made to re-unite these severed aspects of life, which create, almost automatically, radical divisions and disharmonies in the personality; but the way to achieve this is not to go back to an earlier primitive form, but to create a new form, as different from the workshop-household as from the grimly isolated business or factory district of Victorian pride.

Seeking some such integration, the authors of *Communitas* have suggested that houses and factories should be united around 'city squares.' As Messrs. Philip and Percival Goodman have described it, this would seem to restore a wilfully archaic pattern of close association; whereas the problem is to create a modern equivalent. The equivalent, I suggest, is to introduce into the industrial zones of our towns, either by renovation or by new design, the domestic and social functions appropriate to the working day: accessible playgrounds, for example, for physical recreation during the lunch hour and at other intervals; a diversity of dining halls to replace the canteen; meeting halls and committee rooms, usable not by a single plant but by the whole area, for conducting the political affairs of both the management and the worker; school buildings and museums, so that vocational preparation and part time study of a non-vocational nature might be encompassed with a minimum waste of time and effort. There are single industrial plants, like that Cadbury complex at Bournville, where these functions—and medical services as well, have been incorporated in the working structure: what we need now is to organize a whole industrial quarter on the same principles, with further functional and visual clarification.

The same principle holds, of course, for business quarters. Everyone knows the immense recreational value of even a small patch of ground such as St. Paul's Churchyard or the happy social effect of Princes Street in Edinburgh, with the shopping area thrown on one side and the park on the other: but for all that too few business districts are planned with any recognition of the need for recreation space near at hand; in fact, one of the first marks of 'progress,' in America at least, is the cutting down of trees on the main shopping street. The great contribution of Haussmann's new boulevards in Paris was their unification of business and recreation and social entertainment: perhaps nowhere else have the functions of an adult been kept so fully unified as in the heart of Paris. The mechanical segregation of functions practised in the interest of purely mechanical efficiency does not produce an interesting social life or fully animated personality. That is why so many of the desirable things in a community usually occur only through a breakdown or a lapse in its normal functions.

Maturity: Domestic Phase. When our society provides a young couple with a dwelling house and a garden, placed among a thousand other dwelling houses, we feel that we have accomplished much for family life, and we have. When such homes can be achieved, without absorbing too much of the annual family income, a long step is taken toward rehabilitating family life; for who can doubt that Victorian domesticity, among the upper half of the middle classes, was encouraged by all the comforts and conveniences, the sense of internal space and peace, that brought the Victorian father back nightly to his snug household; with the reading circle, the games, the sentimental and amatory singing, that attended, so often, the family gathering. But mere domestic closeness is not enough; the ingrown family tends to become self-absorbed, isolationist, exclusive, hostile to the further development of its members. Something more, therefore, is required for the success of family life: companionship and common interests outside the home, first on the part of husband and wife, then such companionship as may take in, directly or indirectly, the younger members of the family. Here is a place where the city planner must invent public ways of performing economically what the old, three-generation bourgeois family once privately encompassed.

Not the least contribution of the Peckham Health Center is, beyond doubt, the opportunity that it gives a family for having a common meeting place, outside the confines of its home, where the varied age groups, now so often thrust apart by the variety and intensity of individual interests, can become united again, or at least go about their work or play within view of the other members. This business of being 'within view,' though not necessarily in active association, is one of the community-binding attributes that we have too often neglected in modern planning: it is what enhances, for many of us, the value of musical performance in a concert hall, as opposed to its reception by radio in an individual home, though technically the second performance may be as perfect as the first. This visible being together, again, is one of the attractions of a crowded street. Perhaps the most elementary definition of a community is that it is a collection of people who live within sight of each other: in a country hamlet, even to see a neighbor's light at night is to have a special sense of security and sociability. For parents and children to be constant companions is far from advisable; but there is much more likely to be good family relations if each have some idea of what the other is doing—instead of having their activities so separated that they live in different worlds.

In reaction against formidable conditions of overcrowding and physical disorganization, modern planners are naturally tempted into a uniformity of openness which may undermine the social sense as much as brutal congestion. Here Mr. Winston Churchill's wise words about the new House of Parliament building, that it should not be big enough to hold all it members at one time, applies to many other activities. One of the things to be said in favor of a compact shopping center, like the medieval market place or like one of the new markets in Los Angeles, as opposed to the interminable old-fashioned shopping avenue is that it concentrates and so multiplies the occasions for informal meeting and greeting: minimal social activities which, like the formal calls of an older day and order, tend to renew neighborly and friendly relationships. It is better to risk occasional overcrowding in such compact areas than to plan them so spaciously that they will hold the maximum conceivable load without discomfort—which means that they will be physically time-wasting and socially bleak on normal occasions.

The Settlement House, the Community Center, and the Health Center are all worthy attempts to find some point of focus for special activities outside the home. In America, the tendency is to place most of the functions served in such centers into the neighborhood school or the secondary school; for most adult activities occupy parts of the day when the school is not used by children, and auditoriums, swimming pools, gymnasiums, and workshops need not be kept inviolate for scholastic use, provided they are restored to working order before the children arrive next morning.

But the adult life needs, to begin with, an even simpler form of meeting place: as simple as a room capable of holding fifty people seated, where neighborhood discussions may take place, and where occasional social festivities—on a scale too populous for the home—may take place. One of Patrick Geddes's happiest suggestions, in his report on Dunfermline, was for the setting apart of a handsome historic house to be rented at a nominal fee by any family in town, where a big party might be held. (Even a single large room with appropriate kitchen facilities would meet this need.) In Brooklyn, such houses, run by commercial caterers, used to be available and filled an important function in the domestic life of the middle class in that very home-minded city. In a community of five thousand people, I had rather see five of these rooms, functioning in each precinct than have the same facilities concentrated in a single community center. In England, where the pub has a solid place in the community, there is no reason why such community rooms sometimes should not, for simplicity of administration and service, be attached to—though perhaps not fully incorporated into—the pub itself.

Maturity: Phase of Social Interaction. The phase I would deal with under this head could be more properly called citizenship, if we meant by that term the art of living together in a city. The city, when it fully performs its functions, is a representative of the world at large: containing a diversity of products, people, organizations, associations, customs, and beliefs not ordinarily found in any single environment of a more specialized order. Whereas a village, properly, emphasizes likenesses and kinships—and the city in its neighborhood aspect does likewise—the city as a developed form must emphasize—and reconcile—varieties, differences, even antagonisms. A good plan will multiply the spontaneous occasions for mingling and mixing.

In our time, two forces have broken down the capacity of the city to foster the maximum interplay of capacities and functions among its members: that interplay which is necessary to personal growth, and without which men become more solitary, brutish, and ungovernable. One of these forces is the tendency of our mechanical inventions, from the railroad to modern radio and television, to disperse the members of the community over a wider and wider area: a large part of their activities consists in doing business with people they never meet, listening to voices they never see, participating as members of an invisible audience in activities that were once inconceivable in isolation. Actually, these instruments bring into working partnership thousands and even millions of men: multiplying the fact of sociality. But at the same time the sense of sociality becomes dim —until it is restored temporarily, in a gross form, for example, in the crowds in a football stadium.

The other force that has attenuated the social functions of the city, particularly in great conurbations, is the tendency toward segregation: a tendency accentuated by the seemingly progressive function of zoning, which in the United States, often segregates classes and income groups as well as races, into identifiable quarters, whose members have relatively little to do with those of higher or lower status. As a result, each group, each class, each social caste lives in a world which, in both its architectural and its social arrangements, denies the manifold cooperations of all human communities. In the United States, a good deal of our technically most progressive planning, like the great parkways and viaducts that tempt to further suburban expansion, merely break down what traces still remain of a common life at the center; while the suburban pattern of loose open planning in turn increases, even in a country teeming with motor cars, the difficulties of getting together. As a result social isolationism tends to increase directly with area and population.

Now from the standpoint of citizenship, the office of planning must be to maximize the instruments of positive and negative cooperation. The planner must provide visual aids for the realization of the true nature of the common life today: reminders that must be made dramatically effective precisely because, without the intervention of planner and architect, they would in such a large degree remain invisible. Further a good plan will multiply the occasions of an accidental and unpremeditated character, such as those that take place in compact market areas and in public eating places. Though the department store at Welwyn Garden City, is no doubt, out of scale with the community itself, it has, in combination with its great dining-room, provided an indispensable point of focus for the common life, otherwise neglected in the original plan for the community. Thinking in these terms, the planner will multiply the internal spaces of the city, where people may meet for diverse purposes, marketing, eating, drinking, talking, debating, instead of merely multiplying the occasions for escaping from sight and contact with other people or of massing together to perform a single function. A plan that does not further a daily inter-mixture of people, classes, activities, works against the best interests of maturity. In our efforts to do away with the unseemly congestion and disorder of the overgrown city, we must beware of swinging so far in the other direction that we loosen the social bond.

Maturity: Personal Phase. Througout this analysis, I have been indicating the necessity for developing public forms for activities which, among people of imagination and means, have hitherto been performed privately: activities which one now seeks to distribute throughout the whole community. Emerson stated the case for the public assumption of household duties long ago, when he pointed out that he needed books, but did not want to become a librarian, that he valued pictures, but he did not want to be a curator of paintings. Even the relatively wealthy members of the community today cannot content themselves with having only a moiety of the real wealth that is available to them as members of a community.

This rule holds true, not only for those functions which must be socialized, but for those that must be de-socialized: solitude for example. One of the marks of maturity is the need for solitude: a city should not merely draw men together in many varied activities, but should permit each person to find, near at hand, moments of seclusion and peace. The function of withdrawal, so far from being segregated as in the medieval cloister, must be recognized as a daily human need. One of the great attractions of a crowded center, like Westminster, is the ease with which a solitary walker may lose himself in the maize of little streets that twist and dodge behind the main thoroughfares. In new communities, smaller in scale, with lower density, one must use art to accomplish the same results. In the parks that bound neighborhood units, for example, one might leave wider graded paths on the outside, to tempt the sociable, while any footpaths would thread through the inner area. It should not be necessary to pass beyond the boundaries of a community in order to find, for a few minutes or a few hours, an adequate retreat. Too much of our thinking, both in modern architecture, with its open plan, and in modern city design, has been of an entirely extraovert order: admirable for public and social occasions, but life-defeating for those introverted moments when withdrawal, brooding, innerness, require some special sustenance from the physical environment. Just to the extent that we break down the privacy of the traditional wall and the hedge in domestic planning, when we exchange the free standing upper class suburban villa for the worker's terrace house, must we replenish the opportunity for privacy and solitude in the collective plan of the city.

Final Phase: Senescence. Perhaps no part of life has been so neglected by our civilization—and so by the planner himself—as old age. In the course of the last half century, throughout the Western World, the old three generation family has been reduced to the two-generation family: indeed, sometimes, in an effort to maintain spurious standards of youth on the part of the parents, afraid to acknowledge their years, to a one-generation family. The sign of this change has been the increase in the number of separate households, even at a time when the birthrate was drastically falling off. But while the number of old people has increased in every progressed country, thanks to the improvements in hygiene and medical care, no commensurate effort has been made either to build new old people's homes, on the old pattern, or to find some new and better means of providing for their care. Old age pensions are no compensation for their increasing social destitution. Unwanted in the small home, even when they are loved, and too often unloved because they are unwanted, the aged find their lives progressively curtailed and meaningless, while their days are ironically lengthened.

In the general replenishment of family life, which is one of the objectives of good planning, the restoration of the aged to a position of dignity and use becomes one of our principal aims. How shall it be brought about? The first thing to realize is that, if we can not, and probably should not, try to restore the three generation family in its more patriarchial form, we can and should restore the three generation community: this mixture of age groups is as essential to good life as the mixture of economic and social classes. Now there are many important social functions that the aged, so long as their mental faculties are not impaired, may perform to everyone's benefit: the women are capable of participating in the household arts, sewing, mending, knitting, crotcheting; old men, though sometimes too slow in pace to earn a full day's wages, can nevertheless remain effective gardeners, doers of odd jobs and repairs, caretakers and overseers. No community can get along without such minor but important services. Moreover, the aged have a natural affiliation with the young, which often works out reciprocally: as experienced baby-tenders and patient 'sitters' their presence would relieve the parents of the awful confinement of twenty-four hour attendance upon the young.

Because of their immense usefulness here, no community should be considered well-laid out, and no housing adequate, unless it provides special accommodation for the old. A small one-story unit, of from five to ten couples, or a score of individuals, not segregated in any way from the rest of the housing development, is a far more adequate provision for the aged till they need continuous professional care in a nursing home. Such units should be placed, preferably, near playgrounds or schools or neighborhood markets, for the old want most of all the reassuring presence of life, to overcome the loneliness and the growing sense of alienation or frustration that age itself brings with it. Like the admirable home for the aged at Wythenshawe, the quarters for the aged should be on ground level and minimize the efforts and dangers of climbing steps; but unlike that home, the aged, instead of facing inward upon themselves, should be diverted by the bustle and activity of the life outside. Housed under such conditions the aged could be near their families, near enough at hand for affectionate supervision or occasional nursing; best of all, capable of participating without a sense of being burdensome, in the lives of their children or their neighbors; useful, blessed with a purpose in life, even as their days narrow, as is possible under no other condition. Whether run publicly or privately, whether for the hale or for the cripple and the infirm, in need of special nursing service, the important part about the adequate design of accommodations for the old is that they should avoid segregation and institutionalization: even the ministrations of visiting nurse should not diminish the friendly, intimate scale of these arrangements. Here again the principle of being 'within view' is an important one to re-establish, as the basis of a score of little intimacies, adventures, stimuli, that even the magnificent housing quarters, if too segregated or too grandiose in scale, do not provide.

All this suggests that an organic conception of city planning, dealing with all the phases of life as well as all the functions of a community, may devise many solutions that have heretofore been ignored in a more specialized approach. In restoring balance within the urban community, one must think of establishing balance in time through inter-relationship between the phases of life, for each plateau of life has its own special requirements, which can be well served only when the co-ordinate needs of other age groups are taken into account. What perhaps is most needed, as a canon of such design, is the return to the human scale: to units of manageable size, to an order at once visible to the naked eye, to a conception of community less as a maze of organization to be treated by wholesale provisions, than as a constantly varying combination of a multitude of associative activities, varying in intensity and duration, and progressing through the life-cycle, from birth to death.

[Reproduced with the kind permission of the author and the editor of the *Town Planning Review.*]

PARLIAMENTARY DEBATES

United Kingdom. House of Lords. 1962. Vol. 242. Col. 989, 991–6

The Earl of Albemarle rose to ask Her Majesty's Government what basic principles they consider should sanction high-rise building silhouettes in urban landscapes. . . .

LORD SILKIN (5.12 p.m.): My Lords, before the noble Earl answers this Question, I should like to intervene for a very short time. First, I would thank the noble Earl for having put this Question, which is of great interest to all Londoners particularly, and for trying to elicit a reply from Her Majesty's Government, if they will give one. I think it is particularly opportune to ask this Question, because there is no doubt that high buildings, particularly in London, are on the increase, and it is right that we should try to get some declaration of principle as to what kind of high buildings are in the public interest and what are not.

We are very much behind other countries in regard to high buildings. Noble Lords will know that in the United States, in South America, and in many other countries, they are prevalent and are growing much faster than they are here. In some of what I may call the twilight countries, countries that are emerging into modern civilisation, the number of high buildings is regarded as a symbol of their prosperity, civilisation, and so on. We are very much behind, but, as I have said, our numbers are increasing. The question about which we have to make up our minds is whether we should encourage this increase in high buildings or resist it. There is no doubt that high buildings offer a considerable number of advantages. It makes it possible, if the building is properly sited, to provide much better-lighted accommodation than in buildings of traditional height, and there is no interference from these buildings with views of other buildings. There is less over-shadowing, and it adds interest—I stress that—in areas which are generally comprised of low-lying buildings.

The noble Earl has referred to a report of the London County Council on this question. In that report, the London County Council take the view that it is not desirable to have high buildings in areas which are generally of traditional height. There I absolutely disagree. Having lived in two of the areas that are referred to as areas of traditional low buildings, I would say that one of the disadvantages of those areas is that they are dull and uninteresting, and that a few high buildings would add considerable interest, certainly for the residents. At one time in Dulwich there was the Crystal Palace, which was a landmark and of great interest to us all. We deplored the day when that building came down. Another advantage is that it is accepted that by putting up a high building you do not increase the volume of the building. I think that would be undesirable. This is not a means of getting more accommodation; it is merely a means of using the space in rather a different way. By putting up a high building of the same cubic content as a traditional building, you have more land available around the building, which could be a very desirable thing, especially if the site is sufficiently large.

I have read and considered very carefully the report of the London County Council which sets out the policy they will adopt in the future. I am bound to say that I rather deplore it. The report seems to me, and is indeed, avowedly biased against high buildings, just as are the noble Lord, Lord Bossom, and, I gather, the noble Earl who has just spoken. The London County Council and the noble Lords say that unless there is an advantage in high buildings it should not be allowed—in other words, putting the onus of proof on those who want to put up high buildings. I think that is an unfair onus to impose upon a developer. We have to recognise that this question of the erection of high buildings, once you have introduced all the necessary safeguards—safeguards against over-shadowing, blocking out desirable views, interference with views, particularly of public buildings, and so on—is largely a matter of taste. Some noble Lords may not like high buildings. I personally do, but I should not wish, therefore, to impose high buildings on the noble Lord, Lord Bossom, or on the noble Earl. And I hope they would not impose their views on me.

We are living in an age when individual developers carry out development on their land, and are permitted to do so, subject to their complying with the normal town planning requirements, which, of course, contain in design all the safeguards for the community which can be desired. But I think it is quite wrong that any one generation should wish to impose its particular taste upon the community as a whole; a taste which may be unsatisfactory, which may not even be the taste of the public as a whole and may be based on experience in the past.

Some of the most beautiful buildings in the world to-day are those which, at the time they were built, were regarded as ugly and undesirable; and fashions do change even in taste. I believe there are people to-day who regard the Albert Memorial as a very beautiful building. When I was a boy it was regarded as the last word in ugliness. I do not know what the noble Lord, Lord Bossom, who is going to follow me in addressing your Lordships, thinks about the Albert Memorial. I would say the same about the Central Hall, Westminister. I have heard that praised most highly in the last year or two. Nobody would have dared to stand up in public and praise the Central Hall, Westminster, fifteen years ago, but to-day there are many people to be found who would regard such buildings as very delightful. I believe that the Houses of Parliament, when they were first built, were not regarded as the last word in beautiful architecture. Indeed, it would have been difficult to justify the design of the Houses of Parliament in that they are mock Gothic and represent no contemporary kind of architecture at all. But today we regard the Houses of Parliament as one of the most beautiful buildings in the world.

All these things are matters of taste: and I think it is wrong, therefore, solely on the grounds of aesthetics to impose one's ideas of these high buildings. By all means, let us satisfy ourselves on proper requirements of siting, views, ease of fire-fighting and overshadowing, and see that all the necessary protective by-laws, and all the rest of it, are complied with. But I think that when it becomes a matter of taste we must be very sure before we interfere.

Of course, I do not wish to go right to the extreme of my argument—I hope I never shall in any argument—but one has to have regard to the nature of the materials that are used. Obviously, in a building of that kind one has to use the right kind of material, which will harmonise with the area, but I take that for granted. I take it that the real objection, if there is one, regarding high buildings is to the fact that they are high and not in accordance with the tradition of building in this country; and one has to make out a case—as this report says, an extremely powerful case—to establish that a building of traditional height is less desirable than the high building one wants to put up. I think that is a wrong onus and a wrong emphasis, and my own view is that it would be far better to do what this report says has already been done: to let London grow and to develop in a natural way, perhaps somewhat fortuitously and casually, and so long as each building is right and good so will the total emerge.

I want to conclude by referring to a conception of Venice. Venice is a city which has grown over many centuries. Buildings of different generations and different styles, by different architects, have all helped to build up Venice; yet the total ensemble of Venice is one of the most beautiful in the world, and the reason is that each building is harmonised with every other. There has been no attempt to suppress any particular design. It has not been suggested that because many buildings are Gothic, therefore only Gothic buildings must be permitted. Every building is a gem of its own. I would submit that if we can put up attractive buildings which are of attractive materials, the right materials, not interfering with the views, prospects or with other buildings, we should allow a great deal of freedom in the erection of high buildings. I hope the Government will not seek to impose any kind of dead level or standard or create a difficult onus on people to make it impossible for them to provide these high buildings.

There is one more thing I want to say, and that is that this report says how many high buildings there are in London; and if the standards that the London County Council lays down today had been approved, I doubt whether any of these buildings would have been put up at all; I doubt whether any one of these high buildings satisfies the standards which the London County Council themselves lay down. And yet they have given planning permission for the erection of every one of them. I think it is time we cleared our minds over the subject, and I am very glad indeed that the noble Earl has put this Question so that we may have an opportunity of discussing it and heading the views of the Government.

LORD MOLSON (5.26 p.m.): My Lords, I should have been surprised to hear the speech that we have just listened to coming from any Member of the Opposition Front Bench, but my surprise became astonishment when this speech fell from the lips of the noble Lord, Lord Silkin, the father and drafter of the Town and Country Planning Bill, and the Minister who was responsible for commending that Bill to the House of Commons, and who successfully put it upon the Statute Book. The logic of this argument is that since taste varies so completely it is impossible to have any criterion, that anything which interferes with the free enterprise of even the most irresponsible developers should be eyed with the greatest distrust. He covered himself by saying that he did not want to push his argument to extreme, but I hardly know how the argument could have been more extreme than the form in which he put it forward. . . .

ANONYMOUS COUNCILLOR. 1953. Bedale. Yorks. England: "The charm of Bedale's High Street lies in its higgledy-piggledeness and you can't plan higgledy-piggledeness."

FULLER, "AMERICAN LEGAL PHILOSOPHY AT MID-CENTURY." 1954. 6 Journal of Legal Education 457. "[A] serious gardener . . . would set about observing trees under various growing conditions so that he would learn how to help a tree be what it is."

HANS BLUMENFELD. 1957. Lac Beauport, Quebec: "You can't make an old shoe."

JULIAN WHITTLESEY. 1957. Lac Beauport, Quebec: "You can't design a second-hand car."

KOSMOS KAGOOL. 1962. Toronto: "In a democracy you get what you deserve."

ARISTOTLE, POLITICS
(Jowett translation)

First among the materials required by the statesman is population; he will consider what should be the number and character of the citizens, and then what should be the size and character of the country. Most persons think that a state in order to be happy ought to be large; but even if they are right, they have no idea what is a large and what a small state. For they judge of the size of the city by the number of the inhabitants; whereas they ought to regard, not their number, but their power. A city too, like an individual, has a work to do; and that city which is best adapted to the fulfilment of its work is to be deemed greatest. . . . And even if we reckon greatness by number, we ought not to include everybody, for there must always be in cities a multitude of slaves and sojourners and foreigners; but we should include those only who are members of the state, and who form an essential part of it. The number of the latter is a proof of the greatness of a city; but a city which produces numerous artisans and comparatively few soldiers cannot be great, for a great city is not to be confounded with a populous one. Moreover, experience shows that a very populous city can rarely, if ever, be well governed; since all cities which have a reputation for good government have a limit of population. We may argue on grounds of reason and the same result will follow. For law is order, and the good law is good order; but a very great multitude cannot be orderly: to introduce order into the unlimited is the work of a divine power—of such a power as holds together the universe. Beauty is realized in number and magnitude, and the state which combines magnitude with good order must necessarily be the most beautiful. To the size of states there is a limit, as there is to other things, plants, animals, implements; for none of these retain their natural power when they are too large or too small, but they either wholly lose their nature, or are spoiled. For example, a ship which is only a span long will not be a ship at all, nor a ship a quarter of a mile long; yet there may be a ship of a certain size, either too large or too small, which will still be a ship, but bad for sailing. In like manner a state when composed of too few is not, as a state ought to be, self-sufficing; when of too many, though self-sufficing in all mere necessaries, as a nation may be, it is not a state, being almost incapable of constitutional government. . . . Clearly then the best limit of the population of a state is the largest number which suffices for the purpose of life, and can be taken in at a single view. Enough concerning the size of a state.

Much the same principle will apply to the territory of the state: every one would agree in praising the territory which is most entirely self-sufficing; and that must be the territory which is all-producing, for to have all things and to want nothing is sufficiency. In size and extent it should be such as may enable the inhabitants to live at once temperately and liberally in the enjoyment of leisure. . . .

It is not difficult to determine the general character of the territory which is required (there are, however, some points on which military authorities should be heard); it should be difficult of access to the enemy, and easy of egress to the inhabitants. Further, we require that the land as well as the inhabitants of whom we were just now speaking should be taken in at a single view, for a country which is easily seen can be easily protected. As to the position of the city, if we could have what we wish, it should be well situated in regard both to sea and land. This then is one principle, that it should be a convenient centre for the protection of the whole country: the other is, that it should be suitable for receiving the fruits of the soil, and also for the bringing in of timber and any other products that are easily transported. . . . [Book VII, chs. 4, 5.]

We have already said that the city should be open to the land and to the sea, and to the whole country as far as possible. In respect of the place itself our wish would be that its situation should be fortunate in four things. The first, health—this is a necessity; cities which lie towards the east, and are blown upon by winds coming from the east, are the healthiest; next in healthfulness are those which are sheltered from the north wind, for they have a milder winter. The site of the city should likewise be convenient both for political administration and for war. With a view to the latter it should afford easy egress to the citizens, and at the same time be inaccessible and difficult of capture to enemies. There should be a natural abundance of springs and fountains in the town, or, if there is a deficiency of them, great reservoirs may be established for the collection of rainwater, such as will not fail when the inhabitants are cut off from the country by war. Special care should be taken of the health of the inhabitants, which will depend chiefly on the healthiness of the locality and of the quarter to which they are exposed, and secondly, on the use of pure water; this latter point is by no means a secondary consideration. For the elements which we use most and oftenest for the support of the body contribute most to health, and among these are water and air. Wherefore, in all wise states, if there is a want of pure water, and the supply is not all equally good, the drinking water ought to be separated from that which is used for other purposes.

As to strongholds, what is suitable to different forms of government varies: thus an acropolis is suited to an oligarchy or a monarchy, but a plain to a democracy; neither to an aristocracy, but rather a number of strong places. The arrangement of private houses is considered to be more agreeable and generally more convenient, if the streets are regularly laid out after the modern fashion which Hippodamus introduced, but for security in war the antiquated mode of building, which made it difficult for strangers to get out of a town and for assailants to find their way in, is preferable. A city should therefore adopt both plans of building: it is possible to arrange the houses irregularly, as husbandmen plant their vines in what are called 'clumps'. The whole town should not be laid out in straight lines, but only certain quarters and regions; thus security and beauty will be combined.

As to walls, those who say that cities making any pretension to military virtue should not have them, are quite out of date in their notions; and they may see the cities which prided themselves on this fancy confuted by facts. True, there is little courage shown in seeking for safety behind a rampart when an enemy is similar in character and not much superior in number; but the superiority of the besiegers may be and often is too much both for ordinary human valour and for that which is found only in a few; and if they are to be saved and to escape defeat and outrage, the strongest wall will be the truest soldierly precaution, more especially now that missiles and siege engines have been brought to such perfection. To have no walls would be as foolish as to choose a site for a town in an exposed country, and to level the heights; or as if an individual were to leave his house unwalled, lest the inmates should become cowards. Nor must we forget that those who have their cities surrounded by walls may either take advantage of them or not, but cities which are unwalled have no choice. . . . [Book VII, ch. 11.]

The city of Hippodamus was composed of 10,000 citizens divided into three parts—one of artisans, one of husbandmen, and a third of armed defenders of the state. He also divided the land into three parts, one sacred, one public, the third private:—the first was set apart to maintain the customary worship of the gods, the second was to support the warriors, the third was the property of the husbandmen. . . . [Book II, Ch. 8.]

NOTE. For a short account of town planning by the Greeks, see Stewart, *A Prospect of Cities* (1952), Chapter 1, City State, pp. 4-20.

BIBLIOGRAPHY. Literature on planning is voluminous and a much more extensive bibliography was attempted in the revised temporary edition of this casebook. (See pages 297–301.) The following titles are suggested either because they are very good longer works, or as good as can be expected in much shorter space. Books that have been quoted from elsewhere in this volume are not listed in these notes on bibliography.

Lewis Mumford, *The Culture of Cities* (1938) and *The City in History* (1961), are encyclopedic, and well worth critical study. Jane Jacobs, *The Death and Life of Great American Cities* (1962), contains the germ of a good idea, but it need not have taken 452 pages to say it, and her interpretation of other planners' views is better postponed until the other planners' views have been examined at first hand. Another book with a good idea, but written in quite unnecessary jargon, is Kevin Lynch, *The Image of the City* (1960), attractively printed, with good illustrations. Among the short books the best by far is Thomas Sharp, Town Planning (1940), an out of print Penguin. Another short account is Patrick Abercrombie, *Town and Country Planning* (3rd ed., 1959). Thomas Sharp, Frederick Gibberd and W. G. Holford, *Design in Town and Village* (1953), is an excellent short account, well illustrated, published by H.M.S.O. Every student of planning should read Ebenezer Howard, *Garden Cities of Tomorrow* (1898, reprinted 1946), but since it makes little mention of the motor car (which is more understandable in Howard than it is excusable in Jacobs, writing in 1962) Wilfred Owen, *The Metropolitan Transportation Problem* (1956), should be regarded as a necessary complementary piece, although it lacks the charm of the earlier work. Speaking of charm, Steen Eiler Rasmussen, *Towns and Buildings* (1951), is a beautiful book, and also worth reading. Of the historical books, Siegfried Giedion, *Space, Time and Architecture* (3rd ed., 1956) is a well illustrated account of cities in history. Christopher Tunnard, H.H. Reed, *American Skyline* (1955), available in paperback edition, is a more specialized history. Jacob Spelt, *The Urban Development in South-Central Ontario* (1955), is even more specialized.

CHAPTER 3

PLANNING AND LAND VALUE

The value of land does not express the reward of production . . . It is not in any case the creation of the individual who owns the land; it is created by the growth of the community. HENRY GEORGE

1. THE RIGHT TO COMPENSATION

EXPERT COMMITTEE ON COMPENSATION AND BETTERMENT: FINAL REPORT
United Kingdom. 1942. Cmd. 6386

20. . . . For convenience we refer in this Chapter of our Report to built-on land as developed land and to land not built-on as undeveloped land. Agriculture is a highly important form of land development, but the terms as we have defined them are now in common use and their meaning is well understood.

22. It is clear that under a system of well-conceived planning the resolution of competing claims and the allocation of land for the various requirements must proceed on the basis of selecting the most suitable land for the particular purpose, irrespective of the existing values which may attach to individual parcels of land. A coastal area, a beauty spot, the fringe land round existing towns, may all have a high building value for residential or industrial development, yet it may be in the national interest to forbid building whether for reasons of amenity or because the soil is highly fertile and suited for agriculture. Similarly, it may be in the national interest to prevent some of our existing large cities from expanding further. This will involve sterilisation from building of much land which, if unrestricted, would continue to command a high price for development.

Action such as this is practically impossible under the existing planning legislation on account of the liability placed on the local planning authority for compensating all the landowners concerned for deprivation of development value. In this connection two well-recognised facts must be borne in mind. The first is that potential development value created by the expectation of future development is spread over many more acres than are actually required for development in the near future or are ever likely to be developed. The second is that wisely imposed planning control does not diminish the total sum of land values, but merely redistributes them, by increasing the value of some land and decreasing the value of other land. These principles of "floating value" and "shifting value" respectively are of prime importance in connection with the amount of compensation payable, both in respect of the imposition of restrictions on the use of land and also in respect of its acquisition, for the result is not only that compensation has, in the aggregate, to be paid for in excess of the real loss but that payment has to be made for land values that are not really destroyed at all.

Floating Value

23. Potential development value is by nature speculative. The hoped-for building may take place on the particular piece of land in question, or it may take place elsewhere; it may come within five years, or it may be

twenty-five years or more before the turn of the particular piece of land to be built upon arrives. The present value at any time of the potential value of a piece of land is obtained by estimating whether and when development is likely to take place, including an estimate of the risk that other competing land may secure prior turn. If we assume a town gradually spreading outwards, where the fringe land on the north, south, east and west is all equally available for development, each of the owners of such fringe land to the north, south, east and west will claim equally that the next development will "settle" on his land. Yet the average annual rate of development demand of past years may show that the *quantum* of demand is only enough to absorb the area of one side within such a period of the future as commands a present value.

24. Potential value is necessarily a "floating value," and it is impossible to predict with certainty where the "float" will settle as sites are actually required for purposes of development. When a piece of undeveloped land is compulsorily acquired, or development upon it is prohibited, the owner receives compensation for the loss of the value of a probability of the floating demand settling upon his piece of land. The probability is not capable of arithmetical quantification. In practice where this process is repeated indefinitely over a large area the sum of the probabilities as estimated greatly exceeds the actual possibilities, because the "float," limited as it is to actually occurring demands, can only settle on a proportion of the whole area. There is therefore overvaluation. . . .

25. Unquestionably the greatest obstacle to really effective planning has been the fear on the part of planning authorities of incurring indefinite liabilities in the matter of compensation if the extreme step of forbidding development is taken and the almost unanimous opinion expressed in the evidence submitted to us is that the factor of "floating value" plays a large part in the unwillingness of authorities to incur claims for compensation. . . .

Shifting Value

26. The public control of the use of land, whether it is operated by means of the existing planning legislation or by other means, necessarily has the effect of shifting land values: in other words, it increases the value of some land and decreases the value of other land, but it does not destroy land values. Neither the total demand for development nor its average annual rate is materially affected, if at all, by planning ordinances. If, for instance, part of the land on the fringe of a town is taken out of the market for building purposes by the prohibition of development upon it, the potential building value is merely shifted to other land and aggregate values are not substantially affected, if at all. Nevertheless, the loss to the owner of the land prohibited from development is obvious, and he will claim compensation for the full potential development value of his land on the footing that, but for the action of the public authority in deciding that development should not be permitted upon it, it would in fact have been used for development. The value which formerly attached to his land is transferred and becomes attached to other land whose owners enjoy a corresponding gain by reason of the increased chance that their land will be required for development at an earlier date.

A similar shift of values takes place if part of the land is taken out of the market for building purposes by being purchased for a public open space or other public purpose.

27. In theory, in view of these considerations, it should be possible to

compensate all owners whose land is decreased in value by restrictions on development out of a "betterment" fund levied from owners the value of whose land is thereby increased. No scheme has, however, yet been devised under which in actual practice compensation and betterment can be equated in this way. In ascertaining the betterment there immediately arises the difficulty the amount by which a particular parcel of land has increased in value as the direct consequence of the restriction imposed on the other land and not from other causes....

Summary

28. These, in outline, are the factors which, as regards undeveloped land in particular, constitute the key to the difficulties of compensation and betterment which have hampered planning. If land with potential development value is purchased by a public authority or is restricted against development or certain forms of development, compensation has to be paid for individual loss of land values which have not in fact been destroyed but which have only shifted to other land. In addition, where the land belongs to a number of owners, the aggregate of values claimable by individual owners when separately assessed, owing to the factor of "floating value," greatly exceeds the real loss of the claimants taken as a group. On the other hand betterment cannot be collected to any substantial degree in respect of the shifted values because it is impossible to say with certainty whether, and to what extent, a given land value is attributable to a given cause.

30. The requirements and difficulties of replanning the developed areas ... differ considerably from those applicable to undeveloped land and the interference with existing users and existing buildings is necessarily on a much larger scale. As in the case of undeveloped land, however, it is apparent that if the improvement or rebuilding of cities is to be carried out on the basis of a scientifically prepared plan, the planning authority must be in a position to proceed with a single aim of ensuring utilization of the land to the best national advantage. An examination of the Town Planning maps of some of our most important built-up areas reveals that in many cases they are little more than photographs of existing users and existing layouts, which, to avoid the necessity of paying compensation, become perpetuated by incorporation in a statutory scheme irrespective of their suitability or desirability; for even if the scheme provides for certain alterations of existing users and declares certain buildings to be out of conformity with the scheme, the present legislation preserves the right of the owner to rebuild within two years of demolition or destruction and to continue the previous user unless he is compensated for any loss or limitation of his rights.

31. At present a proper allocation of land for the various uses required may involve either restriction of an owner's rights of user or public acquisition of his entire interest. As we have shown in paragraph 26, the effect of such an action is not to decrease the total demand for land. It will increase the competition for the available land within the area and will usually result in expansion on the perimeter or diversion of demand to other areas. Nevertheless, the compensation or purchase price payable for the land of each individual owner has to be determined by reference to its most profitable potential use. Moreover the price of land in the big towns and cities runs into very high figures. The effect is usually to make it impossible for the local authority concerned to carry out desirable improvements or impose any effective control of user with the limited resources at their command....

In addition to having to compensate on the basis of the value attaching to the land, acquisition in developed areas involves payment for the value of existing buildings which need to be demolished, and compensation to a trader for his removal expenses and for disturbance to his business. All these items have to be purchased before the land can be used for the purpose required in the interests of good planning.

32. Bfore proceeding further, it is necessary to consider the general principles underlying payment of compensation for State interference with the use of private property.

Ownership of land involves duties to the community as well as rights in the individual owner. It may involve complete surrender of the land to the State or it may involve submission to a limitation of rights of user of the land without surrender of ownership or possession being required. There is a difference in principle between these two types of public interference with the rights of private ownership. Where property is taken over, the intention is to use those rights, and the common law of England does not recognize any right of requisitioning property by the State without liability to pay compensation to the individual for the loss of his property. The basis of compensation rests with the State to prescribe. In the second type of case, where the regulatory power of the State limits the use which an owner may make of his property, but does not deprive him of ownership, whatever rights he may lose are not taken over by the State; they are destroyed on the grounds that their existence is contrary to the national interest. In such circumstances no claim for compensation lies at common law. Cases exist where this common law principle is modified by statute and provision is made for payment of compensation. The justification is usually that without such modification real hardship would be suffered by the individual whose rights are affected by the restrictions, but there is no right to compensate unless that right is either expressly or impliedly conferred by statute.

33. For the last hundred years owners of property have been compelled to an increasing extent, without compensation, to comply with certain requirements regarding their property such, for example, as maintaining or improving its sanitary equipment, observing certain standards of construction, providing adequate air space around buildings and streets of sufficient width. The underlying reason for such provisions is, obviously, that compliance with certain requirements is essential to the interests of the community and that accordingly the private owner should be compelled to comply with them even at cost to himself. All the restrictions, whether carrying a right to compensation or not, are imposed in the public interest, and the essence of the compensation problem as regards the imposition of restrictions appears to be this—at what point does the public interest become such that a private individual ought to be called on to comply, at his own cost, with a restriction or requirement designed to secure that public interest? The history of the imposition of obligations without compensation has been to push that point progressively further on and to add to the list of requirements considered to be essential to the well-being of the community. It is unnecessary to trace this progress in detail; it may, however, be remarked that the view of the Legislature on these essential requirements for the well-being of the community has passed beyond the field of health and safety to that of convenience and amenity, as witness bye-laws in regard to advertisements and petrol filling stations.

35. The difference in treatment as regards compensation may be rested on the difference between expropriation of property on the one hand and restric-

tion on user while leaving ownership and possession undisturbed on the other. If the question be asked "Does ownership of land necessarily carry with it the right to turn it to any use which happens to be most profitable to the owner?", a negative answer must clearly be given. As we have seen, some restrictions may clearly be imposed—and would be accepted unquestionably by any landowner—without any suggestion of hardship or of giving rise to any just claim for compensation. They are both reasonable and necessary in order that other persons should not be injured in the legitimate enjoyment of their own rights. The principle is at its lowest that of "live and let live" and advances so as to comprehend all the obligations which according to the social standards of the day are regarded as due to neighbours and fellow citizens. But, as the scope of these restrictions increases by the operation of planning, a stage is reached at which the restrictions imposed will be said to go beyond the claims of "good neighbourliness" and general considerations of regional or national policy require so great a restriction on the landowner's use of his land as to amount to a taking away from him of a proprietary interest in the land. When this point has been reached, the landowner will claim to be fairly entitled to compensation, such compensation to be computed upon the principles applicable where other rights of property are taken away from him. . . .

36. The question is whether any kind of restriction at all imposed in the public interest on the use of land by private owners should carry a right to compensation. The mere regulation of the use of land in the interests of the community would not, if the common law were followed out, involve any such payment and an owner could therefore, consistently with the common law, be required to refrain from using his land for purposes specified by the State. Obedience to such a direction would not entitle him to compensation. To some, indeed, it would appear that the acceptance of this common law rule is inevitable if no other satisfactory solution to the difficulties can be found. But it must, we think, be recognized that the full application of such a policy would result in hardship in many cases and, moreover, would involve inconsistent treatment as between individuals. The owner whose land was zoned for agriculture might suffer a loss of potential building value for which he had paid when purchasing the land; the owner whose land was earmarked for factory development would be able to secure a high price and retain the proceeds for his own use, unless special taxation measures were brought into operation.

The extent to which the common law principle ought to be modified by statute in favour of the subject is a matter of policy upon which the decision rests with Parliament. . . .

37. The outline we have given above indicates the main features of the problem presented by our terms of reference. It shows that the compensation difficulty exists because planning, which is directed to securing the best social use of land, tries to operate within a system of land ownership under which there is attached to land a development value depending on the prospects of its profitable use. If there is to be a completely satisfactory basis for planning which gets rid of the difficulty that system itself must be revised, for difficulties which arise out of a system are not solved by framing a new code for assessing compensation and collecting betterment which operates within that system.

38. On the problem of compensation and betterment, the main conclusions we have drawn in the course of our analysis may now be summarised as follows:—

(*a*) The present statutory provisions, which have not proved satisfactory in the sphere of local planning, would be altogether inadequate for application to the circumstances created by planning conceived as a national operation. If measures of post-war reconstruction are not to be prejudiced a method must be found for removing the difficulties and providing an efficient basis for the future.

(*b*) The existence of the compensation-betterment problem can be traced to two root causes:—

(i) The fact that land in private ownership is a marketable commodity with varying values according to location and the purposes for which it is capable of use.

(ii) The fact that land is held by a large number of owners whose individual interests lie in putting their own particular piece of land to the most profitable use for which they can find a market, whereas the need of the State and of the community is to ensure the best use of all land of the country irrespective of financial return. If planning is a necessity and an advantage to the community, as is undoubtedly the case, a means must be found for removing the conflict between private and public interest.

(*c*) It is in the sphere of "development value", whether attaching to land already developed by building, as in urban areas, or to land suitable for development in the predictable future, as in the case of fringe land around towns and cities, that the compensation difficulty is acute. Development values as a whole, however, are dependent on the economic factors that determine the *quantum* of development of various types required throughout the country, and as planning does not reduce this *quantum* it does not destroy land values but merely redistributes them over a different area. Planning control may reduce the value of a particular piece of land, but over the country as a whole there is no loss.

(*d*) In theory, therefore, compensation and betterment should balance each other. In practice they do not. The present statutory code is limited in operation and is not designed to secure balance, and we are convinced that within the framework of the existing system of land ownership it is not possible to devise any scheme for making the principle of balance effective. It is only if all the land in the country were in the ownership of a single person or body that the necessity for paying compensation and collecting betterment on account of shifts in value due to planning would disappear altogether.

It is evident from these conclusions that an adequate solution to the problem must lie in such a measure of unification of existing rights in land as will enable shifts of value to operate within the same ownership, coupled with a land system that does not contain within it contradictions provoking a conflict between private and public interest and hindering the proper operation of planning machinery. We do not imagine that this theoretical conclusion leaves much room for dispute; any difference of opinion that may arise is more likely to be in regard to the most suitable method of translating theory into practice.

47. . . . *First.* Land nationalisation is not a policy to be embarked upon lightly, and it would arouse keen political controversy. A change of view upon the topic of land nationalisation calls for more than a rearrangement of prejudices. Delay, to say the least, would result. *Second.* It would involve financial operations which in the immediate post-war period might, as

we see the matter, be entirely out of the question. *Third.* Land nationalisation would involve the establishment of a complicated administrative machinery equipped to deal with the whole of the land of the country.

49. We recommend the immediate vesting in the State of the rights of development in all land lying outside built-up areas (subject to certain exceptions) on payment of fair compensation, such vesting to be secured by the imposition of a prohibition against development otherwise than with the consent of the State accompanied by the grant of compulsory powers of acquiring the land itself when wanted for public purposes or approved private development. . . .

Shortly the scheme we recommend involves four points:—

(*a*) The placing of a general prohibition against development on all undeveloped land outside build-up areas and immediate payment to owners of the land affected of compensation for the loss of development value.

(*b*) Unfettered determination through planning machinery of the areas in which public or private development is to take place, the amount and type of development being determined as regards development for public purposes by national needs and, as regards private development, by private demand.

(*c*) Purchase by the State of the land itself if and when required for approved development whether for public purposes or for private purposes.

(*d*) In the case of approved development for private purposes the leasing of such land by the State to the person or body undertaking the development.

A scheme on these lines has been much canvassed and has been commonly described as a purchase by the State of the development rights. That is not, in truth, the transaction: it is the result of the transaction. For, when the land itself is purchased for development purposes, the price then payable excludes the development value. It is, indeed, valuable to describe the scheme as a purchase of the development rights as emphasising that the object of the scheme is to secure development, not to prevent development, and for purposes of statement it is a convenient phrase which we use. The control of development passes from the individual to the State. Just as a prohibition against dishonesty finds its real meaning as an inspiration to honesty, so a prohibition against uncontrolled development should inspire ordered development.

It is apparent, therefore, that the scheme involves neither dual ownership of the land nor divided control. Until the land itself is wanted for purposes of development the owner remains in possession and control save only that he may not develop.

Although the administrative requirements are considerable in the early stages they are mainly concerned with the initial tasks of ascertaining the property concerned and distributing the compensation. Once these matters have been carried through the administrative necessities will in the main be confined to the relatively simple and straightforward tasks of effecting legal transfer to the State of the fee simple as and when the progress of development requires and fixing and collecting whatever rents or premiums may be charged to persons granted permission to use the land for development purposes. . . .

50. We recommend the conferment upon public authorities of powers of purchase, much wider and simpler in operation than under existing legislation. . . .

51. . . . The main defect in the structure of our scheme is that increased values may still accrue in part to land which for the time being remains to the full in private ownership.

We therefore recommend a scheme for the imposition of a periodic levy on increases in annual site value, with the object of securing such betterment for the community as and when it is realised, enjoyed or realisable. The method we suggest is, in our view, the only effective way of collecting betterment without hampering individual enterprise in the development of land. The levy will not be payable in respect of land, the development rights in which are to be acquired under the "development rights scheme", so long as such land remains undeveloped. . . .

NOTE. This report is sometimes called the Uthwatt Report (Mr. Justice Uthwatt was Chairman of the Committee) and is one of a trilogy including the Scott Report (Lord Justice Scott, Chairman) of the Committee on Land Utilisation in Rural Areas (1942, Cmnd. 6378) and the Barlow Report (Sir Montague Barlow, Chairman) of the Royal Commission on The Distribution of the Industrial Population (1940, Cmnd. 6153), which set out the basic planning problems of modern England.

NOTE. The Uthwatt Report was followed by the *Town and Country Planning Act, 1947* (10 & 11 Geo. 6, Ch. 51), which nationalized development value of all land and compensated the owner, who retained the existing use value, for the development value, but in turn charged the ultimate developer with a development charge. For an account of its workings, written from the point of view of an American legal scholar, see Haar, *Land Planning Law in a Free Society* (1951). See also Garner, *The Public Control of Land* (1956), for a short English account, especially pages 13–42; and Heap, *An Outline of Planning Law* (1960, 3rd ed.), for a longer account.

VON HAYEK, BOOK REVIEW OF HAAR, LAND PLANNING LAW IN A FREE SOCIETY. 1952. 19 U. of Chicago L.R. 620, at pages 622–24: "[The Uthwatt] report developed a curious theory of 'floating' and 'shifting' values which, though I doubt whether it is taken seriously by a single reputable economist, appears to have made a considerable impression on town planners and administrators. It is based on the assumption that the total value of all the land in a country is a fixed magnitude, independent of the uses to which the individual pieces of land are put, and that, in consequence, the control of the use of land has only 'the effect of shifting land values: in other words, it increases the value of some land and decreases the value of other land, but it does not destroy land values' (p. 99, quoted from the Uthwatt Report). Now this is not merely, as Mr. Haar suggests, a theory which 'may be open to question on the ground of lack of empirical proof' (ibid.). It is sheer nonsense which empirically could neither be proved nor disproved. There is no useful meaning of the term value of which it could possibly be true. The situation is not much better with regard to the theory of 'floating value': the assertion that as a rule the expectation of impending development will affect the value of more land than will in fact be developed and increase it by more than the value of the actual developments. Yet even though it may occasionally be true that the market value of land on the margin of a town may be based on expectations which cannot all be valid, this surely is a difficulty which could be met by appropriate principles of valuation and which does not justify complete disregard of market values.

"All this does not mean that we want to belittle the difficulty caused by the fact that while the cost of planning through reducing the value of some land is not too difficult to recognize and the bearers of the loss certain to claim compensation, the 'betterment,' i.e., the increases in the value of land due to the same planning measures are much more difficult to ascertain. Nor can there be much question that, so far as specific betterments of this kind are ascertainable, it is desirable that the beneficiaries should be made to contribute to the cost of planning in proportion. There is much to be said for taxing away increments of land value which are demonstrably due to public activity. Indeed, of all kinds of socialism, the nationalization of land would have most to recommend itself if it were practicable to distinguish the value of the Ricardian 'indestructable and permanent powers of the soil,' to which the argument alone applies, from that value which the efforts of the owner have contributed. The difficulties here are essentially of a practical nature: the impossibility of distinguishing between these two parts of the value of a piece of land, and the problem of so adjusting rent contracts as to give the user of the land the appropriate inducements for investment. However, though 'only' practical, these difficulties have nevertheless proved insuperable.

"In effect, this was recognized by the Uthwatt Report which, by a 'bold departure from precedent' on which the authors specially prided themselves, started a new development which in the end perverted that reasonable but impracticable idea of the taxation of betterment values into its opposite: instead of using the taxation of land values as a means of forcing the owners to put their land to the best use, the *Town and Country Planning Act* of 1947, under the name of the Development Charge, in effect imposed a penalty amounting to the whole gain to be derived from it, on any one putting land to better use. This transformation of the initial idea began with the Uthwatt Committee's decision 'to cut the Gordian knot by taking for the community some fixed proportion of the whole of any increase in site values without any attempt at precise analysis of the causes to which they may be due' (p. 98, quoted from the Uthwatt Report). The further steps leading from this to the 1947 Act were that this principle, which the Uthwatt Report intended to apply only to yet undeveloped land, was extended to include all redevelopment of land already used for non-agricultural purposes; that, instead of making the value at a fixed date the basis for determining the increment, the value of any piece of land in the particular use to which it was devoted at any given time became the measure of the 'gain' due to a change in that use—apparently even if the 'existing use value' had fallen to zero; and finally that, after the measure had been passed by Parliament in the general belief that some 75 or 80 per cent of the difference between the value in the old use and the value in the new use would be taxed away, the minister empowered to fix the percentage decided that it should be 100 per cent. The result is that, as the law now stands, the Central Land Board, entrusted with levying the Development Charges, is instructed to make it a condition for permitting any development on land that the whole gain derived from it be handed over to the government. It would not seem unfair to sum up this curious evolution by saying that, since what might have made sense theoretically proved to be practically impossible, and since we must have planning whatever the cost ('even only fairly good planning is to be preferred over the past chaos'

—p. 169), even the most nonsensical principle, if it is only administratively feasible, must be adopted.

"It will now be clear that what the British government has undertaken is no less than to remove the incentive from practically any changes in industrial and commercial activity which involve any substantial change in the use of land (the exceptions are so insignificant that we can disregard them for the present purpose). This is a task which cannot rationally be consummated unless the government takes responsibility for practically all investment decisions. If it were to be consistently carried out, land planning would in the end mean central direction of all commercial and industrial activity. No private person or corporation would have any interest in putting a piece of land to better use or in starting anything new on British soil, because the gain, which can only be obtained by using some British land for new purposes, would have to go to the government. Even worse is the fact that since the prospective value of the development must be paid for in cash before the development can be started, the risk of any uncertain venture will be greatly increased."

DUNHAM, *ibid.* 626, at pages 628–30: "[The] author swallows a little too easily the delightfully simple explanation of the 'development charge'—as merely a change of payees. It is argued by the sponsors of this scheme that formerly a developer paid a landowner a price consisting of existing use value plus potential use value and that now it pays the same amount but to two payees instead of one—existing use value to the landowner and the potential use value to the government. This explanation ignores the factor of full knowledge by the only seller (i.e. the government) of the buyer's intended use, and it also ignores the fact that part of a developer's incentive to change from one land use to another arises from his ability to obtain for his own advantage part or all of this 'development value' by acquiring the land at its old and less profitable use value.

"Mr. Hayek's assertion, in his review of this book and in other writings, that under a 'free market' system all advantage of a change in use of a piece of land goes to the developer of the new use and that under the British Planning Act all such advantage will go to the government is unsound in both aspects. While it is true, as Mr. Hayek suggests, that lawyers and other administrative professions need a little more understanding of economics, Mr. Hayek's sweeping generalizations demonstrate that the 'principle riding' economists likewise need a little more understanding of the operation of legal and economic institutions.

"Lawyers have used the term 'market value' for centuries, and its legal meaning probably does not depart widely from the conventional meaning of the term. Public or private agencies with the power of condemnation usually have been unsuccessful in convincing a trier of fact that Mr. Hayek's theory means that the 'market value' payable to a landowner on condemnation is solely existing use value. Few landowners (none in the United States) resisting a valuation made by the tax assessor have been successful in establishing that Mr. Hayek's free market means that the 'market value' on which taxes are payable is a capitalization of the land's earnings. Valuation proceedings in mortgage foreclosures, rate making, damage actions, security issues, arbitration proceedings and in hosts of other legal proceedings produce the same conclusion about the operation of the institution of 'market value.' In each instance, the trier of fact, aided and abetted by economists acquainted with the institution of the urban land market has insisted that 'market value' includes to the seller something representing prospective use value.

"To the extent that market value does include for the seller something representing its prospective use value, Mr. Hayek is wrong in saying that the seller receives from a purchaser converting from one use to another only its existing use value in the free market. Too much consideration of the institution of the free market in land has gone into this legal and practical conclusion to permit acceptance of Mr. Hayek's ancient but untested generalization. In any event, the British Act takes from the exisiting landowner this element of market value and now requires the developer to buy this part of value from the state instead of the former owner.

"Neither am I as certain as Mr. Hayek seems to be that the development charge results in taxing all of the gain on the change of use to the benefit of the government and that it leaves none of the gain for the developer. The development charge is, as Mr. Hayek says, the difference between 'refusal value' and 'consent value.' But it is not clear that 'consent value' makes no allowance for the developer's profit or his risk taking on changing uses."

AMBLER REALTY CO *v.* VILLAGE OF EUCLID, OHIO. 1924. 297 F. 307 (Ohio, United States District Court). An early zoning by-law was held void. WESTENHAVER D.J.: "... The argument supporting this ordinance proceeds, it seems to me, both on a mistaken view of what is property and of what is police power. Property, generally speaking, defendant's counsel concede, is protected against a taking without compensation, by the guaranties of the Ohio and United States Constitutions. But their view seems to be that so long as the owner remains clothed with the legal title thereto and is not ousted from the physical possession thereof, his property is not taken, no matter to what extent his right to use it is invaded or destroyed or its present or prospective value is depreciated. This is an erroneous view. The right to property, as used in the Constitution, has no such limited meaning. As has often been said in substance by the Supreme Court: 'There can be no conception of property aside from its control and use, and upon its use depends its value.' ... The plain truth is that the true object of the ordinance in question is to place all the property in an undeveloped area of 16 square miles in a strait-jacket. The purpose to be accomplished is really to regulate the mode of living of persons who may hereafter inhabit it. In the last analysis, the result to be accomplished is to classify the population and segregate them according to their income or situation in life. The true reason why some persons live in a mansion and others in a shack, why some live in a single-family dwelling and others in a double-family dwelling, why some live in a two-family dwelling and others in an apartment, or why some live in a well-kept apartment and others in a tenement, is primarily economic. It is a matter of income and wealth, plus the labor and difficulty of procuring adequate domestic service. Aside from contributing to these results and furthering such class tendencies, the ordinance has also an esthetic purpose; that is to say, to make this village develop into a city along lines now conceived by the village council to be attractive and beautiful. The assertion that this ordinance may tend to prevent congestion, and thereby contribute to the health and safety, would be more substantial if provision had been or could be made for adequate east and west and north and south street highways. Whether these purposes and objects would justify the taking of plaintiff's property as and for a public use need not be considered. It is sufficient to say that, in our opinion, and as applied to plaintiff's property, it may not be done without compensation under the guise of exercising the police power."

[This decision was reversed on appeal to the United States Supreme Court in *Village of Euclid* v. *Ambler Realty Co.* (1926), reproduced below at p. 472.]

BELFAST CORPORATION *v.* O.D. CARS LTD.

Northern Ireland. House of Lords. [1960] 2 W.L.R. 148

The respondents owned in fee land at Alexandra Park in Belfast on which they had carried on the business of garage proprietors. In 1954 they sought permission from the Belfast Council to erect lock up shops and factories or warehouses on their land. It was refused on the ground that the zoning called for shops with dwellings over them to a minimum height of 25 feet, and that the factory or warehouse development proposed was for an area zoned for residential use. The respondents claimed compensation for injurious affection. Section 102 of the *Planning and Housing Act (Northern Ireland), 1931* provided that property should not be deemed to be injuriously affected by reason of planning scheme restrictions prescribing the height or character or use of buildings or the spaces about them, and section 6(4) of the *Planning Interim Development Act (Northern Ireland), 1944* (under which the respondents applied) provided that where interim development permission was refused the applicant was entitled to such compensation for injurious affection as he could get under the 1931 Act.

Section 5(1) of the *Government of Ireland Act, 1920* provided, in part, that "In the exercise of their power to make laws neither the Parliament of Southern Ireland nor the Parliament of Northern Ireland shall make a law so as either directly or indirectly to . . . take any property without compensation." The respondents' application for compensation went to arbitration. The arbitrators stated a case for the High Court, who held against the respondents. The Court of Appeal of Northern Ireland reversed the High Court. Only part of the judgments of the House of Lords on the appeal as to the constitutional issue is reproduced.

VISCOUNT SIMONDS: . . . I come then to the substantial questions: What is the meaning of the word "take"? What is the meaning of the word "property"? What is the scope of the phrase "take any property without compensation"? . . .

I hope that I do not over-simplify the problem, if I ask whether anyone using the English language in its ordinary signification would say of a local authority which imposed some restriction upon the user of property by its owner that the authority had "taken" that owner's "property". He would not make any fine distinction between "take," "take over" or "take away." He would agree that "property" is a word of very wide import, including intangible and tangible property. But he would surely deny that anyone of those rights which the aggregate constituted ownership of property could itself and by itself aptly be called "property" and to come to the instant case, he would deny that the right to use property in a particular way was itself property, and that the restriction or denial of that right by a local authority was a "taking," "taking away" or "taking over" of "property."

I do not seek to qualify in any way what has been said in such cases as *Central Control Board (Liquor Traffic)* v. *Cannon Brewery Co. Ltd.* (1919).

I have no right to do so. It is, no doubt, the law that the intention to take away property without compensation is not to be imputed to the legislature unless it is expressed in unequivocal terms. But this principle, upon which learned counsel for the respondents so vigorously insisted, seems to me to have no bearing upon the question what is the meaning of the phrase "take property without compensation" is a constitutional instrument such as the *Government of Ireland Act.* If, indeed, I must have recourse to any broad principle of law for the construction of these few simple words, I should remind myself that from the earliest times the owner of property, and in particular of land, has been restricted in his free enjoyment of it not only by the common law maxim sic utere tuo ut alienum non laedas, but by positive enactments.limiting his user or even imposing burdens upon him. I do not therefore approach this question of construction with any predisposition to enlarge the scope of the vital words. For, my Lords, I would here point out that, if such restrictions as the Acts of 1931 and 1944 impose cannot be enforced without the payment of compensation, the practical effect must be to deprive the Parliament of Northern Ireland of the power to legislate, not only in this particular field in a manner recognised as necessary to its proper fulfilment in Great Britain, but in numerous other fields also in which it has been widely realised that the rights of the individual must be subordinate to the general interest. Learned counsel for the respondents were constrained to admit that their success in this argument might lead to the invalidation of numerous Acts whose validity has been hitherto unchallenged. It would not be easy to reconcile this result with the power accorded to the Parliament by section 4 of the Act to make laws for the peace, order and good government of Northern Ireland. It is right, however, that in the interpretation of constitutional instruments guidance should be sought from those courts whose constant duty it has been to construe similar instruments, if only because, as it appears to me, a flexibility of construction is admissible in regard to such instruments which might be rejected in construing ordinary statutes or inter partes documents. The courts of Northern Ireland have not hesitated to adopt this course and have found assistance in their task of construing their own constitution from the manner in which great judges among the English-speaking peoples overseas have dealt with kindred problems. I do not think that any better examples can be found than in the passages cited by the Lord Chief Justice from the judgments of Holmes J. and Brandeis J. Thus, when Brandeis J. says in the passage quoted by the Lord Chief Justice from his judgment in *Pennsylvania Coal Co.* v. *Mahon* (1922): "Every restriction upon the use of property imposed in the exercise of the police power deprives the owner of some right theretofore enjoyed, and is, in that sense, an abridgment by the State of rights in property without making compensation. But restriction imposed to protect the public health, safety or morals from dangers threatened is not a taking. The restriction here in question is merely the prohibition of a noxious use," that very learned judge indicated in clear terms the distinction which should guide us in determining whether or not legislation which diminishes the owner's free enjoyment of his own property is a "taking" of that property. It is clear that such a diminution of rights can be affected without a cry being raised that Magna Carta is dethroned or a sacred principle of liberty infringed.

I will say only one thing more about the American cases. The day may come when it will be necessary to consider the relevance to the constitution of Northern Ireland of the observation of Holmes J. in the case already cited: "The general rule at least is, that, while property may be regulated to a certain extent, if regulation goes too far it will be recognised as a taking." If the question is one of degree, I am clearly of opinion that the day did not arrive with section 10 (2) of the Act of 1931. . . .

LORD RADCLIFFE: . . . The fundamental question, as I see it, is whether the prohibition of taking any property without compensation contained in section 5(1) of the Government of Ireland Act, 1920, bars the enactment by law of such restrictions on the user or development of property as are referred to in section 10(2) of the *Planning and Housing Act (Northern Ireland), 1931,* unless compensation is provided. In my opinion, it does not, because it seems to me that the word "taking" when used in this context does not extend to cover the act of imposing restrictions of that kind.

I do not see how you can give a meaning to this phrase, "taking without compensation," except by reference to the general treatment of the subject in the law of England and Ireland before 1920. A survey would, I think, discern two divergent lines of approach. On the one hand, there would be the general principle, accepted by the legislature and scrupulously defended by the courts, that the title to property or the enjoyment of its possession was not to be compulsorily acquired from a subject unless full compensation was afforded in its place. Acquisition of title or possession was "taking." Aspects of this principle are found in the rules of statutory interpretation devised by the courts, which required the presence of the most explicit words before an acquisition could be held to be sanctioned by an Act of Parliament without full compensation being provided, or imported an intention to give compensation and machinery for assessing it into any Act of Parliament that did not positively exclude it. This vigilance to see that the subject's rights to property were protected, so far as was consistent with the requirements of expropriation of what was previously enjoyed in specie, was regarded as an important guarantee of individual liberty. It would be a mistake to look on it as representing any conflict between the legislature and the courts. The principle was, generally speaking, common to both.

Side by side with this, however, and developing with increasing range and authority during the second half of the nineteenth century came the great movement for the regulation of life in cities and towns in the interests of public health and amenity. It is not an adequate description of the powers involved, so far at any rate as the United Kingdom is concerned, to speak of them as "police powers." They went far beyond that. Their chief sphere was in the delegated legislation conceded to local authorities, though in some cases they arose from the direct legislation of Parliament itself. Achieved by one means or the other, there is no doubt at all that the effect of them was to impose obligations and restrictions upon the owner of town land which impaired his right of development, prohibited or restricted his rights of user, and, in some cases, imposed monetary charges upon him or compelled him to expend money on altering his property. Generally speaking, though not without exception, these obligations and restrictions were treated as not requiring compensation, though, of course, in a sense they expropriated certain rights of property.

A persual of the Public Health Act, 1875, will be sufficient to make the point. It shows how extensive interference could be, even at that date. Only in a few special cases is compensation provided for the consequence of interference. No one, so far as I know, spoke of this as a "taking of property" or treated the general principle of "no taking without compensation" as applicable to the case. For instance, by-laws, which have to be "reasonable," i.e., not manifestly unjust, if the courts are to sustain them, were upheld, even though seriously restricting the user of property without affording any compensation for the restriction (see *Slattery* v. *Naylor* (1888) a case from Australia).

When town planning legislation came in eo nomine in 1909 the emphasis had no doubt shifted from consideration of public health to the wider and more debatable ground of public amenity. It may possibly have been for this reason, I do not know, that the Act of 1909 included a comprehensive, though not exhaustive, "injurious affection" section, the effect of which was to give property owners whose rights were interfered with in the cause of town planning a right to compensation for any damage that they suffered, subject to counter-claims for betterment and certain exclusions. This "injurious affection" embraced an altogether wider category of injury than the "injurious affection" that had been the subject of compensation under the Lands Clauses Act, 1845. In fact, as we know, section 59(2) of the Housing, Town Planning, etc., Act, 1909 (which did not itself extend to Ireland), excluded compensation for injurious affection in respect of several of the same heads of restriction as those which are found in section 10(2) of the 1931 Act in Northern Ireland. I do not think that this last circumstance has any bearing on the present issue: the Westminster legislature with its full soereignty might be able to exclude compensation in cases where the Northern Ireland Parliament under its constitutional limitations could not. What is important, I think, is to recognise that though interference with rights of development and user had come to be a recognised element of the regulation and planning of towns in the interest of public health and amenity, the consequent control, impairment or diminution of those rights was not treated as a "taking" of property nor, when compensation was provided, was it provided on the basis that property or property rights had been "taken," but on the basis that property, itself retained, had been injuriously affected.

These considerations lead me to the following conclusions: (1) The taking of property referred to in section 5(1) of the Government of Ireland Act, 1920, ought not to be treated as applying to the imposition of restrictions on user and development under town-planning powers. (2) It is within the competence of the Parliament of Northern Ireland to decide on what occasions and to what extent compensation is to be afforded for injury suffered under such restrictions. (3) Section 10(2) of the Act of 1931 is accordingly a valid enactment. . . .

I do not imply by what I have said that I regard it as out of the question that on a particular occasion there might not be a restriction of user so extreme that in substance, though not in form, it amounted to a "taking" of the land affected for the benefit of the public. It is not very easy to imagine such a restriction being imposed by a responsible authority or surviving the test of the Ministry's approval, the more so as the Act deals separately with open spaces as a subject of acquisition, not without compensation. But given that such a case might hypothetically occur, the question for us is whether that possibility in itself is sufficient to invalidate section 10(2), the natural subject of which is restrictions and not "takings." I do not think that it is. It seems to me the wrong way to treat the constitutional provision. To my mind, it does more injustice to its intent if a restriction which is in substance a taking, should one ever occur, is attacked ad hoc as not within the true meaning and scope of section 10(2) than that the whole subsection should be thrown on the scrap-heap as constitutionally an outlaw.

REGINA AUTO COURT *v.* REGINA (CITY)
Saskatchewan. Queen's Bench. 1958. 25 W.W.R. (N.S.) 167

The plaintiff owned part of parcel B, plan C.D. 2799 in the city of Regina. In October, 1956 the city gave notice of its intention to amend its Zoning By-law to put the whole of parcel B, then zoned 2nd density residential (R2), into park zone (P). In due course the amending by-law was read and passed.

GRAHAM J.: . . . In its amended statement of claim the plantiff alleged that the city "wrongfully" gave such notice and readings of and to such amended by-law. It asserts that the city should have acquired the property referred to in par. 1 of the statement of claim either by purchase, exchange, agreement with the plaintiff or by expropriation proceedings before having introduced the by-law to rezone the said property for park purposes and that the plaintiff suffered damages inasmuch as it lost the "equitable ownership" of the said property. In the alternative the plaintiff alleges it had been unable to sell or make any other disposition of the property by reason of the action of the city council and has therefore suffered damages. In support of this allegation the plaintiff tendered evidence with regard to the contract referred to in par. 1 of this judgment. . . .

I have found it difficult to fully understand the plea of the plaintiff that it has lost the "equitable ownership" of the said land, but I assume that the plaintiff suggests it has lost certain rights of its ownership as a result of the rezoning of the property.

It is true that any zoning by-law restricts the full and complete user of any property affected thereby. The right to continue to use the property and any buildings thereon for purposes for which it was being used prior to the passing of the by-law is provided for in the by-law as required by *The Community Planning Act*. The plaintiff is still the registered owner of the property and of course can dispose of it but the property would remain subject to the provisions of the zoning by-law.

The fact that it is to some extent confiscatory in nature does not in my opinion affect the validity of the by-law or the right of the city to enact such by-law. As Meredith, J.A. says in *Re Dinnick and McCallum*:

"The legislation is confiscatory in its character although, of course, it is intended to be put in force for the general benefit—including the benefit of each owner generally only."

Zoning by-laws are relatively new but I think it is well known and accepted that it is necessary for any growing city to pass such a by-law in planning the future development of such city.

The city is not required before passing the by-law or any amendment thereafter to negotiate for the purchase or exchange of any property affected thereby or to secure the consent of the owner thereof or to take steps to expropriate such property. It is true, of course, that should the city any time in the future decide to take over the property for public-park purposes it would be necessary then for it to reach an agreement with the owner for the purchase or exchange of the property or failing this to expropriate the property under the appropriate Act.

In my opinion therefore none of the actions of the city as complained of by the plaintiff was "wrongful" and the plaintiff's action must therefore be dismissed with costs.

QUESTION. If the city should decide to take over the property for public park purposes, would the compensation be based on the value of the land as zoned (P)?

THE TOWN PLANNING ACT
Manitoba. Revised Statutes. 1954. Chapter 267

19. (1) Any person whose property is injuriously affected by the making of a town planning scheme, shall, if he makes a claim in respect of the injury within the time, if any, limited by the scheme, not being less than three months after the date when notice of the approval of the scheme is published in the manner prescribed by regulations made by the minister, be entitled to obtain compensation in respect thereof from the responsible authority.

(2) Any person whose property is injuriously affected by the execution of works carried out under a scheme, in respect of any matter or thing that has not been the subject of compensation in connection with the making of the scheme, shall, if he makes a claim in respect of the injury within twelve months after the completion of the works or any section thereof affecting his property, be entitled to compensation in respect thereof from the responsible authority.

(3) A person shall not be entitled to obtain compensation under this section on account of any building erected on, or contract made or other thing done with respect to, land included in a scheme after the time at which the application for authority to prepare the scheme has been made, or after such other time as the minister may fix for the purpose.

(4) Subsection (3) does not apply as respects any work done before the date of the approval of the scheme for the purpose of finishing a building begun or of carrying out a contract entered into before the application was made.

(5) Where, by the making of a town planning scheme, property is increased in value, the responsible authority shall, if it makes a claim in respect of the increase within the time, if any, limited by the scheme, the time not being less than three months after the date when notice of the approval of the scheme is first published in the manner prescribed by the regulations, be entitled to recover from any person whose property is so increased in value an amount determined by the scheme, being not more than one-half of the amount of the increase.

(6) Where by the execution of works under a scheme property is increased in value, the responsible authority may recover from the owner an amount determined by the scheme, being not more than one-half of the increase in respect of any matter or thing for which it has not recovered any amount in connection with the making of the scheme, if it makes a claim for the purpose within twelve months after the completion of the work or any portion of the work affecting the property, as the case may be.

(7) Any question as to whether any property is injuriously affected or increased in value within the meaning of this section, and as to the amount and manner of payment, whether by instalments or otherwise, of the sum that is to be paid as compensation under this section, shall be determined by three arbitrators, one appointed by the responsible authority, one appointed by the person or persons whose property is affected, and one appointed by the other two arbitrators appointed as aforesaid unless the parties agree on some other method of determination.

(8) The Arbitration Act, *mutatis mutandis,* applies to arbitration proceedings instituted under this section.

(9) Any amount due under this section as compensation to a person aggrieved from the responsible authority, or to a responsible authority from a person whose property is increased in value, may be recovered as a civil debt by action in any court of competent jurisdiction.

(10) Where a town planning scheme is revoked by an order of the minister under this Act, any person who has incurred expenditure for the purpose of complying with the scheme shall be entitled to compensation in accordance with this section in so far as any such expenditure is rendered abortive by reason of the revocation of the scheme.

20. (1) Where property is alleged to be injuriously affected by reason of any provisions contained in a town planning scheme, no compensation shall be paid in respect thereof if or so far as the provisions are such as could have been enforced without compensation if they had been contained in by-laws made by the local authority.

(2) Property shall not be deemed to be injuriously affected by reason of the making of any provisions inserted in a town planning scheme, that, with a view to the proper use and development of land for agricultural purposes, and with the object of securing the amenity of the area included in the scheme or any part thereof and proper sanitary conditions in connection with the buildings erected thereon, prescribe the space about buildings or the percentage of any lot that may be covered with buildings, or limit the number of buildings to be erected or prescribed the height, character, location, or use of buildings, or the use of land that the minister, having regard to the nature and situation of the land affected by the provisions, considers reasonable for securing the above purposes.

(3) Where a person is entitled to compensation under section 19 or under this section in respect to any matter or thing, and he would be entitled to compensation in respect to the same matter or thing under any other enactment, he shall not be entitled to compensation in respect of that matter or thing both under this Act and under that other enactment, and he shall not be entitled to any greater compensation under this Act than he would be entitled to under the other enactment.

NOTE. Section 19 (1) and (3) bear a striking resemblance to section 7 (1) and (3) respectively of the *First Draft of Town Planning Act* in 1914, prepared by a Committee on Town Planning and Housing Legislation appointed by the Commission of Conservation, Ottawa. Even earlier, in New Brunswick and Alberta, by S.N.B. 1912, c. 19, section 5 (1) and (3), S.A., 1913, c. 18, s. 5 (1) and (3) similar provisions were introduced into their actual legislation. Nova Scotia followed in 1915, S.N.S., c. 3, Manitoba in 1916, c. 114, Saskatchewan in 1917 (2d session), c. 70. These provisions seem largely to have been dead letters. The editor has so far found no evidence that either the state or a citizen has benefited from them. The saving clause, Manitoba, section 20 (1), which had counterparts in the other Acts, probably robs the provision as a whole of any real protection.

The compensation and betterment provisions undoubtedly had their origin in the *Housing, Town Planning, &c. Act, 1909,* being chapter 44 of the statutes of the Imperial Parliament of that year. See Section 58 (1) and (3) and section 59 (1).

THE TOWN AND RURAL PLANNING ACT
Alberta. Revised Statutes. 1955. Chapter 337

85. (1) No person is entitled to compensation by reason of
  (a) the passing or making of a zoning by-law,
  (b) any provisions contained in a zoning by-law, or
  (c) any lawful action taken under the provisions of a zoning by-law.
 (2) Where a person claims that he is entitled to compensation
  (a) by reason of the passing of a by-law adopting a general plan or development scheme or by the passing or making of an interim development order or by-law, or
  (b) by reason of the carrying out of a provision of a general plan or development scheme,

he is not entitled to compensation if the provisions of the plan, scheme, order or by-law are such as might have been contained in or enforceable by means of a zoning by-law.

THE COMMUNITY PLANNING ACT, 1957
Saskatchewan. Statutes. 1957. Chapter 48

47. Property shall not be deemed to be injuriously affected by reason of the passing of a zoning bylaw under the authority of this Act or by reason of any amendment to or revision of such bylaw.

NOTE. A similar provision is conspicuously absent in Ontario.

2. The Calculation of Compensation

UNITED STATES *v.* MILLER
United States. Supreme Court. 1943. 317 U.S. 369.

Roberts J. delivered the opinion of the Court: The United States condemned a strip across the respondents' lands for tracks of the Central Pacific Railroad, relocation of which was necessary on account of the prospective flooding of the old right-of-way by waters to be impounded by the Central Valley Reclamation Project in California. For many years a proposal to initiate state reclamation works in this vicinity had been before the people of the state. In 1932 they voted approval and authorization of the project. It was, however, subsequently adopted by the United States as a federal project....

Portions of respondents' lands were required for the relocated right-of-way. Alternate routes were surveyed by March 1936 and staked at intervals of 100 feet. Prior to the authorization of the project, the area of which respondents' tracts form a part was largely uncleared brush land. In the years 1936 and 1937 certain parcels were purchased with the intention of subdividing them and, in 1937, subdivisions were plotted and there grew up a settlement known as Boomtown, in which the respondents' lands lie. Two of the respondents were realtors interested in developing the neighborhood. By December 1938 the town had been built up for business and residential purposes.

December 14, 1938, the United States filed in the District Court for Northern California a complaint in eminent domain against the respondents and others whose lands were needed for the relocation of the railroad....

1. The Fifth Amendment of the Constitution provides that private property shall not be taken for public use wihout just compensation. Such compensation means the full and perfect equivalent in money of the property taken. The owner is to be put in as good position pecuniarily as he would have occupied if his property had not been taken.

It is conceivable that an owner's indemnity should be measured in various ways depending upon the circumstances of each case and that no general formula should be used for the purpose. In an effort, however, to find some practical standard, the courts early adopted, and have retained, the concept of market value. The owner has been said to be entitled to the "value," the "market value," and the "fair market value" of what is taken. The term "fair" hardly adds anything to the phrase "market value," which denotes what "it fairly may be believed that a purchaser in fair market conditions would have given," or, more concisely, "market value fairly determined."

Respondents correctly say that value is to be ascertained as of the date of taking. But they insist that no element which goes to make up value as as at that moment is to be discarded or eliminated. We think the proposition is too broadly stated. Where, for any reason, property has no market, resort must be had to other data to ascertain its value; and, even in the ordinary case, assessment of market value involves the use of assumptions, which make it unlikely that the appraisal will reflect true value with nicety. It is usually said that market value is what a willing buyer would pay in cash to a willing seller. Where the property taken, and that in its vicinity, has not in fact been sold within recent times, or in significant amounts, the application of this concept involves, at best, a guess by informed persons.

Again, strict adherence to the criterion of market value may involve inclusion of elements which, though they affect such value, must in fairness be eliminated in a condemnation case, as where the formula is attempted to be applied as between an owner who may not want to part with his land because of its special adaptability to his own use, and a taker who needs the land because of its peculiar fitness for the taker's purposes. These elements must be disregarded by the fact finding body in arriving at "fair" market value.

Since the owner is to receive no more than indemnity for his loss, his award cannot be enhanced by any gain to the taker. Thus, although the market value of the property is to be fixed with due consideration of all its available uses, its special value to the condemnor as distinguished from others who may or may not possess the power to condemn, must be excluded as an element of market value. The district judge so charged the jury, and no question is made as to the correctness of the instruction.

There is, however, another possible element of market value, which is the bone of contention here. Should the owner have the benefit of any increment of value added to the property taken by the action of the public authority in previously condemning adjacent lands? If so, were the lands in question so situate as to entitle respondents to the benefit of this increment?

Courts have had to adopt working rules in order to do substantial justice in eminent domain proceedings. One of these is that a parcel of land which has been used and treated as an entity shall be so considered in assessing compensation for the taking of part or all of it.

This has begotten subsidiary rules. If only a portion of a single tract is taken, the owner's compensation for that taking includes any element of value arising out of the relation of the part taken to the entire tract. Such damage is often, though somewhat loosely, spoken of as severance damage. On the other hand, if the taking has in fact benefited the remainder, the benefit may be set off against the value of the land taken.

As respects other property of the owner consisting of separate tracts adjoining that affected by the taking, the Constitution has never been construed as requiring payment of consequential damages; and unless the legislature so provides, as it may, benefits are not assessed against such neighboring tracts for increase in their value.

If a distinct tract is condemned, in whole or in part, other lands in the neighborhood may increase in market value due to the proximity of the public improvement erected on the land taken. Should the Government, at a later date, determine to take their other lands, it must pay their market value as enhanced by this factor of proximity. If, however, the public project from the beginning included the taking of certain tracts but only one of them is taken in the first instance, the owner of the other tracts should not be allowed an increased value for his lands which are ultimately to be taken any more than the owner of the tract first condemned is entitled to be allowed an increased market value because adjacent lands not immediately taken increased in value due to the projected improvement.

The question then is whether the respondents' lands were probably within the scope of the project from the time the Government was committed to it. If they were not, but were merely adjacent lands, the subsequent enlargement of the project to include them ought not to deprive the respondents of the value added in the meantime by the proximity of the improvement. If, on the other hand, they were, the Government ought not to pay any increase in value arising from the known fact that the lands probably would be condemned. The owners ought not to gain by speculating on probable increase in value due to the Government's activities.

In which category do the lands in question fall? The project, from the date of its final and definite authorization in August 1937, included the relocation of the railroad right-of-way, and one probable route was marked out over the respondents' lands. This being so, it was proper to tell the jury that the respondents were entitled to no increase in value arising after August 1937 because of the likelihood of the taking of their property. If their lands were probably to be taken for public use in order to complete the project in its entirety, any increase in value due to that fact could only arise from speculation by them, or by possible purchasers from them, as to what the Government would be compelled to pay as compensation. . . .

. . . If, in the instant case, the respondents' lands were, at the date of the authorizing Act, clearly within the confines of the project, the respondents were entitled to no enhancement in value due to the fact that their lands would be taken. If they were within the area where they were likely to be taken for the project, but might not be, the owners were not entitled if they were ultimately taken, to an increment of value calculated on the theory that if they had not been taken they would have been more valuable by reason of their proximity to the land taken. In so charging the jury the trial court was correct. . . .

WOODS MANUFACTURING CO. LTD *v*. THE KING
Canada. Supreme Court. [1951] 2 D.L.R. 465

RINFRET C.J.C. delivered the judgment of the Court: The appellant was the owner of a large property situated in the City of Hull, on the east side of Laurier St., and extending to the Ottawa River. The frontage on Laurier St. is 456 ft., and the total area is 6.53 acres, of which an unopened street constitutes 0.75 acres, leaving a net area of 5.68 acres. The appellant is a Canadian corporation with head office in Montreal, and operates mills at St. Lambert, Toronto, Winnipeg, Calgary, Ogdensburg, Welland and Hull. At the site expropriated is located the clothing and canvas division, where for many years prosperous operations have been carried on, the operating profits before income tax, having been in 1947, $183,435.

Pursuant to s. 9 of the *Expropriation Act*. R.S.C. 1927, c. 64, the respondent initiated expropriation proceedings on May 19, 1944, and on May 7, 1946. The first covered the vacant land having an area of 4 acres situated to the south, and the second affected a piece of land contiguous to the north, having an area of 1.6 acres, and on which several buildings are erected.

The action was heard before the Exchequer Court [[1949] Ex. C.R. 9], and on December 23, 1948, the President fixed the compensation at $45,800 for the first expropriated property, with interest at the rate of 5% from May 19, 1944, and at $350,000 for the second expropriated property without interest. The appellant claims that these amounts are inadequate. It is claimed that a total amount of $726,262.58 should have been awarded. By the information, a sum of $329,791.73 was offered for total compensation, including all loss and damage if any, arising out of the expropriations.

While the principles to be applied in assessing compensation to the owner for property expropriated by the Crown under the provisions of the *Expropriation Act,* and under various other Canadian statutes in which powers of expropriation are given, have been long since settled by decisions of the Judicial Committee and this Court in a manner which appears to us to be clear, it is perhaps well to restate them. The decision of the Judical Committee in *Cedars Rapids Mfg. & P. Co.* v. *Lacoste* where expropriation proceedings were taken under the provisions of the *Railway Act* of 1903, determined that the law of Canada as regards the principles upon which compensation for land taken was to be awarded as the same as the law of England at that time and the judgment delivered by Lord Dunedin expressly approved the statement of these principles contained in the judgments of Vaughan Williams and Fletcher Moulton, L.JJ. in *Re Lucas & Chesterfield Gas & Water Bd.* The subject-matter of the expropriation in the *Cedars* Rapids case consisted of two islands and certain reserved rights over a point of land in the St. Lawrence River, the principal value of which lay not in the land itself but in the fact that these islands were so situate as to be necessary for the construction of a water power development on the River. It is in this case that the expression appears that where the element of value over and above the bare value of the ground itself consists in adaptability for a certain undertaking, the value to the owner is to be taken as the price which possible intended undertakers would give and that that price must be tested by the imaginary market which would have ruled had the land been exposed for sale before any undertakers had secured the powers or acquired the other subjects which make the undertaking as a whole a realized possibility. That decision was followed in the same year by a second judgment of the Judicial Committee in the case of *Pastoral Finance Ass'n* v. *The Minister,* where Lord Moulton, in considering a claim for compensation for properties taken by the Government of New South Wales under the *Public Works Act,* 1900, of that state, said that the owners were entitled to receive as compensation the value of the land to them and that probably the most practical form in which the matter could be put was that they were entitled to that which a prudent man, in their position, would have been willing to give for the land sooner than fail to obtain it.

These statements of the law have been followed consistently in the judgments of this Court. . . .

We are unable to avoid the conclusion that the learned President did not apply these principles in the case at bar. In his reasons for judgment he says [p. 14]: "Where an owner makes a claim for property taken from him section 47 [*i.e.*, of the *Exchequer Court Act*] permits compensation to him only to the extent of the value of such property."

Later, he expresses the following views [pp. 41–2]: "It is only the form of the property that is changed; instead of the land, the owner has its money equivalent. It is also clear that the money equivalent referred to is the *market value of the land,* that is to say, the amount of money the owner could turn it into *if he offered it for sale."*

He also states [p 43]: "In the case of *In re Lucas and Chesterfield Gas and Water Board,* in which Fletcher Moulton stated that the money equivalent of the land was estimated on the value to the owner, and not on the value to the purchaser, it was clear that even although the land had special adaptability for a particular purpose its value to the owner was confined to its market value. That means that it cannot be more than it would fetch in the market."

And finally, referring to his own judgment in *R.* v. *Lawson & Sons Ltd.,* he says [p. 46]: "I then expressed the opinion that this definition of 'value to the owner' is essentially the same as that of 'fair market value'."

With deference, we are unable to agree with these statements which, in our view, are not the true expression of the law.

With regard to the property first expropriated we think that, applying the principles laid down by the majority of this Court in *Diggon-Hibben Ltd.* v. *The King* an allowance of 10% for compulsory taking should be added to the value of the land and buildings expropriated, but that apart from this the appellant has not made out its claim that the compensation allowed in respect of such property was inadequate. In the result the amount allowed should be increased from $45,800 to $48,880.

As to the second expropriation, the learned President valued the land at $9,000 per acre, because in his view, during the period that extended between the two expropriations, the land increased in value and, as the area covers 1.68 acres, he awarded $15,120. He found that the reconstruction cost of all the buildings was $478,032 less depreciation amounting to $188,296, leaving a depreciated value of $289,736. To these items he added $435 for fixtures, making a grand total of $305,291. The appellant produced a statement showing a loss of $76,920.96 plus an item of $2,550 as the depreciation in value of certain chattels, making a total claim for loss by disturbance, amounting to $79,470.96. The learned President was of opinion that even if it were conceded that the owner of the expropriated property had a right to compensation for loss by disturbance of his business, the amount of the appellant's claim under this head was difficult to determine as the appellant was left in possession and continued its operations for the time being. He also took the view that even if the defendant were entitled to compensation for loss by disturbance it had no right at the time of the judgment to receive the full amount of its claim for a loss that will happen only in the future, if it happens at all. The learned President, while expressing the opinion that the appellant was not entitled to more than the present value of such prospective loss, reached the conclusion that the evidence supported the claim that the appellant's loss by reason of disturbance, would amount to $79,470.96.

The learned President concluded that the maximum amounts at which he would estimate the various items of the appellant's claim on the second expropriation, if he were required to do so, item by item, would be $15,120 for the land, $289,736 for the buildings and mechanical equipment, $425 for the fixtures, and $79,470.96 for the loss by disturbance of business, making a total of $384,761.96. He held, however, that the valuation should not be made piecemeal, but as a whole, and for the second expropriation he awarded a lump sum of $350,000. It was his view that this amount would adequately cover every factor or element of value, including that of loss by disturbance of business, that could properly be taken into account, and at the same time meet the tests of value to which he referred in this judgment.

It cannot be determined how the $350,000 awarded is distributed amongst the items above set out. Assuming that the whole of the reduction from the total of $384,761.96 was applied to the claim for disturbance the amount would be made up as follows:

Land	$ 15,120
Depreciated value of the buildings and mechanical equipment	289,736
Fixtures	435
Loss by disturbance	44,709
	$350,000

In determining whether or not the total awarded is adequate it is necessary to consider the evidence in some detail. The buildings on the lands secondly expropriated were four in number, a main factory building of stone and brick construction, a tarpaulin and waterproofing building, a garage and an auto shelter or shed. The main factory building was constructed in 1907. It was established in evidence that the building was well suited for the type of manufacturing carried on there and which the company operating also at Montreal and elsewhere in Canada was desirous of continuing. In these premises the company had carried on operations which realized substantial profits, with the exception of the year 1938, during the period 1937 to 1945 inclusive. While the expropriation vesting title in the Crown took place in the spring of the year 1946, the company was permitted to remain in possession and its operations in that year and the year following resulted also in substantial profits. The site on Laurier Ave., in the residential portion of Hull, possessed for the owner the great advantage of being close to a large and available supply of labour suitable for employment in the company's operations and being not far distant from one of the principal bridges across the river leading to the City of Ottawa. While the company, in anticipation of being required to yield possession of the premises, had endeavoured to find a suitable property in Hull for the carrying on of their operations, they had not been able to find any and, according to Mr. E. S. Sherwood, a real estate broker having a wide experience in this district, no comparable buildings for an operation of the magnitude of the Woods Mfg. Co. were available either in Ottawa or Hull and he considered that it was doubtful that any such property would become available. The company had purchased land for a site in Overbrook in the Township of Gloucester, lying to the east of the City of Ottawa and a distance of six miles from its then location, but upon consideration had concluded that it was too far from a suitable supply of labour and had abandoned the idea of building there. Apparently inquiries in the immediate neighbourhood of Hull had not resulted in the company finding a suitable site there and, while some were available further down the Ottawa River, operations there would be faced with difficulty in getting the necessary help. The company's desire to continue its operations in Hull or its immediate vicinity was made plain.

There was a divergence of opinion among the experts as to the value of the property. For the company, Mr. W. H. Bosley, a real estate agent with wide experience in valuations and real estate operations generally, in answer to a question by the learned trial Judge, expressed the opinion that if the owners were desirous of disposing of the property on the market they could have obtained $280,000 for it. Having said this, however, he said that if he were representing a purchaser he would not feel that the property could have been bought at that figure, assuming the owner wished to continue in business, and expressed his inability to give an opinion as to what amount a purchaser might have paid to obtain it, but said that if such a purchaser needed the property urgently he would advise him to pay 10% more than that figure. As to the position of the owner, however, he said that he would advise the Woods Mfg. Co. not to accept such a figure since it could not hope to reinstate itself for that amount. Mr. Sherwood considered that at the relevant time he could have sold the property on the market for $315,000, but said that he would have advised the owner, assuming that it was intended to continue the business, to refuse such an amount "or anything like it". As to a prospective purchaser, assuming the property suited his requirements, he would have advised him to pay 10% in excess of this amount, but would have advised the appellant to refuse such an offer. Mr. R. B. Moffit, the vice-president and comptroller of the appellant said that in his opinion, having regard to the suitability of the plant for the operations and the profit realized, he would have advised against selling for less than $700,000.

Mr. A. B. Doran, a contractor with some 20 years' experience in building construction, estimated the cost of replacing the buildings on the property at $474,873 on the basis of the prices for material as of the date of the expropriation. The main building had been constructed in the year 1907 but had been very well maintained and he computed the depreciation at the sum of $94,631, expressed otherwise, he said that if his firm had been given the contract to rebuild the plant the new building would be worth about $95,000 more than the building as it stood in May of 1946.

The evidence for the Crown as to the reconstruction cost of the main and subsidiary buildings varied but little from that tendered by the owner. Mr. James Adam, an architect and civil engineer of long experience, estimated the cost of replacement at $478,032 and this figure was accepted by the learned President. While declining to estimate the probable future useful life of the building, he considered that since its erection it had deteriorated in the neighbourhood of 35%. Mr. J. A. Coote, an assistant professor of mechanical engineering at McGill University, and a consultant for a firm of engineers in Montreal, had examined the buildings at the request of the Crown. Accepting the reconstruction cost at the amount of the estimate of Mr. Adam and others employed for the purpose by the Crown, he considered that the depreciated value of all the buildings was $287,736. Mr. Coote had never constructed or tendered on the construction of a building and, admittedly, did not have experience with industrial plants of the kind operated by the company and his evidence as to the extent of the accumulated depreciation and of the future useful life of the building appears to have been based upon theories expressed by others on the subject. When counsel for the Crown directed questions to him to establish his qualifications as an expert on the question of depreciation, he said that he had been studying the theory for 25 years, that he had lectured to students in accounting and engineering and had read widely on the subject and considered that a useful life of 60 years was the utmost that could be assigned to the main building. He, however, also said that although the building was practically 40 years old in 1946 it was as a structure in excellent condition, that it was an "extra good building", well constructed and in general very well maintained, and then said in part:

"The question is: how many more years is it good for? Now nobody can tell, sir; I want to agree with the sentiment expressed here yesterday that nobody can tell how long a building is good for."

a statement which he repeated later, saying that "nobody knows what the useful life of that building is going to be". On cross-examination, when asked his opinion as to what condition the building would be in when it had reached 60 years of age, he said that:

"As a structure, I should say it would probably be pretty fair."

but that the maintenance cost then would be much higher and that obsolescence would become an increasingly important factor. He did not say, however, that it would cease to be an effective building for the company's purposes at that time. In answer to a question by the learned trial Judge he made it clear that his opinion on this point was not based upon his own experience, saying that he wished to emphasize that nobody could tell what condition the building was going to be in at age sixty but that:

"Relying upon recorded experience, the experience of other people with buildings of that age, I say that I could not honestly give this building as a piece of productive equipment a life beyond sixty years."

It will be observed that expressed in percentages the depreciation in the main building in the opinion of Mr. Coote was 43.8%, in that of Mr. Adam 35%, and in that of Mr. Doran 22.3%. There appears to be considerable support for the appellant's submission that the learned President was in error in placing the depreciation at the highest of these figures in view of Mr. Coote's admission that his whole calculation was based on the assumption that the useful life of the building was limited to 60 years.

For the Crown the evidence, in so far as it related to the buildings as distinct from the land, was limited to the cost of replacing them. Replacement cost is, of course, a material factor for consideration in determining the value to the owner. In some circumstances it may well represent that value while in others it may greatly exceed it or be materially less. In the present case we are satisfied upon the evidence that the value of the property to the owner was in excess of the value of the land, plus the depreciated value of the buildings. In endeavouring to come to a conclusion as to what amount the owner, presumably directed by prudent business men, would have been prepared to pay for the property in May, 1946, rather than to be forced to give up title and possession, the situation in the business world at that time is to be considered. The second World War had terminated and in consumers' goods of all kinds there existed what is commonly described as a seller's market, due to various factors including accumulated shortages during the war. The Woods Mfg. Co. during the years 1940 to 1946 both inclusive had made an average annual operating profit before income taxes in their Hull plant slightly in excess of $213,000. As there were available then no suitable factory buildings in Ottawa or Hull or the vicinity and the company, if it was to continue in business, was faced with the necessity of constructing new suitable buildings on an appropriate site, there can be no doubt in our opinion, that had the buildings now under consideration then been situated on a site one or two miles down the Ottawa River and available for purchase at the depreciated value of the buildings, plus the value of the site, the company would have purchased without hesitation. To fail to do so under such circumstances would indicate a lack of ordinary business judgment. A substantial further value to the owner is to be attributed to being permitted to remain in undisturbed possession of its property in Hull, with its added advantage of immediate proximity to an adequate labour supply. . . .

The learned President has allowed only the bare value of the land, the lowest depreciated value placed upon the building by any witness and a portion of the proven claim for disturbance. He has declined to consider the value to the owner as distinguished from the market value or to allow 10%, or any amount, for compulsory taking. We are all of opinion that on the evidence the amount awarded is clearly inadequate. The amount to which the appellant is entitled cannot be determined with mathematical accuracy. Keeping in mind the principles stated above and after a careful consideration of all the evidence we are of opinion that the amount of compensation for the property secondly expropriated inclusive of any allowance for compulsory taking should be fixed at the sum of $450,000.

There is this to be added. It is fundamental to the due administration of justice that the authority of decisions be scrupulously respected by all Courts upon which they are binding. Without this uniform and consistent adherence the administration of justice becomes disordered, the law becomes uncertain, and the confidence of the public in it undermined. Nothing is more important than that the law as pronounced, including the interpretation by this Court of the decisions of the Judicial Committee, should be accepted and applied as our tradition requires; and even at the risk of that fallibility to which all Judges are liable, we must maintain the complete integrity of relationship between the Courts. If the rules in question are to be accorded any further examination or review, it must come either from this Court or from the Judicial Committee.

The appeal will be allowed with costs. The amount of compensation for the property first expropriated will be fixed at $48,880 with interest at the rate of 5% per annum from May 19, 1944. The amount of compensation for the property secondly expropriated will be fixed at $450,000 without interest.

THE QUEEN *v*. SUPERTEST PETROLEUM CORPORATION LTD. [1954] 3 D. L. R. 245. (Canada. Exchequer Court). THORSON P.: ". . . I must refer to the second last paragraph of the reasons for judgment of the Supreme Court of Canada in *Woods Mfg. Co.* v. *The King*, which reads as follows: [The President then quoted the paragraph which is reproduced above, and continued:]

"This is a remarkable statement. While there will be general agreement with most of its sentiments it is subject to objection on several counts. It was neither necessary nor relevant to the decision in the case. Consequently, its admonitions, being *obiter dicta,* have no binding effect. That being so, the easier course to follow would be to let them pass without comment but, in view of the circumstances, it would not be proper to do so.

"The implications in the statement have caused me deeper concern than I care to express. For, while the reason for making it is not apparent on its face, there is no doubt that it was because of the fact that I have disagreed with some of the opinions expressed by individual Judges of the Supreme Court of Canada in certain expropriation cases. . . .

"The only real problem in this case is the value of the land. . . .

"It is thus plainly evident that the law on this vexatious question is, to say the least, in a very unsatisfacory state and it is very doubtful that any clarification by judicial decision is possible. Under the circumstances, I have come to the conclusion that it is essential to the fair administration of this branch of the law that there should be a statutory definition of value. It was found necessary in the United Kingdom, as long ago as 1919, to lay down such a definition for use in the case of all lands compulsorily acquired by a Government Department or a local or public authority. This was accomplished by the *Acquisition of Land (Assessment of Compensation) Act,* 1919, c. 57. In my opinion, similar action should be taken in Canada.

"In view of this recommendation it would not be out of order to express my opinion on what would be the most desirable definition even although this will involve critical comment on some of the tests of value that have been laid down. My first comment must, with respect, be on the test stated in the *Diggon-Hibben* case, and adopted in the *Woods Mfg. Co.* case. This is a novel one for which there is no precedent in England. But the criticism of the test is not on the ground of its novelty. I think it will be conceded that it is the most expansive test that has been laid down. My experience in expropriation cases makes me fearful that attempts to apply it will result in excessive awards through the difficulty of avoiding duplication in the weighting of the various factors of value that should be taken into account just as there has been duplication in the defendant's claim for the value of the land in the present case. But whether there is such danger or not there is a more serious objection to the test, namely, the difficulty of applying it. For my part, I must frankly confess that I do not understand it and I am at a loss to know how to operate it. Is the market value of the land to be wholly disregarded? How is the amount which the assumed owner would be willing to pay to be determined? Whose opinion of this subject, if it is not left to the owner to decide, will be available to the Court? Real estate experts will not be able to give it any help. During the trial I put the test to Mr. Bosley, one of the most experienced and reliable real estate experts in the country, but he would not assist the Court in arriving at an answer to it. He explained that he could not apply the test because he could not know what was in the owner's mind. In his opinion, it was only the owner who could decide how much he would be willing to pay. While the wording of the test lends itself to such an opinion it could not have been intended that the owner should be the arbiter of his own entitlement. Under these circumstances it seems to me that in view of the difficulty of applying this test a search should be made for a more easily applicable one. . . .

". . . [It] seems to me that the best definition of value would be that which was actually adopted by the Parliament of the United Kingdom in the *Aquisition of Land (Assessment of Compensation) Act*, 1919, in which one of the rules governing the assessment of compensation by an official arbitrator was put in part by s. 2 (2) of the Act as follows: 'The value of land shall . . . be taken to be the amount which the land if sold in the open market by a willing seller might be expected to realise.' This definition would have several advantages. It would be of general application and readily applicable by real estate experts who could thereupon give realistic and reasonably certain opinions of value and it would be conducive to precise and fair awards. In my judgment, the adoption of this definition would go a long way towards the solution of the problem under discussion. Certainly, it would be of great assistance to this Court in carrying out its duty. . . .

"Having thus summarized the various valuations put forward I must now come to my estimate of the value of the land. It is obvious from my confession that I do not understand the test laid down in the *Diggon-Hibben* case and adopted in the *Woods Mfg. Co.* case and do not know how it operates that I cannot apply it. That being so, I apply to the determination of the value of the land the principles laid down by the Judicial Committee of the Privy Council in the three decisions which I have cited and by Fletcher Moulton L.J. in the *Lucas & Chesterfield Gas & Water Bd.* case. I take the term 'prudent man in their position' in Lord Moulton's formula in the *Pastoral Finance Ass'n* case not as referring to a prudent owner but as meaning a 'prudent purchaser in a position similar to that of the owners'. Such a purchaser could, for example, be another oil company which might be assumed to have full knowledge of all the advantages of the land and the use that could be made of it with its facilities. The value should be the price that a purchaser of this sort might be expected to be willing to pay. In making this statement I am not overlooking the fact that what the Court must estimate is not the value of the land, buildings and equipment, separately found and then added together, which would make for a high estimate, but the value of the land as it stood at the date of the expropriation with the buildings and equipment on it, less the equipment that was removed. In addition, the Court must take into account the factors of value to the owner involved in the defendant's claim for disturbance with which, as Rand J. put it, a purchaser is not concerned. On this basis, I proceed to my estimate. . . .

"I next come to the defendant's claim of $23,355.62 for disturbance. It is interesting to note that there is no express provision in the *Lands Clauses Consolidation Act,* 1845 (Imp.), c. 18, giving compensation for disturbance. That Act recognized only two kinds of compensation to the owner of land compulsorily acquired under it, namely, for the value to him of the land that was taken and for injurious affection to his remaining land. Similarly, there is no express statutory provision in Canada for compensation for disturbance. But, as Scott L.J. put it in *Horn* v. *Sunderland Corp.*, the 'judicial eye' has discerned the right to compensation for disturbance in the owner's right to 'the fair purchase price of the land taken'. Similarly in Canada it is now settled that the right of the owner of expropriated property to compensation for disturbance is included in his right to compensation for the value to him of the expropriated property. It is also interesting to note that when the Bill leading to the *Acquisition of Land (Assessment of Compensation) Act,* 1919, was introduced into the British House of Commons there was no provision in it for any claim for disturbance. So that if it had passed in the form in which it was introduced the owner of the land would not have been entitled to any compensation for disturbance. But Rule 6 was added to s. 2 of the Bill when it was before the House of Lords in the following terms: 'The provisions of Rule (2) shall not affect the assessment of compensation for disturbance or any other matter not directly based on the value of land.'

"The effect of this provision was considered in the interesting case of *Horn* v. *Sunderland Corp.* It does not give a separate right of compensation in addition to the value of the land. If a statutory test of value of expropriated property is laid down by the Parliament of Canada, it is important that provision should also be made for compensation for disturbance but care should be taken that such provision does not result in profit to the owner such as would be the case if the right to compensation to the owner were made a separate and independent cause of action. . . . And care should likewise be taken to guard against such an award of compensation for disturbance as was made in the *Woods Mfg. Co.* case where a claim for $78,000 for disturbance was allowed for a disturbance that has thus far not happened, the owner still being in undisturbed occupation of the property almost 8 years after the date of its expropriation. There is something wrong with a principle that allows such a claim for a loss that has not happened and may possibly never happen. . . .

"I now come to the defendant's claim for a 10% additional allowance for compulsory taking. I dealt at length with the question of this allowance in *The Queen* v. *Community of Sisters of Charity of Providence* and incorporate herein what I said on the subject in that case. There I reviewed the jurisprudence on the additional allowance in England and in Canada and pointed out that neither in England nor in Canada has there ever been any Act of Parliament authorizing it or any rule of law requiring it and that its grant in Canada is based on a practice adopted from a similar practice in England. But the fact is that although the granting of any allowance for compulsory taking was expressly prohibited in England by the *Acquisition of Land (Assessment of Compensation) Act,* 1919, in all cases where land was compulsorily acquired by any Government Department or any local or public authority, the practice of granting it still persists in Canada, under certain circumstances, as the result of recent decisions of the Supreme Court of Canada, in cases under the *Expropriation Act* even although such expropriations are by the Crown in right of Canada. Thus the practice still prevails in Canada under the circumstances referred to in cases where in analogous cases in England it would not be applicable.

"The reason for the prohibition of the allowance by the *Acquisition of Land (Assessment of Corporation) Act* 1919, in the cases to which it applies is clear. The granting of the allowance was one of two prime causes of excessive awards under the *Lands Clauses Consolidation Act*, 1845, the other being excessive valuations of land, which militated against the success of many important public projects requiring the acquisition of land. There was such widespread objection on the part of the public to these excessive awards that when the Bill leading to the Act was before the British Parliament for consideration the provision prohibiting any allowance for compulsory taking was almost unanimously approved. This was a worth while reform in the public interest.

"In my opinion, it would have been competent for the Courts in Canada to accomplish a similar reform in cases under the *Expropriation Act* without any legislative action since the English practice on which the Canadian practice was said to depend had ceased to exist in analogous cases, but it has been decided by the Supreme Court of Canada that under certain circumstances there should be an additional allowance for compulsory taking over and above the value of the expropriated property. . . .

"It is anachronistic to apply the philosophy that the compulsory taking of property is in the nature of trespass to the conditions of the present times when it frequently happens that the property of individuals has to be expropriated for important public purposes. There is no element of tort or delict in an expropriation under the *Expropriation Act*. It is the lawful exercise by the Crown in right of Canada of its right of eminent domain under the authority of an enactment of the Parliament of Canada. All that the owner is entitled to is such compensation as Parliament has decreed. There is no value in sweeping generalizations of inherent right to compensation. . . .

"Under these circumstances, I have never been able to see why the owner of expropriated property should receive more than his property is worth. And since there was no Act of Parliament or rule of law compelling me to make an additional allowance for compulsory taking I could not see any reason for applying in Canada a practice borrowed from England which had ceased to exist there in analogous cases, particularly when I considered the additional allowance for compulsory taking an improper one. I, therefore, never allowed it in any expropriation case coming before me until after the decision of the Supreme Court of Canada in *Diggon-Hibben Ltd.* v. *The King*, in which an appeal from my judgment was allowed because I had refused to grant any additional allowance and an additional allowance of $10,000 was added to the amount of my award. . . ."

DREW *v*. THE QUEEN

Canada. Supreme Court. 1961. 29 D.L.R. (2d) 114

JUDSON J.: I agree with the reasons of the Chief Justice in these appeals except that I would reject the claim for the allowance of 10% for compulsory taking on different grounds.

There appears to be little doubt that *Diggon-Hibben Ltd.* v. *The King* has been regarded as introducing a new principle as a basis for the award of 10% for compulsory taking—"circumstances presenting difficulty or uncertainty in appraising values." This is far removed from the principle of the judgment of Fitzpatrick, C.J., in *The King* v. *Hunting, Barrow & Bell* (1916), where it was said that it had "become so thoroughly established a rule from the innumerable cases both here and in England in which it has been awarded almost as a matter of course, that I certainly should not be prepared to countenance it being questioned in any ordinary case". I will postpone examination of the cases to test whether the award ever was a matter of course in the Canadian Courts and proceed immediately to an examination of the cases subsequent to *Diggon-Hibben* to see what has been the effect of the application of a rule based on difficulty or uncertainty in appraising values.

Almost immediately in *The King* v. *Lavoie*, December 18, 1950 (unreported), the uncertainty rule was restated in slightly different language but the allowance was refused. Since then in all cases in the Supreme Court of Canada the 10% has been allowed with little or no discussion.

In Ontario in thirteen reported cases since 1951 the award has been made in every case except two. In Quebec in all of the cases reported in the Court of Appeal since 1948 the allowance has been made in every case except in *Bellerose* v. *Talbot* (1957). In three recent Nova Scotia decisions the allowance has been made at 5%. The Manitoba Court of Appeal in its most recent decision has made the allowance.

With respect, there appears to be reason to question whether a rule based upon difficulty or uncertainty in valuation is working satisfactorily when it is found that the award is made in nearly every case. This may mean that, notwithstanding the form in which the rule is stated, what is really happening is that the old matter of course rule is being applied. Difficulty and uncertainty can be found in almost every assessment of damages no matter what the cause of action may be. But this affords no logical basis for the addition of 10% when the tribunal of fact, whether Judge, jury or arbitrator, has given full consideration to a claim and made every allowance for the constituent elements that enter into the assessment. The course taken by the decisions may also indicate that the rule is being used as a formula to review an award on a question of *quantum*. . . .

[Judson J. next considered whether "the practice ever grew up in this country to justify a statement that the allowance was a matter of course based on long established practice".]

. . . It is therefore possible to find within the last 50 years that there have been at least three principles followed from time to time in this Court, first, an allowance as a matter of course, second, no allowance where value to the owner has been ascertained and, third, an allowance in special circumstances. It cannot be said that these principles have been satisfactory from the standpoint of logic, definition or application and in my opinion the door is wide open for a reconsideration of the whole problem, particularly when what was obviously the foundation of the rule—and a very insecure one—disappeared in the country of its origin over 40 years ago. . . .

. . . The judgment in *The Queen* v. *Sisters of Charity of Providence* contains a complete historical and critical survey of the application of the supposed rule of the allowance for compulsory taking both in England and Canada and I am content to adopt this survey as part of my reasons along with the criticism that there is no statutory basis for the allowance and no rule of law requiring it. With the restatement of the value to the owner rule in *Woods Manufacturing Co.* v. *The King*, it seems to me that the anomalies have become more strongly emphasized. The rule is that " 'the owner at the moment of expropriation is to be deemed as without title, but all else remaining the same, and the question is what would he, as a prudent man, at that moment, pay for the property rather than be ejected from it' ".

In fixing the amount of an award there are often factors, other than the market value of the property expropriated, which must be taken into account but which are not easily calculated. In such cases the tribunal of fact may decide that compensation for such factors can best be appraised in the form of a percentage of the market value. This is but a part of the process of determining value to the owner. Once that value has been assessed in accordance with the rule in the *Woods* case it represents full compensation and the owner is not entitled to an additional amount for compulsory taking.

[Cartwright, Fauteux, Abbott, Martland and Ritchie JJ. concurred. Locke J. wrote a separate opinion in which, subject to his own comments, he agreed with Judson J. Kerwin C.J.C., on the question of the 10% allowance, said only:

"It was not laid down in the *Lavoie* decision or in any other decision of this Court that mere difficulty in arriving at the value to the owner of the property expropriated, because of difference of opinion among the experts, would be sufficient to grant the 10%. The fact that the witnesses for the Crown and the witnesses for the owner differ as to the value is not a valid reason. In my view it is now settled that the ordinary rule is that the allowance is not to be made and that in order to justify it there must be special circumstances. Undoubtedly the facts in one case will differ from those in another but it is impossible to lay down the rule in any more express terms. Here there are no special circumstances."]

METROPOLITAN TORONTO *v.* LOWRY. 1961. 30 D.L.R. (2d) 1 (Ontario. Supreme Court of Canada). Metropolitan Toronto expropriated land for the Don Valley Parkway including a strip 2,000 feet long and 200 feet wide, more or less, containing about 30 acres, bisecting the respondent's farm, which contained about 240 acres. The municipality offered the respondent $12,500 an acre, but the offer was refused and the matter went to arbitration. In calculating the compensation the arbitrator rejected the proposal of $12,500 an acre, the price at which the respondent had sold the two parts of his farm before the expropriation. Instead, he allowed $15,000, a figure named in the agreements for sale of the two parts, as the price at which each of the purchasers agreed to purchase the adjoining half of the about to be expropriated strip at any time within three years if called upon by the respondent. The options were not taken up before the land was expropriated. (How the respondent knew of the expropriation in advance of it is not disclosed.) The arbitrator also allowed 5% for compulsory taking. The Ontario Court of Appeal dismissed an appeal against the value, but allowed an appeal against the 5%. The Supreme Court of Canada allowed the appeal against the value and fixed the rate at $12,800 an acre. The respondents served notice that they would move that they were entitled to 10% for compulsory taking, but the Court dismissed the motion following the *Drew* case. ABBOTT J.:

"There are concurrent findings of fact as follows: (i) That the best use to which the lands in question could be put was industrial development; (ii) that their market value for this purpose was $12,500 per acre; (iii) that the agreements entered into by the respondents under which they had a right exercisable within 3 years to compel the purchasers to purchase the lands which have now been expropriated at $15,000 per acre were *bona fide* and enforceable agreements.

"Moreover the following further matters appear to be clear on the evidence and indeed were not seriously disputed: (i) That before the agreements in question were entered into the respondents' advisors knew what part of the land was going to be expropriated; (ii) that it was of course possible but extremely improbable that there would be any change in the proposal to expropriate; (iii) that the commercial value per acre for the lands to be expropriated was certainly not more than the average per acre of the whole block of land owned by the respondents; (iv) that the purchasers under the agreements were willing, if necessary, to pay a total price equivalent to an average of $12,800 per acre for all the land owned by respondents; (v) that the clauses in the agreements under which the purchasers could be compelled to pay $15,000 per acre for the parkway lands were designed with the imminent expropriation in mind and for the purpose of fixing a 'floor price' which would be payable by the expropriating authority.

"No evidence was called to show the reason why the purchasers agreed to this unusual term, but it was obviously a matter of indifference to them how the total price which they were willing to pay, if necessary, was calculated.

"Shortly stated, the respondents' contention is that the value of the parkway lands to them could not be less than $15,000 per acre, the amount which they were entitled to receive under the agreements, and that contention was accepted by the learned arbitrator and by the majority in the Court below.

"It is undisputed that the respondents are entitled to receive from the expropriating authority the value of the land to them at the date of expropriation. On the uncontradicted evidence it also cannot be disputed that—except for the effect of the agreements in question—the highest value to respondents of the lands in question was $12,500 per acre.

"The form of words used in the agreements could therefore have no other purpose than to assure to respondents a total price worked out on the basis of $12,800 per acre for all their lands.

"While the respondents were free to make any bargain the purchasers were willing to agree to, in my opinion they could not by attributing a higher value to the strip to be expropriated and at correspondingly lesser value to the balance of their property, thereby throw upon the expropriating authority the obligation to pay out of public funds more than the expropriated lands were in truth worth to the respondents as owners."

ROBERTS AND BAGWELL *v*. THE QUEEN. 1956. 6 D.L.R. (2d) 305 (Canada. Supreme Court). This case raises an interesting question concerning the compensation to be paid under the *Toronto Malton Airport Zoning Regulations* (1953) P.C. 546; 1 S.O.R. Consolidation 1955, 37, which were made under section 4 of the *Aeronautics Act,* R.S.C. 1952, c. 2, as amended in 1952 and published in Volume V of the R.S.C. 1952, c. 302. Section 4(8) provides that "Every person whose property is injuriously affected by the operation of a zoning regulation is entitled to recover from Her Majesty, as compensation, the amount, if any, by which the property was decreased in value by the enactment of the regulation, minus an amount equal to any increase in the value of the property that occurred after the claimant became the owner thereof and is attributable to the airport". Proceedings to recover under this section have to be commenced within two years after the deposit of the regulation. The *Zoning Regulations* prescribed height limitations, and s. 4(2) authorized the Minister to order the owner or occupier of land containing a building or structure that exceeds the limitation to demolish or remove the building or structure. Section 5 prohibited the use of any device that the Minister considered a hazard to navigation, after the Minister had notified the person involved. The Minister made no order and gave no notice, and sections 4(2) and 5 were revoked in 1955 by S.O.R. 55—331 and S.O.R. 55—402. In 1951 a proposed plan of subdivision for industrial and commercial use was given "draft approval" under *The Planning Act,* R.S.O. 1950, c. 277, subject to a condition that the owner observe height limitations shown on the plan. The plan was never registered. There is no provision for compensation for injurious affection under *The Planning Act.* The following quotation deals with the effect of the repeal of the provision for compensation and the existence of the question of height limitation contained in the draft approval on the claim for compensation. NOLAN J.:

"Two questions present themselves for determination in connection with the two Regulations. In the first place, the appellants contend that they are entitled to compensation for the diminution in value due to the effect of these revoked Regulations.

"It was argued by counsel for the Crown that, until an Order was actually made by the Minister, the property could not be said to have been 'injuriously affected'. Under s. 23 of the *Expropriation Act* (R.S.C. 1952, c. 106), injurious affection can result only from some positive act by the Crown, but that is because of the language contained in the section itself, which provides that the injurious affection must be caused by the 'construction' of a public work. Under s. 4(8) of the *Aeronautics Act,* compensation is to be awarded to every person whose property is injuriously affected 'by the operation of a zoning regulation'. The question arises whether there can be injurious affection giving rise to a claim for compensation when no order has actually been made by the Minister. If this question were answered in the negative, the Minister, by forbearing to make an Order within two years, could effectually deprive an owner of compensation for what might render his land almost valueless. The purpose of the statute is clear. Vertical Regulation is necessary in the vicinity of airports and the vesting of the powers mentioned operates with an immediate effect on the use and value of the land. It becomes at once a burden on the land and the resulting diminution in value is a proper subject for compensation.

"The second question for consideration is, what is the effect of the revocation of the two Regulations in 1955 on the compensation?

"In determining the extent of loss in value due to the Regulations, in my view, the Regulations as a whole should be considered, and not the extent of loss produced by one particular section such as s. 5, and it would be impossible to attempt to distribute the diminution in value among individual Regulations. It is quite clear that the subsequent revocation of the Regulation could not give rise to a claim against the owner for a return of any part of compensation already paid and that result cannot, in effect, be reversed by withholding compensation until after the particular burden has been removed. In any event, the revocation did not affect the *quantum* of the award of compensation in the present case, as the learned President states specifically that the revocation of ss. 4(2) and 5 was not taken into account in making the award. . . .

"A cross-appeal was made by the Crown against the award on the ground, to put it shortly, that at the time of the enactment of the restrictive Regulation there was already, on a portion of the land, a provincial height limitation which, on the evidence, reduced the value of the whole radically and to little more than was paid for it. This contention makes it necessary to go into the facts in some detail. . . .

"Here an Official Plan for the Township of Toronto Gore was approved by the Minister on March 5, 1951, and in an appendix to the map and as part of the plan it was stipulated as Item B.1.: 'Special height regulations are shown on the plan of the Department of Transport for one flightway and may be extended to others if required by the Department of Transport. These will apply to all structures. A maximum height limitation will be imposed on the whole urban area of 40 feet, to be measured from the present ground level to the highest point of the roof, not only as a flight safety factor, but also as a means of reducing the ultimate cost of fire fighting equipment.' Although the maximum height limitation 'will be imposed on the whole urban area', it would seem that this is a specific feature of the plan and that it is as effective as if it were embodied in a by-law of the council or an order of the Minister. . . .

". . . [The] appellants, in September, 1951, applied to have about 950 ft. of this land, running back from the Airport Road, brought under a plan of subdivision. On October 24, 1951, the approval of the Minister to a draft plan was given, subject to certain conditions, among which was a height restriction endorsed on the plan. This fixed a maximum building height of 19 ft. at a distance of 50 ft. from the street line, of 24 ft. at 275 ft., and of 34 ft. at 725 ft. It was argued that these restrictions were beyond the power of the Minister to impose, but this would seem to be without substance in view of s. 26(4), which provides that in considering a draft plan of subdivision regard shall be had by the Minister to (f), 'the restrictions or proposed restrictions, if any, on the land, buildings and structures proposed to be erected thereon and the restrictions, if any, on adjoining lands'. Moreover, the Minister, as already mentioned, under s. 25 (1) (*a*) [re-enacted 1951, c. 65, s. 4], has all the powers of a council under s. 390 of the *Municipal Act* and the imposition of the limitation here comes within the scope of that power. It was suggested that the limitation was in conflict with the Official Plan and so far violated s. 25 (1) (*a*) which requires such an order to conform with the Official Plan. As the latter establishes only a maximum height of 40 ft., the limitations within that maximum made by the Minister are in conformity with it.

"Although I have expressed my views on the legal questions raised, it is not necessary to make a definitive holding on them. It is sufficient for the purposes of this appeal that the Official Plan, the by-law and the restrictions on the draft plan of subdivision were in *de facto* existence with a strong presumption of their validity at the time of the imposition of the Dominion restrictions. That fact itself was sufficient to cast such a cloud upon what has been claimed to have been free land as to affect the market value almost as significantly as if their validity were unchallenged....

"It was a necessary step in ascertaining the amount of compensation in this matter to determine, first, the value of the land to the owners, freed of the restrictions. The principle to be applied is as it is stated in the judgment of this Court in *Woods Mfg. Co.* v. *The King*. The question is as to what amount a prudent person in the position of the owners, being in possession of the property but without title to it, would be willing to give sooner than fail to obtain it. The learned President has not applied this principle, but rather the one stated by him in his judgment in *The Queen ex rel. A.-G. Can.* v. *Supertest Petroleum Corp.*, decided since the date of the *Woods* judgment. I am, however, of the opinion that the amount determined upon as the value of the property is adequate and that the sum of $40,000 allowed as compensation for injurious affection is sufficient."

METROPOLITAN TORONTO AND REGION CONSERVATION AUTHORITY *v.* VALLEY IMPROVEMENT CO., LTD. 1962. 35 D.L.R. (2d) 315 (Ontario. Supreme Court of Canada). This complicated case involved a parcel of land comprising floodland, embankment and tableland owned by the respondent, part of which, the floodland and enbankment, was expropriated by the appellant in the course of executing a flood control program. The Ontario Municipal Board fixed the compensation at $3,370 and the Ontario Court of Appeal increased the sum to $77,313. At the time of the expropriation the whole parcel was zoned as "Greenbelt", which permitted only very sparse development for residential purposes (one house to the acre) and commercial uses were prohibited altogether. A year before the Township had passed a flood zone by-law that prohibited residential and commercial use of the floodland owned by the respondent. The by-law was approved for a limited time only and had expired before the expropriation. It was re-enacted in similar terms after the expropriation. Nevertheless the respondent was preparing .9 acres of the floodland for a parking lot in connection with a restaurant known as the Old Mill, operated on the tableland as a lawful, but non-conforming, use established before the by-law was passed. The respondent also had plans for the erection of a motel on the tablelands, but it recognised that it would be necessary to procure a rezoning of the land before that work could proceed. The possibility of rezoning to permit apartment houses was also considered. The Municipal Board said, in part, "The respondent accepts the value of $739 per acre for the lower lands and called no evidence of value in this regard. He takes the position that the flood zone by-law of the township passed November 5, 1956, had the effect of making the subject lands a separate entity and they cannot thus be considered as adjunct or part of the appellant's remaining lands at the top on the date of expropriation, in spite of the fact that the Corporation did not apply for a further time extension. This course was followed he contends, because the Conservation Authority had not decided what lands they wanted covered and were negotiating with certain parties for acquisition of land. Meanwhile expropriations by the Authority were taking place up and down the river. Since the expropriation of the subject lands, however, a new flood zone by-law was passed on the 4th day of May, 1959." The appellant appealed to the Supreme Court of Canada, which effectively reversed the Court of Appeal and directed the Municipal Board to reconsider the amount. CARTWRIGHT J.: "... The Ontario Municipal Board based its award on a valuation of $739 per acre for the 3.47 acres taken (plus an allowance of $500 to cover the expenditure in preparing the .9 acres for parking and an additional 10% for forcible taking). There was evidence to support the figure of $739 per acre, unless it should be held either (i) that the lands taken might have been rezoned to permit the erection of the proposed motel building or (ii) that the 'table lands' might have been rezoned to permit the erection of apartment houses. In the latter alternative the ownership of the lands taken would have added to the value of the 'table lands' as, under the existing by-laws, the number of apartment suites which were permitted to be constructed on a parcel of land was proportional to the area of that parcel. It was stated in argument that had the tablelands been rezoned to permit the erection of apartments, the ownership of the expropriated lands would have permitted the building of 76 more suites than would be permitted lacking that ownership. I did not understand this statement to be challenged.

"The Ontario Municipal Board came to the conclusion 'that there was not a reasonable probability of the desired zoning being realized' and added nothing to the compensation on the ground of possible rezoning.

"The Court of Appeal was of opinion that if the respondent's lands were rezoned to permit the erection of apartment houses all of its lands except the .85 acres of the embankment would have a value of $40,000 per acre, but that this value should be discounted by 33⅓% because of the 'uncertainties and delays implicit in the necessity of obtaining appropriate rezoning'....

"The witness Davis, who gave the value of $739 per acre, made it clear that in his opinion the lands taken were worth very many times that amount to the respondent and that the answer in which he gave the figure $739 was based on the premise, which counsel's question required him to accept, that the respondent could never acquire or use them....

"The fact that the Board fixed the value of the lands taken at $739 per acre shows that it did give to itself the direction [that the flood zone by-law had the effect of making the floodlands an entity entirely separate from the rest of the respondent's land].

"In my opinion, it erred in law in so doing. The giving of this direction would inevitably have the effect of rendering it unnecessary for the Board to give the consideration it would otherwise have given to the question of what estimate a prudent man in the position of the respondent would have made, on the date of expropriation, of the probability or possibility of the 'table-lands' being rezoned to permit the erection of apartment houses. If the value of the lands taken was to be determined on the assumption that the respondent could never use or acquire them it would be a matter of indifference whether there was any possibility of the 'table-lands', as distinguished from the lands taken, being rezoned. If, on the other hand, it was kept in mind that the mere fact of ownership of the lands taken would, in the event of the 'table-lands' being rezoned, permit the erection of an additional 76 suites, the duty, already alluded to, of taking into consideration and estimating the probability or possibility of amendment of the zoning by-law in regard to the 'table-lands' would assume great importance."

JUDSON J. dissenting in part: "I agree with the judgment of Cartwright J., except on question 1. As stated in his reasons, the Board found 'that there was no reasonable probability of the desired zoning being realized'. If the reasons of the Board are taken as a whole, I do not think that the mention of severance means anything more than the lack of this reasonable probability of rezoning the whole area including the expropriated land. This is not error in law. The respondent's artificial structure of hypothesis collapses when it is realized that it depends upon getting such a decision. These expropriated lands could only have value to the owner of the amount assigned to them by the respondent if they remained part of the whole and were rezoned.

"The respondent seeks to build up value in this way. First, there are plans for a motel to be operated in conjunction with its established restaurant. This would involve putting supporting pillars on the lands in question. When expropriation makes this impossible, the motel must be placed on the tablelands, which otherwise would be used for an apartment building. Then the loss of the bottom lands destroys much of the value of the tablelands for an apartment site because the area of the bottom lands could be used as part of the computation of the land required for such a purpose and thus make possible the building of more suites.

"The foundation for all this disappears with the finding of fact made by the Board. I would answer question 1 in the negative."

WILSON *v.* LONG BRANCH

Ontario. Court of Appeal. 1957. 10 D.L.R. (2d) 473

ROACH J.A. delivered the judgment of the Court: This is an appeal by the claimant, Mrs. M. Wilson, by leave of this Court granted on April 17, 1957, from the order of the Ontario Municipal Board, dated May 18, 1956, awarding her the sum of $6,050 on the expropriation by the respondent of lands owned by her.

By the order granting leave to appeal, the appeal is limited to the following questions of law: (a) That the Ontario Municipal Board failed to apply the proper legal standards of valuation in view of the admission by counsel for all parties that the lands in question had no market value at the date of the expropriation. (b) That the Ontario Municipal Board used upon this arbitration evidence of value in another arbitration for different lands. (c)

That the Ontario Municipal Board applied improper principles in arriving at the value of the lands in question in that, there being admittedly no market value, it attempted to place upon the lands a market value, rather than a value to the owner and in particular the replacement value to the owner.

The lands in question are in a low-lying area near the mouth of the Etobicoke River. The area is flat and on several occasions over the years has been flooded when the river overflowed its banks. Remedial measures had been undertaken from time to time to guard against that hazard but they proved inadequate. On October 15, 1954, as the result of Hurricane Hazel the river again overflowed its banks and the water rushed over the area causing substantial property damage and loss of life. In all 43 houses were totally destroyed, 60 others seriously damaged and several lives were lost. The hazard of flooding with its consequential destruction was then recognized as being so great that the lands in the area were declared unfit for residential purposes and on December 15, 1954, the respondent passed By-law 1502 expropriating a large part of the area including the land and premises of the claimant.

The Board awarded the claimant for land and building the sum of $6,050, made up as follows:

Value of land	$1,250.00
Value of building	4,250.00
10% for forcible taking	550.00
	$6,050.00

The Board also awarded the claimant her costs fixed at $150. . . .

In agreeing that the property in question had no market value as of the date of the expropriation, both parties took a reasonable and realistic view. Market value is the price that a purchaser willing to buy would pay to a vendor willing to sell. In the existing circumstances it is a reasonable conclusion that no person would be willing to purchase this property. The hazard of future flooding was so great that no one would risk it. That, however, did not reduce the value to the claimant to nil. It continued to have a value to her as a place in which to live, subject, of course, to that hazard; and, having been compelled to part with it, she was entitled to be compensated on the basis of its value to her. The principle as restated in *Cedar Rapids Mfg. & Power Co.* v. *Lacoste*, still applied.

Mr. Starr submitted that in the circumstances the principle of equivalent reinstatement applied. That principle is described in Cripps on Compensation, 8th ed., pp. 180–1, thus: "This principle is that the owner cannot be placed in as favourable a position as he was in before the exercise of compulsory powers, unless such a sum is assessed as will enable him to replace the premises or lands taken by premises or lands which would be to him of of the *same* value." (The italics are mine.)

Applying that principle the claimant would be entitled to be compensated by a sum equal to the replacement value of the house plus the cost of acquiring a comparable lot. It would be possible to determine the replacement value of the house; it would be more difficult, if not impossible, to determine the cost of a comparable lot. A comparable lot would be one so located as to enjoy equal services including under that heading, sewers, water, electricity, schools, churches, shopping areas and transportation facilities; but it would be one also suffering from a comparable blight, *viz.*, the hazard of floods. It would have to be a lot so located that if the claimant's house stood upon it the whole would have no market value. It might be possible to find such a lot in Metropolitan Toronto but I should think the odds against finding such a lot would be very great. Moreover, if there is such a lot in Metropolitan Toronto on which the counstruction of a residence would be permitted and the plaintiff were willing to purchase it and the vendor willing to sell it would immediately thereby acquire a market value, *viz.*, the price that the willing purchaser would be prepared to pay to the vendor who would be willing to accept it. Searching for such a lot would be almost like searching for a will-o'-the-wisp.

In an effort to apply the principle Mr. Starr introduced evidence that the replacement value of the claimant's house was $5,160 and the cost of the cheapest lot in Metropolitan Toronto was $50 per foot frontage, *viz.*, $2,500, making the total sum to which the claimant would be entitled $7,660. The witness who gave evidence of the so-called cheapest building lot in Metropolitan Toronto must have had in mind the "going price" of such a lot and there cannot be a "going price" unless there are sales and there cannot be sales without persons willing to buy. Therefore, the building lots this witness had in mind must have been lots that had a market value. To put it otherwise he must have had in mind lots that were not blighted by physical conditions such as marred the claimant's property.

In my opinion the Board was right in refusing to accept the evidence of that witness as the absolute measuring stick by which the claimant should be compensated. The claimant was not entitled to compensation in a sum that would enable her to acquire another property that would be more valuable to her than the one that was expropriated. . . . In my opinion since such an owner is parting with his property under compulsion rather than doing so willingly any doubts that may arise in determining the compensation should be resolved in his favour.

In my opinion, in the exceptional circumstances of this case, the Board proceeded on a basis that was practical and fair to the claimant, *viz.*, that she should be awarded a sum equal to the replacement value of the house plus the cost of a lot comparable in size and enjoying services equal to those enjoyed by the land compulsorily taken from her less a sum that would represent the difference in value between such a property and hers due to the absence of the blight that affected her property. That was a most difficult assignment for the Board and I concede that it required the Board, by reference to evidence, to put some value on the lot expropriated even though in fact it had no market value. Whether or not the Board reached the correct figure in its application of that formula is a question of fact with which this Court is not concerned.

Since, in my opinion, the Board applied a proper formula the appeal should be dismissed with costs.

QUESTIONS. What does Roach J.A. mean when he says that "the lands in the area were declared unfit for residential purposes"? Declared by whom? Compare *The Planning Act*, R.S.O., 1960, c. 296, s. 30(1) para. 3. This power to prohibit the erection of a building or structure for residential or commercial purposes on land that is "subject to flooding" was introduced by S.O. 1955, c. 48, s. 40(3). What is the effect of such a by-law on the compensation for land subject to the by-law?

NORTH YORK BOARD OF EDUCATION *v.* VILLAGE DEVELOPMENTS LTD.

Ontario. Supreme Court of Canada. 1956. 3 D.L.R. (2d) 161

LOCKE J.: This is an appeal from a judgment of the Court of Appeal for Ontario which dismissed the appeal of the present appellant from an award made by His Honour Judge Forsyth as compensation for certain lands expropriated by the appellant under the provisions of the *School Sites Act,* R.S.O. 1950, c. 348.

The lands taken, 10.4 acres in extent, formed part of a larger tract of 18.4 acres purchased by the respondent from one Harry Mendel in September, 1952. In July, 1951, Mendel had had prepared a plan of a subdivision of the property, dividing the portions not required for streets into 94 lots designed for use as residential property. In September of that year, this plan was submitted to the Department of Planning and Development for approval as required by s. 26 of the *Planning Act,* R.S.O. 1950, c. 277. The Minister had referred this plan to the Planning Board of the township for its consideration. That Board decided that it should not recommend the approval of the plan for two principal reasons, namely, the township's inability to supply the property with water and because of the school problem in the area. These recommendations were forwarded to the Minister on May 13, 1952, and the plan was not approved.

The respondent is engaged in the business of dealing in subdivisions and in general construction work. After purchasing the tract, on its instructions the town planning consultant who had prepared the plan for Mendel prepared a new plan showing what was substantially the east half of the property as a high school site, the balance being divided into building lots and streets upon which the lots fronted. In March of 1953 this plan was submitted to the Planning Board and on April 30, 1953, the Board decided that it would recommend its approval upon certain conditions. The principal of these was that the respondent should enter into an agreement with the council of the township regarding the installation of services such as the supply of water and for the disposal of sewage, payment of taxes and other related matters. For reasons which are not explained in the evidence, the agreement, the making of which was made a condition precedent to obtaining the recommendation of the Planning Board for the plan, was not settled until March 24, 1954. While so dated a by-law authorizing its execution by the township was not passed until May 10, 1954.

In the interval, negotiations had been carried on for the purchase of the required lands, the appellant by an offer in writing dated February 26, 1954, offering the sum of $100,000 upon conditions stated in a schedule to the offer. One of these specified that the appellant should have the right to retain $10,000 of the purchase-price to insure completion by the respondent of certain specified works by May 1, 1955. While the amount offered was acceptable to the respondent, the condition mentioned was not and the negotiations collapsed.

On March 22, 1954, the appellant passed a resolution expropriating the lands in question, describing them by metes and bounds. The area taken included 9 building lots shown on the prepared plan along the west side of the school site, which the respondent had theretofore assumed to sell, and an area shown as Block A lying along the south border of the part there designated as a high school site. The resolution did not in terms require immediate possession of the lands taken and on May 17, 1954, a second resolution was adopted that immediate possession be required and taken. The respondent, apparently following the settlement of the terms of its agreement with the township dated March 25, 1954, had a new plan prepared giving effect to the changes agreed to, and this was approved by the Planning Board and thereafter by the Minister on May 13, 1954, and registered.

The learned Judge, in determining the amount of the compensation, proceeded upon the basis that the owner was entitled to receive the amount he would have realized from the expropriated property if it had been sold in building lots, as contemplated by the proposed plan rejected by the Minister in 1952, less the amount it would have been necessary to expend upon the property for the provision of the services called for by the agreement of March 25, 1954, and a further deduction for the carrying charges, for interest, legal fees, taxes, selling commissions and other related expenditures. Estimating that there would have been realized from the sale of the lots, less these deductions, an amount of $129,708, he allowed the owner this amount, with interest from March 22, 1954. He further found that the property was excellently situated for subdivision purposes and that that was the most advantageous purpose to which the land could be put and that the lots could have readily been sold after the registration of the plan. While these findings are clearly supported by the evidence, I think, with respect, there was an error in the principle applied in determining the question to be decided.

It appears to have been assumed in making the award that the respondent was entitled as of right to register the plan prepared in 1951 and to sell the lots shown upon it as building lots. With respect, there is no basis for any such assumption. . . .

The risk that the Planning Board of the township, and the Minister of Planning and Development on its recommendation, would decline to approve a plan of subdivision of the property in question into building lots, was one to which the area of 18.4 acres purchased by the respondent in 1952 was subject, in common with all other vacant lands in the township. Before the passing of the expropriation resolution on March 24, 1954, it had been made clear to the respondent that the plan of subdivision as originally proposed in 1952 would not be recommended by the Planning Board to the Minister or approved by him, and it was in consequence of this that the second plan setting aside the area as a high school site was prepared. It cannot, therefore, be said that, as of the date of the expropriation and by reason of it, the respondent was deprived of its right to sell the property as building lots. There was no such market then available or in prospect since the land could not be sold in lots without the approval and registration of the plan. It was not the action of the appellant which deprived the respondent of such a market but the inability of the latter to obtain the recommendation of the Planning Board and the approval of the Minister of the plan of subdivision. It is not, of course, suggested that either that Board or the Minister acted otherwise than in the manner they considered to be in the public interest in discharging their statutory duties.

The owner of property subject to zoning restrictions is not, if the land be expropriated, entitled to compensation on the basis of its value to him if used for some purpose forbidden by the Regulations. The contrary of this proposition was asserted and rejected as long ago as 1870 in *Stebbing* v. *Metropolitan Bd. of Works*. The owner of property suitable for use as licensed premises situate in a place where Part II of the *Canada Temperance Act,*

R.S.C. 1952, c. 30, is in force cannot, if it be compulsorily taken, assert a value based on the profits which he would derive from the sale of liquor.

The fact that there was but one available purchaser for the property does not, of course, affect the right of the respondent to be compensated to the full extent of the value of the property to him as of the date of expropriation, in accordance with the principle so often stated in this Court and restated in *Woods Mfg. Co.* v. *The King.*

The evidence directed to establishing this, while considerable in extent, is not, in my opinion, entirely satisfactory. . . .

There is, however, concrete evidence as to an amount which the present respondent apparently considered to be the value to it immediately preceding the expropriation and that this amount of $100,000 was an amount which the appellant was prepared to pay, subject to conditions which need no longer be considered.

I have come to the conclusion that the proper course to be followed is to settle the amount of remuneration in this Court rather than to refer the matter back.

While it is to be presumed that the respondent offered to accept this amount at a time when it was fully informed as to its legal rights, it should be borne in mind that, being aware that the property was subject to expropriation at a price to be fixed by arbitration, it might well, in order to escape the delays, costs and uncertainty of arbitration and perhaps thereafter litigation, accept less than the full value of the property to it. In the circumstances, I think it proper to add 10% to the above-mentioned figure for the compulsory taking. I would accordingly allow this appeal and fix the amount of the compensation at $110,000, with interest at the legal rate from March 22, 1954.

I would allow the appellant its costs in this Court and in the Court of Appeal. I would not interfere with the order made as to the costs of the hearing before His Honour Judge Forsyth.

[The opinions of Rand and Cartwright J. J., who agreed, and Abbott J., who dissented, are omitted. Taschereau J. concurred with Cartwright J.]

HEWETT *v.* TORONTO

Ontario. Court of Appeal. 1962. 35 D.L.R. 2d 290

Hewett owned a parcel of land with a north/south frontage of 235 feet on Mount Pleasant Road in the city of Toronto, running back in an easterly direction 291 feet, the first 180 feet of which was zoned R2V1, which permitted apartment houses. The remaining 111 feet was in an R1V1 zone and was mostly ravine land although there was some level land. An apartment building in the R2V1 zone could not, without a Committee of Adjustment permission, encroach into the R1V1 zone to the rear, nor could the area in the R1V1 zone be used in computing the permitted size of the apartment that could be built in the R2V1 zone. On December 11, 1954 Hewett agreed to sell the entire parcel to one Stulberg for $88,000. The agreement provided: "It is understood that the west 180 feet of this land is zoned R2V1 and the east 111 feet more or less in R1V1. It is agreed that the Vendor will covenant not to oppose application to rezone R1V1 section to R2V1 within one year from closing." The vendor was aware that the purchaser intended to build an apartment house. Before this deal was closed the city, probably prompted by the complaints of neighbouring ratepayers, passed amending By-law 19,394 to make the depth of 180 feet R1V1 but the by-law was invalid for procedural reasons under *Bondi* v. *Scarborough* (1959) and in any event, it had not been approved by the Municipal Board when the city, in 1955, expropriated the rear 111 feet. Notwithstanding the expropriation, the contract was not immediately terminated, and the parties kept extending it from time to time until August, 1957, when it was cancelled. By-law 19,394 had still not been finally dealt with by the Municipal Board by October, 1961, when Hewett's executrix and the city contested the compensation.

RISK Q.C. Official Arbitrator: . . . It is obvious that the purchaser did not want the property unless it could be used for an apartment site, and Mr. Kaplan's unwillingness to close the transaction on the original date is easy to understand. This, however, does not answer the question whether the vendor had an enforceable contract or whether he did not. All we know is that the time for closing was extended. Surely the purchaser could not have been compelled to close after the expropriation, regardless of the precise reasons which made him reluctant to close earlier. As Mr. Starr graphically put it in his oral argument: "He was just lucky the City laid it right in his mitts so he could get out by expropriation."

The fact that Hewett did not take action against the purchaser shortly after April 1, 1955, is not fatal to the Claimant's contention. The vendor was not obliged to take court action immediately, and chose instead to agree to an extension of time, which is a not unusual course.

After the expropriating By-law was passed no court would have decreed specific performance of the agreement, or even damages. It is not reasonable to believe that Stulberg could have been forced to take the property, or pay damages, after June 21, 1955.

One of the submissions made by Counsel for the Claimant in his written argument was that "equity will not allow a statute to be made an instrument of fraud," and therefore the City should not be allowed to take advantage of the effect of its zoning By-law in destroying the value of the property shortly before expropriation. No effect will be given to this argument. It is not within the jurisdiction of an Official Arbitrator to question or even examine the reasons or motives of the municipal corporation in this or any other case. . . .

Moreover it is just not reasonable to value the Mount Pleasant frontage as if it could be sold for an apartment site. Technically the zoning may not have been changed from R2V1 right down to the present time, because By-law 19,394 has apparently never been approved by the Municipal Board. It cannot be conceived, however, by any stretch of the imagination, that a purchaser would buy this land and pay for it as an apartment site as long as this By-law was "on the books of the City", as Mr. Langer said. Apart from the special situation created by the agreement between Hewett and Stulberg, there was no market for the Mount Pleasant land except for single family residences from the time the re-zoning By-law was passed until the present. Reference of course is made to a real market and not to remote possibilities which might interest persons willing to gamble on the repeal of the By-law. . . .

As to the lands included in the Stulberg offer, the Claimant's contention is that the expropriation spoiled a sale for $88,000.00—there is some evidence that this was a fair price—while the lands remaining, even though fronting on Mount Pleasant, were only worth $29,375.00. Therefore, it was urged, the owner lost the difference between these two figures, namely $58,625.00. This amount looks ridiculous if treated as the market value of the rear lands which were expropriated. If considered as a separate unit, these side hill and ravine lands may not have been worth more than Mr. Bunston's figure of $4,434.00. The proper method, though, is to find the value of the entire piece to the owner before expropriation and the value to him of the part remaining afterwards.

It does not quite follow that the Claimant should be awarded precisely $58,625.00 for the taking of the part at the rear of the Mount Pleasant lands. It is all very well to say that Hewett had an enforceable agreement, but that is not the same thing as having Stulberg's money in his pocket. Quite possibly litigation might have been necessary to enforce the vendor's rights, and a reasonable man in Hewett's position would have made some allowances for the anxiety and delay which would have been caused by a lawsuit, however successful. Having regard to all the circumstances, and attempting to view the situation as Hewett should have done as a prudent man, I find that the value to the owner of the entire parcel covered by the Stulberg offer was $80,000.00 at the moment of the expropriation and $30,000.00 afterwards. . . .

[The city appealed to the Court of Appeal.]

LAIDLAW J.A.: . . . It is plain to me that the error in the award made by the learned arbitrator lies in his assessment of the value to the owner of the part of the . . . parcel not expropriated by the city. He proceeded erroneously on the basis that By-law 19483 [sic] had full force and effect and that the part of the . . . parcel which was not expropriated could be used only for the erection of private dwelling houses. He ought to have treated By-law 19483 as a nullity. . . .

However, in determining the value to the owner of that part of the land an arbitrator could properly take into consideration the probability or the possibility that that part of the land might be rezoned. . . . The evidence now before the Court does not justify a finding that the Ontario Municipal Board would certainly give approval to a rezoning by-law changing the part of the land which was not expropriated from zone R2V1 to R1V1. [After referring to the test in the *Woods* case, his Lordship continued.] . . . It would be wholly unreasonable and without any justification whatsoever to find on that basis that parcel number one expropriated by the city had a value to the owner of $50,000. No prudent person in the position of the owner would pay that amount for the rear portion of the . . . parcel rather than be dispossessed of it. . . .

A court might hold that substantial performance of the contract by the vendor was possible and that it was proper, just and equitable to compel performance of it by the purchaser. However, I find it unnecessary to decide that question now because, as I stated, there is no evidence in this case that the owner of the land suffered any loss or damage in addition to the true value to him of the parcels of land expropriated or that he suffered any injury to the remaining part of his land by reason of the expropriation. . . .

[The opinion of McGillivray J.A., who agreed, is ommitted. McGillivray J.A. accepted the Official Arbitrator's view that the contract "had been rendered unenforceable by the action of the city." Gibson J.A. agreed with Laidlaw J.A.]

NOTE. It should be remembered that the *Bondi* case, so strongly relied on by the Court of Appeal in the *Hewett* case, was decided four years after the expropriation took place, and in 1955 By-law 19,394 would have been regarded by most lawyers (and by the land market) as only wanting in one respect, the approval of the Ontario Municipal Board. Has the Official Arbitrator not assumed the validity of the R2V1 zoning in accepting $80,000 as the value of the entire parcel and the validity of the R1V1 zoning in finding the value of the remaining parcel at only $30,000? If the frontage was worth only $30,000 could the whole parcel still be worth $80,000? Is the assumption valid if the contract was lost by the expropriation? What value would the Official Arbitrator have reached on the test of "market value"?

DICKINSON *v*. TORONTO. 1962. Unreported. Risk Q.C. Official Arbitrator. The city of Toronto expropriated No. 14, DeLisle Avenue, owned by the late Mr. Dickinson, on September 12, 1960. The property had a frontage of 67 feet by a depth of 122 feet. DeLisle Street runs west from Yonge Street one block north of St. Clair Avenue and No. 14 is about 165 feet west of Yonge Street. The intersection of Young and St. Clair is an important commercial area. No. 14 was in an R2 zone, which excluded commercial uses except for parking accessory to a commercial use in the nearby C zone and for a *municipally owned* parking lot. The city intended to use the lot to extend its own parking lot situated at the time of the expropriation immediately to the north and east of No. 14. On the west side the adjoining property was owned by a church and was formerly a manse. On the south side of DeLisle Street property was being acquired by Miles Parking Limited to be used as a parking lot accessory to the commercial use of adjacent land by the A.W. Miles funeral establishment on the north side of St. Clair Avenue. These properties had been recently acquired and using their sales prices as a basis of calculation, one witness for the owner valued No. 14 at $67,000 but the Arbitrator objected that the value was peculiar to the purchaser who was able to use these lots for a commercial use. Two witnesses for the city of Toronto valued the parcel at $27,000 on the assumption that it could be used at best, under R2 zoning, for two triplexes. Neither of the city's witnesses considered the possibility of rezoning. The owner's witnesses appear to have disregarded the R2 zoning altogether and considered the property as suitable for either an office building or a parking lot. RISK Q.C.: "In order to determine this matter, it is necessary to form some opinion, on the basis of the evidence, concerning the chances of re-zoning. . . .

"I have come to the conclusion that there was a reasonable possibility, at the time of the expropriation, that the property would have been re-zoned for commercial use had it not been for the compulsory taking. The history of the zoning, the rejection of certain other applications for re-zoning, and the residential character of DeLisle Avenue west of the subject property have not been overlooked. There are several factors, however, which lead to the conclusion above mentioned:

"(a) The area is 'dominated' by the Yonge-St. Clair business district, as one witness said. The question is, where should the line between commercial and residential be logically drawn.

"(b) The property itself was bounded on two sides by a municipal car park, which is in substance a commercial use. While the house immediately to the west is a former manse, the church property itself forms a natural barrier between the subject property and the rest of the north side of DeLisle Avenue.

"(c) Across the street a 'parking station' has been or will be created. This may be an 'accessory' use, and, therefore, legally permissible, but it is a car park none the less.

"(d) The property was taken for the enlargement of the municipal parking lot. If this could be imagined as a possibility rather than an accomplished fact, the owners of the church property might have been quite willing to consent to its use for a small office building rather than a parking lot, as the lesser of two evils. . . .

"The late Peter Dickinson purchased the property in October, 1959, (his deed being registered on November 2nd) for $40,000.00, payable $7,000.00 in cash and $33,000.00 by mortgage given back to the vendors. Ordinarily the price paid by an owner whose land is subsequently expropriated is not a factor of special importance in determining the value, although it may be taken into consideration along with the prices paid for comparable properties and other relevant facts. In this particular case, however, the purchase by Mr. Dickinson has more than usual significance. He was one of the leading architects in Canada, especially noted for the design of a number of well known commercial buildings. He was a man of great ability. The fact that he was willing to pay $40,000.00 for a property which was demonstrably worth less than $30,000.00, if used in conformity with the existing zoning, is of some importance. He may have made a bad bargain, but on the other hand, he may have had a keen appreciation of the possibilities of the site.

"Although re-zoning for commercial use (more particularly for an office building) was a very real possibility, it was by no means a certainty. It does not seem practicable in this matter to estimate the chances at some percentage of the value if re-zoned. . . . Having regard to all the evidence, the compensation to which the Claimant is entitled will be fixed at the sum of $50,000.00. Interest should be added at the rate of 5 per cent per annum from October 26, 1960, the approximate date when possession was surrendered."

SISTERS OF CHARITY OF ROCKINGHAM *v*. THE KING
Nova Scotia. Privy Council. [1922] 2 A.C. 315

The appellants, who operated a girls' boarding school, owned two small promontories of land on the edge of Halifax harbour separated from the rest of their land by a public road and a railway. They had no right of way across the railway but they had, for many years, crossed it freely to the promontories, on one of which, 220 square feet in area, they had built a bathing house and on the other, 1220 square feet in area, a wharf and esplanade. They had only a prescriptive title to these parcels. The Canadian government expropriated the two parcels and paid compensation, the amount of which, some $8,000, is not in dispute. The land was taken to enable the government to establish a shunting yard for its railway at this point, and in addition to the appellants' land, other land was taken and part of the harbour filled. The present claim is for injurious affection to the land on the other side of the tracks, where the school was located and which was affected by the proposed use of the railway shunting yards. Cassels J. in the Exchequer Court refused the claim. The Supreme Court of Canada upheld him.

LORD PARMOOR: . . . Compensation claims are statutory and depend on statutory provisions. No owner of lands expropriated by statute for public purposes is entitled to compensation, either for the value of land taken, or for damage, on the ground that his land is "injuriously affected," unless he can establish a statutory right. The claim, therefore, of the appellants, if any, must be found in a Canadian statute. . . . Their Lordships have applied the English decisions, so far as they are applicable, in the construction of the Canadian statute.

The *Exchequer Court Act* (R.S. Can., 1906, c. 140) by s. 20 gives exclusive jurisdiction to the Exchequer Court to hear and determine every claim against the Crown, either for property taken for any public purpose or for damage to property "injuriously affected by the construction of any public work." The words "injuriously affected by the construction of any public work" are to be found in ss. 22, 26 and 27 of the *Expropriation Act* (R.S. Can., 1906, c. 143). . . .The real questions, however, to be determined in the present appeal are whether under the special circumstances of the case the appellants can maintain a claim for damage to their property on the west side of the railway, on the ground that it has been injuriously affected by the construction of a public work over the two promontories, and, if so, what is the principle to be applied in assessing the amount. The actual amount, if any, is for the decision of the Exchequer Court, and cannot be raised before their Lordships.

If the railway shunting yard, of which complaint has been made, had been constructed on land, no part of which had been expropriated from the appellants, the appellants would not have been entitled to claim compensation, although, in fact, such construction had seriously depreciated the value of their property on the west side of the railway. Where no land of the same owner has been taken, the words "injuriously affected" only include damage or loss which would have been actionable but for statutory powers, and such damage or loss must be occasioned by the construction of the authorized works, as distinct from their user. . . . If, therefore, the land taken for the shunting yard had belonged wholly to some owner other than the appellants, the appellants could not have claimed compensation on the ground that their property on the east side of the railway had been "injuriously affected"; but part of the land so taken was the property of the appellants, and it is on this ground that the appellants base their claim to compensation.

The first of the reported English decisions which deals with the question of injuriously affecting lands by the construction of public works, where the mischief of which complaint is made is caused by what is done on lands taken from the same owner, is *In re Stockport, Timperley and Altringham Ry. Co.* That decision has been considered in a number of subsequent cases. For a time it gave rise to considerable difference of judicial opinion, but the law as applied by Crompton J. has been twice considered, and approved in the House of Lords: *Duke of Buccleuch* v. *Metropolitan Board of Works*; *Cowper Essex* v. *Acton Local Board.* In the *Stockport Case* a company had taken land, the property of L., and proposed to make their railway so close to a cotton mill belonging to him, that, by reason of the proximity of the railway, and the danger of fire from trains using the line, the building could only be insured at an increased premium, and was rendered of less saleable value. Crompton J. stated the principle as follows: "Where the damage is occasioned by what is done upon other land which the company have purchased, and such damage would not have been actionable as against the original proprietor, as in the case of the sinking of a well and causing the abstraction of water by percolation, the company have a right to say, 'We had done what we had a right to do as proprietors, and do not require the protection of any Act of Parliament; we, therefore, have not injured you by virtue of the provisions of the Act; no cause of action has been taken away from you by the Act.' Where, however, the mischief is caused by what is done on the land taken, the party seeking compensation has a right to say, 'It is by the Act of Parliament, and the Act of Parliament only, that you have done the acts which have caused the damage; without the Act of Parliament, everything you have done, and are about to do, in the making and using the railway, would have been illegal and actionable, and is, therefore, matter for compensation according to the rule in question.' "

The rule to which Crompton J. refers is that an owner is not entitled to compensation, except for matters which, but for statutory powers, would have given a right to action, and he brings the case before him within this rule. In assessing the amount of compensation due to an owner of lands for damage, caused by the construction of works on other land taken from him, Crompton J. justified the inclusion of mischief which arises both in the making and using of the railway, on the ground that but for the Act of Parliament both the making and the using of the railway would have been illegal, and that he was only applying the general principle already established to the circumstances of the case before him.

The principle stated by Crompton J. in the *Stockport Case* was considered in *Duke of Buccleuch* v. *Metropolitan Board of Works,* and a distinction was drawn between that case and the cases of the *Hammersmith Ry. Co.* v. *Brand,* and *City of Glasgow Union Ry. Co.* v. *Hunter.* Lord Chelmsford, referring to these cases, said: "In neither of these cases was any land taken by the railway company connected with the lands which were alleged to have been so injured, and the claim for compensation was for damage caused by the use and not by the construction of the railway. But if, in each of the cases, lands of the parties had been taken for the railway, I do not see why a claim for compensation in respect of injury to adjoining premises might not have been successfully made on account of their probable depreciation by reason of vibration, or smoke, or noise, occasioned by passing trains."

If that decision is applied to the circumstances of the present appeal, it would, in the opinion of their Lordships, sanction a claim to compensation for the probable or apprehended use of the two promontories as part of a railway shunting yard. No doubt a difficulty arises in the assessment of amount where the mischief complained of arises, not only on the land which has been taken from the appellants, but also on land over which they had no ownership claim; but this is no reason for refusing to entertain a claim, so far as the damage claimed can be shown to arise from the apprehended legal use of the lands taken from them.

The subsequent case of *Cowper Essex* v. *Acton Local Board* cannot be differentiated from the case under appeal. It accepts the decision of Crompton J. as an accurate exposition of English compensation law. When that case was before the Court of Appeal, it was held that the intervention of a railway, which was wholly the property of the railway company and in which the claimant seeking compensation had no interest, made a valid distinction from the *Stockport Case,* and that that case ought not to be extended. The Master of the Rolls further expressed an opinion that the *Stockport Case* was in itself wholly wrong. When the case came before the House of Lords, the principle of the *Stockport Case* was confirmed and approved, Lord

Macnaghten saying that, in his opinion, it had stood the test of criticism, that in practice he believed it had always been followed, and that it was perfectly right. As in the present case, the land taken was separated from the lands alleged to be injuriously affected by a railway, and there is no evidence that there was any right of way over the railway between the lands of the same owner on either side. It was held, however, to be sufficient that the lands taken and the lands alleged to be injuriously affected, were held by the same owner under such conditions that the unity of ownership conduced to the advantage of the property being comprised in one holding. Lord Watson, after referring to previous cases, said: "It appears to me to be the result of these authorities, which are binding upon this House, that a proprietor is entitled to compensation for depreciation of the value of his other lands, in so far as such depreciation is due to the anticipated legal use of works to be constructed upon the land which has been taken from him under compulsory powers." In a further passage Lord Watson says: "I am prepared to hold that, where several pieces of land, owned by the same person, are so near to each other, and so situated that the possession and control of each gives an enhanced value to all of them, they are lands held together within the meaning of the Act, so that if one piece is compulsorily taken, and converted to uses which depreciate the value of the rest, the owner has a right to compensation."

In the same case the Lord Chancellor says that where the future use of the part of a proprietor's land taken from him may damage the remainder, then such damage may be injuriously affecting the proprietor's other lands, though it would not be injurious affection of the land of neighbouring proprietors, from whom nothing has been taken for the purpose of the intended works.

Applying then the principle of this decision to the case under appeal, it is clear that the possession and control of the two promontories did give an enhanced value to the land of the same owners on the west side of the railway, and that so far as the depreciation of the value of the lands on the west side of the railway is due to the anticipated legal use of works which may be constructed over the two promontories, the appellants are in the position of owners whose land has been injuriously affected by the construction of public works. It appears that before the hearing of the case the railway shunting yard had been laid out, and that the actual use of the land comprised in the two promontories was inconsiderable. In the opinion of their Lordships, however, actual user at the time when the compensation case is heard is not the basis on which the amount of compensation should be assessed. It may be that at the time when the compensation case is heard no works have been constructed, and in any case the appellants are entitled to claim compensation, which must be claimed once for all, for depreciation in the value of their lands on the west side of the railway, in so far as such depreciation is due to the anticipated legal use of authorized works which may be constructed upon the two promontories. The limitation of the amount of compensation to the anticipated construction of authorized works upon lands actually taken from the appellants has a special importance in a case like the present, where the shunting yard has been largely laid out on land which has not been taken from the appellants, and which has never been part of their property. This limitation, which is plainly expressed in all the leading English decisions, is again restated in *Horton* v. *Colwyn Bay Urban Council,* in which it was held that as the acts of user, the contemplation of which caused the depreciation, would be done on lands not the property of the claimant, the claimant was not entitled to any compensation.

The problem of applying the above principles in a case where the mischief complained of has arisen partly on lands taken from the claimants, and partly on other lands outside their property, can only be settled by a consideration of all the circumstances in a particular case. Clearly in this case the appellants are entitled to a less amount of compensation than if all the lands taken in the laying out of the shunting yard had belonged to them, but on the other hand, the fact that other lands are comprised in the scheme in addition to the lands taken from the appellants, does not deprive the appellants of their right to compensation, so long as their claim is not extended beyond mischief which arises from the apprehended legal user of the two promontories as part of a railway shunting yard.

It is not possible on the information available before their Lordships to give further assistance on the assessment of the amount of compensation due to the appellants.

Their Lordships will humbly advise His Majesty that the judgments of the Exchequer Court and the Supreme Court of Canada should be reversed, and that the case be remitted to the Exchequer Court, and that the costs of this appeal and in the Courts below be paid by the respondent.

THE MUNICIPAL ACT

Ontario. Revised Statutes. 1960. Chapter 249

337. (1) Where land is expropriated for the purposes of a corporation, or is injuriously affected by the exercise of any of the powers of a corporation under the authority of this or any general or special Act, unless it is otherwise expressly provided by such general or special Act, the corporation shall make due compensation to the owner for the land expropriated and for any damage necessarily resulting from the expropriation of the land or, where land is injuriously affected by the exercise of such powers, for the damages necessarily resulting therefrom, beyond any advantage that the owner may derive from any work for the purposes of or in connection with which the land is injuriously affected.

(2) The amount of the compensation, if not mutually agreed upon, shall be determined by arbitration.

(3) Where fencing or additional fencing will become necessary, owing to land having been expropriated, the cost of it shall be included in the compensation.

(4) Where part only of the land of an owner is expropriated, there shall be included in the compensation a sum sufficient to compensate him for any damages directly resulting from severance.

THE PUBLIC WORKS ACT

Ontario. Revised Statutes. 1960. Chapter 338

21. The Minister shall make to the owner of land entered upon, taken or used by him or injuriously affected by the exercise of any of the powers conferred by this Act due compensation for any damages necessarily resulting from the exercise of such powers, beyond any advantage that the owner may derive from the contemplated work, and any claim for such compensation not mutually agreed upon shall be determined as hereinafter provided.

25. If the Minister is of opinion that he can obtain the whole of a lot or parcel of land of which a part may be expropriated by him at a more reasonable price or to greater advantage than by acquiring part only, he may expropriate the whole of the lot or parcel and also any right of way thereto if the right of way is separated from the public work, and may afterwards sell and convey the land or right of way or any part thereof as he deems expedient.

WARNING NOTE. The observation of Lord Parmoor in the *Sisters of Charity* case that compensation claims are statutory only should be kept especially in mind in calculating the set off of advantages. Sometimes the amount can be set off against the compensation for injurious affection only, sometimes against the compensation for the land that is taken as well. This set off is the closest thing to "betterment" to be found in Canada in practice.

NOTE ON BIBLIOGRAPHY. There are many standard texts on compensation, both English and American. In Canada, see Challies, *The Law of Expropriation* (1954). Stewart, *Real Estate Appraisal in a Nutshell* (1962) is a useful and "simplified restatement of the theory and practice of appraising with particular reference to the Canadan scene" (from the author's preface) See also Todd, "Winds of Change and the Law of Expropriation" (1961), 39 *Canadian Bar Review* 542.

THE ACQUISITION OF LAND (ASSESSMENT OF COMPENSATION) ACT, 1919
England. Statutes. 1919. Chapter 57

2. In assessing compensation, an official arbitrator shall act in accordance with the following rules:

(1) No allowance shall be made on account of the acquisition being compulsory:

(2) The value of land shall, subject as hereinafter provided, be taken to be the amount which the land if sold in the open market by a willing seller might be expected to realize: Provided always that the arbitrator shall be entitled to consider all returns and assessments of capital value for taxation made or acquiesced in by the claimant:

(3) The special suitability or adaptability of the land for any purpose shall not be taken into account if that purpose is a purpose to which it could be applied only in pursuance of statutory powers, or for which there is no market apart from the special needs of a particular purchaser or the requirements of any Government Department or any local or public authority: Provided that any bona fide offer for the purchase of the land made before the passing of this Act which may be brought to the notice of the arbitrator shall be taken into consideration:

(4) Where the value of the land is increased by reason of the use thereof or of any premises thereon in a manner which could be restrained by any court, or is contrary to law, or is detrimental to the health of the inmates of the premises or to the public health, the amount of that increase shall not be taken into account:

(5) Where the land is, and but for the compulsory acquisition would continue to be, devoted to a purpose of such a nature that there is no general demand or market for land for that purpose, the

compensation may, if the official arbitrator is satisfied that reinstatement in some other place is bona fide intended, be assessed on the basis of the reasonable cost of equivalent reinstatement:

(6) The provision of Rule (2) shall not affect the assessment of compensation for disturbance or any other matter not directly based on the value of land.

DRAFT EXPROPRIATION ACT
Ontario Branch. Canadian Bar Association

(2) The compensation shall be limited to:
- (a) the market value of the land including any buildings and improvements thereon;
- (b) damages occasioned by the taking to any business established previous to the expropriation;
- (c) damages to land, buildings *etc.*—injurious affection;
- (d) the cost of fencing or additional fencing . . . together with 10 per cent of the amount of compensation so determined and 5 per cent per annum by way of interest from the date possession is obtained to the date payment of compensation is made to the owner.

NOTE. When the draft Act was presented to the Select Committee of the Ontario Legislature on *The Land Compensation Act,* the clause reproduced above was omitted. The submission said, "The (sub) committee recommended that there be a list of specific headings of compensation comparable to those which form the basis of awarding compensation in the United Kingdom. . . . The Ontario members of the Canadian Bar Association, after deliberation, deleted the above-mentioned recommendation primarily upon the ground that any statement of the headings of compensation would serve to create new uncertainties and confusion rather than clarify the law."

See now, *The Expropriation Procedures Act, 1962–63*, S.O., 1962–63, c. 43 (effective January 1, 1964), which provides for "due compensation", including compensation for injurious affection where no land was expropriated.

RISK, MEMORANDUM TO ONTARIO COMMITTEE ON LAND EXPROPRIATION (1961)

(a) The concept of "value to the owner" has become firmly embedded in our case law. We should at least take a fresh look at it, disregarding for the moment the legal wars and skirmishes of the recent past. Nowadays when claimants come before an arbitrator it is quite usual to find them stressing features of their properties which make them particularly valuable to the owners, and testifying that they would pay amounts far in excess of the market value rather than be ejected. I do not say that these people are necessarily insincere. I do say that the concept of value to the owner has increased the natural tendency of human beings to exaggerate their losses. The idea of compensation according to market value has its advantages, among which is the fact that it is easier for both parties to ascertain.

(b) On the other hand, the law as declared by our courts has deprived claimants of other damages to which by any normal standards of fairness they are entitled. I refer to damages which are not part of the value of the real estate itself, but which are the direct consequence of the expropriation.

This is a subject which would have to be considered with great care, and much might be said about the dangers of it, yet for the present I shall say only that the law as it now stands results in injustice in some cases.

(c) As to enumerating the different elements on which compensation is to be based there are of course practical difficulties. To specify the items will be to invite new legal arguments and refinements. Nevertheless, I am inclined to feel that it is worth a try. As one member of the Committee put it when these problems were being discussed by an eminent legal expert, "If the lawyers can't agree we shall have to spell it out—one, two, three, four."

3. PLANNING AND LOCAL TAXES

The present system of local taxation in most parts of Canada rests on the value of land so completely that an examination of planning and land value cannot ignore the effect of the tax system on land use and indirectly on planning.

Typical of local taxation Acts is *The Assessment Act*, R.S.O. 1960, c. 23, section 31(1) of which provides that, subject to special provision "land shall be assessed at its actual value." In ascertaining the "actual value" consideration is to be given to "the present use, location, rental value, sale value and any other circumstances affecting the value" (Subsection 2). The value of land with buildings is to be ascertained by consideration of the same factors and the "cost of replacement." The value of the buildings is the amount by which the value of the land and buildings exceeds the value of the land. The value of the land and the value of the buildings so ascertained are to be set down in separate columns in the assessment roll, and "the assessment shall be the sum of such values" (Subsection 4).

It may be assumed that "actual value" means "market value" and not "value to the owner". See *Sun Life Assurance Co.* v. *Montreal* (1950), where Rinfret C.J. said, "I need not insist on the point that a municipal valuation for assessment purposes is not to be made in accordance with the rules laid down with regard to the valuation of a property for expropriation purposes. One main ground why such a course should not be followed is that the expropriation of a property means the permanent divesting of the owner and should legitimately, therefore, take into account the present value and all the prospective possibilities of the property, while the municipal valuation is, generally speaking, only made for one year, or, in the case of the City of Montreal, for three years, with certain provisions for modification if certain events happen, such as alteration, improvement, fire, etc. . . . In the yearly valuation of a property for purposes of municipal assessment there is no room for hypothesis as regards the future of the property. The assessor should not look at past, or subsequent or potential values. His valuation must be based on conditions as he finds them at the date of the assessment." That case dealt with the meaning of the words "actual value" in the Charter of the City of Montreal. Compare earlier Ontario cases, for example, Meredith C.J.O. in *Re Ontario and Minnesota Power Co. Ltd. and Fort Francis* (1916), "That the same principle [as in the expropriation cases] must be applied in ascertaining the 'actual value' of land for the purpose of assessment . . . is not, I think, open to question." Hodgins J.A. disagreed; he said, " . . . the fact that the municipality appraises the land each year as it then is, and in that way gets the benefit, from time to time, of each realised possibility as it occurs, must be considered. The reason for the rule in compensation cases that 'all advantages which the land possesses, present or future,' must be paid for, is that the land is finally taken, and the owner loses both those present and future advantages, and the taker gets them.

"In the case of assessment the situation is so different that I prefer to place my decision in refusing the application upon the ground that the actual value in this case may properly include the advantageous position of this lot in relation to the other works. Consequently, the propriety of the amount fixed is at best a question of fact."

In order to ascertain the amount of tax to be collected from landowners, the municipality first calculates its needs and then allocates the total amount amongst the landowners according to their assessment. In some provinces there may be added to the "actual value" a "business assessment" either determined by the Council as a percentage of the assessed value, or set by statute, as in Ontario, where, for example, a distiller is assessed an extra 150 per cent, a brewer 75 per cent and a professional man 50 per cent.

One of the peculiarities of assessment, in Ontario at least, is that assessed "actual" values are rarely more than a quarter of the market value of the assessed land and buildings.

It must not be assumed that land and buildings (or improvements) are the only source of revenue for Canadian municipalities although they are the chief tax base. There are substantial contributions to municipalities from the provincial governments. In Ontario highways and education are subsidized by as much as fifty per cent in some cases.

There are other systems of land tax in use elsewhere and the effect of the common Canadian system may be seen by an examination of an alternative, site value taxation, material on which follows. A third system has been in use in England since 1601, the annual rental system. Both land and buildings are taxed under the annual rental system, but the assessment is based on the rental income, or potential income rather than the market value.

RAWSON, PROPERTY TAXATION AND URBAN DEVELOPMENT

Washington, D.C. 1961. Urban Land Institute Research Monograph 4

The analysis of values presented in this part of the study is directed to demonstrating what the difference in the tax load on various types of use and development in a particular city would be in two cases (a) the taxation of land and improvements equally and (b) the taxation of land only.

In considering this question two points should be borne firmly in mind. In any city the value of land per unit area is very much higher at central points than in the outskirts. And, for fully improved sites, the ratio of land value to improvement value is generally much higher at the central points of the city than in the outskirts.

In Burnaby, for example, the point of highest value occurs on the Kingsway commercial strip between Sussex and Nelson Avenues—$210 per front foot unit; the lowest values, from $2½ to $5 per front foot unit, are to be found on the slopes of Burnaby Mountain and in parts of the peat flats near the Fraser River. . . . The differences in value between central and and peripheral lands in a city are much more striking in more densely populated cities serving metropolitan or region-wide functions. In Vancouver, Burnaby's western neighbour, assessed values run from $4 per front foot unit at the lowest points to $3600 at the point of highest values in Vancouver's central business district. The peak value in the dominant metropolitan city, Vancouver, is several times the peak value in any of the surrounding municipalities.

The second point is that different urban land uses, even when the land is well improved and fully used, exhibit on the average different ratios of improvement to land values. Ratios of improvements to land may run in the neighbourhood of 6 or 7 to 1 in good residential development. In commercial and industrial areas the ratio is generally lower—3 or 4 to 1, and in the central business districts, even though the sites may support well constructed multi-story buildings, the ratio may be 2, or even 1 to 1 because of the very high element of the site value in the total value of the property.

The point of these generalizations is that to shift taxation from buildings and land to land alone would bring a shift in the tax load from the peripheral to the central areas, and probably from residential to industrial and commercial properties. It is worth noting that a low ratio of improvement may mean that a site is not well developed, or it may mean simply that the land, although used intensively, is of very high value. The ratio itself, without reference to the use of the site and to its location in the general topography of values in a city, would not be a good guide to determining the quality of improvements in a given property. . . .

In 1957 Burnaby raised $3,049,000 for general municipal purposes by the tax on real estate. For purposes of illustration it has been assumed that that Burnaby required $3,500,000 for general purposes in 1959, to be raised by the property tax. This would have required either (a) a mill rate of $18.60 per thousand dollars of assessed valuation of land and improvements, or (b) a mill rate of $72.30 per thousand dollars of land value. These mill rates have been used throughout this analysis wherever a comparison of taxes has been made.

Three simple examples will serve to show how different ratios of improvement will result in different tax burdens if land alone is taxed. In each of these constructed cases the total value of the property is the same—$10,000. If land and improvements are taxed at an equal rate the tax each property pays will be $186 (18.6 mills × $10,000). If land alone is taxed, at a rate of 72.3 mills, the different portions of land value in the total value, as indicated by the ratio, will result in different tax burdens:

i. Land value $2000: Improvement value $8000: Total value $10,000.
Ratio of Total value to Land value 5:1
Taxes @72.3 × $2000 = $144.60

ii. Land value $8000: Improvement value $2000: Total value $10,000
Ratio of Total value to Land value 1.25:1
Taxes @ 72.3 × $8000 = $578.40

iii. Land value $2580: Improvement value $7420: Total value $10,000
Ratio of Total value to Land value 3.88:1
Taxes @ 72.3 × $2580 = $186.50

Where the ratio of the property stands in relation to the *average ratio* of improvement for the city reveals both the magnitude and the direction of the change in taxes which that property would bear under a changed system of levy.

It is not meant to imply that the average ratio of improvement has particular significance as indicating the type or quality of building development in Burnaby as a whole, or that conclusions could be drawn about another city's development by comparing its average ratio to that of Burnaby. The validity of comparisons of this kind remains to be tested. The average ratio is used in this analysis merely as a quick point of reference for judging whether a given property will pay higher or lower taxes under the two systems of taxation being examined. . . .

The larger the portion of value in a property attributable to the land, the more likely the property's tax would be higher if all improvements were exempted. Obviously vacant properties would pay much more, as would the near-vacant properties used for parking lots and billboards (see Figure 11). Typical of this kind are vacant lots in sample block 20B where taxes would rise from $10 to $41, and in sample block 17B from $16 to $64. In sample block 18B, where the vacant lots are interspersed among commercially used lots, taxes would rise from $28 to $109. . . .

Used car lots, gas stations with extensive blacktopped areas, and lots "used" only to support billboards are common in Burnaby. Commercial lots of this kind show improvement ratios on the order of 1.04:1 and 1.06:1 (billboards); 1.98:1 and 1.36:1 (gas stations). The four properties just mentioned would have their taxes raised substantially if improvements were exempt—the billboard lots from $70 to $262, and from $128 to $469; the gas stations from $308 to $604, and from $996 to $2843. These are typical cases. . . .

In the first instance the tax burden would shift partially from residential property toward commercial and industrial property and toward vacant and under-used land. The initial shift in tax burden would be followed by secondary and tertiary shifts in values but their direction and placement cannot readily be forecast.

Two main factors would be at work—the increased pressure on land and the absence of tax pressure on improvements. The one tends to lower land prices, to bring sites into use, in effect to increase the supply of land. The other, which makes building a more attractive investment, will increase the demand for land. These pressures acting at the same time, one pushing down and the other pulling up, may cancel one another out in affecting land prices. But pressures tending toward efficiency of development would continue to be exerted in each category of land use irrespective of price. The word "tend" is used advisedly since these pressures in the main would have immediate results only on marginal properties.

The third-stage effect, or result third-removed, should be a further increase of pressure on the lowest-ratio development as a result of the gradual improvement and consolidation of development; that is, of a rise in the average ratio of improvement for the city.

An improvement in assessment would likely reinforce rather than counter the tax shifts described. For one thing industrial land is presently underassessed relative to residential land. For another, vacant residential land is underassessed relative to improved residential land. The shift which would take place from residential to industrial and from improved to vacant land, as revealed by the analysis of assessed values, is therefore probably underestimated in terms of the true market values. On the other hand, residential buildings appear to be overassessed in some areas relative to the sites they occupy. Increases in land assessment might lessen somewhat the general advantage residential property has, unless under-assessment of land relative to buildings is equal for all categories of land use.

Considerations such as these in no way affect the validity of the tax shifts which would occur on the basis of present assessments. They do indicate however that a slightly different pattern of shift might be found in other taxing jurisdictions. And they show that assessment practice can have as important an effect as the tax system and the tax rate—that it may either emphasize or nullify a policy of taxing land at a higher rate than buildings. In any case, no matter what the tax system, the need to aim for equity in assessment remains.

CLARK, SITE VALUATION AS A BASE FOR LOCAL TAXATION
Canadian Tax Foundation. 1961. Conference Report.

... I shall now turn to an analysis of the six advantages claimed for site taxation to which I have previously referred. In this analysis I shall assume that we are dealing with a proposal for complete site taxation so that improvements will be entirely exempted. I also wish to assume that site taxation is to be introduced as intelligently as possible and I shall therefore postulate that it is proposed to change over to site taxation very gradually over a period of years and that the change is to be compulsory for all taxing jurisdictions within a province. Alternative assumptions would present particular problems with which there is not time to deal.

The first advantage which I have listed for site taxation is that it would greatly reduce speculation in land by imposing such a heavy tax burden on unused land that the unearned increment would largely disappear. This argument contains some truth but, in my opinion, the possible effects of site taxation on true speculation are greatly exaggerated. The greatest boom in land values ever to occur in Western Canada took place during the years 1909–13 when site taxation was at its zenith. The reason is not hard to find; profits from land speculation can be very large in relation to holding costs and the tripling or quadrupling of land taxes, as might occur under a change to site taxation, could be a relatively minor consideration—especially where it is anticipated that the land will be held for only a short period of time.

It will be true, of course, that under site taxation, the added carrying charges for many vacant pieces of land would make the cost of holding them prohibitive. In many instances, however, it is a mistake to assume that vacant land is being held for speculative reasons. Thus, land may be held by a business for future expansion, by a home-owner to ensure a quiet neighbourhood, by an entrepreneur because he does not consider the time economically propitious for the type of development he has in mind, as well as for other reasons. Vacant land held for these reasons generally would be more likely to be affected by site taxation than land held for speculation.

I would also like to suggest that speculative gains from land are not as harmful as commonly believed. In the first place, land speculators may actually perform a useful service to the community by combining various parcels of land into a single tract suitable for a type of development to which the individual parcels could not have been put. The mere act of holding vacant land over a period of years may also prove a boon to the community which suddenly finds that it has a great need of vacant land for some particular use—whether public or private. I would furthermore like to observe that a considerable proportion of the profit on land today goes to the person who actually develops the land. Thus, in every large Canadian city we have seen builders who have themselves acquired large tracts of farm land on the city outskirts, who have subdivided that land and then sold it with fully serviced homes. In this particular instance, there is a large profit on the sale of the land but it has gone to the person who actually developed that land. Is this an unearned increment or an earned increment? In my opinion it is part of each. This leads me to one very important conclusion; it is the anticipated profit on land which is one of the strongest contributing forces to urban development today. If it were possible to transfer the capital gains on land from private individuals to society at large (and site taxation emphatically does not do this), a great many urban developments now taking place would never have seen the light of day.

One further point should be made; if it is really considered to be a desirable public policy to curtail the existing volume of land speculation—and I am not contending that this is the case—then, in my opinion, this could be done far more effectively by means of a capital gains tax on land than through the adoption of site taxation.

The second advantage claimed for site taxation is that it would lessen the economic evil of unused and undeveloped land because of the increased tax burden on such property. I would certainly agree that the number of vacant parcels of land in a city would be lessened and I would also agree that there would be a tendency to the more intensive use of land. This would presumably result in a more compact urban development which would reduce certain overhead costs involved in running a city. It would, however, bring another set of difficulties in its wake—namely those associated with higher urban densities. Thus, there would be tendencies to construct taller buildings and to place them on smaller lots; the latter would apply especially in residential areas. These forces, in turn, would intensify existing traffic problems and detract from the spaciousness of our new residential areas. It may be contended that population density problems could be controlled by rigid zoning restrictions and by limitations on building heights and lot sizes. This would prevent the worst excesses of high density from occurring, but I am sceptical of any claim that, in a democracy, building restrictions could prevent a considerable overall rise in the density of urban development if there were strong economic forces at work to bring this about.

A third, and most important, advantage claimed for site taxation is that it would stimulate building development by driving down the price of land and by putting a major expenditure on property, i.e., property taxes, on a basis where it no longer increases with the size and value of the improvement. I would have to question the first point here that land prices be driven down. In my opinion, some land would go up in value while other land would decline. It is quite easy to see how the price of a particular parcel of land could rise following the introduction of site taxation if one understands the income residual process by which investors establish land values. Let us assume, for example, that there is a vacant lot in an apartment area and that the highest and best use of the land under composite taxation is for a two-storey apartment. Let us further assume that the net income before depreciation attributable to the property is $7,000, that the building would cost $60,000 and have an economic life of 50 years so that the rate of depreciation would be 2%, and that the rate of return on capital invested in apartments is 8%. On the basis of these assumptions, the required return on the building would be 10% of $60,000 or $6,000 and the residual income attributable to land would be $7,000–6,000 or $1,000. The capitalized value of the land would be $1,000/0.08=$12,500. Now let us assume that site taxation is introduced, and that the only change is that the total property taxes are reduced by $200. The net income before depreciation would then increase to $7,200, the return on the building would remain at $6,000, the residual income attributable to land would increase to $1,200, and the capitalized value of the land would be $15,000, ($1,200/0.08) in place of

$12,500. If you take a further assumption that the highest and best use of the site under site taxation would not be a two-storey apartment but rather a three-storey one, you would likely find that the investment value of the lot was well above $15,000.

The foregoing illustration is based on accepted appraisal theory. The British economist, Ralph Turvey, arrives at a similar conclusion in chapter VII of his book, *The Economics of Real Property,* using a highly sophisticated economic analysis. In conclusion, my own opinion is that following the introduction of site taxation, land values would tend to fall in those areas where taxes would rise—notably in the downtown area, and that land values would tend to rise in those areas where taxes would fall—notably in outlying residential areas. Overall, I am not convinced that there would be any fall in the general level of land values: Looking at this in another way, the value of land, as of other commodities, is determined by forces of supply and demand and can be reduced only if the supply increases or the demand decreases. The introduction of site taxation could not increase the supply of land and surely would not decrease the demand. It therefore follows that the general level of land values would not decline.

The other half of the argument concerning the effects of site taxation on building development is that the optimum capital outlay on any given site would be higher than under composite taxation because property taxes would no longer increase with the size and quality of the building. I think that this argument is generally valid although there is room for disagreement on the degree of stimulus which would be given. My principal observation is that site taxation reduces taxes for old buildings as well as for new ones and that economic development would probably receive greater encouragement from a measure designed to assist new buildings only. If additional stimulus for building development is required—and I am not arguing that it is—I would much prefer the device of a statutory exemption for all new buildings for a period of say five years.

The fourth advantage claimed for site taxation is that property owners could no longer shift a part of their property taxes on to the occupants of their property. Subject to certain qualifications, this contention appears to be correct. I am not competent to discuss all of the intricacies of tax shifting and will content myself with limited observations. First, the significance of this argument is limited greatly on this continent because so many properties are owner-occupied. Secondly, if you assume that site taxation is to replace composite taxation, it is unrealistic to expect that tenants are suddenly going to be able to reduce their rents by the amount of shifted taxes which they have previously been bearing. It is obvious that the process of unshifting would be a long one. The matter is complicated partly because, for many properties under long term lease, the lease provides that property taxes shall be paid by the tenant. While we may recognize that taxes on land do in the long run fall upon owners, we should also recognize that in many cases a shift of taxes from occupant to owner will result in considerable hardship for the latter. Thus while the owner may receive a large economic rent from a given property it is possible that he paid a very large capital sum for the right to receive that rent and that the imposition of site taxation will substantially increase his taxes thereby sharply reducing his income from the property as well as its resale value.

The fifth advantage listed for site taxation is that it would shift a considerable amount of the tax burden off home-owners and place it on downtown commercial property and that this would stimulate housing construction. This is generally true. It is, indeed, the explanation of why site taxation has received strong popular endorsement in countries such as Australia and New Zealand where its use has been determined by local option. It was evidently apparent to most of the homeowners concerned in these countries that their taxes would be lower under site taxation than under composite taxation and they were easily able to out-vote the persons who would lose under site taxation.

I should point out here, however, that a very considerable number of home owners would not really gain from the introduction of site taxation. In the first place, it seems probable that the price of residential land would be higher under site taxation than under composite taxation. Secondly, in the metropolitan areas of Canada, there are large populations living in dormitory municipalities where a very high proportion of the real estate consists of housing and where there is no valuable commercial land which could bear the brunt of a reduction in residential taxes. Thirdly, there would in every municipality be a minority of owner-occupied homes where the improvement-land ratios would be below the general average for all types of real estate and where the introduction of site taxation would mean an increase in taxes. Most of the latter homes would, I submit, belong to low income people living in small old homes on valuable land. Frequently the homes were originally out in the countryside until the city expanded to surround them. One might designate many of these properties as undesirable slums but they differ from the usual concept in that they are owner-occupied and tend to be widely scattered rather than concentrated in one area. There would also be some exceptions in the downtown commercial area; taxes would decline on a minority of these properties, particularly for multi-storied office buildings situated off the main street. There would, in addition, be some benefit from a tendency for central land prices to fall.

I would nevertheless agree that most home-owners would benefit and most downtown property owners would lose from site taxation. This does not dispose of the matter, however, because there are reasons for believing that the predicted results would, on balance, be harmful rather than beneficial. One thing which concerns me is that site taxation would contribute to the further commercial decentralization of our cities—a process which has already gone too far in most cities and is creating serious problems. I do not mean by this that site taxation would contribute to a general decentralization of our cities, but it would foster a decentralization of downtown commerce because it would be so hard hit by the tax change. In other respects, site taxation would oppose decentralization because of its tendency to encourage more compact urban growth. The overall result, however, would be to weaken the city centre which is unfortunate because our cities are in great need of retaining a strong central core.

I am also concerned over the additional subsidization of residential property which would result from site taxation. In general, the value of municipal services received by home-owners is already far in excess of the taxes which they pay. A reduction in these taxes would create further imbalance and lead to demands for more and more services to be paid for largely at other people's expense. I agree that under certain circumstances, the additional subsidization of residential accommodation is desirable. However, such subsidies should be directed to the low income groups whereas site taxation mainly benefits the middle and upper income groups, i.e., those living at the periphery of the city. There are undoubtedly urban areas where shelter needs are critical and something should be done; other means exist for doing this, however, than the drastic expedient of introducing site taxation.

The sixth advantage which I have listed for site taxation is that it would contribute to the redevelopment of blighted areas. In my opinion there is very little to substantiate this claim. Two principal means by which site taxation could encourage redevelopment of blighted areas would be by increasing the taxes on slum properties and thus making them less profitable to hold or by reducing land values in blighted areas. On the basis of my previous analysis, I strongly disagree that either of these results would take place to any significant degree. I have, however, previously accepted that site taxation does provide a general stimulus to development in that property taxes would no longer increase with the size and quality of the building. This point would apply to blighted areas as well as to others.

The site taxation argument concerning blighted areas sometimes suggests that the restriction of taxes to land alone would weigh so heavily upon owners of slum property that they would be forced to redevelop their properties and that they would do so with little or no public assistance. My own belief is that slum property owners would do virtually nothing if subjected to site taxation. I would go further and say that there is almost nothing they could do even if they wanted to because the only answer to the problem is to redevelop the entire neighbourhood which requires powers of expropriation, public funds, public approval and public direction. It is utterly naive to suggest that owners of individual properties within a slum area will attempt to improve their own properties when all around them is sordid blight. I conclude that the slum problem is so enormously costly and involved that site taxation could make only a minute contribution to the solution of it.

No discussion of site taxation would be complete without reference to the very important question of how this method of taxation conforms to the fundamental principles of equity and soundness of taxation. We must particularly ask, therefore, if site taxation meets these criteria as well as composite taxation does. I believe that the comparison is unfavourable to site taxation with regard to three very important principles—ability to pay, benefits received, and stability.

The argument concerning ability to pay is simple. Surely, if you have two identical parcels of land side by side, and one supports a ten-storey office building while the other is merely an unimproved parking lot, the ability to pay taxes is considerably greater in the case of the improved property. Composite taxation recognizes this; site taxation does not, or, if it does, it is only because land assessment is based on the inexcusable theory that the value of land is normally determined by what sort of improvements are situated on it.

I do not find that site taxation conforms nearly as well to the benefits received principle as does composite taxation. Some municipal services do relate more closely perhaps to land value than to building value; in many cases these services are largely financed by local improvement charges based on land frontage or by private developers rather than by regular property taxation. Other services which are financed by property taxation do not seem to bring any direct benefit to land at all; I am thinking here of police protection, fire protection and garbage collection. These services do, of course, affect the selling price of land and therefore benefit it indirectly. Probably most municipal services relate more to people than they do to either land or buildings. This would certainly be true of the two most costly local services—education and roads. It is surely obvious, however, that the number of people living in or working at a property is normally far more closely associated with the value of the building than the value of the land. Thus the cost of providing and maintaining roads, bridges, and public transportation for the thousands of people working in a downtown skyscraper can be enormous; surely the benefits received theory of taxation would require that a heavy tribute should be exacted from the owner of such a monster on a basis which would clearly differentiate between him and the owner of a property with a mere handful of persons in it. Again, I submit that composite taxation is the more equitable method.

The third principle of taxation to be considered is stability. It is difficult to think of a more unstable tax base than an object such as land which is completely fixed in supply and which is therefore subject to the most violent fluctuations in price. It is this fact, of course, which largely explains the dismal failure of site taxation in western Canada during the years since 1913. This largely explains, for instance, why assessed land values of taxable properties in Edmonton declined from $191.3 million in 1914 to $61.6 million in 1921, why taxable land values declined from $120.8 million in Calgary in 1913 to $49.4 million in 1921 and why they declined from $54.5 million in Saskatoon in 1913 to $23.9 million in 1921. It largely explains why the city of Vancouver had tax arrears of $5.5 million at December 31, 1918 equal to 124% of the current tax levy. It further explains why we find the following sentence in Commissioner Goldenberg's 1947 report on Provincial-Municipal Relations in British Columbia:

"It is well to note in this connection that of the six municipalities which defaulted on their debts in the nineteen-thirties, Prince Rupert, Burnaby and Merritt had continued to exempt inprovements until 1932, the district of North Vancouver until 1931, and the City of North Vancouver until 1930."

Following these disastrous experiences, there was a widespread and continuous retreat from site taxation in western Canada and a formidable list of royal commissions, economists, provincial and municipal officials declared themselves against any degree of site taxation whatever.

I am prepared to accept, on the other hand, that the experiences in the west would have been somewhat less catastrophic if site taxation had been administered more soundly—particularly with regard to principles of land assessment. I would also concede that violent fluctuations in the general price of land are much less likely to occur today than several decades ago. When account is taken of the fact that site taxation has proven administratively practicable in countries such as Australia, New Zealand, and Denmark, one is forced to examine closely the question of whether site taxation, whatever its merits, would actually work in Canada today. I do not believe that we can answer this question conclusively because it is not possible to make meaningful comparisons between Canada and the countries where site taxation is in effect. The difficulty is that the real property tax carries a much heavier load in Canada than in these other countries, either because municipal responsibilities are much greater in Canada or because, in these other countries, municipalities have access to major tax fields other than the real property tax. Thus it is commonly said of Australia that the role of municipal government there is narrower than in any other English speaking country. Both education and law enforcement are the direct responsibilities of the state governments and the latter have assumed a major role in connection with hospitals, local transportation and water supply. It is not surprising therefore to find for 1957–58, the latest year available, that the total expenditures of all Australian municipalities were only 118.3 million Australian pounds which is equivalent to about $260 million, which scarcely compares with net general expenditures by Canadian municipalities of $1.5 billion in 1957 and $1.6 billion in 1958. Even allowing for population differences, the Canadian level of expenditures is several times higher on a per capita basis and this is reflected in the property tax levies for the two countries—72.9 million Australian pounds in Australia for 1957–58, equal to $160 million, as compared with $916 million in Canada in 1957 and $997 million in 1958. The level of local government expenditures is also low in New Zealand largely because education and law enforcement are national services in that country. Turning to Denmark, we find that site taxation plays an even smaller role. For 1957–58, again the latest year available, out of total current revenues for all municipalities of 2.836 billion kroner, no less than 1.839 billion kroner came from income taxes, and only 0.581 billion kroner came from property taxes, of which slightly over 60% consisted of taxes on land.

The truth of the matter seems to be that the use of site taxation inevitably forces municipalities to turn to other sources of revenue than the real property tax. This has even happened in western Canada where a number of cities have for many years derived large revenues from utility profits.

To conclude this discussion of tax stability, the changeover to site taxation flies directly counter to what tax experts have been counseling with increasing vigour in recent years, in that it sharply narrows the tax base and places intense pressure on a very restricted area. Published statistics for Ontario cities indicate that the exemption of improvements would remove approximately 75% of the existing property tax base. This means that tax rates under site taxation would approximately quadruple if revenue loss was to be avoided. I am sure that no one would suggest that the income tax or any other major Canadian tax could regularly continue to yield its present level of revenues if 75% of the base were to be removed. Yet this is the proposition which the advocates of site taxation put before us. I must emphasize that the narrow tax base which would result from the adoption of site taxation would lead to very high rates of taxation, highly imaginative efforts to avoid or reduce the tax and increased arrears. If economic difficulties set in for a particular community, as, for example, where a large factory closes down, it is easy to envisage the appearance of the alarming cycle of high tax rates leading to increased tax arrears, leading in turn to a narrower tax base, ever higher rates, greater arrears and finally a financial breakdown. I submit, therefore, that what is needed to improve the Canadian property tax is not a narrower tax base but rather a broader one in which most existing exemptions of real property would be removed and which would reach out to a few kinds of personal property such as automobiles.

Before concluding this paper, I shall mention briefly several other aspects of site taxation which disturb me. We have lived on this continent for generations with composite taxation and millions of people have paid money for properties in the expectation that the level of their tax liabilities will continue as in the past and millions of leases have been entered into on the same assumptions. To change this, except over a very long period of time, could produce great hardship in individual cases and, even where the change is effected over many years, the future tax changes would be anticipated and capitalized in any property transactions bringing immediate losses to property owners unfortunate enough to have low improvement-land ratios. On the other hand, owners of land with high improvement-land ratios would reap a new kind of unearned increment from a tax which is supposed to reduce unearned increments.

Site taxation presents one other difficulty which should not pass unnoticed, namely, the very real technical problem for municipal assessors of achieving equity in land valuation in urban areas where there would—especially under site taxation—be virtually no vacant lots to provide evidence of market value. The only sound basis for arriving at land value would then be by means of capitalizing the residual income left after attributing an estimated income to the building, or, more correctly, to the building representing the highest and best use of the land. These residual techniques are very difficult to apply.

Summary and Conclusions. My overwhelming conviction is that site taxation would fail to accomplish most of the things claimed for it, that other objectives which it would achieve either could be implemented more effectively by alternate policies or are not worth striving for. Our modern cities are the products of immensely powerful economic forces and the impact of site taxation on these forces would generally be very slight. If the result of site taxation were to reduce sharply the general level of land prices, I would have to modify several of my most important conclusions. However, I can see no basis, theoretical or empirical, that this is the case and I challenge the protagonists of site taxation to produce objective evidence showing that land values are lower in cities which have site taxation than in comparable cities where composite taxation prevails. I am, finally, apprehensive that some of the incidental results of site taxation would be very harmful such as the narrowing of the tax base, the increased taxes for some farmers and some industries, and the decentralization of urban commerce. My final conclusion, therefore, is that while our property tax system is greatly in need of strengthening, this purpose would not be achieved by the adoption of site taxation.

NOTE. Mr. Clark's paper, part only of which is reproduced, was given as part of a panel on Site Valuation as a Base for Local Taxation at the Fifteenth Conference of the Canadian Tax Foundation (1961). Also taking part was Mr. H. Bronson Cowan, who took a more sympathetic view of the site value tax base. He said, on the effect of site value taxation on speculation, "Between 1903 and 1913 western Canada, under the capital [or land and buildings] system, experienced a boom of disastrous proportions. . . . During the boom both rural and urban municipalities, in a frantic but belated effort to check it, began to adopt the site value system. It was too late. All four provinces reeled under the shock of the depression. There was a disastrous crash in both land and improvement values. Its effect lasted well into the thirties. During this period some municipalities increased their taxes on improvements in part. It has been claimed that these developments prove that the site value system was a failure. The facts are that in its early days it never had a chance to succeed. Most of the urban municipalities have continued to exempt improvements from taxation by percentages that range from small to as high as 70."

THE ASSESSMENT AMENDMENT ACT, 1955
Ontario. Statutes. 1955. Chapter 4

8. (2) The said section 33 is amended by adding thereto the following subsection:

(2*a*) For the purposes of subsection 2, in ascertaining the sale value of farm lands used only for farm purposes by the owner thereof whose principal occupation is farming, consideration shall be given to the sale value of such lands for farming purposes only and no consideration shall be given to the sale value of lands in the vicinity to which this subsection does not apply.

NOTE ON AMENDMENTS. In the 1960 session by Chapter 3, s. 3(1) the words "and buildings thereon used solely for farm purposes, including the residence of the owner and of his employees and their families on the farm lands" were added, with other minor necessary changes. With the publication of the R.S.O., 1960, the amendments were incorporated as section 35 (3) of Chapter 23. In the 1960–61 session, by Chapter 4, s. 4(1) the words "or used only for farm purposes by a tenant of such an owner" were added. By s. 4(2) a new subsection 3a was added. In the 1961–62 session, by Chapter 6, s. 4(1) the words "whose principal occupation is farming" were struck out of subsection 2 and subsection 3a was amended so that the subsections now read as follows:

"(3) For the purposes of subsection 2 and 4, in ascertaining the sale value of farm lands used only for farm purposes by the owner thereof or used only for farm purposes by a tenant of such an owner and buildings thereon used solely for farm purposes, including the residence of the owner or tenant and of his employees and their families on the farm lands, consideration shall be given to the sale value of such lands and buildings for farming purposes only and no consideration shall be given to the sale value of lands and buildings in the vicinity to which this subsection does not apply.

"(3a) Where the owner of farm lands entitled to the benefit of subsection 3 dies or retires, the sale value of the lands and buildings in respect of which subsection 3 applies shall be ascertained in the manner provided in subsection 3 in assessing such lands during the period the lands are held by him after his retirement or held by his estate after his death, but in no case beyond the two years immediately following the owner's death or retirement unless such lands are occupied by the surviving spouse of the deceased owner or by the retired owner."

CHAPTER 4

THE LEGAL EFFECT OF MASTER PLANS

The best laid schemes o'mice and men
Gang aft a-gley.

ROBERT BURNS

A critical study of the legal effect of master plans brings the law student face to face with one of the pressing problems of planning theory, a problem suggested by the materials in Chapter 3 but postponed for full investigation until it could be studied in a legal context. A reading of planning literature quickly reveals two fairly distinct notions of planning. One notion is of the plan as a rather finished document suitable for publication in hard covers with attractive illustrations. Sharp's *Oxford Replanned* is perhaps the prime example. The other notion sees planning as an extended *process,* possibly without any "plan" at all. The disciples of this school shun what some people call "physical design," or "three dimensional planning."

The two notions tend to manifest themselves in two kinds of legal effect given the "plan" by the local law. The material in section one of the chapter should be read with this dichotomy or at least distinction of view in mind. In the case of the British legislation it is possible to trace a decline in legal effect of the master plan at about the time that under the British Columbia legislation it was increased.

Another way of looking at these two notions is by examining the degree of flexibility in the plan. It is here that the lawyer can make his contribution—in drafting a plan that shows a nice balance between stability and flexibility. It is not in the legal effect alone that either of these qualities is established, although the enabling legislation plays an important role. The properly drafted plan, based on careful analysis of the purposes sought, can frequently assure a degree of stability in objectives at the same time that a useful flexibility of application is secured. To the lawyer at least, if not to the planner, this paradox should present no novelty.

The lawyer is primarily interested in the form of the plan and it is regrettable that libraries in Canadian law schools have so few specimens on their shelves. One reason for this is that the plan that takes the form of *Oxford Replanned* is a rarity. Plans usually consist of not one but a series of documents. In Ontario, for instance, the reasons that a municipality plans are complex, and the first plan that suits one purpose will soon require supplementation. Hence the power or duty to review, revise and amend the plan results in rather cumbersome documents. In Saskatchewan, where a zoning by-law amendment requires approval of the Minister of Municipal Affairs the Minister may refuse his approval when in his opinion it would be expedient to consolidate the by-law and its multiplicity of earlier amendments. No such guide is provided in respect of the plan although that province does call for a periodic review of plans.

In order to assess a plan, individually or as a legal device, it is of first importance to try to understand what it attempts to do. The following matters are offered as a basis for your reflection and class discussion. No one would pretend that the purposes of a master plan, as distinct from what might be called the *process* of planning, are universally understood and accepted. Many lawyers regard plans frankly as little more than a nuisance. Here are some possible uses. Do you think they are of any practical importance?

1. The plan as a *constitution,* in the American sense of the word. Most enabling Acts prohibit a municipality that adopts a plan from entering upon any public works program that does not conform with the plan. In most Canadian provinces municipal government is divided amongst several local units (thus creating difficulties of divided jurisdiction within the municipality): the council, the public utility commission, the school board, etc. A master plan may conceivably be a unifying agency in the hands of the council. Some enabling Acts also prohibit the passing of by-laws that do not conform. This is obviously a very important restriction, but since plans can be amended, it may mean only that by-laws in effect have to be passed twice. Even that low a view of the plan means that a council must take second thought.

2. The plan as a *guide to private development*, which is usually very dependent upon public works programs. This is of great importance to the subdivider and developer of land. He may learn where and when water, sewers, roads, schools, garbage disposal, hydro, telephones, etc., will become available.

3. The plan as a *guide to administrative adjustment of zoning*. Most modern statutes authorizing zoning by-laws also provide some means of modifying the harshness of the by-law in hard cases. Sometimes a plan can operate as a guide to the tribunal created for the purpose.

4. A question of great importance is the *effect a plan has on private interests*.

These four suggestions indicate the areas of primary concern to the lawyer. What can the lawyer do to contribute to the fulfilment of these purposes in a plan? The lawyer, as an advocate of both public and private interest, should have a much more prominent role than he plays in 1963.

5. The plan as a piece of *propaganda*. People who have had much experience with the political problems of planning and development have observed the effect of lack of public understanding and support for planning programs. Whether or not a board or commission should be the primary director and promoter of planning in the municipality there seems to be general agreement that it can serve a valuable purpose in enlightening the citizenry. Plans should be examined very carefully with this function of communication and inspiration in mind. They could represent a goal for community effort which general understanding and acceptance might make more attainable. In this connection a comparison (contrast?) of Professor Gordon Stephenson's *A Redevelopment Study of Halifax, Nova Scotia 1957* with any official plan in Ontario may be instructive. The current English legislation requires the publication of master plans at a reasonable price. Although not prepared under the 1947 Act, Thomas Sharp's *Oxford Replanned* and *Exeter Phoenix* may be mentioned as outstanding examples.

The value of public education and participation in matters of civic improvement was stressed a half a century ago by Sir Patrick Geddes. See his *Cities In Evolution* (1915, edited, revised and reprinted in 1949), especially at pp. 75–96 and 118–123 for text material, and the illustrated "Cities Exhibition" on pp. 163–194. (All page references are to the 1949 edition.)

Despite its recent republication *Cities In Evolution* does not seem to be as widely read today as its penetrating insights would seem to justify.

1. Legislative Policies and Planning Concepts

(a) *Legal Effect on Public Agencies and Private Interests*

THE URBAN AND RURAL PLANNING ACT, 1953
Newfoundland. Statutes. 1953. Number 27

27. From the time when a Municipal Plan or any further plan or scheme prepared for the purposes of a Municipal Plan and approved and brought into effect by or under this Act takes effect it shall be as binding upon the authorized Council and upon all other persons, partnerships, associations or other organizations whatsoever to all intents and purposes as if the Municipal Plan or further plan or scheme was contained in regulations made under Section 61.

THE COMMUNITY PLANNING ACT, 1957
Saskatchewan. Statutes. 1957. Chapter 48

27. (1) The adoption by the council of a community planning scheme shall not commit the council to undertake any of the projects therein suggested or outlined, but shall prevent the undertaking by the council of any public improvements within the scope of the scheme in any manner inconsistent or at variance therewith.

(2) The initial implementation by the council of a community planning scheme shall prevent an owner from erecting any building or structure that is inconsistent or at variance with the scheme or would prejudice the carrying into effect of the scheme.

THE PLANNING ACT
Ontario. Revised Statutes. 1960. Chapter 296

15. (1) Notwithstanding any other general or special Act, where an official plan is in effect, no public work shall be undertaken and, except as provided in subsections 2 and 3, no by-law shall be passed for any purpose that does not conform therewith.

(3) The Municipal Board, upon the application of the council of a municipality for which an official plan is in effect, may by its order declare that a by-law of such municipality shall be deemed to conform with the official plan, if the Municipal Board is of opinion that the by-law conforms with the general intent and purpose of the official plan.

OFFICIAL PLAN: METROPOLITAN TORONTO PLANNING AREA (DRAFT)
Ontario. Metropolitan Toronto Planning Board. 1959.

Existing Non-Conforming By-Laws. Section 179(7) (c) of *The Municipality of Metropolitan Toronto Oct. 1953,* was quoted earlier ["no public work, as defined in *The Planning Act, 1955,* shall be undertaken and no by-law shall be passed, by any municipality or local board within The Metropolitan Toronto Planning Area, that does not conform therewith"].

This section makes clear that a non-conforming undertaking of a public work, or enactment of a non-conforming by-law, by any municipality in the Planning Area, is illegal. However, the legislation fails to define the procedure by which a by-law, enacted prior to the adoption of the Official Plan, is to be amended to make it conforming or to define the obligation of a municipality to enact a by-law enforcing conformance to the Official Plan in an area which is not covered by any zoning by-law.

One aspect of the question of conformance of a by-law with the Official Plan is dealt with by Section 16 of The Planning Act which reads:

"A by-law that conforms with an Official Plan shall be deemed to implement the Official Plan whether the by-law is passed before or after the Official Plan is approved."

This section relieves a council from the responsibility to re-enact a conforming by-law. It states explicitly that a by-law that *does conform may remain* on the statute books. However, it fails to state explicitly that a by-law that *does not conform may not remain* on the statute books.

It is hoped that the question of the procedure for the rescinding or amendment of non-conforming by-laws and for the enactment of conforming by-laws in areas not previously covered by any zoning by-law will be definitely clarified, either by decision of the Municipal Board or of the courts, or by legislative enactment.

RE MARCKITY AND FORT ERIE
Ontario. High Court. [1951] O.W.N. 836

SPENCE J. (orally): This is an application for an order of mandamus compelling the respondent Burger, as building inspector of the Municipal Corporation of the Town of Fort Erie, to issue a building permit upon the application of the Marckity brothers, the applicants herein. It was agreed between counsel that in this case there is no by-law presently effective which affects the issuance of the said permit, and therefore, following *Re Bridgman and The City of Toronto* and *Re Greene and The City of Ottawa* the applicants are entitled to a mandamus to compel the issuance of the permit unless the respondent municipal corporation is entitled to have the Court exercise its discretion by adjourning the application, so that the procedure to make effective a town plan may be carried to its conclusion.

The Court, in the two cases cited, determined that the respondents had not shown a valid case for the exercise of the Court's discretion. Here, however, in my opinion the situation is different. Since at least the year 1948 the adoption of a town plan, under the provisions of *The Planning Act,* R.S.O. 1950, c. 277, has been under consideration, and on the 4th June 1951 the plan was presented to the municipal corporation by the planning board of the Town of Fort Erie, and was adopted by the municipal council. Counsel for the municipality has informed me that, due to the procedural requirements, particularly that the plan should be signed in a large number of copies, it took from then until the 1st October 1951 for the necessary copies of the plan to be made, putting on separate sheets the drawings and the text, and that on the 1st October 1951 the plan, which was in essence the same plan as that approved by the council on the 4th June, was signed in the necessary copies by the mayor and clerk.

In the meantime, on the 11th September 1951, the applicants, together with their engineer, V. C. Thomas, filed an application for a building permit.

The applicants and the said V.C. Thomas allege—and it is not denied—that they were then informed that no by-law prohibited the issue of such a permit. Burger, however, alleges—and it is not denied by the applicants—that he stated to the applicants that the proposed location was in a residential area, as shown on the plan adopted by the municipal council, and that one of the two applicants replied: "There is no plan at present."

Under these circumstances I am of the opinion that the case is exactly opposite to that considered by Mr. Justice Ferguson in *Re Greene and The City of Ottawa,* where he said, at p. 676: "There is no indication that the City had any plans for the area when the application for a permit was filed." In this case there is indication, in fact certainty, that the Town had a plan for the area and that the plan, if and when effective, would prevent the use of these lands for the erection of a "motel" as proposed by the applicants.

I am, therefore, of the opinion that this is such a case as would justify the exercise by the Court of its discretion in refusing to grant the mandamus applied for, and that the proper course is for the Court to adjourn the motion *sine die,* so that it may be determined whether or not the municipal plan will become an official plan under the provisions of the said *Planning Act,* and will effectually prevent the erection of a "motel", and, therefore, would justify the municipality in refusing a building permit for such a building.

In the circumstances, of course, there will be no order as to costs. The application may be brought on by either party upon seven days' notice, when the procedure in reference to the approval of the plan under the provision of *The Planning Act* has been carried out.

NOTE. Do you agree with Spence J.'s basic principle that if the plan is approved it "would justify the municipality in refusing a building permit for such a building?" Is there any direct authority for this view in *The Planning Act, 1955*? Is this an effect the official plan should have? Why are non-conforming *public* works expressly prohibited? If the official plan is to have this specific restrictive effect on *private* land owners, is the procedure established for securing the official plan satisfactory? The next chapter on administration of the planning process, raises this last question.

REGINA *v.* GIBSON, EX PARTE CROMILLER. [1959] O.W.N. 254 (Ontario. High Court). An application for a building permit to erect a church was refused on April 30, 1959. Zoning by-law 11,777 was passed on May 19 prohibiting the erection of a building on land already (and before April 30) shown on the official plan of the Township of Etobicoke as a proposed road or on any land indicated as a road on the zoning map in the by-law. By-law 11,777 had not been approved by the Municipal Board when the applicant applied for an order in lieu of mandamus directed to the building commissioner, to compel the issue of the permit. Schatz J. held the by-law invalid for reasons not here material, and then allowed the mandamus without commenting on the fact that independently of the by-law the official plan showed part of the land on which the church was to be built as a road. The *Marckity* case was not cited.

RE STEVE POLON LTD. AND METROPOLITAN TORONTO LICENSING COMMISSION (1961), 29 D.L.R. (2d) 620 (Ontario. High Court). MCLENNAN J.: "As a result of a perusal of ss. 10 to 20 of the *Planning Act,* R.S.O. 1960, c. 296, I am of the opinion that the Official

Plan adopted by the respondent municipality is little more than a statement of intention of what, at the moment, the municipality plans to do in the future. Provisions for the amendment of an official plan make it clear that the municipality is not bound to carry out that intention and may from time to time as circumstances develop make such changes as appear desirable. The Official Plan is not therefore an effective instrument restricting land user."

NOTE. The official plan in Ontario also has rather unusual legal effects in the way of enabling extraordinary municipal powers. See especially section 19, which authorizes a municipality, with the approval of the Minister of Municipal Affairs, to expropriate land "for the purpose of developing any feature of the official plan". This power has been rarely used, partly because the Minister is said to be reluctant to resort to it if the municipality is otherwise authorized to expropriate the land required. In Ontario a municipality that is authorized to "acquire" land may, by virtue of section 5 of *The Municipal Act,* R.S.O. 1960, c. 249, expropriate it. Is the Minister's position justified? Section 20 of *The Planning Act* authorizes elaborate redevelopment schemes that may be undertaken only by a municipality that has an official plan. The official plan, although required to be approved by the Minister, is probably not binding on the Crown, since the Crown is not expressly bound by *The Planning Act,* but the Minister, in considering a draft plan of subdivision, shall have regard to "whether the plan conforms to [sic] the official plan . . ." (section 28 (4)) and a planning board in determining whether consent to transfer land is to be given under section 26 shall likewise have regard to the official plan. Formerly a committee of adjustment, which is authorized to grant minor variances from a zoning by-law, could only be appointed by a municipality that had an official plan, but in 1962 (S.O., 1961–62, c. 104, s. 4) this limitation was repealed. Where there is an official plan, however, the committee must still be of the opinion that notwithstanding the variance the general intent and purpose of the official plan is maintained (see now section 32*b*). The special power of the council to control in each case the location of hazardous land uses by delegation to the committee of adjustment or the planning board is still dependent upon the existence of an official plan (section 30(3)). A little used power available to a planning board is to be found in section 33, where a board is authorized to restrain the contravention of any by-law that implements an official plan, and the board may even restrain the council that created it, if that council (or any local board) attempts to pass a by-law or undertake a public work that does not conform with the official plan.

THE TOWN AND RURAL PLANNING ACT
Alberta. Revised Statutes. 1955. Chapter 337

66. When a general plan has been adopted
  (a) the council shall proceed with the enactment of a zoning by-law to regulate the use and development of land in the manner prescribed and within the area or areas referred to in the general plan, and
  (*b*) the council or other public authority shall not commence any undertaking or public project that is inconsistent or at variance with the proposals contained in the general plan.

[Section 66 is reproduced as amended by S.A., 1960, c. 107, s. 15]

BILL 57
Alberta. 14th Legislature. 5th Session. 1963.

Explanatory note. General. This is a Bill to repeal and replace The Town and Rural Planning Act, being chapter 337 of the Revised Statutes of Alberta, 1955. The proposed new Act is a revision of the existing Act with numerous alterations, additions and omissions. The section references in the notes to each clause are to the sections of the existing Act from which the proposed new sections are taken. [Bill 47 is now *The Planning Act*, S.A., 1963, c. 43, and came into force August 1, 1963.]

91. Any zoning by-law, development control by-law, development scheme, general plan or replotting scheme prepared and adopted or confirmed, and any action taken or powers exercised by a council pursuant to Part 4 shall be in conformity with any preliminary regional plan or any regional plan that is being prepared or has been adopted under this Part and is subject to any conditions or restrictions imposed under this Part.

[Part 4 includes provisions for zoning and development control.]

MUNICIPAL ACT
British Columbia. Revised Statutes. 1960. Chapter 255

698. (1) The Council shall not enact any provision or undertake any works contrary to or at variance with the official community plan or a plan adopted under Division (6) of this Part. [Division (6) deals with regional planning.]

(2) Subsection (1) does not empower the Council to impair, abrogate, or otherwise affect the rights and privileges to which an owner of land is otherwise lawfully entitled.

699. (1) An official community plan does not commit the Council or any other administrative body to undertake any of the projects therein suggested or outlined.

(2) The adoption of a community plan does not authorize the Council to proceed with the undertaking of any project except in accordance with the procedure and restrictions laid down therefor by this or some other Act.

[Sections 698 and 699 are reproduced as amended by S.B.C., 1961, c. 43, ss. 39 and 40.]

TOWN PLANNING ACT
Nova Scotia. Revised Statutes. 1954. Chapter 292

5. The adoption by a council of an official town plan shall not commit the council to undertake any of the projects therein suggested or outlined, but shall prevent the undertaking by the council of any public improvements within the scope of the official town plan in any manner inconsistent or at variance therewith.

TOWN AND COUNTRY PLANNING ACT, 1947
England. Statutes. 1947. Chapter 43

14. (1) Subject to the provisions of this and the next following section, where application is made to the local planning authority for permission to develop land, that authority may grant permission either unconditionally or subject to such conditions as they think fit, or may refuse permission; and in dealing with any such application the local planning authority shall have

regard to the provisions of the development plan, so far as material thereto, and to any other material considerations.

(3) Provision may be made by a development order for regulating the manner in which applications for permission to develop land are to be dealt with by local planning authorities, and in particular—

(b) for authorizing the local planning authority, in such cases and subject to such conditions as may be prescribed by the order, or by directions given by the Minister thereunder, to grant permission for development which does not accord with the provisions of the development plan;

NOTE: The *Town and Country Planning General Development Order and Development Charge Applications Regulations, 1950,* S.I., 1950, No. 728 provides, in part:

Article 8. A local planning authority may in such cases and subject to such conditions as may be prescribed by directions given by the Minister under this order grant permission for development which does not accord with the provisions of the development plan.

TOWN AND COUNTRY PLANNING (DEVELOPMENT PLANS) DIRECTION, 1954

England. 1954. Ministry of Housing and Local Government.
Circular No. 45/54

The Minister of Housing and Local Government in exercise of the powers conferred on him by articles 5, 6 and 8 of the Town and Country Planning General Development Order, 1950, hereby directs as follows:

1. A local planning authority is hereby authorised to grant permission for development of land which does not accord with the provisions of the development plan in any case where in their opinion the development authorised by the permission, if carried out in accordance with the conditions, if any, to be imposed, would neither involve a substantial departure from the provisions of the plan nor injuriously affect the amenity of adjoining land.

2. (1) In any other case, before granting permission for development which does not accord with the provisions of the development plan a local planning authority shall send to the Minister a copy of the application made to them and of any plans and drawings which accompanied it, together with a statement of the reasons for which they desire to grant the permission and of the conditions, if any, which they propose to impose, and shall not grant permission for that development until the expiration of 21 days (or such shorter period as he may in any particular case appoint) from the date on which such copy is received by the Minister.

(2) Failing any direction from the Minister within the said period the local planning authority shall be authorised to grant permission for that development at the expiration of that period.

3. It shall be a condition of the authorisation given by the preceding paragraphs of this direction that where the permission is to be granted by a council to whom functions of a local planning authority are for the time being delegated, the concurrence in writing of the local planning authority shall be obtained before the grant of such permission, and in a case falling under paragraph 2 shall be notified to the Minister with the other matters referred to in that paragraph.

4. As soon as may be after granting any permission for development

which does not accord with the provisions of the development plan, the authority shall furnish to the Minister a copy of such permission.

A STANDARD CITY PLANNING ENABLING ACT
United States Department of Commerce. 1928

9. *Legal Status of Official Plan.* Whenever the commission shall have adopted the master plan of the municipality or of one or more major sections or districts thereof no street, square, park, or other public way, ground, or open space, or public building or structure, or public utility, whether publicly or privately owned, shall be constructed or authorized in the municipality or in such planned section and district until the location, character, and extent thereof shall have been submitted to and approved by the commission:

Provided, That in case of disapproval the commission shall communicate its reasons to council, which shall have the power to overrule such disapproval by a recorded vote of not less than two-thirds of its entire membership:

Provided, however, That if the public way, ground, space, building, structure, or utility be one the authorization or financing of which does not, under the law or charter provisions governing same, fall within the province of the municipal council, then the submission to the planning commission shall be by the board, commission, or body having such jurisdiction, and the planning commission's disapproval may be overruled by said board, commission, or body by a vote of not less than two-thirds of its membership.

The failure of the commission to act within 60 days from and after the date of official submission to the commission shall be deemed approval.

[The paragraphing is the editor's. The commission referred to is the planning commission, an appointed body separate from the council, or legislative body.]

(*b*) *Compulsory Review*

THE URBAN AND RURAL PLANNING ACT, 1953
Newfoundland. Statutes. 1953. Number 27

35. (1) Every Municipal Plan shall be reviewed by the authorized Council on the expiration of every five years from the date on which the Municipal Plan came into effect and revised as necessary according to the developments which can be foreseen during the next ten years.

(2) Where a revision of a Municipal Plan becomes necessary it shall be amended in accordance with this Act.

THE COMMUNITY PLANNING ACT, 1957
Saskatchewan. Statutes. 1957. Chapter 48

28. Every community planning scheme shall be reviewed by the council whenever the council, having regard to developments since the scheme was adopted, deems it advisable to do so but in any event at least once every five years.

TOWN AND COUNTRY PLANNING ACT, 1947
England. Statutes. 1947. Chapter 43

6. (1) At least once in every five years after the date on which a deve-

lopment plan for any area is approved by the Minister, the local planning authority shall carry out a fresh survey of that area, and submit to the Minister a report of the survey, together with proposals for any alterations or additions to the plan which appear to them to be required having regard thereto.

(c) Amendment

THE PLANNING ACT
Ontario. Revised Statutes. 1960. Chapter 296

14. (1) The provisions of this Act with respect to an official plan apply *mutatis mutandis* to amendments thereto, or the repeal thereof, provided that the Minister may, subject to subsection 2, approve any amendment or repeal that may be proposed by the council of any municipality.

(2) Before approving an amendment or repeal initiated by a council, the Minister may require that a report of the planning board be obtained in respect of the proposal and if the planning board does not concur in the proposal the Minister shall not approve the amendment or repeal unless it has been adopted by a vote of two-thirds of all the members of the council.

(3) Where any person requests the council to initiate an amendment to the official plan and the council,

(a) refuses to propose the amendment; or

(b) fails to propose the amendment within thirty days from the receipt of the request,

such person may request the Minister to refer the proposal to the Municipal Board.

(4) Upon receipt of the request, the Minister may require a report on the proposal from the planning board and may refer the proposal to any public authority that may be concerned therewith and he may refuse the request or refer the proposal to the Municipal Board.

(5) When a proposal is referred to the Municipal Board under subsection 4, the Municipal Board may reject the proposal or direct that the council cause the amendment to be made in the manner provided in the order. [Subsections (1) and (2) are reproduced as amended by S.O., 1961–62, c. 104, s. 3(1) and (2).]

NOTE. The Canadian planning Acts generally require amendments to be adopted by the same procedure that is required for the original adoption, and the Ontario rules are exceptional in two respects. One, the council is authorized to initiate an amendment or repeal, although it cannot initiate an original plan, which must be proposed by the planning board. And two, the citizen has a privilege peculiar to Ontario, of requesting the council to initiate an amendment and the further privilege of requesting the Minister to refer his proposal to the Municipal Board, but he cannot insist on it. If the Minister wishes to refuse the request he may, but he may not approve it. If he thinks it should be approved he can only refer it to the Board and hope for the best.

Compare the corresponding right, in section 30 (19) to appeal to the Municipal Board for an order directing a council to amend a zoning by-law.

And compare the privilege of a person to appeal to the Provincial Planning Advisory Board in Alberta for an amendment to a district general plan or a preliminary district plan. Statutes of Alberta 1957, c. 98, s. 21 as amended by S.A., 1959, c. 89, s. 21.

2. The Content Of The Master Plan

(a) Some Lawyers' Observations

BASSETT, THE MASTER PLAN (1938)

A master plan should show the elements of a community plan. These have been discussed in Part I under the headings streets, parks, sites for public buildings, public reservations, zoning districts, routes for public utilities, and pierhead and bulkhead lines. . . . [p. 65]

Each of the elements of the plan set forth in this book relates to land areas; has been stamped on land areas by the community for community use; can be shown on a map.

If a subject does not conform to these three requirements it does not come under the head of community land planning. . . . [p. 50]

Budgeting and fixing the time for beginning various improvements are said by some to be part of a plan. We doubt this. . . . [p. 51]

. . . a public building is not included because it is transitory. When it is destroyed by fire or otherwise it ceases to be. The elements of a community plan cannot be destroyed by fire or an act of God. A building could not be shown on a dynamic plan although it would undoubtedly be part of a static plan or map. It is an architectural structure and comes within the field of architecture rather than within that of community planning, but there must be an intimate correlation between a building and its site. . . . [p. 45]

An objection may here be raised that thus far the main thing has been omitted, that is, design in the plan. To some all discussion on the subjects mentioned is futile if it does not dwell upon good design. There is a possible good as well as a possible bad design to every street, every park, and every other element of a plan. . . . Design is something effected by a good workman or a good artist. If a community with the advice of good workmen and good artists can establish sound fundamentals, these will be the bases of good design. [p. 46]

The writer's view has been that a master plan should not be adopted by any official body except by a planning commission. If finally so adopted copies can well enough be given to the various municipal departments, but if it needs to be adopted by the local legislative body it becomes to a certain extent hardened. Then when the commission desires to alter certain features in it the legislative body must first be persuaded to authorize the change. This is certain to work disastrously because as soon as a plan ceases to be plastic it becomes a quasi-official map which has not been prepared and executed with the care and precision that the law requires in the case of official maps. [pp. 61–2]

HAAR, "THE CONTENTS OF THE GENERAL PLAN"
Washington. 1955. 21 Journal of the American Institute of Planners 66

The theories concerning the proper scope and contents of the master plan on the whole demonstrate what Herbert Spencer was wont to call a development from the simple to the complex. Bassett's perspective seems far too narrow when used for analyzing the complicated industrial city. His basic urge was to separate out community property from private lands. To him, the master plan was primarily a guide to the coordination of the local government's own activities affecting land use—with the anomalous exception of the zoning plan whose inclusion can, perhaps, be explained on the ground of history and familiarity with that device. Such a conception was simply found wanting as experience unfolded in the planning of cities. The trend that may be traced towards Bettman's view of all-comprehensiveness in later enabling acts and in the Federal program is a response to the growing realization of interdependence in modern industrial society of all activities affecting land.

But granted the validity of this general reaction, many issues are raised that remain to be explored by the professional planners. Not everything should go into the master plan. If all the permutations human activity can improvise are to be encompassed by the master plan, it may be rendered diffuse, ambiguous, and meaningless as a base for action when land development and redevelopment actually occur. There is this kernel of wisdom in Bassett's approach, granted that its execution is faulty: recognizing that there are certain elements of city growth which cannot be effectively treated, his solution was to eliminate them.... City planning and the master plan thus become manageable, although limited, functions. Perhaps the pendulum has swung too far in the present-day formulation of the proper contents of the master plan. The "big picture" may be blurred by the insistence on handling all factors.

The main task of the planner does not seem to be to develop a map or graphic description of the community as it now is or will be in its idealized form. Rather, it is suggested, it is the clarification of land-use goals of a generalized nature which, when adopted by the legislature will become the broad framework for further implementation. This seems to be the trend of some of the recent enabling acts: the "master plan" evolving into a series of statements—planning precepts, if you will—encompassing the greater portions of the major land functionings of the community and their critical inter-relationships. It is to the surveys, analyses and formulations of these criteria that the energies of city planners can most properly be dedicated in furthering a "master plan" concept.

DUNHAM, "CITY PLANNING: AN ANALYSIS OF THE CONTENT OF THE MASTER PLAN"

Chicago. 1958. 1 Journal of Law and Economics 170.

...Recent literature on city planning exhibits a marked tendency to depart from the concept of planning as envisaged by Bassett. In part this is due to a tendency of modern planners so to confuse the terms *plan, forecast* and *proposal* that the reader cannot tell whether the author is writing about actions to be taken by government to achieve some stated objective (a plan), or about the developments which will occur without government intervention (a forecast), or about the way in which a city should develop partly as a result of unplanned forces in the economy and partly as a result of interference with such forces by a plan of government action (a proposal). Bassett quite clearly limited his concept of a master plan to actions to be taken by government with respect to public and private land uses.

The essence of the criticism of the Bassett concept is that it is too narrow because it excludes from city planning all development plans (other than location) of public and private users of land resources; too physical because it emphasizes location and thereby ignores numerous socio-economic forces; too rigid because a city is a dynamic place; and too detailed because a master plan ought to be confined more to general principles. It has been suggested that there does not seem to be any logical basis for the items which Bassett includes in, and excludes from, his city plan. A master or general or comprehensive plan ought, it is said, to concern itself with principles of location, not with actual location, and it ought to be conceived of as a constitution, a set of principles to guide public agencies and private owners in development of the city. Thus the comprehensive plan would not provide a general location for a future park; it would establish a principle for location of parks such as a standard that there should be x acres of park for every y number of people so located that the y numbers reside not more than z distance from the park.

It is the thesis of this paper that there is a theory which would support Bassett's conception of the master plan and the Standard City Planning Enabling Act. This is not to say that Bassett held this theory; certainly he did not make it explicit. Rather it is suggested that support for this limitation on the content of the master plan comes from the organization of city government and from constitutional principles drawing the line between interferences with private property for which the government must pay by reason of the condemnation clauses of our constitutions and those interferences for which no payment need be made under the police power of our governments. The question is whether there is a principle which supports a concept of city planning limiting the plan basically to a showing of the location of public works and utilities and of the places or districts where various types of private development should not be located (the zoning plan). . . .

It is this factor of the external impact of one public work upon another that is the key to Bassett's concept of the master plan. The external impact of a public work may be either beneficial or detrimental to other public works and to property of private persons who may or may not be served by the particular public work. This external impact is not a factor which would figure in the calculations of a planner of one of the operating departments charged with the responsibility of maximizing the satisfactions of users (efficiency) and minimizing the public expense (economy). Because of this external impact, it is possible that a less efficient or more costly location of a public work may, in terms of net community benefit, be more advantageous to general welfare than the most efficient and economical site. Since the external impact comes from location, it is essential that the central planners generally locate public works. . . .

In the statutes and the proposals there may be a confusion of *plan* and *forecast*. If all that is proposed is that the central planners show what it is likely that private owners operating through market forces will do uninfluenced by government, that is one thing. To the extent, however, that the statutes mean that the central planners are to recommend that the community take a series of government actions to secure the proposed development of the whole community, they propose government interference with the decisions of private owners on a scale and of a type never before contemplated in our economy and of a type not consistent with the above theory of central planning.

If what is contemplated is that the central planner plan a private development in a particular way in order to make it a better project for the consumers of its services, then this is giving the central planner extraordinary power of meddling with the choices of the sovereign consumer. Given our commitment to a free enterprise economy, there does not seem to be much justification for interference with the market concerning factors (consumer preferences) which are ordinarily reflected in the market. At least it should take a strong showing that the central planner's idea of what the consumers ought to have is essential to the welfare of such consumers before interference is warranted. . . .

Strictly speaking government can induce the conferring of a benefit via a restriction only when the external benefit results from non-use of the private land, as in the case of restricting land use for an open space in order to obtain for the public the benefits of open spaces. In all other cases the only way the restriction can induce a benefit is to cause a change in the market value of the land to a point where the permitted and desired use becomes an economical use for someone. Thus in *Vernon Park Realty Co.* v. *Mount Vernon,* where land, currently used for a parking lot, was zoned for parking use only because the municipality wanted the benefit of such use, rather than the changed use proposed by the owner, the restriction could not compel the benefit as long as the owner had the alternative of discontinuing the parking lot and leaving the land vacant. Only when the impact of the restriction changed the value of the land to a value for a parking lot would a parking lot be likely to continue.

Unfortunately much of the literature and statutes obscure the difference between restricting a private decision concerning land in order to prevent an external harm and restricting a private decision in order to confer a benefit on persons other than the property owner. There would appear to be substantial differences even though it may be said that preventing owner A from harming owner B confers a benefit upon B so that in essence all restriction confers a benefit. Most often the benefit resulting from eliminating a harm does not result in any particular physical use of the land after the restriction is imposed; the benefit comes as much from non-use as from any of the permitted uses. The benefit resulting from a restriction to obtain a benefit, on the other hand, most often results only from physical use of the land in a particular way. No community or external benefit is obtained from zoning land to industrial uses only if the desired industrial use does not result from the decision of some person in the market; but if industrial uses are prohibited in an area in order to prevent a harm, the benefit is obtained from whatever permissible decision the owner makes concerning his land.

More serious, however, is the ethical and political judgment which the public must make when it seeks to compel the owner to confer a benefit. For in effect, government is compelling a particular person to assume the cost of a benefit conferred on others without hope for recoupment of the cost. There is no approximation of equal sharing of cost or of sharing according to capacity to pay as there is where the benefit is obtained by subsidy or expenditure of public funds. The accident of ownership of a particular location determines the persons in the community bearing the cost of increasing the general welfare.

The legislation and literature of the British Commonwealth, where there is no express constitutional provision to compel compensation to owners of property, reflect greater awareness of this problem than that of the United States. The question is when should an owner be compelled to do something for the general welfare without compensation? . . .

In summary central planners may, as a planning function, plan a private development in the community only where there is a desired or unwanted impact of such development on other land in the community. By and large the steps which government can take to secure the desired external impact are steps requiring compensation to the owner whose land is taken for this purpose. Restriction of private decisions in order to compel him to contribute a benefit to the public appears not to be permissible or desirable. On the other hand, government may prevent activity of a private owner which imposes an external cost upon others.

TOWN PLANNING INSTITUTE OF CANADA, SUBMISSION
Ottawa. 1960. Royal Architectural Institute of Canada, Residential Environment Enquiry.

The normal selective function of the market does not operate in the sale of housing. Because housing is far more durable than other consumer goods, current production provides only a small portion of the total supply, insufficient to satisfy the greatly expanded demand during the ascent of the business cycle. In boom periods the housing market is a seller's market and inferior products can and are being sold at a profit. As soon as the housing market becomes a buyer's market, construction stops, and the owner, not the builder, of the inferior product takes the loss. The builder can—and does—enter the new cycle with the same inferior product. A policy which would encourage the building of houses—both single-family and apartment—for permanent investment and use, rather than for sale, could correct this situation. In any event, as long as this situation remains one cannot validly infer from market reports the choice of the buyer if a greater variety of housing were available.

If land were more often held in leasehold rather than in fee simple, there might be a better attitude to long term mortgages and maintenance after the first twenty to twenty-five years of a building's life. The prevalent attitude that whole sections of our cities can be "traded in" every decade or two must give way to an attempt to build for a lifetime or more if we are to see a radical improvement in the residential environment. To the planning profession these questions, involving legal, financial, and government policies, are of the greatest importance but they have frequently been overlooked in the general concern over poor housing and social discomfort.

DUKEMINIER, "ZONING FOR AESTHETIC OBJECTIVES, A REAPPRAISAL." 1955. 20 Law and Contemporary Problems 218: "According to our basic social hypothesis, this intervention [by community officials, e.g. in zoning out ugly structures such as bill boards] should occur only when community values are *seriously* damaged or threatened by specific uses of land." [How do you measure "community values"? How do you know when they are "*seriously* damaged"? Cf. "gross" negligence.]

(b) Legislative Guides

THE PLANNING ACT
Ontario. Revised Statutes. 1960. Chapter 296

1. In this Act,

(h) "official plan" means a programme and policy, or any part thereof, covering a planning area or any part thereof, designed to secure the health, safety, convenience or welfare of the inhabitants of the area, and consisting of the texts and maps, describing such programme and policy, approved by the Minister from time to time as provided in this Act;

(j) "public work" means any improvement of a structural nature or other undertaking that is within the jurisdiction of a council or of a local board.

10. (1) Every planning board shall investigate and survey the physical, social and economic conditions in relation to the development of the planning area and may perform such other duties of a planning nature as may be referred to it by any council having jurisdiction in the planning area, and without limiting the generality of the foregoing it shall,

(a) prepare maps, drawings, texts, statistical information and all other material necessary for the study, explanation and solution of problems or matters affecting the development of the planning area. . . .

TOWN PLANNING ACT
Nova Scotia. Revised Statutes. 1954. Chapter 292

4. (1) Subject to the approval of the Minister any council shall have power:

(a) to prepare a plan or plans for development, either as to the whole or any part or parts thereof, with details of development either endorsed upon the plan or contained in schedules referring to any such plan, which plan or plans and details of development shall be known as "The Official Town Plan";

(b) from time to time make additions and extensions to and alterations in the official town plan;

(c) to prepare co-ordinating plans for the development of harbour, railway and rapid transit and street railway and airport facilities, and to recommend plans so prepared to any railway board or public authority having jurisdiction in the matter, and to any railway or other company concerned therewith, and to use all lawful measures to secure the adoption of such plans and the due co-ordination of terminal, transportation, and other facilities of commerce and traffic within and about the municipality;

(d) to make provision for any street widening project by defining the minimum distance from the centre or side line of existing or projected streets at which buildings or other structures may be erected, placed, constructed or reconstructed;

(e) to make provision for the reservation of land for projected streets or street widening projects, and for parks and other public purposes;

(f) to make provision for the supply of light, water, sewerage, street transit and other facilities to the various parts of the area included in an official town plan;

(g) to prescribe the order in which any part or parts of the development provided for in the official town plan will be carried out and the order in which any designated parts of the area included in the official town plan will be supplied with light, water, sewerage, street transit and other facilities;

(h) to make provision for the method of financing any works and expenses to be incurred in connection with or incidental to the carrying out of the development prescribed in the official town plan or any part or parts of such development.

THE TOWN PLANNING ACT
Manitoba. Revised Statutes. 1954. Chapter 267

SCHEDULE A
Matters to be Dealt with in Town Planning Schemes

1. Fixing building lines on all existing streets and roads to secure, as far as practicable, having regard to the physical features of the site and the

depths of the existing subdivisions, that the distance between the buildings to be erected or buildings likely to be reconstructed on opposite sides of a street or road shall be according to the use of the buildings and the prospective traffic requirements of the streets and roads.

2. Fixing building lines on all new streets and roads to be made in future so that no building shall be nearer to the centre of any road than the use of buildings to be erected and the prospective traffic requirements of such streets and roads may require.

3. Reserving land for new main thoroughfares that it is desired to keep free from buildings, by agreement with the owners of the land and by co-operation between local authorities with regard to the lines, width, and direction, of main thoroughfares which connect adjacent parts of their respective areas.

4. Limiting the number of separate family dwelling houses to the acre and providing for adequate light and air to the windows of each house, so far as reasonable for the purpose of securing the amenity of any area, and proper sanitary conditions in connection with the buildings erected thereon.

5. Prescribing zones within which to regulate the density of building for the purpose of securing amenity and proper sanitary conditions, and fixing the percentage of the area of the lot on which new buildings may be erected or old buildings reconstructed.

6. Prescribing certain areas that are appropriate to be used for agricultural purposes, and also areas that are likely to be used for building purposes, for use for dwelling houses, apartment houses, factories, warehouses, shops or stores, or other purposes, and the height, use, or general character, of buildings to be erected or reconstructed, so far as reasonable for the purpose of securing the amenity of the areas, and proper sanitary conditions in connection with the buildings, and also the proper use and development of land for agricultural purposes.

7. Prohibiting the carrying on of any noxious trades or manufactures or the erection and use of any buildings with inadequate sanitary arrangements or the erection and use of buildings, billboards, or structures for advertising purposes, that are such as to be injurious to the amenity or natural beauty of any area.

8. Providing for variations in the widths of streets to conform to their differing traffic requirements as,

(a) main thoroughfares connecting two populous districts or parts of one district, or forming the principal means of approach to a city or town;

(b) secondary thoroughfares;

(c) other streets.

THE TOWN AND RURAL PLANNING ACT

Alberta. Revised Statutes. 1955. Chapter 337

64. A general plan . . .

(*a*) shall be prepared on the basis of surveys of land use, population growth, transportation and communication needs, public services and social services within the municipality,

(*c*) shall include proposals to

(i) the uses, whether public or private, to be made of the lands within the municipality,

(ii) the classification of lands for agricultural, commercial, residential, industrial and other classifiable uses,

(iii) the provision of roads, public services, public buildings, schools, parks, recreation areas and the reservation of land for these and other public and community purposes,

(iv) the regulations to be made by means of a zoning by-law to ensure that lands will be developed in accordance with the use classifications prescribed by the general plan,

(v) the sequence in which specified areas of land will be developed or redeveloped and in which the public services and facilities referred to in subclause (iii) will be provided in specific areas,

(vi) the financing and programming of public development projects to be undertaken by the municipality or other public authorities under the general plan,

and

(*d*) shall consist of such written statements, maps, charts and drawings as may be necessary to express and illustrate the proposals contained in the general plan.

[Section 64 is reproduced as amended by S. A., 1960, c. 107, s. 15.]

2*a*. The purpose of this Act is to provide means whereby municipalities, either singly or jointly, may plan for orderly and economical development without infringing on the rights of land owners except to the extent that is necessary, for the greater public interest, to obtain orderly development and use of land in the Province.

[Section 2*a* was added by S. A., 1959, c. 89, s. 2.]

TOWN AND COUNTRY PLANNING ACT, 1947
England. Statutes. 1947. Chapter 51

5. (1) As soon as may be after the appointed day, every local planning authority shall carry out a survey of their area, and shall, not later than three years after the appointed day, or within such extended period as the Minister may in any particular case allow, submit to the Minister a report of the survey together with a plan (hereinafter called a "development plan") indicating the manner in which they propose that land in that area should be used (whether by the carrying out thereon of development or otherwise) and the stages by which any such development should be carried out.

(2) Subject to the provisions of any regulations made under this Act for regulating the form and content of development plans, any such plan shall include such maps and such descriptive matter as may be necessary to illustrate the proposals aforesaid with such degree of particularity as may be appropriate to different parts of the area; and any such plan may in particular—

(a) define the sites of proposed roads, public and other buildings and works, airfields, parks, pleasure grounds, nature reserves and other open spaces, or allocate areas of land for use for agricultural, residential, industrial or other purposes of any class specified in the plan;

(b) designate, as land subject to compulsory acquisition by any Minister, local authority or statutory undertakers any land allocated by the plan for the purposes of any of their functions (including any land which that Minister or authority or those undertakers are or could be authorized to acquire compulsorily under any enactment other than this Act);

(c) designate as land subject to compulsory acquisition by the appropriate local authority—

(i) any land comprised in an area defined by the plan as an

area of comprehensive development (including any land therein which is allocated by the plan for any such purpose as is mentioned in paragraph (b) of this subsection), or any land contiguous or adjacent to any such area;

(ii) any other land which, in the opinion of the local planning authority, ought to be subject to compulsory acquisition for the purpose of securing its use in the manner proposed by the plan.

(3) For the purposes of this section, a development plan may define as an area of comprehensive development any area which in the opinion of the local planning authority should be developed or redeveloped as a whole, for any one or more of the following purposes, that is to say for the purpose of dealing satisfactorily with extensive war damage or conditions of bad layout or obsolete development, or for the purpose of providing for the relocation of population or industry or the replacement of open space in the course of the development or redevelopment of any other area, or for any other purpose specified in the plan; and land may be included in any area so defined, and designated as subject to compulsory purchase in accordance with the provisions of subsection (2) of this section, whether or not provision is made by the plan for the development or redevelopment of that particular land.

[The appointed day was July 1, 1948.]

(*c*) *The Survey*

It has long been recognised that a detailed survey of the planning area is essential as a starting point in the planning process. See Geddes, *Cities in Evolution,* pp. 126–133, for an early account of the dangers of town planning before a survey is attempted, and also for an account of how a survey should be undertaken. Professor Stephenson, in his *A Redevelopment Study of Halifax, Nova Scotia* (1957), commences with a review of the city's history. Historical sketches in Ontario plans are rare; that of Barton Township prepared by the Hamilton-Wentworth Planning Board is the only example to come to the editor's attention. The best historical studies of a planning nature in Ontario are to be found in the conservation reports of river valleys produced by the Conservation Branch that was one of the original branches of the old Department of Planning and Development. The Branch is now attached to the Department of Economics and Resources.

Professional planners still debate the desirability of putting the survey data into the plan, but good reasons can be found in the lawyer's experience with legislative history in statutory interpretation for keeping the *travaux preparatoires* available, whether in the main text or in an appendix. If the plan becomes a commonly used document the language will constantly require interpretation and the survey data will be a useful aid.

Another use for the data is to be found in the inevitable critical appraisal of the survey that may take place before some administrative agency when the planners who prepared the plan may be subject to cross-examination. In these instances it is helpful to have not only the data displayed, but the survey techniques explained.

Survey techniques need explanation because both lawyers and administrative agencies are properly concerned with the inaccuracies of shoddy surveys, sometimes made from the front seat of a slow moving car, by the driver or a front seat passenger. Planners sometimes refer to such surveys as "windshield surveys" and their use is quickly exposed by lawyers in cross-examination. The explanation should cover not only the fact-finding techniques, in which hearsay dangers should be minimised, but also the analytical techniques, in order that a proper statistical critique may be made.

Most Canadian Acts indicate the wisdom of making a survey, but none expresses the emphasis of the English Act of 1947. See especially sections 5 and 6 (1). In Ontario the statutory direction is given to the planning board, which must "investigate and survey the physical, social and economic conditions in relation to the development of the planning area" (section 10 (1)), but although the language is mandatory as it is in England, it is doubtful whether it is enforced any more strictly than, say, the Alberta provision in section 64 (*b*), which is permissive only.

ZEISEL, "THE UNIQUENESS OF SURVEY EVIDENCE"
Ithaca. 1960. 45 Cornell Law Quarterly 322

... Accordingly, for our purpose, surveys may be classified into four groups: (1) *Census* surveys *not* involving *verbal statements, e.g.*, surveyors measuring the acreage of an area, and bookkeepers or accountants determining the amount of a designated type of expenditure; (2) *Census* surveys involving *verbal statements, e.g.* the standard job of the U.S. Census; (3) *Sampling* surveys *not* involving *verbal statements, e.g.*, the job of the Food and Drug Administration in examining shipments of merchandise, a survey of car license plates of patrons to determine their geographic distribution, and certain phases of accounting work; and (4) *Sampling* surveys involving *verbal statements, e.g.*, public opinion polls and similar interviewing operations.

The major legal diffiiculties are compounded in surveys of type (4)....

Sample measurements raise interesting legal issues. It might seem disconcerting that no sample measurement can be stated with complete confidence in its accuracy. But, as we pointed out, the law is accustomed to dealing with less than perfect evidence. Both standards of proof, "reasonable doubt" and "preponderance of evidence," allow for imperfections. Rather, it is the positive aspect of sample measurements that raises new issues, *i.e.*, the possibility of actually measuring the degree of uncertainty or certainty through tolerance limits for the measurement at issue.

One way in which the law might deal with the problem is to accept the range of the sampling error because *any* value within its range would fulfill the immediate legal requirements.... Or the result of the measurement, however inaccurate, may clearly fall short of the legal requirement....

In most situations, however, the universe to be measured will be so large that the court will not have the choice between a sample measurement and a census, but rather, would either have to accept a sample measurement or have no measurement at all. In the latter situation the relatively inaccurate sample measurement may provide better evidence than the law now possesses. That a sample value may be inaccurate by some small margin of error could be of less importance than the fact that it *can* provide a measurement as accurate as it does. This possibility becomes particularly important when the measurement refers to the core of the litigated issue, and hence becomes a measure of the soundness of the court's judgment or verdict....

Let us now consider more closely the dangers of insincerity, faulty narration, perception and memory as they pertain to survey evidence. But let us be sure to see the problem in its precise form: the issue is not whether the reliability of interview response would increase if all interviewees could be examined as witnesses in court, since this is not an available alternative. As a rule, it is not possible to bring the universe or its truly representative sample into court. The customary procedure is to call a number of public witnesses who allegedly are representative of the universe. But a distinguished lawyer with broad experience in this field had this to say about such a procedure: "The poisonous feature of the public witness matter is . . . that all too frequently they are selected not impartially but because they will testify the way the party selecting them wants them to testify." The very fact that such witnesses are arbitrarily selected should render their testimony less credible. Even if these public witnesses would, in fact, give a more reliable response in court than to a survey interviewer, their evidence should be rejected on the ground that these individuals do not adequately represent the universe, no matter how many of them are called.

Assuming it were possible to bring a truly representative sample of public witnesses into court, it is doubtful that their answers would always be more reliable than those given to a survey interviewer. The interviewer is in no way connected with the litigants, not even through the tenuous bonds created by being a witness for one side. Moreover, the interviewee will, as a rule, not learn the purpose for which his response is used. In a proper survey routine, to prevent inadvertent disclosure, not even the interviewer is told of the survey's purpose. In addition, since the survey necessarily precedes the trial, less time will have elapsed between the response and the event to be recalled, than between the event and its deposition at the trial. Finally, the court has before it the complete and uniform question schedule in response to which the survey results were obtained. Court witnesses, on the other hand, at times undergo careful individual preparation prior to trial, the form of which does not necessarily come to the court's knowledge.

To be sure, court witnesses may have a heightened awareness of what is at issue and may be more careful and perhaps more perceptive than survey respondents who are completely unaware of the ultimate issues. Cross-examination, too, may prove its value at any time that recollection or narration proves faulty. But even if some of the *individual* survey responses are not, in fact, totally accurate, the group measurement may still be sufficiently accurate within set tolerance limits.

In summary, therefore, the advantages offered by survey responses should at least suffice to protect such evidence from outright disqualification as hearsay. Moreover, the questions propounded in many cases will be so simple, straight-forward and unambiguous that the hearsay dangers must, in fact, be negligible. Hence, survey evidence, if properly procured, is well covered by Wigmore's formulation of the rationale that underlies all exceptions to the hearsay rule: "Where circumstances are such that a sincere and accurate statement would naturally be uttered, and no plan of falsification be formed. . . ."

Improper Universe. There are three critical points at which a survey operation can fail and provide ground for its impeachment. First, the survey may have been directed at a universe which is irrelevant to the litigated issue. In such cases of obvious error, the court will not need expert advice.

". . . [I]nterviewers stopped [the respondents] in front of one of the appellant's stores in San Francisco and asked them in what manner they spoke of 'Lerner Shops.' Obviously the results of such a survey are of little value in determining what knowledge residents of San Jose had of 'Lerner Shops'. . . ."

Or,

". . . [T]he survey, having been limited to retailers, is inadmissible to show that in the market of ultimate consumers the plaintiff's design had acquired a secondary meaning."

Inadequate Sample. It is not always obvious that a survey reflects an improper universe. Sometimes it purports to represent the correct universe but, in fact, does not do so. This is the second point at which a survey may prove inadequate. The universe may be properly selected, but the sample designed to represent it may be faulty. At this point the expert's help, as a rule, will be needed to explain the magnitude of unavoidable flaws or, as the case may be, of any errors in sampling.

The quality of any sampling procedure depends both on its basic design and its execution. The expert will readily discover its deficiencies from the report itself, supplemented by internal documents and such testimony from the survey staff as may be necessary. Questions directed at discovering the manner in which a respondent was selected for interviewing should provide all the information an expert will need. The survey staff, from the director down to the field interviewers, must be available for cross-examination. While cross-examination of *all* interviewers should be avoided, the court should not refuse to hear as many as are needed to clarify the exact modalities under which the survey was conducted.

To detect deviations from instruction will require a more detailed probing, primarily by questioning the supervisory staff and randomly selected interviewers. Questions should be directed at the institutional safeguards against error (substituting, without permission, respondent B for respondent A) and against the admittedly rare occurrence of faking parts or the whole of an interview. These safeguards may include proper recruitment, training, and supervision of the field staff, as well as spot controls and double checks of the particular survey sample.

One of the more easily overlooked sampling traps may arise from what is technically called non-response. There are always some individuals in any sample from whom it is impossible to obtain the desired information, either because they could not be located (*e.g.*, were not at home) or because they refused to answer the questions asked of them. An effort to measure the size of broadcast audiences, for example, must go far astray if it bases its findings only upon the people found at home. It will exaggerate the true audience because such people are more likely to listen to broadcasts than those who are away from home and, hence, omitted from the survey. There are several techniques for dealing with this difficulty, all aimed at an estimate of how the non-respondents would have responded had they been reached and interviewed.

As has been pointed out, however, no sample is ever without shortcomings: the exigencies of costs, accidents, and other circumstances may escape control and introduce bias. It is the expert's preeminent task to enlighten the court as to the relevance of such flaws in respect to the measured issues. The point is an important one, for even though a sample have many flaws, it may be judged sufficient for deciding a particular issue. The surveys of the late Dr. Kinsey are illustrative although, of course, they have not come before the courts. The "Human Male" and "Female" were represented only by those ill-assorted men and women who, by one means or another, could be persuaded to be interviewed.

There is a standard method of estimating the survey's true value from such an improperly selected sample. First, the degree of under- or over-representation of certain sub-groups is determined, *e.g.*, too many college educated, not enough laborers. One then estimates what the over-all, corrected group average *would* have been had the sub-groups been represented in their true, known proportions. While, of course, such estimates lack the precision of probability samples, they will often be satisfactory if the group measure clearly falls beyond the crucial minimum requirement. But more often, if a sample is improperly designed, the expert will be unable to appraise the size of its bias.

However, even a properly designed and well executed sample may prove wanting, simply because it is too small to provide the desired response, *i.e.*, the sampling error may be too great. This difficulty may derive from the fact that a sample can be sufficiently large to answer some questions, but too small to answer others. Here, again, only the expert can advise the court with precision.

Circumstances of the Interview. The third point at which the validity of a survey must be tested is at its line of questioning and the circumstances under which the interview was conducted. Lawyers know that there is more than one way of posing a question and that the response in each case may be different. Such differences may result from the phrasing of the individual questions, from their sequence, or from the questioning situation. There is a body of experience from which the expert will be able to guide the trier of facts. He will detect bias where the layman sees none, he will know where memory failure will tend to underrate and where vanity may have the opposite effect, and he will know also when, at times, the interviewer's personal opinion affects his respondent's answers.

Yet it is axiomatic, in survey technique, that the danger of question bias increases with the complexity and ambiguity of the questions. If their aim is simple and factual, such as determining the make of the respondent's automobile, neither the form nor the sequence of the questions will make much difference. But in the survey question "As a guess, how much wax would you say there was in glass wax . . . ," the court rightly found "a built-in bias.". . .

(*d*) *Some Examples*

The following excerpts from plans may help to make more real the document, or series of documents, known generally as the master plan. With the exception of the last, all the examples are from official plans prepared under Ontario legislation. This selection is not intended to suggest any superiority in the Ontario plans; quite the contrary, the selections have been made chiefly to provide material for criticism. Keep in mind the use that may be made of the plan, and keep in mind the lawyer's special skill as a draftsman. In this respect the short excerpt from the City of Toronto Official Plan contrasts with the excerpt from the draft Metropolitan Toronto Plan. How precisely should the plan be drafted? As a statute? Could there be some care taken with the organization of the plan so that planning proposals are clearly identifiable and easy to locate, without necessarily being couched in the precise language of well drafted statutes?

OFFICIAL PLAN: TOWNSHIP OF CHINGUACOUSY (1951)

The predominant use of land in this township is agricultural at present with a scattering of rural hamlets and some summer cottages.

The township has no available sources of water and those now drawn on by the Town of Brampton indicate that they will be strained to provide for the normal expansion of that town.

In addition to the absence of a suitable water supply the flat clay plain lying around Brampton presents a major drainage problem for any contemplated urban use. The costly diversion and deepening of the Etobicoke in Brampton provides an example which, while necessary for Brampton, the township wishes to avoid at all costs.

The construction of storm sewers and the long connections to an outlet required for any urban scheme would be prohibitive in cost for the township and in fact for any developer. It is important that anyone contemplating development should be forewarned of the impractibility of providing ordinary drainage except for farm purposes.

While there are pressures for housing due to the adjacent industrial development there are other adjacent areas in which the necessary urban services can be more readily provided.

In view of all these circumstances and after careful study of the problems presented, the whole of the Township of Chinguacousy is hereby designated as a rural area in which the density of population shall be such that it will not require the provision by the municipality of a public water supply, storm or sanitary sewerage. *While no urban development in any form will be undertaken, no obstacle will be placed in the way of any landowners who wish to have their lands annexed to the Town of Brampton or who wish to incorporate so as to assume the full responsibilities of urban development.* Some hamlets are now expanding through the construction of suburban homes and new school accommodation is imperative. Immediate steps shall be taken to set these hamlets up as police villages with a view to incorporation later so that these school costs may be assessed locally rather than against farms of the township at large.

[Although entitled "General Land Use Plan" the text reproduced is the entire text of the plan, and was accompanied by one map, which was cut from a sheet of the National Topographical Series covering Peel County.]

AMENDMENTS. The first amendment to the text was approved on May 1, 1956, and replaced in the sixth (last) paragraph, the italicized sentence with two new sentences:

"No urban development in any form will be undertaken under conditions as they now exist. [Provided, however, that if at any future date, the Township lands recently annexed to the Town of Brampton be developed, no obstacle will be placed in the way of any landowners who wish to have their lands annexed to the Town of Brampton or who wish to incorporate so as to assume the full responsibilities of urban development."]

On April 8, 1958 the second amendment was approved. It deleted from the revised sixth paragraph the second sentence added in 1956 and enclosed in square brackets above. Amendment 2 also made elaborate provision for the development of two large areas, one adjoining Brampton in the south and one adjacent to Brampton in the north, as intensively urbanized land. The scheme of the amendment is to keep the urbanized areas from becoming a tax burden on the remaining rural area. This amounts, in effect, to the establishment of a "new town" in the technical sense without benefit of any special legislation.

OFFICIAL PLAN: TORONTO TOWNSHIP (1953)

3. *Basic Assumptions*

The plan is based on a twenty-year period.

(a) *Population—Natural increase*—it is estimated that the increase of population from natural growth over a period of 20 years will be 25,000 to 30,000. This is based on the trends in the Township over the past ten years.

(b) *Population Increase from Immigration*—it is estimated that the increase in the next 20 years from immigration will be approximately 20,000. This is based on the Federal Immigration Policy, permitting 200,000 people per year to enter Canada. Of this figure it is assumed that 40–50% (80,000 to 100,000 will settle in the Metropolitan area of Toronto). It is reasonable to consider that a large portion of these people will be absorbed by the 3 large municipalities Scarborough, North York and Etobicoke which have sufficient land and facilities. For economic reasons we have planned only for the following future population.

Existing population (1952)	30,000 estimated.
Increase of population by natural growth	30,000
Additional population by immigration	20,000
Total estimated population at the end of 20 years	80,000

NOTE. Although the plan amendment was approved in June of 1953, the documents were in the hands of the Minister for about six months and the "existing population" was probably based on the assessment department's 1952 estimate. The following table shows the assessed population as of December 31 of the year mentioned.

Year	*Population*
1953	35,199
1954	40,016
1955	43,232
1956	46,667
1957	48,773
1958	53,219
1959	57,179
1960	60,109
1961	63,280
1962	65,570

The figures were supplied through the kindness of the Assessment Commissioner of the Township.

In a revised draft official plan for Toronto Township prepared by the Board's staff in 1960 the population estimate for 1980 is shown as 269,000. What is the relevance of population at given times to planning? How important is the population estimate? Does it matter to the planning of the Township whether the estimate turns out to be accurate?

The 1953 Official Plan says nothing more about population. The revision, which may be said to share with the draft official plan of Metropolitan Toronto the distinction of being the most sophisticated attempts at planning in Ontario, analyses future development in terms of specific areas that are to be designed to accommodate a maximum number of persons, in terms of the capacity of streets to carry traffic, of pipes to carry water and sewage, of parks to satisfy recreation needs, of schools to accommodate children and so on. These considerations must be related to the number of persons in a given area, and that number is usually described as the *density* of population. It is more helpful, in planning, to speak of *densities*, since the given area will necessarily be less than the whole planning area, and various areas in the planning area may well be planned for development to different densities. On this point the draft plan states as a principle: "The present scattered development in the township is not economically or sociologically satisfactory. The Plan accepts the premise that the density of future development must be carefully regulated and certain minimum densities, designed for the peculiarities of each neighbourhood, maintained." It might also have prescribed maximum densities to avoid the overtaxing of services.

QUESTION. Why do you suppose the two most sophisticated plans in Ontario in 1963 both have to be described as draft, although they are over three years old?

OFFICIAL PLAN: TORONTO TOWNSHIP (1953)

5. *Land use Classes*

The plan divides the total area into the following basic land use classes and does not attempt to define detailed sub-classifications within each of these basic classes.

Classification	*Area*
Residential	19,032 acres
Industrial	5,000
Agricultural	26,798
Commercial	172
Schools (Existing)	160
Open Space	690
Greenbelt	1,920
TOTAL	53,772 acres

6. *Interpretation of the Plan*

(a) The boundaries between classes of land use designated in this plan are general only, and are not intended to define the exact limits of each such class. It is intended, therefore, that minor adjustments may be made to these boundaries for the purpose of any by-law to implement this plan without the necessity of making a formal amendment to the Official Plan. Except for such minor changes, it is intended that no areas or districts shall be created that do not conform with this plan in respect of land use.

(b) It is intended, in order to control the time and location of development within the residential areas, to establish by restricted area by-law, suburban and rural residential zones, where restrictions will be such as to discourage large-scale housing development.

(c) This plan envisages the establishment of local shopping facilities in residential districts, but it is definitely intended that all such commercial development should be concentrated in well designed, properly located shopping centres, and not scattered or mingled indiscriminately with residential land use. In residential districts, it is intended that provision will be made in the implementaton of this plan for determining the location of such shopping centres, as such are developed. . . .

NOTE. The next excerpts illustrate contrasting treatment of the allocation of land use from a drafting point of view. How precisely should the use be defined? How will it affect the drafting of zoning by-laws?

OFFICIAL PLAN: CITY OF TORONTO (1949)

1. *The Generalised Land Use Map*

This map shows the Board's proposals for the division of the City into the three major land use classifications: Residential, Commercial and Industrial, to serve as a basis for the subsequent preparation of a zoning by-law. Such a by-law will not only implement these proposals but subdivide these three areas into smaller areas for the several types of Residential, Commercial and Industrial use such as single and multiple family housing and light and heavy industry. Pending the passing of a zoning or amending by-law, all existing residential by-laws will continue to apply. [For the purpose of this map the term "residential" is intended to include all uses normally permitted in residential areas such as churches and religious institutions generally, schools, hospitals, parks and playgrounds, etc.] . . .

Following the approval of the official plan the Board proposes to submit for approval a comprehensive zoning by-law. The acreages and percentage of the total City area represented by these major classifications are approximately as follows:

	Acres	%
Residential	10,173	45.5
Commercial	1,166	5.25
Industrial	3,184	14.3
Parks	1,393	6.25
Streets	5,651	25.5
Railways	720	3.20
Total Land Area	22,287	100.00

It will be realized that while theoretically land use regulations may be used to establish a functional or working and balanced relationship from the standpoints of both quantity and quality between the diversified land uses inseparable from a large urban community, this is not practicable in a city such as Toronto where virtually every foot of land is already devoted to some use or other and where the quantitative balance has been secured by the spilling over of residential areas into suburban areas. Desirable trends towards changed land use may be assisted but in general established land uses cannot be changed by legislation alone. For these reasons the land use program now proposed and the implementing zoning by-law which will follow, have as their objective stabilization from the standpoint of quantity and improvement from the standpoint of quality.

AMENDMENT. On July 5, 1951, the Minister of Planning and Development approved the following amendment, replacing the words in square brackets in the first paragraph above and substituting:

"For the purposes of this map,

(a) the term 'residential', in addition to its ordinary meaning, includes (i) all those uses usually found or permitted in residential districts such as parks, playgrounds, golf courses, community centres, schools, churches and other religious institutions, hospitals, children's and adults' homes or shelters, libraries, museums, art galleries, private clubs and home occupations, and (ii) offices of professional persons, business administrative offices and administrative offices of non-profit organizations of a religious, educational, recreational, fraternal or philanthropic nature;

(b) the term 'commercial' includes offices, retail stores, service shops and premises, public service, protection and utility premises and undertakings, places of amusement, small workshops, airports and airfields;

(c) the term 'industrial' includes storage and warehousing, manufacturing, transportation operations, junk yards and shops, and offensive, dangerous or nuisance producing uses."

OFFICIAL PLAN: TOWNSHIP OF SCARBOROUGH (1957)

The Land Use Plan establishes the spatial pattern of development for the Township in broad terms.

The municipality is divided into seven major categories, each of which is a group of complementary land uses. The amounts of land in each category are set forth in Table I. These acreages were established after surveys of population growth, potential jobs and labour force, and assessment, as outlined in Appendix I.

TABLE I

Category	*Approximate Acreage*	%
(a) Residential Neighbourhood Uses	24,200	53.8
(b) Industrial Area Uses	8,500	18.9
(c) Community Shopping Area Uses	400	0.9
(d) Highway Frontage Uses	600	1.3
(e) Major Open Space Uses	3,800	8.5
(f) Institutional Uses*	2,900	6.4
(g) Agricultural Area Uses	4,600	10.2
TOTALS	45,000	100.0

*Includes, for calculation purposes, such miscellaneous uses as H.E.P.C. rights-of-way, major roads, etc.

(a) *Residential Neighbourhood Uses*

Essentially composed of single-family detached dwellings, this category also may include other uses which are necessary for the function of the neighbourhood as a unit; semi-detached dwellings, duplexes and double duplexes, multiple family dwellings, schools, parks, churches, public utilities, and Neighbourhood Commercial Uses.

Neighbourhood Commercial uses are those serving mainly the adjacent residential neighbourhood, and may include the following: Automobile service stations, banks, barber shops, beauty parlors, cleaning and laundry collecting agencies, drug stores, food stores, hardware stores, medical centres, restaurants, shoe repair shops, tobacco shops and variety stores.

(b) *Industrial Area Uses*

Essentially composed of warehousing, manufacturing, and storage uses, this category may also include automobile service stations, offices and other commercial uses incidental to industrial operations or suitable to an industrial area. The selection of particular uses and other special zoning restrictions will be enacted in industrial areas near residential areas.

(c) *Community Shopping Area Uses*

Essentially composed of retail commercial uses commonly found in shopping centres, this category may also include professional and business offices, service shops and agencies, and places of entertainment. This category does not include uses which involve manufacturing or processing operations by machinery or the use of land or buildings for the sole purpose of storage.

Community Shopping Areas are shown diagrammatically on the plan as spots and Maltese crosses. The larger markings indicate the places where major business sub-centres will be encouraged to serve groups of communities. The spots indicate locations where a decision has been made as to which side of the street, or which of the four corners of an intersection is intended as the site for the Community Shopping Area. The Maltese crosses indicate places where no such decision has been made.

The ratio of off-street parking space to retail floor space which will be required will be scaled to the size of the shopping area, having a minimum of 3:1 for the smallest centres and exceeding 7:1 in the largest.

(d) *Highway Frontage Uses*

Includes uses which are suitable for a highway frontage location, by reason of the highway's function as a public transportation route, a traffic artery, or the centre of a community. This category, therefore, includes high density residential uses; highway service uses such as garages, service stations, motels, hotels, restaurants; and general commercial uses such as offices, banks, service shops, etc. The extent, location and physical layouts for these groups of uses will be established through detailed site planning employing accepted design criteria.

High density residential uses shall be permitted in this category only after detailed study and approval by Scarborough Planning Board and Council as to the effects of the increased density on community facilities and services.

Parts of the areas designated under this category may be zoned strictly for or against specific uses in this category, the decisions in such cases to be based upon studies conducted by the Planning Board to determine the location and standards of these uses.

As a general policy, neighbourhood retail shopping uses will not be encouraged along major highways, but where such uses are deemed advisable, they will be permitted where adequate parking and traffic arrangements can be provided.

(e) *Major Open Space Uses*

This category includes large township-owned parks, parts of the river valleys, and the lake shore.

The sections of river valley in this category are of sufficient width that they cannot be considered as neighbourhood parks. It is intended that these valley lands will become publicly owned, but in the meantime, commercial, recreation or amusement areas, private clubs, parks, and golf courses will be expected.

The municipality will continue to seek aid from senior governmental levels for shore protection and erosion control works which will enable it to acquire the Scarborough Bluffs.

(f) *Institutional Uses*

Includes public, semi-public and private uses which occupy large tracts of land with low building coverage, and which do not serve a particular neighbourhood or community. Typical uses are cemeteries, golf clubs, hospitals, seminaries, sewage disposal plants, etc. High Schools are shown diagrammatically with circles indicating the approximate locations where 15 acre sites will be acquired. The south half of Lot 26, Concession D is intended to be the site for an institutional and cultural sub-centre for the Township.

(g) *Agricultural Area Uses*

Includes farming, forestry and quarrying. The Scarborough Planning Board, under Section 24 of the Planning Act, 1955, may consent to separations of land for non-farm homes, or for uses associated with a transportation route, but it is intended that such separations will not be encouraged in agricultural areas. . . .

The Community Plan organizes residential lands into neighbourhoods and communities which will give each area an *identity*. It sets out the basic objectives to be obtained through successive planning steps.

(a) The establishment of neighbourhoods and communities will be founded on these two general rules:

(i) Neighbourhoods are centred on the public elementary school (grades 1 to 8). The boundaries are important.

(ii) Communities are centred on the community shopping centre and the main street. The boundaries are not particularly important. . . .

The Roads Plan is intended to serve primarily as a guide to the Planning Board and Council in acquiring land for the improvement of the Township network of trunk roads. . . .

APPENDIX I

Within the Land Use Plan (Schedule A) the *amounts* of land devoted to various uses bear these relationships to expected population, employment, and assessment.

1. *Population*

The following estimates were prepared by the Metropolitan Toronto Planning Board in 1956, and are used as a guide for the population growth in Scarborough Township to 1980:

Year	*Population*	*5 Year Absolute Growth*
1946	28,000	
1951	56,000	28,000
1956	139,000	83,000
1961	215,000	76,000
1966	285,000	70,000
1971	355,000	70,000
1976	425,000	70,000
1981	480,000	55,000

The area designated for urban uses on the Land Use Plan provides for a potential population of about 465,000 persons. However, it is anticipated that the full population potential of this urban area will not be reached until some time after development has spread to its boundaries. Some in-filling, and intensification of uses is expected to follow in the wake of the first wave of expansion.

The actual population of the urbanized area undoubtedly will be lower than the potential population. Thus, the area designated for urban uses by 1980 is regarded as reasonably in line with land requirements based on the population estimates.

2. *Jobs and Potential Labour Force*

The Land Use Plan provides 8,500 acres of industrial land which, at a suburban industrial average of 15 jobs per acre indicates a potential 128,000 industrial jobs.

The Metropolitan Toronto Planning Board has estimated Scarborough's 1980 non-industrial jobs at about 55,000. Adding the two categories gives a total of about 183,000 jobs.

The 1980 estimated population of about 465,000 will provide a labour force of about 186,000, assuming 40% of the population in the labour force.

This indicated balance of jobs and workers does not mean, of course, that all of Scarborough's workers will be employed in Scarborough. Many Scarborough residents will work elsewhere, and many Scarborough workers will live elsewhere. Nevertheless, the plan indicates a reasonable ratio of jobs to population.

It is recognized that possible changes in the rate of growth, in the number of industrial jobs per acre, in the number of workers per family and the like, may substantially modify this ratio over the next 25 years.

These assumptions are expected to be regularly reviewed, and adjustments to the plan made accordingly. Based on current estimates, potential jobs and population appear to be in balance.

3. *Potential Assessment*

Based on current assessment averages per acre, as revealed in a sample survey by the Planning Board the following potential assessment ratio would accrue in the area to be urbanized by 1980:

Land Use	*Acres*	*Total Ass't.* $ x 1 million	%
Residential (@ $22,500/Acre)	24,200	540	57.1
All Commercial (@ $115,000/Acre Inc. Bus. Ass't)	1,000	115	12.2
Industrial (@ $34,000/Acre Inc. Bus. Ass't)	8,500	290	30.7
		945	100.0

A ratio of 57% to 43% between residential and non-residential assessment is indicated. This ratio may be expected to vary in favour of residential after 1980, since the topography of the Agricultural Area presents little opportunity for industrial land uses. Changing bases of assessment, and varying costs of services required by each type of land will necessitate continuing review of these estimates.

NOTE. In the description of (c) *Community Shopping Area Uses* there is a reference to "Spots" and "Maltese Crosses" on the accompanying maps, and in (f) *Institutional Uses,* to "circles", indicating approximate locations. The use of this technique to indicate a necessary land use that cannot be certainly located when the plan is first published is becoming increasingly popular. Contrast this drafting technique with the relatively rigid boundaries of areas prescribed for Toronto Township above.

OFFICIAL PLAN: TOWNSHIP OF ANCASTER (1957)

The urban area has been subdivided into two classes; the primary development area and the secondary development area. It is the intent of the plan to encourage urbanization to take place first in the areas indicated as primary and subsequently into the areas indicated as secondary. This is to avoid costly extension of services to remote subdivision.

NOTE. This rather inadequate provision is believed to be the first expression of a policy of timing or phasing the development of land to be found in an Official Plan in Ontario. The plan was recommended by the Hamilton-Wentworth Planning Area Board July 20, 1955, and adopted by the Council of Ancaster Township on October 12, 1955. Subject to some amendment (not affecting the above passage) it was approved by the Minister on March 26, 1957. Compare clause 6(b) in the Official Plan of Toronto Township above, approved in 1953, where the staging of development is postponed to the zoning by-law, a rather odd place to find planning policy.

OFFICIAL PLAN: TOWNSHIP OF SCARBOROUGH (1957)

The Development Plan introduces the element of time into the Official Plan. It is intended as a framework for the township Capital Works Program, which in turn, will guide the rate and direction of urban expansion.

The Capital Works Program will include the provision of school accommodation, electric power, water, roads, sanitary sewers, storm drainage, parks, conservation works, erosion control, public housing, fire, police, library and other administrative facilities.

Of these services, sanitary and storm drainage works control the rate and direction of growth most effectively, since these must be progressively constructed commencing at the low point in a watershed. Successive extensions of sanitary sewers and storm drainage works create *Servicing Areas.*

The Township is divided into three broad *Phases of Development*, each Phase being composed of a group of Servicing Areas.

Phase I The urbanized area of the Township lying generally south of Highway No. 401, in which Servicing Areas have been established.

Phase II The area to be urbanized north of Highway No. 401 in which Servicing Areas have not yet been established.

Phase III Area designated for Agricultural Uses, for which no services are contemplated during the period covered by this plan.

Within each Phase, the Council, through its Capital Works Program, will schedule and undertake works in the various Servicing Areas in line with these objectives:

(a) Priority is to be given to the filling in of partially developed communities.

(b) Priority is to be given to the servicing of urbanized areas which are now unserviced, or only partially serviced.

(c) Servicing Areas are to be undertaken in combinations which provide for residential and industrial growth in reasonable balance. The basis for determining such a balance in terms of industrial vs. residential acreage is set out in Appendix II.

(d) Servicing Areas are to be undertaken in combinations which provide for complete development of residential communities.

The following five principles are inherent in the Development Plan:

(a) New Phases of Development will not be commenced before Servicing Areas have been established and assigned priorities in the Capital Works Program.

(b) No intensive urban development will be permitted before essential services are available.

(c) No artificial transfer of sanitary drainage from one watershed to another will be permitted except in the case of minor drainage basins flowing directly into the lake or across Township boundaries, or except in an area where senior governmental levels are prepared to underwrite the costs of full services in advance of progressive development as directed by the Township.

(d) Package plants and other temporary methods for treating sanitary drainage in advance of the progressive extension of trunk sewers from main disposal plants will not be permitted.

(e) Phases of development will be substantially complete before successive Phases are commenced.

The *sequence* of the phases is the essence of the Services Plan, rather than the relationship of each phase to particular points in time. However, Table II is presented to indicate the relationship between time and development based on trends in 1956:

TABLE II

ESTIMATED POPULATION IN EACH PHASE OF DEVELOPMENT AT 5 YEAR INTERVALS

(*Indicates Full Growth Reached at This Point)

Year	1956	1961	1966	1971	1976	1981
Phase	Population (x1000 Persons)					
I	133	205	250	275	290	296*
II	6	10	35	80	135	168*
Agricultural Area	—	—	—	—	—	16
	139	215	285	355	425	480

1956–61—Main development in Phase I (72,000 persons)—infill in Phase II (4,000 persons).

1961–66—Main development in Phase I (45,000 persons)—and when past 75% of capacity commence Phase II (25,000 persons).

1966–71—Phase I slowing down (25,000 persons)—main development in Phase II.

1971–76—Infill development of Phase I (15,000 persons)—main development in Phase II (55,000 persons).

1976–81—Phase I slowly completed to capacity (6,000 persons) completion of Phase II (33,000 persons) start development of agricultural area about 1980 (16,000 persons).

NOTE. The table above may appear to be unnecessarily rigid with its five year programs, but the text passage in clause (e) suggests greater flexibility.

METROPOLITAN TORONTO PLANNING BOARD, OFFICIAL PLAN (DRAFT, 1959)

Rapid transit . . . In conformity with plans envisaged by the Toronto Transit Commission, the Official Plan provides for the extension of the existing Yonge Street Subway to Sheppard Avenue and a number of new lines.

The 8 mile Bloor-Danforth line, to be completed within ten years, will replace the most heavily travelled street car line which now carries almost 200,000 passengers daily. The terminals of the line at Keele Street and Woodbine Avenue were selected for economic reasons. As soon as financially feasible, this line should be extended westward to Royal York Road and eastward to Warden Avenue. Several important arteries converge on these two points at which transfer terminals can be established similar to the Yonge Street terminal at Eglinton Avenue. Planning and land acquisition for these extensions should be initiated in the near future.

The two-mile University Avenue line, now under construction, and the Yonge Street Subway provide north-south access to the downtown area. From the St. George transfer station on the Bloor-Danforth line, the University line is to be extended northwest along Spadina Road and the alignment of the proposed Spadina Expressway to Wilson Avenue, where a terminal yard is to be located. This line would be effectively fed by a number of heavily travelled east-west roads, Wilson Avenue, Highway 401, Lawrence, Eglinton and St. Clair Avenues, and Dupont Street. It would also attract traffic to and from the proposed Yorkdale shopping centre during off peak hours and in the reverse direction during peak hours. As this line would be located, for most of its length, in the median of the proposed Spadina Expressway, construction would be relatively cheap and should, if possible, be timed to coincide with the construction of that road commencing in 1962. With relatively large intervals between stations, this line will provide a fast and direct connection between the northwestern section of Metropolitan Toronto and the central business district. Because of the high ratio of car ownership in that section ample parking space should be provided at the outlying stations of this line.

A line is also proposed on or close to Queen Street. Such a line has been under discussion for many years. While traffic on the Queen Street car line has been decreasing, the total number of passengers carried on Queen, King and Adelaide-Richmond Streets still considerably exceeds the load on the Bloor-Danforth line. With the continuing growth of the traditional central business district anticipated by the Official Plan, travel demand on a Queen Street Subway line is expected to remain heavy. The western terminus of this line would be at Sunnyside, west of which a separate right-of-way for surface transit already exists on Queen Street West. To the east this line would follow the alignment of Queen Street to the neighbourhood of Leslie Street, then swing due north to an interchange station with the Bloor-Danforth Subway and to a terminus at O'Connor Drive. At this terminus passengers would converge from the northeast via O'Connor Drive, from the north via the Don Valley Parkway and Don Mills Road, and from the northwest via the Leaside Viaduct. Passengers from the east would transfer to this line at stations along the north-south leg of the line.

The total length of the proposed rapid transit system, as outlined above and shown on Plate 43, would be about 37 miles. It would provide adequate service for the major part of the population anticipated at 1980 and presents the maximum that could be financially undertaken within 20 years. Experience during this period will indicate which parts of the more extensive plan of ultimate development envisaged by the Transit Commission should be initiated after 1980.

NOTE. Some planners, particularly those with architectural backgrounds, think that a plan should present some sort of "image" or "picture" or "goal" which the planner seeks. While the goal may be idealistic and unattainable, it is thought to be necessary to give proper focus to the program projected in the plan. Although idealistic, the plan need not be and should not be abstracted beyond all real meaning. To say that a plan's goal is to produce a "viable community" as one planner did before a professional gathering in Toronto, is to substitute meaningless jargon for specific purpose. The phrase quoted was not used alone, of course, it happens to be the only one that remained in the editor's memory, but the others only added the sin of verbosity to the sin of vacuity. Although idealistic, the plan need not be divorced completely from realism. Idealism and realism need not be polar extremes. The dichotomy is as false as the dichotomy between the theoretical and the practical. What is good theory is probably most practical if the theorist has been trying to work out a practical scheme. There are, of course, some elements in the growth of a community that cannot be controlled but that doesn't mean the planner must resign himself to some kind of economic determinism in a spirit of planning defeatism.

Admittedly it is not easy to work out a plan that makes specific recommendations for land use, roads, water, sewers, public buildings, public parks and open spaces and the other matters planners are concerned with, but the price for planning paid by the public in red tape and delay is great, and the public should have something better than more red tape and delay in return.

The plans from which the excerpts reproduced above have been taken are rather short on "proposals", or what is sometimes called "three dimensional planning." The following excerpt from Sharp's *Oxford Replanned* is intended to provide a contrast and introduce one of the best essays on the master plan in the English language. The book is not only a delight to read, it is instructive as well.

SHARP, OXFORD REPLANNED

[The following Summary of Main Recommendations is taken from pages 213–215 of Dr. Sharp's plan for Oxford published for the Oxford City Council by the Architectural Press, London in 1948.]

Note. This list does not suggest any order of priority: it follows the order in which the recommendations occur in the text.

1. The character of Oxford is a matter of national as well as local concern. The future of the city must be settled in the light of its place in the national economy, and not merely out of a consideration of the internal needs of Oxford alone or out of the desires of the majority of its inhabitants. (p. 73)

2. In the interest both of the city's social well-being and of its historical character, the great Nuffield and the Pressed Steel works should be removed from the city to some other part of the country. (p. 79)

3. New factories, of the right kind, in the right proportion, and in comparatively small units, will need to be brought into the city to employ those workers who do not migrate with the migrating works. (p. 80)

4. The city should at the most, grow no bigger than its present population of 100,000 and should preferably decline in size to a population of 90,000 or slightly less. (p. 81)

5. The prime function of the future city should be as a university city and a county and regional capital: but though manufacturing should not be a prime function, there should nevertheless be sufficient well-diversified industry to assure its social health and material well-being. (p. 81)

6. New territorial growth should be by way of consolidation within the present urbanized area rather than any extensive building over of new land. (p. 86)

7. There should be no further building, except for rural purposes, in the country-side immediately around the city. (p. 88)

8. If the building of satellites to Oxford becomes necessary, they should be established at least ten miles away. (p. 88)

9. The system of by-pass roads should be completed by the construction of new links from Botley to Kidlington (p. 100) and from the Abingdon Road Bridge to Wheatley. (p. 100)

10. An improved system of radial roads should be developed by the construction of a new western approach from Botley (p. 104); the use of the Headington Old Road continued round the foot of Shotover to the London Road (p. 104); and the use of the Abingdon Road, through the provision of a new bridge over the Thames near Iffley, to relieve the Iffley Road. (p. 104)

11. A middle ring road should be developed to take cross-town traffic (p. 110)

12. New inner city roads, to relieve High Street and Cornmarket Street, should be built running from the Plain, alongside Broad Walk, to St. Aldate's: thence, through St. Ebbe's, to the western end of Queen Street: thence through the grounds of Frewin Hall and the University Union to Baker's corner (p. 114). A new road to relieve George Street should be built across Gloucester Green. (p. 116)

13. No bus service should run on High Street, Queen Street, Cornmarket Street or the upper part of St. Aldate's, excepting a 'shuttle service' along High Street between the Plain and the Stations. Vehicles of over 2 tons should be banned from these streets, and there should be a maximum speed limit of 20 miles per hour upon them. (p. 117)

14. The present railway stations should be rebuilt as one, with a new bus station alongside, the whole constituting a main transport station. (p. 120)

15. Public stands (including two multi-storey buildings) should be provided for about 3,300 cars. (p. 127). Car standing should not generally be permitted in the streets between Cornmarket Street and Magdalen Bridge. (p. 127)

16. All flying immediately over the city should be banned. (p. 129)

17. The conception of a development of 'twin cities' of Oxford and Cowley, with the main administrative and shopping centres transferred to Cowley, is unsound and should be dropped. (p. 131)

18. Since the absence of any knowledge of the plans and intentions of the University is a serious obstacle to the proper planning of the city as a whole, the University and the colleges should be required to produce, at an early date, a responsible statement of their needs and intentions. (p. 133)

19. The main zone of University expansion should be west of St. Giles. (p. 135)

20. It is essential that the foil between collegiate and domestic buildings in the historical city should be retained. Ship Street is an example of this foil: the pre-war plans for its demolition should be abandoned, and the street rehabilitated (p. 136). Similarly the proposed demolition by the University of part of Beaumont Street to make room for further extensions to the Ashmolean should be forbidden. (p. 136)

21. The new University Union should be built on the site of the markets, (p. 137)

22. The proposal by Magdalen College to put large new buildings on the site of the Botanic Gardens buildings should be stopped. (p. 137)

23. Monumental planning will be wholly out of character with the historical city, and should be avoided. (p. 138)

24. The development of a single monumental Civic Centre would be a grave mistake; instead, public buildings should be sited singly or in small related groups at salient and suitable points. (p. 138)

25. The new Town Hall and Municipal Offices should be built at the Mac Fisheries corner. (p. 139)

26. The old Conduit, removed from Carfax in 1795, should be brought back to stand in the square in front of the new Town Hall. (p. 140)

27. The new County Council Offices, Municipal College, Law Courts and City and County Museum should be built along the new western approach to the city centre between Queen Street and Oxpens Road. (p. 140)

28. The new Assembly Halls and City Library and Art Gallery should be built facing the new road across Gloucester Green. (p. 142)

29. The main Health Centre and Youth Centre should be built beyond an open space established eastwards of the Plain. (p. 144)

30. The new streets west of Cornmarket Street and St. Aldate's (see para. 12 above) should become new shopping streets. A shopping arcade should be built between the new street and Cornmarket Street. Cornmarket Street should be made a one-way street (traffic travelling northwards) and its pavements widened. (p. 149)

31. The end portions of George Street should be made into pedestrian promenades. (p. 150)

32. The Market should be moved to a site on the square in front of the new Town Hall. (p. 150)

33. The Cattle Market should be moved to the other side of Oxpens Road. (p. 151)

34. An area near to the stations should be zoned for warehouses. (p. 151)

35. The new Telephone Exchange should not be built as has been intended, between the Police Station and Folly Bridge, but (to a height of three stories) on the west side of the new square below Christ Church. (p. 151)

36. The city should double its hotel capacity in the next few years. New hotels should be built on the east side of St. Aldate's north and south of the river at Folly Bridge. (p. 151)

37. A workshop area should be developed near the stations and (possibly) in the southern part of St. Ebbe's. (p. 152)

38. Extension of the Gas Works on their present site should be prohibited, and the works should be removed altogether to a new site at Cowley. (p. 153)

39. The Electricity Works should be removed to Cowley. (p. 154)

40. Three-storied flats should be built in St. Ebbe's and Jericho. (p. 154)

41. A public footpath and garden strip should be laid out under the Longwall Street section of the city walls. New College should be persuaded to give a right of way along the Slipe so that the outer side of the city walls there can be seen by the public. (p. 155)

42. A green barrier should be established east of Magdalen Bridge. (p. 156)

43. When the property between the Cherwell and St. Clement's Street is

pulled down the site should remain open as public riverside gardens. (p. 156)

44. The city outside the centre should be organized into fourteen neighbourhoods, each more or less self-contained for essential everyday services. (p. 165)

45. Many new playing-fields should be provided. (p. 167)

46. A system of connected open spaces should be developed between neighbourhoods, running from the city centre out into the open country. (p. 168)

47. The Thames riverside is at present quite unworthy of the city. It should be improved and generous riverside open spaces made available to the public. (p. 168)

48. The city's main industrial area should remain at Cowley. (p. 169)

49. New buildings in the historical city should be faced in ashlar, plaster, stucco, or similar material. The use of stone rubble or brick should be avoided. (p. 172)

50. Careful attention should be given to building heights in the city centre. (p. 175)

51. New tree-planting should be undertaken in the suburbs; and unskilled lopping of trees in public places should be stopped. (p. 176)

52. The riverside areas of the Thames between Christ Church and Iffley shoud be given an open park-like treatment; unsatisfactory development such as that along the Iffley Road should be screened by planting new trees. (p. 179)

DON MILLS PUBLICITY

Don Mills Developments Limited: Information Centre

[The following statements are taken from an advertising folder published by the authors of one of Canada's most ambitious development programmes: the building of a balanced community at Don Mills, in the Township of North York, northeast of the City of Toronto. This programme had, of course, to be fitted into the planning laws of the local government and the Province but as an experiment is has certain features peculiar to single ownership, a characteristic present in most of the fine planning of ancient and modern cities, towns and villages of England and Europe.]

Don Mills, located seven miles northeast of downtown Toronto, comprises 2,200 acres of rolling land straddling the upper Don Valley. The direct connection which already exists to all parts of the city is soon to be improved with the completion of the Eglinton Avenue Extension (now under construction) and the Don Valley Parkway. Present driving time of 25 minutes to downtown Toronto will be cut to 12 minutes when the Parkway is built. The Bypass, less than a mile away, permits easy access to northern resorts, eastern and western Ontario and international throughways.

From the beginning, the planners and developers, and the architects and builders of Don Mills have striven to obtain the harmonious blend of homes, shops, schools, churches, parks, industry and other ingredients that go to make a properly balanced community. Their aim has been the creation of a setting for happy living. This goal has been reached. Today's purchaser of a Don Mills home safeguards his investment in a well-designed, well-sited residence by the investment he makes in a new, vigorous, intelligently zoned community. Here are modern homes of almost endless variety on lot frontages of 60 to 100 feet. . . . Here, for those who prefer renting, are modern apartments and garden court homes. . . . Here, for the convenience of residents, stores and medical offices are situated in the very heart of the community. . . . Here, the finest of modern schools are located to eliminate dangerous crossings and long walks by pupils. . . . Here, harmony and convenience are kept in mind in providing land for churches and for activities relating to culture and recreation. . . . Here are provided parklands for every neighbourhood and green-belts for community use. . . . Here are offered services unsurpassed in the Metropolitan area—paved roads, curbs, water, storm and sanitary sewers, street lighting and street signs. . . . Here, thriving modern industry, properly zoned, assists in holding down residential tax bills. . . . And, here, streets are designed to add to pleasant community appearance and, by discouraging through traffic, to increase community safety. *This is Don Mills—the best-planned community in all Canada . . . designed for safer and better living.*

Don Mills has been growing so rapidly it is estimated the population will reach 8,000 by Christmas, 1955 (the first new resident moved into his Don Mills home in October, 1953). Matching this rise in population has been the growth of community spirit and friendly neighborliness. Largest of the many citizens' clubs and organizations, the Don Mills Community Association, stresses family membership. Its purpose, enunciated in the first of its semi-monthly bulletins: To make Don Mills the best place in Canada in which to live, by building a strong and happy community through neighborly participation.

BIBLIOGRAPHY. The best way to discover the content of master plans is to look at them. It is a good idea for anyone interested in town planning to get to know thoroughly one town or city, and to examine its master plan (if it has one) critically and constructively. The following plans, or advisory planning reports, are noteworthy; either because they are good plans, or because they are of historical interest. Patrick Abercrombie, *Greater London Plan* (1944) and J. H. Forshaw and Patrick Abercrombie, *County of London Plan* (1943), are good. So are Thomas Sharp, *Exeter Phoenix: A Plan for Rebuilding* and C. M. Holden and W. G. Holford, *The City of London: A Record of Destruction and Survival* (1947). Amongst the growing number of Canadian titles, Gordon Stephenson, *A Redevelopment Study of Halifax, Nova Scotia* (1957) and Gordon Stephenson and George Muirhead, *A Planning Study of Kingston, Ontario* (1960) are outstanding. Vancouver Town Planning Commission, *A Plan for the City of Vancouver, British Columbia, including a general plan of the region* (1928), prepared by Harland Bartholomew and Associates, is one of the earliest professionally prepared plans in Canada. Jacques Gréber, *Plan for the National Capital* (1950), is a more recent example.

CHAPTER 5

THE MACHINERY OF PLANNING

Faith in machinery is, I said, our besetting danger.
Matthew Arnold

If we may assume, as many observers think we must, that planning will not produce ideal or perfect plans, and that with or without a plan, planning will remain a process, it may be as important to understand who works the process as to understand what it is doing. The materials in this chapter invite consideration of the people in planning and how they get their authority, by election, by appointment, or by qualification. Should elected representatives plan for their constituents? Or should the process be primarily in the hands of appointed people? If so, who should appoint them? What is the role of the professional planner? How does he get along with his political masters? How can this relationship be improved? How are private interests protected?

1. LOCAL PLANNING AGENCIES

MUNICIPAL ACT
British Columbia. Revised Statutes. 1960. Chapter 41

696. The Council may have community plans prepared or revised from time to time, and they may be expressed in maps, plans, reports, or otherwise.

697. (1) The Council may, by by-law adopted by an affirmative vote of at least two-thirds of all the members thereof, designate any community plan prepared under section 696 as the official community plan or as a part of the official community plan.

[Sections 696 and 697(1) are reproduced as amended by S.B.C., 1961, c. 43, s. 36.]

THE TOWN AND RURAL PLANNING ACT
Alberta. Revised Statutes. 1955. Chapter 337

63. A council, by resolution, may authorize

(*a*) the preparation of a general plan describing the manner in which the future development of the municipality may best be organized and carried out within a specified period of time, having regard to considerations of orderliness, economy and convenience, and

(*b*) the carrying out of such investigations, surveys and research and the preparation of such reports, maps and other documentary material as may be necessary for the purpose of preparing a general plan.

64. A general plan

(*a*) shall be prepared under the direction of qualified planning officers or qualified planning consultants, who shall be appointed by and be responsible to the council, . . .

[Section 63 and 64 (*a*) are reproduced as amended by S.A., 1960, c. 107, s. 15.]

NOTE. The Alberta Act does not define the words "qualified planning" directors or consultants, but see Section 2 below.

TOWN PLANNING ACT

Nova Scotia. Revised Statutes. 1954. Chapter 292

2. (1) Every council or councils where more than one is interested may create a board consisting of the mayor or warden (*ex officio*) and six other persons of whom not less than three shall be members of the council.

3. (2) The board may appoint such town planning engineers, consultants, or other officers as may be necessary for its work and may expend such funds as may be furnished by the council.

(4) The officers of a municipality shall at the request of the board do and perform all such duties under this Act as they, or any of them, would do and perform for the council if the board had not been appointed.

4. (1) Subject to the approval of the Minister any council shall have power:

(a) to prepare a plan . . . which . . . shall be known as "The Official Town Plan". . . .

(2) Before adopting, varying or revoking an official town plan, or passing, amending or repealing a zoning by-law, or taking any official action in regard to any matters pertaining to town planning, a council shall, if a board has been established under this Act, request the board to make a report thereon.

NOTE. The Nova Scotia Act is typical of most Canadian planning legislation in giving the power to plan to a council but giving it the privilege of setting up a special agency if it wishes. In most cases the councils seem to prefer to appoint a special agency.

The British Columbia Act provides for an Advisory Planning Commission to be created by the council by "an affirmative vote of at least two-thirds of all the members thereof" and the Commission members "shall serve without remuneration and . . . shall advise the Council on such matters coming within the scope of this Part [XXI Community Planning] as may from time to time be referred to the Commission by the Council." The Council may otherwise determine the constitution of the Commission.

The Alberta Act, which provides for an even greater clutter of planning agencies than Ontario, but which gives the council the initiative, also provides for a municipal planning advisory commission whose constitution is largely left to the council to determine. The commission members "shall represent the council, the citizens at large, and any organization concerned with planning and orderly development in and about the municipality, or any of them." (Section 14*d* as amended S.A., 1960, c. 107. s. 8). Cf. *The Community Planning Act, 1957*, S.S. 1957, c. 48, ss. 9–16, as amended by S.S. 1959, c. 107, ss. 2–4; *The Town Planning Act,* R.S.M. 1954, c. 267, s. 9; and the *Community Planning Act,* S.N.B., 1960–61, c. 6, ss. 5–12.

PRINGLE *v.* VICTORIA

British Columbia. Supreme Court. [1951] 3 D.L.R. 334

MACFARLANE J.: Rule to show cause why By-law 3601 otherwise known as Zoning By-law Amendment By-law (75) 1951 of the Corporation of the City of Victoria should not be quashed in its entirety.

The grounds on which the rule was granted are shortly (1) that the notice of the amending by-law was deceptive; and (2) that the City Council passed the amending by-law before it received the report of the Town Planning Commission. . . .

. . . The second ground of objection raises the question as to the duty of the Council when it has referred to the Town Planning Commission, the application for amendment for consideration and report and either no action is taken by the Commission or the report is equivocal. Here the Commission advised the Council that it had received the application and had laid it on the table until the first day of February, when it was hoped that more definite information might be available to the Commission which would enable a decision to be reached. This letter was written on December 19, 1950. It is only fair to say that it followed other correspondence and an informal joint meeting of members of the Council and the Commission and followed also the refusal by the commission to approve a like application. It is not for me, however, to enter into a discussion of the merits or demerits of the policy under discussion. All I have to decide is whether after an application is referred to the Commission for consideration and report the Council must wait for any report of the Commission. The statute makes no provision for any period of time. It is, I think, unquestionable that the Town Planning Commission is an advisory body only and I think it follows in the absence of some provision in the statute that the Council is free to act, that is, to pass its amending by-law without waiting for some time that the Commission may specify, at the conclusion of which the Commission will consider that it may have more information which it may desire to have before making a recommendation. Of the two, the Council is the sovereign body responsible to the electors and if not satisfied to wait for a specified time, other than sufficient for the Commission to say it approves or does not approve or is not in a position to do either, I see nothing in the statute that requires it to wait.

I wish it clearly to be understood that I am not discussing and do not think it is within my province to discuss, the matter otherwise than as it is affected by the provisions of the statute. On that basis, I do not think the by-law can be quashed and the rule to show cause should be discharged with costs.

NOTE. When this case arose the British Columbia *Town Planning Act*, R.S.B.C. 1948, c. 339 had a section similar to s. 4(2) of the Nova Scotia Act reproduced above.

Should there be a statutory requirement that the Council wait at least, say, two weeks, or a month, for the report of the Commission before taking action? What variations on this theme can you suggest?

THE PLANNING ACT

Ontario. Revised Statutes. 1960. Chapter 296

11. (1) The plan as finally prepared and recommended by the planning board shall be submitted to the council of the designated municipality.

(2) The council of the designated municipality may adopt the plan by by-law.

NOTE. Since a planning board may be appointed to plan an area including not only the whole or part of one municipality but also adjoining municipalities and adjoining territory without municipal organization, one municipality is "designated" as the municipality that appoints the board members and adopts the plan.

Under the Ontario Act there is no power in a council to adopt a plan of its own preparation, it is limited to the adoption of the plan prepared by the planning board. The council can, however, adopt an amendment to the plan on its own initiative, but since one of the duties of the planning board set out in section 10(1) (*f*) is to "review the official plan from time to time and recommend amendments thereto to the council . . . for adoption" it seems clear that the planning board is contemplated as a continuing advisory body.

A board may consist of four, six, or eight members "who are not employees of a municipality or of a local board", except school teachers. The members of the planning board who are "members of *a* municipal council" shall not constitute a majority. This provision ensures that the council does not dominate the board, but it also prevents even members of councils of other municipalities not in the planning area but who live there from assuming a dominant position by sheer numbers. The head of the designated council is *ex officio* a member of the planning board and with the approval of the council he may appoint a substitute to act for him from time to time.

CUMMING, "THE PROVINCE AND THE PLANNING BOARD"

Toronto, Ontario. 1962. 12 *Community Planning Review*, No. 3, 18

. . . A few months ago, a rough classification was made of the 350 planning areas in existence in Ontario at the beginning of this year . . .

The figures indicate that planning boards are inactive or non-existent in more than 70 of these 350 planning areas, and we have no record of any planning activity on the part of a further 80 planning boards, although the appointment of members is being kept up to date in this latter group. Another 50 planning boards appear to be confining their activities to granting consents for transfers [or] leasing of land in areas of subdivision control.

About 60 more planning boards have full-time staff without any formal technical qualifications to the best of our knowledge, or they nominally employ a planning consultant—or have full-time staff *and* a consultant—but we have no indication of any significant planning programme being conducted. Only the remaining 80 or 90 planning boards seem to be embarked upon a positive planning programme, and only 23 of these employ full-time, technically qualified planning staff.

As I have indicated, the classification we made was based on incomplete information and incorporated a considerable element of subjectivity, hence the figures it produced are only approximations. *They are close enough, however, to indicate an unsatisfactory level of planning activity—both in terms of quantity and quality—on the part of planning boards in this Province.* While we can point to over 350 planning areas having been defined now, embracing over 80% of the population of Ontario, only about one-quarter of these seem to be carrying out an effective planning programme and less than 7% employ a full-time, technically-qualified planning staff. Admittedly, most of the large centres are included in this group, so that a substantial part of the population of the Province has some technical planning service.

I want to emphasize the importance of technically qualified staff. Some people say that planning is simply the application of common sense, but there is more to it than that. An effective planning programme for most communities that are undergoing any significant change requires the know-how that can be obtained only by thorough training or by long experience—or both. I appreciate that the hiring of planners with the requisite professional qualifications costs money, but planning is sufficiently important to warrant the spending of money on it. Anyway, I have no doubt that a sound planning programme, properly implemented, will save the community far more money than the programme will cost. . . .

NOTE ON THE BUDGET AND THE PLANNING STAFF. Section 4(10) of the Ontario Act provides that "the planning board shall appoint a secretary-treasurer, who may be a member of the planning board, and may engage such employees and consultants as is deemed expedient." The provision in the Nova Scotia Act requiring the officers of a municipality to work for the planning board appeared in the predecessor of the Ontario Act, but was not repeated in the present Act when it was first enacted as Chapter 71 of the 1946 Statutes. The British Columbia Act provides in s. 701(3) that the council "shall" include in the annual budget such sums as are necessary to defray the expenses of the Commission. No such explicit duty is imposed on the councils in other provinces. An Ontario planning board is a separate body corporate from the municipal corporation, but like all special planning agencies in Canada it has no power to raise money by borrowing or by taxation. It is, therefore, wholly dependent on the largesse of the council, which controls the purse strings. This power has led to a number of indirect measures by councils in Ontario to exert a pressure on the board or its staff. Three examples of which the editor has personal knowledge may be cited.

In 1954 the council of a township approved a budget for its planning board save only the item of $6,000 for the salary of the secretary-treasurer, which was set by the council at $5,200 per annum (the prevailing rate) for the first four months and then at $4,000 for the remaining eight months. The secretary-treasurer resigned and within six months occupied what might be called the highest municipal planning post in Canada.

The same council, a few years later, was asked to approve a planning board budget of $58,000. It approved a budget of $8,000 for the board, which coincided with the item for the secretary-treasurer's salary, and then it voted an item on the municipal budget of $50,000 for "planning". The intent apparently was to denude the planning board of its real control of its staff, but still retain the board as an official planning agency. Pressures that can only be described as "political" were brought to bear on the council and it ultimately approved the board's budget for the original amount.

A joint planning board in Ontario received 80% of its funds from the designated council and 10% from each of the other two constituent councils. After some years of operation the designated council announced that it intended to contribute nothing but that it would employ the board's staff in its own establishment. No outside pressures, if any, were effective, and the staff moved over to the council.

These three cases illustrate something of the friction that seems to be fairly common in the administration of planning in Ontario. There would seem to be room for some sort of "constitutional convention" between the council and the board, at which, before crises arise and attitudes are struck and faces have to be saved, many of the known causes of friction could be discussed calmly and a satisfactory working arrangement agreed upon. What clauses should go into such a constitution?

NOTE. See *The Planning Service Act*, S.M., 1960, c. 49, which provides for agreements between the Minister of Industry and Commerce and a municipality whereby the Minister covenants to assist the municipality in planning matters. The municipality must covenant to pay each year (for a period of not less than five years) to the government an amount to be fixed in the agreement. If the municipality is the responsible authority under *The Town Planning Act*, it must appoint an advisory commission.

A short account of the forerunner of *The Planning Service Act* is given by S. George Rich, in *Community Planning Review*, the journal of the Community Planning Association of Canada, March, 1958, at pages 16–18. Mr. Rich attributes the "reform" of technical planning assistance provided by the province to some extent to the efforts of the Manitoba Division of the C.P.A.C. In 1957 the legislature first introduced an amendment to *The Metropolitan Planning Act* R.S.M., 1954, c. 164, amended S.M., 1957, c. 42, which provided for provincial planning service to be given under the direction of the Metropolitan Planning Commission. Under the agreement between the province and the municipality the Minister guaranteed that the planning service would perform the planning functions outlined in *The Metropolitan Planning Act*. The standard of service was to be that provided by the Commission to the member municipalities in Greater Winnipeg. At that time the cost to the municipality was assessed at twenty cents per capita for each year of the agreement, which had a minimum term of three years. Mr. Rich describes this cost as representing a "fair share" of the cost of the service and the balance was to be borne by the province.

The province of Alberta contributes to district planning commissions an amount said, by Denis Cole, in "Alberta's District Planning Commission" in *Community Planning Review*, Volume XI, Number 4, p. 10 (undated; c. 1961) to be twenty-five cents per capita or 0.10% of the provincial budget and 0.15% of the total capital invested by private enterprise in new buildings plus municipal expenditures on capital works. In one district (Red Deer) the cost per capita contributed by the municipalities was: one city, 87 cents, seven towns, 73 cents, four villages, 51 cents, and four rural municipalities, 21 cents. That district embraces 8,000 square miles and has a total population of 69,849, or less than nine persons per square mile.

Ontario provincial assistance to local planners has largely been delivered in kind. The staff of the department holds conferences designed to bring professional planners in local government together to hear special lectures, to work out problems and to discuss questions in small seminars or workshops. There has been one such conference held for planners in private consulting practice and one for committees of adjustment. No direct financial aid is given to smaller communities, such as summer resort areas where planning is considered necessary but not, apparently, within the reach of the local tax resources.

The Metropolitan Toronto Planning Board, like the Winnipeg Commission, provides technical services for any municipality within the planning area.

COMMUNITY PLANNING ACT
New Brunswick. Statutes. 1960–61. Chapter 6

5. A council may, by by-law, establish a planning commission consisting of not less than five and not more than fifteen members.

6. (1) The council may, by resolution, appoint members to serve on the commission and, with the consent of the commission, remove any member.

(2) Subject to this section, the term of office of members . . . is three years. . . .

NOTE. The other Acts are silent on this question of removal of members. In Ontario, where the relations between the council and the planning boards are sometimes strained, councils have been known to "remove" all the board members despite the duration of their terms, and appoint new incumbents. The Act provides that the members "shall hold office for three years" (except, of course, councillors) and the terms are staggered. *The Interpretation Act*, R.S.O., 1960, c. 191, s. 27 (1) provides that unless the contrary intention appears, "words authorizing the appointment of a public officer or functionary, or a deputy, include the power of removing him, . . . from time to time in the discretion of the authority in whom the power of appointment is vested." Is a planning board member a "functionary"?

NOTE ON AGENCY MEMBERS' QUALIFICATIONS. There would appear to be no readily available data in any of the provinces about the qualifications of the persons who are appointed to planning agencies in this country. An old study in the United States, Walker, *The Planning Function in Urban Government* (2d ed. 1950) reports on the make up of thirty-one planning commissions having a total of 208 members (c. 1935). Thirty-five percent, or 73, were business men, the largest group, 55, being otherwise unclassified. Fifteen percent, or 32, were "realtors", that is, business men engaged in the buying and selling of real estate for others; 11%, or 23, were lawyers; 10%, or 21 were architects; and 7.7%, or 16, were engineers. The table is headed "occupational analysis" and 10 members rejoiced in the occupation of being "women". The editor, not being an angel, hazards the guess that somewhat fewer "realtors", lawyers, architects and engineers find their way to Canadian planning agencies.

It is interesting that the thirty-one commissions examined by Walker had no professional city planners amongst their members. It may be doubted whether any professional man, least of all a city planner, makes the best kind of member. If the function of the commission is to make a "democratic" decision on planning issues presented by the professional staff, the planner, engineer and architect especially, and the lawyer to some extent, are likely to dominate the discussion and subdue the mild mannered and perhaps highly intelligent amateur with refreshing ideas. The place for the professional is, perhaps, on the staff side, or as adviser or advocate in formal processes of hearings and the like. In small communities the lawyer member may find himself in the embarrassing position of having to "retire" because of his professional concern over some matters involving his client's land.

TOWN AND COUNTRY PLANNING ACT, 1947
England. Statutes. 1947. Chapter 51

5. (1) As soon as may be after the appointed day, every local planning authority shall . . . not later than three years after the appointed day, or within such extended period as the Minister may in any particular case allow, submit to the Minister . . . a plan (hereinafter called a "development plan"). . . .

NOTE. This provision is unusual in "western democracies" in that it makes planning compulsory. Fifteen years later the *Town and Country Planning Act, 1962* (S.U.K., 1962, c. 38) was passed revising and consolidating the

1947 Act as amended in the interval. Section 4 of the 1962 Act refers to "any local planning authority who have not submitted to the Minister a development plan for their area" and charges that authority with the duty "within such period as the Minister may in any particular case allow." In his annual report for 1959 the Minister reported that by the end of 1959, the first development plans, theoretically due on July 1, 1951, had not all been approved. Sixty-four county plans, and 76 county borough plans and 2 planning board plans had been approved and 12 plans, or part plans were outstanding.

The "local planning authority" is the county council (for the county) and the county borough council for the county boroughs. A planning board may be established for an area embracing more than the territory of a local planning authority. Only two such boards have been established, one for the Lakes Park and one for Peak Park. In Canadian terms a "county borough" may be approximated to a city of 100,000 or larger. There were altogether 145 planning agencies created by the 1947 Act, replacing over 1400 under the preceding legislation.

BROWN, PLANNING ADMINISTRATION
1954. 4 *Community Planning Review* 24

. . . In Great Britain, the control of all local government functions is jealously guarded by local councils. There we find senior officers appointed by council and reporting directly to the appropriate committees who are largely responsible for transacting the business of the municipality. Technical aspects of planning, except in the large county councils, are usually the responsibility of the City Engineer or City Architect as an addition to his other duties. This arrangement has been the subject of much crticism, since planning does not then receive the undivided attention of the senior official. However, the planner operates in an atmosphere of mutual co-operation with his colleagues which is traditional to the British local government service and inculcated by many years of established custom. Although no special arrangements are devised to ensure coordination, the system (or lack of system) appears to operate successfully in many cases to a remarkable degree, particularly where the ability and personality of the planner is dominant. Nevertheless we must realize that the system is probably operating under ideal local government conditions with council retaining full autonomous power in respect of all local government functions.

In the United States, the situation would seem to be entirely different because of the tendency to set up separate committees or boards to administer certain municipal governmental functions. We often find divorced from the council such responsibilities as education, parks, housing, redevelopment, transportation, and many other important matters. It is difficult to generalize, of course, since there is a great number of variations between the several states and cities. However, it is almost universal to find the planning function exercised by a town planning commission with the commission planning for a variety of proposals often with little regard to the work of the other municipal governmental groups.

Under such an arrangement, not only is coordination basically more difficult because of the divided responsibilities, but the commission's work itself is in no way integrated with municipal government machinery. The planners are not unaware, of course, of the situation, and we find the commissions and their staffs struggling to surmount these conditions and to establish some sort of coordinating procedure.

Traditionally Canada operates somewhere between these two administrative arrangements. We find in the larger cities that planning is normally a municipal function, and the tendency is toward more planning by municipal government than planning by commission. Where commissions operate, their role is less executive and more advisory.

Vancouver is the third largest City in Canada and has been actively engaged in the planning field since 1926. Nevertheless, in one respect it has lagged behind other larger cities since it established its civic planning department less than two years ago, and that department has been fully operative for little more than 12 months.

Since it is one of the newest of the civic planning departments, it might be worthwhile to examine the form of administration which the city decided to adopt, since that decision was made comparatively recently in the knowledge of the changing functions of planning and with the experience of others in mind. The form of administration was established following a report to the City Council prepared by Professor Harold Spence-Sales and Professor John Bland of McGill University. With certain minor modifications in the light of experience, it appears to operate exceedingly well, and would seem to pass the tests which have been mentioned earlier.

Under this system a Technical Planning Board has been established comprising the eight senior departmental heads:

Director of Planning
City Comptroller
City Engineer
Corporation Counsel
Building Inspector
Supervisor, Lands and Rentals
Superintendent, Board of Trustees
Superintendent, Board of Park Commissioners.

The Director of Planning is Chairman of the Board, and the secretarial work is the responsibility of his Department.

The meetings of the Board are not held in public and the members thus are enabled without external pressures of any sort to thrash out on a realistic and factual basis the several problems concerning the development of the City upon which they have been required to report.

Their terms of reference are "to advise Council on the development plan for the City and to coordinate all matters relating to city development." In practice, however, the City Council have been sending to the Technical Planning Board an increasing number of problems of wide variety for their consideration and report. This increasing amount of work is perhaps a measure of their success.

It should be noted that the Technical Planning Board has representatives sent from the Board of School Trustees and the Board of Park Commissioners and forms, therefore, the major operative linkage between those independently elected and operated boards and the City Council.

It is customary for the Director of Planning to prepare his draft reports for the Board in close consultation with those officials who are directly concerned with the particular problem submitted to the Board. For example, a simple issue such as the location of a joint school and park site may involve, in addition to the officials of the School and Parks Boards, the City Engineer and the Supervisor of Lands and Rentals. Although most of the technical and clerical work is carried out by the Planning Department, the other departments make significant contributions as the necessity arises.

Perhaps the classic example of the Technical Planning Board's work was the preparation of a five-year plan of capital works which was approved by the City Council in the Fall of 1953 and endorsed by the electors in a plebiscite in December, 1953. Under the terms of the Vancouver City Charter, the City Council is enabled to submit to the electorate a program of capital development for a period of not more than ten years. In this particular instance the Technical Planning Board, largely through the Planning Department, was in contact with every spending agency, such as the Airport Board, Police Commission, Fire Department, Library Board, Museum Committee, and General Hospital, in addition to the departments represented on the Board itself. This resulted in a program of work for which estimates were prepared or checked, sites provisionally chosen, and the whole generally processed by the Technical Planning Board. It is perhaps worthwhile noting as an example that the City Council, on the recommendation of the Board, decided to build a new central jail and other police facilities as part of the Five-Year Plan in preference to adaption of an existing structure, as originally decided. The consequential saving was some $15,000, with, of course, more modern accommodation.

In submitting their initial report to the City Council, the Technical Planning Board recommended a target figure of total expenditure which was very much below the total compiled from the initial departmental estimates. The City Council instructed the Board to submit a revised program totalling more closely to the target figure, and it was this final program which was accepted by Council with only minor amendments. The absolute co-operation received from all parties concerned, and the co-ordination of works which such a program represented, could be termed an acid test for the administrative arrangements which the Technical Planning Board represents. . . .

Clearly there is considerable advantage to the City Council in receiving from a very experienced group of officials a factual report with an unbiased recommendation. It is perhaps equally important, however, that all development projects are designed on a co-operative basis and all officials concerned participate in a scheme from its earliest stages. Inevitably this must result in economy in devising solutions to current problems and in their execution. Furthermore it builds up a general spirit of departmental collaboration. It is not suggested that all recommendations of the Board have been acceptable to the City Council, but it does mean that decisions of Council are reached in the full knowledge of the several factors which should govern such decisions.

The Spence-Sales-John Bland report indicated that the establishment of a Technical Planning Board would free the Town Planning Commission from complicated technical and administrative matters so as to enable the Commission to concentrate on the broader policy issues. In this connection it is generally recognized that there is a tendency for a town planning commission to get involved too deeply in matters of technical and administrative detail, leaving them too little time for the consideration of the major planning problems. . . .

THE TOWN AND RURAL PLANNING ACT

Alberta. Revised Statutes. 1955. Chapter 337

14c. (1) The council of a city or town having a population of more than fifteen thousand may by by-law establish a board to be known as a technical planning board for the purposes of

(*a*) advising and assisting the council, and

(*b*) co-ordinating the activities of the various departments and agencies of the city,

with regard to the planning and orderly development of the city or town.

(2) The technical planning board shall consist of officials of the city or town appointed by the council in the manner set out in the by-law.

(3) The council may delegate to the technical planning board such powers as it deems necessary for the purposes for which it is established, other than the power of raising money or expropriating land.

(4) The by-law may authorize the technical planning board to retain the services of such special consultants as are necessary for any of its purposes.

(5) The by-law shall provide for the holding of meetings, the keeping of minutes and any other matters pertaining to the organization of the technical planning board and the transaction of its business.

(6) A certified copy of the by-law and any amendments thereof shall forthwith be deposited with the Director.

[Section 14*c* is reproduced as amended by S.A., 1960, c. 107, s. 8.]

NOTE. The Saskatchewan Act provides for a similar "technical planning board." By section 18,

"The board shall consist of:

"(a) one or two members of the council, the commissioners, if any, the solicitor, the engineer, if any, the planner, if any, and such other officers and employees of the city as are designated in the bylaw; and

"(b) at the option of the council, one member or employee of each school board, each hospital board, the parks board, the library board, any other board appointed under *The City Act* and each organization operating a public utility within the city, or of any of them."

2. Professional Persons in Planning

The Alberta Act requires the general plan to be prepared under the direction of "qualified" planners. The Toronto Township (Ontario) Official Plan, which was prepared by a consultant, modestly states, in clause 4(b), under the heading of "Method of preparing the Plan": "in order to have the advice of an expert staff, the Board has retained the services of a competent Town Planner, who has guided the Board and Council in the preparation of the plan."

Who is a "qualified" or "competent" town planner? This question is far from academic, since the increasing use of hearing procedures in which planners offer expert testimony means that more and more frequently the lawyer must establish his own expert's qualifications and know how to attack the opposing expert. The following materials are intended as the basis of discussion and constructive criticism.

ARISTOTLE, POLITICS. (Jowett translation) 325 B.C. "Hippodamus, the son of Euryphon, a native of Miletus, the same who invented the art of planning cities, and who also laid out the Piraeus—a strange man, whose fondness for distinction led him into a general eccentricity of life, which made some think him affected (for he would wear flowing hair and expensive ornaments; but these were worn on a cheap but warm garment both in winter and summer); he, besides aspiring to be an adept in the knowledge of nature, was the first person not a statesman who made inquiries about the best form of government."

BASSETT, THE MASTER PLAN. 1938. "There has been much discussion about the qualifications of the community land planner. He is a person experienced and skillful in co-ordinating streets, parks, sites for public buildings, zoning districts, routes of public utilities and harbour lines."

SUBDIVISION AND TRANSFER REGULATIONS

Alberta. Regulations. 1960. No. 185/60 O.C. No. 926-60.

2. In these Regulations,

(22) "planner" means a person who is a member or associate member of the Town Planning Institute of Canada;

NOTE ON THE T.P.I.C. The Alberta subdivision regulations are believed to be the only place where any official recognition is given to the Town Planning Institute of Canada as the body of professionally qualified planners in Canada. The T.P.I.C. was founded in 1923, with the well known planner, Thomas Adams, earlier a founder and first president of the Town Planning Institute in Great Britain, as its first president. Until recently its requirements for membership were rather loose, and the "grandfather clause" admitted the established planners without a very close examination of their qualifications. The organization was moribund during the 1930's and the war and post war years, but during the early 1950's regained some strength. Its membership qualifications now call for some training and experience, usually a university degree or diploma course in planning, with *one* year of responsible planning work, or a degree in a related discipline, such as geography, sociology, architecture or engineering with *three* years' responsible planning work, followed by a written examination, which now takes the form of a thesis. Persons without university education can become members after six years of training and examination under a system not unlike one once common in legal education, but now almost wholly abandoned in Canada. The T.P.I.C. is incorporated under the Dominion Companies' Act and is in no sense a licensing body. Nevertheless many planning agencies today specify membership in the T.P.I.C. as a qualification for their senior planning posts. There are about 400 members in the T.P.I.C. and there is no other professional group that could be said to embody the profession. In Quebec the Quebec Society of Professional Town Planners and in British Columbia the Planning Institute of British Columbia have almost common requirements for, and a considerable overlapping of membership.

RODWIN, "THE ACHILLES HEEL OF BRITISH TOWN PLANNING"

Appendix A in *The British New Towns Policy* (1956)

The Planner's Background. In the past, British planners have been recruited primarily from three professions: engineering, architecture, and surveying (real estate). The reason, as the *Report of the Committee on the Qualifications of Planners* (Schuster Report) states, is that the profession was founded when the conception of planning was mainly local and restrictive, and when the main skills required were those of the architect, engineer, and surveyor. The report also records the findings of a recent survey of 153 planning authorities of all types. It was pointed out that "senior planning responsibility was held in 81 cases by engineers, in 34 by architects, in 32 by surveyors, and in 6 by members of the Town Planning Institute who have qualified through the examinations of the Institute without having the basic professional qualifications."

The composition of the Ministry of Town and Country Planning is not markedly different. Most of the planning officers are qualified planners who were originally educated as architects, engineers, and surveyors. Most of the research staff were admittedly not conducting research. They gathered the operating physical, economic, and social data. This group comprised primarily planners, geographers, and geologists. There are very few, if any, economists or sociologists now on the staff.

The London County Council has the largest local planning organization in England. More than 260 persons were employed in June 1952. Twenty-four persons were on the "research" staff. Almost all these persons gathered facts for informational purposes or current administrative assignments. The chief of research was trained as a surveyor. The research staff comprised surveyors, geographers, architects, one or two statisticians, and "perhaps" a sociologist. There were no economists on the staff.

Manchester prepared its development plan with a staff of approximately forty-six persons. The top positions were held by engineers. No social scientists were employed. . . .

Until very recently planning curricula in the universities provided almost no training in the social sciences. Consider, for example, the Department of Civic Design of the University of Liverpool the oldest in this field. . . .

In short, the emphasis was on physical planning or practical professional routines. The planner was taught to think physically, visually, technically. He still does. He was only crudely, if at all, familiar with the nature and use of research and scientific method. He knew little of the thinking or of the applicability of the social sciences, particularly economics and sociology. These observations may not apply to the rare individuals who personally educated themselves to overcome these deficiencies. But there is no question that the few statistics presented above accurately depict the present formal training and qualifications of most British planners.

Why this was so is easy to explain. The town planner's duties were formerly quite circumscribed. At best, they involved the layout of streets, roads, utilities, squares, and parks. Technical knowledge and three-dimensional expression were required. In the past, moreover, architects and engineers were not so highly specialized: they were broad-gauge men familiar with design, engineering, and developments in other fields.

Social sciences didn't exist as separate disciplines. Ignorance of the scattered fragments could not really constitute a dangerous gap in knowledge. When the first school of civic design was established, sociology was hardly known. Economics was considered a "dismal" and highly abstract science which still had to develop meaningful empirical tests and analyses of significant propositions. It never occurred to most economists, sociologists, or students of the social sciences that the problems of city planning were and would increasingly become problems of applied social science. Most development decisions were made by private entrepreneurs. Government activity was relatively minor. The market, through the price mechanism, guided activities, instead of the planners. To most planners of the period, with rare exceptions, research in social science was considered scarcely relevant or necessary.

This technical approach was perpetuated by the town-planning schools, guided largely by architects and engineers, and by the Town Planning Institute, the professional organization that set the seal on technical qualifications. . . .

Consequences of the Planner's Background. Few universities with schools of architecture in the United States and Great Britain have adequate research facilities or research training. Many staff members are employed part time, with the remaining time generally spent in professional practice. While there is deep interest on the part of students and staff alike in new designs, new materials, new construction techniques, more efficient utility and heating systems, and the like, these researches are generally conducted by other departments or outside organizations. Direct university research by architects has been quite limited.

When the architect becomes interested in planning, some of this approach and these habits of thinking are carried over. Many town-planning faculty members are also part-time practitioners. When they teach, the work on the drafting board commands major attention. Most of the other aspects tend to be side issues. In general, the same holds true for engineers and surveyors in the field. This emphasis in education, thinking, and teaching, coupled with very limited financial resources, largely explains why university planning departments have not engaged in much research.

Universities, however, ought to make a major contribution to the advancement of knowledge. Actually, few contributions are made in this field. Discussion and general thinking there are aplenty: look at any journal of town planning. Deepening and broadening of insights from professional practice also occur, and indeed are quite valuable. Teaching without such experience would soon go stale. There is also some penetrating historical research. But none of these activities are substitutes for careful and sustained inquiries into the problems, including the social and economic problems, confronting the profession. . . .

Social scientists, on the other hand, were concentrating on the development of the concepts, methodology, and core problems of their disciplines. Urban, regional, and national land-planning problems were specialized peripheral issues, and they neglected them. Occasional stray researchers might get absorbed in questions like the location of industry, the urban neighborhood, and the history of cities. But there the matter ended. As a consequence, there was scarcely any recognition of common denominators. Interdisciplinary studies were unusual. Collaboration between departments rarely occurred. Each department and school went its own way.

New Trends. Signs of a change are evident and not unexpected. . . .

Some Unsolved Problems. . . . But is town planning a separate discipline? Does it have special techniques, concepts, and perspectives? Or can one only practice and make a contribution as a specialist planner? What, indeed, could such a nonspecialist planner do? Persons educated in an undergraduate program as town planners would specialize in making and helping to put into effect comprehensive land-use plans for neighborhoods, towns, and regions. The core function would be to organize transportation, utilities, housing, playgrounds, schools, shops, industrial areas, and other land uses into an efficient physical whole. To do so involves intimate understanding of the tools, concepts, and potential contributions of other disciplines. It also presupposes collaboration with many specialists, such as geographers, economists, sociologists, political scientists, architects, engineers, and surveyors. But the town planner also has distinctive tools and approaches that can exercise crucial influence on the process and the final product of town planning.

Properly taught, this discipline should deepen insight and develop humility concerning the limits and potential contributions of the town-planning profession and the equally vital contributions of others; and it should above all encourage the fundamental team attitude that would help to produce economically efficient, socially desirable, and visually satisfying streets, neighbourhoods, and towns. A person might well be able to master this profession without going through the whole of an architectural, engineering, or surveying course.

Is a planning course too narrow? Does it represent too specialized a perspective? Ought it to be preceded by a more general education, as is the case with law and medicine? Certainly not at present; nor in the future if present trends continue.

ROYAL COMMISSION ON CANADA'S ECONOMIC PROSPECTS, FINAL REPORT (1957)

. . . For some persons, planning is a magic word; for others, it is an obnoxious one. Our own view is that trained, professional town planners are valuable people indeed (they are also, incidentally, very scarce people just at present), provided they are put to work in the right context. They have special skills and techniques; they are apt to possess as well a highly desirable comprehensiveness of outlook. But too much should not be expected of them. They cannot simply be hired and relied upon to produce glittering solutions from their mysterious boxes of tricks. To paraphrase Clemenceau, planning is too important a thing to be left entirely to planners–and with this, most planners would heartily agree. The most successful examples of planning have involved a method of approach, a way of doing things, which has permeated just about every aspect of the municipality's operations, including—this is especially important—the financial aspect. Good municipalities and school corporations have always done a considerable amount of planning, with or without professional assistance. To them, much of what modern proponents of planning now advocate will seem merely an enlarged and more formalized version of what they have been doing all along. At the risk of being caught in the crossfire of contending schools of thought, let us attempt to summarize what the "new look" broadly is. When an area has been subjected to a thorough and continuing survey; when, on the basis of that survey, a zoning, land-use and capital improvements plan has been drawn up, flexible yet resistant to capricious or doubtfully motivated alterations; when to this have been added a zoning by-law, another by-law controlling subdivision, and a long-term capital budget; and when the whole thing has been examined, discussed and accepted by department heads, council and the public—then there is planning, in the full, mid-twentieth-century sense of the term. . . . [page 301]

THE PROFESSIONAL STATUS OF A PLANNING DIRECTOR

Report of Committee on Professional Services, American Institute of Planners. 1955

The planning profession, as represented by the American Institute of

Planners, undertakes in this statement of policy, to identify the position of planning director.

Definition

The Planning Director is the professional and official officer carrying the chief planning responsibility, and is the administrative head of the staff.

Qualifications

The Planning Director must have the capacity to organize the use of specialists of many kinds. He should be able to fit together a number of aims and activities into an harmonious whole. He should especially be able to develop ideas of his own and be willing and able to select and utilize those of other departments in his organization, as well as of other public authorities and private individuals. He must be able to arrange and direct necessary surveys. He must be competent to advise his agency upon the interpretation of the information so obtained, as well as upon the solutions of the problems disclosed and upon policies to be adopted in respect to them. He must have the ability and knowledge to secure the preparation of a plan which proposes the means for carrying out those solutions in a practical manner, paying full regard to economic, social, functional and aesthetic considerations. He must be able to organize the carrying out of the plan. Finally, he must see all these complicated and inter-related stages as one whole and continuous process, with far-reaching social and economic objectives.

These abilities demand a creative or imaginative faculty of mind, a power of synthesis, a broad human understanding, sound sense of values, mature judgment and a high degree of intelligence. A university training in planning and related subjects is a desirable background. Notable accomplishments in professional practice serve as an acceptable equivalent. Both, in combination, are desirable.

Administrative ability and a capacity for good public relations are also prerequisites.

Minimum technical training and experience should be at least that which is required for full membership in the American Institute of Planners.

The Planning Director should possess,

1. Certain innate qualities of intellect and character.
2. A sound basic educational discipline.
3. Some specialized education for planning and an understanding of the component disciplines: engineering, architecture, economics, law and the social sciences.
4. Practical training and experience.

Functions and Duties

To the Planning Commission or Board:

The Planning Director serves his commission or board in two directions. Initially it is his responsibility—

(a) To formulate and present to the commission or board a comprehensive planning program suited to the needs and potentialities of the community;

(b) To frame and recommend specific planning policies for the guidance of the commission or board;

(c) To advise the commission concerning appropriate action on specific projects or proposals coming before the commission or board in the performance of its functions, or which should desirably be initiated by the commission or board itself.

His second responsibility to the commission or board is to serve as its representative in securing the integration of its decisions into plans, policies and program of the jurisdiction which it serves. In discharging this responsibility, the Planning Director is the ambassador of the commission or board, and as such should subordinate his personal advocacies to those of the commission or board.

To Other Government Agencies:

The Planning Director serves as the principal co-ordinating agent, and in three directions:

1. As chief liaison officer for the planning department, it becomes his responsibility to draw upon all other government agencies for information pertinent to planning;

2. It becomes his responsibility to aid in correlating specialized projects or policies represented by separate agencies by sharing information on evolving comprehensive plans from which are often revealed relationships that otherwise would not always be apparent;

3. To represent the commission or the board and its recommendations before the legislative body, or other public agency if there be such, which under local law has authority to review and decide.

To the General Public:

The Planning Director should have the authority and responsibility for providing public information on the content and progress of the planning program under his jurisdiction, always consistent with official policies or directives of the commission or board, and to interpret plans and their objectives to the public.

To the Staff:

The Planning Director, as the highest staff authority and as staff representative of the agency which the staff serves, has the authority and responsibility for organizing the work agenda, assigning duties, establishing lines of authority within the staff, delegating responsibility and related authority and maintaining the dignity of his own position by adhering to his chain of command. He should instruct his staff in the purpose of their tasks and in the techniques for performing them.

To the Consultant, if any;

The Planning Director remains the technical and administrative head of the department if a consultant is engaged. It is the director's responsibility to acquaint the consultant with the agenda, the data, the policies and the accomplishments of his department. He should endeavour to secure from the consultant every possible assistance and should be free to advance his own policies and opinions in his associations with the consultant.

[This committee report is not an official document of the A.I.P.]

QUESTIONS. Does the A.I.P. statement deal sufficiently with the relationship of the planning director with his board and with his council under Ontario legislation? How should a planning director act in the following situations? 1. He is asked by the council for his opinion on a planning matter when he knows that he disagrees with his board? 2. He is asked by the Ontario Municipal Board to give his own opinion in circumstances similar to those in the first situation? 3. He is asked by a press, radio or television representative for his opinion on a current planning problem?

Should the planning director aspire to that "passion for anonymity" that is said to characterize a good civil servant?

NOTE ON CONSULTANTS. Many planning agencies hire consultants, either because they view their task as one not justifying a full time professional staff or because the full time staff is unable to handle a particular problem at a particular time. Some difficulties inherent in this practice should be considered here.

The journeyman consultant sometimes offers the poorly staffed agency a "package plan" which he prepares largely with the aid of his own employees. If care is not taken, the consultant may leave behind him a plan no one will properly understand. Some consultants, to avoid this difficulty, use the local civic employees as much as possible, and by participating in the survey and analysis they may increase their understanding, not only of the plan itself, but of their own day to day work. Before dealing with the consultant, the agency should ascertain what kind of staff the consultant has and how, if at all, he intends to work with the local staff and the local staff and agency members should cooperate fully with the consultant for their mutual advantage.

As to the competence of the consultant, the same questions arise that have been raised in the preceding materials. In Canada there is no completely satisfactory guide to competence in planning although membership in the Town Planning Institute of Canada is rapidly becoming a minimum qualification. Since planning legislation is peculiar to each province and differs considerably from the American and English systems, it is wise for a planning agency to make sure that the consultant is familiar with the local legislation or that competent legal advice is available to the consultant, and that he uses it. Before entering into a contract for consulting services the course of prudence would appear to be full investigation into the training, reputation and previous work of the possible candidate.

The previous work may indicate one very important qualification that should be insisted upon, that the consultant leave behind a fully comprehensible report supported by complete copies of all statistical data and reports of all sorts. It is a sad situation to discover that the consultant has fully informed himself about the probable growth and development of a municipality and then exercises exclusive control of the data.

The contract of employment should prescribe clearly that the agency, or the agency and the consultant severally, has full rights to all materials prepared in connection with the consultant's work.

Many professional planners refuse to "tender" for a planning job. Is "tendering" unprofessional? Why?

NOTE ON ETHICS. Mr. Ronald Haggart in his column in the *Toronto Daily Star* on October 31, 1962, remarked that "A city employee in New York is prohibited from discussing future employment with a private concern that has business before his agency. And politicians and employees may not appear before public agencies for two years after they leave office on matters they handled or knew about while they were in public service." Is this a necessary precaution? Is a judge who resigns from the bench precluded from arguing a case before his former colleagues? Should he be?

A proposal was put before the Council of the Town Planning Institute of Canada that its Code of Ethics be amended to provide: "No staff member of a planning board or council who is a member of the Institute shall appear before the board or council on any matter that he was responsible for or knew about while he was such a staff member for two years after he has left the office of the board." Is this proposal desirable? Should it apply equally to consultants who are members of the T.P.I.C.?

BILL: AN ACT RESPECTING THE ENGINEERING PROFESSION OF SASKATCHEWAN

Saskatchewan. Legislative Bill. 1961. No. 58

2. In this Act:

6. "professional engineering" or "the practice of professional engineering" means reporting on, advising on, valuing, measuring for, laying out, designing, directing, constructing or inspecting any of the works or processes set forth in Schedule A. . . .

50. Every person who, not being being the holder of a subsisting certificate of registration [as an engineer] . . .

(a) engages in professional engineering; . . .

is guilty of an offence. . . .

SCHEDULE A. (*Section 2, par. 6*)

11. Land use planning, community planning and resource use planning.

SUBMISSION TO THE SELECT STANDING COMMITTEE ON LAW AMENDMENTS AND DELEGATED POWERS: SASKATCHEWAN LEGISLATURE

The Community Planning Branch, Department of Municipal Affairs, Government of Saskatchewan. 1961.

Bill No. 58, being an Act respecting the Engineering Profession in Canada seeks to include the practice of land use planning, community planning and resource use planning within the definition of professional engineering. This end is sought through the combined effect of Section 2.6 of the Bill, which defines "professional engineering" or "the practice of professional engineering," and item 11 of Schedule A to the Bill which sets out the types of work or activities which may be undertaken under Section 2.6.

If passed in its present form, the Act would permit any member of the Association of Professional Engineers of Saskatchewan to practice planning as itemized in Schedule A.

The practice of the kinds of planning listed in item 11 of Schedule A requires more specialized skills than are required for membership in the Association. Eligibility for membership in the Association is quite rightly extended to those properly qualified in any branch of engineering, including electrical engineering, mechanical engineering, aeronautical engineering, and so on. However, training in none of these disciplines is intended to provide an appropriate background or the necessary skills for the practice of community planning. Even a training in civil engineering, by itself, is not considered adequate preparation for the practice of planning. Every technically advanced country has acknowledged this fact by the recognition of professional organizations of town or community planners.

In Canada the Town Planning Institute of Canada is the official organization of the professional planners. Eligibility for membership in this Institute requires not only a degree in a basic discipline such as engineering, but also a qualification in planning as such, whch may only be had by post-graduate studies, or an appropriate period in the full-time practice of planning, coupled with the successful completion of the Institute's examinations. There are four universities in the country which offer courses in planning, and in every case these are post graduate courses leading to either a Master's Degree or a Diploma. The same rigid qualifications obtain for membership in the professional planning institutes of Great Britain, the United States, most European and African countries. This is some indication of the order of training which is considered necessary to develop a basic competence in physical planning.

One of the great and growing problems of our times is the continuing deterioration of our urban environment. Recently there has been a great deal of attention focussed on the problems of traffic congestion, slum clearance, street layout, urban sprawl, and so on. If we are to succeed in our efforts to create orderly urban communities then we must not permit them to be planned by those whose training equips them admirably for other kinds of work, but not for the practice of community planning.

Engineers have always participated in the processes of urban development, but at their appropriate level. Their skills are indispensable for the design and carrying out of engineering works. But the planning of a community requires skills ranging from those of the engineer and architect on the one hand to those of the economist and sociologist on the other. To identify community planning specifically with the practice of engineering would do a grave injustice to both engineering and planning, and to accept the engineering training as adequate for the practice of planning could jeopardize the ultimate successful solution of our urban development problems.

Accordingly, it is strongly recommended that item 11 of Schedule A of Bill No. 58 be deleted.

[Item 11 was deleted.]

QUESTION. Would the argument of the above submission have the same validity, if any, if it were applied to architects in the event, however unlikely, that the architectural profession attempted to claim the same privilege for the architects?

NOTE. After the preceding material and the note on the T.P.I.C. on page 204 were set the editor received a copy of Bill 40 of the Saskatchewan Legislative Assembly (1963), which establishes the Association of Professional Community Planners of Saskatchewan, a member of which has the exclusive right to assume verbally or otherwise the title of member of the association, or to use any abbreviation of it, or any title or designation that might lead the public to believe that he is a member, or to act in such a manner as to lead to the belief. A person not registered under the Act may not hold himself out to the public as a professional community planner (as defined in the Act). Section 18 provides that every person, whether or not he is a resident, who is a member of the T.P.I.C. shall be admitted as a member of the Association upon due application and payment of fees.

The editor also received a copy of Bill 215 of the Quebec Legislative Assembly (1963), which establishes the Corporation of Urbanists of Quebec, a member of which has the exclusive right to use the title "urbanist" or "town planner" or "city planner" or to lead anyone to believe he is a member of the corporation. No recognition is made of T.P.I.C. members residing outside the province, but a person who had a university degree in architecture, landscaping architecture, surveying, engineering, law, social sciences, geography or any other subject approved by the Council and who holds a degree in town planning at the date of the coming into force of the Act or who acquired a degree within two years thereafter, may become a member if he applies in writing within one year after the coming into force of the Act. These requirements would exclude many qualified planners who are members of the T.P.I.C. The "grandfather clause" would admit any person who similarly applied and who since January 1, 1940, has during a period of five consecutive years practised as an urbanist for at least two years, one of which may be after the coming into force of the Act. This clause would include most T.P.I.C. members if they applied within the year.

Both bills have since become law.

NOTE ON THE LAWYER'S ROLE IN PLANNING ADMINISTRATION. The planning process may be viewed as the making of plans or the carrying out of plans, or both. In this chapter the emphasis has been on the making. The carrying out of plans is more likely to involve legal relations than the making of them and the lawyer's role in the latter is more obvious than in the former. In each case, however, he is primarily concerned to know when, where and how he can appeal to some person or agency on behalf of his client. In the making of plans his appeal may be either informal or formal, probably both. Informal appeals, or consultations, frequently take place with the planning officials. Wise administrators of planning will seek out the owners of land to learn their intentions so far as they are prepared to disclose them.

On the formal side, enabling legislation usually provides some kind of hearing procedure. The adequacy of this procedure should be critically examined and the materials in the next section are intended to provide this opportunity.

It is, however, long past the day when it could be said that the lawyer's role in administration is confined to the legal question possibly arising in subsequent litigation: have the statutory and "natural law" requirements of the hearing procedure been properly observed? Important as this question is, and the lawyer must of course ask and answer it, the lawyer must also, today, concern himself very much with the planning issues themselves. It is no excuse for him to say that he is not a planner. His client's interests require protection and the lawyer must supply that protection, even if he only consults a professional planner. On the general question of planning appeals in Ontario, see Milner, Administrative Appeals Under Planning Legislation in *Municipal Law* 117 (The Law Society of Upper Canada Special Lectures pt. 2, 1956).

3. Hearings. The Institutional Decision

TOWN PLANNING ACT
Nova Scotia. Revised Statutes. 1954. Chapter 292

6. (1) The council shall, before adopting, varying or revoking an official town plan, give notice of its intention so to do by advertisement inserted at least once a week for two successive weeks in a newspaper published or circulating in the area affected, the first of such notices to be published at least three clear weeks before the date fixed for the consideration of objections.

(2) The notice shall state a place where, and the hours during which, the official town plan may be inspected by any interested person and the time and place set for the consideration by the council of written objections to the adoption, variation or revocation of the official town plan.

(3) The council shall make suitable provisions for inspection of the official town plan by interested persons, and before its adoption, variation or revocation shall consider and determine all written objections thereto.

QUESTION. Does this provision enable a land owner affected by the proposed plan to present oral arguments to the council?

THE PLANNING ACT

Ontario. Revised Statutes. 1960. Chapter 296.

10. (1) Every planning board shall . . .
   (*b*) hold public meetings and publish information for the purpose of obtaining the participation and co-operation of the inhabitants of the planning area . . .

34. (1) When under this Act the approval or consent of the Minister is applied for, the Minister may, and upon application therefor shall, refer the matter to the Municipal Board in which case the approval or consent, as the case may be, of the Municipal Board has the same force and effect as if it were the approval or consent of the Minister.

NOTE. The Minister's approval is required of an official plan and the matter may therefore be referred to the Municipal Board. The Board will hold a hearing. What is the legal subject referred to in the words "and upon application therefor"? Must the applicant have some special status? Can he be a total stranger to the matter for which consent or approval is required? Can he be a Nosey Parker?

Apart from section 34(1) the Ontario Act makes no express provision for a hearing in connection with the official plan. The hearing at the stage of ministerial approval is, of course, after the plan has been settled by the planning board and adopted by the council. By this time it may be very difficult to introduce "new evidence" or shake the views of professional men or politicians who feel the normal desire to defend their position and the normal reluctance to admit to having made a mistake. Can section 10(1) (*b*) be invoked to compel a hearing?

What difference might be intended between a "public meeting" and a "public hearing" as the words are used in, for example, section 30(11*a*) of the Ontario Act, which requires the Municipal Board to hold a public hearing in respect of its approval of certain zoning by-laws? Are the same talents required to conduct each?

NOTE ON PLANNING BOARDS AND THE PUBLIC. The duty to hold "public meetings" imposed on the planning boards puts in some doubt the duty of the board to hold its regular meetings in public. The practice throughout Ontario varies a bit, but many planning boards seem to consider it legally necessary or practically wise to admit at least the press during its general sessions. Is there any legal necessity? Is this a desirable practice? Can a planning board member "think" most effectively while he is being watched? Is a planning board a kind of inner cabinet of policy making for the council? Are cabinet meetings public? What board functions, if any, should be performed in public?

THE URBAN AND RURAL PLANNING ACT, 1953

Newfoundland. Statutes. 1953. Number 27

16. When an authorized Council has adopted a Municipal Plan by resolution in accordance with Section 14 the Minister shall, subject to this Act and upon application of the authorized Council set a day, hour and

place for the holding of a public hearing to consider any objections to the Municipal Plan or any part thereof which may be raised by any person, partnership or association; and the date shall be fixed sufficiently far in advance to allow the authorized Council a reasonable time in which to arrange for the first publications of the notice referred to in Section 15 at least two months before the date of the public hearing, and the public hearing shall be held at some place within the jurisdiction of the authorized Council.

17.—(1) Subject to subsection (2) the public hearing referred to in Section 16 shall be held by a Commissioner to be appointed by the Minister and the Minister shall appoint such other persons as he may deem necessary to assist the Commissioner in holding the public hearing and completing his report thereon and the Minister shall fix the remuneration to be paid to the Commissioner and to such other persons.

(2) Before a day, hour and place for a public hearing is fixed or a Commissioner is appointed under this section by the Minister, the authorized Council shall deposit with the Minister such sum as in the opinion of the Minister is necessary to defray all of the costs of and incidental to the public hearing including without limiting the generality of the foregoing, the remuneration of the Commissioner and such persons as may be appointed by the Minister to assist him and shall further give to the Minister an undertaking in writing under seal to pay to the Minister, within thirty days from receipt of notice from the Minister so to do, any additional sum that may, upon the completion of the public hearing, be found necessary fully to defray the total cost of and incidental to the public hearing.

18. Any partnership, association or person who desires to have his objections to the Municipal Plan or any part thereof considered at the public hearing to be held under Section 19 shall, at least five days before the date set for the public hearing, deposit with the clerk or secretary of the authorized Council two copies of a statement of his objections in writing signed by him and verified by affidavit.

19. On the day and hour and at the place fixed by the Minister under this Act, the Commissioner appointed for the purpose shall proceed to conduct the public hearing and shall hear all objections taken in accordance with this Act in the order in which they were deposited thereunder.

20.—(1) A Commissioner appointed under this Act for the purposes of a public hearing has power to summon any witness and to require him to give evidence orally or in writing upon oath or upon solemn affirmation and to produce such documents and things as may be deemed requisite to the public hearing.

(2) A Commissioner referred to in subsection (1) has the same power to enforce the attendance of witnesses and to compel them to give evidence as is possessed in any court of law in civil cases, and any false statement made by any witness on oath or solemn affirmation is punishable in the same manner as wilful and corrupt perjury.

21.—(1) When any public hearing held under this Act is completed, the Commissioner conducting it shall forward to the Minister a written report thereof in duplicate together with two copies of all the evidence taken at the public hearing.

(2) In the written report to be forwarded by the Commissioner under subsection (1) he shall set forth in full detail his recommendations respecting all objections considered by him at the public hearing together with his reasons therefor and a statement showing all objections which came to his

notice but which were not considered by him together with the reasons why they were not so considered.

23. The Minister may, upon considering a Municipal Plan, together with a report of the public hearing relating to it and the evidence taken at the public hearing, approve or disapprove the Municipal Plan, or may approve it subject to such amendments as may appear to him to be necessary or desirable.

[Section 23 is reproduced as amended by S.N., 1961, No. 9, s. 3.]

ERRINGTON *v.* MINISTER OF HEALTH. [1935] 1 K.B. 249. (England. Court of Appeal). In connection with the confirmation of a "clearance order" made under the *Housing Act, 1930,* the Minister appointed an Inspector to conduct a local inquiry at Jarrow. Inquiries were held in June and September 1933, at which objections were taken that the houses on the land were not unfit for habitation, that the expense of demolition and redevelopment was too expensive for Jarrow to meet, that provision of adequate housing for the dislocated inhabitants was impossible within the time specified in the order for the premises to be vacated, and some discussion took place about making repairs to the satisfaction of the Medical Officer of Health. Some agreement was reached between the owners and the local officials, but the Council insisted that its order be confirmed. In November the officials met with Ministry officials including the Inspector, when it was suggested that repairs in some cases amounting to reconstruction should be required of the owners, failing which, the Minister would confirm the order. In January, 1934, the Council asked the Minister to receive a deputation to try to convince him to confirm the order as it stood. A Ministry official wrote "semi-officially in reply," refusing the meeting—"In view of the quasi-judicial function which the Minister has to exercise there would be considerable difficulty in the way of receiving a formal deputation representing one side only." The Council continued to insist on its order, and a meeting was arranged between the deputation and the Ministry Officials including the Inspector at Jarrow late in January. The meeting was suggested by the Ministry officials as "of advantage" and no representatives of the owners were present. The group inspected the area in question.

In February the Town Clerk wrote to the Ministry reporting that the Borough Engineer, who had not testified at the Inspector's inquiry, advised that the houses were in such a state of disrepair that they could not be reconstructed into dwelling houses fit for human habitation. In March the Minister confirmed the order. In May the appellants moved under section 11 of the Act, for an order from the High Court to quash the clearance order as confirmed. Swift J. upheld the order and conceded that if the Minister conducted an inquiry and considered the report, he "might inform his mind in any way that he liked and arrive at his decision in any way which seemed good to him." The Court of Appeal reversed him. GREER L.J.: "Now it seems to me that if, as I think, the Ministry were acting in a quasi-judicial capacity they were doing what a semi-judicial body cannot do, namely, hearing evidence from one side in the absence of the other side, and viewing the property and forming their own views about the property without giving the owners of the property the opportunity of arguing that the views which the Ministry were inclined to take were such as could be readily dealt with by means of repairs and alterations to the buildings.... The borough engineer had not been called at the public inquiry. Those who represented the owners had not had the opportunity of cross-examining him, testing the value of his opinion, and representing to the Minister through the Inspector that no weight should be attached to his view. . . . That is a view which is hardly consistent with the view which had been expressed on behalf of the Borough Council by the barrister who appeared for them at the inquiry. It is an additional reason being urged by the Council on the advice of the borough engineer in order to put pressure upon the Ministry to confirm the order which had been made by them. . . .

"[A] quasi-judicial officer in exercising his powers must do it in accordance with the rules of natural justice, that is to say, he must hear both sides and must not hear one side in the absence of the other."

TOWN AND COUNTRY PLANNING ACT, 1947

United Kingdom. Statutes. 1947. Chapter 51

10. (3) If as the result of any objections or representations considered, or local inquiry or other hearing held, in connection with a development plan or proposals for amendment of such a plan submitted to or prepared by the Minister under this Part of this Act, the Minister is of opinion that the local planning authority or any other authority or person ought to be consulted before he decides whether to approve or make the plan either with or without modifications, or to amend the plan, as the case may be, he shall consult that authority or person, but shall not be under any obligation to consult any other authority or person, or to afford any opportunity for further objections or representations or to cause any further local inquiry or other hearing to be held.

[See now, the 1962 Act, chapter 38, s. 10(3).]

COMMITTEE ON ADMINISTRATIVE TRIBUNALS AND ENQUIRIES, REPORT

England. 1957. Cmnd. 218

347. One of the main causes of dissatisfaction at this stage [The Minister's decision] is that after the enquiry, when the parties no longer have any further influence upon the course of events, fresh evidence or new opinions may be sought by or placed before the Department of the deciding Minister, and that this new matter may well determine the final decision. Many who do not adopt the extreme position of advocating that the Minister should, in deciding, be restricted to what has been brought before the enquiry nevertheless consider that fair play requires that any new factual evidence should be submitted to the parties for comment. This is also generally conceded by official witnesses, although they point out that what is obtained after the enquiry is more often advice on technical matters or on policy than evidence of new facts.

348. We have already recommended that the case for the acquiring or planning authority should be properly notified in advance and supported at the enquiry, and also that statements of ministerial policy should, whenever possible, be made available before the enquiry. The purpose of these recommendations is to bring to the attention of the parties, before a decision is made, as much as possible of the material upon which the Minister is likely to base his decision.

349. The dissatisfaction caused by the feeling that new factual evidence may be introduced after the enquiry makes it desirable to go one step fur-

ther. This step relates to new factual evidence and not to policy. In our view it is not reasonable to expect the Minister to be absolutely bound by his prior statement of policy. His policy will not often undergo a relevant change in the course of one of these procedures, but he should be free to change it or to review its application to the particular case if he thinks fit. Similarly he must be free to consult fellow Ministers and his official advisers on questions of policy after the enquiry.

350. We think, however, that it is both desirable and possible to draw a distinction at the post-enquiry stage between new factual evidence on the one hand and advice on policy on the other. We recommend that the Minister should be under a statutory obligation to submit to the parties concerned, for their observations, any factual evidence, whether from his own or another Department or from an outside source, which he obtains after the enquiry. In the definition of factual evidence for the purposes of this recommendation we include expert opinion on matters of fact but not expert assistance in the evaluation of technical evidence given at the enquiry. There may be cases in which it is clearly desirable to give the parties an opportunity to cross-examine on the new evidence.

THE KING *v.* THE LOCAL GOVERNMENT BOARD. EX PARTE ARLIDGE. [1914] 1 K.B. 160 (England. Court of Appeal). On January 12, 1911, the local authority of Hampstead made an order prohibiting the use of a dwelling house, No. 83, Palmerston Road, owned by one Arlidge, for human habitation, until in the authority's judgment it was rendered fit for that purpose. All procedural requirements of the *Housing, Town Planning &c., Act, 1909* were complied with, "a public local inquiry" was held by the Local Government Board, and the order was duly confirmed. No appeal was taken. On July 11, 1911, Arlidge applied to the local authority to determine the closing order on the ground that the necessary repairs had been carried out. The authority disagreed, and refused to determine the order. Arlidge appealed. Again all the procedures were complied with. An inspector held another "public local inquiry" at which Arlidge was represented by his solicitor. He was called as a witness on his own behalf and a full opportunity was given to bring forward any material evidence or argument. After the hearing the inspector, accompanied by representatives of Arlidge and of the authority, personally examined the premises. He then reported privately to the Local Government Board, which, on February 26, 1912, confirmed the refusal. Arlidge applied to a Divisional Court of the King's Bench Division (Lord Coleridge, Ridley and Bankes JJ.) for a rule nisi to show cause why a writ of certiorari should not be issued against the Board. The rule was discharged, but this appeal was brought. Buckley L.J. remarked of the case, "With the importance of this case upon its facts I am not impressed at all, but its importance upon the general question which it raises can scarcely be overestimated." He and Vaughan Williams L.J. reversed the Divisional Court on the ground that the inspector's report of the "public local inquiry" was a public document that should have been disclosed and Arlidge should have been able to put his case, at least in writing, before the "personal judge" who was going to pronounce a decision. HAMILTON L.J. (dissenting): "Formally the decision is to be that of the Local Government Board, and in this case it is so expressed and is correct in form. Practically I will assume that it is the decision of some particular official, duly deputed for the purpose. The appellant asks who he was. He complains that he was never told. What does this matter? Curiosity apart, there seem to be only two reasons why an appellant should seek, as it is put, 'to know his judge.' One is to hold him up to public criticism; this may be quite right but it is none of our business. The other is in order that he may be able to shape his arguments in accordance with the deciding official's personal equation. I think, therefore, that this claim is only part of the general claim for a 'hearing' coram judice, for a viva voce appeal, for the right to stand in person before the judgment seat. In my opinion, the question whether the deciding officer 'hears' the appellant audibly addressing him or 'hears' him only through the medium of his written statements, is in a matter of this kind one of pure procedure. The practice of the High Court, past and present, as to hearing motions on affidavits and taking evidence before special examiners or the examiners of the Court, shews that there is nothing universally essential in the judge's seeing and hearing the witnesses for himself. One must remember what the subject-matter of these appeals is. Under this jurisdiction only two questions can come before the Local Government Board on appeal, first 'on such and such a day was the appellant's house fit or unfit for human habitation?' second, 'since the closing order was made, has it or has it not become or been made fit?' . . .

"The provision that a public local inquiry must be held in a certain event suggests that the Legislature contemplated that the other proceedings might be private. It is said that a written argument is an illusory thing, that there is no eloquence or at least no persuasion but in speech. Parliament should know something about that, and it has left the matter to the Board. I find the contention bewildering. Are reasoning and writing mutually exclusive processes? The appellant desires to enjoy what Mr. Upjohn felicitously calls 'the bound and rebound of ideas and arguments between the Bench and the Bar.' This invests with authority a practice (or should I say a foible) of judges, which I had believed to be pardonable and hoped to be not without its uses, but I am unable to see that it is the very pith of the administration of natural justice. . . .

"The real and the only difficult question before us is this. Before he gave his decision the officer of the Board saw what the appellant never saw, the inspector's reports. The officer considered them; can his decision stand? . . . I assume on the evidence that the officer considered Inspector Leonard's report of the first inquiry as well as of the second, and, failing production of them, that, in addition to reporting the evidence, they stated his opinion on the case, his impression of the witnesses, and the observations which he made on his visits to the premises. Prima facie, if a deciding officer considers documents containing material statements and not mere matters of form or repetitions of what is already substantially and fully known to the appellant, he should give the appellant the opportunity of dealing with them before he decides the appeal. Had this been done, the Board's invitation to the appellant, dated January 8, 1912, would have been a real and not a merely illusory proceeding.

"The Board's case, however, is that in treating the inspector's reports as confidential it followed an old and well-known practice. I make no doubt that it did so for reasons which it honestly deemed sufficient, some of which it is easy to surmise and to appreciate. As the inspector does not perform any judicial function in reporting, the privilege which he could claim for his statements, if sued for libel, would be a qualified privilege only and not absolute. If the appellant, and I suppose the local authority, are ultimately to see it, the inspector might hesitate to express himself in his report as frankly as might be desirable for the guidance of the Board. But in addition to practice the Board relies on the language of the statute as warranting this practice when truly construed. Accordingly two questions arise, what is the true construction of the statutes, and, if the statute itself does not authorize the practice, is it, as part of the procedure adopted by the Board, so 'contrary to natural justice' as to vitiate the decision? . . .

"In requiring that in a certain event the Local Government Board should hold a public local inquiry the Legislature was requiring to resort to a proceeding quite well known and in common use, to which was incident the Board's practice to treat the reports made thereon as confidential. The practice is stated in Lumley's *Public Health Act* (7th ed., p. 636), and it was commented on, unfavourably but without effect, by Farwell J. in *Attorney-General* v. *Nottingham.* It was enacted by s. 76 of the Act of 1909 that the Act should be construed as one with the Act of 1890, an Act under which this practice had prevailed. I think it is a sound inference, to be drawn as a matter of construction, that the Legislature, aware, as I take it to have been, of the practice as to these inquiries and its incidents, intended that the local inquiry, which it prescribed, should be the usual local inquiry, and that the usual incidents should attach in default of any special enactment, including the incident that the Board would treat the report as confidential. . . .

"So much for the question of construction, but, if I am wrong in this, . . . What standard of natural justice has been recognized in judicial proceedings? Does it require the procedure now contended for? . . .

"I cannot but feel deeply impressed by these object-lessons in toleration with regard to the procedure of other tribunals. I cannot but feel that all that can be urged against the Local Government Board might be still more forcibly urged against the Court of Criminal Appeal. Though in the long run I must decide for myself, I cannot but be impressed by the unanimous decision of the Divisional Court in the present case. The decisions which I have cited shew that acts done in judicial proceedngs, various in form but all obnoxious to the same kind of objection as is urged here, and all contrary to a first impression of natural, if that means ideal, justice, have still been regarded as entirely consistent with our law. There is no place here for a phrase which was used in argument, namely, the appellant's 'common law right' to stand before his judge. There is no question here of rights attaching at common law to common law Courts. The Local Government Board here is a statutory tribunal, anomalous as compared with common law Courts, created by the Legislature for a special class of appeals and endowed by it with the power of formulating its own procedure. We must assume that a department which the Legislature has trusted will be worthy of the trust. The judgment of such a tribunal, regular on its face, is surely entitled to as much credit as that of a foreign Court. . . . We are bound to remember that this is an appeal upon a concrete case, and we cannot decide it upon any abstract principle or upon any assumption beyond the facts of the case itself. The issue on this appeal was excessively simple. The only difficulty was to make out what the appellant could have to say for himself. The question of the propriety of the closing order had been concluded against him. It must be deemed to have been rightly made, for the purposes of this appeal against the local authority's refusal to determine it. I assume for the purposes of this case both the good faith and the reasonableness of the appellant, but he made it quite plain on the inquiry that his case was that the closing order ought never to have been made at all. He had done nothing to cure the alleged dampness of the house—he said that it was not damp. He therefore enjoyed at the inquiry the fullest opportunity of knowing what he had to meet and of meeting it. The inspector's report could not be really material to the conduct of his appeal and if the deciding officer was wrong, as I think he was not, in considering the reports without first communicating them to the appellant and hearing him upon them, the error was unsubstantial and could not reasonably affect his decision. In the language of Order XXXIX, r. 6, no 'substantial wrong or miscarriage has been thereby occasioned.'. . ."

LOCAL GOVERNMENT BOARD *v.* ARLIDGE. [1915] A.C. 120 (England. House of Lords). The Court of Appeal decision noted above was unanimously reversed, judgments being delivered by Viscount Haldane L.C., and Lords Shaw of Dunfermline, Moulton and Parmoor. LORD SHAW: "My Lords, it is here (and the matter is not a strictly legal one) that I venture to hold an opinion somewhat different from that of Lord Sumner [Hamilton L.J.]. I incline to hold that the disadvantage in very many cases would exceed the advantage of such disclosure. And I feel certain that if it were laid down in Courts of law that such disclosure could be compelled, a serious impediment might be placed upon that frankness which ought to obtain among a staff accustomed to elaborately detailed and often most delicate and difficult tasks. The very same argument would lead to the disclosure of the whole file. It may contain, and frequently does contain, the views of inspectors, secretaries, assistants, and consultants of various degrees of experience, many of whose opinions may differ but all of which form the material for the ultimate decision. To set up any rule that that decision must on demand, and as matter of right, be accompanied by a disclosure of what went before, so that it may be weakened or strengthened or judged thereby, would be inconsistent, as I say, with efficiency, with practice, and with the true theory of complete parliamentary responsibility for departmental action. This is, in my opinion, implied as the legitimate and proper consequence of any department being vested by statute with authority to make determinations."

UNITED STATES *v.* MORGAN. 1941. 313 U.S. 409 (United States. Supreme Court). In June, 1933, the Secretary of Agriculture issued an order setting maximum rates to be charged by market agencies for their services at the Kansas City Stockyards. The market agencies brought an action to set aside the order. In a protracted series of actions the case reached the Supreme Court for the fourth time. One issue involved the question of the Secretary's familiarity with the record, which consisted of about 10,000 pages of transcript of oral evidence and over 1,000 pages of statistical exhibits (Hughes C.J. in the second time round in the Supreme Court; Frankfurter J. in the fourth case refers to "1,340 printed pages and thousands of pages of additional exhibits.") Objection was also taken to the "bias" of the Secretary evidenced by his criticism in a letter to the *New York Times* newspaper of the second Morgan decision. The Secretary later wrote "a patently sincere denial of bias." On these two matters, FRANKFURTER J.: ". . . the letter did not require the Secretary's dignified denial of bias. That he not merely held but expressed strong views on matters believed by him to have been in issue, did not unfit him for exercising his duty in subsequent proceedings ordered by this Court. As well might it be argued that the judges below, who had three times heard this case, had disqualifying convictions. In publicly criticizing this Court's opinion the Secretary merely indulged in a practice familiar in the long history of Anglo-American litigation, whereby unsuccessful litigants and lawyers give vent to their disappointment in tavern or press. Cabinet officers charged by Congress with adjudicatory functions are not assumed to be flabby creatures any more than judges are. Both may have an underlying philosophy in approaching a specific case. But both are assumed to be men of conscience and intellectual discipline, capable of judging a particular controversy fairly on the basis of its own circumstances. Nothing in this record disturbs such an assumption.

"And so we conclude that the order of the Secretary furnishes 'the appropriate basis for action in the district court in making distribution of the fund in its custody'. . . . But, finally, a matter not touching the validity of the order requires consideration. Over the Government's objection the district court authorized the market agencies to take the deposition of the Secretary. The Secretary thereupon appeared in person at the trial. He was questioned at length regarding the process by which he reached the conclusions of his order, including the manner and extent of his study of the record and his consultation with subordinates. His testimony shows that he dealt with the enormous record in a manner not unlike the practice of judges in similar situations, and that he held various conferences with the examiner who heard the evidence. Much was made of his disregard of a memorandum from one of his officials who, on reading the proposed order, urged considerations favorable to the market agencies. But the short of the business is that the Secretary never should have been subjected to this examination. The proceeding before the Secretary 'has a quality resembling that of a judicial proceeding'. . . . Such an examination of a judge would be destructive of judicial responsibility. We have explicitly held in this very litigation that 'it was not the function of the court to prove the mental processes of the Secretary'. . . . Just as a judge cannot be subject to such a scrutiny, . . . so the integrity of the administrative process must equally respected. . . . It will bear repeating that although the administrative process has had a different development and pursues somewhat different ways from those of courts, they are to be deemed collaborative instrumentalities of justice and the appropriate independence of each should be respected by the other. . . ."

COMMITTEE ON ADMINISTRATIVE TRIBUNALS AND ENQUIRIES, REPORT

England. 1957. Cmnd. 218

327. The evidence presented to us has paid more attention to inspectors' reports than to any other aspect of the procedure. The main question is whether these reports should be published, and on this the evidence which we have received, other than the evidence from Government Departments, has been overwhelmingly in favour of some degree of publication. Before discussing publication, however, we express certain views on the form which these reports should take. A number of Departments have made available to us at our request copies of reports by inspectors in typical cases. Most of these reports were not written for publication and they have not therefore been included in our published evidence. To judge by these samples the reports of inspectors are useful and well constructed documents for the purpose in view.

The contents of the report

328. The first part of an inspector's report should summarise the relevant evidence and set out his findings of fact and inferences of fact thereon. The second part should set out the reasoning from those facts, including the application to the particular case of any considerations of policy, and should normally conclude with recommendations for the Minister's action. The inclusion of recommendations is important, since the inspector hears the evidence at first hand and has an opportunity of immediately relating what he hears to the physical facts of the case, by personal inspection of the land. We recognise, however, that there will be cases where the element of policy is so large that it would not be reasonable to insist on recommendations being given.

The case for publication

329. Most of the evidence in favour of publication has advocated publication of the full text, and the Report of the Donoughmore Committee has been cited in support of this view. A close reading of the relevant parts of that Report indicates, however, that in relation to enquiries of the kind with which we are immediately concerned the Committee was not in favour of the publication of the whole of the inspector's views, since it specifically stated: ". . . we see no objection to the tendering by separate report or otherwise of such advice as the Minister may call for on any questions of Ministerial policy which may be involved." We propose to treat publication as a matter for consideration afresh. We first set out the main arguments for and against publication without specifying the extent of publication contemplated, and follow with our conclusions.

330. The first argument advanced in favour of publication is that fair play for the citizen requires that he should know how the inspector has reported to the Minister the course of the enquiry and the inspector's assessment of the case in the light of the enquiry. It is at the enquiry that the individual citizen has his "battle" with authority–or, if the expression were not somewhat misleading in this context, his "day in court"—and it is argued that there is little point in providing for a special procedure in these cases if the process is thereafter secret except for the Minister's final decision.

331. The second argument is that publication would serve to make these procedures and the ministerial powers which lie behind them better understood and more acceptable to the public generally, since the degree of openness would be increased and the application of national policy to particular local circumstances would be more easily appreciated.

332. The third argument is that the deciding Minister might be expected to seek to reduce as far as possible the chances of having to disagree with the published findings or recommendations of the inspector and would consequently be inclined to present at the enquiry evidence which, it is suggested, is now withheld until the later and secret stage.

333. Fourthly, it is argued that publication, particularly if it took place before the decision and the parties were given an opportunity to seek to correct alleged mistakes of fact in the report, would negative the argument for a formal appeal on fact against the Minister's decision. Several witnesses who in their memoranda of evidence had proposed such an appeal agreed in subsequent oral evidence that in these cases prior correction of fact would be preferable.

334. Fifthly, it has been pointed out that since the Ministry of Education, whose practice it is to publish inspectors' reports, does not appear to

suffer any embarrassment thereby and has no wish to change the practice, it is not easy to see why other Departments cannot follow suit.

The case against publication

335. The main arguments against publication are follows. First, it is argued that the report of the inspector, though clearly of great importance, is but one of perhaps many matters which the Minister must take into consideration in arriving at his decision, and that to publish this alone would give a misleading impression and indeed might increase public dissatisfaction in those cases where the Minister found it necessary to differ from the inspector's recommendations.

336. Second, it is argued that publication would tend to transform the inspector's recommendations into a provisional decision, which the public could then set against the final decision of the Minister, and that the Minister ought not to be exposed to the difficulty and embarrassment which would arise from the disclosure of differences between his decision and the recommendations of the inspector. Even if inspectors were placed under the general charge of the Lord Chancellor they would remain civil servants, and emphasis is laid upon the importance of preserving the confidential relationship between Ministers and their official advisers. Any argument based on the practice of the Ministry of Education in publishing reports is, it is said, irrelevant, since its enquiries are carried out by persons from outside the Government service. Moreover, the issue at its enquiries is generally one of site and not of policy, the need for a school having already been separately established.

337. The third argument is that there is in fact no evidence of widespread demand by the public to see inspectors' reports and that the expense of publication in all cases would consequently not be justified. It is admitted, however, that if publication were thought desirable on important grounds of principle it would not be right to allow expense to be a decisive consideration.

338. Fourth, it is argued that the knowledge that their reports would be published might lead inspectors to be less frank and therefore less helpful to the Minister in their comments and recommendations. Reports might also be completed less promptly because of the greater care needed in drafting.

339. The fifth argument is that since a report must necessarily involve considerable summarisation, its publication would be unlikely to satisfy all parties that they had been adequately reported.

343. Our general conclusion is that the right course is to publish the inspector's report. Apart from the arguments in favour of publication to which we have referred we are impressed by the need for some further control beyond that which Parliament, in theory, though not always in practice, can exercise. There is no doubt that publicity is in itself an effective check against arbitrary action. On the assumption that these cases will continue to be decided by Ministers after an enquiry, complete publicity at all stages is impossible, but we think that is should be insisted upon whereever it is possible. Moreover, the publication of the report seems to flow naturally from the fact that the enquiry itself is held in public.

344. Accordingly we recommend that the complete text of the inspector's report should accompany the Minister's letter of decision and should also be available on request centrally and locally.

345. Additionally, we recommend that the parties should have an op-

portunity, if they so desire, to propose corrections of fact to what we have described in paragraph 328 as the first part of the inspector's report before the report is tendered to the Minister. . . .

351. There is a consensus of opinion that the final letter of decision from or on behalf of the Minister should contain full reasons for the decision. The practice of giving properly reasoned decisions has grown noticeably in recent years. Decision letters sent on behalf of the Minister of Housing and Local Government seem to us to be admirable, but the standard of performance among other Departments is unequal. It is not sufficient for a deciding Minister merely to assure the recipients of his letter that he has considered the evidence at the enquiry and the (confidential) report of the inspector. It is a fundamental requirement of fair play that the parties concerned in one of these procedures should know at the end of the day why the particular decision has been taken. Where no reasons are given the individual may be forgiven for concluding that he has been the victim of arbitrary decision. The giving of full reasons is also important to enable those concerned to satisfy themselves that the prescribed procedure has been followed and to decide whether they wish to challenge the Minister's decision in the courts or elsewhere. Moreover, as we have already said in relation to tribunal decisions, a decision is apt to be better if the reasons for it have to be set out in writing because the reasons are then more likely to have been properly thought out.

352. Accordingly we recommend that the Minister's letter of decision should set out in full his findings and inferences of fact and the reasons for the decision. Since the letter will be accompanied by the full text of the inspector's report it will inevitably reveal where, if at all, the Minister differs from the inspector's findings or inferences of fact or recommendations and also reveal the reasons for those differences. Copies of the letter of decision, together with the full text of the inspector's report, should be made available on request centrally and locally.

NOTE AND QUESTIONS. Despite the striking degree of judicial agreement in *Arlidge's* case, back in 1914–15 (eight judges against two) academic opinion at least has been fairly critical, and the report of the Franks Committee on Administrative Tribunals and Enquiries was followed by legislative and administrative adoption of the recommendation that the inspector's report be published along with the decision. Just what value the "reform" has had is not easy to appraise. In the Report of the Ministry of Housing and Local Government for 1959, at page 99, it is reported that "The number of occasions on which the Minister's decision differed from the Inspector's recommendation remained at about 5 per cent of the total number of decided appeals, the same percentage as in 1958. (This percentage indeed held good for all types of planning inquiries.)"

What advantage is there in having the Inspector's report along with the Minister's decision? Would it not be more useful if it were published before the Minister decides, and an opportunity were given to argue further before the Minister (or "deciding officer," as Hamilton L.J. put it)? Are the Inspector's reasons better than the Minister's? Of what use are the Minister's if there is no appeal from his decision? Does the Franks Committee overvalue the publication of the Minister's reasons? Giving reasons has a possible value to the Ministry in that it may compel the deciding officer to direct his mind more closely to what he is doing. But is it necessary to require reasons in all cases? Do judges always give reasons? Are all "reasons" equally useful for any or all purposes for which "good" reasons may be useful?

Would a statement of the Minister (or the deciding officer) in which he tried to explain what he was trying to do be of more general use? What does Professor Fuller mean by the expression "the collaborative articulation of shared purposes"? See Fuller, "Human Purpose and Natural Law" (1956) 53 *Journal of Philosophy* 697, reprinted (1958) 3 *Natural Law Forum* 68. Could the occasional report of the Minister's reasons help newcomers to planning to get a better understanding of what the Minister is trying to do? Is this a function of the lawyer's idea of precedent?

FRANKLIN *v*. MINISTER OF TOWN AND COUNTRY PLANNING
England. House of Lords. [1948] A.C. 87

LORD THANKERTON: My Lords, the appellants, who are the owners and occupiers of dwelling-houses and land situate at Stevenage, challenge the validity of the Stevenage New Town (Designation) Order, 1946, made on November 11, 1946, by the respondent, under the *New Towns Act, 1946*, which had received the Royal Assent on August 1, 1946. . . .

There does not appear to be much dispute as to the facts, but a great deal rests on the proper inference to be drawn from these facts. On January 21, 1946, a committee appointed in 1945 by the respondent, as Minister of Town and Country Planning, and the Secretary of State for Scotland, known as the "Reith Committee," made an interim report, dated January 21, 1946. The committee recommended: "Arrangements should be made for setting up immediately a public corporation for the development of a new town at Stevenage to proceed with the necessary work in advance of legislation." The New Towns Bill was introduced by the respondent in the House of Commons on April 17, 1946, and was ordered to be printed. On or about April 24, 1946, the respondent sent letters to one hundred and seventy-nine owners of land at Stevenage inquiring whether they were prepared to sell land to the respondent, with a view to the development of the area as a garden city, as provided by s. 35 of the *Town and Country Planning Act, 1932*. There is no evidence that any land was acquired by the respondent as the outcome of these letters, and we are entitled to assume that the Minister was acting on the suggestion of the Reith Committee, and that the proposal was superseded by the passage of the *New Towns Act*. On May 6, 1946, the respondent attended and spoke at a public meeting in Stevenage Town Hall, called to consider a proposal for designating an area of land in the neighbourhood of Stevenage as the site of a new town. The appellants base their case mainly on the statements made in an advance press notice issued by the respondent prior to the meeting, and statements made by the respondent in the course of his speech as evidence that the respondent had by that time completely made up his mind that the designation of Stevenage as a new town would be carried through, whatever was said at the meeting or subsequently. . . .

In my opinion, no judicial, or quasi-judicial, duty was imposed on the respondent, and any reference to judicial duty, or bias, is irrelevant in the present case. The respondent's duties under s. 1 of the Act and sch. I thereto are, in my opinion, purely administrative, but the Act prescribes certain methods of or steps in, discharge of that duty. It is obvious that, before making the draft order, which must contain a definite proposal to designate the area concerned as the site of a new town, the respondent must have made elaborate inquiry into the matter and have consulted any local authorities who appear to him to be concerned, and obviously other departments of the Government, such as the Ministry of Health, would naturally require to be consulted. It would seem, accordingly, that the respondent was required to satisfy himself that it was a sound scheme before he took the serious step of issuing a draft order. It seems clear also, that the purpose of inviting objections, and, where they are not withdrawn, of having a public inquiry, to be held by someone other than the respondent, to whom that person reports, was for the further information of the respondent, in order to the final consideration of the soundness of the scheme of the designation; and it is important to note that the development of the site, after the order is made, is primarily the duty of the development corporation established under s. 2 of the Act. I am of opinion that no judicial duty is laid on the respondent in discharge of these statutory duties, and that the only question is whether he has complied with the statutory directions to appoint a person to hold the public inquiry, and to consider that person's report. . . .

My Lords, I could wish that the use of the word "bias" should be confined to its proper sphere. Its proper significance, in my opinion, is to denote a departure from the standard of even-handed justice which the law requires from those who occupy judicial office, or those who are commonly regarded as holding a quasi-judicial office, such as an arbitrator. . . .

Coming now to the inference of the learned judge from the respondent's speech on May 6, that he had not then a mind open to conviction, the learned judge states it thus: "If I am to judge by what he said at the public meeting which was held very shortly before the Bill, then published, became an Act of Parliament, I could have no doubt but that any issue raised by objectors was forejudged. The Minister's language leaves no doubt about that. He was not only saying there must and shall be satellite towns, but he was saying that Stevenage was to be the first of them." It seems probable that the learned judge's mind was influenced by his having already held that the respondent's function was quasi-judicial, which would raise the question of bias, but, in any view, I am clearly of opinion that nothing said by the respondent was inconsistent with the discharge of his statutory duty, when subsequently objections were lodged, and the local public inquiry took place, followed by the report of that inquiry, genuinely to consider the report and the objections. The only passages in the speech quoted in the appellants' case are contained in the third quotation I have made from the speech, and are as follows: "I want to carry out in Stevenage a daring exercise in town planning (*jeers*). It is no good your jeering: it is going to be done. . . . After all this new town is to be built in order to provide for the happiness and welfare of some sixty thousand men, women and children. . . . The project will go forward, because it must go forward. It will do so more surely and more smoothly and more successfully with your help and co-operation. Stevenage will in a short time become world famous. People from all over the world will come to Stevenage to see how we here in this country are building for the new way of life." The only two additional passages founded on by the appellants' counsel at the hearing before this House were the sentence in my first quotation, "In anticipation of the passage of the Bill—and I have no doubt that it will go through," and, in my fourth quotation, "But we have a duty to perform, and I am not going to be deterred from that duty. While I will consult as far as possible all the local authorities, at the end, if people become fractious and unreasonable I shall have to carry out my duty—(*Voice*: Gestapo!)." My Lords, these passages in a speech which was of a political nature, and of the kind familiar in a speech on second reading, demonstrate (1.) the speaker's view that the Bill would become law, that Stevenage was a most suitable site and should be the first scheme in the operation, and that the Stevenage project would go forward, and (2.) the speaker's reaction to the hostile interruptions of a section of the audience. In my opinion, these passages are not inconsistent with an intention to carry out any statutory duty imposed on him by Parliament, although he intended to press for the enactment of the Bill, and thereafter to carry out the duties thereby involved, including the consideration of objections which were neither fractious nor unreasonable. I am, therefore of opinion that the first contention of the appellants fails, in that they have not established either that in the respondent's speech he had forejudged any genuine consideration of the objections or that he had not genuinely considered the objections at the later stage when they were submitted to him. . . .

REX *v*. SUSSEX JUSTICES. EX PARTE McCARTHY. [1924] 1 K.B. 256 (England. King's Bench). HEWART C.J.: "It is said, and, no doubt, truly, that when that gentleman (the deputy clerk) retired in the usual way with the justices, taking with him the notes of the evidence in case the justices might desire to consult him, the justices came to a conclusion without consulting him, and that he scrupulously abstained from referring to the case in any way. But while that is so, a long line of cases shows that it is not merely of some importance but is of fundamental importance that justice should not only be done, but should manifestly and undoubtedly be seen to be done. The question therefore is not whether in this case the deputy clerk made any observation or offered any criticism which he might not properly have made or offered; the question is whether he was so related to the case in its civil aspect as to be unfit to act as clerk to the justices in the criminal matter. The answer to that question depends not upon what actually was done but upon what might appear to be done."

THE ONTARIO MUNICIPAL BOARD ACT

Ontario. Revised Statutes. 1960. Chapter 274

92. (1) In determining any question of fact the Board is not concluded by the finding or judgment of any other court in any action, prosecution or proceeding involving the determination of such fact, but such finding or judgment is, in proceedings before the Board, *prima facie* evidence only.

(2) Except as otherwise provided in this Act, the pendency of any action, prosecution or proceeding in any other court involving questions of fact does not deprive the Board of jurisdiction to hear and determine the same questions of fact.

(3) The finding or determination of the Board upon any question of fact within its jurisdiction is binding and conclusive.

93. (1) The Board may, at the request of the Lieutenant Governor in Council, or of its own motion, or upon the application of any party, and upon such security being given as it directs, state a case in writing for the opinion of the Court of Appeal upon any question that, in the opinion of the Board, is a question of law.

(2) The Court of Appeal shall hear and determine the special case and remit it to the Board with the opinion of the Court thereon.

94. The Lieutenant Governor in Council may, at any time, upon petition of any party, person or company interested, all parties interested first having been heard, vary or rescind any order, decision, rule or regulation of the Board whether such order or decision is made *inter partes* or otherwise, and whether such regulation is general or limited in its scope and application, and any order that the Lieutenant Governor in Council may make with respect thereto is binding upon the Board and upon all parties.

95. (1) Subject to the provisions of Part IV, an appeal lies from the Board to the Court of Appeal upon a question of jurisdiction or upon any question of law, but such appeal does not lie unless leave to appeal is obtained from the Court within one month after the making of the order or decision sought to be appealed from or within such further time as the Court, under the special circumstances of the case, shall allow after notice to the opposite party stating the grounds of appeal.

(2) Upon such leave being obtained, the Registrar shall set the appeal down for hearing at the next sittings, and the party appealing shall, within ten days, give to the parties affected by the appeal, or the solicitors by whom such parties were represented before the Board, and to the secretary, notice in writing that the case has been so set down, and the appeal shall be heard by such Court as speedily as practicable.

(3) On the hearing of any appeal, the Court may draw all such inferences as are not inconsistent with the facts expressly found by the Board and are necessary for determining the question of jurisdiction or law, as the case may be, and shall certify its opinion to the Board and the Board shall make an order in accordance with such opinion.

(4) The Board is entitled to be heard, by counsel or otherwise, upon the argument of any such appeal.

(5) The Supreme Court has power to fix the costs and fees to be taxed, allowed and paid upon such appeals, and to make rules of practice respecting appeals under this section, and until such rules are made the rules and practice applicable to appeals from a judge of the Supreme Court to the Court of Appeal shall be applicable to appeals under this Act.

(6) Neither the Board nor any member of the Board is in any case liable to any costs by reason or in respect of any appeal or application under this section.

(7) Save as provided in this section and in sections 42 and 94.

(a) every decision or order of the Board is final; and

(b) no order, decision or proceeding of the Board shall be questioned or reviewed, restrained or removed by prohibition, injunction, *certiorari* or any other process or proceeding in any court.

96. (1) The costs of and incidental to any proceeding before the Board, except as herein otherwise provided, shall be in the discretion of the Board, and may be fixed in any case at a sum certain or may be taxed.

(2) The Board may order by whom and to whom any costs are to be paid, and by whom the same are to be taxed and allowed.

(3) The Board may prescribe a scale under which such costs shall be taxed.

97. Every person summoned to attend before the Board or before any inspecting engineer, or person appointed to make inquiry and report, shall, in the discretion of the Board, receive the like fees and allowances for so doing as if summoned to attend before the Supreme Court.

12. (1) Except as provided in section 15, two members of the Board form a quorum and are sufficient for the exercise of all the jurisdiction and

powers of the Board and not less than two members shall attend at the hearing of every application.

(2) All orders, rules, regulations, certificates and other documents made or issued by the Board may be signed by any member of the Board or the secretary of the Board or any officer of the Board designated by the Lieutenant Governor in Council as a signing officer.

15. (1) The chairman may authorize one member of the Board to conduct the hearing of an application and to report to the Board, and such member has all the powers of the Board for the purpose of such hearing.

(2) The report of such member may be adopted as the order of the Board by two other members of the Board, one of whom shall be the chairman or a vice-chairman, or may be otherwise dealt with as the Board deems proper.

CURRIE v. INLAND REVENUE COMMISSIONERS. [1921] 2 K.B. 332 (England. Court of Appeal). SCRUTTON L.J.: "There has been a very strong tendency, arising from the infirmities of human nature, in a judge to say, if he agrees with the decision of the Commissioners, that the question is one of fact, and if he disagrees with them that it is one of law, in order that he may express his own opinion the opposite way. Undoubtedly the less a judge has tried cases with juries, the greater is the tendency on his part to think that the view he forms on the evidence is the only possible one; but when he has tried innumerable cases with juries and continually finds twelve reasonable and intelligent men taking a different view of the evidence from that which he himself takes, he becomes more and more convinced that there may be in many states of facts more than one possible view of the evidence, and that the fact that he would have taken a different view himself does not show that the view taken by the twelve persons was necessarily wrong."

DRISCOLL *v.* CHURCH COMMISSIONERS FOR ENGLAND. [1956] 3 All E.R. 802 (England. Court of Appeal). DENNING L.J.: "A person who is aggrieved by the decision as being erroneous in point of law may bring the matter up to this court. I would not wish those words unduly to hamper an appeal from the tribunal, and I do not think they do, because it is well settled that the question whether or not there is any evidence to support a particular finding is a question of law. It is also well settled that the question whether an inference drawn from primary facts is a legitimate inference is also a question of law. There have been before the Divisional Court several cases of dangerous driving where the Lord Chief Justice and his colleagues, having had primary facts stated, have held that the justices were not justified in dismissing the charge and have directed them to convict. . . .

"In this case, therefore, we have to see what are the facts which the tribunal has found, and to see what are the conclusions which it has drawn from those facts. Then we have to see whether the conclusions which it has drawn are reasonable conclusions for it to draw."

VALLEY IMPROVEMENT CO. LTD. *v.* METROPOLITAN TORONTO AND REGION CONSERVATION AUTHORITY. 1961. 29 D.L.R. (2d) 593 (Ontario. Court of Appeal). KELLY J.A.: "It is clear, I think that the Board has not applied the correct principles in determining the amount to be paid to the appellant by the authority. Normally, therefore, the matter would be remitted to Board for reconsideration. In the case at bar, however, there appear to be cogent reasons militating against this course. Relevant legislation entrusts to the Board a number of different duties to be discharged by it in various capacities; the combined result is really an embarrassment to the Board and such as to make it extremely difficult for it to proceed objectively to determine the compensation to be payable to the appellant or to anyone in a position similar to that of appellant. The Board, by virtue of certain sections now to be found in the *Planning Act* was required to pass upon the zoning and flood-control by-laws of the township before they became effective. The Board would also be required to review and pass upon any future by-law of the township to vary the zoning of appellant's subject property and of the other properties owned by the appellant adjacent thereto. One of the questions to be determined in settling the amount of compensation is the probability, as of the date of expropriation, of the change in the zoning regulations to permit appellant's contemplated uses. In another capacity the Board will be called upon to approve capital expenditures to be borne by the township as a result of its obligation to furnish funds to the Authority for its flood control and conservation works; thus the very amounts payable by the Conservation Authority as compensation to the appellant will fall in part to be borne by the township and will be the subject-matter of an application by the township to the Board for its approval *qua* capital borrowing. In these circumstances it simply does not have the appearance of justice that the Board be required as arbitrator to determine the compensation arising from the action of the Authority in expropriating appellant's lands. It is in no sense a criticism of the Board to state that the Legislature, in placing the Board in these various capacities, has demanded of it a standard of detachment beyond that reasonably to be expected of any tribunal. Consideration of these matters, coupled with the fact that the Board's decision is not grounded upon a conflict in the evidence as to value or upon the credibility of witnesses, impels me to the conclusion that this Court should determine the compensation to be awarded. . . ."

[Of this view Cartwright J. in the Supreme Court of Canada said, "With respect, I have reached the conclusion that, in the case at bar, the Court of Appeal had no jurisdiction to fix the amount of the compensation."]

RE OTTAWA BY-LAW 155-62. 1962. N. 3617-62 (Ontario. Municipal Board). This was an application by the City of Ottawa for approval of its amending by-law changing the permitted uses from single family to apartment buildings. J. A. KENNEDY Chairman and MILBURN Member: "The only objection taken to approval of the by-law is that these lands shoulds not be used as a building site at all or in any event not for a high density building. The objectors contend this parcel should be added to the adjacent park as they claim that the park is not large enough to serve the needs of the area. At the request of the Board Alphonse Dulude, Commissioner of Recreation and Parks for the City of Ottawa, was called as a witness. His evidence was that this neighbourhood is served with park space sufficient for the city's own activities.

"It is not the duty or the function of this Board to interfere with the policy adopted by city council as to how much land it should acquire and operate for park purposes. The only way in which the question of park facilities can be material on this application is to determine whether the proposed use of the subject lands will overtax the park facilities and other related services. In the light of all the evidence and in the light particularly of the evidence of Mr. Dulude the Board is unable to make such a finding. For these reasons the by-law should be approved." [Why did the city not call Mr. Dulude? Was it proper for the Board to call him?]

RE DIAMOND AND THE ONTARIO MUNICIPAL BOARD

Ontario Court of Appeal. 1962. 32 D.L.R. (2d) 103.

SCHROEDER J. A. delivered the judgment of the Court: This is an application by way of a case stated in writing by the Ontario Municipal Board for the opinion of this Court upon the questions therein set out pursuant to s. 93 of the *Ontario Municipal Board Act,* R.S.O. 1960, c. 274. The case stated by the Board is in the terms following:

"This application came on for hearing before the Board at the City of Toronto on the 27th day of October, 1961 at which time the Board was attended by counsel appearing for the applicant, A. E. Diamond, by counsel appearing for the Corporation of the Township of North York and by counsel appearing for certain other interested persons.

"At the hearing, Murray Jones, who is Commissioner of planning for the Metropolitan Toronto Planning Board, appeared in answer to a subpoena issued at the request of the applicant, A. E. Diamond, and was sworn. He was asked by counsel for the said applicant the following question:

"Q. 'Would you please give your opinion to this Board as to the highest and best use of this property which we have been discussing.'

"Mr. Jones answered:

"A. 'My instructions are not to express a personal opinion.'

"The Board is informed that this witness and other employees of the Metropolitan Toronto Planning Board have been directed by that board not to give a personal opinion if asked to do so when giving evidence as a witness before the Ontario Municipal Board.

"This Board was urged by counsel for the applicant that it should exercise the same powers as those of the Supreme Court by virtue of section 37 of *The Ontario Municipal Board Act.* Because this situation is so serious for this witness and for others who may appear before this Board under similar circumstances and because this matter is of vital importance to this Board in the discharge of its duties under the law, it seems appropriate instead of presuming to interpret the law, which this Board may or may not have power to do in these circumstances, that this Board should seek an opinion on certain questions of law in order that it may be guided by such opinion in dealing with the matter now before it.

"Accordingly the Board states, pursuant to the provisions of Section 93 of *The Ontario Municipal Board Act,* the following questions for the opinion of the Court of Appeal, which this Board deems to be questions of law:

"1. Has the Ontario Municipal Board the power to compel witnesses before it to answer questions as to fact?

"2. Has the Ontario Municipal Board the power to compel witnesses before it who are qualified to give opinion evidence to answer questions as to their opinion?

"3. If the answer to question Number 1 or Number 2 is in the affirmative has the Ontario Municipal Board the power to commit a witness to jail for refusing to answer any such question?

"4. Has the Metropolitan Toronto Planning Board the right to prevent professional planners in its employ from giving their opinions in evidence when called as witnesses before the Ontario Municipal Board?

"5. Has the Ontario Municipal Board the power, after due notice, to order any individual or group of individuals to withdraw any instructions or direction given to any other individual to refuse to answer any question before this Board?

"6. If the answer to Number 5 is in the affirmative has the Ontario Municipal Board power to commit to jail for failure to comply with such an order?"

It becomes important at the outset to determine the real nature of this tribunal and of the functions which it discharges. It is, of course, a creature of statute and possesses only those powers and can discharge only those functions authorized by the statute which created it. . . .

The duties which devolved upon the Board in the present case involved the hearing of an appeal under the provisions of s. 30(19) of *The Planning Act,* R.S.O. 1960, c. 296, following the refusal or the failure of a municipal council to make a requested amendment to a restrictive by-law, and it is not contended that the powers which it was required to exercise in this instance were judicial rather than administrative. The question raised is whether under the terms of the *Ontario Municipal Board Act*, contempt power has been conferred upon the Board to enable it to perform its functions, and in particular, to enable it to compel obedience to an order requiring a witness to answer a question put to him in proceedings before it.

The power to fine or imprison for a contempt committed in the face of the Court is a necessary incident to every Court of justice and a witness who refuses to be sworn or to affirm (as the case may be) or who, having been sworn or having affirmed, refuses to answer, is guilty of contempt and may be fined or imprisoned. . . .

It is necessary in many cases for the Board, in discharging its functions, to ascertain the facts with which it has to deal, and in the conduct of its enquiries it is essential that it possess incidental powers commonly associated with a Court of justice. If it were not invested with the power to punish a witness who refuses to be sworn or to affirm (as the case may be) or who, having been sworn or having affirmed, refuses to answer a question when directed to do so, the administrative machinery of the Board would soon grind to a halt, for the most effective direct sanction commonly available to compel obedience to such an order or direction is the power to hold a recalcitrant witness in contempt and, as a means of coercion, to commit him to prison. The necessity of conferring such power upon the Board was recognized by the Legislature, and it was doubtless the appreciation of this particular need which led to the enactment of ss. 33 and 37 of the *Ontario Municipal Board Act*, which provide as follows:

"33. The Board for all purposes of this Act has all the powers of a court of record and shall have an official seal which shall be judicially noticed.

"37. The Board for the due exercise of its jurisdiction and powers and otherwise for carrying into effect the provisions of this or any other general or special Act, has all such powers, rights and privileges as are vested in the Supreme Court with respect to the amendment of proceedings addition or substitution of parties, attendance and examination of witnesses, production and inspection of documents, entry on and inspection of property, enforcement of its orders and all other matters necessary or proper therefor."

It was contended by counsel for the respondents that the Board not being in fact a Court of Record, has not the capacity to receive powers essentially judicial in their nature, or alternatively that the contempt power, the abuse of which involves such grave consequences to the liberty of the subject, should not be attributed to an administrative body or agency created by statute unless that power has been conferred in the clearest and most unambiguous language.

There is not much authority in point, but any case law bearing upon the question fails to support that contention. [Schroeder J. A. then considered *Turcotte* v. *Beique & Whelan* (1891), *Re Singer* (1929) and *Toronto* v. *York Township* (1938) and continued:] . . .

It is not contended that the language of s. 37 of the *Ontario Municipal Board Act* when read with s. 33 which declares that the Board for all purposes of the Act has all the powers of a Court of record, is not sufficiently broad in its scope and effect to give the Board the power to issue subpoenas to secure the attendance of witnesses. By the provisions of s. 37 the Board was given all such powers as were vested in the Supreme Court with respect to

"attendance and examination of witnesses, production and inspection of documents, entry on and inspection of property, enforcement of its orders and all other matters necessary or proper therefor."

This language is admittedly very broad and reasonably construed it must be held to include by necessary implication such powers as are vested in the Supreme Court for the punishment of disobedience of its orders but subject to the restrictions mentioned later. That would, in my opinion, carry with it the authority to fine or commit to prison, or both, for contempt committed in the face of the tribunal.

The practical reason for conferring contempt power is the Board's need, if its machinery is to function smoothly and efficiently. It is a power which is indispensable to the proper conduct of the proceedings before it. But notwithstanding the general language used in s. 37, since those essential powers are given to that body only to facilitate the procedure before it, to the extent of its reasonable requirements, they are not unrestricted in scope. The words are capable of a wide and a narrow construction, but I would consider that the principle to be deduced from the judgment of Bowen L.J., in *Wandsworth Bd. of Works v. United Telephone Co.* (1884), can appropriately be applied here. That learned jurist stated:

". . . if a word in its popular sense, and read in its ordinary way, is capable of two constructions, it is wise to adopt such a construction as is based upon the assumption that Parliament merely intended to give such power as was necessary for carrying out the objects of the Act and not to give any unnecessary powers."

The power to fine or commit for contempt should be restricted to a degree adequate to the end intended to be served by the legislation, for although the powers, rights and privileges which are vested in the Supreme Court are, as to certain aspects of procedure and enforcement, conferred upon the Board and it has been given the powers of a Court of Record, it is nevertheless an inferior tribunal, and its administrative processes are subject to the general supervisory and appellate powers of the Supreme Court of Ontario. At common law, an inferior Court of Record may commit to prison or fine for a contempt committed *in facie curiae*, but not for a contempt not committed in the Court's presence. That power is possessed only by superior Courts of Record. If the Board's contempt power is held to be equal to that possessed by an inferior Court of Record the real object of the enactment will be adequately met and its effectiveness not impaired. The words should, in my view, be construed accordingly.

Our attention was also directed to ss. 47 and 51 of the *Ontario Municipal Board Act* wherein specific powers of enforcement of certain orders or directions given by the Board are provided for. Section 52 is a general section which confers further powers respecting enquiries made by the Board or the inspecting engineer, or any person appointed under the Act to make any enquiry and report, and confers in such instances "the like power to summon witnesses and enforce their attendance, and compel them to give evidence and to produce books, papers or things that they are required to produce, as is vested in any court in civil cases."

In my view, the latter section adds nothing to the combined effect of the provisions of ss. 33 and 37 as they affect the power of the Board to control the proceedings before it.

Counsel for the respondents conceded that if it should be held that the Board had power to compel witnesses to answer questions as to fact, it had the like power to compel witnesses, qualified to give opinion evidence, to answer questions as to the opinion of such witnesses. That accords with my own view and having regard to counsel's admission, no good purpose will be served by my giving extended reasons to support it.

It follows from the foregoing that I would answer Qq. 1, 2 and 3 affirmatively. I refrain from answering Q. 4, since that question is too general in its scope and effect and perhaps somewhat academic. Question 5 is a rather odd question. For a Court or an administrative body to do what that question contemplates, is, to say the least, rather unorthodox procedure. Question 6 necessarily falls into the same pattern and it, too, should not be answered. Perhaps it is sufficient to say that if a witness lawfully summoned before the Board, is bound to answer questions put to him if ordered to do so, persons attempting to dissuade any such witness from giving evidence or to interfere with his testimony may well come within the purview of those sections of the *Criminal Code*, 1953–54 (Can.), c. 51, which are designed to prevent attempts to obstruct, pervert or defeat the course of justice. As I have stated, the Board, in my opinion, does not possess the contempt powers of a superior Court of Record, and it would have no power to deal with any contempt of its authority not committed in its presence. In that view, the content of Qq. 4, 5, and 6 becomes irrelevant.

It should be remembered that while the power to punish summarily for contempt is considered necessary for the proper administration of justice, it is a power which, as has been said, should be used cautiously and sparingly; from a sense of duty and under the pressure of the public necessity, and not to vindicate the Judge or administrative officer as a person, but rather to prevent undue interference with the administration of justice.

The special case should be remitted to the Board with the opinion of this Court expressed in accordance with the foregoing. I would make no order as to costs.

NOTE: The litigation reported hardly touches the problem that concerned the Metropolitan Planning Board when it finally asked its principal officer to refuse to testify as to his personal opinion before the Municipal Board. If it were the case that the Planning Board wanted to keep from the Municipal Board any disagreement between the Planning Board and its experts on its staff, there would seem to be a fair case for the Municipal Board to have the advantage of all the advice it can get. There is no reason to suppose that the Municipal Board is in any way bound to take the advice of the Planning Board, or that it should ignore the advice of that Board's expert if he differed. Nor is there any reason to think that the Planning Board had the slightest desire to keep from the Municipal Board the opinions of its expert, no matter how much they may have disagreed.

On the other hand, the Planning Board was aware that as the views of its staff became known, it became possible for anyone to subpoena a member of the staff and he could then count on an expert witness at a minimum fee to support his case. In *Diamond's* case it was the applicant Diamond who wanted the Board to hear Mr. Jones' opinion. And if Diamond can get Mr. Jones' time away from the Planning Board, so can any number of other applicants. Will this availability of the Planning Board's staff at the beck and call of private citizens be inimical to the proper functioning of the staff? Could the Municipal Board have properly permitted Mr. Jones to refuse to answer? Can the public interest be served by the Board submitting a statement of its views and its staff's views without its staff being called as a witness? Does "natural justice" demand that someone be cross-examined on such a statement? In answering the question put to him in *Diamond's* case is Mr. Jones acting as a witness or as an advocate?

4. Provincial Supervision of Planning

MUNICIPAL ACT
British Columbia. Revised Statutes. 1960. Chapter 225

697. (2) A by-law [designating a community plan as the official community plan] does not come into force and effect until it has received the approval of the Lieutenant-Governor in Council.

[Section 697(2) was amended by S.B.C., 1961., c. 43, s. 38.]

THE COMMUNITY PLANNING ACT, 1957
Saskatchewan. Statutes. 1957. Chapter 48

26. (1) . . . the scheme shall have no effect until approved by the minister.

(3) The minister may refuse to approve a community planning scheme where in his opinion the provisions contained therein are not in conformity with good community planning practice.

["good community planning practice" is not defined in the Act.]

TOWN PLANNING ACT
Nova Scotia. Revised Statutes. 1954. Chapter 292

7 An official town plan adopted, varied or revoked by a council shall not have effect unless and until approved by the Minister.

COMMUNITY PLANNING ACT
New Brunswick. Statutes. 1960–61. Chapter 6

50. (4) The council shall send a copy of every by-law passed under this Act; . . . to the Director within ten days of its being passed. . . .

["Director" means the director of the community planning branch of the Department of Municipal Affairs. The purpose of section 50(4) appears to be to inform the director. He has no power to approve or disallow.]

THE PLANNING ACT
Ontario. Revised Statutes. 1960. Chapter 296

12. (1) Upon adoption, the plan shall be submitted by the council that adopted it to the Minister who may refer the plan to any department of the public service of Ontario that may be concerned therewith and to The Hydro-Electric Power Commission of Ontario, and, in the case of a joint planning area, the Minister shall refer the plan to the council of every municipality in the planning area that the Minister considers is affected by the plan, and if modifications appear desirable, the Minister shall settle such modifications as far as possible to the satisfaction of all concerned and cause the plan to be amended accordingly.

(2) The Minister may then approve the plan, whereupon it is the official plan of the planning area.

NOTE. If the Minister approves the plan he may be said to have made an institutional decision, the characteristics of which were suggested by some of the materials reproduced in section 3 above.

Section 34(1) of *The Planning Act* in Ontario, which is reproduced above, enables the Minister to substitute the Ontario Municipal Board in his place and the local council, or, indeed, any citizen, or at least any interested citizen, may require him to do so. There is likely to be a difference in the approach of the Municipal Board from that taken by the Minister. The Board's decision can hardly be regarded as an institution decision. The Board has no staff and it tends to regard itself as having more of the characteristics of a court. It makes no claim to "expertise", although some members, through experience, must have acquired a high degree of familiarity with planning theories. This fact alone suggests that the Board, which normally sits with a quorum of two members, is likely to give decisions with varying degrees of knowledge of planning background. The Board follows the adversary system and with one important exception, "knows" only what is presented in "evidence" before it. Whether the presentation of a case is successful depends, presumably, on the qualifications of the advocates in charge. The Board does not insist that only barristers may appear, and indeed almost any person may be heard in some types of case. The Minister of Municipal Affairs, who refers the planning question to the Board does not send along a representative from the Attorney General's Department, or even his own Departmental Solicitor. If a qualified planner appears, he is more likely to be treated as a witness than as an advocate, although it is not always clear what facts he has to testify about and his task would seem often to be one of advocacy of the public interest. It is not without some justification that some wit remarked that the administrative process is one where the witnesses argue and the lawyers testify.

The one exception referred to above arises out of the relation of the Board to the Community Planning Branch of the Department of Municipal Affairs. When a plan has been referred to the Minister and voluntarily or otherwise he in turn refers it to the Board, he sends along with the plan the departmental files relevant to the plan, for the Board's information. The Board is thus informed to some extent of the same matters that would have entered into the Minister's "institutional decision", but the free play of informal inquiry between the Minister and his staff is, of course, missing.

The Board takes the view that any such material must be disclosed to the public at the hearing and presumably any matter of fact can then be contested by calling witnesses. Is the Board's practice necessary for a "fair hearing"? Will the same frankness be displayed by the Department in what is sent to the Board if it knows that the Board will disclose the material to the "parties"?

THE DEPARTMENT OF PLANNING AND DEVELOPMENT ACT, 1944

Ontario. Statutes. 1944. Chapter 16

3. The Minister shall collaborate with the Ministers having charge of the other departments of the public service of Ontario, with the Ministers having charge of the departments of the public service of the Dominion and of other provinces, with municipal councils, with agricultural, industrial, labour, mining, trade and other associations and organizations and with public and private enterprises with a view to formulating plans to create, assist, develop and maintain productive employment and to develop the human and material resources of the Province and to that end shall co-ordinate the work and functions of the departments of the public service of Ontario.

NOTE. When this Act was introduced the then Premier of Ontario privately announced his intention of becoming the first Minister of the Department, thus retaining the collaborative function in the First Minister. He was prevailed upon not to assume this extra burden and the post was in fact given to a newcomer to the Cabinet.

The Department of Planning and Development administered *The Planning Act, 1946,* and subsequent amendments and consolidations. In 1961 *The Department of Planning and Development Act,* by then R.S.O., 1960, c. 99, was repealed. See S.O., 1960–61, c. 18. Chapter 18 set up a new Department of Commerce and Development and section 3, above, was enacted as section 3 of Chapter 18. The Minister charged with collaboration under the section became the Minister of Commerce and Development. Later the name was changed to the Department of Economics and Development. Meanwhile, in 1960, the functions of the Community Planning Branch of the old Department of Planning and Development had been transferred to the Department of Municipal Affairs and the "Minister" in The Planning Act became the Minister of Municipal Affairs.

EXPERT COMMITTEE ON COMPENSATION AND BETTERMENT: FINAL REPORT

United Kingdom. 1942. Cmd. 6386

359. We have stated our assumptions that planning is intended to be a reality and a permanent feature of the administration of the internal affairs of the country, and that the system of planning assumed is one of national planning with a high degree of initiation and control by the Central Planning Authority, which will have national as well as local consideratons in mind, and that such control will be based on organised research into the social and economic life of the country and be directed to securing the use and development of land to the best advantage.

We have further stated that the Central Planning Authority we have in mind is an organisation which does not yet exist, and that "planning" has a meaning not attached to it in any legislation nor, until recently, in the minds of the public. Put shortly, National Development is added to planning. We propose in this Chapter to use the term National Development.

Having set forth a scheme which will bring under the control of the Central Planning Authority all undeveloped land in the country outside town areas (and undeveloped land cannot be considered by the Central Planning Authority in isolation from land inside town areas), we ought to state our views as to the form the Central Planning Authority might properly assume.

360. However the Central Planning Authority is constituted and whatever departmental arrangements are made, it is essential that there should exist means by which the requirements of agriculture, transport, public services and defence, as well as housing, industrial location, town siting and other matters, can be given proper weight and considered as a whole. Co-ordination at the centre as respects the various Government Departments interested in particular aspects of planning is necessary. Without this the general lines on which National Development should proceed cannot be properly determined, nor the lands properly managed in the interests of National Development.

361. It is clear at the outset that the settlement of the broad principles of policy, the making of the schemes necessary to carry out that policy and the execution of the schemes are distinct matters.

362. In our view it would be a mistake if there were created a Government Department concerned with National Development, which would rank with existing Government Departments. What is wanted is thought at the centre, an informed vision, unified control of land use and co-ordination between the existing Departments.

We think that this can only be secured if there is set up a Minister—we call him the Minister for National Development—who should be specially charged with National Development. He should have no departmental cares, but he should have the advantage of a highly qualified staff informed as to the economic conditions and needs of the country, competent to put forward proposals for consideration and to advise on the economic and other questions (other than technical questions) arising out of schemes for development.

363. The broad principles of policy would, we apprehend, be settled by the Cabinet after consideration by a Committee of Ministers presided over by the Minister for National Development. The making of schemes necessary to carry out that policy would fall to the Committee of Ministers presided over by the Minister for National Development. Upon those schemes the Committee would have the assistance of the various Government Departments.

The actual execution of the schemes and formulation of detailed plans would fall to the Government Department concerned.

364. The planning functions of the Minister of Works and Planning under the present legislation appear to us to fall directly within the sphere of the Minister for National Development. Clearly the control of the "development rights scheme" and the exercise of the powers arising under it also fall within the sphere of the Minister for National Development. In our view general matters connected with development of land should be kept under the one hand and should be under the personal direction of the Minister for National Development.

365. The next question is what organisation should, consistently with the principles set out in the previous paragraph, be set up so as to secure that the Minister is not concerned with matters of day-to-day administration,

that administration is properly handled and that local authorities, private developers, and landowners have ready access to informed advice and authoritative direction. In our view a suitable organisation would be a Commission on the lines of the War Damage Commission. To the Commission so set up definite powers—including the powers arising under the Town and Country Planning Act and the "development rights scheme" should be given. The control of the Minister for National Development—and, with that, Parliamentary control—should be secured by empowering the Minister to give directions to the Commission.

366. We would make only two observations upon the composition of the Commission. First, it is necessary that there should be a full-time Chairman and that it should include a member of the economic staff of the Minister. Second, it would be an advantage if no other members were full-time members. The opportunity should be seized of securing the service upon the Commission of persons who, by their experience of public affairs, their knowledge of the needs of industry or their knowledge of land utilisation, will ensure common sense administration, and command for the Commission the confidence of the public.

TOWN AND RURAL PLANNING ACT
Alberta. Revised Statues. 1955. Chapter 337

83. (7) No by-law [adopting a general plan] has any force or effect unless it has been approved by the Board. . . .

NOTE. The "Board" means the Provincial Planning Advisory Board established pursuant to section 5 of the Act. It consists of the Director, who is its executive member, and such representatives of the departments of the provincial government concerned with any aspects of urban and rural development within the province as may be appointed by the Lieutenant-Governor in Council. The Act expressly provides that no Minister of the Crown shall be appointed to the Board. The Board acts as a hearing body in a number of situations and there is an appeal to a judge of the Supreme Court of Alberta on any question of jurisdiction or law. Otherwise there is no right of appeal or review by the prerogative writs.

The Board is directed to report to the Minister who may be charged with the administration of the Act, but on one matter only, the "regulations to be made to control and regulate the subdividing of land," the Board "advises the Lieutenant-Governor in Council."

By Bill 57 the name is changed to Provincial Planning Board.

5. Regional Planning

(a) Metropolitan Planning and the Territory of Governments

BLUMENFELD, THE FORM OF THE METROPOLIS (1958)

The Rise of the Modern Metropolis. The Metropolis as we know it today is a new phenomenon. We may still talk of the big city and of suburbs, but these words have lost their original meaning. We are dealing with different parts of a single new unit, an entirely new form of human settlement, which is neither city nor country, and which, for lack of a better term, we may call a Metropolitan Area, or Metropolis, for short.

This fundamental change of the pattern of human settlement is, of course, a product of the industrial revolution. The industrial revolution in the fields of transportation and communication has proceeded in two distinct phases. During the first phase it created highly efficient means for long-distance, inter-urban communication; steamships and railroads; and a highly efficient means of long distance communication, the electric telegraph. Long-distance transportation removed the limitation of the growth of a city which dependence on the food production of the surrounding region had previously imposed.

In the second phase the industrial revolution reached intra-urban transportation and communication and transformed them radically; transportation first by electric traction, applied to street cars, rapid transit, and suburban trains, and then by the internal combustion engine, applied to trucks, buses and private automobiles; communication by the telephone, followed with lesser effect so far by radio and television.

The revolution in intra-urban transportation and communication broke the barriers which kept the 19th century city confined within limits set by travelling time by foot or hoof, roughly within a radius of three to five miles–and has led to its transformation into the modern metropolitan area. We are only in the beginning of this process.

Metropolitan Population Movement. The two aspects of the revolution in transportation and communication have produced two opposite population movements. The development of inter-urban transportation and communication, still continuing and reinforced by the development of aviation and of a nation-wide express highway network, produces the movement from farms and small towns to metropolitan areas and a growing concentration of the population of the nation in such areas. Nine tenths of the growth of the population in the United States since 1950 has occurred in metropolitan areas. Within these areas the population spreads further and further out. The inflowing country-to-city migration is accompanied by an outflowing city-to-suburb migration.

I have traced this development in the eight county area which now constitutes the Philadelphia metropolitan area, for the years 1860 to 1950, dividing it into 3 periods: the railroad age, 1860–90, the streetcar age, 1890–1920 and the automobile age, 1920–50. It may be noted that the rate of population growth was only half as great in the third as in the two preceding periods, about 35% versus over 70%. During the first, and to a slightly lesser degree during the second period, the periphery of the area lost population. However, during the third period, even the most distant parts of the area showed an increase. In other words, the outgoing city-to-suburb wave had overflowed the incoming country-to-city wave.

For the half-century 1900–1950 it is possible to trace population changes by concentric circles of one mile width up to 10 miles, of two mile width up to 18 miles, and for the balance of the area up to 25 miles, that is up to a line beyond which the influence of the neighboring centers of Trenton, Allentown-Bethlehem, and Reading modifies the picture. An amazingly regular pattern emerges. Density decreases consistently from the center to the periphery, and the pattern becomes more consistent from decade to decade. More and more the population distributes itself in relation to the center. It is therefore a double-edged process which implies centralization as well as decentralization; increased dominance of the center over an increasingly decentralized population. Formerly independent towns become satellites, and former satellites are submerged in the metropolitan flood. The whole process might best be described as Metropolitan Integration.

In this process the wave of population growth has a definite crest—the zone of the highest ratio of poulation increase, which is also characterized by the highest average value of homes and the highest percentage of home ownership. This crest of the wave has moved outward quite regularly, through depression as well as through boom periods, at a rate of about a mile per decade. It is therefore misleading to talk about an "explosion" set off by the automobile. We are dealing with a gradual, consistent, secular trend. And the trend is definitely toward a decreasing range of densities, towards a more even distribution of the population over the entire Metropolitan Area.

I have dwelt at some length on these historical developments in order to emphasize their deep-rooted, consistent, inexorable character. There is still a lingering notion that this whole development was an avoidable mistake, a sinful fall from grace, from the lost paradise of the presumably good old days of small-town life. The evidence is all to the contrary. The Metropolis is our fate. The question is not *if* we want want it to be, but *how* we want it to be.

Requirements of the Metropolis. We may try to define the characteristics which make this new form of human settlement, the Metropolis, different from the city as we have known it for 5000 years.

1. It combines the traditional function of the city as a leading center with the traditional function of the countryside as the main focus of production.
2. As a result it contains a much larger population, both as a percentage of the nation and in absolute numbers.
3. This population spreads out at increasingly lower densities and therefore covers an incomparably larger area.
4. This area contains both areas of "urban" development and "open" areas, such as large parks, golf courses, and country clubs, air fields, large institutions, even agricultural areas.
5. Place of work and place of residence are separate, and many of the places of work are large, both in terms of area and in terms of people employed.

The last point leads back to the basic reason for the existence of these evergrowing concentrations of people: division of labor. For the Metropolis and its precursor, the large industrial city, came into being not primarily as places for living, but as places for making a living. Primarily the Metropolis is a large labor market. People come to the Metropolis because it offers them a wide choice of employment opportunities; and places of employment establish themselves in the Metropolis because it offers them a wide choice of skills, both for direct employment, and in other establishments on whom they can call for supply of materials and parts, as well as for all kinds of services: repair and maintenance, finance, marketing, technical and legal advice, etc. Places of employment attract workers, as well as each other, and the availability of workers attracts places of employment. The process feeds on itself. It is dependent on mutual accessibility which defines the essence as well as the limits of the Metropolis.

The role of the Metropolis as a place for making a living calls for mutual accessibility between place of residence and place of work. This results in a pair of contradictory requirements: distance between residence and work should be minimized; and even the most distant places of work and residence should be mutually accessible. Expressed differently: minimum need for commuting and maximum opportunity for commuting. The former calls for an approximate balance between places of employment and labor force in each section of the metropolitan area; the latter for a form which minimizes time distances between all parts of the area.

The role of the Metropolis as a place for living also calls for a pair of contradictory requirements. Ebenezer Howard defined city and country as the "two magnets" which attract people seeking the good life. People have sought access to both by moving to the suburbs. But as more and more people moved to the suburbs, they moved farther and farther away from the city, and the country moved farther and farther away from them. The process defeated itself. Yet the goal remains valid. The center, as the point accessible to most people, is the logical place for all those facilities which are the hallmark of the "city" because they can exist only when supported by a large population. And the more urban the environment, the greater the need for relaxation "away from it all" in the open country. Hence our second pair of contradictory requirements: access to the center and access to open country.

The division of place of residence and place of work and the specialization and differentiation of types of work and, to some extent, also of types of residence, have led to a need of separation of different functions into separate areas. This has been largely accomplished by zoning. But we now find that "good" residential zoning protects the residents of such a zone—in particular the children who rarely leave it—not only from all kinds of "nuisances" but from most experiences of life itself. They see nothing of the working life of the community and little of other classes of people than their own. Separation becomes segregation. Hence a third pair of contradictory requirements: separation and integration of functions.

Integration into a unit as vast as the Metropolis may seem remote and meaningless. It is widely felt that people need integration and identification with a smaller and more comprehensible unit, a neighbourhood or community. But you identify most easily with people who are like yourself; and, saying "we" of the "in-group" means saying "they" to all others. Strong neighbourhood identification may lead to isolation from the larger community. In his study of Park Forest, Herbert Gans found that the most neighbourly blocks contributed little to the life of the community, and that the community leaders were persons who had relatively little contact with their immediate neighbours. We can thus formulate a fourth pair of contradictory requirements: identification with the neighbourhood and identification with the Metropolis as a whole.

Finally, people need a feeling of identity not only in space, but even more in time: they need stability. But the Metropolis is a highly dynamic entity, constantly growing and changing and every one of its parts must be able to adjust to these changes. Hence another and most vexing pair of contradictory requirements: stability and flexibility.

Basic Elements of the Metropolis. In trying to satisfy these pairs of contradictory requirements, the form of the Metropolis must accommodate four basic elements, each of which may, of course, be further broken down into sub-categories.

As already stated, the modern Metropolis continues, enlarges, and intensifies the central functions of the traditional city—commercial, administrative, cultural. All those functions which serve the entire metropolitan area and the surrounding region must be at the point best accessible to all, in the central area. The central area epitomizes the essence of the Metropolis: mutual accessibility. All those who need frequent mutual contact to carry on their business, congregate in the Central Business District. It can serve this contact function best if it is highly concentrated. Generally it is the only area with a sufficiently high concentration of people to be served by rapid transit, and the relation to such lines in turn strongly influences the pattern of the surrounding area.

The function of the Metropolis as an organizing center competes both for space and for labor force with its function as place of production. Originally many factories and warehouses were located in the center, but as Ernest Jurkat has shown for Philadelphia, establishments dealing with goods gradually give way to establishments dealing with persons. Modern manufacturing and warehousing and the related transportation facilities require extensive areas. These industrial areas form the second basic element of the Metropolis. They should be accessible to as many residential areas as possible to the center, and preferably also to each other.

The residential areas constitute the third, most extensive and important, element of the Metropolis. They should have access to some industrial areas, to the center, and to open areas for recreation. These open areas finally are the fourth basic element. The shape and distribution of these four basic elements and their relation to each other determine the pattern of the Metropolis.

Patterns for the Metropolis. In most cases the pattern which has developed spontaneously can be described as undifferentiated concentric sprawl. In a small pre-industrial town this pattern was adequate. Every residence was close both to the center with its market place, town hall, and cathedral, and to the surrounding countryside. As the workshop was part of the home the problem of locating industrial and residential areas did not exist.

With the growth of the city this pattern produced all the familiar problems: lack of open space, amorphous neighbourhoods, confused traffic, indiscriminate mixture of industry and residence. With further sprawl into the suburbs this mixture was usually avoided—to be replaced by the opposite one of long distances from suburban residence to any place of work.

"Suburban sprawl" or "scatteration" has often been condemned. Yet, at least one proposal carries the idea of scatteration even further. Frank Lloyd Wright's "Broadacre City" where every house will have a lot of an acre or more and people will travel by private automobiles to factories, shops, schools, scattered here and there.

At the opposite extreme is Le Corbusier's "Radiant City" with a business center consisting of a group of office towers, surrounded by residential areas, consisting of elevator apartments, both surrounded by lawns and trees.

Another scheme was developed by Milyutin during the Russian first 5-year plan. He proposed a transportation ribbon consisting of railroad and and highway, in a green buffer strip, with industry on one side and residences on the other, each workers' settlement opposite its industry, and separated by open space from the next industrial-residential unit.

The satellite towns now being built in Great Britain are yet another pattern; each town is self-contained, its residents working in local industry and its size strictly limited; home and work are close and open space is nearby. A modified version of the satellite scheme could be planned with continuous "fingers" of "satellites" radiating from the center, with "green wedges" left open between the fingers; this would greatly improve mutual accessibility while preserving the main advantages of the greenbelt-satellite scheme.

The pattern of Metropolitan Philadelphia, like that of most metropolitan areas, does not correspond to any of these schemes, but has elements of most of them. Originally, the city grew as a solid mass from the center outward. Then fingers developed along the street car lines, and longer ones along the suburban railroads. With the coming of the automobile most of the former, and to a lesser extent, the latter, were submerged by a new suburban sprawl. Satellite towns are clearly part of the pattern. On the other hand, the most intensive development has taken place in a ribbon along the Deleware.

Distribution of Residential Densities. In the various patterns of existing metropolitan areas there is an enormous range of density. While it would be futile to attempt to define the ideal density, it is possible to define a range beyond which densities may be regarded as excessively high or excessively low.

In the older areas excessively high densities remain the main problem because of lack of light, air, sunshine, and privacy and acute shortage of space for open air recreation and for parking. But in many of the newer suburbs there are only 6 or less houses per net acre, resulting in densities of about 5,000 persons per square mile. This has several serious disadvantages.

1. The total developed area becomes very extended; the residents of the outer sections have to travel long distances to the center, and those of the inner sections are far removed from open country. Costs of transportation and of utilities become very high.

2. The number of people living within easy walking distance is too low to support either an effective bus service or a school or shopping facilities. Thus the residents become dependent on the private automobile. When the head of the family uses the car to drive to work, the housewife is isolated.

3. The cost of the house as well as of transportation limits the population groups who can afford to live in such suburbs and thereby increases class segregation.

Thus there is a strong case for favoring somewhat higher densities in the suburbs. There appears to be no sound reason to increase population density in the older, inlying areas, from say 25 to 50 dwelling units per net acre. An increase of suburban density, from say 5 to 10 units per net acre will do five times as much to limit "sprawl." It might be well to realize that one-third of the land within a circle of 25 miles radius, built up at 8 dwelling units per net acre, would accommodate over ten million people. Raymond Unwin's slogan "nothing gained by overcrowding" is still true. But something might be gained by building fewer detached single-family houses and more row or group houses and apartments in suburban developments.

The Visual Form of the Metropolis. In talking of the form of the Metropolis we have so far been thinking of the two-dimensional pattern which can be read on a map. But there is no particular virtue in a neat or interesting pattern on a map if it cannot be perceived on the ground.

Cities are perceived in two ways: from the outside as a silhouette, and from the inside as a sequence of spaces of streets and squares. A metropolitan area is so extensive that it can rarely be seen as a whole from the outside; and it is far too vast to be perceived as a sequence of streets and squares. It can only be dealt with as an urban landscape, with the silhouette of the built-up sections surrounding the open park or water areas. The center stands out strongly in American cities by the silhouette of its skyscrapers, but the balance of the area tends to be formless. It can be organized, socially as well as formally, only around subsidiary community centers. In the planned suburb of Vallingby near Stockholm apartment towers surround the community center, in which public and shopping facilities are grouped next to the suburban railroad station. This may point the direction in which a Metropolis as a whole could be given a visible form. A second approach is relation to a "leitmotif" which unifies the entire area. In Greater Philadelphia the relation to the two rivers might be developed into such a leitmotif.

We have a few—far too few–examples of neighbourhoods which have a tangible form with which their residents can identify themselves. To find a form for the entire Metropolis which its citizens could perceive as a thing of pride and joy remains a task for the future.

NOTE. Mr. Blumenfeld's text, reproduced above with his permission, was first delivered as an address at the Philadelphia Housing Association's Forum on Neighbourhoods in 1958 in Philadelphia, which accounts for the illustrative material from Philadelphia and its metropolitan area. Mr. Blumenfeld was at the time Deputy Planning Commissioner for the Metropolitan Toronto Planning Board. His account of the "Patterns for the Metropolis" also appears in the Metropolitan Toronto draft official plan, part of which is reproduced below, and in which Mr. Blumenfeld naturally had a hand. Other material indicates the scope of the metropolitan problem in Canada, and its similarity to the North American, if not western world situations generally.

OFFICIAL PLAN: METROPOLITAN TORONTO PLANNING AREA (DRAFT)

Ontario. Metropolitan Toronto Planning Board. 1959

The Toronto Scheme. The situation of the Metropolitan Toronto Planning Area presents some analogies with that of Stalingrad. A broad urban ribbon has in fact, developed from Hamilton to Oshawa, far beyond the boundaries of the Planning Area. Basically the plan's conception of this area is that of an urban ribbon, bounded on the south by Lake Ontario and a park strip along the lakeshore, which is to be developed to the maximum possible extent; and to the north by a substantially rural area; with the stream valleys running from the rural area down to the lake developed as parks, corresponding to the perpendicular green ribbons of the Ribbon Scheme; and tied together by road and rail facilities generally paralleling the lakeshore.

There are strong reasons for discouraging major urban development to spread indefinitely to the north, quite aside from the idealistic one of preserving open farm and forest lands accessible to the metropolitan residents. While there are fair sources of groundwater supply in this area, extensive urbanization would have to rely on water supply from Lake Ontario, involving costly water mains, pumping stations, and reservoirs. The greatly increased runoff of storm water from paved surfaces and roofs would increase the flood danger in the intensely developed lower reaches of the stream valleys cutting through the developed areas. Most critical is the problem of sewage disposal. It is hardly feasible to extend trunk mains for many miles from the lake. If, on the other hand, local disposal plants are built upstream, their effluent threatens to pollute the creeks and rivers further downstream in the urbanized area, in particular when these plants suffer a breakdown or become overloaded.

All these considerations support the concept of an urban ribbon of limited depth, extending east and west along the lakeshore.

The "open" area to the north is not to consist solely of farms and forests. It is a suitable location for many urban uses of a non-intensive character; parks, golf courses, and country clubs, cemeteries, institutions on large grounds. Also, in suitable locations, airfields and areas for open storage, and for residential development on large lots, generally of one acre or more, for which a growing demand is expected. In addition, villages existing within this area, are, of course, recognized and should be equipped with all necessary facilities.

While the basic concept of the plan is that of a broad urban ribbon, this is substantially modified by the existing urban development which has generally spread out from the core in the form of a semi-circle. From this compact urban area a "finger" extends to the north along Yonge Street and will reach up to and merge with the existing "satellite town" of Richmond Hill. To the northwest and northeast of the semicircular urban area, the villages of Woodbridge and of Markham are to develop into small "satellite towns" of strictly limited size, close to, but not merging with the compact urban area.

The Ajax-Pickering area, located east of the deep and broad valley of the Rouge River, may also be regarded as a fairly large satellite town. At the opposite end of the Planning Area, west of the Credit River, several large developers have assembled an area totalling about 10 square miles and are developing plans for a "New Town" in cooperation with the local and Metropolitan Toronto Planning Boards. However, this will not be a completely isolated satellite town, but will be contiguous with the urban ribbon at the western end of the Panning Area near Clarkson.

If the schematic sketch presented in Plate 2, Fig. 4 [not reproduced] is read not as a map of the urbanized area, but inversely as a map of open areas, it shows, in addition to the park strips along the lake and in the valleys, two broad "green wedges." To the east the valleys of the two branches of the Rouge River and the land between them separate the urban areas of Scarborough and Pickering. To the west a wedge of open country extends southward to the H.E.P.C.'s high tension line between the Etobicoke Creek and the Credit River. There are two reasons for keeping this area out of urban development. First, it is in line of the main approach to Malton Airport and will be strongly affected by the noise of jet planes. Second, it is cut by half a dozen small, parallel valleys, a topography which makes the estabishment of a sewage system extremely difficult.

The existence of these two broad green wedges will enhance the attractiveness and value of the residential areas which surround them on three sides.

Summing up, the Toronto scheme may be interpreted as a combination of the ribbon, finger, and satellite schemes. It has been derived however, not from any preconceived notion of an ideal scheme, but from a realistic interpretation of the basic factors of geography and history.

[This passage is taken from Chapter II, "General Concept of the Plan".]

METROPOLITAN AREAS IN CANADA. The following table has been made up from census data published by the Dominion Bureau of Statistics.

The concept of a "metropolitan area" is obviously not a universally agreed concept, as witness the fact that both Metropolitan Toronto and Metropolitan Winnipeg have smaller areas than the census metropolitan area in each case.

Metropolitan Area		Population 1961	1956	1951
Montreal, Que.	(M.A.)	2,109,509	1,745,001	1,471,851
(50)	(C.)	1,191,062	1,109,439	1,021,520
Toronto, Ont.	(M.A.)	1,824,481	1,502,253	1,210,353
(13)	(Metro.)	1,618,787	1,358,028	1,117,470
	(C.)	672,407	667,706	675,754
Vancouver, B.C.	(M.A.)	790,165	665,017	561,960
(15)	(C.)	384,522	365,844	344,833
Winnipeg, Man.	(M.A.)	475,989	412,248	356,813
(14)	(Metro.)	474,374		
	(C.)	265,429	255,093	235,710
Ottawa, Ont.	(M.A.)	429,750	345,460	292,476
(12)	(C.)	268,206	222,129	202,045
Hamilton, Ont.	(M.A.)	395,189	338,294	280,293
(12)	(C.)	273,991	239,625	208,321
Quebec, Que.	(M.A.)	357,568	311,604	276,242
(30)	(C.)	171,979	170,703	164,016
Edmonton, Alta.	(M.A.)	337,568	254,800	176,782
(5)	(C.)	281,027	226,002	159,631
Calgary, Alta.	(M..A.)	279,062	201,022	142,315
(5)	(C.)	249,641	181,780	129,060
Windsor, Ont.	(M.A.)	193,365	185,865	163,618
(9)	(C.)	114,367	121,980	120,049
Halifax, N.S.	(M.A.)	183,946	164,200	133,931
(9)	(C.)	92,511	93,301	85,589
London, Ont.	(M.A.)	181,283	154,453	128,977
(3)	(C.)	169,569	101,693	95,343
Kitchener, Ont.	(M.A.)	154,864	128,722	107,474
	(C.)	74,485	59,562	44,867
Victoria, B.C.	(M.A.)	154,152	133,829	113,207
(6)	(C.)	54,941	54,584	51,331
Sudbury, Ont.	(M.A.)	110,694	97,945	73,826
	(C.)	80,120	46,482	42,410
St. John, N.B.	(M.A.)	95,563	86,015	78,337
(6)	(C.)	55,153	54,491	50,779
St. John's, Nfld.	(M.A.)	90,838	79,153	68,620
(10)	(C.)	63,633	57,078	52,873

[The number in brackets under the name of the area is the number of municipalities within the area according to the 1956 census figure. The 1961 figures were not available when this material was prepared, but the census metropolitan area had been enlarged in some cases, and the earlier figures have been adjusted to make them comparable.]

The *National Housing Act*, R.S.C., 1952, c. 188, defines a "metropolitan area" for the purposes of that act to mean "a city together with one or more adjacent municipalities in close economic relationship with the city." The word "city" is not defined. It may safely be said that for the lawyer the legal problems of metropolitan government begin whenever the population of a "community" reaches beyond the boundary of one municipality into another. The size of the first municipality is irrelevant. Thus a town or village in Ontario may be part of a "metropolitan area" if its population spreads into the adjoining township of which the town or village was once a part. For many purposes the inhabitants of the community will not distinguish between the town or village and that part of the township that is socially closely connected with it. Yet for tax purposes the two are quite separate and the quality of services found in the town may be much better than that of the township. There are, in short, two governments governing one "community." The next materials illustrate how local governments have grappled with this problem, which is made difficult chiefly because of the strange loyalties that develop for a municipal government the existence of which one would think was really only brought home to most citizens when they receive their tax bills.

Usually a sense of "belonging" is to be found in any closely knit group of people, and when the metropolitan area has "growed" over a long time various groups have developed within it, each with some notion of a vested interest it doesn't want to lose, but which it thinks it will if its historically accidental boundaries are disturbed. This sense of "belonging" is greatly enhanced by the political boundaries in many cases, while in others many inhabitants couldn't say where the boundaries are, and couldn't care. The Toronto Argos and Maple Leafs hardly "belong" only to the city.

Only about twenty-five to thirty-five per cent of the qualified electors vote at municipal elections (less than half the national election average). Yet most residents seem to fear that any change of their municipal boundaries will inevitably result in a tax increase. Since municipal taxes seem to be slowly but steadily increasing anyway, the fear is a difficult one to assuage.

One device that has received little publicity, but has been fairly frequently applied, is the intra-municipal sale of services. Thus a larger, established municipality might "wholesale" water to a suburban municipality. The contract device has never proved adequate for a large metropolitan area. The need is for some way of providing the central municipality with an elastic boundary!

RE BRANTFORD ANNEXATION
Ontario. Municipal Board [1954] O.W.N. 834

CUMMING Q.C. Chairman and YATES Q.C. Member, signed the decision of the Board. [After the nature of the application and the preliminary steps are described, the decision continues:] . . . In previous annexation decisions the Board has laid down the principle that when a municipality seeks to extend its boundaries and to bring under its jurisdiction substantial areas administered by one or more neighbouring municipalities it must assume the general burden of proof. The removal of any large area, whether developed or undeveloped, from the jurisdiction of one municipality and its addition to another is always a serious matter, and the decision in each case cannot depend upon the mere application of arbitrary rules or rigid tests. In the opinion of the Board, the applicant municipality must first establish the fact that the growth and development of the area within its jurisdiction and the area sought to be annexed has reached a point which requires some readjustment of the municipal boundary. It must then proceed to show why this readjustment should take the form of an immediate transfer to the applicant of the specific areas described in the application. The Board does not consider that it would be justified in ordering important boundary-changes merely because existing boundaries might appear at first glance to be unrealistic or of uncertain origin. If, on the other hand, after a full and exhaustive public hearing and after respectful attention to the views of residents and officials of the municipalities concerned and an exhaustive study of the past development and present position of the municipalities involved, the Board in its best judgment considers that the time for a change in boundaries has arrived, it seems clear that the Legislature has imposed upon it the duty of ordering such a change in the best interests of the present and future residents and ratepayers of both the applicant municipality and the areas affected.

The first question, therefore, which must be decided is whether the growth and development of the City on the one hand and of the adjoining areas on the other has now reached a stage which justifies a substantial extension of the City's boundaries. Another aspect of the same problem is the question whether the inter-municipal relationships of the City, the Township and the County have reached a point calling for some change in their respective areas of jurisdiction in order to provide more efficiently and economically the municipal services which are the responsibility of these local governments. An answer to this question requires some review of the development of the municipalities since the existing boundaries were established, and a matter of particular importance is the extent, location and apparent trend of population-growth in that period. The municipalities comprising the present county of Brant were originally part of the counties of Oxford, Halton and Wentworth and were formed into a separate county in 1852 with the town of Brantford as the county town. It was then and still is one of the smallest and most compact counties in the Province. Brantford, the county town, then comprised about 800 acres of land with a population of some 3,000 persons. Notwithstanding the advantages of the location on main transportation routes, the growth of the town was slow and it was not until 1877 that it attained a population of more than 10,000, which then entitled it to elevation to the status of a city. This was accomplished by a special Act of the Legislature and at the same time the area was increased to approximately 3,000 acres. Then, as now, the erection of the City resulted in automatic separation from the County for municipal purposes and it is interesting to note that this particular case involved a drastic change in the economy of the County, which lost about one-third of its total population and more than one-quarter of its total assessment. In the succeeding 75 years the population growth in the City was steady, if not spectacular, reaching approximately 37,000 in the year 1952 immediately preceding the hearing. By the same year the population of the County had increased to about 33,000, of which almost 18,000 was in the Township. During the entire period no extension of the City's boundary occurred with the exception of the annexation of 300 acres from the Township in 1920.

The growth of population in the Township is shown graphically in various exhibits and in the opinion of the Board is extremely significant. At the time of the incorporation of the City the populaton in the Township was approximately 6,800. In the following 60 years there was practically no growth in the Township population but in the 15-year period beginning with the year 1937, and especially in the years following the conclusion of the second world war, there was a heavy influx and in 1952 the Township had a population of nearly 18,000 persons, almost half the total population of the City. In the year 1949 alone there was an increase in the Township population of more than 18 per cent and in the 15-year period between 1937 and 1952 the overall increase was 134.7 per cent as compared with a 17 per cent increase in the City in the same period. This recent development in the Township is in striking contrast to the extremely slow rate of growth during the previous 60 years. It is also important to remember that during the past 5 years, when the Township has experienced its greatest growth, the City has apparently reached its maximum population and a trend towards a slight decrease is already evident. The official statistics for the year 1953, published since the conclusion of the hearing, indicate a City population of 36,526 and a population in the Township of 18,662. During the same 15-year period none of the other municipalities in the County, including even the town of Paris, seems to have experienced any great increase in population.

Although it is evident from the most casual inspection that a very large part of the new population in the Township has become established in the immediate vicinity of the City, it was urged on behalf of the Township that this development did not indicate that the City was running out of residential sites or that it could not accommodate a larger population within its present limits. The weight of the evidence does not support this contention. In addition to the considered opinions of the assessment commissioner and other witnesses there was uncontested evidence to show that the present density of population in the City, on the basis of assessed acreage, is much higher than in most Ontario cities of comparable size excepting those which have recently extended their boundaries by major annexations. The suggestion that the City could provide for a larger population within its present borders by reducing its housing standards and permitting population densities approaching those to be found in such cities as Toronto and Hamilton does not commend itself to the Board. The Board does not find that the City's present zoning by-law imposes any unreasonably high standards and there was no evidence of the existence of any large areas which by redevelopment could accommodate a larger population. The Board is in complete sympathy with the evident desire of the great majority of the City's residents to maintain existing values in the older established residential districts and to avoid the undesirable social and economic effect of overcrowding. The existing population-density of more than 20 persons per assessed acre appears to be high for a city of this size. On the whole, the Board finds that this branch of the City's case has been well established and that if reasonably good standards are to be maintained the City cannot accommodate a greater population within its present limits.

With respect to the contention that the City lacks space for further industrial and commercial expansion or for public purposes, counsel for the Township practically conceded that this was the case. He claimed, however, that this did not necessarily justify the annexation of additional lands. Conceding the importance of a high percentage of industrial and commercial assessment in order to lighten the burden of local taxation upon residential property, he pointed out that the City, having attained a very favourable balance of assessment, should not seek further improvement of this ratio by the addition of potential industrial lands located in the Township and that, in effect, the City should now permit the Township to obtain its fair share. It was very evident throughout the proceedings that, although there has been in the past a very commendable degree of co-operation in seeking to attract industry to the area, competition between these two political divisions of the same urban community in this respect is still strong. The two municipalities share equally the cost of maintaining a joint industrial commission and considerable success has been achieved in attracting new industries. However, it has been difficult to persuade new industries to take up locations in the Township where necessary services are not immediately available and the officials of the Township seem to feel that the City should be obliged to extend services beyond its borders so that the Township can improve its competitive position. The importance of industry in the economy of the region is obvious. In the 10-year period during and immediately following the second world war there was a tremendous increase in industrial production and employment. The extent of this expansion is shown in the following statistics placed in the record.

MANUFACTURING

	Production	Employees
1939	$ 25,708,393.	6,549
1949	128,461,371.	15,360 (including Brantford and environs)

Both the City and the Township hope that a high rate of industrial expansion will continue and both are anxious to exploit the many advantages of the area as an industrial location. There was definite evidence, however, that in the immediate past desirable industries have been lost to the other localities as a direct result of the lack of suitable serviced land in either the City or the Township, and notwithstanding the high degree of co-operation already referred to, the Board is forced to conclude that the present division of political jurisdiction is to some extent responsible and that in the interests of the present and future citizens of the area something more than a desire to co-operate is required.

With respect to the development in the City and the Township of municipal services generally, the evidence was unusually complete. Both municipalities have shown a very high degree of efficiency and intelligence in attacking the problem of providing for their residents the municipal and educational services which are the responsibility of local governments and in adjusting and expanding their administrative organizations to meet the needs of the areas under their jurisdiction. The nature of the service problem faced by the two municipalities has differed in many important respects. The present City, formerly the Town of Brantford, has throughout been a typical urban municipality based on an industrial economy and its rate of population growth has been reasonably steady. Except during the depression years, when extensive and long-continued unemployment imposed severe strains upon the municipal financial structure, the City has been able to provide an urban type of service for its inhabitants without serious difficulty. It now has the administrative organization and the financial capacity required to undertake future expansion.

The service problem which has been faced by the Township, particularly in recent years, has been typical of the problems encountered by other suburban municipalities adjoining rapidly-growing industrial centres. In a comparatively short period it has been required to provide for a large increase in the size and an important change in the nature of the population requiring municipal and educational services. The service requirements of the new residents in the areas adjoining the City are essentially urban, whereas most of the land under its jurisdiction is still rural and used for farming purposes. As a result the Township has been compelled within a comparatively brief span of years to make fundamental changes in its municipal organization and to undertake heavy capital expenditures for the purpose of providing typical urban services in the area surrounding the City without imposing upon the rural ratepayers an impossible burden of taxation for services which they neither need nor desire. At the same time the Township has not had the benefit of any high percentage of non-residential assessment comparable to that enjoyed by the City, and for this reason it has been compelled to plan and control its development and to limit the extension of urban services, and, in effect, the rate of population-growth, in order to avoid serious financial difficulty. The elected and appointed officials of the Township have consistently recognized the nature of their problem and have made use of all available means of controlling and directing the development of the suburban areas. On the evidence, the Board must find that the Township has throughout been remarkably successful in dealing with a complex and difficult problem and that it has provided the utmost service possible to its new residents having regard to its available resources and the basic disadvantages inherent in the present situation. Nevertheless, the Township is now facing serious service problems including the planning and construction of a costly sewage and drainage system to serve almost the entire area. The topography of the region requires that this system be closely related to the existing system in the City for the reason that no other outlets are available. The evidence in this case discloses an unusual degree of unification and co-ordination of services achieved by the City and the Township by means of voluntary agreements. Costs are shared either on the basis of actual use or on a *per capita* basis, or by the payment of rates which may include an allowance for capital costs.

Although these agreements cover a wide range of services and reflect a commendable spirit of co-operation and goodwill, the Board is unable to agree with the suggestion of counsel for the Township that they can or should be extended to the entire field of municipal and educational services and operations which concern both municipalities. It was not denied that negotiations preceding the making or renewal of some of these agreements have often been lengthy and in some cases contentious, particularly where there were sincere differences of opinion with respect to the degree of benefit to be obtained or the location of proposed buildings intended for joint use. The Board has no wish to discourage the efforts of adjoining municipalities to solve their common problems by voluntary joint-service agreements but it cannot ignore some of the fundamental disadvantages of this method which are well known to experienced municipal officials and to the Board. The validity of most agreements of this type cannot extend beyond the life of existing councils even when heavy capital expenditures are incurred by one of the contracting parties. For example, the City might construct a school large enough to serve the needs of the City and the Township, but there can be no assurance that the Township board will not decide, before the school has been paid for, to construct its own school and thus terminate its obligation to pay non-resident pupil fees to the City board. Another common difficulty is the lack of any right to representation on the board or body owning and operating a project designed to serve both municipalities. For these and other reasons the usefulness of voluntary inter-municipal agreements is limited, especially where it is impossible to measure accurately the respective degrees of benefit and the cost of the project must be recoverable wholly or in part from general taxation.

Notwithstanding the considerable amount of evidence devoted to this subject and the persuasive arguments of counsel for the Township, the Board finds itself in agreement with the contention of counsel for the City that in a case such as this, where there has been a very substantial development and it is necessary to plan and construct costly municipal works and schools designed to serve both the city and the suburban areas, an equitable distribution of costs can be obtained only by means of area-wide assessment and taxation imposed by a single authority.

Before leaving the subject of services it should be noted that the City on its part has already planned and undertaken the construction of extensive improvements and enlargements of its basic service plant and facilities for the purpose of providing for the needs of the expanding population on its borders. Conspicuous examples of this far-sighted policy are to be found in the enlargement of the filtration-plant, the construction of new feeder-mains and costly trunk-sewers and the planning of a second large secondary school.

Having referred briefly to some of the most significant features of the development and the present position of the two municipalities most vitally concerned in the present application, and having also reviewed with great care the entire body of evidence, the Board is of the opinion that on the whole a strong case for the extension of the City's political boundary has been shown unless effect is to be given to one or more of the objections raised on behalf of the respondent municipalities and vigorously supported in argument. It is now proposed to discuss these submissions. In this case they extend over a very wide field, and some of them range far beyond the local problems which gave rise to the present application.

The most serious objection to the proposal was undoubtedly the contention that annexation of the proposed area to the City would have a serious and, in fact, a disastrous effect upon the organization and economy of the remaining Township and the entire County and that for this reason alone, regardless of the indicated needs of the City and the surrounding suburban area, either the application should be dismissed in its entirety or the annexation should be confined to a much smaller area. It was pointed out that the Township of Brantford from the beginning has been the largest municipality in the County, and since the erection of the City in 1877 the Township has been the chief source of County revenue. In 1952 it contributed about 50 per cent of the entire County budget. It was shown that as a result of the proposed annexation the Township would lose 63.5 per cent of its total assessment and the County would lose nearly 32 per cent of its total equalized assessment. The largest item of County expenditure is the maintenance and improvement of 123.5 miles of county and suburban roads of which only 8 miles are within the area proposed to be annexed. The 1953 County budget provided for a total expenditure of approximately $450,000 which, after the deduction of available revenues including road grants and subsidies, resulted in a County levy of about $225,000. Approximately $105,000 of this amount represented the County's net expenditure on its road-system.

There can be no doubt that if the proposed annexation becomes effective the economy of the County will be seriously affected and drastic readjustments will be necessary. Although elaborate computations intended to show the financial effect upon the County and its constituent municipalities were presented in evidence, the Board for reasons which will soon be apparent does not propose to make, at this time, a detailed analysis of these exhibits or an exact estimate of the probable effect of the proposed annexation on the finances of the County and its constituent municipalities. Assuming for the present that the financial effect will be serious due to the size of the area with relation to the present taxable resources of the County and the Township, is this sufficient reason for the dismissal of the application?

After full consideration of the implications of this objection, which was raised in various forms throughout the entire hearing, the Board has come to the conclusion that it is essentially unsound in principle. It appears to be based upon a conception of the nature of municipal institutions and the division of the Province into various areas for municipal purposes which is inconsistent with the entire history of the legislation and the development of the present system. The division of the Province into various areas for municipal purposes is and always has been an important responsibility of the Provincial Government. Although it may be true that in the southern portion of the Province such divisions have remained substantially unchanged for more than a century, it is a serious error to assume that they were then fixed and determined for all time and that the Legislature in its wisdom will not from time to time, as a matter of Provincial policy, make such changes as may be necessary in the light of greatly changed conditions. Moreover, notwithstanding such divisions the Province has always reserved to itself and has frequently exercised the power to alter the boundaries between existing municipalities. Under the present legislation it has delegated this important responsibility to this Board, subject to the conditions and limitations set forth in *The Municipal Act*, R.S.O. 1950, c. 243, as amended. Nothing in the existing or antecedent legislation can be found to justify the suggestion that municipal boundary-changes should be confined to minor additions or readjustments. Nor can the Board find any expressed or implied limitation of its powers suggesting that annexations should be confined to cases where there will be no substantial effect upon the economy of existing counties. The legislation permits the enlargement of any municipality by means of annexation, including cities and separated towns as well as urban municipalities within a county. When any large town within a county attains the necessary population it is permitted to become a city, notwithstanding the consequent transfer of what may be a very large proportion of the assessment of the county in which it is located. The Board has already drawn attention to the fact that this very County sustained a serious loss of assessment when Brantford became a City in 1877. It is prepared to concede, as a matter of course, that in dealing with any particular application due consideration must be given to the effect of a proposed annexation upon the county and the remaining municipalities within the county, especially where large areas are involved. Nevertheless, in the opinion of the Board, the policy of the Legislature throughout, clearly apparent from its various enactments, has been to impose no rigid and artificial restrictions upon the growth and expansion of the thriving towns and cities of the Province in order to preserve the fixed boundaries, or even the existence, of adjoining municipalities including counties. In the result, the Board must decline to give effect to this objection on the substantial ground that it would require the Board to assume responsibilities and determine policies which are completely beyond its jurisdiction.

It seems desirable at this point to draw attention to a recent important change in the legislation which, in the opinion of the Board, removes much of the force of the objection which has just been discussed. Under the new Part I of The Municipal Act, enacted by 1954, cc. 56 and 57, the Board was given a new and significant ancillary power with respect to annexations where an adjoining municipality or a county will lose by annexation 15 per cent or more of its assessment and in the opinion of the Board an undue burden will be placed upon it as a result. The Board may now authorize and direct compensating grants to be paid by the annexing municipality during a period of not more than five years after the effective date of the annexation, for such amounts as may be agreed upon or, failing agreement, as the Board may deem equitable. This allows municipalities and counties sustaining a substantial loss of taxable resources as a result of annexation a reasonable time to reduce their respective organizations and expenditures and to consider their position. It would appear that in the light of the evidence presented to the Board on this application both the County and the Township have a *prima facie* case for relief under this legislation, but it is unnecessary and undesirable that the Board should attempt to exercise this new power at this time. It is hoped that the City, the Township and the County, in view of their fine past record in negotiating voluntary agreements on similar matters, will be able to reach a satisfactory agreement on this question. If this proves to be impossible within a reasonable time, the Board upon application will determine the matter after a supplementary hearing and due notice thereof.

As a second main objection it was submitted on behalf of the Township that even if the City had used all the area now within its boundaries, it had achieved "a reasonable balance of assessment" and did not need the lands in question. The Township, on the other hand, it was claimed, urgently required the lands for additional industrial and commercial assessments to enable it to provide economically the services needed for its new and expanding residential areas. It is true that the area sought by the City includes not only much of the existing industrial assessment located in the Township but also large areas designated as future industrial sites. Nevertheless, it seems to the Board that this line of argument ignores the basic facts of the situation.

Admittedly the urgency of the Township's need for additional non-residential assessment is due to the disproportionate amount of its residential development in recent years and the resulting demand for urban services in the areas where that development has occurred. But with the existing and potential industrial areas which the Township is so anxious to retain the City also proposes to annex practically the whole of the adjacent urbanized area where residential development has already taken place or is in prospect. The Township would certainly have a sound basis for objection if it were deprived of its present or potential industrial assessment and left with an extensive residential development requiring urban service. The proposal now before the Board, however, when carefully examined, would appear to be entirely fair to the remaining Township. In the opinion of the Board, the responsibilities to be transferred to the City are at least equal to, if not much greater than, the probable increase in tax-producing resources. If, on the other hand, the argument is based on the theory that the urbanized areas in the Township have now been provided with all the services they need or should have, and that the Township can now look forward to a general reduction in the tax-burden on homes and farms alike as a result of an ever increasing industrial development, the Board cannot accept such an optimistic view. In its experience the percentage of industrial and commercial assessment in suburban townships such as this seldom approaches that of the adjacent central city, while the demand for additional services from the expanding residential areas almost invariably outruns the ability to supply them. As for the very considerable agricultural area in the Township, there is nothing in the evidence to justify the view that it requires the alleged benefit of industrial assessment in addition to favourable consideration in the matter of Provincial grants and subsidies.

From another point of view it seems to the Board that the Township's alleged "need" of the area is based on a misconception frequently encountered in annexation applications. A municipal corporation does not exist for its own sake. It is created primarily to provide and maintain essential local services required by the area which, for the time being, is included in its boundaries. It has no claim to the lands in that area which is comparable to the interest of an owner. If conditions in the area change to the extent that the municipal services required can be more efficiently or economically provided by an adjoining municipality, nothing is lost or gained except the duty and responsibility of providing necessary services. If the cost of supplying those services is less than the tax revenue derived there may be a loss in one sense, but is it a loss which gives the remaining municipality any just cause for complaint? In the opinion of the Board, in the present case the vital question is not whether one municipality or the other has a greater "need" of the area in question. It is much more a question whether the area needs one of the municipalities more than the other. When the evidence is reviewed from this point of view, the Board is forced to the conclusion that the area has reached a stage in its development when its present and future service-needs can best be supplied by the City. This conclusion is supported by the opinions of the majority of the Township residents who appeared at the hearing and by the highly unusual circumstance that there was no evidence of widespread organized opposition to the City's proposal on the part of the ratepayers in the affected area. Those who appeared voluntarily to support the application almost invariably mentioned their need for services which the Township has so far been unable to supply.

The third major objection advanced on behalf of the Township was to the effect that the City's application was made too late, and that it should have taken steps to extend its boundaries before the Township had built up a new urban community outside the City. On behalf of the City it was admitted that annexation proceedings might well have been commenced some years ago and in explanation of the delay reference was made to an accumulation of City problems at the end of the war and a failure to foresee the extent of post-war expansion common to nearly all the industrial cities in the Province. This argument is familiar to the Board as a result of previous hearings. The proper timing of an annexation application presents many practical problems and the question whether annexation should take place before or after the urban development in the adjacent areas has commenced gives rise to sincere difference of opinion. In the present case the Board agrees that, in the light of what has happened, the City should have taken steps to provide for its outward expansion long before it did. The Board does not agree, however, that this delay justifies a dismissal of the present application. This contention of the Township implies that it should now be permitted to surround the City with what is, in effect, a new town or city that will be practically identical with the existing City in everything but its name and its political organization. In the opinion of the Board, the undesirable results of such a development are too obvious to require further mention. The urban growth of the Township is part and parcel of the growth of the City and on the evidence there was no basis for the contention that it was or is an independent phenomenon. The municipal services now required by the area are substantially identical with those required and supplied in the City and in the interests of efficiency and economy alone they should be planned, constructed and financed by a single authority. In advancing the present application, the City has recognized its obligation to provide for its own growth by making the financial and other resources of the present City available to assist in the development of the adjoining area. In the opinion of the Board, notwithstanding the objections of the Township authorities, it is still not too late to undertake this task.

By way of defence, and against the objections of counsel for the City, counsel for the respondents suggested certain alternative proposals which they contended might provide a solution for the problem before the Board. The Board does not propose to discuss the merits of these alternatives for the main reason that all of them appear to require either far-reaching changes in the whole municipal structure or special legislation designed to meet the problems of this particular area and this particular County. It was seriously suggested, for example, that the Board should dismiss the present application and then seek the co-operation of various Provincial departments in undertaking extensive investigations with a view to the setting-up of a new system of county government to include as a basic feature the inclusion of cities within the county structure and a very considerable enlargement of county functions. A section of the Township's official brief proposed the establishment of "a consolidated municipal corporation set up for the purpose of providing those services which are needed by the whole of the area." It suggested the financing of this structure by a uniform assessment and the establishment of a "consolidated council." These and other alternatives were obviously presented on the assumption that the Board would find that a definite and serious problem existed requiring some immediate solution, and in the hope that the Board would see fit to reject the solution proposed by the City. In view of the evidence disclosed the assumption, at least, was justified. So far as the alternative solutions are concerned it is sufficient to say that in the opinion of the Board it is not called upon to deal in this application with proposals involving a fundamental change in Provincial policy or matters, however important and interesting, which are clearly beyond its jurisdiction.

Returning now to the basic question whether the City, as applicant, has sufficiently satisfied the onus of showing the need for a substantial extension of its boundaries into the neighbouring Township, the Board, after full consideration of both the evidence and the substantial objections raised on behalf of the respondents, is quite satisfied that the answer must be in the affirmative. It has studied with some care the course of development of the municipalities concerned including the County, and especially the nature of the areas now sought to be annexed. It is well aware of the difficulties and problems which follow a major readjustment of municipal boundaries and is fully conscious of its responsibilities in dealing wth an application of this kind. The comparatively recent expansion in this area is undoubtedly a product of great changes which have occurred in the economy of the Province and the entire nation during and since the second world war and it is not surprising that in this important industrial area the City's boundaries, established so many years ago, have been found to be inadequate. Moreover, in the opinion of the Board there is a serious danger that the growth and prosperity of the entire area will be halted or checked by a failure to establish a more realistic boundary as a necessary part of the reorganization and improvement of municipal services which are necessary if the Brantford area is to take its proper place in the expanding economy of the Province. It may be true that annexation is not always feasible or even desirable as a solution of the problem of City growth. In the present case, however, the Board has found no good reason why this normal and logical method of providing for the growth of such a city as Brantford should not be resorted to.

There remains, however, the question whether the location and extent of the area proposed to be annexed should be approved. It was strongly urged on behalf of the Township that the area sought greatly exceeded any conceivable present or future needs of the City and at first glance it might appear that the proposal to add an area more than twice as large as the existing City is unduly ambitious. On closer examination, however, it is apparent that the City council had, in fact, given long and careful consideration to the problem of the location of the new boundaries and that it had also obtained a survey and report from a competent professional consultant before coming to a decision. Without reviewing in detail the opinions of the consultant, who gave evidence on behalf of the City and whose views and conclusions were the subject of vigorous cross-examination, the Board is of the opinion that, on the whole, sound and well-recognized planning principles have been followed in determining the location of the proposed new boundaries. Although the total area is 7,900 acres as compared with a present City of 3,292 acres, a very considerable quantity of lowlying land lying south of the City is included chiefly for the purpose of recognizing the river as a natural southern boundary. In addition railway lands and lands occupied by tax-exempt institutions require approximately 300 acres and it is estimated that the developed residential areas have already taken up 2000 acres of the remainder. As a result less than half of the area proposed to be annexed, or some 3,800 acres, will be available for present and future industrial use and future residential expansion, including the lands required for parks, streets, schools and public buildings. Some 1,400 acres are to be set aside for industrial and commercial use, including the lands now used or held for such purposes. This will leave an area of about 2,500 acres available for future residential development, which will be sufficient to provide for an additional population of about 30,000 persons with a density of 11.5 persons per acre.

The question whether such a great increase in population should be expected and provided for depends to some extent upon an appraisal of factors affecting the probable rate of industrial expansion in this part of the Province, and other matters beyond the scope of this inquiry. It may well be that the City will not be called upon to provide for such a large increase in population for many years, However, it must be remembered that the problem has grown to its present proportions chiefly because of a failure to recognize the implications of a pronounced shifting of the population of the country from rural to urban centres and a very considerable increase in immigration since the war, coupled with a serious underestimate of the extent of post-war expansion. In the opinion of the Board the decision of the council to apply for sufficient territory to provide for its growth over a lengthy period is to be preferred to a policy of frequent piecemeal annexations. Physical and topographical features of the area clearly impose natural geographic limitations upon the City's growth not only to the west and to the south but also to the north. The presently undeveloped lands to the east and north-east of the present City are definitely in the path of development and will eventually require services which the City alone can supply. Their inclusion within the City at the present time should lead to no injustice in the matter of assessment and taxation if well-established principles of equitable assessment are followed and services are not prematurely extended. This applies particularly to the lands now used for farming purposes and the holdings of the rather considerable number of veterans who have purchased under The Veterans' Land Act and who are not yet in a position to sell or subdivide their lands. Although the area intended for future residential and industrial growth is undoubtedly large consideration must be given to changing standards of desirable population density, an increasing demand for more open space in residential neighbourhoods, more parks and public places and the demand for larger industrial sites to accommodate modern plants and ample off-street parking and loading facilities. Of paramount importance is the necessity for avoiding for a long period of years a repetition of the confusion and controversy involved in another major annexation proposal and the serious interference with the orderly administration of local municipal affairs which cannot be avoided when important boundary-changes are made. For these reasons the Board has concluded that on the whole evidence the entire area described in the application should be annexed to the City. This should not interfere with such minor readjustments of the proposed boundary as may be agreed upon by the respective councils in order to meet any practical difficulty which has become apparent since the hearing. It is desirable, however, that any amendment of this nature should be brought before the Board prior to the preparation and issue of a formal order.

As to the date when the annexation should become effective, the Board is firmly of the opinion that in view of the length of time which has elapsed since the matter first became the subject of serious discussion in the community the effective date should not be postponed for another year. In the Board's view the problems giving rise to this application are in urgent need of solution and no good purpose will be served by further delay. The effective date will therefore be the 1st January 1955. In accordance with the existing legislation, after the expiration of 28 days from the official mailing of copies of this decision a formal order will be issued providing for the annexation to the City of Brantford of the portions of the Township of Brantford described in the application and in Schedule "A" to this decision to be effective on 1st January 1955. However, for all the purposes of the annual election of the councils and local boards of the City and the Township, including the qualifications of electors and candidates, the nomination and election of candidates who will hold office during the year 1955, the formal order will provide for an earlier effective date, and if necessary will fix the dates for the nomination and election of candidates in both municipalities. In the meantime, and during the waiting-period, there would appear to be no reason why the officials of the municipalities concerned should not commence the preparation of supplementary voters' lists for the purpose of the December elections. As the material before the Board does not include any proposed redivision of the City into wards, the Board's order will direct that for the purposes of the 1954 election in the City the boundaries of the existing wards are to be extended on their present courses to the newly-established boundary of the enlarged City. All adjustments of assets and liabilities as between the municipalities, including the County, affected by this order will be made as of 1st January 1955, but, as previously indicated, the amounts of the compensating grants to be paid by the City to the Township and the County should be the subject of a special supplementary application and hearing if the parties are unable to agree.

In accordance with the Board's usual policy there will be no order as to costs except that the City will be required to pay the Board's fees, in an amount to be fixed at a later date, together with the cost of reporting the proceedings.

RE TORONTO AND MIMICO
Ontario. Municipal Board. 1953

CUMMING Q.C. Chairman and MOORE O.L.S. Vice-Chairman, signed the decision and recommendations of the Board: ... [The] council of the city on February 2, 1950 adopted its by-law Number 17,847 authorizing an application to the board for an order amalgamating the city with Forest Hill, Long Branch, Swansea, Leaside, Mimico, New Toronto, Weston, East York, North York, York and substantial portions of Etobicoke and Scarborough. [The City of Toronto and the Town of Mimico were applicants, the other municipalities and the County of York and the Township of Toronto were respondents.]

In a written decision dated May 8, 1950 the board ruled that it could not proceed with the Toronto application on the ground that the enabling legislation did not authorize an order for the amalgamation of one or more municipalities with parts of adjoining municipalities. Following this decision the council of the city on May 15, 1950 passed the by-law authorizing the application now before the board.... The city seeks an order "amalgamating" the city with the twelve respondent municipalities and there seems to be no doubt that under the legislation relied upon, the board has sufficient power to issue such an order notwithstanding its far-reaching implication.... It seems to be quite clear that in requesting an order for amalgamation the city is asking for the complete dissolution of all thirteen existing municipal corporations and the creation in their stead of a new city, under a name to be chosen by the board, having jurisdiction over the entire geographical area now included in the existing municipalities. The creation of such a city would result in the separation of the twelve suburbs from the County of York so that the present county is vitally interested in the issues raised by the application....

In direct contrast to the city's proposal for complete dissolution of the existing muncipalities, the Mimico application proposes that they should continue but with reduced powers and responsibilities and that there should be created an entirely new authority for the joint administration of a number of services specified in the application. The area sought to be included is almost the same as the area proposed for amalgamation but parts of Scarborough and Etobicoke are omitted. The Mimico application was opposed throughout by all the other municipalities including the city and the county. Counsel for Mimico made it very clear that his municipality preferred the wider proposal of the city but asked that the board grant the order sought in the Mimico application if the city's application should not succeed.... The public hearing of both applications commenced on June 19, 1950 and proceeded steadily notwithstanding a number of unavoidable adjournments and delays until the conclusion of oral argument on June 7, 1951 when the board's decision was reserved....

Prior to the opening of the public hearing counsel for the city filed with the board an admirable written summary of the case for amalgamation and the facts which he hoped to prove in support of the city's application. The central theme was the contention that the entire area had become a single community in every respect except its form of local government and that the existing division of jurisdiction was impeding or blocking its progress. He referred to the lack of adequate community planning on an area basis, the need for unified control of water supply, sewage and drainage disposal, public transportation and arterial highways, and the failure of the municipalities to agree upon such matters as parks and low cost housing projects. An additional series of submissions referred to the alleged advantages of unification of administrative and operating civic departments in the interests of efficiency and economy. The third and perhaps the most important part of the city's case as summarized in the submission and developed throughout the hearing involved the proposal for sharing of resources and all responsibilities by means of complete amalgamation. Reference was made to the fact that certain municipalities have a preponderance of industry while others have little or none and to the resulting variations in the burden of taxation falling upon the owners and occupants of homes and in the standards of education and other services supplied. The present and future financial problems of the area were referred to at length and it was contended on behalf of the city that "the financial fabric of the thirteen municipalities should be available for the provision of public services for the entire community."

In their formal submissions counsel for the respondents for the most part recognized the need for co-ordination of certain services but vigorously denied that it was necessary to abolish the local governments to obtain the benefit of co-ordinated action. They also doubted the alleged efficiency and economy of administrative centralization and attacked the proposal for an overall sharing of resources and responsibilities. Each respondent claimed that its residents were satisfied with the prevailing standard of service or were in any event unwilling to pay higher taxes to secure higher standards, and local variations in service requirements were emphasized. Throughout the hearing the respondents made a concerted attempt to show errors, extravagance and inefficiency on the part of the city in handling its own problems and claimed that these alleged faults of the existing city government would spread throughout the area in the event of amalgamation. Moreover, all the respondents contended that amalgamation would result in increased overall taxation without any corresponding improvement in municipal service.

In the evidence given at the hearing and in the subsequent argument, the alleged advantages and disadvantages of amalgamation as a solution of the metropolitan problem were developed at great length. The board in this decision cannot attempt any lengthy review of its consideration of the facts and arguments relied upon by the contending parties. The board has attempted to study the whole question fairly and impartially in the light of the evidence and argument, and has reached certain general conclusions which will be stated as briefly as possible.

In the opinion of the board there are certainly many obvious advantages in a completely centralized and consolidated form of local government which would follow an outright amalgamation of the thirteen municipalities. The substitution of one municipal government for thirteen would remove all existing divisions of jurisdiction and would undoubtedly expedite the planning, construction or acquisition of adequate co-ordinated water supply and sewage disposal systems, urgently needed arterial highways, major parks and recreational areas, an extended public transportation system and other physical needs of the area. Similarly amalgamation would provide a drastic solution to all problems attributable to the existing inequitable and illogical distribution of taxable resources and would make such resources available to provide the service needs of the entire region. All borrowing powers would be concentrated in a single authority and capital expenditures could be planned and undertaken on a priority basis according to need and would be secured by the combined assets and tax paying powers of the entire area. There can be no doubt that a single government could provide the type of centralized control which is essential to the adoption and implementation of a sound program of capital expenditure and the need for such a program in view of the important capital improvements required in almost every part of the area is self-evident. Again under a single government the development of the area could be directed and controlled by a single authority according to a sound comprehensive regional plan and conflicting official or unofficial local plans of development could be harmonized.

These outstanding and important advantages of the city's proposal were clearly established by the evidence and skilfully and ably developed in the supporting arguments of counsel for the applicants. Nevertheless, the board after giving the most earnest consideration to the whole evidence has come to the conclusion that there are a number of serious objections to the proposal for amalgamation which, in the humble opinion of the board, are sufficient to outweigh its manifest advantages as a possible solution of the local government problem in the Toronto area at this time.

In the first place the Board has been forced to conclude that the issue of any order for the amalgamation of these thirteen municipalities comprising a very large and important city, four towns, three villages and five townships would result in immediate and prolonged administrative confusion of the most serious kind. Only those familiar with the great complexity of the administrative machinery developed by urban municipalities under modern conditions are in a position to appreciate the probable results of any attempt to compel the merger of the great variety of local services now provided by the city and its suburbs. Throughout the hearings, the board was impressed with the very considerable variation in administrative organizations and procedures in the various local governments. Departments having the same name perform different functions in different places. In the city, as might have been expected, divisions and subdivisions of departmental activity have apparently been carried to the extreme and the number of agencies and officials performing specialized functions is very large. In many of the suburbs procedures and methods of administrative accounting have been improvised and developed to meet local needs. In the field of education almost every type of school board permitted under existing legislation has been established and there are greatly varying degrees of centralization of authority and equally varied methods of administration. Undoubtedly this complex organization could in time be re-organized and adapted to serve the purposes of a vast consolidated city government, but, in the opinion of the board, the process of adjustment would be immensely complicated by sectional differences, ignorance of local conditions and a great number of difficult personnel problems which would prolong the period of adjustment almost indefinitely. In the meantime administrative conditions could easily become chaotic.

In the second place, in the opinion of the board, the immediate creation of a single municipal government would result in a substantial increase of taxation due to the practical necessity of bringing all suburban wage and salary scales and working conditions up to city levels, which in most cases are higher than in the suburbs. In addition, residents of various parts of the metropolitan area would be inclined to insist upon being provided services equivalent to those enjoyed in other areas and a single municipal council or board of education would find it difficult, if not impossible, to resist the pressure of these demands. In the light of the evidence and statistical information available the board is also inclined to agree with the contention of the respondents that in the larger municipalities with complex administrative problems costs tend to increase with the size of the municipality, chiefly because of the larger number of employees per unit of population; and that per capita costs in general tend to increase with the size of the municipality. Moreover, the popular notion that a large city is able to pay more than a small one and to afford an almost endless list of desirable but unnecessary expenditures regardless of its true financial position cannot be ignored in any consideration of the probable cost of amalgamation.

A third and very serious objection to the scheme of local government proposed by the city is the proposed concentration of all municipal duties and responsiblities in a single all-powerful council which would be expected to deal wisely and adequately with both local and metropolitan problems. The board heard from many witnesses factual accounts of the actual operations of the local councils and it was impressed with the time expended in detailed consideration of a great variety of local problems and the nature and volume of the business transacted in numerous and lengthy meetings of the councils and their various committees. In theory municipal councils may be said to be primarily policy forming bodies and the detailed administration of the affairs of the municipality according to the policies determined by the councils should be left to the operating departments and the appointed civic officials. In practice, however, as the evidence adduced before the board showed very clearly, a great amount of time is required for the consideration of long detailed committee reports, the hearing of individuals and delegations, and the discussion of a great variety of purely local problems and conditions. This type of local government involving direct and personal contacts between the electors and the elected representatives in regular or special meetings of the council or of its committees, and at ratepayers' meetings and by means of personal interviews or telephone messages, is considered to be the right and privilege of local taxpayers and the primary function of local councils and elected bodies. Even in the existing organization the political necessity of providing this kind of service all too often prevents adequate consideration of major matters of policy affecting the entire municipality. It is almost common knowledge that nearly all locally elected bodies, large or small, are compelled, with or without their consent, to operate in a similar manner. It seems to the board that under these circumstances it is unrealistic to expect that any single municipal council can be expected to undertake the burdens and responsibilities of the existing local governments in this area and, at the same time, to give sufficient consideration to the many difficult problems confronting the metropolitan area as a whole and to provide the kind of leadership it requires. The proposal of the city assumes that a single city council can cope with all the local, sectional and regional problems of the present local governments in an area of more than two hundred and forty square miles with a present population of well over a million persons. The board cannot accept this fundamental assumption. On the contrary, it is convinced that one essential of a sound metropolitan government for the Toronto area must be the separation of local and metropolitan municipal functions and duties.

A fourth serious objection to the city's proposal has been the subject of anxious consideration by the board throughout the hearing. Briefly stated, the board has entertained grave doubt whether the need for reform of local government in this area justifies and requires the complete dissolution of the existing municipal institutions and the creation of a form of government which appears to be bitterly opposed by eleven of the thirteen local municipalities concerned. The applicants attempted to persuade the board that the respondents' opposition to the proposal for outright amalgamation was more formal than real and that it did not represent the views of the great majority of ratepayers now residing in the suburbs. The board considers it extremely significant that this contention was not supported by formal or informal submissions which would justify a finding that the objecting municipal councils did not substantially represent the views of their ratepayers. Nor can the board in any way agree with the somewhat cynical view that the appointed and elected officials of the local municipalities who, notwithstanding widely publicized contrary opinions, appeared before the board to explain carefully and intelligently their views on this very controversial issue, and voluntarily submitted themselves to vigorous cross-examination, were, after all, merely protecting their own positions.

The board heard the evidence and observed the demeanour of a succession of apparently competent and intelligent local municipal leaders and officials and it is convinced on the whole evidence that they were all genuinely alarmed at the prospect of the complete dissolution of a form of government which, whatever its deficiencies with respect to the needs of the larger area, was in their view serving an important and useful purpose in providing the kind of local government needed and desired by the local communities. In brief, they could not bring themselves to believe that the form of metropolitan government desired by the city could be properly called a local government. To them the complete loss of their local autonomy meant domination by the central city through its concentrated voting power regardless of any system of representation by population or any proposed division of the proposed new city into wards. On the whole, the board must agree with the main contention of the respondents that although the type of government proposed by the city might be strong, efficient and well organized, it would not be a local government.

The board fully appreciates that any major proposal for alteration of local municipal boundaries brings a strong emotional reaction and an illogical resistance to change in any form. It has not hesitated in the past to exercise the very wide discretionary powers entrusted to it by the legislature and to order substantial annexations in the best interests of the great majority of persons concerned, nothwithstanding the objections of a minority. In the present case the board is charged with the grave responsibility of determining whether the city's proposal is the only acceptable solution of the local government problem in this area, and that it must therefore be forced upon the unwilling local municipalities. The practical and technical advantages of complete consolidation must be frankly admitted. They are comparable with similar advantages in a completely centralized totalitarian form of national government. Local government in a democracy, however, at least to the great majority of Ontario people, means a government which is very close to the local residents and is carried on by duly elected local leaders who offer their services from time to time in the interests of their local community and who learn at the same time something of the duties and responsibilities of public office. The applicants have failed to convince the board that this traditional method of handling local affairs has no place in an acceptable plan for a better form of metropolitan government in the Toronto area, and that outright amalgamation is the only answer. The city's application must therefore be dismissed.

The form of metropolitan organization proposed in the Mimico application is in direct contrast to the single centralized city government requested by Toronto. It is based upon a plan provided for in Section 22 of The Municipal Act (first enacted in 1946). The first subsection is in the following words:

"22. (1) Upon the application of a municipality as defined in *The Department of Municipal Affairs Act* for the creation of an area consisting of the applicant municipality or a part thereof and one or more other municipalities or parts thereof for the joint administration therein of education, fire and police protection, planning, highways, sewers, sewage disposal, garbage disposal, public health including hospitals and hospitalization, welfare including unemployment relief, parks or any public utility as defined by *The Department of Municipal Affairs Act,* the Municipal Board may by order on such terms as it deems expedient create such area or a greater or smaller area for any or all of such purposes."

Pursuant to this legislation the town council, by a by-law passed on February 4, 1947, authorized an application for an order

"for the creation of an area for the joint administration therein of education, fire and police protection, administration of justice, health and welfare, planning, sewage disposal and public utilities including transportation and main highways."

The by-law proposes that the area of joint administration should include the city, New Toronto, Mimico, Long Branch, Weston, Swansea, Forest Hill, Leaside, York and East York in their entirety, and "the urban sections" of Etobicoke, North York and Scarborough. The portions of the three last mentioned townships to be included in the area are not described in the by-law and it must therefore be assumed that the town expects the board to define the limits of the "urban sections" in any order to be issued as a result of the application. The question whether the board has jurisdiction to supplement an application by the addition of detailed descriptions not included in the authorizing by-law was not discussed by counsel on the hearing. It should also be pointed out that although the board clearly has jurisdiction under the legislation to create an area for any or all of the purposes set out in the section there does not appear to be any power to include "administration of justice" as requested by Mimico, and it may be doubted whether there is any power to confine the joint management of highways to "main" highways only.

Notwithstanding these technical objections the proposal must be carefully examined on its merits as a possible approach to the problem of providing a better form of local government in the Toronto area. The question to be decided, in the light of the evidence and the enabling legislation, is whether this scheme of metropolitan government can be expected to meet the needs of the thirteen municipalities as an alternative to the proposal for outright amalgamation made by Toronto. What, then, are the most important advantages and disadvantages of the Mimico proposal?

At the outset it seems clear that the joint management plan would meet most of the objections to amalgamation which were based upon the proposed dissolution of the existing municipalities and their local boards. It assumes the continued existence of the local units and the full exercise of their present powers with respect of all matters except those which are to be jointly administered. In direct contrast to the concentration in a single elected authority of all municipal powers with respect to both local and metropolitan affairs, the legislation definitely accepts the principle that there should be a separation of the powers and duties which are deemed to be the concern of the area as a whole from the purely local responsibilities left with the existing councils . . . Although the intended relationships of the new authority to existing municipal and educaitional institutions are not too clear it seems to this board that the proposal to retain local councils for local purposes must be acknowledged to be a definite advantage of the plan now under consideration.

In the second place the board feels that the joint management plan might be reasonably expected to remove most, if not all, of the difficulties which are the result of the present division of jurisdiction between the thirteen independent municipalities with respect to the administration of the important group of services named in the application. . . .

Turning now to the disadvantages of the joint management scheme proposed by Mimico, the board is compelled to resort to a more detailed analysis of the legislation in the absence of any guidance from the results of actual experience. The legislation has been in force for more than five years but, so far as the board is aware, it has been invoked only once, when the Town of Burlington in 1947 applied for and obtained an order for the creation of an area, including the town and part of the adjoining Township of Nelson, for the joint management of a public water system. The board does not have available sufficient information to describe or evaluate in detail the results of that interesting experiment which was limited to the operation of a single self-supporting utility. Nevertheless, basic defects in the legislation were clearly indicated.

The most serious objection to the joint management plan outlined in Section 22 is found in the first subsection quoted above, which refers only to the joint *administration* of certain specified services, and is apparently limited to facilities and services existing on the date of the creation of the area. The Board of Management, although it is to be an elected body with power to impose levies for its purposes similar to that possessed by a county, can only "administer." It is given no power to plan or construct extensions or improvements of existing services or to build new schools, public works and other projects which might be needed throughout the area. It would therefore be quite powerless to provide the most urgent requirements of the metropolitan area during the present period of rapid expansion. . . . If debenture financing is required, the by-laws must apparently be passed and the debentures issued by the existing municipalities. It is hardly necessary to say that in view of the need for new capital works and extensions in the Toronto metropolitan area the vague and limited powers given to a board of management under the legislation are entirely inadequate.

A number of other objections cannot be ignored. For example, the term of office of the elected members is limited to two years and the election must be by wards. It is at least doubtful whether either of these provisions can be expected to provide a satisfactory board of management in view of the special problems of a very large metropolitan area, the need for long range policies and the desirability of attracting intelligent, public-spirited candidates free from local affiliations and interested primarily in the problems of the entire area. It is also quite possible that the administration of some self-supporting utilities might well be committed to an appointed commission but no provision is made in the legislation by which the Board of Management can delegate any of its functions or duties. . . .

After weighing all the possible advantages and disadvantages of the Mimico proposal, the board has concluded that, on the whole, the application must be denied. . . .

NOTE. The discussion of "The Evidence", on pp. 9–22, provides an excellent summary account of the Toronto metropolitan area. In the last fifty pages of its "decisions and recommendations" the Board proceeded to outline its views of a proper solution for the metropolitan Toronto problems, to be reached by special legislation. The Board's decision is dated January 20, 1953. Contemporaneously the province was preparing "Bill 80," which was passed as S.O., 1953, c. 73, *An Act To Provide for the Federation of the Municipalities in the Toronto Metropolitan Area for Certain Financial and Other Purposes.* The scheme of the Act is to create a "county" with much broader powers than ordinary counties in Ontario enjoy. An Ontario county is essentially a federation of the constituent municipalities. For a comparison of the Board's recommendations and the Act, see Milner, "The Metropolitan Toronto Plan," (1957) 105 *U. of Pa. Law Rev.* 570, especially at pp. 577–587.

THE MUNICIPALITY OF METROPOLITAN TORONTO ACT, 1953
Ontario. Statutes. 1953, Chapter 73

179. (1) The Minister of Planning and Development shall define a planning area under *The Planning Act*, which shall include the Metropolitan Area and such other municipalities or parts of municipalities as in his opinion constitute a complete planning unit, and the name of the planning area shall be The Metropolitan Toronto Planning Area.

(2) The Metropolitan Corporation shall be the designated municipality within the meaning of *The Planning Act* for the purposes of the said planning area.

(3) The planning board for the planning area shall be constituted as provided in *The Planning Act* except that the membership of the board shall at all times include two persons recommended by the Metropolitan School Board and approved by the Minister of Planning and Development.

(4) Subject to subsection 5, all planning areas and subsidiary planning areas heretofore established, which are included in The Metropolitan Toronto Planning Area, shall be subsidiary planning areas within the said planning area.

(5) On the day The Metropolitan Toronto Planning Area is defined, the planning area constituted under *The Planning Act* and consisting of the whole of the County of York, and the Toronto and York Planning Board, are hereby dissolved.

(6) Nothing in subsection 4 shall affect any official plan in effect in any subsidiary planning area.

(7) When the Minister has approved an official plan adopted by the Metropolitan Council,

(a) any official plan then in effect in a subsidiary planning area affected thereby shall be amended to conform therewith;

(b) no official plan of a subsidiary planning area shall be adopted that does not conform therewith;

(c) no public work, as defined in *The Planning Act*, shall be undertaken, and no by-law shall be passed, by any municipality or local board within The Metropolitan Toronto Planning Area, that does not conform therewith.

181. The scope and genneral purpose of the official plan for The Metropolitan Toronto Planning Area shall include,

(a) land uses and consideration generally of industrial, agricultural, residential and commercial areas;

(b) ways of communication;

(c) sanitation;

(d) green belts and park areas;

(e) public transportation,

and such other matters as the Minister of Planning and Development may from time to time define under *The Planning Act*.

182. Except as provided in this Part, the provisions of *The Planning Act* shall continue to apply.

NOTE. The Minister defined the area embraced by the Municipality of Metropolitan Toronto, that is, Toronto plus the twelve suburbs, *and* the townships adjoining the metropolitan area municipalities, together with the municipalities contained within the outer limits of the townships. This definition added thirteen more municipalities to the thirteen area municipalities, making a total of twenty-seven municipalities in the Metropolitan Toronto Planning Area, if the Metropolitan Municipality is itself counted separately.

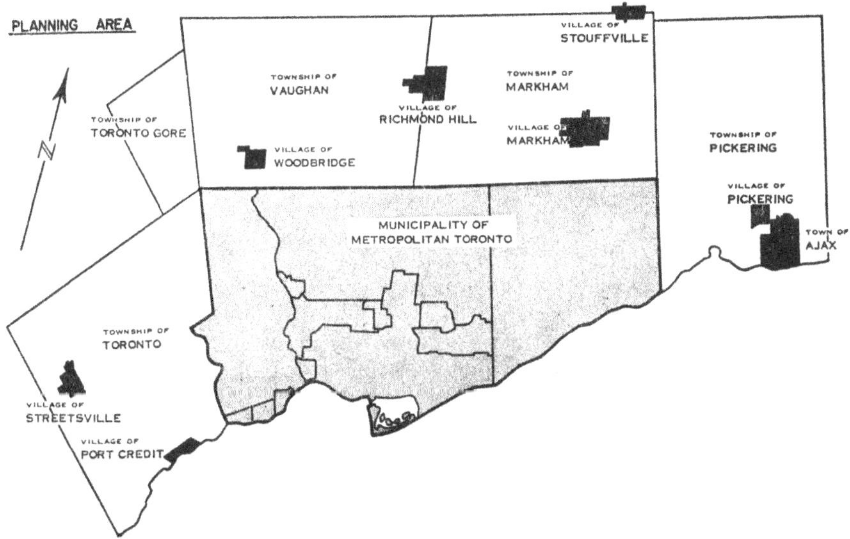

NOTE ON NOVA SCOTIAN METROPOLITAN PLANNING COMMISSIONS. By the addition of Part V to the *Planning Act* introduced by S.N.S., 1956, c. 43, s. 2, provision is made for metropolitan planning commissions to be established by Ministerial order upon application of two or more councils. The order specifies, among other things, "the cities, towns and municipalities which shall be represented on the commission," the area over which the commission has power, the number and qualifications of members to be appointed by "each participating unit" and the number to be appointed by the Minister, and, their terms of office. The area and its representation may be altered by the Minister upon application by a council seeking representation or by the commission itself, to compel representation or to alter the area. The commission may, among other things, prepare and recommend to the council of any participating unit an official town plan, a plan for the orderly development of the metropolitan area or any part thereof, and a zoning by-law. A commission displaces a town planning board in respect of its activities in the metropolitan area, except that it retains its administrative powers presumably to enable it to continue to exercise its powers (if any) apart from metropolitan matters.

(*b*) *The Larger Region*

The planner would probably regard the metropolitan planning area as something less than a *regional* planning area, although he might have some difficulty with his fellow planners in agreeing on *the* definition of a region. One cynical observer has suggested that a region is the next largest area after the last one the planner failed to conquer. It is not difficult to show that many of the factors that influence the growth and change of a city lie outside its boundaries, and even outside the boundaries of the adjacent municipalities. Just where to draw the line is another question. The Town of Port Credit, in Ontario, lies at the mouth of the Credit River, on Lake Ontario. If one were designing an ideal sewer system one might regard the Credit River Valley as the region, except that the northern reaches are economically unimportant to Port Credit and the Valley would be of little interest beyond the sewer system. Port Credit's "region" is hardly likely to stop at the outer boundaries of Toronto Township, which surrounds it except on the Lake side. Port Credit lies roughly between Toronto and Hamilton. Its region could, therefore, be the area between, but excluding those two cities. But the influence of those cities are not to be neglected, so its region might well embrace both. At the present time (1963), the Community Planning Branch has under way a regional study of the area bounded by Oshawa on the east and Hamilton west and south, which is approximately 2,500 square miles. Port Credit is at the centre and mustn't be overlooked. The Oshawa-Hamilton area is the commercial and secondary industrial heart of Ontario, and *its* region could be Ontario, but of course Ontario can hardly be regarded as not subject to country-wide influence, so that Ontario's region is Canada, and of course we would have to include the United States and England, where live the presidents of the great corporations that have wholly owned subsidiaries in Toronto. It is perhaps understandable that some early students of Town Planning Law in the United States have ended up teaching International Law!

Although agreement on the identity of ideal regions may be lacking, there is a general acceptance of the need for a planning area somewhere between the city and the province or state. How should the boundaries of this region be determined? By whom? What kind of planning agency should be established? Is the formula intended for metropolitan complexes good enough for the larger region? Is a regional plan necessary? What form should it take? What legal effect should it have? How should it be adopted?

THE TOWN AND RURAL PLANNING ACT

Alberta. Revised Statutes. 1955. Chapter 337

10. The Board, on its own motion, or upon receiving an application of a district planning commission or of a council made by resolution and after making such inquiries and holding such hearings as it deems sufficient may recommend to the Lieutenant Governor in Council

(*a*) the establishment of a district planning commission,
(*b*) the representation of a municipality on a commission,
(*c*) the withdrawal of a municipality from a commission,
(*d*) the establishment or alteration of a district planning area,
(*e*) the amendment of an order establishing a commission and of the regulations governing a commission, and
(*f*) the establishment of regulations governing a commission.

11. Upon the recommendation of the Board the Lieutenant Governor in Council may by order

(*a*) establish a district planning commission,
(*b*) establish regulations governing a commission,
(*c*) provide for the representation of a municipality on a commission,
(*d*) establish or alter a district planning area,
(*e*) withdraw a municipality from a commission, and
(*f*) amend an order establishing a commission and the regulations governing a commission.

12. (1) The order establishing a commission shall specify

(*a*) the municipalities that are to be represented on the commission and the name of the commission,
(*b*) the area, to be known as the district planning area, with respect to which the commission shall exercise its powers,
(*c*) the number of members to be appointed to the commission by each represented municipality, and
(*d*) the number of members to be appointed to the commission by the Board to represent the Province.

(2) The order may provide that two or more municipalities shall be represented on the commission by the same member who shall be appointed by the councils of those municipalities, jointly or in rotation as the order may prescribe.

14. A commission may

(*a*) study the resources and development of the district planning area with a view to preparing a general plan for the area,
(*b*) advise and assist the council of any municipality represented on the commission
 (i) in the planning and orderly development of the municipality, and
 (ii) on matters affecting planning and orderly development that are of common concern to the municipality and any other municipality or the Province.
(*c*) prepare and recommend to the council of any municipality represented on the commission a general plan, development scheme and zoning by-law, or any of them,

(*d*) promote public interest in the planning and orderly development of the district planning area,

(*e*) appoint such planning engineers, consultants and other officers as are necessary for any of the purposes of the commission.

(*f*) expend such funds as are furnished by the municipalities represented on the commission and the Province for any of the purposes of the commission, and

(*g*) exercise such rights and powers and perform such duties as may be

(i) vested in it by the Lieutenant Governor in Council, or

(ii) delegated to it by a council of a municipality represented on the commission.

(3) The order establishing a commission shall include regulations

(*a*) governing the organization of the commission, the holding of its meetings and the transaction of its business in general, and

(*b*) prescribing the proportion in which the funds required to meet the expenses of the commission shall be contributed by the Province and by the represented municipalities, and

(*c*) requiring the commission to submit annually to its members and to the Board a report on its operations during the preceding year concerning district planning, municipal planning, subdivision approvals, income and expenditure, and any other matters of major importance.

101. (1) A commission shall prepare and adopt a district general plan to secure the orderly and economical development of the district planning area as a whole.

(2) By a district general plan the commission shall

(*a*) divide the district planning area or any part thereof into zones of permitted land use categories, including low density agricultural, high density agricultural, small-holding, country residence, highway commercial, district recreational, general urban, new general urban and major industrial zones, or any of these and such other zones as the commission may deem necessary and essential for the purpose of the plan,

(*b*) define, within the limits and for the objectives established by this Part, the uses of lands and buildings permitted within each zone, in the same manner that a council might do by a zoning by-law in accordance with subsections (3) and (4) of section 80,

(*c*) establish the stages, sequence, or order of priority of development for and within each zone, and prohibit the development of any zone otherwise than in accordance with the established stages, sequence, or order of priority for that zone,

(*d*) prescribe the nature of, and the minimum regulations made pursuant to clauses (*a*) and (*b*) of subsection (6) of section 80 that are required to be contained in any zoning by-law to be put into effect within the territory of a municipality, to ensure that development therein will proceed according to the district general plan, and

(*e*) make proposals relating to roads, services, public buildings, schools, parks and other open spaces, their location and the reservation of land for these and other similar purposes.

102. A commission may study and recommend to the proper authorities concerned proposals relating to

(*a*) the adjustment of boundaries between municipalities and the annexation of territory by municipalities,
(*b*) the supply of water and the provision of sewerage facilities to the municipalities,
(*c*) the conservation of the natural resources, the prevention of the pollution of streams, the control of flooding, and the best utilization of land and resources of the district planning area, and
(*d*) the location, attraction, development, diversification, and dispersal of industry within the district planning area.

109. (1) A district general plan comes into effect upon being confirmed by the commission.

(2) When a district general plan comes into effect, every council shall
(*a*) forthwith enact and maintain in effect such a zoning by-law as may be required to give effect to the provisions of the district general plan as they affect the territory of its municipality,
(*b*) take such other action within its powers as may be necessary to give effect to, or to remove an inconsistency with, the district general plan as it affects the territory of its municipality, and
(*c*) thenceforth refrain from enacting a by-law, taking any action or undertaking a public work that conflicts with or is inconsistent with the district general plan.

113. During the interim period prior to the coming into effect of a district general plan, development occurring within the district planning area shall be guided and controlled by each municipality in accordance with a preliminary district plan which shall be prepared and adopted by a commission as soon as possible after the commission commences operation pursuant to this Part.

114. A preliminary district plan shall consist of
(*a*) a map showing the district planning area or part thereof divided into such zones or any of them as are defined in this Part and such other similar zones as the commission may deem essential for the purposes of the preliminary plan, and
(*b*) for each zone, a schedule of permitted, restricted or prohibited uses.

116. A preliminary district shall not be adopted except upon the affirmative vote of two-thirds of the members present and voting upon the resolution.

117. (1) When a preliminary district plan comes into effect every council shall
(*a*) where there is in effect in the municipality an interim development order and by-law made pursuant to Part II, cause the preliminary district plan to be used as a guide for the issuing of permits for development under the provisions of the order or by-law, and notwithstanding anything contained in the order or by-law, ensure that no permit is issued that would permit a land use at variance with or in contravention of the preliminary district plan,
(*b*) where there is in effect in the municipality a zoning by-law, forthwith amend the by-law to the extent necessary to remove any inconsistency with or variance with the preliminary district plan, or
(*c*) where there is no by-law in effect, forthwith enact a zoning by-law or commence the exercise of interim development control so

as to ensure that the provisions of the preliminary district plan are carried out within the municipality.

(2) A preliminary district plan comes into effect upon being adopted by the commission and being approved by the Board.

123. A person may appeal to the Board

(*a*) where he has requested the commission to amend a district general plan and the amendment has been refused by the commission although the council of the municipality concerned has recommended that the amendment be approved, or

(*b*) where he has requested the commission to amend a preliminary district plan and the amendment has been refused by the commission.

126. The Board, in disposing of an approval, having regard to the provisions of this Part, to the general scope and intent of the district general plan, or preliminary district plan, and to the merits and circumstances of the particular case, may

(*a*) settle the content of a preliminary district plan or district general plan and of any by-law made in conformity therewith by a council,

(*b*) determine whether a by-law, action or public work of a municipality, as in effect or as proposed, conforms to a preliminary district plan or district general plan,

(*c*) determine whether a council is conforming to, enforcing, or properly administering the provisions of a preliminary district plan or district general plan and the by-laws relevant thereto,

(*d*) require a commission to amend a preliminary district plan or district general plan, and

(*e*) require a council to adopt, amend, enforce, or administer a by-law in a manner that will cause conformity with a preliminary district plan or district general plan.

127. Except on questions of law, a decision of the Board shall be final and binding upon all parties concerned in an appeal.

99. In this Part, . . .

(*b*) "country residence zone" means a zone, characterized by special scenic qualities, in which land is used or is to be developed for groups of permanent dwellings of good construction on large sites;

(*c*) "district recreational zone" means a zone in which land is or is proposed to be provided for the recreational use of the general public in the district planning area, and in which land is used or is to be developed for summer cottages, recreational and associated uses, as well as for institutional purposes and those uses permitted in a low density agricultural zone;

(*d*) "general urban zone" means a zone in which land is used or is to be developed for general urban purposes including housing, industry other than major industry, retail and wholesale business, public or quasi-public uses, institutions, or any of them;

(*e*) "high density agricultural zone" means a zone in which land is used or is to be developed for farming, institutional, and recreational purposes, and in which land may not be subdivided into parcels of less than ten acres except in exceptional circumstances;

(*g*) "highway commercial zone" means a zone in which land may be used only for those purposes that provide essential services to the highway traffic, including service stations, garages, motels, tourist camps, roadside restaurants and refreshment stands and uses of a like nature;

(*h*) "low density agricultural zone" means a zone in which land is used or is to be developed for forestry, grazing, ranching, farming or institutional purposes or for purposes incidental to those purposes, and in which land may not be subdivided into parcels of less than twenty acres in area except in exceptional circumstances;

(*i*) "major industrial zone" means a zone in which land is used or is to be developed for manufacturing or industrial warehousing uses, and where any use that will produce, directly or indirectly, by reason of noise, odors, fumes, dust, appearance or otherwise, such effects as may be detrimental to other land uses in or outside the zone, is restricted to particular parts of the zone or is subject to special regulations, or both;

(*j*) "new general urban zone" means

(i) an area proposed by a commission as the site for the development of a new town under the provisions of *The New Towns Act*, or

(ii) an area proposed by a commission as the site of general urban development but which is at the time of zoning adjacent to but not included within the boundaries of an urban municipality,

and within which zone the permitted uses are such as may conveniently be permitted without prejudicing the later development of the area for general urban purposes;

(*k*) "small-holding zone" means a zone in which land is used or is to be developed for the same purposes as in a high density agricultural zone but within which land may be subdivided into groups of parcels of small size suitable for market gardening and similar small scale agricultural pursuits;

NOTE. A district general plan may be adopted by a vote of two-thirds of the members present and voting on the resolution, but only after thirty days notice of motion. The plan must then be confirmed by publication and the hearing of representations "by property owners and other interested persons." The confirmation must also be by a vote of two-thirds of the members present and voting on the resolution. Unless the order establishing a commission under section 12(3) (a) prescribes a quorum, presumably a vote of two of only three voting members present could adopt and confirm a district general plan. Although a preliminary district plan requires the approval of the Board, a district general plan does not.

NOTE ON DISTRICT PLANNING COMMISSIONS IN ALBERTA. There are seven District Planning Commissions in Alberta:

Peace River District	95,000 sq. mi.
Edmonton District	5,300
Calgary District	9,300
Red Deer District	8,700
Oldman River District	14,000
Medicine Hat District	11,000
Battle River District	10,700

The total area included in all districts is 154,000 square miles. The area of the province is 255,000 square miles more or less and when the proposed Athabasca River District, of 18,600 square miles, and North Saskatchewan River District, of 20,400 square miles, more or less, are established as presently proposed, about three quarters of the area of the province will be included in district planning areas. Section 100 (a) (i) limits the application of Part IV of the Act to districts having a municipality represented that has a population of over 50,000, which means only Edmonton and Calgary. Under paragraph (ii) the Lieutenant-Governor in Council, on the recommendation of the Board, may declare the Part to apply to other districts. In 1962 the Oldman River District was brought under the Part. Unless the Part applies the Commission is limited to its privileges under section 14, and it has no *duty* to plan.

The Alberta regional planning system is briefly described by Denis Cole in 11 *Community Planning Review* No. 4, (undated, c. 1961) pages 10–11, where he gives the composition of the Red Deer District, which contains the city of Red Deer (pop. 20,000), seven towns (total pop. 14,700), four rural municipalities (total pop. 33,363). The total population of the District, about 70,000, has a gross density of 9 persons per square mile.

MUNICIPAL ACT

British Columbia. Revised Statutes. 1960. Chapter 255

720. (1) On petition by the Councils of two or more municipalities in a region, the Lieutenant-Governor in Council may declare any area, including unorganized territory within the region, a planning area and define the boundaries of the area.

(2) The Lieutenant-Governor in Council may, as deemed expedient, extend, reduce, or otherwise alter the boundaries of any area declared as aforesaid.

(3) Where a planning area is declared under subsection (1), the Lieutenant-Governor in Council shall establish a board under the name of "The Regional Planning Board."

(4) The Board shall consist of one member of Council appointed by the Council of each municipality within the area and one member appointed by the Lieutenant-Governor in Council who shall hold office during pleasure.

(5) The first members of the Board shall be so appointed within one month after the establishment of the Board, and thereafter each Council shall annually, in the month of January, appoint its member for a term of one year.

(6) The term of office of each Council member, except for the initial appointment, is for one year or until his successor is appointed.

(7) The Board shall, from its own members, elect a Chairman, and shall determine its own procedure.

(8) The members of the Board shall serve without remuneration.

(9) In the case of the inability of the appointee of a municipality to perform his duties as a member of the Regional Planning Board because of illness, absence, or temporary disability, the Mayor, Reeve, or Chairman of the Council which appointed him may appoint another representative to act for the time being in place of such member.

721. (1) It is the duty of the Board to prepare regional plans applicable to the planning area, and for this purpose may appoint and employ such

planning engineers or consultants and such other persons as may be necessary, whose salaries and other remuneration shall be paid from the general funds of the Board.

(2) The Board may undertake community planning work for a member municipality on such terms and conditions as are mutually agreed upon.

722. (1) In the month of January in each year the Board shall adopt, subject to the approvals required under subsection (2), a budget of expenditures for the current year, and the budget shall be submitted to the Council of each member municipality for approval not later than the thirty-first day of January.

(2) Each Council aforesaid shall approve or reject the budget of the Board not later than the last day of February; and if at least two thirds in number of the Councils of the member municipalities approve the budget, it shall be the budget for the current year, and the Board shall not incur any liability beyond the budget. If the budget does not receive the required approvals, the Board shall amend and resubmit the amended budget to the Councils, which shall deal with the matter as expeditiously as possible.

723. (1) The Board may, by an affirmative vote of at least two-thirds of all the members thereof, adopt as the official regional plan for the planning area any regional plan prepared under section 721.

(2) Any official regional plan so adopted is in force and effect when approved

(a) by at least two-thirds in number of the member municipalities; and

(b) by the Lieutenant-Governor in Council.

(3) If, upon application of a member municipality for an amendment to the approved official regional plan, the proposed amendment fails to obtain the requisite approval of the Board, or of the member municipalities, or both, the member municipality may appeal, and the matter shall be decided by three arbitrators to be forthwith appointed as hereinafter provided; namely, the Council of the said municipality shall appoint one, the Board shall appoint another, and such two arbitrators shall appoint a third arbitrator within ten days after their appointment; but in the event of such two arbitrators not appointing a third arbitrator within the time aforesaid, the Minister shall, on application of either party, appoint such third arbitrator.

NOTE ON REGIONAL PLANNING IN BRITISH COLUMBIA. There are two regional planning boards in British Columbia. The Lower Mainland Regional Planning Board includes 28 municipalities and some unorganized territory (an unusually large part, about one-third, of the population of British Columbia lives in "unorganized territory," that is, provincial territory with no local government). The population in the region, which includes the city of Vancouver, is about 880,000.

The other region is that of the Capital Region Planning Board, consisting of six municipalities and some unorganized territory. It includes the capital city of Victoria and has a population of about 150,000.

No plans have been approved under section 723, but both boards have published a number of useful studies of planning problems in their respective regions.

NOTE ON REGIONAL PLANNING IN ONTARIO. There is no specific provision for regional planning under the Ontario Act, but from the beginning "joint planning areas" have been possible and there has been considerable use of this device, although it is used for the most part as a way of solving the metropolitan, rather than the regional, planning problem. At the end of 1961 there were 74 joint planning areas in Ontario.

The Minister of Municipal Affairs may either upon his own initiative or upon application by a council or councils, define a planning area that includes the whole or parts of two or more municipalities and theoretically such an area could be "regional" in scope, if the Minister was of the opinion that it constituted a complete planning unit. One of the municipalities is designated by the Minister and that municipal council appoints the members of the planning board for the joint planning area, subject to the approval of the Minister, who presumably takes care that the membership is to some extent representative of the whole area and not just of the designated municipality. Notwithstanding this requirement, however, the Metropolitan Toronto Planning Board had no representation for several years from the outer fringe municipalities that were within the planning area but not in the metropolitan municipality. The size and constitution of a board for a joint planning area is governed by the same sections that govern boards for single areas, but section 5 virtually authorizes the Minister to amend the Act with respect to the constitution and functions of a planning board, and he can easily enlarge the Board to any size he considers suitable for a regional planning area.

A joint planning area does not preclude local planning, but the smaller area is known as a subsidiary planning area, and may have its own planning board. The danger of overlapping jurisdiction is supposedly avoided by the Minister under section 2 (6) defining in the case of a joint planning area "the scope and general purpose of the official plan of the planning area and the functions of the planning board thereof." Misunderstanding has arisen at times.

A planning board for a joint area must submit its estimates to each council and when they are approved by the councils representing more than one-half the population of the joint planning area, they are binding on all the councils, but the apportionment may be contested before the Municipal Board by any council.

NOTE ON REGIONAL PLANNING AND REPRESENTATION. One of the most frequently raised criticisms of planning agencies in Canada, and especially in Ontario, is the removal of the planning function from the elected council into the hands of appointed planning boards or commissions. In all provinces except Ontario the choice is largely left to the council, but in Ontario the planning board is a *sine qua non* to the adoption of an official plan. This shift of initial responsibility in planning (even in Ontario the elected council has to adopt the plan before its becomes official) is said to be justified on two grounds. One is that the term of the elected council in Ontario is only one, or at best, two years, and the longer term of the appointed board member gives him a security that encourages him to take a longer view of things. The other ground is that planning should be done by people somewhat removed from the pressures of day to day government. This second ground comes suspiciously close to the often stated ideal of "taking planning out of politics", a rather remarkable ambition in a democracy dedicated to the principle of the supremacy of parliament. It is perhaps more understandable in the United States, where the democratic principle seems to be founded, in part at least, on the supremacy of the judiciary.

Whatever the justification, there seems to be a low but chronic pressure to restore planning to the elected council. But this desire is clearly unattainable in Ontario or in any other province if the planning area embraces more than one municipality. There is no elected council established for the purpose of regional planning. The problem of settling on a suitable regional planning agency may therefore be considered in part as the problem of finding the most satisfactory substitute for the elected council as the regional agency.

One possible agency in Ontario is the county council. Ontario county councils are not elected directly—the county is a kind of federation of towns, villages and townships within its boundaries (cities and "separated towns" are not "in" the county) and the county council is drawn from the local councils. The objection to the county as a regional planning unit is that the county boundaries were determined many years ago, doubtless for very legitimate purposes, but they are not suitable for contemporary planning purposes in most cases.

Another possible agency suggested for regional planning is the provincial legislature. According to this suggestion it would be feasible for the legislature to divide the province into regions and instruct its civil service to prepare "official plans" for each region, to be adopted by the house, or a committee, after approval by the Minister. The obvious objection to this procedure is the absence of any guarantee of consultation with the municipalities, whose planning would be limited to their own territory in each case. To meet this need it has been suggested that for each region a consultative committee be established, consisting of the members of the legislature for the region and representatives of the provincial departments concerned and the local councils. It might also be possible, so the suggestion goes, to co-opt representatives from federal departments and from private business. What are the advantages and disadvantages of this suggestion?

BIBLIOGRAPHY. The current popularity for regional planning has outstripped the literature on the subject, but some titles may be mentioned. In North American terms the English experience and writing on regional planning is hardly remarkable, notwithstanding that Patrick Geddes, in his *Cities in Evolution* was an early advocate of regional planning. More recently W. A. Robson (ed.), *Great Cities of the World* (1954), presents some interesting accounts of the problems of metropolitan government. See also the *Report of the Royal Commission on Local Government in Greater London 1957–60* (1960, Cmd. 1164). The Editors of Fortune, *The Exploding Metropolis* (1958), available in a paperback edition, is a collection of essays of interest. A recently published source of interesting Canadian material is the four volume set of the background papers for the "Resources for Tomorrow" Conference (1961). See especially Gertler, "Regional Planning and Development—Aims, Problems and Methods," Volume 1, pp. 393–407, including a short bibliography; Slater, "Regional Growth and Decline," Volume 1, pp. 409–417; and Hugo-Brunt "Environment as an Aspect of Regional Planning and Development," Volume 1, pp. 419–443, with photographs. On the sociological side see Greer, *Governing the Metropolis* (1962) and Carver, *Cities in the Suburbs* (1962).

(c) *New Towns*

LASH, "THE ALBERTA NEW TOWNS ACT"
Toronto. 1957. 12 University of Toronto Law Journal 98

THE Alberta New Towns Act (S.A. 1956, c. 39) provides a form of local government suited to the peculiar needs that arise when an urban centre is suddenly created where none existed before. The need for such a form of government has been felt in Alberta for a number of years. Since the end of the war, as a result of the rapid expansion of the province's economy, there has been at least one new urban community arise in each year. Until the passage of the New Towns Act, the local government needs of these new communities were provided for in a number of ways. In two cases the industrial companies concerned took responsibility for the townsite. In one case, a special act of the legislature was passed. In some other cases, the communities were left to grow as hamlets, unwanted children of rural municipalities, without any local responsibility and with a resultant lack of planning and economical development.

The problem of new towns is not peculiar to Alberta, but more in this province than in others these communities have been growing up in settled areas as well as in frontier mining or logging regions. Most other provinces have dealt with this problem by the use of special provisions in the legislation that deals with mining areas or remote and unorganized parts of their provinces. In Alberta, it was realized that the growth of a new community, because of sudden resource development or because of the decentralization of a metropolis, might occur anywhere.

Although a new town has its own peculiar local government needs and problems, it was felt desirable to fit the organization as closely as possible into the existing framework of local government in the province. Municipal organizations in Alberta are either rural or urban, and they do not overlap in boundaries or in functions. An urban municipality is either a village, town, or city and its boundaries rarely include any more than the settled subdivided lands. A rural municipality rarely includes any subdivided areas, and has few of the powers needed to provide the facilities that urban areas normally require.

Because of this basic division in the structure of local government in Alberta, it was not possible to adopt the solution used in Britain and provide for the formation of new town corporations that are not really local government units at all. In Britain, the new town corporation sees that the land is developed and built on, doing it all itself if necessary, while the existing local authority assumes the local government functions until it becomes necessary to create an urban district. In Alberta there is need for a new local authority in the first instance. At the same time, it has not often been necessary for government to undertake the functions of a development corporation. There seems to be no lack of private development corporations willing to develop and build towns; in fact some of the new towns of Alberta are the direct result of proposals originally made by such private companies.

The ordinary legislation dealing with towns and cities is valueless for the establishment of new towns because that ordinary legislation presupposes the existence of a resident population in a built-up area. Under ordinary legislation the amount of money that a council may spend or borrow for its future needs is limited by its present assessment or by what the proprietary electors are willing to assent to in annual elections. To provide adequately for new towns, however, vast programmes of capital development have to be embarked on before there is any assessment and often before there are any residents who can qualify to vote. Even after a new town has been established its assessment will not reflect its future or even its present assets, because of the lag of assessment behind development. At the same time the residents have had so little opportunity to form a cohesive society and to select their leaders that it is sometimes impossible to provide for an elected council.

The New Towns Act provides that any area of the province can be established a new town by order of the Lieutenant-Governor-in-Council. Before such an order is made, however, the proposal will be investigated by the Provincial Planning Advisory Board, whether the proposal is made by a private development company, by an existing local authority, or by an industry proposing a new development project and requiring townsite accommodation. In the course of its studies the Provincial Planning Advisory Board will find out whether the planning makes for economy and fair charges to prospective purchasers of dwellings. To do so, the Board will hold hearings, have special studies made, and perhaps call upon the Board of Public Utility Commissioners to investigate the financial aspects of the proposal.

If the Executive Council agrees with a favourable recommendation made by the Provincial Planning Board, the new town will be created, its boundaries will be set out, and a Board of Administrators will be appointed. Members of the Board of Administrators may be civil servants of the province, persons resident in the area of the new town, or representatives of organizations or companies in the vicinity of the town. If it is considered desirable, the Lieutenant-Governor-in-Council may provide that some members of the Board of Administrators should be elected. This provision is of assistance in cases where there is already some settlement in the area, and should also be of assistance in the latter stages of the life of the new town organization in providing a gradual transition from new town status to the status of an ordinary town or city.

The Lieutenant-Governor-in-Council also appoints the chairman of the Board of Administrators who is the chief executive of the town. The Board operates the new town with all the powers of an ordinary town, together with some added powers. The Board may, for example, acquire land by expropriation for any purpose whatsoever. They may expend money and issue debentures for all the purposes that a city may do. They are especially empowered to enter into agreements with owners of land and with developers regarding the subdivision of land, the provision of utilities, the prices of lots, and the methods of selling lots. They can prohibit an owner from selling or subdividing his land until such an agreement has been entered into. They can, of course, develop the town themselves without the assistance of private development companies, and they can provide temporary housing and shelter for construction workers and new residents of the town.

The Board of Administrators cannot do any of these thing, however, until they have submitted and had approved (1) comprehensive proposals for the planning and orderly development of the town, and (2) a financial programme, including an annual estimate of revenue and expenditure, the estimated amount of population growth and development, the consequent value of assessable property, and the anticipated revenues and expenditures in future years. The planning proposals have to be approved by the Provincial Planning Advisory Board, and the financial programme has to be approved by the Board of Public Utility Commissioners once in each year. Naturally, the financing proposed must be consistent with the approved development proposals, which may be changed from time to time with the approval of the Provincial Planning Board.

Once the Board of Administrators have received approval of their proposals for planning, developing, and financing the town, they may issue debentures and spend money according to the programme that has been approved. The amount of debentures is not limited to any proportion of their assessment nor to the amount of the current tax levy. The Board of Administrators also have access to a special fund of one million dollars established by the legislation. The Provincial Treasurer may make grants, or make a special loan or advance to the new town from that special fund.

For all other purposes the new town is an ordinary town, and the provisions of other acts of the legislature which have reference to towns also apply to a new town. Nevertheless, no vote of the proprietary electors takes place so long as it remains a new town, nor is there any election held other than for the purpose of electing a member of the Board of Administrators. The Act provides a procedure for turning a new town into a normal urban municipality; it is implied that a new town should not remain such any longer than necessary. However, before the new town can become an ordinary urban municipality, it must repay to the province any loans or advances received and the Board of Public Utility Commissioners and Provincial Planning Advisory Board must once again grant their approval to the change of status.

Since the Act came into force at the end of March, 1956, seven applications for the creation of new towns have been received by the Provincial Planning Advisory Board. Three of these represent townsites in the Pembina oil fields, and one is from a town developing as a result of the establishment of a new pulp mill. One was received from an existing village feeling the effects of oil development, one is an existing town within "satellite" distance of Edmonton, and one is a new satellite of Edmonton proposed by a private development company. Four of these applications have been granted and one has been refused. Two others are still under consideration and investigation by the Board.

BIBLIOGRAPHY. The new town concept stems mainly from Howard, *Garden Cities of Tomorrow* published in 1898 and reissued in 1946. The current popularity of the concept in England produced the New Towns legislation, which is critically examined in Rodwin, *The British New Towns Policy* (1956). An early disciple of Howard, Clarence Stein, applied the idea in North America in a number of places, including Kitimat in northern British Columbia. His earlier experiences are recounted in Stein, *Towards New Towns for America* (1957). For an account of Kitimat, see Clark, "Kitimat—A Saga of Canada," 49 *Canadian Geographical Journal*, 152 (1954). On the region, see Richardson, "The Kitimat Region," background papers for the "Resources for Tomorrow" Conference, Vol. 1, page 445 (1961).

CHAPTER 6

SUBDIVISION CONTROL

Jerusalem is builded as a city that is compact together.

Psalm 122

The growth of cities, which has been graphically pictured in the Royal Commission Report on Canada's Economic Prospects, and confirmed by the metropolitan area census data, is inevitably accompanied by the conversion of farm land and forests into partially or fully serviced urban building lots. This radical change in the boundaries of privately owned land may take place in various ways. Until recently the only control was the market. Although the local government played its part, it too was largely governed by the market in that it had to pay market prices or more for land and it had to borrow from the private money lending market. It could, of course, resort to expropriation for streets. The results of this "natural" or "uncontrolled" growth need no further comment. More recently, and particularly since the end of the Second World War, more conscious attempts at government control have been made. A century and a half ago the settlers and early governors in what is now Canada divided the forest up into township lots and major roads. This was the first *division* of land, and any later division within this early framework has been called a *subdivision*. The materials in this Chapter illustrate some of the problems involved in this subdivision and the techniques of control that have been devised.

Subdivision on a large scale, either of a neighbourhood or a new town, naturally raises planning problems of the kind involved in master planning, although the scale is smaller, more comprehensible and manageable. If there is a good master plan for the area, the planning problems in the details of subdivision will naturally be easier, but if there is a poor plan or no plan at all, then the subdivision plan itself may have to be preceded by a plan for a wider area, so that streets will not be designed that ultimately dead end unintentionally because there is no sensible way of connecting them to major streets subsequently built. Not only will streets have to be planned in the wider context, but so also will all municipal services as well as neighbourhood services normally, in this country, privately supplied: shops, churches, prekindergarten schools and the like. The "extra-legal" materials reproduced here are therefore intended to supplement the materials examined in Chapter 3.

The most common legal problems in subdivision control arise out of the conflicts over design and the supply of services. Naturally the land owner is anxious to get as many lots from his land as he can. Because it cannot afford sewers the municipality is likely to be looking for larger lots (therefore fewer) with park space and school yards. It comes as a surprise to many subdividers to learn that good design frequently cuts down the length of the roads and increases the number of lots, at the same time producing adequate traffic routes. Wide streets also add to the expense of a development and narrower streets are sometimes quite feasible for certain purposes but they are not popular with municipal engineers. Since streets may cost as much as $70 a foot when all services are included, the savings may be quite impressive.

The services themselves can vary widely. A fully serviced subdivision includes, underground: water, sanitary and storm sewers, gas, hydro and telephone lines; and above ground: asphalt streets, concrete curbs, sidewalks, sodded boulevards and street lighting. At the other extreme, development might be permitted on lots with wells and septic tanks, open ditches along the roads instead of storm sewers, and gravelled surfaces on the roads. The cost could vary from $10 to $80 a foot. Municipalities like to have at least storm and sanitary sewers, and while the open ditch, when properly graded and sodded, is not unattractive, its maintenance by the municipality is very expensive. The problems raised by the materials in this chapter centre largely about these conflicting interests.

"Subdivision of land" is generally thought of as the dividing up of say a hundred acre farm into 400 building lots. The expression is also used to refer to the division of a parcel containing 12000 square feet into two parcels each containing 6000 square feet. Modern planning legislation usually provides a state control over subdivision whether the number of parcels resulting be two or two thousand. The control may, of course, vary in form, but since separating the ownership of a hundred acre farm into two, one owner having one acre and the other ninety-nine, will possible create design difficulties later on and services difficulties even then, some control is generally considered necessary from the start. The study of subdivision control, therefore, must be made in this varying context, from one or two lots to the setting up of a whole neighbourhood or even a new town.

The controls may be exercised locally or centrally, by *ad hoc* decisions or by general regulations, and on the same or a different basis depending on the number of lots involved. These alternatives should also be examined, to see the advantages and disadvantages of each.

1. The Growth of Urban Areas

EXECUTIVE COUNCIL, MINUTES AND YORK REPORT (1796)

The Committee begs leave likewise to recommend to yr Excellency that every Applicant for a Town Lot shall be obliged by his Licence of Occupation to lay down his House on a line which shall be marked for him by the Surveyor, which Line in the front of the First Range shall be retired twelve feet from the Edge of the Street, in order to allow a space for Pallisadoes, or other Ornaments in front of the Buildings at the Pleasure of the Occupant, and that the front of all other back buildings shall be on an exact line with the sides of the Streets—

It is also recommended that the Occupants of the Front Range of Houses shall be obliged by their Tenure to give them a front of at least forty six feet, which may be extended, but not diminished; And as it [is] hoped that the Occupants of the front Row of Houses will make a Point of raising such Buildings as shall be an Ornament to the Town and worthy of so beautiful a Situation, it is recommended to allow three Years for the Completion of their Plan before Officers of Government shall be considered as having forfeited their claim to the Douceur of 100 Acres in the first Concession as proposed by Your Excellency.

RICHARD CARTWRIGHT, LETTER TO ISAAC TODD (1793)

You will smile perhaps when I tell you that even at York, a Town Lot is to be granted in the Front Street only on Condition that you shall build a House of not less than 47 Feet Front, two Stories High & after a certain

Order of Architecture; in the second Street they may be somewhat less in Front, but the two Stories & mode of Architecture is indispensible; and it is only in the back Streets and Allies that the Tinkers and Taylors will be allowed to consult their own Taste and Circumstances in the Structure of their Habitations upon Lots of 1/10 of an Acre. Seriously our good Governor is a little wild in his projects. . . .

PETER RUSSELL, LETTER TO JOHN ELMSLEY C.J. (1797)

After having your opinion, Sir, and those of the other Officers of Government, I endeavored so to benefit from each, that by improving and adding to what Genl. Simcoe had done, I might give to the Town of York every Beauty and Convenience which its situation is capable of;—But without limits there can be no perfection,—When you proposed to me therefore to extend the Town to the Garrison Reserve, I strongly objected to it, for the reasons which still operate with me. In such an extent it would be impossible to prevail upon the Inhabitants to build near each other, and years might elapse in Consequence before the place would assume even the appearance of a Town.—The present Plan of York, which indeed exceeds in Extent my original Design that I might Comply with your wishes to add to the number of front Lots occupies a full mile in length and more than half that in breadth.—a space much larger than we have any probability of filling with Inhabitants for many years. The Expence therefore of making Streets and public Sewers and keeping them in repair will fall heavy upon those who shall have Houses even in this confined space; but should the Town be extended as you desire, and the Houses not increased in proportion, the Expense to the thinly scattered Inhabitants would be doubled and Trebled, or the Town might remain for ever an Ugly, Miry, unhealthy Swamp.—However as the Reserve extends to the Garrison, the Town may be hereafter enlarged as the Population may call for it, the doing it sooner shall never receive my concurrence.—It is my wish in the meantime that this reserved Land (after Deducting an Area of five hundred Yards square for Military purposes) may be divided into Ten Acre Lots, and let the Inhabitants of the Town not having 100 Acre Lots for Parks (resumable at pleasure) at an Annual Rent of one Dollar each to make them some Amends for their being deprived of Park Lots, by the land in the rear of the Town being all engrossed by the Officers of Government.

PETER RUSSELL, LETTER TO D. W. SMITH (1797)

. . . It is very much my wish that the Rear Lots in the old part of the Town of York are filled up before a single rear Lot shall be given away in the new Part. . . .

[The preceding minutes and letters are selected from Firth (ed.), *The Town of York* (1962), a collection of documents of early Toronto.]

MOBILITY—SOME FACTS AND SUGGESTIONS
Ontario. 1958. 5 *Ontario Planning* No. 1

A cartoon in a popular magazine not long ago showed a man standing in the back yard of his home, an arm around his son's shoulders.

The house was one of a row of box-like single family homes, each on its own fenced lot.

"Son", the father was saying, with a gesture that would have suited a feudal estate or a ranch in the Alberta foothills, "someday this will all be yours." The boy didn't look too impressed; perhaps he was thinking it was about time he got back to his homework. . . .

[It] is far from certain when the time comes for father, or mother, to dispose of what the law calls the "estate", that either of them will still own or be living in the same place. In fact, in some parts of Ontario, the property may have changed hands half a dozen times and the family itself have made as many moves. And even if father does stay put, that certainly doesn't mean that son will want to, or be able to.

One group that has recently compiled some interesting information on this subject is the Round Table on Man and Industry, sponsored by the School of Social Work at the University of Toronto. . . .

Briefly, the survey suggests a strikingly high degree of mobility, not only in the areas selected for study, but elsewhere in the Province as well. According to a report by the Round Table's research director, Dr. George M. Hougham, 60 per cent of the families interviewed in five of the areas surveyed last summer had moved into their dwellings in the previous four years. A full 15 per cent had lived in their present homes less than six months. At the other extreme, only 15 per cent of the families had not moved at all since the end of the war. In the "most stable" of the five communities surveyed, only half of the people had lived in their present homes for over four years. . . .

Some school enrolment and transfer figures for the whole of the Province obtained from the Ontario Department of Education would seem to corroborate roughly the findings of the Round Table. Out of approximately 912,000 children enrolled in public and separate elementary schools throughout the Province in September, 1956, over 210,000—more than one in five—transferred to another elementary school in Ontario during the year ending September, 1957. The proportion of secondary school transfers during the same period was considerably lower—about 16,000 out of a total of 186,000, or a little more than one in twelve. . . .

Assuming that a fairly high degree of mobility is characteristic of our communities at present and seems to continue to be so, it would seem worth considering some of its implications for community planning, and especially those aspects of land use planning with which local planning agencies are concerned.

For example:—Can a local planning agency assume that, if an area is initially well laid out and protected by an adequate zoning by-law, new families moving in will, on the average tend to have about the same number of school age children, the same needs for commercial facilities, parks etc. and that, consequently, so far as the area's physical characteristics are concerned, it matters little whether the average length of occupancy is four years or 24 years?

In weighing expressions of public opinion for or against a proposed change in zoning or a variance, is the likely length of occupancy of *all* interested parties a relevant factor to consider?

Could a high rate of mobility in a community indicate a need for more rental housing, public or private, whether in the form of single detached homes or row housing and apartments?

Does a high rate of mobility necessarily mean a lack of responsible interest and participation on the part of residents in neighbourhood or community affairs?

Is a high degree of anticipated mobility on the part of residents of an area likely to make their demands for civic improvements and amenities more, or less, urgent?

People may feel that their life work demands a fairly high degree of mobility. At the same time, they may be doubtful of their ability to meet this demand. Is it possible that such people may stress or even overemphasize the value of physical stability, as symbolized by home ownership?

Is there any reason to assume that a physically stable person or family is more emotionally stable, neighbourly, trustworthy, useful, etc. than a comparatively mobile one?

Although questions such as these probably warrant formal study and investigation, they would appear well worth considering also simply in the light of everyday local experience.

NOTE. It is sometimes suggested that the "suburbs" are populated by people fleeing from the "city." Is this generalization accurate? If a stranger comes to work in a large community will he necessarily find an attractive vacant house in the "city", or will he have to look in the "suburbs"? Where will a house cost him more? If a young man living at his parents' home in the "city" marries a young lady living in her parents' home in the "city", will the young couple, who may want to live near their parents, necessarily find an attractive vacant house in the "city"? Will they be "fleeing from the city" if they buy a house in the nearest "suburb"? Is there a stock of empty houses, attractive or otherwise, in the "city"? If the population of a "city" fills the available houses, where will a newcomer go who wants to live in the "city"? How do you distinguish between the "city" and the "suburbs"?

The notion that one family in four moves every year may be statistically true, but what does it mean in social terms? Could it mean that three quarters of the families in any area with such a rate of turnover in fact "put their roots down" for a much longer period?

BLUMENFELD, "TRANSPORTATION IN THE MODERN METROPOLIS"

Kingston, Ontario. 1961. 67 *Queen's Quarterly* 640; 649, 652–3.

In Metropolitan Toronto, in 1959, about two-thirds of all trips were made by private car and one-third by transit. However, while only one out of five trips for social and recreational purposes was made by transit, two out of five of the trips from home to work were transit trips. Of the trips most highly concentrated in space and time, the rush hour trips to and from the C.B.D. [the central business district], transit still accounted for over 70 per cent, the same percentage as in 1929. . . .

Cost and benefits of public and private transportation. Both private and public transportation require substantial investments and large operating cost, and these have to be weighed in assessing their respective rôles.

According to the Gordon Commission, the total cost of a passenger car-mile averaged 10.5 cents. If a transit fare of 15 cents is assumed, this indicates that driving a car without passengers is cheaper for distances up to 1½ miles, with 1, 2, or 3 passengers up to 3, 4½ and 6 miles, respectively. It is therefore evident that in a considerable number of cases it is cheaper for the individual to drive than to ride, even if he figured the total cost. However, about three-quarters of the cost of operating an automobile consists of more or less fixed costs; and, in practice the driver counts only the "out-of-pocket" costs of operation which averages 2.8 cents per mile. So, except when he has to pay for parking, from the point of view of the individual car owner it is always cheaper to drive.

On the other hand, one bus lane carries during a peak hour 5 times, one street-car track 10 times, and one rapid transit track up to 50 times as many persons as an ordinary street lane. About 12 expressway lanes would be required to carry the volume of passengers now carried during peak hours by the Toronto subway. Transit vehicles travel 2½ to 5 times more miles annually than passenger cars. While a private automobile performs about 15,000 person-miles annually, a bus (excl. inter-urban) averages over 500,000, a street-car over 800,000, and a subway car about one and a half million person-miles annually. Thus, despite its underuse during all but the 20 peak hours of the week, one subway car performed as many person-miles as 100 passenger cars—and required no parking space.

These comparisons indicate strongly that the market may not allocate resources in the most rational way to private and public transportation, respectively. As indicated above, the greater part of the cost of operating an automobile consists of fixed costs. If public transportation is to compete with the private car, a substantial portion of its cost will also have to be transformed into fixed costs. The only practical way of doing this is by covering them out of general tax revenues. It might be objected that it is unfair to ask the auto driver to pay for a service which he does not use. However, he benefits from the fact that the transit rider, by leaving his car at home, frees the street for the driver.

Support of public transit out of tax revenues underwrites a deficit, obviously an undesirable procedure; or it assumes responsibility for all or part of the capital cost, in particular of rapid transit lines, while the operating agency must cover the operating cost out of user charges. This militates against a rational weighing of capital versus operating costs and may lead to a curtailment of surface feeder lines which frequently can only be run at an operating loss and to subsequent underutilization of the rapid transit lines and of the capital invested in them. The only sound procedure is for the municipality to pay in accordance with the service performed, that is per passenger-mile or seat mile. This method has now been adopted by the state of New Jersey for subsidizing suburban railroad service.

A strong case could be made for operating public transit as a public service free of charge. This would permit considerably faster loading of buses, resulting in greater speed and consequent economies of operation. There is a precedent for this in vertical public transportation. The entire cost of elevator service in office and apartment buildings is always assessed as a "fixed cost" as part of the rent, regardless of the amount of use of the service by the various tenants.

The question of the relative costs and benefits of the competing modes of transportation requires further research in order to develop a comprehensive transportation system which allocates to each mode its appropriate rôle.

FIRESTONE, RESIDENTIAL REAL ESTATE IN CANADA (1951)

17. *International Fluctuations of House Building.* During the pre-war period, fluctuations in housing building were more severe in the United States than in either Canada or the United Kingdom. Dwellings started in the United States, excluding farm areas, declined by 90 per cent from a peak of 937,000 in 1925 to a low of 93,000 in 1933. On a similar basis, house

building in Canada fell off by 66 per cent from a peak of 61,000 dwellings completed in 1929 to 21,000 in 1933. In the United Kingdom there was a corresponding decline of only 20 per cent from 255,000 completions in 1927 to 203,000 in 1931, and from this low house building in the United Kingdom recovered to reach an all-time peak of 365,000 units completed in 1936. In the United States and Canada, house building in the 'thirties never reached the peak levels of the 'twenties. The situation was reversed in the post-war period when North American countries were able to expand house building activity much more rapidly than the United Kingdom. The after-effects of World War II, which fell more heavily on the United Kingdom than on the United States or Canada, were mainly responsible for this (pp. 75–76).

19. *Increase in the Value of Residential Real Estate*. Between 1921 and 1949 the value of residential real estate in Canada rose from $5.3 billion to $15 billion, an increase of 56 per cent in volume and 127 per cent in price (pp. 77–79).

21. *Value of Housing Completions*. Construction work involved in building the 91,000 dwellings *completed* in 1949 was estimated at $709 million, or an average of about $7,800 per unit. The $709 million figure includes the value of work performed on units started in 1948 but completed in 1949. New residential construction work *put in place* was slightly higher in 1949, amounting to $716 million, because housing starts continued to exceed completions in that year (pp. 83–86).

3. *Age of Housing*. About three-fifths of the housing stock was less than 40 years of age, one-fifth between 40 and 60 years, and the remaining fifth over 60 years. Since the life expectancy for the average Canadian house has been estimated as 60 years for a farm home and 75 years for an urban dwelling, some 400,000 houses in Canada were over age. Many of these are slum and substandard homes in need of replacement (pp. 46–49).

[The numbered paragraphs are from the Summary of Analysis.]

NATIONAL HOUSE BUILDERS ASSOCIATION, SUBMISSION

Canada. 1962. Royal Commission on Banking and Finance

4.50 *Refinancing of Existing Houses*. The *National Housing Act* provides for the insuring of mortgages by approved lenders on new houses only. It does not provide, in any way, for insured mortgage loans on existing dwellings. Many owners of existing houses are confined to accommodation which has become inadequate or unsuitable for their present needs because of their inability to adequately refinance such dwellings for resale. By adequate refinancing we mean financing to the same extent and under the same terms as that provided for new housing under the *National Housing Act*. There is a vast amount of our housing stock virtually frozen in this manner because the only available mortgages are conventional mortgages limited to 66⅔% of the value of the property—possibly supplemented by a second mortgage at a high rate of interest.

4.51 Under the *National Housing Act* a home owner may now finance a new house with an insured first mortgage based on 95% of the first $12,000 of lending value and 70% of the remainder, up to certain specified limits for each dwelling unit, depending on type and size. This sort of financing allows low initial down payments, particularly since the term of the mortgage may extend for 35 years. Interest, which is now set at 6¼% per annum is moderate and probably as low as could reasonably be expected, considering other prevailing interest rates.

4.52 Since this sort of financing is not available on existing houses, it is much easier for the prospective home owner with limited means to buy a new house than it is to purchase an existing house. Because new houses are generally built in the suburbs, it follows then that new home owners are almost automatically forced to move further and further from the centres of our cities, while home owners wishing to dispose of their houses in more central locations have great difficulty in finding buyers capable of meeting the high down payments which are required.

4.53 In order to supplement the smaller conventional mortgages, a thriving market in second mortgages has been created. Interest rates on second mortgages are frequently higher than on first mortgages, the term is generally shorter and there is usually a substantial bonus to be paid in addition. The actual interest rate, when all this is considered, can run as high as 40% on some second mortgages and often does exceed 20%. Unfortunately many unsuspecting home purchasers, when buying older houses, assume second mortgages which they later find great difficulty in carrying and not a few lose their entire investment as a result.

4.54 If refinancing were permitted under the *National Housing Act*, the original lender could supply a new mortgage at the current NHA interest rate, based on the appraised or actual current value of the property. The lender could retire the present loan and supply merely the difference to bring it up to the amount of the new loan. Since some earlier loans carry interest rates below the current rate, the lender probably would be agreeable to the refinancing. The new loan could carry the usual mortgage insurance protection which would be paid for by the 2% mortgage insurance fee as in the case of loans on new houses. It seems only sensible to continue to utilize existing houses in the older parts of our cities, where schools exist and where the streets and sewers are installed, rather than let neighbourhoods gradually deteriorate through disuse.

4.55 Shortly after the Second World War a great many inexpensive houses were built. The owners of these, in many cases, have families which have outgrown their accommodation. Like the owners of the older houses, these people cannot resell because of their inability to refinance their homes. If this were possible, there would be a tremendous supply of low cost dwellings available for persons of low income. These buildings cannot be reproduced at their initial cost in today's market. Prospective purchasers here too must look to the suburbs to fill their housing needs. Our whole financial structure under the *National Housing Act* forces people to the outskirts in search of new houses with low down payments, whereas many might prefer to purchase in more central locations if refinancing was available.

4.56 If the home owner cannot resell his house in order to buy a new one, the builder likewise cannot take it in on trade because he finds himself in a similar situation when he comes to dispose of it. In effect then, without NHA refinancing there is no real trade-in market for used houses. This prevents people who wish to do so from purchasing new houses since the builder cannot take in the present house and they cannot sell it. They are locked in.

4.57 An effective trade-in market should be an essential element in the housing industry. The freedom to exchange old and new houses is one of the necessary ingredients to movement and healthy activity within the industry.

4.58 In the United States, under the Federal Housing Administration, new and existing houses are financed under exactly the same terms. A great deal of experience has been accumulated since 1934 when this legislation came into effect. So important is the refinancing of existing buildings that last year FHA insured loans on older properties amounting to 63% of its total commitments, while those of new properties amounted to only 37%.

2. THE TECHNIQUES OF CONTROL

THE CITY AND SUBURBS PLANS ACT
Ontario. Statutes. 1912. Chapter 43

2. Where any person is desirous of surveying and subdividing into lots with a view to the registration of a plan of the survey and sub-division, any tract of land lying within or within five miles of a city, having a population of not less than 50,000, he shall submit a plan of the proposed survey and subdivision to "The Ontario Railway and Municipal Board" for its approval.
3. (2) Nothing in clause (a) shall authorize the laying out of any road or street, less than 66 feet in width.

NOTE. The City and Suburbs Plans Act was repealed by *The Planning and Development Act,* S.O., 1917, c. 44, which defined an "urban zone" as five miles around the outside of a city and three miles around towns and villages. The local council was authorized to adopt a "general plan" that had no other legal significance except that it was to be "regarded" when plans of subdivision were approved by the Ontario Railway and Municipal Board. Plans of subdivision were to be referred by the council to the municipal engineer, who was to have regard to specified matters including conformity with the general plan. Provision was made for town planning commissions, at the option of the council, to take over the duties of the council under the Act, and to use the council's staff. The Act was repealed by *The Planning and Development Act,* S.O., 1918, c. 38, which continued the "urban zone" system of extraterritorial control until the 1918 Act was repealed by *The Planning Act, 1946,* the forerunner of the current legislation.

MUNICIPAL ACT
British Columbia. Revised Statutes. 1960. Chapter 43

711. (1) The council may regulate the subdivision of land, and for that purpose may by by-law
- (a) regulate the area, shape, and dimensions of parcels of land and the dimensions, locations, alignment, and gradient of highways in connection with the subdivision of land, and may make different regulations for different uses and for different zones of the municipality;
- (b) prescribe minimum standards with respect to the matters contained in clauses (a) and (d);
- (c) require that a proposed subdivision
  - (i) be suited to the configuration of the land being subdivided; and
  - (ii) be suited to the use to which it is intended; and
  - (iii) shall not make impracticable the future subdivision of the land within the proposed subdivision or of any adjacent land;

(3) Every approving officer shall give due regard to and take cognizance of any official community plan when dealing with applications for the approval of any plan of subdivision.

711A. (1) Where a physical examination of lands is required, the approving officer may, at the cost of the owner of the land proposed to be subdivided, personally examine or have an examination or report made on the proposed subdivision, but the owner shall not be charged an amount greater than one-tenth of one per centum of the assessed value of the land included in the subdivision as shown on the real-property assessment roll at the time of subdivision.

(2) If the subdivision plan is not approved, the owner is not liable to be charged.

[Sections 711 and 711A are reproduced as amended by S.B.C., 1961, c. 43, s. 45, and 1962, c. 41, ss. 31 and 32.]

RE DISTRICT OF DELTA

British Columbia. Supreme Court. 1960. 27 D.L.R. (2d) 65

VERCHERE J.: This is an appeal under s. 98 [re-enacted 1950, c. 36, s. 5] of the *Land Registry Act*, R.S.B.C. 1948, c. 171 from the refusal by the Approving Officer of the Corporation of the District of Delta to approve a plan of a proposed subdivision of a portion of Lot 9, Block C, of Lots 1 and 2 of timber Lot 7, sections 3 and 4, Township 5, Plan 18497, New Westminster District. It is agreed by counsel that the appeal was properly launched.

The Approving Officer's reasons for not approving the subdivision plan submitted to him on July 6, 1960 are contained in his letter dated August 1, 1960 addressed to Mr. George Hodgins, which reads as follows:

"Re: Application to subdivide a portion
of—Lot 9, Block C of Lots 1 and
2 of T.L. 7, Section 3 and 4, Twp. 5

"The above application has been considered and in view of the unique physical conditions of the site and the apparent potential problems that might arise from the slipping or erosion of the bank it would not appear advisable to approve this subdivision unless adequate information regarding the stability of the bank is submitted by a qualified soil mechanics engineer.

"I would point to s. 96 of the *Land Registry Act* which states in part—

" 'In considering an application before him for subdivision approval, the Approving Officer may refuse to approve the subdivision if in his opinion the anticipated development of the subdivision would be against the public interest.'

"It is apparent that there are potential dangers if this subdivision is approved and it is possible that some special works might prevent the possibility of sliding or erosion in this area. Again, a report from a qualified soils mechanic engineer is necessary in this respect.

"I would state that without the report of a qualified soils engineer regarding this site, I am of the opinion it would not be in the public interest to approve this subdivision."

Section 96 of the *Land Registry Act*, R.S.B.C. 1948, c. 171, in its present form was re-enacted in 1954, c. 18, s. 6 and reads as follows:

"In considering an application before him for subdivision approval, the approving officer may hear objections from any interested persons, and may refuse to approve the subdivision if in his opinion the anticipated development of the subdivision would injuriously affect the established amenities of adjoining or adjacent properties or would be against the public interest."

That part of Lot 9 which is sought to be subdivided lies on the Tsawwassen Bluff and runs from a private road forming the west boundary of Lots 1 to 8, Block C, Plan 18497, steeply down to the sea. The general slope was described as being approximately one of 40%, slightly more, it was said, than the angle of repose of well-drained crushed rock, but it is not a continuous slope as the surface is formed into three benches. The area is thick with brush and trees, some of which were said to be approximately 300 years old. The private road forming the west boundary, with water mains beneath its surface, had been installed by the petitioner during the past year at a cost of approximately $15,000 to service the lots to be created by the subdivision of the portion of Lot 9 aforesaid. The area had been zoned by the municipality for residential purposes.

Counsel for the municipality stated that the public interest sought to be protected by the Approving Officer was the interest of the unascertained purchasers of the several lots to be created by the proposed subdivision plan. He contended that the *Land Registry Act* gives to the Approving Officer a discretionary power over proposed subdivisions which in this case had been exercised reasonably and in good faith in view of the topography of this land and the nature of the soil.

The evidence indicated that the area was very desirable as a building site because of the view it afforded but that it was unsuitable for building sites generally because it was unstable. It did not, however, seem to me that the expert opinions submitted ruled out the use of this land as a site or sites for every kind of residence. The deputy municipal engineer was of the opinion that the land sought to be subdivided was unstable and unsuitable for use as a building site and the Approving Officer's evidence indicated that it was partly as a result of this advice that he refused approval and told the applicant it should obtain and submit a soil report. But Mr. Ripley, an engineer consultant in soil mechanics and foundations, was not, it would seem of the same opinion. A copy of his letter to Mr. Hodgins dated August 11, 1960 was introduced in evidence and this letter, stated to be written after a "superficial examination of the property by Mr. Ripley," said:

"The property under consideration consists of the seaward slope of the Point Roberts peninsula just north of the International Boundary Line. The lots in general extend from the high water mark of Georgia Strait up the very steep bank to the top edge of the plateau. The total vertical height of the hillside is of the order of 170 ft. Speaking of the Tsawwassen area in general, a condition of potential instability exists on the exposed banks. This is attributable to the type and disposition of the foundation soils occurring in the area and to other site characteristics such as steep topography, wave action, ground and seepage water conditions. The general physical condition of the bank is such that in its natural state it exists at a rather delicate state of equilibrium which can be disturbed by relatively minor actions. When disturbed by removal of vegetation and grading, erosion and slide blocks may develop on the bank slopes and the bank recedes inland. Disturbance of the slopes can result in undermining and physical damage to any houses or cottages built on the slopes or to the housing development on the plateau above. Because the proposed development occurs on the steep slope portion of the peninsula it is the most critical area. Therefore, concern for the stability of the bank is a vital and fundamental factor which must be taken into account in the use of this site.

"While it is our opinion that stability of the bank can be most readily assured by leaving the bank in its natural undeveloped condition with trees and vegetation undisturbed, it is recognized that the property has considerable scenic value and that it is desirable to utilize it for this reason. In view of the stability problem we consider that the land could be best and most safely utilized for a temporary comparatively low-cost summer cottage type development rather than for permanent higher cost type houses. It is understood that you contemplate selling the lots in question for summer cottage development. It is the tentative opinion of this firm, based on the superficial examination, that light summer-type cottages could be successfully constructed on the subject benches and occupied for a period approximating their normal economic life, provided that all measures necessary for the maintenance of the delicate natural equilibrium of the slopes are applied and rigidly enforced at all times."

I take it from the foregoing that cottages of light construction could be successfully and economically constructed on these lands but measures should be taken to ensure that the existing degree of support for the slope is maintained.

Further, Mr. Ripley stated that the factors tending to bring about instability in the bank were erosion by waves at the shore, denuding the bank of cover, escape of water from the top of the bank and the human element in constructing paths, walks and buildings. He added that the indiscriminate use of the bank by the public could, in his opinion, be more dangerous than its use for the construction thereon of houses.

The evidence also indicated that Lot 10, as shown on the plan of the proposed subdivision, had in fact already been created by a subdivision plan which was approved by the Approving Officer on August 28, 1959. According to the Approving Officer, the subdivision plan creating Lot 10 was approved by him in ignorance of the nature of the equilibrium of the bank. The plan for which approval is sought will create three other parcels within the property, namely, Lots 11 and 12 and the residue of Lot 9. It was established that Lot 11 had been purchased by Mr. Moral Cleugh presently residing in close proximity to it on the east, subject to the vendor being able to procure approval of the subdivision plan and pass title. Mr. Cleugh said that he was in no way dissatisfied with his bargain and that in his opinion it was a very desirable building lot on which he intended to build when he could afford it. Mr. Hodgins, an officer of the petitioning company, said he intended to retain Lot 12 for his own use as the site of a boat house, and that the future of the residue of Lot 9 was undecided although his purpose, frankly stated, was to sell it at a profit.

It seems apparent that although the ultimate use of the land cannot be precisely stated, such use will have to comply with the residential use to which it is restricted by the zoning by-law, and that some form of this use can be successfully and economically adopted. The question then is whether or not the public interest referred to in s. 96 of the *Land Registry Act* can include the interest of subsequent purchasers who might find that some but not every residential use they contemplate cannot be permitted by the nature of the terrain.

In Westminster Corp. v. London & North Western Ry., (1905), Lord Macnaghten said this:

"There can be no question as to the law applicable to the case. It is well settled that a public body invested with statutory powers such as those conferred upon the corporation must take care not to exceed or abuse its powers. It must keep within the limits of the authority committed to it. It must act in good faith. And it must act reasonably. The last proposition is involved in the second, if not in the first. But in the present case I think it will be convenient to take it separately."

Further in *Re Dist. of Surrey* (1959), my brother Wilson, with whom I respectfully agree, said this:

"The right to subdivide real property, to sell a part rather than the whole is an ordinary incident of ownership. Various restrictions limiting this right have been established by statute, for the salutary reason that the unrestricted exercise of such a right can create hardship to other landowners and to municipal corporations. No one can question the necessity for such controls. Nevertheless, such restrictions are in derogation of common law rights and, where they are sought to be imposed by municipal by-law, clear statutory authority must be shown."

In *Re Land Registry Act, Re Plan of Subdivision* (*South Saanich Dist.*) (1955) Coady, J., as he then was, pointed out that:

"There are many reasons why municipal corporations should have and are given a measure of control over proposed subdivisions and the court should not on appeal lightly interfere with the decision of the approving officer."

But in that case he also said this:

"If the future owners of these lots cooperate, it would not seem that any difficulty will arise. If they do not co-operate, then that is primarily their problem. To seek to protect them in a contingency that may never arise is to assume a position that is too paternalistic and unreal in the circumstances."

In the present case it seems to me that the Approving Officer's concern, in the public interest, for the unascertained purchasers of the lots created by the plan for which approval is sought is "too paternalistic and unreal in the circumstances". The evidence indicates that the land can be satisfactorily utilized for "a temporary comparatively low-cost summer cottage type development" and it may well be that purchasers will have to confine themselves to this type of development. While it is possible that some future owner may not do this, it does not seem to me that this contingency, speculative as it is, is one which can or will injuriously affect the interests of the municipality or the public generally. That being the case it cannot, I think, be said that the Approving Officer has acted reasonably in concluding that the interest of the unascertained purchasers is, in fact, a public interest.

I would therefore allow the appeal and direct that the plan be registered, it being otherwise in order. As to costs, the Approving Officer having acted in the exercise of his best judgment and on what he considered sufficient grounds, the municipality should not be condemned in costs. There will therefore be no order as to costs, see *Re Land Registry Act, Re Plan of Subdivision* (*South Saanich Dist.*).

TOWN PLANNING ACT

Nova Scotia. Revised Statutes. 1954. Chapter 292

27. (1) Where no special Act of the Legislature applies with respect to sub-divisions in a city, town or municipality, the Minister may prescribe regulations respecting subdivisions of land including:

(c) procedure to be adopted for approval of final plans by the council . . .

(5) Unless a board has been appointed by a municipality, no subdivision shall be made in that municipality in respect of lands situated within three miles of a city or two miles of a town, as the case may be, unless the approval of the board of such city or town is first obtained, provided that where such a subdivision is within the limits mentioned of more than one city or town, the approval of the board of the nearest city or town in which a board has been appointed shall be sufficient compliance with the provisions of this subsection; provided further that whenever a board appointed by a municipality approves of a subdivision of lands which are situated within three miles of a city or two miles of a town, the board shall forthwith furnish to the clerk of the said city or town or to the clerk of the city or town nearest to the subdivision, if there is more than one city or town, a true copy of the plan of the subdivision as approved, and such city or town may, within thirty days after receipt of such copy of the plan of subdivision, appeal to the Minister from the approval of such board and shall give to such board notice of appeal.

(9) A board, with the approval of the council and of the Minister may prescribe additional regulations respecting subdivisions of land within its jurisdiction. . . .

THE URBAN AND RURAL PLANNING ACT, 1953
Newfoundland. Statutes. 1953. Number 27

61. (1) . . . the Advisory Board may, subject to the approval of the Lieutenant-Governor in Council, make . . . regulations

(b) prohibiting the subdivision of any land which is situated outside of the City of St. John's and outside of areas held or administered by the St. John's Municipal Council, except with the approval in writing of the Director;

(f) prescribing that in a Municipal Area or a Joint Planning Area the authorized administrator may approve a proposed subdivision where a number of building lots not exceeding seven are involved in the subdivision;

(g) prescribing standards for subdivisions;

(h) providing that no conveyance, transfer or agreement to convey or transfer an interest in any land situated in any Municipal Area or Joint Planning Area which did not hitherto pass as a separate parcel by conveyance, transfer, assignment, gift or operation of law shall be effectual to pass any interest in the land either at law or in equity unless the conveyance, transfer or agreement to convey or transfer is first approved by the Minister or by some person designated by him, and prescribing that the Registrar of Deeds shall not register any such document unless such approval is obtained; . . .

[Section 61 is reproduced as amended by S.N., 1955. No. 19, s. 6.]

SUBDIVISION AND TRANSFER REGULATIONS
Alberta. Regulations. 1960. 185/60; Order in Council 926–60

4. (1) When a person proposes to carry out a subdivision to which these regulations apply, he shall make application for approval of the subdivision in the manner hereinafter provided;

(2) In the case of land lying within the area of jurisdiction of an approving authority as set out in the First Schedule, the application shall be submitted to and the approval thereof shall rest with that approving authority;

(3) In all other cases applications shall be submitted to and the approval thereof shall rest with the Director;
[The approving authorities are the technical planning boards of Edmonton or Calgary and the district planning commissions.]

7. (1) Before approving an application [the Director or approving authority (other than a technical planning board) shall request comments of municipal authorities, local health authorities, etc.]

(2) The Director or the approving authority shall give due consideration to the comments of other bodies or authorities to whom an application has been referred, but shall not be bound by them.

(3) After thirty days from the date of reference under Regulation 7(1), the application may be dealt with by the Director or the approving authority without further delay, whether or not the comments have been received.

8. (1) If the subdivision as proposed complies, to the satisfaction of the Director or approving authority, with the requirements of these regulations, the application shall be approved.

9. If a decision on an application is not made within ten weeks from the date of receipt of the application in its complete and final form, or within such longer period as the applicant may consent to in writing, the application shall be deemed to be refused, and the applicant may appeal under Regulation 11 as though he had been sent a refusal at the end of that period.

11. (1) When the Director or an approving authority refuses an application or approves an application subject to specified conditions, the applicant may appeal the decision to the Board within thirty days of the date of mailing of the notice of decision;

(3) In determining an appeal, the Board shall not be bound by these regulations, but may waive or modify any requirement herein or any condition of approval specified in the decision, having regard to all the circumstances related to and all the consequences that may issue from the development and use of the land within the proposed subdivision.

12. (1) Where the Director or an approving authority is of the opinion that compliance with a provision of these regulations is impracticable or undesirable because of circumstances peculiar to the subdivision, the Director or the approving authority may recommend that the applicant be relieved in whole or in part from complying with such a provision;

THE PLANNING ACT

Ontario. Revised Statutes. 1960. Chapter 296.

28. (1) When land is to be subdivided for the purpose of being sold, conveyed or leased in lots by reference to a registered plan of subdivision, the owner of the land . . . [shall apply] for approval, to the Minister [of Municipal Affairs].

[Section 86(2) of *The Registry Act*, R.S.O., 1960, c. 348 and section 161(1) of *The Land Titles Act*, R.S.O., 1960, c. 204, provide that no plan of survey or subdivision to which *The Planning Act* applies shall be registered unless approved under that Act.]

(3) The Minister may then confer with officials of municipalities and departments of the public service, commissions, authorities and any others who may be concerned and shall settle a draft plan that, in his opinion, will meet all requirements.

(4) In considering a draft plan of subdivision, regard shall be had, among other matters, to the health, safety, convenience and welfare of the future inhabitants and to the following:

(a) whether the plan conforms to the official plan and adjacent plans of subdivision, if any;
(b) whether the proposed subdivision is premature or necessary in the public interest;
(c) the suitability of the land for the purposes for which it is to be subdivided;
(d) the number, width, location and proposed grades and elevations of highways, and the adequacy thereof, and the highways linking the highways in the proposed subdivision with the established highway system in the vicinity, and the adequacy thereof;
(e) the dimensions and shape of the lots;
(f) the restrictions or proposed restrictions, if any, on the land, buildings and structures proposed to be erected thereon and the restrictions, if any, on adjoining lands;
(g) conservation of natural resources and flood control;
(h) the adequacy of utilities and municipal services;
(i) adequacy of school sites;
(j) the area of land, if any, within the subdivision that, exclusive of highways, is to be conveyed or dedicated for public purposes.

(11) Upon settlement of the draft plan, the Minister may give his approval thereto, and may in his discretion withdraw his approval or change the conditions of approval at any time prior to his approval of a final plan for registration.

(13) Upon presentation by the person desiring to subdivide the Minister may, if satisfied that the plan is in conformity with the approved draft plan and that the conditions of approval have been or will be fulfilled, approve the plan of subdivision and thereupon the plan of subdivision may be tendered for registration.

(14) When a final plan for registration is approved by the Minister under subsection 13 and is not registered within one month of the date of approval, the Minister may withdraw his approval and may require that a new application be submitted.

29. Every person who subdivides and offers for sale, agrees to sell or sells land by a description in accordance with an unregistered plan of subdivision is guilty of an offence and on summary conviction is liable to a fine of not more than $500.

26. (1) The council of a municipality may by by-law designate any area within the municipality as an area of subdivision control and thereafter no person shall convey land in the area by way of a deed or transfer on any sale, or mortgage or charge land in the area, or enter into an agreement of sale and purchase of land in the area or enter into any agreement that has the effect of granting the use of or right in land in the area directly or by entitlement to renewal for a period of twenty-one years or more unless,

(a) the land is described in accordance with and is within a registered plan of subdivision; or
(b) the grantor, mortgagor or vendor does not retain the fee or the equity of redemption in any land abutting the land that is being conveyed or otherwise dealt with; or
(c) the land is ten acres or more in area and the land remaining in the

grantor, mortgagor or vendor abutting on the land conveyed or otherwise dealt with is also ten acres or more in area; or

(d) the land or any use of or right therein is being acquired or disposed of by Her Majesty in right of Canada or Her Majesty in right of Ontario or by any municipality, metropolitan municipality or county; or

(e) the consent,

(i) of the planning board of the planning area in which the land lies, or

(ii) where the land lies in more than one planning area, of the planning board designated by the Minister from time to time, or

(iii) where there is no planning board, of the Minister, is given to the conveyance, mortgage, charge or agreement.

(2) The council may in the by-law designate any plan of subdivision, or part thereof, that has been registered for eight years or more, which shall be deemed not to be a registered plan of subdivision for the purposes of subsection 1.

(3) The council of a municipality may by by-law provide that this subsection applies to land in the municipality that is within a plan of subdivision registered before or after the passing of the by-law, or is within such registered plan or plans of subdivision, or part or parts thereof, as is or are designated in the by-law, and thereafter no person shall convey [etc., as in subsection 1]).

(4) An agreement, conveyance, mortgage or charge made in contravention of this section or a predecessor thereof does not create or convey any interest in land, but this section does not affect an agreement entered into, subject to the express condition contained therein that such agreement is to be effective only if the provisions of this section are complied with.

(5) A by-law passed under this section is not effective until the requirements of subsections 6 to 11 have been complied with.

(6) Two certified copies of every by-law passed under this section shall be lodged by the clerk of the municipality in the office of the Minister, where they shall be available for public inspection during office hours.

(13) A planning board and the Minister in determining whether a consent is to be given under this section shall have regard to the matters that are to be had regard to under subsection 4 of section 28 in considering a draft plan of subdivision and may impose such conditions as it or he considers necessary to ensure that such matters are effectively provided for and maintained and, in addition, may require that any or all of such conditions be fulfilled prior to the granting of a consent.

(14) Where, on an application to a planning board for a consent under this section, the consent is refused or is given subject to one or more conditions or where the planning board refuses or neglects to make a decision on the application within sixty days after the receipt by the planning board of the application, the applicant may appeal to the Municipal Board and the Municipal Board shall hear the appeal and make such disposition thereof as to it may seem proper, but the Municipal Board does not have power to rescind a consent that has been given by a planning board but may vary or rescind any condition that has been imposed on the granting of a consent.

(15) An agreement, conveyance, mortgage or charge is not in contravention of this section if a consent has been given, although such consent

is subject to a condition that has not been complied with at the time such agreement, conveyance, mortgage or charge is made.

[As to the history of subsection 4, see Notes in (1961), 39 *Canadian Bar Review* 461 and (1959), 37 *Canadian Bar Review* 636.]

NOTES AND QUESTIONS. Prior to the 1960–61 session, there was no eight year limitation on the power of the council to deem a registered plan not to be a registered plan of subdivision. Why is the protection extended only to plans approved within the preceding eight years? Subdivision control in its present form started in 1946, with the new *Planning Act*. In 1963 a plan registered in good faith in 1954 would not be entitled to the protection. Why? Is there any reason for setting arbitrarily a period during which mistakes cannot be corrected?

Must the plan that is "deregistered" under section 26(2) be designated in the same by-law that designates the subdivision control area under section 26(1)? Note that "part lot control" under section 26(3) may be introduced "by by-law," but "deregistration" may be designated "in *the* by-law."

If a council designates a plan to be deemed not to be a plan by an amending by-law, does that by-law require the Minister's approval? Does such a change amount to an *alteration* or *dissolution* of an area of subdivision control under section 26(12)?

Suppose that Smith owns 100 acres of land in a remote part of a rural township on the fringe of a rapidly growing city. He manages in 1952 to get a plan of subdivision with 100 foot lots approved by the Minister. In 1963 only one-third of the lots have been sold. The council passes an amendment to the subdivision control by-law deeming the Smith plan not to be a plan. The requirements of subsections 5 to 11 are complied with. Can Smith ignore the by-law until it is approved by the Minister? Can he require the Minister to refer the matter to the Municipal Board if his approval is applied for? Could Smith attack the by-law in the High Court? On what ground? Suppose the by-law had merely instituted part lot control, when Smith had hoped to sub-divide his 100 foot lots each into two 50 foot lots? Would you give the same answer to the questions above?

RE CARDINAL AND O'MALLEY. [1952] O.W.N. 817 (Ontario. High Court). It was unsuccessfully argued in this case that the Minister's approval was not required for a plan of subdivision where there was no official plan in force. JUDSON J.: "The interrelation of the proposed subdivision plan and the official plan is only one of the many matters that the Minister is required to consider and he does not lose his powers under the section because of the non-existence of an official plan." An appeal was dismissed.

3. PHYSICAL DESIGN

(*a*) *The planner's idea*

ADAMS, RURAL PLANNING AND DEVELOPMENT (1917)

We have seen that some of the worst results of the present rectangular system, as a basis of development, are shown in the building subdivisions in rural areas lying adjacent to cities and towns. It is there that the plan of the country and the plan of the city influence and control each other; and it is there that the most inconvenient forms of development and some of the worst sanitary conditions are to be found in Canada. The same is true of the outer suburbs of cities in the United States. The proper planning of these suburban areas is of the utmost importance in connection with the future development of Canadian life. These are the districts which are more in need of control under proper planning and development schemes than any other. At present subdivisions are laid out without regard being paid to the best lines and widths of main lines of communication, to physical conditions or to convenience.

But even if we were tied to the rectangular system for township and farm boundaries, that is no reason for not replanning within these boundaries to suit proper and economic building development as soon as the time arrives for the farm land to be converted into building land. In settled districts we may be compelled to continue to put up with the inconvenience caused by farm roads approaching lakes, hills and escarpments at right angles, and crossing ravines where the maximum of cost is required to be incurred to overcome physical obstacles; but, as soon as building subdivision takes place, a new set of conditions arise and an entire change of plan is needed. Proper planning will give more convenient means of communication between the country and the town, a matter of great importance in connection with cheapening the cost of production and making farming more profitable. This question of communication by road is part of the large problem of transportation and distribution which is dealt with in the succeeding chapter. [pp. 67–8.]

Those who contend that the fixed system of surveying in Canada, in which the land is divided into sections without regard to its quality and character, is at least suitable for level and unbroken country, do not take into consideration, first, the importance of classifying land and arranging the sizes of the divisions according to its suitability for different kinds of farming; second, the need for linking up the homesteads with the village centres, and, third, the importance of the plan of development as distinct from the surveyor's plan of measurement.

Another objection to the rectangular system as now carried out is that it forces the subdivision of land and the laying out of streets to follow the cardinal lines of the compass. For purposes of measurement this method ensures accuracy, but it adds to the evils caused by the rigidity of the system, in regard to both farm boundaries and building subdivisions. Lines which run due east and north and have no regard to watersheds and water courses, cause fertile valleys and meadow land to be cut up into awkward shapes and sizes for farming purposes. In regard to building subdivisions it is undesirable for purposes of health that buildings should stand squared by the four cardinal points. Building land should be laid out north-east and south-west and north-west and south-east instead of north-south and east-west, which is the worst disposition in which to place buildings in order to obtain the best distribution of sunlight.

Owing to the rectangular system in rural districts being the foundation for the checkerboard lay-out of cities and towns it is unfortunate that the direction of streets is fixed according to a rule which has no regard to orientation. [p. 71.]

The present unscientific system of fixing the alignment of roads is accompanied by an equally unscientific system of fixing road widths. Most roads are too wide and many are too narrow, and those that are too narrow are restricted in width by reason of the law which requires the others to be too wide. It may be claimed that, both in rural and urban territory, a general average of 66 feet is wide enough for all purposes and that no community, even when comparatively closely settled, can afford to lay out and pave streets of a greater average width. This question may not affect the farmer except insofar as he may have to contribute towards an inconvenient and expensive road system in connection with the urban development in rural territory. It is in this connection that the grievance of bad road planning becomes acute. First, as already shown, the alignment is fixed without regard to contours, and, second, the width is determined on a minimum basis for all roads no matter for what purpose they are to be used.

The minimum standard in Ontario and elsewhere is 66 feet. This standard applies to the main arterial thoroughfare required to carry heavy traffic and to the short residential street required for purely domestic needs of a few houses. In many districts acres of macadam, asphalt and concrete are laid in a few streets and might with advantage be used over twice the length of street now paved. One consequence of this irrational and expensive method is that the cost of local improvements to the local councils in many localities is so great that money is not available for necessary purposes of public sanitation. Another is that the tax burden on the property owners is so heavy that they are proportionably limited in the capital available for making their houses sanitary and durable in construction, and they are compelled to crowd their land with buildings in order to put it to economic use.

But even at this late day, with all the lessons we have had of waste of land and unnecessary expenditure of capital in providing for too wide roads for purely local traffic—in providing many miles of road space where it is not needed at all, and in thus lessening the ability of provincial and local authorities to obtain the space and provide the means to construct main arterial highways where these are required—there are those who regard any suggestion to make streets narrower than 60 or 66 feet as reactionary. Yet there are few who will deny that it is impracticable, in any community where the density of building is comparatively open, as in Canada, to provide land and make satisfactory roads or streets to a greater average width than 66 feet. What happens is that the land is provided for roads or streets, as the law requires, but that few of the roads or streets are ever properly constructed, the reason being that there is too much road surface for the population, even when the land is closely settled. *Excessively wide streets, instead of securing more air space, cause congestion, e.g., in the erection of apartment houses in towns because without such congestion the frontages could not afford to meet the cost of local improvements.* This has been proved in Germany, Sweden, and other countries where the tenement system prevails, and it is being proved in Canada where the tendency towards the tenement building is being created by the wide street. In the rural districts, although land is plentiful and cheap, it stands to reason that all roads should not be of the same width, and that there should be variation to suit the requirements of traffic.

What happens in practice is that our by-laws fix a width, not according to scientific theory, nor yet on any practical basis, but simply because of the convenience of making a hard and fast rule in accordance with some custom. The 66 feet width of Ontario seems to have no other justification than the fact that it is the length of a chain. It is about half the width that should be provided for some main arteries, and about twice what is necessary for the short, tributary streets. It is true that, in the absence of proper development schemes, we must have a system of regulations fixing a general standard in these matters—that is the inevitable weakness of the by-law system—but it is quite as absurd to regulate the width of a street according to a fixed by-law standard as it would be to prescibe that all sewers and water mains should be of the same diameter. [pp. 88–90.]

STEIN, TOWARD NEW TOWNS FOR AMERICA (1957 Revised ed.)

'The Radburn Idea' to answer the enigma 'How to live with the auto,' or, if you will, 'How to live in spite of it,' met these difficulties with a radical revision of relation of houses, roads, paths, gardens, parks, blocks, and local neighborhoods. (Figs. 19, 20 and 21. [Fig. 20 is omitted. The map of St. James's precinct, from John Rocque's *Map of London*, 1746, has been inserted by the editor as an interesting historical antecedent of the Radburn idea.]). For this purpose it used the following elements:

1. The Superblock in place of the characteristic narrow, rectangular block.
2. Specialized Roads Planned and Built For One Use Instead of For All Uses: service lanes for direct access to buildings; secondary collector roads around superblocks; main through roads, linking the traffic of various sections, neighborhoods and districts; express highways or parkways, for connection with outside communities. (Thus differentiating between movement, collection, service, parking, and visiting.)
3. Complete Separation of Pedestrian and Automobile, or as complete separation as possible. Walks and paths routed at different places from roads and at different levels when they cross. For this purpose overpasses and underpasses were used.
4. Houses Turned Around. Living and sleeping rooms facing toward gardens and parks; service rooms toward access roads.
5. Park as Backbone of the neighborhood. Large open areas in the centre of superblocks, joined together as a continuous park.

Geddes Smith described Radburn compactly in 1929 as: 'A town built to *live* in—today and tomorrow. A town "for the motor age." A town turned outside-in—without any back doors. A town where roads and parks fit together like the fingers of your right and left hands. A town in which children need never dodge motor-trucks on their way to school. A *new* town—newer than the garden cities, and the first major innovation in town-planning since they were built.'

None of the elements of the plan was completely new. The distinctive innovations of Radburn were the integrating superblocks, specialized and separated means of circulation, the park backbone, and the house with two fronts. Radburn interwove these to form a new unity, as a practical and attractive setting for the realities of today's living.

There were precedents for all the elements.

Superblocks with great green interiors had been built in America. Before 1660, the Dutch in Nieue Amsterdam (New York) built their homes around the periphery of large blocks, with farms behind and sometimes with a great garden core. However, throughout the nineteenth century and the early twentieth, most city growth was based on the repetitious geometric gridiron; a plan for facile plotting, surveying, legal recording—but not a plan for living. So Henry Wright and I went to Britain, on a special investigation to study superblocks with culs-de-sac, before we started planning Radburn. We concluded that, because of the greater use of the automobile in America, we were justified in increasing the size of super-blocks over those at Welwyn, Letchworth and Hampstead Garden Suburb. The Radburn blocks were 30 to 50 acres in size. Their outlines were determined

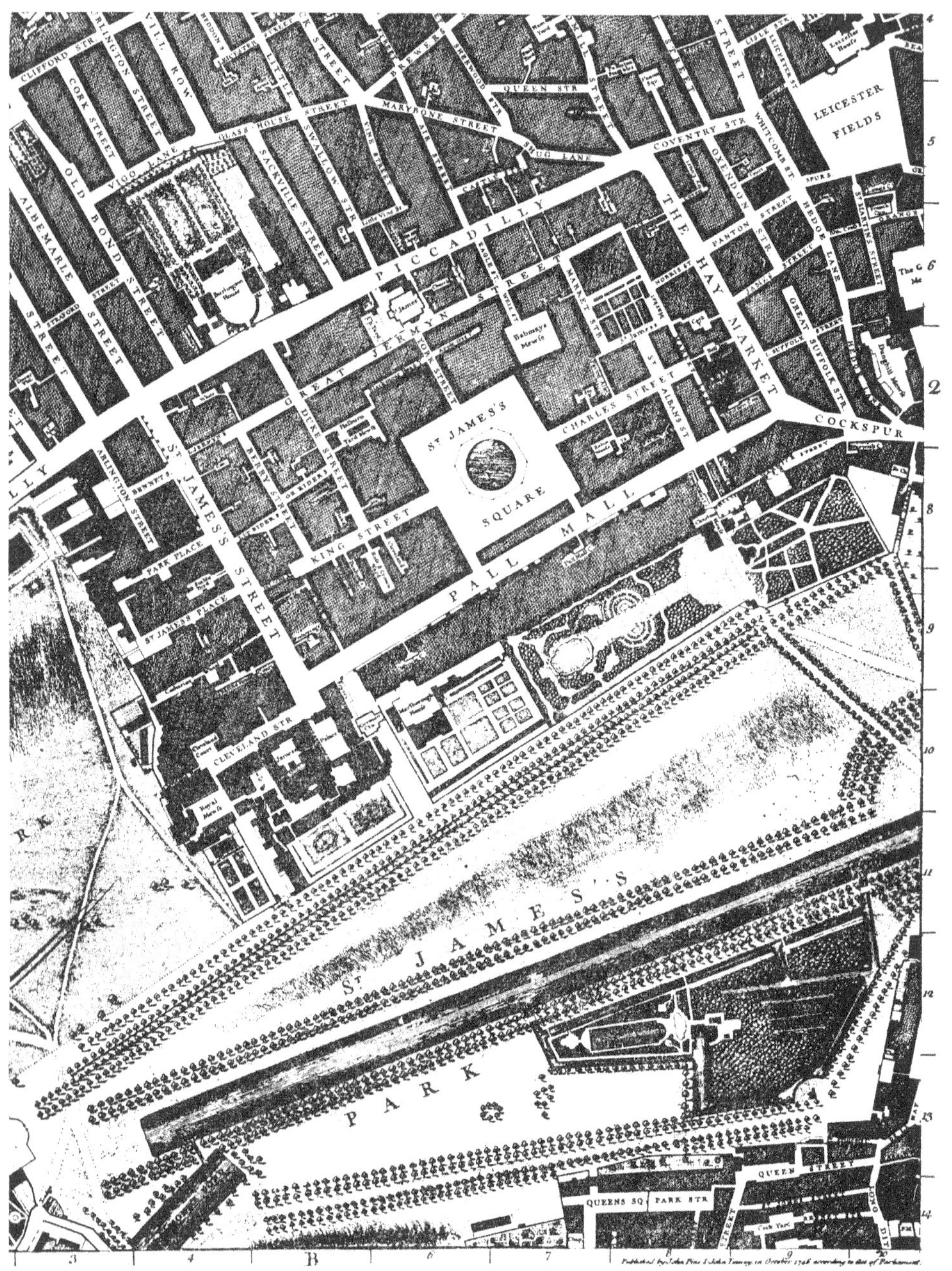

St. James's precinct, London, 1746. An early "Radburn plan"?

by their internal needs and by topography. Because of our heavier automobile traffic we faced fewer houses on main highways than most of the British examples. The English experiences helped us greatly, but if the superblock had not existed logic would have forced us to invent it. A rational escape from the limitations of the checker-board plan in which all streets are through-streets, with the possibility of a collision between auto and pedestrian every 250 feet, compelled it.

Fig. 21—Plan of the residential districts, dated November 1929.

Culs-de-Sac.—The dead-end lane had served in England for peacefulness and for economy of roads and utilities. Culs-de-sac had been used occasionally in our colonial villages. But the typical early American arrangement of houses was along the main, and sometimes only, road. This was more neighborly, and it was easier to shovel snow away in winter. The costliness of through street pavement and main line utilities was not yet a factor of economic importance. Later the extravagance was not understood. Real estate and municipal engineering customs perpetuated obsolete forms. I have already spoken of our experience with courts opening off streets at Sunnyside.

Separation of Different Means of Communication had an excellent nearby precedent, Central Park in New York. Here, almost half a century before the invention of the automobile, Frederick Law Olmsted and Calvert Vaux planned and executed what they described in 1851 as: '... A system of independent ways; 1st, for carriages; 2nd, for horsemen ... ; 3rd, for footmen; and 4th, for common street traffic requiring to cross the Park. By this means it was made possible ... to go on foot to any district of the park ... without crossing a line of wheels on the same level ... '

The automobile has multiplied the need of separating antagonistic uses of streets. The need is recorded in the statistics of automobile accidents—

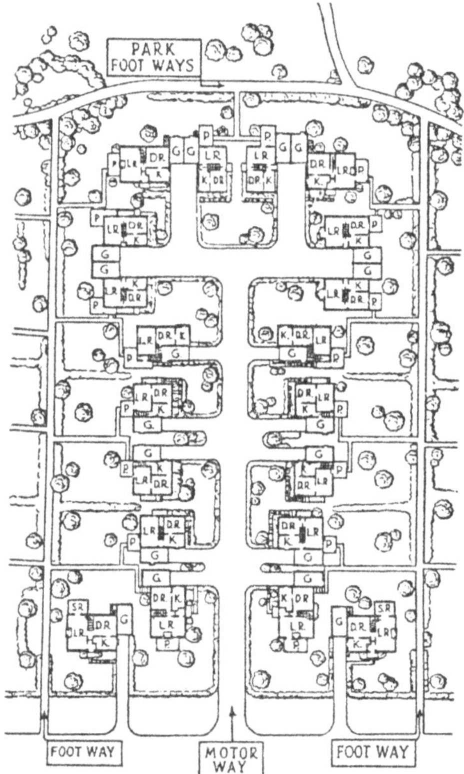

Fig. 19—Plan of a typical "lane" at Radburn. The park in the center of the superblock is shown at the top; the motor ways to the houses are at right angles to the park.

33,410 deaths in 1946, to say nothing of the million or more cripples. At Radburn we proposed to unscramble the varied services of urban streets. Each means of circulation would take care of its special job and no other: through traffic only on the main highways; with street intersections decreased about two-fold; most parking as well as garages, delivery, and other services, on the lanes; walks completely separated from autos by making them part of a park instead of a street, and by under- or over-passing the roads; finally, children's play spaces in the nearby park instead of in busy roads.

Specialized Highways were in their infancy in the U.S.A. at the time that Radburn was conceived. There was not much more than the differentiation of parkways and pseudo-expressways from the ordinary city or town street. To plan or build roads for a particular use and no other use required a predetermined decision to make specialized use permanent or rather long-lived. That was contrary to the fundamentals of American real estate gambling, to serve which the pattern of ordinary highways had become the basis of city planning. I say this in spite of the fact that the 1920's were the heyday of zoning. None of the realtors, and few city planners who accepted zoning as their practical religion, seemed to have faith enough in the permanency of purely residential use to plan streets to serve solely that use. No, not even when the economy of so doing was clearly proved by Henry Wright and Raymond Unwin. Zone for dwellings? Yes, but don't give up the hope that your lot may be occupied some day by a store, gas station, or other more profitable use.

The Radburn Plan proposed to protect the residents, 1st, by planning and building for proposed use, and no other use; 2nd, by private restrictions rather than by wishful zoning.

The House Turned Round.—The creation of the Radburn Idea and of the Radburn Plan was a group activity. It was not merely the conception of its architect-planners. It took form out of actual experience at Sunnyside. It was influenced by the character and diversified abilities and experience of the technicians and the staff of the City Housing Corporation. But there can be no question that the seed from which the Radburn idea grew was conceived by that imaginative genius Henry Wright. Luckily we have in his own words 'The Autobiography of Another Idea'—that is, the Radburn idea.

'In 1902, as an impressionable youth just out of architectural school . . . at Waterford . . . Ireland, . . . I passed through an archway in a blank house wall on the street to a beautiful villa fronting upon spacious interior gardens. That archway was a passage to new ideas . . . I learned then that the comforts and privacy of family life are . . . to be found . . . in a house that judiciously relates living space to open space, the open space . . . being capable of enjoyment by many as well as by few.'

From that time on Henry started 'to face kitchens and service rooms toward the street, and living-rooms inward toward the garden.' At Sunnyside we both wanted to turn all the houses that way, as we ultimately did at Radburn, but conservative opposition only permitted placing some of the porches on the lovely garden side.

Economy of the Radburn Plan.—The parks that formed the interior core of the Radburn superblocks were secured without additional cost. Or rather the savings in expenditure for roads and public utilities at Radburn, as contrasted with the normal subdivision, paid for the parks. The Radburn type of plan requires less area of street to secure the same amount of frontage. In addition, for direct access to most houses, it uses narrower roads of less expensive construction, as well as smaller sized utility lines.

The superblock of 35 to 50 acres is surrounded by wide streets, but it replaces the greater number of wide broad streets of the normal checkerboard plan with service roads only 18 to 20 feet wide. The use of these is limited to 15 or 20 families living on each cul-de-sac, and they carry no through traffic going elsewhere. Therefore they can be of lighter construction, and sewers and water lines are of lesser size and cost than the main lines on the through highways. In fact the area in streets and the length of utilities is 25 per cent less than in the typical American street plan.

The saving in cost of these not only paid for the 12 to 14 per cent of the total area that went into internal parks, but also covered the cost of grading and landscaping the play spaces and green links connecting the central block commons. The greater part of this expenditure was improvement. The land itself—in spite of its value for spinach-growing—cost only six cents a square foot. What makes subdivided land costly, even with the financing, carrying charges, taxes, and profits, is not the land itself. It is the roads and walks, sewers, water lines, electric, gas and other utilities that surround it. This land in lots along streets or lanes costs 6 cents gross or 10 cents per square foot, but an additional 25 cents must be added to pay its share of the improvement that lead to it. A park or playground in a regular town surrounded directly by improved streets would cost as much as it would with houses as a frontage. But not at Radburn—there land is just land (except for surrounding walks). There are no streets. So before landscaping the land, the cost of the parks was less than a fifth of what it would have been had dangerous highways encircled it. [pp. 41–48.]

[Mr. Stein's complete book should be consulted. The above passages have been reproduced with his kind permission and the approval of the Reinhold Publishing Corporation to show the basic "Radburn Idea" which, together with Howard's *Garden Cities* has had a widespread influence on subdivision development in North America even where the idea has been very much misunderstood in the development of suburbia.]

FIRESTONE, RESIDENTIAL REAL ESTATE IN CANADA (1951)

11. *Single and Multiple Dwellings.* Three out of four dwellings built in Canada in 1949 were single units, reflecting the preference of Canadians for self-contained homes constructed as single units, and the effects of government measures encouraging home ownership. In the 'twenties and 'thirties the number of single units built was proportionately smaller, between one-half and seven-tenths of the total (p. 65).

12. *Variations in Fluctuations of Houses Built for Rent and Owner Occupancy.* Over the last three decades, building for rental purposes shows for certain parts of the pre-war period wider fluctuations than building for owner occupancy. Among the reasons for this difference in the amplitude of fluctuations should be included the fact that individual householders and businessmen are affected by different degrees of optimism and pessimism about future prospects, the personal element which enters into the decision of the individual family man to build or to buy a new home but which is absent when an entrepreneur makes up his mind to embark on a rental housing project, and the prevalence of "speculative" house building (pp. 65–69).

64. *Single and Multiple Housing Completions.* About nine out of every

ten houses built in 1949 were single units in all the provinces except Quebec. In this province however, only one out of every three units was of a single house type. The preference for rental accommodation in metropolitan Montreal is mainly responsible for this (pp. 172–175).

[The numbered paragraphs are from the Summary of Analysis.]

NATIONAL HOUSE BUILDERS ASSOCIATION SUBMISSION

Canada. 1962. Royal Commission on Banking and Finance

6. 1 *The Increase in Multiple Family Units.* Since the termination of the last war, there has been a steady change taking place in the form of housing being built in Canada. The single family house was once the predominant type. Back in 1948, for instance, 80% of the units were single family and only 11% were apartments. However, by 1951, multiple family units had risen to 25.9% and the figure was higher in 1961 when it reached 34.2% —over 1/3 of all construction in the housing field.

6. 2 In areas of 5,000 population and over, multiple family units made up 48% (including semi-detached) of the home building activity in 1961. In Metropolitan Toronto, 76% of residential construction last year was of the multiple family type. As we progress as a nation and as more and more of us move into our cities, our housing requirements change. In the older Canada before the war more people lived in rural areas and in smaller communities. The cities into which they have migrated are becoming large and sprawling. Many people are finding single detached houses less suited to this urban life and hence duplexes, semi-detached houses, town houses, apartments and other forms of communal accommodation are gaining favour. Builders have recognized this shift in the market and have gradually changed their operations to the multiple housing field.

6. 3 Multiple housing may be rental accommodation or it may be owned co-operatively. There is a whole new field of opportunity opening up for home ownership in multiple projects. Low wage earners can hardly aspire to owning a single detached house in many of our urban communities. Land costs are too great and can best be overcome by increasing the number of families which occupy an acre of ground. Builders, designers and architects have been working on this problem of increased density and there are now numerous examples of excellent solutions involving multiple housing units which are attractive, economical and vastly better than the living accommodation presently provided for those in the very limited income groups.

6. 5 It is anticipated that the 20–29 year age group which is to show such an increase in this decade will be in the market for multiple family and low-cost housing. They will not be earning large salaries, will probably not have large, if any, down payments to make on expensive houses, but will require low cost housing. The multiple unit, either owned or rented, is apparently the best answer on the horizon today. It is the only form of housing able to overcome the high cost of serviced land. By use of increased density, that is more persons per acre of land, the land cost per unit of accommodation comes down. Serviced land costs for single family houses meanwhile are continuing upward at an astounding rate—a rate whihc cannot be matched by improved building techniques and reduced construction costs.

6. 6 The other group, the 70 years plus group, which is also to increase in the 1960's is another for which multiple family housing is very appealing. Older persons find the responsibilities of single detached houses with their

extensive home care less and less attractive. They are demonstrating this by their acceptance of the special forms of housing which have been constructed with their particular needs in mind. We have only scratched the surface of housing for the elderly.

CHURCHES IN NEW SUBDIVISIONS

Ontario. 1955. 2 *Ontario Planning* No. 5

In the planning of a new subdivision the situation of the church is often over-looked, or perhaps more accurately, deliberately by-passed. Perhaps the foremost reason for this is that the church has no unified voice when it is approached with the problem of choosing a site in advance of an immediate congregation being available.

Educational authorities are organized into school boards at the local level, and at the very most, the planner has three groups with which to consult, but more probably there will be only one. In direct contrast to this, is the difficulty of consulting numerous religious groups when attempting to plan for a future congregation of unknown religious affiliations. Thus, the first problem is—who is to be consulted—obviously it is impractical to provide sites for all religious denominations.

The usual course of events is for an area to develop and then a religious body will attempt to find an appropriate site—often at rather high cost to itself, and the adjoining area.

If a site is chosen for the church of one particular denomination, it may automatically restrain members of other religious beliefs from locating in that neighbourhood. Because of this, a developer is reluctant to set aside land for religious purposes.

The lack of literature on church location is indicative of the dearth of research in this field. The developer, having no basis upon which to proceed, nor the time for original research, takes the path of least resistance, and provides no site.

No one would deny that the church has a rightful place in every plan and is an essential part of the community. A community spirit is often based essentially upon the church symbol and activities, and is an important basis for the neighbourhood. The church role is not confined to religion, but plays its part in the social and cultural life of the people.

The population necessary to support a church building has been estimated to be from 1,000 to 4,000 or about 700 families. The 1953 Conference Extension in Philadelphia suggested one church for 1,500 to 2,500 population of Protestant preference. For Roman Catholics the figure has been set at approximately 3,500. In Levitt Town allowance was made for one church per 750 families—the denomination of each being determined by a "running total" of the population of the area.

"Churches have proved undesirable when located among residences largely because of the automobile parking problem. Activities are going on continually in the modern church. Church sites adjacent to shopping centres have been found satisfactory where they act as a buffer between residential and business uses and where parking is provided nearby which will reduce the damaging effect of excessive parking on residential streets. However, churches should not be so located as to monopolize parking areas in shopping centres at times when shops are open for business. Off-street parking should always be provided on the church site. Church sites necessarily must be from 3 to 5 acres or more in area." (Community Builders Handbook, 1954, p. 89.)

"In developing a new community, church sites should not be selected adjacent to a shopping centre just to take advantage of the parking facilities although there are other good reasons for such a location. There is an overlapping of uses of parking. (Churches should be built on sites sufficiently large to incorporate space for their own needed parking). While churches might be in the general neighbourhood of the shopping centre, don't put them in it. In any event, provide enough parking space to avoid interfering with your merchants." (Community Builders Handbook, 1954, p. 203.)

"Where neighbourhoods are composed of very diversified religious groups, churches may often be grouped with other community facilities at the district level, such as high schools and civic centres, as they then serve a rather widely scattered population. In these cases location of the church on or near a primary traffic artery is important, and land allocations for churches should be considered a district rather than a neighbourhood problem." (Public Administration Service, Planning The Neighbourhood, p. 50).

" . . . characteristics of modern church activity. The amount and nature of their activities will vary widely with the denomination and extent of its program . . . In nearly all cases . . . one or more services will be held on Sunday morning. Sunday evening services and meetings on Wednesday and Thursday are usually the other major meetings regularly scheduled. In addition to meetings of various groups held each week, some churches will have bazaars, dinners, plays, fashion shows, dances and even bingo games scheduled throughout the year. These functions generate a considerable amount of traffic to and from the church. Even in the so-called small neighbourhood church, a substantial proportion of the attendants use automobiles even though they may live less than one-half mile away." (Home Builders Manual for Land Development, p. 200.)

"Land values and building densities customary, or allowed, vary greatly from the heart of a large city to the fringe of a small one, have a decided bearing on lot size. However, the following standards are helpful in deciding the space requirements for the average church based on a seating capacity for 50% of its members.

(1) Worship unit of 10 to 12 square feet per person
(2) Fellowship unit of 12 to 15 square feet per person
(3) Educational unit of 20 square feet per person
(4) Off-street parking at one car space for each three in attendance or 100 square feet per person;

Another method of space computation is as follows: (a) Up to 400 members—a minimum of one acre (2 is better) (b) 400 to 800 members—a minimum of two acres (3 to 5 is better) (c) 800 to 1200 members—a minimum of three acres (d) 1200 or more members—a minimum of four acres (William H. Claire, The Church in the City Plan, Journal of the American Institute of Planners, Fall 1954; p. 177.)

"If the Church is to be properly located in the American community, three needs must be met on national level: (1) Ideally, Protestant, Roman Catholic and Jewish forces should unite in an approach to planners. If this ideal is impossible, the Protestant denominations must unite and move forward alone. This concept of united ecumenical action requires a whole new strategy. Services of worship, united study projects, joint social action are not enough. There must be a strategy for dividing responsibility, or territory, or people. The importance of this suggestion should not be minimized, for it proposes a division that can determine the future life and strength of a denomination. As a strategy, it calls for more than the comity procedures of the past. It calls for a regional distribution of churches, for the safe-guarding of minorities, for the recognition of majorities, for the protecting of religious freedom, and for taking into account the sociological and psychological factors of the community. This is, in effect, a strategy that calls for a new attitude, and thus, a new profession—for a Church equivalent of the American Institute of Planners, or perhaps for a Church Chapter of the American Institute of Planners. (2) The second emerging need is for a realistic approach to the professional planner, an approach that will present the Church as a uniting force in the building of a community. The burden of perfecting a technique and demonstrating its power to unite people rests with the Church, and when it has succeeded, planners will make planning for the Church one of their primary concerns. In the same way, the Church must first unite and then demonstrate that its denominations are component parts in a united body of public opinion that will support those projects that include adequate church planning. (3) The third need is for the reduction to an approved body of statistical information, such data as will enable planners to determine how many churches are needed, where they should be located, and what acreage is required for churches in any neighbourhood or community they plan. This is an undertaking of considerable magnitude, for not only must the churches gather the data, but they must unite in determining the formula by which the data are to be used. Nevertheless, it must be done." (John H. Shope, "The Need for Church Planning," Journal of the American Institute of Planners, Summer 1954, pp. 123, 124.)

It is obvious from the above that finding a location for a church involves more than just setting aside some land. It concerns the location in relation to the population it is to serve, the type of activities it will sponsor, and the amount of land necessary to accommodate the building and the accessory uses in keeping with the amenities of the neighbourhood. Thus, the location of churches should be viewed in a similar manner to the location of schools in regard to the official plan. And again, in view of the numerous activities and needs of a church it should be restricted by restricted area by-laws as to amount of parking space, front, side and rear and permissible activities and accessory buildings.

SUBDIVISION DESIGN: GOOD, GRID AND GIMMICKY

Ontario. 1958. 5 *Ontario Planning* No. 8, p. 1

The following illustrations were prepared by the Community Planning Branch for a departmental exhibit at the Canadian National Exhibition. The text captions and comparative analysis are taken from *Ontario Planning*, the departmental publication.

Unplanned Neighbourhood
Grid Iron Pattern

Streets—No distinction is made between streets as to their function. Each is potentially a through traffic route. A total of 91 intersections—71 of them cross-intersections—means a high accident hazard. Unrestricted highway access impedes through highway traffic and creates further accident hazard. Acreage devoted to streets is almost double that in the planned subdivision. (See COMPARATIVE ANALYSIS.) Topography of the site has been ignored and gridiron pattern over-runs natural features, such as

pond and watercourse, which are preserved in the planned layout. Owing to the excessive length of streets, service costs are increased.

Housing—Housing is all single family and building lines are not varied, creating a monotonous effect. Some building lots are long, narrow and poorly shaped.

Neighborhood Facilities—School, church, shops and community centre are largely dispersed and off-street parking facilities are inadequate or lacking altogether.

Industry—Light industrial uses are situated within the residential area and there is no buffer between heavy industrial and residential uses.

"Can of Worms"
Bad Curvilinear Pattern

Although numerous criticisms may be made of this layout, the chief one is that the arbitrarily imposed curved street pattern creates confusion of traffic movement. No single street has a clear destination and there is no collector

street serving as a logical and convenient link both within the neighborhood and to the highway.

Planned Neighbourhood Good Curvilinear Pattern

Streets—The neighbourhood is surrounded by major transportation routes, Interior streets are laid out in a curved pattern, fitted to the topography of the site, in such a way as to discourage through traffic and, at the same time, provide for good interior circulation and economic servicing. Elimination of cross-intersections and the use of T-intersections reduces accident hazard. An *interior collector street* ensures convenient flow and distribution of traffic in the residential area. Altogether, there are only 53 intersections, compared with 91 in the gridiron plan. Access to the highway is limited and intersections with the highway are designed with grade separation—to keep through traffic moving safely and quickly.

Housing—Provision is made for various housing types—apartments, row housing and semi-detached, as well as single-family detached. This creates added social and esthetic interest and value, as well as ensuring economic use of land. Set-backs of one- and two-family units are varied to create visual interest.

Neighborhood Facilities—School, community centre, park, church and shopping facilities, together with adequate parking space for these uses, are centrally located and grouped for the maximum convenience of all residents of the neighborhood.

Industry—Heavy industry is located next to the railway line and highway. Light industrial sites adjacent to the residential area are screened by open space and trees.

COMPARATIVE ANALYSIS OF SUBDIVISION DESIGN

LAND USES (areas in acres except where mentioned)	*UNPLANNED* (Gridiron Pattern)	*"CAN OF WORMS"* (Bad Curvilinear Pattern)	*PLANNED* (Good Curvilinear Pattern)
Internal Roads Length (Linear feet)	60,760	43,578	38,270
Internal Roads Area	95.0	66.0	53.0
Neighborhood Shopping Area	9.2	8.1	5.7
Open-Space Area	8.1	19.5	27.5
Community Center Area	3.7		2.8
Primary Schools Area	4.4	9.0	10.5
Churches	4.3	9.4	10.0
Multiple Dwellings Area		23.0	32.0
Total Residential Area — Excluding Roads	205.3	218.0	220.5
Total Area of Subdivision	330.0	330.0	330.0
RESIDENTIAL USES			
Total Number of Residential Lots	1,110	840	1,140
Multiple Dwellings Area Converted Into Lots (5 Lots Per Acre)		115	160
Total Number of Lots	1110	955	1300
RESIDENTIAL USES			
Number of Single Family Dwellings	1110	840	912
Number of Semi-Detached Dwellings			228
Number of Row-Housing Units			106
Number of Apartment Units		650	675
Total Number of Units	1110	1490	1921
POPULATION			
Single Family Dwellings 4 Persons Per Unit	4440	3360	3648
Semi-Detached Dwellings 4 Persons Per Unit			912
Row Houses—4 Persons Per Unit			424
Apartments—3 Persons Per Unit			2025
Total Population	4440	5310	7009

DENSITY (Dwellings per acre except where mentioned)	UNPLANNED (Gridron Pattern)	"CAN OF WORMS" (Bad Curvilinear Pattern)	PLANNED (Good Curvilinear Pattern)
Gross Density (Total Number of Dwellings Divided By Total Acreage of Scheme)	3.35	4.5	5.8
Net Density (Total Number of Dwellings or Persons Divided by Total Residential Acreage Including Roads)	3.7	5.2	7.0
Or Persons	17.0	18.4	25.5

(*b*) *The legislator's view*

MUNICIPAL ACT
British Columbia. Revised Statutes. 1960. Chapter 43

712. (1) Subject to subsection (2), the Council may by by-law prescribe the minimum frontage which any parcel of land in any proposed subdivision may have with respect to the highway upon which the parcel fronts, but, whether so prescribed or not, no parcel of land in any proposed subdivision shall have less than one-tenth of its perimeter fronting on such highway.

(2) The Council may, by an affirmative vote of at least two-thirds of all the members thereof, exempt a person proposing to subdivide land from any prescribed minimum frontage or from the limitation provided under subsection (1).

SUBDIVISION AND TRANSFER REGULATIONS
Alberta. Regulations. 1960. 185/60; Order in Council 926–60

20. (1) There shall be direct access to every lot or parcel from a public street, roadway or walkway, and also if the Director or the approving authority so requires from a service roadway, lane or utility right-of-way;
28. (1) Streets included in or adjacent to a subdivision shall be classified with regard to present and future traffic requirements, adjoining uses and topography, and the minimum widths of streets in each class shall be provided as follows:

Urban highway or arterial roadway	132 feet
Main through town roadway	100 feet
Secondary through roadway or residential collector street	80 feet
Minor or residential street	50 feet
Service roadway adjacent to or intersecting a controlled highway	66 feet
Service roadway adjacent to an arterial roadway	50 feet
Service roadway in lieu of lane	30 feet
Cul-de-sac (with 50 foot turning radius)	50 feet
Half street	one-half of the street or roadway ultimately required
Walkway in lieu of front street	50 feet

provided, however, that no street or roadway shall be less than 66 feet wide where storm sewers are not provided.

(2) Where definite proposals for future traffic circles or other major street intersections have been adopted, land for these shall be provided in addition to any land required pursuant to clause (1).

29. The length of a street or roadway measured between successive intersections shall not be excessive having regard to convenience of vehicular access, and in the cases of culs-de-sac and loop service roadways, their lengths shall not exceed 300 feet and 1,500 feet respectively unless in a specific case a greater length is approved by the Director or the approving authority.

36. (1) The side lines of all lots and parcels shall be as nearly as possible perpendicular to the street lines, except as may be required for reasons of topography or aspect;

(2) A lot shall not have frontage on two parallel or approximately parallel streets;

37. (1) In a subdivision which will be served by a public sewer and water system:

- (a) each lot in a "street and lane" or in a "walkway and service roadway" system to be used for a single family dwelling shall have:
  - (i) a mean width of not less than 40 feet for internal lots and not less than 50 feet for corner lots, provided that the average width of any group of adjoining internal lots shall be not less than 45 feet and provided that the lot widths are reasonably varied;
  - (ii) a mean length of not less than 110 feet; and
  - (iii) an area of not less than 5,000 square feet.
- (b) each lot in a "street and utility right-of-way" system to be used for a single family dwelling shall have:
  - (i) a mean width of not less than 55 feet;
  - (ii) a mean length of not less than 100 feet;
  - (iii) an area of not less than 5,500 square feet.
- (c) each lot to be used for a duplex dwelling shall have an area of not less than 3,500 square feet for each dwelling unit;
- (d) each lot to be used for a row house dwelling shall have an area for each dwelling unit of not less than:
  - (i) 2,500 square feet for an interior lot;
  - (ii) 3,500 square feet for an end house lot.

(2) In a subdivision which cannot be served or is not intended to be served by a public sewer or public water system, each lot to be used for a single family dwelling or a duplex dwelling shall have:

- (a) (i) a mean width of not less than 80 feet for internal lots and not less than 100 feet for corner lots;
  - (ii) a mean length of not less than 125 feet; and
  - (iii) an area of not less than 10,000 square feet; or
- (b) such greater dimensions and area as the Director or the approving authority may require after consideration of the recommendation of the local Board of Health, in relation to the nature of the site.

(3) The depth or length of any lot or parcel shall bear a reasonable relationship to its width.

38. (1) Lots or parcels intended for use as dwelling sites shall not be located within distance and direction as the Director or the approving authority may specify from the right-of-way of an operating railway line, the

right-of-way of a controlled highway, any airport or airfield runway, or any heavy industrial site, dam, reservoir or aqueduct.

NOTE. The provisions of section 37 and 38 are frequently found in zoning by-laws and the extent to which the subdivision regulations regulate land use and open space may be seen from the next parts (not reproduced), which deal with subdivisions for commercial use, industrial use, country residences, small holdings, resorts, in the vicinity of highways and highway commercial use. Each part regulates the "permitted locations" and thus the use of land.

NOTE ON STREET WIDTH IN ONTARIO. Nothing in *The Planning Act* in Ontario sets a standard for street widths, but it is generally believed, and subdivisions are therefore designed on that belief, that the Minister will not approve a plan that provides for streets narrower than 66 feet. It is also believed that the Department of Highways, which makes annual grants for the maintenance of streets by townships, will not provide its largesse for streets under 66 feet in width. In addition to this real or imagined obstacle, *The Municipal Act*, R.S.O. 1960, c. 249, in section 466(2), provides that "No highway less than 66 feet in width, or, except in a city or town, more than 100 feet in width shall be laid out by the council of the municipality without the approval of the Municipal Board or by any owner of land without the approval of the Council of the municipality and of the Municipal Board." Section 466 does not affect *The Planning Act*.

4. Municipal Services

THE INSTALLATION OF MUNICIPAL SERVICES

Ontario. 1954. 1 *Ontario Planning* Nos. 6 and 7. Supplements.

The physical improvements required by a municipality for a subdivision are closely related to the stage of existing or anticipated urban development within the municipality, or within that portion of the municipality in which the subdivision is located. In more remote areas such as resort properties with lot sizes of one acre or more and suitable water and soil conditions, the only improvement required may be an access road. On the other hand, in subdivisions within or adjacent to built-up urban municipalities with lot areas as low as 5,000 square feet, all urban services and amenities may be required. The standard subdivision agreement of the Township of North York, which is located within the municipality of metropolitan Toronto, contains clauses covering the following services which, where considered necessary, must be installed by the subdivider: (a) roadways including asphalt surfacing; (b) watermains; (c) sanitary sewers; (d) storm sewers; (e) sidewalks; (f) street lighting; (g) street signs.

The agreement also contains clauses setting forth conditions relating to the following matters: (a) hydro-electric installations; (b) existing and final grades and contour; (c) clearance for building lots prior to issuing building permits; (d) lands for municipal purposes; (e) payment of taxes; (f) notification to purchaser as to services; (g) drainage works; (h) financial arrangements with the township; (i) registration of the subdivision agreement.

Methods of Financing Services. When the services and improvements to be installed in the subdivision have been determined by the municipality, the question of the method of financing is raised. The municipality may charge the cost of the improvements to the following sources or a combination of them:

(a) the general tax rate to be paid for by taxpayers as a whole and utility rates to be paid for by utility users;

(b) a local improvement rate under *The Local Improvement Act* [Now R.S.O., 1960, c. 223] to be charged in part to owners of properties abutting the properties and in part to the corporation's share. In a township the corporation's share may be levied against an Area;

(c) the subdivider, who would shift the cost to the purchaser of the property.

The first method is seldom used except in combination with the second. The traditional method of financing municipal services is under *The Local Improvement Act* where a large percentage of the cost is charged to owners of abutting properties by a special frontage rate and the remainder for flankages, intersections and non-taxable properties to the general tax rate. Local improvement debentures sold under the provisions of *The Local Improvement Act* are amortized over a period of years depending on the service and the internal economy of the municipality. The additional width for a street widening or the centre strip of a street and the additional cost incurred from installations over and above the size needed to service the adjoining properties may be charged to the general tax rate on the assumption that these are improvements which benefit the community as a whole.

The rapid and extensive scale of land development in recent years has placed a strain on the financial position of some municipalities which must build large-scale capital works such as sewage treatment plants and trunk sewers, water pumping and filtration plants and trunk mains, arterial roads and schools, etc. This problem may be better understood when it is realized that the population of the Province which is reaching 5 million is increasing at a rate of 150,000 per year, with the increase confined largely to urban areas and their semi-urban fringe.

In order to accommodate an increase in population of 150,000 per year a land area equivalent to the whole of the metropolitan area of Windsor or the combined built-up areas of Belleville, Owen Sound, Brantford, St. Catharines and Sarnia must be developed and serviced each year. In 1953, 1200 applications for subdivision, a high percentage of which were located in or adjacent to the larger towns and cities, were submitted for the approval of the Minister. In the circumstances there would be an unrelenting pressure to develop the land for more intensive uses. In the absence of legal instruments of control and appropriate guidance according to good planning principles, random development, land speculation and subdivision would likely grow to proportions which would plunge the municipality into financial difficulties in the event of even a minor economic recession.

Where services are installed under local improvement provisions and the only costs incurred by the subdivider are the purchase price of the land and the preparation of the plan should the demand for building land be active, speculative land subdivision is encouraged. On the other hand where the subdivider must install the services and risk a larger financial outlay, he is forced to assume a more prudent outlook. Because speculation is reduced the financial position of the municipality is safeguarded.

Development Costs Cause of Concern. Municipalities which must undertake extensive capital development programs have been reluctant to provide local services in subdivisions as well. They have hesitated to add to their debenture debt where the speculative element in the subdivision is strong and the subdivider stands to profit from the installation of services. In such situations they usually require the subdivider to install and pay for all services on his land. An Ontario municipality of 13,000 which this year adopted a policy of having subdividers pay for services discovered that had the policy been initiated a year previously the issue of local improvement debentures would now be reduced from $100,000 to $35,000.

The practice of having the subdivider install services which was very rare until the end of the war when municipalities had little difficulty in borrowing money for works is becoming more frequent. In 1949 mainly as a result of the financial policy adopted by the Government of Canada the funds available to municipalities were reduced and by 1951, in the face of a further demand for funds for federal government purposes and a related general increase in interest rates, municipalities were able to market their debentures only if they too were willing to pay the higher interest rates. A growing number of municipalities then ceased to be willing to increase their debenture debt in order to finance services under *The Local Improvement Act* and called upon builders when developing their lands to install their own services.

Advantages and Disadvantages of Builder Installed Services. It would appear that although advantages result to municipalities from this practice, subdividers may experience some inconvenience when required to install services. Some of the advantages and disadvantages may be summarized as follows:

(a) By keeping their debt to a minimum and reducing borrowing requirements municipalities benefit on the money market;

(b) Under circumstances where the municipality is unable to supply all builders and home owners with the benefits of *The Local Improvement Act,* objection may be raised against the credit of a municipality in a difficult money market situation being extended for the benefit of a restricted and limited number of builders and home owners requesting such assistance. In certain instances the limited ability of the municipality to install services under *The Local Improvement Act* has had the effect of creating a significant premium on serviced land and a monetary advantage for those builders who were fortunate enough to have their applications for local improvements approved by the Municipal Council. If the municipality under *The Local Improvement Act* is able to proceed with only a fraction of the municipal services being demanded in areas where all or partial services are required it is placed in a difficult position;

(c) Municipalities have claimed that developers who subdivide for profit should pay for all services at current prices and no portion should be charged to general rates as is the case when financing is under *The Local Improvement Act.* They, therefore, require developers to install all services within the entire project, including flankages and intersections which were formerly charged to the general rate;

(d) Use of this new method may prove more satisfactory than *The Local Improvement Act* in that less strain is placed on the municipality. To the extent that a larger portion of improvement costs are financed under the mortgage the financial position of the municipality is protected;

(e) Where the services are installed by the municipality under *The Local Improvement Act* the lapse of considerable time between registration of the plan and installation of services is unavoidable. After registration of the plan under present circumstances as a matter of policy at least 25 per cent of the lots must be improved prior to the passing of the local improvement by-law and the approval of the Ontario Municipal Board must be granted prior to the sale of the debentures. The municipality is also placed in the unfavourable position of issuing permits for lots where the installation of services is problematic. Furthermore, this procedure is not convenient in new subdivisions, particularly to builders who are also subdividers and are anxious to build on a large number or all lots in the project at one operation in order to reduce their building costs;

(f) The builder and land developer when required to install services are affected in a manner different from the municipality. The home purchaser, upon whom the builder shifts the additional cost of services, must finance in whole or in part, depending on the basis of his mortgage financing, a corresponding increase in the purchase price;

(g) The builder and land developer have greatly increased working capital requirements and must restrict the size of their operations accordingly. The larger builders in strong credit positions may manage but the smaller builders find it increasingly more difficult to undertake both building and land development;

(h) There is some question as to the desirability of having each builder install services within his own subdivision even where they are inspected by the municipal engineer. There appears to be merit in having services installed under the direct supervision of the municipality. In spite of the best efforts of municipal engineers, instances have been reported where builder-installed services were unsatisfactory and substandard in quality, design and construction;

(i) It has been claimed that the new home owner would be at a disadvantage in receiving less favourable terms than the people who built within the municipality in earlier years, particularly where there is a difference in the portion of services charged against local rates;

(j) The net effect of the subdivider's installing services is a higher down payment required from prospective home owners even where 80 per cent of services are financed by a *National Housing Act* loan;

(k) Where there is comprehensive planning and zoning within the municipality, theoretically, there should not be variations in the completed subdivisions. However, it has been claimed that, in practice, because the builder is interested only in the lands which he owns, there is a tendency toward piecemeal development and a lesser degree of integration in the services when considered from the standpoint of the community as a whole.

Municipalities are in the position of having to assess the relative merits of builder-installed as opposed to municipally-installed services and to weigh the advantages and disadvantages of each method. The method of financing is a matter of local policy which must be decided by the municipal council.

Comparison of Cost Structures. When the cost structures of houses having local services installed by the subdivider and by the municipality under *The Local Improvement Act* are compared, although the down payment required of the home purchaser is usually higher in the first instance, the annual charge, because it is amortized over a period of 20 to 25 years, is considerably lower. In contrast, because local improvement debentures are repayable in a shorter period of 10 to 15 years, the owner pays a greater amount per year but a lesser amount in total interest. The lower sale price made possible by *Local Improvement Act* provisions, in spite of higher carrying charges, is generally preferred by house owners over having the services installed by the builder and the cost consolidated into the mortgage debt.

When based on theoretical calculation there may be little difference in the aggregate cost whether the municipality or the builder installs the services, under actual market conditions, where the municipality undertakes to install or has already installed services on a local improvement basis, due to the natural increment in land values which results from the development, there is a stronger tendency to incorporate the cost of the land in the sale price at a figure considerably in excess of the cost of the raw land . . .

[A detailed discussion of the methods of financing the housing project has been omitted. There is a comparison of conventional mortgage lending by private lenders and by private lenders under The National Housing Act and under the N.H.A. with an agreed sale provision.]

Where a municipality upon receipt of a petition under the provisions of *The Local Improvement Act* undertook to install the services there was a strong tendency for far too much land, often poorly selected and requiring expensive grading and filling, to be subdivided. On the other hand, where the subdivider installed the services at his own expense, because of the greater financial outlay, it has been found that he acted more carefully and exercised greater prudence in the selection and development of land. Being responsible for his own risks, he restricted his operations to producing a commodity which would sell on a competitive market.

Where a subdivider is charged for services either of two methods of payment may be used:

(a) He may be required to make a direct payment to the municipality for engineering and inspection fees and all construction costs and have the services designed and installed by the municipality according to standards specified in the subdivision standards by-laws; or

(b) He may enter into an agreement with the municipality to undertake the engineering and installation of services according to plans and specifications approved by the municipality. The services when constructed, inspected and approved would be assumed by the municipality. The specifications for services contained in the agreement would be outlined where one has been passed as required by the subdivisions standards by-law.

Statutory Authority for the Charges. The view has been expressed that authority for municipalities to charge subdividers for municipal services should be explicitly expressed by statute as is done in some American states. It is agreed that where there is a statutory rule the municipality, should it so wish, may order the subdivider to install local improvements such as roadways, pavements, curbs, gutters, sewers, watermains, street lights, etc. as a condition of the approval of the final plan of subdivision, or as an alternative because of the practical considerations, authorize the filing of a performance bond to cover the cost of the services.

American Experience. In American planning literature where model subdivision statutes are suggested the general rule is to include provisions requiring the subdivider to install or arrange for the amenities such as:

Grading and paving streets; installation of street lighting; installation of curbs; installation of gutters; installation of street trees; installation of water mains; installation of sanitary sewers; installation of storm drains.

As early as 1928 the U.S. Department of Commerce in their *Standard City [Planning] Enabling Act* included sections which provided for arrangements to be made by municipalities with owners for grading and improving streets, installation of water mains and sewers, and other services, precedent to approval of the subdivision. Provisions were also included for acceptance of performance bonds. . . .

The foregoing would indicate that in American experience the practice of charging local improvement costs directly to subdividers as a condition of approving the plan

(a) is not a recent innovation, and

(b) has now been adopted in areas of rapid development to the extent of becoming almost universal.

Ontario Practice. Under *The Planning Act* of Ontario, pursuant to the provisions of subsections (3), (4), (6) and (8) of section 26, the Minister has, as a matter of policy, accorded to municipalities prior to approval of the final plan, the privilege of entering into agreements with subdividers to provide for local improvements. . . .

Under subsection (4) and the procedural provisions of subsections (6) and (8), municipalities may recommend to the Minister conditions of approval of the draft plan. The conditions as recommended are usually accepted by the Minister and required of the subdivider prior to approval of the final plan. While the plans are formally approved by the Minister, because he confers with the municipalities and usually awaits and accepts their recommendations, by informal arrangement, the process of approving plans of subdivision is made a co-operative joint effort of the Minister and the municipalities.

As part of their role in this joint process subdivision examination and approval a number of municipalities have passed subdivision standards by-law which, in fact, are formal declarations of policy, to outline standards and specifications regarding widths, grading and surfacing of roadways, installation of water mains and sewers, etc., which have uniform application to various areas within the municipality. At the request of the municipality, the Minister may at his discretion direct that the standards specified in the by-law be enforced in specific instances by an agreement or undertaking to be given by the subdivider to the municipality.

Where the services are designed and installed under the supervision of the municipal engineer and the works department, the subdivision agreement usually charges the subdivider with a fee equivalent to five per cent of costs. If engineering designs and supervision are provided by a firm of consulting engineers on behalf of the subdivider usually the charge is only for inspection.

The content of by-laws and agreements containing standards and specifications is usually determined by the stage of development in the municipality. As mentioned previously, in the Toronto Metropolitan Area, the largest number of services possibly are covered by the Township of North York subdivision agreement. For purposes of reference, the agreement is reproduced as Appendix "A".

Charges for Capital Improvements off the Subdivision. Improvements such as roads, water mains, sewers and sidewalks located within the boundaries of the subdivision as a general rule are installed and paid for by the subdivider. Certain items such as storm sewers and asphalt pavements when installed after the subdivision has been built up have at times been financed as local improvements. These local services are, however, but a part of the total cost of development and must be connected, in order to be made operative, to capital works and services built off the site. The cost of capital works which are of general benefit to the municipalities, has presented a serious financial problem to rapidly developing municipalities. Pumping stations, filtration plants, trunk mains and sewers, sewage treatment plants, new schools, etc., must be financed and built in municipalities which were until recently entirely agricultural in their economy.

In order to meet the financial burden of some of these capital improvements certain municipalities have made charges on subdividers on a uniform per lot or other area basis. A study of the capital charge practices of some ten municipalities in the Toronto area leads to the conclusion that no standard pattern has yet been adopted which is applicable to all municipalities, but charges are levied by each municipality in a manner to meet its own financial problems. There are also instances within one municipality where charges are made on the basis of the special problems created by the subdivision and not according to a uniform policy applicable to all subdivisions.

The survey showed that of the ten municipalities two did not make a practice of capital charges except in special circumstances where charges had been made for schools and sewage treatment plants in large subdivisions. Five municipalities made regular charges for either special or general purposes ranging from $500 per acre to $550 per lot. Three other municipalities were intending to charge but as yet, being without a uniform policy, charged only in very special instances.

NOTE. The North York agreement has been omitted. It is reprinted as well in (1960) *Special Lectures of the Law Society of Upper Canada* on the *Sale of Land*, pages 164–179. The agreement should be consulted for its terms.

5. The Equitable Distribution of Servicing Costs

(a) Parks and recreation

SUBDIVISION AND TRANSFER REGULATIONS

Alberta. Regulations. 1960. 185/60; Order in Council 926–60

22. (1) When land that exceeds two acres in area is subdivided, such parcels as the Director, the approving authority, or the Board may designate and as may be specified by the other provisions of these regulations shall be reserved for provincial and municipal government use and other public purposes, and for parks, school sites and other community purposes.

(2) The provision of a reserve under clause (1) may be deferred, only when the newly created parcels in the proposed plan of subdivision are in excess of 20 acres each, and where a written covenant is made by the owner to the effect that he will provide the required reserve at a later date. Such covenant shall run with the land and shall specify:

(a) the area of the reserve, the provision of which is being deferred;
(b) the parcel from which the reserve is to be provided; and
(c) the circumstances in which the reserve shall be provided.

23. (1) Except as otherwise provided herein, the total area of a reserve or reserves provided shall be not less than ten percent of the whole area to be registered under the plan of subdivision.

(3) For the purpose of determining the area of the reserves to be provided in any subdivision, land previously donated or sold for a nominal

sum by the applicant and permanently reserved for school, park or other public or community purposes within or adjacent to the land which is to be subdivided may, with the concurrence of the Director or the approving authority, be deemed to be a reserve within the subdivision.

(4) Notwithstanding the other provisions of this regulation, the provision of reserves of lesser area may be authorized by the Board if the total area of the reserves, public streets, roadways, lanes and walkways otherwise required to be provided in a subdivision would be more than forty per cent of the area of the land being subdivided.

24. (1) The location of each reserve shall be to the satisfaction of the Director, the approving authority, or the Board and, in the case of reserves provided for provincial government use, to the satisfaction of the Director of Surveys.

(2) The land contained in each reserve shall be suitable for the use for which it is intended and shall, as to the average conditions of its topography and the nature of its soil, be of the same general character and quality as the remainder of the land in the subdivision.

(3) Notwithstanding Regulation 23, where the land to be subdivided contains waste land or ravines, swamps, natural drainage courses, or other areas which in the opinion of the Director or the approving authority are unsuitable for building sites or other private use, the Board, upon recommendation of the Director or the approving authority, may require that those areas be reserved for park or other public purposes in addition to such reserves as are provided pursuant to Regulation 23.

25. Each reserve shall be designated on the plan of subdivision as either Community Reserve or Public Reserve and, in cases where the specific future use of a reserve is known, such use may also be specified under the main designation of the reserve.

THE COMMUNITY PLANNING ACT, 1957
Saskatchewan. Statutes. 1957. Chapter 48

67. (1) The Minister may make regulations not inconsistent with the provisions of this Act for controlling the subdivision of land. . . .

68. Regulations under section 67 shall

(d) require that, if the land to be subdivided is to be subdivided for residential purposes and it is intended that the number of families that are to reside on the land is equal to or greater than the product of four multiplied by the number of acres contained in the land, provision be made for the dedication to the public use, other than for streets and lanes, of ten per cent of the land and that in all other cases provision be made for such dedication of five per cent of the land to be subdivided; provided that, in the case of a townsite or the first subdivision within a quarter section, the parcel of land so reserved shall be at least two acres in area; . . .

COMMUNITY PLANNING ACT
New Brunswick. Statutes. 1960–61. Chapter 6

29. (1) Subject to this Act, the council may, by by-law to be known as a subdivision by-law, control the subdivision of land in the municipality, and without limiting the generality of the foregoing, a subdivision by-law may

(e) require as to any subdivision or any class of subdivision that land
   (i) to an amount indicated in the by-law, not exceeding ten per cent of the area of the subdivision, and
   (ii) at such location as may be approved by the commission,

shall be conveyed to the council for public purposes as a condition of approval of a subdivision plan by the commission;

(f) provide that, in the discretion of the commission, there shall be paid to the council, in lieu of a conveyance of land under a provision passed under paragraph (e), such sums as may be indicated in the by-law, not exceeding one-twelfth of the market value of land in a subdivision exclusive of the streets intended for public use;

THE PLANNING ACT

Ontario. Revised Statutes. 1960. Chapter 296

28. (5) The Minister may impose such conditions to the approval of a plan of subdivision as in his opinion are advisable and, in particular but without restricting in any way whatsoever the generality of the foregoing, he may impose as a condition,

(a) that land to an amount determined by the Minister but not exceeding 5 per cent of the land included in the plan shall be conveyed to the municipality for public purposes other than highways or, if the land is not in a municipality, shall be dedicated for public purposes other than highways;

(8) Where the land is in a municipality and an official plan, indicating the amount and location of the land to be ultimately provided for public purposes, is in effect in the municipality, the Minister may authorize, in lieu of the conveyance for public purposes other than highways required under subsection 5, the payment to the municipality of a sum of money not exceeding the value of 5 per cent of the land included in the subdivision.

(9) Land conveyed to a municipality under subsection 5 shall be held and used by the municipality for public purposes, but may be sold with the approval of the Minister.

NOTE. The Minister may be asked by a municipality to require a subdivider of land to convey up to five per cent of the land in a subdivision to the municipality for parks and recreational purposes, but where the five per cent is such a small area that it would be useless for such purposes, the municipality used to ask the subdivider to contribute cash instead. As this practice increased, subsection 8 was passed to regularize it, and the effect may have been to increase pressure on a council to establish a planning board and adopt an official plan. But when it became apparent that the five per cent was of the value of the land in the subdivision before the services were added, grasping municipalities returned to their earlier practice of asking for land. When the plan was prepared, the local authority could say to the subdivider, we want lots 5, 6 and 7 on the plan for a park. Although the council had no intention of putting a park where lots 5 to 7 were shown on the plan, they nevertheless could ask the Minister to require that these lots be conveyed to the municipality. After the subdivider had serviced the land in his plan, the municipality, with the Minister's approval under subsection 9, could sell these lots back to the subdivider at the going price for serviced lots.

Is such a practice within the intent of section 28 (5)? Should the municipality contribute to the cost of servicing its lots? Would the municipality have to pay for serviced land elsewhere when it used the money to buy park land? Should the Minister give his approval to the sale? Could the subdivider require the Minister to refer the application for his approval to the Municipal Board? What sort of park policy does this section contemplate?

Is the Ontario formula of a percentage of the land satisfactory? Would a formula based on density of development be more appropriate?

(b) Street services and schools

MUNICIPAL ACT

British Columbia. Revised Statutes. 1960. Chapter 43

711. (1) The Council may [by by-law] . . .

(d) require that the highways within the subdivision be cleared, drained, and surfaced to a prescribed standard, but excluding the construction of sidewalks and boulevards;

(e) where the municipality has a sewage-disposal system, require that a sewage-collection system be provided in accordance with standards set out in the by-law, make provision for the connection of the system with the established sewage-disposal system of the municipality, and provide that the lands included in the subdivision shall be exempt from, but only from, the charges imposed in the municipality for works of a like nature for a period of time calculated to be sufficient to amortize the actual cost of the collection system computed at an interest rate not exceeding four per centum per annum; but if the municipality requires that any main of such collection system be of a diameter in excess of that required to service the subdivision the municipality shall assume and pay the cost providing the excess capacity.

(2) Subject to section 713, the owner of land being subdivided shall provide, without compensation, land for highways in accordance with a by-law under subsection (1).

(5) In addition to any other powers exercisable or exercised under this Act, the Council may by by-law require that where the nearest boundary of any land proposed to be subdivided is two thousand feet or more in distance, or such greater distance specified in the by-law from an established trunk water-main or a trunk sanitary sewer, or both, provision be made by the owner of the land for the installation of water-mains or sanitary sewers, or both, including trunk water-mains or trunk sanitary sewers, or both, from such established trunk water-main or trunk sanitary sewer, or both, in and to the proposed subdivision, according to minimum standards prescribed in the by-law.

(6) A by-law under subsection (5) may provide for the sharing of the cost, or any portion thereof, of any trunk water-main or trunk sanitary sewer, or both, between the municipality and the owner of the land proposed to be subdivided.

(7) Where land proposed to be subdivided is in an area of the municipality zoned for agricultural, rural, or industrial use, an appeal lies to the Zoning Board of Appeal from the enforcement of any provisions of a by-law enacted under subsection (5), and the provisions of clause (c) of subsection (1) of section 709 shall, mutatis mutandis, apply.

713. Where land is being subdivided, the owner shall not be required on subdivision to provide without compensation

(a) for the purpose of a highway allowance within the subdivision, land exceeding in depth sixty-six feet; or

(b) for the purpose of widening a highway that is less than sixty-six feet in width and that borders or is within the subdivision, land of a depth exceeding thirty-three feet or the difference between sixty-six feet and the width of the highway, whichever is the lesser.

SUBDIVISION AND TRANSFER REGULATIONS

Alberta. Regulations. 1960. 185/60; Order in Council 926–60

21. (1) Upon the written request of the municipal authority, the Director or the approving authority may approve a proposed subdivision on the condition that all or any

(a) roads, streets and lanes;

(b) drainage ditches, culverts, storm sewers, dikes and land fill;

(c) sidewalks, walkways, curbing and boulevards, and;

(d) necessary services,

be provided or constructed.

(2) Where a municipality requests that all or any of the works and services referred to in clause (1) be constructed or provided at the expense of the owner or partially at the expense of the owner, the Director or the approving authority may approve a proposed subdivision on the condition that the applicant enter into an agreement in writing with the municipal authority stating:

(a) the respective obligations to be assumed by him and the municipal authority with reference to the construction, installation, operation, repair and maintenance of the specified works and services;

(b) the manner in which the costs of the same are to be met or recovered;

(c) the standards of construction to be adopted and complied with;

(d) the periods of time within which specific items of construction or installation work are to be completed in relation to the general development of the subdivision.

(3) The applicant shall file a certified copy of such agreement with the Director or the approving authority prior to or upon submission of the plan of subdivision, who may require a caveat to be placed upon the land to be registered within the subdivision.

(4) If a subdivision which is the subject of such an agreement is later included within the limits of another municipality, the respective obligations set forth in the agreement shall remain in effect as between the applicant and that municipality.

COMMUNITY PLANNING ACT

New Brunswick. Statutes. 1960–61. Chapter 6

29. (1) . . . a subdivision by-law may

(h) require that persons proposing to subdivide land shall install at their expense or contribute to the extent described in the by-law in providing the facilities mentioned in subparagraph (ii) of paragraph (j);

(j) provide that no approval shall be given of a subdivision plan unless, in the opinion of the council,
 (i) the council will be able in the forseeable future to provide the proposed subdivision with light, water, streets, schools, recreational areas, transit, sewage lines or other facilities, or the person proposing the subdivision makes satisfactory arrangements for providing such facilities; and
 (ii) the owner of the land has made satisfactory arrangements to install at his own expense, or to assist to the extent required by the by-law in installing streets, curbing, sidewalks, culverts, drainage ditches, water and sewage lines and other facilities deemed necessary by the council or delivers a performance bond acceptable to the council in an amount sufficient to cover such expenses, or pays such sum as may be provided in the by-law, if required by the council so to do, to provide such facilities.

THE PLANNING ACT
Ontario. Revised Statutes. 1960. Chapter 296

28. (5) The Minister . . . may impose as a condition [to the approval of a plan of subdivision],
 (b) that such highways shall be dedicated as the Minister deems necessary;
 (c) when the subdivision abuts on an existing highway, that sufficient land, other than land occupied by buildings or structures, shall be dedicated to provide for the widening of the highway to such width as the Minister deems necessary; and
 (d) that the owner of the land enter into one or more agreements with the municipality dealing with such matters as the Minister may consider necessary, including the provision of municipal services.

(6) Every municipality may enter into agreements imposed as a condition to the approval of a plan of subdivision.

(7) Where the owner of the land or the municipality in which the land is situate is not satisfied as to the conditions imposed or to be imposed by the Minister or by the municipality, as the case may be, he or it may, at any time before the plan of subdivision is approved, require the matter to be referred to the Municipal Board by written notice to the secretary of the Board and to the Minister in which case the matter shall be deemed to be referred to the Board under section 34.

G. S. SHIPP AND SON LTD. *v.* TORONTO TOWNSHIP. [1952] O.W.N. 793 (Ontario. High Court)). A township by-law attempted to require a subdivider to erect at his own expense all the necessary poles and wires for hydro-electric power along new highways. The court could find no authority in the legislation and held the by-law invalid. AYLEN J.: "The municipality not only attaches a purely arbitrary and irrelevant condition but goes further and attempts to dictate the terms upon which the power lines are to be erected and who shall erect them." [Why is the by-law "arbitrary"? To what is the condition "irrelevant"?]

RE TORONTO TOWNSHIP AND G. S. SHIPP AND SON LTD. [1952] O.W.N. 775 (Ontario Muncipal Board). The Minister of Planning and

Development referred a plan of subdivision to the Board for its consideration. The Township objected to approval of the plan on the ground that it was "premature": the cost of its services was beyond its means. It was willing to recommend approval if Shipp would give the Township $750 a lot as a donation toward future capital cost of schools. All future subdivision plans were to be subject to this requirement. The Board approved the plan because the Township "had gone too far with its approval of the subdivision before asking for the extra conditions". MOORE and ROWLAND Vice Chairmen: "As to the provision whereby the subdivider was asked to pay the Township $750 per lot to help pay the capital cost of new schools, and also with respect to hydro lines and sewage disposal, the Board does not see that asking for this is in any different class from asking for the provision of water-mains, grading and surfacing of roadways, and the building of storm sewers, except that the subdivider was also to undertake that the lands would still be liable for the same rate of school tax as those of others who had not made a similar contribution. . . . If we can say so here we must reiterate that in the Board's opinion any more residential subdvisions in the Township of Toronto would be premature at the present time, and by this we mean that the Township should have time to consolidate its position financially and otherwise and not because there is a lack of demand for housing. . . ."

NOTE ON PREMATURITY. The Board's reiteration that Toronto Township plans would be premature (see section 28(4) (b) of *The Planning Act* above) not because there was a lack of demand for housing, but because the Township should have time to consolidate its position financially and otherwise illustrates a change in the meaning of "premature" as the word is used in the Act. It originally referred to the market conditions. During the depression years of the 1930s many plans of subdivision lay vacant although municipal services had been installed by the municipality which was paying for them on a local improvement basis. Had the plan not been approved until there was better evidence of a market, the houses built on the lots would have increased the assessment and the ratepayers would have contributed to the payment for the servicing. A "premature" subdivision, therefore, was one for which there might be no market and hence little help from new taxpayers to pay for costs made necessary by the plan.

The Board's new meaning made a major change in the philosophy of the Act. The Board was saying that a municipality was entitled to regard a plan as premature, and so to recommend to the Minister, if its financial position was such that it could not pay for necessary municipal services even if they were off the plan. The prime example was, and still remains, the school costs. Residential rates rarely pay for schools. If it is assumed that a residential tax rate of $200 to $300 is average to high average, and that it costs a municipality (or school board, which is usually a separate corporate body) $150 to $200 a pupil a year, it is clear that the municipality must find some other source of revenue. Apart from provincial subsidies it must either borrow or tax its residents. Since borrowing power depends on a healthy financial position, the matter inevitably resolves itself to one of the ratio of residential assessment to industrial and commercial assessment. The latter represents more valuable, or higher assessment, and it has the enviable characteristic of not needing schools. The tax from the industrial and commercial assessment shows, as it were, a profit which can be deflected into paying the losses on schools.

In Ontario it has been assumed without very much published critical analysis, that ideally a municipality should have a "balanced assessment," that is, the ratio of residential to industrial and commercial assessment should be 50–50. This has frequently proved unattainable, and 60 (residential) to 40 (industrial and commercial) is widely accepted.

BOARD OF EDUCATION (ETOBICOKE TOWNSHIP) *v.* HIGHBURY DEVELOPMENTS LTD. 1958. 12 D.L.R. (2d) 145 (Ontario. Supreme Court of Canada). The Municipal Board refused to approve Highbury's plan of subdivision on the ground that it was "premature" because the School Board and Highbury could not agree on the price the Board was to pay for school sites shown on the plan. In effect the School Board wanted to pay the price of the "raw land", thus requiring Highbury to subsidize it to the extent of the costs of the services that Highbury had installed on the streets on which the school sites were located. The question on appeal was whether the Minister or the Board could withhold approval solely on the ground advanced. The Court of Appeal and the Supreme Court of Canada thought not. CARTWRIGHT J. quoted with approval Aylesworth J.A.'s remarks in the Court of Appeal: " '. . . . the error in the [Board's] decision proceeds from failure to distinguish in the application of the Act between acquisition of school sites, which is not dealt with, and adequacy of school sites, which is, from a misapplication of the term "premature" as applied in the Act to a "proposed subdivision" and to a certain confusion of thought as between the terms, school sites and school facilities, the latter of which also is not within the purview of the Act.' " [Aylesworth J. A. also said, of the meaning of the word "premature", after quoting from two dictionaries, ". . . it is clear to me that 'premature' as used in cl. (*b*) means that a proposed subdivision may be premature in the sense that it is presented too soon for any real need or demand for housing of the type contemplated or is perhaps put forward before finalization of a pending official plan as defined by the Act or before final determination of zoning provision under current consideration in a municipality. I make no attempt completely to define the application of the word—merely to illustrate the meaning which I think it ought to be given within the context of the Act."]

RE DICKSON PARK DEVELOPMENTS LTD.
Ontario. Municipal Board, 1957. P.F.M. 6085–57

J. A. KENNEDY, Q.C. Vice-Chairman and R. L. KENNEDY Member, signed the decision of the Board: This is an application by Dickson Park Developments Limited for approval under the provisions of *The Planning Act* of a proposed subdivision of certain lands in the Township of Toronto being part of Lots 2, 3, 4 and 5, according to Registered Plan Number D-22 for the County of Peel. The application has been referred to the Board by the Minister of Planning and Development. The proposed draft plan contains eighteen lots intended for residential development.

The hearing of the application commenced before the Board on the 2nd day of July, 1957. The applicant appeared by counsel in support of the application and the Corporation of the Township of Toronto appeared by counsel in opposition.

Early in the hearing it became apparent that while the Township had some objections to certain features of the proposed plan, a resolving of these difficulties had never been attempted by negotiation for the reason that the Township had a fundamental objection to this plan as well as to a number of others. This objection seems to have been fairly stated in a resolution passed by the council of the Township of July 23rd, 1956, in the following terms:

"Whereas by reason of the rapid growth of population of the Township, the demand for municipal services has increased the taxes to an alarming extent;

"Therefore, be it resolved that all proposed residential subdivisions of land in the Township are premature unless

"(a) the applicant provides within the same Township school area or public school section industrial assessment at least equal in amount to the anticipated residential assessment in his proposed subdivision;

"(b) the applicant provides all necessary municipal physical services to and within his proposed industrial and residential lands;

"(c) the applicant enters into the then current engineering and financial agreements with the Corporation;

"(d) the applicant satisfies such further requirements as may be appropriate in the circumstances."

The Board decided that the hearing should proceed first to determine the validity of the position taken by the Township as disclosed by this resolution before proceeding to deal with other objections for the reason that should the Township's position be upheld as to the general policy, then it would not have served any purpose to deal with the details now.

Evidence was adduced on behalf of the Township that there are pending before the Minister of Planning and Development applications for subdivision of lands in the Township aggregating some six thousand residential lots. The evidence of the treasurer of the Township was that the present proportion of assessment in the Township between residential and industrial-commercial is 60–40 and that level has been maintained for some time past. A rough calculation of the increase in the residential assessment that would be caused if the whole of the six thousand lots were approved for immediate development and so developed would show a change in this proportion between residential and industrial-commercial to about 70–30. The treasurer felt that any appreciable increase in the present proportion of residential over industrial-commercial would sharply increase the proportion of school costs, although no setup was presented showing this by actual calculation. He stressed even more that in his opinion it would then become impossible for the Township to sell debentures for future capital projects in the open market. No evidence was adduced to support his opinion as to this.

The total assessment in the Township for the year 1956 was given as \$62,040,291. The present net debt of the Township is approximately \$11,000,000. This would be increased by projects approved, but not yet debentured, and other projects intended for the immediate future to a total of about \$16,000,000. This would bring the Township debt to rather a high percentage of its assessment in the year 1956, but there was evidence before the Board of increases in the assessment to June 30th of this year of \$3,732,290. There was also evidence of some further substantial items of assessment that will, in all probability, be included in this year's assessment roll. Of the new assessments coming in this year up to June 30th a proportion was given as residential forming 25%, commercial 8% and industrial 67%. It will be seen that the increase for this year is very heavily on the industrial-commercial side, but of course it may be that this should be attributed at least in part to the policy with respect to residential development which the Township appears to have been following.

It is clear from a study of the *Planning Act* that even though every other requirement of that Act could be met the Minister or the Board should not approve a plan of subdivision if it is premature. The real question before the Board, then, is whether the municipality is permitted by the Act to prevent residential development as premature simply because the advent of such development would create problems, however difficult, for the municipality. The Board finds that it should not refuse approval to a plan of subdivision as premature unless it has been clearly demonstrated by proper evidence that the acceleration of residential development above the level of some enlightened policy or program definitely established would create for the inhabitants of the municipality an unfair hardship or burden through taxation or some other cause.

The applicant in this case sought to establish that the type of house planned for each of the eighteen lots in question would be of such a value as to produce in taxes a sufficient amount to pay any increase in the tax burden on the municipality resulting from the services required. The Board finds it impossible to accept this as the specific or only test to be satisfied for the approval of a plan of subdivision. No policy should be adopted which would mean that residential development for houses valued at $25,000 and over would be permitted while houses costing, say $10,000 would be prohibited. The Board does not conceive that the municipality possesses such a power. The practice, on its face, would be contrary to public policy.

On the other hand, it seems obvious that the development of the eighteen lots now in question would not, of itself, be felt at all by the municipality. If the Board finds the general policy adopted by the Township is not sound or has not been sufficiently justified by the evidence adduced on this application, no harm will be done by approval of the plan now before the Board, and the Township will still have an opportunity at a future hearing on a subsequent application to justify its present policy or to justify such new policy as it may hereafter adopt.

The Board feels, with respect, that the policy presently followed by the Township should not be supported for two reasons:

In the first place it is unwise to allow the indusrial or commercial development of the Township to depend on a measure of quid pro quo such as that contained in the resolution quoted above. Such a premium placed on industrial development removes from the hands and control of the municipality the power to make decisions on perhaps the most important questions in its development. To be placed in a position, for example, where residential development in a certain area would be approved ahead of such development in another area more mature for such development by reason of location, services, etc., would clearly not advance or promote the greatest common good. To give to any intending residential developer the opportunity to make deals with some intending industrial developer and thereby gain a priority over others actually more entitled to develop or whose development would be for the greater good of the community, is unwise and might even lead to abuse.

The other reason which the Board has for being unable to support the Township at this time in rigid control of residential expansion is that the Township does not appear now to have any over-all plan as to where development should first occur and where it would be most advantageous to the public good. If there is such a plan, it was not presented at the hearing.

If the requirement of such a policy is not stated in so many words in the *Planning Act* it seems clear that such is the intention and scheme of the Act. It is appropriate and necessary that an immediate study should be made and an orderly program set up in the light of present development, existing services, and an over-all plan as to extension of services, which latter the Township possesses, no doubt, at the present time. If it does not, then such a plan is a very urgent necessity. When consideration, then, is based on such a plan for development, an orderly program could be set up to govern consents to approval of plans of subdivision. Due regard would be had in this way to increases in industrial and commercial assessments and any balance between these and residential assessments shown to be necessary could be maintained. Such a program would be supported by this Board.

Another weakness in the position of the Township on this application is that it has not been established by evidence that further residential development beyond the proportion which the Township is now prepared to permit would create hardship or unfair burden on the inhabitants of the community. It is important that a municipality should be protected against development which would make it impossible in the result for the debentures of that municipality to be sold in the open market. Such circumstances would in turn make it impossible for the municipality to provide essential services for its inhabitants. It seems clear, also, that a municipality should be protected against any development which would result in the natural course in oppressive taxes on its inhabitants. The fact that these or other similar conditions would result, however, would have to be established by sufficient evidence upon which the Board could make such findings.

In the result the Board finds that this proposed subdivision should not be delayed because of the general policy established by the Township and embodied in the resolution above quoted.

This application will be adjourned for a period of three months during which the applicant and the municipality will negotiate and endeavour to resolve the specific objections to this proposed plan. If they are resolved within that time, the Board should be advised and the plan will be approved. If they are not resolved within that time either the applicant or the municipality may apply further to the Board for directions.

At the hearing Gerald M. Bickey, 2084 Linchmeyer Avenue, Toronto Township, appeared and made objections to the dead end feature in certain streets in the proposed plan. The Board expects that the municipality will consider Mr. Bickey's objections in this regard and that a report will be furnished as to the result of such consideration.

QUESTIONS. Has the Board adequately explained why the eighteen Dickson Park lots should be preferred over the 6,000 residential lots pending before the Minister? Is the approval of this plan consistent with the Board's complaint that there is no "over-all" plan as to where development should first occur? Would the policy of favouring developers, regardless of the location of their land, if they provided new industrial assessment, result in any more haphazard development than the Board's approval here? What "evidence" could the Township Treasurer adduce to support his opinion that if the assessment ratio dropped to 70–30 the Township could not sell its debentures? Should the Board have postponed this application until the Treasurer produced the necessary "evidence" if he could, and the Planning Board produced the necessary plans? Has the developer some "right" to have a decision at this point of time? Why?

STEPHANIE *v.* VILLAGE OF STREETSVILLE. [1953] O.W.N. 261

(Ontario. Municipal Board). On March 12, 1952, Stephanie wrote asking the Streetsville council whether it had any objection to his proposed subdivision of his twelve acres. On April 10 the village clerk replied stating, "So long as the by-laws of this Village regulating the opening of subdivisions are conformed with, the Council has no objections in you subdividing your property." On April 21 Stephanie submitted his plan to the Minister. Between then and June 3, when Stephanie attended a meeting at which the reeve of Streetsville and the medical officer of health were present and he was told everything was in order, Stephanie's plan was examined by various provincial and county authorities and it was acceptable to all but the Peel County health unit, who on May 30 had written recommending that the area be not developed without sanitary sewers. The medical officer of health evidently did not agree. On June 11 the Minister's office stated it was unable to recommend the plan to the Minister in view of the objections of the village authorities reported by the clerk. The principal objection was to the septic tank sewage disposal. The Board agreed to approve the plan when (1) water mains had been installed, (2) roads had been graded and gravelled on the new streets in the plan, (3) surface drainage with necessary easements was opened up to the satisfaction of the village engineer, and (4) Stephanie conveyed 5 per cent of the acreage to the village. MOORE Vice-Chairman and YEATES Member: ". . . The objection that the streets are 'dead-ended' is one that has some merit when looked at from the point of view of the authority charged with maintenance of the streets, but if it were sustained it would effectually stop all pioneering work in land development.

"It was stated that the proposed subdivision is situated between two industrial plants and that the Village authorities believe the land should be used for industrial purposes and not for housing. There are, however, seven houses on the south side of Thomas Street and west of the sash and door factory, and the village has no zoning by-law.

"The village clerk stated that on 11th May he took an agreement to Stephanie to be signed. This agreement was not filed with the Board and no details of its provisions were given, except that it was in accordance with the Village by-laws. No by-law was filed, but the Board assumes that the one that is meant is By-law 979, 'A by-law to provide for the payment by subdivision owners for services prior to the installation of such services.' A copy of this by-law and the draft agreement attached to it was filed as an exhibit in another application now before the Board. The agreement provides for the construction of ditches for the disposal of surface water, the building of houses according to the standards established by the village engineer, and that the owner consents to a by-law restricting the use of the land. It does not provide for the construction of sanitary sewers or water mains, or for the grading and surfacing of streets. Stephanie says that the only condition imposed on him by the Village authorities was that he was to convey to the Village 5 per cent of the land, exclusive of highways, and to construct a water main. There is a water main along Thomas Street in front of his property.

"The evidence produced and the chronology of events from 12th March to 4th June 1952 leads the Board to believe that the Village authorities were, during the greater part of that interval in favour of having the Stephanie subdivision approved, and had given that impression to the owner.

"[It] is the opinion of the Board that when, as in this case, a subdivider is told that he may proceed under certain conditions, those conditions should not be drastically changed after he has spent a lot of time, effort and money. It is thought that Stephanie could have been told at the start that in the opinion of the health unit his land was not suitable for development without sanitary sewers, and that the nearest sanitary sewer outlet was one-half mile away from his property. Similarly, he could have been told that the public school was crowded and that since more residential subdivisions meant more children to educate and new classrooms to be built, thus creating more debenture-debt, the municipality would not approve his plan. . . ."

QUESTIONS. As to the objection that the streets were "dead-ended", could the Board properly have rejected the plan of subdivision until the village had prepared an official plan by which dead ending could have been related to future planned development? Should Stephanie have to wait? Should Stephanie have to wait until the village passes a zoning by-law? How did the Board get to look at By-law 979 which it "assumed" was referred to? Should the Board be able to look at material before it in other cases? Is this consistent with its function as an "adjudicative body"?

BEAVER VALLEY DEVELOPMENTS LTD. *v*. TOWNSHIP OF NORTH YORK

Ontario. Court of Appeal. 1960. 23 D.L.R. (2d) 341

The appellant developer entered into an agreement with the defendant Township to pay to the Township $5 per foot frontage on 4,831 feet on lots on a plan of subdivision, making a total of $24,155. The Minister in his draft approval of the plan had set as a condition that "the owner agrees to satisfy all the requirements [of the Township authorities] . . . re . . . installation of services . . ." and prior to the signing of the final plan that he be advised that the conditions had been carried out to their satisfaction.

MORDEN J. A.: . . . In this action, which was instituted in February 1957, the plaintiff claimed—

"(a) A declaration that the convenant I have quoted providing for the payment of $24,155.00 is unenforceable,

"(b) a declaration that the guarantee bond given by the Dominion Insurance Company is unenforceable and,

"(c) an order setting aside the covenant and directing that the guarantee bond be delivered up to the plaintiff and be cancelled."

The defendant township by its defence denied that the plaintiff was entitled to the relief it claimed and by its counterclaim sought judgment against the plaintiff for $24,155. Mr. Justice Aylen, after the trial of the action, delivered judgment dismissing the action with costs and allowing the counterclaim, also with costs.

Counsel for the plaintiff in this Court made a very vigorous attack upon the learned trial Judge's reasons in the course of which many interesting points of law were argued. Briefly, his submissions were as follows: that the negotiations with respect to sewage facilities leading up to the subdivision agreement of December 10, 1955, were based upon the possibility that the Glendale Sewage Disposal Plant would have to be enlarged because of the expected increased demands upon that plant which would be caused by sewage originating in the plaintiff's lands; that the plaintiff's covenant to pay the township $5 a foot frontage was to reimburse the township for the cost of this contemplated extension of the sewage plant; that this plant had been owned or operated by the Municipality of Metropolitan Toronto since January 1, 1954; and that the construction of a main trunk sewer by the Municipality of Metropolitan Toronto through the west branch of the Don River and extending to Ashbridges' Bay obviated any probability that the Glendale Plant would ever be enlarged. Upon these submissions he argued that the sum the plaintiff covenanted to pay was no longer required by the township for any sewage facility to be provided by it and therefore this sum was a levy by the township in the nature of a tax for which there was no statutory authority. At this point it should be mentioned that the township, by agreement with Metropolitan Toronto, undertook not to approve any plans of subdivisions within the township unless the subdivider agreed to pay the township $5 a foot frontage upon all residential lands which sums were to be paid over to Metropolitan Toronto to defray the costs incurred by that body for or in connection with sewage works under its jurisdiction. This agreement, although executed after the agreement between the parties to this action, was being negotiated at about the same time as the subdivision agreement. It should also be noted that the *Municipality of Metropolitan Toronto Act*, provides by s. 66(1): "No municipality or person shall connect any local work, local watercourse, private drain or private sewer to a metropolitan work or watercourse without the approval of the Metropolitan Council."

In my opinion, it is unnecessary for the proper disposition of this appeal to decide whether counsel's attack upon the judgment below has merit and whether the learned trial Judge's reasons can be supported. I have come to the conclusion that Mr. Justice Aylen's judgment must stand because the agreement between the parties, of December 1955, has been immune from attack since the enactment of the following section of the *Planning Act*, 1959 (Ont.), c. 71: "4(3) Every muncipality shall be deemed to have always had authority to enter into agreements imposed as a condition to the approval of a plan of subdivision and all such agreements entered into before this section comes into force are hereby validated and confirmed and declared to be legal, valid and binding."

This section came into force on March 26, 1959, the day after judgment was handed down in this action. It is plainly retrospective in its operation and applies to the agreement which is in issue here. . . .

Section 4(3) is all embracing in its terms; it contains no conditions or qualifications. The agreement dated December 10, 1955 is clearly a subdivision agreement. The Minister had imposed by his letter of November 8, 1955 as a condition of his approval of the draft plan of subdivision that the plaintiff was to satisfy all the requirements, financial and otherwise, of the township and the agreement did satisfy the township and thus met the Minister's condition. Mr. Manning argued that the only agreements which were validated by s. 4(3) were those which restricted in their scope to matters mentioned in s. 26 of the *Planning Act*, 1955 (Ont.), c. 61, But s. 4(3) contains no such qualification or limitation and it would be an unwarrranted extension of the judicial function for a Court to gloss the section by interpreting it as if it had such a limitation. Counsel then argued that the interpretation I have now placed on the section would validate subdivision agreements containing highly unreasonable terms. However, under the *Planning Act*, 1955, a municipality is not given any power to impose terms or conditions—that power resides in the Minister. A subdivider who is dissatisfied with terms proposed by a municipality can apply to the Minister for relief or require him to refer the matter to the Ontario Municipal Board under s. 29 of the *Planning Act.* The plaintiff was dissatisfied with the covenant in question before it executed the agreement but it did not see fit to seek relief from it by an application under s. 29.

Counsel for the appellant then submitted that assuming the agreement to be valid, nevertheless, the frontage charge of $5 a foot was payable for specific purpose—the cost of enlarging the Glendale Sewage Disposal Plant —and as that work has not been done and may never be done, the purpose for which the covenant was exacted has failed and the plaintiff is therefore freed of its obligation under it. I do not interpret the covenant in that limited sense. Although it bears the caption "Sewage Disposal Plant Charge" the language does not in my view import that the payments exacted are to be devoted to any particular project or work or are to be held by the township upon trust for any particular purpose. Proper arrangements had to be made for the carrying away and disposition of sewage which in the future would originate on the plaintiff's lands. Such arrangements had to be made before any plan of subdivision could or would be approved by the Minister. Such arrangements were in fact made and the plan was approved. I fail to appreciate how the details of sewage disposal eventually decided upon and which may be changed from time to time in the future can in any sense affect or modify the plaintiff's liability under the covenant.

Counsel also submitted that the charge of $5 a foot frontage was an indirect tax which was beyond the constitutional power of the Ontario Legislature to validate. When this point was argued, all members of the Court expressed their opinion that that charge was not an indirect tax and I do not consider it necessary to consider it further.

For these reasons, I am of the opinion that the plaintiff's appeal should be dismissed with costs.

THE MUNICIPAL ACT

Ontario. Revised Statutes. 1960. Chapter 297

299 (1) Where a contribution is received by a municipal corporation in consideration of the expense incurred or to be incurred by the corporation as a result of a proposed subdivision of land, such contribution shall be used only to meet expenditures for work done within the subdivision or for the benefit or use of the occupiers or subsequent occupiers of the land within the subdivision or to meet expenditures incurred wholly or in part by reason of the subdivision of such land and, where a contribution is made for a specific purpose, it may be used only to meet expenditures for such purpose.

(3) Notwithstanding subsection 1, if any of the contributions referred to in subsection 1 are not required or likely to be required for the purposes mentioned in subsection 1, they may, with the approval of the Department, be expended for some other purpose.

[Introduced by S.O., 1958, c. 64, s. 20.]

(c) *Proposals to shift the burden*

CANADIAN FEDERATION OF MAYORS AND MUNICIPALITIES, SUBMISSION

Ottawa. 1962. Royal Commission on Banking and Finance.

P. *FUTURE MUNICIPAL CAPITAL REQUIREMENTS*

. . . The Need for a National Municipal Borrowing Program

(i) It is in this context [of the best possible fiscal and administrative arrangements for community development] that we see the necessity for an effective partnership between all levels of government for the purpose of providing and facilitating the capital borrowing needs of municipal governments in the period ahead.

(j) Another reason for such a partnership is the physical inter-relationship between housing, urban transportation, harbour and airport facilities, federal and provincial works, municipal utility services, water conservation and the provision of recreational space for a rapidly increasing urban population. All such facilities are inter-related parts of the physical development which constitutes a new or redeveloped city (or region). No part can be considered in isolation from the others. Each is an essential segment of the urban pattern which must, for the purpose of design and financing, be seen as a whole.

(k) Another reason why joint responsibility is essential is that the burden of cost which community growth and development imposes upon all levels of government is so great as to require the closest possible collaboration between them: first, in the programming of such works and, second, in the mobilizing of capital for the entire program.

(l) In recent federal legislation (allowing federal loans for long-terms based on the federal government's borrowing rate) and in the urban renewal legislation (allowing a direct federal investment of 50% of the cost of acquiring and clearing land for redevelopment) the federal government has taken important steps toward assisting in investment in essential community development.

(m) The experience with the sewer legislation illustrates clearly the significance of federal initiative and cooperation in solving the problem of borrowing for basic community facilities. The eagerness of the local governments in taking advantage of the direct long-term sewer financing is convincing evidence that their need—as far as basic municipal works are concerned—is for federal assistance in arranging the capital financing of such projects.

(n) They require such assistance because of the handicaps under which they operate insofar as capital borrowing is concerned. These handicaps arise, at least in part, from the fact that the magnitude of municipal borrowing needs—in these times—has strained the limitations dictated by a municipal tax revenue structure which was never conceived to meet capital needs of these proportions.

(o) It is not that our urban communities are poor. There are some exceptions; but, in the main, the productive wealth of the nation is concentrated in them and is continuing to increase. Most of this wealth, however, is already pre-empted for tax purposes by the senior governments so that municipal governments have no access to it. As a consequence, municipalities are unable to command sufficient income from the total taxable wealth resources of the community to support the growing burden of costs involved in undertaking the community improvements which are needed.

(p) A further consideration affecting municipal improvement programs is that the ability of municipal governments to borrow is by no means uniform throughout the country. The larger municipalities are in the most preferred position, although even they have their difficulties. The smaller municipalities are in the worst position. It is frequently difficult to market the debentures of a smaller municipality and, at times, there is no market receptivity for such issues at all.

(q) Moreover, during recurrent periods in recent years, the capital market for municipal bonds has tightened considerably. Because of the general shortage of capital investment funds the market has been more selective with interest rates reflecting the competition of both private and public borrowers for a share of the limited supply. The cost of borrowing has soared to the point where in 1961 new municipal bond issues of even high-rated municipalities were being offered at a yield price of 6.30% to 6.35%, with the yield price of smaller municipalities being offered at as much as 7.75%.

(r) While effective yield prices of 6 to 7 percent and more may not present any grave financing problem to private borrowers who require capital for productive business and industrial purposes, the same cannot be said for municipal governments whose capital borrowings are used, in the main, for socially useful community improvements. . . . As shown by the following table, every percentage point increase in the costs of municipal borrowing adds substantially to the overall debt carrying charges which the municipality has obligated itself to repay.

COSTS OF MUNICIPAL BORROWING

AMOUNT	*ANNUAL COST FACTOR*
$1 MILLION FOR 20 YEARS AT 5%	$ 80,242.59
$1 MILLION FOR 20 YEARS AT 6%	87,184.56
$1 MILLION FOR 20 YEARS AT 7%	94,392.93
$1 MILLION FOR 20 YEARS AT 8%	101,852.27

Q. *NATIONAL MUNICIPAL LOAN FUND*

(a) The recurrent major fact which emerges from this submission is that municipal governments are experiencing difficulty with respect to their capital borrowing requirements. The difficulty is becoming increasingly acute and, in the view of the Federation—speaking for the municipal governments of Canada—there are good and sufficient reasons why the Federal Government, in cooperation with the provinces, should establish a National Municipal Loan Fund for the purpose of facilitating the capital borrowing needs of municipal governments.

(b) There is nothing novel about the principle of this proposal. Municipal loan agencies of this sort have existed in Europe since before the turn of the century. The "Crédit Communal" of Belgium was formed in 1860 and has been operating successfully ever since. Similar banks or institutions are in existence in the Netherlands, Spain, Denmark, Norway, Italy, Switzerland, Israel and Turkey; and in the United Kingdom the Public Works Loan Board is in effect a municipal loan bank. (1)

(c) A National Municipal Loan Fund or Municipal Development Bank (the name is less important than the purpose of the agency) could be established by the Federal Government with the concurrence and coopertion of the provinces. In order to assure the constitutional position of the provincial governments, loans to any municipality would require the final approval of the province in which the borrowing municipality is located.

(d) The creation of such a federally-initiated municipal loan fund would relieve municipalities from exposure to some of the vagaries of the market and would reduce their borrowing costs. Federal financial assistance to municipalities has been increasing in recent years and has taken the form of grants for hospitals, vocational and technical schools, housing and sewer projects. The purpose of the loan fund would be to maintain and extend federal financial participation in such durable municipal work requirements. While the Bank would be a new form of intervention, it would be a way of acknowledging that municipalities do have special financing difficulties and would be a useful vehicle for channelling to the municipalities any assistance that federal or provincial authorities might provide to reduce municipal borrowing costs. Its primary purpose, however, would be to marshal the capital funds required by municipal governments and make such funds available to the municipalities.

(e) A possible source of federal funds to enable municipalities to obtain their borrowings at a cost lower than the market rate would be to apply the federal revenues received from the taxation of interest on municipal bonds to municipal loans contracted through the proposed loan agency.

(f) As the municipalities see it, the proposed agency would issue its own securities with a federal guarantee and use the resulting funds for loans to municipal governments at interest rates comparable to those obtained by the Federal Government (less the proposed municipal interest tax subsidy) and thereby make it feasible for any municipality, large or small, to finance the cost of municipal capital works.

(g) In effect, the municipalities are saying that, in their importance as basic community needs, municipal capital works are of equal priority with those of the senior governments. It would, therefore, be fair and equitable to enable municipal governments to have the same advantages as senior governments in respect to the capital market.

(h) The establishment of such a Fund would not preclude municipalities from seeking capital funds elsewhere; but it would offer an alternative source of funds at more reasonable rates of interest than those now available to all but a few of the larger and better rated municipalities. Moreover, it would have the desirable effect of maintaining a reasonable flow of capital funds to municipal governments during a period of tight money pressure; and, during a recession, could be a buffer against the tendency of the market to shy away from municipal bond borrowing.

(i) Another purpose which a national municipal lending agency would serve would be to facilitate borrowing within Canada for Canadian needs. It would therefore be a positive means of implementing the federal government's policy of encouraging reliance upon domestic savings.

(j) For three impelling reasons, therefore, a Municipal Development Bank is a missing link

(1) in upgrading municipal capital requirements to the equal status which they deserve with those of the federal and provincial governments;

(2) in facilitating—for the purpose of assuring soundly based national growth and development—the constant review and coordination of public investments; and

(3) in implementing, to the advantage of the entire national economy, the policy of drawing to the utmost upon Canadian savings for our capital investments.

(k) The Federation feels that the equalization of the capital needs of municipal governments—in their approach to the capital market—will be in the interest of all governments concerned and will be a major step forward in the common effort toward national growth and stability.

(l) The introduction of such inter-governmental cooperation in borrowing would further strengthen democratic government at the local level. The municipalities would retain the initiative—and would indeed be in a better position than now to exercise the initiative—in the planning and execution of comprehensive programs of capital works. Already more and more of our local governments are preparing long-term capital works budgets based upon carefully-considered programs of physical development. Their principal concern is whether they can finance such undertakings and at what cost. The establishment of a national municipal lending agency, by removing one of the most frustrating obstacles to municipal development, would give a sharp incentive to the forward planning of growth and redevelopment. It would help greatly to keep constantly before each urban area a planned capital development program which would not only provide work but would direct such work to the satisfaction of basic community needs.

(m) This reliance in a democratic manner upon municipal initiative is important. For it is only at the level of the local community that a balanced program representing the needs and desires of local citizens can be developed. Even a large proportion of Federal and Provincial works (such as roads, bridges, harbour installations, airports and office buildings) must fit into a workable community program in the interest of all concerned.

(n) Municipal responsibility for such programming must therefore be acknowledged and must of course be fully exercised by the municipalities themselves if they are to take advantage of a more favourable relationship to the capital market which a federal lending agency would make possible.

(o) The municipal governments contend that there is a strong and clearly defined need to establish such a National Municipal Loan Agency in Canada and that it is in the national interest to do so. Since the proposal was first put forward there has been a growing body of informed support in favour of the proposal. Certainly, so far as the municipal governments are concerned, it would enable them to initiate and carry through needed programs of local improvements and redevelopment for which the urgency is now very considerable and which in many municipalities, without such a facilitating loan agency, are likely to be indefinitely delayed.

KING, "*LEASEBUY*—A MARKETING METHOD FOR RESIDENTIAL LAND" (1961)

The most significant change in the price of residential properties (house and land) has resulted from the increase in the degree of municipal servicing which the purchaser must buy and pay for at the time of purchase. The variation in the unit cost of the house alone parallels very closely the changes in cost of other commodities, or the change in value of the purchasing currency. The new pattern now forces the home-buyer to include another commodity in the purchase, i.e. full municipal services. The effect of this added item varies inversely as the price of the complete property; as price increases the effect of the servicing component decreases; as price decreases the effect of the servicing component increases and is further heightened by the general adoption of minimum lot sizes per housing unit.

The new servicing requirements have been imposed fairly quickly. There has been no development of a method of financing to replace the discarded local improvement financing, until quite recently. The development of a useable form of leasehold title will now provide terms to a purchaser which equal or improve upon those available through local improvement financing. It also offers a solution to the new problems of the developer. . . .

There can be no valid criticism levelled at a venture simply because it is operated to produce a profit commensurate with the risks attendant on it. However, if a choice exists between two methods of operation which will each produce that profit, one method producing better results or causing less damage than the other, then failure to use the better method will justify both criticism and public concern. Such a choice becomes available through the introduction of the use of leasehold title which can preserve or enhance the profit earned without necessitating the risk of long term damage to a community or its residents. . . .

The enquiry led inevitably to the conclusion that the problem created by the land could be solved by the land and that the solution lay in the proper use of a long-term leasehold title to that land. It led also to a determination of the basic requirements of such a title if it were to be of practical value. These are:—

(a) payment for all or part of the serviced land value must be deferred indefinitely.
(b) rental must be fair, competitive and avoid any element of purchase.
(c) a lessee must have an option to purchase.
(d) title must be mortgageable under the *National Housing Act.*
(e) title must be freely assignable by the lessee.
(f) lease terms must be profitable to the lessor.

As a result of such an enquiry a company, Leasebuy Limited, was incorporated several years ago for the purpose of investigating and developing the practical use of such a title. It has developed a very simple form of leasehold title in land, known [as] a—Leasebuy title—which embodies all the basic requirements listed. This form of title has now been put into use on a so-far limited scale, to prove its practical value. One of the principal objections raised during the development stages was a doubt as to acceptance by the home-buying public. It has now been demonstrated that it is acceptable if it is available, as a means whereby a purchaser may defer the capital cost of full services without in any way diminishing his enjoyment of a home or his choice within his means. With such a title to land a property can be "low-cost" and be available to a greatly expanded market. It can offer freedom from the present limitation of choice to the "too expensive, too cheap, or too crowded".

Leasebuy title is not a magic formula which suddenly and of itself alone solves all of the problems connected with the development and marketing of residential properties. It is a specific financing tool designed to fill the gap caused by the shift away from local improvement financing; it permits the acquisition of a property without the assumption of all of the capital costs charged against the land.

Leasebuy title is established by the execution, delivery and registration of a form of ground lease agreement which has a term of 99 years and contains an option to purchase the title in fee simple at any time. The rental and option price are stated by schedule for the full term, so that both parties are aware of all applicable terms throughout the whole life of the lease. The lessee is also assured of the right to exercise the option and thus terminate the lease, without penalty or bonus, at any time that he deems it desirable. . . .

Before embarking on an explanation of the economics of the Leasebuy process it is desirable to establish the relationships which are created by such a ground lease. The lease is an agreement between the Lessor (the owner of the serviced land) on the one hand, and the Lessee (the owner of the house which occupies that serviced land) on the other. Each party to the lease is the owner of a valuable real asset; such ownership is subject, in each case, to the continued existence of the lease. The Lessor, while he owns the title in fee simple to the land has, through the lease, granted all the rights to the use of the land to the Lessee on condition that the rent specified be paid. The Lessee, having acquired all that rights to use the land, cannot be disturbed in his enjoyment of them so long as he pays the agreed rental. Since the house is subject to the Lessor's right of reversion in the event of default it is a more than adequate guarantee that the rent will, in fact, be paid. . . .

To outline the Leasebuy process and demonstrate the manner in which the varied requirements of the participants are satisfied, an actual case is analysed. It is not presented as an ideal example, nor as an ultimate example, but simply as an actual transaction involving a property for which all the factors have been determined. Costs, values, sales prices, loan amounts etc. are known and have been crystallized.

The transaction analysed relates to the sale of a house with leasehold interest in the lot, financed through an NHA mortgage of the leasehold. The property consists of:— a 3 bedroom, brick veneer bungalow, with attached garage, fireplace, partially finished recreation room, full basement; situated on a 69′ x 123′ lot and serviced by sanitary and storm sewers, water, paved roads, curbs and gutters, sidewalks, buried hydro and telephone services, all installed and paid for. The contract cost of the completed house is $13,150. The mortgage financing is for a 30 year term at 6.75% and is NHA insured.

The property was offered for sale with a choice of terms as shown below; either would be accepted. The actual purchase was made on the Leasebuy offering. The alternate offerings were:

	FREEHOLD (1)	LEASEBUY (2)
Selling Price —		
initial	$18,039	$14,611
deferred to option	nil	3,600
final	$18,039	$18,211
NHA mortgage, including insurance fee	$14,484	$13,050
Down payment	$ 3,555	$ 1,561
Monthly payments:		
Mortgage prin & int	$ 93.05	$ 83.84
Taxes	30.14	30.14
Ground rent	nil	19.00
Total per month	$ 123.19	$ 132.98
Qualifying income	$ 5,475	$ 5,910

The ground lease requires payment of a rental of $228.00 per year and grants an option to purchase for $3600. These amounts are fixed for the first 30 years and increase slightly after that time. The purchaser's reasons for choosing this offering are obvious, less cash at time of purchase, the right to terminate the lease through the option, low-cost financing in the interim, freedom from compulsion to pay off land value.

It is important to show that this choice does not involve the purchaser in hidden costs nor does it expose him to future balloon financing. This may be shown by a comparison of the total or final cost of this property to a purchaser by either a freehold or a Leasebuy purchase at the outset. In this comparison it is assumed that at the end of 30 years the NHA mortgage is discharged and the land is owned in fee simple. For simplicity the loss of earnings on principal payments are ignored; sufficient to state that they are less in the Lease-buy case because of the smaller principal amount borrowed. Such a comparison shows:—

	FREEHOLD (1)	LEASEBUY (2)
Total of monthly payments of mortgage principal and interest	$33,498	$30,182
Loss of earnings on down payment, @ 3½% compounded annually	$ 9,978	$ 4,381
Ground Rent	nil	$ 6,840
Purchase Option exercised	nil	$ 3,600
Total cost incurred	$43,476	$45,003
Initial saving in down payment	nil	$ 1,994
Net final cost incurred	$43,476	$43,009
Net saving	nil	$ 467

It is rather startling to find that, through the use of Leasebuy title, the purchaser *who does not have* the extra $1994 needed to make a freehold purchase will effect a saving of $467 in addition to the use of the property. The corollary is evident; the purchase *who does have* the extra $1994, may, through the use of Leasebuy title still retain that amount for other use as he sees fit. Its value at 3½% compounded annually over 30 years amounts to $5,597. Such a purchaser could effect a total saving of $4070 by a Leasebuy rather than a freehold purchase. While it is presently unusual for a purchaser to consider the final cost of his property it may well become an important factor as the savings are demonstrated. The benefits enjoyed by a home purchaser through the use of Leasebuy title are obvious and readily apparent; they are therefore significant marketing features. To have practical value the Leasebuy process must, while creating the above benefits, also generate the costs and profits required to compensate the other participants.

The requirements of those other participants are fully expressed by a statement of the prices to be paid for the goods and services they provide. In the case under examination it is possible to reduce this to a statement of two such prices. The serviced land has cost the developer $3,300 with all charges for land, servicing, administration, financing and sale included. The house, complete and delivered, costs $13,150 with all charges for materials, labour, administration, financing and builder's profit included. With the loan application fee of $35.00, the mortgage insurance fee of $256.00 and sales commission of $452 the total cost of the finished property as sold, amounts to $17,283. This includes a builder's profit but does not include a profit in the land which is not sold. A freehold sale at the price of $18,039 will produce such a profit in the amount of $756 after payment of all costs. We are concerned with the realisation of $17,283 to pay necessary expenses, through the Leasebuy process. . . .

It would be well to consider the effect of using a second mortgage instead of a lease to reduce the down payment. For a reduction of $1994 it is usual for a bonus to be required. Assuming a bonus of $550, the second mortgage would be for a principal amount of $2494 and the initial price is increased to $18,539. Assuming that interest only need be paid, at 7½%, and a term of five years, monthly charges would be increased to $138.03. By the use of this device the purchaser may defer the need for the additional capital

for the five year period. Suitable arrangements to repay this short term loan are a necessary and integral part of the purchaser's security of tenure. As he has assumed a debt and pledged his equity of redemption he must either pay off the debt, refinance it on the lenders terms, or suffer foreclosure. The very significant benefit of Leasebuy is the freedom from need to pay off the leased value; in fact it need never be paid if the lessee finds it more convenient or advantageous to continue the lease. There is no real comparison between the security offered the purchaser by the two methods of reducing the down payment, with Leasebuy there is long term security, with a second mortgage there is doubtful security for a short term. In addition to these considerations the income requirement with a disclosed second mortgage is very much increased. . . .
[The quoted material is from a mimeographed copy of the paper kindly supplied by the author.]

BIBLIOGRAPHY. Subdivision control has been the subject of two series of Special Lectures of the Law Society of Upper Canada, 1956, Part II *Municipal Law* (see especially Steele, "Municipal Controls on Subdivisions" and Conlin, "Agreements and Plans of Subdivision"); and 1960, *Contracts For the Sale of Land* (see especially Tucker, "Lawyer's Role in the Development of a Subdivision").

The old Ontario Department of Planning and Development in 1958 published a *Subdivision Approval Manual*, which is still available without charge from the Community Planning Branch of the Municipal Affairs Department. Ontario practice is well outlined. Notes and articles in *Ontario Planning*, apart from those reproduced above, are too numerous to mention. Useful accounts of subdivision, rather than subdivision control, are presented in Spence-Sales, *How to Subdivide* (1950) and Kostka, *Planning Residential Subdivisions* (1954) and *Neighbourhood Planning* (1957). All three are difficult to obtain.

CHAPTER 7

LAND USE CONTROL BY PRIVATE ARRANGEMENT

Private deed restrictions can preserve . . . common green areas which are likely to disappear if protected solely by zoning.

CLARENCE S. STEIN.

1. LEASEHOLD: CONTROL BY OWNERSHIP

SPENCER'S CASE

England. Court of King's Bench. 1583. 5 Co. 16a; 77 E.R. 72

Spencer and his wife brought an action of covenant against Clark, assignee to J. assignee to S. and the case was such: Spencer and his wife by deed indented demised a house and certain land (in the right of the wife) to S. for a term of 21 years, by which indenture S. covenanted for him, his executors, and administrators, with the plaintiffs, that he, his executors, administrators, or assigns, would build a brick wall upon part of the land demised, &c. S. assigned over his term to J. and J. to the defendant; and for not making of the brick wall the plaintiff brought the action of covenant against the defendant as assignee: and after many arguments at the Bar, the case was excellently argued and debated by the Justices at the Bench: and in this case these points were unanimously resolved by Sir Christopher Wray, Chief Justice, Sir Thomas Gawdy, and the whole Court. And many differences taken and agreed concerning express covenants, and covenants in law, and which of them run with the land, and which of them are collateral, and do not go with the land, and where the assignee shall be bound without naming him, and where not; and where he shall not be bound although he be expressly named, and where not.

1. When the covenant extends to a thing *in esse*, parcel of the demise, the thing to be done by force of the covenant is *quodammodo* annexed and appurtenant to the thing demised, and shall go with the land, and shall bind the assignee although he be not bound by express words: but when the covenant extends to a thing which is not in being at the time of the demise made, it cannot be appurtenant or annexed to the thing which hath no being: as if the lessee covenants to repair the houses demised to him during the term, that is parcel of the contract, and extends to the support of the thing demised, and therefore is *quodammodo* annexed appurtenant to houses, and shall bind the assignee although he be not bound expressly by the covenant: but in the case at Bar, the covenant concerns a thing which was not *in esse* at the time of the demise made, but to be newly built after, and therefore shall bind the covenantor, his executors, or administrators, and not the assignee, for the law will not annex the covenant to a thing which hath no being.

2. It was resolved that in this case, if the lessee had covenanted for him and his assigns, that they would make a new wall upon some part of the thing demised, that for as much as it is to be done upon the land demised, that it should bind the assignee; for although the covenant doth extend to a

thing to be newly made, yet it is to be made upon the thing demised, and the assignee is to take the benefit of it, and therefore shall bind the assignee by express words. So on the other side, if a warranty be made to one, his heirs and assigns, by express words, the assignee shall take benefit of it, and shall have a *warrantia chartae*. But although the covenant be for him and his assigns, yet if the thing to be done be merely collateral to the land, and doth not touch or concern the thing demised in any sort, there the assignee shall not be charged. As if the lessee covenants for him and his assigns to build a house upon the land of the lessor which is no parcel of the demise, or to pay any collateral sum to the lessor, or to a stranger, it shall not bind the assignee, because it is merely collateral, and in no manner touches or concerns the thing that was demised, or that is assigned over; and therefore in such case the assignee of the thing demised cannot be charged with it, no more than any other stranger.

3. It was resolved, if a man leases sheep or other stock of cattle, or any other personal goods for any time, and the lessee covenants for him and his assigns at the end of the time to deliver the like cattle or goods as good as the things letten were, or such price for them; and the lessee assigns the sheep over, this covenant shall not bind the assignee, for it is but a personal contract, and wants such privity as is between the lessor and his assigns of the land in respect of the reversion. But in the case of a lease of personal goods there is not any privity, nor any reversion, but merely a thing in action in the personalty, which cannot bind any but the covenantor, his executors, or administrators, who represent him. The same law, if a man demises a house and land for years, with a stock or sum of money rendering rent, and the lessee covenants for him, his executors, administrators, and assigns, to deliver the stock or sum of money at the end of the term, yet the assignee shall not be charged with this covenant: for although the rent reserved was increased in respect of the stock or sum, yet the rent did not issue out of the stock or sum, but out of the land only; and therefore as to the stock or sum the covenant is personal, and shall bind the covenantor, his executors and administrators, and not his assignee: and it is not certain that the stock or sum will come to the assignee's hands, for it may be wasted, or otherwise consumed or destroyed by the lessee, and therefore the law cannot determine at the time of the lease made, that such covenant shall bind the assignee. . . .

6. If lessee for years covenants to repair the houses during the term, it shall bind all others as a thing which is appurtenant, and goeth with the land in whose hands soever the term shall come, as well to those who come to it by act in law, as by the act of the party, for all is one having regard to the lessor. And if the law should not be such, great prejudice might accrue to him; and reason requires, that they, who shall take benefit of such covenant when the lessor makes it with the lessee, should on the other side be bound by the like covenants when the lessee makes it with the lessor. . . .

HOUGH, "THE LIVERPOOL CORPORATE ESTATE". 1950. 21 *Town Planning Review*. 226 (University of Liverpool). In this article the author traces the history of the city of Liverpool in respect of its ownership and leasing of land on long term leases (now usually 99 years) for private development. "As will be seen from the accompanying map, the corporate estate comprises the major part of the central area of the City, extending over a built up area of about 750 acres. It comprises almost all classes of property, including departmental stores, shops, theatres, cinemas, office blocks, factories, warehouses, churches, hotels and dwellinghouses (Fig. 17)." The estate includes about one third of the area of the city, 8,100 acres out of 27,364, and 7,800 acres outside the city. "This tendency to the extensive civic ownership of land is not peculiar to Liverpool but applies to most of our large cities, and is due in the main to their statutory obligations to provide houses, schools, parks, cemeteries and all the other services which progressive municipalities require today." Liverpool's estates are amongst the largest civically owned estates in Britain.

"It is due to no fault of our predecessors that areas such as these [residential areas laid out with squares early in the nineteenth century], the development of which was such a tribute to their foresight, constitute today one of the major problems in the management of the corporate estate. At the time of the original development in the early part of the nineteenth century, the houses in these districts were built for the prosperous commercial and profesional classes, but in the course of time, with the provision of improved methods of transport and an altered mode of life, these people gradually migrated to the outskirts of the City, and further afield. The effect on the older residential areas was a steadily increasing and continuous deterioration, and the stage has now been reached when, from an estate management point of view, the position is becoming serious. The main short term remedy, which is being actively pursued by the Estate Committee of the Council, appears to be to regain control of as many houses as possible, and to exercise a rigid control over the letting, at the same time maintaining the houses pending redevelopment, in as good condition, both externally and internally, as is possible, having regard to their age and the supply of labour and materials. The problem is rendered more difficult by the present housing shortage, but meanwhile a considerable contribution towards satisfying the demand for housing has been and is still being made by the conversion of some of the houses into small self-contained flats.

"The long term policy of the Estate Committee is to redevelop this inner residential part of the City by the erection of blocks of varying types of flats, but obviously this policy cannot be implemented until, with the easing of the housing shortage, it is possible to obtain vacant possession of suitably sized blocks of property to enable a start to be made on rebuilding." Although the redevelopment of these areas may be a "major problem", the cost of the land on which the redevelopment is to take place is no part of it. In Toronto today land expropriated for redevelopment costs about $300,000 an acre.

BENNETT, "SHOPPING CENTRES: PROBLEMS CONFRONTING LANDLORDS AND TENANTS"

1957. *Canadian Bar Association Annual Meeting: Papers*

It is my purpose in this paper to discuss those problems of a legal character confronting landlords and tenants arising out of the basic difference between the modern shopping centres which have recently come into being in most of our large cities, and the old fashioned shopping districts as they exist in every urban municipality.

A shopping centre has been defined as a type of partnership between the developer, a lending institution, merchants, and municipal and other governmental authorities. Each of these partners possesses a definite interest in the resulting development.

Shopping centres are the logical and inevitable outgrowth of our modern way of life. The rapid increase in the number of automobiles on the road

Fig. 17—Land in Corporation ownership, including land within the areas of neighbouring local authorities.

each year has created almost insuperable problems of parking for everyone, especially the shopper. In addition, the problem is emphasized by new suburban districts adjoining large urban centres which have mushroomed almost over night. Provincial and municipal legislative bodies, taking cognizance of this trend, have enacted legislation and by-laws for the zoning, regulation and control of various types of construction, including of course, commercial construction. This type of construction, if planned on the highest level and conforming to all by-laws applicable thereto, must result in the development of the modern shopping centre. The better the centre is planned, the easier it becomes to secure desirable tenants who will pay rentals commensurate with the volume of business done in their respective stores, the rentals being generally on the basis of a fixed percentage of the gross intake with a minimum monthly guarantee. The interest of both the landlord and the tenant is substantially identical. It is therefore in their best interest not only to work together in the planning of the shopping centre but also in the management and operation thereof. In fact, the shopping centre in many respects resembles a large department store. The major difference, of course, is that in a department store each department is managed by a department manager, subject to the control of the head management, while in a shopping centre each unit is operated by individual management. It therefore becomes the responsibility of the landlord to make sure that in some way most of those things necessary to provide central authority and control which is provided by the head management of the department store, are provided.

The instrument which creates the relationship between the landlord and the tenant is the lease. The lease should include a provision requiring the tenant to become a member of an association to be incorporated as a non-profit corporation under the Companies Act and to comply with all the regulations and by-laws adopted by the association, and also provide that failure to do so, and to pay the necessary dues imposed by the association on its members, should be regarded as a breach of the conditions contained in the lease, entitling the landlord to the same remedies as if a breach were made in any of the other conditions contained in the lease.

By the terms of the lease the association should be given jurisdiction to deal with the following, among other matters:

1. The regulation of the hours when all the stores in the shopping centre should be kept open for business.

2. The supervision and right to censor the advertising of the tenants so as to prevent any misrepresentations in such advertising and the prohibition of auction sales, fire sales or other objectionable practices.

3. The right to prohibit signs projecting on the sidewalk or erected over a roof of any store and also regulating facia signs and placards. The lease itself may also deal independently with these matters and give the landlord the same authority as is given the association.

4. The association may be given authority with regard to the lighting of the store windows and even in respect of the window dressing.

5. The association should be required to take out public liability insurance to protect each of the members as well as the landlord against possible claims by persons suffering injury to property or to person while in the parking lot or on any of the grounds forming part of the shopping centre. In some leases the tenants are required to indemnify the landlord against claims of this nature, but it may prove difficult to establish which tenant should assume responsibility for an accident on the parking lot over which all the tenants have common rights.

6. The association should deal with the promotional and general advertising for the benefit of the shopping centre as a whole. This is probably one of the most important functions of the association as well as being the most costly one, and the degree of the success of the centre depends largely on the extent and quality of the advertising.

7. There may be many other matters which should be delegated to the association such as maintaining and supervising a playground on a portion of the grounds—looking after shrubbery and trees on the grounds—Christmas decorations, arranging of religious services which may be carried on on the parking lot on Sundays, public dances on the grounds when it may be regarded as desirable and the supply of popular music from a public address system.

8. The association should also have authority with regard to the supervision and control of the parking lot, the assessment to be imposed on each tenant for the cost of its maintenance, supervision, lighting and removal of the snow therefrom. The landlord should also be a member of the association and have a right to vote.

9. The lease should also provide that if in the landlord's opinion any resolution or by-law adopted by the association is unfair or unreasonable, he should have the power of vetoing such resolution or by-law. The reason for this seemingly arbitrary provision is that the obligation of the tenant to meet the various items of cost is apportioned on the basis of the ratio of area of merchandising space occupied by each tenant to the total merchandising space of the whole centre. It could thus happen that in some instances the larger number of tenants occupying small areas would take advantage of the fewer tenants occupying large areas of merchandising space by using their majority power to compel the tenants of larger stores to embark on heavy expenditures against their own inclinations. The landlord is thus in a position to prevent any injustice from being carried out by one group against another group.

In a carefully planned shopping centre every type of business should be represented, including stores providing certain types of services (distinguished from sale of merchandise) such as hairdressing salons, shoe repair shops and watch repair shops. It is of the utmost importance that supermarkets operated by large chains, and at least one large store and several more either large or small stores dealing with ladies' ready to wear, should form part of the shopping centre. These types of business have exceptional power to attract customers who, once they come to the centre, will likely patronize the other stores as well. It is also a known fact that women are not as likely to shop in a centre where they cannot compare prices of women's apparel in the different stores in the same vicinity.

The tenant would be concerned to know the amount of competition to be expected in the same centre by other tenants and the appearance and location of the stores operated by competitors. A clause embodying the representations in respect of these matters may be required to be included in the lease by the tenant. The landlord, on his part, should require an undertaking from the tenant, not to carry on a business other than his usual type of business in the centre or within a specified distance from the centre. This would protect the other tenants in the centre as well as protect the centre from undue competition in its vicinity. In drafting this clause it might be advisable to read the decision of *Stop & Shop* v. *Independent Builders Limited* (1933), in order to avoid the pitfalls which may arise by reason of the fact that the same type of merchandise may be sold by tenants carrying on different types of business.

The landlord, in planning a centre, should also be careful to locate the stores having a strong popular appeal certain distances apart from each other so that no one section of the centre will become more or less valuable than any other section. It is therefore important for each tenant to know who his neighbours will be, and he may insist on a stipulation to that effect in the lease. These suggestions are made on the assumption that the negotiations for the lease are carried on prior to the completion of the shopping centre as happens in most cases.

The clause with respect to the assigning or sub-letting of the lease by the tenant is a matter of considerable importance in a shopping centre. The landlord, in order to be sure that the statements of gross receipts by tenants are accurate, must satisfy himself that the proposed assignee or sublessee is a person of integrity. Above all, the substitute tenant must be one who is acceptable to the other tenants in the centre since the successful operation by each contributes to the successful operation by all. On the other hand, tenants generally are reluctant to have clauses which restrict their right to assign or sub-let. The following is an arrangement with respect to this problem which is acceptable to many tenants for inclusion in the lease:

(a) that the landlord reserve the right to arbitrarily withhold his consent to any assigning or sub-letting, notwithstanding any provision in the Landlord and Tenant Act for say, the first three years of the term,

(b) thereafter, if he wishes to assign or sub-let, the tenant notifies the landlord, giving him the full information as to the identity of the proposed assignee or sub-tenant.

(c) the landlord then can either consent or withhold his consent.

(d) if he consents, then the guaranteed minimum rental provided by the lease is altered so that it becomes the average annual rental paid by the tenant during the preceding three years or the minimum as originally provided in the lease, whichever is the higher.

(e) if the landlord refuses to consent, then in such event he is obligated to release the tenant from further liability.

(f) if the landlord refuses to consent, the tenant is given the right within a limited time to withdraw his application for approval by the landlord to the proposed assigning or sub-letting. In that event the lease continues in effect.

The clause with regard to the right of the tenant to use the parking lot is also a subject which requires careful treatment. Shortly after the shopping centre is completed, some tenants may find their operation so successful that they may desire to extend the depth of the stores, or the landlord may wish to add more stores to the centre. The landlord should, therefore, not give the tenant more than a license in common with any other tenants from time to time, to use the parking lot, which license can be modified. The landlord should stipulate that he has the right to add a specified distance to the depth of any store and also to add more stores to the shopping centre if he compensates by providing additional parking space in the immediate vicinity. He should also have the right to change or alter the entrance and exits of the parking lots, laneways and sidewalks in what he considers the best interest of the centre.

Another important problem confronting the landlord and the tenant is that pertaining to the rental payable by way of percentage of the gross sales with a minimum guaranteed rental. First of all, the landlord has to guard himself against the possible dishonesty of a tenant who may falsify his sales records and furnish wrong statements. These are very rare happenings, but the landlord will nevertheless try to protect himself against this contingency. The lease should, therefore, provide:

1. That the tenant keep accurate records of all sales.
2. That sales statements be furnished monthly and at more infrequent intervals, say each six months, certification of these statements be made by a chartered accountant.
3. That the landlord should have access to the books and records of the tenant for a period of at least three months after each statement is delivered.

Another aspect of the same problem is in regard to the definition of the words "gross sales." It should be defined as including all sales of merchandise from the premises whether wholesale or retail, cash or credit, or for any other consideration, including all deposits not refunded and from all sales conducted on the premises by any sub-tenant, assignee, licensee or concessionaire. No credit is to be given to tenant for uncollected or uncollectable accounts. On the other hand, deduction should be made for returned merchandise for which cash has been refunded and of any amount collected from customers for provincial or municipal sales taxes. Instalment sales are to be treated as full sales as of the time the sales were effected.

If the arrangement of the tenant is that he is to pay a fixed percentage of the gross sales or a guaranteed minimum, whichever is the higher, no problem arises in the event of an interruption of business due to a fire or other cause. On the other hand, a problem would arise if an interruption of business takes place and the tenant's obligation is to pay one rate on the gross annual sales up to a fixed amount and then another rate on the volume of business in excess of that amount. Obviously by reason of the interruption of business the volume of business for the whole year would suffer and the landlord would not receive his fair rental for the portion of the year when business is carried on. The simplest way of avoiding this pitfall is to establish these various amounts on a monthly instead of a yearly basis, and also provide for an adjustment on a per diem basis.

A prudent landlord will insist on having the tenant pay any increase in realty taxes. In Ontario our assessors are required to assess each store separately in order to enable the municipality to establish the business tax payable by the tenant of each store. It is therefore not difficult to arrive at the increase which may take place in the taxes in Ontario, but in the other provinces where the assessors generally do not make separate assessments of each store and taxes increase for the whole shopping centre, such increase should be proportioned in the ratio that the merchandising area of each store bears to the total merchandising area of the whole shopping centre.

There are tenants such as banks who do not pay any percentage of the volume of business done by them. In that case, the tenants usually are required to pay all the taxes in respect of their demised premises.

With respect to the repair clause, apart from the usual provisions in the usual form of lease, the landlord should require the tenant to assume responsibility for repairing broken plate glass and vitrolite and repaint the interior of the premises whenever required.

With respect to the fire clause, there should be no cancellation provision even in the event of total destruction, except perhaps during the last two years of the term of the lease, at the option of the landlord, but the landlord must covenant to restore the premises as speedily as practicable.

This clause is essential in order to enable the landlord to fulfill his representations to each tenant in respect of the identify of the other tenants in the centre throughout the term of the lease.

In a shopping centre, heat is generally supplied from a central plant and the tenant is required to pay a proportionate cost of such heating on the same basis as maintenance of the parking lot. The landlord should stipulate that he should not be responsible for any loss of business or damage caused by the tenant while repairs are being carried on in the usual way.

The landlord should also reserve the right to promulgate new rules and regulations which in the course of time are found reasonable and necessary for the proper operation of the centre.

One of the most difficult matters concerning shopping centres, particularly in the Province of Ontario, is caused by the *Factory, Shop and Office Building Act*. This act was enacted in 1913 primarily for the purpose of protecting employees from being exploited by their employers in regard to the number of working hours each day. The Act of 1913 was an amalgamation of two earlier acts which dealt with shop and factories separately. These earlier acts passed in the late nineteenth century were aimed principally against child labour. Under this Act, municipalities are permitted to enact by-laws regulating the hours and days when shops must close. The council of each municipality has the power to enact by-laws on its own initiative, or following a petition presented to it by a certain percentage of merchants in any category of business. In the latter event, it is mandatory for the council to pass an early closing by-law. As it happens, most of the by-laws in Ontario municipalities are based on petitions presented by different categories of business and the only way to change or repeal by-laws enacted in this way is by the submission of another petition by the merchants of such category requesting the change or repeal. It is a well known fact that in most municipalities these by-laws are anachronisms permitting night shopping only on Saturdays or before certain holidays. Relatively few people work on Saturdays these days and Friday has taken the place of Saturday for most shoppers. Furthermore, most women prefer to do their shopping in the evening when the family car is available and they can be accompanied by their husbands and sometimes by the rest of the family. Public opinion polls have been taken and it has been established that a large majority of shoppers prefer to have shops open for business at least two nights a week. The opposition to the changing of these by-laws comes mostly from the merchants of the old shopping district who are waging a constant battle against the inroads of the modern shopping centre. It is generally the opinion held by most people who are familiar with this situation, that even the merchants in the old shopping districts would benefit by being permitted to keep open a few nights a week and certainly Friday night instead of Saturday night.

There are also a number of anomalies in these by-laws. One of the most glaring examples of this was revealed recently in the City of Ottawa. This city has early closing by-laws adopted following petitions in accordance with the provisions of the *Factory, Shop and Office Building Act*. Subsequently the city annexed a suburban area where there were no early closing by-laws. The merchants in the annexed area automatically became subject to the by-laws that were in force in the City of Ottawa, without being consulted in any way. If the merchants in the suburbs were against these by-laws, it is quite possible that their votes might have prevented the by-laws from coming into effect in the whole city. These by-laws, of course, are restricted to the territorial limits of the municipality enacting them and there are any number of instances where one shopping district may be partly in two municipalities. The stores in one municipality may be permitted to keep open in the evenings while other stores in the same area may be prohibited from so doing. This results in discrimination. Since most of these by-laws were enacted many years ago, some of the categories covered by these by-laws have somewhat altered the type of business being carried on by them. In the result, certain types of merchandise may be sold in the evenings by one category of merchants and not by another.

There are many other instances of unfairness in these by-laws. The main purpose of the act was to protect employees against being required to work too long hours. This is no longer the factor as most merchants in shopping centres have their stores closed a portion of a day during the week to compensate the employees for a time worked in the evenings, or they employ additional help. In any case the *Hours of Work and Vacations with Pay Act* which applies to retail shops, effectively protects the employees. In the opinion of important authorities and one which the writer shares, the law in Ontario should be repealed and a new one enacted on a provincial basis, keeping in mind the modern trend of living.

[The text of Mr. Bennett's paper is reproduced with his permission from "Papers presented at the Annual Meeting, Banff, 1957", of the Canadian Bar Association. See also Landis, "The Drafting of Percentage Leases," (1955) 11 *University of Toronto Law Journal* 43.]

2. Restrictive Covenants: Control by the Vendor

TULK *v.* MOXHAY

England. Chancery. 1848. 2 Ph. 774; 41 E.R. 1143

In the Domestic Papers for 1630: "Henry Earl of Manchester, Lord Privy Seal, Thomas Earl of Arundel and Surrey, and Secy. Dorchester to the king, have viewed the place and heard the parties interested, and to accommodate the Earl of Leicester and benefit the parish of St. Martin's, have set down fit limits for the wall, and appointed a way across the fields, and set apart a portion thereof to be turned into walks and planted with trees, and spaces left for the inhabitants to dry their clothes. These alterations to be made at the earl's expense, besides which he is to pay to the parish a perpetuity £3 per annum in recompense of the Lammas common to which the parishioners were entitled."

Sometime around 1640 Leicester House was erected and thereafter Leicester Fields or Gardens or Square came into existence. The property remained in the Sidney family for some years but after the death of the last earl (about 1750) the estate, consisting of the family mansion house and gardens and numerous houses in the square and streets adjoining, descended upon two Sidney sisters who held undivided moieties. The moiety of one of the sisters had become the property of Sir George Yonge and was conveyed by him to James Stuart Tulk in 1772. In 1786 partition proceedings were commenced and by the certificate of the commissioners the Tulk family had allotted to them the "piece of ground called Leicester Square, as the same was then enclosed with iron railings, and kept and used as a garden or pleasure ground," and as owners and proprietors they were to keep and maintain for ever afterwards "the said square garden or pleasure ground, and the railings round the same in sufficient and proper

LEICESTER FIELDS. From A SURVEY OF LONDON in the Reign of Queen Elizabeth by RALP AGAS.

LEICESTER SQUARE & ITS SURROUNDINGS in 1658. FROM FAITHORNE'S MAP of LONDON & WESTMINSTER.

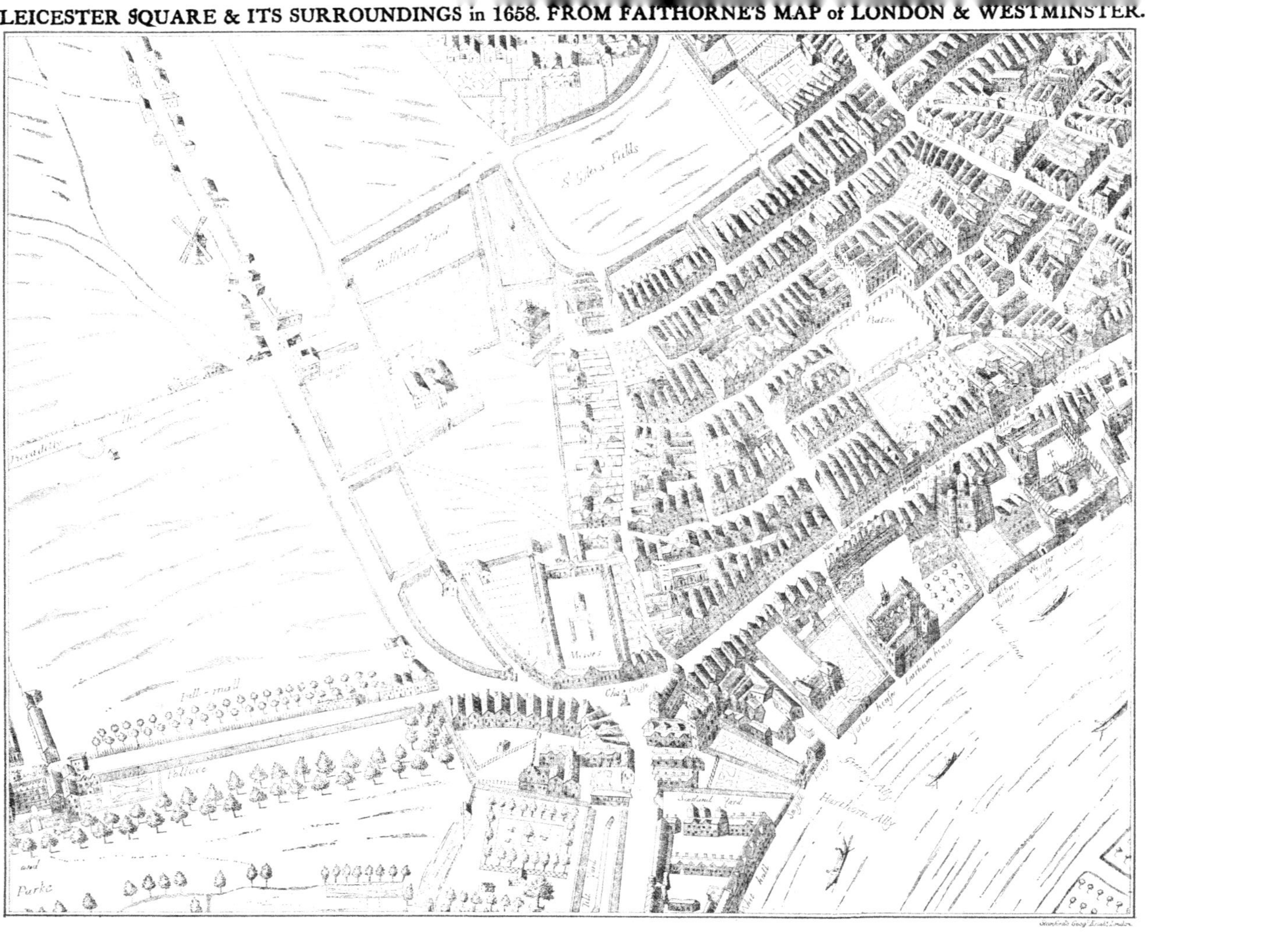

repair as a square garden or pleasure ground, in like manner as the same then was." (The complete history of the title is set out briefly (in about seventeen pages) in *Tulk* v. *The Metropolitan Board of Works* (1867), in 49 numbered paragraphs.)

In 1808 the square and several of the houses were held in fee simple by Charles Augustus Tulk, who had taken from his father and given him a covenant to keep the garden in its then form uncovered by any buildings. On July 15, 1808, Tulk conveyed to Charles Elms for £210, and the deed contained the following covenant:

"And the said Charles Elms, for himself, his heirs, executors, administrators and assigns, both covenant, promise and agree, to and with the said Charles A. Tulk, his heirs, executors and administrators, in manner following; that is to say, that he, the said Charles Elms, his heirs and assigns, shall and will, from time to time and at all times hereafter, at his and their own proper costs and charges, keep and maintain the said piece or parcel of ground and square garden, and the iron railing round the same, in its present form, and in sufficient and proper repair, as a square garden and pleasure ground, in an open state and uncovered with any buildings, in a neat and ornamental order; and shall not nor will take down, nor permit or suffer to be taken down, or defaced, at any time or times hereafter, the equestrian statue now standing or being in the centre of the said square garden, but shall and will continue and keep the same in its present situation, as it now is; and, also, that it shall and may be lawful to and for the inhabitants of Leicester Square aforesaid, tenants of the said Charles A. Tulk and of John A. Tulk, his father, their heirs and assigns, as well as the said Charles A. Tulk and John A. Tulk, their heirs and assigns, on payment of a reasonable rent for the same, to have keys (at their own expense), and the privilege of admission therewith annually, at any time or times, into the said square garden and pleasure ground."

By 1839 the property had come into the hands of one Inderwick, who had bought from one Barron to whom he had covenanted in the terms set out above. On April 25, 1839, the property was put up for sale by auction pursuant to the following particulars of sale:

"Particulars of a very valuable plot of freehold ground, consisting of the extensive pleasure-grounds forming the open plot of the whole of Leicester Square, namely, the valuable land lying within the railing, and containing 3,926 square yards, or three-quarters of an acre and ten perches (be it more or less). There is *malheureusement,* a covenant which restrains the possessor of the fee-simple from building on this grand and unrivalled open space; an Act of Parliament, however, might remedy the difficulty; and it will perhaps be difficult for an enterprising character to withstand the temptation; but the leading feature is the certainty that, in the immense improvements which are in full progress, this square must necessarily be required, or, failing to make suitable terms with the possessor of this valuable land, an extinguisher must, of course, be at once placed upon the ground plan, which is now upon the point of adoption, namely, to communiciate Covent Garden with Piccadilly, thus opening a grand thoroughfare to the City of London, and giving to Her Majesty a decent and proper line of road when she honours our national theatres with a visit."

One Hyam Hyams attended the sale and bought the property for £451 10s. He later assigned his interest under the contract to Moxhay. Moxhay refused to sign the covenant demanded by Inderwick and Inderwick refused to convey without it. In due course Moxhay sued for specific performance (See *Moxhay* v. *Inderwick* (1847)) and was awarded a decree on condition that he either indemnify Inderwick against any breach by Moxhay of the covenants contained in the deed of 1839 between Inderwick and Barron, or enter into a similar covenant as requested by Inderwick, which would be a sufficient indemnity.

Moxhay elected to give the indemnity and he became the purchaser without having covenanted, but obviously with notice of the existence of the covenant of his vendor's part. Moxhay apparently paid £120 and gave a bond of £1000 to one Gisby and his wife, the former Harriet Gibson, who had received all Barron's real and personal estate at his death, and who then released Inderwick from his covenant.

Moxhay having finally acquired title without the covenants in August, 1848, shortly proceeded to cut down trees and shrubs, remove part of the iron railing, and erect a hoarding upon the grounds. Charles Augustus Tulk then applied to the Master of the Rolls (Lord Langdale) for an *ex parte* injunction restraining Moxhay, which was granted. Moxhay moved, on December 5, 1848, before the Master of the Rolls, to dissolve the injunction. In continuing the injunction the Master of the Rolls said, in part (from 18 L.J. Ch. 83 at pp. 85–86):

"Now the defences which are set up in this case are of this kind. First of all, that there is such a change of circumstances that performance of the covenant ought not to be required. It was likened to the case of *The Duke of Bedford* v. *The Trustees of the British Museum* (1822). I think Mr. Palmer, with the ability and sense with which he has conducted the whole of this business, did not press that strongly in his reply: and he was perfectly right in doing so, because there is a manifest and plain difference between the two cases. In the case of *The Duke of Bedford* v. *The Trustees of the British Museum* the party who was seeking against the other the performance of the covenant, had himself, by his own acts, placed the property under such different circumstances that it was perfectly manifest there was no reciprocity; the parties were not in any way in the same situation; but in the reply it went rather upon a different footing. There has been, not a difference with regard to the original argument, but a difference with regard to a particular point; it was said that a passage was made through the north side of Leicester Square, and consequently (although according to an act of parliament) that that of itself would vary the covenant. I am clearly of opinion that that could not be so. It is said that an act of parliament has been forced upon all these parties for a new street, not touching the property in question, but thereby making a great thoroughfare, having a tendency to alter the sort of persons who might like to inhabit that particular place. But that thoroughfare through the upper part of it does not alter it at all in this respect to persons residing in the square; it does not follow that they might not desire to have a pleasant garden in the middle of the square. I do not think it in the least alters that.

Then the reply turned upon the point of acquiescence. In 1808 this covenant was made. Looking at the particular meaning of that deed, I can only conjecture—I will not place any weight upon it, but I should have supposed that the purchaser of that piece of ground, under such a deed as this, had apprehended it was worth his while to pay the money he paid, hoping to get some revenue from it by means of the garden and the keys. Manifestly one thing is plain; if such were the case his only hope to induce persons to get admission into the garden was to keep it in a neat and ornamental condition, so as to entice people to come out of their houses, and having gone to the expense of having keys, to pay for them. But it has been grossly neglected; it has become, what is called in the eloquent language of Chancery pleading in the answer, "a disgrace and reproach to the neighbourhood, and that boys broke in," and I do not know what they did there. This has been done with the permission of those who have been the owners of the place, and who had power over it, and not with the permission of Mr. Moxhay, as he only became owner (although he had a right of contract previously) in the month of August last. However, for a long series of years from the description I have received, it has been in such a condition that nobody would give a farthing to go into it, and they would be very anxious to avail themselves of the right to stop out of it. This being the condition of the place, the argument is, that the inhabitants of the square have never come and offered to pay their money; they have never asked the defendant or anybody else to keep it in order. I cannot say that that seems to me to be a reason why this injunction should be refused. That is the argument here, that there has been such an acquiescence, that the Court, even if it saw right to interfere on other grounds, ought not interfere upon this ground. I think that I cannot act upon that. I do not think the grounds stated are grounds why the Court should not exercise the jurisdiction, if it has jurisdiction, which I must, in the present state of authority, conceive the Court has. . . ."

On December 21, Moxhay moved before the Lord Chancellor that the order of the Master of the Rolls might be discharged.

LORD COTTENHAM: That this court has jurisdiction to enforce a contract between the owner of land and his neighbor purchasing a part of it, that the latter shall either use or abstain from using the land purchased in a particular way, is what I never knew disputed. Here there is no question about the contract: the owner of certain houses in the square sells the land adjoining, with a covenant from the purchaser not to use it for any other purpose than as a square garden. And it is now contended, not that the vendee could violate that contract, but that he might sell the piece of land, and that the purchaser from him may violate it without this Court having any power to interfere. If that were so, it would be impossible for an owner of land to sell part of it without incurring the risk of rendering what he retains worthless. It is said that, the covenant being one which does not run with the land, this Court cannot enforce it; but the question is, not whether the covenant runs with the land, but whether a party shall be permitted to use the land in a manner inconsistent with the contract entered into by his vendor, and with notice of which he purchased. Of course, the price would be affected by the covenant, and nothing could be more inequitable than that the original purchaser should be able to sell the property the next day for a greater price, in consideration of the assignee being allowed to escape from the liability which he had himself undertaken.

That the question does not depend upon whether the covenant runs with the land is evident from this, that if there was a mere agreement and no covenant, this Court would enforce it against a party purchasing with notice of it; for if an equity is attached to the property by the owner, no one purchasing with notice of that equity can stand in a different situation for the party from whom he purchased. There are not only cases before the Vice-Chancellor of England, in which he considered that doctrine as not in dispute; but looking at the ground on which Lord Eldon disposed of the case of *The Duke of Bedford* v. *The Trustees of the British Museum*, it is impossible to suppose that he entertained any doubt of it. . . .

With respect to the observations of Lord Brougham in *Keppell* v. *Bailey* (1834), he never could have meant to lay down that this Court would not enforce an equity attached to land by the owner, unless under such circumstances as would maintain an action at law. If that be the result of his observations, I can only say that I cannot coincide with it.

I think the cases cited before the Vice-Chancellor and this decision of the Master of the Rolls perfectly right, and, therefore, that this motion must be refused with costs.

NOTE ON THE SUBSEQUENT HISTORY. *Tulk* v. *Moxhay* was decided on December 21, 1848. Charles Augustus Tulk died on January 16, 1849. Edward Moxhay died on March 19, 1849, having by his will devised the Square to his widow, Phoebe Moxhay. Mrs. Moxhay conveyed the Square to James Wyld for £3000, for the purpose of erecting a large building to house a model of the earth. Representatives of the Tulk family then called upon Wyld to repair and reinstate the Square in compliance with the covenants of 1807, but no proceedings were taken in view of an arrangement then entered into, permitting Wyld to erect his globe for a period of 10 years from April 25, 1851, but clearly excepting the project from the covenants, which were to remain in effect. And Wyld agreed further that Lydia Tulk her heirs and assigns could purchase an undivided half of the Square at any time within one year after the term expired, and Augustus Henry Tulk could similarly purchase the other moiety, or the other members of the family on his failure. Six houses on the north side of the Square never belonged to the Tulk family, and one was owned by Henry Webb at the time of this agreement. Webb, the Tulks and Wyld negotiated about the "globe" but no agreement was reached. Wyld carried out his project in the succeeding 10 years without the consent of Webb, and during this time Wyld paid the rates on the Square. In 1861 John Augustus Tulk, a grandson of Charles A. Tulk, became owner of one moiety in the Square pursuant to the agreement, upon payment of £500.

Tulk and Wyld were tenants in common in fee in January, 1865, when the Metropolitan Board of Works acting in pursuance of *An Act for the protection of certain garden or ornamental grounds in cities and boroughs* ((1863), 26 Vict. c. 13), took charge of the Square, alleging that it was in a "dilapidated and neglected state" (which was in subsequent litigation admitted to have been the fact).

Tulk brought action against the Metropolitan Board of Works in 1865 for trespass, and at the trial a verdict was found for the plaintiff, subject to a special case, which was argued before Cockburn, C. J., Mellor and Lush JJ. on Nov. 12 and 15, 1867. See *Tulk* v. *Metropolitan Board of Works* (1867).

The question turned solely on the interpretation of section 1 of the Act, the case of which referred to "any enclosed garden or ornamental ground [that] has been set apart otherwise than by revocable permission of the owner thereof, in any public square, crescent, circus, street, or other public place, for the use or enjoyment of the inhabitants". Where such a garden has been neglected, the Board could "take charge" of it under detailed conditions and procedures. (The section contains one sentence of 615 words and is a model of bad drafting style but should be read as an illustration of the device used to preserve London gardens and squares.)

The Court held that the section did not apply. Cockburn C.J. discussed the origin and devolution of title in some detail. He said, in part, at p. 118,

"I can therefore see no trace of irrevocability. Until we come to the grant or conveyance to Elms of the open ground in 1808, I can see no trace of any mention of 'inhabitants,' or a reference to the right, or the permission, if I may so call it, for it is rather a permissive right on the part of the inhabitants to use the piece of garden for the purpose of recreation, arising from the covenant, which is attached to or forms part of the conveyance of the property. That cannot be said to be irrevocable; for the person who has secured it to the public or inhabitants of a given district, can at any time release it; and then there would be no obligation on the part of the person to whom the estate has been conveyed to allow the public to have any such use of it.

"The case, therefore, seems to me to fail on both points. It fails in shewing that there has been any permission to use, or any conveyance to the use and enjoyment (I mean in the popular sense of the word use, not in the legal sense) of the inhabitants, and still less does it shew that there has been any irrevocable permission.

"Now, it may be said to what does the first section apply? I think only to a case where there has been what, in the popular sense, may be called a dedication to a portion of the public. It is admitted that is not a phrase that can be used as a term of art in legal phraseology, yet one understands perfectly well what is meant by it."

TAYLOR, LEICESTER SQUARE (1874)

Throughout the reigns of Elizabeth, James, Charles I., and the Protector, the authorities, local and central, had done their best to discourage building in and about London. The repeated attacks of plague, between 1590 and the most famous outbreak of 1665, [there were outbreaks in 1592, 1603, 1625, 1636 and 1665] were no doubt the chief reason for this desire to limit the natural increase of London.

Elizabeth's first proclamation against new building, dated 7th July, 1582, assigns for reasons, "1st, the difficulty of governing a more extended multitude, without device of new jurisdiction and officers for the purpose; 2ndly, the improbability of supplying them with food, fuel, and other necessaries of life at a reasonable rate; and 3rdly, the danger of spreading plague and infections throughout the realm." But the proclamations for the same purpose, after the accession of James I., were more numerous and more stringent. There is a recorded saying of that sapient monarch, "that the growth of the capital resembled that of a rickety child's head, in which an excessive influx of humours drained and impoverished the extremities, and at the same time generated distemper in the overloaded part." He would not allow his nobles to remain in London the year through without special licence, and, Lord Bacon tells us, would sometimes say to them, "Gentlemen, at London you are like ships in a sea which show like nothing; but in the country villages you are like ships on a river, which look like great things." An Act of 1657 shows that in this point Cromwell was not less disposed to believe in both the expediency and efficacy of restriction than his predecessors. The preamble recites that the excessive number of new buildings in the suburbs of the City, and parts adjoining, is very mischievous and inconvenient, and that "the said growing evil is of late so much multiplied and increased, that there is a necessity for some further and speedy course for the redress thereof." The statute imposed a fine of £100, and a continuing penalty of £20 a month, on every one building a house or cottage on a new foundation, in or within ten miles of the suburbs; and enacted that every building erected since 1620, and not having four acres of land attached to it, should pay a fine of one year's rent. This was in relief of offenders, for, under the existing law, such houses were liable to be pulled down. Exemptions from penalties to the amount of £7,000 under the Act were allowed to the Earl of Bedford and his brothers, in respect of the buildings in Covent Garden parish; and the builders of Lincoln's Inn Fields were exempted from forfeits in regard to new buildings erected on three sides of the square, before the 1st of October, 1659, provided they paid a fine of one full year's value for every house within a month of its erection, and conveyed the residue of the Fields to the Society of Lincoln's Inn, "for laying the same into walks for common use and business."

In spite of this strenuous discouragement, London without the walls continued to grow. In Faithorne's map (1658), the quarter between Chancery Lane and the Haymarket, east and west, and Holborn and the Strand, north and south, which in Aggas's map (1592) was open fields, is seen covered for the most part with houses. Lincoln's Inn Field and Covent Garden Piazza are complete, stately squares, planned and built from the designs of Inigo Jones. . . . [pp. 21–25]

Between the Restoration and the Revolution, Castle Street, Newport Street, Cranborn Alley, and Bear Lane had been built; the square had been surrounded by houses, and had assumed its present dimensions. The buildings on the south side were finished in 1671, the north and east having been built before, and including the best houses. The ground in the centre of the square was railed round before the end of the century, and served for duels, like other open space in those days of swords and sudden quarrels. . . . [p. 151]

No part of London has outlived a century without curious vicissitudes. The odder the vicissitudes, the richer the crop of memories. Leicester Square certainly yields to no rival of its own day and generation—Lincoln's Inn Fields, Covent Garden Piazza, Soho or Golden Square—in the strangeness of its changes and the variety of its associations. What a kaleidoscopic series of permutations and combinations does the Square present as we turn Time's glass,—whether in its residences, from the home of the Sidneys and the last resting-place of the Queen of Hearts, the nursery and court of the first three Princes of Wales of the Hanoverian line, to the tavern and table haunts of republican refugees and out-at-elbows exiles; in its famous inhabitants, from the Sidneys and Sunderlands, Newton and Swift, the Marquis of Caermarthen and Speaker Onslow, Hogarth, Reynolds, and Sir George Savile, John Hunter, Cruikshank, and Charles Bell, Kosciusko and La Guiccioli, to Barber and Burford of the Panorama, and Dibdin of the Sea-Songs; in its architecture, from the stately Jacobean Leicester House of 1636, of the school, if not from the design, of Inigo Jones, to the bastard Byzantine of Wylde's Great Globe and the gingerbread Moresque of the Alhambra; in its social gatherings, from Sir Joshua's famous dinner-table, focus of all that was most distinguished for art and literature, wit and wisdom, science and social distinction, in the most brilliant circles of the most brilliant epoch of English society, to the cheap restaurants and subterranean "shades" of a later generation, haunts of the most questionable company, native and foreign, round repasts as questionable: its exhibitions from Sir Ashton Lever's Holophusicon—no contemptible rival of the British

Museum—to the Invisible Girl and the Industrious Fleas: its metamorphoses, as of Hogarth's house, at the sign of the Golden Head, into Archbishop Tenison's schools; of John Hunter's mansion and museum into the dingy office of the "*International, Journal Quotidien Francais*," below, and the head-quarters of the First Middlesex Artillery Volunteers above; or of Sir Joshua's studio into Puttick and Simpson's sale-rooms: its failures, from the high-reaching educational aims of the Cosmos Institute, to the more frivolous but still ambitious project of the promoters of the Alexandra Theatre and Winter Garden, whose notice-board still impends the charred ruins of Savile House: its antiquities, from Miss Linwood's musty and mournful gallery, still remembered by survivors of the last generation, to that deplorable horse and his rider, whose long martyrdom of ridicule and insult has at length come to a close. . . .

It is true that the vicissitudes of a London quarter usually follow a downward road. And the more easterly it lies, the more decidedly downwards its tendency. From being fashionable, it may become professional, and hold there, as Lincoln's Inn Fields does: or it may resign itself to come down from mansion houses to hotels, as Covent Garden Piazza has done: or may fall still lower, as Golden Square has fallen, to lodging and boarding-houses of the cheaper and more cosmopolitan kind: or may become frankly industrial, like Soho Square. Even if situated within the charmed circle of the West End the London square is not safe from vicissitude. Clubs and Institutions will gradually elbow out noblemen's residences; and this change, already consummated over more than half of St. James's Square, may in time spread to other and, as yet, unassailed centres of fashion further and further west, driving the upper ten, at last, altogether into the outlying regions of Belgravia and Bromptonia, Kensingtonia and Tyburnia. In the downward tendency of its successive changes Leicester Square is in no way exceptional. The exception in its case is that as regards its central enclosure, at least, there has been vouchsafed to it a late revival; the usual motto of metropolitan neighbourhoods once on the decline being *vestigia nulla retrosum.*

The march of London fashion and population, like that of empire according to the poet, has been westward. As the ocean of bricks and mortar has rolled from the East it has left its seamarks behind it, telling of earlier stages of society, and other conditions of manners, as the real sea leaves its record of strata and fossils.

No portion of London shows these changes more strikingly than the part built between the Restoration and the Hanoverian succession, one of the periods of quickest expansion in our metropolitan history. This may be roughly described as the area bounded north by the line of Oxford Street and Holborn; south, by the Strand; east, by the line of Chancery Lane; and west, by that of Bond Street. . . . [pp. 1–5]

In January, 1873, an aquarium company offered £50,000 for the enclosure, then in the lowest depths of degradation and neglect. As the first step towards possession a hoarding had been already erected, when a meeting of the House-holders in the Square was convened, a Defence Committee formed, and Mr. Henry Bickers, jun., chosen chairman. A Bill was at once filed in Chancery, through Mr. Webb, one of the freeholders, to compel the removal of the hoarding, and to restrain any erection on the enclosed ground. The injunction was granted as prayed for. A deputation of the inhabitants then waited on the Board of Works, urging the Board to apply for Parliamentary powers to purchase the square, with all the existing rights. A Bill was introduced by the Board, the standing orders were suspended in its favour, and it became law in due course.

In the meantime, Baron Albert Grant had been applied to for his aid in raising the capital of the company created for purchase of the enclosure. This first called his attention to the place. When the company's operations were arrested by injunction, the ground was offered to him as a building speculation. He found, on taking legal opinion, that it was unavailable for building purposes, and then conceived the idea, now so happily carried into effect, of buying out the shareholders who claimed rights in that ill-used quarter of an acre, converting the space into an ornamental garden, and handing it over to the Metropolitan Board of Works for the enjoyment of the public. The interests were bought out for £13,000, eight of fourteen shares, held by the representatives of the Tulks, easily, the other six after long and troublesome negotiation. The last was purchased from an owner, whose agent arrived from New Zealand only a few days before the completion of the works.

Baron Grant employed Mr. James Knowles as his architect. The laying out of the garden was entrusted to Mr. John Gibson, jun., to whom with his father the public is indebted for the tasteful planting and arrangement of Battersea Park.

The principal ornament of the new Square is a white marble fountain, surmounted by a statue of Shakespeare, also in white marble, the figure being an exact reproduction, by Signor Fontana, of the statue (designed by Kent and executed by Scheemacker), on the Westminster Abbey cenotaph. The water spouts from jets round the pedestal, and from the heads of dolphins at each of its corners, into a marble basin. Flower beds surround this central mass, and the enclosure, so long a squalid and sordid waste, is now a gay and peaceful garden of flowering shrubs, green plots, inlaid with bright flower-beds, and broad, gravelled paths. The iron railing outside is waist high, elaborately designed, and executed by the Coalbrooke-dale Company. In each angle of the garden is a bust of white marble on a granite pedestal. To the south-east, stands Hogarth, by Durham; to the south-west, Newton, by Weekes; to the north-east, John Hunter, by Woolner; to the north-west, Reynolds, by Marshall. Only Hogarth and Reynolds could be placed in juxtaposition to their houses in the Square.

The idea which the designer of the central fountain wished to convey (I use his own words) was of the Poet, standing isolated and colossal, cut off from the rest of the world by the quasi Castalian spring, which rises at his feet, but brought close to all men in his works, symbolized by the grass and flowers which spring round the margin of the fountain, and which its water bedews and nourishes. The dolphins playing close below him imply his Arion-like attraction for the "sane and simple" animal part of us, and those memorable words to which his finger points—"There is no darkness but ignorance"—his deep, sympathetic insight into our brighter nature and its needs.

The modified repetition of the figure in the Abbey was chosen for the statue, partly because it has become the traditional figure of Shakespeare in this country, and is recognizable by everybody at a glance; partly because, if not a great, it is certainly not a mean work of art; and partly because the difficulties of selection would have made the production of an original work impossible in the time at command.

On Thursday, the 2nd of July, 1874, the garden was formally handed over by the donor to the Metropolitan Board.

A brilliant day, and the interest of the occasion, combined to attract a great crowd. Spectators filled the open windows, and fringed the roofs where ever there was a balustrade to secure them. Within the hoarding pavilions

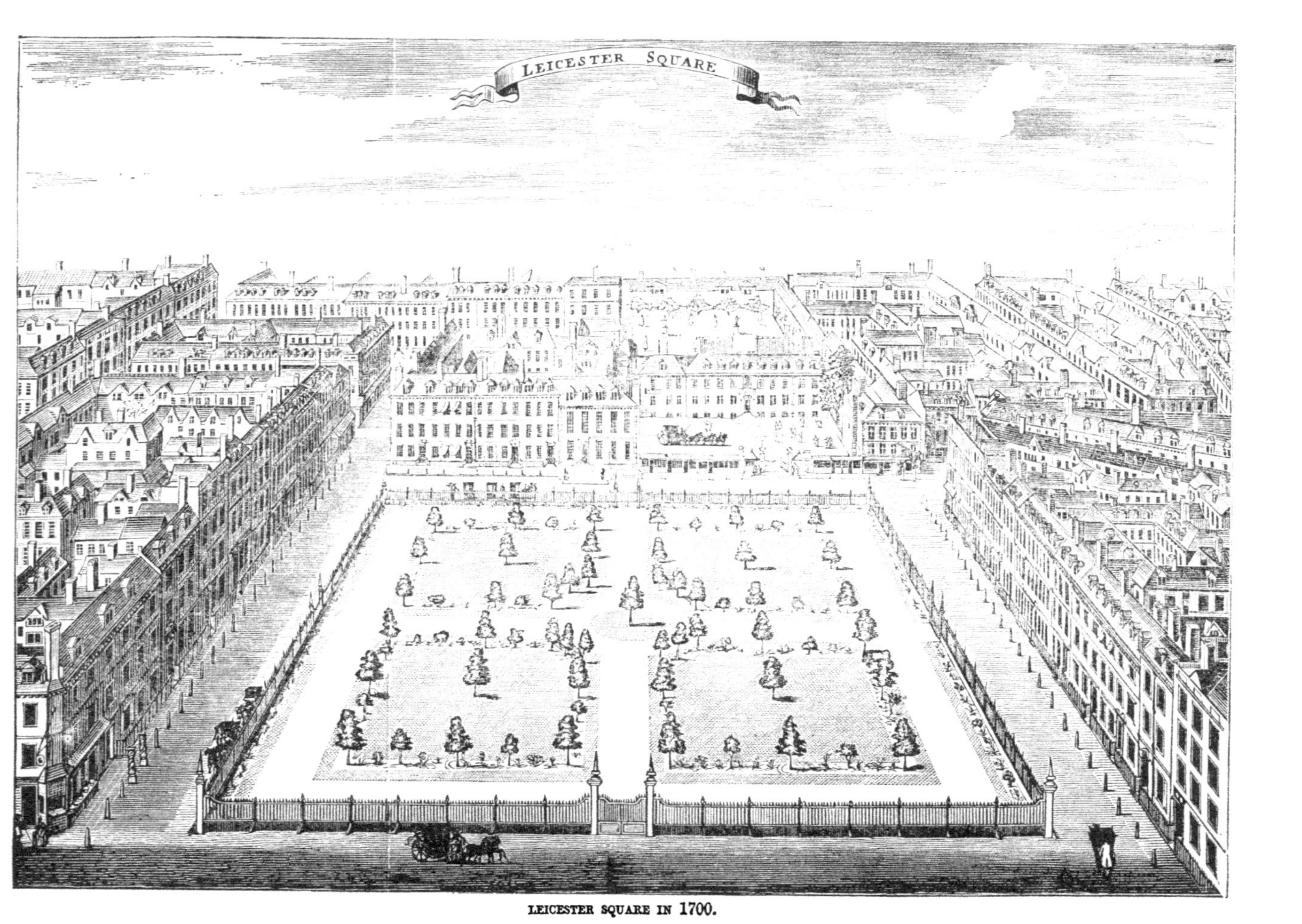

LEICESTER SQUARE IN 1700.

LEICESTER SQUARE IN 1874.

were arranged round for the accommodation and refreshment of more than 2,000 invited visitors, and the shelter, meant as a protection against showers, was available against sunshine.

At three o'clock the transfer of the garden took place, after Baron Grant had told the story of his purchase, had thanked the Leicester Square Defence Committee for the local influence they had exerted on their recalcitrant neighbours, and had explained the considerations which had influenced him in choosing Shakespeare for the central figure of the Square, and in deciding on the claims to pedestals at its angles. He apologized to Dr. Johnson for disappointing him at the last moment. The marble which was now the famous Anatomist had been meant for the great Moralist. The whole cost of the gift, purchase of the ground and collateral expenses, legal, architectural, horticultural, and artistic, was stated by the donor to have been £28,000. Baron Grant then signed the deed of conveyance which transferred the garden formally to the Metropolitan Board of Works. In the involuntary absence of the Chairman, the Board was represented by Mr. Richardson, who thanked Baron Grant for his gift in the name of the Board and of the public of the metropolis, and exchanged a deed of acceptance for the deed of transfer.

Mr. Bickers presented this address to Baron Grant from the Defence Committee:

"SIR,—We, the members of the Leicester Square Defence Committee, and the inhabitants generally, desire to offer you this expression of our sincere and heartfelt thanks for the munificent gift which has this day been inaugurated. We feel sir, that in this matter you have not merely conferred on us a great local boon, but at the same time have wiped out a very serious blot on our municipal management, and one that almost reached the proportions of a national disgrace. We have long felt that the late condition of the Square was not only a very serious detriment to its immediate neighbourhood, but was such as to make it a laughing-stock to our neighbours; and yet so much difficulty surrounded the case that for a considerable time it seemed impossible to mend matters. You, sir, by a great act of generosity, have surmounted these obstacles, and have converted that which was a filthy wilderness into a blooming garden and a thing of beauty. We trust, sir, that you may be long spared to see how your gift is appreciated; and, moreover, that you may see your example followed, and many of our squares, which are unsightly and useless, converted into charming gardens, decorated by works of art, and thus made to minister to the health and to the elevation of the tastes of the people."

(Signed by the Committee, and dated "Leicester Square, July 2, 1874.")

Mr. Richardson then proceeded to unveil the central statue and set the fountains playing. After making the tour of the gardens and successively uncovering the busts at the four corners, Baron Grant and the members of the Board returned to the central pavilion, where Mr. Richardson formally declared the gardens open, thenceforward and for ever, as a pleasure ground for the people. [pp. 477–484]

[Leicester Square is now owned and maintained by the London County Council and is open to the public.]

NOTE ON THE ILLUSTRATIONS. The reproductions of Agas's map and Faithorne's map are from *Leicester Square*, as are the two drawings of the square, in 1700 and in 1874. The reproduction of the Bloomsbury area, from John Rocque's map of London, 1746, is taken from *London*

200 Years Ago by W. Crawford Snowden, a charming collection of photographs, old prints and map sections.

NOTE. The similarity of the problems facing the government of Queen Elizabeth I and those facing the Ontario government in 1963, resulting from the overspill of the central city population, is remarkable. So also is the similarity of means adopted to meet the problems. The illustrations help to show the need for some organization of the growth and change of a city.

NOTE ON LONDON SQUARES. What the Earl of Leicester was trying to do in setting up Leicester Square was fairly typical of his times, and the Tulk family were acting in the best tradition in extracting the covenant they did and attempting to enforce it. The *Report of the Royal Commission on London Squares* (1928, Cmd. 3196), suggests that "high class residential development in squares commenced in the 17th century with the erection of houses in St. James's Square (Westminster), Leicester Square and Bloomsbury Square" and by the end of the century eight more squares had been formed. In 1928 the Royal Commission found 461 "enclosures" with a total of 400 acres, varying in size from a few square yards, "mere strips in front of houses" to large squares up to 7 acres. The Earl of Leicester probably had in mind open space and gardens enclosed by private residences with Leicester House and gardens dominating on the north, although the drawing in 1700 hardly suggests domination. The prevalence of the "plague" may have encouraged open space designs, but the chief objective seems to have been the establishment of pleasant surroundings to suit the tastes of the upper classes in Stuart and Georgian England. Planners sometimes refer to such pleasant surroundings as "amenities," a rather overworked and underdefined word in their jargon.

Today the land uses around Leicester Square are entirely commercial; offices, shops, theatres, cinemas and restaurants. The Square, now, in fact, fulfills quite a different, but equally desirable planning purpose. It provides a pleasant bit of green and open space in the very heart of the theatre land and the Piccadilly shopping area of the west end. Oddly, an essential feature of successful "open space" is a sense of enclosure which a square attains if it is built upon all four sides. See Sharp, Gibberd and Holford, *Design in Town and Village, Part III, Chapter III* "The Enclosed Place" (pp. 97–109) for a discussion of relevant planning concepts, complete with plans, maps, diagrams and some excellent photographs.

Perhaps the most interesting of the three pioneer developments is St. James's Square and its environs, originally laid out by Henry Jermyn, the first Earl of St. Albans about 1663. Sir John Summerson, in his *Georgian London* (1945), suggests that St. Albans was inspired by the Place Royale at Paris or the Belle Cour at Lyons. Originally he planned a small group of very large homes, but in the building boom after the great fire (1666) he increased the number of lots and developed the whole area between Pall Mall and Piccadilly west of the Haymarket. An examination of the original layout reveals most characteristics of a "modern" neighbourhood unit. The area is enclosed by wide main traffic routes, with narrow and quiet internal streets. There are houses for the wealthy and the poor, a market place (shopping centre), a church (designed and built by Wren 1684) and, of course, the Square itself. *Georgian London* provides a delightful account of the development of London over the next century and a half.

By no means all of the squares in London were developed by restrictive covenants. See the Royal Commission Report for the varieties of legal devices from leasehold to public ownership, with varying degrees of public control. St. James's Square for example was owned in 1928 by the St. James's Square Trustees, and restrictions on use were provided by public statute, 12 Geo. I, c. 25 (1726). The Trustees maintain the Square out of rates levied on the occupiers of houses in the Square. The area has degenerated somewhat into a club land, and the building of Lower Regent Street and Waterloo Place has destroyed the neighbourhood unit character of the original. See Wheatley and Cunningham *London Past and Present* (1891) for short histories of the area and its inhabitants.

ROGERS v. HOSEGOOD. [1900] 2 Ch. 388 (England. Court of Appeal). In 1869 four partners, including Rogers, one of the plaintiffs, were engaged as builders and were owners in fee (subject to a mortgage) of some land at Palace Gate in London, which they had laid out in plots suitable for the building of large private dwelling houses. In that year two of the plots were conveyed by the partners and their mortgagees to the Duke of Bedford who covenanted, with intent that the covenant might so far as possible bind the premises conveyed, into whosoever hands they might come, and might enure to the benefit of the four partners, their heirs and assigns and others claiming under them, to all or any of their lands adjoining or near to the premises, that the premises should be used for a private residence only and that no trade or business should be carried on.

By a deed dated March 25, 1873, Sir John Millais purchased one plot from the partners. He gave a covenant similar to the Duke's. At the date of this conveyance Sir John had no knowledge of the covenants contained in the deeds of 1869 and his own deed contained no assignment of the benefit of the covenants beyond the conveyance of "all the rights, easements, or appurtenances belonging or reputed to belong thereto."

In 1872 the Duke of Bedford died and the defendant Hosegood purchased the Bedford plots with notice of the covenants. Notwithstanding he proposed to erect on the plots one large apartment dwelling.

In 1896 Sir John Millais had died, and his surviving trustees, William Henry Millais and George Gray, with Rogers, one of the original partners, sought an injunction restraining the defendant from erecting the building. Farwell J. granted the injunction to the Millais trustees but dismissed the action by Rogers for reasons immaterial here. Hosegood appealed, but his appeal was dismissed. COLLINS L. J.: "The real and only difficulty arises on the question—whether the benefit of the covenants has passed to the assigns of Sir John Millais as owners of the plot purchased by him on March 25, 1873, there being no evidence that he knew of these covenants when he bought. Here, again, the difficulty is narrowed, because by express declaration on the face of the conveyances of 1869 the benefit of the two covenants in question was intended for all or any of the vendor's lands near to or adjoining the plot sold, and therefore for (among others) the plot of land acquired by Sir John Millais, and that they "touched and concerned" that land within the meaning of those words so as to run with the land at law we do not doubt. Therefore, but for a technical difficulty which was not raised before Farwell J., we should agree with him that the benefit of the covenants in question was annexed to and passed to Sir John Millais by the conveyance of the land which he bought in 1873. A difficulty, however, in giving effect to this view arises from the fact that the covenants in question in the deeds of May and June, 1869, were made with the mortgagors only, and therefore in contemplation of law were made with strangers to the land, to which, therefore, the benefit did not become annexed. That a court of equity, however, would not regard such an objection as defeating the intention of the parties to the covenant is clear; and, therefore, when the covenant was clearly made for the benefit of certain land with a person who in the contemplation of such a court was the true owner of it, it would be regarded as annexed to and running with that land, just as it would have been at law but for the technical difficulty . . . [When] as here, it has been once annexed to the land reserved: the presumption must be that it passes on a sale of that land, unless there is something to rebut it, and the purchaser's ignorance of the existence of the covenant does not defeat the presumption."

ROGERS *v*. HOSEGOOD. [1900] 2 Ch. 388 (England. King's Bench). The trial judge had to decide whether the covenant that "every messuage to be erected on the two plots, or either of them or any part thereof, should at all times thereafter be adapted for and used as and for a private residence only," would be violated by the erection of the apartment house. On this point, FARWELL J.: ". . . In my opinion, a flat such as is proposed is not one messuage or dwelling-house, but several. I cannot see any substantial difference for the purposes of a covenant of this nature between a terrace of adjoining residences, separated from one another vertically, and a pile of residences, separated from one another horizontally. If the building of the defendant was carried no higher than the ground-floor it would, in my opinion, be impossible to contend that each of the residences opening onto the inner area was not a separate house, and I cannot see that the superposition of seven other rows of residences can make any difference. . . . In my opinion, a large building which is to be used as thirty or forty separate residential flats does not answer the description of a messuage to be used as and for a private residence. But if the whole structure could be regarded as a private residence only, it is difficult to see how thirty or forty different families and establishments can find place therein, unless the owner of the entire messuage is carrying on the trade of letting apartments. . . . "

RENALS *v*. COWLISHAW. 1878. 9. Ch. D. 125 (England. Chancery Division). HALL V. C.: "It appears to me that . . . in order to enable a purchaser as an assign (such purchaser not being an assign of all that the vendor retained when he executed the conveyance containing the covenants, and that conveyance not shewing that the benefit of the covenant was intended to enure for the time being of each portion of the estate so retained or of the portion of the estate of which the plaintiff is assign) to claim the benefit of a restrictive covenant, this, at least, must appear, that the assign acquired his property with the benefit of the covenant, that is, it must appear that the benefit of the covenant was part of the subject-matter of the purchase. Lord Justice Bramwell, in *Master* v. *Hansard* (1876), said: 'I am satisfied that the restrictive covenant was not put in for the benefit of this particular property, but for the benefit of the lessors to enable them to make the most of the property which they retained.' In the present case I think that the covenants were put in with a like object. If it had appeared in the conveyance to Bainbrigge that there were such restrictive covenants in coneyances already executed, and expressly or otherwise that Bainbrigge was to have the benefit of them, he and the plaintiffs, as claiming through him, would have been entitled to the benefit of them. But there being in the conveyance to Bainbrigge no reference to the existence of such covenants by recital of the conveyances containing them or otherwise, the plaintiffs cannot be treated as entitled to the benefit of them."

QUESTION. Does this principle mean that there is a type of case where the vendor may make the restriction effective by express assignment at his option, where the restriction benefits the vendor personally, at least primarily?

LONDON COUNTY COUNCIL *v*. ALLEN
England. Court of Appeal. [1914] 3 K.B. 642

SCRUTTON J. (sitting ad hoc in the Court of Appeal): In this case the London County Council, on January 24, 1907, entered into an indenture with one Morris Joseph Allen, a builder, describing himself as "the owner in fee simple of certain land," by which he

"doth hereby for himself, his heirs and assigns, and other the persons claiming under him, and so far as practicable to bind the land and hereditaments herein mentioned into whosesoever hands the same may come, covenant and agree with the council that he and they will not erect or place, or cause or permit to be erected or placed, any building, structure, or other erection upon the land shewn by green colour on the said plan, without the previous consent in writing of the council so to do, and that on every conveyance, sale, charge, mortgage, lease, assignment, or other dealing with the land herein mentioned, or any part thereof, he will give notice of the aforesaid covenant in every conveyance, transfer, mortgage, charge, lease, assignment, or other document by which such dealing is effected."

The plots coloured green were two plots intended to be reserved for the making of roads. On plot No. 1, in July, 1911, three houses were built by Mrs. Allen; on plot No. 2 a wall was built by Allen. The London County Council thereupon issued a writ claiming a mandatory injunction to pull down the houses and wall respectively. Thereupon it was alleged that as to Plot No. 1 the legal estate was in one Norris as mortgagee, and the equity of redemption in Mrs. Allen, who had taken title from Mr. Allen and Willcocks, his mortgagee, who had no notice of the restrictive covenant; and it was contended (1) by way of demurrer that as the London County Council were not neighbouring landowners, or grantors of the plot in question, a covenant by Allen in their favour was only a personal covenant, and could not affect the land when in the hands of assigns of Allen, whether they had notice of the covenant or not. It was said that to affect them the right must be in the nature of a negative easement; that an easement required both a dominant and a servient tenement; and that as the council had no land to which the benefit of the covenant could attach, there could be no dominant tenement, and therefore no negative easement binding on a servient tenement, but only an easement in gross, which did not bind assigns of the land. (2) It was alleged that the defendants Mrs. Allen and Norris could prove they were purchasers for value of the legal estate without notice of the covenant, and therefore not bound by it. Avory J. found on the second contention as a fact that Mrs. Allen and Norris had not satisfied him they had not notice, actual or constructive, of the covenant. On the first contention he said: "It was contended before me that this restrictive covenant, being in the nature of a negative easement, the action would not lie except at the suit of a covenantee who was at the time of the covenant in possession of land which required protection; and that the plaintiffs were not at the time in possession of any such land. But having regard to the powers vested in the London County Council, under ss. 7 and 9 of the London Building Act, 1894, and to the admission made in the argument before me that the conditions imposed in this case were not ultra vires, I think this contention fails." He apparently treated the duty and interest of the County Council in the matter of new streets as sufficient to make the covenant bind the land in the hands of assigns from Allen. This Court determined to decide the first contention before hearing argument on the second, and we have now to decide on the first contention.

Counsel on each side agreed that the burden of this covenant would not run with the land at law, so as to bind assigns, for the reason stated in the notes to *Spencer's Case* that "there appears to be no authority which has decided, apart from the equitable doctrine of notice" (by which is meant, as hereinafter explained, the doctrine identified with the case of *Tulk* v. *Moxhay*) "that the burden of a covenant will run with land in any case except that of landlord and tenant." . . .

The question then is whether it is essential to the doctrine of *Tulk* v. *Moxhay* that the covenantee should have at the time of the creation of the covenant, and afterwards, land for the benefit of which the covenant is created, in order that the burden of the covenant may bind assigns of the land to which it relates. It is clear that the covenantee may sue the covenantor himself, though the former has parted with the land to which the covenant relates: *Stokes* v. *Russell* (1790). To answer the question as to the assigns of the covenantor, and the land in their hands, requires the investigation of the historical growth of the doctrine of *Tulk* v. *Moxhay*. Though the covenantee in that case did hold adjacent land, there is no trace in the judgment of Lord Cottenham of the requirement that the covenantee should have and continue to hold land to be benefited by the covenant. I read Lord Cottenham's judgment as proceeding entirely on the question of notice of the covenant, and on the equitable ground that a man purchasing land with notice that there was a covenant not to use it in a particular way would not be allowed to violate the convenant he knew of when he bought the land . . .

Up to 1881, when counsel in *Haywood* v. *Brunswick Permanent Benefit Building Society* stated that *Tulk* v. *Moxhay* had been applied in fifteen cases, I cannot trace, nor could counsel before us discover, that *Tulk* v. *Moxhay* had been based on anything but notice of the covenant by the assignee. In the case cited, in which the Court of Appeal refused to extend the doctrine to an affirmative covenant to repair, Lindley L. J. said "The result of these cases is that only such a covenant as can be complied with without expenditure of money will be enforced against the assignee on the ground of notice." Brett L.J. said "That case" (*Tulk* v. *Moxhay*) "decided that an assignee taking land subject to a certain class of covenants is bound by such covenants if he has notice of them, and that the class of covenants comprehended within the rule is that covenants restricting the mode of using the land only will be enforced." Cotton L.J., after citing Lord Cottenham that "No one purchasing with notice of that equity can stand in a different situation from the party from whom he purchased," said "This lays down the real principle that an equity attaches to the owner of the land."

Meanwhile in *De Mattos* v. *Gibson*, in 1858, Knight Bruce L.J. had put the principle as applying to all property thus: "Reason and justice seem to prescribe that, at least as a general rule, where a man, by gift or purchase, acquires property from another, with knowledge of a previous contract, lawfully and for valuable consideration made by him with a third person, to use and employ the property for a particular purpose in a specified manner, the acquirer shall not to the material damage of the third person, in opposition to the contract and inconsistently with it, use and employ the property in a manner not allowable to the giver or seller," resting the matter on knowledge of the previous contract, that is notice.

In *Catt* v. *Tourle*, in 1869, A., a brewer, had sold land to B. with a covenant that he should have the exclusive right to supply all ale consumed in any public-house erected on the land. C., with knowledge of the covenant, bought part of the land from B., erected a public-house on it, but did not take his beer from A. The Court of Appeal, citing *De Mattos* v. *Gibson*, restrained C., treating the covenant as negative, and resting the judgment on the ground that C. "clearly purchased with notice of the present covenant, and . . . cannot be heard to say that he is now entitled to disregard its provisions." It is to be noted that A. is not stated to have owned any land, and as he might brew beer anywhere, the covenant could not relate to any particular land of his.

In *Luker* v. *Dennis*, in 1877, A., a brewer, granted a lease to B. of public-house X., with a covenant that B. should take from him all beer consumed not only in X., but also in public-house Y., which B. held of a different landlord. C. took public-house Y. from B. with notice of the covenant, and did not take his beer from A. It was argued before Fry J. that notice was not enough unless the covenantee had some interest in the land bound by the covenant, either as vendor or lessor. That learned judge refused to accede to this argument, and, citing *De Mattos* v. *Gibson*, and *Catt* v. *Tourle*, granted the injunction, giving, as he said, "effect to the equitable doctrine of notice." I think up to this point the doctrine has been rested on notice, and did not depend on the covenantee having land in favour of which the covenant was created.

The first departure from this position occurs in the judgment of Jessel M.R. in *London and South Western Ry. Co.* v. *Gomm*, in March, 1882. The contract to be enforced was one to reconvey land on notice, and clearly therefore an affirmative covenant, and, as such, within the doctrine laid down in *Haywood's Case*, in December, 1881, excluding such contracts from the doctrine of *Tulk* v. *Moxhay*. The Court also held that the sale was ultra vires the railway company, and void for remoteness. But Sir George Jessel, holding that the covenant did, but for its being ultra vires and void, create an interest in the land, discussed the nature of the right. He said: "The doctrine of that case," (*Tulk* v. *Moxhay*) "rightly considered, appears to me to be either an extension in equity of the doctrine of *Spencer's Case*, to another line of cases, or else an extension in equity of the doctrine of negative easements; such, for instance, as a right to the access of light, which prevents the owner of the servient tenement from building so as to obstruct the light. The covenant in *Tulk* v. *Moxhay* was affirmative in its terms, but was held by the Court to imply a negative. Where there is a negative covenant expressed or implied, as, for instance, not to build so as to obstruct a view, or not to use a piece of land otherwise than as a garden, the Court interferes on one or other of the above grounds. This is an equitable doctrine, establishing an exception to the rules of common law which did not treat such a covenant as running with the land, and it does not matter whether it proceeds on analogy to a covenant running with the land or on analogy to an easement. The purchaser took the estate subject to the equitable burden, with the qualification that if he acquired the legal estate for value without notice he was freed from the burden. That qualification, however, did not affect the nature of the burden; the notice was required merely to avoid the effect of the legal estate, and did not create the right, and if the purchaser took only an equitable estate he took subject to the burden, whether he had notice or not."

It will be noticed that the equitable estate or burden was held to arise independent of notice; which I respectfully think was contrary to the previous authorities; and that in Sir George Jessel's view it did not matter whether it was by analogy to covenants running with the land, or on analogy to an easement. Both, however, had this in common, that some land belonging to the covenantee was required, either from him to let, that the covenant might run with the land, or as a dominant tenement for the easement, an easement in gross being merely a personal right. Whether the "analogy" or "extension" spoken of by Sir George Jessel involved this condition as to land is not discussed. . . .

[After discussing *Rogers* v. *Hosegood*, Scrutton J. observed, "This again appears to me to treat land as essential, on both sides of the covenant, to affect assigns whether of the benefit or burden." and continued:]

This view seems to me to be adopted also by the Court of Appeal in *Formby* v. *Barker* (1903). A., the owner of the land, conveyed all his land with a restrictive covenant against its being used in particular ways to B., who assigned it to C., who had notice of the covenant. A. died; C. began to use the land in a way forbidden by the covenant; the administratrix of A., who had no land, sued C. It was argued that the right to enforce such a covenant depended entirely on notice; members of the Court suggested in argument that the benefit of the covenant, if not pursued by the covenantee, must follow some land; and this was the argument put forward for the defendant, that without land the covenant was only one in gross. Romer L.J. asked "Is there any case in which it has been held that such a covenant purporting to bind land for ever is valid except for the protection of an estate?" and counsel for the plaintiff did not refer him, as they might have done, to *Catt* v. *Tourle* and *Luker* v. *Dennis*, in neither of which cases had the plaintiff an estate, but only a trade. In the judgments, Vaughan Williams L.J. points out that A. conveyed his whole estate and had no contiguous estate which would be benefited by the covenant in question. . . . Romer L.J. thought that the assign of a covenantee could not sue unless the covenant related to or concerned some ascertainable property belonging to him or in which he was interested. Stirling L.J. while saying that different considerations would apply if the covenantee sued, a remark which leaves it doubtful whether he thought the covenantee could, though owning no land, have sued assigns of the land restricted, rested his judgment on the ground that damages, not injunction would be the appropriate remedy.

The doctrine was again considered, and I think further developed, in *In re Nisbet and Potts' Contract*, in 1905. The owner of certain land had entered into restrictive covenants with the vendor, who owned an adjoining estate. A squatter, without notice of those covenants, acquired a title, by adverse possession, and sold to A., who did not require a forty years' title, which would have disclosed the restrictive covenants. A. sold to B., who, having reason to believe there were restrictive covenants, declined to complete. B. took out a summons for a declaration that the title was not one which he ought to be compelled to accept. Farwell L.J. treated the nature of the right of action created under the doctrine of *Tulk* v. *Moxhay* as analogous to an equitable charge on real estate, not depending in any way on notice for its validity, but only defeated by a legal estate acquired for value and without notice. He held therefore that the squatter, though he had no notice and had the legal estate, was bound by the restrictive convenants, as apparently he only took the land subject to the equitable interest in it, and that as the purchaser from the squatter of the legal estate for value would, if he had required a forty years' title, have had notice of the covenants, he had constructive notice and was bound by the covenants. In the Court of Appeal, the appellant argued that notice was part of the cause of action, the respondent that the doctrine rested on an interest in land, binding on the land itself, with a dominant and servient tenement. The Court of Appeal adopted the latter argument, and held that the restrictive covenant was an equitable interest in the land, whether the occupier of the land had notice of it or not, unless he had purchased the legal estate for value without notice. They do not expressly refer to the necessity of there being a dominant tenement to enforce the interest, but there was in fact such a dominant tenement in the case.

Lastly, in *Milbourn* v. *Lyons* (1914), where a person who had agreed to sell with a restrictive covenant died, and his personal representatives, having sold all their land, conveyed with a similar restrictive covenant, Neville J. enforced the title against a purchaser who knew of the restrictive covenant, and therefore objected to complete, on the ground that there was no restriction against him, as the vendors, at the date of the covenant, had no land to which the benefit of the covenant could be attached, and the Court of Appeal affirmed his judgment on similar grounds.

I think the result of this long chain of authorities is that, whereas in my view, at the time of *Tulk* v. *Moxhay* and for at least twenty years afterwards, the plaintiffs in this case would have succeeded against an assign on the ground that the assign had notice of the covenant, since [these last] three decisions of the Court of Appeal, the plaintiffs must fail on the ground that they have never had any land for the benefit of which this "equitable interest analogous to a negative easement" could be created, and therefore cannot sue a person who bought the land with knowledge that there was a restrictive covenant as to its use, which he proceeds to disregard, because he is not privy to the contract. . . . It may be, if the matter is considered by a higher tribunal, that tribunal may see its way to revert to what I think was the earlier doctrine of notice, or at any rate to treat it as co-existing with the later refinement of "an equitable interest analogous to a negative easement" binding on persons who are ignorant of it. The remarks of Lord Selborne in *Earl of Zetland* v. *Hislop* are not favourable to the too rigid development or enforcement of the latter alternative; and the observations of Lord Macnaghten, Lord Davey, and Lord Lindley in *Noakes & Co.* v. *Rice* (1902), seem to suggest that the doctrine of *Tulk* v. *Moxhay* may well be reconsidered and put on a proper footing. For I regard it as very regrettable that a public body should be prevented from enforcing a restriction on the use of property imposed for the public benefit against persons who bought the property knowing of the restriction, by the apparently immaterial circumstance that the public body does not own any land in the immediate neighbourhood. But, after a careful consideration of the authorities, I am forced to the view that the later decisions of this Court compel me so to hold.

In my opinion, therefore, the demurrer of Mr. Morris and of Mrs. Allen succeeds.The action against Mr. Morris must be dismissed with costs. I regret that I do not see my way to depriving Mrs. Allen of her costs, as, whatever may be her equitable rights, I am not at all favourably impressed with her conduct as a good citizen. I see no reason for interfering with the judgment against Mr. Allen in respect of plots No. 1 or No. 2 and his appeal must be dismissed with costs.

[The judgment of Scrutton J. has been considerably cut and the judgments of Buckley and Kennedy L.JJ. are omitted.]

NOTE. From the statement of facts set out by Buckley L.J. it appears that the defendant, M. J. Allen, had applied to the L.C.C. for their permission under s. 7 of the *London Building Act, 1894*, to lay out a new road, called Galloway Road, running from south to north, and a further small portion of road at the northern end of Galloway Road running from east to west in continuation of a road called Dunraven Road. The L.C.C. gave their permission upon terms including the covenant recited by Scrutton J. Both Galloway Road and Dunraven Road now exist and intersect and are shown on current street maps of London.

Sections 7 and 9 of the *London Building Act, 1894* gave the L.C.C. certain powers of control over land which the owner proposes to form or lay out in streets, but the L.C.C. at the date of the covenant had no estate or interest in any land adjoining or in any manner affected by the observance or non-observance of the covenant contained in the deed. It is not common in England for the local government to hold the fee in the streets.

See now, *The Housing Act, 1936*, 26 Geo. 5 & 1 Edw. 8 c. 51, s. 148, which provides: Where . . . (b) an owner of any land has entered into a covenant with the local authority concerning the land for the purposes of any of the provisions of this Act; the authority shall have the power to enforce the covenant against the persons deriving title under the covenantor, notwithstanding that the authority is not in possession of or interested in any land for the benefit of which the covenant was entered into, in like manner and to the like extent as if they had been possessed of or interested in such land.

RE McKILLOP AND CITY OF VANCOUVER
British Columbia. Supreme Court. [1954] 3 D.L.R. 63

WHITTAKER J.: This is a petition under s. 234 of the *Land Registry Act*, R.S.B.C. 1948, c. 171, by the City of Vancouver, for an order directing the Registrar of Titles to register certain charges, registration of which had been applied for by the City, and refused by the Registrar.

The owners (hereinafter referred to as "the McKillops") of certain lots on Marine Drive in the City of Vancouver, on February 2, 1953, sold the lots by agreement of sale to C.R.D. Company Ltd. (hereinafter called "the Company"). The Company duly applied to register the agreement of sale.

The lots are in a part of the City zoned as a three-storey multiple-dwelling district. The McKillops asked the City to re-zone the area, changing it to a six-storey light industrial district, this change being for the benefit of the company as well as of the McKillops. The City agreed to re-zone, on condition that the McKillops agree to certain stipulations as to the user of a portion of the lots 40 ft. in width immediately adjoining Marine Drive.

An agreement dated February 18, 1953, was accordingly entered into between the McKillops as grantors and the City as grantee, whereby the City agreed to re-zone the area as requested, and the McKillops covenanted: (a) That they would not any time thereafter erect any building or structure on the said 40-ft. strip; . . .

The covenants of the grantors were expressed to be made "with intent to bind all persons in whom the said lands or any portion thereof shall for the time being be vested but not so that the grantors—shall be personally liable for breach of any covenant contained herein by any person other than the grantors, except in respect of such portion of the said lands as shall at the time of such breach be owned or occupied by the grantors."

The agreement further provides that the "rights, grants, easements and licences given or granted by these presents shall be and at all times shall be deemed to be for the benefit and advantage of the said portion of Marine Drive aforesaid, that is to say, the portion thereof which immediately adjoins the northerly boundary of the said lands."

The covenants were expressed to be "covenants running with the said lands forever" and to enure to the benefit of and to be binding upon the parties and their heirs, executors, administrators, successors and assigns, and to have effect only "during the lives and life of the living descendants of His late Majesty King George the Fifth, and the last survivor of them, and such further period as shall be consistent with the laws against perpetuity."

The C.R.D. Company Ltd. was not a party to the agreement, but the Company, by agreement under seal dated April 8, 1953, hereinafter called "the priority agreement" agreed with the City, its successors and assigns, that "the within re-zoning agreement (which was attached) shall be an encumbrance upon the within-described property prior to the said agreement (that is the agreement by which the Company purchased the lands) in the same manner and to the same effect as if it had been dated and registered prior to the said agreement.". . .

The learned Registrar's refusal to register the building restriction as a restrictive covenant (see (a) above) is based on a number of grounds:

1. That the agreement does not indicate that any land is benefited.

If a public street can be said to be benefited by a building restriction, then I think that the agreement sufficiently indicates that the restrictive covenant is intended to be for the benefit of Marine Drive.

2. That neither the City in its ownership of the street, nor the street itself *qua* street, can be touched or concerned, and hence a restrictive covenant cannot be annexed.

The learned Registrar admits there is no reported decision supporting this contention and suggests that I break new ground. I do not feel inclined to do so. In these days when ever more attention is being paid to spaciousness and beauty of prospect, it would seem desirable that cities and municipalities should have the right, by agreement with adjoining owners, to provide that a space free of buildings shall be left adjoining streets and highways. A municipality holds its streets as trustee for the public: *Vancouver* v. *Burchill*, [1932], 4 D.L.R. 200 at p. 205, S.C.R. 620 at p. 625. The purpose of this particular building restriction, combined with the covenant to landscape the area, is to enhance the enjoyment to be derived by the public from the use of the street. This enhanced enjoyment of user of the street by its real owner, the public, is such that I think it can be said that the restrictive covenant touches or concerns the street. The dominant land in *Tulk* v. *Moxhay* was not a street, but the covenant there was similar to the one in question here in that its purpose was to secure for the owner of the dominant land what might be called pleasure of prospect. The Court held that the covenant created an equitable interest in the servient land and that the covenant could be enforced against a subsequent purchaser having notice of the equity.

3. That the City has no freehold estate in Marine Drive save as to a strip 17 ft. in width.

It is unnecessary to explore this interesting contention of the learned Registrar. The 17-ft. strip, it is conceded, does belong to the City. It is a substantial part of Marine Drive and immediately adjoins the servient land.

4. That there is no covenant by C.R.D. Company Ltd.

I think that the priority agreement makes it sufficiently clear that the Company makes itself a party to the creation of whatever charges are created by the agreement of February 18, 1953. . . .

NOTE. Whittaker J. was reversed on other grounds in the Court of Appeal, *sub nom., Vancouver* v. *Registrar Vancouver Land Registration District*. See also *Re Daly and City of Vancouver* (1956), where Lord J. adopts the reasoning of the principal case.

NOTE. Compare section 8(4) of *the Town Planning Act*, R.S.B.C. 1948, c. 339, which provides,

"(4) In lieu of acquiring title to any such lands [adjacent or neighbouring lands to lands essential to the carrying out of a town planning project] the council may by agreement with the owner or by expropriation, acquire the right to cause to be imposed upon the lands or to be created such building restrictions or easements as might have been imposed or created if the municipality had acquired the title." *The Town Planning Act* was repealed by the *Municipal Act, 1957* (B.C.) c. 42, s. 896.

ONE TWENTY-FIVE VARSITY ROAD LTD. *v.* TOWNSHIP OF YORK

Ontario. Court of Appeal. 1960. 23 D.L.R. (2d) 465

MORDEN J.A. delivered the judgment of the Court: The appellant company appeals from the order of King J. dated December 2, 1959, dismissing the appellant's application for (a) a mandatory order directing the township and its building inspector to issue a permit authorizing the construction of eight pairs of semi-detached houses on Lots 18 to 25, Plan 5052, fronting on Clairton Crescent and (b) an order declaring cl. 4 in an agreement, dated May 15, 1956, between Exclusive Development Co. Ltd. and the township is invalid, illegal and *ultra vires*, and does not affect the lands therein mentioned nor bind any subsequent purchasers of them.

The lands comprising Plan 5052 prior to the registration of the plan were owned by Exclusive Development Co. Ltd. As a necessary step towards the approval of this plan under the *Planning Act*, 1955 (Ont.), c. 61, that company, as owner, entered into the agreement already mentioned. The clause in question is:

"(4) THE OWNER hereby further covenants and agrees with the TOWNSHIP that he will endeavour to obtain the consents of the owners of the lands abutting to the east of lots 18 to 24 inclusive, as shown on the proposed plan, to the removal of the ridge of earth along the rear parts of the said lots 18 to 24 inclusive and on lots abutting to the east thereof and having received such consents to have this ridge removed to grades satisfactory to the Township Engineer. Failing to obtain the said consents the OWNER agrees not to erect buildings on the said lots 18 to 24 inclusive."

The plan was, in due course, approved by the Minister of Planning and Development and then registered. In February, 1959, the owner sold certain lots as shown on the plan including Lots 18 to 25 to H. D. Hume Construction Co. Ltd. and that company in April entered into an agreement of sale of the lots in question to the appellant.

Both the appellant's predecessors attempted without success to obtain consents from the owners of the abutting lands to the removal of the ridge of earth mentioned in the agreement. In May, 1959, the appellant filed with the township building inspector plans of the dwellings it proposed to erect upon Lots 18 to 25. That official told the president of the appellant company that there was no purpose to be gained by making a formal application for permits because there had been no compliance with cl. 4. The plans of the proposed dwellings apparently conform to the township's building code and zoning by-law. The only ground advanced by the township for refusing to receive an application for a building permit is the non-compliance with the clause.

Upon the first return of the appellant's application, Aylen J. ordered that the persons, now represented by Mr. Erichsen-Brown, be added as respondents to these proceedings and adjourned the application 1 week. These persons, numbering fifteen in all, are the owners of lands fronting on Woodgate Drive and abutting to the east on Lots 18 to 24 inclusive. In my respectful opinion, they were properly added in view of the appellant's attack upon cl. 4 of the agreement. It would have been open to them to contend that they had the benefit of that clause. However as will be seen, their counsel both before King J. and this Court did not claim that they had a right to enforce the covenant but on their behalf claimed substantive relief of a far-reaching nature.

As I have said, King J. dismissed the appellant's application. The reasons of the learned Judge were not recorded. In this Court Mr. Laidlaw argued that the restriction in cl. 4 did not run with the lands and is not binding upon or enforceable against the purchasers subsequent to Exclusive Development Co. Ltd., upon the short ground that the township did not exact the covenant as owner of any land to which the benefit of the covenant could be attached either at the time it was exacted or by assignment of the benefit by the township to purchasers of such land. In support of this submission he relied upon *London County Council* v. *Allen* (1914), and *Re Hunt & Bell* (1915).

The covenant, of course, was valid and binding under the law of contract between the parties to the agreement of May 15, 1956. Once, however, the burdened lands pass to another owner, then, before the covenant can be enforced against him, it must satisfy the stringent conditions laid down by a long series of cases having their origin in *Tulk* v. *Moxhay* (1848), which has lent its name to this particular branch of the law of equity. Since that decision the doctrine has been refined and qualified considerably. I do not consider it necessary to discuss at any length the development of this genus of equitable interests. It is sufficient to say that there are two conditions necessary for enforceability of the covenant against appellant both of which are absent. The first is that the covenant must have been exacted for the benefit of ascertainable lands of the covenantee; the second is that the benefit in some manner must have become annexed to such lands. As stated in many cases, the right to enforce the covenant is analogous to a negative easement and there must be a dominant as well as a servient tenement. . . .

The absence of a dominant tenement to which the burden of the covenant could be annexed was the decisive reason for the failure of the plaintiff to succeed in enforcing the covenant against a subsequent purchaser in *Can. Construction Co.* v. *Beaver (Alberta) Lumber Ltd.* (1955).

In the appeal now under consideration the township did not exact the covenant in cl. 4 for the benefit of any of its lands; it could not exact such a covenant for the benefit of the lands which it did not own—the lands of Mr. Erichsen-Brown's clients. The covenant is one *in gross*.

Mr. Shanoff, on behalf of the township, in the course of a frank argument, did not in any way question the validity of the cases relied upon by Mr. Laidlaw. He urges us to extend the doctrine of *Tulk* v. *Moxhay* to the situation now before us. The doctrine as therein originally stated was based upon notice and there is no doubt that in this case the appellant had notice of the covenant. I should point out, however, that the plaintiff in *Tulk* v. *Moxhay* had lands capable of being benefited by the covenant at the time he exacted it and when he sought to enforce it. Altogether apart from this consideration and assuming that the result in that case was based solely upon notice, it is, not only undesirable but in my opinion, too late now for this Court to return to the position as it was in 1849 and give countenance to a development of the doctrine along such substantially different lines; we ought, I think, to adhere to the greatly restricted scope of the doctrine in *Tulk* v. *Moxhay* as evidenced by the numerous decisions subsequent to that case. A restrictive covenant enforceable between persons other than the original parties is, in effect, an equitable interest in property. It is well recognized that decisions affecting real property upon the basis of which titles are passed and accepted should not lightly be disturbed; this is one branch of law which requires stability. As Middleton J.A. said in *Re Hazell* (1925):

"It is a well-established principle of real property law that questions such as this, once placed at rest, should not be again agitated, even if it should be shewn that the earlier decisions are not in all respects satisfactory."

Mr. Shanoff argues alternatively that we should find within the meaning of the cases I have mentioned, what would amount to a dominant tenement in the township's interest and duty, under the *Planning Act* and the *Municipal Act*, R.S.O. 1950, c. 243, to regulate and control the use of land for the benefit and welfare of the township's inhabitants. I decline to take this venturesome step and would point to the failure of a similar argument in *London County Council* v. *Allen* and, to what is, perhaps, more pertinent, that the restriction the township now seeks to enforce could have been incorporated in the plan itself before it was approved and registered or appropriate restrictive by-laws could have been passed. The agreement in question was not the only method open to the township to protect its inhabitants if it so desired.

Finally, Mr. Shanoff seeks aid for his case in the recent amendment to the *Planning Act*, 1955. I refer to 1959, c. 71, s. 4(3) which says: "Every municipality shall be deemed to have always had authority to enter into agreements imposed as a condition to the approval of a plan of subdivision and all such agreements entered into before this section comes into force are hereby validated and confirmed and declared to be legal, valid and binding."

The agreement containing cl. 4 is, in my opinion, a subdivision agreement within the meaning of this subsection. The subsection is by its terms retrospective in its operation (and this Court so decided in *Beaver Valley*

Developments Ltd. v. *North York Tp.* (1960) and the agreement therefore comes within its ambit. The purpose of the section was, in my view, to remove doubts which had arisen as to the power and authority of municipalities to make agreements with subdividers which required the subdividers to provide certain services, to pay moneys to the municipality, or satisfy other conditions as consideration for the concurrence by the municipality with a proposed plan. It would be extending to an unwarranted degree the scope and application of the subsection to hold that it rendered building restrictions binding upon subsequent purchasers of the subdivided lands. Such restrictions can only be imposed by a municipal by-law passed under Part III of the *Planning Act*, 1959, or by private agreement in the manner sanctioned by the present operation of the doctrine in *Tulk* v. *Moxhay*. I cannot attribute to the subsection the long term and, perhaps, perpetual effect upon the use of land for which the township's counsel contends.

Upon this branch of the case, therefore, I am of the opinion that cl. 4 of the agreement did not justify the township or its building inspector in refusing to grant the appellant the building permit it seeks.

I now come to the consideration of Mr. Erichsen-Brown's submissions on behalf of his clients. . . .

I would allow the appeal. . . .

SEABEE HOMES LTD. *v.* TOWN OF GEORGETOWN
Ontario. High Court. 1961. 31 D.L.R. (2d) 705

GALE J. (orally):—In my opinion this application ought to be dismissed. Having regard to the lateness of the hour my reasons will be understandably short, but I do wish to express the foundation for the decision which I have reached and have just expressed.

In or about 1954 Delrex Developments Limited, which apparently is a creation of one Heslop and which I will hereafter refer to as "Delrex", entered into an agreement or agreements with the Town of Georgetown concerning the future development of some 600 or 700 acres outside the limits of the town. Under these the town undertook to annex the land in question, to agree to the plans submitted by Delrex and to provide the necessary services for development. It also agreed that it would release for residential development, upon the application of Delrex, lands zoned for residential purposes, provided that at the time of each application for release the ratio of the assessment value of all residential lands lying within the municipal limits of the town, as against the combined assessment value of the industrial and commercial lands lying within the municipal limits, should not be greater than 60 to 40.

Until this year relations between Delrex and the town were maintained on a friendly basis and from time to time lots were released by the town. However, prior to June Rex Heslop Homes Ltd., another of the Heslop ventures, purchased, or purported to purchase, Lot 209, Plan 622, which was one of the plans embraced by the agreements to which I alluded, and when a building permit was not granted to it—since the ratio of assessment was at that time leaning too heavily in favour of residential properties—launched an application for *mandamus*. That application was dismissed by Mr. Justice McLennan in June of this year whereupon an appeal was launched by Rex Heslop Homes Ltd., which appeal was likewise dismissed by the Court of Appeal on the 23rd of last month. Both Mr. Justice Mc-

Lennan and the Court of Appeal refused to exercise their discretion in favour of the applicant on the ground that the relationship between Delrex and Rex Heslop Homes Ltd. was so close as to indicate that the sale to the latter and the application for its building permit was a patent device to circumvent the covenants of Delrex in the agreements to which I have made reference.

On or about October 4th, and while the appeal was pending, this applicant, Seabee Homes Ltd., which is controlled by two brothers by the name of Zorge, purported to purchase Lots 213, 214 and 215, which are also on Plan 622 and close to Lot 209. Seabee Homes Ltd. is a building construction firm, as I understand it, doing business generally in the vicinity of Georgetown. It is to be noted, too, that that company owned other lots on Plan 622. The usual plans and specifications in respect of the residence to be erected on Lot 213 were duly submitted to the Building Inspector of the town and they were all in order. However, the Inspector and the council of the town refused to issue the necessary permit on the ground that to do so would be to give aid to a plan on the part of Delrex to avoid its obligations under the 1954 agreement.

When this matter came on for argument Mr. Laidlaw conceded that the material leading up to the application for the permit was in order, that the 1954 agreement was a private one as between Delrex and the town, and that the applicant Seabee Homes Ltd. was not bound by it. It was also shown, however, that the officers of Seabee Homes Ltd. had prior knowledge of the 1954 and other relevant agreements and also had knowledge of the proceedings which terminated in the Court of Appeal on November 23rd to which I have already made reference. In those circumstances Mr. Laidlaw contended that as a *mandamus* is a discretionary remedy it ought not to be granted here because, in the first place, to do so would in effect amount to assistance by the Court to Delrex to perpetrate a breach of its contract with the town and a breach of trust with resulting great hardship on the town since many other lots could be similarly processed, and, secondly, that in the situation shown to exist the application is not being made by a *bona fide* applicant but rather is part of a general intent or device to assist Delrex in circumventing the 1954 agreement. He conceded that unless the Court could reasonably infer from the circumstances proved that Seabee Homes Ltd. was not an "arm's length" purchaser from Delrex, the town would be bound by the effect and reasons to be found in the decision of the Court of Appeal in *One Twenty-five Varsity Rd. Ltd.* v. *Tp. of York* (1960), upon which counsel for the applicant relied heavily.

I am of the opinion, accepting as I do without reservation and indeed willingly that which was enunciated in the *York Tp.* case, that it does not govern the circumstances which have been shown to exist in this instance and that the discretion of the Court ought not to be exercised in favour of this applicant by the granting of an order of *mandamus*. I quite concede that, while the awarding or withholding of an order of *mandamus* is a matter of discretion in the Court, that discretion must be applied judicially and not out of pique or caprice or without good reason. But even imposing that restriction, as I do, upon the exercise of a discretion in this case, I am of the opinion that the circumstances will reasonably support the inference which I draw to the effect that the applicant was not acting at arm's length with Delrex in respect of this purchase and that it does not come here in good faith but rather is an instrument to avoid the obligations and covenants of Delrex. In other words, I am satisfied that Seabee Homes Ltd. is sufficiently identified with Delrex as to suggest to me that the Court ought not to give the former the equitable relief which it here seeks.

The circumstances which support my conclusion were referred to by Mr. Laidlaw. He pointed, for example, to the timing of the purchase and the launching of this application. It will be recalled that the purchase was made on or about October 4th by Seabee Homes Ltd., while the appeal to the Court of Appeal was pending, and arranged by an officer who admittedly had knowledge not only of the 1954 agreement but of those proceedings. The details of the purchase are also extremely interesting. In the offer to purchase the applicant offered to buy the three lots which I have mentioned for the sum of $11,700, stipulating that it was to be accepted by October 4th and that the sale was to be completed on October 10th. I find it strange that a transaction of that magnitude would be set up in that way, particularly when Mr. Weinstein, who is the solicitor for the company, has acknowledged that the applicant did own other lots on Plan 662. I hasten to add, however, that in no sense do I attribute any improper conduct to Mr. Weinstein.

The actual terms of the offer are peculiar. As already mentioned, the price to be paid was $11,700. Of that amount only $585 was to be paid in cash with the balance to be secured by a mortgage back of $11,115, in respect of which interest was not to begin to run until March 28, 1962. When questioned about that feature of the matter Mr. Zorge failed to offer any explanation. It is to be noted too, that the agreement contains no commitment on the part of Seabee Homes Ltd. to build or otherwise develop the lands. Mr. Laidlaw points out that the time before which interest is payable is just about sufficient to allow these proceedings to be concluded.

I also am puzzled by and draw the inevitable inference from the fact that although the officers of Seabee Homes Ltd. had knowledge generally of the 1954 agreement and of the then pending proceedings which had resulted disastrously—so far as Delrex was concerned—before Mr. Justice McLennan, apparently they had no discussion with those in charge of Delrex about the former agreements or the failure of Rex Heslop Homes Ltd. to obtain a permit, and the agreement for purchase between Seabee Homes Ltd. and Delrex was not conditioned in any way upon the procuring of a building permit by the former.

The circumstances as to the selection of the lots purchased by the applicant are also interesting. It is quite true that the applicant is a building contractor engaged in that area and that Mr. Zorge explained the reason for seeking 60-ft. lots. His evidence, however, as to how these particular three lots were purchased is far from satisfactory. At one stage of his cross-examination he said that he had decided upon these particular lots before he went to see Mr. Bairstowe of the Delrex company, and at another stage that they were picked out as a result of his discussion with Mr. Bairstowe. If the latter is true then, of course, it suggests that the selection was not independent of that officer of the Delrex company. Mention was also made of the fact that the area in which these lots are found is relatively undeveloped, is remote from the open roads and services and that Mr. Zorge admitted he had no buyer in mind for the houses which he intended to build.

Taken individually probably none of those circumstances are of decisive effect; but taken cumulatively they leave me with the definite impression—and I think it is a reasonable one—that this was not a *bona fide* purchase of these lots by the applicant from Delrex Developments Ltd., but rather was the next step beyond the abortive attempt by Delrex, in purporting to sell to Rex Heslop Homes Ltd., to avoid the obligations and undertakings into which it had entered in 1954, and that the applicant, by assisting Delrex in such attempt has not made this application in good faith. Accordingly the judgment in the *York Tp.* case, *supra,* does not require me to issue the *mandamus*. . . .

Mr. Rotenburg also contended that an aura of suspicion would not be enough to forestall the applicant and I am inclined to agree with him. However, it is my conviction that the circumstances here suggest much more than a mere aura of suspicion.

He also contended that any purchaser buying from Delrex would necessarily be put into the same difficult position. I do not agree. It would depend upon the circumstances of the particular transaction. If, as for example in the *York Tp.* case, a *bona fide* purchaser, even with knowledge of the 1954 agreements, purchased a lot in good faith and with no ulterior intention of assisting Delrex to circumvent its contracts, he would be entitled, as it seems to me, to a *mandamus* in the event that the town refused him a building permit.

Mr. Rotenberg also argued, ingeniously, that if there had been any want of integrity in the background or purpose of this transaction then Delrex and Seabee Homes Ltd. would have arranged matters so that it could not have been detected. I express no opinion upon that save to say that the conclusion for which he contends does not necessarily follow.

The application will be dismissed with costs.

IN RE BALLARD'S CONVEYANCE. [1937] 1 Ch. 473 (England. Chancery Division). A conveyance contained a covenant in the following terms: "The said Herbert Cassin Wright doth hereby covenant with the said Emily Harriet Ballard, her heirs and assigns and successors in title owners from time to time of the Childwickbury Estate of the said Sir John Blundell Maple that he the said Herbert Cassin Wright, his heirs and assigns, will perform and observe the conditions and stipulations set forth in the schedule hereto so far as the same relate to affect or concern the said premises hereinbefore expressed to be hereby conveyed."

The schedule contained provisions forbidding erection of buildings other than a private dwelling-house on the property, and forbidding erection of buildings except garden or farm buildings otherwise than of red brick and in conformity with plans and specifications previously submitted to and approved of in writing by the vendor or her surveyor; also provisions laying down the minimum value of the houses to be erected and the minimum area of land to be attached to each house; also provisions against user of the property, or any building erected on it, for certain specified purposes or for any purpose which should be or tend to become a nuisance or annoyance to the vendor or the owners or occupiers of any other part or parts of "the above-mentioned estate" or any of them, or for any trade or business; and condition 4 prescribed that any question as to the value of any house built or otherwise under or in connection with the stipulations should be determined by the vendor's surveyor for the time being. Then followed a restriction against burning bricks and against permitting movable dwellings and deposit of rubbish.

By condition 6 it was provided that nothing in the conditions or in the conveyance contained was to oblige the vendor to enforce the foregoing stipulations or any of them in respect of any part of the property, or preclude her from waiving or varying, by licence or otherwise, such stipulations or any of them in respect of any part of the property, and she was to be at liberty, if she should think fit so to do, effectually to release any part of the property from such stipulations or any of them.

Condition 7 provided that in the stipulations "the property" meant the entire property shown in the plan (i.e., the property conveyed and also Lot 1 already mentioned): and condition 8 provided that the expression "the vendor" was to be deemed to include Mrs. Ballard, her successors in title owners of any part of "the above-mentioned estate" for the time being remaining unsold, and that the expression "the purchaser" should include the applicant, his heirs and assigns.

The applicant, who owned 18 acres subject to the building restrictions, by his summons under s. 84 of the *Law of Property Act, 1925*, asked for a declaration that no part of the property in question was any longer affected by any of the restrictions contained in the conveyance of June 28, 1906; or in the alternative that it might be declared whether the said restrictions or any of them were at the date of the summons enforceable and if so, by whom. The declaration was granted. CLAUSON J.: "That land [the property in question] is an area of some 1700 acres. It appears to me quite obvious that while a breach of the stipulations might possibly affect a portion of that area in the vicinity of the applicant's land, far the largest part of this area of 1700 acres could not possibly be affected by any breach of any of the stipulations.

"Counsel for the respondents asked for an adjournment in order to consider whether they would call evidence (as I was prepared to allow them to do) to prove that a breach of the stipulations or of some of them might affect the whole of this large area. However, ultimately no such evidence was called.

"The result seems to me to be that I am bound to hold that, while the covenant may concern or touch some comparatively small portion of the land to which it has been sought to annex it, it fails to concern or touch far the largest part of the land. I asked in vain for any authority which would justify me in severing the covenant and treating it as annexed to or running with such part of the land as is touched by or concerned with it, though as regards the remainder of the land, namely, such part as is not touched by or concerned with the covenant, the covenant is not and cannot be annexed to it and accordingly does not and cannot run with it. Nor have I been able through my own researches to find anything in the books which seems to justify any such course."

QUESTIONS. What is meant by "touching and concerning" land? How can you tell whether in fact a covenant touches or concerns particular land? Is the statement of the covenantor or the covenantee that the covenant is for the benefit of described land sufficient? Does a covenant require "consideration"? If condition 6 is taken literally, is there mutuality of consideration? Will "equity aid a volunteer"? See the text part for a discussion of the power to vary a covenant.

ZETLAND *v.* DRIVER. (1939) Ch. 1 (England. Court of Appeal). In April, 1935, Driver purchased property known as No. 200 Lord Street in Redcar, Yorks, with knowledge of a covenant, Clause 2 of which provided: "The purchaser to the intent and so as to bind as far as practicable the said property hereby conveyed into whosesoever hands the same may come and to benefit and protect such part or parts of the lands in the Borough Township or Parish of Redcar, in the North Riding of the County of York, now subject to the settlement (a) as shall for the time being remain unsold or (b) as shall be sold by the vendor or his successors in title with the express benefit of this covenant, covenants with the vendor that the purchaser will at all times observe, perform and keep the said stipulations contained in the Second Schedule hereto." The Second Schedule provided "(a) that the property hereby conveyed shall not (except with the previous consent in writing of the vendor, which expression in this Schedule includes where the context admits his successors in title) be used for any other purpose than the erection of a shop and dwelling-house . . . (d) that no intoxicating or spirituous liquors shall be sold from the premises and in particular that no part of the land hereby conveyed shall be used for the purposes of a club and that no act or thing shall be done or permitted thereon which in the opinion of the vendor may be a public or a private nuisance or prejudicial or detrimental to the vendor and the owners or occupiers of any adjoining property or to the neighbourhood." Notwithstanding the covenant Driver and one Wilson operated an eating-house for the consumption of fried fish and other food. In April, 1936, the business was extended to include the sale of fried fish for consumption off the premises. As a result of complaints about the extension, the Marquess of Zetland, who claimed to be entitled to enforce the covenant, formed the opinion that such sales were detrimental to the amenities of the neighbourhood and to his own property. Driver and Wilson refused to give up the business and the Marquess brought this action to restrain the defendants from frying fish for consumption off the premises or from doing any other act which in the opinion of the Marquess or other the successor in title of the late Marquess his father, who took the covenant, might be a public or private nuisance. The parties agreed that the lands benefited by the covenant included scattered parcels with houses and certain land part of which was more than a mile away. Held, for the Marquess. The objection that the Marquess' opinion was unreasonable and capricious and that he was acting in a quasi-judicial capacity and should have given defendants a hearing was flatly rejected. FARWELL J.: "Such covenants can only be validly imposed if they comply with certain conditions. Firstly, they must be negative covenants. No affirmative covenant requiring the expenditure of money or the doing of some act can ever be made to run with the land.

"Secondly, the covenant must be one that touches or concerns the land, by which is meant that it must be imposed for the benefit or to enhance the value of the land retained by the vendor or some part of it, and no such covenant can ever be imposed if the sale comprised the whole of the vendor's land. Further, the land retained by the vendor must be such as to be capable of being benefited by the covenant at the time when it is imposed.

"Thirdly, the land which is intended to be benefited must be so defined as to be easily ascertainable, and the fact that the covenant is imposed for the benefit of that particular land should be stated in the conveyance and the persons or the class of persons entitled to enforce it. The fact that the benefit of the covenant is not intended to pass to all persons into whose hands the unsold land may come is not objectionable so long as the class of persons intended to have the benefit of the covenant is clearly defined.

"Finally, it must be remembered that these covenants can only be enforced so long as the covenantee or his successor in title retains some part of the land for the benefit of which the covenant was imposed. Applying those conditions to the present case, the covenant sued upon appears to comply with them. . . .

"It is said, however, on behalf of the respondents, that this covenant is not one which can run with the land because it is imposed for the benefit, not only of the unsold land of the vendor, but also for the benefit of the adjoining owners and the neighbourhood. If that were the true construction of the covenant, that might be so; but in our judgment reading the covenant as a whole, it cannot be so construed. The paramount purpose of the covenant, as appears from the conveyance itself, is to benefit and protect the unsold land of the vendor. . . . Then it was said that it was open to objection as offending the rule against perpetuities, but in our judgment there is no ground for such contention. The formation of an opinion by a successor in title of the original vendor at whatever time cannot operate to create any new estate or revest the land and, consequently, the rule against perpetuities has no application.

"Under those circumstances, there does not appear to be any ground on which the appellant can properly be refused the relief which he seeks; but Bennett J. took the opposite view and held that the benefit of the covenant had not passed to the appellant. In coming to that conclusion he founded himself upon a decision of Clauson J. in *In re Ballard's Conveyance*, which he considered to be exactly in point and binding upon him. In our judgment the learned judge was wrong in thinking that *In re Ballard's Conveyance* was an authority in this case. It is not necessary for us, and we do not propose, to express any opinion as to that decision beyond saying that it is clearly distinguishable from the present case, if only on the ground that in that case the covenant was expressed to run with the whole estate, whereas in the present case no such difficulty arises because the covenant is expressed to be for the benefit of the whole or any part or parts of the unsold settled property.

"It is to be noticed in the present case that the benefit of the covenant is not intended to pass to a purchaser without express assignment. It is not necessary for us to express any opinion as to what would be the effect of a sale of part of the settled property with an express assignment of the covenant; but, if such a purchaser could enforce the covenant, it could only be for so long as some successor in title of the original covenantee retained some part of the settled property, since such a person alone can form the requisite opinion."

QUESTIONS. What or who is a "successor in title"? Is a purchaser a successor in title? See *Stroud's Judicial Dictionary*, (3rd ed.) Vol. 4, under the item "Successor": 'Successor in title.' Where a purchaser covenants to do nothing which the vendor or his successors in title consider injurious to the adjoining land, it seems that 'successors in title' means successors in title otherwise than by sale (*Zetland (Marquis)* v. *Driver*)" Is this proposition justified by the case reproduced above? Why should the court make this curious limitation of the "ordinary meaning" of successors in title?

3. Restraint of Competition

KEPPELL *v.* BAILEY. 1834. 2 My. & K. 517; 39 E.R. 1042 (England. Chancery). In 1795 a company was formed to construct the Trevil Railroad to carry limestone from the Trevil Quarry to the furnaces and ironworks of various members of the Company. Each covenanted to procure all the limestone he required from the Trevil Quarry and to ship it on the Trevil Railroad. One furnace at Beaufort changed hands in 1833 and the new owners, with full knowledge of the covenants of 1795, commenced building a new railroad from the Beaufort Ironworks to a quarry east of Trevil Quarry. The shareholders of the Trevil Railroad filed a bill to restrain the defendant owners of Beaufort Ironworks from using the new railroad. An *ex parte* injunction having been obtained, on motion it was dissolved. LORD CHANCELLOR BROUGHAM: ". . . There are certain known incidents to property and its enjoyment; among others, certain burthens wherewith it may be affected, or rights which may be created and enjoyed over it by parties other than the owners; all which incidents are recognised by the law. In respect of possession, the property may be in one, while the reversion is in another; in respect of interest, the life estate in one, the remainder in tail in a second, and the fee in reversion in a third. So in respect of enjoyment; one may have the possession and the fee-simple, and another may have a rent issuing out of it, or the tithes of its produce, or an easement, as a right of way upon it, or of common over it. And such last incorporeal hereditament may be annexed to an estate which is wholly unconnected with the estate affected by the easement, although both estates were originally united in the same owner, and one of them was afterwards granted by him with the benefit, while the other was left subject to the burthen. All these kinds of property, however, all these holdings, are well known to the law and familiarly dealt with by its principles. But it must not therefore be supposed that incidents of a novel kind can be devised and attached to property at the fancy or caprice of any owner. It is clearly inconvenient both to the science of the law and to the public weal that such a latitude should be given. There can be no harm in allowing the fullest latitude to men in binding themselves and their representatives, that is, their assets real and personal, to answer in damages for breach of their obligations. This tends to no mischief, and is a reasonable liberty to bestow; but great detriment would arise and much confusion of rights if parties were allowed to invent new modes of holding and enjoying real property, and to impress upon their lands and tenements a peculiar character, which should follow them into all hands, however remote. Every close, every messuage, might thus be held in a several fashion; and it would hardly be possible to know what rights the acquisition of any parcel conferred, or what obligations it imposed. The right of way or of common is of a public as well as of a simple nature, and no one who sees the premises can be ignorant of what all the vicinage knows. But if one man may bind his messuage and land to take line from a particular kiln, another may bind his to take coals from a certain pit, while a third may load his property with further obligations to employ one blacksmith's forge, or the members of one corporate body, in various operations upon the premises, besides many other restraints as infinite in variety as the imagination can conceive; for there can be no reason whatever in support of the covenant in question, which would not extend to every covenant that can be devised. . . ."

NORCROSS *v*. JAMES. 1885. 2 N.E. 946 (Massachusetts. Supreme Court). The defendants bought land with notice of a covenant by a predecessor in title that he would not use his land as a quarry. He had sold six adjoining acres to a predecessor in title of the plaintiffs who intended to operate a quarry and apparently wanted protection from competition. The defendants nevertheless commenced quarrying and the plaintiffs brought this bill to restrain them. Held, for the defendants. HOLMES. J.: "[The covenant] does not make the use or occupation of it more convenient. It does not in any way affect the use or occupation; it simply tends indirectly to increase its value, by excluding a competitor from the market for its products. If it be asked what is the difference in principle between an easement to have land unbuilt upon . . . and an easement to have a quarry left unopened, the answer is that, whether a difference of degree or of kind, the distinction is plain between a grant or covenant that looks to direct physical advantage in the occupation of the dominant estate, such as light and air, and one which only concerns it in the indirect way which we have mentioned. The scope of the covenant and the circumstances show that it is not directed to the quiet enjoyment of the dominant land.

"Again, this covenant illustrates the further meaning of the rule against unusual incidents. If it is of a nature to be attached to land, as the plaintiff contends, it creates an easement of monopoly,—an easement not to be competed with,—and in that interest alone a right to prohibit one owner from exercising the usual incidents of property. It is true that a man could accomplish the same results by buying the whole land and regulating production. But it does not follow because you can do a thing in one way that you can do it in all; and we think that if this covenant were regarded as one which bound all subsequent owners of the land to keep its products out of commerce, there would be much greater difficulty in sustaining its validity than if it be treated as merely personal in its burden. Whether that is its true construction as well as its only legal operation, and whether, so construed, it is or is not valid, are matters on which we express no opinion."

NOTE. Compare Holmes J.'s view with *Catt* v. *Tourle* and *Luker* v. *Dennis* referred to by Scrutton J. in *L.C.C.* v. *Allen,* and *Keppel* v. *Bailey.*

CANADIAN CONSTRUCTION CO. LTD *v.* BEAVER (ALBERTA) LUMBER LTD. [1955] S.C.R. 682 (Alberta. Supreme Court of Canada). The Beaver Lumber Company sold six lots (which may be called Parcel A) to one Henderson, who covenanted that "the said lots or any part thereof shall not for the period of twenty-five (25) years from the date hereof be used for the purpose of manufacturing, storing, buying, selling or otherwise acquiring or disposing of any lumber or building materials of any kind whatsoever." Henderson also covenanted that "the said restriction and condition shall be binding upon each of the said lots hereby conveyed for the benefit of the vendor . . ." The contract concluded with the words "These presents shall enure to the benefit of and be binding upon the successors and assigns of the vendor and the heirs, executors, administrators and assigns of the purchaser." No other land of the Beaver Lumber Company was mentioned in the agreement but in fact at the time of the sale the Company owned Parcel B, four blocks north and one block east of Parcel A (about one thousand feet away), to which it had removed its business from Parcel A some time before. Parcel A passed through several owners and the defendant, Canadian Construction Company, finally acquired it with notice of the covenants, which the Construction Company contested. Three interesting questions arose, only one of which was necessarily decided by the Supreme Court. The first dealt with the admissibility of oral evidence to show the existence of Parcel B owned by the Beaver Lumber Company but not described or even mentioned in the carefully drawn agreement to sell. The second question concerned the necessity of their being land "touched and concerned" and whether, assuming the evidence of Parcel B was admissible, it met the requirement. Egbert J. at the trial thought it would. The Supreme Court found it unnecessary to decide this question. The third question was whether the covenant was for the benefit of the land or purely personal to the vendor. The Supreme Court was agreed that the proper interpretation of the agreement was that the covenants were personal. The Court said nothing to indicate whether if the covenants had been made expressly for the benefit of Parcel B they would have been enforceable.

NEWTON ABBOTT CO-OPERATIVE SOCIETY LTD. *v*. WILLIAMSON AND TREADGOLD LTD. [1952] Ch. 286 (England. Chancery). The vendor owned premises known as "Devonia" in Bovey Tracey, Devon, where she carried on the business of an ironmonger. She also owned premises on the opposite side of the street which she sold subject to a covenant that the purchasers would not carry on certain specified trades or any business competing with the ironmongery business. A dispute arose over the covenant between successors in title of the vendor and the purchaser. It was argued that the covenant was taken solely to protect the goodwill of the business carried on at Devonia (which was not mentioned in the contract), that it had no reference to the land itself, and that it was not taken for the benefit of such land—in brief, that it was a covenant in gross incapable of assignment. Although such a covenant would benefit the business in that an enhanced price could be obtained for the business, no such enhanced price could be obtained for the land. Upjohn J. felt entitled to look at "surrounding circumstances" to define the land touched and concerned, and he concluded that by taking the covenant the vendor was thereby enabled to sell her premises, or her business, to better advantage as she thought fit. For a critical discussion of this case see *Restrictive Covenants Affecting Freehold Land* by Preston and Newsom (2nd ed), Excursus B, pp. 70–77 dealing with the propriety of using restrictive covenants to restrain competition.

RE BOWES CO., LTD. AND RANKIN. 1924. 55 D.L.R. 601 (Ontario Court of Appeal) A covenant not to use premises as a canning factory without the consent of the vendor or his successors or assigns was held enforceable. The vendor retained two other canning plants in the same village but not on adjoining land. The covenant would appear to have been primarily, if not exclusively, in restraint of trade rather than for the benefit of land. MIDDLETON J. A.: "... although [the covenant] relates to the business to be carried on by the purchaser, and is intended to protect the business carried on by the vendor, it must be kept in mind that on each parcel of the vendor's property there was a canning factory, and that the benefit of the covenant, if it passed upon any sale, would tend to enhance the price to be obtained."

QUESTIONS. Is there a valid distinction between a covenant benefiting "land" and one benefiting "things done on land"? Has land any significance apart from the things one do over, on or under it?

4. Discrimination Against Social Groups

NOBLE AND WOLF *v.* ALLEY

Ontario. Supreme Court of Canada. [1951] 1 D.L.R. 321

KERWIN J.: This is an appeal against a judgment of the Court of Appeal for Ontario affirming the judgment of Schroeder J. on a motion under s. 3 of the *Vendors and Purchasers Act*, R.S.O. 1937, c. 168. That section, so far as relevant, provides that a vendor of real estate may apply in a summary way to the Supreme Court in respect of any requisition or objection arising out of, or in connection with, a contract for the sale or purchase of land. The motion was made by the present appellant, Mrs. Noble, as the vendor under a contract for the sale by her to the purchaser, her co-appellant Bernard Wolf, of land forming part of a summer resort development known as the Beach O'Pines.

This land had been purchased in 1933 by Mrs. Noble from the Frank S. Salter Co. Ltd., and in the deed from it to her appeared the following covenant:

"And the Grantee for himself, his heirs, executors, administrators and assigns covenants and agrees with the Grantor that he will carry out, comply with and observe, with the intent that they shall run with the lands and shall be binding upon himself, his heirs, executors, administrators and assigns, and shall be for the benefit of and enforceable by the grantor and/or any other person or persons seized or possessed of any part or parts of the lands included in Beach O'Pines Development, the restrictions herein following, which said restrictions shall remain in full force and effect until the first day of August, 1962, and the Grantee for himself, his heirs, executors, administrators and assigns further covenants and agrees with the Grantor that he will exact the same covenants with respect to the said restrictions from any and all persons to whom he may in any manner whatsoever dispose of the said lands. . . .

"(f) The lands and premises herein described shall never be sold, assigned, transferred, leased, rented, or in any manner whatsoever alienated to, and shall never be occupied or used in any manner whatsoever by any person of the Jewish, Hebrew, Semitic, Negro or coloured race or blood, it being the intention and purpose of the Grantor, to restrict the ownership, use, occupation and enjoyment of the said recreational development, including the lands and premises herein described, to persons of the white or Caucasian race not excluded by this clause."

Although the deed was not signed by Mrs. Noble, I assume that she is bound to the same extent as if she had executed it.

Each conveyance by the company to a purchaser of land in the development contained a covenant in the same form. The present respondents, being owners of other parcels of land in the development, were served with notice of the application either before Schroeder J. or the Court of Appeal, and they and their counsel affirmed the validity of the covenant, its binding effect upon Mrs. Noble, and that any of the respondents are able to take advantage of the covenant so as to prevent by injunction its breach. While before the Judge of first instance the vendor and purchaser apparently took opposite sides, each of them appealed to the Court of Appeal and, there, as well as before this Court, attacked the contentions put forward on behalf of the respondents.

In the Courts below emphasis was laid upon the decision of MacKay J.

in *Re Drummond Wren* (1945) and it was considered that the motion was confined to the consideration of whether that case, if rightly decided, covered the situation. The motion was for an order declaring that the objection to the covenant made on behalf of the purchaser had been fully answered by the vendor and that the same did not constitute a valid objection to the title or for such further and other order as might seem just. The objection was: "Required in view of the fact that the purchaser herein might be considered as being of the Jewish race or blood, we require a release from the restrictions imposed in the said clause (f) and an order declaring that the restrictive covenant set out in the said clause (f) is void and of no effect."

The answer by the vendor was that the decision in *Re Drummond Wren* applied to the facts of the present sale with the result that clause (f) was invalid and the vendor and purchaser were not bound to observe it. In view of the wide terms of the notice of motion, the application is not restricted and it may be determined by a point taken before the Court of Appeal and this Court, if not before Schroeder J. . . .

Whatever the precise delimitation in the rule in *Tulk* v. *Moxhay* may be, counsel were unable to refer us to any case where it was applied to a covenant restricting the alienation of land to persons other than those of a certain race. . . .

It was a forward step that the rigour of the common law should be softened by the doctrine expounded in *Tulk* v. *Moxhay* but it would be an unwarrantable extension of that doctrine to hold, from anything that was said in that case or in subsequent cases, that the covenant here in question has any reference to the use, or abstension from use, of land. Even if decisions upon the common law could be prayed in aid, there are none that go to the extent claimed in the present case.

The appeal should be allowed with costs here and in the Court of Appeal. There should be no costs of the original motions in the Supreme Court of Ontario.

RAND J.: Covenants enforceable under the rule of *Tulk* v. *Moxhay* are properly conceived as running with the land in equity, and, by reason of their enforceability, as constituting an equitable servitude or burden on the servient land. The essence of such an incident is that it should touch or concern the land as contradistinguished from a collateral effect. In that sense, it is a relation between parcels, annexed to them and, subject to the equitable rule of notice, passing with them both as to benefit and burden in transmissions by operation of law as well as by act of the parties.

But by its language, the covenant here is directed not to the land or to some mode of its use, but to transfer by act of the purchaser; its scope does not purport to extend to a transmission by law to a person within the banned class. If, for instance, the grantee married a member of that class, it is not suggested that the ordinary inheritance by a child of the union would be affected. Not only, then, is it not a covenant touching or concerning the land, but by its own terms, it fails in annexation to the land. The respondent owners are, therefore, without any right against the proposed vendor.

On its true interpretation, the covenant is a restraint on alienation . . . [I]t becomes necessary to deal with the question whether for the purposes of specific performance the covenant is unenforceable for uncertainty.

[After quoting the covenant, Rand J., continued]

If this language were in the form of a condition, the holding in *Clayton* v. *Ramsden* (1943), would be conclusive against its sufficiency. In that case the House of Lords dealt with a condition in a devise by which the donee became divested if she should marry a person "not of Jewish parentage and of the Jewish faith" and held it void for uncertainty. I am unable to distinguish the defect in that language from what we have here: it is impossible to set such limits to the lines of race or blood as would enable a Court to say in all cases whether a proposed purchaser is or is not within the ban. As put by Lord Cranworth in *Clavering* v. *Ellison* (1859) the condition "must be such that the Court can see from the beginning, precisely and distinctly upon the happening of what event it was that the preceding vested estate was to determine."

The effect of the covenant, if enforceable, would be to annex a partial inalienability as an equitable incident of the ownership, to nullify an area of proprietary powers. In both cases there is the removal of part of the power to alienate; and I can see no ground of distinction between the certainty required in the one case and that of the other. The uncertainty is, then, fatal to the validity of the covenant before us as a defect of or objection to the title.

I would, therefore, allow the appeal and direct judgment to the effect that the covenant is not an objection to the title of the proposed vendor, with costs to the appellants in this Court and in the Court of Appeal.

ESTEY J.: . . . This restrictive covenant literally construed would prohibit any person possessing the slightest degree of race or blood specified purchasing any land in this area. So construed, it would be necessary to determine whether it constituted such a substantial restraint upon alienation as to make the clause void "as being repugnant to the very conception of ownership": Cheshire's *Modern Real Property*, 6th edition at page 523.

It is, however, submitted that the parties never intended that the language should be so construed strictly. Once, however, another or more liberal construction be given the issue becomes one of what degree or race or blood would be permitted. As to what degree, the contract is silent. A judge, therefore, called upon to determine this issue, finds in the contract no standard or other assistance that would constitute a basis upon which the issue might be determined.

[The opinion of Kerwin J. is the judgment of Kerwin and Taschereau JJ. and the opinion of Rand J. is the judgment of Rand, Kellock and Fauteux JJ. The opinion of Locke J., who dissented on a procedural point, is omitted. The opinion of Estey J. proceeded along the lines taken by Kerwin and Rand JJ.]

QUESTIONS. What is the defect in the covenant here? Is it only uncertainty of language? Could a more precise form of words effectually exclude purchasers or occupiers of a certain race, creed or colour?

Does the court hold that a restraint on alienation does not run with the land? Is either Kerwin J. or Rand J. justified in saying that the covenant here has no reference to the use, or abstention from use, or mode of use, of land? Read the text of the covenant again.

A restrictive covenant in a deed provides: "And the purchaser further agrees that he will not subdivide or sell any part of the lot hereby conveyed to the intent that the size of the lots in the subdivision will remain constant." Does the decision in the principal case affect this clause?

Is it socially desirable that the defect in the covenant in the principal case should be overcome? Compare MacKay J. in *Re Drummond Wren* where a similar covenant was held unenforceable as against public policy. Why did the Supreme Court ignore the public policy issue? What is the public policy? Is the exclusion of certain persons from a particular group necessarily anti-social? Is there any way to regulate segregation so that the benefits (if any) are retained and the disadvantages avoided?

CONVEYANCING AND LAW OF PROPERTY ACT

Ontario. Revised Statutes. 1960. Chapter 66

22. Every convenant made after the 24th day of March, 1950, that but for this section would be annexed to and run with land and that restricts the sale, ownership, occupation or use of land because of the race, creed, colour, nationality, ancestry or place of origin of any person is void and of no effect.

NOTE. Section 21 was introduced in 1950 before the decision in the principal case was handed down. If the Supreme Court could be said to have held that a covenant restricting sale, etc., on grounds of race, creed or colour does not run with the land, does s. 21 have any effect to avoid a clause, even as between the original covenantor and covenantee?

Litigation over racial restrictive convenants in the United States involves issues of due process and equal protection under the Fourteenth Amendment, but the cases are frequently helpful on public policy issues. Compare *Shelley* v. *Kraemer* (1948), 334 U.S. 1 and *Charlotte Park and Recreation Commission* v. *Barringer* (1955), 88 S.E. 2d. 114.

GALBRAITH *v.* MADAWASKA CLUB LTD.

Ontario. Supreme Court of Canada. 1961. 29 D.L.R. 2d 153

The Madawaska Club was incorporated for the purpose of protecting, preserving and propagating fish and game and pursuing hunting, capturing and taking fish and game on the lands of the Club, and to conduct experimental work in forestry biology and other branches of natural science. The share capital was $2,000 divided into 80 shares of $25 each. Membership was limited to graduates or under-graduates of the University of Toronto or of the School of Practical Science or any officials connected with either and all other persons were expressly excluded from the right to acquire and hold shares in the Club. The Club obtained grants on several islands in Georgian Bay, one of which, No. 122, was sold in fee to Ella Firth who covenanted that she would not convey the land to anyone not a member of the Club, and that she would observe the by-laws. By-law 19 provided that occupation of a dwelling or premises by persons who are not members of the Club shall only be by special permission of the Board of Directors. Firth conveyed to Galbraith who covenanted in the same terms. Galbraith conveyed to himself and his wife in a deed without the covenants. In this action Galbraith claimed a declaration that the restraint on the transfer of the shares was void and that No. 122 was not subject to certain by-laws. The trial judge held that the by-laws restricting the transfer shares were invalid but he also held that By-laws 18, 19 and 28 were valid and ran with the land. Galbraith appealed only as to By-law 19. The defendant cross-appealed. The Court of Appeal dismissed the appeal, and allowed the cross-appeal.

Galbraith appealed to the Supreme Court of Canada which held the transfer restrictions and By-laws 18 and 28 valid.

JUDSON J. delivered the judgment of the Court on the question of By-law 19: I agree with the reasons of the Chief Justice on the first branch of the case that the appellant fails in his claim for a declaration concerning the restrictions on the transfer of shares. I also agree that the appellant and his wife are joint tenants in fee simple of the land and not licensees as the Court of Appeal held. In my opinion the result of this litigation is that the plaintiff is bound only by the restrictions contained in By-laws 18 (a) and (b) and 28 but not by By-law 19 and to this extent I would modify the judgment of the learned trial Judge.

After a trial in which he was largely successful, Galbraith appealed to the Court of Appeal on one point only—whether he was bound by By-law 19. He was, of course, a purchaser with notice. By-law 19, so far as it is applicable, reads: "Occupation of a dwelling or premises by persons who are not members of the Club shall only be by special permission of the Board of Directors." The club cross-appealed on all points. The Court of Appeal held, as a result of a point raised before them for the first time in the litigation, that Galbraith was a licensee of the land and not an owner in fee simple and consequently subject to all the restrictions. On appeal to this Court, he seeks to have the judgment at trial restored with the above-mentioned modification as to not being bound by the restrictive covenant contained in By-law 19. He has never appealed against the declaration that he is bound by By-law 18 (a) and (b) and 28.

The chain of title in this case is short. The club acquired the fee simple to the land in question by grant from the Dominion of Canada. I mention this because other club lands were acquired by grant from the Province of Ontario. The provincial grant contains special conditions limiting the persons who may become interested in the lands and nothing that I say in these reasons has any application to the lands contained in the provincial grant. In 1945 the club granted in fee simple to Ella R. Firth part of island 122. The grantee covenanted in the following terms:

"to the intent that the burden of these covenants may run with the lands aforesaid during the Corporate existence of The Madawaska Club Limited, the said Grantee for herself, her heirs, executors, administrators and assigns, DOTH COVENANT AND AGREE with the said Grantor its successors and assigns as follows: that she the said Grantee, her heirs, executors, administrators and assigns.

"(a) Will not nor will any of them transfer said land by Deed of Ownership or any similar agreement to any person *not a member of the Club*, and that any such sale, lease or transfer to any person not a member of the Club, or attempted alienation of the said land to take it out of the control of the by-laws of the Club shall be null and void. . . .

"(d) Will observe and carry out the by-laws of The Madawaska Club Limited, annexed hereto marked "A" and will hold the said land subject to the terms herein contained and subject to the terms and conditions imposed upon the said land by the said by-laws."

By-law 19, which was the main subject-matter of argument on this branch of the appeal, is thus introduced by way of covenant (d) contained in the deed.

In 1947 Mrs. Firth conveyed in fee to Galbraith and took from him the same covenants. In 1951 Galbraith conveyed to himself and his wife as joint tenants and this deed did not contain the covenants. Thus, notwithstanding the fact that the action is one brought by Galbraith for a declaratory judgment, the dispute is really one between the club as the original covenantee and a subsequent purchaser of the restricted land who takes with notice but claims to be free of the covenant.

If Galbraith, as assignee of the servient land taking with notice, is to be bound by this covenant, certain essential requirements must be satisfied. I will take it that the covenant is negative in substance, if not form, for the negative implication is very clear. The requirements are that this covenant must touch and concern the dominant land, that the club as covenantee must retain land capable of being benefited by the covenant and that there must be express annexation of the covenant to the dominant land. In my opinion all three requirements are lacking in this case.

The juridical basis for the enforcement of these covenants has undergone a marked change since *Tulk* v. *Moxhay* (1848). The doctrine of of notice was the decisive factor in that case. The presently developed theory of enforceability is that expressed by Rand, J., in *Noble & Wolf* v. *Alley* (1951). . . .

Assuming for the moment that there has been an annexation of this covenant to some land of the club capable of being benefited at the time of the conveyance to Mrs. Firth, does this covenant relating to occupation of the servient land touch or concern the dominant land for it is that land which must be "touched or concerned" (*Rogers* v. *Hosegood* (1900))? There is no privity of contract between Galbraith, as owner of the restricted land, and the club. The club has parted with the fee simple. If the club is to enforce the covenant against Galbraith, it must be done for the benefit of land retained by the club at the date of the covenant. It is this protected land which must be touched and concerned by the covenant, within the classic definition of Farwell J., in *Rogers* v. *Hosegood*: "the covenant must either affect the land as regards mode of occupation or it must be such as per se, and not merely from collateral circumstances, affects the value of the land."

The covenant in question here gives the club the right to choose the persons who shall occupy the servient land, if the owner wishes to go outside the club membership. This has nothing to do with the use to which the land may be put, but relates only to the kind of person who may be given occupation. It is imposed by the vendor for its own benefit as a club. It does not touch or concern the land, as being imposed for the benefit of or to enhance the value of land retained by the club. It calls into being the exercise of an unfettered personal discretion by the club management and its plain purpose is to preserve the amenities of the club. That such a covenant does not touch or concern the dominant land is concluded in this Court by the decision in *Noble & Wolf* v. *Alley*. . . .

It was held that [the covenant in that case] was not a covenant touching or concerning the land and I can see no possible ground for any distinction between a covenant restricting alienation and one restricting occupation.

There is nothing in the conveyance from the club to Mrs. Firth which attempts to annex the benefit of the covenant to any land retained by the club. Further, there is no evidence anywhere in the record to indicate whether the club had any such land capable of being benefited. The grantee simply covenants for herself, her heirs, executors, administrators and assigns, with the grantor, its successors, and assigns, to the intent that the burden of the covenants should run with the lands during the corporate existence of the club but nothing is said about any other lands. This fails to meet what I think must be regarded as the minimum requirements that the deed itself must so define the land to be benefited as to make it easily ascertainable (*Zetland* v. *Driver* (1939)).

There was exactly the same situation in *Can. Construction Co.* v. *Beaver (Alta.) Lumber Ltd.* (1955)....

However, the plain implication in the judgment of this Court in affirming the trial judgment [in that case] was that a restrictive covenant contained in an agreement which omits all reference to any dominant land, although it sets out the restrictions placed upon the servient land, is unenforceable by the covenantee against a successor in title of the covenantor, since such an agreement expresses no intention that any other lands should be benefited by the covenant. A covenant running with the land cannot be created in this manner and in the absence of any attempted annexation of the benefit to some particular land of the covenantee, the covenant is personal and collateral to the conveyance as being for the benefit of the covenantee alone.

5. Neighbourhood Planning: The Building Scheme

Although the doctrine of *Tulk* v. *Moxhay* as defined in the later cases did a great deal to free property owners from the restrictions of the general contract rule against third party beneficiaries, and many well planned projects of civic design were made possible, there was still a basic weakness. The restrictive covenants could only be enforced by the original covenantee, his express assigns, or the successor in title of land to which the covenant had been annexed and in fact touched and concerned. There was, however, another very similar device developing at the same time, that provided the necessary reciprocity of right to sue, which put all the covenantors in as good a position as the covenantee. This device came to be known as the building scheme. The following cases illustrate its attributes and raise some nice problems of its creation and scope. While the modern planner, in setting up a building scheme, ought to be able to avoid the problem of creation by proper drafting, the problems of scope will remain.

Looming large among the problems of creation is the question of evidence, for it seems to be clear that a deed is not essential, nor, apparently, is even writing an essential, notwithstanding the Statute of Frauds. The rights of owners to enforce mutual covenants do not seem necessarily to arise in contract and seem rather to have a quality of property, but the intention to create a scheme is essential, regardless of whether it is determined by evidence of express provision in all conveyances, by interpretation of the provisions, by the fact that all conveyances have similar (or the same) covenants, although silent as to the existence of the scheme, or perhaps even by reference to the advertising of the scheme.

REID *v.* BICKERSTAFF. [1909] 2 Ch. 305 (England. Court of Appeal). COZENS-HARDY M.R. . . . "The case of the plaintiffs rests upon two alternative propositions, either of which, if established, will entitle them to the relief they claim: (1) There was a building scheme affecting the estate of the common vendors, and each purchaser became under an implied covenant or obligation to every other purchaser to conform to and obey the provisions of the scheme, which included the restrictive covenant in question. (2) Apart from any building scheme, the plaintiffs, or some of them, are entitled to the benefit of the restrictive covenants which were entered into. Different considerations apply to these two propositions, and it will be convenient to deal with them separately.

"(1) What are some of the essentials of a building scheme? In my opinion, there must be a defined area within which the scheme is operative. Reciprocity is the foundation of the idea of a scheme. A purchaser of one parcel cannot be subject to an implied obligation to purchasers of an undefined and unknown area. He must know both the extent of his burden and the extent of his benefit. Not only must the area be defined, but the obligations to be imposed within that area must be defined. Those obligations need not be identical. For example, there may be houses of a certain value in one part and houses of a different value in another part. A building scheme is not created by the mere fact that the owner of an estate sells it in lots and takes varying covenants from various purchasers. There must be notice to the various purchasers of what I may venture to call the local law imposed by the vendors upon a definite area.

"(2) If on a sale of part of an estate the purchaser covenants with the vendor, his heirs and assigns, not to deal with the purchased property in a particular way, a subsequent purchaser of part of the estate does not take the benefit of the covenant unless (a) he is an express assignee of the covenant, as distinct from assignee of the land, or (b) the restrictive covenant is expressed to be for the benefit and protection of the particular parcel purchased by the subsequent purchaser. In the case of (a) of course, the subsequent purchaser can sue. In the case of (b) the benefit of the covenant passes to the purchaser, whether he knew of its existence or not. It is in the nature of an easement attached to his property as the dominant tenement. But unless either (a) or (b) can be established, it remains for the vendor to enforce or abstain from enforcing the restrictive covenant. For example, I sell a piece of land with a covenant that no public-house shall be erected thereon. I sell the adjoining lot to a purchaser who is ignorant of the existence of the covenant. I am at full liberty to release the covenant, or to assign the benefit of it to any particular purchaser, or to deal with the rest of my land as I think fit. It is irrelevant to urge that the performance of the covenant would be greatly for the benefit of the adjoining land. The benefit of a covenant capable of being annexed to land, but not expressed to be so annexed, either by the deed containing the covenant or by some subsequent instrument executed by the covenantee, does not pass as an incident of land on a subsequent conveyance. . . ."

RE WHEELER. 1926. 59 O.L.R. 223 (Ontario. Appellate Division). The Northern Realty Company in 1909 conveyed a number of adjacent but not all adjoining lots to one Gillis, who did not sign the deed, which contained a restrictive covenant running for 21 years, limiting the use to one detached dwelling house, with no stable on lots narrower than 50 feet, costing not less than $3,500 of brick or stone or both with a front yard of 15 feet and side yards of 6 feet. Northern Realty conveyed other lots on the same street in the same area with differing covenants, $4,500 as the minimum cost in one, $3,000 in another, some side yards were 3 feet, one permitted the erection of a stable, another a "house for an automotor", one permitted one house or two houses on two lots with a "house for an automotor". The last parcel sold by Northern exacted no covenant. The Gillis lots were conveyed without any covenant. This was an action by subsequent purchasers of five adjoining Gillis lots to quiet their titles. The respondents, owners of the seven lots in the same block oppose the appellants. Held, for the appellants. MIDDLETON J.A.: "Nothing is said in the material filed by either party indicating the circumstances under which the property was subdivided. There is nothing to shew that there was a building scheme unless it is to be inferred from the conveyances.

"Upon the motion for relief under the statute the appellants further shew that there has been in some instances, violation of the building restrictions; that duplex houses have been erected; and, further, that upon the portion of the reserve adjacent to the appellants' lands an apartment-house is being erected; and that on all the surrounding streets many buildings have been erected upon small lots, and entirely out of harmony with the requirements of the covenants referred to. . . .

"In the case of *Elliston* v. *Reacher* (1908) Mr. Justice Parker thus sums up the requisites of a building scheme p. 384):

" 'It must be proved (1) that both the plaintiffs and the defendants derive title under a common vendor; (2) that previously to selling the lands to which the plaintiffs and defendants are respectively entitled the vendor laid out his estate, or a defined portion thereof (including the lands purchased by the plaintiffs and defendants respectively), for sale in lots subject to restrictions intended to be imposed on all the lots, and which, though varying in details as to particular lots, are consistent and consistent only with some general scheme of development; (3) that these restrictions were intended by the common vendor to be and were for the benefit of all the lots intended to be sold, whether or not they were also intended to be and were for the benefit of other lots retained by the vendor; and (4) that both the plaintiffs and the defendants, or their predecessors in title, purchased their lots from the common vendor upon the footing that the restrictions subject to which the purchases were made were to enure for the benefit of the other lots included in the general scheme whether or not they were also to enure for the benefit of other lands retained by the vendor.'

"Here there is no real attempt to shew a building scheme on the part of the Northern Realty Company. So long as they had lots remaining on their hands, they exacted varying covenants extending over varying times, for all that appears, entirely for their own benefit. There is nothing to shew that there was any intention on the part of that company to secure any benefit to the owners of lots once sold. This may be gathered from the fact that when they came to sell the last remaining parcel they exacted no covenant at all . . . Then again the varying nature of the covenants goes far to shew that there was no real building scheme at all. . . .

Nor can I agree with the learned judge that a building scheme has been established with reference to the lands conveyed to Gillis, and resold by him. It has to be borne in mind that these did not constitute a compact and consolidated parcel. . . .

"Nor did Gillis in selling the different lots seek to impose any restrictions. All his deeds are deeds absolute in form without any qualification. It may well be that those who took under him with knowledge of his obligations in the deed from the Northern Realty Company to him would be bound to observe his negative covenant, and that the Northern Realty Company would have been entitled to enforce it against them; but, when it sold its last lot, it lost the right to invoke the equitable jurisidiction of the Court; and Gillis, being himself in no peril, would have no right to call upon his purchasers to observe the covenant. . . ."

RE LORNE PARK

Ontario. High Court. 1913. 30 O.L.R. 289

MIDDLETON J.: By letters patent dated the 16th July, 1886, the Toronto and Lorne Park Summer Resort Company was incorporated by the Province of Ontario, for the purpose of acquiring by purchase, owning, improving, and managing as a summer resort, the property known as "Lorne Park," with power to make improvements and alterations, erect and construct all kinds of buildings, wharves, piers, etc., and to maintain roads, streets, avenues, lanes, etc., with the power to sell, mortgage, or exchange any part of the park, to establish a line of ferries, and to makes contracts for the purpose of providing entertainment.

Thereafter the company duly acquired the park in question, and, after having had a survey made, subdivided a certain portion of it, as shewn by a plan registered on the 7th August, 1886. On this plan were shewn a number of streets, and building lots laid out and fronting thereon. There are two large blocks that were not in any way subdivided. Free access to these blocks appears to have been afforded by Longfellow, Sangster, and Burns Avenues, which are shewn as communicating with them, and Tennyson

Avenue, shewn as passing between them. In 1888, the plan was amended by the company by the laying out of Roper Avenue at right angles to Tennyson Avenue, so subdividing the larger of these two parcels. Upon the amended plan, these three blocks appear entirely enclosed by the street lines and without any name, mark, or label of any kind to indicate their purpose. For convenience upon the reference, they had been marked "X", "Y," and "Z" for the purpose of identification.

These undesignated blocks or places contain, it is said, about 25 acres, approximately one-third of the whole parcel.

Literature was issued by the company indicating its intention in dealing with the park property. It is said in the circular of 1889:—

"The domain of the company has recently been considerably extended toward the north-east, and this delightful resort now embraces about 90 acres, more than half of which has been reserved for terrace, avenues, plea-

sure-grounds, and woodland rambles, the residue being laid out into cottage lots"—a statement which would only be true if the three blocks in question are regarded as forming part of the reserve.

"The ball ground has been considerably enlarged so as to give ample space for lacrosse and baseball. Lawn bowls, quoits, lawn tennis, croquet, swings, etc., have been provided."

"Picnic Grounds.

"The condition of the picnic grounds (about 25 acres in extent) has been much improved since last season, and every opportunity is afforded societies and schools for enjoying their annual outings. Rustic pavilions and dining-halls, with kitchens attached, are provided . . . A stable and driving-shed may be found on entering the park by those visitors who drive from the city or neighbourhood."

In another circular, exhibit 4, a plan is also printed in which the blocks in question and the space taken for Roper Avenue are shewn, with a distinctive colouring on the larger parcel, on which a building is indicated marked "pavilion."

In this circular it is said: "In the first place, the design was to unite quietness for private residences with complete sporting grounds for public amusement. This has been done by the admirable adaptation of the grounds for separating the two. A splendid square of about 25 acres has been set apart for picnics and sports."

On the faith of statements contained in this literature and made orally, a number of the lots were sold. The individual lots were described simply by their number according to the registered plan. Each conveyance contained the following clause:—

"And it is hereby agreed that the party of the second part, his heirs, executors, administrators, and assigns, and his or their families, subject to the by-laws of the company, shall have free access to all the streets, avenues, terraces, and commons of the said park; and shall have free ingress and egress for himself and themselves, his and their family or families, servants and agents, with horses and carriages, or other vehicles, to and from the said lands by any of the streets or avenues in the said park; and, subject as aforesaid, shall have free ingress and egress to and from the said park at any wharf or wharves in front thereof."

And also the following provisions:—

"And it is hereby declared and agreed that the said lands are granted by the parties of the first part to the party of the second part, subject to the following provisoes and conditions, which shall be deemed to run with the land:—

"1. No intoxicating or spirituous liquors or beverages shall be sold or bartered upon the said lands, nor shall any be used thereon except for medicinal purposes.

"2. No business is to be carried on upon the said lands, nor is the same to be used for any other purpose than as a private dwelling, without the consent, in writing, under seal, of the said company.

"3. The party of the second part, his executors, administrators, or assigns, shall before the 1st day of July, 1888, erect and complete a neat and respectable house or cottage on the said lands for a private dwelling, which will cost not less than $400.

"4. Only one dwelling shall be erected on the said lands, and no building shall be erected or placed on said lands till the plans thereof have been approved by the president and two directors of the said company.

"5. No part of such dwelling or of any verandah or porch in front thereof shall be placed nearer than twenty feet from the front of said lot.

"6. No cess-pools or filth of any kind shall be allowed on the said lands. No fence on the said lands shall be higher than six feet, and all fencing within fifty feet from the front of said lands shall be wire or iron and not more than three feet high.

7. All water-closets or privy-pits must be approved by the company before being erected, and must be kept clean and free from offensive odours.

"8. No animals or fowl shall be kept on said lands.

"9. No conveyance or lease of said lands or any part thereof shall be made or be valid without the consent, in writing, under seal, of the said company.

"10. And the parties of the first part shall have the right to pass by-laws and make regulations for the construction of sewers, drains, watercourses, waterworks, and for all kinds of street improvements, in streets, avenues, terraces, and commons adjacent to the said lands, and also for lighting all or any of the streets, avenues, terraces, or other public parts of said park adjacent to said lands; and the lands hereby granted and the owners thereof, to the extent of the value of said lands, shall be liable to contribute to the cost of all the above named improvements equally with all other lands that are adjacent to the streets, avenues, terraces, and commons wherein said improvements are made, such contributions to be assessed equally against each lot so situated."

The different claimants now claim title under these conveyances. Their contention is, that the effect of the conveyances is to give them some right with respect to the three parcels which I have mentioned, which prevent the present owner from being declared to be the owner in fee simple without some qualification.

The learned Referee held that the claimants had established their rights with reference to the parcels lying north-east of Tennyson Avenue, but had failed with reference to the parcel of the south-west of that street. The right of the claimants to the streets, avenues, and unenclosed portions of the park has been conceded, and need not be discussed.

The first question calling for consideration is the meaning of the expression contained in the deed by which it is stipulated that the grantee "shall have free access to the streets, avenues, terraces, and commons of the said park." The claimants contend that this word "commons" should be taken to include the three parcels in question. The owner, on the other hand, contends that this is not the true meaning of the word, and that it is amply satisfied by referring it to the unenclosed space upon the plan, more particularly to the wide strip along the lake shore marked "Boustead Terrace." I think this contention is somewhat militated against by the fact that the clause provides for ingress and egress to and from the lots sold "by any of the streets or avenues in the said park." As the lots fronting on the lake shore face Boustead Terrace, this is apparently regarded as a street or avenue rather than the commons.

It is quite true that this word "commons" is not used in its more strict and literal sense, but it is a flexible word; and in *Municipal Council of Sydney* v. *Attorney-General for New South Wales* (1894) the Privy Council had no difficulty in giving it a meaning wide enough to cover that which is contended for by the claimants here. There certain lands had been dedicated as a permanent common. The question was, whether this created a common or pasturage only. It was held that it did not. Lord Hobhouse says: "The word 'common,' it is true, has a technical meaning in England and in New South Wales; though what kind of enjoyment it may indicate, and for what persons, cannot be understood without something more. Standing alone it is an ambiguous term which requires explanation, and which may be explained by circumstances. But further, it is very often used, though inexactly and in popular parlance, to denote land devoted to the enjoyment of the public or of large numbers of people. And the question is whether it has not been so used in this instance. It appears to their Lordships that there are several considerations, some more and some less cogent, all bearing the same way . . . The omission to name commoners, or in any way to define the nature of the common, is more consistent with the intention of leaving the enjoyment a variable thing and open to all comers, than to give it to a defined class which, even if a large one, must be limited. The contiguity of the land to a populous city suggests that other modes of enjoyment are more suitable than pasturage."

Much was said upon the argument as to the nature of the right claimed, if any. I do not think that it is necessary to define the exact nature of the right. In an early case, *City of Toronto* v. *McGill* (1859), Spragge V.-C., said: "Whether these acts would amount to a dedication to the public, or an equity in the nature of an easement would have arisen to purchasers, it is not necessary to say."

It may be that the term "dedicate" is only appropriate where the right is conferred upon the public; here no public right was contemplated, nor do I think it was given, because those to be benefited were not the public but the purchasers of the different lands; indeed, I think it would be unprofitable to enter into a discussion to ascertain whether the right claimed can properly be called an easement, or whether it created an implied obligation in the nature of a restrictive covenant, because it seems to me that all this is more a question of terminology than of real substance. The main question remains: was it the intention of the parties that these three parcels should be set apart and held as recreation grounds for the use of those who might buy lots upon the faith and strength of the scheme put forward by the vendors?

In 13 *Cyc.* 455, it is said: "Where the owner of real property lays out a town upon it, and divides the land into lots and blocks, intersected by streets and alleys, and sells any of the lots with reference to such plan . . . he thereby dedicates the streets and alleys to the use of the public." This in some countries, as here, depends upon statutory provisions, but it is also true at common law. The writer then proceeds (p. 457): "The owner will be held to have dedicated to the public use such pieces of land as are marked on the plan or map as squares, courts, or parks. The reason is that the grantor by making such a conveyance is estopped, as well in reference to the public as to his grantees, from denying the existence of the easement." The reason underlying this statement is well illustrated by the case of *Clark* v. *City of Elizabeth* (1878), "Of the propriety of the rule there can be no question. It is based on the most obvious principles of fair dealing: the principles which require the vendor to deliver to his vendee that which the latter has bought and paid for—the principles which hold men to their lawful bargains."

This principle has been applied in our own Courts in the case of *Town of Guelph* v. *Canada Co.* (1853) where the Canada Company, after having laid out the town of Guelph, shewing upon the registered plan a block marked "market square," sought to sell off the square in town lots. Esten

V.C. says: "The American cases which were cited throw much light on this branch of the law. There can be no doubt that if the owner of land lay out a town or village upon it, containing streets, squares, and other public places, and exhibit maps and plans of such intended town or village so laid out, and people settle in the place upon the understanding that such public thoroughfares and places exist, and no effectual alteration is made, and the place grows under such circumstances into a town or village, there is a complete dedication of such thoroughfares and places to the public use." See, also, *Attorney-General* v. *Town of Brantford* (1858).

I quite appreciate that there is room for distinction between cases in which there has been a dedication to the public, and the public right is being asserted, and cases such as this, where there is not in strictness any public right; but the allegation is that a private right has been conferred upon the individuals who purchase relying upon the scheme propounded by the vendors. It may well be that these cases may well be more aptly likened to the class of cases in which the Court has been called upon to deal with building schemes.

In *Reid* v. *Bickerstaff*, [1909] 2 Ch. 305, the principle underlying these cases is discussed in the Court of Appeal. All that is there regarded as essential appears to me to exist here. There is a defined area within which the scheme is operated; there is the reciprocity which is said to be the foundation of the idea of a building scheme; there is the local law imposed and yet to be imposed by the vendors over the whole area; for the extracts from the deed which I have quoted shew the co-operative nature of the whole undertaking. In the defined area of this park, the cottagers are to erect suitable dwellings. The lands are not to be conveyed or leased without the consent of the company, and the company is to have the right to pass by-laws providing for the construction of sewers, waterworks, etc., and all necessary improvements and lighting in streets, avenues, terraces, and commons, and other public parts of the park, to which the owners must contribute the cost.

Numerous cases can, no doubt, be found where the plaintiff has failed to establish a valid building scheme or to prevent the user of the lands in a way inconsistent therewith. In none of these cases where the plaintiffs have failed, have I found the principle laid down opposed to that upon which I am now acting. For example, at first sight, what was said by Kekewich, J., in *Whitehouse* v. *Hugh* (1906) might appear inconsistent where he says: "A purchaser from a building owner is not entitled to say 'On that plan you see a vacant space, and therefore I can insist as part of my bargain that the vacant space shall remain vacant.' " This, it will be noticed, is spoken of a case in which there is nothing more shewn than the vacant space, and the case, therefore, resembles *City of Toronto* v. *McGill*. Here much more is shewn; and, when one reads the evidence shewing the conduct of the parties and the rights which it was assumed by both parties the purchasers had with respect to the lands in question, one cannot fail to be impressed with the idea that this is a case where the whole scheme was that of a group of summer residences surrounding ample recreation grounds.

Mackenzie v. *Childers* (1889) is an effective answer to the suggestion that it is impossible to conceive that the promoters intended to sterilise for all time the 25 acres in question, and that all these statements are consistent with a mere expression of intention and the absence of obligation on the part of the vendors. Kay, J., there says what is equally applicable here: "I have no doubt that it was the best and most lucrative mode of dealing with the estate, and that they have received much more under it than could have been made by sale of the land in any other way. I have no reason to suppose that the conditions imposed were depreciatory. I should infer just the contrary."

The cases cited mostly arise upon plans, but the principle is of wider application, and includes all cases in which the land is sold upon what mav be called a "building scheme," a scheme by which a part of the entire tract is set apart by the vendors for the benefit of the purchasers. When this is shewn, either by indications found upon a plan used in making the sales or otherwise, the vendors cannot depart from the plan or scheme which was the foundation of the sales. This may be regarded as an implied covenant, an implied grant of an easement, an equity in the nature of an easement, or it may rest on the principles of estoppel. In any case, the property so dedicated or quasi-dedicated is rendered subject to the rights held out to the purchaser as an inducement to purchase. These rights may exist in perpetuity . . .

If the conduct of the parties and mode of user of the land in question can be looked at, the evidence conclusively shews that the three blocks were intended as the "commons" referred to in the deed.

The right to use these parcels is not an exclusive right conferred upon the lot-owners, but is subject to the right of the vendors themselves to use and to lease or license for picnic purposes.

Reliance was placed on the Registry Act as avoiding the claimant's rights under the deeds in question. No evidence was given to shew that the present owner is a purchaser for value without notice. On the contrary, he took with knowledge of the infirmity of title, and cannot complain.

I cannot see any reason for confining the judgment to the two parcels. All three seem to me to be in the same position.

The result is, that the petitioner's appeal fails, and the claimants succeed, and I cannot see any reason why costs should not follow.

[Affirmed on appeal (1914), 33 O.L.R. 51.]

QUESTION. Do the accepted principles of building schemes properly apply to a case such as this, where the purchasers are given positive rights over land not included in the grant in fee to them? Compare the analytical approach of the English courts in the next cases.

RE ELLENBOROUGH PARK. [1955] 3 All E.R. 667 (England. Court of Appeal). A conveyance provided, in part, that the purchaser should have "also the full enjoyment . . . at all times hereafter in common with the other persons to whom such easements may be granted of the pleasure ground set out and made in front of the said plot of land intended to be hereby granted in the centre of the square called Ellenborough Park . . . but subject to the payment of a fair and just proportion of the costs charges and expenses of keeping in good order and condition the said pleasure ground."

The judgment of the Court of Appeal was delivered by Sir Raymond Evershed M. R., who affirmed the decision of Dankwerts J. who had held that the right conveyed was an easement. The judgments in both courts are lengthy, and carefully reasoned, and should be referred to for their terms. The line of analysis is merely indicated by the following excerpts, as an alternative to the analysis offered in the principal case. SIR RAYMOND EVERSHED M.R.: "The substantial question raised in this appeal is whether the respondent, or those whom he has been appointed to represent, being the owners of certain houses fronting on, or, in some few cases, adjacent to, the garden or park known as Ellenborough Park in Weston-super-Mare, have any right known to the law, and now enforceable by them against the owners of the park, to the use and enjoyment of the park to the extent and in the manner later more precisely defined. Both the premises now belonging to the respondent, or to the owners for whom he acts as champion, [who will be referred as the 'owners of the houses'] and also the park itself, were originally part of an estate known as the White Cross Estate. The houses in question were built and the park laid out in the middle of the last century. None of the owners of the houses is an original grantee from the proprietors of the White Cross Estate. Similarly, the present owners of the park are the successors in title of the original grantors of the premises of the house owners . . .

"The exact area of 'the White Cross Estate' was not proved; but Ellenborough Park (that is the pleasure ground) and the road round it (Ellenborough Crescent or Crescent Road) is a rectangular area measuring about 350 yards from east to west and about one hundred yards from north to south, its western boundary facing the sea. The right was granted to the purchasers of each of the plots of lands, the houses on which face inwards round the Crescent Road into the park; but it was also granted in respect of some nine or ten other plots not actually facing into the park but separated from the Crescent Road only by houses so fronting. There appear to be no private ways from the houses built on these other plots direct to the Crescent Road and the Park. Access in these cases to the park has to be obtained by the short distance over the ordinary roads in no case more than about 150 or 200 yards. It does not appear what, if any, special obligations were imposed on the original purchasers of these last few houses as regards the character of the houses and the like . . .

"The original common vendors were engaged on a scheme of development of this part of the White Cross Estate designed to produce a result of common experience; namely, a row of uniform houses facing inwards on a park or garden which was intended to form, and formed in fact, an essential characteristic belonging, and properly speaking 'appurtenant,' to all and each of them. In substance, instead of each house being confined to its own small or moderate garden, each was to enjoy in common, but in common exclusively with the other houses in the crescent, a single large 'private' garden . . .

"It is clear . . . that if the owners of the houses are now entitled to an enforceable right in respect of the use and enjoyment of Ellenborough Park, that right must have the character and quality of an easement as understood by, and known to, our law. It has, therefore, been necessary for us to consider carefully the qualities and characteristics of easements, and for such purpose to look back into the history of that category of incorporeal rights in the development of English real property law. It may be fairly assumed that in *Duncan* v. *Louch*, the Court of Queen's Bench, in 1845, and particularly Lord Denman, C.J., who delivered the first judgment in the court, was of opinion that such a right as the owners of the houses claim was capable of fulfilling the qualifying conditions of an easement. Buckley, J., in 1904 in *Keith* v. *Twentieth Century Club, Ltd.* answered certain questions which Byrne, J., had ordered to be set down to be argued before the court, themselves depending on the assumption that such a right could exist in law. On the other hand, Farwell, J., a judge peculiarly experienced and learned in real property law, on two occasions, namely in 1903 in *International Tea Stores Co.* v. *Hobbs*, and in 1905 in *A.-G.* v. *Antrobus,* used language appearing to treat as axiomatic the proposition that a right which should properly be described as a *jus spatiandi* was a right excluded by English law, as by Roman law, from the company of servitudes . . . Although the existence of gardens surrounded by houses, the owners or occupiers of which enjoy in practice the amenities of the gardens, is a well-known feature of town development throughout the country, no other case appears to have come before the courts in which the validity of the rights in fact enjoyed in the gardens has even been tested.

"For the purposes of the argument before us counsel were content to adopt, as correct, the four characteristics formulated in Dr. Cheshire's *Modern Real Property* (7th Edn.), p. 456 et seq. They are (i) There must be a dominant and a servient tenement: (ii) an easement must accommodate the dominant tenement: (iii) dominant and servient owners must be different persons: and (iv) a right over land cannot amount to an easement unless it is capable of forming the subject-matter of a grant.

"Two of the four may be disregarded for present purposes, viz., the first and the third. If the garden or park is, as it is alleged to be, the servient tenement in the present case, then it is undoubtedly distinct from the alleged dominant tenements, viz., the freeholds of the several houses whose owners claim to exercise the rights. It is equally clear that if these lands respectively constitute the servient and dominant tenements, then they are owned by different persons. The argument in the case is found accordingly to turn on the meaning and application to the circumstances of the present case of the second and fourth conditions; i.e., first, whether the alleged easement can be said in truth to 'accommodate' the dominant tenement, in other words, whether there exists the required 'connection' between the one and the other; and, second, whether the right alleged is 'capable of forming the subject-matter of a grant.' The exact significance of this fourth and last condition is, at first sight perhaps, not entirely clear. As between the original parties to the 'grant' it is not in doubt that rights of this kind would be capable of taking effect by way of contract or licence. But for the purposes of the present case, as the arguments made clear, the cognate questions involved under this condition are: whether the rights purported to be given are expressed in terms of too wide and vague a character; whether, if and so far as effective, such rights would amount to rights of joint occupation or would substantially deprive the owners of the park of proprietorship or legal possession; whether, if and so far as effective, such rights constitute mere rights of recreation, possessing no quality of utility or benefit; and on such grounds cannot qualify as easements."

[The court accepted *Duncan* v. *Louch* as "authoritative in favour of the the recognition by our law as an easement of a right closely comparable to that now in question which, if it involves in some sense a '*jus spatiandi*', is nevertheless properly annexed and appurtenant to a defined hereditament."]

NOTE ON THE SUBSEQUENT HISTORY OF THE LORNE PARK PROPERTY. The following facts are gathered from a statutory declaration prepared by a solicitor in connection with a matter not relevant here.

Lorne Park Estates Limited was incorporated in 1919 and on the 9th of June, 1919, Sidney Small, the purchaser, at a sale by auction under power of sale when default was made under second mortgage on the unsold lands, conveyed the property to the Lorne Park Estates Limited. The Company at no time received an assignment of the covenants contained in the various conveyances granted by the original company, The Toronto and Lorne Park Summer Resort Co., requiring among other things, that the consent of the original Company, The Toronto and Lorne Park Summer Resort Co., in writing, must be given to any conveyance.

In 1922 Lorne Park Estates Limited amended Plans B-88 and C-89 by closing up certain of the streets, opening new streets and the new plan was registered as No. A-23, which plan also resubdivided many of the lots.

In the year 1948, the Lorne Park Estates Limited conveyed all the unsold lots on Plans B-88, C-89 and A-23 to Stanley Stuart Mills and Vincent Walter Price, Trustees of the Estate of Mary Louise Clarke, and by Supplementary Letters Patent changed its name to Lorne Park Estates Association, surrendered its share capital and became a corporation without share capital and not operated for gain. The Lorne Park Estates Association remained the owner of the private roads and commons in the Park.

During the years following the acquisition of the property by Lorne Park Estates Limited in 1919, that Company provided certain services to the property owners in the Park and attempted to collect fees for the cost of the services. Substantial difficulty arose in enforcing the collection because the Company did not hold an assignment of the covenants held by the original Company, The Toronto and Lorne Park Summer Resort Co.

In some cases Lorne Park Estates Limited joined as a party in certain conveyances from private owners to purchasers of lots in the Park giving its consent to the sale. The consents were given either in connection with undertakings and arrangements for the provision of Park services to the purchasers, or because the consents were requested, although Lorne Park Estates Limited did not assert that such consents were necessary. The consents were given by Lorne Park Estates Limited only after the proposed purchaser had signed a service agreement with Lorne Park Estates Limited and in some cases the purchasers of lots in the Park declined to sign the agreement for services and in such cases the sales were completed without the consent of Lorne Park Estates Limited.

The Lorne Park Estates Association is now running into a difficult problem of raising money to pay for the maintenance of the roads, which have not been taken over by the Township of Toronto. Consideration has been given to a proposal to introduce a private bill before the Ontario Legislature, making it compulsory for all residents to contribute to the upkeep of the roads.

6. Flexibility: Private Power To Vary Restrictions

RE ZIERLER

Ontario. High Court 1957. 8 D.L.R. (2d) 189

Wilson J.: This is an application for an order declaring that the restrictive covenants contained in the deeds numbered 4752 and 5149 for the Village of Point Edward in the said County, are not now binding on Lots 40, 41, 42 and 43 and that part of Lot 39 in the Village of Point Edward in the said County, according to registered Plan No. 7 for the village as more particularly described in the deed 99616, for the County of Lambton.

The lands comprising the subdivision were registered as Plan No. 7 on July 5, 1948. They consist of lots numbered 2 to 89, and an unnumbered triangle of land at the north-east corner of the subdivision. There is no Lot No. 1. All of the necessary parties, owners and mortgagees have been served.

The applicant is opposed by the owners of eleven of the lots, Nos. 20, 26, 30, 32, 35, 36, 38, 44, 66, 77, 84. The point to be decided is whether there is a building scheme applicable to this subdivision. The applicant contends there is not, those who oppose the application contend there is.

After perusing the material filed in support of this application, I have come to the conclusion that when the plan of subdivision was registered the owners contemplated selling most of the lots for residential purposes with the same restrictions throughout, namely, that a house costing not less than $6,500 and other restrictions mentioned would apply to each lot with certain exceptions. It was always the intention to transfer two lots to the village for park purposes, and that Lots 12 to 17, both inclusive, were to be transferred to the Crown for highway purposes, and, putting a construction most favourable to the respondents upon the material before the Court, a gasoline service station was to be erected on the triangle already referred to above. I find that this intention was not carried out and that the conclusion to be drawn from the material filed is that the owners failed to exact restrictions in respect of all lots sold, save those referred to in such a manner as to indicate that they were under no obligation to any purchaser or purchasers to impose restrictions in respect of lots remaining unsold and hence there could not be a building scheme under the third requirement as laid down in the well known case of *Re Wheeler* (1926). This is quite clear when an examination is made of the chronological order of the sales.

The first sale according to the plan was registered on November 1, 1949, to the Government of Lots 12 to 17 already mentioned, and in addition a small corner of Lot 39 and the whole of Lot 40. There were no restrictions on any of these lots. The next sale appears to have been Lots 18 to 40 on June 1, 1950, all subject to restrictions. Then followed four conveyances of 8 lots subject to restrictions, and on May 19, 1952, a conveyance to one Chrapko of Lots 71 and 72 at the north-east corner of the plan with no building restrictions and there were five conveyances of 5 lots with restrictions. Then on July 21, 1952, Lots 2 to 11 and part of Lot 75 were conveyed to the Government of the Province of Ontario for highway purposes and on this conveyance there were no restrictions. Only parts of these lots were so used and the remainder are being sold by tender. No one knows to what use they may be put. Then there were five more conveyances of 5 lots with restrictions. On September 9, 1952, one Phelps bought Lot 76 with no restrictions. On November 25, 1952, Lots 73 and 74 and part of Lot 75 were sold with no restrictions. Following this there were fourteen conveyances of 23 lots in all containing restrictions and finally on March 9th, 1955, the last conveyance consisted of Lots 61 and 62 to the Village of Point Edward with no restrictions. There are no lots unsold now and the trustees have disbanded. It is my understanding that these lots are to be used for park purposes, but the question of whether or not the village may sell them or use them for other purposes is not before me and I have not sufficient information concerning this aspect to justify the expression of any opinion concerning the use of these 2 lots. There are no restrictions registered against them.

The land was held by trustees, under circumstances which need not be recounted here, for realization, and the decision to sell this land as a residential subdivision was arrived at by them. The title to all the lands was registered in the name of one Kenny, who received his instructions from the trustees and he in turn gave instructions to one Nelson who was also a trustee, and, as I understand it, the only person who had any communication with the public. I understand that the form of deed used is that which appears by the conveyance from William H. Kenny to Lyle Stanley Horner dated May 26, 1950. This is ex. D to the affidavit of Wilfred Ray Oliver, sworn on November 23, 1956. It is in the form usually used when an absolute owner conveys an estate in fee simple, and contains the usual covenants. It is not the form usually used by trustees. The land is referred to in that deed as being Lots 18 to 49 and is a grant to the grantee in fee simple, and I now quote: "To the intent that the burden of this covenant may run with the land, the Grantee doth hereby covenant and agree on behalf of himself, his heirs, executors, administrators and assigns, with the Grantor, that the Grantee, his heirs, executors, administrators and assigns will henceforth observe and comply with the stipulations, restrictions, and provisions hereinafter set forth in respect of the land hereby conveyed and that nothing shall ever be erected, fixed, placed or done upon the land in breach or violation or contrary to the fair meaning of the said stipulations, restrictions and provisions but this covenant is not to be held binding upon the Grantee or any other person except in respect of breaches committed or continued during their, his or her joint or sole seisin of or title to the lands upon or in respect of which such breaches have been committed."

I think it is fair to say that many, if not all of the purchasers, who purchased subject to restrictions, thought they were buying land which was adequately protected by the building restrictions. On the other hand, neither the trustees, nor Kenny personally in the deeds, ever placed themselves in the position where they were bound to impose restrictions on any or all lots. In Kenny's cross-examination upon his affidavit filed upon the motion the conclusion is plain that the trustees could instruct him at any time and in respect of any lot or lots that restrictions were not to be imposed, and that is apparently what happened concerning Lots 2 to 14, part of Lot 39, all of Lot 40, Lots 73, 74, 76 and part of Lot 75. This was probably deliberate. The trustees had held these lands for 20 years and they were endeavouring to salvage what they could from their investment.

It is well known that the profit or loss on a subdivision comes out of the sale of the last lots which are sold and if a subdivision does not sell well, and if the vendor is bound by the building restrictions which he has put on, so that he can not change the conditions he may very well have a loss on his hands as in so many subdivisions. The restrictive covenants, therefore, do not always give the purchaser all the protection that he expects that he is going to receive. I think that there was no obligation as of the time that the subdivision was put on the market to exact the same covenants from all the purchasers or substantially all of the purchasers who would in future buy the lots. That is a fair deduction after considering all the evidence. There are some very strong statements to the contrary in the affidavits which have been filed on behalf of the owners who are opposed to this application, but considering those affidavits in the light of the cross-examinations upon them I have come to the conclusion that the vendors were entitled to leave open the question of what restrictions they would exact. I must say that I have a good deal of sympathy for the residents who are opposed to this application but the drafting of building restrictions is not a matter to be done lightly and indeed requires a good deal of care if a building scheme is to be effectively established. In my opinion, however, the arguments as presented by Mr. Jamieson should be adopted. Both counsel have carefully prepared their arguments which have been full and exhaustive, but I must say that I have come to the conclusion that this motion may be decided under the law as stated in the leading case of *Elliston* v. *Reacher* [Wilson J. cited the report of the case in the trial court.]

There was vagueness in the minds of the trustees as to what was to be the defined portion to which the residential restrictions were to be made to apply. It is clear, as I have already indicated, they considered they could give a deed to any lot or any number of lots without any restrictions and that they did so. In order to establish a building scheme, the respondents must prove what the scheme was. In this they have failed. The trustees appear to have had a general plan in mind but it did not amount to a building scheme at the time the subdivision was put on. I think they were leaving themselves an escape when they decided that in their discretion the restrictions in any particular case were not to be inserted in a deed and that this was their policy.

I think there are other grounds upon which the opposition to this motion fails, but, in the circumstances it is unnecessary to discuss them.

In the result the applicant is entitled to the order which he asks. The applicant is not asking for costs as I understand it and I make no order as to costs.

RE LANKIN. [1951] O.W.N. 821 (Ontario. High Court). AYLEN J.: "... It is my view that since The Canada Permanent Trust Company reserved the right to waive the restrictions with respect to any particular lot, the restrictions in question never constituted a building scheme which is now enforceable ... There was no common scheme as a result of which these building restrictions were imposed, for the simple reason that the trust company could, at any time, waive the restrictions with respect to any particular lot. Apart from that fact, there was such a break in the imposition of the restrictions that there is no one who can now enforce them. ..."

WHITEHOUSE *v.* HUGH [1906] 1 Ch. 253 (England. Chancery Division). KEKEWICH J.: "... But, further, the conveyance, as I have said, was subject to certain conditions, and by the ninth condition 'the vendors reserve to themselves the power of allowing a variation of the plans and conditions.' In none of the cases which have come before the Court has there been a reservation of any power of that kind, but reference has been made to the possibility of sustaining such a reservation, and it has been assumed that it would be perfectly good. Now the relation between the parties in all these building scheme cases is contractual. The question is as to the enforcement of a bargain which is to be found in some statement or representation from which the Court has implied a contract that certain conditions shall be observed. Directly that conclusion is come to, the question is one of contractual relation, and if one of the parties has put in a reservation of power to alter the contract, then that reservation becomes part of the contract itself, whether that contract is expressed or implied. In other words, if the plaintiff is bound by part of the contract he is equally bound by the whole of it, including the reservation. The difficulty is to make the reservation fit in with the circumstances of this case. The ninth condition is not happily worded. The condition is that the vendors may allow others to make variations in the plans and conditions; not that they themselves may make variations. I do not think that this condition would enable the vendors to vary the plans and conditions to any extent they please. Take a critical instance. By the sixth condition the vendors must make the roads specified in the scheme. It seems to me it would be impossible to allow the vendors to say, 'We will not make the roads,' or 'We will not make all of them,' or 'We will make them differently,' or 'We will alter them when made.' The language of the condition is not very apt, but I think that it means this: The vendors having represented that the houses should be built in a certain way, they allow a purchaser to build in a different manner—as, for instance, two houses on a plot instead of one, or a shop instead of a dwelling-house, or to make other similar variations. If that is the meaning of it, why should they not allow a purchaser to build on this vacant space?. . . "

WHITEHOUSE *v*. HUGH. [1906] 2 Ch. 283 (England. Court of Appeal). Kekewich J. was affirmed on appeal. VAUGHAN WILLIAMS L.J.: " . . . The answer to that contention is that that might have been true if it had not been for the fact that the 9th condition, subject to which the appellant took his conveyance, gave the society an absolute power to alter the scheme by closing the road in question. I am not sure whether that condition gave the society power to make any alteration in the scheme which they pleased, such as what counsel for the appellant, in the course of his argument, called a radical alteration, but it is clear that at any rate it covers the closing of this road . . . "

ELLISTON *v*. REACHER. [1908] 2 Ch. 665 (England. Court of Appeal). COZENS-HARDY M. R.: " . . . The plaintiff says there was a building scheme affecting this estate, which was divided up into lots. . . . including the restriction on building an hotel without the consent of the vendors, . . . Lest it should be supposed that I have forgotten, I will say there is also added at the end a provision that the vendors reserve a right to deal with any part of the estate not disposed of without reference to these conditions. . . .

"Then it is said that the whole scheme is inconsistent and cannot have been intended, because there was power in the vendor to deal with property undisposed of without reference to this deed. That is an argument which has not been brought forward for the first time here. So far as I am aware it is an argument that has never prevailed. I do not deny that the insertion of such a power is an element to be considered, but out of many building schemes which I have seen I think I am right in this remark, that it is altogether exceptional not to see some power reserved to the vendor to abstract certain property from the scheme. On the face of the scheme, which all the parties were content with, they were told that they entered into this building scheme with the knowledge that the vendors might, if they were so advised, on the one hand give consent to the erection of a public-house next door to the man who bought a lot, and on the other hand release any unsold property from the covenants. I cannot see that that has any real importance in the case."

ZETLAND *v*. DRIVER. [1939] Ch. 1 (England. Court of Appeal). The covenant provided that no act or thing should be done or permitted on the land which in the opinion of the vendor might be prejudicial or detrimental to him and the owners or occupiers of any adjoining property or to the neighbourhood. The vendor formed an opinion that selling fish and chips for consumption off the premises was detrimental to the amenities of the neighbourhood and to his own property. He was challenged on procedural grounds. FARWELL J.: "They further say that the opinion of the appellant was wholly unreasonable and capricious and that in forming an opinion he was acting in a quasi-judicial capacity and was, therefore, bound to give the respondents an opportunity of being heard before coming to any conclusion and that this he has failed to do. In addition, they plead laches and acquiescence as a bar to the relief sought.

"It will be convenient to dispose at once of those last mentioned pleas. In our judgment, there is no foundation for the plea of laches or acquiescence, nor is there anything in the evidence to support the contention that the opinion which the appellant formed as to the respondents' business was capricious or other than a bona fide opinion formed after a proper consideration of the facts. In forming his opinion the appellant was in no sense performing a judicial or quasi-judicial function, and he was, therefore, under no obligation to give the respondents an opportunity of being heard. . . ."

QUESTIONS. If an opportunity to be heard is not required, is the discretion of the vendor quite unfettered? What effect can be given to the implication that his discretion must not be "capricious or other than a bona fide opinion"?

RESTRICTIVE COVENANTS. 1958. Don Mills Developments Ltd. Schedule A. Clause 24: Provided always that notwithstanding anything herein contained, the Grantor and its successors shall have power by instrument or instruments in writing from time to time to waive, alter or modify the above covenants and restrictions in their application to any lot or lots, parcel or parcels of land comprising part of the said lands without notice to the owners of any other lot or lots, parcel or parcels of land on the said plans. [Is this clause such that the "building scheme" is defeated? How would you have drafted it?]

Clause 26. To the intent that the burden of this covenant shall run with the said lands for a period of forty years from the 1st day of February, 1954, the Grantee, for himself and his heirs, executors, administrators, successors, and assigns, covenants and agrees with the Grantor, its successors and assigns that the grantee's successors in title from time to time of all or any part or parts of the said lands, will observe and comply with the stipulations, restrictions and provisions set forth in Schedule A herein. [Why is clause 26 in the schedule rather than in the text of the agreement? Is this clause sufficient to create a building scheme? The agreement provides that "The Purchaser agrees . . . to observe and comply with the . . . restrictions . . . set forth in Schedule A hereto, and every deed from the Vendor to the Purchaser shall contain a covenant to such effect and be executed by the Purchaser." Does this clause help to establish a building scheme?]

RE PINEWOOD ESTATE, NEW IDEAL HOMESTEADS, LTD *v.* LEVACK

England. Chancery Division. [1957] 2 All E.R. 517

WYNN-PARRY J.: There is no doubt that the applicant is bound by the terms of the deed of 1899, so far as the burden of the covenants therein contained is concerned. The question which I have to determine is whether the respondent or anybody else is entitled to enforce those covenants.

I propose first to consider whether there is in existence what is conveniently known as a building scheme affecting this area of land clearly ascertained; because if there is an existing building scheme fulfilling the conditions laid down by Parker, J., in *Elliston* v. *Reacher*, the covenants attach, and the respondent and the other persons interested will have the benefit of the covenants in the deed.

It is rightly conceded that immediately prior to the execution of this deed on Dec. 21, 1899, there was such a building scheme. There was a common vendor, the Capital & Counties Bank, Ltd., which was dealing with land which had been laid out, for the purpose of development in lots, and the bank sold the lots to the persons who were parties to the deed of 1899. It is also clear that in the conveyances to these parties the bank imposed certain restrictions, with the terms of which I am not concerned. The purchasers from the bank were apparently not satisfied with the restrictions which had been imposed on them respectively by the bank, and therefore they entered into the deed of 1899 for the purpose of bringing into existence a new set of restrictions.

The question arises (and this, of course, is a question of construction) what was the effect of what they did? Was it merely, as has been contended by the respondent, to alter the terms of the building scheme so far as regards the restrictions, or was the effect, as is contended for on behalf of the applicant, to destroy the building scheme and put in its place this document as constituting the entirety of the rights of the parties against each other?

In the first place it is to be observed that the bank is not a party to the deed. The bank, it is agreed, had conveyed to the four parties to the deed of 1899, all the land in the neighbourhood in which it had been interested. No doubt it was therefore thought there was no need to make the bank a party. The document recites the interest of the respective parties and says that the land conveyed to them was conveyed on the basis of it being subject to the observance and performance of certain restrictive stipulations contained in the schedules to the respective documents by which their shares in the land were conveyed to them. Then there appears this recital:

"And whereas the parties hereto have agreed to release each other from the said restrictive stipulations which are scheduled to the four several hereinbefore recited indentures of conveyance and in consideration of such release, to enter into the covenant hereinafter contained for the observance and performance of the restrictive stipulations contained in the schedule to these presents it being intended that the restrictive stipulations contained in the schedule to these presents shall supersede the aforesaid restrictive stipulations which are scheduled to the four several hereinbefore recited indentures of conveyance."

In the operative part that intention was carried out in this language:

"Now this indenture witnesseth that in consideration of the premises the parties to these presents do hereby mutually release and discharge each other and their respective heirs and assigns and the freehold hereditaments and premises to which the same relate from the restrictive stipulations which are scheduled to the four hereinbefore recited indentures of conveyance and in consideration thereof each of the parties to these presents doth hereby covenant for himself or herself, his or her heirs and assigns with each other party hereto and every two and three of them, his, her or their heirs and assigns, and with intent to bind the land to which the restrictive stipulations contained in the schedule to these presents relate into whosesoever hands the same may come . . . to observe, perform, fulfil and keep the restrictive stipulations contained in the schedule to these presents so far as the same relate to the hereditaments and premises of and belonging to the respective covenantors."

Let me comment on that language: In the first place, both in the recital and in the operative part the word "release" is used, and, indeed, in the operative part the phrase "release and discharge" is used; so that what was done—and there can be no doubt about this—was that the pre-existing set of restrictive stipulations was abolished, and the parties and each of them were discharged therefrom. Then with deliberate intent there was brought into existence a number of new restrictive stipulations which were set out in the schedule to the deed, to the language of which I need not refer.

As was pointed out by counsel for the applicant, if this document had been expressed to be supplemental to the four pre-existing documents there might have been some ground for the argument that this document should be treated merely as a modification of an existing scheme, but it was not so expressed to be supplemental. In view of the language which is used, it is a document which, to my mind, wipes out the past so far as the restrictions as to user are concerned and which brings into existence as between these four parties for all purposes a new set of restrictive stipulations. The parties by the language which they have used, must be taken to have determined that for the future their rights as between each other would depend on and be found only in this deed of Dec. 21, 1899. I therefore conclude that there is no building scheme, within the meaning of that phrase as used in *Elliston* v. *Reacher*, in existence, and that therefore the respondent cannot assert with success that she can obtain the benefit of the restrictive stipulations by virtue of this document.

What, then, is her position? It is admitted by counsel for the applicant that she could claim the benefit of the restrictive covenants if it could be shown either that the benefit had been annexed by proper words of annexation or that there was a complete chain of assignments of the benefit of the covenants; but it is conceded on behalf of the respondent that there are no words of annexation, and it is conceded that the chain is not complete. In those circumstances, the respondent says that she is entitled to the benefit of the restrictive provisions because it is a deed which shows clearly by its language an intention that the parties should be mutually bound by the restrictions and that that element of mutuality is enough to carry the benefit of the restrictive stipulations. That means that she is endeavouring to set up a further method by which the benefit of the restrictive stipulations can be transferred. She relies on *Whatman* v. *Gibson* (1838); but on examination it will be found that in that case there was a common vendor, and I think that that decision can be supported on the basis that, notwithstanding the fact that it was decided so long ago, it really contains the essential elements which Parker, J., required in *Elliston* v. *Reacher*. Therefore, I do not think that it affords the respondent any support.

The real question is: Is there a fourth class at all? The first class is the *Elliston* v. *Reacher* type of case; the second consists of cases where there are proper words of annexation; the third consists of cases where there is a continuous chain of express assignments. But is there a fourth class?

In *Osborne* v. *Bradley* (1903) Farwell J., said:

"This is an action on a covenant in a deed made between the plaintiff, Mr. Osborne, and Mr. Bavin. Mr. Bradley, the defendant, was a purchaser from Bavin. The conveyance was made expressly subject to the covenants contained in the conveyance from Osborne to Bavin. It is a conveyance in fee. Negative covenants in conveyances in fee restricting the right of the purchaser to use the land purchased may for the purposes of a case like the present be considered as falling under three classes: (i) where the covenant is entered into simply for the vendor's own benefit; (ii) where the covenant is for the benefit of the vendor in his capacity of owner of a particular property; and (iii) where the covenant is for the benefit of the vendor, in so far as he reserves unsold property, and also for the benefit of other purchasers, as part of what is called a building scheme."

I am not concerned with the first class, and the third class is obviously the *Elliston* v. *Reacher* type of case. Counsel for the applicant submitted, and I think he was right, that the second class stated by Farwell J., is really to be sub-divided into two classes, namely, annexation and continuous chain of assignment. That, I think, emerges from *Re Union of London & Smith's Bank, Ltd.'s Conveyance, Miles* v. *Easter* (1933). The judgment of the Court of Appeal was delivered by Romer L.J., who said:

"That the plaintiff is bound by the covenants in question is not disputed, in view of the fact that he purchased his lands with notice of them. What is in dispute is the question whether the defendants are entitled to the benefit of such covenants. Now the defendants are not the original covenantees, and it therefore becomes necessary to ascertain what person other than the original covenantee is entitled to the benefit of a restrictive covenant affecting land. This question was put to himself by Hall, V.-C. in *Renals* v. *Cowlishaw* (1878) and the answer was given in a judgment so well known that it is unnecessary to refer to it at length. It is a judgment that has received the approval both of this court and of the House of Lords, and has always been regarded as a correct statement of the law upon the subject. Stated shortly, it laid down this: that, apart from what are usually referred to as building scheme cases (and this is not a case of that sort), a purchaser from the original covenantee of land retained by him when he executed the conveyance containing the covenant will be entitled to the benefit of the covenant if the conveyance shows that the covenant was intended to enure for the benefit of that particular land. It follows that, if what is being acquired by the purchaser was only part of the land shown by the conveyance as being intended to be benefited, it must also be shown that the benefit was intended to enure to each portion of that land. In such cases the benefit of the restrictive covenant will pass to the purchaser without being mentioned. It runs with the land. In all other cases the purchaser will not acquire the benefit of the covenant unless that benefit be expressly assigned to him—or, to use the words of the vice-chancellor, 'it must appear that the benefit of the covenant was part of the subject-matter of the purchase'."

In my view, that passage establishes the other two classes. But I can find no authority, certainly none was cited to me, which establishes the fourth class suggested. In my opinion, therefore, it is not open either to the respondent or to anybody else on this line of reasoning to rely on these restrictive covenants. . . .

In the result, I propose to make a declaration in accordance with para. 1 of the summons.

NOTE AND QUESTIONS. The applicant, the owner of part of the Pinewood Estate, sought a declaration that its land was not affected by the covenants in the deed of 1899. The respondent, the owner of other land in the Estate, contended that she was entitled to the benefit of the covenants.

Could the difficulty here be got over by the interested owners conveying to a trustee on trust to reconvey subject to the agreed covenants? If so, is there any purpose in refusing to recognize the device used in this case?

SHARP *v.* QUINN. 1931. 4 P. 2d. 942 (California. Supreme Court). The following clause was held valid:
"That at any time after sixteen (16) of the lots in said Outside Land Block No. 220 have been sold and conveyed by the said parties of the first part, their heirs and successors or assigns, the several restrictions, conditions and covenants aforesaid may be abrogated, rescinded, or annulled, in whole or in part, by the owners of not less than sixteen (16) of the lots in said block, evidenced by an instrument in writing executed by the said owners in the manner provided by law for the conveyance of real property, and duly recorded in the office of the county recorder aforesaid."

7. Group Control of The Restrictions

The attempts of the purchasers in the *Pinewood Estate* case to "control their own destiny", and the setting up of the Lorne Park Estates Association as a non-profit corporation to hold the "common land" point to a need for some refinement of the building scheme whereby the inhabitants as a group can exercise the power to vary the restrictions as they choose. Some developers deliberately avoid setting up a building scheme because they feel that many house buyers are reluctant to live in an area where neighbour may be set against neighbour and each man is his own policeman. If the only alternative to a building scheme is the *Tulk* v. *Moxhay/L.C.C.* v. *Allen* type of covenant, that type carries with it the handicap that the control may stop when the vendor sells the last lot. Two practices that overcome this handicap are growing in popularity.

The first practice is typified by the Don Mills development. The fact that the development corporation remains the owner of the land on which the shopping centre stands ensures the existence of a person legally capable of enforcing the covenants and a person with a real incentive to keep the area in a good state since it will maintain or increase his shopping centre profits. If there is no building scheme, however, and the covenants have benefited only the land retained by the developer there is still the objection that the developer may not always be as alert as he should be or will exercise his discretion in an unpopular way. And there is also the objection that the developer's control is too autocratic.

The second practice is represented by the Lorne Park Estates Association, where the autocratic developer is replaced by an association of the inhabitants. In the Lorne Park situation there would seem to be little difficulty, since the "Association" is a corporation and has the same property interest in the covenants as the developer who preceded it. Can the result be obtained by arrangements short of incorporation to acquire the developer's remaining interest in the name of an association of the inhabitants?

NEPONSIT PROPERTY OWNERS' ASSOCIATION, INC. *v.* EMIGRANT INDUSTRIAL SAVINGS BANK

New York. Court of Appeals. 1938. 15 N.E. (2d) 793

Lehman J.: The plaintiff, as assignee of Neponsit Realty Company, has brought this action to foreclose a lien upon land which the defendant owns. The lien, it is alleged, arises from a covenant condition or charge contained in a deed of conveyance of the land from Neponsit Realty Company to a predecessor in title of the defendant. The defendant purchased the land at a judicial sale. The referee's deed to the defendant and every deed in the defendant's chain of title since the conveyance of the land by Neponsit Realty Company purports to convey the property subject to the covenant, condition or charge contained in the original deed. . . .

It appears that in January, 1911, Neponsit Realty Company, as owner of a tract of land in Queens county, caused to be filed in the office of the clerk of the county a map of the land. The tract was developed for a strictly residential community, and Neponsit Realty Company conveyed lots in the tract to purchasers, describing such lots by reference to the filed map and to roads and streets shown thereon. In 1917, Neponsit Realty Company conveyed the land now owned by the defendant to Robert Oldner Deyer and his wife by deed which contained the covenant upon which the plaintiff's cause of action is based.

That covenant provides:

"And the party of the second part for the party of the second part and the heirs, successors and assigns of the party of the second part further covenants that the property conveyed by this deed shall be subject to an annual charge in such an amount as will be fixed by the party of the first part, its successors and assigns, not, however exceeding in any year the sum of four ($4.00) Dollars per lot 20 x 100 feet. The assigns of the party of the first part may include a Property Owners' Association which may hereafter be organized for the purposes referred to in this paragraph, and in case such association is organized the sums in this paragraph provided for shall be payable to such association. The party of the second part for the party of the second part and the heirs, successors and assigns of the party of the second part covenants that they will pay this charge to the party of the first part, its successors and assigns on the first day of May in each and every year, and further covenants that said charge shall on said date in each year become a lien on the land and shall continue to be such lien until fully paid. Such charges shall be payable to the party of the first part or its successors or assigns, and shall be devoted to the maintenance of the roads, paths, parks, beach, sewers and such other public purposes as shall from time to time be determined by the party of the first part, its successors or assigns. And the party of the second part by the acceptance of this deed hereby expressly vests in the party of the first part, its successors and assigns, the right and power to bring all actions against the owner of the premises hereby conveyed or any part thereof for the collection of such charge and to enforce the aforesaid lien therefor.

"These covenants shall run with the land and shall be construed as real covenants running with the land until January 31st, 1940, when they shall cease and determine."

Every subsequent deed of conveyance of the property in the defendant's chain of title, including the deed from the referee to the defendant, contained, as we have said, a provision that they were made subject to covenants and restrictions of former deeds of record.

There can be no doubt that Neponsit Realty Company intended that the covenant should run with the land and should be enforceable by a property owners association against every owner of property in the residential tract which the realty company was then developing. The language of the covenant admits of no other construction. Regardless of the intention of the parties, a covenant will run with the land and will be enforceable against a subsequent purchaser of the land at the suit of one who claims the benefit of the covenant, only if the covenant complies with certain legal requirements. These requirements rest upon ancient rules and precedents. The age-old essentials of a real covenant, aside from the form of the covenant, may be summarily formulated as follows: (1) It must appear that grantor and grantee intended that the covenant should run with the land; (2) it must appear that the covenant is one "touching" or "concerning" the land with which it runs; (3) it must appear that there is "privity of estate" between the promisee or party claiming the benefit of the covenant and the right to enforce it, and the promisor or party who rests under the burden of the covenant. Clark on *Covenants and Interests Running with Land,* p. 74. Although the deeds of Neponsit Realty Company conveying lots in the tract it developed "contained a provision to the effect that the covenants ran with the land, such provision in the absence of the other legal requirements is insufficient to accomplish such a purpose." *Morgan Lake Co.* v. *New York, N.H. & H.R.R. Co.* In his opinion in that case, Judge Crane posed but found it unnecessary to decide many of the questions which the court must consider in this case.

The covenant in this case is intended to create a charge or obligation to pay a fixed sum of money to be "devoted to the maintenance of the roads, paths, parks, beach, sewers and such other public purposes as shall from time to time be determined by the party of the first part [the grantor], its successors or assigns." It is an affirmative covenant to pay money for use in connection with, but not upon, the land which it is said is subject to the burden of the covenant. Does such a covenant "touch" or "concern" the land? These terms are not part of a statutory definition, a limitation placed by the State upon the power of the courts to enforce covenants *intended* to run with the land by the parties who entered into the covenants. Rather they are words used by courts in England in old cases to describe a limitation which the courts themselves created or to formulate a test which the courts have devised and which the courts voluntarily apply. . . . In truth such a description or test so formulated is too vague to be of much assistance and judges and academic scholars alike have struggled, not with entire success, to formulate a test at once more satisfactory and more accurate. "It has been found impossible to state any absolute tests to determine what covenants touch and concern land and what do not. The question is one for the court to determine in the exercise of its best judgment upon the facts of each case." *Clark, op. cit.* p. 76.

Even though that be true, a determination by a court in one case upon particular facts will often serve to point the way to correct decision in other cases upon analogous facts. Such guideposts may not be disregarded. It has been often said that a covenant to pay a sum of money is a personal affirmative covenant which usually does not concern or touch the land. Such statements are based upon English decisions which hold in effect that only covenants, which compel the covenanter to submit to some *restriction on the use* of his property, touch or concern the land, and that the burden of a covenant which requires the covenanter to do an affirmative act, even on his own land, for the benefit of the owner of a "dominant" estate, does not run with his land. *Miller* v. *Clary*. In that case the court pointed out that in many jurisdictions of this country the narrow English rule has been criticized and a more liberal and flexible rule has been substituted. In this State the courts have not gone so far. We have not abandoned the historic distinction drawn by the English courts. So this court has recently said:

"Subject to a few exceptions not important at this time, there is now in this state a settled rule of law that a covenant to do an affirmative act, as distinguished from a covenant merely negative in effect, does not run with the land so as to charge the burden of performance on a subsequent grantee [citing cases]. This is so though the burden of such a covenant is laid upon the very parcel which is the subject-matter of the conveyance." *Guaranty Trust Co. of New York* v. *New York & Queens County Ry. Co.*, opinion by Cardozo, Ch.J.

Both in that case and in the case of *Miller* v. *Clary* the court pointed out that there were some exceptions or limitations in the application of the general rule. Some promises to pay money have been enforced, as covenants running with the land, against subsequent holders of the land who took with notice of the covenant. Cf. *Greenfarb* v. *R. S. K. Realty Corp.*; *Morgan Lake Co.* v. *New York, N.H. & H.R.R. Co.* It may be difficult to classify these exceptions or to formulate a test of whether a particular covenant to pay money or to perform some other act falls within the general rule that ordinarily an affirmative covenant is a personal and not a real covenant, or falls outside the limitations placed upon the general rule. At least it must "touch" or "concern" the land in a substantial degree, and though it may be inexpedient and perhaps impossible to formulate a rigid test or definition which will be entirely satisfactory or which can be applied mechanically in all cases, we should at least be able to state the problem and find a reasonable method of approach to it. It has been suggested that a covenant which runs with the land must affect the legal relations—the advantages and the burdens—of the parties to the covenant, as owners of particular parcels of land and not merely as members of the community in general, such as taxpayers or owners of other land. *Clark*, *op. cit.* p. 76. Cf. Professor Bigelow's article on "The Contents of Covenants in Leases," 12 *Mich. L. Rev.* 639; 30 *Law Quarterly Review*, 319. That method of approach has the merit of realism. The test is based on the effect of the covenant rather than on technical distinctions. Does the covenant impose, on the one hand, a burden upon an interest in land, which on the other hand increases the value of a different interest in the same or related land?

Even though we accept that approach and test, it still remains true that whether a particular covenant is sufficiently connected with the use of land to run with the land, must be in many cases a question of degree. A promise to pay for something to be done in connection with the promisor's land does not differ essentially from a promise by the promisor to do the thing himself, and both promises constitute, in a substantial sense, a restriction upon the owner's right to use the land, and a burden upon the legal interest of the owner. On the other hand, a covenant to perform or pay for the performance of an affirmative act disconnected with the use of the land cannot ordinarily touch or concern the land in any substantial degree. Thus, unless we exalt technical form over substance, the distinction between covenants which run with land and covenants which are personal, must depend upon the effect of the covenant on the legal rights which otherwise would flow from ownership of land and which are connected with the land. The problem then is: Does the covenant in purpose and effect substantially alter these rights?

The opinion in *Morgan Lake Co.* v. *New York, N.H. & H.R.R. Co.* foreshadowed a classification based upon substance rather than upon form. It was not the first case, however, in which this court has based its decision on the substantial effect of a covenant upon legal relations of the parties as owners of land. Perhaps the most illuminating illustration of such an approach to the problem may be drawn from the "party wall" cases in this State which are reviewed in the opinion of the court in *Sebald* v. *Mulholland*. The court there pointed out that in cases, cited in the opinion, where by covenant between owners of adjoining parcels of land, "a designated party was authorized to build a party wall, the other agreeing to pay a portion of its value when it should be used by him," the court was constrained to hold that "the agreement was a present one. The party who was to build and the one who was to pay were expressly designated, and the covenant to pay was clearly a personal one". At the same time, the court also pointed out that such covenants must be distinguished from the covenants (passed upon by the court in the earlier case of *Mott* v. *Oppenheimer*, "by which the parties conferred, each upon the other, the authority to erect such [party] wall, and dedicated to that use a portion of each of their lots, with an agreement that, if either should build, the other might have the right to use it by paying his share of the expense". In such a case, it was said by the court: "It was not and could not then be known who would build, or who was to pay when the wall was used. The agreement was wholly prospective, and its purpose was to impose upon the land of each, and not upon either personally, the burden of a future party wall, and to secure to the land, and thus to its subsequent owners, a corresponding right to the use of the wall by paying one-half of its value.... In that case the character of the agreement, its obvious purpose, its prospective provisions, and the situation of the lands when the agreement was made, all concurred in showing an intent that its covenants should run with the land, and clearly justified the court in so holding".

Looking at the problem presented in this case from the same point of view and stressing the intent and substantial effect of the covenant rather than its form, it seems clear that the covenant may properly be said to touch and concern the land of the defendant and its burden should run with the land. True, it calls for payment of a sum of money to be expended for "public purposes" upon land other than the land conveyed by Neponsit Realty Company to plaintiff's predecessor in title. By that conveyance the grantee, however, obtained not only title to particular lots but an easement or right of common enjoyment with other property owners in roads, beaches, public parks or spaces and improvements in the same tract. For full enjoyment in common by the defendant and other property owners of these easements or rights, the roads and public places must be maintained. In order that the burden of maintaining public improvements should rest upon the land benefited by the improvements, the grantor exacted from the grantee of the land with its appurtenant easement or right of enjoyment a covenant that the burden of paying the cost should be inseparably attached to the land which enjoys the benefit. It is plain that any distinction or definition which would exclude such a covenant from the classification of covenants which "touch" or "concern" the land would be based on form and not on substance.

Another difficulty remains. Though between the grantor and the grantee there was privity of estate, the covenant provides that its benefit shall run to the assigns of the grantor who "may include a Property Owners' Association which may hereafter be organized for the purposes referred to in this paragraph." The plaintiff has been organized to receive the sums payable by the property owners and to expend them for the benefit of such owners. Various definitions have been formulated of "privity of estate" in connection with covenants that run with the land, but none of such definitions seems to cover the relationship between the plaintiff and the defendant in this case. The plaintiff has not succeeded to the ownership of any property of the grantor. It does not appear that it ever had title to the streets or public places upon which charges which are payable to it must be expended. It does not appear that it owns any other property in the residential tract to which any easement or right of enjoyment in such property is appurtenant. It is created solely to act as the assignee of the benefit of the covenant, and it has no interest of its own in the enforcement of the covenant.

The arguments that under such circumstances the plaintiff has no right of action to enforce a covenant running with the land are all based upon a distinction between the corporate property owners association and the property owners for whose benefit the association has been formed. If that distinction may be ignored, then the basis of the arguments is destroyed. How far privity of estate in technical form is necessary to enforce in equity a restrictive covenant upon the use of land, presents an interesting question. Enforcement of such covenants rests upon equitable principles . . . and at times, at least, the violation "of the restrictive covenant may be restrained at the suit of one who owns property or for whose benefit the restriction was established, irrespective of whether there were privity either of estate or of contract between the parties, or whether an action at law were maintainable." *Chesebro* v. *Moers*. The covenant in this case does not fall exactly within any classification of "restrictive" covenants, which have been enforced in this State (Cf. *Korn* v. *Campbell*) and no right to enforce even a restrictive covenant has been sustained in this State where the plaintiff did not own property which would benefit by such enforcement so that some of the elements of an equitable servitude are present. In some jurisdictions it has been held that no action may be maintained without such elements. But cf. *VanSant* v. *Rose*. We do not attempt to decide now how far the rule of *Trustees of Columbia College* v. *Lynch* will be carried, or to formulate a definite rule as to when, or even whether, covenants in a deed will be enforced, upon equitable principles, against subsequent purchasers with notice, at the suit of a party without privity of contract or estate. Cf. "Equitable Rights and Liabilities of Strangers to a Contract" by Harlan F. Stone, 18 *Columbia Law Review,* 291. There is no need to resort to such a rule if the courts may look behind the corporate form of the plaintiff.

The corporate plaintiff has been formed as a convenient instrument by which the property owners may advance their common interests. We do not ignore the corporate form when we recognize that the Neponsit Property Owners' Association, Inc., is acting as the agent or representative of the Neponsit property owners. As we have said in another case: when Neponsit Property Owners' Association, Inc., "was formed, the property owners were expected to, and have looked to that organization as the medium through which enjoyment of their common right might be preserved equally for all." *Matter of City of New York, Public Beach, Borough of Queens*. Under the conditions thus presented we said: "It may be difficult, or even impossible, to classify into recognized categories the nature of the interest of the membership corporation and its members in the land. The corporate entity cannot be disregarded, nor can the separate interests of the members of the corporation." Only blind adherence to an ancient formula devised to meet entirely different conditions could constrain the court to hold that a corporation formed as a medium for the enjoyment of common rights of property owners owns no property which would benefit by enforcement of common rights and has no cause of action in equity to enforce the covenant upon which such common rights depend. Every reason which in other circumstances may justify the ancient formula may be urged in support of the conclusion that the formula should not be applied in this case. In substance if not in form the covenant is a restrictive covenant which touches and concerns the defendant's land, and in substance, if not in form, there is privity of estate between the plaintiff and the defendant. . . .

HALSALL *v.* BRIZELL. [1957] Ch. 169 (England. Chancery). In this case the court had to decide on the validity of a clause in a building scheme set up in 1851 requiring the purchasers of lots in the scheme to pay the expenses incurred in maintaining roads and a sea wall promenade to which they had access. The roads and promenade were vested in the vendors in trust. The deed provided for annual meeting of owners for the time being of the lots at which the levies were determined. The defendants were executors of a purchaser who took subject to the covenants. UPJOHN J.: " . . . In so far as the deed of 1851 purports to make the successors of the original contracting parties liable to pay calls, is it valid and enforceable at all? I think that this much is plain: that the defendants could not be sued on the covenants contained in the deed for at least three reasons. First, a positive covenant in the terms of the seventh covenant does not run with the land. Secondly, these particular provisions with regard to the payment of calls plainly infringed the rule against perpetuities. Of course, these parties are not parties to the contract. Finally, it is conceded that the provision for distraining on failure to pay is not valid. A right to distrain can only be annexed to a rent charge which this certainly is not. It is, however, conceded to be ancient law that a man cannot take benefit under a deed without subscribing to the obligations thereunder. If authority is required for that proposition, I refer to one sentence during the argument in *Elliston* v. *Reacher* where Sir Herbert Cozens-Hardy M.R., said 'It is laid down in *Coke* on *Littleton,* 230b, that a man who takes the benefit of a deed is bound by a condition contained in it though he does not execute it.'

"If the defendants did not desire to take the benefit of this deed, for the reason that I have given they could not be under any liability to pay the obligations thereunder. They do desire, however, to take the benefit of this deed. They have no right to use the sewers which are vested in the plaintiffs, and I cannot see that they have any right, apart from the deed, to use the roads of the park which led to their particular house, No. 22 Salisbury Road. The defendants cannot rely on any way of necessity nor on any right by prescription, for the simple reason that, when the house was originally sold in 1851 to their predecessor in title, he took the house on the terms of the deed of 1851 which contractually bound him to contribute a proper proportion of the expenses of maintaining the roads and sewers, and so forth, as a condition of being entitled to make use of those roads and sewers. Therefore, it seems to me that the defendants here cannot, if they desire to use their house, as they do, take advantage of the trusts concerning the user of the roads contained in the deed and the other benefits created by it without undertaking the obligations thereunder. On that principle it seems to me that they are bound by this deed, if they desire to take its benefits. . . . "

QUESTION. Could shareholders in a non-profit corporation attempting to control a private development be prevented from selling their shares to persons not owning or residing on land within the scheme? See *The Corporations Act*, R.S.O. 1960, c. 71, sections 101, 106, 111, 39, and see *Ontario Jockey Club Ltd.* v. *McBride* (1927) and *Galbraith* v. *Madawaska Club Ltd.* (reproduced on another, but related, point, above).

8. JUDICIAL INTERPRETATION AND APPLICATION

In the next section cases are presented raising problems in the modification or discharge of covenants under summary statutory procedures. In this section something of the same judicial control of covenants is apparent without legislative assistance. One of the earliest examples of the "discharge" of a covenant is to be seen in the *British Museum* case. How can obstructive covenants be challenged?

SMITH *v.* EGGERTSON

Manitoba. Court of Appeal. 1922. 66 D.L.R. 774

FULLERTON J.A.: The plaintiff and defendant are the owners of adjoining lots of land in the same subdivision. The plaintiff, relying upon a restrictive covenant binding on the defendant, asks in his statement of claim for an injunction restraining the defendant from continuing to erect stores on his lot. The material part of the covenant reads as follows:

"The party of the second part agrees with the party of the first part that any building or dwelling-house which he shall erect upon said lot . . . shall be of the value of at least twenty-five hundred dollars ($2,500) actual cash spent and that the front of the said house, verandah or porch or the projection nearest the street shall be at least twenty (20) feet back from Arlington Street frontage of said lot."

Macdonald J., who heard the motion, granted the injunction, being of the opinion that the covenant in question prohibited the construction of any building other than a dwelling-house. I am unable to agree with the view taken by the Judge.

Counsel for the plaintiff contended that the wording of the provision dealing with the location of the structure to be erected on the lot shewed clearly that a dwelling-house only was intended to be referred to and for that reason the words "any building or" in the earlier part of the clause should be treated as surplusage. The elimination of these words, however, would not help the plaintiff. The covenant would then be confined to the value and location of a dwelling-house. The argument of counsel for the plaintiff amounts in effect to this—although there are no express words in the covenant prohibiting the construction of a store on the lot, there are certain surrounding circumstances which point to the conclusion that the parties intended to make the district residential and, therefore, the Court should import into the covenant words which will carry out such intention. To accede to this argument the Court would have to make a new contract for the parties, which of course it cannot do.

QUESTIONS. Does this decision put the location of "any building" other than a dwelling house beyond the control of the covenant? Why should the original grantor be concerned about the location of the one but not the other? Could "any building" refer to buildings accessory to a dwelling-house? How would you redraft the covenant to produce the effect the plaintiff wanted?

RE COSGRAVE AND DELTA PARK LTD.
Ontario. High Court. [1936] O.W.N. 617

MACKAY J., in a written judgment, said that this was a motion, made under Rule 604, to determine the rights of the parties dependent on the interpretation of a restrictive covenant contained in a deed dated the 29th day of November, 1912, and a deed dated the 23rd day of April, 1923, being of lots 53 and 54 of Plan 548, registered as No. 30526 N.S. and No. 250789 N.S. respectively, Hamilton, Ontario.

The restriction to which lot 53 is subject, is as follows:

"No more than one building shall be erected on said lot and such building shall be of brick, stone or cement material and of the cash value of not less than thirty-five hundred dollars. The said lot shall be used for residential or store purposes only."

Lot 54 is subject to the following restriction:

"Any buildings erected on said lot shall be of brick, stone or cement material and of the cash value of not less than thirty-five hundred dollars each."

It is proposed to erect one building costing $5,000 on both lots, and it is maintained by counsel for the adjacent property owners that, while the owners of Lots 53 and 54 are at liberty to erect one building of the cash value of $3,500 on lot 53 and one or more buildings of the cash value of $3,500 on lot No. 54, the restriction is violated by the erection of a single building costing $5,000 partly on one lot and partly on the other.

The learned Justice said that, having regard to the general purpose and intention of the restrictions contained in the deeds, he was of the opinion that if, as is the fact, one building may be erected on lot 53 of cash value of not less than $3,500, and a building or buildings of like value may be erected on lot 54, the construction of part of such building (that is a single building of cash value of not less than $3,500) on one lot and the remaining part on the other, is not a breach or violation of the restrictions contained in the deeds of lot 53 or lot 54.

QUESTIONS. Can you tell the "general purpose and intention of the restrictions" from what is reported in this case? What further evidence would you require? Would such evidence be admissible?

How would you redraft these covenants to achieve the "general purpose"? As a matter of style, could you safely omit the words "said" and "such"? Does the word "said" ever add anything to the clarity of "legal English"? Is the word "the" not always precisely as accurate?

PAGE *v.* CAMPBELL. 1921. 61 S.C.R. 633 (Ontario. Supreme Court of Canada). The appellant tried to restrain the respondents from erecting a church on the corner of Moy Avenue and Niagara Street in Windsor on the ground that it would be contrary to building restrictions applicable to all the lots fronting on Moy exacted by the appellant when he sold the land. The respondents purchased with notice of the restrictions and first tried to get the consent of their neighbours, who instead of consenting petitioned the appellant to commence this action. The appellant had sold all the land in Plan 579 on which the corner was located, and all the lots on Plan 591, which was a continuation of the subdivision of the farm commenced in Plan 579, and projected Moy Avenue further, as did Plan 648, the third to be registered on the original farm. The appellant owned Lots 228 and 229 on Plan 579 at the start of the action but he had sold them by the time of the trial. Throughout the litigation he owned Lot 605 on Moy Avenue on Plan 648, but the majority of the Supreme Court of Canada found that he held no land to which the covenants were annexed. Moreover, he was slow in bringing this action. IDINGTON J.: "In conclusion the acquiescence and delay from at least some time in November until the 24th January, whilst the church was being built, should debar him seeking any injunction when the building was almost completed.

"The purpose of so building was evident in October and if an injunction was to be the remedy, it should have been applied for promptly.

"The covenant does not run with the land and hence the only possible remedy was in equity which does not countenance such a course of conduct." BRODEUR J. (who dissented): "In the present case the appellant is still the owner of a lot situate on Moy Avenue. He is himself under restrictive obligations. He is then entitled to rely on *Tulk* v. *Moxhay*, and to ask that the respondents, the subsequent purchasers of the lots 138 and 139 on Moy Avenue, be ordered to demolish the buildings which they have erected contrary to the covenant contained in their vendor's title.

"The respondents contended also that the plaintiff should not succeed because when the church was constructed he stood by and allowed the respondents to complete their building. The work began in December and the plantiff almost immediately saw the respondents and made his objections to the building being erected. Correspondence was exchanged between the parties until January and, not being able to agree, the present action was instituted on the 16th of January. It cannot be contended in those circumstances, that the respondents may effectively say that the plaintiff stood by."

RE SECOND CHURCH OF CHRIST SCIENTIST AND DODS. 1920. 18 O.W.N. 409 (Ontario. High Court). A conveyance contained the following "conditions and restrictions": "(1) No building or erection shall be placed upon the land except a detached private dwelling house. . . . (6) The purchaser will commence within one year from this date and complete within a reasonable time thereafter a dwelling house upon the said lands conforming with the above restrictions. . . ." The Second Church of Christ Scientist purchased two lots with notice of the restrictions and proceeded to build a church. There was nothing in any of the deeds to show that the benefit of the restrictions was to run with any land, but Dods, as the original grantor was held entitled to enforce them. It was argued that by waiving clause (6) Dods had lost his right to enforce clause (1). ORDE J.: "Standing by and allowing a purchaser to erect a building which did not comply with restriction (1) might constitute a waiver or estoppel; but the grantor might, if he wished, expressly waive no. (6) without waiving no. (1). A tacit waiver could hardly go further than an express one—and the grantor may yet take steps to enforce no. (6)." [What steps could he take? Is Clause (6) specifically enforceable? Is the Church's title subject to a condition?]

EVANGELICAL LUTHERAN CHURCH *v.* SAHLEM
New York. Court of Appeal. 1930. 172 N.E. 455

CARDOZO C.J.: The plaintiff, a religious corporation, has sued the owner of a parcel of real property in the village of Snyder, the owner's wife being joined with him as a defendant, to procure a declaratory judgment adjudging that restrictive covenants affecting the use of a parcel belong to the plaintiff are no longer in effect, with a prayer for general relief.

The Supreme Court at Special Term refused to declare that the covenants had spent their force, adjudged, on the contrary, that they were valid and subsisting, but coupled that adjudication with one to the effect that the defendants were not entitled to hinder the projected use through the aid of an injunction, and were to be limited in respect of remedies to an action for damages at law.

The Appellate Division unanimously affirmed, but certified the case for the judgment of this court.

In September, 1923, a tract of land in the village of Snyder, divided into 128 lots, was subjected to restrictive covenants whereby the only building to be erected on any of the lots was to be "one single-family dwelling with its usual private barns, garages or other out-buildings to be used only for private residential purposes." The covenants were so framed as to run with the land in respect of benefit and burden and were to continue in force for a term of twenty years.

The defendant Philip Sahlem, who will hereafter be referred to as the defendant, became the owner of two of these lots, and placed upon them a private dwelling in which he made his home. The dwelling had been standing there for years when the plaintiff, a Lutheran Church, conceived the plan of building a church edifice upon part of the restricted tract. Before purchasing its lots, which are directly opposite to those owned by the defendant, the plaintiff, knowing of the covenants, made application to the lot owners to vary the restrictions. The defendant, though a member of the same religious communion, would not consent to the variance. He took the position that he had bought his lots for the purpose of a home, and that his peace and comfort would be disturbed by a meeting house across the way with the parking of cars, the tooting of horns and the invasions of privacy attendant upon crowds. All the other lot owners were willing to modify the covenants by permitting the church to be erected, and signed consents accordingly.

The plaintiff, armed with these consents, decided to take title to the land and bid defiance to its neighbor. It signed a contract of purchase in February, 1928, and gave written notice to the defendant that the church would be erected. The defendant retorted with a warning that the builder would go forward at its peril. A deed of conveyance was accepted the next month. It recited the restrictions, and stated that the title to be conveyed to the grantee was subject thereto. The grantee promptly thereafter caused plans to be made for a parish house and church, made a contract with a builder for the construction of the parish house, and began the work of excavation. At this point, apparently, its courage began to fail. Once more it wrote to the defendant, insisting that, with all the other lot owners compliant, the defendant "ought" not to have the right to hinder the progress of an institution attempting to do humanitarian work." Once more the defendant stood his ground. Self-help was succeeded at this stage by combat in the courts. The plaintiff, renouncing its attitude of defiance, checked the progress of the work, and invoked the aid of the judicial process for a declaration of its rights.

The judgment rendered in its favor eviscerates the restrictive covenants while declaring them alive. It does this on the ground that the damages occasioned to the defendant by the building of a church will be "slight and inconsequential" in comparison to those occasioned to the plaintiff if the use shall be enjoined. There is neither finding nor proof that the character of the neighborhood has so changed as to defeat the object and purposes for which the restrictions were imposed. Business has moved to some extent into blocks not far away which once were used for dwellings. The tract subjected to these covenants remains, however, what it has been since the restrictions were established, a place for homes exclusively. Indeed, there is no claim by any one that the plaintiff is at liberty, ignoring the covenants altogether, to devote the land in its ownership to business uses generally. By concession, its immunity will end if its building is not a church. The basis of this judgment, denying to the defendant owner the aid of equitable remedies, is not the presence of changed conditions extracting from the covenants their original vitality and reducing them to barren archaisms. The covenants are as useful in preserving to this tract the quality of a home section as they were at the beginning. The basis of this judgment is a holding that an owner, anxious to improve his land in knowing violation of a covenant still subsisting, may have the judgment of a court of equity advising him in advance that, so far as equity is concerned, he may go forward with impunity if only on a balancing of losses the loss to the wrongdoer appears to be greater than his victim's.

By the settled doctrine of equity, restrictive covenants in respect of land will be enforced by preventive remedies while the violation is still in prospect, unless the attitude of the complaining owner in standing on his covenant is unconscionable or oppressive. Relief is not withheld because the money damage is unsubstantial or even none at all. "If the construction of the instrument be clear and the breach clear, then it is not a question of damage, but the mere circumstance of the breach of covenant affords sufficient ground for the Court to interfere by injunction." . . . "The parties had the right to determine for themselves in what way and for what purposes their lands should be occupied irrespective of pecuniary gain or loss, or the effect on the market value of the lots." Inequity there may be in standing on the letter of covenant when the neighborhood has so altered that the ends to be attained by the restriction have been frustrated by the years. Inequity there may be in a demand for a mandatory injunction that will tear a completed building down, when the builder has acted in good faith, the covenant is presently to expire, and the havoc wrought by demolition will be disproportionate, in a degree shocking to the conscience, to any corresponding benefit. Few formulas are so absolute as not to bend before the blast of extraordinary circumstances. In the award of equitable remedies there is often an element of discretion, but never a discretion that is absolute or arbitrary. In equity, as at law, there are signposts for the traveler. "Discretion . . . 'must be regulated upon grounds that will make it judicial.' "

Here, in the case at hand, no process of balancing the equities can make the plaintiff's greater when compared with the defendant's, or even place the two in equipoise. The defendant, the owner, has done nothing but insist upon adherence to a covenant which is now as valid and binding as at the hour of its making. His neighbors are willing to modify the restriction and forego a portion of their rights. He refuses to go with them. Rightly or wrongly he believes that the comfort of his dwelling will be imperiled by the change, and so he chooses to abide by the covenant as framed. The choice is for him only. Neither at law nor in equity is it written that a license has been granted to religious corporations, by reason of the high purpose of their being, to set covenants at naught. Indeed, if in such matters there can be degrees of obligation, one would suppose that a more sensitive adherence to the demands of plighted faith might be expected of them than would be looked for of the world at large. Other owners may consent. One owner, the defendant, satisfied with the existing state of things, refuses to disturb it. He will be protected in his refusal by all the power of the law.

If there is nothing in the defendant's conduct that should serve to banish him from equity, the question must still be met whether something in the plaintiff's conduct, some element of mistake or misadvanture or even intolerable hardship, may work a like result. Nothing of the kind appears. Before taking a deed and even before signing the preliminary contract, the plaintiff knew of the restriction and knew that the defendant would not consent to any variance. It decided to ignore him. In the face of a covenant too plain to be misread, with conditions in the restricted tract the same as they had been when the covenant was made, it signed a contract with a builder for the construction of a parish house, reserving for the future the contract for the church, and dug some spadefuls of earth as a sign that building had begun. At this point it prudently desisted and invoked the blessing of the law. With the building still a project, it induced a court of equity to advise it that there would be no hindrance by injunction if operations were resumed. Destruction of the defendant's easements, or rights analogous to easements, would proceed with safety and in order.

Neither principle nor precedent supports the decree of absolution thus granted to a wrongdoer. Here is no case of irreparable hardship, shocking to the conscience, as where a mandatory injunction would destroy a finished building to vindicate a doubtful right. Here is a case where the building is yet a plan, the work on it preliminary, the outlay unsubstantial, the act to be absolved still waiting for the doer. His path has been made easy by a judicial declaration that the wrong may go on without annoying interference.

The judgments of the Appellate Division and the Special Term should be reversed, and judgment rendered in favor of the defendants declaring the restrictive covenants described in the complaint to be enforceable at law and in equity, with costs in all courts.

[Pound, Crane, Lehman, Kellogg and Hubbs JJ. concurred; O'Brien J. dissented. The citations of cases have been entirely deleted.]

THE DUKE OF BEDFORD *v*. THE TRUSTEES OF THE BRITISH MUSEUM. 1822. 2 My. & K. 552; 39 E.R. 105 (England. Chancery). In 1675 Ralph Montagu purchased from the wife of William Russell (afterwards Lord Russell) a piece of land in Bloomsbury containing about seven acres, on which he covenanted that in case he should build, he would build "one fair and large messuage and dwelling-house, fit for him and his family to inhabit". He also covenanted that if he should build "northward beyond the range and building of Southampton House, situate near thereunto", other than accessory buildings he should forfeit and pay £3 a day so long as the building remained. There were numerous other covenants. In due course Montagu erected Montagu House which burned down, was rebuilt, and in 1753 was taken over by the British Museum. The estates of Lady Russell had become vested in the Duke of Bedford and houses had been erected and streets formed on the north, east and west sides, adjacent to the Museum. The original house, Southampton House, later called Bedford House, was pulled down in 1800 to make way for streets and buildings which were erected on its site.

The bill was filed for the purpose of obtaining an injunction to restrain the Defendants, the trustees of the British Museum, from proceeding to raise in the gardens certain additional buildings which they had it then in

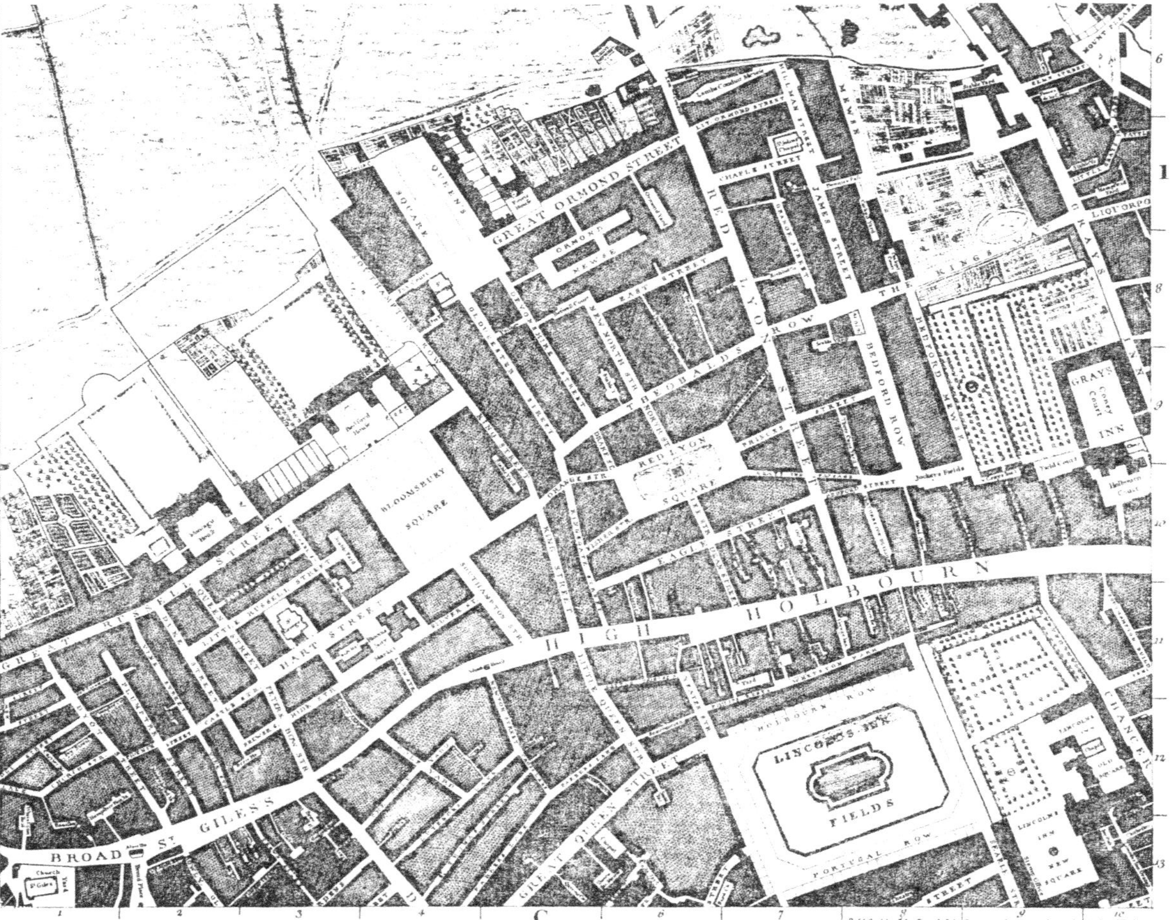
GREAT ORMOND STREET
QUEENS SQUARE
ORMOND MEWSE
RED LYON STREET
JAMES STREET
BEDFORD ROW
BEDFORD MEWSE
THE KINGS WAY
GRAYS INN
Coney Court
THEOBALDS ROW
RED LYON SQUARE
ORANGE STR
EAGLE STREET
BLOOMSBURY SQUARE
SOUTHAMPTON ROW
GREAT RUSSELL STREET
HART STREET
HIGH HOLBOURN
LINCOLNS INN FIELDS
HOLBOURN ROW
PORTUGAL ROW
LINCOLNS INN NEW SQUARE
CHANCERY
GREAT QUEEN STREET
BROAD St GILES
1
C

contemplation to erect. The intended additions were designed for the reception of statues and other monuments of ancient art brought from Greece by the Earl of Elgin. They were to consist of a wing sixty feet in height, joining the principal building at the eastern extremity, and extending from it into the garden northwards to the distance of two hundred and ninety feet. On the western side a similar wing had been built about the year 1805, extending northwards about one hundred and forty feet; it was designed to lengthen the latter, so as to correspond with that to be built on the east. These wings, if erected, would extend northward considerably beyond what had been the line of the range and building of Southampton House. The injunction was refused. LORD CHANCELLOR ELDON: "Now, in determining how a Court of Equity ought to proceed, it is proper to consider not only what would be done in the actual matter before it, but what the Court would do in other cases falling within the same principle. Suppose that after Mr. Montagu had built this house ranging with all the surrounding buildings that belonged to the Duke of Bedford, and ranging with Powis House and other large mansions standing in Great Russell Street; suppose that after the summer house and banqueting house had been erected (which clearly would not have affected the prospect from Bedford House), and after the garden wall (on which the feoffee was not to place three additional bricks) had been built, the Duke of Bedford had said, 'there is nothing to restrain me; I will place a sugar house on one side and a soap house or gas works on the other side;' or rather, suppose, which is a handsomer way of putting it, that the Duke had built a row of houses close to the wall, and afterwards Mr. Montagu had said he did not like to have his gardens overlooked by his neighbours' servants, and he would therefore, notwithstanding the covenant, build this wall twice as high as it was before: though I admit that the Duke of Bedford might have had a proper ground of action, would this Court have granted an injunction? My answer is, no: for upon looking to authority, I find the law to be as Lord Kenyon has laid it down. If this deed is permitted to be urged against what I must call, not the legal, but the actual intention of the parties, and if you have the means of obtaining any remedy, you may have recourse to your deed; but you cannot under such circumstances come into a Court of Equity for a remedy which the Court never grants except in cases where it would be strictly equitable to grant it. It is impossible to state, as the doctrine of a Court of Equity, that the Court will carry into execution a specific covenant in all cases where the legal intention of the deed is found. A doctrine like that would be widely inconsistent with general practice, and would directly contradict the daily and hourly experience of us all.

"The deed proceeds further, and states as a distinct covenant that if the said Ralph Montagu, his heirs or assigns, or any of them, shall at any time thereafter erect any building of what nature soever on the north end of the said piece of ground, and which shall extend northward beyond the range and building of Southampton House, situate near thereunto, other than one or more summer house or other houses for the accommodation of the garden, he and they shall forfeit and pay, &c.—. Now what would it have signified as between these parties, in the consideration of such a case as this, whether a house was or was not built in the range of Southampton House, if there were placed between this house and Southampton House three or four streets excluding the smallest possible view from Southampton House of anything north of this mansion, and by the acts of the Bedford family themselves destroying the very purpose for which this covenant was here inserted? . . . "

VAN KOUGHNET *v.* DENISON

Ontario Court of Appeal. 1884. 11 O.A.R. 699

HAGARTY C.J.O.: . . . The remedy here sought is . . . an application to the Court's power to hold the defendant, as the original vendor, to the due performance of the agreement which formed part of the consideration for the purchase, viz., that "Bellevue Square was always to remain unbuilt upon, except one residence with the necessary out-buildings, including porter's lodge." This deed was in 1860.

It contained the further agreement on vendee's part, his heirs, assigns, &c., not to permit any business of a public nature such as a tavern, &c., to be carried on on the property conveyed.

A burden is thus imposed on the property sold, and on this adjacent property of the vendor. Any purchaser of either property with notice, would be held bound by these respective provisions . . .

When Bovell bought from the defendant in 1860, the whole of the property was in mortgage to a building society. Bovell's lot was released therefrom. Down to 1869 the property was beyond his control, except by his paying off the mortgage. It was sold under power of sale in 1866 to Mr. Coate, and in 1869 was conveyed by Coate's vendee to the defendant. In 1869, and before reconveyance to defendant, a street as a continuance of Denison Avenue, was opened from south to north about through the centre of the block said to be Bellevue Square, but we do not see at what date. The west half or part thus cut off from the rest was sold in lots and built on by various persons.

Until about 1872, no attempt seems to have been made to sell or use portions of the remaining eastern part, and then plaintiff gives the notice of March, 1872.

Nothing further seems to have been done till shortly before the filing of the bill in this case.

I do not see how plaintiff could have interfered at any earlier period, nor can I see how the alienation of the western portion can affect his rights. He has done nothing to bring himself within the principle so clearly set forth in *Duke of Bedford* v. *Trustees of the British Museum* . . .

I do not think that defendant can be released from the legal consequences of his original agreement by any of the facts shewn in evidence arising from the sale and alienation of large portions of the property originally called Bellevue Square, by title paramount, created by himself prior to his agreement. . . .

OSLER J.A. . . . The defendant is not in a position to invoke against the plaintiff the rule laid down in the leading case of *The Duke of Bedford* v. *Trustees of the British Museum*. . . . Because the acts upon which he relies as having changed the character and circumstances of the square, and the surrounding property are acts to which the plaintiff was no party, in which he has not acquiesced, and which he was powerless to prevent. There does not appear to be any less valid reason, apart from the hardship of the case (which is not a reason), why so much of the original square as remains and can be ascertained, should not still be subject to the defendant's covenant, than there was for fastening it upon the whole square twenty years ago . . .

[The opinions are greatly curtailed and those of Burton and Patterson JJ.A. are omitted. In the court below Boyd C. said in part: " . . . It was not shown that any appreciable injury arose to the plaintiff or Dr. Bovell from the occupation of the western part of the square . . ."]

COWAN *v.* FERGUSON

Ontario. Court of Appeal. 1919. 45 O.L.R. 161

MEREDITH C.J.O. read the judgment of the Court: The appellants are the owners of two lots on the hydraulic canal in the city of Galt, being lots 8a and 8b as shewn on a plan prepared by Deputy Surveyor Kerr in or about the month of February, 1842, and the respondent is the owner of lots 6a and 6b and 7a and 7b according to the same plan.

The action is brought to restrain the respondent from erecting any building for a foundry and from carrying on the business of a foundry on her lots.

The right to this relief is based upon a covenant contained in an agreement between Robert Dickson, the then owner of these and other lots, and one Fisher, dated the 15th February, 1842, by which Dickson covenanted with Fisher, his heirs and assigns, that in sales and agreements for sale by Dickson or his heirs or assigns of water-lots or lots of land in the village of Galt, with the privilege of using water-power thereon, there should be inserted in the instrument or instruments evidencing such sale or agreement for sale, a clause restraining and prohibiting "such purchaser or purchasers or person or persons from carrying on the business of a foundry on the land so sold or agreed to be sold to him or them as aforesaid." . . .

When the covenant was entered into, Galt was a small country village, and water-power was that used in manufacturing industries. Galt has now become a thriving industrial city, having within its limits many manufacturing establishments, and stream and electrical power have to a very large extent replaced water-power.

When Fisher purchased from Dickson and established his foundry business, it was, no doubt, important to him that he should not be subjected to the competition of other foundries; and the covenant was, doubtless, entered into for the purpose of protecting him from such competition by persons who should thereafter purchase Dickson's lots on the canal.

The case, is, therefore, one I think, for the application of the principle which my brother Latchford applied—that where, after the entering into of a covenant restricting the use to which the land comprised in a building scheme may be put, there has been a general change in the character of the neighbourhood, the Court will not enforce the covenant.

Dealing with this principle, Sargeant J., said in *Sobey* v. *Sainsbury* (1913), referring to *Knight* v. *Simmonds* (1896):

"The effect would, but for the principles applied in the cases I have referred to, have been to stereotype and perpetuate, far beyond the real intention of the contracting parties, and to the prejudice of successive generations, restrictions which had in the course of time become obsolete and meaningless. And, having regard to the great number of persons who in the case of building schemes may be originally entitled to enforce these covenants, it would, I think, be an undue limitation of the discretion of the Court to refuse specific performance of the covenant if the refusal should be restricted to cases where there was some personal or individual default on the part of the plaintiff or his predecessors in title. This might easily result in the enforcement of such restrictions after long intervals of time and under totally changed conditions from motives of spite or caprice, or from a desire to make money out of the relaxation of technical but obsolete restrictions. And it is for reasons of this kind that I understand James L.J., and Lindley L.J., to have carefully stated that the Court may refuse to specifically enforce such obligations in an altered state of circumstances: 'Whatever the explanation of the altered state of things may be.' "

While the change of circumstances in the case at bar differs from those which had taken place in the case just referred to, the principle enunciated by Sargeant J. is equally applicable.

It was contended by counsel for the appellants that this principle was applicable only when the party seeking to enforce the covenant or his predecessor in title had been a party to making the changes; but the contrary is emphatically stated by Sargeant J., in the passage from his judgment which I have quoted, and the observations of James L.J., and Lindley L.J., support his view, for they speak of the doctrine applied by Sargeant J., as being applicable not only where the changes have been permitted or acquiesced in, but also where they are the result of "a long chain of things."

The judgment of my brother Latchford may also, I think, be supported upon the ground that the appellants, knowing that the respondent was erecting a building to be used as a foundry, acquiesced in what she was doing and even made suggestions as to the mode of constructing part of the building.

It is, besides, conceded that the appellants have not sustained and will not in the future sustain any injury from the use to which the respondent has put her property.

For these reasons, in my opinion, the case is not one in which the Court should interfere to enforce the covenant; and I would affirm the judgment and dismiss the appeal with costs.

SHAUGHNESSY HEIGHTS PROPERTY OWNERS' ASSOCIATION v. CAMPBELL AND CAMPBELL. [1951] 2 D.L.R. 62 (British Columbia. Supreme Court). An example of "covenants" enacted in a private act. Wilson J. enjoyed the operation of a catering business in the statutory private dwelling house area. It was shown that out of 450 houses in the area, 150 were in violation of the act, but 96% of the "violations" were justified under temporary (war-time and transitional) emergency legislation which permitted conversion to multiple dwellings. Of the remaining 4% of violations, one was a home for the aged operated by the British Columbia government. Since the lawful "doubling up" by conversion to rooming houses and boarding houses was temporary, there was no showing of more than a temporary "change in the character of the neighbourhood" which the residents did not necessarily acquiesce in as they were powerless to prevent it.

9. Modification and Discharge under the Statutes

THE CONVEYANCING AND LAW OF PROPERTY ACT
Ontario. Revised Statutes. 1960. Chapter 66

62. (1) Where there is annexed to any land any condition or covenant that the land or a specified part of it is not be built on or is to be or not to be used in a particular manner, or any other condition or covenant running with or capable of being legally annexed to land, any such condition or covenant may be modified or discharged by order of a judge of the Supreme Court or of the judge of the county or district court of the county or district in which the land or any part of it is situate.

(2) Where an application under subsection 1 is made to the judge of a county or district court, a respondent may, by notice served on the applicant and on the other respondents, if any, and filed with proof of service thereof with the clerk of the county or district court not later than two days preceding the day of return of the application, require the proceedings to be removed into the Supreme Court.

(3) Upon the filing of the notice and proof of service thereof, the clerk of the county or district court shall forthwith transmit the papers and proceedings to the proper office of the Supreme Court in the county or district in which the application is made.

(4) When the papers and proceedings are received at the proper office of the Supreme Court, the proceedings shall *ipso facto* be removed into the Supreme Court.

(5) Before making any such order, the judge shall cause notice of the application to be given to such persons as appear to him to be interested in the relief sought, either by personal service, advertisement or by registered mail as he directs.

(6) An appeal lies to the Court of Appeal from the decision of a judge under subsection 1.

(7) Nothing in this section applies to building restrictions imposed by by-law passed under *The Municipal Act* or *The Planning Act*.

NOTES AND QUESTIONS. To whom must the notice required by subsection (2) be given? Do the "private law" concepts of "annexation" and "touching and concerning" have any relevance? Should notice be limited to owners of land contained within a building scheme? If a person could not enforce a covenant, should he be heard in opposition to its modification? Is there some general equity that would require hearing the neighbours who own land that is not legally affected by the covenants? Consider the following passage by Bowen L.J. in *Blount* v. *Layard* (1891):

" . . . nothing worse can happen in a free country than to force people to be churlish about their rights for fear that their indulgence may be abused, and to drive them to prevent the enjoyment of things which, although they are matters of private property, naturally give pleasure to many others besides the owners, under the fear that their good nature may be misunderstood . . . "

See, on the somewhat similar English legislation, s. 84(2) of the *Law of Property Act*, 1925, Maugham J., in *Re Sunnyfield* (1932): "When such an order as this is asked for, the court ought to make every effort to see that all persons who may wish to oppose the making of the order have the opportunity of being heard, stating their objections in argument before the court, and inviting the court to refuse to exercise its powers. In the present case it seems that every effort has been made to give notice to all persons having a probable interest in the property, and accordingly I ought not to refuse to proceed to the hearing of the matter."

Does Maugham J. refer to a legal, equitable or social "interest in the property"?

Section 84(1) of the English Act provides for hearing before a special tribunal, now the Lands Tribunal, which may be composed of a single member, either a lawyer or a surveyor (a somewhat more broadly qualified person than a Land Surveyor in Canada and not to be confused.) "The Tribunal normally orders the putting of notices on the site and the insertion of advertisements in the press." See Newsom, *The Discharge and Modification of Restrictive Covenants* (1957), p. lxiii.

RE BEARDMORE

Ontario. Court of Appeal. [1935] O.R. 526

MASTEN J.A. delivered the judgment of the court: This is an appeal from the order of Rose C.J.H.C. dated July 15th, 1935, amending certain building restrictions as to lands on Orchard View Boulevard in the City of Toronto.

The original restrictions which the respondents applied to modify are contained in two orders made by Middleton J., the one being dated 9th May, 1923, and the other the 21st December, 1923. The result of those orders, so far as they affect the lands here in question, is to declare that the restrictions form part of a general building scheme and are annexed to the land proposed to be sold and to provide as follows:

"No building shall be erected or placed upon the said lands or any part thereof (except as to Lots 1 to 17 inclusive, Plan M–380 fronting on Eglinton Avenue) any portion whereof (including verandahs, porches or bay windows) is nearer to the street line in front thereof than 15 feet or nearer either of the side lines of the land used in connection therewith than 18 inches or which is not (unless it be an outbuilding, appurtenant to a residence) a detached one family residence constructed as to external walls thereof wholly of brick and/or stone and/or stucco (or cement plaster) on brick or tile, and erected on a parcel having at least 24 feet frontage. No building shall be erected on Lots 1 to 70 all inclusive or 127 to 143 all inclusive Plan M–380 or on Lots H, I, and J., Plan M–325 costing less than $4,500.00 exclusive of the land; and no building shall be erected on Lots 71 to 81 all inclusive or 121 to 126 all inclusive according to said Plan M–380 or on Lots B to G all inclusive, except the west 50 feet thereof, according to Plan M–425 costing less than $3,000.00 exclusive of the land." Provided however that "a club house the plans whereof are satisfactory to the City Architect of the City of Toronto, and such appurtenances and outbuildings as are usual or incidental or necessary for the purpose of a club (and in particular of a Hunt club) but excluding stables and kennels, may be erected on Lots 71 to 81 both inclusive, Plan M–380, and on Lots K and J, Plan M–425 or on some or on any of said lots."

The respondents by their present application ask for an order modifying the above conditions in order that it may become lawful to erect "double duplexes and four-family dwellings constructed as to the external walls thereof wholly of brick and/or stone and/or stucco or cement plaster on brick or tile and costing not less than $12,000.00 exclusive of the land, together with a garage or garages used in connection therewith, upon a parcel having a frontage of not less than 45 feet inclusive of mutual side drive on Lots 71 to 81 inclusive, Plan M–380, or on some or any of said lots or any part or parts thereof."

The lots in relation to which the amendment of the restrictions is sought are situate on the south side of Orchard View Boulevard. The Eglinton Hunt Club premises lie immediately to the north of Orchard View Boulevard and abut on its northerly boundary; the lands of the majority of the appellants are situate on the north side of Willowbank Boulevard and their gardens and rear premises abut on the lands in question.

In his reasons for judgment the learned Chief Justice said:

"The experts called on behalf of the applicants, who are well-known and, I imagine, competent men, expressed the opinion that if the buildings proposed were erected the selling value of the objectors' properties would not be diminished; but I thought that, however that might be, the buildings with the exterior stairways and platforms would be something of an eye-sore, and would be a very distinct eye-sore if the tenants used the platforms in the way suggested. I said, therefore, that I should not make an order permitting the erection of these four-family dwellings unless that particular objection could be removed. There was another adjournment, and Mr. Walker, counsel for the applicants, has now produced amended plans which show no exterior stairways, nothing in the rear walls but the windows of bedrooms and bathrooms; and as the case has gone on the applicants have modified their original application by agreeing that any houses that may be erected shall be of the value, including the garages, of at least $15,000.00 each, and at my suggestion, have agreed that no house shall be closer than six feet to the side line of the parcel on which it is erected, and that the garages to be constructed, which will be close to the north line of the objectors' premises, shall be of a limited height, the rear wall not more than nine feet high and the total height of the building to the ridge to be not more than fifteen feet from the level of the ground.

"With these modifications I think, although counsel for the objectors do not agree, that the serious objections have been met."

In pursuance of that view the order now in appeal was issued . . .

The application of the respondents is based upon the ground that in consequence of the existing restrictions they are experiencing great difficulty in realizing upon the vacant lands in question; that they have obtained an offer for the purchase of certain of these lands conditionally upon the right on the part of the purchaser to erect on them what is known as double duplexes or four-family dwellings, and that the relaxation of the restrictions as they stand at the present time will not appreciably prejudice the appellants. The application is supported by the opinion of two experts of undoubted eminence.

The appellants, who resisted the application in the Court below, say that they purchased, or most of them purchased, after investigation of the restrictions to which the lands in question are subject, that but for the restrictions they would not have purchased, and they object very strenuously to large buildings such as these "four-family" dwellings and to garages designed for the use of tenants of such buildings, and that if the application is refused and existing restrictions are continued, the access to them of air from the north will be much better than would be possible if large four-family dwellings were constructed. They allege that the order appealed from will depreciate the value of their property and will destroy certain amenities which they now possess. Their contentions are supported by three experts.

This application is brought under the provisions of *The Land Titles Act*, R.S.O. 1927, c. 158, s. 79 and *The Conveyancing and Law of Property Act*, R.S.O. 1927, c. 137, s. 57.

The Land Titles Act empowers the registered owner of freehold lands to place restrictions on the register, and subsec. 4 of sec. 79 reads as follows:

"Any such direction may at any time be withdrawn or modified at the instance of all the persons for the time being appearing by the register to be interested in such direction, and shall also be subject to be set aside by the Court."

Section 57 (1) of *The Conveyancing and Law of Property Act* is as follows:

"Where there is annexed to any land any condition or covenant that such land or any specified portion thereof is not to be built on or is to be or not to be used in a particular manner, or any other condition or covenant running with or capable of being legally annexed to land, any such condition or covenant may be modified or discharged by order of a judge of the Supreme Court."

The provision was originally enacted by 1922, 12 Geo. V, ch. 53 (Ont.), and then contained in addition to the present provision the following words which appeared at the end of the subsection: "On proof to his satisfaction that the modification will be beneficial to the persons principally interested." These words were omitted at the time of the revision of the Statutes in 1927.

I agree with the view expressed by Sedgewick J. in *Re Crocker* (1931) where he says:

"This amendment does not make it any easier for an applicant to succeed in amending building restrictions. The rule still should be that the order should not be made unless the benefit to the applicant greatly exceeds any possible detriment to the respondents."

I think the effect of the change is to confer upon the Court an untrammelled judicial discretion to be exercised in accordance with recognized principles of law and equity and that the phrase used by the Court in the case of *Re George* (1926), that "the Judge must satisfy himself that the balance of convenience is in favour of granting the application" is by no means the only test to be applied under the existing statutory provisions. I shall refer to this again at a later stage. . . .

The cases decided under the Act are consistent in making plain the extreme caution with which the jurisdiction in question is to be exercised. I refer first to the case of *Re George*. That was an application to remove a restriction prohibiting the erection of more than two detached dwelling houses on some five acres of land in Rosedale. Those opposing the applicants were neighbouring residents who alleged that the interference with their view across a ravine might be destroyed by the erection of more houses as proposed. The applicants argued that the benefits to them so outweighed the damage. if any, to the respondents that the case was brought within the words "beneficial to the persons principally concerned." In delivering the judgment of the Court, Middleton J.A., said at p. 577:

"The meaning that has been given to the expression in practice is that the Judge must satisfy himself that the balance of convenience is in favour of granting the application, having regard to the rights and interests of both parties, and I think it may safely be said that the order should not be made unless the benefit to the applicant greatly exceeds any possible detriment to the respondents."

This application (*Re George*) took place before the change in the Statute and to some extent was based on the words "balance of convenience", since eliminated.

Re George was followed shortly afterwards by the case of *In re Ontario Lime Co. Ltd.* (1926). The application was refused and Middleton J.A., delivering the judgment of the Court, said:

"It has been more than once pointed out that under this statute there is no power to make compensation to a landowner who is prejudicially affected, and the jurisdiction is one to be exercised with the greatest caution, and an order should seldom, if ever, be made which will in truth operate to the prejudice of the adjacent landowner who has any real rights. The true function of the statute is to enable the Court to get rid of a condition or restriction which is spent or so unsuitable as to be of no value and under circumstances when its assertion would be clearly vexatious."

I am not aware of any modification or variation of the law so declared and settled and, as already observed, I think the change in the Statute tends to increase the burden resting on the applicant to establish a case warranting the intervention of the Court.

In my opinion the applicant must by his evidence completely satisfy the Court that if the proposed modification is allowed the injury to the neighbouring owners, who object, will be negligible. Whether the evidence does or does not go far enough to establish such a case involves a conclusion of fact on which different minds may naturally take different views. With profound respect for any opinion expressed by the learned Chief Justice, I find myself, after careful perusal and consideration of all the evidence, unable to agree with his conclusion.

At least two different states of fact may appear on such an application. If the lands of the applicant and of the respondent both remained vacant, then a consideration of relative financial values and of the relative benefits and injuries to the several parties might well be a matter for consideration. But I think that a view looking to other than financial results ought to be taken by the Court where, in reliance upon a restriction, lands of the objecting party have been acquired and built upon and are in actual occupation and enjoyment by him of certain amenities which he prizes.

The leaning of the Court against any interference with such amenities is illustrated by the principal established in equity in regard to a life tenant without impeachment for waste who will be restrained from cutting ornamental timber. See *Kerr on Injunctions*, 6th ed., p. 74 and following.

I think the Court should in such a case as this be reluctant to interfere with the vested rights of the present appellants in the enjoyment of the amenities which induced them to buy, build on and occupy their lands.

Dealing with the matter therefore on the basis that this Court is bound to arrive at its own conclusions, all I can say is that the evidence falls short of assuring my mind that the appellants' lands will not be to some real extent lessened in value by the order now in appeal. But over and above this ground, I am bound to say that the evidence entirely fails to satisfy me that the order in appeal does not deprive the appellants of existing amenities, the vested rights in which are not negligible.

I would therefore allow the appeal with costs here and below, payable by the respondents to the appellants.

RE DINNICK. [1933] O.W.N. 55 (Ontario. High Court). Building restrictions imposed in 1900 limited buildings to private residences. On an application for discharge so that an apartment could be built it was established that "the character of the neighbourhood . . . had greatly changed" but McEvoy J. could not bring himself to the conclusion that this alone justified an order: "... [There] could be no doubt that a great advantage would accrue to the applicant if he were permitted to build an apartment house upon this land, but that it was equally plain that the building of an apartment house would materially and largely injure the value of the Gooderham property as residential property." [Query, how do you prove the change in "character" of a neighbourhood? What is the "neighbourhood"? Should it comprise land not affected by the covenants? Is an increase of value (because of the demand for commercial or high density residential use) evidence of a change?]

RE MOODY

Ontario. Court of Appeal, [1941] O.W.N. 167

MIDDLETON J.A., in a written judgment, said that pursuant to sec. 60 of *The Conveyancing and Law of Property Act*, R.S.O. 1937, c. 152 Della Moody obtained an order from Hope J. dated the 18th day of February, 1941, wherein the restrictions, covenants and conditions annexed to or running with Lot 29 on the south side of Eglinton Avenue, in the Village of Forest Hill in the County of York, according to Plan Number 2350 registered in the Registry Office for the East and West Riding of the County of York, were modified so as to permit the erection of a funeral home upon the said lot. From this order Samuel Senyk and Anna Senyk, who are the owners of the corner lot No. 13 on the south side of Eglinton Avenue immediately opposite Lot 29, appeal. Between these lots Warren Road proceeds southerly.

Della Moody is a widow, who inherited from her husband Lot 29, and she held the lands for about eight years and has been unable to obtain a satisfactory purchaser. She has arranged now to sell the land for the purpose of erecting an undertaker's establishment and a funeral home on it, and hence made the application which has been granted.

Senyk is the owner of a barber shop across Warren Road, and resides in the apartments above his store with his family. He purchased the store for $10,600 about ten years ago, and is violently opposed to the granting of the application. He says that he would not have purchased the store or the dwellings above it except in reliance upon the covenant that he had upon the conveyance to him, and he has been ever since in residence above the store. His opposition to the granting of the order is supported by some eight or nine residents who authorized Mr. Beaudoin to appear for them as opposed.

The statute warranting the application . . . authorizes the making of an order by a Judge of the Supreme Court vacating any restrictive covenant which is annexed to and runs with the legal title, but enjoins the Judge before he makes the order to cause notice to be given to such persons as shall appear to him to be interested in the relief sought. The statute contains no provision for compensation to those adversely affected, and so is in no sense of an expropriatory nature. For this reason the statute is not entitled to any wide effect, and is only to be used where the character of the neighbourhood is so changed that an order can be made without doing violence to the rights of other land owners . . .

Eglinton Avenue as it goes westward ceases to be a purely business street. The Baldwin Estate originally owned the entire parcel and dedicated the Eglinton Avenue frontage as a location for stores, nearly all of which have business quarters below and residential quarters above. But this dedication was not wide open. The deeds contained covenants upon the whole Eglinton Avenue frontage prohibiting the erection of any buildings except for use as stores and with residential quarters. Mr. Justice Orde, under circumstances that are not disclosed here, permitted the erection of duplex and apartment houses upon the said lands, but did not otherwise interfere with the restrictions. This funeral home, as it is called, is described by Mr. Beaudoin's client as constituting a very serious detriment to his property across the road, and as a dark spot in the midst of a bright and well-lighted commercial district. The objection is not fanciful, for many would object to live next door to an undertakers' establishment where funerals are an almost daily occurrence.

The appeal should be allowed with costs and the application dismissed.

FISHER J.A., in a written dissenting judgment, said that the Legislature in enacting sec. 60 of *The Conveyancing and Law of Property Act* must have had in mind that radical changes would take place in the future in cities expanding and extending out into restricted areas, and also that restrictive covenants should not be lightly interfered with because of the fact that the section specially provides that notice is to be given to such persons as might appear to the Judge to be interested before any amendment was heard by the Court; and thus giving to the Court wide discretionary powers in making or refusing an order. For these reasons sec. 60 should not be given a restrictive, but a liberal meaning. Apart from the applicant only one party who owns the property immediately to the east of the property in question, appeared and objected to an order being made.

It appears that counsel opposing intimated on the argument before Hope J. that there were others opposing, but no material is on file, and, therefore, objections from that source cannot be considered.

The main objections to the establishment of a funeral home are that it will have a depressing effect upon the appellant's business, being that of a barber on the opposite side of a street, and on his tenants who live above the barber shop; that a funeral always brings gloom into the district where it is being conducted; that it will be the means of bringing a large number of motor vehicles and there will be difficulties experienced in parking; and also that it will depreciate the value of the appellant's property.

The question is, are these objections fatal to the order made? The learned Justice of Appeal said that in his opinion they are not. It is frankly admitted by all that since the restrictive covenant was made the whole district in which the property in question is situate has undergone a radical change. It must also be admitted that because of widespread areas, paved streets, and with the ever increasing motor traffic, cities in recent years have been created within cities, and that large and active commercial districts have been established in formerly quiet residential districts. It must also be admitted that changing conditions have brought the erection of a large number of apartment houses throughout the city. The material on this application discloses the fact that an order was made some years ago by Orde J., permitting the erection of an apartment house in this district. Some of the outstanding radical changes in the district since the covenant was made are large blocks of shops, gasoline stations, a fire hall, a police station, and, no doubt, moving picture establishments. All these would bring a largely increased motor traffic with the usual difficulties in parking. With all these changes the respondent wants to add one more, the establishment of a funeral home. It is common knowledge that in recent years funeral homes have been established all over the city, and it would appear that they have come to stay. These funeral homes are provided with seating capacity, and the funeral services are conducted therein; and, no doubt, they have been established because of the many citizens now who, for convenience or other reasons, use funeral homes instead of their own homes.

There is lack of evidence in the material before the Court of objections of any kind being made by persons living in districts where funeral homes have been established. No one questions the fact that the presence of a funeral home brings an atmosphere of gloom and solemnity. No one by choice would favour a funeral home being established near their property any more than one would favour a gasoline station being established near their property because of the fact that there are smells of gas and oil from such a place, and also the fact that multitudes of motor vehicles come and go during the day and night; and also no one by choice would favour the proximity of apartment houses because these draw all kinds of people and largely increase motor traffic during the day and night. Funerals are conducted from churches into which the bodies are taken, and it is difficult to see what difference there is between a funeral being conducted from a church into which bodies are taken and one conducted from a funeral home where these same things are done, so far as an atmosphere of gloom is concerned.

The learned Justice of Appeal said that he could not conceive of a customer of the barber shop situate on the opposite side of the street refusing to enter that shop for a shave or a hair cut simply because he happened before entering to notice there was a funeral home across the street and that he might witness through the window of the shop a funeral being carried on, or that any of his tenants of the flat above would refuse to stay in the flat because they might at odd times witness a funeral. One can understand objection to a funeral home being established in a purely private residential district, but not to one established in a mixed active commercial and residential district such as this one is. It seems that the dominant purpose of the Act is to grant relief if the presiding Judge is satisfied on the material before him to grant relief. The question is largely one of fact, and the learned Judge, whose order is appealed, came to the proper conclusion. There is no reason for interfering with the discretion exercised by him in making the order, and the appeal should be dismissed with costs.

[McTague J.A. agreed with Middleton J.A.]

RE SECTION 51 LAND TITLES ACT (GRIEVE'S APPLICATION)

Alberta. Supreme Court. 1953. [1954] 1 D.L.R. 301

EGBERT J.: This is a petition by Annie Charlotte Grieve that the covenants and conditions contained in a certain agreement for sale be modified or discharged so as to permit the erection of an apartment house upon certain lands owned by the petitioner. . . .

The petitioner derived title from one William Bell Grieve, who, in turn, derived title from the C.P.R. Both Grieve's and the petitioner's titles were expressed to be subject to the Anderson caveat, [notice of a restrictive covenant limiting use of the land to the erection of a single dwelling house only] but there was no express assignment to either from the C.P.R. or from William Bell Grieve of any benefits or burdens arising under the C.P.R.—Anderson agreement aforesaid.

The petitioner has arranged to sell her lots to one Griffith on condition that a modification or discharge of the restrictive covenants can be obtained so as to permit of the erection on the land by Griffith of an apartment house.

Notice has been served by the petitioner on all interested parties (in accordance with an order made by this Court) and no one opposes the petition except one Blundun, who is the owner of the lot immediately adjoining the petitioner's property on the west, and who lives in a single-family dwelling-house, erected thereon. . . .

. . . Blundun is one of the persons who is entitled to enforce the covenants contained in the 1911 agreement and is properly before the Court. The question which remains, then, is whether, despite Blundun's opposition, I should modify or discharge the covenants, by virtue of the statutory authority conferred upon the Court by the provisions of s-s. (3) of s. 51

of the *Land Titles Act*, R.S.A. 1942, c. 205, which, as amended by 1950, c. 35, s. 2, reads in part as follows:

"(51(3) . . . but any such condition or [restrictive] covenant may be modified or discharged by order of the Court, on proof to the satisfaction of the Court that the modification will be beneficial to the persons principally interested in the enforcement of the condition or covenant, or that the condition or covenant conflicts with the provisions of a zoning by-law, official plan or scheme of development under *The Town and Rural Planning Act* and the modification or discharge is in the public interest.". . .

The situation here is that it is proposed to build on the land now owned by the petitioner a modern apartment building containing fifteen suites or apartments at a cost of approximately $150,000. As part of a general scheme, and under the provisions of Interior Development By-law No. 4271, the use classification of all lands in the City of Calgary was revised, and the present classification of the petitioner's land is "R.3", *i.e.*, classified for multiple-family dwellings. Mr. Martin, employed by the City of Calgary as City Planner, states that he verily believes there is a housing shortage in Calgary, and, in his belief, it would be in the public interest to permit the erection of an apartment building on these lands. He further says that an application has been received, and approved by the City Planning Department for the erection of the said apartment block, and permit therefor will issue subject to the Anderson caveat being removed. The apartment, if built, would accordingly comply with the zoning by-laws or regulations of the City of Calgary.

The first situation in which the Court may discharge or modify covenants such as these, is where the modifications will be beneficial "to the persons principally interested in the enforcement" thereof. It seems to me that the application cannot be based on that ground. That provision seems to contemplate the case where all those persons principally interested in the enforcement of the covenant are agreed that a modification of it will be to their mutual interest, and not to the case where some of those persons are persuaded it is in their interest while some of them are equally persuaded it is not in their interest, and refuse to consent to such modification. It seems to me that it was never intended that the Court should act the part of a benevolent despot and say to this latter class, "A modification of this covenant is in your interest whether you think so or not; and you are going to have it whether you want it or not". It would undoubtedly be in the interest of the petitioner, as she would receive a better price for her now vacant lots than she would otherwise receive, but there is no evidence before me that it would be in the interest of Blundun or of any other of "the persons principally interested in the enforcement" of the covenants, which incidentally appears to me to be a question quite different from the question of whether or not a modification might be in the public interest. . . .

It is urged here on behalf of the petitioner that a housing shortage exists in the City of Calgary, and that it would be in the public interest to alleviate that shortage by permitting the erection of an apartment building on those lands. Unless I take judicial notice of the nation-wide housing shortage, there is practically no evidence before me of the alleged housing shortage in Calgary, and even if I take judicial notice of such shortage, there is no evidence whatever before me that that shortage cannot be better and more fully alleviated by the erection of apartment houses on locations other than the petitioner's property.

The onus is surely on the petitioner to prove that the public interest will be peculiarly or particularly furthered by the modification which she proposes. This onus has not been in any way discharged. There is no evidence whatsoever that the character of the neighbourhood has been materially changed, so that an order can be made without doing violence to the rights of other landowners. There is no proof whatever that the covenant is spent, that it is so unworkable as to be of no value, or that the circumstances are such as to make its assertion clearly vexatious. . . .

The petition will, accordingly, be dismissed. . . .

RE EGLINTON AND BEDFORD PARK PRESBYTERIAN CHURCH. 1927. 61 O.L.R. 430 (Ontario. Court of Appeal). The Ontario Act still required that the modification be beneficial to the persons principally interested and the covenants, which had about two years to run, prohibited a church and any building within fifteen feet of the street line. MIDDLETON J.A.:

"But, if it is necessary to make the finding suggested, I am here prepared to make it. It appears to me to be greatly to the interest of all those principally concerned to have this corner-lot, adjacent to Yonge Street, occupied by a substantial and worthy edifice, not devoid of architectural charm and beauty, standing 20 feet from the street-line, rather than to leave the land vacant and an eyesore, subject to the jeopardy of the erection of residences on the street-line of Glenview Avenue and the peril of the erection in 2 years time of stores or of the ugly abomination called an apartment house which might cover the whole lot and might well assume the proportions of a skyscraper.

"It may sound harsh to be party to the forcing upon the residents something which they do not desire and to say that this is really in their best interests, but there is much in the material and in what took place during the course of the argument to indicate that some of the opposition to the proposition in reality arises from differences of opinion concerning matters of policy in connection with the church itself.

"The form of the order modifying the restriction should be to permit the erection of the church upon the lots in question, and there should be a provision in it that until the 2nd May, 1930, no part of the building shall be erected upon that portion of the 80 feet nearest to Mr. Carter's house, which is shewn upon the sketch as vacant land, and that the church should be no nearer Glenview Avenue than shewn in the plans."

RE ST. TIMOTHY'S CHURCH. 1930. 39 O.W.N. 93 (Ontario. Chambers). The restrictions permitted only the erection of residences on the land covered by a plan. The application to vary, made by the church, was opposed by three owners on the grounds that the neighbourhood was residential and its character would be destroyed by the church, traffic would be greatly increased and their properties would depreciate in value. It was reported of Middleton J.A.: "Those opposed to the scheme are convinced of the soundness of their objection; but, after having weighed the matter, the learned Judge has come to the conclusion that the objection has not anything like the substance which these owners think it has. In the first place, while the restriction is wide enough to require its amendment before the church can be built, it is impossible to believe that the erection of a church was intended to be excluded from the building scheme. What was the intent was the establishing of a residential district and the exclusion of factories, stores, warehouses, hotels, apartment houses, and other like buildings, which were inappropriate to a residential neighbourhood. It can never have been thought that a church would be regarded as objectionable. The particular edifice contemplated is of an artistic design and will be an ornament to the neighbourhood. It is not extraordinarily large so as to overshadow the surrounding buildings, and adequate land space has been provided. Nor is it the type of structure which will result in the great increase of traffic contemplated. It is a mere parish church intended to serve the people of the neighbourhood. It is not the type of a church which will attract many from a long distance so as to bring about much vehicular traffic. The suggestion that the erection of this church will result in the diversion of the heavy traffic from Yonge Street appears to be fanciful.

"In all the circumstances the order sought should be made.

"Upon the argument nothing was said as to the possibility of a church-bell causing a nuisance. If so desired by the respondents, a term may be inserted in the order providing that the church authorities must undertake that a bell will not be installed in the building. The noise from a bell is often rightly regarded by those in the immediate neighbourhood as objectionable."

LAW OF PROPERTY ACT, 1925
England. Statutes. 1925. Chapter 20

84. (1) The Authority hereinafter defined shall (without prejudice to any concurrent jurisdiction of the court) have power from time to time, on the application of any person interested in any freehold land affected by any restriction arising under covenant or otherwise as to the user thereof or the building thereon, by order wholly or partially to discharge or modify any such restriction (subject or not to the payment by the applicant of compensation to any person suffering loss in consequence of the order) on being satisfied—

(a) that by reason of changes in the character of the property or the neighbourhood or other circumstances of the case which the Authority may deem material, the restriction ought to be deemed obsolete, or that the continued existence thereof would impede the reasonable user of the land for public or private purposes without securing practical benefits to other persons, or, as the case may be, would unless modified so impede such user; or

(b) that the persons of full age and capacity for the time being or from time to time entitled to the benefit of the restriction, whether in respect of estates in fee simple or any lesser estates or interests in the property to which the benefit of the restriction is annexed, have agreed, either expressly or by implication, by their acts or omissions, to the same being discharged or modified; or

(c) that the proposed discharge or modification will not injure the persons entitled to the benefit of the restriction:

Provided that no compensation shall be payable in respect of the discharge or modification of a restriction by reason of any advantage thereby accruing to the owner of the land affected by the restriction, unless the person entitled to the benefit of the restriction also suffers loss in consequence of the discharge of modification, nor shall any compensation be payable in excess of such loss; but this provision shall not affect any right to compensation where the person claiming the compensation proves that by reason of the imposition of the restriction, the amount of the consideration paid for the acquisition of the land was reduced.

[The "Authority" is now the Lands Tribunal.]

(2) The court shall have power on the application of any person interested—

(a) To declare whether or not in any particular case any freehold land is affected by a restriction imposed by any instrument; or

(b) To declare what, upon the true construction of any instrument purporting to impose a restriction, is the nature and extent of the restriction thereby imposed and whether the same is enforceable and if so by whom.

(3) The Authority shall, before making any order under this section, direct such enquiries, if any, to be made of any local authority, and such notices, if any, whether by way of advertisement or otherwise, to be given to such of the persons who appear to be entitled to the benefit of the restriction intended to be discharged, modified, or dealt with as, having regard to any enquiries notices or other proceedings previously made, given, or taken, the Authority may think fit.

DRISCOLL *v*. CHURCH COMMISSIONERS FOR ENGLAND
England. Court of Appeal. [1956] 3 All E.R. 802

DENNING L.J.: In the years between 1865 and 1870 the predecessors of the Church Commissioners for England granted leases of certain premises in Croydon at a ground rent for ninety-nine years, and those leases are due to expire in 1964 and the succeeding years. (I expect that they were building leases at a ground rent.) In those leases the commissioners put a restrictive covenant. The usual form was,

"the premises shall not be used for any trade or business or otherwise than as a private dwelling-house save with the previous written consent of the lessor"

Large houses were built—ten-roomed or even twenty-roomed houses—and there is no doubt that at the date when the covenant was made it was contemplated that those houses would be occupied by persons of wealth and position with sufficient servants to keep such large houses going for use for a single family. In the course of years—and particularly since the wars, when it has become almost impossible to get servants to staff houses of this size—the Church Commissioners have readily granted consents to these houses being used, not for single private dwelling-houses, but to be converted into flats or as guest houses and so forth.

We are concerned with a number of these houses, the leaseholds of which were brought by the applicant, Mr. Terence John Driscoll, a few years back. We were told that when he bought them, some were used as boarding houses, others were self-contained flats, and two or three were still used for single private dwelling-houses. The applicant turned them into hostels and residential clubs for people from overseas. He had not, however, consent for this user of the premises, so he applied in 1949 to modify those restrictive covenants.

[Denning L.J. then referred to section 84 of the *Law of Property Act, 1925*, and continued:]

The Church Commissioners, when he sought a modification, did not turn it down altogether. There was a letter in September, 1949, in which the solicitors to the Church Commissioners, writing to the solicitors for the applicant, said:

"In certan cases licences have been granted permitting houses on the commissioners' estate to be used as guest houses, but the terms of the licences are such as to preserve character of the neighbourhood . . . We are prepared to take our clients' intructions with regard to the granting to Mr. Driscoll of a similar licence. The terms on which Messrs. Clutton would advise the granting of such a licence are as follows. . . ." Then it sets out a number of conditions: that each house should have its own resident matron or supervisor, that it is to be properly furnished, that it is to be kept outwardly as a private residence, that the number of persons occupying each house is to be restricted, that wireless sets are not to be audible outside, and so forth; and the licence was to be "revocable at the commissioners' pleasure and to be personal to" the applicant. Then the applicant has to make good within twelve months all the dilapidations.

So the Church Commissioners offered to grant him permission on those conditions. He did not see his way to agree to those conditions; and one can well see that they were rather stringent. There were negotiations, and he eventually determined to go to the tribunal to see if the tribunal would modify the restrictions. Before he got there, the commissioners issued writs for forfeiture in respect of six out of the eight leases . . .

Putting that matter on one side, the applications came before the president of the tribunal, Sir William FitzGerald. He sat himself to hear the case, he heard the evidence, and he went and inspected the site. He refused to modify the restriction. The applicant appeals to this court.

I must first say a word about appeals from the Lands Tribunal. Parliament has now enacted, in the *Lands Tribunal Act, 1949*, s. 3(4): "A decision of the Lands Tribunal shall be final"; but then there is this proviso:

"Provided that any person aggrieved by the decision as being erroneous in point of law may, within such time as may be limited by rules of court, require the tribunal to state and sign a case for the decision of the court . . ."

That is the provision under which the matter is brought before us. A person who is aggrieved by the decision as being erroneous in point of law may bring the matter up to this court. I would not wish those words unduly to hamper an appeal from the tribunal, and I do not think they do, because it is well settled that the question whether or not there is any evidence to support a particular finding is a question of law. It is also well settled that the question whether an inference drawn from primary facts is a legitimate inference is also a question of law. There have been before the Divisional Court several cases of dangerous driving where the Lord Chief Justice and his colleagues, having had primary facts stated, have held that the justices were not justified in dismissing the charge and have directed them to convict. Such was *Bracegirdle* v. *Oxley* (1947). It is for the tribunal of facts to find the primary facts, but having done so, the inferences from those facts are matters on which an aggrieved person can appeal.

In this case, therefore, we have to see what are the facts which the tribunal has found, and to see what are the conclusions which it has drawn from those facts. Then we have to see whether the conclusions which it has drawn are reasonable conclusions for it to draw. So far as the facts are concerned, the Church Commissioners agreed that there were changes in the neighbourhood. Mr. Clutton, their chartered surveyor, said:

"It is true that the houses were now too large for single occupation, but the commissioners would always agree to their conversion into flats or to other uses subject to such conditions as they considered fit to impose to maintain what they consider a proper standard for the neighbourhood."

The president of the tribunal made these findings:

"I was of opinion that, although there were changes in this area of Croydon, those changes were only to the extent that they reflected the change in regard to the size of private residences. It is true that few people could afford to keep these rather large houses as private residences today and consequently most of them have been converted into flats or guest houses, but I came to the conclusion that it is still essentially a residential area and that the owners and lessees of the houses in the area were entitled to the amenities which they enjoyed when they entered into their leases. One of those amenities was the benefit of a covenant that no trade or business should be carried on in the area and that premises should not be used otherwise than as a private dwelling-house save with the previous written consent of the lessor. I cannot regard that provision as obsolete today and I came to the conclusion that if those amenities were to be preserved the Church Commissioners should still retain the control which can be exercised by giving or withholding their consent, subject to the proposed conditions referred to in para. 11 above which I found as a fact reasonable. Furthermore, it was clear to me that the gravamen of the objection, which the evidence and my inspection satisfies me is valid, of the Church Commissioners is the manner in which the applicant conducts these clubs and the dilapidated condition into which he allowed the premises to fall. I do not hesitate to say that the applicant's failure in these respects does injure both the Church Commissioners and the other objectors [the other residents]. The only conclusion that I can draw is that the applicant's object in making this application is to free himself altogether from the reasonable fetters which the Church Commissioners consider necessary to maintain the character of this neighbourhood. The applicant failed to satisfy me on any of the grounds set out in s. 84 of the Act as a condition precedent for the discharge of modification of the covenants . . . In these circumstances I felt unable to exercise my discretion to grant this application."

So we have those primary facts (if I may so call them) in regard to these premises. When the premises were originally let in 1865 or 1867 it was undoubtedly contemplated that they should be used as single private dwelling-houses only; but at the present day, if they are to be used at all, there has to be a departure from that purpose which was originally contemplated; they must be turned into flats or into guest houses. In one sense, therefore, the covenant is obsolete, because it can be said no longer to serve the purposes originally contemplated; but, as Sir William FitzGerald says, the covenant still serves a useful purpose in another way: it enables the landlords, the Church Commissioners, to keep control over the use to which these houses are put. It enables the landlords here, the Church Commissioners, to keep the area as a residential area, instead of its being used, as it might have been, for commercial purposes. It seems to me that, so long as the landlord uses this covenant reasonably for a useful purpose, then, even though that purpose goes beyond what was contemplated ninety years ago, the covenant is not obsolete; whereas, if the covenant is shown no longer to serve any useful purpose, then, of course, it is obsolete. And in considering whether it still serves a useful purpose, I think that it is very important to see how the landlord, or whoever is entitled to the benefit of the covenant, has used it in the past and seeks to use it in the present. If he uses it reasonably, not in his own selfish interests but in the interests of the people of the neighbourhood generally, as, for instance, when he gives his consent for any sensible change of user, then it will serve a useful purpose. I should have thought that if he uses it unreasonably, for instance, to exact a premium as a condition of his consent; or if he refuses consent altogether when he ought to give it, as, for instance, for turning it into flats, it would no longer serve a useful purpose. In short, so long as the landlord uses the covenant reasonably in the interests of the public at large it is not obsolete, but, if he seeks to use it unreasonably, then it is obsolete.

The same result is reached by another line of reasoning. Assume that the covenant is obsolete because the premises cannot be used for single dwelling-houses. Nevertheless I am clearly of opinion that the tribunal has a discretion whether to discharge or modify these restrictions. We have been referred to *Julius* v. *Bishop of Oxford* (1880), which lays down the circumstances in which permissive words in a statute can be treated as compulsive. Counsel for the applicant urged us to say that the power given by the words "the authority shall have power by order wholly or partially to discharge or modify any such restriction" is not only a permissive power but also imposes a duty on the tribunal to modify the restriction in some way or other, though it has a discretion as to the precise way to be adopted. I do not agree with that view. It seems to me that this section does give a discretion in the tribunal whether to modify the restriction at all. In this case the President of the Lands Tribunal, having considered the matter and seen the premises, has said that in his discretion he does not think it is reasonable to modify it in the way proposed or sought by the applicant. I see no reason to suppose that he exercised his discretion wrongly.

I would only add that, before the tribunal, the applicant sought to make a case on the second limb of s. 84 (1) (a):

> "that the continued existence thereof [of the restriction] would impede the reasonable user of the land for public or private purposes without securing practical benefits to other persons . . ."

The president of the tribunal found that that was not made out. On the facts which I have stated, it seems to me that he was well justified in so saying. The continued existence of this restriction does not impede the reasonable user of the land when we know that, on the findings of the tribunal, the Church Commissioners have given their consent freely and reasonably to all reasonable changes of user, such as enabling the houses to be turned into flats or into guest houses, subject to conditions which they have felt it necessary to impose in order to preserve the residential character of the area.

I can find no fault in point of law with the reasoning of the tribunal, and I would dismiss the appeal accordingly.

[The opinions of Hodson and Morris L.JJ., who agreed or at least reached the same conclusions, are omitted.]

RE BERRIDGE'S APPLICATION

England. Lands Tribunal. 1954. Reference No. LP/34/1953

BAILEY Esq.: This is an application by the owners of a piece of land situate in Yardley Woods Road, in the City of Birmingham, for the discharge or modification of a restrictive covenant.

The land is situated on the west side of Yardley Wood Road, at a distance of about 200 yards from the junction of Wake Green Road. It contains about 7,000 square yards, with a frontage to Yardley Wood Road of 156 feet. Part of the land is back land lying behind the gardens of four houses, Nos. 239, 241, 253 and 245, Yardley Wood Road. It has been laid out and cultivated as a garden and is at present being used in that way.

The applicants are the representatives of the Third Church of Christ Scientist at present established at Camp Hill, Birmingham. The premises which they occupy there have become unsuitable because that part of the city has become almost entirely industrial. They purchased the land in question early in 1953, a site considered by them to be well suited for their purposes.

The conveyance by which the land was transferred to them is dated March 23, 1953, and the transfer is subject to the following restrictive covenants originally imposed when what was known as the Willmotts' Wake Green Estate was sold in building plots in 1903. . .

The applicants ask that these restrictions should be modified so as to permit the erection of buildings of a temporary or permanent nature to be used as a church and Sunday school and reading room and for other church purposes.

Objections to the application were lodged by ten parties.

Of these parties four are the owner-occupiers of the four houses—Nos. 239, 241, 243 and 245 Yardley Wood Road—behind which lies the back land already referred to.

Three are interested in a vacant piece of land fronting on to the west side of Yardley Wood Road adjoining the south boundary of No. 245.

One is the owner-occupier of a house and garden situated further down Yardley Wood Road on the west side and numbered 257.

One is the owner of a house—Heathercroft, No. 8 St. Agnes Road. This house and garden is situated at the back of the land in question; the garden boundary forming part of the west boundary of the "back" land referred to.

The other objector is Mrs. Nellie Pratchett Chattock, now living at Budleigh Salterton, Devon, who is the sole surviving representative of the Trustees of Willmotts' Wake Green Estate. This is a formal objection lodged in pursuance of the Trustees' duty towards the several purchasers of building plots to encourage the preservation of the amenities for the common good of all residents on the estate.

The owners of Nos. 239, 241 and 243 Yardley Wood Road withdrew their objections at the hearing in consideration of an agreement by the applicants to sell to them a piece of land 21 feet wide adjoining their back fences and the back fence of No. 245, so that the privacy of their gardens should be protected by the screen of trees and shrubs growing on the land.

I have considered the evidence given before me as to changes which have taken place in the neighbourhood since the restrictions were imposed and I have been round the roads affected with which I already had acquaintance.

There have been changes in the neighbourhood in the way of a new use for some of the residences, some of which are now being used as nursing homes and offices. On the other hand I find that these changes are not such as to render the restriction obsolete and I have felt myself bound to hesitate before passing from a consideration of that precedent condition to decide whether the application should be granted for other reasons.

A large part of the land in question is back land which has been used as an extension of the garden to a house in St. Agnes Road—No. 6—next door to "Heathercroft," the house belonging to one of the objectors. I find that the continued existence of the restriction will impede the reasonable user of this land, because I am satisfied that in future the cost of keeping up a garden of this size attached to a house of the character of No. 6 St. Agnes Road or any other house in the neighbourhood will make it unlikely that any future occupant of any of these houses would retain the land as a garden.

And I further find that the use as a Christian Science church is as good a use for the land as is likely to be devised as far as can be seen into the future.

It remains to consider whether the objectors will be injured by the modification. I find that no injury will be suffered by Mr. Duncan Ronald Thomas, of 257 Yardley Wood Road, nor to Alfred Henry Higgins, William Henry Arthur Horton, or Francis Henry Simpson in respect of their interests in the vacant land between Nos. 245 and 255 Yardley Wood Road, nor to the same Francis Henry Simpson in respect of No. 255 Yardley Wood Road.

I also find that Miss Ena Marjorie Bartley will not be injured in respect of her interest in "Heathercroft," No. 8 St. Agnes Road.

The objectors who are most affected are those who are the owner-occupiers of Nos. 239, 241, 243 and 245 Yardley Wood Road.

The first three of these have withdrawn their objections on terms.

The owners, Mr. George Herbert Yule and Mrs. Evelyn Yule, of No. 245 Yardley Wood Road, have not seen their way to join in the agreement for the purchase of the strip of land which has been agreed to be transferred to the other three owners, their neighbours. They will be protected by this transfer in the same way as their neighbours and I do not find that their property will be injured. If the application is not granted there is the possibility that the back land will lie derelict for many years which would be a serious detriment to them.

I therefore decide that this application should be granted, subject to the following conditions:

1. The land to be used for the erection of a Christian Science church and Sunday school and reading room, with normal offices and rooms, and subsidiary buildings.

2. Such building or buildings to be of a permanent structure, subject to the possible erection of a temporary building for three years in accordance with the letter dated September 11, 1952, addressed to the Secretary of Sites and Buildings Committee, Third Church of Christ Scientist, from the Birmingham City Engineer and Surveyor.

3. The buildings to be single storey buildings with no galleries and no tower and to be placed approximately in the position shown on the plan produced to the Tribunal prepared by the Architects' Department of the Bournville Village Trust and marked "Drawing No. 150 /1 Scale 1/500 JSR 16. 7. 52."

4. The buildings are not to be used for week-day clubs, bazaars, entertainments or social functions.

5. Land not covered by buildings to be laid out and maintained as a garden or orchard, save that if the applicants so decide some part of it to be used as a car park.

6. The agreement for the transfer of the land to a width of 21 feet adjoining Nos. 239, 241, 243 and 245 Yardley Wood Road to be completed . . .

NOTE. Apart from its intrinsic interest this decision is reproduced as an illustration of the Lands Tribunal at work when the member is qualified as a surveyor rather than as a lawyer. Mr. Bailey is described as a B.Sc., a Member of the Institute of Civil Engineers and a Fellow of the Royal Institute of Chartered Surveyors. The decision is edited from the version reproduced in Newsom, *The Discharge and Modification of Restrictive Covenants* (1957), a valuable text on the subject as it is now being developed by the two professions in England.

10. Private and Public Control in Conflict

RE SECTION 51 LAND TITLES ACT (GRIEVE'S APPLICATION). [1954] 1 D.L.R. 301 (Alberta. Supreme Court). The facts of this case are set out above at page 446. On the question whether "the condition or covenant conflicts with the provision of a zoning by-law, official plan or scheme of development under *The Town and Rural Planning Act* . . ." EGBERT J.: "I can find nothing in the material before me to indicate that the conditions or covenants sought to be modified conflict with the provisions of any zoning by-law, official plan or scheme of development. It is true that Mr. Martin, City Planner, says in his affidavit that 'as part of a general scheme and under the provisions of the Interior Development By-law, Number 4271, the use classification of all lands in the City of Calgary was revised and that the present classification of Lots 11 and 12, Block 233, Plan 5700 A.G., is R. 3, that is classified for multiple family dwellings'. But surely all that means, all it can possibly mean is that insofar as the City of Calgary is concerned, its zoning by-laws or regulations have been altered so as to permit of multiple-family dwellings being erected in an area where only single-family dwellings might have been erected before. There is nothing whatsoever to suggest that the present classification is obligatory, that only multiple-family dwellings may be erected in the area, and that the erection of further single-family dwellings is prohibited. How then can it be said that a covenant enforceable by and against each individual owner in the area conflicts with a provision which is merely permissive and not obligatory? The city has said 'In this area you may, at your discretion, build either multiple or single family dwellings', to which the owners promptly reply 'We have already agreed among ourselves that we will build only single-family dwellings'. How can it be said that there is anything conflicting between the two statements?

"If I am right in my opinion that no conflict exists such as is contemplated by the statute, the matter is disposed of as the second part of the subsection is not then applicable, but if I am wrong in this opinion, I must still consider whether the proposed modification or development is in the public interest. . . ."

NOTE. The requirement that regard be had to conflict with *The Town and Rural Planning Act* in Alberta is not to be found in most provinces. The issue is squarely raised where the restrictive covenant permits, say, *only* single family houses, and the zoning permits, say, *only*, multiple dwelling buildings such as high rise apartments. One or the other of the controls must give way, or the land is effectively sterilized. The private control could be modified or discharged in jurisdictions having legislation similar to the Ontario and English Acts reproduced in the last section, and the equity jurisdiction dating at least from the *British Museum* case (1822) could probably be invoked otherwise, although probably only discharge and not modification is possible under the cruder rule of the Chancery Courts.

There would seem to be little ground for preferring the private choice over the public choice if collision is unavoidable. Nevertheless in Ontario where the legislation is silent on this point, under *The Planning Act*, s. 30(19) a person who seeks an amendment to a zoning by-law and is refused by the Council may appeal to the Municipal Board for an order directing the Council to amend the by-law. In deciding whether to direct an amendment should the Board consider the private restrictions? Both English and American courts have had to deal with this conflict and some instances are next noted.

RE LEESHORE CONSTRUCTION COMPANY. 1955. Unreported (Ontario. High Court). This case was an attempt by the Leeshore Construction Company in Etobicoke, Ontario, to free itself of covenants requiring it, among other things, to build only one two storey or one storey and a half private dwelling house on each of its lots. Leeshore wished to build "duplexes" and "double duplexes" on the property, which was then zoned by Etobicoke Zoning By-law 7673 as "second density".

An application was made for the amendment of the By-law rezoning the land to the "fifth density". On September 8, 1954, the Etobicoke Council passed By-law 9224 to accomplish this purpose, and added a rider that "the erection of duplexes and double duplexes shall be the only uses permitted under the Fifth Density residential classification". Before By-law 9224 was approved by the Ontario Municipal Board the Council changed its mind and passed By-law 9329 amending By-law 9224 to allow only duplexes.

Thereafter Leeshore secured a formal refusal from the Council to amend the By-law so as to permit "double duplexes", or "quadriplexes" and an appeal was launched to the Municipal Board under what is now section 30 (19) of *The Planning Act*. The appeal was allowed and the amendment directed.

In his affidavit in support of the application to have the restrictive covenants discharged the president of Leeshore deposed that the directed amendment would allow "only the building of 8 double duplexes and 1 duplex as shown on the attached plan and in the event that this application to discharge or vary the restrictions against title is not approved of, the Company will be unable to use the lands in question".

Notwithstanding that the sterility of the lands by the operation of the zoning by-law and the restrictive covenants was self imposed Young Co. Ct. J. granted an order discharging the covenants as requested. Counsel in the case reports that the oral argument proceeded on the ground that the private right should give way to the public interest.

MARSHALL *v*. SALT LAKE CITY. 1943. 141 P 2d 704 (Utah. Supreme Court). LARSON J.: "... 3. We come now to the matters involved in plaintiff's second cause of action, which raises issues beyond those discussed above. This relates to the Gibbs property on Hubbard Avenue, and the effect on the issues involved in this action, of the building restrictions imposed by the deed conveying those lands from the Douglas Heights Improvement Company to the Hubbard Investment Company. The Gibbs property, together with other lands adjoining and abutting it, were in 1913 owned by the Douglas Heights Land and Improvement Company. It conveyed the land by warranty deed, recorded in February of that year, to the Hubbard Investment Company, which deed contained certain building restrictions, one reading "nor shall any building for business purposes be erected on said land". As far as the record shows these restrictions have never been abrogated or modified. The zoning ordinance provides that its provisions do not abrogate or annul any covenants running with the land. The trial court held that these restrictions in the deed ran with the land and therefore Gibbs could not build, and the city could not permit him to build business structures on the land. The city complains of this ruling because: First, Gibbs was not made a party to the suit; second, plaintiff was not a party, nor an assignee of a party, to the covenant; that is, he did not own any of the lands covered by the covenant. In the interest of Gibbs, Attorney E. A. Walton filed in this court a brief *amicus curiae* in which he further assails the holding of the trial court because the record shows that Gibbs does not deraign his title through the parties to the covenant, but adversely to them, in that Gibbs claims through a tax title, which, it is contended, wiped out, or is free from, the restrictions of the covenant. "That zoning ordinances cannot override, annul or relieve land from building restrictions, or covenants placed thereon by deed is well settled, and in fact is not controverted by the parties before the court.

"But in the case before us, plaintiff was not the owner of, or interested in, any lands covered by the covenant. It is elemental that such covenants as run with the land are only enforceable by the parties thereto or their assigns. Only such parties can claim the benefits of the covenant. Since plaintiff has no right to enforce the covenant, he is in no position to complain of its violation. As to what rights, if any, an owner of property covered by the covenants may have against Gibbs, or the right of any such person to enjoin the erection of a business building on Gibbs' property, is not before us and we express no opinion thereon." [All citations omitted.]

DAVID *v*. BOWEN. 1941. 12 S.E. 2d. 873 (Georgia. Supreme Court). An action to restrain the use of house as a boarding house contrary to a restrictive covenant not to use for "any commercial or manufacturing establishment or factory or apartment house of any kind" and "Not to build more than one residence on said lot".

ATKINSON J.: "Construed strictly and most strongly against the grantor, the covenant is not violated by the defendant, successor in estate to the grantee, by occupying the dwelling-house on the lot as a residence and permanent home for herself and family, and using the same for a boarding house from which she earns her livelihood. . . . It does not affect the case that the property is located in a zoned district provided by municipal ordinance regulating the keeping of boarders, and that the defendant had applied for a license for carrying on such business."

MARTEN *v*. FLIGHT REFUELLING, LTD. [1961] 2 All E. R. 696 (England. Chancery Division). Land later made subject to a restrictive covenant that it was not to be used for other than agricultural purposes without the consent of the grantor was first requisitioned by the Air Ministry in 1942 under its emergency powers. In 1942 a farm containing some 562 acres of which 200 acres of the land requisitioned was sold to its agricultural tenant subject to the covenant. At the end of the war the Air Ministry did not give up the land, but continued to use it for Ministry purposes. Flight Refuelling, Ltd. occupied part of the land in 1942 and carried out work for the Ministry under contract, as well as servicing of Belgian government aircraft, nuclear work for the Atomic Energy Administration, and work on flight refuelling equipment which was of general use to industry. The covenant was not said to be for the benefit of any particular land, but the Court accepted Upjohn J.'s view in the *Newton Abbott* case (noted above on page 393) that "attendant circumstances" might be looked at, and indeed to refuse to would "have involved not only an injustice but a departure from common sense". The 200 acres, on the whole 562 acres formed part of the Cricket Estate, in Dorset, consisting of some 7,500 acres, and it was objected that the covenant could hardly benefit the whole area. *Re Ballard's Conveyances* was referred to. The Court decided that that case turned upon the absence of any evidence to show how a large area might be benefited, and in this case three witnesses were called, two of whom the court found "clear and convincing". The covenant was declared to be enforceable by Martin, the original covenantee, but an injunction would not lie to restrain the Ministry's authorized use, although the activity of Flight Refuelling, Ltd., in respect of the Belgian aircraft servicing, and the nuclear research not for the Ministry, was restrained. WILBERFORCE J.: "The basic statute is the Defence Act, 1842, and by subsequent legislation the powers of this Act have been made available to the Secretary of State for Air. These powers may be used for the purposes of the Air Force or the defence of the realm. The Acts provide, as one would expect, for the acquisition of land by purchase, but do not, so it appears, provide for such acquisition to be free from any restrictive covenant formerly binding the land. In fact, the land was conveyed to the Air Ministry, it was so conveyed subject to the covenant, so far as valid and subsisting. This being the position as regards acquisition of the land, the Attorney-General claims that, although the covenant may not actually be extinguished, the court cannot interfere with any user of the land for the purposes for which the land could be acquired, that is to say, the service of the Air Force or the defence of the realm. He relies, for authority to support this, on *Hawley* v. *Steele* (1877). . . .

"[T]he Air Ministry having acquired this land for use as an aerodrome, the court cannot criticise the ministry's choice and say that some other land might just as well, or better, have been chosen; nor can it interfere with any reasonable use of the land for that purpose. Further, Sir George Jessel M.R., appears to me to have decided [in *Hawley* v. *Steele*] that the protection of the Act applies not only to the Secretary of State himself but to individuals acting under his authority, certainly to his own officers, and possibly to other individuals, provided that they are carrying out for him those functions which the Act authorises him to carry out. That case, therefore, gets me to this point: that the court cannot interfere with the use by the Air Ministry of the land as an aerodrome, or for any of the statutory purposes for which the land has been acquired. Indeed, the plaintiffs, by their counsel, disclaimed any intention so to do. . . .

From the initial period when possession of the airfield was taken for indisputably defence purposes, one passes gradually over fifteen years, to a stange when the Air Ministry, no longer needing the airfield for immediate operational purposes, desires to have it available for any emergency and decides that the most economical method of so doing is to make use of a commercial company which is willing to pay a substantial rent for the right to use the airfield and its facilities for its own purposes, some of those purposes being of direct and others of indirect interest to the ministry itself. . . .

"It would be unreasonable, in my judgment, and not in accordance with the principles stated so clearly in *Hawley* v. *Steele* to permit the company to store any products made surplus to the requirements of the services while forbidding it to sell them to other consumers. It is a question of degree, no doubt, at what point the company's production assumes the dimensions of a separate activity, but I am content to hold that on its present scale that portion of the flight refuelling activity which is beyond what is needed for service purposes ought not to be prohibited.

That leaves the nuclear work and that done for the Belgian Air Force. Neither of these, in my judgment, falls within the statutory protection, even when extended as generously as I have thought right to extend it. . . ."

WYLD *v*. SILVER. [1961] 3 All E.R. 1014 (England. Chancery Division). In this case, notwithstanding that planning permission under the 1947 Act to erect five bungalows had been given, and work commenced, an injunction was granted to restrain the building when an ancient public right to hold a fair on the parcel was established. The right was recited in an Enclosure Award made in 1803 under a private Act of Parliament of 1799, c. 118. The award recited that "a due compensation hath been made by the said commissioners on the quantity of earth of the said allotments." No fair had been held within living memory, but the May 29, 1875 issue of the "Windsor and Eton Express" referred to the annual pleasure fair being held at Wraysbury in that month.

CHAPTER 8

CONSTITUTIONAL AUTHORITY TO REGULATE LAND USE

When all else fails, try the Constitution.

ANON.

1. IN CANADA

No attempt has been made in this section to reproduce all the cases on Canadian constitutional law, nor to point out all the occasions where conflict exists in potential, if not actual, land use regulation by the Dominion and the provinces. Instead, illustrations have been selected from one area of regulation that is basic to modern planning techniques. The illustrations could, however, be multiplied many times. It should be kept in mind that whenever a government (or legislature) is authorized to develop land it has, implicitly, a power to plan, as well as carry out that plan. In the discussion on shopping centres, no consideration was given to the possibility of having banks and post offices located in the centres, yet most operators of shopping centres are anxious to have banks and a post office to add to the convenience of shoppers. Both institutions are, of course, subject to Dominion legislative power. Both institutions can go where Parliament sends them and the provincial legislature cannot keep them out.

The area that has been selected for somewhat more detailed study is transportation. For a comprehensive treatment of constitutional questions in transport and communication see Laskin, *Canadian Constitutional Law*, (2nd ed. 1960) ch. IX. Particularly since the advent of the motor car, transport has been perhaps the most crucial factor in planning a modern community. In planning for the motor car one has to plan not only the size and location of roads in relation to surrounding land uses, one has also to consider the alternative means of transport, for people and goods continue to be moved in significant numbers and quantities by means of railways, ships and aircraft. Section 92 (10) of the *British North America Act* makes it fairly clear that railways are a Dominion concern (although railway hotels, a more profitable aspect of Canadian railway operation (?), would appear to be within provincial control, at least for labour regulation: *C.P.R.* v. *Attorney General of British Columbia* (1950) holding that the Empress Hotel in Victoria, B.C. was not a part of the C.P.R. works and undertaking connecting British Columbia with other provinces and had not been declared a work for the general benefit of Canada. The *Hours of Work Act*, R.S.B.C. 1948, c. 154 therefore applied to the Empress Hotel.

Less clear is the position of roads themselves. While every province assumes control over its highways, which it shares to some extent with various levels of local government, there would seem to be ample authority for the Dominion to build and regulate the use of highways, at least those that could be called "Undertakings connecting the Province with any other or others of the Provinces." But even a local road could be built for national defence purposes. Compare, as to the operation of a bus line between Nova Scotia and New Brunswick, and into the State of Maine, *Winner* v. *S.M.T. (Eastern) Ltd.* (1951). And see, following the Supreme Court's decision, the *Motor Vehicle Transport Act*, 1953–54 (Can.) c. 59, which effectively delegates Dominion jurisdiction to existing provincial boards. Even when the province assumes control over its highways a conflict with Dominion jurisdiction arises every time the highway crosses a railway.

Canada is an important shipping nation and the provinces of British Columbia, Ontario, Quebec, New Brunswick, Nova Scotia and of course the island provinces of Prince Edward Island and Newfoundland, all have harbours connecting with international trade routes. Even Manitoba has, for a short season, an important harbour at Churchill. Control of harbours would appear to be implicit in legislative power with relation to "shipping and navigation", and the conflict of this power with municipal government, the lowest of our three tiers of government, is evidenced by the *Montreal Harbour Commissioners* case below. In connection with the navigation power, it is important to remember that a power to regulate shipping on a navigable river necessarily involves a power to control the location, construction and maintenance of a bridge over that river. The most recent Dominion undertaking under this power is the highly publicized St. Lawrence seaway project. See the *St. Lawrence Seaway Authority,* R.S.C. 1952, c. 242, as amended.

Dominion authority over aerial transport was recognized in 1932, in *Re Regulation and Control of Aeronautics.* The conflict with municipal government again is evident from *Johannesson* v. *West St. Paul,* below. As to administration of legislation respecting transport of goods by rail and water, see the *Transport Act,* R.S.C. 1952, c. 271.

Telephone and radio communication are also within Dominion jurisdiction and in *Toronto* v. *Bell Telephone* (1905) the Privy Council upheld the right of the Bell Company to dig up the streets of the City of Toronto and lay cables under them.

BRITISH NORTH AMERICA ACT

91. It shall be lawful for the Queen, by and with the Advice and Consent of the Senate and House of Commons, to make Laws for the Peace, Order and Good Government of Canada in relation to all Matters not coming within the Classes of Subjects by this Act assigned exclusively to the Legislatures of the Provinces; and for greater certainty, but not so as to restrict the Generality of the foregoing Terms of this Section, it is hereby declared that (notwithstanding anything in this Act) the exclusive Legislative Authority of the Parliament of Canada extends to all Matters coming within the Classes of Subjects next hereinafter enumerated, that is to say: . . .

5. Postal Service.
6. The Census and Statistics
7. Militia, Military and Naval Service and Defence . . .
10. Navigation and Shipping . . .
15. Banking . .
16. Savings Banks . .
24. Indians and Lands reserved for the Indians . . .
28. The Establishment, Maintenance and Management of Penitentiaries.

92. In each Province the Legislature may exclusively make Laws in relation to Matters coming within the Classes of Subjects next hereinafter enumerated; that is to say: . .

5. The Management and Sale of the Public Lands belonging to the Province, and of the Timber and Wood thereon . . .

8. Municipal Institutions in the Province.
9. Shop, Saloon, Tavern, Auctioneer, and other Licenses, in order to the raising of a Revenue for Provincial, Local, or Municipal Purposes.
10. Local Works and Undertakings, other than such as are of the following Classes—
    (a) Lines of Steam or other Ships, Railways, Canals, Telegraphs, and other Works and Undertakings, connecting the Province with any other or others of the Provinces, or extending beyond the Limits of the Province:
    (b) Lines of Steamships between the Province and any British or Foreign Country:
    (c) Such Works as, although wholly situate within the Province, are before or after their Execution declared by the Parliament of Canada to be for the general Advantage of Canada or for the Advantage of Two or more of the Provinces . . .
13. Property and Civil Rights in the Province . . .
16. Generally all matters of a merely local or private nature in the Province.

93. In and for each Province the Legislature may exclusively make Laws in relation to Education . . .

95. In each Province the Legislature may make Laws in relation to Agriculture in the Province, and to Immigration into the Province; and it is hereby declared that the Parliament of Canada may from Time to Time make Laws in relation to Agriculture in all or any of the Provinces, and to Immigration into all or any of the Provinces and any Law of the Legislature of a Province, relative to Agriculture or to Immigration, shall have effect in and for the Province as long and as far only as it is not repugnant to any Act of the Parliament of Canada.

96. The Governor-General shall appoint the Judges of the Superior, District and County Courts in each Province, except those of the Courts of Probate in Nova Scotia and New Brunswick.

HODGE *v.* THE QUEEN. 1883. 9 App. Cas. 117 (Ontario. Privy Council). LORD FITZGERALD: "It appears to their Lordships, however, that the objection thus raised by the appellants is founded on an entire misconception of the true character and position of the provincial legislatures. They are in no sense delegates of or acting under any mandate from the Imperial Parliament. When the *British North America Act* enacted that there should be a legislature for Ontario, and that its legislative assembly should have exclusive authority to make laws for the Province and for provincial purposes in relation to the matters enumerated in sect. 92, it conferred powers not in any sense to be exercised by delegation from or as agents of the Imperial Parliament, but authority as plenary and as ample within the limits prescribed by sect. 92 as the Imperial Parliament in the plenitude of its power possessed and could bestow. Within these limits of subjects and area the local legislature is supreme, and has the same authority as the Imperial Parliament, or the Parliament of the Dominion, would have had under like circumstances to confide to a municipal institution or body of its own creation authority to make by-laws or resolutions as to subjects specified in the enactment, and with the object of carrying the enactment into operation and effect.

"It is obvious that such an authority is ancillary to legislation, and without it an attempt to provide for varying details and machinery to carry them out might become oppressive, or absolutely fail. . . . It was argued at the bar that a legislature committing important regulations to agents or delegates effaces itself. That is not so. It retains its powers intact, and can, whenever it pleases, destroy the agency it has created and set up another, or take the matter directly into his own hands. How far it shall seek the aid of subordinate agencies, and how long it shall continue them, are matters for each legislature, and not for Courts of Law to decide."

CITY OF MONTREAL *v.* MONTREAL HARBOUR COMMISSIONERS. [1926] A.C. 299 (Quebec. Privy Council). The Commissioners are a corporation which from before 1867 controlled the harbour of Montreal. The harbour became the property of the Crown in right of Canada at Confederation, and in subsequent years it was extended by Dominion statute down the river. The town of Maisonneuve (later annexed to Montreal) had a sewer on First Avenue that emptied into the river where the Commissioners proposed to erect an embankment, and in the ensuing conflict over the respective rights of Maisonneuve, Quebec Province and the Commissioners, Maisonneuve commenced an action against the Commissioners for damages for interference with their right to empty sewage into the river. The action was later adopted by Montreal who claimed further damages for the Commissioners' unlawful interference with the construction of an extension of the sewer across the harbour boundaries. The action was dismissed. The Privy Council distinguished between the Commissioners' proprietary rights in the harbour and the Province's proprietary rights in the river apart from the harbour, and the city's right, which was a mere license from the Province as owner of the river. VISCOUNT HALDANE: "Now there is no doubt that the power to control navigation and shipping conferred on the Dominion by s. 91 is to be widely construed. . . . But while this is so, it does not appear to their Lordships that the right of the Dominion extends so as to authorize them to vest in a body like the Commissioners an exclusive right to occupy property of the Province without compensation and to erect upon it permanent works, such as quays, docks and railways. . . .

"But this by no means disposes of the case. It was undoubtedly within the power of the Province of Quebec, with a view to the improvement of the harbour of Montreal, to waive her strict legal rights and expressly or by inference to sanction the works undertaken for that purpose, and it must be considered whether such a sanction is to be inferred in the present case. In their Lordships' opinion it is. . . . It was not until the year 1919, when the works were far advanced, that the Attorney-General of Quebec intervened; and although at the time of his intervention he claimed to have the Commissioners excluded from possession of their works, he has at no time insisted on the claim, and is content to have the legal rights in the bed and foreshore of the river determined. Having regard to all these facts, their Lordships are satisfied that the Provincial authorities have waived any claim to interfere with the existing works, and that, so far as they are concerned, they are bound by what has been done. . . . The only right of the City to discharge their sewage into the river rests on the licence of the Provincial authorities, which was itself (as the statute of 1911 shows) made subsidiary to the proceedings of the Harbour Commissioners. The appeal of the City therefore fails."

QUESTIONS. Does the holding in the Montreal case mean that the Dominion Parliament cannot confiscate land without compensation? Or is the holding limited to confiscation of provincial land? Is the power to make laws in section 91 or 92 not broadly enough stated to authorize confiscation? Is there to be implied some "bill of rights" here?

NOTE. See now the *National Harbours Board Act*, R.S.C. 1952, c. 187, which sets up a Board with jurisdiction over the harbours of Halifax, Saint John, Chicoutimi, Quebec, Three Rivers, Montreal and Vancouver, and all other harbours that the Governor in Council may choose to transfer to it. By section 10(1), "When previously authorized by the Governor in Council, the Board may acquire, hold, possess, sell, dispose of, or lease real and personal, movable and immovable property; and may either by itself or in co-operation with others construct, maintain and operate roads, railways, vessels, plant and equipment; and generally do such things and exercise such powers as it deems necessary for the efficient administration, management and control of the harbours, works and other property under its jurisdiction."

Apart from the *National Harbours Board Act* there is special legislation relating to individual ports and harbour commissioners. See, for example, the *Port Alberni Harbour Commissioners Act*, S.C., 1947, c. 42; the *Belleville Harbour Commissioners Act.*, S.C., 1952, c. 34; the *Hamilton Harbour Commissioners Act*, S.C., 1951, c. 17.

The *Toronto Harbour Commissioners Act* was passed by the legislature of the former province of Canada, in 1850 (See c. 80). Of the Toronto Harbour Commissioners, the Toronto *Municipal Handbook* for 1960 had this to say:

"The opening of the new St. Lawrence Seaway system in 1959 commenced a new era for the Port of Toronto and the City it serves. Ocean vessels of over 500 feet in length became a common sight along the waterfront. Cargoes of sugar from Mauritius, automobiles from Europe, and steel from the United Kingdom moved into the area, while exports of soya bean meal and scrap metal moved to foreign markets. In addition to these single type cargoes, the entire direct overseas business took a tremendous upsurge with almost a 200 per cent increase taking place. With the expeditious handling of ships and cargo, the result was that the port gained a reputation of being the finest on the Great Lakes.

"A Municipal Airport located at Toronto Island is one of the ten busiest airports in Canada. It has a seaplane base in addition to land runways. It is administered by the Toronto Harbour Commissioners for and at the expense of the City. The same arrangement is in force with regard to the Toronto Harbour Police. This Marine Police Force, equipped with speedboats and lifeboats, patrols the more than 40 miles of waterways that exist in the harbour limits."

THE MUNICIPAL ACT
Ontario. Revised Statutes. 1960. Chapter 249

377. By-laws may be passed by the councils of all municipalities:

43. For making, improving and maintaining public wharves, docks and slips, and for preserving shores, bays, harbours, rivers or waters and the banks thereof.

44. For regulating harbours.

JOHANNESSON *v.* WEST ST. PAUL

Manitoba. Supreme Court of Canada. [1951] 4 D.L.R. 609

ESTEY J.: The appellants submit that s. 921 of the *Municipal Act,* R.S.M. 1940, c. 141 is legislation in relation to aeronautics and, therefore, beyond the competency of the Legislature of Manitoba to enact.

"921. Any municipal corporation may pass by-laws for licensing, regulating, and, within certain defined areas, preventing the erection, maintenance and continuance of aerodromes or places where aeroplanes are kept for hire or gain."

The facts out of which this issue arises are as follows:

The appellant, Konrad Johannesson, has been engaged in commercial aviation in northern Manitoba and Saskatchewan since 1928. He desired an airport at Winnipeg and on September 27, 1947, obtained an option upon, and on April 20, 1948, purchased a portion of River Lot 33 Pl. 3992 in the respondent municipality for the purpose of equipping and maintaining it as an aerodrome.

The respondent municipality, under date of May 27, 1948, passed By-law No. 292, by virtue of the foregoing s. 921. The effect of this by-law may be briefly expressed: (a) As to Lots 1 to 33, Pl. 3992, in the respondent municipality, the erection or maintenance of any aerodrome or machine shop for testing or repairing aircraft is entirely prohibited; (b) in the remaining portion neither of the foregoing may be erected or maintained without a licence from the respondent municipality.

The appellants, on October 22, 1948, asked the Court to declare s. 921 ultra vires of the Legislature of Manitoba and the enactment of By-law 292 by the respondent municipality a nullity.

Campbell J. held that the provincial Legislature had jurisdiction to enact s. 921 and that the by-law was valid. His judgment was affirmed by a majority of the Court of Appeal in Manitoba, Coyne J.A. dissenting.

The Attorneys-General for Manitoba and the Dominion (the latter for the first time in this Court) have intervened and contended respectively that the Province has and has not competent authority to enact s. 921.

The judgments in the Court below proceed upon the basis that the Aeronautics Convention in Paris, ratified on behalf of the British Empire on June 1, 1922, was still in effect. Mr. Varcoe, on behalf of the Attorney-General of Canada, however, informed the Court that this Convention had been abrogated by the Civil Aviation Convention in Chicago in 1944, which became binding on Canada on April 4, 1947. This is important as the Chicago Convention, unlike the Paris Convention, is signed by Canada in her own right and, therefore, s. 132 of the *B.N.A. Act* has no application in determining the jurisdiction of the Parliament of Canada and the provincial Legislatures in relation thereto: *Radio* case, (1932), *Labour Conventions* case, (1937). This does not, however, mean that the *Aeronautics* case (1932) is of no importance in a consideration of the present issue.

In that case the Judicial Committee considered three questions:

"(1) Have the Parliament and Government of Canada exclusive legislative and executive authority for performing the obligations of Canada, or of any Province thereof, under the Convention entitled 'Convention relating to the Regulation of Aerial Navigation'?

"(3) Has the Parliament of Canada legislative authority to enact, in whole or in part the provisions of s. 4 of the *Aeronautics Act,* R.S.C. 1927, c. 3?

"(4) Has the Parliament of Canada legislative authority to sanction the making and enforcement, in whole or in part, of the regulations contained in the *Air Regulations, 1920*, respecting:...

"(c) the licensing, inspection and regulation of all aerodromes and air stations?"

The Paris Convention, drawn up at the Peace Conference in Paris and dated October, 1919, was ratified by His Majesty on behalf of the British Empire June 1, 1922. Canada already had enacted in 1919 the *Air Board Act*, (1919 (Can.), c. 11), amended it in 1922 (1922 (Can.), c. 6), and styled it the *Aeronautics Act* (R.S.C. 1927, c. 3). It will be observed that the *Air Board Act* was enacted in the same year that the Paris Convention was drawn up, no doubt with the Convention in mind, but the latter is not mentioned and the comprehensive language of the statute deals with aeronautics in all its phases. This is evident from the following provisions:

"3. It shall be the duty of the Air Board—

"(a) to supervise all matters connected with aeronautics;

"(f) to prescribe aerial routes;

"(k) to investigate, examine and report on all proposals for the institution of commercial air services within or partly within Canada or the limits of the territorial waters of Canada;

"(l) to consider, draft, and prepare for approval by the Governor in Council such regulations as may be considered necessary for the control of operation of aeronautics in Canada or within the limits of the territorial waters of Canada; and,

"(m) to perform such other duties as the Governor in Council may from time to time impose."

It was this legislation that the Privy Council had before it in the *Aeronautics* case. Moreover, it should be noted that while Q. (1), as submitted by the Governor in Council, dealt with the legislative jurisdiction of Canada in relation to the Paris Convention, Qq. (3) and (4) concerned the legislative jurisdiction of the Parliament of Canada to enact s. 4 of the *Aeronautics Act* and the Regulations thereunder without regard to the Convention.

In the course of the judgment itself their Lordships stated: "The determination of these questions depends upon the true construction of ss. 91, 92 and 132 of the *B.N.A. Act*."

Their Lordships suggest that it may come under s. 91 (2), (5) and (9), but expressly state that it does not come under s-s (10) (Navigation and Shipping). They also point out that it does not come under Property and Civil Rights (s. 92 (13)) and then state: "Transport as a subject is dealt with in certain branches both of s. 91 and of s. 92, but neither of those sections deals specially with that branch of transport which is concerned with aeronautics."

Then, after discussing s. 132, they conclude: "To sum up, having regard (a) to the terms of s. 132; (b) to the terms of the Convention which covers almost every conceivable matter relating to aerial navigation; and (c) to the fact that further legislative powers in relation to aerial navigation reside in the Parliament of Canada by virtue of s. 91 (2), (5) and (7), it would appear that substantially the whole field of legislation in regard to aerial navigation belongs to the Dominion. There may be a small portion of the field which is not by virtue of specific words in the *B.N.A. Act* vested in the Dominion; but neither is it vested by specific words in the Provinces. As to such small portion it appears to the Board that it must necessarily belong to the Dominion under its power to make laws for the peace, order and good government of Canada. Further their Lordships are influenced by the facts that the subject of aerial navigation and the fulfilment of Canadian obligations under s. 132 are matters of national interest and importance; and that aerial navigation is a class of subject which has attained such dimensions as to affect the body politic of the Dominion."

Their Lordships, apart from s. 132, and in support of their answers to Qu. (3) and (4), were of the opinion that legislation in relation to aeronautics was within the competence of the Parliament of Canada. The remark of Viscount Dunedin, in the *Radio* case, that "the leading consideration in the judgment of the Board was that the subject fell within the provisions of s. 132 of the *B.N.A. Act*." and that of Lord Atkin in the *Labour Conventions* case that "The *Aeronautics* case concerned legislation to perform obligations imposed by a treaty between the Empire and foreign countries," particularly when read in relation to their context, do not detract from the foregoing, while the observations of Viscount Simon L. C. in the *Canada Temperance Federation* case (1946) would appear to support the foregoing view when he states: "In their Lordships' opinion, the true test must be found in the real subject-matter of the legislation: if it is such that it goes beyond local or provincial concern or interests and must from its inherent nature be the concern of the Dominion as a whole (as for example in the *Aeronautics Case* and the *Radio Case*), then it will fall within the competence of the Dominion Parliament as a matter affecting the peace, order and good government of Canada, though it may in another aspect touch upon matters specially reserved to the Provincial Legislatures."

The Judicial Committee having decided that legislation in relation to aeronautics is within the exclusive jurisdiction of the Dominion, it follows that the Province cannot legislate in relation thereto, whether the precise subject-matter of the provincial legislation has, or has not already been covered by the Dominion legislation.

It is then submitted that if aeronautics is within the legislative competence of the Parliament of Canada, including the power to license and regulate aerodromes, it would not include the location and continuation of aerodromes, which would be a provincial matter under Property and Civil Rights. With great respect, it would appear that such a view attributes a narrower and more technical meaning to the word "aeronautics" than that which has been attributed to it generally in law and by those interested in the subject. Indeed, the definition adopted by Dysart J.A. as he found it in 2 Corpus Juris Secundum, pp. 900–1, "The flight and a period of flight from the time the machine clears the earth to the time it returns successfully to the earth and is resting securely upon the ground" contemplates the operation of the aeroplane from the moment it leaves the earth until it again returns thereto. This, it seems, in itself makes the aerodrome, as the place of taking off and landing, an essential part of aeronautics and aerial navigation. This view finds support in the fact that legislation in relation to aeronautics and aerial navigation, not only in Canada, but also in Great Britain and the United States, deals with aerodromes, as well as the Conventions above mentioned. Indeed, in any practical consideration it is impossible to separate the flying in the air from the taking off and landing on the ground and it is, therefore, wholly impractical, particularly when considering the matter of jurisdiction, to treat them as independent one from the other.

The submission that in the granting of the licence the sufficiency of the location will always be considered and might even be the controlling factor in the granting or refusing of a licence, in so far as it may be of assistance, emphasizes the importance of the location of the aerodrome and of the essential part the aerodrome plays in any scheme of aeronautics. Legislation which in pith and substance is in relation to the aerodrome is legislation in relation to the larger subject of aeronautics and is, therefore, beyond the competence of the provincial Legislatures.

It is submitted that s. 921 is zoning legislation, as that term is now understood in municipal legislation. The general provisions for the enactment of zoning by-laws are contained in ss. 904, 905 and 906 of this statute. As notwithstanding this general provision such legislation may be enacted under other sections, it is necessary to determine the nature and character of the provisions of s. 921. The foregoing ss. 904, 905 and 906 are typical of legislation authorizing zoning by-laws. The end and purpose of zoning legislation, as the name indicates, is to authorize the municipality to pass by-laws in respect of certain areas and make those areas subject to prohibitions and restrictions designed to provide uniformity within those particular areas. The Legislature, in enacting s. 921, provided that, without regard to the nature and character or the use and purpose made of the area, the municipality may prohibit entirely, or permit only under a licence issued by it, an aerodrome within certain areas. Such legislation is in pith and substance in relation to aerodromes and, therefore, in relation to aeronautics rather than to zoning.

The appeal should be allowed with costs to the appellants, Konrad Johannesson and Holmfridur M. E. Johannesson, against the respondent municipality.

LOCKE J.: . . . It has been said on behalf of the respondents that the by-law is merely a zoning regulation passed in exercise of the powers vested in the municipality elsewhere in the *Municipal Act* and I understand the section referred to is that portion of s. 896 which, under the heading "Zoning Trades", empowers a municipal corporation to pass by-laws for preventing the erection of certain specified buildings and the carrying on of certain occupations within defined areas, these including the erection, establishment or maintenance of machine-shops which would presumably cover those designed for the repair of aircraft. The by-law, in so far as it prohibits the erection, maintenance or continuation of aerodromes, must depend for its validity upon s. 921: s. 3 is apparently based upon cl. (h) of s. 896. The inclusion of the prohibition of the erection or maintenance of a machine shop, however, is obviously for the purpose of preventing the use either of the strip of land fronting upon the river or the surface of the river adjoining to the east as an effective aerodrome. Section 921 was undoubtedly passed for the purpose of enabling municipal corporations to prohibit or to license or regulate the activity of aeronautics in and upon the lands and the waters within their boundaries, and not merely as an addition to the powers of zoning trades assumed to be given by s. 896. Had this been intended, and irrespective of any question as to its validity, no doubt it would have been done by amendment to cl. (f) or cl. (h) of s. 896. The powers sought to be conferred upon the municipal council appear to me to be in direct conflict with those vested in the Minister of National Defence by the *Aeronautics Act*. Section 3 (a) of that statute imposes upon the Minister the duty of supervising all matters connected with aeronautics and prescribing aerial routes and by s. 4 he is authorized, with the approval of the Governor in Council, to make regulations with respect to, inter alia, the areas within which aircraft coming from any place outside of Canada are to land and as to aerial routes, their use and control. The power to prescribe the aerial routes must include the right to designate where the terminus of any such route is to be maintained, and the power to designate the area within which foreign aircraft may land, of necessity includes the power to designate such area, whether of land or water, within any municipality in any Province of Canada deemed suitable for such purpose.

If the validity of the *Aeronautics Act* and the *Air Regulations* be conceded, it appears to me that this matter must be determined contrary to the contentions of the respondent. It is however, desirable, in my opinion, that some of the reasons for the conclusion that the field of aeronautics is one exclusively within federal jurisdiction should be stated. There has been since the First World War an immense development in the use of aircraft flying between the various Provinces of Canada and between Canada and other countries. There is a very large passenger traffic between the Provinces and to and from foreign countries, and a very considerable volume of freight traffic not only between the settled portions of the country but between those areas and the northern part of Canada, and planes are extensively used in the carriage of mails. That this traffic will increase greatly in volume and extent is undoubted. While the largest activity in the carrying of passengers and mails east and west is in the hands of a Government-controlled company, private companies carry on large operations, particularly between the settled parts of the country and the north and mails are carried by some of these lines. The maintenance and extension of this traffic, particularly to the north, is essential to the opening up of the country and the development of the resources of the nation. It requires merely a statement of these well recognized facts to demonstrate that the field of aeronautics is one which concerns the country as a whole. It is an activity, which to adopt the language of Viscount Simon in *A.-G. Ont.* v. *Canada Temperance Federation*, must from its inherent nature be a concern of the Dominion as a whole. The field of legislation is not, in my opinion, capable of division in any practical way. If, by way of illustration, it should be decided that it was in the interests of the inhabitants of some northerly part of the country to have airmail service with centres of population to the south and that for that purpose some private line, prepared to undertake such carriage should be licensed to do so and to establish the southern terminus for their route at some suitable place in the Municipality of West St. Paul where, apparently, there is an available and suitable field and area of water where planes equipped in a manner enabling them to use the facilities of such an airport might land, it would be intolerable that such a national purpose might be defeated by a rural municipality, the council of which decided that the noise attendant on the operation of airplanes was objectionable. Indeed, if the argument of the respondents be carried to its logical conclusion the rural municipalities of Manitoba through which the Red River passes between Emerson and Selkirk, and the City of Winnipeg and the Town of Selkirk might prevent the operation of any planes equipped for landing upon water by denying them the right to use the river for that purpose. . . .

[Opinions of Rinfret C.J.C., Kerwin and Kellock JJ. have been omitted. The decision of Locke J. has been severely cut. All the judges agreed in the result.]

NOTE ON AERONAUTICAL CONTROL: ZONING. Section 4 of the *Aeronautics Act*, R.S.C., 1952, c. 2, was amended in 1952 (see Volume V.

of R.S.C., 1952, c. 302) to authorize the Minister to "make regulations with respect to

(j) the height, use and location of buildings, structures and objects, including objects of natural growth, situated on lands adjacent to or in the vicinity of airports, for purposes relating to navigation of aircraft and use and operation of airport, and including, for such purposes, regulations restricting, regulating or prohibiting the doing of anything or the suffering of anything to be done on any such lands, or the construction or use of any such building, structure or object.

Section 4 was also amended in other respects, providing for so-called "zoning regulations" under paragraph (j) set out above. Subsections (8) and (9) provided:

(8) Every person whose property is injuriously affected by the operation of a zoning regulation is entitled to recover from Her Majesty, as compensation, the amount, if any, by which the property was decreased in value by the enactment of the regulation, minus an amount equal to any increase in the value of the property that occurred after the claimant became the owner thereof and is attributable to the airport.

(9) No proceedings to recover any compensation to which a person may be entitled under subsection (8) by reason of the operation of a zoning regulation shall be brought except within two years after a copy of the regulation was deposited pursuant to subsection (6) or (7).

Under this authority the Governor General in Council on the recommendation of the Minister of Transport approved *The Toronto Malton Airport Zoning Regulations* (1 S.O.R. Consolidation 1955, 37.)

The *Regulations* provide in part:

3. These regulations apply to all lands adjacent to or in the vicinity of Toronto Airport, Malton, Ontario, including public road allowance, as more particularly described in the Schedule hereto.

4. (1) No person shall erect or construct, on any land to which these regulations apply, any building, structure or object or any addition to any existing building, structure or object, the highest point of which exceeds in elevation the elevation at that point of such of the surfaces hereinafter described as project: immediately over and above the surface of the land upon which such building, structure or object is located, namely,

(a) a horizontal surface, the outer limits of which are at a horizontal radius of 13,000 feet more or less;

(b) the approach surfaces abutting each end of the strip designated as 10–28, the strip designated as 14–32 and the strip designated as 05–23, and extending outward therefrom, the dimensions of which approach surfaces are 600 feet on each side of the centre line of the strip at the strip ends and 2,000 feet on each side of the projected centre line of the strip at the outer ends, the said outer ends being 200 feet above the elevations at the strip ends, and measured horizontally, 10,000 feet from the strip ends; and

(c) the several transitional surfaces, each rising at an angle determined on the basis of a ratio of one foot vertically for every seven feet measured horizontally from the outer lateral limits of the strips and their abutting surfaces.

as shown on a Plan No. T724 dated December 17, 1952, and revised February 20, 1953, of record in the Department of Transport.

(2) Where any building, structure or object on any land to which these regulations apply exceeds the limits in elevation specified in subsection (1), the Minister may order the owner or occupier of the land to remove, demolish or modify such building, structure or object or do any act or thing necessary to ensure that such building, structure or object complies with the limits in elevation so specified and may, in any such order, specify the time within such removal, demolition, modification, act or thing shall be done.

5. No person shall operate or cause to be operated on any lands to which these regulations apply any machine, device, contrivance or thing after being notified by the Minister that, in the opinion of the Minister, the machine, device, contrivance or thing causes or is likely to cause, by the emission of light, smoke, noise or fumes, a hazard or obstruction to aircraft using the airport.

[The short title and interpretation sections and the schedule describing the lands have been omitted. Section 4 (2) and section 5 were revoked by S.O.R. /55–331 and S.O.R. /55–402]

QUESTIONS. How should the Dominion and the Municipality co-operate in this zoning, if at all? Is the meaning of "injuriously affected" quite clear? Is a person whose property is "injuriously affected" by a by-law passed under the Municipal Act in Ontario entitled to any compensation? Why not?

2. The American View

(*a*) *The zoning power*

VILLAGE OF EUCLID *v*. AMBLER REALTY CO.

Ohio. Supreme Court of the United States. 1926. 272 U.S. 365

Sutherland J. delivered the opinion of the Court: The Village of Euclid is an Ohio municipal corporation. It adjoins and practically is a suburb of the City of Cleveland. Its estimated population is between 5,000 and 10,000, and its area from twelve to fourteen square miles, the greater part of which is farm lands or unimproved acreage. It lies, roughly, in the form of a parallelogram measuring approximately three and one-half miles each way. East and west it is traversed by three principal highways: Euclid Avenue, through the southerly border, St. Clair Avenue, through the central portion, and Lake Shore Boulevard through the northerly border in close proximity to the shore of Lake Erie. The Nickel Plate railroad lies from 1,500 to 1,800 feet north of Euclid Avenue, and the Lake Shore railroad 1,600 feet farther to the north. The three highways and the two railroads are substantially parallel.

Appellee is the owner of a tract of land containing 68 acres, situated in the westerly end of the village, abutting on Euclid Avenue to the south and the Nickel Plate railroad to the north. Adjoining this tract, both on the east and on the west, there have been laid out restricted residential plats upon which residences have been erected.

On November 13, 1922, an ordinance was adopted by the Village Council, establishing a comprehensive zoning plan for regulating and restricting the location of trades, industries, apartment houses, two-family houses, single family houses, etc., the lot area to be built upon, the size and height of buildings, etc.

The entire area of the village is divided by the ordinance into six classes of use districts, denominated U-1 to U-6 inclusive; three classes of height districts denominated H-1 to H-3, inclusive; and four classes of area districts, denominated A-1 to A-4, inclusive.

Appellee's tract of land comes under U-2, U-3 and U-6. The first strip of 620 feet immediately north of Euclid Avenue falls in class U-2, the next 130 feet to the north, in U-3 and the remainder in U-6. The uses of the first 620 feet, therefore, do not include apartment houses, hotels, churches, schools or other public and semi-public buildings, or other uses enumerated in respect of U-3 to U-6 inclusive.

The uses of the next 130 feet include all of these, but exclude industries, theatres, banks, shops, and the various other uses set forth in respect of U-4 to U-6 inclusive.

The lands lying between the two railroads for the entire length of the village area and extending some distance on either side to the north and south, having an average width of about 1,600 feet, are left open, with slight exceptions, for industrial and all other uses. This includes the larger part of appellee's tract. Approximately one-sixth of the area of the entire village is included in U-5 and U-6 use districts. That part of the village lying south of Euclid Avenue is principally in U-1 districts. The lands lying north of Euclid Avenue and bordering on the long strip just described are included in U-1, U-2, U-3 and U-4 districts, principally in U-2.

The enforcement of the ordinance is entrusted to the inspector of buildings, under rules and regulations of the board of zoning appeals. Meetings of the board are public, and minutes of its proceedings are kept. It is authorized to adopt rules and regulations to carry into effect provisions of the ordinance. Decisions of the inspector of buildings may be appealed to the board by any person claiming to be adversely affected by any such decision. The board is given power in specific cases of practical difficulty or unnecessary hardship to interpret the ordinance in harmony with its general purpose and intent, so that the public health, safety and general welfare may be secure and substantial justice done. Penalties are prescribed for violations, and it is provided that the various provisions are to be regarded as independent and the holding of any provision to be unconstitutional, void or ineffective shall not affect any of the others.

The ordinance is assailed on the grounds that it is in derogation of section 1 of the Fourteenth Amendment to the Federal Constitution in that it deprives appellee of liberty and property without due process of law and denies it the equal protection of the law, and that it offends against certain provisions of the Constitution of the State of Ohio. The prayer of the bill is for an injunction restraining the enforcement of the ordinance and all attempts to impose or maintain as to the appellee's property any of the restrictions, limitations or conditions. The court below held the ordinance to be unconstitutional and void, and enjoined its enforcement.

Before proceeding to a consideration of the case, it is necessary to determine the scope of the inquiry. The bill alleges that the tract of land in question is vacant and has been held for years for the purpose of selling and developing it for industrial uses, for which it is especially adapted, being immediately in the path of progressive industrial development; that for such uses it has a market value of about $10,000 per acre, but if the use be limited to residential purposes the market value is not in excess of $2,500 per acre; that the first 200 feet of the parcel back from Euclid Avenue, if unrestricted in respect of use, has a value of $150 per front foot, but if limited to residential uses, and ordinary mercantile business be excluded therefrom, its value is not in excess of $50 per front foot.

It is specifically averred that the ordinance attempts to restrict and control the lawful uses of appellee's land so as to confiscate and destroy a great part of its value; that it is being enforced in accordance with its terms; that prospective buyers of land for industrial, commercial and residential uses in the metropolitan district of Cleveland are deterred from buying any part of this land because of the existence of the ordinance and the necessity thereby entailed of conducting burdensome and expensive litigation in order to vindicate the right to use the land for lawful and legitimate purposes; that the ordinance constitutes a cloud upon the land, reduces and destroys its value, and has the effect of diverting the normal industrial, commercial and residential development thereof to other and less favorable locations.

The record goes no farther than to show, as the lower court found, that the normal, and reasonably to be expected, use and development of that part of appellee's land adjoining Euclid Avenue is for general trade and commercial purposes, particularly retail stores and like establishments, and that the normal and reasonably to be expected use and development of the residue of the land is for industrial and trade purposes. Whatever injury is inflicted by the mere existence and theatened enforcement of the ordinance is due to restrictions in respect of these and similar uses; to which perhaps should be added—if not included in the foregoing—restrictions in respect of apartment houses. Specifically, there is nothing in the record to suggest that any damage results from the presence in the ordinance of those restrictions relating to churches, schools, libraries and other public and semi-public buildings. It is neither alleged nor proved that there is, or may be, a demand for any part of appellee's land for any of the last named uses; and we cannot assume the existence of facts which would justify an injunction upon this record in respect of this class of restrictions. For present purposes the provisions of the ordinance in respect of these uses may, therefore, be put aside as unnecessary to be considered. It is also unnecessary to consider the effect of the restrictions in respect of U-1 districts, since none of appellee's land falls within that class.

Building zone laws are of modern origin. They began in this country about twenty-five years ago. Until recent years, urban life was comparatively simple; but with the great increase and concentration of population, problems have developed, and constantly are developing which require, and will continue to require, additional restrictions in respect of the use and occupation of private lands in urban communities. Regulations, the wisdom, necessity and validity of which, as applied to existing conditions, are so apparent that they are now uniformly sustained, a century ago, or even half a century ago, probably would have been rejected as arbitrary and oppressive. Such regulations are sustained, under the complex conditions of our day, for reasons analogous to those which justify traffic regulations, which, before the advent of automobiles and rapid transit street railways, would have been condemned as fatally arbitrary and unreasonable. And in this there is no inconsistency, for while the meaning of constitutional guaranties never varies, the scope of their application must expand or contract to meet the new and different conditions which are constantly coming within the field of their operation. In a changing world, it is impossible that it should be otherwise. But although a degree of elasticity is thus imparted, not to the meaning, but to the application of constitutional principles, statutes and ordinances, which, after giving due weight to the new conditions, are found clearly not to conform to the Constitution, of course, must fall.

The ordinance now under review, and all similar laws and regulations, must find their justification in some aspect of the police power, asserted for the public welfare. The line which in this field separates the legitimate from the illegitimate assumption of power is not capable of precise delimitation. It varies with circumstances and conditions. A regulatory zoning ordinance, which would be clearly valid as applied to the great cities, might be clearly invalid as applied to rural communities. In solving doubts, the maxim sic utere tuo ut alienum non laedas, which lies at the foundation of so much of the common law of nuisances, ordinarily will furnish a fairly helpful clew. And the law of nuisances, likewise, may be consulted not for the purpose of controlling but for the helpful aid of its analogies in the process of ascertaining the scope of the power. Thus the question whether the power exists to forbid the erection of a building of a particular kind or for a particular use, like the question whether a particular thing is a nuisance, is to be determined, not by an abstract consideration of the building or of the thing considered apart, but by considering it in connection with the circumstances and the locality . . . A nuisance may be merely a right thing in the wrong place—like a pig in the parlor instead of the barn. If the validity of the legislative classification for zoning purposes be fairly debatable, the legislative judgment must be allowed to control. . . .

There is no serious difference of opinion in respect of the validity of laws and regulations fixing the height of buildings within reasonable limits, the character of materials and methods of construction, and the adjoining area which must be left open, in order to minimize the danger of fire or collapse, the evils of over-crowding, and the like, and excluding from residential sections offensive trades, industries and structures likely to create nuisances.

Here, however, the exclusion is in general terms of all industrial establishments, and it may thereby happen that not only offensive or dangerous industries will be excluded but those which are neither offensive nor dangerous will share the same fate. But this is no more than happens in respect of many practice-forbidding laws which this Court has upheld although drawn in general terms so as to include individual cases that may turn out to be innocuous in themselves. The inclusion of a reasonable margin to insure effective enforcement will not put upon a law, otherwise valid, the stamp of invalidity. Such laws may also find their justification in the fact, that, in some fields, the bad fades into the good by such insensible degrees that the two are not capable of being readily distinguished and separated in terms of legislation. In the light of these considerations, we are not prepared to say that the end in view was not sufficient to justify the general rule of ordinance, although some industries of an innocent character might fall within the proscribed class. It cannot be said that the ordinance in this respect "passes the bounds of reason and assumes the character of a merely arbitrary fiat." Moreover, the restrictive provisions of the ordinance in this particular may be sustained upon the principles applicable to the broader exclusion from residential districts of all business and trade structures, presently to be discussed.

It is said that the Village of Euclid is a mere suburb of the City of Cleveland; that the industrial development of that city has now reached and in some degree extended into the village and, in the obvious course of things, will soon absorb the entire area for industrial enterprises; that the effect of the ordinance is to divert this natural development elsewhere with the consequent loss of increased values to the owners of the lands within the village borders. But the village, though physically a suburb of Cleveland, is politically a separate municipality, with powers of its own and authority to govern itself as it sees fit within the limits of the organic law of its creation and the State and Federal Constitutions. Its governing authorities, presumably representing a majority of its inhabitants and voicing their will, have determined, not that industrial development shall cease at its boundaries, but that the course of such development shall proceed within definitely fixed lines. If it be a proper exercise of the police power to relegate industrial establishments to localities separated from residential sections, it is not easy to find a sufficient reason for denying the power because the effect of its exercise is to divert an industrial flow from the course which it would follow, to the injury of the residential public if left alone, to another course where such injury will be obviated. It is not meant by this however, to exclude the possibility of cases where the general public interest would so far outweigh the interest of the municipality that the municipality would not be allowed to stand in the way.

We find no difficulty in sustaining restrictions of the kind thus far reviewed. The serious question in the case arises over the provisions of the ordinance excluding from residential districts, apartment houses, business houses, retail stores and shops, and other like establishments. This question involves the validity of what is really the crux of the more recent zoning legislation, namely, the creation and maintenance of residential districts from which business and trade of every sort, including hotels and apartment houses, are excluded. Upon that question this Court has not thus far spoken. The decisions of the state courts are numerous and conflicting; but those which broadly sustain the power greatly outnumber those which deny altogether or narrowly limit it; and it is very apparent that there is a constantly increasing tendency in the direction of the broader view. We shall not attempt to review these decisions at length.

As evidence of the decided trend toward the broader view, it is significant that in some instances the state courts in later decisions have reversed their former decisions holding the other way.

The decisions enumerated in the first group cited above agree that the exclusion of buildings devoted to business, trade, etc., from residential districts, bears a rational relation to the health and safety of the community. Some of the grounds for this conclusion are—promotion of the health and security from injury of children and others by separating dwelling houses from territory devoted to trade and industry; suppression and prevention of disorder; facilitating the extinguishment of fires, and the enforcement of street traffic regulations and other general welfare ordinances; aiding the health and safety of the community by excluding from residential areas the confusion and danger of fire, contagion and disorder which in greater or less degree attach to the location of stores, shops and factories. Another ground is that the construction and repair of streets may be rendered easier and less expensive by confining the greater part of the heavy traffic to the streets where business is carried on.

The matter of zoning has received much attention at the hands of commissions and experts, and the results of their investigations have been set forth in comprehensive reports. These reports, which bear every evidence of painstaking consideration, concur in the view that the segregation of residential, business, and industrial buildings will make it easier to provide fire apparatus suitable for the character and intensity of the development in each section; that it will increase the safety and security of home life; greatly tend to prevent street accidents, especially to children, by reducing the traffic and resulting confusion in residential sections; decrease noise and other conditions which produce or intensify nervous disorders; preserve a more favourable environment in which to rear children, etc. With particular reference to apartment houses, it is pointed out that the development of detached house sections is greatly retarded by the coming of apartment houses, which has sometimes resulted in destroying the entire section for private house purposes; that in such sections very often the apartment house is a mere parasite, constructed in order to take advantage of the open spaces and attractive surroundings created by the residential character of the district. Moreover, the coming of one apartment house is followed by others, interfering by their height and bulk with the free circulation of air and monopolizing the rays of the sun which otherwise would fall upon the smaller homes, and bringing, as their necessary accompaniments, the disturbing noises incident to increased traffic and business, and the occupation, by means of moving and parked automobiles, of larger portions of the streets, thus detracting from their safety and depriving children of the privilege of quiet and open spaces for play, enjoyed by those in more favored localities—until, finally, the residential character of the neighborhood and its desirability as a place of detached residences are utterly destroyed. Under these circumstances, apartment houses, which in a different environment would be not only entirely unobjectionable but highly desirable, come very near to being nuisances.

If these reasons, thus summarized, do not demonstrate the wisdom or sound policy in all respects of those restrictions which we have indicated as pertinent to the inquiry, at least, the reasons are sufficiently cogent to preclude us from saying, as it must be said before the ordinance can be declared unconstitutional that such provisions are clearly arbitrary and unreasonable, having no substantial relation to the public health, safety, morals, or general welfare.

It is true that when, if ever, the provisions set forth in the ordinance in tedious and minute detail, come to be concretely applied to particular premises, including those of the appellee, or to particular conditions, or to be considered in connection with specific complaints, some of them or even many of them, may be found to be clearly arbitrary and unreasonable. But where the equitable remedy of injunction is sought as it is here, not upon the ground of a present infringement or denial of a specific right, or of a particular injury in process of actual execution, but upon the broad ground that the mere existence and threatened enforcement of the ordinance, by materially and adversely affecting values and curtailing the opportunities of the market, constitute a present and irreparable injury, the court will not scrutinize its provisions, sentence by sentence, to ascertain by a process of piecemeal dissection whether there may be, here and there, provisions of a minor character, or relating to matters of administration, or not shown to contribute to the injury complained of, which if attacked separately, might not withstand the test of constitutionality. In respect of such provisions, of which specific complaint is not made, it cannot be said that the land owner has suffered or is threatened with an injury which entitles him to challenge their constitutionality.

The gravamen of the complaint is that a portion of the land of the appellee cannot be sold for certain enumerated uses because of the general and broad restraints of the ordinance. What would be the effect of a restraint imposed by one or more of the innumerable provisions of the ordinance, considered apart, upon the value or marketability of the lands is neither disclosed by the bill nor by the evidence, and we are afforded no basis apart from mere speculation, upon which to rest a conclusion that it or they would have any appreciable effect upon those matters. Under these circumstances, therefore, it is enough for us to determine, as we do, that the ordinance in its general scope and dominant features, so far as its provisions are here involved, is a valid exercise of authority, leaving other provisions to be dealt with as cases arise directly involving them.

And this is in accordance with the traditional policy of this Court. In the realm of constitutional law, especially, this Court has perceived the embarrassment which is likely to result from an attempt to formulate rules or decide questions beyond the necessities of the immediate issue. It has preferred to follow the method of a gradual approach to the general by a systematically guarded application and extension of constitutional principles to particular cases as they arise, rather than by out of hand attempts to establish general rules to which future cases must be fitted. This process applies with peculiar force to the solution of questions arising under the due process clause of the Constitution as applied to the exercise of the flexible powers of police, with which we are here concerned.

[Van Devanter, McReynolds and Butler JJ. dissented, but did not record their reasons. All citations have been omitted.]

NOTE. This case not only illustrates the kind of constitutional problem that bedevils American legislation about zoning—a problem you must understand if you are to evaluate American decisions properly for consideration in Canadian settings—it also illustrates what rational basis the lawyers and judges in this case were able to find for a kind of legislation becoming very common in Canada. This rational basis should be examined critically.

What is meant by "the police power"? Does the existence of this label in any way clarify the decision of the court? Note the reference to this "power" in the cases below. Do you think it desirable that a court should be able to quash legislation on the ground that it is "clearly arbitrary and unreasonable"?

THE MUNICIPAL ACT

Ontario. Revised Statutes. 1960. Chapter 249

243. Every council may pass such by-laws and make such regulations for the health, safety, morality and welfare of the inhabitants of the municipality in matters not specifically provided for by this Act as may be deemed expedient and are not contrary to law, and for governing the proceedings of the council, the conduct of its members and the calling of meetings.

MORRISON *v*. KINGSTON. [1937] 4 D.L.R. 740 (Ontario. Court of Appeal). MIDDLETON J.A.: "By-laws which may be passed under the general power are to be for the 'health, safety, morality and welfare,' of the inhabitants 'in matters not specifically provided for by this act,' and which are 'not contrary to law.'

"Dealing with the subject-matter of the enactment authorized one finds that matters of 'health' are generally regulated by the *Public Health Act*, R.S.O. 1927, c. 262; matters of 'safety' are covered by a multitude of Acts of which the *Highway Traffic Act* . . . will serve as examples; matters of 'morality' are generally dealt with by the Parliament of the Dominion. The Criminal Code deals with most moral questions. More specific questions are dealt with by the *Opium and Narcotic Drug Act*, R.S.C. 1952, c. 201, and other familiar legislation. These topics are entirely removed from the sphere of legislation of municipal councils. The power to legislate for the 'welfare' of the inhabitants is too vague and general to admit of definition. It may mean so much that it probably does mean very little. It cannot include powers that are otherwise specifically given, nor can it be taken to confer unlimited and unrestrained power with regard to matters in which a conditional power only is conferred upon the subsidiary Legislature."

(*b*) *Zoning for aesthetics: design control*

ST. LOUIS GUNNING ADVERTISEMENT CO. *v.* CITY OF ST. LOUIS

Missouri. Supreme Court. 1911. 137 S.W. 929

WOODSON J.: . . . The purpose of this suit was to test the validity of a certain ordinance, enacted by the municipal assembly of the city of St. Louis, in so far as it purports to regulate and control signs and billboards within the limits thereof, and to enjoin the city and its officers from enforcing it against the plaintiff . . .

This trial took a somewhat unusual course, in that the Court heard evidence as to the necessity for the enactment of the ordinances in question, and as to the existence or non-existence of the evils which they were designed to abate. The evidence of the case, under the stipulation before set out consisted of the petition, answer, and the affidavits filed in the cause by the plaintiff and defendants; and it is necessary for proper consideration of the cause that we have the pleadings and evidence before us, and as they cannot be materially abridged, we copy them in full . . . [The petition, the answer, the plaintiff's affidavits and the defendant's affidavits, which occupy nine two column pages, are omitted.]

Speaking generally, plaintiff's business consists of outdoor advertising, displayed at conspicuous points and places by means of pictures, signs and letters. The more conspicuous and public the place the greater is the desire to cover it with that class of advertisements. The privacy of the home, places of public resort, retreats for rest and recreation, seats of learning and even the sanctity of the church are as much within the shadow of the structures hereinafter described as are the vacant lots and commanding views along the public thoroughfares of the city. The walls and roofs of many residences and business houses are not exempt from this intrusion. While all kinds of business and merchandise are advertised by this means of display, yet observation and common experience teach us that probably the greater per cent. thereof proclaim the newest and choicest brands of liquors, tobacco, cigars and cigarettes, and announcements of various plays which are to be presented at the various theatres. These, however, are interspersed with information regarding the comforts and necessities of life. These billboards are temporary affairs, consisting of upright timbers or posts set in the ground at various distances from each other, braced from the rear, with stringers running from one to the other and there secured by means of nails or bolts. These stringers are then covered with boards standing on ends and nailed thereto and thereby presenting a smooth vertical surface upon which the various announcements are made or displayed. In this general statement, we might also add that there is but one virtue connected with this entire business and that is the advertising itself. This is a legitimate and honorable business if honorably and legitimately conducted, but every other feature and incident thereto have evil tendencies and should for that reason be strictly regulated and controlled. The signboards and billboards upon which this class of advertisements are displayed are constant menaces to the public safety and welfare of the city; they endanger the public health, promote immorality, constitute hiding places and retreats for criminals and all classes of miscreants. They are also inartistic and unsightly. In cases of fire they often cause their spread and constitute barriers against their extinction; and in cases of high wind their temporary character, frail structure and broad surface render them liable to be blown down and to fall upon and injure those who may happen to be in their vicinity. The evidence shows and common observation teaches us that the ground in the rear thereof is being constantly used as privies and dumping ground for all kinds of waste and deleterious matters, and thereby creating public nuisances and jeopardizing public health; the evidence also shows that behind these obstructions the lowest form of prostitution and other acts of immorality are frequently carried on, almost under public gaze; they offer shelter and concealment for the criminal while lying in wait for his victim; and last but not least, they obstruct the light, sunshine and air which are so conducive to health and comfort. House signs and sky signs are similar to billboards and are used for the same purposes except they are attached to the walls of buildings or are constructed upon the roofs thereof. They endanger the public safety only in being liable to be blown down and injure people in their fall. They also assist in the spread of fire and greatly interfere with their extinction. The amount of good contained in this class of this business is so small in comparison to the great and numerous evils incident thereto that it has caused me to wonder why some of the courts of the country have seen fit to go as far as they have in holding statutes and ordinances of this class void, which were only designed for the suppression of the evils incident thereto and not to the suppression of the business itself. While advertising as before stated, is a legitimate and honourable business, yet the evils incident to this class of advertising are more numerous and base in character than are those incident to numerous other businesses which are considered mala in se; and which for that reason may not only be regulated and controlled, but which may be entirely suppressed for the public good under the police power of the state. My individual opinion is that this class of advertising as now conducted is not only subject to control and regulation by the police power of the state, but that it might be entirely suppressed by statute, and that too, without offending against either the state or federal Constitution . . .

The record shows that the reason why the municipal assembly enacted the ordinance prohibiting billboards from being erected nearer the street lines than that mentioned was for the purpose of protecting pedestrians and others upon the streets from injury in case said billboards should be blown down by high winds.

Common observation and experience teach us that generally when such structures are blown down the upright posts supporting them only partially break, near the ground, thereby permitting the entire structure to fall prone upon the ground with the lower parts scarcely displaced from their natural position while the top parts thereof reach out upon the ground the full number of feet that the boards are high. If they are 14 feet in height, as the ordinance permits them to be, then in falling they would fall upon and injure anyone who should be passing along the street within 14 feet of the base line of such billboards. From this it must be seen that the city wisely forbade the erection of such boards nearer than 6 feet to the side line of lots fronting upon the street and nearer than 15 feet to the front line thereof. The ordinance would have been wiser and better if it would have prohibited all such structures from being erected nearer than 15 feet to the line of any street, avenue or any other public thoroughfare . . .

It is also in keeping with common knowledge that the natural tendency of all such structures is to create and maintain just such nuisances as the record in this case shows these billboards have done in this case. Their ordinary and natural conditions and tendencies are nuisances in character, if I may so coin that word.

In answer to these suggestions, counsel for plaintiff argue that the same nuisances might be committed behind fences and in buildings. While that is possible, yet it is not probable; nor does the erection and maintenance of a building or a fence along the lines of private property bordering upon public streets have the natural tendency to create any such nuisance as those mentioned. Buildings and fences are erected for the purpose of inclosing grounds and excluding therefrom strangers and trespassers; and common experience teaches us that they are effectual for that purpose, which is inconsistent with the idea that they promote and harbor nuisances, as billboards do, which rarely if ever, inclose the grounds upon which they stand. That is not the purpose of their erection. Generally they are built along only one end or side of a lot or plot of ground, but occasionally upon two sides, and in rare instances, upon three, but I have never seen or heard of a lot being inclosed upon all four sides by billboards. The end of the lot fronting upon an alley is almost invariably left open for the simple reason that the alley is not conspicuous in the public eye, and for that reason it would be useless to display advertisements at such places where they could not be seen. The nearer the lot of ground is inclosed by such structures, provided there is a sufficient opening for ingress and egress, the greater will be the nuisances committed behind them and the more dangerous they become to public health and safety . . .

[Only a small portion of the decision has been reproduced. The Court continued in the same vein for another 20 pages.]

GRAVES J. dissented: . . . To my mind the ordinance strikes at the use of a structure rather than the character of the structure. This I gather from the very definition of a billboard as given in the ordinance . . .

If this definition does not condemn the structure of whatever material upon the sole ground of the use to which it is to be put, rather than upon the fact of its being safe, then I have studied English awry. If this definition has reference to public morals, I fail to see it. If it refers to public health, I fail to see it. If it refers to public safety or the general welfare, I fail to see it. Yet the lawmaking power of St. Louis has said to this court by its own definition what structure it had in mind. It has not said a word in the definition about public safety, public health, public morals or general welfare—the only wards of the police power. Instead of so doing it has adopted the aesthetic view of a civic league or confederation of civic leagues and undertakes to condemn structures on the basis of the use to which they are to be put. The use of safe private structures for advertising purposes is a lawful use. Such lawful use cannot be stricken down to please the eye. Of course, under the police power the character of the advertising could be scrutinized. Further, the character of the structure as to public safety, health and morals may be regulated, but such are the limits of the police power.

To illustrate the ordinance under question, a few examples or supposed cases will not be out of order. If I own a corner lot 20 feet wide, I can maintain and put up a brick or stone wall on the building line, provided I do not use, or propose to use such brick or stone wall for the painting thereon of display signs or advertisements. If I build the same stone or brick wall and advertise my mercantile, real estate, or other legitimate business thereon, I would have to tear it down. Counsel for the city in oral argument admitted as much. . . .

NOTE AND QUESTIONS. Note Graves J.'s reference to the aesthetic ground. Why cannot aesthetic considerations fall within the expression "public welfare"—a traditional part of the "police power" formula? Note the use of the formula in section of the *Municipal Act*. Is this section restrictive of by-law making power in Ontario?

MURPHY INC. *v*. TOWN OF WESTPORT

Connecticut. Supreme Court of Errors. 1944. 40 A 2d. 177

MALTBIE C.J.: The named plaintiff is a corporation engaged in the business of outdoor advertising, and the other plaintiff, Backiel, is the owner of land in the defendant town which the corporation had leased and upon which it proposed to erect a billboard. The town has adopted a zoning ordinance and the land leased to the plaintiff is in a "business district" as defined in it. The plaintiffs brought the action to restrain the defendants from enforcing a provision in the ordinance forbidding in a business zone such a billboard as the corporation proposes to construct and to compel the issuance of a building permit for its erection. The trial court held the provision of the ordinance in question void and gave judgment for the plaintiffs. The defendants have appealed.

The zoning ordinance divided the area of the town into residence districts and business districts. In the residence districts all advertising signs are forbidden except that, where the premises are used for certain home occupations or offices, signs giving notice of the use not exceeding two square feet in area may be displayed, and that signs not exceeding eight square feet in area may be erected for the purpose of advertising the particular land or premises upon which a sign stands. In business districts such signs are also permitted, but the ordinance provides that "Billboards or advertising signboards are prohibited in all business districts except as they refer to business conducted on the property on which the billboard stands.". . .

Since about 1905 there has been a considerable volume of litigation involving the right of a state or municipality to regulate or prohibit billboards, and generally speaking, there has been a growing tendency to regard the power more broadly . . . In the earlier cases, courts apparently did not realize as clearly as they do now, as the result of facts found upon various trials, that billboards may be a source of danger to travellers upon highways through insecure construction, that accumulations of debris behind and around them may increase fire hazards and produce unsanitary conditions, that they may obstruct the view of operators of automobiles on the highway and may distract their attention from their driving, that behind them nuisances and immoral acts are often committed, and that they may serve as places of concealment for the criminal . . .

The earlier cases were more prone to regard esthetic considerations as the predominating motive of the restrictions or prohibitions and for that reason to condemn the regulations as not within the police power of the state; and there are a number of fairly recent decisions which hold that, where esthetic considerations afford the sole ground for the enactment of laws or ordinances affecting the individual's use of his land, they are void . . .

. . . [S]uch esthetic considerations as are involved in the regulation or prohibition of signboards cannot be divorced from material and economic factors; the presence of signboards near property may definitely affect its value and the comfort of those who may be living upon it . . .

Whether or not esthetic considerations in themselves would support the exercise of the police power, there can be no question that, if a regulation finds a reasonable justification in serving a generally recognized ground for the exercise of that power, the fact that esthetic considerations play a part in its adoption does not affect its validity . . .

As stated by the Court of Appeals of New York:

"Beauty may not be queen; but she is not an outcast beyond the pale of protection or respect. She may at least shelter herself under the wing of safety, morality, or decency.". . .

If . . . we turn to the case before us, we are struck by the absence of any finding in regard to those circumstances which, as we have pointed out, other courts have considered in passing upon the validity of similar regulations. This action was brought by the corporation seeking to erect the billboard and by the owner of the land on which it was to be placed, and the burden of proof to sustain their right to relief rested upon them. This burden is emphasized by the principle that, in considering legislative action taken under the police power, it is the duty of the court, "in the exercise of great care and caution, to make every presumption and intendment in favor of the validity of the statute, and to sustain it unless its invalidity is beyond reasonable doubt." . . .

As the trial court did not have before it sufficient facts to enable it to determine whether or not the plaintiffs were entitled to relief, we must remand the case for further proceedings.

There is error, the judgment is set aside and a new trial is ordered.

[In this opinion the other Judges concurred.]

NOTE. On the method used to establish the background, or "legislative facts," note the contrast between Maltbie C.J., who is "struck by the absence of any findings" and Woodson J., who several times said "common observation and experience teaches us . . .". How do you think material of this sort ought to be proved to a court?

GENERAL OUTDOOR ADVERTISING CO. INC. *v.* DEPT. OF PUBLIC WORKS

Massachusetts. Supreme Judicial Court. 1935. 193 N.E. 799

Fourteen suits were directed against the Department of Public Works to obtain decrees that all and certain parts of the rules and regulations promulgated by the Department and a by-law adopted by the Town of Concord are unconstitutional. In a long decision (26 two column pages) the various rules, regulations and the by-law were upheld. Only a very short part of the opinion is reproduced, mainly the part dealing with the evidence of the effect of billboards taken by the master.

RUGG C.J.: . . . The cases were consolidated into a single cause for hearing and were referred to a master under a rule "to hear the parties and their evidence, and to report his findings . . . together with such facts and questions of law and portions of the testimony as any party may in writing request." The master heard the parties and their evidence on one hundred and fourteen days and took a view of signs, billboards and advertising devices in different sections of the commonwealth, travelling approximately a thousand miles with counsel for that purpose. The record consists of five large printed volumes. The master filed a comprehensive report and reported a great amount of evidence, comprising many hundreds of printed pages . . .

The master made this finding:

"Billboards are designed to compel attention. The advertising matter displayed upon them in words, pictures or devices, is conspicuous, obtrusive and ostentatious, being designed to intrude forcefully and persistently upon the observation and attention of all who come within the range of clear normal vision. The only real value of a sign or billboard lies in its proximity to the public thoroughfare within public view. The advertising signs or billboards of the complainants, and others, are always located within public view, and almost invariably along or adjacent to boulevards, main roads, avenues and streets, in populated areas, where traffic of all kinds is heaviest. They are also located along the highway in rural or open sections and along the lines of railroads. In a very few instances, certain of the complainants own the fee in the premises where their signs or billboards are erected. For the most part, however, the complainants erect their signs or billboards on premises under a lease or licence for definite terms."

The finding is abundantly supported by reported evidence. In essentials, it is almost, if not entirely, a matter of common knowledge. The object of outdoor advertising in the nature of things is to proclaim to those who travel on highways and who resort to public reservations that which is on the advertising device, and to constrain such persons to see and comprehend the advertisement. It does not appeal alone to the desire or consent of such persons: it is forcibly thrust upon the attention of all such persons whether willing or averse. For such persons who strongly wish to avoid advertising intrusion, there is no escape; they cannot enjoy their natural and ordinary rights to proceed unmolested . . .

[T]he particular facts as found by the master may be summarized.

The business of outdoor advertising is to-day a nation-wide industry employing a large amount of capital and supporting a large number of employees, and is utilized by manufacturers and merchants as a valuable means—by signs, electric displays and posters—of directing attention to the goods, wares and merchandise which they are offering for sale and which may be or may become the subject-matter of interstate and foreign commerce. It is recognized as an established business and an important advertising medium possessing advantages not found in any other. The most important of these advantages are dominant size, continued visibility, attention value through the employment of colour, and repetition capacity of the advertising message. The plants and equipment of the plaintiffs are not adapted for any other industry. Although the signs, billboards and other devices as maintained by the plaintiffs fall into seven groups, viz., poster boards, painted bulletins or signs, wall boards, painted walls, roof boards, spectacular signs and illuminated signs, the greater part of their outdoor advertising business is in the display of advertisements upon poster boards. These are thin walls or screens having a sheet iron surface over a wooden framework with supports set in the ground. Upon the smooth surface lithographed or printed sheets of paper are posted bearing a brief pictorial or other message. Painted bulletins or signs are similar but are constructed entirely of wood and the advertisement is painted directly upon the face of the structure. The estimated market value as of January 1, 1924, of the combined plants, including in that term all kinds of outdoor advertising devices, interests in land, structures, licenses and permits, equipment, offices and repair shops of the plaintiffs was five million dollars. Signs and billboards in large part are erected and maintained without regard to standards of size or safety in construction, location or maintenance. The master further found: "In some isolated cases, certain signs and billboards in this Commonwealth have been used as screens to commit nuisances, hide law breakers, and facilitate immoral practices. Around some few filth has been allowed to collect, and some have shut out light and air from dwelling places. In and around others, rubbish and combustible materials have been allowed to collect, which to some degree tends to create a fire hazard. Those instances were all so rare, compared with the total number of signs and billboards in existence, that I am unable to find upon the evidence that signs and billboards, in general, as erected and maintained in this Commonwealth, have screened nuisances or created a danger to public health or morals or facilitated immoral practices, or afforded a shelter for criminals, or created or increased the danger of fire, or hindered firemen in their work." ...

The master found that beauty in the sense intended and employed in the framing and administration of the rules and regulations has in fact a real and substantial economic value to the commonwealth and to its citizens ...

The master also found that signs and billboards when erected or maintained in districts of an indisputably business character have no depreciating effect upon property values. In a neighbourhood of homes, such commercial intrusions are offensive to the sight and obnoxious to ordinary reasonable persons who may own or occupy those homes. Because of the serious aversion to such signs and billboards, they substantially and materially annoy and disturb the occupants and interfere with the comfortable enjoyment of their homes. The introduction of signs and billboards into such a neighbourhood tends seriously to injure and depreciate the value of the property. In urban districts of a mixed character, which are neither distinctively business nor residential, the effect of signs and billboards is rarely, if ever, seriously objectionable to the occupants of houses, or appreciably detrimental to property values; in rural communities when signs or billboards are located in proximity to homes not occupied by persons deriving revenue from such signs, the master was unable to find upon the evidence that they are less obnoxious than in a community of homes elsewhere ...

I find that billboards, signs and advertising devices when erected in sections or locations chiefly of historic interest or possessing natural beauty of landscape, pleasant or agreeable situation, prospect, view and attractive or picturesque surroundings or character, are inharmonious with and disfigure the same, and affect injuriously the benefits to be derived therefrom, and the enjoyment of the public therein, as also the economic value thereof to the Commonwealth and its citizens."...

The master states in his original and supplemental reports that his findings are based on all the evidence. Confessedly, all the evidence is not reported in full, notwithstanding the voluminous record. Very much of the testimony is not printed. The testimony of divers witnesses reported at the request of the plaintiffs is not complete but is stated only in part. As already pointed out, the original rule to the master required him to report "his findings to this Court together with such facts and questions of law and portions of the testimony as any party may in writing request." This form of reference was designed to relieve the court of the duty of reviewing all the testimony in order to test the accuracy of the findings of the master. . . .

The settled rule with respect to the report of a master without a full report of the evidence is that his findings of fact based upon oral testimony are accepted as true unless mutually inconsistent and plainly wrong . . .

After careful consideration . . . we are of opinion that the plaintiffs are not entitled to relief.

QUESTIONS. Is the method of taking evidence in this case satisfactory? Is this procedure consistent with the adversary system? Is this "legislative" or "adjudicative" evidence?

BERMAN *v.* PARKER

District of Columbia. Supreme Court of the United States.
1954. 348 U.S. 26

DOUGLAS J. delivered the opinion of the Court: This is an appeal from the judgment of a three-judge District Court which dismissed a complaint seeking to enjoin the condemnation of appellants' property under the *District of Columbia Redevelopment Act of 1945*, 60 Stat. 790, D.C. Code 1951, sections 5-701 to 5-719. The challenge was to the constitutionality of the Act, particularly as applied to the taking of appellants' property. The District Court sustained the constitutionality of the Act.

By section 2 of the Act, Congress made a "legislative determination" that "owing to technological and sociological changes, obsolete layout, and other factors, conditions existing in the District of Columbia with respect to substandard housing and blighted areas, including the use of bulidings in alleys as dwellings for human habitation, are injurious to the public health, safety, morals and welfare, and it is hereby declared to be the policy of the United States to protect and promote the welfare of the inhabitants of the seat of the Government by eliminating all such injurious conditions by employing all means necessary and appropriate for the purpose."

Section 2 goes on to declare that acquisition of property is necessary to eliminate these housing conditions.

Congress further finds in section 2 that these ends cannot be attained "by the ordinary operations of private enterprise alone without public participation" that "the sound replanning and redevelopment of an obsolescent or obsolescing portion" of the District "cannot be accomplished unless it be done in the light of comprehensive and coordinated planning of the whole of the territory of the District of Columbia and its environs"; and that "the acquisition and the assembly of real property and the leasing or sale thereof for redevelopment pursuant to a project area redevelopment plan . . . is hereby declared to be a public use". . .

The first project undertaken under the Act related to Project Area B in Southwest Washington, D.C. In 1950 the Planning Commission prepared and published a comprehensive plan for the District. Surveys revealed that in Area B, 64.3% of the dwellings were beyond repair, 18.4% needed major repairs, only 17.3% were satisfactory; 57.8% of the dwellings had outside toilets, 60.3% had no baths, 29.3% lacked electricity, 82.2% had no wash basins or laundry tubs, 83.8% lacked central heating. In the judgment of the District's Director of Health it was necessary to redevelop Area B in the interests of public health. The population of Area B amounted to 5,012 persons, of whom 97.5% were Negroes . . .

Appellants own property in Area B at 712 Fourth Street, S.W. It is not used as a dwelling or place of habitation. A department store is located on it. Appellants object to the appropriation of this property for the purposes of the project. They claim that their property may not be taken constitutionally for this project. It is commercial, not residential property; it is not slum housing; it will be put into the project under the management of a private, not a public, agency and redeveloped for private, not public, use. That is the argument; and the contention is that appellant's private property is being taken contrary to two mandates of the Fifth Amendment (1) "no person shall . . . be deprived of . . . property without due process of law"; (2) "nor shall private property be taken for public use without just compensation." To take for the purpose of ridding the area of slums is one thing; it is quite another, the argument goes, to take a man's property merely to develop a better balanced, more attractive community . . .

The power of Congress over the District of Columbia includes all the legislative powers which a state may exercise over its affair . . . We deal, in other words, with what traditionally has been known as the police power. An attempt to define its reach or trace its outer limits is fruitless, for each case must turn on its own facts. The definition is essentially the product of legislative determinations addressed to the purposes of government, purposes neither abstractly nor historically capable of complete definition. Subject to specific constitutional limitations, when the legislature has spoken, the public interest has been declared in terms well-nigh conclusive. In such cases the legislature, not the judiciary, is the main guardian of the public needs to be served by social legislation, whether it be Congress legislating concerning the District of Columbia . . . or the States legislating concerning local affairs . . . This principle admits of no exception merely because the power of eminent domain is involved . . .

Public safety, public health, morality, peace and quiet, law and order—these are some of the more conspicuous examples of the traditional application of the police power to municipal affairs. Yet they merely illustrate the scope of the power and do not delimit it . . . Miserable and disreputable housing conditions may do more than spread disease and crime and immorality. They may also suffocate the spirit by reducing the people who live there to the status of cattle. They may indeed make living an almost insufferable burden. They may also be an ugly sore, a blight on the community which robs it of charm, which makes it a place from which men turn. The misery of housing may despoil a community as an open sewer may ruin a river.

We do not sit to determine whether a particular housing project is or is not desirable. The concept of the public welfare is broad and inclusive . . . The values it represents are spiritual as well as physical, aesthetic as well as monetary. It is within the power of the legislature to determine that the community should be beautiful as well as healthy, spacious as well as clean, well-balanced as well as carefully patrolled. In the present case, the Congress and its authorized agencies have made determinations that take into account a wide variety of values. It is not for us to re-appraise them. If those who govern the District of Columbia decide that the Nation's Capital should be beautiful as well as sanitary, there is nothing in the Fifth Amendment that stands in the way.

Once the object is within the authority of Congress, the right to realize it through the exercise of eminent domain is clear. For the power of eminent domain is merely the means to the end . . . Once the object is within the authority of Congress, the means by which it will be attained is also for Congress to determine. Here one of the means chosen is the use of private enterprise for redevelopment of the area. Appellants argue that this makes the project a taking from one businessman for the benefit of another businessman. But the means of executing the project are for Congress and Congress alone to determine, once the public purpose has been established . . . The public end may be as well or better served through an agency of private enterprise than through a department of government—or so the Congress might conclude. We cannot say that public ownership is the sole method of promoting the public purposes of community redevelopment projects. What we have said also disposes of any contention concerning the fact that certain property owners in the area may be permitted to repurchase their properties for redevelopment in harmony with the over-all plan. That, too, is a legitimate means which Congress and its agencies may adopt, if they choose.

In the present case, Congress and its authorized agencies attack the problem of the blighted parts of the community on an area rather than on a structure-by-structure basis. That, too, is opposed by appellants. They maintain that since their building does not imperil health or safety nor contribute to the making of a slum or a blighted area, it cannot be swept into a redevelopment plan by the mere dictum of the Planning Commission or the Commissioners. The particular uses to be made of the land in the project were determined with regard to the needs of the particular community. The experts concluded that if the community were to be healthy, if it were not to revert again to a blighted or slum area as though possessed of a congenital disease, the area must be planned as a whole. It was not enough, they believed, to remove existing buildings that were insanitary or unsightly. It was important to redesign the whole area so as to eliminate the conditions that cause slums—the overcrowding of dwellings, the lack of parks, the lack of adequate streets and alleys, the absence of recreational areas, the lack of light and air, the presence of outmoded street patterns. It was believed that the piecemeal approach, the removal of individual structures that were offensive would be only a palliative. The entire area needed redesigning so that a balanced, integrated plan could be developed for the region, including not only new homes but also schools, churches, streets, parks and shopping centres. In this way it was hoped that the cycle of decay of the area could be controlled and the birth of future slums prevented . . . Such diversification in future use is plainly relevant to the maintenance of the desired housing standards and therefore within congressional power.

The District Court below suggested that if such a broad scope were intended for the statute, the standards contained in the Act would not be sufficiently definite to sustain the delegation of authority . . . We do not agree. We think the standards prescribed were adequate for executing the plan to eliminate not only slums as narrowly defined by the District Court but also the blighted areas that tend to produce slums. Property may of course be taken for this redevelopment which, standing by itself, is innocuous and unoffending. But we have said enough to indicate that it is the need of the area as a whole which Congress and its agencies are evaluating. If owner after owner were permitted to resist these redevelopment programs on the ground that his particular property was not being used against the public interest, integrated plans for redevelopment would suffer greatly. The argument pressed on us, is, indeed, a plea to substitute the landowner's standard of the public need for the standard prescribed by Congress. But as we have already stated, community redevelopment programs need not, by force of the Constitution, be on a piecemeal basis—lot by lot, building by building.

It is not for the courts to oversee the choice of the boundary line nor to sit in review on the size of a particular project area. Once the question of the public purpose has been decided the amount and character of land to be taken for the project and the need for a particular tract to complete the integrated plan rests in the discretion of the legislative branch . . .

The District Court indicated grave doubts concerning the Agency's right to take full title to the land as distinguished from the objectionable buildings located on it. We do not share those doubts. If the Agency considers it necessary in carrying out the redevelopment project to take full title to the real property involved, it may do so. It is not for the courts to determine whether it is necessary for successful consummation of the project that unsafe, unsightly or unsanitary buildings alone be taken or whether title to the land be included, any more than it is the function of the courts to sort and choose among the various parcels selected for condemnation.

The rights of these property owners are satisfied when they receive that just compensation which the Fifth Amendment exacts as the price of the taking.

The judgment of the District Court, as modified by this opinion, is affirmed.

QUESTIONS. This case interprets the Fifth Amendment rather than the Fourteenth which is applicable to the States. Does this decision put an end to doubts in the various States? What meaning may a State constitution put on its own "due process" clause?

(c) Back to Canada (and England)

THE MUNICIPAL ACT
Ontario. Revised Statutes. 1960. Chapter 249

379. (1) By-laws may be passed by the councils for local municipalities:

122. For prohibiting or regulating the erection of signs or other advertising devices and the posting of notices on buildings or vacant lots within any defined area or areas or on land abutting on any defined highway or part of a highway.

THE MUNICIPAL ACT
Manitoba. Revised Statutes. 1954. Chapter 173

895. (1) Any municipal corporation may pass by-laws, subject to the provisions of The Town Planning Act applicable thereto,

(e) for controlling and regulating the advertising of any business conducted in any zone or district and for appointing an official to the approval of whom any such advertising must conform;

COMMUNITY PLANNING ACT

New Brunswick. Statutes. 1960–61. Chapter 6

19. The council may, by by-law . . .
   (a) regulate as to any district
      (xiv) the public display of advertisement; . . .

66. (1) Subject to the approval of the Lieutenant-Governor in Council, the [Provincial Planning] Board may make regulations
   (d) respecting billboards, posters and other advertising signs and devices;

CITIES AND TOWNS ACT

Quebec. Revised Statutes. 1941. Chapter 233

426. The Council may make by-laws:

1. . . . to divide the municipality into zones . . . to prescribe the architecture, dimensions, symmetry, alignment and destination of the structures which may be erected therein . . .

[Section 426 was revised and consolidated by S.Q., 1960, c. 76, s. 17.]

THE PLANNING ACT

Ontario. Revised Statutes. 1960. Chapter 296

30. (1) By-laws may be passed by the councils of municipalities:
   4. For regulating the . . . external design . . . of buildings or structures . . .

TORONTO TOWNSHIP ZONING BY-LAW 2813 (1959)

29. (1) No person shall erect on lots in any block within a housing project dwellings more than twenty per cent of which are alike in external design with respect to size and location of doors, windows, projecting balconies and type of surface materials.

(2) Not more than three buildings alike in external design shall be built upon adjoining lots that front on the same street.

MINISTRY OF HOUSING AND LOCAL GOVERNMENT, REPORT (1959)

Appeals concerned with design excite a good deal of interest although they form only a small proportion of the total. Particulars follow of two typical cases.

The Leicestershire County Council refused permission for a house to be built on the main street of the small, charming village of Swithland within Charnwood Forest—an area described in the development plan as one of outstanding landscape value. The grounds for refusal were that the materials chosen for this building—straw coloured bricks and purple roofing tiles—were unsuitable in a place where the traditional materials were Swithland stone and slate. The council said that they would be ready to give permission if the walls were finished in stucco or colourwash, the roof clad in grey slates, and some features finished in local stone.

At the local inquiry it was obvious that the proposal had aroused strong feeling on the part of residents, especially those who had incurred extra cost in building houses in local materials. The appellant argued that a previous appeal concerning a house he was building on an adjacent plot had been allowed by the Minister, although the council had stipulated exactly the same conditions about building materials. Local stone and slate would add materially to the cost of the house. The village, he considered, was very drab and needed brightening up.

The Minister did not agree that the two cases were identical. In allowing the previous appeal he had said that grey bricks and tiles were not out of keeping with the character of the village; this proposal was concerned with straw-coloured bricks and purple tiles. The design, which was similar to that of the other house, was suitable for a single isolated dwelling, but if the three adjoining plots were developed in the same style, the design of the buildings as a group would be out of harmony with the rest of the village. The present designs were more suitable for an urban than a rural background. The Minister therefore dismissed the appeal and suggested that a fresh proposal should provide for developing the site with 3 detached houses as a unified whole to harmonise with the village architecture.

The village of Trimley St. Mary, near Ipswich, has no special architectural character, but the local planning authority thought that a proposed house of modern design would be out of keeping with its surroundings, though the design in itself was satisfactory. The most notable feature was the emphasis on horizontals, with a flat roof and horizontal timber cladding on the upper floor. A silver-grey finish was proposed for the timber. The three existing properties nearby all had pitched roofs. Two were of recent construction, built of purple-brown brick with a dark brown tiled roof. The third, Trimley House, dated from the early 19th century. It had long rendered walls painted a light shade, and a slate roof.

On appeal, the Minister took the view that there would be no greater contrast architecturally between the proposed house and the two recent ones than there was between them and Trimley House—with which the new house would blend as far as line and colour were concerned. He considered that the setting, particularly the tall trees behind the buildings, would continue to have a unifying effect on the scene. The appeal was accordingly allowed.

3. The English View

FRIEDMANN, LEGAL THEORY (3rd ed. 1953)

The use of natural law ideas in the development of English law revolves around two problems: the idea of the supremacy of law, and, in particular, the struggle between common law judges and Parliament for legislative supremacy on one hand, and the introduction of equitable considerations of "justice between man and man," on the other.

The first ended in a clear victory for parliamentary supremacy and the defeat of higher law ideas; the latter, after a long period of comparative stagnation, is again a factor of considerable influence in the development of the law.

Coke, as Chief Justice, vigorously asserted supremacy of common law over Acts of Parliament in his famous dictum in *Bonham's Case* (1610) having, in his previous career, as a Crown lawyer, magnified the State and the prerogative with equal vigour.

"It appears in our books that in many cases the common law will control Acts of Parliament and sometimes judge them to be utterly void, for when an Act of Parliament is against common right or reason or repugnant or impossible to be performed the common law will control it and adjudge such Act to be void."

Here, as in other cases, higher law is invoked for the legitimation of a bitter political struggle, which has its parallel, although with very different results in the struggle between the American legislature and the Supreme Court. Coke's dictum is generally recognized as having had little basis in the actual administration of law, and Professor Holdsworth asserts that from the sixteenth century onwards—and beyond any shadow of doubt after the revolution of 1688–supremacy of law and supremacy of Parliament had merged, not to be challenged again until the present day. Lip-service continued to be paid, however, to the idea of natural law. The following passage in Blackstone's *Commentaries* might well have come from St. Thomas himself:

"This law of nature being coeval with mankind and dictated by God Himself is, of course, superior in obligation to any other. It is binding over all the globe, in all countries, and at all times; no human laws are of any validity if contrary to this . . . Upon these two foundations the law of nature and the law of revelation depend all human laws. . . ."

This statement does not prevent Blackstone from asserting the absolute legislative supremacy of Parliament. Since then higher law doctrines have fallen into disrepute in England. In some branches of modern English law, principles of natural justice are openly invoked as the test of validity of legal acts, although that test cannot, of course, be applied to any Act of Parliament. The most important examples are the supervision of administrative acts and decisions by the law courts, the recognition of foreign judgments and the recognition of custom.

NOTE. For an exciting account of the implications of "positivism" and "natural law" see Hart, "Positivism and the Separation of Law and Morals" 71 *Harv. Law Rev.* 593 and Fuller, "Positivism and Fidelity to Law—A Reply to Professor Hart" *ibid.* p. 630.

CHAPTER 9

NON-CONFORMING USES: RETROACTIVITY

I returned, and saw under the sun, that the race is not to the swift. . . .

Ecclesiastes

What to do with land the development and use of which has already been established when a program of planning or regulation is commenced has plagued every planner and state authority where planning or regulation or both has been undertaken in the twentieth century. Most people would agree that retroactive legislation is unpopular, if not immoral, and respect for vested interest is dearly held in a modern democracy. But beyond the high sounding phrases about "ex post facto" laws and "democratic rights" there is a very difficult question of drawing the line between the right of the individual and the right of other individuals or the totality of individuals comprising the state or municipality. The materials here presented give a picture of the actual laws in effect in several jurisdictions, and there is a sufficient variety of views to enable you to work out your own formulae or solutions if you wish. But what is completely lacking in the legislative provisions is any indication of the "philosophy," or basic purpose, to be served by them. Without an understanding of purpose intelligent interpretation is impossible, as cases like the *Oakwood Stadium* case and the *Central Jewish Institute* case make abundantly apparent.

Read the following materials, keeping in mind that the inevitable result of zoning so as to create so-called "non-conforming uses" is to create a monopoly in the land use continued despite the restriction as to future use. What evil, if any, results from creating a monopoly in land use? How does zoning generally affect property values? Why does property increase in value? What part does the owner play in the increase?

1. THE PROTECTION OF VESTED "RIGHTS": ESTABLISHMENT AND DISCONTINUANCE

REGINA *v*. ON HING

British Columbia. Supreme Court. 1884. 1 B.C.R. (II) 148

Certiorari to bring up a conviction for that On Hing "unlawfully altered a wooden building within the fire limits of the City of Victoria, to wit: on Government Street, without the written permission of the Inspector of buildings, approved by a majority of the Fire Wardens, contrary to the form of the by-law in that case made and provided," whereby he was adjudged to pay a fine of $50 within one week, in default distress, in default of distress one month's imprisonment.

BEGBIE C.J.: Several grounds were relied on for quashing the conviction. The first objection was that against the validity of the building by-law under which the conviction was had. That by-law, No. 98 (which was produced and proved before the magistrate), by section 23 provides that "no wooden building within the fire limits shall be altered without the written permission of the Inspector and majority of the Fire Wardens" previously obtained. This provision was defended as being authorized by the Municipalities Act, 1881, c. 16, s. 104, sub-sec. 78, which empowers the municipality to make by-laws (*inter alia*) "to regulate the erection of wooden buildings, notwithstanding any Act or law in force in the Province," and sub-sec. 58, "the prevention of fires." The applicant contends that this statute does not authorize any by-law respecting alterations of existing buildings, but only by-laws respecting new erections. And upon this, the only point of general interest, we are not left without authority. Both the statute and the by-law are very similar in effect to a statute and by-law in Ontario relating to similar matters, which have been considered and decided in the case of *R.* v. *Howard*. There the statute authorized a municipality to make by-laws against fires, and for "regulating the erection of wooden buildings and preventing the erection of wooden buildings or additions thereto and wooden fences" in specified parts of the city. A by-law was made, under that supposed authority, ordering that all roofs of shingle should have the shingles laid in half an inch of mortar. The defendant, the owner of a wooden house of several years' standing, proceeded to re-shingle it without mortar; and being convicted of a breach of the by-law, the conviction was quashed, for that the statute only authorized the passing of a by-law to regulate new erections, and did not authorize a by-law to interfere with existing wooden buildings; that "the statute only applied to the erection, or creation as it were, of new buildings or additions thereto, or the removal and placing of a wooden building in a new locality within the fire limits." And the powers given under the statute to make by-laws "for the prevention of fires" were held not to affect the decision.

I feel quite disposed to follow the reasoning of Hagarty C.J., in that case; and this case is in many respects stronger; the words in italics in the Ontario Statute not being contained in the B.C. Statute. In addition to the grounds there adopted by the Court, it is to be considered that a by-law (dealing with matters of this sort) cannot go beyond the words of the statute; and the statute here gives no power whatever to regulate alterations; so that this by-law is quite unauthorized.

MUNICIPAL ACT

British Columbia. Revised Statutes. 1960. Chapter 255

705. (1) A building or structure lawfully under construction at the time of the coming into force of a zoning by-law shall, for the purpose of that by-law, be deemed to be a building or structure existing at that time.

(2) A lawful use of premises existing at the time of the adoption of a zoning by-law, although such use does not conform to the provisions of the by-law, may be continued; but if such non-conforming use is discontinued for a period of thirty days, any future use of those premises shall, subject to the provisions of this section, be in conformity with the provisions of the zoning by-law.

(3) A lawful use of a building or structure existing at the time of the adoption of the zoning by-law, although such use does not conform to the provisions of the zoning by-law, may be extended throughout the building or structure, but no structural alterations except those required by Statute or by-law or those allowed by the Zoning Board of Appeal shall be made therein or thereto.

(4) Where any building or structure the use of which does not conform to the provisions of any applicable zoning by-law is damaged or destroyed to the extent of seventy-five per centum or more of its value above its foundations, as determined by the building inspector, whose decision shall be subject to review by the Zoning Board of Appeal, it shall not be repaired or reconstructed, except for a conforming use in accordance with the zoning by-law.

(5) A change of tenants or occupants of any premises or building or structure shall not be deemed to affect the use of the premises or building or structure within the meaning of this section.

THE TOWN AND RURAL PLANNING ACT

Alberta. Revised Statutes. 1955. Chapter 337

82. (1) A non-conforming building shall not be enlarged, added to, rebuilt or structurally altered except

(*a*) as may be required by statute or by-law,

(*b*) as may be necessary to make it a conforming building, or

(*c*) as may be deemed necessary by the council, or an agent or servant of the municipality designated by the by-law, for the routine maintenance of the building.

(2) If a non-conforming building is damaged or destroyed by fire or other causes to an extent of more than seventy-five per cent of the value of the building above its foundation, the building shall not be repaired or rebuilt except in conformity with the provisions of the by-law.

(3) A non-conforming use may be continued, but if the use is discontinued or changed any future use shall conform to the provisions of the by-law.

(4) Subject to subsection (1) a non-conforming use may be extended throughout the building in which it was permitted under subsection (3) in respect of a part of the building, but the building, whether or not it is a non-conforming building, shall not be enlarged or added to and no structural alterations shall be made therein.

(4*a*) Where a non-conforming use is being made of part of a parcel and the use is being continued pursuant to subsection (3), the use shall not be extended to any other part of the parcel and no additional building shall be erected upon the parcel while the non-conforming use continues.

(5) The use of land or buildings shall be deemed not to be affected by reason only of a change of owners, tenants or occupants of the land or buildings.

[Section 83 is reproduced as amended by S.A., 1959, c. 89, s. 12.]

TOWN PLANNING ACT

Nova Scotia. Revised Statutes. 1954. Chapter 292

18. (1) Any building lawfully under construction at the time of the first publication of the advertisement of intention to pass a zoning by-law shall, for the purpose of that by-law, be deemed to be a building existing at the time of the passing of a zoning by-law.

(2) The lawful use of premises existing at the date of the first publication of the advertisement of intention to pass a zoning by-law under this Act, although such use does not conform to the provisions of the by-law, may be continued; but if such non-conforming use is discontinued, any

future use of those premises shall be in conformity with the provisions of the zoning by-law.

(3) The lawful use of a building existing at the time of the passing of a zoning by-law under this Act, although such use does not conform to the provisions of the zoning by-law, may be extended throughout the building, but no structural alterations except those required by statute or by-law shall be made therein while such use continues.

(4) Where no structural alterations are made in a building of a non-conforming use, such use may be changed to a use of similar character, with the consent of the council.

(5) A change of tenants or occupants of any premises or building shall not be deemed to affect the use of the premises or building within the meaning of this Section.

(6) If any building which is by this Act deemed to be a building existing at the time of the passing of the zoning by-law is damaged or destroyed by fire or other causes to an extent of more than fifty per cent of the value of the building above its foundations, and if at the time of its damage or destruction the use thereof is not in conformity with the provisions of the zoning by-law, the non-conforming use shall not be continued in respect of the building upon its repair, rebuilding or reconstruction without the approval of the council.

19. Prior to the passage of a zoning by-law or prior to the passage of an amendment of a zoning by-law if application therefor has been made, the council may for a period not exceeding two months withhold a building permit for any building, or the council may impose such conditions on the granting of the building permit as may appear to the council to be in the public interest.

THE PLANNING ACT

Ontario. Revised Statutes. 1960. Chapter 296

30. (7) No by-law passed under this section applies,

(a) to prevent the use of any land, building or structure for any purpose prohibited by the by-law if such land, building or structure was lawfully used for such purpose on the day of the passing of the by-law, so long as it continues to be used for that purpose; or

(b) to prevent the erection or use for a purpose prohibited by the by-law of any building or structure the plans for which have, prior to the day of the passing of the by-law, been approved by the municipal architect or building inspector, so long as the building or structure when erected is used and continues to be used for the purpose for which it was erected and provided the erection of such building or structure is commenced within two years after the day of the passing of the by-law and such building or structure is completed within a reasonable time after the erection thereof is commenced.

NOTE ON THE HISTORY OF SECTION 30 (7). The earliest form of this section appears in S.O., 1904, c. 22, s. 19, which added s. 541a to *The Consolidated Municipal Act, 1903*. Section 541a is reproduced on page 605 and authorized limited restrictions. The last paragraph read:

"Provided that this section shall not apply to any buildings now erected or used for any of the purposes aforesaid so long as they continue to be used as at present."

The words "now" and "at present" apparently referred to the date of Royal Assent to the amendment, on April 26, 1904.

The paragraph quoted survived minor amendments (see pp. 606–7) extending the subject matter over which municipal control might be exercised until 1913, when *The Municipal Act, 1913*, c. 43, consolidated the various provisions as s. 409, of which paragraph 2, sub-paragraph (b) read:

"This paragraph shall not apply to a building which was on the 26th day of April, 1904, erected or used for any of such purposes, so long as it is used as it was used on that day."

The paragraph remained unchanged in the R.S.O., 1914, c. 192, s. 409, heading 2. For a current interpretation of that version see *Toronto* v. *Presswood* (1944).

In S.O., 1917, by c. 42, s. 18, paragraph 2c was added to s. 409. It read:

"The passing of a by-law under this section shall not prevent the extension or enlargement of any building used for any of the purposes mentioned in this section at the time of the passing of the by-law."

This appears to be the first introduction of the notion that the permissible retroactivity should be limited to the date the by-law was passed rather than to the date when enabling power was conferred on the municipality. When S.O., 1921, c. 63, s. 10, introduced s. 399a which authorized general zoning, the provision, sub-paragraph (a) of paragraph 2, read:

"No by-law passed under this section shall apply to any land or building which on the day the by-law is passed is erected or used for any purpose prohibited by the by-law so long as it continues to be used for that purpose, nor shall it apply to any building in the course of erection or to any building the plans for which have been approved by the city architect prior to the date of the passing of the by-law, so long as when erected it is used for the purpose for which it was erected."

Prior to 1921, a by-law could have been retroactive for seventeen years, but the new provision seriously limited the power. However, s. 399a did not repeal the old s. 541a, it was an additional power to control land use. The provisions of s. 541a as amended persisted in the legislation until S.O., 1941, c. 35, s. 15, when they were repealed. See R.S.O., 1937, c. 266, s. 420, paragraphs 2 to 10. The retroactivity of a by-law passed under paragraph 2 was limited only by reference to use on April 26, 1904. Paragraph 3 referred to May 1, 1914; paragraph 4 to May 1, 1916, and paragraph 2c of s. 409 introduced in 1917 (see above) was retained as subparagraph (b) of paragraph 4; paragraph 6 to April 1, 1918; paragraph 7 to May 1, 1919; paragraph 9 to April 1, 1928; and paragraph 10, which was introduced in 1934, referred to the day the by-law was passed. The provisions, or such of them as had already been passed, appeared in the R.S.O., 1927, c. 233, as s. 411, paragraphs 2 to 8.

Meanwhile the provision that first appeared as s. 399a in 1921 was retained, with no radical change in principle, until 1955.

In the consolidation of 1922, s. 399a (2) (a) reproduced the 1921 version except that the words "building in the course of erection or to any" were deleted, presumably because it was considered that plans would have been approved and a permit would have been issued for any building in the course of erection, and would so be protected by the next part of the provision. The 1922 consolidation also introduced an ungrammatical change by substituting the word "buildings" for the word "building" so that it read, "No by-law passed under this section shall apply to any land or buildings which . . . is erected or used . . ." This deviation from grammatical standards, if it is one, persisted until 1941. The 1922 version was re-enacted in the R.S.O., 1927, c. 233, as s. 398 (2) (a); in the R.S.O., 1937, c. 266, as s. 406 (2) (a).

The Statutes of Ontario 1941, c. 35, s. 13, re-enacted the section with very slight changes: the clause "which on the day the by-law is passed" became "which, on the day of the passing of the by-law"; the words "is erected or used" were revised to read "is used or erected"; and the words "city architect" were changed to "municipal architect or building inspector."

The Statutes of Ontario, 1946, c. 60, s. 50 (6) introduced the words "or structure" after the word "building" wherever it appeared. Doubtless the word "building" was inapt to describe a gasoline pump in a service station, or a fence, etc. This amended version appeared in the R.S.O., 1950, c. 243, as s. 390 (6).

The first major change was enacted in 1955, when the protection of non-conforming land and buildings was possibly reduced by a radical rearrangement of the section. By c. 48, s. 40 (4) the section was divided into its present two paragraphs and instead of excluding the by-law from any application to non-conforming land, buildings or structures, the by-law merely did not apply so as to prevent their use.

The 1955 amendment represents a concerted attack on the unsatisfactory state of the law, which is widely recognised, but for which no quite satisfactory amendment has yet occurred to the legislators. The materials below will emphasize the unsatisfactory state and will perhaps suggest some improvements to the thoughtful student.

In 1956, c. 50, s. 16 inserted the word "lawfully" in clause (a) so that protection was clearly available only for land, buildings or structures lawfully used on the day the by-law was passed.

The Statutes of Ontario, 1957, c. 76, s. 23 (2) added the words "and provided the erection of such building or structure is commenced within two years after the day of the passing of the by-law and such building or structure is completed within a reasonable time after the erection thereof is commenced" at the end of clause (b). In the S.O., 1959, Chapter 71 transferred the entire section 390 of *The Municipal Act* to *The Planning Act, 1955*, as section 27*a*. In the R.S.O., 1960, c. 296, it appeared as section 30, and sub-section (7) it remained and remains (1963) unchanged since 1957.

PROBLEM. The shift of emphasis in the 1955 amendment to what is now section 30 (7) of *The Planning Act*, so that the by-law now applies, but not so as to prevent the use of the land, has created a difficulty of some practical importance. Under the 1921 law it was clear that the by-law simply did not apply to land in non-conforming use on the day the by-law was passed. Under the 1955 amendment it is at least arguable that the by-law applies to such land in every respect save that it cannot prevent the non-conforming use of the parcel. How is this use determined?

Suppose that a service station at the intersection of two major highways is in non-conforming use, and that vehicles can be and are driven on to the station lot right at the point of intersection. The by-law making the station non-conforming requires that land that is used for a service station is to be laid out with curbing clearly marking off access ramps not more than 25 feet wide and a "daylight corner" that is curbed back fifty feet in each direction from the intersection. The object of these requirements is to control traffic. Do these requirements apply to the existing station? The application of these new standards clearly would not prevent the lot from being used as a service station, but clearly would prevent the intersection from being used as an access.

If the regulation applies, although the prohibition doesn't, there is still a difficulty of enforcement. In the case of the new use, the by-law may say, and usually does, that no person shall use land or erect or use a building or structure for a service station unless he builds the prescribed curbs. If he fails to build the curb he may be restrained by an injunction from using the service station. In the case of the non-conforming use, presumably this power to restrain is not available, since the by-law cannot be applied so as to prevent the use. Can the regulation be enforced by fine or imprisonment? Effectively?

NOTE. Compare the 1917 amendment adding paragraph (2c) to s. 409 set out above, which in effect permits the extension or enlargement of the particular non-conforming buildings dealt with in that section with *Re Wilmot and Kingston*, below, and see also s. 30 (18), first introduced in S.O., 1943, c. 16, s. 11 (2), applicable to land or buildings, by 1946, c. 60, s. 50 (7) made applicable to land, buildings or structures, and in 1950, by c. 46, s. 19 (2) slightly revised to its present form. Section 30 (18) of *The Planning Act* now reads:

(18) Notwithstanding any other provision of this section, any by-law passed under this section or any by-law deemed to be consistent with this section by subsection 3 of section 13 of *The Municipal Amendment Act, 1941*, may, with the approval of the Municipal Board, be amended so as to permit the extension or enlargement of any land, building or structure used for any purpose prohibited by the by-law if such land, building or structure continues to be used in the same manner and for the same purpose as it was used on the day such by-law was passed.

RE WILMOT AND KINGSTON

Ontario. Court of Appeal. [1946] 3 D.L.R. 790

LAIDLAW J.A.: The Corporation of the City of Kingston appeals from an order of Urquhart J. dated October 22, 1945, made upon motion in Court on behalf of the respondents. The Court ordered and adjudged "that the Corporation of the City of Kingston do forthwith issue to the plaintiffs a building permit, permitting them to alter and enlarge the buildings now standing on parts of Lots 580 and 581 on the west side of Frontenac Street in the City of Kingston, as shown on a Plan . . . and to build new buildings thereon in accordance with the plans and specifications filed on the application for permit dated June 26th, 1945."

The question to be decided by the Court is whether the provisions contained in by-law No. 184, passed by the Council of the Corporation of the City of Kingston on December 15, 1941, are effective in law to prohibit the respondents from (a) altering and enlarging the buildings in use by the respondents at the time the by-law was passed for purposes contrary to the provisions thereof, and (b) building new buildings on land likewise used for such purposes at that time.

It will be convenient to reproduce relevant parts of By-law No. 184 and also certain sections of the *Municipal Act*, R.S.O. 1937, c. 266, as amended:

BY-LAW NO. 184

A By-law for the Zoning of the City of Kingston passed December 15th, 1941.

Section 1. General

1.1 Scope of this By-law.

Within the City of Kingston, no dwelling, business, trade or industry shall be located, nor shall any building or structure be erected, altered or used, nor shall any land be used, except in conformity with the regulations of the By-law.

1.2. Use Zones.

For the purposes of this By-law the municipality is hereby divided into 'Use Zones'. . .

1.3. Classification of Use Zones.

The Use Zones are: . . .

C. Multiple-family dwelling zone.

Section 6. Regulations Governing Zone 'C'

6.1. General

Except as hereinafter provided, all structures and parts thereof erected or altered in Zone 'C' shall conform to the regulations of this Section.

6.2. Permissible Uses

No building or part thereof and no land shall be used for purposes other than: . . .

(c) A retail store or shop.

6.5. Percentage of Lot Occupancy.

(a) subject to Clause (b), no building shall occupy more than sixty per cent of the area of the lot upon which it is situated if an interior lot, nor more than seventy-five per cent of the area if a corner lot.

Section 9. Supplementary Regulations

9.3. Non-Conforming Uses.

9.3.1. Existing Structures.

Subject to Item 9.3.2. a building, which, at the date of enactment of this By-law, is used for a purpose not permissible within the district in which it is located, shall not be enlarged, extended, reconstructed, or altered structurally, unless such building is thereafter to be used for a purpose permitted within such district, provided that the interior of such building may be reconstructed or altered, in order to render the same more convenient or commodious for the same purpose for which, at the date of enactment of this By-law, such building is used.

9.3.2. Partial Destruction of Existing Buildings.

A building which is damaged to the extent of fifty per cent or more of its value (exclusive of walls below grade) as at the date of the damage and as determined by fair building standards, and which does not conform with the requirements of this By-law in respect of use, lot occupancy or height, shall not be restored except in conformity with the regulations for the use zone in which such building is located. . . .

9.3.3. Extension of Non-Conforming Uses.

Any use made of buildings or lands at the date of enactment of this By-law may be continued, although not conforming with the regulations of the use zone in which they are located, or such use may be extended throughout the building, provided, in either case, that no structural alterations, other than those provided in Item 9.3.1., or as may be required by existing law or by-law, are made therein, and that no new building or extension to such building is erected.

10.4.5. Use, Non-Conforming.

'Non-conforming use' shall mean any use of a building or premises that does not conform to the regulations of the use zone in which such building or premises is located.

. . . Before and on the date By-law No. 184 was passed, the respondents carried on the business of a dairy on part of Lots 580 and 581 on the west side of Frontenac St. in the City of Kingston. The main plant was situated on Lot No. 580 and consisted of a dairy building, in which an office was located, a detached stable and a detached garage. They sold milk and a chocolate beverage over a counter on the premises and by retail sale directly to the householders throughout the city.

On June 2, 1944, the respondents became owners by deed of the westerly 50 ft. of the south half of Lot No. 581. On or about November 16, 1944, they applied to the City Engineer of the City of Kingston for a building permit to construct a cement block building, 27 ft. by 37 ft., to be used in connection with their business. The building was to be constructed on the part of Lot No. 581 acquired by the respondents in June, 1944. The permit was refused on the ground that the proposed building contravened the by-laws of the City of Kingston. A motion was thereupon made to the Court on behalf of the respondents for a mandatory order that the city issue a permit as applied for. The motion was dismissed by an order of Mackay J. by an order dated February 19, 1945, and an appeal therefrom to this Court was dismissed by an order dated June 7, 1945. In reasons for the order of the Court of Appeal, as given by Roach J.A. the view is expressed that s-ss. 9.3.1, 9.3.2 and 9.3.3 of By-law No. 184 were *ultra vires*. The formal order of the Court does not contain such a declaration as part of the judgment of the Court. Nevertheless, counsel relies upon the opinion and urges that effect ought to be now given to the views expressed by the learned Justice of Appeal in the earlier proceedings. It ought to be borne in mind, however, that the motion before the Court, and the question to be determined in those proceedings, were substantially different from those in the present proceedings. The respondents previously proposed to erect a building on land which was not acquired by them until after By-law No. 184 was passed and not used by them for any prohibited purpose prior to or at that time. The permit which they sought to obtain from the city included that building, and the real question to be determined by the Court was whether under those circumstances the proposed plan of construction was in contravention of the provisions of the by-law. The respondents altered their plans, and now are endeavouring to obtain a permit for the alteration and enlargement of buildings in use on the date the by-law was passed for purposes contrary to its provisions, and for the creation of new buildings on land use at that time for the same purpose. I think that the question to be now decided is not concluded by the judgment of this Court in the former proceedings. I give to the views expressed by Roach J.A. my most serious consideration and respect, but do not feel bound by them in the matter now in controversy between the parties. The question may be approached in two steps: Firstly, what legislative power did the council of the municipality possess to prohibit the things which the respondents seek to do? Secondly, if such power existed, has it been effectively exercised by By-law No. 184?

Section 406 (1) of the *Municipal Act*, as amended in 1941, covers two classes of property: (1) land and (2) buildings. The restriction in respect of each class of property is the subject of a separate provision. The prohibition as to land is against the use of it, and as to buildings is against the erection or use. There is no limitation imposed directly by the provisions of the statute upon the legislative power vested in the councils of the municipalities by s. 406, but the scope of application of the by-law is expressly limited by s-s. (2) thereof. That subsection excepts from the application of such a by-law certain lands particularly described, and also certain buildings particularly described, which I enumerate as follows: (1) land which is used on the day of the passing of the by-law for any purpose prohibited by the by-law, so long as it continues to be used for that purpose; (2) any building which is used or erected on the day of the passing of the by-law for any purpose prohibited by the by-law, so long as it continues to be used for that purpose; and (3) any building, the plans for which have, prior to the passing of the by-law, been approved by the municipal architect or building inspector, so long as the building when erected is used for the purpose for which it was erected.

Thus, if land is used on the day of the passing of a by-law for a purpose prohibited thereby, that use may continue and such a by-law by express statutory provision is not applicable to that land so long as it continues to be used for that purpose. If the use for that purpose ceases, the by-law thereupon becomes applicable and the land cannot thereafter be used for a prohibited purpose. In the same manner, and to the same extent, the use of any building in existence at the time a by-law is passed for a purpose prohibited by the by-law may continue. But the right of a property owner or user at the date of the passing of such a by-law is fixed and limited in consequence thereof. It is thereafter subject to the provisions of any by-law enacted in the proper exercise of the legislative powers of the council of the municipality. The effect of such an enactment is to prohibit the erection of any building after the date of the passing of the by-law on premises which on that date were used for purposes prohibited thereby. This is made plain, I think, by the reasons given by Viscount Cave L.C. in *Toronto* v. *R.C. Separate Schools Trustees*. Thus, in my opinion, it was within the power of the appellant municipality to pass a by-law the provisions of which would effectively prohibit the erection by the respondents of a building on land used by them at the date of the passing of the by-law for purposes prohibited thereby and notwithstanding such use at that time. The council of a municipality could not, of course, make such a by-law applicable to a building for which plans had received the specified approval at the date of the passing of the by-law. That case is not now in question. I am of opinion also that a by-law passed in proper form by the council of a municipality, pursuant to the powers contained in s. 406 (1) of the *Municipal Act*, must be construed so as to include a prohibition against any alteration or reconstruction of any existing building by way of addition, enlargement or extension to it. The fact that a separate section of a by-law makes express provision for work of that nature does not, in my opinion, make such sections void or *ultra vires*; nor does that particularization affect the validity of the by-law as a whole. Alteration or reconstruction of that kind is nonetheless within the language of the statute, "erection . . . of buildings." Finally when one reads and gives proper effect to s. 406 (9), as enacted in 1943, and as read together with s-ss. (1) and (2), it becomes plain that a by-law passed under the general powers of a council, as contained in s. 406 (1), extends to prohibit the "extension or enlargement" of any land or building used for any purpose prohibited by the by-law on the day such by-law was passed, excepting works of erection for which plans have received the specified approval prior to that date. The council of the municipality may (with the approval of the Municipal Board) amend such a by-law to permit such "extension or enlargement." In the absence of such an amendment, the provisions of the by-law are operative and effective, with only the exceptions mentioned, and it does not in such circumstances lie within the power of the council to permit such work.

Have the powers contained in s. 406 of the *Municipal Act* been exercised by By-law No. 184 effectively to prohibit the proposed work of construction on the premises of the respondents? Section 1.1 expressly provides, *inter alia*, that no building shall be erected within the City of Kingston except in conformity with the regulations of the by-law. The premises in question are subject to Regulations Governing Zone "C", as set forth in s. 6 of the by-law. By section 6.1, all structures and parts thereof erected or altered in that zone (with certain exceptions) shall conform to the regulations of the section. Section 6.2 provides that "No building or part thereof and no land shall be used for purposes other than: . . . a retail store or shop." I do not discuss at length the question whether any building now erected or proposed falls within the exception "a retail store or shop." I am certain that it does not. The reasons given by Roach J.A. in *Wilmot* v. *Kingston* (1945), are abundantly clear and satisfying on this point.

Section 9.3.1, in my opinion, covers particular classes of structural work, namely, enlargement, extension, reconstruction or alteration, all of which, in my opinion, fall within the meaning of the language "erection of buildings", as used in the statute. They add nothing to the effective prohibition found in s. 1.1 and s. 6, nor do they nullify or detract from the effect of those sections. Likewise, in s. 9.3.2 the use of the word "restored", in connection with a building damaged by fire, is within the scope and meaning of the words "erection of buildings." Section 9.3.3 is perhaps intended to express and give effect to the exceptions from application of the by-law, as contained in s. 406 (2) of the statute, but does not affect the validity of the by-law. There is no other appropriate provision for the statutory exceptions, but such a provision is not essential to the validity of the by-law: *Re Toronto R.C. Separate Sch. Bd. & Price* (1923), referred to by Roach J.A. in *Wilmot* v. *Kingston*.

I add my view in accordance with that of the Honourable The Chief Justice of Ontario expressed in *Chatham* v. *Sisters of St. Joseph et al.* (1941), that it is doubtful whether the Court can properly hold one part or parts of the by-law to be ultra vires and the remainder to be valid, because of the express requirements of the statute in s-ss. (3), (4), (7) and (8) as to approval by the Municipal Board.

My conclusion is that By-law No. 184 effectively prohibits the alteration and enlargement of the buildings now standing on the lands particularly described in the judgment of the Court below and the erection of new buildings thereon.

Consequently, this appeal ought to be allowed with costs. The judgment of Urquhart J. ought to be set aside and in place thereof the order should be that the motion be dismissed with costs.

[The opinion of Hogg J.A., which discussed the *Separate School Board* case at some length, is omitted. Robertson agreed to the result.]

WILMOT *v.* KINGSTON. [1945] 4 D.L.R. 291 (Ontario. Court of Appeal). ROACH J.A.: ". . . Counsel for the appellants argued, first, that the by-law was *ultra vires* because it purports to apply to land or buildings which, on the day of the passing of the by-law were used or erected for a purpose prohibited by the bylaw, even though they continued to be used for that purpose, and, therefore, that it contravenes s-s. (2) of s. 406 of the *Municipal Act*.

"The municipality being the creature of the Legislature, can exercise only those powers which the Legislature confers upon it. Focusing attention on ss. 9.3.1, 9.3.2 and 9.3.3 of By-law 184, what does the respondent corporation purport to do in the exercise of the power conferred upon it by the Legislature? I think it is plain that it purports to do exactly what the Legislature by s-s. (2) of s. 406 has said it shall not do, viz., to make the by-law apply to land and buildings which at the date of the passing of the by-law were used for a purpose prohibited by the by-law, even though those lands and buildings continue thereafter to be used for that purpose. Those sections demonstrate this excess of jurisdiction very plainly. By them the corporation purports to exercise a restrictive authority over land and/or buildings, the use of which as of the date of the passing of the by-law, was not in conformity with the restrictions in the by-law, even though the use thereafter continues to be the same as before.

"The use to which the appellants' original lands and buildings—this does not include the Casselman land—was put as of the passing of the by-law has continued to be the same from the passing of the by-law to date, and the use to which the remodelled or additional structures on the original lands will be put hereafter is the same use, viz., for the operation of a dairy business. For these reasons By-law No. 184, despite ss. 9.3.1. and 9.3.3. has no application to those lands and buildings if, as I understood during the argument was the case, the appellants desire to modernize those buildings by altering or adding to them or razing or reconstructing some or all of them, By-law No. 184 does not stand in the way.

Sections 9.3.1, 9.3.2 and 9.3.3 are *ultra vires* but that does not make the whole by-law invalid. . . ."

REGINA *v.* CAPPY AND SMITH

Ontario. Court of Appeal [1953] 1 D.L.R. 28

HENDERSON J.A. (dissenting): An appeal from His Honour Judge Factor of the County Court of the County of York upon a trial *de novo* on September 28, 1951, who quashed the convictions of the respondents by Magistrate O. M. Martin, dated June 18, 1951, whereby the respondent Norman Smith was convicted for that on the 19th day of May, 1951, he did in the said County of York "use the lands known as the Oakwood Stadium in the Township of York being part of Township lot 29 Concession 3 from the Bay and other lands described in Township of York by-law No. 13,249 for the purpose of holding and carrying on thereon Stock Car Races, contrary to York Township by-law No. 13,249", and whereby the said Norman Smith was adjudged to forfeit and pay a fine of $50 and costs amounting to 87c and in default to serve a sentence of ten days, and whereby the respondent Joseph Cappy was convicted that he did on the 19th day of May, 1951, in the said County of York "use the lands known as the Oakwood Stadium in the Township of York being part of Township lot 29 Concession 3 from the Bay and other lands described in Township of York By-law No. 13,249 for the purpose of holding and carrying on thereon

Stock Car Races, contrary to the Township of York By-law No. 13,249", and was adjudged to pay a fine of $50 and costs amounting to 88c and in default to serve a sentence of ten days in the common gaol.

This appeal is by special leave of Roach J. of February 6, 1952, upon the ground that a question of law is involved in the appeal.

On April 5, 1948, the Township of York passed its By-law 13249 pursuant to what was then s. 406 of the *Municipal Act*, R.S.O. 1937, c. 266, as re-enacted by 1941, c. 35, s. 13 (1), and amended by 1946, c. 60, s. 50. The section, in the same form as it was on the date of the passing of the by-law now appears in R.S.O. 1950, c. 243, as s. 390. The by-law provides that the lands known as Oakwood Stadium may not be used "for any other purpose than that of a detached or semi-detached private residence, duplex, triplex, double duplex or apartment house with suitable outbuildings therefor." The by-law contains the following exemption, which is the exemption that is applicable by reason of what is now s. 390 (6):

"This By-law shall not apply to any land or buildings which on the day the said By-law is passed is erected or used for any purpose prohibited by this By-law so long as it continues to be used for that purpose."

On February 15, 1951, the respondents purchased the lands known as Oakwood Stadium and on May 19, 1951, they began to promote and conduct in the stadium stock car races.

Oakwood Stadium consists of an oval open space upon which there is sitting accommodation partly in open stands and partly in a covered stand. This stadium at the time of the passing of the by-law in 1948 and prior to the occupation of the respondents in February, 1951, was suitable for permitting members of the public to witness various kinds of sport contests including the playing of soccer, rugby and track and field events. Prior to February, 1951, there was a cinder track 18 ft. wide around the perimeter of the playing field suitable for foot-races.

On May 19, 1951, the exhibition or contest of stock car races was held. This contest consists of a number of races of a designated number of laps in which six or eight cars take part. The playing-field area of the stadium is used as a repair pit for the cars involved and as a place to store them when they are not actually engaged in a race. A race commences when six or eight cars are lined up two abreast on the track. They complete one or two circles of the track at a slow speed and then the starter's flag commences the race. The cars endeavour to complete the designated number of laps in the shortest possible time, passing each other from time to time.

The cars used are motor cars manufactured prior to 1939 and modified by their owners to increase the power, reduce the weight and increase the strength of the top, so that accidents are less likely to injure the occupants.

During the progress of the race the cars give off very loud noises from their exhaust and from the screeching of wheels and the clanging and banging when the cars collide with each other. There are also extensive fumes from the exhaust.

Shortly after the occupation of the premises by the respondents began in February, 1951, substantial changes were made in the Oakwood Stadium at a cost of from $5,000 to $9,000. The major changes made were as follows:

(a) The track was increased in width from 18 ft. to 40 ft.

(b) The four lower rows of seats were removed from the bleachers and a safety-rail consisting of a fence, the posts of which were in the form of concrete-filled boilers, was substituted.

(c) The cinder track was covered with sand and gravel and oiled. The ends of the track were banked to provide an inclined turn and the banked portions were covered with asphalt.

The evidence of Mr. Crang, the former owner, is that prior to 1948 the stadium management had experimented with automobile and motorcycle racing as follows: (a) a midget-car racing, one week in 1932 and one week in 1934; (b) racing cars, two one-week meets about two years apart; (c) motorcycles, once and one race at a carnival. Also that the former owners had reached the conclusion prior to April, 1948, that the premises were unsafe for the racing of cars, midget cars or motorcycles and this use had been abandoned for the reason that the premises would require an expenditure of money on them to make them safe for car, midget car or motorcycle races.

[After quoting s. 390 (1) 1 and (6), Henderson J.A. continued.]

The learned County Court Judge in his reasons for judgment came to the conclusion that since at the time of the passing of the by-law the premises were used for a non-residential purpose, they could continue to be used for any non-residential purpose. In his opinion the effect of the qualifying clause "so long as it continues to be used for that purpose" is the same as "so long at it continues to be used for a non-residential purpose." In other words, if the premises had been used as a store at the time of the passing of the by-law they could be used as a factory, since both are non-residential purposes.

Also in his reasons he finds that the use being made of the lands prior to the by-law and the use being made on the date of the conviction were "for a similar purpose." He also finds that the changes made in the premises were substantial but "the character of the use of the buildings and lands was not substantially changed."

I am unable to agree with the conclusion of the learned County Court Judge or with his reasons therefor. In my opinion the change made in the character of the premises so as to adapt them for motor-car racing is in direct conflict with the provisions of the by-law and of the statute under which it was passed.

Prior to the date of the passing of the by-law the premises in question were not used and were not adapted or suitable for use for motor-car racing and it required a substantial expenditure of money and complete reconstruction of the facilities so as to enable motor-car racing to be carried on.

In presenting his appeal Mr. Mason properly referred to the facts only as they were presented by the respondents, and based his appeal purely upon the question of law.

I am of opinion that the judgment of the learned County Court Judge should be reversed and that the convictions by the Magistrate should be restored, and that the respondent should pay the costs of the appeal to His Honour Judge Factor, of the motion before Roach J.A. for leave to appeal, and of this appeal.

LAIDLAW J.A.: . . . The appeal to this Court is on a question of law alone but it is necessary first to set forth the material facts. A company named Oakwood Securities Ltd. was incorporated under the provisions of the Ontario *Companies Act* by letters patent dated October 31, 1925. The purposes and objects of that company stated briefly, are in part:

"(b) to carry on generally the business of furnishing amusement to the public; to carry on the business of operating a hippodrome, circus, race course, amusement park, theatre and exhibition and of presenting performances of all kinds, in all its branches and in particular to lay out and prepare any lands or emplacements for the running of horse, automobile, motorcycle, bicycle, aeroplane and all kinds of races . . . to construct grand or other stands . . . and other erections, buildings and conveniences whether of a permanent or temporary nature which may seem directly or indirectly conducive to the Company's objects;

(c) to conduct, hold and promote race meetings and athletic sports, matches of all kinds."

After incorporation, the Company proceeded to carry on its business on the lands and premises known and referred to as the Oakwood Stadium situate in the Township of York. It used the stadium for motorcycle races, midget-car races, automobile races, dog races, rodeo carnivals and, according to the Secretary-Treasurer, "tried nearly everything we thought would draw the public." There was a quarter-mile race-track about 18 ft. in width surrounding a playing field. The track was suitable for foot-races but unsafe for motorcycle, stock-car or midget-car races. The Company was not willing to spend the money to make the track safe for races of that kind and partly for that reason gave up having them but continued to carry on its activities of other kinds on the property until it was sold by the Company to the respondents in 1951.

Pursuant to the powers contained in what is now s. 390 of the *Municipal Act* the council of the Township of York passed By-law 13249 dated April 5, 1948, which was approved by an order of the Ontario Municipal Board on April 27, 1948. . . .

On February 15, 1951, the respondents purchased the property and commenced to use it for soccer, football matches, boxing matches, baseball games, "track-meets" and for "stock-car races." A stock car is described as "a car you might buy on a lot or drive on the street . . . to differentiate from special racing cars." Changes were made by the respondents to make the track suitable for stock-car races. The width was increased from 18 ft. to about 40 ft., the surface was treated, the corners were banked higher, safety rails were erected and a substantial sum of money was expended for the work.

Counsel for the appellant maintains that the learned Judge in the Court below ought to have held that the use of the property by the respondents for stock-car racing was contrary to the provisions of By-law 13249. He argues that the use of the property for that purpose was abandoned, or at least discontinued, prior to the passing of the by-law and that in consequence, cl. 3 of the by-law is not applicable so as to afford the respondents a good answer to the charge against them. That clause corresponds with s-s. (6) of s. 390 of the *Municipal Act* and limits the scope of the by-law by express provision that it shall not apply to any land, building or structure of the character described therein. It will be observed that there are two classes of property covered by the subsection, namely, land and a building or structure. It will be observed also that there are two specifications set forth in the clause. Firstly, in the case of land it must be in use on the day of the passing of the by-law for a purpose prohibited by the by-law, and in the case of a building or structure it must be erected on that day for such a purpose. Secondly, the use of the land or of the building or structure for a purpose prohibited by the by-law must continue. Thus, if the use of either the land or a building or structure for a purpose prohibited by the by-law has commenced either before or after the day of the passing of the by-law and thereafter has been discontinued, the property thereupon ceases to meet the specifications contained in the clause and the by-law becomes applicable to it. In the present case both the land and structures comprised in Oakwood Stadium were used for the same purpose, and the use commenced many years before the by-law was passed. There can be no doubt that the use of the whole property was for a purpose prohibited by the by-law.

The cardinal question for consideration is whether or not the use for that purpose was discontinued before the day of the passing of the by-law. That question can be answered only after considering and determining what was the purpose for which the property was used. In my opinion that purpose was a general one. It comprehended the use of the stadium for public amusement and entertainment and for public exhibitions and performances of all kinds. The purpose must be regarded collectively as a whole and cannot properly be divided into parts. Thus it cannot be said the purpose for which the property was used on the day of the passing of the by-law was for football games or for foot-races or for any other particular kind of public entertainment, exhibition or performance. It was for one and all of that kind of activity. It follows that, in my opinion, the purpose for which the property was used at the time of the passing of the by-law did not change and the use of the property for that purpose did not cease merely because the users of it were unwilling at one time, prior to the passing of the by-law, to spend the money necessary to make part of the property suitable and safe for one particular kind of activity within the general class, and for that reason in part discontinued that particular kind of public entertainment or performance. Nor did the fact that at a later date the users of the property decided to spend the money and thereafter made the changes in the property necessary to make it suitable and safe for stock-car races have the effect of changing the purpose for which the property was used. I think that the purpose for which the property was used at all times before and after the passing of the by-law was the general one as I have described it above, and that the use for that purpose was not at any time discontinued. Therefore, I hold that the by-law was not applicable to the land, building or structure known as Oakwood Stadium on the day of the alleged offence. Accordingly, the appeal should be dismissed.

[Aylesworth J.A. agreed with Laidlaw J.A.]

QUESTIONS. Does this decision repudiate, accept or ignore the view expressed by Factor Co. Ct. J. in the County Court? What bearing has the objects clause of a corporation on the actual use made of land owned by the corporation? Is intent to use equivalent to actual use? Does subsection (6) refer to actual use?

What is the proper meaning of "any purpose" and "that purpose"? How would you classify the purpose the land here was used for on the day the by-law was passed? Spectator sports? Games? Quiet sports? Something an audience or spectators hear or see? Football?

What is the effect, if any, of writing subsection (6) into the By-law? Is this a good idea?

NOTE. See now, so far as the merits of the principal decision are concerned s. 379 (1) paragraph 59 of the *Municipal Act* (Ontario), introduced by S.O., 1952, c. 63, s. 16 (3).

Paragraph 59 provides:

"For prohibiting, or for licensing, regulating and governing, the racing of motor vehicles or motorcycles, or one or more defined classes thereof, in the municipality or one or more defined areas thereof; and for prohibiting, or for licensing, regulating and governing, the holding of motor vehicle or motorcycle races, or one or more defined classes thereof, in the municipality or one or more defined areas thereof."

GAYFORD *v.* KOLODZIEJ

Ontario. Court of Appeal, 1959. 19 D.L.R. (2d) 777.

ROACH J.A. delivered the judgment of the Court: In my opinion this appeal fails and should be dismissed with costs.

Two submissions were made on behalf of the appellant. . . . second, that prior to the passing of By-law 1159 and By-law 1135 to which it was an amendment the lands in question had been used as a tourist home and had continued to be so used without interruption down to the date of these proceedings and therefore that they do not come within the by-law even if it is valid.

By-law 1135 was passed by the municipal council on June 5, 1948 and By-law 1159 on August 9, 1949. Both by-laws were approved by an order of the Municipal Board dated August 26, 1949. . . .

By-law 1159 is entitled "A By-law to Amend By-law No. 1135 of the Township of North Gwillimbury." It contains this recital: "Whereas representations have been made to the Council that the defined area to which by-law 1135 applied was too large and that the restrictions imposed by the said by-law should apply to a smaller area." That recital speaks for itself. In response to those representations the municipal council decided to narrow the area. . . .

The property in question is within the narrower area covered by By-law 1159. On the date when By-law 1135 was passed it was being used as a resort and tourist home and continued to be so used until the summer of 1953. The defendants purchased it in June 1954 and they have operated it as a resort and tourist home since they first acquired it. It is not disputed that such use of lands to which By-law 1159 applies is thereby forbidden. The defendants' immediate predecessor in title was one Edna Street. In the last summer during which she was the owner, *viz.* the summer of 1953, she leased it for use as a private residence from the middle of July to the middle of September and during that period to her knowledge it was used, not as a resort catering to the public, but exclusively as a private residence. The property is in a summer colony on the shore of Lake Simcoe. The tourist season in that area covers only the summer months and I agree that discontinuance of user as a lodge or tourist home catering to the public during the major part of the summer season is tantamount to discontinuance for the whole year.

In my opinion there was such a lapse in or discontinuance of the non-conforming user in 1953 as to remove from the property the cloak that up to that time exempted it from the by-law, and the appellants' second submission also fails.

QUESTIONS. Why does it matter whether discontinuance of user during the summer season "is tantamount to discontinuance for the whole year"? Why the *whole* year? Why a *year*?

O'SULLIVAN FUNERAL HOME LTD. *v.* CITY OF SAULT STE. MARIE AND EVANS

Ontario. Supreme Court. 1961. 28 D.L.R. (2d) 1

FERGUSON J.: This is an application for an order by way of *mandamus,* directed to the Corporation of the City of Sault Ste. Marie and to its issuer of building permits requiring the city [or] its licence issuer to issue a permit to the plaintiff to make certain alterations at the plaintiff's premises, 1009 Queen St. East, Sault Ste. Marie, Ontario, in accordance with plans filed and approved, in short, substantially to change a residence into a funeral parlour. The City of Sault Ste. Marie was zoned pursuant to the powers vested in the municipality by s. 390 (1) and (2) of the *Municipal Act,* R.S.O. 1950, c. 243. The Zoning By-law, No. 2367, was passed by the City Council on October 17, 1955, and approved by the Municipal Board on June 12, 1956. The area in question surrounding the above-mentioned property belonging to the applicant is zoned as residential. . . .

The question then for decision on this motion is, whether the building was "on the day of the passing of the by-law used for any purpose prohibited by the by-law". The applicant submits that it was used as a funeral parlour or funeral home at the date of the passing of the by-law and for some time prior thereto. The city's objection to the issue of the permit is that the building was never substantially used as a funeral parlour and indeed such use as it was put to was only incidental to its use as a residence. . . .

The applicant has carried on business as an undertaker in the west end of Sault Ste. Marie since the year 1950. In November, 1954 the applicant company purchased 1009 Queen St. East in the city. Queen St. is the principal business street in the City of Sault Ste. Marie and business premises extend along that street for a considerable distance from the centre of the city easterly followed by residences of the type shown in the photograph, ex. A, to the affidavit of Dennis O'Sullivan, which is the building we are concerned with on this motion. The Zoning By-law, s. 16(6), prohibits the use of the land or buildings after the effective date of the by-law except as permitted by the by-law and where the lands have been used before the effective date of the by-law for a nonconforming use, such use shall not be enlarged, reconstructed or exteriorly altered unless such building structure or land is thereafter used only as permitted by this by-law.

I think the order for *mandamus* must go. The company obtained title to the property on November 12, 1954. Some alterations were made to enlarge the kitchen on the ground floor. It is said that a promise was made by one McGee, an employee of the applicant, through whom the property was purchased by the company, that the building would not be turned into a funeral parlour. The promise, if given, was not a corporate act of the company and binding on it. Even if it were a corporate act its materiality with reference to the present application is not shown.

On March 23, 1955 a funeral was held from the premises, another on May 30th of that year. Again on September 2nd and October 4th, 1955 and on September 13, 1956 and on October 28, 1956 funerals were held from the premises. The by-law, it will be remembered, was not passed by the council until October 17, 1955. It appears that an information and complaint were laid against the company for carrying on a funeral parlour contrary to the by-law before the local Magistrate some time after the by-law was passed. The result of the prosecution is really not material; presumably the charge was dismissed. It is, however, important that subsequently the City of Sault Ste. Marie assessed the company for business tax for years 1958, 1959 and 1960, which tax was paid. I think it is now too late for the city to say that the use of the premises prior to June, 1956 was only incidental to its use as a residence. If the applicant were an individual engaged in some other employment such use might be incidental and not connected with a business, but in this case the applicant was an undertaker and the use of the building to expose a corpse for viewing by relatives and friends was part of the applicant's business. The use had an individuality of its own, quite apart from the use of the business as a residence.

In view of the decision of the Supreme Court of Canada in *Central Jewish Institute* v. *Toronto* (1947), the fact that only a part of the premises was used for the undertaking business purposes does not constitute an objection to the application on the ground that such use was not the most substantial use to which the building was put. In that case it was held that if on the date of the passing of the by-law a part of the building is used for a purpose prohibited by the by-law, the building as a whole is exempt. The fact that the building was used in the limited way that I have indicated is not in dispute in this case, but it is argued that that is not such a use as constitutes an exemption. In my opinion this argument is effectively disposed of by the case which I have just now cited. . . .

It is urged that because no funeral was held from 1009 Queen St. East between October, 1955 and September, 1956 the exemption was lost for lack of continuous user. But the evidence is that the main alterations were made on the main floor, wallpaper was put on the walls suitable for funerals, and the place rewired for funerals. There is no evidence that the main floor was at any time turned back into living quarters. It does not seem to be valid to say that because no funeral was held in the building for 11 months that user of the building as a funeral home ceased when it is shown by the evidence that it continued to be owned by an undertaker and remained equipped to receive funerals. And it is not shown that it was used for any other purpose.

My opinion is that the city's objection to the application fails and the *mandamus* must go. The city must pay the costs of the motion.

FEJER *v.* WELLWOOD

Ontario. Court of Appeal. 1963. Unreported

In 1960 the applicants bought a garage sandwiched between two dwelling houses on Brunswick Avenue in Toronto in a R.4 V.1 Zone. The garage had been operated for some forty years by its previous owner and in particular when the Toronto Zoning By-laws were passed in 1953 and 1959 respectively. In May of 1962 a fire destroyed the building. Fejer, a son of the applicants, in his affidavit described the damage as "substantial" but the building "was not demolished or destroyed." In his affidavit the defendant, the Commissioner of Buildings said, "I am informed by one of the building inspectors employed by my department that the garage building erected on the lands was damaged by fire to the extent of 80% of its value before the fire." In cross-examination on his affidavit Fejer was asked "In terms of percentage, how much of the building was destroyed?" He answered, "I don't know how many per cent."

In his affidavit Fejer deposed that the applicants had found it possible, notwithstanding the fire, to carry on the business of a public garage on the premises, "and in the partially demolished building" but some of the operations previously carried on therein were not possible and would not be possible until the building was "repaired". The "business office" had been continually used and some of the office was used for storage. During the four months following the fire the applicants performed work and services on motor vehicles in the public garage business to the value of about $2,000. On cross-examination Fejer said there was a forty foot space in front of the building on which the applicants did repair work, and there was cleared space outside the "partially demolished" building at the back, on which more work was done. Apparently no garage work was done inside the building.

The Toronto Building By-law 9868, Article 4 provides that "Repairs and alterations to any building to the extent of over 50% of the value of such building, as it was before such repairs and alterations were necessary, shall be considered a re-erection of such building and subject to the provisions of this By-law."

The applicants applied for a building permit to erect a new garage into which would be incorporated from the original building only part of a masonry wall still standing after the fire and after demolition made necessary because of the unsafe condition of the building after the fire, or because of the plans to rebuild. The remaining wall was about forty feet long out of a former (and proposed) ninety foot wall. The permit was refused because the new building would not conform with the Zoning By-law. This action for an order of *mandamus* followed. Donnelly J. gave the order but his reasons, if any, were not preserved. The City appealed.

AYLESWORTH J.A. at the conclusion of the argument: In this case of Fejer and Wellwood, the Corporation of the City of Toronto appeals from an order of mandamus directed to its building inspector, issued by Donnelly J. on the 21st of December last.

Much has been said as to the proper interpretation and application of the relevant sections of The Planning Act and in particular, section 30, subsection of that Act. Many, in fact all of the authorities to which the Court has been referred, deal with or are sought to be applied to facts which we are of the opinion are not analogous to the facts in the instant case. It is our view and apparently it was that of the learned trial Judge of first instance, although we have not the benefit of his reasons, that on the facts of this particular case the applicant for the building permit here seeks to renovate and restore to complete use the building existing before the fire. Admittedly, the building which will emerge is not precisely the same building or a building even with the same appearance in many respects but in essence, as I have said, the "it" mentioned in section 30 of the statute, that is the building, sufficiently remained after the fire to permit of its restoration to full use the permit sought by the applicant therefor. This is evidenced, we think, by the fact that, although admittedly in a limited way, the building after the fire continued in use. The restoration and renovation in contemplation does not constitute either an enlargement or extension of the building. Taking the view we have taken of the particular facts, it becomes unnecessary for the disposition of this appeal to enter into any analysis of the precise effect of the authorities cited to the Court. In the result the appeal is dismissed with costs.

REGINA *v.* RUTHERFORD'S DAIRY LTD.
Ontario. High Court. [1961] O.W.N. 146

This was an appeal by way of a case stated by a magistrate after conviction of the accused for unlawfully using certain lands for a use forbidden by a zoning by-law.

In 1942 the accused or its predecessor in title acquired certain lands fronting on Kennedy Rd., in Scarborough twp. In 1950 it acquired other lands to increase its total holding to a parcel of approximately 4 acres having a frontage on Kennedy Rd. of around 200 ft. by a depth of 900 ft. All of this land during the relevant period was used for dairy purposes and the dairy building itself at that time stood about half way back in the parcel from Kennedy Rd. In 1955 a plan of subdivision of the land was registered in the registry office and later the same year the land on the plan with the exception of the front part of it was zoned for residential purposes. In 1958 the accused built a new building nearer to the Kennedy Rd. but it continued to use all of the front portion of the land designated on the plan as block B, for dairy purposes using the land in the rear of the new building as a parking lot for its motor vehicles. The charge was laid in respect of this land in the rear of the new building which under the zoning by-law was zoned for residential purposes only. In the stated case the magistrate stated as follows:

"In the operation of the business from 1942 until after the by-law was passed 12th September 1955, ingress and egress was obtained by a means of a paved driveway across the lands from Kennedy Rd.; water was obtained by a 6 inch water main under the land from Kennedy Rd.; hydro was obtained by a power line and poles over the lands from Kennedy Rd.; and sanitary drainage was provided by a drainage ditch over the land to Kennedy Rd. Each of the foregoing passed under or over the lands in question."

After the new building was built in 1958, the land in question in this proceeding was no longer needed or used for the purpose of the services mentioned by the magistrate but was used for parking motor vehicles used by the accused in its business. The accused claimed that the land in question was exempt from the zoning by-law being used for a legal non-conforming use said use having been established prior to the passing of the by-law.

McRuer C.J.H.C.: On the finding of the magistrate the inescapable conclusion is that the land in question was used in connection with the operation of the company's business at the time the by-law was passed. In fact, the operation of the company's business was dependent on the road and services that passed over or under this land.

Counsel for the municipality argued that the land in question did not continue to be used for the same purpose as at the time the by-law was passed within the meaning of *The Planning Act*, R.S.O. 1960, c. 296, s. 30(7). I do not think this section is to be given the restricted meaning contended for by counsel for the appellant. The true test is, was the land used in connection with the operation of the dairy at the time the by-law was passed? The character of the user may now be different but unless it is shown there was an abandonment of the user in connection with the operation of the dairy the land might be put to some other use than was the case at the time the by-law was passed.

In *Reg.* v. *Cappy*, Laidlaw, J.A., in giving the judgment of the majority of the Court is noted as having said,

"The cardinal question for consideration is whether or not the use for that purpose was discontinued before the day of the passing of the by-law.

That question can be answered only after considering and determining what was the purpose for which the property was used. In my opinion that purpose was a general one. It comprehended the use of the stadium for public amusement and entertainment and for public exhibitions and performances of all kinds. *The purpose must be regarded collectively as a whole and cannot properly be divided into parts.* Thus it cannot be said the purpose for which the property was use on the day of the passing of the by-law was for football games or for foot-races or for any other particular kind of public entertainment, exhibition or performance. It was for one and all of that kind of activity." (Emphasis added.)

I think the language of Laidlaw, J.A., may be applied with even greater force to this case. The purpose for which the land here in question was used was for the purpose of operating a dairy and the dairy could not have been operated in the location in which it was without using the land in question. There was no abandonment of the use of the land for the purpose of the operation of the dairy but the character of the user was merely changed. I cannot think that on a proper interpretation of the by-law land which had been used as a passageway for motor vehicles in connection with the operation of the dairy cannot now be used as a parking place for motor vehicles. The use of the land at the time of the operation was for the purpose of the whole undertaking and likewise a use of space for parking motor vehicles is part of the whole undertaking.

Having come to this conclusion, it is not necessary for me to decide the question that arises out of another interesting aspect of this case. On 6th February 1956, the township passed by-law 6754 to amend by-law 6523 which had the effect of exempting the whole of block B from the operation of the original by-law and zoning it commercially. This by-law was approved by the municipal board, 15th March 1956, and 19th March 1957, the approval was rescinded by an order of the board. By-law 8067 was passed by the township 17th February 1958, to amend by-law 6754. By the terms of this by-law the southerly 50 ft. of the westerly 100 ft. of block B was zoned for residential purposes or to be planted with shrubbery and the rest of the westerly 100 ft. of block B was exempt from the original by-law and zoned for commercial purposes with certain conditions with respect to fences and shrubbery. This by-law was approved by the municipal board 27th February 1958, but the order was rescinded, 26th May 1958, by a subsequent order of the board.

It may be that in March 1956 a non-conforming use was obtained by the appellant when by-law 6754 was passed and approved and that this non-conforming use could not be lost by the subsequent rescission of the approval by the municipal board. Likewise, in 1958 when by-law 8067 was passed and approved the appellant enjoyed a non-conforming use between February and May 1958, when the order of the board was rescinded. If it was necessary for me to come to a conclusion with respect to the interesting questions raised by this novel situation it might be necessary for me to send the matter back to the magistrate for more definite findings of fact with respect to the use at the relevant dates. In view of the decision that I have arrived at with respect to the main point argued this course is unnecessary.

The appeal will be allowed with cost.

[Her Majesty appealed, [1961] O.W.N. 274:]

AYLESWORTH J.A. delivered the judgment of the Court of Appeal at the conclusion of the argument: We are all of the opinion that the appeal fails.

In our view, upon the stated case before McRuer C.J.H.C., and applying the words of the statute to the facts as disclosed before him in that stated case, there was from the very inception of the township by-law a legal non-conforming use of all of block B and in the circumstances of this case we do not think that that non-conforming use can be restricted either in terms or in area as submitted by the appellant. As I have said, in our opinion, on the facts, and I do not seek to be exhaustive with respect to the facts, namely, the existence of the roadway, the purchase at a time when the use was unrestricted by the appellant progressively of the two parcels, the existence of the other services of which mention has been made, the placing of the sign on block B, all establish a legal non-conforming use of all of block B. This use, in our view, continued uninterrupted until the occupation by the respondent of the new dairy building on block B. We view the move from the old to the new dairy building site as a constriction, if you will, of the legal non-conforming use as it had applied to that date to the whole of B and also to C merely to B and we think that there was at all times a sufficient and full use of all of B to remove that use from the prohibition of the by-law. For these reasons we would therefore dismiss the appeal with costs.

SOME BACKGROUND FACTS IN REGINA *v.* RUTHERFORD'S DAIRY. The land contained in Registered Plan 4802 was once owned by Rutherford who operated a dairy on what is now Block C, but who sold the land to Pugh Bros. Construction Ltd., who subdivided it. The plan was, in the normal course, preceded by a draft plan which the Minister approved on January 17, 1955. The draft plan contained significant differences from the final Plan 4802. Instead of Blocks A and B fronting on Kennedy Road there were three Blocks, A, F and B, none of which extended through to Ellendale Drive. Behind Block F was Block E, fronting on Ellendale Drive and evidently an old road allowance. In any case Blocks E and F were 66 feet wide. Behind Block B, fronting on Ellendale Drive, were three smaller lots, numbered 15, 16 and 17, and clearly intended for houses.

Among the conditions of approval set by the Minister on January 17, 1955, were:

"1. That the owner consents in writing to a by-law restricting the land uses of this subdivision in a manner satisfactory to the Township of Scarborough, but of not less standard as to set-backs and side yards than the requirements of the C.M.H.C.

"5. That Blocks D and E shall contain only single family dwellings.

"6. Blocks A, B, C and F to be subject to a site plan to be approved by the Scarborough Planning Board.

"7. That the owner enters into an agreement with the Township of Scarborough binding on himself and his heirs and successors in title that there will be no re-division of the blocks shown on this plan save by a new application to this Department pursuant to the provisions of Section 26 of the Planning Act.

"10. That prior to the signing of the final plan by the Minister we are to be advised by the Township of Scarborough that the conditions above have been carried out to their satisfaction."

Plan 4802 was approved by the Minister on May 25, 1955. On August 15, 1955, the Community Planning Branch wrote to the owner drawing attention to the fact that the final plan did not match the draft plan and commenting "This discrepancy was not noticed by this Department and in

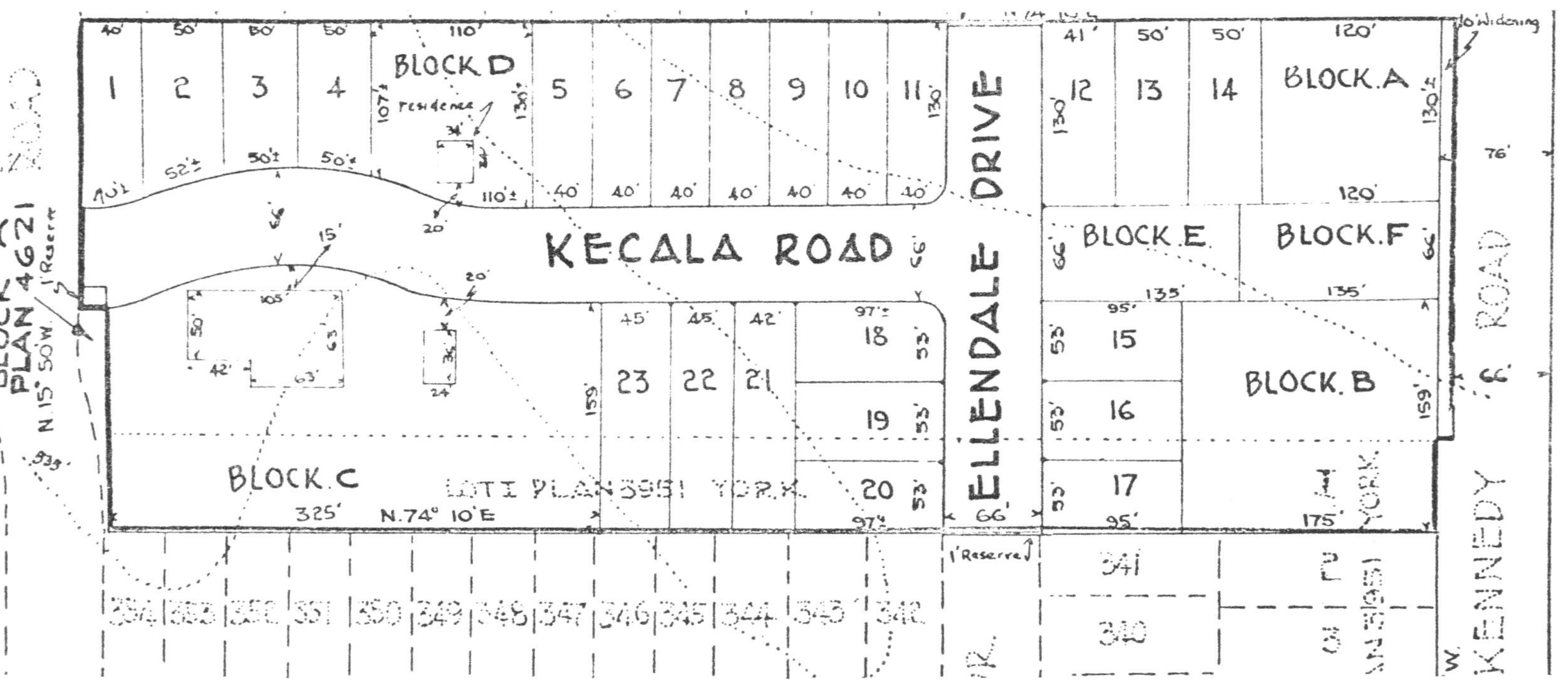

Draft Plan (4802) as approved

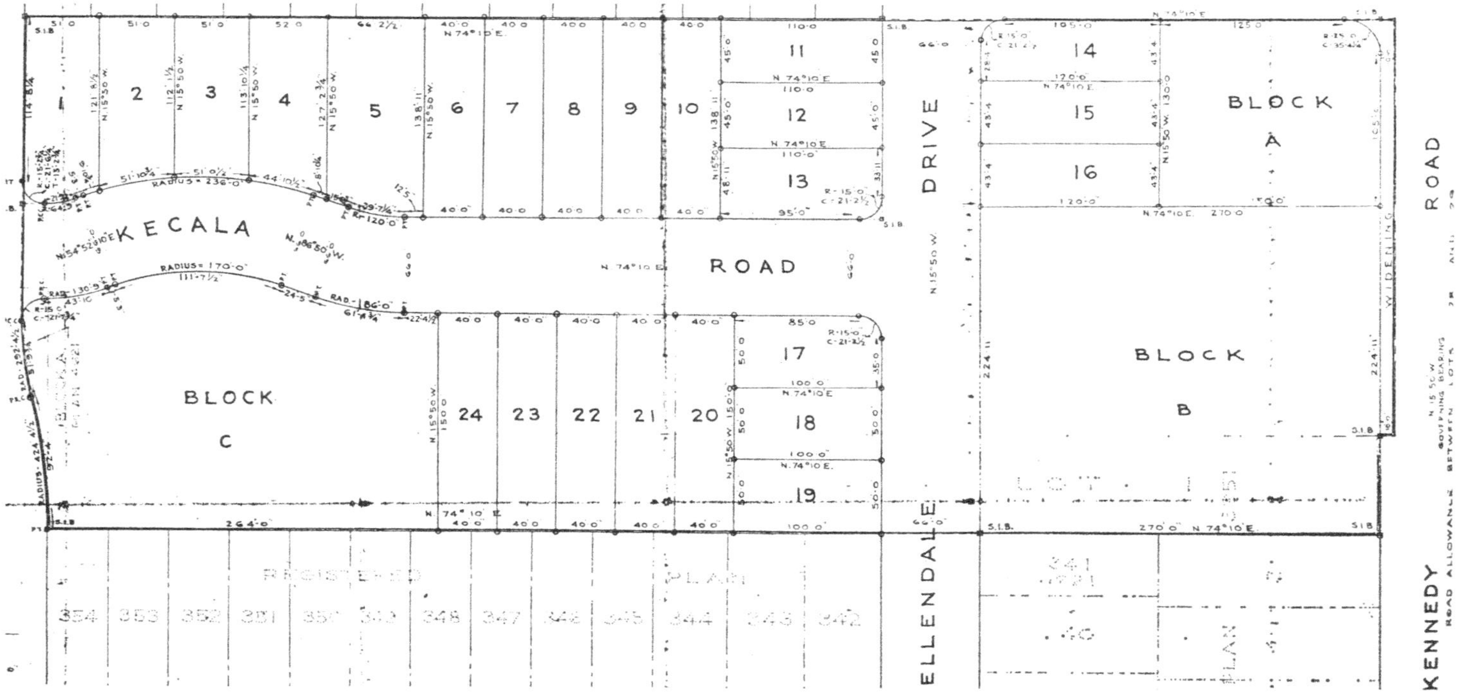

KECALA ROAD

DRIVE

ELLENDALE

KENNEDY ROAD

ROAD WIDENING

BLOCK A

BLOCK B

BLOCK C

REGISTERED PLAN

LOT

Final Plan (4802) as approved

actual fact the final plan should not have been recommended to the Minister for his signature in its present form." No further action was taken by the Branch.

On September 12, 1955, By-law 6523 was passed reserving the westerly 100 feet of Block B and lots 14, 15 and 16 for residential use. Section 2 of By-law 6523 provided that "except as hereinafter in this by-law provided, no person shall use any land in the defined areas except for residential purposes and no person shall erect or use any building for any purpose other than as a single family dwelling."

Section 9 provided that "one dwelling only shall be erected or placed on one lot as shown on the plan".

Section 11 provided that "single family dwellings may be erected on . . . the W. 100′ of Block B according to Plan Number 4802 provided that each dwelling has appurtenant thereto an area of land with at least 5,000 square feet and a frontage on a public street with at least 40′0″."

Section 13 provided that "the following land may be used for commercial uses including residential (living units on second floor of commercial buildings) subject to 50% of the area of each parcel being allocated for off street parking. . . .

"(c) Blocks A, C and the easterly 170′ of Block B, Plan 4802. . . ."

On February 6, 1956, By-law 6754 was passed amending By-law 6523 and permitting all of Block B and lots 14, 15 and 16 to be used for "commercial uses". Block C was rezoned from commercial to residential use. The Municipal Board instructed that the owners of properties within 200 feet of the proposed changes be notified of the hearing on the By-law. None of the residents within 200 feet of Block B received a notice and if a notice went to the residents within 200 feet of Block C they would hardly be likely to object since the By-law heralded the removal of the Rutherford Dairy from Block C to Block B. There was no opposition to the By-law on March 15, 1956, and the Board gave its approval.

When the residents within 200 feet of Block B later discovered the amendment they appealed to the Council, who prevailed upon the Municipal Board to rehear the case. Blocks B and C were conveyed by Pugh Bros. Construction Ltd. back to Rutherford. Lots 14, 15 and 16, despite the approval of By-law 6754 zoning them for commercial use, were sold and houses were built on them and sold. By February 26, 1957, when the Board conducted its rehearing, the new houses on lots 14, 15 and 16 were occupied by new owners. One of the residents who attended the rehearing described it as having been conducted under "most adverse conditions, in that pneumatic drills were being used outside the Municipal Board's chambers making it extremely difficult to hear during large parts of the proceedings."

On March 19, 1957, the Board rescinded its earlier approval of By-law 6754, which presumably had the effect of reviving the original By-law 6523. On March 22, 1957, the Board wrote that it "is prepared to approve this by-law [6754] when it is amended" so as to establish a part of Block B, in the south west corner, 42 feet wide fronting on Ellendale Drive by 120 feet deep as residential, to create a buffer lot next to the existing house on Ellendale Drive immediately south of Block B and not on Plan 4802. The rest of Block B was to be fenced and landscaped along its south, west and north sides. The result would have been that lots 14, 15 and 16, by then in residential use, and most of Block B, would have been zoned for commercial use. No by-law was then passed in the terms suggested by the Board.

Instead, on April 18, 1957, Rutherford was granted a building permit for a new dairy on the easterly 170 feet of Block B, within the "commercial" zone created by the valid and subsisting By-law 6523. Whether a dairy was a "commercial" use was not put in issue.

On April 11, 1957, the Scarborough Council adopted its official plan, which was approved by the Minister on December 18, 1957. Under the official plan the land fronting on Kennedy Road included in Plan 4802 was placed in the category of "Highway Frontage Uses", none of which clearly and necessarily included a dairy. The area so categorized on the Land Use Plan did not cover the whole depth of Block B, or lots 14, 15 and 16, and while some plan zones might be supposed to have only indefinite borders, the official plan prescribed expressly that the boundaries of Highway Frontage Uses on the Land Use Plan should not be extended except by formal amendment of the plan.

On February 3, 1958, the Scarborough Council gave first reading to a by-law to amend By-law 6523 and extend the commercial zoning to cover the whole of Block B save for the buffer "lot" required by the Municipal Board. Despite angry protests from residents near Block B, the Council gave the amendment second reading on February 10, and passed the amendment as By-law 8067, on February 17. By-law 8067 amended By-law 6754 substantially in accordance with the Municipal Board's dictate of March 22, 1957, save that the residential area reserved in the south west corner of Block B was made 50 feet wide (probably to be consistent with the width of lots opposite on the other side of Ellendale Drive) and 100 feet, rather than 120 feet deep. Since By-law 6523 only reserved a depth of 100 feet in the residential part of Block B, this may be consistent with that by-law. On the other hand, lots 14, 15 and 16 are 120 feet deep.

Consistently with its letter of March 22, 1957, the Municipal Board approved By-law 8067 without a hearing on February 27, 1958. On May 26, 1958, at the request of some of the residents living near Block B, the Municipal Board set aside its approval, thus restoring By-law 6523 to full operative affect. In the notice of application the grounds for rescinding the approval were suggested that (a) no public hearing had been held on By-law 8067 and (b) By-law 8067 did not conform with the official plan. The Board directed a rehearing but no rehearing was held. Some attempts at a negotiated solution were made through an intermediary representing the residents. No direct negotiations seem to have taken place.

On July 25, 1959, By-law 9507 was passed, re-enacting By-law 6523 insofar as it affected Plan 4802 and it was approved by the Municipal Board save as to Block B, and the Board directed that Rutherford should have until April, 1960 to decide whether he wanted a full scale hearing regarding Block B. On April 21, 1960 Rutherford was charged with the offence described. The date of the offence was April 6, 1960.

In a statement prepared in 1958 for the residents near Block B the following comment appears: "That is the history of Plan 4802 and By-law 6523 to date. To a reader not directly involved it must seem like a comedy of errors. To those who have been involved, it is a tragedy of injustices".

TOWNSHIP OF TORONTO *v*. NEWMAN. 1960. Unreported (Ontario. Supreme Court). This was an action to restrain the carrying on or operation of a pit or quarry on the defendant's land. The defendant opened a gravel pit about June, 1958 and removed 1,600 yards of gravel during the summer while he continued to operate part of the land as a farm. After 1958 he gave up the farm but continued to remove gravel until a restraining order was issued in January, 1960. The lands were zoned for residential use and quarrying was prohibited. The by-law was passed in April, 1953 and re-enacted in 1959. Under what is now paragraph 118 of section 379(1) of *The Municipal Act*, R.S.O. 1960, c. 249, first enacted by S.O. 1959, c. 62, s. 18, the council passed By-law 2775 which prohibited the enlargement or extension of a pit or quarry "beyond the limits of the land owned and used in connection therewith on the first day of January, 1959." The action was dismissed with costs. MOORHOUSE J.: "The legislation in my opinion is clear and free from doubt and does not authorize the confiscation of the defendants' rights as suggested on behalf of the plaintiff. The removal of any sand or gravel from a pit extends or enlarges it. The removal of quantities to the extent permitted by exhibit 2 does not extend or enlarge the operation beyond the limits or boundaries of the defendants' lands. Upon the evidence before me I find there are no ditches, fences, fields, natural or artificial boundaries within the whole area of the defendants' lands. Witnesses for the plaintiff have suggested, by diagrams prepared by them and filed, that limits of the operations might be established within the boundaries of the lands. To do so would in my opinion amount to a confiscation of rights not authorized by the legislation. There is no evidence before me which would enable me to determine where a line should be drawn around the site of operations and in effect say 'this is the limit of the land used by the defendants for a gravel pit on either 1st January . . . 1959'.

"Upon the facts of this case I conclude the word 'limits' in the statute is synonymous with the word 'boundaries'. The application of the meaning suggested by the able argument of counsel for the plaintiff in my opinion would prohibit the continuance of the operations and that the Legislature has not authorized." [Does Moorhouse J.'s interpretation make the words "used in connection therewith" redundant? Could the effect of such words be to reduce the protection of the non-conforming use to something less than the land owned? Compare the jurisdiction of the committee of adjustment under section 32*b* (2) (i) of *The Planning Act*. For the history of the 1959 amendment to *The Municipal Act* see *Pickering* v. *Godfrey*.]

THE PLANNING ACT

Ontario. Revised Statutes. 1960. Chapter 296

30. (1) By-laws may be passed by the councils of municipalities:

6. For prohibiting the making or establishment of pits and quarries within the municipality or within any defined area or areas thereof.

NOTE. Paragraph 6 was added to the predecessor of section 30(1) in 1959 by S.O., c. 71, s. 5. In 1958 paragraph 115 of section 388(1) of *The Municipal Act*, which had been repealed by S.O., 1957, c. 76, s. 21(11), was replaced in its present form, by Chapter 64, s. 29(6). Paragraph 115 is now paragraph 119 and is reproduced on page 23. In 1959, by Chapter 62, s. 18(3), paragraph 114*a* was added, and is now paragraph 118, reproduced on page 23.

2. THE ELIMINATION OF NON-CONFORMING USES: PURCHASE AND AMORTIZATION

THE PLANNING ACT
Ontario. Revised Statutes. 1960. Chapter 296

30. (6) The council may acquire any land, building or structure used or erected for a purpose that does not conform with a by-law passed under this section and any vacant land having a frontage or depth less than the minimum prescribed for the erection of a building or structure in the defined area in which such land is situate, and the council may dispose of any of such land, building or structure or may exchange any of such land for other land within the municipality.

NOTE. This provision has had little actual use. Since some non-conforming uses are "injuriously affected" by their status, councils usually avoid purchasing any to avoid pressure to purchase all of them. Is this political view valid?

EXPERT COMMITTEE ON COMPENSATION AND BETTERMENT: FINAL REPORT
United Kingdom. 1942. Cmd. 6386

241 . . . The question whether the right to maintain, replace, extend and use an existing building is to subsist in perpetuity, notwithstanding that the building does not conform to the provisions of the scheme (and it must be remembered that non-conformity may consist in excess density as well as incongruity of use), is fundamental in relation to the replanning of built-up areas. On the one hand, it would not be equitable, without compensation, at any time and for any reason to remove, or to prohibit the maintenance, replacement, extension or use of an existing building. On the other hand, an unqualified right, unless compensation is paid, to replace non-conforming buildings and to maintain existing uses permanently is inconsistent with the present conception of planning.

The problem is one of finding a proper balance between the two considerations, and, before putting forward our recommendations for its solution, it is necessary to draw attention to certain other matters.

242. In the first place, planning law has never admitted that an owner is, in all circumstances, entitled to compensation for the disappointment of expectations however reasonable. Thus, when undeveloped land is "zoned" under a planning scheme for future development (i.e., when the scheme imposes limitations on the type of building which may be erected on the land) or when a scheme limits the density at which dwelling houses may be built upon it, the owner has no right to compensation merely because the same land *might* have been used for a more profitable type of building or for the building of houses at a higher density than that prescribed. That being so, we see no logical reason why an owner should be entitled to compensation if, on his buildings being demolished in the ordinary course and by his own volition, he is not allowed to rebuild for the same use as before and at the same density as before where his proposals are out of conformity with the planning scheme. Where new and essential public standards are set up in the interests of health and amenity, there is, in our view, nothing unreasonable in expecting owners (on rebuilding at any rate) to conform with these necessary standards without being compensated.

243. Second, an argument of some weight in favour of limiting the right to non-conforming user, etc., is that the owner is himself enjoying the benefits of town planning and of conformity by *other people*. The benefits may not be limited to amenity; they may in some cases result in giving one individual an advantage over his fellows by removing competition.

244. Third, the existing provisions of the [1932] Act appear to accept the principle that in certain cases the detriment to the public interest of replacing a building in a particular location may be so great that compensation should not be payable in respect of a restriction on replacement. This is the case, for example, in regard to buildings on land unsuitable for development by reason of danger and injury to health (see Section 19 (1) (*e*)). A similar principle is applied to the continuance in a new building of a noxious or offensive use (see Section 19 (2) (ii) (*d*)). The Act, however, draws a sharp line between uses so detrimental that no compensation is payable, and other uses in which the right to continue the user is absolute. This sharp differentiation of treatment does not correspond to realities. Detriment is a matter of degree, and there may be much detriment to the general interests of a locality although the use could not be said to be noxious or offensive within the meaning of the Statute.

245. The hampering effects on reconstruction and redevelopment of the present provisions for the protection of existing buildings and uses have been the subject of strong representations to us, and various suggestions for solving the problem have been put forward. Generally they proceed on the view, which we think is a right one, that a building or existing use should not, if contrary to the provisions of the scheme, be given a perpetual right of maintenance or continuance. In short, a "life" should be placed on any "non-conforming" building or use, and the right to maintain, replace, extend or use a building would be subject to that "life". What the "life" should be would depend on the circumstances of each case, and among the factors to be taken into account should be:—

(i) The probable effective physical life of the building in view of its age and condition;

(ii) Its probable effective economic and income-producing life, having regard to the possibility of the site being put to a more profitable use by rebuilding (that is, the actual income being received should be compared with what a new building would produce);

(iii) The degree and nature of non-conformity or of the detriment caused by the particular building or user.

246. Again, a distinction should be drawn between buildings which in some way or other are themselves unsatisfactory (as, for example, where the lay-out is too crowded) and buildings to which the only objection is that they conflict with some object of a scheme, such as an open space, or a road. Take the case of a building on the line of a proposed new road which otherwise conforms to the provisions of a scheme and which, therefore, if it were in a slightly different position, would be subject to no limit of life. If a limited life is placed on the building, then, at the end of it, the right of maintenance and replacement having gone, the owner loses not only the "bricks and mortar" value of his building, but also the building value of the site, which the local authority would then acquire at a much reduced cost. This would be inequitable for, *ex hypothesi*, his building conforms to requirements and it is in no sense his fault, but a mere accident, that it happens to be on the line of a road which has been planned.

It would not appear, therefore, that the principle of a life for buildings could properly be applied to properties which contravene the scheme only because they stand in the way of a public improvement, though, if on other grounds a life could be placed on the property if it were in a contiguous zone, the principle would be applied.

247. Our recommendations for dealing with the matter are as follows:—

(A) (1) If a non-conforming use of a building has ceased for a period of one year, or if a non-conforming building is wholly or substantially demolished by the voluntary action of the owner, the use of the building or of any new building and the erection of a new building must conform to the scheme, no compensation being payable. (We deal at (B) and (C) below with cases of buildings destroyed by accident and by enemy action respectively.)

(2) Subject to (1) above, the planning authority should have power by notice to be given at any time to require conformity with the planning scheme, without compensation, as regard (a) any non-conforming use or (b) any non-conforming building (except a building which contravenes the scheme only because it stands in the way of a public improvement), such requirement not to be enforceable until after the expiration of such period (the "life" of the use or building) as the authority may determine (subject to an appeal to the Official Arbitrator who may allow or refuse the appeal or may reduce or increase the period) after taking into consideration all the circumstances, including (a) the probable effective physical life of the building having regard to its age and condition, (b) its probable effective economic and income-producing life, and (c) the degree and nature of the non-conformity.

(3) If after a "life" has been determined under (2) above, the planning authority considers it necessary to enforce conformity before the expiration of such "life", the authority should be empowered to do so, but any compensation payable should be assessed with due regard to the fact that conformity would otherwise have been enforceable without compensation at the end of such period.

(4) In lieu of the provisions of Section 19 (2) (ii) (b) of the Act of 1932, as to reasonable alterations and extensions of existing non-conforming buildings, there should be a new provision that no such work may be carried out without the consent of the planning authority, which may be withheld or be given subject to conditions, and should be subject to appeal to the Central Planning Authority, but whatever may be the decision no compensation should be payable.

248. (B) If a non-conforming building is destroyed involuntarily (otherwise than by enemy action)—

(1) the owner should have the right to rebuild only in conformity with the scheme, and no compensation should be payable by reason of the prohibition of the re-erection of a non-conforming building.

(2) The new conforming building should be allowed to be used for the pre-existing non-conforming use (if any) during the unexpired portion of the "life" applicable to the old building destroyed, but if the planning authority requires this non-conforming use to cease before the end of that "life" compensation should be payable on the basis laid down at (A) (3) above.

250. Non-conforming uses and buildings are so various in character and extent that we do not suggest that there should be a statutory definition of the "degree or nature of non-conformity" for the purposes of our proposals in the foregoing paragraphs. Indeed, we think that the question of what is

"non-conformity" must be left to be determined by reference to the provisions of each particular scheme.

251. Although we are concerned in this Chapter only with the question of compensation for town planning restrictions, it is clear that, as regards the basis on which compensation should be calculated there is no difference in principle, in the case of a non-conforming building or use, between the enforcement of conformity and the public acquisition of the property. We have therefore recommended in paragraph 228 of Chapter VII that, where a "life" has been placed on a non-conforming building or use under our recommendation (A) (2) in paragraph 247 above for the purposes of securing conformity, the compensation payable on the public acquisition of the property shall be assessed by reference to the remainder of the "life" still outstanding.

CITY OF LOS ANGELES *v*. GAGE

California. District Court of Appeal. 1954. 274 P. (2d) 34

VALLÉE J.: This appeal involves the constitutionality of the provisions of a zoning ordinance which require that certain nonconforming existing uses shall be discontinued within five years after its passage, as they apply to defendants' property.

Plaintiff brought this suit for an injunction to command defendants to discontinue their use of certain property for the conduct of a plumbing business and to remove various materials therefrom, and to restrain them from using the property for any purpose not permitted by the comprehensive zoning plan provisions of the Los Angeles Municipal Code. The cause was submitted to the trial court on admissions in the pleadings and a stipulation of facts. Defendants will be referred to as "Gage."

In 1930 Gage acquired adjoining lots 220 and 221 located on Cochran Avenue in Los Angeles. He constructed a two-family residential building on lot 221 and rented the upper half solely for residential purposes. He established a wholesale and retail plumbing supply business on the property. He used a room in the lower half of the residential building on lot 221 as the office for the conduct of the business, and the rest of the lower half for residential purposes for himself and his family; he used a garage on lot 221 for the storage of plumbing supplies and materials; and he constructed and used racks, bins, and stalls for the storage of such supplies and materials on lot 220. Later Gage incorporated defendant company. The realty and the assets of the plumbing business were transferred to the company. The case is presented as though the property had been owned continuously from 1930 to date by the same defendant. The use of lots 220 and 221 begun in 1930, has been substantially the same at all times since.

In 1930 the two lots and other property facing on Cochran Avenue in their vicinity were classified in "C" zone by the zoning ordinance then in effect. Under this classification the use to which Gage put the property was permitted. Shortly after Gage acquired lots 220 and 221, they were classified in "C-3" zone and the use to which he put the property was expressly permitted. In 1936 the city council of the city passed ordinance 77,000 which contained a comprehensive zoning plan for the city. Ordinance 77,000 re-enacted the prior ordinances with respect to the use of lots 220 and 221. In 1941 the city council passed Ordinance 85,015 by the terms of which the use of a residential building for the conduct of an office in connection with the plumbing supply business was permitted. Ordinance 85,015 prohibited the open storage of materials in zone "C-3" but permitted such uses as had been established to continue as nonconforming uses. The use to which lots 220 and 221 was put by defendants was a nonconforming use that might be continued. In 1946 the city council passed Ordinance 90,500. This ordinance reclassified lots 220 and 221 and other property fronting on on Cochran Avenue in their vicinity from zone "C-3" to zone "R-4" (Multiple dwelling zone). Use of lots 220 and 221 for the conduct of a plumbing business was not permitted in zone "R-4." At the time Ordinance 90,500 was passed and at all times since, the Los Angeles Municipal Code (§ 12.23 B & C) provided: "(a) The nonconforming use of a conforming building or structure may be continued, except that in the 'R' Zones any nonconforming commercial or industrial use of a residential building or residential accessory building shall be discontinued within five (5) years from June 1, 1946, or five (5) years from the date the use becomes nonconforming, whichever date is later.

* * *

"(a) The nonconforming use of land shall be discontinued within five (5) years from June 1, 1946, or within five (5) years from the date the use became nonconforming, in each of the following cases: (1) where no buildings are employed in connection with such use; (2) where the only buildings employed are accessory or incidental to such use; (3) where such use is maintained in connection with a conforming building."

Prior to the passage of Ordinance 90,500, about 50% of the city had been zoned. It was the first ordinance which "attempted to zone the entire corporate limits of the city." Prior to its passage, several thousand exceptions and variances, were granted from restrictive provisions of prior ordinances, some of which permitted commercial use of property zoned for residential use, "and in some cases permitted the use of land for particular purposes like or similar to use of subject property which otherwise would have been prohibited." Under Ordinance 90,500, the uses permitted by these exceptions and variances that did not carry a time limit may be continued indefinitely.

The business conducted by Gage on the property has produced a gross revenue varying between $125,000 and $350,000 a year. If he is required to abandon the use of the property for his business, he will be put to the following expenses: "(1) The value of a suitable site for the conduct of its business would be about $10,000; which would be offset by the value of $7,500 of the lot now used. (2) The cost incident to removing of supplies to another location and construction of the necessary racks, sheds, bins and stalls which would be about $2,500. (3) The cost necessary to expend to advertise a new location. (4) The risk of a gain or a loss of business while moving, and the cost necessary to reestablish the business at a new location, the amount of which is uncertain."

The noise and disturbance caused by the loading and unloading of supplies, trucking, and the going and coming of workmen in connection with the operation of a plumbing business with an open storage yard is greater than the noise and disturbance that is normal in a district used solely for residential purposes. . . .

The right of a city council, in the exercise of the police power, to regulate or, in proper cases, to prohibit the conduct of a given business, is not limited by the fact that the value of investments made in the business prior to any legislative actions will be greatly diminished. A business which, when established, was entirely unobjectionable, may, by the growth or change in the character of the neighborhood, become a source of danger to the public health, morals, safety, or general welfare of those who have come to be occupants of the surrounding territory. . . . The effect of zoning restrictions may be to depreciate sharply the value of a particular parcel. The mere fact that some hardship is experienced is not material since "Every exercise of the police power is apt to affect adversely the property interest of somebody.". . . An individual cannot complain of incidental injury if the police power is exercised for proper purposes of health, safety, morals, or general welfare, and if there is no arbitrary and unreasonable application in the particular case. . . . Damage caused by the proper exercise of the police power is surely one of the prices an individual must pay as a member of society.

A nonconforming use is a lawful use existing on the effective date of the zoning restriction and continuing since that time in nonconformance to the ordinance. A provision permitting the continuance of a nonconforming use is ordinarily included in zoning ordinances because of the hardship and doubtful constitutionality of compelling the immediate discontinuance of nonconforming uses. . . .

It is generally held that a zoning ordinance may not operate to immediately suppress or remove from a particular district an otherwise lawful business or use already established therein. 58 Am.Jur. 1022, § 148.

No case seems to have been decided in this state squarely involving the precise question presented in the case at bar. Until recently zoning ordinances have made no provision for any systematic and comprehensive elimination of the nonconforming use. The expectation seems to have been that existing nonconforming uses would be of little consequence and that they would eventually disappear. See 9 *Minn.L.Rev.* 593, 598. The contrary appears to be the case. 35 *Va.L.Rev.* 348, 352; *Wis.L.Rev.* (1951) 685; 99 *Univ.Pa.L.Rev.* 1019, 1021. It is said that the fundamental problem facing zoning is the inability to eliminate the nonconforming use. 17 *Ill. Munic.Rev.* 221, 232. The general purpose of present-day zoning ordinances is to eventually end all nonconforming uses. . . . There is a growing tendency to guard against the indefinite continuance of nonconforming uses by providing for their liquidation within a prescribed period. . . . It is said, "The only positive method of getting rid of nonconforming uses yet devised is to amortize a non-conforming building. That is, to determine the normal useful remaining life of the building and prohibit the owner from maintaining it after the expiration of that time." Crolly and Norton, "Termination of Nonconforming Uses," 62 *Zoning Bulletin* 1, Regional Plan Assn., June 1952.

Amortization of nonconforming uses has been expressly authorized by recent amendments to zoning enabling laws in a number of states. Ordinances providing for amortization of nonconforming uses have been passed in a number of large cities. The length of time given the owner to eliminate his nonconforming use or building varies with the city and with the type of structure. . . .

The theory in zoning is that each district is an appropriate area for the location of the uses which the zone plan permits in that area, and that the existence or entrance of other uses will tend to impair the development and stability of the area for the appropriate uses. The public welfare must be considered from the stand-point of the objective of zoning and of all the property within any particular use district. . . . It was not and is not contemplated that preexisting nonconforming uses are to be perpetual. . . . The presence of any nonconforming use endangers the benefits to be derived from a comprehensive zoning plan. Having the undoubted power to establish residential districts, the legislative body has the power to make such classification really effective by adopting such reasonable regulations as would be conducive to the welfare, health, and safety of those desiring to live in such district and enjoy the benefits thereof. There would be no object in creating a residential district unless there were to be secured to those dwelling therein the advantages which are ordinarily considered the benefits of such residence. It would seem to be the logical and reasonable method of approach to place a time limit upon the continuance of existing nonconforming uses, commensurate with the investment involved and based on the nature of the use; and in cases of nonconforming structures, on their character, age, and other relevant factors.

Exercise of the police power frequently impairs rights in property because the exercise of those rights is detrimental to the public interest. Every zoning ordinance effects some impairment of vested rights either by restricting prospective uses or by prohibiting the continuation of existing uses, because it affects property already owned by individuals at the time of its enactment. . . . In essence there is no distinction between requiring the discontinuance of a nonconforming use within a reasonable period and provisions which deny the right to add to or extend buildings devoted to an existing nonconforming use, which deny the right to resume a nonconforming use after a period of nonuse, which deny the right to extend or enlarge an existing nonconforming use, which deny the right to substitute new buildings for those devoted to an existing nonconforming use—all of which have been held to be valid exercises of the police power. . . .

The distinction between an ordinance restricting future uses and one requiring the termination of present uses within a reasonable period of time is merely one of degree, and constitutionality depends on the relative importance to be given to the public gain and to the private loss. Zoning as it affects every piece of property is to some extent retroactive in that it applies to property already owned at the time of the effective date of the ordinance. The elimination of existing uses within a reasonable time does not amount to a taking of property nor does it necessarily restrict the use of property so that it cannot be used for any reasonable purpose. Use of a reasonable amortization scheme provides an equitable means of reconciliation of the conflicting interests in satisfaction of due process requirements. As a method of eliminating existing nonconforming uses it allows the owner of the nonconforming use, by affording an opportunity to make new plans, at least partially to offset any loss he might suffer. The loss he suffers, if any is spread out over a period of years, and he enjoys a monopolistic position by virtue of the zoning ordinance as long as he remains. If the amortization period is reasonable the loss to the owner may be small when compared with the benefit to the public. Nonconforming uses will eventually be eliminated. A legislative body may well conclude that the beneficial effect on the community of the eventual elimination of all nonconforming uses by a reasonable amortization plan more than offsets individual losses.

The ordinance in question provides, according to a gradual periodic schedule, for the gradual and ultimate elimination of all commercial and industrial uses in residential zones. These provisions require the discontinuance of nonconforming uses of land within a five year period, and the discontinuance of nonconforming commercial and industrial uses of residential buildings in the "R" zones within the same five-year period. These provisions are the only ones pertinent to the decision in this case. However, it may be noted that other provisions of the ordinance require the discontinuance of nonconforming billboards and, in residential zones, the discontinuance of nonconforming buildings and of nonconforming uses of nonconforming buildings, within specified periods running from 20 to 40 years according to the type of building construction.

We have no doubt that Ordinance 90,500, in compelling the discontinuance of the use of defendants' property for a wholesale and retail plumbing and plumbing supply business, and for the open storage of plumbing supplies within five years after its passage, is a valid exercise of the police power. Lots 220 and 221 are several blocks from a business centre and it appears that they are not within any reasonable or logical extension of such a center. The ordinance does not prevent the operation of defendants' business; it merely restricts its location. Discontinuance of the nonconforming use requires only that Gage move his plumbing business to property that is zoned for it. Such property can be found within a half mile of Gage's property. The cost of moving is $5,000, or less than 1% of Gage's minimum gross business for five years, or less than half of 1% of the mean of his gross business for five years. He has had eight years within which to move. The property is usable for residential purpose. Since 1930 lot 221 has been used for residential purposes. All of the land within 500 feet of Gage's property is now improved and used for such purposes. Lot 220, now unimproved, can be improved for the same purposes.

We think it apparent that none of the agreed facts and none of the ultimate facts found by the court justify the conclusion that Ordinance 90,500, as applied to Gage's property, is clearly arbitrary or unreasonable, or has no substantial relation to the public's health, safety, morals, or general welfare, or that it is an unconstitutional impairment of his property rights.

It is enough for us to determine and we determine only that Ordinance 90,500 of the city of Los Angeles, insofar as it required the discontinuance of Gage's wholesale and retail plumbing business on lots 220 and 221 within five years from the date of its passage, is a constitutional exercise of the police power.

The judgment is reversed, and the superior court is directed to render judgment for plaintiff as prayed for in the complaint.

3. The Claim of Protection for Vesting "Rights"

CITY OF TORONTO *v.* WHEELER
Ontario. High Court. 1912. 4 D.L.R. 352

MIDDLETON J.: By sec. 10 of the *Municipal Act*, 1912, 2 Geo. V. ch. 40, sec. 541a of the Municipal Act, 1903, as amended by 4 Edw. VII. ch. 22, sec. 19, was further amended by conferring upon cities the power "to prohibit, regulate, and control the location on certain streets, to be named in the by-law of . . . garages to be used for hire or gain." This statute was assented to on the 16th April, 1912.

A by-law in the terms of the statute was passed on the 13th May. Prior to the coming in force of the statute, the defendant, desiring to erect a garage upon one of the streets subsequently included in the by-law, entered into treaty with the owner of the lands in question, and, contemporaneously, plans of his proposed building were prepared and submitted to the City Architect for his approval, under the requirements of the building by-law. On the 17th April, the defendant received a building permit, authorizing the construction of the building in accordance with the plans and specifications submitted. He thereupon completed his purchase of the land and proceeded to make contracts for the erection of the buildings, and at the present time has the excavation well under way.

The sole question is, whether the municipality can at this stage interfere with what was sanctioned by the permit issued on the 17th April.

With reference to legislation of this kind, it is, I think, a sound principle that the Legislature could not have contemplated an interference with vested rights, unless the language used clearly required some other construction to be given to the enactment.

The language here used is by no means free from difficulty and ambiguity. What is prohibited is not, as in sub-sec. (b), the "location, erection, and use of buildings," for the objectionable purpose, but the "location" only; and, I think, it may fairly be said that what had been done previous to the enactment of the by-law in question constituted a complete location of the garage. The context indicates that "location" is used in some sense differing from "erection and use."

It would be manifestly most unfair so to construe the statute as to leave the defendant in the position in which he would find himself if, on the faith of the municipal assent indicated by the building permit, he had purchased the lands and entered into contracts for the erection of his building, and was then enjoined from the completion of the work already entered into upon the ground.

For this reason, I think the action fails, and must be dismissed with costs.

CITY OF TORONTO *v.* WILLIAMS
Ontario. Divisional Court. 1912. 8 D.L.R. 299

BOYD C.: This lot was purchased by the defendant in May, 1911, for $10,000, at the rate of $100 a foot. Land in the neighbourhood is now held at $200 per foot.

On the 1st October, 1911, a permit was obtained for building on it a two-storey and attic dwelling (a bungalow); and, for the purpose of that project, a cellar was dug, 26 by 60 feet and 4 feet deep, and a small load of stone hauled there in the latter part of that month.

On the 31st January, 1912, a permit was obtained to erect an apartment house on the same lot (which would supersede the other permit); but no work was done in pursuance of the scheme till the 18th July, 1912, when a new excavation was begun on the north side of the lot, and more or less work done.

Before this last work on the lot, the defendant knew of a by-law being passed by the city on the 13th May, 1912, forbidding the erection of apartment houses on residential streets, which included this locality, and that former permits would cease and become invalid; and there was a letter received by him from the City Architect notifying him that the permit was withdrawn. Prior to this, the only work done on the place was referable to the abandoned bungalow scheme.

This by-law was pursuant to the powers given to cities by the statute 2 Geo. V. ch. 40, sec. 10 (assented to 16th April, 1912); and it follows the words of the Act. The prohibition is against "the location" on the street named of apartment houses.

The argument before us was, that the location of this apartment house (coupled with the defendant's intention to build thereon) had attached or had been completed when the permit was obtained, and that all the prior and subsequent work done on the lot was referable thereto, and having been so acted upon, it was inequitable and incompetent for the city to recede or to revoke the location.

But it is to strain the meaning of the word "location" to give it this scope. No doubt, the word is used with a technical or conventional import when used in connection with lines of railway and other undertakings, as pointed out by Strong C.J., in *The Queen* v. *Farwell* (1887). But there is nothing in the statute to interfere with its etymological and ordinary meaning: *City of Toronto* v. *Ontario and Quebec R.W. Co.* (1892).

The word "location" is used in the statute in its primary and proper import, as given in Latham's Johnson's Dictionary (sub voce), namely: "Situation with respect to place; act of placing; state of being placed." Read the clause with this substitution of words: "Prohibit the situation with respect to place of an apartment house on the street." "Prohibit the site of house being placed on the street." Any of these substitutes brings out the meaning, which is forbidding the *locus* being used for the purpose of putting an apartment house thereon.

The context and intent of the statute and by-law is to forbid the placing of an apartment house on that site. The preparation of the plans and specifications was no more than a preliminary to the application for a permit; and the permit, when granted, was merely to erect the proposed building, i.e., to locate it on the site. No outlay has been incurred since the granting of this permit up to the date of its revocation, and no case of estoppel can be made out. The permit to build may be regarded as a license to build; but that the owner might withdraw from, as might also the city, in case the situation was not changed, in pursuance of the license. No such change is proved here; the only change appears to be a steady increase in the value of the land.

We cannot mistake the policy of the Legislature; the plaintiffs, as a public body, are called on to enforce it in proper residential neighbourhoods. While it may bear hardly on the individual owner, who is hampered in the free enjoyment of his property, still it is one of the effects of advancing civic life and amenity that, for the sake of preponderating advantages to the whole locality, one proprietor may have to suffer deprivation.

This is said to be a test case, involving a score of other permits; and, this being so, and the point being without authority, it seems fitting, while we reverse the decision in appeal, to do so without costs.

The injunction is continued indefinitely while the prohibition continues.

MIDDLETON J.: In *City of Toronto* v. *Wheeler* matters had so far advanced that when the by-law was passed the building had been begun—the defendant had given "to airy nothing a local habitation" as well as a "name."

I fully appreciate that any prohibition of the owner's common law right to use his land as he sees fit, so long as no nuisance is committed, may in individual cases be regarded as a hardship, but this case must be determined upon the construction of the statute and the by-law, which is in the words of the statute.

It must not be forgotten that there is another side to the question of hardship. The statute is remedial, and is for the protection of those who, in residential districts, have built houses and laid out gardens which would be much depreciated by the erection of large and often unsightly buildings completely overshadowing them.

Even if it be admitted that the word "location" might mean something less than an actual placing upon the ground, and that it might be used to indicate the choice of a site for a projected building, it is clear that this is not what the Legislature meant to prohibit. That which is prohibted and rendered penal is not the mental process, the intention to use the land for the prohibited purpose, but the actual use of the land for that purpose. The extent of the prohibition may be gauged by the liability to the penalty.

The permit cannot be regarded as an estoppel, as at the time it was issued the city officials had no option. The statute, not then passed, could not be deprived of its effect by their action.

For this reason, the appeal must be allowed. It is not a case for costs.

[The decision of Lachford J., who agreed, is omitted.]

CRIDLAND *v*. CITY OF TORONTO

Ontario. Supreme Court. 1920. 55 D.L.R. 384

MIDDLETON J.: The applicants desire to erect a factory in a district not declared to be "residential," and have filed plans, etc., in accordance with the provisions of the building by-law.

By by-law 8284, the building by-law was, on the 15th December, 1919, amended by adding clause 12, reading as follows:

"12. When an application or the drawings or specifications accompanying the same relate to property on a street residential in character but not so declared by by-law, the inspector of buildings shall forthwith report the particulars thereof to the committee on property, which shall consider the advisability of declaring the whole or some part of the property on said street residential, and report the matter to the council, and pending the decision of the council thereon the inspector shall withhold the issuing of a permit and shall act in accordance with the decision of the council."

The inspector of buildings, deeming the street to be residential, refuses to issue a permit pending the decision of the council on the question of declaring the street or some part to be residential.

For some reason the matter has not been reported to the property committee, but the board of control has directed that a permit be not issued.

It is said that the building inspector should not have found this "street residential in character," as at the part where this factory is to be placed there are large city stables and other buildings of a commercial character. I do not think I should enter upon the discussion of this matter.

I think the amending by-law is beyond the power of the municipality. No doubt it can declare a district residential and so prevent the erection of a factory, but it has no power to compel a land-owner to refrain from the exercise of his rights under the law as it is to-day, so as to enable the city council to consider the enactment of a law which will make that unlawful which is to-day lawful. The citizen desiring to build is entitled to do so if he complies with the law as it is to-day as to building, and the building by-law must not be used as a means of delaying him until the council considers a question which arises under an independent section of the statute.

The amending by-law is also objectionable from another point of view.

The council has power to pass laws binding on all those who are subject to its jurisdiction; but an attempt to regulate the conduct of any individual rather than to pass a general law is bad. This situation indicates that the council does not really intend to pass a law setting apart a residential district, but to prohibit this factory because this particular industry may prove to be a nuisance to the owner of the adjoining premises.

I think the mandatory order sought may go, and that costs should be awarded against both respondents.

The validity of the city by-law being attacked, the city corporation is a proper party to these proceedings; and, as the civic officer was acting in obedience to the by-law, the city corporation ought to bear the costs.

TOWN AND COUNTRY PLANNING ACT, 1947
England. Statutes. 1947. Chapter 51

78. (1) Subject to the provisions of this section, where any works for the erection or alteration of a building have been begun but not completed before the appointed day, then if immediately before that day those works could have been completed in conformity with the provisions of a planning scheme or of permission granted thereunder, or in accordance with permission granted by or under an interim development order, and if any permission required under the Restriction of Ribbon Development Act, 1935, for the carrying out of those works was granted, planning permission shall, by virtue of this section, be deemed to be granted under Part III of this Act in respect of the completion of those works.

26. (1) Without prejudice to the provisions of this Part of this Act with respect to the service of enforcement notices, if it appears to a local planning authority that it is expedient in the interests of the proper planning of their area (including the interests of amenity), regard being had to the development plan and to any other material considerations—

(a) that any use of land should be discontinued, or that any conditions should be imposed on the continuance thereof; or

(b) that any buildings or works should be altered or removed,

they may by order require the discontinuance of that use, or impose such conditions as may be specified in the order on the continuance thereof, or require such steps as may be so specified to be taken for the alteration or removal of the buildings or works, as the case may be:

Provided that no such order shall take unless it is confirmed by the Minister, and the Minister may confirm any order submitted to him for the purpose either without modification or subject to such modifications as he considers expedient.

(7) Where the requirements of any order under this section will involve the displacement of persons residing in any premises, it shall be the duty of the local planning authority, in so far as there is not other residential accommodation suitable to the reasonable requirements of those persons available on reasonable terms, to secure the provision of such accommodation in advance of the displacement.

27. (1) Where an order is made under the last foregoing section requiring any use of land to be discontinued, or imposing conditions on the continuance thereof, or requiring any buildings or works on land to be altered or removed, then if, on a claim made to the local planning authority within the time and in the manner prescribed by regulations under this Act, it is shown that any person has suffered damage in consequence of the

order by the depreciation of any interest in the land to which he is entitled or by being disturbed in his enjoyment of the land, that authority shall pay to that person compensation in respect of that damage; and any compensation payable under this subsection in respect of the depreciation in the value of an interest in the land shall be assessed in accordance with the provisions of the Fourth Schedule to this Act. . . .

UNFINISHED BUILDING WITHIN S. 78

The following is an extract from the letter of the Minister of Town and Country Planning dated July 22, 1950, dismissing an appeal against the determination of the Reigate Borough Council that planning permission is required for the erection of two pairs of semi-detached houses on the appellant's land in London Road, Redhill.

"Approval was given by the Council on May 18, 1932, for the erection of three pairs of houses on the appeal land. One of these three pairs was completed before the war in accordance with this interim development permission, and certain works were done in connection with the erection of the remaining two pairs, namely,

(a) the demolition of a substantial building, at the time standing on the site, and the clearing of the site;

(b) the laying of approximately 40 ft. of drain across the site;

(c) the construction of an inspection pit with connections to take the drainage from the house proposed to be erected on Plot No. 4;

(d) the construction of an inspection pit with intercepting trap and connections to take the drainage from the houses proposed to be erected on Plots No. 1, 2 and 3.

It was claimed that the above works are works within the meaning of s. 78(1) of the Act, and that these works could have been completed in conformity with the provisions of a planning scheme, or of permission granted thereunder, and that therefore, in accordane with s. 78(1), planning permission under Part III of the Act should be deemed to be granted in respect of the completion of the two pairs of semi-detached houses to be erected on Plots 1, 2, 3 and 4.

After careful consideration of all the facts and representations before him, it appears to the Minister that the erection of the dwelling-houses in question has not in fact been commenced, and he cannot accept the contention that the construction of works connected with the drainage and sewering of the houses when erected, are works for the erection of the houses."

(By courtesy of the County Planning Officer of the Surrey County Council.)

NOTE. The extract from the Minister's letter is reproduced as it appears in [1950] Journal of Planning and Property Law 897. For a comment see Leach, "Unfinished Buildings," [1951] J.P.L. 143. Has the laying of drains any other purpose in view than the erection of the houses?

SHAUL *v*. JASPER PLACE. 1953. 10 W.W.R. (N.S.) 268 (Alberta District Court). BUCHANAN C.J.D.C.: ". . . Holding as I do that the effect of sec. 26(1) of the [*The Town and Rural Planning*] *Act* is to exclude from the operation of the by-law (and from the operation of any building regulations, restrictions or requirements promulgated by virtue of the by-law's provisions) 'any building lawfully under construction' at the time named and by inference to include within the operation of the by-law any building not lawfully under construction at the said date, it remains to determine whether the excavation of a 'dug-out' for each building proposed to be erected can be deemed adequate to justify the application thereto of the phrase 'a building under construction.' Can a hole in the ground be described as a 'building under construction'? Although details are not before me I am justified, I believe, in assuming that the plans and specifications filed by the plaintiffs with the defendant as a condition precedent to the issue of the permits indicated that a "dug-out" basement would be the initial step in the construction of the two dwellings authorized by the permits. In other words, before the framework of the dwellings could be erected the 'dug-outs' must necessarily be excavated. The excavation of the 'dug-outs' was a necessary step in the construction of the dwellings for which the permits were issued. I hold therefore that the buildings contemplated by the plaintiffs could reasonably be described as 'lawfully under construction' at the date prescribed by sec. 26(1) of the Act. . . ."

NOTE. Section 26(1) provides:

"Any building lawfully under construction at the time of the first publication of the advertisement of intention to pass a zoning by-law, shall for the purpose of that by-law be deemed to be a building existing at the time of the passing of a zoning by-law."

TORONTO *v*. ROMAN CATHOLIC SEPARATE SCHOOL BOARD

Ontario. Privy Council. [1926] A.C. 81

VISCOUNT CAVE L.C.: This appeal raises some important questions as to the relative rights of a School Board acting under the Separate Schools Act of Ontario and a City Council acting under the Municipal Act of that Province. By virtue of the Separate Schools Act, the Board of Trustees of the Roman Catholic Separate Schools for the city of Toronto (who will be referred to in this judgment as the "School Board") have power to acquire or rent school sites and to build and carry on schools. By virtue of the Municipal Act, the Corporation of the city of Toronto is empowered to prohibit by by-law the use of land or the erection or use of buildings within any defined area for any purpose other than that of a private residence. The question is whether, in the circumstances of this case, a by-law made by the Corporation under the latter statute is enforceable in respect of a site purchased by the School Board for school purposes.

In the year 1921 the School Board, having been evicted for the purpose of a street improvement from their school in St. Vincent Street, purchased two adjoining houses with gardens, being Nos. 14 and 18 Prince Arthur Avenue, Toronto, with the object of transferring their scholars to a new school to be erected on that site. No. 14 Prince Arthur Avenue was vacant, and the School Board obtained possession of that property on August 19, 1921; but No. 18 was let to tenants who were subject to a two months' notice to quit, but actual possession of that property was not obtained until the month of April in the following year. Immediately on obtaining possession of No. 14, the School Board, without depositing plans as required by the municipal by-laws then in force, made some structural alterations in the building with a view to adapting it for temporary use as a school; and subsequently—namely, on September 6 and 9, they deposited plans for these temporary alterations. Prince Arthur Avenue is a residential street and on September 14 the residents in that street, having heard of the proposal to open a school there, appealed to the Board of Control to intervene; and that Board referred to the City Council the question of making a by-law preserving the residential character of the street, and instructed the city architect to withhold his approval of the plans deposited by the School Board pending the consideration of this question by the Council. The School Board thereupon acted with great promptness. On September 15 their architect deposited with the city architect plans for the erection of a school extending over the site of Nos. 14 and 18 Prince Arthur Avenue, and on the same day the School Board applied to the Court for a mandamus directing the city architect to consider these plans and to grant a permit both for the temporary alterations and for the erection of a school building upon the entire site. They also opened a school in No. 14 as altered, and by agreement with the tenants of No. 18 obtained possession of a part of the garden at the rear of that house, and caused it to be used as a playground for the scholars.

On September 26 the City Council met and under the powers conferred upon them by s. 399a of the Municipal Act, passed a by-law (No. 8834) in the following form:

"I. No person shall use the land fronting or abutting on either side of Prince Arthur Avenue, between Avenue Road and Huron Street, or erect or use any buildings on the said land for any other purpose than that of a detached private residence.

"II. Any person convicted of a breach of any of the provisions of this by-law shall forfeit and pay, at the discretion of the convicting magistrate, a penalty not exceeding (exclusive of costs) the sum of $50 for each offence.

"III. This by-law shall take effect upon, from and after receiving the approval of the Ontario Railway and Municipal Board."

This by-law was approved, after arguments on both sides, by the Railway and Municipal Board. The application for a mandamus, having been adjourned in the meantime, was thereupon dismissed by Middleton J.; and an appeal to a Divisional Court against this dismissal was adjourned by that Court sine die to enable the School Board to take proceedings to get the by-law quashed.

Accordingly, on March 10, 1922, the School Board brought an action against the City Council and their architect, claiming to have the by-law declared invalid or inapplicable and consequential relief. On April 19, 1922, the City Council commenced an action against the School Board, claiming an injunction to restrain that Board from using in breach of by-law No. 8834 the part of its land not used for school purposes prior to the passing of the by-law, being the front part of No. 18 Prince Arthur Avenue. The two actions were consolidated, and were tried by Middleton J., who dismissed the action brought by the School Board and granted an injunction as asked by the City Council. An appeal to the Appellate Division of the Supreme Court of Ontario against this judgment, and against the refusal of Middleton J. and the Divisional Court to grant a mandamus, was dismissed. The School Board applied for leave to appeal against the decision of the Appellate Division to the Supreme Court of Canada, and such leave was granted on an undertaking by the School Board to abandon as a ground of appeal any contention that the form of the by-law in question in this action, if it was completely enacted, did not correctly follow the statute pursuant to which it was passed, and also any contention that the Municipal Council in passing the by-law acted in bad faith.

On the hearing of the appeal to the Supreme Court of Canada, that Court (Idington J. dissenting) allowed the appeal and made an order that the city architect should consider the application of the School Board for a permit to erect a school building upon the premises Nos. 14 and 18 Prince Arthur Avenue, and should grant a permit for the erection of that building in accordance with the plans and specifications left with the city architect by the Board or as the same might be amended in compliance with the by-laws of the city of Toronto respecting buildings. The reasons for this decision are to be found in the judgment delivered by Duff J. on behalf of the majority of the Court, from which it appears that the decision was based mainly upon the proviso marked (*a*) contained in s. 399a of the Municipal Act of 1921. That section, after enacting that by-laws might be passed by the councils of cities and other municipalities for prohibiting the use of land or the erection or use of buildings within any defined area or areas abutting on any defined highway or part of a highway for any other purpose than that of a detached private residence, provided as follows: "(*a*) No by-law passed under this section shall apply to any land or building which on the day the by-law is passed is erected or used for any purpose prohibited by the by-law so long as it continues to be used for that purpose, nor shall it apply to any building in course of erection or to any building the plans for which have been approved by the city architect prior to the date of the passing of the by-law, so long as when erected it is used for the purpose for which it was erected."

After referring to this proviso, the learned judge said (1): "The right of the owner of land, therefore, to make use of it, subject to the existing by-laws, in the erection of such buildings upon it as he thinks proper to erect, is preserved inviolate down to the point of time when the restrictive by-law is actually passed; and thereafter, in the limited degree prescribed, in the special cases mentioned. That right, as Middleton J. held in the case already cited, includes the right to receive the necessary permit for the erection of a building proposed to be erected in conformity with the law in force for the time being. It is quite manifest that in the result, if effect be given to the judgments of the Ontario Courts, this right is denied the appellants. The by-law producing this result cannot, in view of the circumstances, in our opinion, be sustained as a valid exercise of the authority given by the statute. The protection of the existing status is a substantive element in the purpose of the enactment. The by-law, passed in the circumstances in which it was passed, necessarily had the effect (and it was so designed) of depriving the appellants of the benefit of a status of which the statute guaranteed the protection. That, in our opinion, is not according to the tenor of the authority created."

The learned judge concluded by expressing a hope that, with the co-operation of all parties concerned, it might be possible to make other arrangements which would relieve the residents of the street of the very grave detriment and hardship arising from the presence of the school, the existence of which was not disputed.

With the greatest respect for the opinion of the learned judges composing the majority of the Supreme Court, their Lordships are unable to concur in this reasoning. No doubt it is true that, unless and until a by-law restricting the building upon any land is passed, the owner of the land has a right, subject to the existing by-laws, to erect upon it such buildings as he may think proper. But the whole object and purpose of s. 399a is to empower the city authority, acting in good faith, to put restrictions upon that right with a view to the protection of neighbouring owners against that "grave detriment and hardship" to which the learned judge referred; and the "status" or proprietary right of the owner is limited by the powers of the city to be exercised for the protection of his neighbours. If the reasoning of the learned judge is to be taken literally, then in every case the "status" of the building owner is to prevail, and that whether he has or has not deposited plans with a view to building upon his land; and even if the sentences quoted refer only to a case where plans have been deposited before the by-law is passed, they yet go beyond the express terms of the statute. The operation of proviso (*a*) is confined to cases where at the date of the passing of a by-law either (1.) a building is erected or used for a purpose prohibited by the by-law, or (2.) a building is in course of erection, or (3.) the plans for a building have been approved by the city architect; and it would appear to their Lordships to be a necessary inference from the express terms of the proviso that where plans have been deposited but not yet approved, and the building is not in course of erection, the operation of the by-law is not excluded. There may be a prima facie right to have the deposited plans approved; but if so, that right is negatived by the passing and approval of the by-law. It was suggested that the by-law was defective on the ground that the limitations contained in proviso (*a*) to the section should have been but were not embodied in the by-law itself; but having regard to the undertaking given by the respondents to abandon any contention that the form of the by-law did not correctly follow the statute, this argument was not open to the respondents on this appeal, and their Lordships accordingly express no opinion upon it . . .

[Part of the opinion is omitted. The Judicial Committee held that a School Board could only exercise its powers subject to the zoning by-law and that the *B.N.A. Act* did not prevent a municipality from zoning against denominational schools.]

QUESTIONS. The by-law in this case "shall take effect upon, from and after receiving the approval of the Ontario Railway and Municipal Board." What significance has subsection (7) of the present s. 30 when this commencement clause is used? Since the plans were deposited prior to the passing of the by-law and perhaps long before its approval, at which time of approval it was to "take effect", why was the School Board not entitled to mandamus? How long can the building inspector "hold up" plans before approving them? In the absence of a zoning by-law, what possible grounds for delaying the approval could be raised?

CENTRAL JEWISH INSTITUTE *v.* TORONTO

Ontario. Supreme Court of Canada. [1948] 2 D.L.R. 1

KERWIN J. delivered the judgment of himself and LOCKE J.: The appellant, Central Jewish Institute, is the defendant in an action brought by the respondent, the Corporation of the City of Toronto, claiming an injunction restraining the appellant from using certain premises known as 561 Avenue Rd., in the City of Toronto, as a school or as a nursery school, contrary to the provisions of By-law 16654, passed by the council of the corporation on July 24, 1946, and approved by the Municipal Board, September 24, 1946. This by-law was passed and approved in conformity with the provisions of s. 406 of the *Municipal Act* . . .

The appellant had for some years operated on University Ave. in the City of Toronto what is described in the evidence as a "progressive" school for children from two to ten years of age. According to one of the teachers, the term "progressive" indicates that the children "are allowed to progress at their own speed, they are allowed a little more freedom." The classes ran from nursery, pre-school (junior kindergarten and kindergarten) to grade school. No summer school had ever been held there. It became necessary for the appellant to acquire new premises for its school and by a written document of June 25, 1946, the appellant offered to purchase the premises known as 561 Avenue Rd., Toronto, from one Greenhill with the purpose of carrying on its school there. This offer was accepted on June 27, 1946, at which date the property was not subject to any restrictions nor was the use to which it might be put limited in any way by any by-law. Greenhill was then using the house on the premises as a boarding house or rooming-house, described in the evidence as a guest-house. One thousand dollars was paid as a deposit, a mortgage of $26,500 was to be assumed and the balance was to be paid on September 1, 1946, when possession was to be taken.

Presumably hearing of an agitation by adjoining owners to have the council of the corporation pass a restrictive by-law, the appellant, on July 12, 1946, made a supplementary agreement with Greenhill by which the deposit on the property was increased by $5,000, which was immediately paid. Clauses 2, 3 and 4 of the supplementary agreement provide as follows:

"2. Possession of the whole of the premises without prejudice to the rights of the Parties to be given to the Purchaser July 15th, 1946, with right to remodel in its discretion; provided that the present occupants of the premises may be allowed to remain undisturbed until the 1st day of August, 1946.

"3. Mr. Greenhill to be allowed the use and occupancy of one room and kitchen and garage apartment for his personal use and such space in addition as he may require for furniture, etc., until the 31st day of August, 1946.

"4. Date for closing this transaction to be August 31st, 1946."

In accordance with cl. 2 of this supplementary agreement, a number of children and three teachers went on the property on July 15, 1946, and from then until the by-law was passed, the grounds and part of the building were used by teachers and children as a nursery school for very young children. As the trial Judge finds, at least five children were brought to the premises, although some witnesses put the attendance between the relevant dates as high as fifteen or eighteen, and what was conducted was really a summer school—most of the time being spent outdoors and only inside when the weather was inclement. The trial Judge states: "Certain of the defendant's witnesses gave evidence to the effect that prior to July 24, 1946, the kitchen and a ground floor was used. Their demeanour, however, does not impress me. Furthermore during this time the vendor was still carrying on a guest-house with a full complement of furniture in the house." There is no doubt that Greenhill still had a considerable part, if not all, of his furniture in the house but he was disposing of it from time to time and, at the most, there were only about three to five guests and they were under notice to leave. Furthermore, in addition to the witnesses for the appellant, Mrs. Ferguson, called by the respondent, testified that when it rained she thought there was a basement to which the children went.

The appellant argued that the use made by the appellant of the premises should be taken to be that of the date of the approval of the by-law by the Municipal Board. If that contention were sound, it would be sufficient to dispose of the matter and allow the appeal because it is not denied that by September 24, 1946, the date of the Municipal Board's order, the appellant was using the premises for every kind of a school conducted by it. It has been assumed in all the cases to which we were referred that the important date was the passing of the by-law. That this is the proper conclusion is apparent in my view from a comparison of the provisions of ss. (2) and (3) of s. 406 of the Act. The former refers to the use of any land or building on the day of the passing of the by-law, while the latter provides that no part of any such by-law passed under the section shall come into force without the approval of the Municipal Board.

The trial Judge and the Court of Appeal seem to have proceeded on the ground that the principal use of the premises on July 24, 1946, the date of the passing of the by-law, was as a residence and guest-house and that, therefore, the appellant was not within the exception ss. (2) s. 406 of the *Municipal Act*. Mr. Justice Hogg, speaking for the Court of Appeal, states: "That building, No. 561 Avenue Rd., was used to a very limited extent for school purposes on July 24, 1946; the principal use of the house was, on that date, that of a rooming-house or guest-house."

In my view this is not the determining factor. The extent of the user of premises as a school would vary from time to time and in the months of July and August it is well known that the pupils in the ordinary classes are on vacation. It is true that the appellant had not conducted a summer school on University Ave. but there was nothing to prevent it commencing such a school as part of its curriculum. According to the evidence,, a nursery school is part of the course provided by the appellant and the mere fact that no grade classes were held on the Avenue Rd. premises prior to the date of the passing of the by-law does not prevent the application of ss. (2) of s. 406 of the *Municipal Act*. It is not necessary that the entire premises, that is every room in the building, be used. While a *bona fide* intention to use is not sufficient, as has been decided by the Judicial Committee in [*Toronto* v. *Separate Schools*] it is an important element in considering the evidence as to actual user. There is no doubt, in the present case, as to the purpose of the appellant in purchasing the premises nor, I think, is there any real doubt on the evidence as to what it did. This is not a case of disturbing concurrent findings but of accepting the facts as found and of drawing the proper legal conclusions therefrom. The appellant took steps during the summer vacation, in an endeavour to bring itself within ss. (2) of s. 406 of the Act and, in my opinion, has succeeded in so doing. It actually used the premises as a school and the mere fact that it was a nursery summer school does not prevent the appellant increasing the number of pupils or enlarging the scope of its activities so as to conduct classes not in operation at the relevant time. We are not concerned, in the present appeal, with any question of erecting new buildings.

A similar result was arrived at by Middleton J., in *Re Hartley and Toronto* (1924), and his decision was affirmed by the Court of Appeal for Ontario (1925). It is argued that this decision is in conflict with that of the Privy Council already mentioned but I am satisfied that this is not so. The *Separate Schools* case had also been decided in the first instance by Middleton J., and his judgment had been affirmed by the Court of Appeal, when the *Hartley* case came before him and he found no conflict. Later, the decision was reversed in this Court and to some extent at least the decision of the majority of the Court of Appeal in the *Hartley* case, delivered by Hodgins J.A., was based upon the reasons for judgment of this Court. This latter judgment was subsequently reversed by the Judicial Committee. However, there is no conflict between the judgment of the Privy Council and the decisions of the trial Judge and the Court of Appeal in the *Hartley* case and in my opinion the latter were correctly decided. In any event, I can find nothing inconsistent between what I have suggested is the proper construction of the word "used" in ss. (2) of s. 406 of the *Municipal Act* and the reasoning and decision of the Judicial Committee. In fact the latter were concerned with a separate piece of property that was fenced off from the remainder of what had been purchased by the trustees, and that was in the separate possession of a third party and that had not been used at all at the relevant time by the trustees.

There remains but to add that in my view the decisions referred to in the judgment of the Court of Appeal as to the meaning of the words "actually used and occupied" in various *Assessment Acts* have no application to the present case. The appeal should be allowed and the action dismissed with costs throughout.

RAND J.: . . . The precise language of the statute is important: "No by-law passed under this section shall apply to any land or building which, on the day of the passing of the by-law, is used or erected for any purpose prohibited by the by-law." [s. 406 (2)].

It will be seen that the exemption is not to the existing use but to the building; and there is no implication that it is the whole of the building that must be so used or that the use must be the sole use. The language would be satisfied by a partial use as if, for instance, an owner was carrying on a grocery store on the ground floor and using the second storey for his home: could it seriously be questioned that the use of the lower floor in such a case would be protected by the exemption? If that same business were extended to the upper storey, could it be said that the exemption did not continue or was lost? The building would still be used on the ground floor for the prohibited purpose; the building as a whole would be exempt; and I think it would necessarily follow that no such extension could bring about a forfeiture of the exemption. In any case the question is whether a real use, in good faith, is being made of the building, a use not merely incidental to some other use, but possessing an individuality of its own. The view of the statute seems to me to underlie the decision of both Middleton J. and the Court of Appeal in *Re Hartley*, and I think it sound.

There is substantially no conflict of evidence as to the use here. The appellant purchased the premises for the school activities that were then being carried on in other premises. They consisted of the training of the children from two to ten years of age, and the different stages are denominated nursery or junior kindergarten, kindergarten and grade. Admittedly they had not before been carried on in summer, and I will assume that what was done here in July when the grade department was on holiday, was done to establish rights ahead of the move then under way to bring about the restriction. That was precisely the case in *Re Hartley* and it was treated as the unobjectionable exercise of rights of an owner. But it was part of the existing or intended school establishment, carried on appropriately to the season, and obviously it is not necessary that there be use of all departments contemporaneously.

Mr. Cartwright raised also the point that the by-law itself contains a clause to the effect that it "shall come into force upon receiving the approval of the Municipal Board." That, in substance, is the language of the statute providing that "No by-law passed under this section shall come into force or be repealed or amended without the approval of the municipal board." What the *Municipal Act* contemplates is the "passing of the by-law by the municipality" and its "coming into force" upon the approval of the Municipal Board. Here, the by-law itself contains an endorsement, "Passed July 24, 1946." That shows on its face the distinction between "passing" and "coming into force" and I cannot agree that the clause containing the latter is intended to suspend the time when the by-law is to be deemed to be "passed."

I would, therefore, allow the appeal and dismiss the action with costs throughout.

[The opinions have been considerably shortened and that of Kellock J. has been omitted. Taschereau J. agreed in allowing the appeal.]

QUESTIONS. What does Rand J. mean in the principal case when he says that the exemption "is not to the existing use but to the building"? Has the "general intent and purpose" of the Municipal Act been defeated here? How would Rand J. have regarded the commencement provisions in the Separate Schools case? If A has a shop in the basement of his dwelling-house, could he move out and extend the shop throughout the building? Suppose he is a veterinarian surgeon using the basement of his house for a dog hospital, could he move out and extend the use throughout all floors of the house? Could he use his yard for dog runs?

Do you agree with the observation of Middleton J. in the *Separate Schools* case quoted with approval by Kellock J. in the principal case, that s. 390 (6) "defines precisely the effect of the by-law"? Does this case apply to s. 30(7) of *The Planning Act*?

RE HARTLEY AND TORONTO. 1924. 56 O.L.R. 433 (Ontario. Court of Appeal). FERGUSON J.A. (dissenting): "The matron and inmates of the Home went into use of part of the building on the 26th May, and the by-law was passed a few days thereafter, but Mrs. Taylor remained in the use and occupation of that part of the building not occupied by the matron and the two girls until some time after the by-law had been passed . . .

"The subsection of the statute upon which the respondent bases his claim to exemption from the by-law, takes, in the Act, the form of an exception, and it seems to follow that the onus of establishing that he or his building and lands are within the excepted classes is upon him.

"In my opinion, the facts and circumstances adduced in evidence do not establish that on the day the by-law was passed (the 31st May) the respondent had obtained possession of, and was using, as a detention Home for girls, the downstairs floor of the building or the lands connected with the building, or that he was making a substantial and real use of any part of the building for a detention Home. My conclusion on the evidence is that Mrs. Taylor continued in possession and use of the more substantial part of the building and of the lands, and that on the day of the passing of the by-law the respondent was only in possession of and making a colourable use of the smaller part of the building, and consequently that the respondent has failed to establish any user of the whole property or of the whole building, or such a user of any part thereof as he now desires to make of the whole."

CANADIAN PETROFINA LTD. *v.* MARTIN AND ST. LAMBERT

Quebec. Supreme Court of Canada. 1959. 18 D.L.R. (2d) 761

FAUTEUX J. delivered the judgment of the Court: This is an appeal from a unanimous decision of the Court of Queen's Bench setting aside a judgment of the Superior Court maintaining appellant's petition of mandamus, for the issuance of a building permit for the erection of a gasoline filling station on the southwest corner of Victoria & Woodstock Sts. in the City of St. Lambert.

The events leading to this litigation may be summarized as follows:

The appellant company, a vendor of motor fuels and motor oils and operator of service stations, obtained on November 12, 1954 and accepted on July 27, 1955, an option to purchase, at the location and for the purpose above indicated, a parcel of land, conditional upon it obtaining from the city respondent all necessary permits and approvals. By a letter, dated May 30, 1955 and supported by a plot plan, construction plans and specifications, appellant applied for a gasoline filling station building permit, required under building By-law 392 then in force in the city. Acknowledging receipt of this application in a letter of June 10, 1955, respondent Martin, city manager and building inspector, advised appellant that the building by-law of the city did not allow the erection of a gasoline filling station in that area, which, it may be added, was within what is described in the by-law as district "D". Some ten days later, *i.e.*, in a letter dated June 20th, addressed to the mayor and councillors of the city respondent, appellant asked what specific provisions of the by-law prevented the granting of its application, in answer to which respondent, in a letter of June 29th, referred appellant to By-law 392, s. 5, arts. 87 and 89. On the very date of appellant's letter of June 20th, notice of motion having been duly given, the council of the city passed By-law 405 reading as follows: ...

"1. THAT Article 87 is amended by adding the following paragraphs:

" '87A.–Article 87 was never meant to authorize gasoline filling stations, the erection of which was and is prohibited in District D.

" '87B.—The provisions of section 87A of this By-Law are interpretative and shall take effect as from the first of January 1950.

" '87C.—Gasoline filling stations are prohibited in all Districts within the limits of the City of St. Lambert, except in District F.'

"2. This present By-Law shall come into force according to law."

A month later, on July 20th, appellant's solicitors being seized of the matter, informed the city by letter that they had advised their client that art. 87 of By-law 392, properly interpreted, was ineffective to prohibit the erection of gasoline filling stations in district "D", that the adoption of By-law 405, of which they alleged having been recently apprised, could not defeat the rights already acquired by the company under By-law 392, and that, unless the city was prepared to grant the permit, appropriate judicial proceedings would ensue. This was followed by a letter from the city, dated July 21st, advising that the matter would receive the immediate attention of its legal advisor upon the return of the latter from vacation, and by a further letter, on September 14th, from appellant's solicitors to the city, insisting upon a decision in the matter.

On October 18th, appellant, with the authorization of Challies J., caused a writ of mandamus to issue. In the declaration, served with the writ upon respondents, appellant prays that *articles 87A and B* of By-law 405 be declared null and void and of no force or effect as *ultra vires* and, demanding a declaration of its readiness to pay, on the issue of the permit, such amount as, pursuant to the provisions of the city by-law, might be indicated by the building inspector, that respondent Martin be enjoined to grant appellant the building permit requested.

The trial Judge [ordered the respondent Martin, as building inspector, to grant the appellant's application in accordance with his plans and specifications. The respondent appealed to the Court of Queen's Bench, who reversed the trial judge and the appellant brought the present appeal.]

It should immediately be said that appellant's submission that, in passing By-law 405, the city acted in bad faith and in a manner oppressive and unjust to the company, is not supported. The declared purpose of the by-law is to remove any possible ambiguity as to its interpretation as invariably given in the past by the city. While the declared purpose of a legislation is not always conclusive of its true purpose, in the present case, the fact that the city's interpretation is identical to that of the Court of Appeal supports the sincerity of the purpose indicated in the by-law and that the latter was not adopted to defeat appellant's application for a permit, but for general application.

It should also be noted that, under the statutory powers of the city, the provisions of *article 87C* of By-law 405 are admittedly unassailable and, in fact, in no way assailed by appellant. These provisions constitute a part of the subject-matter of the by-law, which the municipal council manifested its intention to enact irrespective of the rest of the subject-matter and hence a part subject to severance if other parts were invalid.

In this situation, assuming that on any ground raised, it should be held that art. 87 of By-law 392 and arts. 87A and B of By-law 405 in no way affect its rights to erect, in district "D", a gasoline filling station, appellant cannot succeed unless it appears that, contrary to what is the case for any landowner in the district, its rights are not subject to the restrictive provisions of *article 87C*.

Appellant's contention must be that, having made the application for a a permit and deposited the plans at a time when its right to use the land for the proposed purpose was in no way affected by a by-law, it had an accrued right which could not be defeated by the subsequent enactment of art. 87C of By-law 405.

The merit of this proposition is, I think, implicitly negatived on the reasoning of the Judicial Committee in *Toronto* v. *Bd. of Trustees of R.C. Separate Schools for Toronto*. While the statutory powers of the City of Toronto differ from those of the respondent city, in that any by-law passed pursuant thereto is restricted in its operation, and while the questions of fact arising in that case are, in some respect, at variance with the admitted facts of this case, the basic principle governing in the matter is the same. What was then said by Viscount Cave L.C. may be stated concisely as follows, for the purpose of this case. The whole object and purpose of a zoning statutory power is to empower the municipal authority to put restrictions, in the general public interest, upon the right which a landowner, unless and until the power is implemented, would otherwise have to erect upon his land such buildings as he thinks proper. Hence the status of landowner cannot *per se* affect the operation of a by-law implementing the statutory power without defeating the statutory power itself. Prior to the passing of such a by-law the proprietary rights of a landowner are then insecure in the sense that they are exposed to any restrictions which the city, acting within its statutory power, may impose.

From this it follows that, while the right to erect includes the right to receive the necessary permit for the erection of the building proposed to be erected in conformity with the law in force for the time being, the latter right is not any more secure than the former to which it is incidental. And if the insecurity attending this incidental right has not yet been removed by the granting of the permit, by the municipal authority acting in good faith, as in the present case, such right cannot become an accrued right effective to defeat a subsequently adopted zoning by-law prohibiting the erection of the proposed building in the area affected.

In these views, I find it unnecessary to pursue the matter further.

I would dismiss the appeal with costs.

HAMMOND *v*. HAMILTON

Ontario. Court of Appeal. [1954] 2 D.L.R. 604

ROACH J.A. delivered the judgment of the court: This is an appeal, by leave granted by Ferguson J., from an order of Aylen J., dated November 20, 1953, adjourning *sine die* an application of the appellants herein for an order that the Building Commissioner of the Corporation of the City of Hamilton issue a building permit for the erection of a gasoline service station on the corner of Warren Ave. and Franklin Rd. in the City of Hamilton.

There are no facts in dispute and they are as follows.

The lands on which the appellants desire to build the gasoline service station consist of Lots 1, 2 and 3 in what is known as Norwood Park Survey. Those lots and other lots were purchased by the appellant Violet Hammond on August 10, 1953. The appellant Frank Hammond has no proprietary interest in any of the lots. He is the son of Violet Hammond and apparently acted for his mother in the purchase of the lots and he is the one who will actually build the service station if the permit is granted. Lots 1, 2 and 3 were purchased for the specific purpose of building a gasoline service station thereon.

The lands as laid out in the Norwood Park Survey were formerly in the Township of Barton and were annexed to the City of Hamilton as of January 1, 1952, by order of the Ontario Municipal Board dated July 28, 1952.

On July 25, 1950, the City of Hamilton passed a zoning by-law, No. 6593, which of course did not affect these lands because these lands on that date were outside the City of Hamilton.

In the spring and summer of 1953 a land-use survey was made and tentative zoning was established by the Planning Board of the City of Hamilton for the annexed area.

A series of four meetings was held on August 4th, 5th, 6th and 7th, 1953, at four different centres for the purpose of informing any persons interested and who might attend of the particulars of the proposed zoning. Notices that those meetings would be held for that purpose were published in the local press.

On September 29, 1953, the City Council adopted the following recommendations of the Board of Control: "That the City Solicitor be instructed to prepare a Draft By-law for the consideration of the Hamilton Planning Board and the City Council designed to preserve existing conditions as to the use of lands and buildings in all areas annexed to the City since the passing of the Zoning By-law in 1950 so as to enable the Hamilton Planning Board to prepare a zoning scheme for the annexed area, and further that the Building Inspector be instructed, pending consideration of such by-law, to refrain from issuing building permits for uses which are or might be inconsistent with the present use of lands and premises in the vicinity of any proposed work."

On September 9, 1953, the appellant Frank Hammond filed with the Building Commissioner of the respondent corporation an application for the building permit in question in this action. With that application the plan of the proposed building was submitted. It is not contended by the respondent corporation that there was anything lacking in the application or plan that would justify the application being refused. The plan was approved by the Fire Department, the Police Department and the Board of Health. It was examined by the plan examiner and found satisfactory and stamped by him.

The applicant was then informed that the building permit would not be issued until a licence to operate a service station on that site had first been approved by the City Council. Apparently there is some rule, or regulation, or by-law, that a building permit shall not issue for any structure the occupancy of which requires a licence until after the application for the licence has been thus approved. Had it not been for that requirement the building permit would have issued prior to September 29th.

The applicant promptly applied through the City Clerk for the requisite licence. He was required to advertise that such an application was pending to enable any resident in the area who desired to object to it to do so. The application came before the Property and Licence Committee of the City Council on October 6, 1953. Only one resident appeared in opposition to the granting of the licence. It developed that his opposition was due to a misunderstanding by him of the nature of the business proposed to be operated and he withdrew his opposition. The Property and Licence Committee approved the application and recommended to the City Council that the licence issue.

The recommendation of the Property and Licence Committee was considered by the council at a meeting held on October 13, 1953, and referred back to the committee.

The licence has not been issued, but only because the granting of the licence would be meaningless and useless unless a building permit were also issued and the Building Inspector has been forbidden by the council to issue that permit,

From the foregoing it is clear that there is presently no restriction as to the use of the proposed site for commercial purposes. All that has been done to date by way of zoning the area is tentative and no final decision has been reached and of course no zoning by-law has been passed.

Ferguson J. in his reasons for granting leave to appeal, correctly described the present situation when he said: "In this case someone in the Planning Board offices of the City of Hamilton has drawn a plan, but that plan serves only as a basis for discussion. It may be that when the discussions have been completed the city will decide to do nothing. In other words, to date no decision of any kind has been arrived at, except a decision to discuss the problem."

Aylen J. in his reasons stated that: "It is not known when the broad plans of the municipality affecting the area will be finalized or what might be the ultimate result. Meanwhile the applicants will be deprived of what appears to be their legal rights." However, he concluded that the application for a *mandamus* should be adjourned *sine die* because the area proposed to be zoned is large and it will take time to study and consider and carefully plan the nature of any restrictions to be applied. To give the respondent corporation the necessary time and prevent any interference with whatever overall scheme might eventually be adopted he adjourned the application *sine die*.

In my most respectful opinion, in the circumstances in this case the learned Judge should have exercised his jurisdiction to decide the matter. The applicants were *prima facie* entitled to the relief they sought and there were no circumstances sufficient to justify the matter being adjourned *sine die*.

It is fundamental that in any well-organized system of jurisprudence the law should be certain and every person subject to that system be able at any time to determine what his legal rights are and be entitled to them. Middleton J. gave effect to that fundamental principle in *Cridland* v. *Toronto* . . .

Since the decision in *Cridland* v. *Toronto* a practice has been developing which unless confined to very definite and limited circumstances threatens to make the Courts the medium through which legal rights may be denied. The practice to which I refer is the practice of adjourning a motion for a mandamus, with the result that when the motion eventually comes on for hearing the applicant finds himself faced with a restrictive by-law which has been enacted in the interim. . . .

[After discussing the *Separate School Board* case Roach J.A. continued]:

. . . In *Re Robertson and Toronto* (1934) the facts were that the applicant was *prima facie* entitled to an order of *mandamus* but it appeared that the City Council was proposing to consider that afternoon—the motion was heard in the morning—a by-law imposing a building restriction which would prevent the granting of the permit. In that circumstance counsel for the City asked the Court to exercise a discretion to delay the giving of judgment or the making of an order until after the council had an opportunity of considering the question. Rose C.J.H.C. there said: "In the present case there is nothing to suggest that the City council is taking sides or is proceeding otherwise than in the ordinary exercise of its function to decide what is right, having regard to the interests of all the inhabitants of the street on the one hand and the interests of the particular landowner on the other, and I think it would be unseemly that, when the matter is so soon in the ordinary course to be considered by the council, the Court should do something which would prevent the exercise by the council of the power that has been entrusted to it."

He therefore adjourned the matter *sine die* rather than to a definite date because the council would not be sitting again until September (that was June 25th) and the City Council would probably that day, i.e., June 25th, adjourn the matter for further consideration. He gave leave to either party to bring the motion on for hearing on two days' notice.

The judgment in *Re Greene and Ottawa* (1952) requires consideration. There the application for the permit was made on June 13, 1951. On June 18, 1951, the City passed the restricting bylaw. The by-law was not enforceable until approved by the Ontario Municipal Board. Application to that Board was pending and was due to come on for hearing on July 10, 1951. On July 5, 1951, an application for a *mandamus* came on for hearing before Ferguson J., and was granted. In the course of his reasons he said: "I am asked to adjourn the motion because it is argued that, even if I grant an order of *mandamus* for the issue of a permit, the applicant will not be able to proceed with his building because so long as his plans are not approved—and I understand they are not as yet approved—his right to proceed with the structure will be affected by whatever by-law is approved by the Board; and the judgment of the Privy Council in [*Toronto* v. *Separate Schools*] seems to support that view. On this point, I express no opinion whatever. I am concerned only with whether or not the Court should stay its hand because the Municipal Board may approve the by-law. The argument is fundamentally unsound. This Court is one of universal jurisdiction. Its function is to enforce the presently existing legal rights of the litigants. No one can challenge its right to do so."

In the *Separate School Board* case when the motion for *mandamus* which had been adjourned by Ferguson J.A. was renewed before Middleton J., the by-law had been passed and an application for its approval was pending before the Ontario Railway and Municipal Board. Middleton J. refused to grant the order then. He appears to have made a sort of interim order. What he did is fully set out in the judgment of the Court of Appeal. In effect he held that the final order on the motion for mandamus should await the decision of the Ontario Railway and Municipal Board. If by that decision the by-law should be approved, then the motion before him was to stand dismissed with certain rights reserved to the Separate School Board.

It would seem, from what Ferguson J. stated in that part of his reasons which I have quoted, that had he been presiding when the application in the *Separate School* case came before Ferguson J.A. or when the application in the *Robertson* case came before Rose C.J.H.C. he would not have adjourned the applications as they did.

Decisions by single Judges in a number of other cases were referred to us in argument. In some the Court in the exercise of its discretion adjourned the application: in others it refused to do so. The facts in those cases were not always the same.

The case that comes nearest to the one at bar is *Re Marckity and Fort Erie and Berger*. In that case Spence J. adjourned the application *sine die*. There was no by-law in that case, but a zoning plan under the provisions of the *Planning Act*, R.S.O. 1950, c. 277, had been presented to the Municipal Corporation by the Planning Board and it had been adopted. The facts in the case at bar, without again stating them, are quite different. . . .

In my opinion, the Judge before whom an application is made for a *mandamus* such as was sought by the appellants unquestionably has a discretion to adjourn the application but, as Kerwin J. said in *Re Metro Oil Ltd. & Toronto*, it is "one that should be rarely exercised."

Under what circumstances should it be exercised?

With the utmost respect for those Judges who have previously held otherwise, in my opinion unless the council of the municipality prior to the motion for *mandamus* coming on for hearing before the Judge has clearly made a decision to restrict the land against the type of building described in the application for the permit and the plans submitted therewith, the motion should not be adjourned merely to enable the council to do so.

That decision is usually expressed in a formal by-law duly enacted. If the by-law by its terms imposes the restriction as of the date it was passed and the council is proceeding or has proceeded in good faith and with all reasonable dispatch to have it approved by the Municipal Board then it would be proper to adjourn the motion pending the decision of that Board. In that circumstance the council would have done all it could possibly do.

There may be rare cases in which the council has made the decision but has not actually enacted the by-law. The *Marckity* case is an illustration. A Municipal Council cannot act as swiftly as an individual. Formalities have to be complied with and instructions have to be given to the corporation solicitor who in turn must prepare the by-law. Unavoidable delays in enacting the by-law may occur. If the decision, though not expressed by by-law, is clear and if it appears that the council has proceeded or is proceeding to implement its decision by a by-law with reasonable promptitude having regard to all the circumstances the motion might well be adjourned.

Whether the decision has been expressed by by-law or otherwise it must in all cases be manifested that in making that decision the council has acted in good faith and has taken an unbiased and objective view of the situation and has not taken sides or proceeded otherwise than in the ordinary exercise of its function to decide what is right having regard to the interests of all the inhabitants in the area on the one hand and the interest of the particular landowner on the other. Unless all those conditions clearly appear the motion should not be adjourned.

In the case at bar no such decision had been made by the municipality and in my respectful opinion the applicants were entitled to the order of *mandamus* which they sought. It may be that, as a matter of strict technical procedure, the Building Commissioner of the City of Hamilton should be added as a party, and counsel for the appellants asked that he should be so added. I would add him as a party and order that the corporation should direct him to issue the building permit and that he do so. The Building Commissioner should not have costs awarded against him. In refusing the permit he was acting on instructions from the City Council. The appellants should, however, have their costs on the application to Aylen J. and on this appeal against the respondent corporation.

RE UPPER CANADA ESTATES & MacNICOL. [1931] 4 D.L.R. 459 (Ontario. Supreme Court). Orde J. A.: "If the making of the application and the deposit of the plans are sufficient to give the applicants an unassailable right to the issue of a permit, then the conclusions of the Judicial Committee [in the *Separate School Board* case] are unintelligible. I think it is plain from that judgment that the statutory power conferred upon the council of the municipality to pass a by-law regulating the character of buildings in any defined area in the interest of the public at large is intended to be paramount to the *primâ facie* rights of the individual, and that the question of their respective rights does not fall to be dealt with as of the date of the application and deposit of plans but as of the date when the question comes before the Court for its adjudication.

"The race would seem to be to the swift in these matters, and the goal is not reached merely when the application for the permit is made, or even when the proceedings for a mandamus are launched, but only when the matter comes to be dealt with by the Court."

RE UCCI AND CITY OF TORONTO. [1955] 4 D.L.R. 700 (Ontario. High Court). Smily J.: "It is with the latter part of [s. 390 (6)] that we are now concerned, that is, whether prior to the day of the passing of the by-law the plans had been approved by the municipal architect or building inspector. There have been affidavits filed and cross-examinations on some of the affidavits for the purpose, on the part of the applicants, of establishing that the plans had been approved within the meaning of s-s. (6) prior to the passing of the by-laws in question, and on the part of the City to the effect that the plans had not been approved. The problem is not a simple one, as I view it. It is a question whether the plans have been approved or were approved by the municipal architect or building inspector at the time of the passing of these by-laws.

"There is evidence in the affidavits that the plans had been filed, there is no dispute about that really, and also that they had been considered by members of the staff of the Commissioner of Buildings (possibly they may be described as plan-examiners), and it is contended on behalf of the applicants that members of the staff (one in particular is referred to with respect to each building) indicated that the plans were satisfactory and that a permit would be issued within a few days. Now it might be suggested that until the permit has been issued, it has not been established that the plans have been approved. However, while the issuing of a permit might be good evidence that the plans had been approved, I do not think the fact that the permit was not issued necessarily means that the plans have not been approved.

"On the other hand, I do not think I can assume that the apparent satisfying of the plan-examiner constitutes approval by the Commissioner, for I suppose he does take the place of the man referred to as 'the municipal architect or building inspector' within the meaning of s-s. (6)—at any rate the argument has proceeded on the assumption that the Commissioner of Buildings is the man referred to in that subsection, unless it can be said that the applicants' argument is that the description would apply to a member of the staff who has examined the plans. However, I do not think that that is the case. It might, of course, be different if the plans had been found to be satisfactory by a member of the staff and there were bad faith on the part of the Commissioner of Buildings in not approving of the plans in the regular course of affairs. I do not think that there has been any bad faith shown in that regard here.

"Some question came up as to whether the plans as originally filed, and upon which certain amendments were made, should be considered as sufficient, provided that those plans as amended were satisfactory to the examiners, and whether the filing of revised plans later incorporating the amendments was simply putting on the files a clean set of plans for the convenience of the Department I think it might very well be that approval of the plans would not be considered by the City Architect or building commissioner until revised plans had been filed, or indeed the plans might not be submitted to him for approval by the plan-examiner who had the matter in hand, and it may be that approval by the City Commissioner is more or less contemporaneous with the issue of the permit.

"However that may be, I think there must be approval by the building commissioner or someone whom he has designated to do that. Whether he has the power to delegate this authority need not be considered here, because there is no evidence that he has, so that I would be inclined to be of the view that there should be evidence of approval by the Commissioner of Buildings himself, but I do not know that the applicants are really contending otherwise, possibly they are, but if they are not, then they are contending that that, i.e., approval by the Commissioner, must be assumed from the statements which were made through various persons as indicated in the affidavits filed. I do not think that that is sufficient; in other words, I do not think the statement by the examiner that the plans seem to be satisfactory constitutes an approval. For instance, quoting the statement in the affidavit of one of the applicants where it is said that after changes had been initialled by a draftsman employed by the architect and the plans as amended were again submitted to the Commissioner of Buildings, the person examining the plans said or advised this representative of the applicants that the necessary signatures would then be endorsed on the plans and that the required permit would be issued within the course of a few days, that is not necessarily an approval by the Commissioner. In fact it would almost imply that, at that time at any rate, there was no approval, but that later, in the expectation of this examiner, the approval would be given. That I do not think is enough; I do not think that is the approval required in s-s. (6), nor, in my opinion, is the fact that examination of the plans or amendments or revised plans could be completed by an examiner in a short space of time (reference was made to the admission by the Commissioner that if the plans were examined at that time, the examination could be completed in half a day by an examiner if he devoted all his time to it) sufficient to remove the proposed buildings from the application of the by-laws. I do not think that that indicates that the plans had been approved or that they were in such a position that the approval should be given and failure to give approval would indicate bad faith. Possibly the applicants are not suggesting that there would be bad faith in that circumstance. I might say, so far as the requirement for quantities of building materials is concerned, that I do not think this is important. I think the plans could be approved without having that information, but I do not think that substantial compliance with the requirements of the plan-examiners or the Department of the City is sufficient."

REGINA *v.* TORONTO, EX PARTE 94 CRESCENT ROAD LTD.

Ontario. High Court. [1961] O.W.N. 129

The applicant company erected an apartment house at 94 Crescent Road in the Rosedale area of Toronto in 1955 and it later acquired adjoining property on which it proposed to erect a second apartment house. It applied for a building permit on June 30, 1960. The plans submitted did not conform with the building by-law and the applicant was notified of the defects on July 11, 1960. On December 2 the applicant completed amending and corrective material, but no written specifications were furnished. Meanwhile, on November 7, 1960, the city council had passed By-law 21,101 which would prohibit the proposed apartment. The Municipal Board hearing was scheduled for March 13, 1961. This was an application for an order in the nature of mandamus.

THOMPSON J: . . . From the material before me, I am satisfied that few applications for building permits are full and complete when filed. The evidence further discloses that such applications are processed by the city officials in two stages. First examination is made to determine whether or not the proposed structure will conform to the zoning by-law. If it does, then further examination is made to determine whether or not there is a compliance with the building by-law. Changes and additions are sometimes required and a reasonable opportunity given for strict compliance. Despite by-law 9868, requiring the submission of specifications with the application, it appears that sometimes they are not asked for in practice until the second stage of processing.

In the instant case, apart from the requirements of the by-law, specifications were not demanded, as the application had been processed only through the first stage, when it was then refused allegedly owing to the passing of by-law 21,101. The evidence satisfies me, however, that the application did meet the requirements of the existing zoning by-law 20,623, but not until 5th December.

The applicant was notified by letter of the refusal of the permit 14th December and the reason then given was the passing of by-law 21,101, prohibiting the erection and use of buildings for apartment house purposes in Rosedale.

The applicant was aware of the passing of this by-law as early as 2nd December and on that date made formal demand for the issue of the building permit.

The applicant subsequently requested that the buildings committee reconsider its application for a permit. Accordingly the applicants' solicitor attended a meeting of the committee 18th January 1961, and made certain representations on its behalf. The meeting was adjourned ostensibly for the purpose of consulting the ratepayers in the area concerned and the evidence does not disclose further consideration of the applicant's request. This motion was launched 3rd February 1961.

The respondents now take the position that, by reason of the failure of the applicant to file and submit specifications, it is impossible to approve of the applicant's plans and so to determine that the application for permit conforms to the building by-law. Such position is verified by the affidavit of Milne, the director of building regulations. They further take the position that the applicant has not complied with by-law 9868 in that it has failed to furnish a certificate showing the quantity of cement, brick, stone and plaster to be used. They further object to the vehicle parking facilities proposed. In this latter objection there is no substance. The requirement as to the certificate relating to materials is not of major importance and were I disposed to grant the order sought, I would now permit such certificate to be deposited pursuant to the undertaking of the applicant now given by counsel.

The failure of the applicant to furnish and file specifications is, however, in my view fatal to its success upon this motion. . . .

It is not without some constraint that I conclude that I must refuse this application. The fatal objection has been taken for the first time since the commencement of these proceedings. The reason heretofore given for refusing the permit was the passing of by-law 21,101. It may well be that that was the real reason, or at least the underlying reason for such refusal. Although the applicant was not as diligent as it might have been in pursuing its application, it appears to me that it has been lulled into a sense of false security by the conduct of the respondents.

It becomes perhaps unncessary, in the light of the view I have taken to deal with the application of the city to adjourn. However, as much importance was attached by counsel to this aspect of the motion during the course of the argument, I feel it only fair that I should make some comment upon it.

The principles to be considered in dealing with such an application were fully and carefully dealt with by Roach, J.A., in *Hammond* v. *Hamilton* (1954). Were I now called upon to exercise my discretion having due regard to those principles, although it may now be of small comfort to the applicant, I may say that I would unhesitatingly refuse the adjournment.

The evidence discloses that the city planning board had made a planning appraisal of the Rosedale district and published a report in March 1960, followed by a supplementary report in June 1960, respecting future zoning.

These reports recommended the prohibition of the use of land and the erection and use of buildings for apartment house purposes in large areas of the district. There were, however, certain exceptions recommended. The reports were considered by the buildings committee. Representations were made to the committee in the summer of 1960 on behalf of the S. Rosedale ratepayers' association which was opposed to apartment use and construction throughout the whole area.

A by-law to implement the appraisal reports, and to give effect to them, upon the recommendation of the committee, is now in the stage of preparation and when completed is to be considered by the committee. In the meantime by-law 21,101 was passed on 7th November. I have no hesitation in concluding that by-law 21,101 was enacted as an interim measure and as a stop-gap to satisfy the demands of a group of individuals known as the ratepayers' association, until such time as the recommended by-law is ready. I find it difficult to escape the conclusion that it was aimed at the applicant's lands as its application for permit was the only pending application in the area at the time of its enactment.

The material before me further indicates that there are other residents in the area who are not opposed to apartment use.

In the result, however, for the reasons indicated, the motion will be dismissed, but, under the circumstances, without costs.

RE DAWNBURT AND LONDON. [1961] O.W.N. 239 (Ontario. High Court). An application for mandamus to compel the building inspector to issue a permit to erect two "apartment units" on unzoned land in the city. The land had originally been a part of Westminster Township and the city had annexed the area. The Council by resolution had instructed the building inspector not to issue building permits without the approval of Council pending preparation of a zoning by-law by the planning board. The application was recommended by the public works committee on April 10, 1961. On April 17 the Council refused to adopt the recommendation. This application was commenced on April 21, the notice being returnable on May 5. After the application was commenced it was discovered that plans and specifications had not been properly filed. A complete formal application for a permit was made on April 28. On May 5, on the return the counsel for the city of London asked for and got an adjournment until May 19. KING J.: "It appears that this motion was launched before the plans and specifications had been properly filed. However, it would seem that the committee considering the matter had knowledge of the plans and specifications and at all events they were filed prior to the return of the motion, 5th May 1961, on which date an adjournment was granted at the request of the municipality. I am of the opinion the within motion should be dealt with and that it is not necessary for the applicant to launch a new motion. This is not a proper case for granting an adjournment to the municipality to enable a by-law to be passed and approved because no decision has been arrived at even tentatively as to what type of buildings will be permitted to be built on the lands in question. There is merely a resolution of council preventing any building whatever, presumably until council decides what it should do, if anything, restricting buildings on lands such as those in question. The applicant has a *prima facie* right to have its plans and specifications approved and to be issued a permit, subject however to meeting any reasonable requirements of the city architect as far as footings are concerned. The applicant having started proceedings before filing plans and specifications there will be no order as to costs."

4. NOTICE OF ZONING BY-LAWS

Because part of the evil of retroactivity arises from the fact that to the best of his knowledge the subsequent evildoer was acting innocently at the time when he committed the subsequently illegal act, it is helpful to consider at this point the publicity given to wholly prospectively operating by-laws. If a by-law is not known and cannot be known by reasonable inquiry on the part of the citizen then he is in much the same position as if the by-law were retroactively enacted. Municipal by-laws are notoriously difficult to procure and the suggestion is sometimes made that they should be registered in land registry offices.

TRAFALGAR TOWNSHIP *v.* HAMILTON. [1954] 1 D.L.R. 740 (Ontario. Court of Appeal). A by-law limited certain land to residential uses. The respondent Hamilton purchased property subject to the by-law but she only learned of the by-law later after she had registered her deed. She proposed to use her property as a tourist home, a prohibited use. The *Registry Act*, now R.S.O., 1960, c. 348, by section 76(1), renders void as against subsequent instruments every "instrument affecting the land" unless registered. The respondent successfully contended that the by-law, which was not registered, was an "instrument affecting land". Hogg J.A.: "The language of both ss. 1(d) and 74(1) of the *Registry Act* does not make reference to the title to land being affected. The language of these sections of the statute is confined to an instrument "affecting" the land itself. Land may be affected otherwise than with respect to title alone. In my view, land may be seriously affected, as for instance, in its market value, when its use is restricted.

"It is true that the by-law in question does not create an interest in land, either legal or equitable. . . . It is difficult to conceive how a by-law could affect land to any greater extent than by restricting its use by its owner, unless in the case where the by-law expropriates the land, thereby taking not only the use but the title itself from the owner."

NOTE. As a direct result of the *Trafalgar* case the Ontario Legislature passed c. 83 of the 1954 statutes, amending *The Registry Act*. Section 11 provides:

11 (1) Notwithstanding anything in *The Registry Act*, where a by-law has been passed before the 19th day of March, 1954, under section 390 of *The Municipal Act* or a predecessor of that section and land to which *The Registry Act* and the by-law applies, or a building or structure thereon, was being used on that day, for a purpose prohibited by the by-law, by a person who purchased the land for valuable consideration without actual notice of the by-law, the by-law does not apply to the land, building or structure so long as it continues to be used for that purpose.

(2) Subsection 1 applies only where the purchaser purchased the land,

(a) after the passing of the by-law;

(b) before the 19th day of March, 1954; and
(c) before the registration, if any, of the by-law under *The Registry Act.*

(3) Subsection 1 does not apply where the land, or a building or structure thereon, was being used, on the 19th day of March, 1954, for a purpose prohibited by the by-law, by virtue of regulation 45 of Ontario Regulations 98/52 or by virtue of a by-law passed under *The Rent Control Act, 1953.*

What is a "predecessor" of s. 390? Is s. 541a of *The Consolidated Municipal Act, 1903* a predecessor?

At the same time, by c. 56, s. 11 *The Municipal Act* was amended by the addition of s. 234 (1a), which provides:

(1a) The clerk shall keep an index book in which he shall enter the number and date of,

(a) every subsisting by-law heretofore passed under section 390 or a predecessor of that section;
(b) every by-law hereafter passed under section 390;
(c) every other subsisting by-law, and every other by-law hereafter passed, that affects land but does not directly affect the title to land.

On the operation of these amendments, see *Regina ex. rel. Courneyea* v. *Girvin* (1956) and *Regina ex. rel. Courneyea* v. *Waters* (1957). If a purchaser of land protected by the provision retains a solicitor to search title and the solicitor does not check for by-laws with the municipal clerk, should his knowledge of the by-law be presumed? And imputed to the purchaser?

The 1954 amendments are not universally regarded as satisfactory and some pressure is being exerted to require that by-laws be deposited in registry offices without necessarily being registered against each property. How would you devise such a scheme?

CHAPTER 10

LAND USE AND BULK CONTROLS

The poor are being zoned into the Atlantic Ocean.
HUGH POMEROY

This chapter attempts to present some typical provisions of zoning by-laws and to raise some of the substantive problems of zoning. While these questions are not "legal" in the traditional sense, they are constantly explored by courts in the United States in a constitutional context, and in Canada by provincial zoning supervisory bodies. The next chapter is concerned with the more traditionally legal questions, usually procedural, of the validity of the by-law.

Zoning by-laws usually do two things. They limit land uses in particular areas or zones and they regulate the permitted uses. The first may be called land use segregation and the second bulk control, since the size and shape of buildings and their location on the land are the usual matters controlled. The word "bulk" seems to be a fairly good word to catch them all. The two sections of this chapter follow this division, but you may find it impossible to consider a problem of use limitation without considering the regulation of that use. You have already experienced this difficulty in the prohibition and regulation of non-conforming uses.

The really fundamental question raised by the materials in this chapter is this: Can zoning and its accompanying regulation be simplified? A distinguished planner once told the editor that all he wanted to control was land use and density. He was an "architect-type" planner and he wanted his fellow architects to be free to design aesthetically attractive buildings and streets. How can density be controlled? Should architects be so freed from state restriction?

1. LAND USE SEGREGATION

CITY OF TORONTO ZONING BY-LAW NO. 18,642 (1952)

3. (1) For the purpose of this by-law and of the maps contained in appendix "A" hereto annexed, herein referred to as "District Maps," the following classes of use district and volume area are hereby established, namely:

Parks District	G
Residential Districts	
— 1st density	R. 1
— 1st density (modified)	R. 1A
— 2nd density	R. 2
— 3rd density	R. 3
— 4th density	R. 4
— 4th density (modified)	R. 4A
Commercial District	C. 1
Industrial Districts	C. 2, C. 3, C. 4
Volume Areas	V. 1, V. 2, V. 3, V. 4

5. (1) No person shall, within any G district, use any lot or erect or use any building or structure for any purpose except one or more of the following G uses, namely:

(a) a public park, including therein one or more athletic fields, field houses, community centres, bleachers, open or closed swimming and wading pools, green houses, botanical gardens, zoological gardens, band stands, skating rinks, tennis courts, bowling greens, boat liveries, bathing stations and refreshment rooms;

(b) a public playground;

(c) a playlot;

(d) a golf course;

(e) any use which is accessory to any of the foregoing uses.

6. (1) No person shall, within any R. 1 district, use any lot or erect or use any building or structure for any purpose except a G purpose or one or more of the following R. 1 uses, namely:

(a) a private detached dwelling house, including the keeping therein of not more than two roomers or boarders;

(b) the office of a physician or dentist, located in the basement or on the first floor of the private detached dwelling house which such physician or dentist regularly uses as his private residence;

(c) a converted dwelling house provided (1) the building by reason of its age and size has become obsolete, unsuitable and unmarketable for single family use, (2) each dwelling unit therein has a floor space of not less than six hundred (600) square feet except in the case of an attic where the permissible floor area per dwelling unit shall not be less than four hundred and fifty (450) square feet, and (3) no exterior addition to or major exterior alteration of any such dwelling house proposed to be so converted is made and the external appearance and general character of the building as a private detached dwelling house is not materially altered;

(d) a municipal community centre, including any appropriate bulletin board;

(dd) a church, provided it is originally constructed for the purpose;

(e) a municipal water reservoir;

(f) a drinking water fountain;

(g) an ornamental structure;

(h) any use which is accessory to any of the foregoing uses including a private garage.

7. (1) No person shall, within any R. 1A district, use any lot, or erect or use any building or structure for any purpose except for any G or R. 1 use or one or more of the following R. 1A uses, namely:

(a) a duplex dwelling house, a double duplex dwelling house or an apartment house designed by an architect and the exterior thereof constructed of burnt brick or natural stone;

(b) a neighbourhood garage;

(c) any use which is accessory to any of the foregoing uses.

8. (1) No person shall, within any R. 2 district, use any lot or erect or use any building or structure for any purpose except for any G, R. 1A use or one or more of the following R. 2 uses, namely:

(a) a one-family dwelling house; a semi-detached dwelling house; a duplex dwelling house; a double duplex dwelling house; a triple dwelling house; a converted dwelling house; group housing;

(b) the keeping of not more than three roomers or boarders in any of the foregoing classes of dwelling accommodation, except in the case of a one-family dwelling house where the family consists of a group of not more than five unrelated persons;

(bb) the letting of a flat in a private detached dwelling house, a one-family dwelling house or a semi-detached dwelling house to a family of two or more persons who are interrelated by bonds of consanguinity, marriage or legal adoption;

(c) the office of a physician or dentist, located in the basement or on the first floor of any of the foregoing classes of dwelling accommodation which such physician or dentist regularly uses as his private residence;

(d) a public school, a day nursery, a nursery school, a church, Bible Institute, Christian Science reading room or religious library or a private academic, religious or philanthropic school, provided that any building used for any purpose mentioned in this paragraph is or was originally constructed for such purpose and has a side yard of at least ten (10) feet;

(e) a parking station;

(f) any use which is accessory to any of the foregoing R. 2 uses.

9. (1) No person shall, within any R. 3 district, use any lot or erect or use any building or structure for any purpose except for any G, R. 1, R. 1A or R. 2 use or one or more of the following R. 3 uses, namely:

(a) a community centre; a student fraternity or sorority house; a boarding or lodging house;

(b) any use which is accessory to any of the foregoing uses.

10. (1) No person shall, within any R. 4 district, use any lot, or erect or use any building or structure for any purpose except for any G, R. 1, R. 2 or R. 3 use or one or more of the following R. 4 uses, namely:

(a) an apartment house; a private hotel; the office of a physician, dentist, osteopath or chiropractor in the portion of an apartment house or private hotel used by him as his regular place of residence if such portion of the building is located in the basement or on the first floor thereof; a public school, a day nursery, a nursery school; a private academic, religious or philanthropic school; a church, Bible Institute, Christian Science reading room or religious library; a branch of the Conservatory of Music; a military academy; a private hospital, public hospital, or psychiatric hospital; a home for the aged; a public or private home for the blind; a maternity boarding house; a children's home; a children's shelter; a boys' home, girls' home, orphanage or infants' home; a monastery, a nunnery or religious retreat; a private club; a public library, public museum, public art gallery or an observatory; a bathing station; Salvation Army, Y.M.C.A., Y.W.C.A., Y.M.H.A., Y.W.H.A.;

(b) any use which is accessory to any of the foregoing uses.

11. (1) No person shall, within any R. 4A district, use any lot or erect or use any building or structure for any purpose except for any G, R. 1, R. 2, R. 3 or R. 4 use or one or more of the following R. 4A uses, namely:

(a) the office of a professional person or persons such as a physician, barrister, engineer, architect, Ontario Land Surveyor; the administrative office of a non-profit organization of a religious, educational, recreational, fraternal or philanthropic nature; a business administrative office; an office building for the accommodation of any foregoing office or offices.

12. (1) No person shall, within any C. 1 district, use any lot or erect or use any building or structure for any purpose except any G or R use or one or more of the following C. 1 uses, namely:

(a) *Public*: a defence project, a police station, a fire hall, a government office, municipal baths and swimming pool; public commercial scales;

(b) *Residential*: an hotel, an apartment-hotel, one or more dwelling units in the upper portion of a C. 1 building;

(c) *Recreational*: a place of amusement, commercial baths and swimming pool, a commercial club, an athletic field other than in a public park, a tavern or public house;

(d) *Stores,* etc.: a retail store, a sample or showroom, a delicatessen shop, a box lunch shop, a caterer's shop, a bake-shop, an eating establishment, an auctioneer's premises, a commercial lending library, a pawnbroker's shop, a photographer's shop, a second-hand shop, a tailor's shop, a pet shop, a sales or hire garage;

(e) *Workshops*: a dressmaker's shop, a motor vehicle repair shop, class "A", a locksmith's or gunsmith's shop, a shoe repair shop, a taxidermist's shop, an upholsterer's shop, a laboratory, class "A", a custom workshop, a private commercial garage;

(f) *Offices, Studios, etc.*: a business office; an office building, a film exchange, an artist's or photographer's studio, a motion picture studio, a commercial school, a clinic, an undertaker's establishment:

(g) *Service Shops, etc*: a service and repair shop, a barber's shop, a ladies' hairdressing establishment, a massage parlour, a dry cleaner's distributing station, a spotting and stain removing shop, a dry cleaning shop, a hand laundry, a shoe shine shop, an automobile service station, a parking lot, a parking station, a taxi cab stand or station, a car washing establishment, a cold storage locker plant, an animal hospital, a duplicating shop, and a printing plant in which not more than ten (10) persons are employed;

(h) *Signs*: a wall sign, window sign, roof-sign, projecting sign, ground sign, a banner sign or other sign, notice or advertising device, except any sign, notice or advertising device, externally displayed or visible from the exterior of any building, respecting or apparently respecting such matters as fortune telling, palmistry or phrenology;

(i) *Miscellaneous*: an air port, an air field, private commercial scales, market gardening;

(j) any use that is accessory to any of the foregoing uses.

13. (1) No person shall, within any C. 2 district, use any lot or erect or use any building or structure for any purpose except for any G or C. 1 use or one or more of the following C. 2 uses, namely:

(a) *Public*: a waterworks plant, a pumping station, a city yard;

(b) *Transportation and Distribution*: a railway, including service and repair yards, a railway station, a bus station, a milk or bread distributing depot, a motor vehicle repair shop, class "B", a commercial stable;

(c) *Sales Outlets*: an open air market; a builders' supply yard, class A; bulk cement storage, batching and mixing of concrete; a lumber yard, a retail coal, coke and wood yard; a retail fuel oil yard provided the fuel oil is stored in underground tanks;

(d) *Workshops, etc.*: a blacksmith's shop, a tinsmith's shop, a bookbinder's shop, a carpenter's shop, a commercial welder's shop, a dry-cleaning establishment, a machine laundry, a contractor's yard or shop, class "A" (provided there is no storage of bulk cement), a workshop or equipment yard of a decorator, interior decorator, display designer or sign erector;

(e) *Storage*: a storage warehouse, class "A", a cold storage plant, including the processing of frozen foods, a natural ice plant;

(f) *Manufacturing*:

(i) an artificial ice plant, a dairy products plant, a wholesale dyeing plant, a printing plant, a bakery, a soft drink bottling works, a brewery, a tobacco factory, a canning factory (fruits and vegetables), a fur goods factory, a pickle factory without curing or storage vats on the premises, a miscellaneous vegetable food products factory, class "A", a prepared horn or bone products factory, a textile factory, a sheet mica factory, an inoffensive gas plant;

(ii) a paper products factory, a wood products factory, a small metal wares factory, an ink factory, a plastic products factory, a miscellaneous industry factory, provided that, in the conduct of any of the classes of factory named in this clause, (1) there is no hammering, stamping, grinding, sawing, drilling or planing or other operation by any means other than manual or electric motor; (2) all heat-processing is powered only by gas, oil or electricity; and (3) no gas or electricity is generated on the factory premises; and provided further, in the case of a plastic products factory, that all fabrication is of previously prepared material.

(iii) packing or packaging any goods, wares, or merchandise, substances, articles or things mentioned in clauses (i) or (ii);

(g) any use which is accessory to any of the foregoing uses.

14. (1) No person shall, within any C. 3 district, use any lot or erect or use any building or structure for any purpose except for any G, C. 1 or C. 2 use or one or more of the following C. 3 uses, namely:

(a) *Public*: public harbour works, including public wharves, lighthouses and beacons;

(aa) *Sales Outlets*: a builders' supply yard, class B;

(b) *Storage*: a contractor's yard, class "B", a grain elevator;

(c) *Manufacturing*:

(i) a pattern shop, a flour or feed mill, a saw mill, a planing mill, a rag mill, a distillery, a winery, a vegetable oils plant, a pea-straw ensilage plant, a candy factory, a pickle factory having curing or storage vats on the premises, a sauerkraut factory, a vinegar factory, a meat products factory, a fish packing plant, a leather goods factory, a wood products factory, a paper products factory, a small metal wares factory, a plastic products factory, a miscellaneous vegetable products factory, a miscellaneous vegetable food products factory, class "B", a miscellaneous industry factory, a pharmaceutical factory, an animal food factory, a non-dangerous or non-offensive metal products factory, a general chemical products factory, a non-dangerous or non-offensive miscellaneous non-metallic minerals factory;

(ii) a ceramics factory if wholly enclosed, and having all heat-processing powered only by gas, oil or electricity and having no gas or electricity generated on the factory premises;

(iii) packing or packaging any goods, wares, merchandise substances, articles or things mentioned in clauses (i) or (ii);

(d) *Miscellaneous*: a cartage, express or truck transport yard or terminal for one or more highway transportation companies or organizations, a shipping, trans-shipping or distributing depot;

(e) any use which is accessory to any of the foregoing uses.

15. (1) No person shall, within any C. 4 district, use any lot or erect or use any building or structure for any purpose except for any C. 1, C. 2 or C. 3 use or one or more of the following C. 4 uses, namely:

(a) *Public*: a sewage disposal plant, a public incinerator or refuse destructor, a garbage dump;

(b) *Storage*: a storage warehouse, class "B", a fuel storage tank, a wholesale fuel supply yard, a salvage yard or shop;

(c) *Manufacturing*: a tannery, a pulp mill, a paper mill, a metal products factory, a primary metals plant, a distillation plant, an animal by-products plant, a wool carbonizing plant, an artificial abrasives plant, a general gas plant, an offensive gas plant, a dangerous gas plant, a ceramics factory, a miscellaneous non-metallic minerals plant, an offensive chemical products factory, a dangerous chemical products factory;

(d) *Miscellaneous*: a slaughter-house, a stock yard, a laboratory, class "B", a pit or quarry, a poultry-killing establishment;

(e) any use that is not permitted in any other class of district but which may be lawfully established in the City of Toronto;

(f) any use which is accessory to any of the foregoing uses.

[Extensive regulatory provisions contained in subsections of the sections reproduced have been omitted. Many of the land uses described here are defined in an interpretation section containing 134 definitions. The provisions are reproduced from the Fifth Revision in the Office Consolidation of 1957.]

THE BUILDING AND ZONING BY-LAW
Nova Scotia. Halifax County. 1958

3. For the purpose of this By-law the following classes of Zones are hereby established, namely:

G.	General Building Area
R. D.	Designed Residential Area
R.	General Residential Area
I.	Industrial Area

6. (1) No person shall erect, alter or repair any building or cause the same to be done in the General Building Area without first obtaining a written Permit therefor from the Inspector.

13. (1) No permit shall be issued where the proposed building, alteration or repair:

(a) does not conform to the requirements of this By-law, the Acts or Regulations respecting protection against fire, or the By-laws of the Municipality;

(b) would be detrimental to the health of the occupants or of the public;

(c) would result in a fire-hazard to the occupants or of the neighbouring buildings;

(d) would neither conform to nor improve the general appearance of the locality;

(e) would occasion a nuisance to the owners or occupants of premises in the vicinity;

(f) would not provide adequate off street parking;

(2) The Inspector may refuse to issue a permit to erect or alter a building so that it may be used as a shop, tavern, restaurant, factory, overnight cabin, motel, apartment house, or for any other industrial or commercial purpose, until he has been furnished with the consent in writing of the majority of the property owners within 1,000 feet of the land or premises.

24. *Zone (RD) Designated Residential Area.*

All provisions of Zone G shall apply to this area with the exception that only houses having the appearance of single family dwellings, schools, churches, community centres and public works buildings shall be allowed. No basement apartments shall be allowed. No commercial or industrial buildings shall be built. This area shall be set up by Council by By-law and

Section 4 amended only on the written application of 75% of the property owners in the area who shall own 75% of the land and on the recommendations of the Halifax County Planning Board. No permit shall be issued for this area until the plans of the building have been approved by the Halifax County Planning Board.

25. *Zone (R) General Residential Area.*

All provisions of Parts II, III, and Appendix "A" shall apply to this area with the exception that single or multiple family dwellings, schools, churches, fire halls, community centres or public works buildings shall be allowed. No commercial or industrial buildings shall be built. This area shall be set up by Council by By-law only on the recommendation of the Halifax County Planning Board.

26. *Zone (I) Industrial or Commercial Use only.*

No building shall be erected in this zone unless it is for industrial or commercial purposes or a fire hall or community centre or a public works building except that where an industry wishes to build houses for its employees such housing may be erected subject to approval of the Council. This area shall be set up by Council by By-law only on the recommendations of the Halifax County Planning Board.

QUESTIONS. The blending of a building and zoning by-law is unusual in Canada. Is it a good idea? What purposes are served by a building by-law? A zoning by-law? Do they mix well? Can they be completely separated?

NOTE ON ZONING OF LAND USE. Zoning and Classification. It is one thing to understand (if that is possible) the classification of land uses in a zoning by-law. But without a zoning map before you, the effect of the classification is at best only half understood. The location of the zone in relation to other zones, the size of the zone and the ease with which the zone may be changed, wholly or partly, vary constantly, and constitute the "dynamics" of zoning. If a small industrial zone, of, say, 12,000 square feet, or about the size of two or three city residential lots, is established in the centre of a residential zone, only a lawyer would say that the residential zone excluded industry. Even the lawyer would admit that the residential *area* included an industry. Yet it is easy to imagine cases where if not an industrial, a commercial use of land might well be so established, as, for example, in cases where service stations are dropped into a residential area.

Competition for Land Use. Industrial land, or land reasonably suitable for economic industrial use, is not just anywhere in a municipality where people do not want to live. Access to road, rail, water and perhaps air transport may be vital, a water supply and a good sewer system are usually necessary, and a labour supply and a market are also convenient unless the industrial process is highly automatic and the product very cheap to transport to a distant market. Because people rarely nowadays want to live within sight of their place of work, or anyone's place of work, it is fashionable to segregate working places from living places. In some communities this segregation may amount to a complete exclusion of working places. See, for example, Forest Hill Village near (next to) Toronto. Something like 90% of the land assessment is residential, 10% commercial or industrial, and there is not much industrial. (For a social study of Forest Hill Village (under a pseudonym) see Seeley, Sim and Loosley, *Crestwood Heights* (1956)).

Is a municipality entitled to zone industry out altogether? Could this be proper in some municipalities and not in others? Has an industrialist a "right" to land where he wants it?

Usually the shoe is on the other foot. The municipality will probably show more industrial land than it needs (or has, in some cases, bearing in mind what makes land useful for industry) because it requires more industry for its economic health.

The Highest and Best Use of Land. Land uses are sometimes classified according to a value scale. Thus, for many years, residential use was considered the "highest" or "best" use of land, and within that use class, the sparsest development was the "highest" or "best" residential use. So you find R1, R2, R3 zones, representing zones increasing in density of use. Socially R1 is the "highest" or "best" class. It even creeps into the "social" consciousness of the inhabitant, who might feel insulted if his land were rezoned from R2 to R3. Somehow a person living in an R2 zone is "better" than a person living in R3. This pathetic spectacle of public ignorance and snobbery is a very real political factor in remedying the gross errors of original zoning, or sin, as the case may be.

Land uses are also sometimes referred to as more or less "compatible", and residential uses are always, fashionably, thought to be "incompatible" with anything smacking of industry (work) or commerce. Despite this, there is on record the complaint of an industrial executive who operated a beautifully landscaped factory in a single storey building of modern architectural design in Don Mills, in North York near (next to) Toronto, who found the practice of the apartment dwellers (the lowest residential use) across the road, of hanging washing on balconies, distasteful. It spoiled the view for his workers! Fashionably, however, shops, gas stations, glue factories, foundries, etc. are "incompatible" with residential uses, and should at least be separated by a strip of open or landscaped land.

Commercial uses, fifty years ago, tended to remain in the centre of town, particularly of small towns. But with the advent of the motor car, and the tendency to urban industrial living, the central business district branched out in a kind of ribbon, or strip, development, along established highways. Current thinking opposes this movement and prefers the "shopping center", a compact development with stores in the centre of a large parking area. Zoning to create shopping centres is difficult, since the value of the land is likely to be increased 200 times by the monopoly rights conferred on the owner of the land in the zone, and the location of such a zone, with its monopoly rights, may be attacked as invalid, as discriminatory, or spot, zoning. In any case, the economic concession is likely to have political repercussions.

This economic factor of monopoly, coupled with the many economic advantages to a community of industrial and commercial land use, has led some writers to the view that industrial use is the "highest" and "best" use of land. This about face is sufficient to indicate the futility of this kind of analysis, if such a classification can be dignified by word analysis. Obviously any modern community is going to need some industrial land, some commercial land, and some residential and recreational. The job of a zoning by-law is to find the "right" place for each area.

VALLEY IMPROVEMENT CO. LTD. *v.* METROPOLITAN TORONTO AND REGION CONSERVATION AUTHORITY. 1961. 29 D.L.R. (2d) 593 (Ontario. Court of Appeal). KELLY J.A.: ". . . the evidence of the witness Wronski, the Planning Director of the Township of Etobicoke

. . . 'Q. Having regard to the land which I have just outlined in the Exhibit, will you tell the Board what is your opinion as to its ultimate and best use from the point of view of the planner and in all the circumstances of land development in this day and age? A. It is an extremely difficult question to answer. One could point out that the present use is one of the best uses because it gives the highest public satisfaction of the land, making land available to the largest number of people. Looking at it from the point of view of the owner of the land, it has higher possibilities and returns financially. The present Etobicoke zoning is residential zoning permitting one dwelling in an acre. The location of the land may indicate from the owner's point of view that there could be better returns because of the suitability of the land for other residential purposes. I do not know instantly the grades and traffic considerations in minute detail but bearing in mind, says the Metropolitan proposal of the extension of the Rapid Transit across from Humber to Bloor, in the final analysis bearing in mind that the existing development in apartment sites on both sides of Bloor Street, supposing the school situation is suitable, I would say that the top lands, the lands the Counsel described, could be suitable for apartments presuming all other factors are equal. It depends from what point of view you are looking at it, of course.' . . ."

PROBLEM CASES. The proper allocation of land use fixed by a zoning by-law is far from a settled matter of established planning principle and even if the principles were not open to argument, the application of them to existing and new towns would still present problems.

The general objective of zoning would appear to be to keep incompatible uses of land well separated. This separation may be achieved simply by setting up large areas zoned for residential use, other areas for shops, other areas for dirty industry. Such, indeed, has been the tradition. But the fashion seems to be changing. Objection is now raised to monotony and conformity as besetting sins. Very difficult choices are being forced on the planner and zoner. How "pure" must he make the residential zone? Can he put in the same zone both detached and semi-detached one family dwellings along with multiple family dwellings, row houses, maisonettes, "walk up" and "high rise" apartments? Can he intrude a discreet amount of local shopping? How large should he make a "pure" residential zone? Note that the size of a zone may be very important. How can you tell whether a zone is too large or too small?

Where should he put the churches? In a residential zone? In, or near, a shopping centre? What about funeral "homes"? Or hospitals? For humans? For dogs? Can a school be put in a "residential" zone? Is a school more fitting in a residential zone of high density than low density? Should the richer inhabitants be "protected" from schools? Do they need greater protection than their poor neighbours? Do they pay more for the protection?

Some land uses may have their location dictated by natural considerations or by economic considerations the planner may find almost equally irresistible. A sand or gravel pit can only be where nature deposited the sand or gravel. If the "use" of land for a gravel pit is not permitted, is the owner entitled to compensation? How should such a use be zoned? Is there any way of assuring that when the economic use is exhausted, the pit will be reinstated in some more compatible use? Is this a part of the job of zoning?

Industrial uses are sometimes put on the east side of a city (in the northern hemisphere) on the theory that the prevailing west winds will blow the obnoxious smoke and dirt out of the city. On to the adjoining farms? Or the adjoining suburbs? Is zoning a sensible way to deal with industrial dirt? Should all industry be segregated? Industries sometimes require heavy duty roads to take the extra traffic, not to mention extra large water pipes and sewage drains. Is it a sufficient reason to segregate industry that the segregation may cut down on the cost of these extra services? What "reasons" are there for segregating shopping uses? Is "convenience to the public" a more important consideration in locating a shop than the initial economic advantage of the landowner who wants to double up his residential use with a small shop? Do other residential users need to be "protected" from such practices?

RE TRAFALGAR TOWNSHIP AND SHELL OIL CO. LTD.

Ontario. Municipal Board. 1957. Unreported

There are two applications before the board. The first is for an amendment to the official plan, changing some 929 acres from agricultural and residential to industrial and open, and the second for approval of an amendment to the zoning by-law in respect of the same lands to implement the change in the official plan and so as to permit refineries of the Shell Oil Co. Ltd. and Cities Service Canada Ltd. to locate on the property. By consent of all counsel, the applications were heard together.

The application was brought before the Trafalgar subsidiary Planning Board, the Joint Planning Board of Oakville-Bronte-Trafalgar and by the Council of the Township of Trafalgar, all of which approved. The Village of Bronte also is in favour of the application. The Town of Oakville, however, appeared and opposed the application. It was argued that, since all the local authorities directly concerned in the matter were in favour of the application, the board should also approve, unless it were clearly demonstrated that these boards had acted in a rash or ill-considered manner or that a minority in these boards had over-ridden the majority by some improper means. The board considers this argument to be persuasive but not necessarily conclusive.

It should be mentioned that in coming to their decisions in the matter the local boards had several meetings with the public and also had various reports submitted by their planning director and also by various consultants considered to be experts in their field.

The objections to the application may be summarized under three general headings: Pollution both air and water. Noise. Disruption of the concept of the official plan and zoning by-law.

Under the first of these general headings, it should be noted that the township has included in its by-law certain standards which the owners of the land will be required to meet and also took the precaution, which may or may not have been necessary, to obtain agreements from the two companies concerned that these requirements would be met. All the expert evidence adduced before the board clearly indicated that these standards were the highest that could be reasonably expected.

In regard to air pollution, it was generally agreed that with the methods which the companies proposed to use there would be nothing in the refining process which would be harmful to the public health. It remains, therefore, to consider if there would be anything which would cause inconvenience or annoyance to the inhabitants of the area. The best evidence on this subject appears to be that with modern methods this would not occur. Mr.

B. C. Newbury, Dr. Katz and Professor Alcott were the experts called in this aspect of the matter and all were agreed that if the standards of the by-law were met the unpleasant odor would be either so small as to be negligible or non-existent.

As to water pollution, Mr. Delaporte of the Ontario Water Resources Commission gave unequivocal evidence that no pollution would be permitted. There was additional evidence as to the proposed method of waste disposal so that any danger in this regard is thought to be more imaginary than real.

Under the second general heading, Noise, the evidence disclosed that while noise was at one time, it is no longer considered to be any problem. This is, of course, clearly provided for in the by-law and in addition the only direct and positive evidence adduced was that of Mr. Burroughs who had made actual tests in the Montreal plant and found that the noise generated at a refinery was about the same as that at a busy street intersection of a city. This was confirmed by Prof. Alcott, whose authority on this question cannot be disputed.

The next general heading was the disruption of the concept of the official plan and the zoning by-law. There appeared to be, on the part of those objecting, a great fear that if the application were granted, it meant the end of all planning and zoning restrictions in the township. This is clearly wrong. The application is for an amendment only and the official plan and by-law are still in force as amended. The granting of any application does not set a precedent, as each application must stand on its own merits and is so considered by the board. It should be observed that there is no change in the law involved, as the board is acting entirely within the limits of the existing relevant statutes.

From a planning aspect, the applicants called Dr. Faludi, a recognized expert, and E. Cumming, the planning director, also well qualified, and both recommended granting the application. Those opposing called Mr. Deacon and Mr. Adamson, both also well qualified. However, Dr. Deacon's main objection was to a so-called chain reaction, through which the industrial area might spread into surrounding residential districts. This, however, was explained to occur only in occupied lands and in the present case the lands surrounding the affected area are all in the main unoccupied. Also there is the natural barrier created by 12-Mile Creek and to the west Nelson Township has already indicated it desires industrial development. Mr. Adamson objected to an extension of an industrial "finger" to the lakeshore. However, this was qualified by him when it was pointed out that the southern portion of the lands were to become open space, to be used as a park, so that the intrusion became in effect negligible, particularly when the extensive buffer zones required under the by-law and agreements are taken into account.

The conclusions that the board has reached are given much support from the experience obtained in regard to the B.A. refinery at Clarkson. Here, despite the fact that the methods used are inferior to those proposed, a subdivision containing expensive and modern homes has developed recently, within 600 feet of the refinery and the owner of the land intervening is most anxious to develop his land for residential uses. A list of a large number of plans of subdivision in Trafalgar already registered was filed with the board, but it is significant that no subdivider appeared to object to the applications. It is also significant that Mr. Hamilton, a member of a syndicate controlling 2,100 acres throughout the township appeared and vigorously supported the application.

There was some mention made of a tract of land at the southwest corner of the township, containing some 50 acres and now zoned residential. In the opinion of the board, this can be adequately serviced in co-operation with Nelson Township and to the board as presently constituted, it is inconceivable that this should ever be changed to industrial, surrounded as it is by residential and open space lands used for park purposes.

For these and other reasons too lengthy to detail, the applications are granted. The board's costs are hereby fixed at $1,000, which shall be paid in equal parts by Cities Service Canada Ltd. and Shell Oil Co. Ltd., which shall also pay the cost of reporting and transcribing the proceedings before the board.

RE NORTH YORK BOARD OF EDUCATION

Ontario. Municipal Board. 1962. N. 2065–61

J. A. Kennedy Chairman and Jamieson Member: This is an appeal by the Board of Education of the Township of North York from a refusal of the council of that township to pass a by-law to change the permitted use of a four acre parcel of land at the southwest corner of Lawrence Avenue and High Point Road to permit the erection thereon of an elementary school containing six to eight rooms. The parcel is within a highly restricted residential area in which only single family residences with accessory buildings are permitted on a minimum lot of two acres and is about the centre of a school attendance area designated by the applicant board of education.

This highly restricted area was created some time prior to 1952 but until that year churches and schools were permitted. In 1952 the special provisions were imported into a new comprehensive by-law for the whole township and in this revision churches and schools were eliminated as a permitted use. The present appeal, if allowed, would clear the way for the school board to construct an elementary school in the approximate centre of the school attendance area, unless certain covenants in deeds which will be mentioned later would prevent this.

Prior to 1952 and especially since that year this special restricted area has been developed by the erection of very high class and very costly residences. It has been described as an area of exclusive country living in the heart of Metro. One architect and planning consultant called by the school board stated that in his opinion there is not another comparable area in the whole of Canada. The owner of one dwelling said his annual taxes are in exess of $4,000 and from about 80 dwellings the township collects substantially in excess of $200,000 a year in taxes. About one-half of this sum goes to schools. Twenty-six pupils who attend North York schools reside in the area at the present time and these do not cost more than $300 each per annum to educate, a total annual cost not exceeding $7,800.

It is a great misfortune, of course, but as so often happens in circumstances of this nature a great deal of heat and emotion have been generated to interfere with calm discussion and appraisal of the real issues.

The only territory in the township to the south of this restricted area from which school population might come is the subdivision known as Glen Orchy. This subdivision was approved recently and is now developing. It appears that if a school site must be chosen north of the restricted area it will be necessary to transport at least the younger pupils from Glen Orchy by bus and this appears to be the compelling reason of the school board to make this appeal after the proposal has been rejected by the planning board and council of the township. Since the prospect of transporting these pupils by bus looms as such an important factor in the position of the school board now, it is difficult to understand why that board, in answer to a questionnaire from the township planning board prior to approval of the Glen Orchy subdivision, reported that no school site would be required in Glen Orchy and that pupils from the subdivision would attend Owen Boulevard School which is a considerable distance north of the restricted area.

It is true that this statement was revised somewhat six weeks later but the first statement can only mean that the school board at that time expected it would transport students from Glen Orchy to the north by bus.

Strong and concerted opposition to any change in these very high restrictions is presented by substantially all the owners in the restricted area. They aver that they were induced to build or buy their homes in this highly exclusive area because of the high restrictions on which they relied and there is nothing in the evidence that would cast any doubt on this. They contend that the present circumstances do not constitute a public need sufficient to compel them to surrender any measure of the protection previously afforded and on the strength of which this development, highly profitable to the township assessment wise, has occurred over the past ten years.

In the opinion of the Board the only question to be determined is whether there is a public necessity sufficiently strong to warrant a change after ten years in these restrictions which have proven beneficial to these owners and to the township as a whole, even to this very school board as indicated by the tax revenue noted earlier in this decision.

The reasons advanced by the school board may be stated briefly as follows:

1: The site proposed is approximately in the centre of the school attendance area.

2: Moving the site north of this restricted area would require transporting at least the younger pupils from Glen Orchy by bus.

This school attendance area is still far from fully developed, especially in the northern part. There is no way of knowing in advance the pattern of development in this area and in the surrounding areas. In a word, the boundaries of school attendance areas are subject to change as development proceeds.

There is, of course, cost involved in the transportation of even a small number of pupils by bus even for a temporary period. According to the evidence there are also certain educational or academic advantages if pupils are within walking distance of their school. The latter, and for that matter the former, do not appear to have been deemed very serious when the school board made the statement prior to approval of the Glen Orchy plan of subdivision that pupils from that subdivision would attend the Owen Boulevard School. In reality the estimated cost of transportation by bus would not be a large item in the budget of this school board nor would it be too much out of line if looked upon as the cost of retaining this restricted area in its present condition, all of which is so beneficial to the township and to the school board from a financial point of view.

There is one further point worthy of some mention. Deeds in this area contain restrictive covenants which appear from the evidence before the Board to be in the nature of a building scheme. The Board is not asked nor has it jurisdiction to decide the validity or effect of these covenants to prevent the erection of a school on the site proposed. It does appear, however, from what has been said by counsel, that the granting of this appeal would open costly and protracted litigation and the Board inclines against costly litigation at public expense if it can be avoided.

For a great many years building schemes established under conveyances and other covenants in deeds have performed a very valuable service in controlling development and maintaining desirable standards of land use. Until recent years this was the only means available for such a purpose. Now, however, land use by-laws passed under the authority of *The Planning Act* and other similar legislation perform this function very well as a part of local government at a level where the greatest common good is paramount rather than the restrictions of a private contract. In the opinion of this Board by-laws passed by local government are a more desirable means of achieving acceptable control of land use.

In a growing line of decisions this Board has followed the principle that it should not presume to interfere with the exercise by a municipal council of the discretion vested in it by the Legislature to the extent of directing the council to amend a land use by-law unless it is established that the council has not made a reasonable exercise of its discretion. In the opinion of the Board the evidence in this case does not establish such a failure on the part of the council. For these reasons the appeal fails and must be dismissed.

QUESTIONS. What harm to the neighbourhood will be caused by the North York School Board? Why is the proposed school resisted by the "strong and concerted opposition"? How would the proposed school affect the market value of the adjacent residential properties? Is there "no way of knowing in advance the pattern of development in this area"? Is determination of such a pattern beyond the scope of planning and land use control authorized under *The Planning Act* in Ontario?

RE CITY OF TORONTO BY-LAW 21,381
Ontario. Municipal Board. 1962. N. 2814–61

McCrae Member: The parcel described in the subject by-law is located at Bloor Street and Castle Frank Road and is commonly known as the Sir Edward Kemp Estate. It is the intention of the Toronto Board of Education to erect a Vocational School on the site should the application be decided favourably. Counsel for the city pointed out that The Ontario Municipal Board decision (P.F.M.–8985–59) dated the 7th day of March, 1960, when the same property was involved in an appeal, makes mention of the evidence at that time as indicating an institutional use as being best for this land. The subject land is located in an Rl Zone and in the City of Toronto schools are not a permitted use in this zoning category. Rather than rezone the parcel to R2 it was decided that it would be more desirable to permit the erection of a School on the designated lands subject to very stringent regulations imposed in the by-law.

The entire parcel is defined by metes and bounds in the by-law. At the same time the area of land to be built upon is described by metes and bounds to control its situation on the property. Provision is made as to gross floor area, height, parking, etc. and there is to be no ingress or egress from the school grounds by way of the easterly end of Castle Frank Crescent.

In his evidence, M.B.M. Lawson, Commissioner of Planning for the City of Toronto stated that the subject site was an ideal one for a school and it would integrate well with the homes located in the area. It was his opinion that a straight redesignation would have allowed the school to be sited anywhere on the property with detrimental effects to the neighbouring homes. This opinion is shared by the pertinent city committees and the Planning Board.

The only opposition to the application came from T. C. Payne and his wife, Ruth Sherrit Payne of 70 Castle Frank Crescent whose home shown in Exhibit 9 will be closest to the proposed school. At the hearing the plans indicated that the school would be forty-five feet away from the Payne lot line but this has since been found to be in error and a letter from F. J. Cornish, counsel for the Board of Education under dating of May 2, 1962, states that surveys taken have reduced this distance to 29.36 feet from the lot line.

The position taken by the Paynes is that the intended work will seriously prejudice the value of their home. While agreeing that the house does not face the school they believe that the blank wall will obstruct the view from the dining and bedroom windows. It was their request that if the building is to be allowed it should be relocated on the property. They also wanted specific provision made for a latticed board fence of the usual type found around school buildings in the metropolitan area since the by-law only mentions suitable fencing and hedge.

When the school was first proposed for the area there was determined opposition by the ratepayers. After many meetings with city officials and boards they agreed that if certain provisions were complied with opposition would be withdrawn. Exhibit 8 is the proposal put forward by the ratepayers and concurred in by the school board, and while there was a legal obstacle involved in guaranteeing to maintain the trees a commitment was given that the majority of the trees will remain except for those to be removed due to school construction.

After carefully considering all of the evidence adduced before me I am of the opinion that the application for approval of the by-law should be granted. I would also recommend that the Board's order should not issue until it has been reasonably satisfied that every effort has been made by the Board of Education, bearing in mind the interests of the other neighbours, to comply with the request of the property owner closest to the work as to type of fence, particularly so since the new information places the school even closer than anticipated to his lot line. Should difficulties arise in this regard, the Board may be spoken to by either party.

[The decision of McCrae Member, was adopted by R. L. Kennedy Vice-Chairman and Milburn Member.]

RE KINDERLAW INDUSTRIES LIMITED

Ontario. Municipal Board. 1962. P.F.N. 770–60; 1230–61

J. A. Kennedy Chairman and Roberts Member: These applications arise out of the same subject matter and seek approval of a proposed amendment to the official plan of the Township of Toronto and also an order directing the council of the Township to amend the zoning by-law. In the result the designated and permitted use of the lands in question would be changed from residential to a commercial use which would permit the erection of a shopping centre. The lands in question comprise 22 acres, are located in the southerly part of the area of Toronto Township known as Cooksville, have a frontage on the west side of Highway No. 10 of some 740 feet and extend to the west some 1300 feet in an area zoned for residential use and now developed in part with single family dwellings.

While The Metropolitan Toronto Planning Area Board resolved in favour of this proposal with certain conditions as to control and routing of traffic, the township planning board and the council of the township both refused the application.

The traffic engineer and the director of land use (planning division) of the Metropolitan Toronto Planning Area Board were called as witnesses under subpoena by counsel for the township and during an extensive examination each gave evidence substantially against approval of these applications.

In the opinion of the Board an important principle is involved in this case. Despite the fact that land use planning is still in its infancy, its basic tenets have become even now not only accepted but demanded from government for the protection and enjoyment of a more abundant life. One important attraction of this science is that it can be made to serve man's basic desire for privacy and related amenities in private dwelling areas. Hardly anyone would suggest that commercial or industrial development in close proximity does not reduce the amenities in a residential district. Common consent of mankind establishes this proposition beyond question.

Recognizing these fundamental truths, this Board will not order changes in zoning that would remove from existing private dwellings a reasonable measure of protection. In the case of new development provision and designation of lands required for commercial and industrial development should be made before adjacent or neighbouring lands are developed for private residential use or for other use that would be affected injuriously by commercial or industrial development in proximity. After residential development has taken place zoning of land should not be changed to permit commercial or industrial use in a proximity or under circumstances that will injuriously affect such residential development.

A study was made of the Cooksville area under the direction of an experienced and capable township planning director. This study was adopted by the township planning board and implemented in council by an official plan amendment and companion zoning by-law both of which were duly approved. By these enactments the lands here in question and a considerable area to the north as well as to the south were designated for residential use. Since that time good quality and very desirable single family dwellings have been constructed on the lands immediately adjoining the site now proposed for commercial use and also on lands extending to the north. With very few exceptions the residents of this area vigorously oppose these applications. The Board finds on the evidence that the enjoyment of these residences would be affected injuriously by the commercial development proposed.

It does not appear necessary to make any findings about the effect of the proposed shopping centre on traffic. Qualified opinion evidence was given that new traffic problems would result from the development and that the site in question was not suited for the development proposed because of lack of sufficient frontage on arterial roads.

Nor is it necessary to make a finding on the question of need for a new shopping centre at this place. While there was evidence that the proposed shopping centre could be supported from residential development existing and anticipated, it did appear that some of these computations included areas within the primary trade areas of other retail shopping centres already established. These applications should be decided on the simple ground that the residential zoning in force should be maintained because those who built or acquired single family dwellings in close proximity relying on that zoning would be injuriously affected by the change now sought.

The application and appeal will be dismissed. This is not a case for costs except that the appellants will pay to the Board an additional hearing fee of $150.00. There will be no other order as to costs.

QUESTIONS. How fundamental is the "truth" that "commercial or industrial development in close proximity" reduces the "amenities in a residential district"? Can commercial districts properly include residential uses?

RE MISSISSAUGA GOLF AND COUNTRY CLUB
Ontario. Municipal Board. 1962. N. 3026–62/N. 2253–61

J. A. KENNEDY Chairman: This is an application by Mississauga Golf and Country Club Limited for approval of a proposed amendment to the official plan of the Township of Toronto and for an order directing the council of the Township of Toronto to pass an amending by-law. These proposals would change the permitted use of a parcel of land at the intersection of the North Service Road and the Mississauga Road from residential to commercial to permit the construction thereon of a gasoline service station which would be owned and operated by Texaco Canada Limited. This parcel is across the Mississauga Road from the Mississauga Golf and Country Club. As indicated above it is bounded on the south side by the North Service Road which is along the north side of the Queen Elizabeth Way. The parcel in question is the most easterly 205 feet of a tract of land owned by the golf club and in the triangle formed by the Mississauga Road and the North Service Road, extending along Mississauga Road westerly a distance of approximately 1400 feet and along the North Service Road a distance of approximately 800 feet. I conducted this hearing under the authority of Section 15 of *The Ontario Municipal Board Act* and now report to the Board.

This large tract is still wholly undeveloped. The owner of the land has proposed a plan of subdivision into residential lots but approval has been refused pending the bringing of services to these lands.

Very strenuous opposition has been presented to this proposed change by owners of residential properties extending for a considerable distance to the west, principally along the Mississauga Road. There is no commercial use in the immediate area and the permitted use of all the land on this side of the Queen Elizabeth Way, with the exception of the golf course, is single family residential. It does appear that certain uses a short distance to the west on Mississauga Road do not accord with this permitted use but while these appear to be what is known as nonconforming uses they do not appear to be creating any trouble or problem.

This application is very strongly supported by the golf club for the reason that the establishment of a service station at this place would provide a very desirable convenience for the members of the club as well as for other residents in the area, and, of course, the golf club is interested in making a sale of this land.

The gasoline service station would be more than 600 feet from any existing residential use along the North Service Road and about 1200 feet from any residence along the Mississauga Road and a much greater distance from any residential use to the east. To the south, as noted, is the Queen Elizabeth Way and to the north the Mississauga Golf Course.

Very strong opposition is presented by the Mississauga West Ratepayers' Association. They are concerned about any intrusion of a commercial use at this place and apparently most concerned that this may be only the thin edge of the wedge making it possible at a later date to extend and expand commercial uses in the area. I find on the evidence that the council refused this application because of the concerted opposition of so many residents in this area, and further, that the council was of the opinion that a service station is not actually needed at this place.

I find on the evidence that this one commercial use at this location would provide a desirable and often necessary convenience to persons frequenting the golf course as well as to a great many other persons who pass this point where well travelled roads converge. The service station would be distant about 600 feet from any residence on the North Service Road and about a quarter of a mile from any residence on Mississauga Road. As noted above, it would be even farther from any residence in the opposite direction. I am satisfied on the evidence that the real reason for the objection which has been mounted against this application is the fear that this change of the permitted use would be merely the forerunner of other changes to commercial use intruded into what has been developed as a very select area except for the gravel pit operations some distance to the west which have occasioned much dissatisfaction and a great many complaints in recent years.

I am of the opinion that a gasoline service station along the lines of the drawing which has been filed and subject to restrictions such as those which have been suggested, would not interfere with the reasonable enjoyment of residences in this area. It would have to be understood, however, that the tract of land in question would be designated as a special use zone and that the remaining lands of this same owner to the west as well as other lands in the area would remain zoned for single family residential use and no other.

I am satisfied that it is possible, by following a suitable design and by imposing appropriate restrictions, to establish a service station at this site where the Mississauga Road meets the North Service Road without doing any damage to the value and amenities of the surrounding residential land. It should be remembered that the golf club is the owner of a considerable tract of land immediately to the west which will have to be developed ultimately and sold for single family residential purposes and that this tract is of more than sufficient extent to serve as an adequate buffer in the event that a buffer might be deemed desirable. This site is at the intersection of two fairly busy roads and overlooks the Queen Elizabeth Way, which is a main Ontario highway. It is very doubtful in my mind whether it would be appropriate as a site for any residential use with the possible exception of a high density residential development which is not appropriate for this location.

I recommend that the proposed change in the official plan be approved and that an order issue directing the enactment by the council of the necessary by-law. There is an opportunity here for the oil company concerned to accomplish an outstanding result in blending this use with the amenities desirable in this area. Having this in mind I suggest that the design and general appointments of the service station, as well as the conditions to be imposed, be left to be further negotiated between the golf club and the township subject to further direction by this Board.

[The foregoing report was adopted by R. L. Kennedy Vice-Chairman and Jamieson Member.]

DUFFCON CONCRETE PRODUCTS, INC. *v.* BOROUGH OF CRESSKILL. 1949. 64 A. 2d 347 (New Jersey. Supreme Court). Cresskill is a small residential community of about 1,300 acres and 2,300 persons. Its zoning by-law provided for three residential districts and a fourth for "commercial districts for business centers." All heavy industry was excluded. Early in 1946 the prosecutor purchased land in a commercial zone abutting on a residential district and two blocks away from a public school. He filled in the land at a cost of $6,000 and commenced the manufacture of concrete slabs in the open. He had forty employees and used a pneumatic drill and a ten horsepower motor to run a cement mixer. After two months he applied for a permit to erect a factory. The permit was refused and he challenged the validity of the by-law by *certiorari.* The former Supreme Court set the by-law aside and the Borough appealed. On this hearing the by-law was upheld. VANDERBILT C.J.: "What may be the most appropriate use of any particular property depends not only on all conditions, physical, economic and social, prevailing within the municipality and its needs, present and reasonably prospective, but also on the nature of the entire region in which the municipality is located and the use to which the land in that region has been or may be put most advantageously. The effective development of a region should not and cannot be made to depend upon the adventitious location of municipal boundaries, often prescribed decades or even centuries ago, and based in many instances on considerations of geography, of commerce, or of politics that are no longer significant with respect to zoning. The direction of growth of residential areas on the one hand and of industrial concentration on the other refuses to be governed by such artificial lines. Changes in methods of transportation as well as in living conditions have served only to accentuate the unreality in dealing with zoning problems on the basis of the territorial limits of a municipality, improved highways and new transportation facilities have made possible the concentration of industry at places best suited to its development to a degree not contemplated in the earlier stages of zoning. The same forces make practicable the presently existing and currently developing suburban and rural sections given over solely to residential purposes and local retail business services coextensive with the needs of the community. The resulting advantages enure alike to industry and residential properties and, at the same time, advance the general welfare of the entire region."

THE PLANNING ACT

Ontario. Revised Statutes. 1960. Chapter 296

30. (1) By-laws may be passed by the councils of municipalities:

1. For prohibiting the use of land . . . within the municipality . . .
2. For prohibiting the erection or use of buildings . . . within the municipality . . .

MUNICIPAL ACT

British Columbia. Revised Statutes. 1960. Chapter 255

702. (2) In making regulations [zoning by-laws] under this section, the Council shall have due regard to the following considerations.

(a) The promotion of health, safety, convenience, and welfare of the public:
(b) The prevention of the overcrowding of land, and the preservation of the amenities peculiar to any zone:
(c) The securing of adequate light, air, and access:
(d) The value of the land and the nature of its present and prospective use and occupancy:
(e) The character of each zone, the character of the buildings already erected, and the peculiar suitability of the zone for particular uses:
(f) The conservation of property values.

THE TOWN AND RURAL PLANNING ACT
Alberta. Revised Statutes. 1955. Chapter 337

80. (1a) The by-law shall be based upon a survey of the existing uses and conditions of land and buildings and an analysis of future needs in the development of the municipality which shall be reported upon to the satisfaction of the Board prior to the passing of the by-law.

THE COMMUNITY PLANNING ACT, 1957
Saskatchewan. Statutes. 1957. Chapter 48

40. In prescribing or establishing a district the council shall have due regard to its character, the nature of the uses of land and buildings in the district and its peculiar suitability for particular uses in relation to the most appropriate use of land throughout the municipality.

2. BULK REGULATION

LIONSHEAD LAKE, INC. *v.* WAYNE TOWNSHIP
New Jersey. Supreme Court. 1952. 89 A. 2d 693

VANDERBILT C.J. delivered the judgment of the Court: The plaintiff, the owner and developer of a large tract of land in the defendant township, commenced this action in lieu of a prerogative writ challenging the validity of the defendant's zoning ordinance in fixing the minimum size of dwellings and in placing certain of its properties in a residential district. On the plaintiff's motion the trial court entered summary judgment in its favor on the first count, setting aside the provisions of the ordinance fixing the minimum size of dwellings (1950). On appeal this judgment was reversed by the Appellate Division of the Superior Court because of the existence of a factual question and the case was remanded for trial.

The Township of Wayne is the most extensive municipality in Passaic County. It covers 25.34 square miles in comparison with the 23.57 square miles of Newark. It has a population of 11,815 in comparison with Newark's 437,857. Only 12% of the total area of the township has been built up. Included within its borders are several sizeable lakes (the one located within the plaintiff's development, e.g., having an area of about 145 acres) and as a result a considerable number of its residences have been built for summer occupancy only. Although a political entity it is in fact a composite of about a dozen widely scattered residential communities, varying from developments like the plaintiff's where the average home costs less than $10,000, to more expensive sections where the homes cost from $35,000 to $75,000. It has but little business or industry.

On July 12, 1949, four years after the plaintiff had commenced the development of its Lionshead Lake properties and after over a hundred houses had been constructed there, the defendant adopted a revised zoning ordinance dividing the entire township into four districts; residence districts A and B, a business district and an industrial district, the last two comprising but a very small proportion of the township's total area. In section 3 of the ordinance pertaining to residence A districts it was provided that:

"(d) Minimum Size of dwellings: Every dwelling hereafter erected or placed in a residence A district shall have a living-floor space, as herein defined: of not less than 768 square feet for a one story dwelling; of not less than 1000 square feet for a two story dwelling having an attached garage; of not less than 1200 square feet for a two story dwelling not having an attached garage."

These minimum size requirements for dwellings were made applicable to residence B districts by section 4(d) of the ordinance, to business districts by section 5(c), and to industrial districts by section 6(b) the result being that the same minimum size requirements for dwellings prevailed throughout the entire township.

Within the entire township only about 70% of all the existing dwellings meet the minimum requirements of the ordinance; in some sections of the township as few as 20% of the existing dwellings comply with the ordinance requirements, in others (among them the plaintiff's Lionshead Lake development) only about 50% are above the prescribed minimum, while in other areas the percentage of compliance is far greater, reaching 100% in some of the more exclusive sections. The low percentage of compliance in certain areas is not particularly significant, however, for the reason that the township is as yet substantially undeveloped. Compliance with the requirements of the ordinance in the future will undoubtedly result in the non-conforming houses comprising but a small minority even in those areas where they are now in the majority. There was testimony to the effect that to build a house for year-round occupancy having the minimum 768 square feet of living space would cost from $10,000 to $12,000, if mass produced, and that only about 30% of the population were financially able to afford such homes. The plaintiff's witness who so testified, a builder and developer, was hardly qualified, however, to express an opinion as to the financial ability of present and potential residents of the township and his opinion as to construction costs was considerably out of line with that of the defendant's expert who testified that homes complying with the ordinance could be and were being built at a cost of $8,500 to $9,200 if for year-round occupancy and $7,500 to $8,200 if for seasonal use only.

To meet the plaintiff's attack on the reasonableness of the ordinance, the defendant produced a recognized public health expert who testified that the living-floor space in a dwelling had a direct relation to the mental and emotional health of its occupants and that he had developed scientific standards for different size families: 400 square feet for one person, 750 square feet for two persons, 1,000 square feet for three persons, 1,150 square feet for four persons, 1,400 square feet for five persons and 1,550 square feet for six persons. These the witness considered as desirable goals rather than legal standards. He conceded that the housing standards prescribed by the agencies of the Federal Government are below those written into the ordinance, as are those of the New Jersey Code of Minimum Construction Requirements for One and Two Family Dwellings, prepared by the Department of Economic Development, Division of Planning and Engineering (1946), which, however, does not have the force of law but is merely advisory. . . .

[After discussing the constitutional and legislative background, Vanderbilt C.J. continued:]

The underlying question before us is whether in the light of these constitutional and legislative provisions the zoning ordinance of the defendant township is arbitrary and unreasonable. That question, moreover, must be answered in the light of the facts of this particular case. We must bear in mind, finally, that a zoning ordinance is not like the law of the Medes and Persians; variances may be permitted, the zoning ordinance may be amended, and if the ordinance proves unreasonable in operation it may be set aside at any time. . . .

The Township of Wayne is still for the most part a sparsely settled countryside with great natural attractions in its lakes, hills and streams, but obviously it lies in the path of the next onward wave of suburban development. Whether that development shall be "with a view of conserving the value of property and encouraging the most appropriate use of land throughout such municipality" and whether it will "prevent the overcrowding of land or buildings" and "avoid undue concentration of population" depends in large measure on the wisdom of the governing body of the municipality as expressed in its zoning ordinance. It requires as much official watchfulness to anticipate and prevent suburban blight as it does to eradicate city slums.

Has a municipality the right to impose minimum floor area requirements in the exercise of its zoning powers? Much of the proof adduced by the defendant township was devoted to showing that the mental and emotional health of its inhabitants depended on the proper size of their homes. We may take notice without formal proof that there are minimums in housing below which one may not go without risk of impairing the health of those who dwell therein. One does not need extensive experience in matrimonial causes to become aware of the adverse effect of overcrowding on the well-being of our most important institution, the home. Moreover, people who move into the country rightly expect more land, more living room, indoors and out, and more freedom in their scale of living than is generally possible in the city. City standards of housing are not adaptable to suburban areas and especially to the upbringing of children. But quite apart from these considerations of public health which cannot be overlooked, minimum floor-area standards are justified on the ground that they promote the general welfare of the community and, as we have seen in *Schmidt* v. *Board of Adjustment of the City of Newark* (1952), the courts in conformance with the constitutional provisions and the statutes hereinbefore cited take a broad view of what constitutes general welfare. The size of the dwellings in any community inevitably affects the character of the community and does much to determine whether or not it is a desirable place in which to live. It is the prevailing view in municipalities throughout the State that such minimum floor-area standards are necessary to protect the character of the community. A survey made by the Department of Conservation and Economic Development in 1951 disclosed that 64 municipalities out of the 138 reporting had minimum dwelling requirements. In the light of the Constitution and of the enabling statutes, the right of a municipality to impose minimum floor-area requirements is beyond controversy.

With respect to every zoning ordinance, however, the question remains as to whether or not in the particular facts of the case and in the light of all of the surrounding circumstances the minimum floor-area requirements are reasonable. Can a minimum of living floor space of 768 square feet for a one-story building; of 1,000 square feet for a two-story dwelling having an attached garage; and of 1,200 square feet for a two-story dwelling not having an attached garage be deemed unreasonable in a rural area just beginning to change to a suburban community? It is significant that the plaintiff admits that of the 100 houses in its development 30 met the minimum requirements when constructed and 20 more by voluntary additions of the owners to meet their individual needs have been enlarged to conform to the minimum requirements of the ordinance, and while this litigation has been pending 20 others have been constructed conforming to the ordinance. If some such requirements were not imposed there would be grave danger in certain parts of the township, particularly around the lakes which attract summer visitors, of the erection of shanties which would deteriorate land values generally to the great detriment of the increasing number of people who live in Wayne Township the year round. The minimum floor area requirements imposed by the ordinance are not large for a family of normal size. Without some such restrictions there is always the danger that after some homes have been erected giving a character to a neighbourhood others might follow which would fail to live up to the standards thus voluntarily set. This has been the experience in many communities and it is against this that the township has sought to safeguard itself within limits which seem to us to be altogether reasonable. . . .

JACOBS J. (concurring): The Township of Wayne is a sprawling residential municipality which is sparsely populated and largely undeveloped. Like many North Jersey communities it is fertile territory for extensive development; unlike less fortunate communities it is still in a position to plan and control its development and avoid the ravages which may be observed in unplanned and unsightly urban, and occasional suburban, municipalities.

In 1946 the township, acting through its planning board, engaged a professional city planner to formulate a master plan. Working with the board and a citizens committee he submitted his plan and included therein a recommendation that every new dwelling in the township have minimum living space of 1,200 square feet. After considerable discussion the township declined to accept the proposed minimum but did provide in its ordinance of July 12, 1949 that one-story dwellings shall have not less than 768 square feet, that two-story dwellings with garages attached shall have not less than 1,000 square feet, and that two-story dwellings without garages attached shall have not less than 1,200 square feet. The figure of 768 feet was approved after weighing all the pertinent factors including the fact that during the preceding year 85% of the applications for building permits were for dwellings containing 768 feet or more in living space and the further fact that the 768 figure would enable the use of "standard size lumber" in 24′ x 32′ houses. The provisions with respect to two-story dwellings were influenced in considerable part by aesthetic considerations which I believe to be entirely proper. . . .

In the light of modern understanding, adequate living space must be considered as having reasonable relation to health, particularly mental and emotional health. See *Report on Planning the Home for Occupancy* issued by the Committee on the Hygiene of Housing of the American Public

Health Association, pp. 1, 17 (1950); . . . During the trial below Dr. Winslow, Professor of Public Health at Yale University for over 30 years, testified forcefully to that effect and also pointed out that "the sense of inferiority due to living in noticeably substandard homes probably does more damage to the health of children than all the unsanitary plumbing." See 60 *Yale L.J.* 507 (1951). His studies have led him to the view that the proper goals for the present are 400 square feet minimum living space for one person, 750 for two, 1,000 for three and 1,550 for four; the average family in Wayne Township contains between three and four persons. It may be noted that there are numerous communities in our State which have comparable minimum living space requirements. Mr. Herbert H. Smith, Chief of the Planning Section of the New Jersey Department of Conservation and Economic Development, testified that of 138 communities replying to his inquiries 64 have such requirements, including 21 which have a single minimum applicable throughout the entire municipality.

The township's ordinance was attacked by complaint filed in the Law Division in August 1950 by the plaintiff, a corporation which had developed Lionshead Lake. Prior to July 1949 it had built approximately 100 houses, including many which contained lesser living space than provided in the ordinance; since the adoption of the ordinance 20 additional houses have been built, all satisfying the prescribed minimum living space requirements. The plaintiff has not at any time sought any exception or variance under R.S. 40:55–39, N.J.S.A.; on the contrary it sought and obtained from the lower court a judgment which determined that the ordinance is "invalid with respect to Residence 'A' and 'B' Districts in which the plaintiff's property is situated, and the same be and is hereby set aside and of no force and effect and for nothing holden."...

A witness for the plaintiff testified that at the time of the adoption of the ordinance, the cost of a house containing 768 square feet of living space, if mass produced, would approximate $9,500 to $10,500. On the other hand, another witness testified "that a year round one-family home, containing 768 square feet in area complying in all respects with the building code of the Township of Wayne would presently cost between $8,500 and $9,200." Applications for permits filed by the plaintiff since the passage of the ordinance indicated that it was constructing such houses at even lesser stated costs. The record contains nothing to indicate the buying power of residents of Passaic County where Wayne Township is located, although the May 10 1952 issue of *Sales Management* (at p. 414) estimates that Passaic County has an average effective buying income per annum of $6,000 per family, and represents the forty-ninth highest county in the United States. In the light of the foregoing I find no basis for the suggestion that the minimum in the ordinance is unreasonably high; in any event it is clearly within the broad range which should be allowed in the interests of social progress. . . .

The further suggestion has been advanced that the ordinance is defective in that it does not differentiate between various sections of the township and is not related to the number of occupants of the dwelling. This ignores the fact that the ordinance prescribes only minimum footage which is small enough to be applicable throughout the entire community. If any neighbourhood ought have a higher minimum perhaps it will be dealt with in a later ordinance; in the meantime no harm is done to it by any of the present restrictions. Similarly, perhaps some later ordinance will attempt to deal with the complex subject of relating minimum living space to actual occupants; in the meantime the prescribed minimum is sufficiently low to be applied generally. No matter what may be the size of the particular family the 768 feet minimum will be a significant step forward when contrasted with the plaintiff's "doll houses." Mathematical precision in the ordinance need not be attained; it is sufficient that its comprehensive provisions are reasonably calculated to achieve ends which are within the broad ambit of proper modern day zoning....

OLIPHANT J. (dissenting): I find I must dissent from the philosophy and the result arrived at in the majority opinion. Zoning has its purposes, but as I conceive the effect of the majority opinion it precludes individuals in those income brackets who could not pay between $8,500 and $12,000 for the erection of a house on a lot from ever establishing a residence in this community as long as the 768 square feet of living space is the minimum requirement in the zoning ordinance. A zoning provision that can produce this effect certainly runs afoul of the fundamental principles of our form of government. It places an unnecessary and severe restriction upon the alienation of real estate. It is not necessary, it seems to me, in order to meet any possible threat to the general health and welfare of the community.

It should be borne in mind that the threat to the general welfare and health of the community usually springs from the type of home that is maintained within the house rather than the house itself. Certain well-behaved families will be barred from these communities, not because of any acts they do or conditions they create, but simply because the income of the family will not permit them to build a house at the cost testified to in this case. They will be relegated to living in the large cities or in multiple-family dwellings even though it be against what they consider the welfare of their immediate families.

My difficulty with the provision in this ordinance is that it applies equally to every part of the 25½ square miles of this township and it applies without any regard to how the various districts of the community have been zoned. It applies to the districts classed Residence A and B, Business or Industrial Districts. While it is conceivable that some municipalities may be of such a cohesive and homogenous character as to warrant the imposition of certain uniform regulations on the entire community, viz., the prohibitions of any industrial plants in a purely residential community . . . the defendant township is certainly not of such character. It is sparsely settled and is made up of a group of widely separated communities or developments, and in some of these developments the minimum living space requirements imposed by the ordinance are easily met by all the existing dwellings while in other sections only a minority of the houses meet the standards imposed, and in the plaintiff's Lionshead Lake development only about 50% of the dwellings comply.

To impose identical living floor space minimums on all the sections of such a municipality is to fail completely to give any consideration whatever to the "character of the district and its peculiar suitability for particular purposes." While zoning regulations may legitimately be imposed in the district to serve the general welfare by "conserving the value of property and encouraging the most appropriate uses of land," such regulations are wholly unreasonable and beyond the zoning power and an unwarranted interference with private property rights if they are designed or operate to change completely, for better or for worse, the very character of the district. Any regulation imposed must bear a reasonable relation to the particular area subject thereto. Insofar as the minimum living floor space requirements of the ordinance under review apply to the entire community and to the plaintiff's properties in particular, they are clearly arbitrary and capricious and were very properly set aside by the trial court as an abuse of the zoning power.

My views on this particular phase of zoning do not prohibit minimum floor space in a house in particular districts or a proper correlation of minimum floor space in the house and the area of the lot or lots in question, but I cannot agree with the majority when they state with respect to this minimum square footage requirements that "whether it will 'prevent the overcrowding of land or buildings' and 'avoid undue concentration of the buildings' depends in large measure on the wisdom of the governing body of the municipality." This is clearly indicative of a lack of standard with respect to this particular phase of zoning in the Zoning Act itself and it assumes that the discretion of the zoning board or governing body of a municipality amounts to wisdom. To buttress their position the majority further states: "We may take notice without formal proof that there are minimums in housing below which one may not go without risk of impairing the health of those who dwell therein." In so stating they inferentially approve certain theories advanced to sustain this ordinance by text writers and certain reports of the Department of Conservation and Economic Development. But it seems to me that the decision as to what the minimum square footage in a particular house should be is essentially within the legislative province, and the Legislature not having spoken it is not within the power of this court or the Department of Conservation and Economic Development to attempt to supply the deficiency in the statute.

I am authorized to say that Mr. Justice Wachenfeld concurs in this opinion.

ADDITIONAL FACTS. Of 68 houses built on the Lionshead Lake, Inc. property before the war, 17 were 484 square feet in area (outside measurements), 18 were something under 600 square feet, and 22 were 676 square feet. The remaining 11 were not specified in the record.

NOTE. For a comment on this case, see Haar, "Zoning For Minimum Standards: The Wayne Township Case," (1953), 66 *Harv. L.R.* 1051. Professor Haar assails the ordinance on the ground of economic segregation and concludes that the New Jersey court "substituted shibboleths for reasoning, and used liberal shibboleths to attain an illiberal result." For a reply to Professor Haar, see Nolan and Horack," How Small A House?—Zoning For Minimum Space Requirements," (1954), 67 *Harv. L.R.* 967. Professors Nolan and Horack provide additional factual material. Professor Haar replies to his critics in "Wayne Township: Zoning For Whom?—In Brief Reply," (1954), 67 *Harv. L.R.* 986.

NOTE ON REGULATIONS IN ZONING BY-LAWS. The *Wayne Township* case, although only likely to arise in Canada in the exercise by the Ontario Municipal Board or a similar provincial supervisory agency in another province of its duty to approve restricted area or zoning by-laws, emphasizes an aspect of zoning that was hinted at in the preceding section. While a municipality may sometimes directly exclude a reasonable but unwanted use, there is a more common danger of excluding a reasonable and wanted use by the severity of its regulations. The *Wayne Township* by-law excluded possible residential users by setting high standards of house size. For several years Toronto Township's By-law 1614 excluded any residential use on a lot smaller than 6000 square feet with a frontage smaller than forty feet and in a house smaller than 720 square feet outside measurement, if only one storey, 550 square feet if a storey and a half, and 500 square feet if two or more storeys. The by-law was, in this respect, not questioned by the Municipal Board. Some more functional solutions to this problem of open space around houses are set out below.

Examples of Regulation. Zoning by-laws introduce an amazing variety of detailed restrictions, any of which, if not complied with, will justify enforcement action to prohibit the use of the land. Restrictions in residential zones usually relate to lot area, frontage, depth of front yard, side yards and rear yards, house area, the percentage of the lot covered by buildings, and height. Residential zones vary with the size of house, the size of the lot, and the number of houses on a lot. Modern taste seems to prefer the single family detached dwelling on a separate lot. It may be that this is a universal desire held by all humans. If so it is a material factor in the shape of the modern city, which lacks the compactness and cohesiveness of its mediaeval predecessor.

Residential restrictions may be, probably inevitably are, partly arbitrary matters, but one has only to read the rationalization in the American cases on the police power to see that some rational element can at least be pretended to be present. Minimum lot and yard sizes help to determine density of development, but they are crude measures that seriously restrict freedom of design. The kind of sewer facilities may matter, since the septic tank has limited use. Sometimes it is said that open development prevents the spread of fire and permits easier movement of fire fighting equipment. The height of buildings is often limited for the same reason. Unless a municipality is prepared to purchase fire fighting equipment equal to the job, it may have to limit height to thirty-five feet. Yet the cost of the equipment is not great enough to prohibit economic use of land for higher buildings, to say nothing of the esthetic limitations. One of the most carefully planned developments in Canada, at Don Mills, is esthetically disappointing because the "civic centre" has no buildings over thirty-five feet high. Whether this is necessary in a municipality like North York, with a population in 1962 of 269,959, is debatable, and if it is necessary, it is little credit to the political achievements of the 1,824,481 who make up the total metropolitan area of which North York is a part.

Regulation is by no means confined to residential areas, although it is perhaps most common in such areas. Toronto Township originally required all commercial areas to be at least 200 feet deep. This meant that the owner of a parcel of land in a commercial area might find his land sterilized, if his parcel was 180 feet deep and the owner of the land behind refused to sell him twently feet, or asked an unreasonable price for it. This "hardship" could also happen to residential land owners, for large parts of the Township had been subdivided and lots sold that had less than 6000 square feet and forty feet in frontage. The original standard as passed by the Council had been 7,500 square feet and fifty feet in frontage. The Municipal Board required the amendment, not because the higher standard excluded poor people, but because, the Board thought, people who had bought smaller lots had a vested interest in their "right to build." Carried to its logical conclusion this reasoning might mean that a municipality had to allow the owner of a lot with 3000 square feet to erect a house. Or on even smaller lots perhaps with smaller houses. Fortunately the Board was not moved by such specious logic, and drew a line at 6,000 square feet, much closer to the Council's standard. Experience with the By-law has shown, however, that many lots existed at its passing that were much smaller than 6000 square feet. Plan C20 in the Township, registered in 1920, contained some forty lots measuring fifty feet by 115 feet, having an area of only 5,750 square feet. Each of the forty lots was effectively sterilized, for Plan C20 was so built up that combining of two of the lots was usually impossible.

One might well ask whether a zoning by-law should be passed without regard to existing property boundaries. On the one hand, the haphazard subdivision of the past should not control the desire for higher standards in the future, and yet the difficulty of acquiring additional land is well known, and some regard must therefore be had for the undersized lots. There is little moral justification for putting a landowner at the mercy of the adjoining landowner, who, by fixing his price beyond his neighbour's reach makes himself rather than the state, the real legislator in the case.

On the question of undersized lots, see the material on "replotting" in Chapter 13.

Parking Space. Parking space has become one of the most important regulatory zoning problems in contemporary society. In many parts of Canada the incidence of the automobile is as high as in the United States, where it is as high as anywhere in the world. Parking space may be required for single family houses, but provision for one space for each house is rarely difficult. By contrast, provision of parking for a "high rise" apartment building may be a very expensive item in the contractor's budget. Requirements are said now to be about three quarters of a car for each apartment in the building, and estimates are said to indicate that in a few years space for one and a quarter cars will be required for each apartment. To draft a provision that will let the contractor off by providing space for three quarters of a car for each apartment now, and yet require him to supplement this until the highest minimum of one and a quarter is reached, is quite a challenge to the municipal lawyer, yet to require the contractor (or owner) to meet the future minimum now may now require him to tie up a good bit of capital for no return.

Clearly all commercial uses do not make equal demands for parking space, and it may be impossible to work out minimal requirements for classes of land use that will have practical utility. Where a warehouse is erected in a commercial zone and parking space is provided adequate only to its needs, if the next owner attempts to convert the warehouse into a mammoth grocery store, the parking almost certainly will be inadequate. Problems of this sort have led developers to cooperate to the extent of producing shopping centres where the parking is related to a total commercial community with a wide variety of commercial uses. In such circumstances formulae can be safely made much more general.

Performance Standards. In the United States many municipalities have experimented with what are known as performance standards. In terms of open space around high buildings, the following extract from the City of Toronto's Zoning By-law is a good illustration. But Canadian municipalities have not yet gone as far as their American counterparts. Performance standards are particularly applicable, or are thought to be by their advocates, in relation to nuisance controls. It is now possible to measure the quantity of sound, or noise, emitted by an industry, and to measure the quantity of solid dirt in the smoke from industrial (and residential) chimneys. Effluent from paper mills can be similarly measured. Electro-magnetic radiation has been measured and controlled for years by the Canadian Broadcasting Corporation and the Department of Transport. Instead of establishing a zone where smoky, dirty, noisy uses are permitted, the degree of smoke, dirt, and noise permitted anywhere is determined by the by-law, and the "zoning" element is reduced to a minimum. Whether this sort of solution produces a really desirable flexibility is still unsettled and planners and politicians are themselves debating the merits. Yet the notion of performance standards underlies a good deal of modern zoning. It is now widely recognized that shopping centres are appropriate in residential neighbourhoods, if proper precautions are taken to isolate or eliminate the undesirable features; for example, if unloading is required to go underground, if off street parking is adequate and pleasantly landscaped, if night lighting is kept within the bounds of good taste and the streets leading to the center are designed to handle the traffic, the shopping centre will be a real convenience to its neighbourhood and not a source of complaint.

Those who advocate performance standards argue that a factory is not undesirable in gross, but certain measurable aspects may be undesirable if present in too great a degree. Some smoke is harmless, too much is quite another matter. So the proposal is to ascertain how much smoke can be tolerated, and allow so much and no more. Similarly with noise. If an industrial process creates 85 decibels of sound at the property boundary, and it is considereed that the neighbours should not have to tolerate more than 70 decibels, the industrial process either stays out, or finds various ways of reducing noise: for example, by soundproofing the factory walls; by acquiring more land; by planting dense shrubbery and trees between the building and the lot line. If the performance standard is the only test, human ingenuity is free to work out any solution it can think up. If rigid zones and rigid regulations are established, then freedom is greatly restricted. In all probability moderate zoning and moderate performance standards will go hand in hand.

No one would pretend that performance standards will be easy to administer. Flexibility is the source of most difficulty in administration. A hard and fast rule can be enforced by a police department. A rule based on measurements of sound, dirt, dust, smoke, etc., will require an efficient engineering department and an intelligent legal approach. Evidence problems will be acute. Expert witnesses will be often needed. Yet if zoning in any form is to continue, and flexibility is to become our modern god, performance standards seem to be the most attractive solution so far.

One unsolved difficulty with performance standards, whose special merit is objectivity of measurement, is to find an objective standard for the degree of noise, smoke and dirt that the individual has to tolerate. So far this degree is wholly subjective and upon the subjective degree rests the whole structure of objective standards. If the subjective degree is to be determined by an elected body, it may be objected that the body will have very little real understanding of the objective standards.

ZONING RESOLUTION OF THE CITY OF NEW YORK (1960)

12–10. Words in the text or tables of this resolution which are *italicized* shall be interpreted in accordance with the provisions set forth in this Section.

23–61 *Definitions* (*repeated from Section 12–10*) An "initial setback distance" is a horizontal distance measured from a *street line* into a *zoning lot* for a depth as set forth in the district regulations.

A "public park" is any publicly-owned park, playground, beach, parkway, or roadway within the jurisdiction and control of the Commissioner of Parks, except for park strips or malls in a *street* the roadways of which are not within his jurisdiction and control.

A "sky exposure plane" is an imaginary inclined plane:

(a) Beginning above the *street line* (or, where so indicated, above the *front yard line*) at a height set forth in the district regulations, and

(b) Rising over a *zoning lot* at a ratio of vertical distance to horizontal distance set forth in the district regulations.

A "narrow street" is any *street* less than 75 feet wide.

A "wide street" is any *street* 75 feet or more in width.

A "street wall' is a wall or portion of a wall of a *building* facing a *street*. The "aggregate width of street walls" at any given level is the sum of the maximum widths of all *street walls* of a *building* within 50 feet of a *street line*. The width of a *street wall* is the length of the *street line* from which, when viewed directly from above, lines perpendicular to the *street line* may be drawn to such *street wall*.

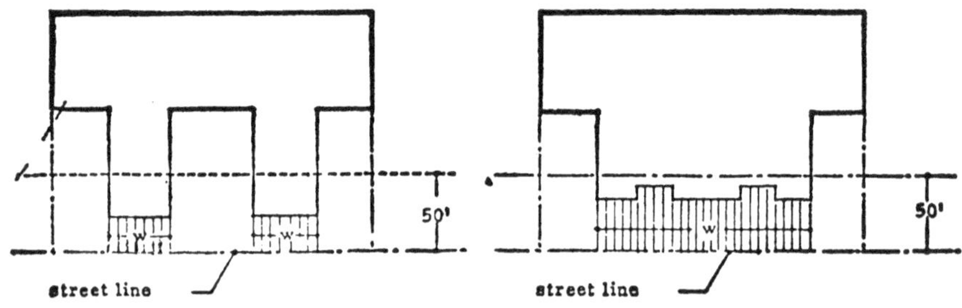

ILLUSTRATION OF AGGREGATE WIDTH OF STREET WALLS
SECTION 23-61

A "front yard line" is a line drawn parallel to a *front lot line* at a distance therefrom equal to the depth of a required *front* yard.

The "front yard line level" is the mean level of that portion of the *front yard line* from which, when viewed directly from above, lines perpendicular to the *front yard line* may be drawn to a *street wall*. On *corner lots*, the *front yard line level* is the mean of the *front yard line levels*.

A "rear yard line" is a line drawn parallel to a *rear lot line* at a distance therefrom equal to the depth of a required *rear yard*.

23–631. Front setbacks in districts where front yards are required

In the districts indicated, where *front yards* are required, the front wall or any other portion of a *building or other structure* shall not penetrate the *sky exposure plane* set forth in the following table:

MAXIMUM HEIGHT OF FRONT WALL AND REQUIRED FRONT SETBACKS
Sky exposure plane

Height above *front yard line* (in feet)	Slope over *zoning lot* (expressed as a ratio of vertical distance to horizontal distance)					
	On *narrow street*			On *wide street*		
	Vertical distance		Horizontal distance	Vertical distance		Horizontal distance
25	1	to	1	1	to	1
35	1	to	1	1	to	1

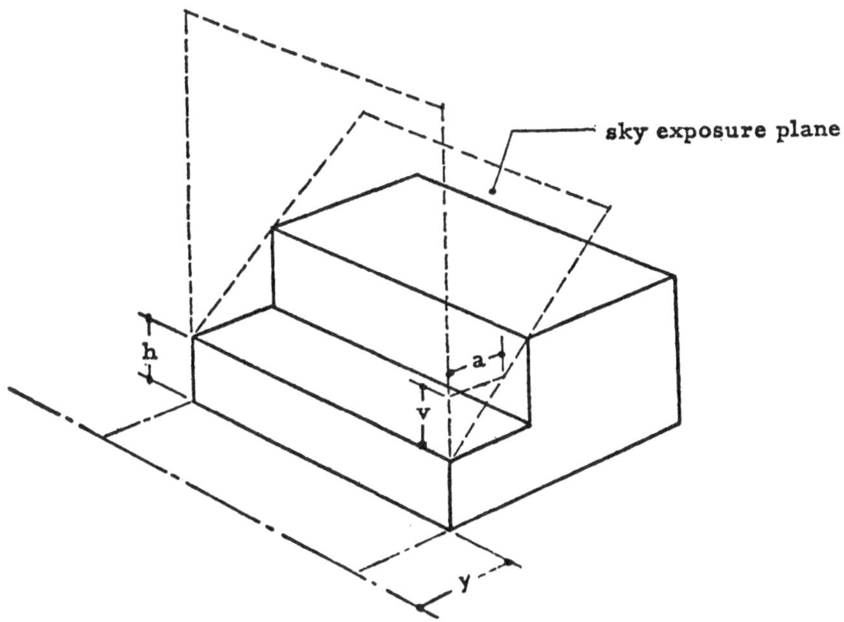

y is the depth of required *front yard*
h is the height of *sky exposure plane* above *front yard line level*
v is the vertical distance
a is the horizontal distance

ILLUSTRATION OF SECTION 23–631

23–632. Front setbacks in districts where front yards are not required
In the districts indicated, where *front yards* are not required, if the front wall or other portion of a *building or other structure* is located at the *street line* or within the *initial setback distance* set forth in the following table, the height of such front wall or other portion of a *building or other structure* shall not exceed the maximum height above *curb level* set forth in the following table. Above such specified maximum height and beyond the *initial setback distance*, the *building or other structure* shall not penetrate the *sky exposure plane* set forth in the following table:

MAXIMUM HEIGHT OF FRONT WALL AND REQUIRED FRONT SETBACKS

Initial setback distance (in feet) On *narrow street*	*Initial setback distance* (in feet) On *wide street*	Maximum height of a front wall, or other portion of a *building*, within the *initial setback distance*	Height above *street line* (in feet)	*Sky exposure plane* — Slope over *zoning lot* (expressed) as a ratio of vertical distance to horizontal distance): On *narrow street* Vertical distance		On *narrow street* Horizontal distance	On *wide street* Vertical distance		On *wide street* Horizontal distance
20	15	60 feet or six *stories*, whichever is less	60	2.7	to	1	5.6	to	1
20	15	85 feet or nine *stories*, whichever is less	85	2.7	to	1	5.6	to	1

23–711. Standard minimum distance between buildings

In all districts, as indicated, except as provided in Section 23–712 (Minimum distance between buildings in high bulk districts), the minimum distance between any two buildings (referred to as *building* A and *building* B) shall vary according to the length and height of such *buildings*. Such minimum distance shall be either 30 feet or the distance required under the following formula, whichever is the greater distance:

$$S = \frac{L_A + L_B + 2\,(H_A + H_B)}{6}, \text{ where:}$$

S = required minimum horizontal distance between any wall of *building* A, at any given level, and any wall of *building* B, at any given level, or the vertical prolongation of either.

L_A = total length of *building* A.
The total length of *building* A is the length of that portion or portions of a wall or walls of *building* A from which, when viewed directly from above, lines drawn perpendicular to *building* A will intersect any wall of *building* B.

L_B = total length of *building* B.
The total length of *building* B is the length of that portion or portions of a wall or walls of building B from which, when viewed directly from above, lines drawn perpendicular to *building* B will intersect any wall of *building* A.

H_A = height of *building* A.
The height of *building* A at any given level is the height above natural grade level of any portion or portions of a wall or walls along the total length of *building* A.

H_B = height of *building* B.
The height of *building* B at any given level is the height above natural grade level of any portion or portions of a wall or walls along the total length of *building* B.
For the purposes of this Section, natural grade level shall be the mean level of the ground immediately adjoining the portion or portions of the wall or walls along the total length of the *building* on the side facing the other *building*.

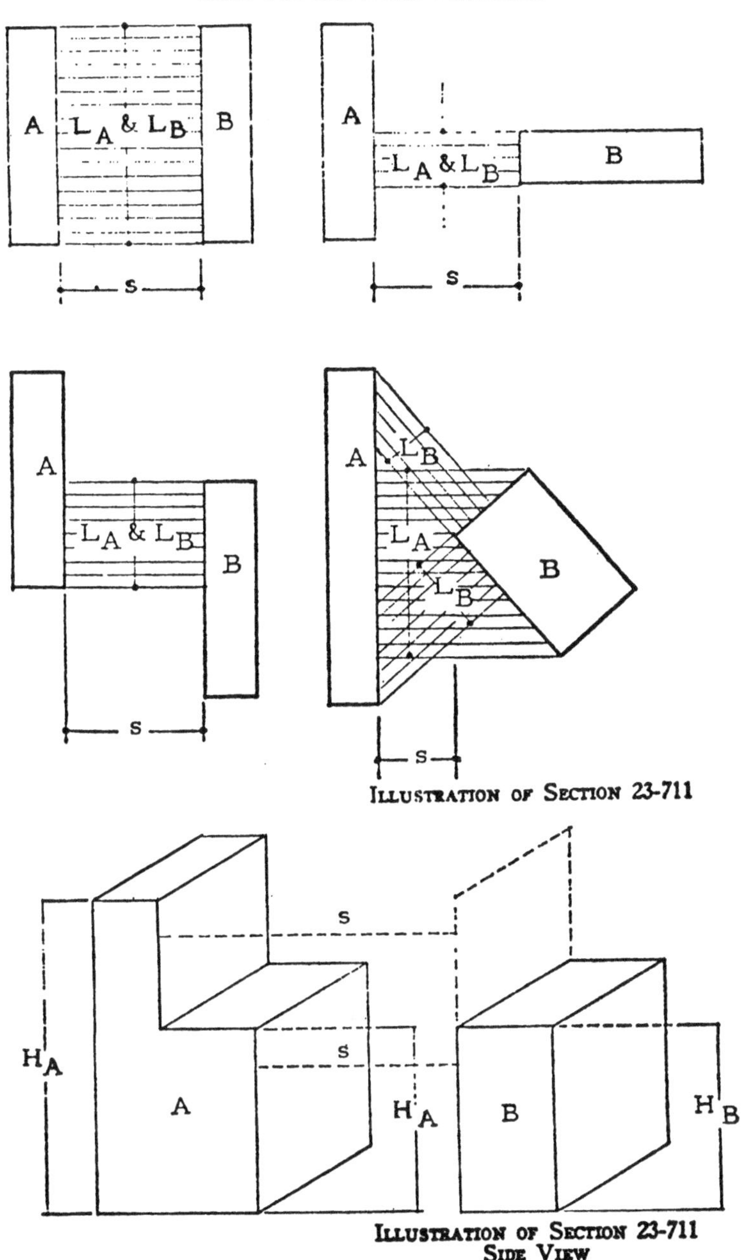

ILLUSTRATION OF SECTION 23-711

ILLUSTRATION OF SECTION 23-711
SIDE VIEW

s is the required minimum distance between a wall of building A and a wall of building B.
L_A is the length of building A, as defined.
L_B is the length of building B, as defined.
H_A is the height of building A, as defined.
H_B is the height of building B, as defined.

If "$L_A + L_B$" is equal to zero, the formula set forth above shall not apply, and the minimum distance shall be 30 feet.

However, the minimum required distance between two *buildings* on a single *zoning* lot as derived from the formula set forth in this Section shall be reduced by 15 percent in the event that:

(a) One of the said two *buildings* has a height of two *stories* or less, and the other has a height of six *stories* or more and

(b) The difference in height between the said two *buildings* is 60 feet or more.

23–712. Minimum distance between buildings in high bulk districts

In the districts indicated, on any single *zoning lot* having a *lot area* of not more than 100,000 square feet, the minimum distance between any two *buildings* shall be either 30 feet or the minimum distance required under the following formula, whichever is the greater distance:

$$S = \frac{L_A + L_B + H_A + H_B}{6}, \text{ where}$$

S, L_A, L_B, H_A, and H_B

shall have the same meaning as in Section 23–711 (Standard minimum distance between buildings).

If "$L_A + L_B$" is equal to zero, the formula set forth above shall not apply, and the minimum distance shall be 30 feet.

However, if neither of two *buildings* exceeds in height nine *stories* or 85 feet, whichever is less, the minimum distance required between such *buildings* need not be more than 80 feet.

NOTE ON THE NEW YORK ZONING RESOLUTION. The above provisions of the Zoning Resolution have been reproduced as an illustration of the drafting devices used to make a complex "by-law" more understandable. Attention is drawn to the repetition of definitions in sections where they are especially relevant, the italicizing of defined words, and the uncommon but very sensible use of line drawings to illustrate the verbal rules. Compare the city of Toronto Zoning By-law below. Could the line drawings published by the Planning Board have been made part of the by-law?

The line drawing illustrating section 23–632 has been deliberately omitted. Can you supply the omission?

CITY OF TORONTO ZONING BY-LAW NO. 20,623 (1959)

4. (3) (a) Subject to the provisions of paragraphs (b), (c) and (d) and of subsections (4) and (6), no person shall, on any *lot* in any R district, erect or use any building or structure any part of which projects beyond any of the angular planes constructed in the manner hereinafter described in this paragraph; but in no case shall any part of a building or structure be erected closer to any *lot* line than the distance of twenty-five (25) feet.

The hereinbefore referred to angular planes shall be constructed over the *lot* from each *lot* line at natural or finished ground level, whichever is the lower, at a vertical angle of sixty (60) degrees above the horizontal and measured perpendicular to the *lot* line or, in the case of a curved *lot* line, perpendicular to the tangents of all points of the *lot* line;

(b) Where a *lot line* of an *inside lot* coincides with a *street* line, the angular plane may be constructed from the centre line of the

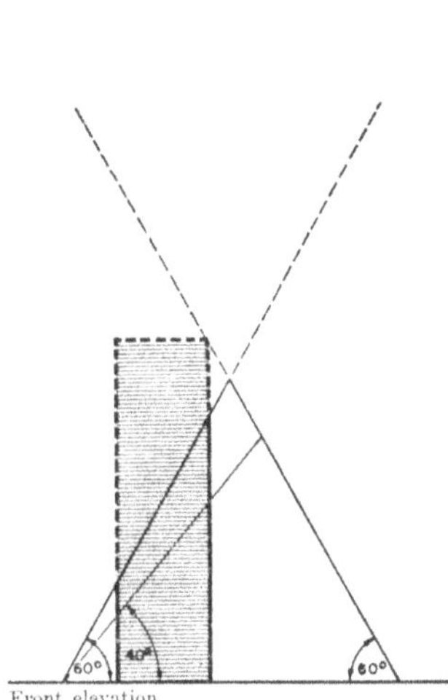

Front elevation

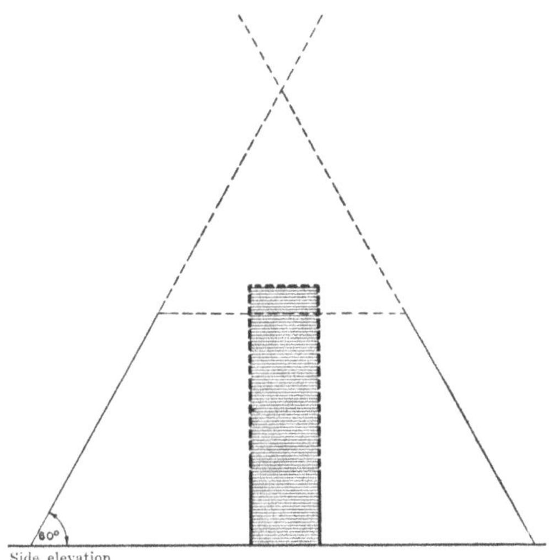

Side elevation

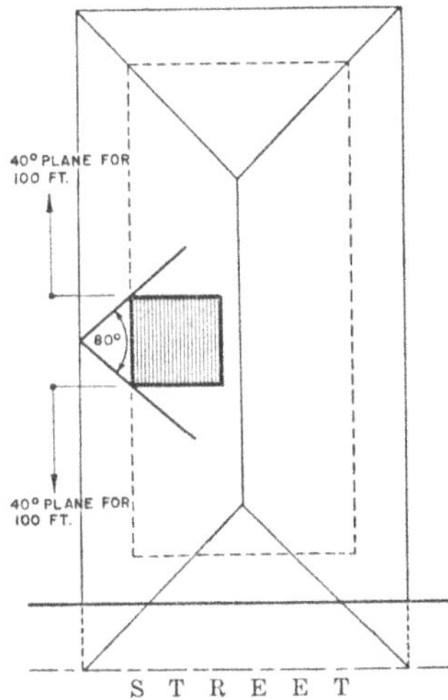

These diagrams are reproduced from *A Guide to the Revised Residential Zoning Standards* published by the City of Toronto and the City's Planning Board (1958). They illustrate "how part of a building may penetrate one of the side angular planes [see section 4(3) (c) and (d)]. No attempt is made to show how other parts of the building, or other buildings, might also be erected on the site, Such building must conform to a plane of 40° for a distance of 100 feet on either side of the tower."

street instead of the *lot* line or from any intervening line parallel to the centre line of the *street* provided that (i) the distance between the line on which the plane is constructed and the *lot* line does not exceed thirty-three (33) feet, (ii) the vertical angle of sixty (60) degrees is constructed perpendicular to the line on which the plane is constructed or, in the case of a curved line, perpendicular to the tangents of all points of the curved line and (iii) in no case shall any part of the building or structure be erected closer to the *lot* line than the distance of twenty (20) feet;

(c) Notwithstanding the provisions of paragraphs (a) and (b) of of this subsection but subject to the provisions of paragraph (d), any part of a building or structure may project beyond any prescribed sixty (60) degree angular plane if, in each case, (i) the projection through the plane subtends a horizontal angle not exceeding eighty (80) degrees formed by lines drawn from a point on the line on which the sixty (60) degree angular plane is constructed opposite to the centre of the projection, (ii) the extremities of the projection are enclosed by the arms of such eighty (80) degree horizontal angle; and (iii) no part of the building or structure is erected closer to any lot line than the distance of twenty-five (25) feet (twenty (20) feet where the *lot* line of an *inside lot* coincides with a *street* line);

(d) Where part of a building or structure projects through the sixty (60) degree angular plane in the manner permitted by paragraph (c), no other part of the building or structure within a distance of one hundred (100) feet of either side of the projection shall project beyond a forty (40) degree angular plane, constructed from the line from which the sixty (60) degree angular plane was constructed and in a manner similar to that prescribed in paragraphs (a) and (b) for sixty (60) degree angular planes, unless the extremities of the projection through the forty (40) degree angular plane are enclosed by arms of the horizontal angle constructed pursuant to paragraph (c).

(4) Notwithstanding anything contained in subsection (3), but subject to the provisions of subsection (6),

(a) where the proposed building or structure is to be erected on an *inside lot* between existing buildings or structures which are distant not more than eighty (80) feet from the respective *side lot lines* of the *lot*, no part of the proposed building or structure shall be erected closer to the *front lot line* than a straight line across the *lot* and connecting the nearest parts of the external faces of the front walls of such existing buildings or structures, but in no event shall any part of the proposed building or structure be erected closer to the *front lot line* than twenty (20) feet;

(b) a *private detached dwelling house*, a *one-family dwelling house*, a pair of *semi-detached dwelling houses* or the end house of *row housing* may be erected on a *corner lot* in an R district with no part of the building closer to the *front lot line* and *flank* of the lot, respectively, than the distance of twenty

(20) feet provided that the said distance from the *flank* may be reduced by one (1) foot, or fraction thereof, for every one (1) foot, or corresponding fraction thereof, that the said distance from the *front lot line* is increased but in no case shall the distance from the *flank* be so reduced to less than eight (8) feet; and, in the case of every other R building erected on a *corner lot* in any R district, the sixty (60) degree angular planes referred to in paragraph (a) of subsection (3) may be constructed, in the manner and to the extent provided in paragraph (b) of said subsection, from the respective centre lines of the streets upon which the *front lot line* and *flank* of the lot respectively abut;

(c) none of the provisions of subsection (3) shall apply to any detached *accessory* building or structure except that no detached *accessory* building or structure shall be erected (1) closer to any residential building than the distance of fifteen (15) feet or (2) closer to the *front lot line* of an *inside lot* or *corner lot* than the distance at which the main building or structure is erected;

(d) in the case of a *lot* in a Zone 2, 3, 4 or 5 area and having a lesser *front lot line* than ninety (90) feet,

(i) the distance from either or both of the *side lot lines* (except where the *side lot line* is the *flank* of a *corner lot*) at which any part of a building, other than a *duplex dwelling house, a double duplex dwelling house, a triplex dwelling house, a double triplex dwelling house* or an *apartment house* in a Zone 2 area may be erected may be not less than three(3) feet for a distance not exceeding thirty (30) feet back from the *minimum front lot line set-back* provided no part of the building that projects beyond the prescribed sixty (60) degree angular plane exceeds thirty (30) feet in *height*; (21,054) (21,295)

(ii) except in the case of a *duplex dwelling house*, a *double duplex dwelling house*, a *triplex dwelling house*, a *double triplex dwelling house* or an *apartment house* in a Zone 2 area, any building may be erected with one or both of its side walls located on the nearest *side lot line* (except where the *side lot line* is the *flank* of a *corner lot*) for a length not exceeding thirty (30) feet back from the *minimum front lot line set-back* provided no such wall contains any door, window or other opening and no part of the building that projects beyond the prescribed sixty (60) degree angular plane exceeds thirty (30) feet in *height*; (21,054)

(iii) any building may be erected with no part thereof closer to the nearest *side lot line* (except where the *side lot line* is the *flank* of a *corner lot*) than the distance of ten (10) feet for a length not exceeding forty-five (45) feet back from the *minimum front lot line set-back* provided no part of the building that projects beyond the prescribed sixty (60) degree angular plane exceeds thirty (30) feet in *height*;

(iv) any building to which clauses (i), (ii) and (iii) apply may be erected combining the *side lot line* set-back exceptions contained in the said clauses, provided the first thirty (30) feet of the building and the side walls thereof comply with the respective requirements of clauses (i) and (ii), the next fifteen (15) feet of the building complies with the requirements of clause (iii) and the part of the building, if any, that is more than forty-five (45) feet back from the *minimum front lot line set-back* complies with the set-back requirements of paragraph (a) of subsection (3);

(e) as an alternative to the provisions of paragraph (d), and in addition, in the case of a *lot* in a Zone 1 area and having a lesser *front lot line* than ninety (90) feet, the distance from either or both of the *side lot lines* (except where the *side lot line* is the *flank* of a *corner lot*) at which any part of a *private detached dwelling house,* a *one-family dwelling house*, a *pair of semi-detached dwelling houses* or the end houses of *row housing* may be erected may be not less than three (3) feet, without any limitation on *height* or distance back from the *minimum front line set-back;*

(f) in the case of a *lot* in any Zone 4 or 5 area and having a lesser *front lot line* than ninety (90) feet, any building may be erected with no part thereof closer to the nearest *side lot* line (except where the *lot line* is the *flank* of a *corner lot*) than the distance of fifteen (15) feet for a length not exceeding forty (40) feet back from the *minimum front lot line set-back* provided that no part of the building that projects beyond the prescribed sixty (60) degree angular plane exceeds sixty (60) feet in *height*;

(g) for the purposes of paragraphs (d), (e) and (f), "*height*" means the vertical distance between the average elevation of the natural or finished level of the ground, whichever is the lower, along the portion of the *side lot line* opposite the part of the building concerned and, in the case of a pitched-roofed building, the mean height level between the eaves and ridge and in the case of any other kind of roof, the highest point of the roof; and "*minimum front lot line set-back*" means twenty (20) feet from the *front lot line* except in a case governed by paragraph (a) when the minimum shall be as therein provided and except when the building is erected on a *corner lot* and the *minimum front lot line set-back* is increased in accordance with paragraph (b) in which case the minimum shall be as so increased; but in no event shall any part of any building to which paragraphs (d), (e) or (f) apply be erected closer to any *lot line*, other than *a side lot line*, than compliance with paragraph (a) of subsection (3) permits.

(5) (a) Subject to the provisions of paragraphs (b) and (c) and of subsection (6), no person shall, on any *lot* in any R district, erect or use any building or structure any part of which projects beyond any of the angular planes constructed in the manner hereinafter described in this paragraph; but in no case shall the distance between any external walls of a building or structure that face each other be less than fifty (50) feet.

The hereinbefore referred to angular planes shall be constructed outwards from the base line of each external wall of each part of the building or structure at a vertical angle of forty (40) degrees above the horizontal and measured perpendicular to the base line or, in the case of a curved *base line*, perpendicular to the tangents of all points of the curved *base line*;

(b) It shall not be necessary to comply with paragraph (a) if no part of the building or structure is erected within the arms of horizontal angles of sixty-five (65) degrees constructed outwards, at the natural level of the ground, from the nearest extremities of external walls that face each other provided that where the two extremities of one wall are, respectively, equidistant from the opposite extremities of the other wall or where the two extremities of one wall are equidistant from the nearest extremity of the other wall, the sixty-five (65) degree horizontal angles may be constructed from either pair of equidistant extremities;

(c) Where two external walls of a building or structure rise from the ground and face and are parallel to each other and neither wall contains any opening except windows that light stairways and not more than two service or emergency or fire exit doors, the distance between the said walls may, subject to compliance with the requirements of By-law No. 9,868, being "A By-law To regulate the erection and provide for the safety of buildings", be not less than six (6) feet, in which case paragraph (a) shall not apply;

4. (12) (a) No person shall, on any *lot*, in any V.1, V.2, V.3 or V.4 area, as the case may be, erect any C. building or C. structure having a greater *gross floor area* than as follows:

V.1 areas	3 times the area of the lot
V.2 areas	5 times the area of the lot
V.3 areas	7 times the area of the lot
V.4 areas	12 times the area of the lot

(aa) No person shall, on any lot in any L.1, L.2, L.3 or L.4 Zone, as the case may be, erect any non-*residential building* or non-*residential structure* having a greater *gross floor area* than as follows:—

L.1 Zones	1.0 times the area of the *lot*
L.2 Zones	2 times the area of the *lot*
L.3 Zones	3 times the area of the *lot*
L.4 Zones	4 times the area of the *lot*

(b) No person shall on any *lot* in any zone 1, zone 2, zone 3, zone 4 or zone 5 area, as the case may be, erect any R. building or R. structure or any residential building or structure having a greater *gross floor area* or so that the *lot* has lesser *landscaped open space* than as follows:

Zones	*Maximum gross floor area*	Minimum *landscaped open space*
zone 1 areas	0.35 times the area of the *lot*	30% of the area of the *lot*
zone 2 areas	0.6 times the area of the *lot*	30% of the area of the *lot*
zone 3 areas	1.0 times the area of the *lot*	30% of the area of the *lot*
zone 4 areas	2.0 times the area of the *lot*	35% of the area of the *lot*
zone 5 areas	2.5 times the area of the *lot*	35% of the area of the *lot*

(c) For the purposes of this By-law,

(i) "*gross floor area*" means, in the case of a C. building or C. structure other than a residential building or structure, the aggregate of the areas of each storey above *grade* measured between the exterior faces of the exterior walls of the building or structure at the level of each storey; and, in the case of an R. building or R. structure or a residential building or structure, means the aggregate of the areas of each floor, whether any such floor is above or below *grade*, measured between the exterior faces of the exterior walls of the building or structure at the level of each floor, exclusive, however, of any part of the building or structure below *grade* which is used for heating equipment, the storage or parking of motor vehicles, locker storage and laundry facilities, children's play areas and other *accessory* uses or used as living quarters by the caretaker, watchman or other supervisor of the building or structure;

(iii) "*landscaped open space*" means open, unobstructed space on a *lot* which is suitable for the growth and maintenance of grass, flowers, bushes and other landscaping and includes the part of a lot unoccupied by any building or structure by reason of the operation of subsections (3), (4) or (5) of this section and any surfaced walk, patio or similar area but does not include any driveway or ramp, whether surfaced or not, any curb, retaining wall, motor vehicle parking area or any open space beneath or within any building or structure.

[The numbers in brackets after some sections are the numbers of amending by-laws. The excerpt is reproduced as it appears in the office consolidation of February, 1962. *Italicized* words are defined in the interpretation section.]

CHAPTER 11

THE LIMITATIONS OF ZONING BY-LAWS

Rigorous law is often rigorous injustice.

TERENCE

Apart from the very important planning powers held at all levels of government arising indirectly from their powers to carry out public works, the most significant power to control land use is, on this continent, exercisable by municipal by-law. The remaining chapters are primarily concerned with the legal problems involved in the exercise of this by-law making power, and with drafting problems implicit in the use of the power to achieve some sort of known goal. There are other methods of land use regulation considered in some jurisdictions to be more sophisticated. The study of these methods has been postponed until the strengths and weaknesses of the traditional method have been fully explored.

1. THE SCOPE OF STATUTORY AUTHORITY

(*a*) *Ultra vires*

DONALD *v.* WHITBY
Ontario. Court of Appeal. [1949] 1 D.L.R. 361

ROBERTSON C.J.O.: This is an appeal by the municipal corporation from the order of Barlow J., dated 16th September 1948, whereby he quashed By-law No. 1780 of the municipal corporation, being "a By-law to regulate the erection of signs or other advertising devices within the Town of Whitby."

The by-law purports to be passed pursuant to the provisions of s.-s. (54) of s. 405 of the *Municipal Act*, R.S.O. 1937, c. 266 [now s. 371(1)¶ 122 R.S.O. 1960, c. 249] The statute authorizes the councils of local municipalities to pass by-laws: "For prohibiting or regulating the erection of signs or other advertising devices, and the posting of notices on buildings or vacant lots within any defined area or areas or on land abutting on any defined highway or part of a highway."

Mr. Justice Barlow did not give any reasons in writing for his order, but we were informed that he proceeded upon the authority of the judgment of the late Mr. Justice Middleton in *Rex* v. *Cullian* (1937). A by-law passed on the authority of the same provision of the *Municipal Act* was in question in that case. Mr. Justice Middleton, in ruling against the validity of the by-law, said:

"I think this present by-law is defective because the municipality is empowered to prohibit or regulate the erection of signs or other advertising devices and the posting of notices, but what the council has undertaken to do is to pass a by-law regulating the erection of signs and other advertising devices, but saying nothing whatever about the posting of notices.

"I think the municipal powers are limited by the precise words of the legislative enactment, and the municipality must do all that is authorized by the *Municipal Act* or leave the subject alone."

The by-law in the present case, like the by-law in the *Cullian* case, purports to regulate the erection of signs and other advertising devices, but says nothing about the posting of notices, and counsel for the respondent relies upon the *Cullian* case as a decision directly in point . . .

We are confronted now with the very question that was decided by Mr. Justice Middleton in the *Cullian* case. We have to determine whether the present by-law is defective, because the council undertook to pass a by-law under s. 405 (54) regulating the erection of signs and other advertising devices, but said nothing whatever in the by-law about the posting of notices.

The jurisdiction of a municipal council to pass by-laws under s. 405 of the *Municipal Act* is a jurisdiction delegated to it by the Provincial Legislature, which has a broad and general jurisdiction to make laws in relation to municipal institutions in the Province, under s. 92(8) of the *B.N.A. Act.* A municipal council has the jurisdiction delegated to it by the Legislature, and no other. The common complaint in attacks upon municipal by-laws is that the council has exceeded its jurisdiction. The complaint here is that the council did not exercise in full the jurisdiction conferred upon it. The complaint is not that the council has put anything in the by-law that it had no power to enact; the complaint is that the council should have proceeded in the same by-law to deal with the posting of notices, or, as expressed by Mr. Justice Middleton in the Cullian case, the municipal council must do all that is authorized by the *Municipal Act*, or leave the subject alone . . .

In my opinion a municipal council has generally a wide discretion as to the manner and the extent of the exercise of its statutory powers, so long as it does not exceed them. I am further of the opinion that the terms in which s. 405 (54) of the *Municipal Act* is expressed plainly indicate that it was the intention of the Legislature that the council should have a wide discretion in the exercise of the powers that it confers, and that it cannot be said that, in passing a by-law under its authority, a municipality must do all that is authorized by the *Municipal Act*, or leave the subject alone. The opening words of clause 54 so indicate. By-laws may be passed for prohibiting or regulating; the council is not to do both, but in the exercise of its discretion in any given case may either prohibit or regulate. No doubt, in the same by-law the council may prohibit some things and may make regulations to govern other things. For example, a by-law may prohibit advertising devices that show a red or a green light near a highway traffic signal, or a large sign that obstructs the view at a dangerous corner. The same by-law may contain regulations that apply to signs or other advertising devices that are not prohibited. Equally within its powers, when prohibiting or regulating where it is deemed necessary, the council may refrain from either prohibiting or regulating signs or advertising devices that, in its judgment, it is not advisable in the public interest, either to prohibit or to regulate.

If the council were required to exercise its powers to the full or "do all that is authorized by the *Municipal Act* or leave the subject alone," it would require to exercise its powers of prohibition or regulation in respect of the erection of all signs and other advertising devices and the posting of all notices on buildings or vacant lots within any defined area or on land abutting on any defined highway or part of a highway, as to which it determined to exercise its powers. The mere fact that it is left to the council to define the area or the highway or portion of a highway to be affected, itself indicates a wide discretion in the council, and not a power restricted to its exercise to its full limit, if exercised at all.

Some support for the attack upon the by-law was sought to be obtained by suggesting possible discrimination by reason of the by-law, in favour of persons who advertised by posting notices, and whose notices are neither prohibited nor regulated. It is impossible to say what character of notices the Legislature had in mind in making the enactment, but this much seems clear, that notices in the nature of advertising were not intended, for "signs and other advertising devices" are already covered by the clause. It is common knowledge that there is much advertising done by signs and advertising devices that, for a variety of reasons, may become objectionable from a public point of view, if it is not controlled by the means that are available to a municipality under s. 405 (54). I am not aware that the posting of notices, other than such notices as would come within the description of "signs or other advertising devices", is commonly so objectionable from a public point of view as to make the omission to prohibit or regulate the posting of such notices a ground for imputing some improper motive or unfair conduct to the municipal council. There is nothing on the record in the present case to support anything of that nature affecting the passing of the by-law under attack.

In my opinion the appeal should be allowed and the motion to quash the by-law should be dismissed. The municipality should have its costs of both the motion and the appeal.

COMMODORE GRILL *v.* DUNNVILLE. [1943] 4 D.L.R. 183 (Ontario. Court of Appeal). The Court conceded the possibility that there might be some special instance to be found where for some exceptional reason, the power delegated by the legislature could be exercised only in the restricted manner indicated by Middleton J.A. in the *Cullian* case.

(*b*) *Prohibition and regulation*

IN RE GLOVER AND SAM KEE
British Columbia. Supreme Court. 1914. 20 B.C.R. 219

MACDONALD J.: The appellant was convicted by the police magistrate of the City of Kamloops upon a charge that on the 26th of July, 1913, "he constructed and used a building for a laundry or wash-house within a certain portion of the City of Kamloops, contrary to the City of Kamloops Laundries or Wash-houses By-law, 1903, No. 50." The appellant was granted a case stated for the opinion of this Court, pursuant to the Summary Convictions Act.

It was admitted that the by-law had been duly passed by the Council of the City of Kamloops, that the property upon which the laundry of the appellant was situated was within the portion of the City of Kamloops specifically referred to in such by-law, and that appellant held himself out to the public and solicited business as proprietor of the laundry.

Several questions were submitted arising out of the objections taken to the validity of the by-law under which the conviction was obtained, but I have only deemed it necessary to deal with the more important grounds.

The statute in force at the time, and under which the by-law purports to have been passed, was R.S.B.C. 1897, Cap. 144, Sec. 50, Subsec. (91). This subsection gives power to each council of every municipality to make by-laws "for licensing and regulating wash-houses and laundries . . . for preventing and regulating the erection or continuance of any laundries or wash-houses which may be proved to be nuisances." This subjection was amended by section 4 of the statutes of 1900, Cap. 23, by inserting after the words "and for naming or defining the streets or limits (as in the case of fire limits) on or within which laundries or wash-houses may be established, maintained or operated."

It was contended that the council had misapprehended its powers, as it had not named or defined the streets or limits within which laundries or wash-houses might be "established, maintained or operated," but had created a restricted district within which buildings or structures for laundry purposes should not be "constructed and used." There is nothing illegal or improper in itself in the establishment, maintenance or operation of a laundry or wash-house. It is a legitimate and necessary business. When any interference by the Legislature is contemplated with such a business or calling, the statutory power conferred upon the municipality must be clearly indicated, and then specifically followed in any by-law passed thereunder. Aside from the unauthorized manner in which the council sought to segregate a district within which laundries or wash-houses might be not constructed and used, I consider the by-law exceeds the statutory power conferred upon the municipality. The Legislature, by the amendment referred to, extended the jurisdiction of the council so that it might be "established, maintained or operated," but it did not confer power of prevention so that "no building or structure of any kind shall be constructed and used for a laundry or wash-house" within a specific portion of the municipality . . .

The contention was made that the by-law was bad, in that it was unreasonable and oppressive and intended to create a monopoly by restraining the trade or calling which it assumed to regulate. I do not think the by-law could have been successfully attacked on this ground. Whatever burden is created or apparent privilege follows from the establishment of an area within the municipality where laundries or wash-houses might only be carried on, it is not a subject for judicial interference. It is a matter purely discretionary with the council of each municipality, and "the Court ought, as far as possible, to support by-laws made by local authorities unless it can be clearly seen that the by-law was made without jurisdiction and was unreasonable." . . .

It was contended that the by-law in its wording was prohibitive and not regulative. There is a great difference between prevention and regulation, and even between restraint and regulation, but I do not consider that the by-law except as to creating a restricted district, bears the construction thus sought to be placed upon it.

It is worthy of mention that the statute in force at the time of the passing of this by-law, and which provided for licensing and regulating of wash-houses or laundries, was amended in R.S.B.C. 1911; see Cap. 170, Sec. 50, Subsec. (117), and now the council of a municipality may pass by-laws for "preventing and regulating the erection and use or continuance of any laundries or wash-houses and for ordering the removal of laundries or wash-houses in a particular locality, when, in the opinion of the council, such laundries are a nuisance or an eyesore to such locality." This amendment greatly extended the powers of the council both as to prevention and regulation.

I consider the by-law bad. The determination of the magistrate was erroneous in point of law and should be reversed, and the conviction of the appellant should be set aside, with costs payable by the respondent.

TORONTO *v.* VIRGO
Ontario. Privy Council. [1896] A. C. 88

LORD DAVEY: This is an appeal from a judgment of the Supreme Court of Canada, reversing by a majority the previous decisions of the Court of Appeal for Ontario, and of Sir Thomas Galt C.J. The question for decision is whether a section of a by-law was competently and validly made by the corporation of the city of Toronto.

The section in question is designated as sub-s. 2a of s. 12 of by-law 2934, in amendment of s. 12 of by-law 2453. The last-mentioned section as amended requires a licence to be taken out by -

"All hawkers, petty chapmen, or other persons carrying on petty trades, or who go from place to place, or to other men's houses, on foot or with any animal bearing or drawing any goods, wares, or merchandise for sale, or in or with any boat, vessel or other craft, or otherwise carry goods, wares, or merchandise for sale: . . ."

Sub-s. 2a is the only part of the by-law now complained of. It is in the following words:

"No person named and specified in sub-s. 2 of this section (whether a licensee or not) shall, after the first day of July, 1892, prosecute his calling or trade in any of the following streets and portions of streets in the city of Toronto."

Then follows an enumeration of eight streets in the city of Toronto. It is stated in the evidence that these streets comprise the busiest and most important thoroughfares of the city.

The statutory power under which the corporation claim to make this by-law is contained in the Municipal Act of Ontario (c. 184 of the Revised Statutes of Ontario of 1887), s. 495, which so far as is material, is in the following words:

"The council of any county, city and town separated from the county for municipal purposes, may pass by-laws for the following purposes . . .

"For licensing, regulating and governing hawkers or petty chapmen, and other persons carrying on petty trades, or who go from place to place or to other men's houses, on foot or with any animal, bearing or drawing any goods, wares, or merchandise for sale, or in or with any boat, vessel, or other craft, or otherwise carrying goods, wares, or merchandise for sale, and for fixing the sum to be paid for a licence for exercising such calling within the county, city or town, and the time the licence shall be in force: . . ."

It appears to their Lordships that the real question is whether under a power to pass by-laws "for regulating and governing" hawkers, &c., the council may prohibit hawkers from plying their trade at all in a substantial and important portion of the city no question of any apprehended nuisance being raised. It was contended that the by-law was ultra vires, and also in restraint of trade and unreasonable. The two questions run very much into each other, and in the view which their Lordships take, it is not necessary to consider the second question separately.

No doubt the regulation and governance of a trade may involve the imposition of restrictions on its exercise both as to time and to a certain extent as to place where such restrictions are in the opinion of the public authority necessary to prevent a nuisance or for the maintenance of order. But their Lordships think there is marked distinction to be drawn between the prohibition or prevention of a trade and the regulation or governance of it, and indeed a power to regulate and govern seems to imply the continued existence of that which is to be regulated or governed. An examination of other sections of the Act confirms their Lordships' view, for it shews that when the Legislature intended to give power to prevent or prohibit it did so by express words. . . .

It is argued that the by-law impugned does not amount to prohibition, because hawkers and chapmen may still carry on their business in certain streets of the city. Their Lordships cannot accede to this argument. The question is one of substance and should be regarded from the point of view as well of the public as of the hawkers. The effect of the by-law is practically to deprive the residents of what is admittedly the most important part of the city of buying their goods of or of trading with the class of traders in question. And this observation receives additional force from the very wide definition given to "hawkers" in the Act. At the same time the "hawkers", &c., are excluded from exercising their trade in that part of the city. There was no evidence, and it is scarcely conceivable that the trade cannot be carried on without occasioning a nuisance. The appellants in their printed case wisely disclaim any intention on the part of the council to discriminate against hawkers and pedlars in favour of permanent shopkeepers. No other explanation of the object of the by-laws is offered. The question, therefore, is reduced to a bare question of power.

Their Lordships on the whole have come to the conclusion that it was not the intention of the Act to give this power to the corporation. They therefore agree with the majority of the judges of the Supreme Court, and will humbly advise Her Majesty that this appeal be dismissed with costs.

QUESTION. Can you use a bare licensing power to determine land use in particular places?

RE McCORMICK AND TORONTO TOWNSHIP
High Court (Ontario) [1948] 3 D.L.R. 70

WELLS J.: This is an application to quash By-law 1364 of the Township of Toronto [licensing and governing trailer camps]. . . .

There was some affidavit evidence before me, which was contradicted by the Township officials, that the real purpose of this by-law was to drive tourist camps out of the township. In so far as this affidavit evidence is concerned, I am not able to come to any conclusion on it, nor do I think that any conclusion could be reached in respect of these alleged intentions of the council without hearing oral evidence, and I do not regard these allegations as constituting a basis for my conclusion. . . .

It would seem to me that the evidence as to the financial results of the licence fees imposed might be one of the factors which, in this case, I should consider. It is not, however, necessarily a conclusive one. What must be looked at is the obvious effect of the licence fees generally, and in my view, looking at the whole matter, and giving it the best consideration I can, there is very little doubt that the fees imposed are in fact prohibitive of the tourist camp business in the township in question.

While it is quite true that it is no longer possible to quash a by-law on the ground of its unreasonableness, some attention must be paid to the power under which the municipality acts. What was given here was a power to pass by-laws for the licensing, regulating and governing of tourist camps. It was not a right to prohibit tourist camps, but to regulate and govern them. Under the guise of a licensing by-law the municipality cannot, in my opinion, impose fees which in effect are confiscatory and prohibitive. The power to license is not a power to destroy; it is a power to govern and regulate. . . .

While the evidence as to the prohibitive nature, from an examination of the accounts of the applicants and the rather bald statement of certain other tourist camp operators, is not too satisfactory, nevertheless I think it must be obvious on its face that the licensing fees imposed are, in effect, prohibitive, and in many cases would absorb more than a very substantial part of the gross revenue of the tourist cabins in any tourist camp. In my view, what the municipality was attempting to do here was not to regulate and govern tourist camps, but to destroy them and drive them out of the township of Toronto. It has not the power to do that. . . . [The licensing clause was quashed.]

REGINA *v.* GIBSON, EX PARTE CROMILLER
Ontario. High Court. [1959] O.W.N. 254

This was an application by way of originating notice for an order in lieu of *mandamus* requiring the respondent, the building commissioner of Etobicoke twp., to issue to the applicant a building permit.

The applicant applied for a building permit 21st April 1959, and was refused by the respondent 30th April 1959. The township council 19th May 1959, passed by-law 11777 providing *inter alia* that no building should be erected on any land shown on the official plan of the township as a proposed road and further that no building should be erected on any roadway indicated as such on the zoning map attached to the by-law. Part of the applicant's land was situated on one of the proposed roadways shown on the amendment of the official plan dealt with by by-law 11777.

SCHATZ J. in a written judgment said that the township had applied for approval of by-law 11777 to the municipal board and he had been asked to adjourn the motion pending the hearing before the board. Before determining the question as to whether he ought to adjourn the application he ought to determine whether by-law 11777 was a valid by-law. The by-law was passed under s. 27a of the Planning Act 1955, c. 6, as enacted by 1959, c. 71, s. 5. Section 27a was similar to s. 390 of the Municipal Act, R.S.O. 1950, c. 243. The learned Judge quoted cll. (1) and (2) of s. 27a (1). These clauses authorised the prohibition of the use of land, or the prohibition of the erection or use of buildings, either for such purposes as might be set out in the by-law or for all purposes except for such purposes as might be set out in the by-law. These two clauses therefore did not authorize by-laws absolutely prohibiting the use of land or the erection or use of buildings but such by-laws might be passed only to limit the type of buildings. It was therefore his opinion that there was no authority in either of the clauses to authorize the passing of by-law 11777. Clause (3) of the said section permitted the total prohibition of the erection of a building or structure for residence or commercial purposes on lands of a certain character but it was clear that this clause would not apply in this matter. He was not therefore called upon to exercise his discretion in either adjourning or refusing to adjourn the motion. . . .

[The application was allowed.]

QUESTIONS. Assuming that Schatz J.'s interpretation of paragraphs 1 and 2 of section 30(1) is right, and there is no power to prohibit all buildings, would a by-law be invalid that prohibited building a house or other structure within 58 feet of the centre line of a road shown on the official plan? Such a regulation would merely ensure the usual set back of 25 feet and would mean that no building or structure could be built on the road. Would a by-law be invalid that limited the use of land to the growing of crops? Such a limitation of use would effectively prohibit all building on the road but would not prohibit all use of the land. Is the Court's interpretation a proper one?

CHAMPION *v.* AMES (LOTTERY CASE). 1902. 188 U.S. 321 (United States. Supreme Court). HARLAN J.: "But it is said that the statute in question does not regulate the carrying of lottery tickets from State to State, but by punishing those who cause them to be so carried Congress in effect prohibits such carrying; that in respect of the carrying from one State to another of articles or things that are, in fact, or according to usage in business, the subjects of commerce, the authority given Congress was not to prohibit, but only to regulate. This view was earnestly pressed at the bar by learned counsel, and must be examined. . . .

"We have said that the carrying from State to State of lottery tickets constitutes interstate commerce, and that the regulation of such commerce is within the power of Congress under the Constitution. Are we prepared to say that a provision which is, in effect, a prohibition of the carriage of such articles from State to State is not a fit or appropriate mode for the regulation of that particular kind of commerce? If lottery traffic, carried on through interstate commerce, is a matter of which Congress may take cognizance and over which its power may be exerted, can it be possible that it must tolerate the traffic, and simply regulate the manner in which it may be carried on? Or may not Congress, for the protection of the people of all the States, and under the power to regulate interstate commerce, devise such means, within the scope of the Constitution, and not prohibited by it, as will drive that traffic out of commerce among the States?

"In determining whether regulation may not, under some circumstances, properly take the form or have the effect of prohibition, the nature of the interstate traffic which it was sought by the act of May 2, 1895, to suppress can not be overlooked. . . .

"If a State, when considering legislation for the suppression of lotteries within its own limits, may properly take into view the evils that inhere in the raising of money, in that mode, why may not Congress, invested with the power to regulate commerce among the several States, provide that such commerce shall not be polluted by the carrying of lottery tickets from one State to another? In this connection it must not be forgotten that the power of Congress to regulate commerce among the States is plenary, is complete in itself, and is subject to no limitations except such as may be found in the Constitution. What provision in that instrument can be regarded as limiting the exercise of the power granted? What clause can be cited which, in any degree, countenances the suggestion that one may, of right, carry or cause to be carried from one State to another that which will harm the public morals? We cannot think of any clause of that instrument that could possibly be invoked by those who assert their right to send lottery tickets from State to State except the one providing that no person shall be deprived of his liberty without due process of law. We have said that the liberty protected by the Constitution embraces the right to be free in the enjoyment of one's faculties; to be free to use them in all lawful ways; to live and work where he will; to earn his livelihood by any lawful calling; to pursue any livelihood or avocation, and for that purpose to enter into all contracts that may be proper. . . . But surely it will not be said to be in part of any one's liberty, as recognized by the supreme law of the land, that he shall be allowed to introduce into commerce among the States an element that will be confessedly injurious to the public morals. . . ."

NOTE. Section 8 of Article I of the United States Constitution provides, in part: "The Congress shall have Power [3] To *regulate* Commerce with foreign Nations, and among the several States, and with the Indian Tribes;" [Emphasis added.]

QUESTION. Should the powers of the United States Congress and a Canadian municipality be tested by different standards despite the identity of words used to describe them?

(*c*) *Pitfalls of interpretation*

ST. CATHARINES *v.* HULSE
Ontario. Court of Appeal. [1936] 2 D.L.R. 453

MIDDLETON J. A.: An appeal by the defendant from the judgment of McEvoy J. enjoining the defendant from carrying on an undertaking business at the premises known as 75 Church St. in the City of St. Catharines contrary to the provisions of By-laws 3428 and 3759 of the said City of St. Catharines.

By a section of the Municipal Act (now found as s. 406(8)) a municipal corporation is entitled to pass a by-law declaring any highway or part of a highway to be a residential street, and to prescribe the distance from the line of the street "in front of it at which no building on a residential street may be erected or placed." Pursuant to this section the municipality passed two by-laws; No. 3428 passed on July 10, 1922, declaring that portion of Church St. from James to Geneva St. is a residential street and that no building or extension of a building at present erected shall hereafter be erected on that part of Church St. within a distance of the north side of 22 ft. from the line to the street in front of it. By a second By-law No. 3759 passed on July 27, 1927, Lyman St. is declared to be a residential street and no building or erection shall be hereafter made on either side of Lyman St. within a distance of 15 ft. from the line of said street.

It nowhere appears in the material when the building in question was erected. It is spoken of as an "old residence" situated at the corner of the two streets. No complaint is made that the building transgresses the building lines laid down by these by-laws, but it is said that the defendant purchased the lands recently; his conveyance bears date May 28, 1935, and was registered on June 15, 1935, and he has made such internal alterations in the structure of the building that he is now intending to use it as an undertaking establishment and funerals are conducted from the premises.

The plaintiffs lost no time in issuing a writ on June 20, 1935, to restrain this, with the result that the injunction appealed from was granted.

The contention of the defendant is that the case falls within s. 398 of the Municipal Act which enacts that a municipality may prohibit the use of any land or the erection or use of buildings within any defined area, except for such purposes as may be set out by the by-law, but this by-law can only be passed after notice to the owners affected, and with the approval of the Municipal Board, and for this reason the original by-laws of 1922 and 1925 have not the effect of prohibiting the carrying on of any business.

The provisions of s. 406(8) are singularly bald. All that the municipality is authorized to do is to declare a part of the highway to be a residential street, and to define a building line beyond which buildings may not be erected. What is meant by a residential street is in no way defined, and I can find little authority to throw light upon it. Murray's Oxford Dictionary speaks of "residential" as adapted to houses of the better class, "a neighbourhood characterized by houses of a superior kind," thus contrasting a residential district with a slum district, although in one sense in a slum there are many residences.

In *Toronto* v. *Foss* (1913) Meredith J.A., speaking of a by-law passed under another section now repealed, says:

"It is quite plain that neither the by-law, nor the legislation upon which it is founded, was intended to be applicable to all kinds of work or trading; neither comprises shops of all kinds, nor businesses of all kinds. If the legislation had been meant to be as comprehensive as the plaintiffs contend for, it should, and doubtless would, have been embodied in very different language.

"No doubt, the purpose of the legislation was to prevent a residential street being turned into a business street; to preserve its residential character, all of which, however, can be done, as the legislation itself indicates, without decreeing that no trade or business of any kind shall be done in any house or building upon it."

It was after this that the municipality were given the power now found in s. 398.

The defendant here contends, and the evidence supports him, that this house is a residence. He intends to use some portion of it as a funeral chapel and in other portions to carry on his occupation as an undertaker. This, he says, is not sufficient to change the character of the street and make it less a residential street.

I agree, and think that the intention to prohibit the use of any buildings in a defined area for any purpose whatsoever must be given effect to under the provisions of s. 398, and is subject to the approval of the Municipal Board.

It is not without significance that the whole neighbourhood is by no means residential in the strict sense. There are in the immediate neighbourhood a Catholic Church, an Anglican Church, a Convent, a Presbyterian Church, a Club House, and a number of other non-residential structures.

In my view the appeal should be allowed, and the action dismissed.

MULOCK C.J.O.: . . . The term "residential" suggests, but does not expressly limit to residence the use of buildings erected on a "residential" street. People reside in private residences, hotels, apartment houses, boarding houses, hospitals, industrial homes, lunatic asylums, houses for the aged and blind, for children, infants, etc. May buildings of these various kinds be erected on residential highways and be used for the purposes for which they are intended? If not, which are excluded? Does "residential highway" mean a highway on which may be erected buildings to be used only as residences, where he may not carry on his calling or business, such as that of a doctor, a dentist, an artist, seamstress, a tailor, a masseur, a teacher, or even an undertaker? The dictionaries do not, with any reasonable degree of certainty, enable one to determine what is a residential highway. It is, I think, a highway substantially, but not exclusively, used for private residential purposes; its residential character being preserved. There are different kinds of residential highways. There may be on one highway none but high class dwellings occupied solely as private residences. Whilst another, although there may be such a proportion of private residences as give a residential character to the street, yet there also may be upon it many places used for other than residential purposes.

The meaning of residential highway as used in the section is vague, and does not warrant its being interpreted as prohibiting the carrying on of a business of undertaker in the defendant's premises.

The Court should not give effect to language of a confiscatory character if its meaning admits of reasonable doubt. . . .

[Fisher J.A. agreed with Middleton J.A.]

RE RELIGIOUS HOSPITALLERS OF ST. JOSEPH OF HOTEL DIEU. [1946] 4 D.L.R. 737 (Ontario. High Court). The Court held that a by-law passed under s. 406(10) of the Municipal Act, R.S.O. 1914, c. 192 (the section concerned in the *Hulse* case) could not prevent the erection and use of a building as a hospital. WELLS J.: "It does probably prohibit the erection and use of buildings for stores, manufacturing plants and processing plants of an industrial nature. I do not think the designation of a street as "residential" however, was meant, nor should it be interpreted, as prohibiting the erection of a hospital on the street."

RE GUEST AND WESTON. [1954] O.W.N. 271 (Ontario. High Court). The Court held that a by-law passed under the same section as in the *Hulse* case could not prevent the erection of a church by the Weston Congregation of Jehovah's Witnesses. WELLS J.: "Counsel for the respondent corporation argued that to permit any building to be erected in the prescribed area there had to be some residential quality about it. With great respect, however, I do not think that is the test. What is required is that anything which is permitted to be erected in the prescribed area shall not destroy the residential character of the neighbourhood, and, in all fairness, I do not think it can be said that the erection of a church has that effect. It is quite true that if a whole line of churches were erected on the street, to the exclusion of other buildings, it would lose its residential character. That is not suggested as being a possibility here, nor are churches commonly erected in that fashion, and I do not think it can be said that the erection of the church here in question will destroy the residential quality of the neighbourhood in which it is built. If it is possible to permit trade or business of the type of an undertaker in the area, I think it is also possible to permit the conduct of worship without altering the residential quality of the neighbourhood."

NOTE ON THE HISTORY OF ZONING ENABLING LEGISLATION IN ONTARIO. Section 398 referred to by Middleton J.A. in the *Hulse* case is a forerunner of the current s. 30. The by-law in *Toronto* v. *Foss*, which forbade the erection or use of buildings as "stores" or "manufactories" was based on s. 541a of *The Consolidated Municipal Act, 1903*, which was introduced by amendment in 1904, c. 22, s. 19. Section 541a provided:

"The councils of cities and towns are authorized and empowered by a vote of two-thirds of the whole council to pass and enforce such by-laws as they may deem expedient;

"(a) To regulate and limit the distance from the line of the street in front thereof at which buildings on residential streets may be built; such distance may be varied upon different streets or in different parts of the same street.

"(b) And in the case of cities only, to prevent, regulate and control the location, erection and use of buildings for laundries, butcher shops, stores and manufactories.

"The location, erection, construction or use of any buildings in contravention of any such by-law may, in addition to any other remedy provided by law, be restrained by action at the instance of the municipality passing such by-law;

"Provided that this section shall not apply to any buildings now erected or used for any of the purposes aforesaid so long as they continue to be used as at present."

The by-law was directed at a ladies' tailor employing four seamstresses in one room of an otherwise private residence.

In 1905, c. 22, s. 21, the words "stables for horses for delivery purposes" were inserted before the word "laundries". In 1907, c. 40, s. 12, the words "blacksmith shops, forges, dog kennels, hospitals or infirmaries for horses, dogs, or other animals" were added. In 1908, c. 48, s. 9 power to "prevent, regulate and control the location and making of pits and quarries" was added, and the municipality given power to restrain a breach of the by-law passed for this purpose. In 1909, c. 73, s. 18 power was added to regulate "the location of stables, garages, barns, outhouses and manure pits." In 1912, c. 40, s. 10, in the case of cities over 100,000, power was added to "prohibit, regulate and control the location on certain streets to be named in the by-law of apartment or tenement houses and of garages to be used for hire or gain." An apartment or tenement was a building containing three or more suites. In 1913, c. 43, there was a revision and consolidation of the 1903 Act and by s. 406 (10) the power of a city or town to declare "any highway or part of a highway to be a residential street", was clarified to the state in which it was used by the municipalities involved in the cases noted above. Section 409 (2) consolidated the various amendments listed here. In 1914, c. 33, s. 409(2) was made to apply to "plumber shops, machine shops, tinsmith shops, moving picture or other theatres and buildings used for the storage of builders' plant." In 1915, c. 34, s. 29, extended the power of s. 406 (10) to villages. In 1916, c. 39, s. 8, s. 409 (2) was made to apply to "private hospitals, public dance halls and undertakers' establishments." In 1917, c. 42, s. 18, s. 409 (2d) was added to enable the prohibition of the "sale of goods, wares and merchandise on any private lands as defined." In 1918, c. 32, s. 10 added s. 409 (2e) making s. 409 (2) apply to "warehouses and gasoline and oil filling stations." In 1919, c. 46, s. 17 added paragraph (2f) to include "tents, awnings, or other similar coverings for business purposes and buildings for the housing of motor trucks or apparatus used in any truck cartage business." In 1920, by c. 58, s. 16 the building line power in s. 406 (10) was extended to townships bordering on a city of 100,000 or more. The same section authorized the townships to require a two foot side yard but the by-law could not apply to a street less than 66 feet in width.

In 1921, c. 63, s. 10 added s. 399a authorizing by-laws "for prohibiting the use of land or the erection or use of buildings within any defined area or areas or abutting on any defined highway or part of a highway for any other purpose than that of a detached private residence." Power was also given generally to regulate "the height, bulk, location, spacing and character of buildings to be erected or altered within any defined area or areas or abutting on any defined highway or part of a highway, and the proportion of the area of the lot which such building may occupy." For the first time, Municipal Board approval was required. Section 409 (2) was not repealed. In 1922 *The Consolidated Municipal Act 1922* retained ss. 399a, 406 (10), 409 (2) and (2a) to (2f); s. 410 retained city control of apartment houses; and s. 411a retained village control of residential streets and building lines. This power in townships bordering on cities of 100,000 or more, was retained in s. 410a (made 410b in 1924, c. 53, s. 22 and applied to townships within ten miles of a city not less than 100,000). In 1924, by c. 53, s. 22 all the powers of s. 399a (2) were given to the adjacent townships.

Finally, in the S.O., 1924, the provision of s. 399a (1) was amended to give it the same generality its successor carries today where by s. 12 of c. 53, it was made to read:

"For prohibiting the use of land or the erection or use of buildings within any defined area or areas or abutting on any defined highway or part of a highway except for such purposes as may be set out in the by-law."

In 1959, by the S.O., c. 71, s. 5, the provision was transferred from *The Municipal Act* to *The Planning Act, 1955.*

TOWNSHIP OF PICKERING *v.* GODFREY
Ontario. Court of Appeal. 1958. 14 D.L.R. (2d) 520

MORDEN J.A.: In this action the plaintiff [appellant] Township claims a perpetual injunction restraining the defendant from digging or transporting gravel and other substances from lands owned by the defendant in Lots 13 and 14, Concession V, Pickering, in contravention of the plaintiff's By-law 2077:

By-law No. 2077 was passed by the Township Council on March 2nd, 1955 and was amended by By-law 2090 on April 25th, 1955 in some particulars which are not relevant to the issue in this action. These By-laws were subsequently approved by the Ontario Municipal Board...

[By-law No. 2077 designated certain areas as "Greenbelt" lands and the "uses permitted" section included these words: "*Commercial* nil" and "*Industrial* nil."]

After the By-laws were passed, the defendant became the owner of certain lands in the Township the major portion of which are situate within the area covered by By-law 2077. The defendant's activities are described in the affidavit of the Township By-law Enforcement Officer as follows:

"I . . . did see a number of loads of gravel and other substances being dug in this area by mechanical equipment and loaded on trucks which were driven away . . . during the working hours on the 2nd and 3rd day of October, 1957 aproximately 100 tons of gravel and other substances were removed from the land described above of which approximately 50% was sold to third parties." The defendant attended a council meeting on September 16th, 1957 and according to the affidavit of the Township Clerk he advised the council:

"that it was his intention to develop the whole of his land . . . as a gravel pit and that it was his intent to remove a large quantity of gravel and other substances therefrom. He proposed either to stockpile the gravel and other substances so removed on unzoned land or to sell the said gravel and other substances."

It was contended on behalf of the plaintiff that the defendant's activities, both present and proposed, on the land, are in violation of the By-law. On the other hand, the defendant's counsel argued that (a) the Township had no power under Sec. 390 (1) of the Municipal Act, R.S.O., 1950, c. 243, to regulate and control the use of land; (b) the By-law does not comply with sec. 388 (1) (115) of the Act; (c) the digging of a pit and the abstraction of gravel and other substances found therein is not a use of land; and (d) these operations are neither "commercial" nor "industrial" activities. Counsel also argued that the By-law is defective in that it uses the language of the Planning Act and does not contain any words of prohibition. . . .

[After setting out the text of s. 390 and s. 399a of 1921, reproduced above, his Lordship continued:]

The matter now to be considered is whether the making of a quarry or a pit falls within the meaning of words "use of land" appearing in s. 390 (1) (i). If it does not, then the plaintiff's By-law is ineffective to prevent the defendant from conducting his operations as described in the affidavits. It is trite law in Ontario that a municipal corporation is the creature of statute and its only legislative powers are those delegated to it by the Legislature. It is also well established that the common law right of every subject to employ himself and his property in a lawful manner can not be taken away, restricted or affected except by statute, or by-law passed pursuant to statutory authority and expressed in clear language; *R.* v. *Stronach* (1928). At the same time, it must be recognized that a by-law passed under s. 390 restricting the use of land is presumably for the general benefit of the inhabitants of the locality and may operate to the detriment of individual property owners in the area and such a result in no way affects the validity of the by-law. Such by-laws which fall within the empowering legislation should be benevolently interpreted and supported; *Toronto* v. *Williams* (1913) and *Montreal* v. *Morgan* (1920).

Counsel did not refer to any decisions interpreting the words "use of land" as they appear in s. 390 and I could find none. The dictionary definitions of "use" are numerous and diverse. An examination of them and some authorities to which I will refer, has led me to the opinion that the word when used in conjunction with such commodities as food and water connotes the idea of consumption, but when applied to more durable forms of property means the employment of the property for enjoyment, revenue or profit without in any way otherwise diminishing or impairing the property itself. For example, in the civil law, usufruct is defined as "the power of disposal of the use and fruits, saving the substance of the thing"; *Stair's Institutes*, (1681) xvi. 327. The same distinction was made by Falconbridge J. in *Re Davis and Toronto* (1891) in interpreting another section of the *Municipal Act*. At p. 247, he is reported as saying:

" 'using' applied to land cannot mean wasting, consuming or exhausting by employment, as, e.g. to use flour, beer or water for food or drink. It means holding or occupying, and so must be read with the rest of the section. . . ."

The gravel and other substances which this defendant is removing from the lands is part of the land itself. If he granted this right to another, it would be a *profit à prendre* and the grant would be a grant of part of the land itself; Armour, *Real Property*, (2nd ed.) 47. It could not be successfully argued that a municipality could by by-law passed under s. 390 lawfully prohibit an owner from selling his land or any part of it. This is illustrated by *Brake* v. *Inland Revenue Commissioners* (1915). Under the *Finance Act, 1910,* land used "bona fide for any business, trade or industry other than agriculture" was exempt from undeveloped land duty. Brake carried on the business of developing and selling land. It was argued on his behalf that this business brought the land within the exemption. Rowlatt J. rejected this argument, saying at p. 733:

"It seems to me to be too clear for argument that the use of land for any business, trade, or industry means the employment of this land as land. That means, of course, its physical employment, not because one reads in the word "physically" before "used" in the statute, but because the use of land means the use of land as land, and that brings in the idea of physical use. The use of it meant by the statute is not the use of it as a saleable article held in a condition in which, regarded as land, it is unused for business, trade, or industry, whether it is so held as a marketable commodity, or as a sample, or as serving any ulterior commercial purpose."

In my opinion the making of pits and quarries is not a "use of land" within the meaning of s. 390 and it therefore follows that a by-law passed under it cannot prevent a landowner from digging and removing gravel or other substances for his lands.

Mr. Dubin submitted that even if the digging of quarry or pit was not "a use of land" within the meaning of s. 390, nevertheless the totality of the defendant's operations–the digging, the extraction, the transportation and eventual sale was a commercial or industrial use of land and therefore fell within the prohibition of the By-law.

The only evidence on the nature of the operations are the above quoted extracts from the affidavits. All that the defendant does on the lands covered by the By-law is to dig up gravel and load it on trucks which carry it away. This is as far as the evidence goes and discloses what might be described as a mining operation, and neither a commercial nor an industrial operation within the common acceptation of those words.

Counsel referred to s. 388 (1) (115) of the *Municipal Act* which empowered local municipalities to pass by-laws "for prohibiting the making of pits and quarries in the municipality or regulating the location of them." . . . Last year, paragraph 115 was repealed by 1957 (Ont.) c. 76 s. 21(11) and now no municipality has the specific power of prohibiting the making of pits and quarries.

The plaintiff's By-law, by its very terms, was not a by-law passed under s. 388 (1) (115). In 1955, it had this power to pass such a by-law but if it had done so, the by-law would have become void before the writ in this action was issued because of the repeal of paragraph 115. . . . If my interpretation of the words "use of land" had been wider and covered the making of pits and quarries, then the fact that a specific power to prohibit such activities existed in 1955 under s. 388 would not in my opinion, disable a municipality from passing a by-law under s. 390 prohibiting the same activities. Many of the matters covered by s. 388 (1) such as factories for the manufacture or storage of explosives (para. 20), slaughter houses (para. 91), gas works, tanneries and distilleries (para. 110), and stables, garages, barns (para. 116) could be prohibited or regulated by a properly worded general by-law under s. 390. In my view the legislative history of paragraph 115 affords no assistance in the interpretation of s. 390 (1).

Having reached the conclusion that a by-law passed under s. 390 can not prohibit the making of a gravel pit, it is unnecessary to consider Mr. Williston's interesting submissions with respect to the form and interpretation of the plaintiff's by-law.

In my opinion, Mr. Justice Barlow properly dismissed the action and the plaintiff's appeal from his judgment should be dismissed with costs.

LEBEL J.A.: . . . The question is essentially one of fact, and, to put the matter bluntly, there are no facts before us, in my opinion, which would justify us in holding that the mere digging down into land and the transporting of gravel and other substances extracted therefrom—even with a view to realizing the value of the gravel or other substance—amounts to a user of land for commercial or industrial purposes. Authority to restrain the use of land for commercial or industrial purposes is not, in my opinion, the same as authority to restrain the sale or other disposition of the land itself or of any of its substances, components or minerals. . . .

[Aylesworth J.A. agreed with Morden J.A.]

RE DAVIS AND TORONTO. 1891. 21 O.R. 243 (Ontario. High Court). A motion to quash a by-law respecting the construction of a sewer, on the ground, *inter alia*, that the city had no power to expropriate an easement. The city purported to act under s. 479 (15) of the *Municipal Act*, R.S.O. 1887, c. 184, which authorized the passing of a by-law "for entering upon, breaking up, taking or using any land in any way necessary or convenient for the said purposes" of drainage or sewerage. [Is *Re Davis in pari materia* with the principal case? Do you agree with the interpretation technique used by Morden J.A.? Is this a "good" approach to a statute? What is the purpose of s. 390? What does its legislative history suggest? Its common law background? Its social history?]

QUESTIONS. The regulation of sand and gravel pits presents a serious problem to a modern suburban municipality. Sand and gravel may be removed in order to prepare rough, hilly land for subdivision. Since many subdividers believe houses may only be built on dead flat land, is this extraction process, which may go on for months and perhaps over a year, the operation of a pit or quarry? What principles, if any, should be invoked in the zoning of a gravel pit?

NOTES AND QUESTIONS. The special treatment of pits and quarries in Ontario raises two serious doubts about the meaning or scope of zoning power in that province, and, to some extent in other provinces.

If extracting sand or gravel is not a use of land, and in Ontario it would appear not to be, since the legislature enacted a special section to deal with it, rather than define the word "use" to include it, is the depositing of sand or gravel elsewhere a use of land? In particular, is the deposit of "clean fill" on vacant land a use of the vacant land? Is the deposit of garbage a use of land? Is a city garbage dump a use of land by the city?

Can a municipality control the contour of land? Can it insist that the subdivider maintain the existing grade? Can it demand a new grade?

If extracting sand and gravel is not a use of land, is cutting and removing a tree a use of land? Can a landowner operate a lumber mill on his land so long as he is only cutting up his own timber growing on the land? Can the stripping of sod be restricted? Is the zoning power available to control removal of vegetation in an effort to require good conservation practice on river banks?

On the meaning on "use" and "purpose" in section 30, consider the significance of paragraph 3, "For prohibiting the erection of a building or structure for residential or commercial purposes on land that is subject to flooding or on land where, by reason of its rocky, low-lying, marshy or unstable character, the cost of construction of satisfactory waterworks, sewage or drainage facilities is prohibitive." Could not such a control be regarded as a prohibiting of the use of land or the erection or use of a building or structure? Why is a separate paragraph necessary? Could a building for industrial purposes be prohibited? Has the municipality no control over the erection of buildings on swampy or flood lands for agricultural, industrial or recreational use?

FULLER, "POSITIVISM AND FIDELITY TO LAW— A REPLY TO PROFESSOR HART" *

Cambridge. 1958. 71 *Harvard Law Review* 630, 661–9

It is essential that we be just as clear as we can be about the meaning of Professor Hart's doctrine of "the core and the penumbra," because I believe the casual reader is likely to misinterpret what he has to say. Such a reader is apt to suppose that Professor Hart is merely describing something that is a matter of everyday experience for the lawyer, namely, that in the interpretation of legal rules it is typically the case (though not universally so) that there are some situations which will seem to fall rather clearly within the rule, while others will be more doubtful. Professor Hart's thesis takes no such jejune form. His extended discussion of the core and the penumbra is not just a complicated way of recognizing that some cases are hard, while others are easy. Instead, on the basis of a theory about language meaning generally, he is proposing a theory of judicial interpretation which is, I believe, wholly novel. Certainly it has never been put forward in so uncompromising a form before.

As I understand Professor Hart's thesis (if we add some tacit assumptions implied by it, as well as some qualifications he would no doubt wish his readers to supply) a full statement would run something as follows: The task of interpretation is commonly that of determining the meaning of the individual words of a legal rule, like "vehicle" in a rule excluding vehicles from a park. More particularly, the task of interpretation is to determine the range of reference of such a word, or the aggregate of things to which it points. Communication is possible only because words have a "standard instance," or a "core of meaning" that remains relatively constant, whatever the context in which the word may appear. Except in unusual circumstances, it will always be proper to regard a word like "vehicle" as embracing its "standard instance," that is, that aggregate of things it would include in all ordinary contexts, within or without the law. This meaning the word will have in any legal rule, whatever its purpose. In applying the word to its "standard instance," no creative role is assumed by the judge. He is simply applying the law "as it is."

In addition to a constant core, however, words also have a penumbra of meaning which, unlike the core, will vary from context to context. When the object in question (say, a tricycle) falls within this penumbral area, the judge is forced to assume a more creative role. He must now undertake, for the first time, an interpretation of the rule in the light of its purpose or aim. Having in mind what was sought by the regulation concerning parks, ought it to be considered as barring tricycles? When questions of this sort are decided there is at least an "intersection" of "is" and "ought," since the judge, in deciding what the rule "is," does so in the light of his notions of what "it ought to be" in order to carry out its purpose.

If I have properly interpreted Professor Hart's theory as it affects the "hard core," then I think it is quite untenable. The most obvious defect of his theory lies in its assumption that problems of interpretation typically turn on the meaning of individual words. Surely no judge applying a rule of the common law ever followed any such procedure as that described (and, I take it, prescribed) by Professor Hart; indeed, we do not normally even think of his problem as being one of "interpretation." Even in the case of statutes, we commonly have to assign meaning, not to a single word, but to a sentence, a paragraph, or a whole page or more of text. Surely a paragraph does not have a "standard instance" that remains constant whatever the context in which it appears. If a statute seems to have a kind of "core meaning" that we can apply without a too precise inquiry into its exact purpose, this is because we can see that, however one might formulate the precise objective of the statute, *this* case would still come within it.

Even in situations where our interpretive difficulties seem to head up in a single word, Professor Hart's analysis seems to me to give no real account of what does or should happen. In his illustration of the "vehicle," although he tells us this word has a core of meaning that in all contexts defines unequivocally a range of objects embraced by it, he never tells us what these objects might be. If the rule excluding vehicles from parks seems easy to apply in some cases, I submit this is because we can see clearly enough what the rule "is aiming at in general" so that we know there is no need to worry about the difference between Fords and Cadillacs. If in some cases we seem to be able to apply the rule without asking what its purpose is, this is not because we can treat a directive arrangement as if it had no purpose. It is rather because, for example, whether the rule be intended to preserve quiet in the park, or to save carefree strollers from injury, we know, "without thinking," that a noisy automobile must be excluded.

What would Professor Hart say if some local patriots wanted to mount on a pedestal in the park a truck used in World War II, while other citizens, regarding the proposed memorial as an eyesore, support their stand by the "no vehicle" rule? Does this truck, in perfect working order, fall within the core or the penumbra?

Professor Hart seems to assert that unless words have "standard instances" that remain constant regardless of context, effective communication would break down and it would become impossible to construct a system of "rules which have authority." If in every context words took on a unique meaning, peculiar to that context, the whole process of interpreation would become so uncertain and subjective that the ideal of a rule of law would lose its meaning. In other words, Professor Hart seems to be saying that unless we are prepared to accept his analysis of interpretation, we must surrender all hope of giving an effective meaning to the ideal of fidelity to law. This presents a very dark prospect indeed, if one believes, as I do, that we cannot accept his theory of interpretation. I do not take so gloomy a view of the future of the ideal of fidelity to law.

An illustration will help to test, not only Professor Hart's theory of the core and the penumbra, but its relevance to the ideal of fidelity to law as well. Let us suppose that in leafing through the statutes, we come upon the following enactment: "It shall be a misdemeanor, punishable by a fine of five dollars, to sleep in any railway station." We have no trouble in perceiving the general nature of the target toward which this statute is aimed. Indeed, we are likely at once to call to mind the picture of a disheveled tramp, spread out in an ungainly fashion on one of the benches of the station, keeping weary passengers on their feet and filling their ears with raucous and alcoholic snores. This vision may fairly be said to represent the "obvious instance" contemplated by the statute, though certainly it is far from being the "standard instance" of the physiological state called "sleep."

Now let us see how this example bears on the ideal of fidelity to law. Suppose I am a judge, and that two men are brought before me for violating this statute. The first is a passenger who was waiting at 3 A.M. for a delayed train. When he was arrested he was sitting upright in an orderly fashion, but was heard by the arresting officer to be gently snoring. The second is a man who had brought a blanket and pillow to the station and had obviousy settled himself down for the night. He was arrested, however, before he had a chance to go to sleep. Which of these cases presents the "standard instance" of the word "sleep"? If I disregard that question, and decide to fine the second man and set free the first, have I violated a duty of fidelity to law? Have I violated that duty if I interpret the word "sleep" as used in this statute to mean something like "to spread oneself out on a bench or floor to spend the night, or as if to spend the night"?

Testing another aspect of Professor Hart's theory, is it really ever possible to interpret a word in a statute without knowing the aim of the statute? Suppose we encounter the following incomplete sentence: "All improvements must be promptly reported to . . . ." Professor Hart's theory seems to assert that even if we have only this fragment before us we can safely construe the word "improvement" to apply to its "standard instance," though we would have to know the rest of the sentence before we could deal intelligenty with "problems of the penumbra." Yet surely in the truncated sentence I have quoted, the word "improvement" is almost as devoid of meaning as the symbol "X".

The word "improvement" will immediately take on meaning if we fill out the sentence with the words, "the head nurse," or "the Town Planning Authority," though the two meanings that come to mind are radically dissimilar. It can hardly be said that these two meanings represent some kind of penumbral accretion to the word's "standard instance." And one wonders, parenthetically, how helpful the theory of the core and the penumbra would be in deciding whether, when the report is to be made to the planning authorities, the word "improvement" includes an unmortgageable monstrosity of a house that lowers the market value of the land on which it is built.

It will be instructive, I think, to consider the effect of other ways of filling out the sentence. Suppose we add to, "All improvements must be promptly reported to . . ." the words, "the Dean of the Graduate Division." Here we no longer seem, as we once did, to be groping in the dark; rather, we seem now to be reaching into an empty box. We achieve a little better orientation if the final clause reads, "to the Principal of the School," and we feel completely at ease if it becomes, "to the Chairman of the Committee on Relations with the Parents of Children in the Primary Division."

It should be noted that in deciding what the word "improvement" means in all these cases, we do not proceed simply by placing the word in some general context, such as hospital practice, town planning, or education. If this were so, the "improvement" in the last instance might just as well be that of the teacher as that of the pupil. Rather, we ask ourselves, What can this rule be for? What evil does it seek to avert? What good is it intended to promote? When it is "the head nurse" who receives the report, we are apt to find ourselves asking, "Is there, perhaps, a shortage of hospital space, so that patients who improve sufficiently are sent home or are assigned to a ward where they will receive less attention?" If "Principal" offers more orientation than "Dean of the Graduate Division," this must be because we know something about the differences between primary education and education on the postgraduate university level. We must have some minimum acquaintance with the ways in which these two educational enterprises are conducted, and with the problems encountered in both of them, before any distinction between "Principal" and "Dean of the Graduate Division" would affect our interpretation of "improvement." We must, in other words, be sufficiently capable of putting ourselves in the position of those who drafted the rule to know what they thought "ought to be." It is in the light of this "ought" that we must decide what the rule "is."

Turning now to the phenomenon Professor Hart calls "pre-occupation with the penumbra," we have to ask ourselves what is actually contributed to the process of interpretation by the common practice of supposing various "borderline" situations. Professor Hart seems to say, "Why, nothing at all, unless we are working with problems of the penumbra." If this is what he means, I find his view a puzzling one, for it still leaves unexplained why, under his theory, if one is dealing with a penumbral problem, it could be useful to think about other penumbral problems.

Throughout his whole discussion of interpretation, Professor Harts seems to assume that it is a kind of cataloguing procedure. A judge faced with a novel situation is like a library clerk who has to decide where to shelve a new book. There are easy cases: the *Bible* belongs under Religion, *The Wealth of Nations* under Economics, etc. Then there are hard cases, when the librarian has to exercise a kind of creative choice, as in deciding whether *Das Kapital* belongs under Politics or Economics, *Gulliver's Travels* under Fantasy or Philosophy. But whether the decision where to shelve is easy or hard, once it is made all the librarian has to do is put the book away. And so it is with judges, Professor Hart seems to say, in all essential particulars. Surely the judicial process is something more than a cataloguing procedure. The judge does not discharge his responsibility when he pins an apt diagnostic label on the case. He has to do something about it, to treat it, if you will. It is this larger responsibility which explains why interpretative problems almost never turn on a single word, and also why lawyers for generations have found the putting of imaginary borderline cases useful, not only "on the penumbra," but in order to know where the penumbra begins.

These points can be made clear, I believe, by drawing again on our example of the statutory fragment which reads, "All improvements must be promptly reported to . . . ." Whatever the concluding phrase may be, the judge has not solved his problems simply by deciding what kind of improvement is meant. Almost all of the words in the sentence may require interpretation, but most obviously this is so of "promptly" and "reported." What kind of "report" is contemplated: a written note, a call at the office, entry in a hospital record? How specific must it be? Will it be enough to say "a lot better," or "a big house with a bay window"?

Now it should be apparent to any lawyer that in interpreting words like "improvement," "prompt," and "report," no real help is obtained by asking how some extralegal "standard instance" would define these words. But, much more important, when these words are all parts of a single structure of thought, they are in interaction with one another during the process of interpretation. "What is an 'improvement'? Well, it must be something that can be made the subject of a report. So, for purposes of this statute 'improvement' really means 'reportable improvement.' What kind of 'report' must be made? Well, that depends upon the sort of 'improvement' about which information is desired and the reasons for desiring the information."

When we look beyond individual words to the statute as a whole, it becomes apparent how the putting of hypothetical cases assists the interpretative process generally. By pulling our minds first in one direction, then in another, these cases help us to understand the fabric of thought before us. This fabric is something we seek to discern, so that we may know truly what it is, but it is also something that we inevitably help to create as we strive (in accordance with our obligation of fidelity to law) to make the statute a coherent, workable whole.

I should have considered all these remarks much too trite to put down here if they did not seem to be demanded in an answer to the theory of interpretation proposed by Professor Hart, a theory by which he puts such store that he implies we cannot have fidelity to law in any meaningful sense unless we are prepared to accept it. Can it be possible that the positivistic philosophy demands that we abandon a view of interpretation which sees as its central concern, not words, but purpose and structure? If so, then the stakes in this battle of schools are indeed high.

I am puzzled by the novelty Professor Hart attributes to the lessons I once tried to draw from Wittgenstein's example about teaching a game to children. I was simply trying to show the role reflection plays in deciding what has to be done. I was trying to make such simple points as that decisions about what ought to be done are improved by reflection, by an exchange of views with others sharing the same problems, and by imagining various situations that might be presented. I was assuming that all of these innocent and familiar measures might serve to sharpen our perception of what we were trying to do, and that the product of the whole process might be, not merely a more apt choice of means for the end sought, but a clarification of the end itself. I had thought that a famous judge of the English bench had something like this in mind when he spoke of the common law as working "itself pure." If this view of the judicial process is no longer entertained in the country of its origin, I can only say that, whatever the vicissitudes of Lord Mansfield's British reputation may be, he will always remain for us in this country a heroic figure of jurisprudence.

I have stressed here the deficiencies of Professor Hart's theory as that theory affects judicial interpretation. I believe, however, that its defects go deeper and result ultimately from a mistaken theory about the meaning of language generally. Professor Hart seems to subscribe to what may be called "the pointer theory of meaning," a theory which ignores or minimizes the effect on the meaning of words of the speaker's purpose and the structure of language. Characteristically, this school of thought embraces the notion of "common usage." The reason is, of course, that it is only with the aid of this notion that it can seem to attain the inert datum of meaning it seeks, a meaning isolated from the effects of purpose and structure.

It would not do to attempt here an extended excursus into linguistic theory. I shall have to content myself with remarking that the theory of of meaning implied in Professor Hart's essay seems to me to have been rejected by three men who stand at the very head of modern developments in logical analysis: Wittgenstein, Russell, and Whitehead. Wittgenstein's posthumous *Philosophical Investigations* constitutes a sort of running commentary on the way words shift and transform their meanings as they move from context to context. Russell repudiates the cult of "common usage," and asks what "instance" of the word "word" itself can be given that does not imply some specific intention in the use of it. Whitehead explains the appeal that "the deceptive identity of the repeated word" has for modern philosophers; only by assuming some linguistic constant (such as the "core of meaning") can validity be claimed for procedures of logic which of necessity move the word from one context to another.

(*d*) *Anglo-Canadian attitudes toward unreasonableness*

KRUSE *v*. JOHNSON
England. Divisional Court. [1898] 2 Q.B. 91

At a court of summary jurisdiction held in and for the division of Bearsted in the same county the respondent, a superintendent of police, preferred an information against the appellant for that he, on the day therein specified, did sing in a certain highway, within fifty yards of a dwelling-house there, after being required by a constable to desist, contrary to a by-law in that behalf made by the county council of Kent.

The by-law in question was made by the county council under s. 16 of the *Local Government Act, 1888*, and was as follows:

"4. No person shall sound or play upon any musical or noisy instrument or sing in any public place or highway within fifty yards of any dwelling-house after being required by any constable, or by an inmate of such house personally, or by his or her servant, to desist."

At the hearing of the information it was proved to the satisfaction of the justices that the appellant, who was conducting an open-air religious service, did on the day in question, together with others, in the parish of Leeds in the county of Kent, begin to sing a hymn within fifty yards of a dwelling-house, and continued so to sing after he had been requested by a constable to desist. It was further proved by the occupier of the dwelling-house that such singing was an annoyance to him; but it was not proved that on the day in question he had requested the constable to ask the appellant to desist. The occupier had, however, complained to the police on previous occasions.

It was contended on behalf of the appellant that the by-law was invalid . . .

LORD RUSSELL OF KILLOWEN C.J.: The county council of Kent, claiming to act under their statutory powers, made the following by-law. [His Lordship read the by-law.]

The appellant was summoned before the magistrates for offending against this by-law, when it was proved that on October 17, 1897, he persisted in singing in a public highway within fifty yards of a dwelling-house, after having been required by a police constable to desist. It was further proved by the occupier of the dwelling-house that the singing of the appellant and those with him was an annoyance to such occupier. The occupier had not, on the day in question, set the constable in motion, but he had on previous occasions complained to the police of the appellant's singing.

The magistrates convicted the appellant, and against that conviction the present appeal is brought.

The question reserved for this Court is whether the by-law is valid. If valid, the conviction is to stand. It is objected that the by-law is ultra vires, on the ground that it is unreasonable and therefore bad. It is necessary, therefore, to see what is the authority under which the by-law in question has been made, and what are the relations between its framers and those affected by it.

But first it seems necessary to consider what is a by-law. A by-law, of the class we are here considering, I take to be an ordinance affecting the public, or some portion of the public, imposed by some authority clothed with statutory powers ordering something to be done or not to be done, and accompanied by some sanction or penalty for its non-observance. It necessarily involves restriction of liberty of action by persons who come under its operation as to acts which, but for the by-law, they would be free to do or not do as they pleased. Further, it involves this consequence—that, if validly made, it has the force of law within the sphere of its legitimate operation.

In the present case we are dealing with a by-law made by a local representative body, namely, the county council of Kent, which is created under the *Local Government Act, 1888*, and is endowed with the powers of making by-laws given to municipal corporate bodies under the *Municipal Corporations Act, 1882*. . . .

Sect. 23 of the Act of 1882 provides that the council of a borough may from time to time make such by-laws as to them seem meet for the good rule and government of the borough, and for the prevention and suppression of nuisances not already punishable in a summary manner, and they may, by such by-laws, appoint such fines, not exceeding £5, as they deem necessary for the prevention of offences against the by-laws. It is under this authority that the by-law in question was framed.

What are the checks or safeguards under which this very wide authority of making by-laws is exercisable? The same s. 23 further provides that no by-law can be made unless two-thirds of the whole number of the council are present; and, when so made, it shall not come into force until the expiration of forty days after a copy thereof has been fixed on the town hall; and it shall not come into force until the expiration of forty days after a copy sealed with the corporate seal has been sent to the Secretary of State; and if within those forty days the Queen, with the advice of her Privy Council, disallow a proposed by-law or part thereof, such by-law shall not come into force. We thus find that Parliament has thought fit to delegate to representative public bodies in town and cities, and also in counties, the power of exercising their own judgment as to what are the by-laws which to them seem proper to be made for good rule and government in their own localities. But that power is accompanied by certain safeguards. There must be antecedent publication of the by-law with a view, I presume, of eliciting the public opinion of the locality upon it, and such by-laws shall have no force until after they have been forwarded to the Secretary of State. Further, the Queen, with the advice of her Privy Council, may disallow the by-law wholly or in part, and may enlarge the suspensory period before it comes into operation. I agree that the presence of these safeguards in no way relieves the Court of the responsibility of inquiring into the validity of by-laws where they are brought in question, or in any way affects the authority of the Court in the determination of their validity or invalidity. It is to be observed, moreover, that the by-laws having come into force, they are not like the laws, or what were said to be the laws, of the Medes and Persians—they are not unchangeable. The power is to make by-laws from time to time as to the authority shall seem meet, and if experience shews that in any respect existing by-laws work hardly or inconveniently, the local authority, acted upon by the public opinion, as it must necessarily be, of those concerned, has full power to repeal or alter them. It need hardly be added that, should experience warrant that course, the Legislature which has given may modify or take away the powers they have delegated. I have thought it well to deal with these points in some detail, and for this reason—that the great majority of the cases in which the question of by-laws has been discussed are not cases of by-laws of bodies of a public representative character entrusted by Parliament with delegated authority, but are for the most part cases of railway companies, dock companies, or other like companies, which carry on their business for their own profit, although incidentally for the advantage of the public. In this class of case it is right that the Courts should jealously watch the exercise of these powers, and guard against their unnecessary or unreasonable exercise to the public disadvantage. But, when the Court is called upon to consider the by-laws of public representative bodies clothed with the ample authority which I have described, and exercising that authority accompanied by the checks and safeguards which have been mentioned, I think the consideration of such by-laws ought to be approached from a different standpoint. They ought to be supported if possible. They ought to be, as has been said, "benevolently" interpreted, and credit ought to be given to those who have to administer them that they will be reasonably administered. This involves the introduction of no new canon of construction. But, further, looking to the character of the body legislating under the delegated authority of Parliament, to the subject-matter of such legislation, and to the nature and extent of the authority given to deal with matters which concern them, and in the manner which to them shall seem meet, I think courts of justice ought to be slow to condemn as invalid any by-law, so made under such conditions, on the ground of supposed unreasonableness . . . I do not mean to say that there may not be cases in which it would be the duty of the Court to condemn by-laws, made under such authority as these were made, as invalid because unreasonable. But unreasonable in what sense? If, for instance, they were found to be partial and unequal in their operation as between different classes; if they were manifestly unjust; if they disclosed bad faith; if they involved such oppressive or gratuitous interference with the rights of those subject to them as could find no justification in the minds of reasonable men, the Court might well say, "Parliament never intended to give authority to make such rules; they are unreasonable and ultra vires." But it is in this sense, and in this sense only, as I conceive, that the question of unreasonableness can properly be regarded. A by-law is not unreasonable merely because particular judges may think that it goes further than is prudent or necessary or convenient, or because it is not accompanied by a qualification or an exception which some judges may think ought to be there. Surely it is not too much to say that in matters which directly and mainly concern the people of the county, who have the right to choose those whom they think best fitted to represent them in their local government bodies, such representatives may be trusted to understand their own requirements better than judges. Indeed, if the question of the validity of by-laws were to be determined by the opinion of judges as to what was reasonable in the narrow sense of that word, the cases in the books on this subject are no guide; for they reveal, as indeed one would expect, a wide diversity of judicial opinion, and they lay down no principle or definite standard by which reasonableness or unreasonableness may be tested.

So much for the general considerations which, it seems to me, ought to be borne in mind in considering by-laws of this class. I now come to the by-law in question.

It is admitted that the county council of Kent were within their authority in making a by-law in relation to the subject-matter which is dealt with by the impeached by-law. In other words, it is conceded, and properly so, that the local authority might make a by-law imposing conditions under which musical instruments and singing might be permitted or prevented in public places; but it is objected that they had no authority to make a by-law on that subject in the terms of this by-law. Further, it is not contended that the by-law should, in order to be valid, be confined to cases where the playing or singing amounted to a nuisance; but the objections are, as I understand them, that the by-law is bad—first, because it is not confined to cases where the playing or singing is in fact causing annoyance, and next, because it enables a police constable to bring it into operation by a request on his part to the player or singer to desist. As to the first of these objections, if the general principles upon which these by-laws ought to be dealt with are those which I have already stated, it is clear that the absence of this qualification cannot make the by-law invalid. But, further, such a qualification in my judgment would render the by-law ineffective. What is to be the standard of annoyance? What may be a cause of annoyance to one person may be no annoyance, and may even be pleasurable, to another person. Again, who is to be the judge in such case of whether there is or is not an annoyance? Is it to be the resident of the house within fifty yards of the playing or singing; or is it to be the magistrate who hears the charge? It is enough to say that, in my judgment, the absence of the suggested qualification cannot make the by-law invalid, even if it be admitted that its presence would be an improvement.

As to the second objection–namely, that the policeman has the power of putting the by-law into operation by requiring the player or singer to desist—I again say that, even if the absence of this power would be an improvement and would make the by-law in the apprehension of some more reasonable, it is not, on the principles I have already stated, any ground for declaring the by-law to be invalid. In support of this objection pictures have, in argument, been drawn—more or less highly coloured—of policemen who without rhyme or reason would or might gratuitously interfere with what might be a source of enjoyment to many. In answer, I say a policeman is not an irresponsible person without check or control. If he acts capriciously or vexatiously, he can be checked by his immediate superiors, or he can be taught a lesson by the magistrates should he prefer vexatious charges. If the policeman persisted in saying that the musician should desist when the people in the neighbourhood desired his music, his gratuitous interference would promptly come to an end. Nor is it correct to say, as has been erroneously stated in some of the cases cited, that the magistrate would be bound in every case to convict where the musician did not desist when called upon. It is clear that under s. 16 of the *Summary Jurisdiction Act, 1879*, the magistrate, if he thinks the case of so trifling a nature that it is inexpedient to inflict any punishment, may, without proceeding to conviction, dismiss the information. The facts of this case are certainly no illustration of the by-law having been gratuitously or vexatiously put in force. The case states that, although it was not proved that the occupier of the house within fifty yards had, on the day in question, requested the constable to require the appellant to desist, yet it was proved that the singing was an annoyance to the occupier, and that he had on previous occasions complained to the police of such singing. Indeed, it was stated during the argument that the conviction here appealed from was the second conviction of the appellant for an offence against this by-law . . .

MATHEW J. dissenting: . . . It was contended on behalf of the appellant that the by-law was not reasonable and was not certain. It forbade, without qualification of any kind, conduct which might be perfectly innocent and unobjectionable. It did not provide, as has been done in similar enactments and in the county council's by-law No. 3, that the Act prohibited should be an annoyance to any one. It contained no exception, and would, according to its terms, condemn all music and singing within fifty yards of a dwelling-house as in the nature of a nuisance. The right to prohibit was conferred on any policeman. Why should liberty of conduct, it was asked, be so interfered with? A policeman has no such authority in the metropolis: Why should a policeman in the country be entrusted with powers so easily abused?

For the respondent it was argued that the by-law was well enough. It had been framed by a representative body, created under recent legislation, whose regulations should be indulgently treated. It must be taken, it was said, that Parliament intended that local authorities should be upheld, and to this end that new canons of construction should be adopted by the Courts to preserve their by-laws from being declared invalid. It was no longer enough to point out that a by-law according to its terms was unreasonable; it should be upheld if it might be reasonably enforced, and it was no longer an objection that it might be unreasonably enforced. It was urged that there were adequate safeguards for the public which, though not expressed, ought to be implied. It was true that any policeman might prohibit acts of which no reasonable man ought to complain; but it was said that confidence might be reposed in the discretion of a policeman, and that he would not be likely to interfere unreasonably. This seems to me too generous a view of the qualifications of the ordinary constable. There was, it was said, a further safeguard, namely, that the county council would not sanction interference by the police unless there was some good cause. But a by-law once made could not be, and ought not to be, controlled in its operation by the members of the council. Further, the policeman who interfered without good cause would, it was argued, be reprimanded by his superiors, or a magistrate would probably refuse to issue a summons. These suggestions imply that there would be cases in which a constable ought not to have the power to prohibit or to prosecute. It seems to me that the public ought to be informed in clear language what these cases were. It would not be satisfactory to a person, who was innocent of any real offence and was summoned as a criminal, to have an apology offered to him on the ground that the policeman had been wanting in discretion. Again, it was said that the magistrate would have the power to refuse to convict, in a trifling case, under s. 16 of the *Summary Jurisdiction Act*; but the by-law affords no security that this power would be exercised. A magistrate might reasonably consider that he was bound to convict; for a by-law once duly published becomes part of the law of the land in the locality to which it applies. It should be remembered that this by-law has been made for the purpose of securing the good rule and government of the district. It would appear not to be well calculated in its present form to secure any such result. The interference of a policeman, which the by-law permits, would not be unlikely, it seems to me, to produce angry altercation, and to lead to a breach of the peace . . . No case has been cited in which there is any trace of the principle now contended for, that such by-laws are to be interpreted with any particular indulgence because of their popular origin. If this view be adopted, it seems to me the judges will be placed in an anomalous position. Where they differ from bodies not popularly elected their jurisdiction to pronounce upon the validity of a by-law would remain unimpaired; but where they differed from bodies like a county council, their position would be altogether different. They would be bound to uphold what in other cases they would be right in condemning. I concur in the view that deference should be shewn by the Courts to the by-laws of a local authority, which may appear to interfere unduly with personal liberty, but where there was reason to suppose that the regulations were called for by the requirements of the particular place. There may be peculiar circumstances in the condition of a borough or part of a county which make stringent regulations as to personal conduct necessary. In that sense, I agree, a by-law ought to receive an indulgent interpretation. But this by-law is not confined to a particular locality; it applies to the whole of rural Kent.

It seems to me that what we are asked to do in this case is not to interpret the by-law, but to frame a new enactment with the necessary safeguards for freedom of conduct. It is practically proposed that we should add a proviso to the by-law as it stands to the effect that it ought not to be unnecessarily or unreasonably enforced. This I consider we have no power to do . . .

[The opinion of Sir F. H. Jeune agreeing with Lord Chief Justice Russell is omitted. Mathew J. and Lord Russell heard the case originally in a Divisional Court and they were unable to agree. The Lord Chief Justice thereupon called together a specially constituted Court to rehear the case. Mathew J. continued to dissent, but those members of the court who didn't deliver separate opinions concurred in the judgment of Russell L.C.J. Besides the judges already mentioned, Chitty L.J., Wright, Darling and Channell JJ. also took part.]

STRICKLAND *v.* HAYES
England. Queen's Bench [1896] 1 Q.B. 290

The appellant was charged at the city of Worcester with unlawfully using obscene language in a public place, contrary to a by-law made by the Worcestershire County Council, and which was in the following terms: "No person shall in any street or public place, or on land adjacent thereto, sing or recite any profane or obscene song or ballad, or use any profane or obscene language."

The evidence proved that the appellant had used the language complained of on a footpath in a field in the presence of a large number of persons. These facts were not disputed; but the appellant contended that the by-law was unreasonable, and therefore bad.

The justices convicted the appellant, but stated this case for the opinion of the Court. . . .

KAY L.J.: I have the strongest desire to uphold this conviction and to support this by-law, since it appears that the appellant, on a public footpath and in the presence of a large number of persons, used obscene language. But the danger of upholding the conviction is this. Here is a by-law made under an Act of Parliament which enables county councils to make by-laws for the better government of their counties. If we were to hold it good, we should have similar by-laws made by county councils throughout the country in completely unrestricted words. If the by-law is contrasted with the provisions of Acts of Parliament dealing with similar subject-matter, it is seen at once that words requiring that the act should be done so as to cause annoyance are omitted. In a town where the offence is regulated by the *Towns Police Clauses Act*, there is no infringement of the regulation unless annoyance is proved. What is the reason that a similar provision should not be imposed in regard to the county? Can it be right that a county council rejecting that restriction should, under an Act of Parliament, make a by-law in these wide terms when they are only empowered to make by-laws for the better government of the county? It would be an infringement of such a by-law if no human being heard the language, and not only if no human being was annoyed by it. If a man were to give himself up and to confess that he had when alone used such language, there would be an infringement of the by-law. It is in much wider terms than any that are usually framed with regard to the subject. It would seem, when it is compared with Acts of Parliament, that the omission of words requiring the condition of annoyance was designed, and that it was intended that the by-law should be much wider than such Acts. I should like to support Mr. Channell's very ingenious argument, that annoyance must be implied from the use of such language; but in spite of it the fact remains that in statutes and by-laws relating to the subject, words are ordinarily found denoting that the annoyance of others is part of the essence of the offence, and that such words are not to be found here. There is force, too, in the contention of Mr. Crump, that a man has a right to claim that his offence should be clearly stated in the by-law, and that if the annoyance of others is part of the offence that should be stated and not merely implied. It seems to me that this by-law forms such a dangerous precedent that I must say that it is too wide, both on account of the words as to land adjacent to a street or public place, and also because it does not contain words requiring that the acts should be done so as to cause annoyance to others. The conviction, therefore, must be quashed; and I will only express the hope that the by-law may speedily be reframed, and in more careful language.

[The opinion of Lindley L.J. to the same effect is omitted.]

THE MUNICIPAL ACT
Ontario. Revised Statutes. 1960. Chapter 249

242. (2) A by-law passed by a council in the exercise of any of the powers conferred by and in accordance with this Act, and in good faith, shall not be open to question, or be quashed, set aside or declared invalid, either wholly or partly, on account of the unreasonableness or supposed unreasonableness of its provisions or any of them.

NOTES AND EXCERPTS ON SECTION 242 (2). Speaking of this section Middleton J. said, in *Rogers* v. *City of Toronto* (1915);

". . . The Courts have no right to interfere with municipal action unless the municipality proposes to transcend the limits of the jurisdiction conferred upon it by the Legislature.

"At one time the Courts assumed jurisdiction to review municipal legislative action, upon the ground that the action was unreasonable. There never was in Ontario any real foundation for such jurisdiction. The supremacy of the municipal legislative authority within the sphere of its delegated jurisdiction was not at first recognized. It was assumed that the municipality occupied some subordinate position, and that the principles applicable to the determination of the validity of by-laws of companies, or the rules and regulations of boards exercising a delegated authority, could be applied to municipal action. This assumed supervisory and paternal jurisdiction of the Courts, although founded in error, became well established, and was only put an end to by the direct action of the Legislature, which enacted that no municipal by-law should be dealt with by the Courts on the ground of unreasonableness or assumed unreasonableness . . ."

But in 1928, Masten J.A., in *Re Howard and City of Toronto*, took a somewhat more critical approach. He said, in part:

"The Court is prohibited from quashing a by-law on the ground of unreasonableness, real or supposed, provided the council in passing it acted in good faith, but the unreasonableness of the by-law may be given in evidence to establish want of good faith in the council who passed it: *Consolidated Municipal Act, 1922*, sec. 249, subsec. 2 (originally enacted in 1913).

"The powers of the council must be exercised *bona fide*, and the action of its members must not be founded upon fraud, oppression or improper motives: *Davis* v. *Bromley Corporation* (1908) and as to refusal to hear interested parties, see *Jones* v. *Township of Tuckersmith*, (1915) and *Re Fenton and County of Simcoe* (1885).

"A by-law may be quashed if the council in passing it was not using its power in good faith in the interest of the public, but simply to subserve the interests of private persons: *In re Morton and City of St. Thomas* (1881) *Jones v. Township of Tuckersmith*, where the principle of *In re Morton and City of St. Thomas* is recognized by the Court of Appeal as continuing unaffected by the statute of 1913.

"What is or is not in the public interest is a matter to be determined by the judgment of the municipal council; and what it determines, if in reaching its conclusion it acted honestly and within the limits of its powers, is not open to review by the Court: *Jones* v. *Township of Tuckersmith*. . . .

"It is not a valid objection to a by-law that it operates to the special benefit of some private individual if at the same time it is in the public interest: *In re Inglis and City of Toronto, Jones* v. *Township of Tuckersmith, United Buildings Corporation Ltd.* v. *City of Vancouver*.

"The question of the relative balance of convenience or detriment to different persons is a matter which the Legislature has committed to the consideration and determination of the municipal council, and their judgment on that question, if *bona fide* exercised in what they believe to be the public interest, will not be interfered with by the Court: *In re Inglis and City of Toronto*. . . .

"Every municipal council, in all matters not specificially provided for by statute, is empowered to regulate its procedure, the conduct of its members, and the calling of meetings (*Consolidated Municipal Act*, 1922, sec. 250).

"Procedure is a matter of internal regulation of business, and in the absence of statutory obligation the council is at liberty to alter or suspend the ordinary procedure: per Osler J. A., in *Re Brewer and City of Toronto* (1909).

"It is well settled that failure to conform with the rules of procedure of a municipal council does not invalidate a by-law passed by it: per Meredith C.J.O., in *Village of Merritton* v. *County of Lincoln* (1917).

"The Court cannot prescribe the procedure to be adopted by the council, and cannot quash a by-law for error in procedure, except in cases where there has been a failure to observe the formalities (by way of notice or otherwise) prescribed by the statute as a condition precedent to the exercise of its powers or unless the proceedings are so inequitable and unfair as to evidence a fraudulent misuse by the council of its powers.

"The applicants must establish the charge of bad faith or improper conduct on the part of the members of the council. The Court must act on the evidence as it stands and cannot speculate about the unascertainable motives of unknown persons: *United Buildings Corporation Ltd.* v. *City of Vancouver*, [1915] A.C. 345, at p. 353.

"In dealing with a proposed by-law which involves a conflict of interests between private individuals who are affected, the council, while exercising a discretion vested in it by statute, acts in a quasi-judicial capacity (*In re Vashon and Township of East Hawkesbury* (1879), 30 U.C.C.P. 194, at p. 203), and its preliminary investigations and all subsequent proceedings ought to be conducted in a judicial manner, with fairness to all parties concerned."

JONES *v*. TOWNSHIP OF TUCKERSMITH. 1915, 33 O.L.R. 634 (Ontario. High Court). MEREDITH C.J.O.: "There is nothing, I think, in the contention that the opponents of the by-law were not afforded an opportunity to state their objections to its being passed. They, or such of them as chose to go to the meeting at which the by-law was to be considered, were heard in opposition to it, and there was nothing to prevent the council as it did at its first meeting in the following year, from coming to a conclusion as to whether or not the by-law should be passed, without giving the opponents of it an opportunity of again being heard. It is true that the respondent Robinson testified that he did not say all that he could have said, but he was not prevented from doing so, and, as he testified, only refrained from saying more because the solicitor for the corporation, who was present at the meeting, advised the council, or stated, that it had power to close any street. Robinson was not asked and did not state what it was that he would have said, and I am very doubtful of his ability to have added anything of importance to the arguments against the passing of the by-law which he and the other opponents of it had adduced."

MUNICIPAL ACT

British Columbia. Revised Statutes. 1960. Chapter 255

703. (1) The Council shall not adopt a zoning by-law until it has held a public hearing thereon, notice of which stating the time and place of the hearing has been published in not less than two consecutive issues of a newspaper published or circulating in the municipality, with the last of such publications appearing not less than three days nor more than ten days before the date of the hearing.

(2) The notice of hearing shall

(a) identify the land or lands deemed affected;

(b) state in general terms the intent of the provisions of the proposed by-law; and
(c) state where and the days and hours during which a copy of the proposed by-law may be inspected.

(3) At the hearing all persons who deem their interest in property affected by the proposed by-law shall be afforded an opportunity to be heard on matters contained in the by-law.

(4) The hearing may be adjourned from time to time.

(5) The Council may without further notice, in the zoning by-law as adopted, give such effect as it deems fit to representations made at the hearing.

704. No zoning by-law shall be amended or repealed except after a hearing under section 703, and except upon the affirmative vote of at least two-thirds of all the members of the Council.

CITIES AND TOWNS ACT

Quebec. Revised Statutes. 1941 Chapter 233

426. The council may make by-laws:

1. . . . to divide the municipality into zones of such number, shape and area as the council deems suitable for the purpose of such regulation . . .

Any by-law passed under this paragraph 1 and any part of such by-law dividing the municipality into zones or into sectors for voting purposes . . . may not be amended or repealed except by another by-law approved in accordance with the following provisions:

The clerk, within three days of the passing of such by-law, shall give public notice thereof and keep it posted up for at least five days.

A public meeting of the electors who are property-owners shall be held, between seven and ten o'clock in the evening, at the place and on the day fixed by the council, between the fifteenth and twenty-fifth day after the passing of the by-law and after a notice of convocation of at least five clear days given by the clerk after the expiration of the delay fixed for presenting the petition contemplated in the last paragraph of this paragraph 1.

Such meeting shall be presided over by the mayor or the acting mayor or, in their absence, by an alderman.

The clerk, acting as secretary of the meeting, shall read the repealing or amending by-law and submit it to the electors present and qualified to vote on such by-law. If, within the hour following the end of the reading of the by-law, six electors present who are property-owners and qualified to vote, or the majority of the electors qualified to vote when their number is less than twelve, demand that the by-law be submitted for approval to the electors who are property-owners, the chairman of the meeting shall fix as polling day a suitable date within the forty days following such meeting; otherwise the by-law is deemed to have been approved by the electors.

If there is a poll, it shall be held on the date fixed by the chairman of the meeting of electors and according to the procedure prescribed by sections 399 to 410. In no case can the by-law be approved by the electors unless one-third of those who are qualified to vote on such by-law and who reside in the municipality have voted. The only persons permitted to vote on the repealing or amending by-law, or on the portion of a by-law respecting such repeal or amendment, are the electors who are owners of immoveables situated in the municipality or, as the case may be, in the zone or sector affected by the said by-law or portion of a by-law.

Nevertheless, the owners of immoveables situated in a zone or sector adjacent to that affected by the by-law or portion of a by-law in question shall also be permitted to vote, upon presentation to the clerk, within the five days following the period of posting of the public notice provided for in the third paragraph of this paragraph 1, of a petition signed by at least twelve electors who are property-owners in the adjacent zone or sector in question, or by the majority of them if their number is less than twenty-four.

[Section 426 was revised and consolidated by S.Q., 1960, C. 76, S. 17.]

(*e*) *Uncertainty*

RE GOLDSTEIN AND CITY OF WINDSOR
Ontario. High Court. 1928. 35 O.W.N. 9

McEvoy J. in a written judgment, said that the applicant was a ratepayer of the city and was the contractor for the building of a large apartment house, the erection of which was about to be begun in the city. Everything was ready for starting work when some ratepayers, whose houses were in the neighbourhood, conceived the idea that an apartment-house in the locality was undesirable and would be detrimental to other residential properties in the neighbourhood.

Upon the 28th May, 1928, by-law No. 3870 was passed by the city council providing that "no person shall locate or erect any apartment or tenement-house or any garage to be used for hire or gain in that portion of the city . . . on both sides of Dougall Avenue, commencing at a point on Dougall Avenue measured 100 feet southerly from the southerly limit of Erie Street and extending to a point on Dougall Avenue measured northerly from Tecumseh Road, and this area so restricted shall be bounded on the east by the alley next east of Dougall Avenue and on the west by the alley next west of Dougall Avenue."

A point measured northerly from Tecumseh Road might be even north of where the apartment-house was to be built. No area is in fact defined by the description.

Section 412 of the Municipal Act, R.S.O. 1927 ch. 233, gives power to pass by-laws for prohibiting the location or erection within any defined area of apartment-houses.

This by-law was illegal because it did not define any area.

The learned Judge said that he had considered the question whether he might not hold that the words "100 feet" were omitted by oversight after the word "measured," and take the by-law to read "measured 100 feet northerly from Tecumseh Road"; but, having in mind all the circumstances, and considering the danger of reading into the by-law any distinct number of feet, 100 or 200, which would result in his deciding what part of the city was to be restricted, instead of the council deciding, he had determined not to adopt the suggestion.

The by-law was also attacked on the ground that it was not passed honestly and in the public interest. Upon this the learned Judge expressed no opinion, as an action has been brought by Goldstein in which the same question is raised. It was said also that the by-law was unreasonable, but that was a matter not for the Court but for the council. The learned Judge expressed no opinion as to whether the by-law was discriminatory.

There should be an order quashing the by-law for illegality, with costs.

RE HARRIS AND HAMILTON. 1879. 44 U.C.Q.B. 641 (Ontario. Queen's Bench). One Harris obtained a rule *nisi* calling on the city of Hamilton to shew cause why By-Law 149 should not be quashed wholly or in part. Clause 3 provided that "On or after the first day of May next after the passing of this by-law no crier or vendor of small wares shall practise his or her calling in the James Street market, or in the public streets adjacent thereto."

ARMOUR J.: "That part of clause three of this by-law, composed of the words, 'or in the public streets adjacent thereto' is, however, bad for uncertainty.

"The statute provides for the prevention of criers and vendors of small ware 'from practising their calling in the market, public streets, and vacant lots adjacent thereto'; that is, vacant lots adjacent to the public streets.

"The by-law could have prohibited the criers and vendors of small ware from practising their calling in the market, and in the public streets, and vacant lots adjacent thereto, that is, adjacent to such public streets, but not, as has been assumed to be done, in the public streets adjacent to the market, without, at all events, particularly describing such streets.

"The third clause of the said by-law must, therefore, so far as the words 'of in the public streets adjacent thereto' be quashed.

"As the applicant succeeds in part and fails in part, there will be no costs."

THE PLANNING ACT

Ontario. Revised Statutes. 1960. Chapter 296

30. (5) Land within any area or areas or abutting on any highway or part of a highway may be defined by the use of maps to be attached to the by-law, and, upon any application, the Municipal Board may require that land mentioned in the by-law be so defined, and the information shown on such maps shall form part of the by-law to the same extent as if included therein.

NOTE AND QUESTIONS. Section 30(5) is reproduced as amended by S. O., 1961–62, c. 104, s. 6(1), which authorized the Municipal Board to require maps. What standard of map should be required? Should the legislature or the Municipal Board determine the standard? Should poor municipalities be required to reach the same standard as the rich ones?

MONTREAL *v.* MORGAN. 1920. 60 S.C.R. 393 (Quebec. Supreme Court of Canada). ANGLIN J.: "It seems to have been practically common ground in the courts below, as it was at bar in this court, that the erection of any building other than a dwelling house fronting on any of the streets named in the by-law would contravene it. I am far from being satisfied, however, that this construction of the words 'for residential purposes' is not too narrow. I rather incline to the view that 'residential' is used in contradistinction to 'business and industrial' and that such buildings as churches and schools would not necessarily be excluded—that buildings not of a business or industrial character, such as are ordinarily found in exclusively residential districts, are not prohibited . . .

"Nor does this imply such vagueness or indefiniteness in the by-law as would render it invalid.

"I fully recognize the force of the general rules that the language of by-laws should be explicit and free from ambiguity, and that by-laws in restraint of rights of property as well as penal by-laws should be strictly construed.

But the very statement of the latter rule implies that a by-law is not necessarily invalid because its terms call for construction—as does also another well recognized rule, viz., that a by-law of a public representative body clothed with ample authority should be 'benevolently' interpreted and supported if possible, *Kruse* v. *Johnson*. It may be a counsel of perfection that in drafting by-laws the use of words susceptible of more than one interpretation should be avoided; but it is too much to exact of municipal councils that such a degree of certainty should always be attained. It would be going quite too far to say that merely because a term used in a by-law may be susceptible of more than one interpretation the by-law is necessarily bad for uncertainty. . . .

"During the course of the argument I directed attention to s.s. 10 of s. 406 of the Ontario *Municipal Act*, which empowers councils of cities and towns to pass by-laws "for declaring any highway or part of a highway to be a residential street," and I put to counsel the question: "Could a by-law passed by the council of an Ontario town in these terms—'B Street is hereby declared to be a residential street'—be successfully attacked as too vague and indefinite to be enforced?" In the application of such a by-law it would of course be necessary to determine just what class of buildings should be permitted in a residential street. But I cannot think that the by-law should therefore be held invalid. That business and industrial establishments are excluded by by-law No. 570 there would seem to be no room for reasonable doubt. Nor can there be any question that a public garage is a business establishment, if indeed it is not industrial as well.

"I am, for these reasons, of the opinion that by-law No. 570 is valid and effectual, as a regulation passed under the first clause of paragraph 44 (a) of Art. 300 of the charter of the City of Montreal, to prohibit the erection on the part of Jeanne Mance Street here in question of a public garage. . . ."

WALKER *v*. STRETTON. (1896). 12 T.L.R. 363 (England. King's Bench). LORD RUSSELL OF KILLOWEN C.J.: ". . . It was undesirable that the Courts should be, so to speak, astute in picking holes in by-laws which dealt with matters which were more familiar to the authorities who framed the by-laws than to the Courts. It was also safe to lay down this general proposition—that, although it was desirable that by-laws should be so free from doubt that 'he who runs may read,' yet as even in the case of higher legislative bodies this was not always attained, the Court should strive to so construe this by-law as to give reasonable effect to the object aimed at. . . ."

RE ELLIOTT. 1896. 11 Man. R. 358 (Manitoba. King's Bench). BAIN J.: ". . . The second objection is, that section three of the by-law is unintelligible. This section is loosely and carelessly drawn, but it cannot be said to be unintelligible. If, however, it is unintelligible, it will be impossible to say whether its provisions are illegal or not, and it will be merely inoperative. . . ."

NOTE ON DRAFTING. Any text book on drafting of statutes will emphasize two aspects of drafting—the composition of legislative sentences and the understanding of the legislative policy. The composition of sentences can fairly easily be mastered in the abstract; this is an aspect of drafting that can be, should be, and has been, reduced to a series of rules and supplementary comment. An understanding of legislative policy cannot be taught so abstractly, but this casebook is designed to demonstrate some of the legal and planning background of any legislation regulating land use. Just as the draftsman requires experience to make him the real master of the drafting rules of composition, so also he requires experience with actual situations to appreciate the full significance of policy analysis and understanding.

Nevertheless, a few words of advice or warning may be offered about policy problems. First of all, the draftsman must fully understand the fact situation with which he is dealing. To whom will the regulation apply? How will it affect him? There is a tendency to dismiss fact investigation as a never ending chore, but while it is never ending, it cannot be dismissed. Within the limits of time available, the fact situation must be thoroughly investigated. In zoning by-laws, perhaps the most important facts are existing land uses and property boundaries. Then one must ask, what limitations are to be imposed, why, and will they work? It is extraordinary how many zoning by-laws, in Ontario at least, are drafted and passed without either the draftsman or the members of the municipal council ever knowing, in reasonable detail, what existing rights they are invading, because no thorough study has been made of existing uses and property limits. When these facts have been obtained, the extent to which the uses are to be redirected can be considered more intelligently.

Along with existing uses, one should learn existing laws. It is dangerous to tamper with existing laws without understanding what is being changed. It is not sufficient to know merely that there is or is not another zoning by-law in effect. The whole legal picture should be known: the possibility of land use regulation by other municipal, provincial or federal bodies; and the common law position including the extent of private control and the effectiveness of these controls.

But what is most important for the draftsman to understand is what it is that the legislative body wants to achieve. This is particularly important when the by-law will be rigid in its terms and possibly even strictly enforced. Sometimes the legislator, or his planner advisor, thinks he wants to establish minimum yards when he really only wants to guarantee that there will be no overcrowding, which can be guaranteed by limiting the percentage of a lot that may be covered by buildings. If the legislator (and draftsman) proceeds to the first objective, he will limit the citizen's free choice of locating his house where he wishes on the lot. If he proceeds to the second objective, he will leave the citizen with a great degree of freedom of choice. It often happens that the more skillful planner wants the best of both objectives, which makes the draftsman's job more difficult. To ascertain the real objective from the generalized instructions of the planner usually requires a cross-examination of the planner by the draftsman after he has made his own analysis of the facts and his instructions.

Finally, the draftsman must have a thorough knowledge of the ways of making laws effective. In this field he cannot, at the moment, do better than study Ernst Freund's *Legislative Regulation*, which, though old (it was published in 1932) is still the most comprehensive text written on the subject. It is comparative in scope, and examines devices in use in the United States, the United Kingdom and in Germany.

COODE ON LEGISLATIVE EXPRESSION (1843)

It is no demerit of modern legislation that it applies itself minutely to special cases. It would, in fact, be the greatest merit of any system of laws that they varied exactly as every case varied in its elements. It is the indiscriminating and general rules of law that make the harshness of a system of law—that make special classes of persons obnoxious to unintended and unforeseen oppression—that require for their mitigation the arbitrary modifications of judicial construction and of courts of equity. The more a legislature is civilized the more it measures and considers the differences in each class of cases, and adjusts the law to their varieties. With every fair enactment for the peculiarities of a special case, the law loses a portion of its rudeness and unbending character. The proper object of legislation is to make certain rules of the utmost possible convenience—not to propound rules of the utmost possible generality. Legislation is not a science, but a practical art. The perfection of a science is reached, when every particular proposition is resolved into or deducible from one general proposition; but the perfection of legislation is attained in proportion as every variety of right, and every corresponding obligation and liability are most specifically determined, and when the least is left to interference from extensive and remote generalities. It is most true that in adjusting its provisions to special differences, the general principles of the pre-existent law should be as far as possible adhered to; mutual consistency having a great value as well as particular aptness; and it is also true in regard to law as in regard to all other things, that a simple general rule is most easily comprehended by those who have no practical acquaintance with the particulars included by it, and this fact is also of practical importance in legislation; but to those who do know the particulars experimentally, as each man knows his own case, the more general the terms of a rule the less certain and close does its application appear—the more specific the terms of a rule, the more easily and precisely is its application seen and understood. Generalizing the expression of the law is more the work of the scholastic professor; specializing the law the proper task of the practical legislator. In this process of modifying and adjusting the law to special cases, the constant action of the legislature and of the judiciary of England has undeniably made a greater and better progress than the institutions of any other country; and to desire a codification or simplification which should destroy these nice adjustments, or diminish in any way the speciality of the law, or to propose arrangements to cramp or obstruct in future the further extension of specific legislation, would be to sacrifice aptness and certainty in the law to verbal generality; and to supplant the beneficent officiousness of the legislator by the despotic formalities of the methodizer.

Nevertheless, this beneficent process of adjusting our law to the partial and various interests of the community has unquestionably, so far as our statute law is concerned, introduced a cumbrousness, intricacy, and confusion, quite without any parallel in the legislation of any other country.

Without some rule for expressing the limitation of the law to its specific occasions, the draftsman first draws an enactment in terms too general for his purpose; he then attempts to detract from its generality by interpolated limitations, qualifications, exceptions, and by that bane of all correct composition, the Proviso. It would indeed be lamentable if the aptness and flexibility of legislation could only be attained by such intricacy and confusion in the expression of the law, as we see resulting from this clumsy process. But there is no necessary connexion in these effects. The law can universally be made, like every other matter, clearer in all its details, and more compact in all its parts, by the orderly specification of those details.

As on the due expression of the legal subject the extent of the law depends, and as on that of the legal action the nature of the law depends; so on the expression of the case, and of the conditions, do the clearness, precision, and form of our statute law mainly depend.

The rule to be observed is of such simplicity as to make its utterance appear almost an absurdity; but simple as it is, it is the most frequently neglected of any rule of composition.

It is, that wherever the law is intended to operate only in certain circumstances, those circumstances should be invariably described BEFORE any other part of the enactment is expressed.

If this rule were observed, nine-tenths of the wretched provisoes, and after-limitations and qualifications with which the law is disfigured and confused, would be avoided, and no doubt could ever possibly arise, except through the bad choice of terms, as to the occasions in which the law applied, and those in which it did not. It is beyond a doubt that the *casus legis*, which can be described in a proviso, or in a phrase interpolated into other matter by way of limitation, can be more easily expressed alone, and at the beginning of the enactment. It is equally beyond a doubt that its proper place is at the beginning, and that it is misleading the reader to commence an enactment as if it were universal, and to wind it up by a parenthetical qualification or proviso which limits it to certain occasions only. . . .

INTERPRETATION ACT
Ontario. Revised Statutes. 1960. Chapter

s. 10. Every Act shall be deemed remedial, whether its immediate purport be to direct the doing of anything which the Legislature deems to be for the public good, or to prevent or punish the doing of anything which it deems to be contrary to the public good, and shall accordingly receive such fair, large and liberal construction and interpretation as will best ensure the attainment of the object of the Act according to the true intent, meaning and spirit thereof.

s. 8. The preamble of an Act shall be deemed a part thereof and intended to assist in explaining the purport and object of the Act.

NOTES. No draftsman can afford not to know thoroughly the *Interpretation Act* of his own jurisdiction. It has rather limited application to municipal by-laws, but a study of its provisions will serve as a reminder of many short hand forms that can safely be used where the Act does apply. Notwithstanding s. 8, the Courts are reluctant to look at preambles, their feeling being that here is more ambiguous language to be construed.

NOTE ON BIBLIOGRAPHY. The whole of the second edition of *Coode on Legislative Expression* is reproduced as an appendix to Driedger, *The Composition of Legislation* (1957), an excellent text on the subject. On the interpretation of statutes, see especially, Willis, "Statute Interpretation in a Nutshell" (1938), 16 *Canadian Bar Review* 1. See also, Kilgour, "The Rule against the Use of Legislative History: 'Canon of Construction or Counsel of Caution'?" In 1948 the Conference of Commisioners on Uniformity of Legislation in Canada published a revision of its *Rules of Drafting and Observations and Suggestions on the Drafting of Legislation*, which it distributes without charge (if copies remain available).

2. Enforcement Problems

THE MUNICIPAL ACT
Ontario. Revised Statutes. 1960. Chapter 249

482. (1) By-laws may be passed by the councils of all municipalities and by boards of commissioners of police for imposing fines of not more than

$300, exclusive of costs, upon every person who contravenes any by-law of the council or of the board passed under the authority of this Act.

483. Where a prosecution is brought by a peace officer or employee of the corporation or of the local board of health, the whole of the fine belongs to the corporation, and in other cases belongs one-half to the corporation and the other one-half to the prosecutor.

[Section 32 of *The Planning Act* makes these provisions applicable to sections 30 and 31 of that Act.]

485. Where a council has authority to direct or require by by-law or otherwise that any matter or thing be done, the council may by the same or by another by-law direct that, in default of its being done by the person directed or required to do it, such matter or thing shall be done at his expense, and the corporation may recover the expense incurred in doing it by action, or the same may be recovered in like manner as municipal taxes, or the council may provide that the expense incurred by it, with interest, shall be payable by such person in annual instalments not exceeding ten years and may, without obtaining the assent of the electors, borrow money to cover such expense by the issue of debentures of the corporation payable in not more than ten years.

ORPEN *v.* ROBERTS

Ontario. Supreme Court of Canada. [1925] S.C.R. 364

A by-law of the city of Toronto, passed under paragraph 10 of section 406 of *The Municipal Institutions Act*, R.S.O., 1914, c. 192, prohibited building on lands "fronting" on the north side of Carlton Street closer to the street line than 25 feet. The respondents built an apartment building "fronting" on Homewood Avenue and closer to Carlton Street than 25 feet. The property consisted of the corner lot abutting on both Homewood Avenue and Carlton Street and additional lots abutting on Homewood Avenue only. Mrs. Orpen owned a dwelling house on the north side of Carlton Street near the apartment building. On hearing of the respondents' application for a building permit Mrs. Orpen applied for an injunction to restrain its construction. Lennox J. refused and she appealed to the Appellate Division, who dismissed the appeal on the ground that since the apartment building did not "front" on Carlton Street the lot did not "front" on Carlton street, hence the by-law did not apply to it. Mrs. Orpen appealed to the Supreme Court of Canada. For the purpose of his judgment Duff J. assumed that there had been an infraction of the by-law.

DUFF J.: . . . But the object and provisions of the statute as a whole must be examined with a view to determining whether it is a part of the scheme of the legislation to create, for the benefit of individuals, rights enforceable by action; or whether the remedies provided by the statute are intended to be the sole remedies available by way of guarantees to the public for the observance of the statutory duty, or by way of compensation to individuals who have suffered by reason of the non-performance of that duty.

In substance, the proposition advanced by the appellant is that any proprietor, whose property might suffer in value by reason of the failure of some other proprietor to observe the building restrictions established by a by-law promulgated under the authority of this enactment, has a right to invoke the jurisdiction of the courts to prevent by injunction the obnoxious act and to recover damages in respect of any loss actually suffered in consequence of it if wholly or partly completed. In effect, if this contention be sound, such a by-law creates in favour of any proprietor who may be prejudicially affected in his property by an infringement of any of the prohibitions of such a by-law, a negative easement (enforceable in the same manner as a restrictive covenant) over the property within the area where the by-law operates.

It is legitimate to observe that this construction if it were to prevail, would be an unfortunate construction. As Meredith C.J. said, in *Tomkins* v. *The Brockville Rink Company* (1899), when one considers the different kinds of acts and conduct which municipal councils in Ontario are by statute permitted to prohibit or to regulate, and the multiplicity of duties they have authority to impose upon property owners and others within their jurisdiction, one is rather startled by the proposition that in each case a duty is imposed for the failure to perform which an action lies by one who is injured owing to the non-performance of it; and it seems highly unlikely, as Farwell J., said in *Mullis* v. *Hubbard* (1903), that the legislature contemplated as the result of this legislation that "the numerous individuals" in the vicinity of a residential area, should be entitled to bring their private actions against a man who had built a few feet in front of the line allowed, even though the municipal authorities themselves should not consider it a proper case for interference.

The question to be decided might possibly have presented greater difficulties had it not been for the history of the enactment and the course of decision upon it and upon analogous provisions of the Act. The statute which was the parent of the legislation now under discussion was first passed in the year 1904; but before examining the language of the enactment of that year, it will be advantageous first to consider the decision in *Tompkins Case* already referred to, and the judgment of Meredith C.J. which was delivered in the year 1899. The action was brought by a ratepayer, who complained that the defendant company, in violation of a fire limits by-law, was erecting a wooden building in the vicinity of his own property, alleging that, in consequence of this breach of the by-law, the premiums payable for the insurance of his own buildings would be increased, and the value of his property diminished. The action was brought to restrain the defendant from proceeding with its building, and for damages. In a judgment which contains an elaborate review of the pertinent decisions, Meredith C.J. held that the authority conferred upon municipalities to establish fire limits and to regulate the construction of buildings within those limits was an authority given in the interests of the public generally, and that the sole remedy in respect of any infraction of a by-law passed under it lay in proceedings for the enforcement of the penalties prescribed by the by-law under the authority of the statute, including, if the by-law so ordained, the liability to have the building removed.

It was, as already mentioned, in 1904 that the legislature, in chapter 22 of the statutes of that year (by sec. 19) first dealt with the subject of establishing residential areas and regulating the construction of buildings in those areas. By the same statute, sec. 20, the legislature dealt also with the subject that had been discussed in *Tompkins' Case* and, in cases of infringement of prohibitions of the kind considered in that case, it was provided that either the municipal corporation or any ratepayer might bring an action, and jurisdiction was conferred upon the High Court to grant an injunction in such a proceeding. It is not immaterial to notice this section, because it seems to indicate that the legislature was legislating with a view to the state of the law ascertained by *Tompkins' Case* as touching the effect of fire limits by-laws.

Section 19 was in these words: ". . . The location, erection, construction or use of any buildings in contravention of any such by-law may, in addition to any other remedy provided by law, be restrained by action at the instance of the municipality passing such by-law; . . ."

In the consolidation of 1913, subsection (*a*) of this section appears in altered form, as quoted above, as subsection (10) of sec. 406, ch. 43, which confers a variety of powers on the councils of cities and towns; while that part of the section which gave a right of action, at the instance of the municipality, for restraining breaches of by-laws passed under the authority of it, is replaced by sec. 501, which is in these words:

"501. Where a building is erected or used, or land is used in contravention of a by-law passed under the authority of this Act in addition to any other remedy provided by this Act and to any penalty imposed by the by-law, such contravention may be restrained by action at the instance of the corporation."

Section 20 of the Act of 1904, which, as already mentioned, gave a special right of action in respect of the contravention of fire limits by-laws to the corporation and to any ratepayer, was not reproduced in the consolidation of 1913 and, indeed, was expressly repealed. The result, therefore, of the changes effected by the consolidation of 1913 was that by virtue of section 501, which appears in Part 22 of the statute under the heading of "Penalties and Enforcements of By-laws," contraventions of by-laws regulating the erection or the use of buildings or land might be restrained by action at the suit of the corporation, while the right of action given by sec. 20 of the Act of 1904 to a ratepayer in respect of violations of the particular class of by-laws with which it dealt (fire limits by-laws) was abrogated.

Section 501, it will have been observed, carefully preserves any other remedy provided by the Act and the liability to any penalty imposed by the by-law. But there is no mention of remedies under the general law; and it seems to proceed upon the assumption that in respect of such contraventions there could be no remedy except such as is given or authorized by the Act. This view is fortified by the inference to be drawn from the contrast between the language of sec. 501 and that of sec. 19 of the Act of 1904, which explicitly preserved "any other remedy provided by law." The change in language is striking, and appears to be most readily explained on the theory that in 1913 the legislature accepted and proceeded upon the opinion to which Meredith C.J. had given effect in *Tompkins' Case*, namely, that, according to the scheme of the Act, as regards by-laws of the character to which sec. 501 applies, the remedial measures available to persons affected by a breach of them are those provided or authorized by the Act, and those alone.

This view of the section seems to have commended itself to Middleton J., when giving judgment in *Mackenzie* v. *City of Toronto* (1915), although, as a decision on the point was not strictly required, he expressed no decided opinion concerning it; and to Orde J. in *Preston* v. *Hilton* (1920). It was after these judgments had been delivered and published that the *Municipal Institutions Act* of Ontario was again consolidated in 1922 as chapter 72 of the statutes of that year, and sec. 501 was re-enacted without change.

Although by sec. 20 of the *Interpretation Act*, R.S.O. [1914], the legislature is not to be presumed by reason merely of having re-enacted a statutory provision without changing its language to have adopted a previous judicial construction of that language, nevertheless, the history of the legislation, when read in light of the course of judicial decision and opinion touching the effect of it, may, independently of the intrinsic weight of such decisions and opinions, afford convincing evidence of the intention of the legislature. There appears to be little room for doubt that in this instance the Appellate Division has accurately interpreted that intention.

The appeal should accordingly be dismissed with costs.

IDINGTON J.: . . . The penalty imposed . . . is only fifty dollars which, as regards the parties hereto, seems so trifling that I am unable to see therein any effective restraint. . . .

There are many actions which have been successfully maintained though founded, in the last analysis, upon what were merely by-laws provided for by statute and well founded thereon, but few, if any, upon our *Municipal Acts*. . . . [It is] impossible to properly hold that the legislature ever intended that the appellant should have the right of action she claims herein.

If that conclusion, coupled with the apparent refusal herein of the city to assist such appellant in maintaining its by-law, renders the enactment of such a by-law rather farcical I cannot help it. . . .

[The judgment of Idington J. has been somewhat abbreviated and the judgment of Duff J. is the judgment of the rest of the Court.]

THE MUNICIPAL ACT
Ontario. Revised Statutes. 1960. Chapter 249

486. Where any by-law of a municipality or of a local board thereof, passed under the authority of this or any other general or special Act, is contravened, in addition to any other remedy and to any penalty imposed by the by-law, such contravention may be restrained by action at the instance *of a ratepayer* or the corporation or local board. [Italics added.]

NOTE. Duff J.'s doubts in *Orpen* v. *Roberts* in 1925 about the wisdom of private enforcement powers seem to have prevailed for some time with the Ontario legislature. The addition of the words "of a ratepayer" to what is now section 486 was not made for nearly twenty years. See S.O., 1944, c. 39, s. 48.

While a fine of $300 is substantial in most cases, there is no guarantee that the convicting magistrate will impose the maximum penalty once, let alone time after time if the offence is repeated, and municipalities have sometimes resorted to the restraining action (which is commenced in a higher court more remote from local politics). Two limitations on this method of enforcement may be noted. First, if there has been what would be called, in the equity cases on injunctions, laches, the court may delay the operation of the injunction. It is also doubtful how far a court will use its discretion when a mandatory injunction is sought that involves removing a building.

TORONTO *v.* HUTTON
Ontario. High Court. [1953] O.W.N. 205

The city brought this action to restrain the defendant from using her property as a nursing home in violation of a by-law restricting its use to that of a private residence.

LEBEL J.: . . . It is unnecessary to review the evidence, for both in the witness-box and in her examination for discovery the defendant has frankly admitted that she is, and has been since 1946, engaged at 27 Walmer Road, in the city of Toronto, as the proprietress of a nursing-home. It is clear from the evidence that this house is really used for the accommodation of aged and infirm people, in many cases persons requiring constant nursing services. She frankly admits, too, that she is engaged in this business for profit, although she says, and I have no doubt she speaks the truth, that the profits are small. It is unquestionably a business, and as such it is being carried on in contravention of the by-law I have mentioned. That by-law of the plaintiff corporation is filed as ex. 1; it was passed on 11th December 1923, and was approved by the body then known as the Ontario Railway and Municipal Board on 24th January 1924.

The object of the by-law was undoubtedly to restrict the use of buildings on either side of Walmer Road, from Bloor Street to Bernard Avenue, in any other way than as detached private residences. There can be no question, on the evidence presented before me, that over the course of the years there has been a material change in the locality covered by the by-law. I must go upon the evidence presented here, and I am satisfied from the defendant's testimony that the area covered by the by-law is now anything but a residential district. That being the case, it must have changed with notice to the plaintiff corporation; it could not be otherwise. I am told that at the present time there is a contemplated zoning of the entire city, but I think it could hardly be said that in any reconsideration of the zones of this city the area covered by the by-law could now be said to be residential in character. Nevertheless, the by-law is still in effect, and still prohibits the use of any building in the area for any purpose other than that of a detached private residence.

I am satisfied that the power to grant an injunction under the provisions of s. 497 of *The Municipal Act*, R.S.O. 1950, c. 243, is a discretionary one with the Court . . .

However, the discretion exercisable by a Court is a judicial discretion. A judge cannot be actuated in exercising his discretion by his own personal feelings or by caprice. I have every sympathy with the defendant in the position in which she finds herself. I accept it as a fact that she leased this house in 1942, that she converted it at very considerable cost into a guest-nursing home, as she calls it, in 1946, and that at neither time did she know or have any means of knowing about the existence of this by-law . . .

I think that the action must succeed, and that costs must follow the event. However, it is within my discretion to postpone or stay the operation of this injunction for some period of time. Counsel for the plaintiff has pointed out that in *The City of Toronto* v. *Beck*, an unreported decision of my brother Barlow, made on 28th November 1949, he granted a stay of two months. In *The City of Toronto* v. *Robinson et al.*, my brother Spence granted a stay of four months. In *The City of Toronto* v. *Torrance*, my brother Barlow granted no stay at all. It is perfectly plain why that was so; it was a very different type of business that my learned brother had to deal with there.

In *The City of Toronto* v. *Rudd and Rudd*, (1952) which dealt with a business somewhat similar to the one now before me, my brother Wells granted a stay of 18 months. His reasons for so doing are to be found on pp. 94–5 of the report. He says: "It is quite clear on the evidence that Dr. Rudd has spent very large sums of money in equipping this dwelling-house as a private hospital and that he is operating it in a perfectly proper and inoffensive manner." The same things are true here. Even though I am not concerned with what was there called a private hospital, the defendant may be said to be carrying on much the same kind of institution.

Mr. Justice Wells also pointed out that he felt that there had been a casual attitude on the part of the plaintiff corporation in connection with the case before him. I think the same is true here, particularly in view of the fact that while he was dealing with a business commenced in 1949, Mrs. Hutton testified in this case that she had established her guest-nursing-home three years before that. And in the other cases I have referred to, the ones dealt with by my brothers Barlow and Spence, the businesses objected to had not been in existence as long as has that of the defendant in this case.

It may well be that the plaintiff corporation has had good reason for its delay in bringing this action. I do not know, so I do not propose to go into it. I am considering the delay only from the standpoint of the difficulty in which the defendant must now find herself, and the hardship that her aged people will suffer if an injunction is granted to take effect immediately. As I pointed out earlier, she had no notice before she started this business that she was acting in defiance of the by-law. She said that she expended something like $22,000 on the property. She also said that at the present time there are some 21 patients there, and this seems to be about the possible accommodation of the place, according to the testimony of Mr. Badley. Taking what he said together with what the defendant herself said, this building at 27 Walmer Road is certainly used for the accommodation of aged people, some of them being bedridden and requiring daily nursing service.

Mr. Joy said that if I granted the injunction he would not oppose a comparatively short stay, and he suggested six months. But he was frank to admit that he knew of no place or other institution the City could recommend for the reception of these people within a six-month period. Surely these poor people must not be made to suffer.

It follows, I think, that in the exercise of its discretion the Court should take everything into consideration, and it should do the best it can, first of all, to make it clear that by-laws such as these must necessarily be obeyed, and secondly, to ensure that in enforcing obedience no real hardship be inflicted upon innocent people.

For these reasons I propose to follow the example set by my brother Wells. I am going to postpone or stay the operation of the injunction for a period of 18 months . . ."

NIAGARA FALLS *v.* MANNETTE. [1943] O.W.N. 599 (Ontario. High Court). The city asked for a mandatory injunction requiring the defendants to remove a "building" that they had dismantled and relocated in a residential section. They had stated in their application for a permit (which was refused) that they intended to use the "building" as a tourist cabin, but in fact used it as a shop for the sale of souvenirs and similar articles. Plaxton J. was of the opinion that the by-laws were validly made and that the defendants had erected a building, and used it, for a purpose in contravention of the by-laws in question, and that a mandatory injunction should be granted. The Court of Appeal dismissed the appeal without calling on counsel for the respondent. No reasons are reported.

NOTE. Whether a request by a municipality to demolish a more elaborate building would be so readily granted is uncertain. Read section 486 of *The*

Municipal Act carefully to see whether a past act, completed before the action is commenced, could be "restrained", or whether only the continuing use could be stopped after the offending building has been erected.

The courts fail to distinguish between an action by a municipality to restrain, as a means of enforcing a statutory penalty, and an action for a private injunction by a citizen against another citizen under equity jurisdiction. In both cases the court will require the usual undertaking that the applicant for an interlocutory injunction pay damages to the defendant if at the trial it should appear that the injunction has been unjustified. If an injunction is sought to restrain a gravel pit operator from digging gravel out of land in an exclusively residential zone, the damages might be quite substantial if ultimately a court adopted the view of Morden J.A. in *Pickering* v. *Godfrey* above. This limitation not only discourages most private citizens from resorting to section 486, it also discourages less well to do municipalities. Is it right that no distinction should be made between equity injunctions and statutory injunctions of a quasi criminal character? Is an innocent man legally but mistakenly charged and gaoled and subsequently acquitted compensated? Should the action to restrain brought by a private citizen under s. 497 be treated differently in this respect from one brought by the municipality?

TCHAPEROFF *v.* CITY OF VICTORIA AND MEMORIAL AIRPARK ASSOCIATION OF GREATER VICTORIA. [1948] 2 W.W.R. 722 (British Columbia. Supreme Court). MACFARLANE J.: "This is an action brought by an owner of residential property in the Gordon Head District, against the city of Victoria, the owner of neighbouring land, and against the Memorial Airpark Association of Greater Victoria, an association with which the city has entered into an agreement permitting the association 'to commence the work of preparation of the grounds for a runway for emergency aircraft.' The defendant association, by its president, admits that it is the intention of the association to carry out its objects on this land when the present work of preparation is completed and these objects include the establishment and maintenance of an airpark for the furtherance of civil aviation. The word 'airpark' seems to have special significance in that it means a field for landing and taking off of light aircraft. A licensed airpark must have runways in excess of the length now available on this particular parcel of ground, but the association hopes to obtain additional land so that eventually at least the field may be licensed. There is no assurance that the field will not be used, to some degree, without licence. So far the work done consists of laying out and levelling the land for two runways, which, so far as present available information goes, will allow aircraft to take off into the prevailing winds when these runways are finished. Since the commencement of the action, the direction of one of these runways has been altered somewhat but, before this was done, the flightways appropriate to this runway would have passed over a part of the plaintiff's property. He fears damage from possible crashes and interruption of the peaceable enjoyment of his property from noise of aircraft, testing and preparing to take off and, after taking off, passing close to his house or at a fairly low altitude, and also annoyance from the general operation of the airpark and from the resort thereto of onlookers and others in numbers attracted by the establishment of the airpark in that locality. The action is based on a claim of violation of his property rights—present and threatened. Although not parties to the action, the plaintiff, it appears from the evidence, has been assisted in the preparation and maintenance of his action by a group of other residents of the area in which there are a number of fairly valuable properties, the owners of which either fear depreciation of the value of their property or are, as neighbours, in sympathy with the protest of the plaintiff, sharing his fear that owing to the limited size of the field accidents may result.

"The claim to violation of the property right of the plaintiff is founded principally on the fact that the area is, and when he purchased his property was, zoned by the municipality of the district of Saanich, the local authority under the provisions of the *Town Planning Act*, R.S.B.C., 1936, c. 287, by by-law of that municipality for single family dwellings. The neighbouring land, when obtained by the city of Victoria from His Majesty the King in right of Canada, was restricted to use for an aerodrome. So far no buildings have been erected and all that has been done is at most the laying out of the runways and the levelling of the ground together with its seeding.

"The injury apprehended in respect of which an injunction is asked is one of possible nuisance. The plaintiff by his statement of claim alleges that the agreement between the two defendants is *ultra vires* of the corporation of the city of Victoria. He asks for a declaration that the agreement is void and has no legal effect. I will deal with these contentions later." [The Court followed *Orpen* v. *Roberts* and held that the by-law gave the plaintiff no enforceable rights.]

"I come then to the question of nuisance apart from any claim under the by-law. On the evidence it is clear that there is nothing to support a claim for nuisance on the facts as they exist at present. The evidence as presented in four days of this trial does not, I think, on the basis of preponderance of probabilities, support the claim of nuisance at least as governed by the particulars given, even in the future. . . . Here I do not think there is any present right in the plaintiff which is being infringed, nor is there the doing of any 'illegal act.' It is true that the plaintiff claims that the agreement between the city and the Memorial Airpark Association is illegal and *ultra vires* of the city, but I fail to see that the plaintiff has any status to attack that agreement and I do not see that I can make that assumption. . . ."

RE TENENBAUM AND LOCAL BOARD OF HEALTH OF TORONTO

Ontario. Court of Appeal. [1955] 3 D.L.R. 330

F. G. MacKay J.A. delivered the judgment of the Court: This is an appeal from the order of Wells J. dated December 31, 1954, whereby he dismissed an application by the appellants by way of *mandamus* to require the Local Board of Health of the City of Toronto either (a) to grant permission in writing to the applicants for the keeping of a plant for the killing and processing of poultry at 182 Brunswick Ave. in the City of Toronto, or (b) in the alternative to direct the Medical Officer of Health to make a report to the Local Board of Health in regard to the approval of the premises not based upon his views as to the restrictive by-laws but based upon the question of health only.

The appellants are the owners of premises at 182 Brunswick Ave., and they made an application under the provisions of s. 9 of the statutory by-law, being Sch. B. to the *Public Health Act*, R.S.O. 1950, c. 306. This section provides: "All slaughter-houses within this municipality shall be subject to inspection under the direction of the local board of health, and no person shall keep any slaughter house unless the permission in writing of the board for the keeping of such slaughter house has been first obtained and remains unrevoked. Such permission shall be granted, after approval of such premises upon inspection, subject to the condition that the slaughter-house shall be so kept as to comply with the regulations of the Department respecting slaughter-houses, and upon such condition being broken the permission may be revoked by the board, and all animals to be slaughtered, and all fresh meat exposed for sale in this municipality shall be subject to like inspection."

Application for the permit was first made by the appellants in July, 1952. On November 13th, 1952, the Secretary of the Board of Health informed the appellants' solicitor by letter that the application would "be given favourable consideration, conditional upon the premises being approved by the Federal Department of Agriculture." Following this letter the appellants spent a considerable sum of money rebuilding their premises.

The facts relating to this application and the Court proceedings following the refusal of the Board to grant the permit are fully set out in the reasons for judgment of Wells J., and it is unnecessary for the purpose of this appeal to repeat them, except to say that the order of this Court on appeal from the order of Spence J. ([1954] O.W.N. 261) directed the Board of Health to give directions that an inspection of the premises of the appellants be made by the Medical Officer of Health, and that after receiving his report the Board should consider whether or not permission in writing should be given by it to the appellants to operate a poultry-processing and slaughtering plant on the premises. Following this order the Medical Officer of Health personally inspected the premises, and made a report in writing to to the Board of Health.

The matter of whether the permit should be granted was considered by the Board at two meetings in January, 1954, and finally on March 23, 1954. The material filed indicates that the Board of Health, in reaching their decision as to whether they should grant or refuse a permit, had before them, and considered, the report of the Medical Officer of Health which contained references to certain zoning or residential by-laws as well as dealing with strictly health considerations and that the Board also considered residential or zoning by-laws that applied to the district in which the premises of the appellants were located. They also heard the representations of the appellants and their solicitors, and a deputation of residents from the district and their solicitor.

The Minutes of the Meeting of the Board of Health held on March 23, 1954, do not set out the reasons of the Board for refusing the application, but an affidavit of one Arthur Hall, who attended the meetings of the Board as clerk and recorded the minutes of the meetings, states that the application was discussed at Board meetings held on January 6th, January 20th, and March 23rd, 1954, the parties who were present at the meetings, and that the application was, in his opinion, refused by the Board "because of the strong opposition to the establishment of the chicken killing business, which was said to be offensive, in a residential area . . . and because of the two by-laws of the City Council, which apparently prohibit carrying on of such business at that location."

I am of the opinion that the Board of Health was bound to consider the effect of the residential by-laws in determining whether it should grant or refuse the permit. I am also of the opinion that it was entitled to consider the representations of those opposing the granting of the permit in so far as the representations related to matters of health, as well as the report of the Medical Officer of Health.

The residential by-laws in question are:

1. By-law 14769, passed on June 7th, 1937. The first paragraph of this by-law is as follows: "No building shall be erected or used for the slaughter of animals or fowl on land abutting on any of the highways or parts thereof nor within any of the areas set forth in the Schedule in Section III of this By-law and no such land shall be used for either of the said purposes." The land of the appellants in respect of which they were requesting a permit is admittedly within the area set forth in the Schedule in s. 111 of the by-law.

2. By-Law 16920, passed on April 28, 1947. This by-law provides that: "No person shall use any land within the area in the portion of the City of Toronto bounded by Bathurst Street, Bloor Street, College Street and Spadina Avenue and Spadina Crescent, hereinafter more particularly described, for any purpose except a private residential purpose." The by-law then contains an exception to this in relation to "light manufacturing" in any "building, the use of which at the date of the passing of this by-law was predominantly commercial, other than a retail store or shop", and a further exception with regard to "the use of any building which at the date of the passing of this by-law was used as a retail store" for certain businesses, including that of a butcher-shop.

In *Hopkins* v. *Swansea Corp.* (1839), Lord Abinger C.B. said: "The by-law has the same effect within its limits, and with respect to the persons upon whom it lawfully operates, as an act of Parliament has upon the subjects at large." This statement was quoted and followed in *Victoria Corp.* v. *Meston* (1905).

In *Re McIntosh & Pontypridd Improvements Co. Arbitration* (1891), it was held that even though the plans for a building had been passed by the local authority the building could not be erected in contravention of any of their by-laws.

That case was followed in *Yabbicom* v. *King* (1899) where it was held that a local authority empowered to make by-laws for the regulation of buildings within its jurisdiction had no power to sanction plans in contravention of by-laws properly made. At p. 448 Day J. said: "The district council could not control the law, and by-laws properly made have the effect of laws; a public body cannot any more than private persons dispense with laws that have to be administered."

On these authorities I think the Board of Health was bound to take into consideration the provisions of the by-laws.

By-law 14769 prohibits the operation, within the area where the appellants' premises are located, of the type of business for which the appellants sought a permit and on this ground alone the Board was entitled to refuse the permit. It was argued by the appellants that By-law 16920 by implication repealed the earlier by-law. By-law 14769 covers a much smaller area than the subsequent bylaw and prohibits only one class of business, that is, the slaughtering of animals or fowl. By-law 16920 is much wider in its terms. Although it may be that the second by-law also clearly prohibits the type of business which the appellants propose, I think it is unnecessary to decide this, because I am of the opinion that the earlier by-law was not repealed. I do not think there is anything inconsistent or repugnant in the two by-laws and I am of the opinion that the reasoning in *R. ex rel. Spence* v. *Gall* (1954) applies in this case.

The appellants also submit that the Board of Health in dealing with such applications may consider only the report of the Medical Officer of Health, and that the Medical Officer of Health must confine his report to the sanitary condition of the premises and whether or not the proposed business would be injurious to health, and if the report is favourable in these repects the Board must grant the permit. It is to be noted that under ss. 80 to 91 of the *Public Health Act*, dealing with nuisances, local Boards of Health and Medical Officers of Health are given wide power to abate any of the conditions enumerated in s. 81 which are or may be a nuisance. Section 92 deals with offensive trades, one of those enumerated being the slaughtering of animals. This section provides that no person may establish any such trade without the consent of the Local Board of Health or the municipal council.

Section 8 of the statutory by-law reads as follows: "No person shall at any time use any house, shop or out-house as a slaughter-house or as a place for the slaughtering of animals or fowl therein, unless such shop, house or out-house is distant not less than 200 yards from any dwelling house and not less than 50 yards from any public street."

This section was repealed by By-law 7521 of the City of Toronto, passed in November, 1915, under the provisions of s. 131 [re-enacted 1953, c. 87, s. 6] of the *Public Health Act*, and the following was substituted therefor: "No person shall at any time use any premises in the City of Toronto as a slaughter-house or as a place for slaughtering of animals or fowls therein, unless such premises have first been approved by the Medical Officer of Health."

I think that these sections of the Act and the by-law make it clear that the Board, in considering applications for a permit of this kind, may take into consideration the question whether the proposed operation of the appellants is likely to be a nuisance or offensive because of its location in close proximity to residential properties. It is to be noted that the report of the Medical Officer of Health does not say that the proposed operation will not be a nuisance or offensive, but only that it will not, in his opinion, be a greater nuisance or more offensive than the business previously carried on by the appellants. This is made clear by the following paragraph from his report:

"It is not to be assumed that the foregoing presages an approval per se. A comparison has been offered of an operation which can go on by unquestioned right and one which apparently cannot. One is not foolhardy enough to suggest that the contemplated operation would be utterly devoid of the potential of menace or offensiveness, but it is clear that the second state would be no worse than the first, probably better, in that reconstruction, whether regularly or irregularly embarked upon, has provided a place which fundamentally will lend itself to more effective surveillance and control."

I think that the effect of s. 9 of the by-law is that the premises must be inspected and approved by the Medical Officer of Health before the Board can grant a permit. This section does not preclude the Board from considering the other provisions of the by-law or the provisions of the *Public Health Act* to which I have referred, or entitle them to ignore a zoning by-law of the municipality. It follows that the Board may, because of the other matters which they are entitled to consider, refuse a permit even if the report of the Medical Officer of Health has approved of the premises.

It was also argued by the appellants that because the report of the Medical Officer of Health referred to matters other than those of health and sanitation, he should make a new report confined to these matters only. It may be that he should have confined his report to these matters only, but the fact that he also referred to other matters does not, in my opinion, invalidate his report and make it necessary for him to submit a new report.

NOTE. Wells J. in the Court below quoted the Medical Officer's report in full. The last paragraph of the report contains the relevant (?) observations about the zoning by-laws. This paragraph reads:

"I now come to my final observation. As Medical Officer of Health I find it impossible to divorce myself from the role of official of the Corporation and, for that matter, member of a local board of health. I cannot believe that I am privileged to form judgment without regard for existing by-laws affecting location and, furthermore, I cannot feel other than that the necessary basic clearance with restrictive ordinances has not been carried out. Until such time as I may appropriately disregard this consideration or until the matter has been conclusively dealt with by amendment of by-laws, or other regularized course, by the authorities whose function it is to do so, I cannot alter my total assessment which at this time prompts me to report that I must decline to give approval to the use of these premises for the purpose of slaughtering fowl."

After quoting the report, Wells J. commented:

"Penetrating as well as one can through the veil of language, the opinion of the Medical Officer of Health, as I gather it, would seem to be that from a sanitary and health aspect, insofar as the building and installations themselves are concerned, the conditions he found were satisfactory, but that, owing to the existence of certain residential by-laws, permission should not be granted until it was clear that the applicants were not bound by these by-laws."

On the issue generally, Wells J. said, in part:

"In the case at bar the Local Board of Health is not, I think, entitled to consider matters that are extraneous to the by-law under which it is acting, in the sense that some fancied or personal objection to the character of the applicants would entitle them to refuse permission; but in my view, it is entitled in considering whether permission should be granted to consider whether that which is sought is in accordance with the other by-laws and regulations of the municipal corporation, and if it is in contravention of them, then until that aspect of the matter is cleared up, the Board is, in my view, entitled to take the whole problem into consideration. It apparently did so in this case. Accordingly, it would be a very empty gesture on my part to direct the Medical Health Officer to bring in a further report confining himself, as he should have done, to the public health aspects of the matter on which he was reporting. It is also not clear to me that the Board was not entitled to take into consideration the location of the proposed slaughter-house from the public health aspect, and they may well have done so. While s. 8 of the statutory by-law was replaced, as I have already stated, it was apparently within the contemplation of the original by-law that slaughter-houses should not be very close to dwelling houses and public streets; and while, owing to the crowded conditions in Toronto, that may be an impossible requirement, particularly in relation to the public street, the matters indicated there are not precluded, in my view, from consideration by the Local Board of Health in deciding whether written permission should be granted or not."

RE RESOLUTION OF COUNCIL, TOWN OF MELVILLE
Saskatchewan. District Court. [1953] 1 D.L.R. 208

McFadden D.C.J.: This is an application by way of notice of motion made by or on behalf of L.O. Langford, Dr. George A. Paille, Chris Perdicaris, Edward Ruhr, Gordon J. Hart, Mervin G. Hart and Sam MacDonald, electors of the Town of Melville, Saskatchewan, to quash in whole for illegality a certain resolution of the council of Melville passed on February 26, 1952, purporting to authorize and instruct the building inspector for the said town to issue a permit to make alterations to the building situated on Lots 7 and 8 in Block 7, Plan T-286 in the said town . . . [The first ground of illegality was]

"(a) That under the provisions of Bylaw No. 578 of the Town of Melville as amended by Bylaw No. 589 of the said town, the building inspector of the said town is the official authorized to enforce the provisions of the said bylaws and the council of the said town has no authority to pass a resolution in respect thereto."...

The application now before me—an application to quash for illegality a resolution of the town—is, or might be, I appreciate the fact, one of great importance to all parties concerned. It is unfortunate that cases such as this do arise from time to time in a community. However, there is a dispute in this case and I am called upon to give, what I consider to be, a decision based on a correct interpretation of the law on the matter in question. I have reached the conclusion that the application should be granted, and that the resolution in question should be quashed in its entirety for illegality. Some reasons for arriving at such conclusion I shall now enumerate . . .

Section 220, para. 81, of the *Town Act*, provides that the council may make by-laws appointing building inspectors and defining their duties. Section 16 of the *Community Planning Act*, 1945 (Sask.), c. 51, empowers the council to pass zoning by-laws. Section 55 of the latter Act is as follows: "For the purpose of carrying out the provisions of this Act and of any by-law or scheme thereunder, every council shall possess and may exercise all the powers conferred upon it by the appropriate municipal Act."

The *Community Planning Act*, s. 16 (2) (c), permits the by-law to make provision designating the uses for which buildings may not be altered or repaired and designating the class of use which only shall be permitted. Such powers appear to have been exercised by the council in the zoning by-law, No. 578. Section 3 of such zoning by-law says that no building shall be erected or altered except in conformity or to conform with the regulations. Section 8 under the heading "Administration" says that such by-law shall be enforced by the building inspector who shall perform such duty in addition to his present duties (presumably under the building by-law) without additional remuneration. It is noted that while s. 8 speaks of "building permits" no specific reference is made to proposed "alterations." I think, however, that as "alterations" are referred to in s. 3 (1) of the by-law it must be assumed that s. 8 applies to alterations as well as to new structures. Mr. Ross has pointed out that the building by-law itself has not been filed and is not before the Court. That, I think, is unfortunate. The record would have been more satisfactory had the applicants filed the building by-law (if there is one in force) but I am of opinion that their failure to do so is not fatal to the application. I feel that I must assume from the contents of By-law 578, particularly s. 8 thereof (and which by-law has not been questioned) that there is a building by-law and that a building inspector was appointed thereunder with duties defined. That I think is clear from s. 8 of Zoning By-law 578 which imposes additional duties on the building inspector in addition to his regular duties as building inspector. It seems clear from the material on file that the property in question herein is in the area of the town known as the general business district and as such is subject to Zoning By-law 578. The administration of Zoning By-law 578 having been placed by s. 8 thereof under the jurisdiction of the building inspector, I am of opinion that the council had not the right to assume jurisdiction and to instruct and authorize (particularly had not the right to instruct) the building inspector to issue the permit as it appears to have done in its resolution of February 26, 1952. The building inspector had refused to issue the permit previous to that time and if he did so without justification it seems to me that the parties applying for the permit might have had the right to commence *mandamus* proceedings compelling the building inspector to issue the permit. *Archibald* v. *The King* (1917), a Nova Scotia case finally decided by the Supreme Court of Canada, is somewhat in point. There, a municipal clerk had refused to issue a licence for fishing on the ground that his council had neglected to pass a by-law setting a fee for such licences as authorized by the *Fisheries Act*. The Act, provided, among other things, that the licences were to be issued by the municipal clerk. Upon the clerk's refusal to issue a licence to the applicant a writ of *mandamus* issued against the clerk. Upon appeal to the Supreme Court of Canada, the Chief Justice said, in part, as follows [pp. 49–50]:

"At first sight I thought, as I suppose anyone would have thought, that this action was misconceived in that the mandamus should have been asked to be directed to the municipality of the County of Halifax rather than to one of the corporation's officials, namely, the appellant, the municipal clerk.

Upon consideration, however, I have come to the conclusion that the judgment appealed from is right."

"The Act not having imposed any obligatory duties on the council but only given permission for the exercise of rights which must be regarded rather in the light of privileges, the duties expressly imposed on the clerk of the council, the named official, must be treated as imperative and addressed to him personally. For the fulfilment of his duties he requires no authority or instruction from the council. The duties are not judicial or discretionary but purely administrative, and that being so I think a mandamus will lie to compel him to perform them and to issue a licence in a proper case." . . .

I find that the applicants are entitled to succeed on the first ground of illegality as set out in (a) of the amended notice of motion, that is, that the council was not authorized to pass the resolution in question.

Now it seems to me that having arrived at the above conclusion based on the first alleged ground of illegality, it is unnecessary to deal with the remaining three grounds of illegality as set out in the amended motion . . .

At the conclusion of the argument on the motion, counsel for the town asked for a stay of proceedings for 30 days should I find in favour of the applicants and at that time I intimated that such stay likely would be granted. However, in looking over certain material on file, it appears that work on the building has been progressing for some time, apparently against the wishes of the applicants, and, under such circumstances, not wishing to further complicate matters, I do not feel that I should grant a stay of proceedings but rather should leave the parties to whatever, if any, legal rights they might have should they wish to pursue them, or, better still, to mutually agree on a stay of proceedings should they feel so inclined. Of course, as aforesaid, the money paid into Court will remain as heretofore provided.

BELLEVILLE *v.* MOXAM. [1953] 4 D.L.R. 151. (Ontario. High Court). McRUER C.J.H.C.: "... It is first to be pointed out that in this letter the real reason for the alleged cancellation of the permit is not set out. It is said that it was issued without proper authority and the applicant is asked to have one issued under the authority of the council and then is asked to make his application to one of the aldermen, the chairman of planning. This procedure is all quite irregular. Permits are not issued by the municipal council. A certain official is clothed with authority to issue the permits and the chairman of planning is not the man who has that authority. . . . "

3. DISCRIMINATION: SPOT ZONING

Spot zoning is an American label and it is therefore suspect in its application to Canadian zoning law for the reason that the constitutional background differs radically. Nevertheless, under the label "discrimination" Canadian and English courts have come to results similar to those reached by American courts interpreting "due process". In the cases that follow the problem of spot zoning is presented from both countries and under both labels. In all cases, remember that in Canada if a legislature authorizes a municipal council to discriminate the council can discriminate. In the United States some question may arise about "due process". It may be that the discrimination attempted by the council and attempted to be authorized by the state legislature is such that the state itself has violated due process. In any event, if there is a violation of "due process" the desirability of the legislative device may be open to question in Canada either legally or as a matter of legislative policy.

MILLER *v.* CHARLESWOOD RURAL MUNICIPALITY
Manitoba. King's Bench. [1937] 3. W.W.R. 686

DYSART J.: This is a motion by a resident ratepayer of the municipality of Charleswood to quash a by-law passed by the council of that municipality. The application is brought under sec. 380 of *The Municipal Act, 1933*, (ch. 57).

The by-law in question was passed on December 21, 1936, No. 378, and amends an earlier by-law which was enacted in 1933 as No. 278, prohibiting the "establishment of farms or ranches for the rearing and maintenance of foxes and other fur-bearing animals" within an area of about 700 acres therein defined. This by-law is known as the "Fur By-Law". The amending by-law No. 378 carves a rectangular portion of about 10 acres out of the said 700 acres of restricted area. The 10 acres in question are in the midst of a small residential district, but the neighbouring residents, with the exception of the two applicants herein, have consented to the amendment.

The motion to quash is based on two grounds: (1) That the by-law was passed without observance of the requirements and conditions imposed by statute; and (2) That it was passed in the interest of a private individual and not of the public . . .

But to quash it on the ground just mentioned might be only temporizing and, as a broader ground is also relied upon, it should be considered. This second ground is that the by-law was passed in private and not in public interest. I think this objection must prevail. The movement to amend the fur by-law was initiated by Percy James, who lives on part of lot 41 in the restricted area, and who, in poor circumstances, desired to keep a fur farm there as a means of a livelihood. This commendable desire on his part had the sympathy and support of seven of his near neighbours, who at James's solicitation signed the petition, upon the strength of which Councillor Hayward, actuated also by laudable intentions, gave notice of motion for this amending by-law.

Fur farming entails something of a nuisance in that it engenders very disagreeable odours, which when wafted by the breezes are very objectionable to residents in the neighbourhood. Evidence of this fact was undisputed. The "fur by-law" was undoubtedly passed in the public interest to protect the residents of the restricted area and the public generally from these odours. The amendment is to permit fur farming in the very heart of a small community in the area so restricted. There can be no public need of such a change. The purpose of the amending by-law is chiefly to benefit Mr. James, who has initiated and pressed the amendment through. Those of his neighbours who have agreed to it have done so only by request of James. Councillor Hayward himself states that he supported the by-law in order that Mr. James might thereby be enabled or allowed to earn a livelihood at fur farming, and so save the municipality the expense of keeping or maintaining James and his family. The petition by which action of the council was initiated has been received in evidence, in the condition in which it comes from the files of the municipality. Attached to it is a memorandum reading as follows:

"Percy James will keep mink on the east side of Lot Forty-one (41) and will see that there is little or no odour."

This is cogent evidence that the by-law was passed to enable James—not the public—to do something which the original by-law prohibited. It seems beyond question then that the purpose of this by-law was to benefit Mr. James directly, and to benefit the municipality only indirectly. Such by-law is invalid.

In the case of *Wallace* v. *Dauphin* (1932) I refer to several cases which recognize this principle. In *In re Waterous and Brantford* (1903) a by-law was passed closing up and diverting a public street to enable a large manufacturing company to erect a building on the portion so closed, the company to reimburse the city for all costs. Although the by-law recited that the diversion of the street would be in the public interest, it was quashed as being passed for private and not for public interest. In *In re Loiselle and Red Deer* (1907) two by-laws were passed to close and sell to the Canadian Pacific Railway a public lane, but the by-laws were quashed as being for the benefit of the railway company. At p. 44 Stuart J. said:

"I think the idea of 'public interest' should be confined to the direct and immediate question of the closing of the highway in itself, and not extended to indirect advantages which may be expected from the persons to whose individual interests it is to have the highway closed."

And in *In re Weir and Calgary* (1907), the same Court, in quashing another such by-law, held that it was passed for the private benefit of a Mr. Hull because "on its face it is expressed to have been passed on his application."

For these reasons I hold that this by-law was passed in private and not public interest, and is therefore invalid and ought to be quashed.

Judgment accordingly. Costs to applicant.

[The part of the opinion dealing with the Council's failure to observe procedural rules set out in the *Municipal Act* is omitted. Dysart J. held the by-law invalid on this ground alone.]

NOTE. A distinction is to be drawn between failure to observe procedural rules set out in the enabling legislation and those established by the Council itself. Apparently the Council may disregard rules of its own creation with impunity, although it should take care either to provide in the rules the procedure for their suspension or to avoid prejudice to any members who may have relied on the rules. In *Rannard* v. *City of Winnipeg* (1935), the council discussed "new matter" without notice, contrary to its procedure By-law 10,192. Although no members objected no vote was taken to suspend the standing rules. Under By-law 10,192 suspension required a vote of two-thirds of the members present. Since the By-law protected only those members present presumably no protected member was prejudiced by the failure to vote in the absence of objection and there was no suggestion in the reported opinion that the common law gave absent members greater protection than the By-law. Perhaps the best view of the case rests on the language of the City Charter, which provided that after reading the minutes "the Council shall then proceed to business in accordance with the by-law regulating the same". In effect the procedure by-law had a statutory status. The case dealt with an early closing by-law, which was quashed on the procedural ground. The by-law seemed to have stirred up considerable controversy. Adamson J. remarked, "I express no opinion as to the unfairness or injustice or the alleged discriminatory character of these by-laws; but it does seem to me that in times like these to make the road of these taxpayers more difficult might be unwise. If it is being done to help their employees, it should be remembered that anything which hurts them will also in the long run hurt their employees."

The Court of Appeal found no fault with the procedure.

SCARBOROUGH TOWNSHIP *v.* BONDI

Ontario. Supreme Court of Canada. 1959. 18 D.L.R. (2d) 161

JUDSON J.: This is an appeal from the judgment of the Court of Appeal for the Province of Ontario which quashed an amendment to a zoning by-law of the Township of Scarborough. The original By-law, 2041, was passed on March 21, 1938 under authority of s. 406 of the *Municipal Act*, R.S.O. 1937, c. 266, now R.S.O. 1950, c. 243, s. 390(1), para. 4. It imposed residential restrictions on certain lands in registered plans 2763 and 1734 and permitted the erection of only one dwelling per 100 ft. of frontage on a public street.

Before the present dispute the by-law had been amended on at least three occasions on the petition of individual property owners so as to permit the erection of dwellings on parcels of land having a frontage of less than 100 ft. on a public street but having large areas. The lands of the respondent comprise the westerly portion of Lot 98 and are approximately 20,000 square feet in area. Lot 98 is a triangular shaped corner lot which has a frontage of 221 ft. on Annis Road and 333 ft. on Hill Crescent. Before the passing of the amending By-law 7203 (the by-law under attack) it would have been possible to erect at least four dwellings because of the frontages on the two streets. The by-law in question here, passed on September 17, 1956, amended By-law 2041 by providing that "Notwithstanding the provisions of this by-law, two single family detached dwellings only may be erected on the whole of lot 98, registered plan 1734". The easterly portion of Lot 98 fronting entirely on Hill Crescent already had a house built on it. The respondent's property, the westerly portion of Lot 98, is still vacant land. It has a frontage of 221 ft. on Annis Road by approximately 100 ft. on Hill Crescent. The perpendicular depth throughout is 100 ft. If therefore, one looks at the by-law before amendment, it would be possible to put two houses on this vacant lot, each having a frontage of

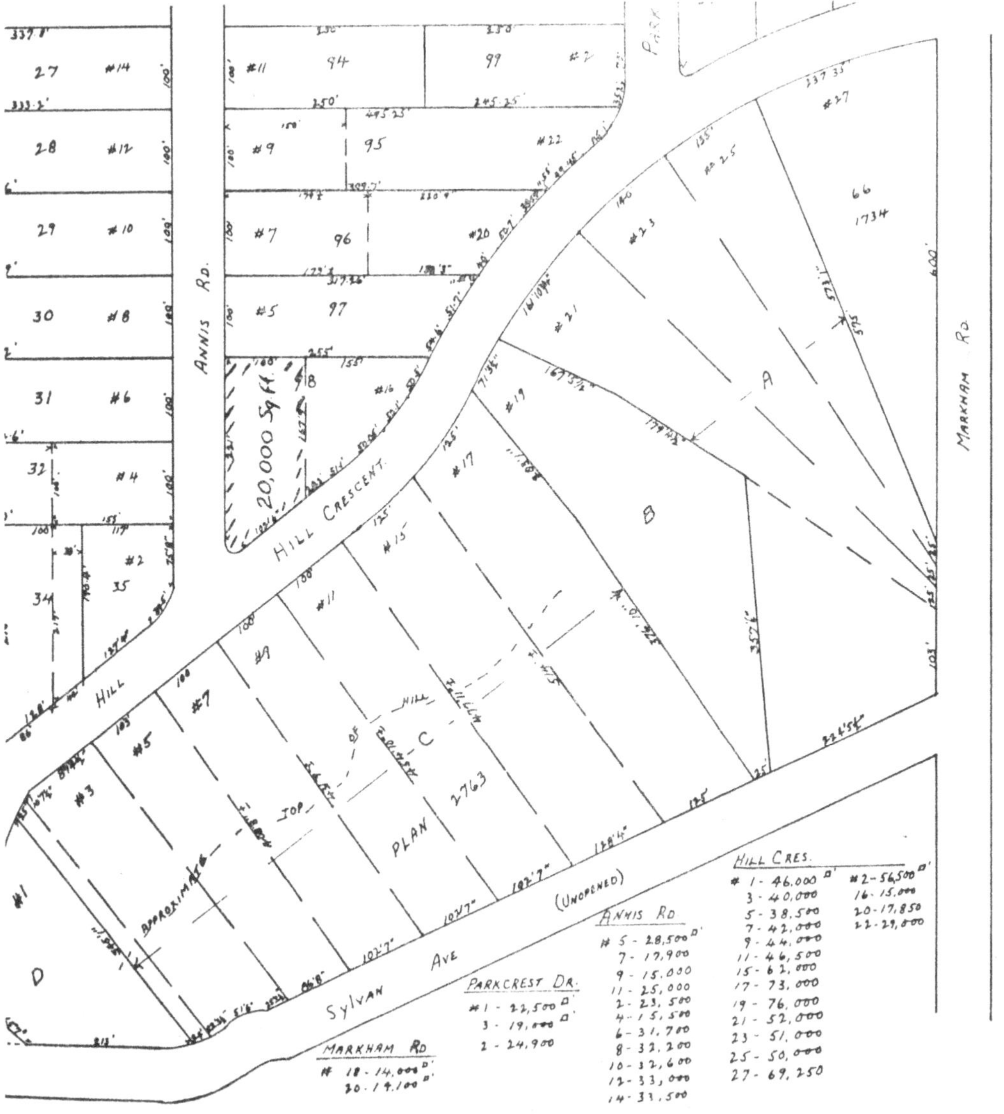

Registered plan 1734 (*Bondi's case*)

110 ft. 6 ins. on Annis Road by a depth of 100 ft. This would give each house an area of approximately 11,000 square feet.

The respondent purchased his property in May of 1951. In July of 1956 he agreed to sell to a third party, who proposed to put two houses on the property, each having a frontage of 100 ft. on Annis Road. It was a condition of the agreement that the purchaser should be able to obtain permission from the municipality to erect these two houses. The agreement came to nothing because property owners in the vicinity petitioned the Township Council to amend the by-law. Their petition pointed out that the average ground area for the houses in this neighborhood was in excess of 45,000 square feet, whereas the two new houses would each have a ground area of approximately 10,000 square feet. The objection to the proposed buildings on comparatively small lots in a neighbourhood such as this is apparent and needs no further comment. The amending by-law was first read on September 17, 1956 and received its second and third readings on September 24, 1956. It came before the Ontario Municipal Board for approval on November 1, 1956. An oral hearing was held at which the respondent was represented and heard. The Board reserved judgment and gave its decision approving the amendment on November 22nd after an inspection of the area. The Board stated that the restriction imposed by the amending by-law was reasonable and in keeping with the general character of the neighbourhood.

The respondent then moved for an order quashing the by-law. The application was dismissed by order dated April 12, 1957. This order was reversed on appeal and it is from this reversal that the present appeal is taken. The Court of Appeal held that even if the amending by-law was passed in good faith, it was discriminatory in scope, application and effect and consequently invalid, being aimed at and applying only to one lot within the defined area.

I do not think that one can characterize this by-law as discriminatory merely because it points to one particular person or lot. The task of the municipality in enacting the original by-law was to impose building restrictions over a fairly wide area. Lot 98, out of which the respondent's property came, was originally triangular in shape at the intersection of Annis Road and Hill Crescent. There was at that time no indication that it would be divided into two parcels so as to leave the respondent with a 221 ft. frontage on Annis Road with a depth of only 100 ft. No other lot in the immediate vicinity has a depth of less than 150 ft. If the municipality had foreseen this subdivision at the time of the enactment of the original by-law, can it be doubted that it could have provided that the 100 ft. frontage should be taken to refer to the frontage on Hill Crescent and not to a division of the 221 ft. frontage on Annis Road? This is all that the amending by-law does, although it does not say so in so many words. The intent and effect of the amending by-law are clear—to compel the respondent to fall in with the general standards of the neighbourhood and prevent him from taking advantage of the district amenities, the creation of the by-law, to the detriment of other owners. Far from being discriminatory, the amending by-law is nothing more than an attempt to enforce conformity with the standards established by the original by-law and which have been observed by all owners in the subdivision with this one exception.

The classic definition of discrimination in the Province of Ontario is that of Middleton J. in *Forst* v. *Toronto* (1923); "When the municipality is given the right to regulate, I think that all it can do is to pass general regulations affecting all who come within the ambit of the municipal legislation. It cannot itself discriminate, and give permission to one and refuse it to another."

Although I have a firm opinion that the original and amending by-laws do not infringe this principle, I share the doubt expressed by the learned Chief Justice whether it can ever afford a guide in dealing with a restrictive or zoning by-law. The mere delimitation of the boundaries of the area affected by such a by-law involves an element of discrimination. On one side of an arbitrary line an owner may be prevented from doing something with his property which another owner, on the other side of the line, with a property which corresponds in all respects except location, is free to do. Moreover, within the area itself, mathematical identity of conditions does not always exist. All lots are not necessarily of the same frontage or depth. The configuration of the land and the shape of the lots may vary. Some lots may have frontages on two streets. These are only some of the considerations which may justify a municipality in enacting these by-laws in exercising a certain amount of discretion.

The power to pass the by-law is contained in s. 390(1) para. 4 of the *Municipal Act*, now R.S.O. 1950, c. 243. It reads:

"390(1) By-laws may be passed by the councils of local municipalities:

"4. For regulating the cost or type of construction and the height, bulk, location, spacing, external design, character and use of buildings or structures to be erected within any defined area or areas or upon land abutting on any defined highway or part of a highway, and the minimum frontage and depth of the parcel of land and the proportion of the area thereof which any building or structure may occupy."

I think that this by-law may be justified under "spacing" and "minimum frontage and depth of the parcel of land". Although the original by-law refers only to minimum frontage and says nothing about the depth of the parcel, the facts are that at that time, long before Lot 98 had been subdivided, there were no lots in the immediate vicinity of the land in question with a depth of less than 150 ft. and in most cases the lots were considerably deeper. Therefore, when the by-law said that a lot should have a minimum frontage of 100 ft., the facts made it mean 100 ft. frontage by a depth of not less than 150 ft. It was at that time impossible to foresee how Lot 98, with its peculiar shape as compared with the rest of the lots, would eventually be subdivided. The municipality dealt with the problem after the subdivision had actually been made and when the owner of the westerly portion proposed to make a use of the lot which was not in keeping with the character of the neighbourhood.

I have no doubt concerning the finding of the learned Chief Justice that the municipality in enacting this amending by-law was acting in good faith and in the interest generally of the area covered by the by-law and that it was not legislating with a view to promoting some private interest, and I am equally satisfied with the finding of the Municipal Board that the amending by-law was reasonable and in keeping with the general character of the neighbourhood. I am therefore of the opinion that it resulted from a valid exercise of the legislative power and that it was not in fact discriminatory against the respondent. . . .

NOTE. In the result of the *Bondi* case, Judson J. agreed with Cartwright J., whose opinion is not reproduced, and with both of whom Taschereau and Abbott JJ. agreed, Locke J. concurring with Cartwright J. that the by-law was void because it was passed by the council *before* it was submitted for approval to the Municipal Board. The Court read the Municipal Act provision requiring that "no part of any by-law passed under this section [now s. 30 of *The Planning Act*] and approved by the Municipal Board shall be repealed or amended without the approval of the Municipal Board" as meaning that unless the Board's approval was given before the by-law was passed it was a nullity and that the Board had no authority to approve that nullity afterwards. This rather unconvincing view was thought to be buttressed by what is now section 39 of *The Ontario Municipal Board Act*, R.S.O. 1960, c. 274, which provides that "where . . . the permission, approval or sanction of the Board is necessary to the exercise of any power or the doing, or the abstention from doing or continuing to do any act, matter, deed or thing, such power shall not be exercised or act, matter, deed or thing be done or abstained from being done or be continued until such permission, approval or sanction has been obtained". Of this provision Cartwright J. said, "The predecessor of this section was first enacted in 1932 by s. 47 of 22 Geo. V., c. 27. Its terms appear to me to be free from ambiguity and to be fatal to the appellant's case." He conceded that this construction, which he thought the Court was compelled by the plain words of the statute to adopt, "may result in great inconvenience".

In fact virtually no council followed the possible practice of giving a by-law two readings, then getting the Board's approval, before giving the by-law a third and final reading. The legislature, however, had had fair warning, because the point successfully taken in the *Bondi* case in the Supreme Court had been mentioned but not decided in the Court of Appeal in 1957. In 1958, by S.O., c. 64, s. 31 (2) the offending section was amended to make it parallel the form of subsection (8) (now s. 30 (10) of *The Planning Act*).

Between 1932 when the requirement of (previous?) approval was introduced, and 1959 when the *Bondi* case was decided in the Supreme Court, the section had been twice reenacted in the R.S.O. 1937 and 1950, and some people might say that the legislature must be taken to know that the almost universal interpretation or application of the section had been that the council could pass the by-law before getting approval. Is there some imperative requirement for disregarding common interpretation if it is a possible although not necessary meaning of the words in the statute?

Cartwright J. quoted Hodgins J.A. in *Re Butterworth and Ottawa* (1918): "I think the Court should not be astute to quash a by-law passed by the municipal council and approved by the Board, just because the method adopted is open to some criticism due to the peculiar wording of the legislation giving authority to make the by-law effective. The only consequence would be to require the parties to try it again in a slightly different way so as to produce a result exactly the same", but he concluded that section 39 of *The Ontario Municipal Board Act* was overwhelming. Do you agree? How should the highest court deal with such a problem? Any differently from a lower court?

NOTE ON THE SUBSTANTIVE POINT IN THE BONDI CASE. It is remarkable that in the Court of Appeal, where the unanimous view was that the by-law was invalid because it discriminated against Bondi, there was little attempt to show why the by-law was unfair in substance rather than form. It is true that the amendment was aimed at the one lot 98, or perhaps even only the westerly half of lot 98, but there was no attempt to show any hardship falling on the owner of that half lot that was not shared in fact by the owners of the other lots to which the by-law being amended applied. The neighbours who requested the legislation had themselves pointed out, as Gibson J.A. noted, in his judgment, that "by crowding two houses on this lot, each house will have a ground area of approximately 10,000 square feet as compared with an average in excess of 45,000 square feet in the neighbourhood. This is certain to detract from the neighbourhood and tend to reduce the value of surrounding properties." In short, the contention of those who supported the by-law amendment was that the Bondi property was being made to conform with an existing standard, instead of continuing to enjoy a special privilege. If this view is correct, does it weaken the otherwise strong statement of Judson J. in the Supreme Court in support of "spot zoning"?

At the trial McRuer C.J. said, "If the original by-law had restricted the building to one house on each lot shown on the plan except Lot 98 on which two houses might be built, I do not think that it could be argued that the by-law was bad on that account. Therefore, it would seem to me to be within the power of the municipality to amend the by-law by providing that two houses and only two houses might be built on Lot 98 . . . ". Would he have said this if Lot 98 had been the same size as the other lots?

McRuer C.J. also said "In considering this argument [about discrimination] I do not think that the cases that deal with discrimination with respect to licensing are governing authorities where the validity of restrictive by-laws is in question."

THE METROPOLITAN STORES LIMITED *v.* THE CITY OF HAMILTON. [1945] O.R. 590 (Ontario. High Court). HOPE J.: ". . . . In reviewing and considering the evidence in the present case, which I have done with great care, and in the light of counsel's argument, I have concluded that the plaintiff has failed to prove that the by-law was passed *mala fide* and not in the public interest. This burden was upon the plaintiff. . . ."

PROBLEM. A council is concerned with two trends, the expansion of its central business area into the adjacent residential area and the "renewal" (repair) of the older houses in the residential area by people who want to live near the downtown area and who are prepared to spend several thousand dollars to renovate run down old houses. At the same time small shopkeepers and professional men are buying the houses for business use. The city council tries to satisfy both groups by proposing a by-law that permits both residential uses and use for "home occupations" including professional offices and small shops, but requires the commercial use to be confined within the building as it exists on the day the by-law is passed, and limits any signs or advertising of any sort to an announcement of the identity of the business and its personnel on a sign not over one square foot in area. It is objected that since one house in commercial use contains 1,000 square feet of floor space and the adjoining house contains 1,500 square feet, the by-law unfairly discriminates among the various buildings. The owner of the 1,000 square feet contends that he is entitled to add to his building another 500 square feet of floor space for commercial use. The object of the by-law is to preserve the residential appearance of the street for the benefit of the residential users, and to preserve the architectural character of the street, which is the best one of its type (late Victorian) in the city. How could the by-law be justified?

RE NORTH YORK BY-LAW 14,067
Ontario. Court of Appeal. 1960. 24 D.L.R. (2d) 12

McGILLIVRAY J.A.: This is an appeal, leave having been given, upon certain questions of law arising from an order of the Ontario Municipal Board, hereinafter referred to for convenience as the Board, refusing approval of a By-law 14,067 passed by the Township of North York.

The by-law in question purported to change from RM3 to RM6 the designated zoning of five lots having a frontage of 250 ft. on the east side of Bathurst St. extending from Lyonsgate Drive to Sandringham Drive. RM3 standards would permit the erection of a four-storey building upon this parcel. RM6 standards would permit a building of five storeys to be erected having double the accommodation of the four-storey building. Lands to the north and south of the area in question are vacant and are zoned RM3.

Previous to the passing of By-law 14,067 the township council, believing that the zoning of lands fronting on Bathurst St. should be reviewed, retained planning consultants to make a study of the situation. These consultants submitted what was known as the "Deacon Report". A portion of this report is summarized by the township planning staff as follows: "The Deacon Report, in dealing with Bathurst Street frontages, pointed out the variation of multiple family zoning in this area ranging from RM3 to RM5 had not permitted sufficient variation in building types. This monotony of building types and sky line was a direct result of the 35′ height limitation in these zones. Therefore, the Deacon Report recommended that an RM6 zoning which requires an increase in side yards when a building is extended in height should be permitted on these lands in an effort to provide a greater opportunity for variation in architectural design."

Since receipt of the Deacon Report the township council has, from time to time, granted applications to change individual parcels of land on Bathurst St., the owners entering into an agreement, in each case, with the council to provide certain facilities considered desirable by the council. In the case under review such an agreement was made between the council and the owner of the lands. I shall refer to its terms later.

By-law 14,067 was passed on May 11, 1959, pursuant to s. 27*a* of the *Planning Act*, 1955 (Ont.), c. 61, which section was enacted by 1959, c. 71, s. 5. Application was then made to the Board, as required by the *Planning Act*, for approval of the by-law and proper notice was given for a public hearing on June 17th in the Board's chambers. On the return of the appointment counsel appeared for the appellant and for the township. No one appeared in opposition and the application was granted.

In some manner undisclosed, ratepayers who had received notice of the hearing were under the belief that the hearing was at a time other than that set by the Board. As a result they failed to appear at the hearing. Subsequently a letter was sent to the Board on June 30th by the solicitor for the township stating that, as these people were prevented from being heard, the township council requested the Board to rehear the application. The Board thereupon, without notice to the parties, by order of July 3, 1959 rescinded its order of June 17, 1959, and new notices were sent out for a hearing on Friday, August 7, 1959, at the Board's chambers. At this hearing the Board, differently constituted than upon the previous occasions, dismissed the application for approval of the by-law and gave its reasons therefor.

Leave to appeal from the Board's order was granted by the Court by order dated September 21, 1959, which directed that the following points of law be argued on this appeal:

"(a) As a matter of law did the Ontario Municipal Board have jurisdiction to rescind their order of the 17th day of June, 1959;

"(b) as a matter of law did the Ontario Municipal Board validly rescind their order of the 17th day of June, 1959;

"(c) as a matter of law did the Ontario Municipal Board have jurisdiction to rehear and/or review the application of The Corporation of the Township of North York;

"(d) as a matter of law did the Ontario Municipal Board validly rehear and/or review the said application;

"(e) as a matter of law did the Ontario Municipal Board err in the construction which it placed on Section 27a of The Planning Act, 1955."

The first four of these points of law may conveniently be dealt with together. Section 46 of the *Ontario Municipal Board Act*, R.S.O. 1950, c. 262, reads as follows: "46. The Board may rehear any application before deciding it or may review, rescind, change, alter or vary any decision, approval or order made by it."

Counsel for the appellant contended that the power given to the Board to rescind under this section could only be exercised upon notice to the parties concerned which method of procedure, had it been followed, would have permitted counsel to submit further argument. As this had not been done he contended that the Board had exceeded its powers and that the order rescinding its previous order was a nullity.

I am unable to give effect to this contention. The Board had power under s. 46 to rescind or rehear the motion. . . .

I conclude that the Board was not in error in any of the first four matters of law addressed to this Court all of which questions should be answered in the affirmative.

I now address myself to the last question of law lettered (e) namely— "as a matter of law did the Ontario Municipal Board err in the construction which it placed on Section 27*a* of The Planning Act, 1955."

The relevant portions of s. 27*a* are:

"27*a*(1) By-laws may be passed by the councils of municipalities. . . .

"4. For regulating the cost or type of construction and the height, bulk, location, size, floor area, spacing, external design, character and use of buildings or structures to be erected within the municipality or within any defined area or areas or upon land abutting on any defined highway or part of a highway, and the minimum frontage and depth of the parcel of land and the proportion of the area thereof that any building or structure may occupy.

"(9) No part of any by-law passed under this section shall come into force without the approval of the Municipal Board, and such approval may be for a limited period of time only, and the Board may extend such period from time to time upon application made to it for such purpose."

In its reasons the Board stated as follows:

"Those opposing approval were not represented by counsel and apparently did not have legal advice. It could be argued that this by-law is not a valid exercise of council's legislative power under the section since it singles out this one parcel of land for the preferred treatment of RM6 zoning while leaving unchanged the zoning of lands on either side, similar in every respect and which, according to the evidence of Mr. Adams, a planning consultant called to support approval, ought to be zoned RM6.

"The Board is of the opinion that such a contention is sound and that accordingly this by-law is not a valid excuse of the power given to the council by the section in question.

"It might be argued on the narrower ground that this individual parcel is not an 'area' as that word is used in the section—that it was not the intention of the Legislature to permit a council to legislate in favour of one individual unless under special circumstances, which are not present in this case, and the board finds that such a contention is also sound.

"But even though these two contentions should be found to be without merit, the board finds that there is a third difficulty in the way of approval of this by-law. The power given to the council under the section is clearly a power to legislate. This is a power to enact provisions, terms and conditions applicable to the construction, etc., of every building of the class in question in the area or areas in question. It is not a power to grant or refuse individual applications for the construction of buildings and to permit a building of a certain class or dimension on condition that the applicant will comply with stipulations there and then improvised and imposed by the council. It is not enough to say that such conditions are in the best interests of the public. It is not enough to say that council believes it is acting in the public interest. There is nothing special or unusual about the present case such as in the case of the *Township of Scarborough* v. *Bondi*, recently decided in the Supreme Court of Canada. It is admitted that there are many other parcels along Bathurst Street in the same circumstances exactly as the one here in question. Counsel for the township frankly admitted that the council wished to deal with these parcels individually so that it might be able to impose in each case such conditions as it would deem desirable and which it might not be possible to impose by a by-law having general application even in a certain area.

"The board is of the opinion that such a course of action is not intended or permitted by the statute. For these reasons the board finds that this by-law is not a proper exercise of the power contained in the statute and, as indicated at the conclusion of the hearing, the application must be dismissed."

As can be seen the Board reaches its results upon a finding that the tract of land here in question is not an "area" because "it was not the intention of the Legislature to permit a council to legislate in favour of one individual unless under special circumstances, which are not present in this case". The tract in question is described as "the whole of lots 1175 to 1179 inclusive, according to Registered Plan 2044". The lots are said to have a frontage of 250 ft. on the east side of Bathurst St. extending from Lyonsgate Drive to Sandringham Drive. No information is before us as to the depth of the lots. The township is empowered by s. 27*a* (1) para. 4 (*supra*) to pass a by-law to regulate the character of structures "to be erected within the municipality or within any defined area or areas upon land abutting on any defined highway or part of a highway".

It is obvious, to begin with, that the tract in question is land abutting on "part of a highway", for a whole township block must be a "part" of a highway. As to the word "area" it has many meanings but there can be little doubt that the word taken in its commonly accepted sense and as used in the section referred to may be a tract of land either large or small.

A similar wording was construed in the case of *Re Wood & City of Winnipeg* (1911). In that case the city charter provided that the city could pass by-laws "for regulating the distance, within specified areas, from the street line" in front of which no building should be placed. Upon this authority a by-law had been passed covering but a few lots, as in the present case, and it was under attack. Perdue J.A. expressed the unanimous opinion of the Court in the following words: "The prohibition permitted by the enactment is to apply to a specified area within the city, but nothing is said as to how extensive or how limited that specified area is to be. . . . This is, it appears to me, a specified area, within the meaning of the clause in the statute."

The Board in the present case, however, considered that the land in question was not an area because it was not the intention of the Legislature to permit a council to legislate in favour of an individual. It is true the words "except under special circumstances" were added but it is apparent that the Board's interpretation of the words was based wholly upon this consideration. It is sufficient to say that the question whether the area involved was controlled by one individual or by one corporation is *nihil ad rem*. Small areas may be zoned as well as large ones and facts as to their ownership or control should have no bearing when consideration is being given to the question of whether or not the area sought to be zoned complies with the general purpose and intent of the legislation.

The *Planning Act* itself appears to contemplate and provide for applications by individuals for re-zoning as will be seen in s. 27*a*(19) where the word "applicant", not applicants, is used.

Section 27*a* deals in great particularity with the character and type of buildings to be constructed in a particular area. Of necessity, in urban municipalities, this must involve, if not spot zoning, at any rate areas quite limited in extent. In this respect by-laws passed under s. 27*a* differ from the common type of general by-law. I am of the opinion that the interpretation of the word "area" in the light assigned by the Board is clearly wrong.

The same may be said of the weight given by the Board to the fact that the township had a collateral agreement with the owner of the lands to be zoned. The agreement in question provided for the erection of fences and planting strips, the character of exterior walls, the construction of pavements and for traffic control. There was no suggestion of bad faith by the township in entering into this agreement. On the contrary it was acknowledged that the township was acting in the interest of its citizens by so doing. This factor of a collateral agreement should be given no weight or consideration by the Board when weighing the desirability of giving its approval to the by-law.

The Board having misdirected itself in these matters, point (e) must be answered in the affirmative.

In doing so, however, some reference should be made to the actual powers of the Board in matters of this kind. In its reasons the Board purports to deal with the validity of the by-law, the exact words being "this by-law is not a valid exercise of the power given to the council by the section in question" and counsel for the township contended that, throughout its reasons, the Board indicated that it was, in effect, declaring the by-law to be invalid. I need hardly say that the Board has no power to deal with the validity or otherwise of a by-law. That jurisdiction can only be exercised by the superior Courts. The Board's power is wholly administrative and it has no concern with whether a by-law is *intra vires* or *ultra vires*. Its sole function is to consider whether or not a by-law is to receive its approval having in mind, the general interest and the intent of the Act under which the by-law was passed. As no by-law passed under the Act became effective until it had received the Board's approval it is obvious that quite a wide field was left to the Board as to matters which it was entitled to review. Among these, of necessity, must have been a consideration of the intent and purpose of the Act and, insofar as this might be a consideration of law, it was nevertheless one which the Board was entitled to exercise as incidental to its administrative functions. It is my opinion that the Board, notwithstanding its words, sought to do no more than that on this occasion and was acting within its powers. I adopt the words of Aylesworth J.A. in *Ontario Teachers' Federation* v. *Duncan*, (1958): "The Committee of Adjustment and in turn the Ontario Municipal Board in carrying out their functions under the *Planning Act*, are performing administrative functions. Incidental to the performance of such functions, they may be called upon to act judicially but such judicial action is necessary to enable each of those bodies to perform the primary administrative duty with which each body respectively is charged. Administratively each body must consider broad questions of policy and expediency. . . .

The Board was thus entitled to consider not the validity of the by-law but whether the by-law represented good and desirable rezoning in the municipality and on the street in question and if it was in accordance with a policy furthering the health, safety, convenience and welfare of the inhabitants of the district. In this respect it was entitled to examine the nature and extent of the proposed variation. It had the right to consider the character of the immediate neighbourhood and any serious objection raised by the adjoining owners. It had a right, in short, to review the general propriety of the proposed change and any other matters relevant to whether or not this by-law should receive approval as being in accordance with the purpose and intent of the *Planning Act*.

The Board's decision unfortunately was not arrived at so much by an application of the above principles as by its interpretation of s. 27*a* of the *Planning Act*, an interpretation which as I have said was an erroneous one.

I would allow this appeal, set aside the order of the Board and remit for consideration of the Board. The order of the Court should certify to the Board that points of law (a), (b), (c), (d) and (e) are answered in the affirmative.

I would make no order as to costs.

THE MUNICIPAL ACT

Manitoba. Revised Statutes. 1954. Chapter 173

894. (1) Any municipal corporation may pass by-laws,

(*a*) for regulating, within the corporation or specified areas thereof, the distance from the street line of any lot or parcel of land, in front of which a building or structure shall not be placed thereon; . . .

(2) It is not necessary that the distance fixed in a by-law passed

under clause (*a*) of subsection (1) shall be the same on all parts of the street.

NOTE. This section is similar in principle to S.O., 1904, c. 22, s. 19, which introduced section 541a of *The Consolidated Municipal Act, 1903.* The section is reproduced on pages 605–6.

THE PLANNING ACT

Ontario. Revised Statutes. 1960. Chapter 296

30. (19) Where an application to the council for an amendment to a by-law passed under this section or a predecessor of this section, or any by-law deemed to be consistent with this section by sub-section 3 of section 13 of *The Municipal Amendment Act, 1941*, is refused or the council refuses or neglects to make a decision thereon within one month after the receipt by the clerk of the application, the applicant may appeal to the Municipal Board and the Municipal Board shall hear the appeal and dismiss the same or direct that the by-law be amended in accordance with its order.

NOTE. Section 30(19) provides an obvious authority for "spot zoning". Its possibilities were referred to by McGillivray J.A. in *Re North York By-law 14,067*. The section enables what is sometimes called an "irate-payer" to take positive action to get what he wants. The provision, if not unique in Canada, is nearly so. Compare section 123 of *The Town and Rural Planning Act,* R.S.A. 1955, c. 337, as amended by S.A., 1959, c. 89, s. 21, which authorizes a person to appeal to the Provincial Planning Advisory Board when he has requested and been refused an amendment to a district general plan, although he was supported by the municipal council concerned, or to a preliminary district plan. The usual practice in Ontario is for the applicant to draft the amendment he desires, so that a specific proposal can be discussed and rejected and, perhaps, ultimately directed by the Board.

Where the proposed amendment does not conform with the official plan the applicant may have some trouble. While section 14 of *The Planning Act* roughly parallels section 30(19), there is one difference. When requested to refer a proposal for a change in an official plan to the Municipal Board the Minister may refuse and he cannot be compelled to refer the matter to the Municipal Board, something which he can be compelled to do in the exercise of virtually every other power he has under the Act.

Presumably the Board, on an application under section 30(19) has no power to direct a by-law in broader terms than the council could have enacted on its own initiative under section 30. The Board could not, therefore, direct a discriminatory by-law, or one that in any other way requires authority not to be found in section 30 or in another Act. On the other hand, the applicant usually seeks an amendment applicable to his own property. Should the section perhaps be taken to apply only to whole zones? Would it be wiser for the applicant to broaden the amendment to cover a whole zone if possible?

What is an "amendment"? If an existing by-law (such as the one in the *Separate School Board* case) applied to only one street, and it is extended to apply to the next street, is the new extension an "amendment" or a separate by-law? Why does the section deal only with amendments? Why does it not permit ratepayers to invoke the Board's aid to secure the protection of a restrictive by-law in the first instance?

RE JENKINS AND BELLEVILLE

Ontario. Municipal Board. 1957. P.F.M. 5179–56

NUNN Member and MILBURN Member: This matter was heard before the Board at the City of Belleville on Tuesday, the 27th day of August, 1957. Mr. E. G. Porter, solicitor for the Appellant, Mr. James W. Jenkins, informed the Board that his client was the owner of a property known as Number 214 Church Street, and that this property was being used as a parking lot to accommodate the guests of the Quinte Hotel, Mr. Jenkins being a shareholder in the hotel. The Appellant had requested the City of Belleville to change the zoning of the lot from Residential to Commercial. This the City refused to do, and they informed him by letter from the City Solicitor, Mr. R. A. Pringle, that the use of this lot for parking was contravening the City's Zoning By-law Number 6495.

Mr. Jenkins then decided to bring this matter before the Ontario Municipal Board, requesting a change in zoning. The Board was also informed that the City Council by resolution appointed three members of the Council to attend the Board's hearing to oppose the rezoning of this lot. The Board was informed that there had been no report from the City Planning Board, and also that at the recent meeting of the City Council a resolution had been proposed to rezone the whole block between Bridge Street and Campbell Street, on the East side of Church Street, which would include the subject property. The Board reserved its decision until a report from the Planning Board could be forwarded, and until the City Council dealt with the proposed resolution.

The Board now has before it a copy of a letter from the Belleville and Suburban Planning Board dated August 29, 1957, which states that "At a meeting of the Belleville and Suburban Planning Board held on Tuesday, May 7th, 1957, this matter was discussed and it was the decision of the Board that approval of the request to amend the area be given." The Board also has before it a letter from Mr. R. A. Pringle which states: "At the regular meeting of Council held on November 4th, the following recommendation was passed which is self-explanatory: Re Rezoning of Certain Street in the City of Belleville—Original recommendation tabled from September 9, 1957 to September 23, September 23 to October 7. October 7 laid over for one month, November 4, 1957—That the Municipal Board be informed that this Council has tabled indefinitely discussion of the matter of rezoning the area north of Bridge Street and South Campbell Street on the east side of Church Street. Yeas – 7, Nays – 5, Absent – 2, Refrained from Voting – Alderman Safe – Carried."

In the light of the evidence and the more recent information indicating that the City was not prepared to rezone this whole block as Commercial, and recognizing that the present by-law does not make provision for dealing with parking lots, and recognizing also that the present request for rezoning would constitute spot zoning of only one lot, the Board dismissed the appeal.

Since the Appellant has already paid the Board's fee, there will be no further costs.

NOTE. What weight, if any, should the Board attach to the Planning Board's recommendation of approval?

The accompanying reproduction of part of the zoning map shows the lands in question. The white area, for residential use, contains a church, a parking lot and vacant land. The reference in the decision to the "east"

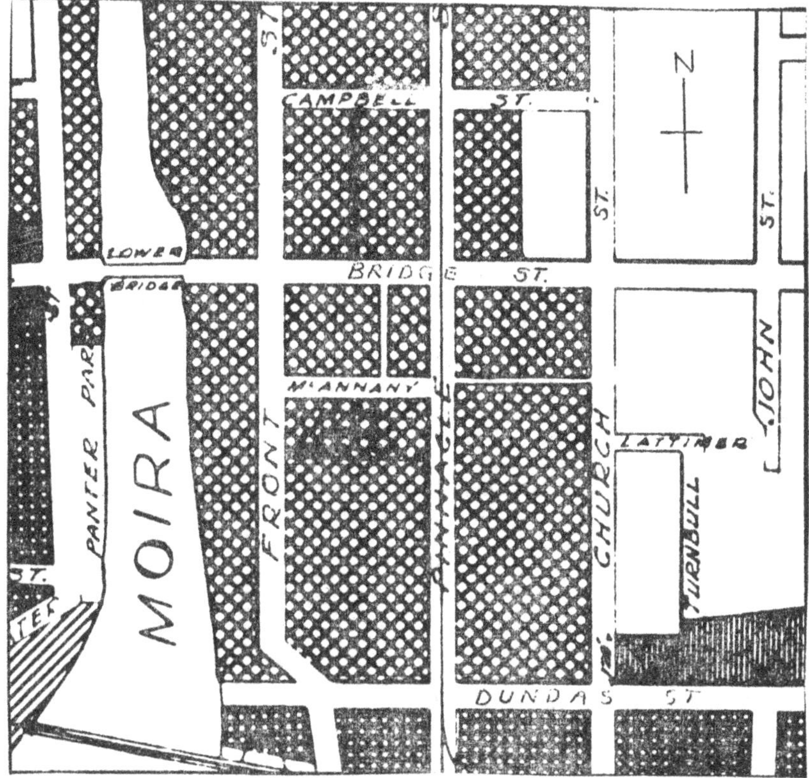

Sketch of part of Belleville

side of Church Street seems to be in error since Campbell Street does not run east of Church Street yet the area is said to be south of Campbell Street. Assuming the area referred to is west of Church Street, would the requested rezoning of the area be offensive as discriminatory?

RE HIGHBURY DEVELOPMENTS LTD. AND ETOBICOKE

Ontario. Municipal Board. 1958. P.F.M. 6685–57

J. A. KENNEDY Vice-Chairman and YATES Vice-Chairman: This is an appeal under the provisions of Section 390 Subsection (17) of The Municipal Act for an order compelling the Council of the Township of Etobicoke to pass a by-law changing the zoning of Block "A", Registered Plan 4992 from R2 to R5. This would be to change the permitted uses from single family only to multiple family dwellings which includes apartments. Block "A" is a parcel of land with a frontage on Kipling Avenue of 950 feet with a depth varying from 160 feet at one end to 210 feet at the opposite end. On the opposite side it fronts on Templar Drive. The lands comprised in this registered plan together with other lands adjoining were all developed by the present applicant, Highbury Developments Limited, and sold to various persons for the construction of residences. Upon the lands immediately surrounding Block "A" in question here there have been constructed single family dwellings. Now this developer seeks to have Block "A" re-zoned to permit the erection of apartment buildings.

At the time of the registration of Plan 4992, Block "A" which contains 3.65 acres, was shown as reserved. The applicant now contends that it was always the intention that this block would be used for apartment buildings, but the Board finds on opinion evidence adduced at the hearing that this block is rather shallow for advantageous development as a site for apartments. When the lands surrounding this block were sold, the block was zoned as R2 permitting use for single family dwellings only. Very vigorous opposition to any change in zoning was put forth by the persons who bought single family dwellings on these surrounding lands. Their evidence was that they had been led to believe by the agents of the present applicant, in some cases that Block "A" would be developed by the construction of single family dwellings and in other cases that it would be developed with certain types of multiple dwellings; but, in no case, according to their evidence, was there any suggestion that this block might be developed as apartment building sites. The Board finds on the evidence that there was a representation made by the present applicant, through its agents, to the purchasers of the lands surrounding Block "A" that this Block would be developed for use other than that of apartment sites, and closer to the use of single family dwellings.

This is an appeal from a decision of the Township Council refusing to grant the application of the present applicant. By Section 390 of The Municipal Act the municipal council is given discretion to pass or not pass a by-law such as that asked for here by the appellant. The Council clearly had jurisdiction to exercise its discretion as it did by refusing the application. The duty of this Board on this appeal is to review that exercise of discretion by the Council and to determine whether there is cause for this Board to interfere. It must be clear that this Board should decline to interfere with the exercise by elected representatives of the discretion given to them by Parliament, except where it is shown that their action is clearly not for the greatest common good, that it creates an undue hardship, that some private right is unduly interfered with or denied, that they have acted arbitrarily, on incorrect information or advice, or otherwise improperly. The only one of these circumstances that might be said to exist here is that a private right has been unduly interfered with.

Now, what is the right of the applicant in this case which it seeks to assert? It can only be the right to apply for a change in the zoning to permit the use of Block "A" as apartment sites. The Board finds that the applicant through the representations made by its agents to purchasers of the surrounding lands has now parted with the right to apply for this change. In the sense that equity sees that done which ought to be done, it would be inequitable now to impose upon those purchasers a condition immediately adjacent to their homes which it was represented to them when they purchased would not be later permitted. In the circumstances, the appeal will be dismissed.

The Board makes no order as to costs.

LEAHY *v.* INSPECTOR OF BUILDINGS

Massachusetts. Supreme Judicial Court 1941. 31 N.E. 2d 436

RONAN J.: The petitioners seek a writ of mandamus to require the respondent, the building inspector, to enforce the zoning ordinance of New Bedford as it was before it was amended on April 8, 1937, whereby a parcel of land located on the corner of County and Mill Streets and owned by one Epstein was changed from a residential to a business district, and to revoke the building permit issued by the respondent for the construction upon said parcel of a building to be used for commercial purposes. The case was heard upon an auditor's report including certain maps which were put in evidence before the auditor. The single justice found the facts as stated by the auditor, and found and ruled that the amendment to the zoning ordinance was invalid in that it was not the same for zones, districts or streets having substantially the same character. He ordered the writ to issue. The case is here on exceptions of both parties to the action taken upon their requests for rulings.

The city had enacted a zoning ordinance in 1926 by which the city was divided into residential, business and industrial districts, and the height, area and use of structures in these districts were regulated. There were three grades of residential districts known as "A", "B" and "C". The Epstein lot was in a residence "A" district. On September 13, 1929, the zoning ordinance was amended, and this lot, together with the adjoining lot abutting on County Street and extending to North Street, was changed from a residence "A" district to a residence "C" district. This changed the locus from one that was in the main an area for single family dwellings to one where dwellings accommodating three or more families were permitted. Thereafter, Epstein filed a petition in the Land Court . . . to determine the validity of the ordinance, claiming he was aggrieved in not having his land included in a business district. The Land Court, by a decision rendered on March 29, 1935, dismissed the petition.

When Epstein purchased this property in 1924 there was a one-family dwelling on the lot. After the 1929 amendment, Epstein moved this house to the rear of the lot, turned the house around to face Mill Street and changed it into a structure to accommodate four families. This left vacant the land at the corner of County and Mill Streets. In February, 1937, Epstein petitioned the city council to change this vacant land from a residence "C" district to a business district, the land measuring about ninety-six feet on County Street and one hundred and twenty feet on Mill Street. The planning board, to whom the petition was referred, held a public hearing and reported to the city council recommending that no change be made in the zoning map as the granting of the petition "would constitute spot zoning and would be detrimental to the best interests of the city." The committee on ordinances held a public hearing and voted to recommend the granting of the petition. On April 8, 1937, the amendment to the ordinance was passed unanimously by the city council and the board of aldermen, and became effective upon the failure of the mayor to approve or disapprove it within ten days after it had been presented to him. The building inspector has issued to Epstein a permit for the construction of a store upon this corner lot and Epstein intends, unless the permit is revoked, to build such a structure.

County Street is one of the main thoroughfares of the city, running north and south, and for several blocks north of Mill Street both sides of the street are included in residential districts. This portion of the street has been for years a fine residential section. The original ordinance was adopted in 1926 to continue the residential atmosphere of the street as it then existed. Both sides of County Street south of the intersection of Mill Street for one half a street block is zoned for residences and then, as one proceeds southerly, both sides of the street are included in business districts. There is a most decided trend toward business in that portion of County Street, but no new business has been located on County Street for a mile or more north of the block south of Mill Street during the last twelve years. Mill Street crosses County Street and runs east and west. A large amount of traffic passes over this street between the western part of the city and Cape Cod. Both sides of Mill Street west of County Street are in residential districts. There is no demand for residential property on County Street. The Epstein lot is practically useless for residential purposes, but in all probability it can be used profitably for business. The auditor found that the zoning for business comes to a complete stop one half a block south of Mill Street and that if the ordinance as amended is valid it will be the first encroachment of business into what was designated and has remained a residential area, and he, therefore, found that the ordinance as amended, if valid, is not the same for zones, districts or streets having substantially the same character . . .

The enabling statute, which is a regulation of the use of structures and land under the police power, expressly recognizes its inherent limitations by authorizing cities to adopt ordinances regulating and restricting the height and size of buildings, the size and width of the lots, the percentage of the lot that may be occupied, and the location and use of buildings and land for trade, industry and residence, if such ordinances are "for the purpose of promoting the health, safety, convenience, morals or welfare of its inhabitants." . . . [1933 (Mass.) c. 269, 1.] provides that such regulations shall be designed for certain enumerated purposes and the ordinances "established hereunder in any city or town shall be the same for zones, districts or streets having substantially the same character." The validity of this amendment must be tested by the terms of the enabling statute.

In the first place, there is nothing contained in the report of the auditor that shows that the amendment was passed to accomplish any of the enumerated purposes set forth in the statute, although some of these purposes are expressed in such general and broad terms that it ought to be comparatively easy to demonstrate that an ordinance that purports to promote the public welfare by changing the zoning regulations serves at least one of these designated purposes . . .

The establishment of zoning districts is based upon the physical characteristics of substantial areas and their suitability for use for certain purposes in view of the present and future requirements of the public health, morals, safety and general welfare . . .

A city council is empowered to amend a zoning ordinance when the character and use of a district or the surrounding territory have become so changed since the original ordinance was enacted that the public health, safety, morals and welfare would be promoted if a change were made in the boundaries or in the regulations prescribed for certain districts; but mere economic gain to the owner of a comparatively small area is not sufficient cause to invoke an exercise of this amending power for the benefit of such owner . . .

The petitioners contend that the action of the city council in establishing as a business district a single corner lot located in what is essentially a residential district is arbitrary and unreasonable and, consequently, is invalid. There are decisions to this effect . . .

The auditor found that the operation of the amendment will not result in uniformity of regulations and restrictions for zones, districts or streets having substantially the same character. That finding was warranted, if not required, by the various subsidiary findings and especially those that set forth to a considerable extent and in much detail the character and use of the various properties in the vicinity of the Epstein lot. The Epstein lot has never been used for business. No business area is any nearer to this lot than it was when the zoning ordinance was first enacted. It remains in a long established residential district where no substantial changes in its character or use have occurred since the zoning ordinance first became effective. The lot in question is not on the edge of a residential district for it is surrounded on all sides by districts zoned for residences. The effect of the amendment is to single out one lot located within what is essentially a residential district and impose restrictions upon this lot that are less onerous than those imposed upon the remaining portions of what is really the same zoning district. [The enabling statutes] prohibit the amendment of an ordinance that accomplishes such a result, and as the amendment was unauthorized by these statutes, it cannot be sustained.

[Ronan J. gave the decision of the court, comprised of Field C.J. and Donahue, Dolan and Ronan JJ.]

4. Delegation

CRAWFORD, CANADIAN MUNICIPAL GOVERNMENT (1954)

A Municipal Council has both legislative and administrative functions and combines in one body the activities which at the other levels of government are divided between Parliament or the legislature and the executive or cabinet. The legislative activities of a council are important but in time a framework of legislation is built up to cover the range of problems requiring major legislative action. While this basic municipal legislation is not, or at least should not be, static, the bulk of current legislation of most municipal councils deals with the amendment or revision of existing by-laws or the passing of by-laws relating to administrative matters. After a municipality has enacted legislation covering traffic, streets, public health, licensing, fire prevention and control, the regulation of building, zoning, and similar matters, most of its legislative activity is of a routine nature arising out of its administrative function.

The administrative activities of councils vary according to the area and population under their jurisdiction and the extent to which functions have been transferred to special purpose bodies. Obviously the activities under a rural or village council will be much fewer than those for which the council of a city must provide. Not only do the powers granted to the more populous municipalities permit more extensive activities, but the need and demand for public services increases as the population concentration increases. This demand has been intensified in recent years by the change in viewpoint of the citizens as to the purpose and function of governments. Hence the legislative function of local government is relatively less important than the administrative function in so far as the day-to-day operations are concerned, and in the extent to which it absorbs the attention of councils. Macdonald, referring to the cities of the United States, stated: 'It is safe to say that nine-tenths of the work of our cities is administration. Only at rare intervals does a vital issue make its appearance.'

The policies arrived at by a council are carried out by paid permanent officials, who may be either full-time or part-time employees, a matter which chiefly depends on the size of the municipality. In total number, considering all the smaller and rural municipalities, the part-time officials probably exceed those on a full-time basis. Council members may personally supervise the carrying out of council policies in the smaller municipalities, but this is impossible in a community of any considerable size to the extent that was possible before skilled techniques and scientific knowledge were such important factors in the operation of municipal services.

Councils in larger municipalities usually assign to each of their standing committees the supervision of one or more of the departments or services. These committees make reports and recommendations to council on the work under their jurisdiction. Usually the responsible official attends the committee meeting to be available for consultation, and he can obtain the committee's advice on his problems, and explain his reasons for any recommendations he may make. As a rule officials in charge of what might be called service departments such as Works, Fire, Parks, and Welfare, do not deal directly with council, unless specifically instructed to do so, but rather work through and with the committees. More frequently those in charge of internal departments, such as the treasurer or clerk, deal directly with council, although in most instances their recommendations go to council through a committee.

It is the council which makes the major decisions as to policy, to build a bridge, to pave a street, or to put the fire department on a three-shift basis. The council is the ultimate authority on all matters, large or small, that may come before it or with which it may choose to deal. To a considerable extent, however, the task of supervising the carrying out of policy and many final decisions in minor matters are left to the committees. The task of actually doing the job as well as many of the detailed decisions are left with the officials.

RUSSELL *v.* TORONTO

Ontario. Court of Appeal. 1907. 15 O.L.R. 484

Action impeaching a purchase assumed to be made on behalf of the city of Toronto at a sale for arrears of taxes held on April 24, 1901, and a deed of conveyance purporting to be made in pursuance of the sale and purchase dated October 1, 1902. Only those parts of the opinions dealing with the delegation of the Council's authority to the Assessment Commissioner are reproduced. In the trial court MacMahon J. quoted section 184(3) of the *Assessment Act*, R.S.O. 1897, c. 224.

MACMAHON J.: . . . "(3) If the council of the local municipality, in which is situate any lot to which sub-sec. 2 refers [ss. (2) refers to land which the treasurer fails to sell at the tax sale for the full amount of taxes due] desire to become the purchasers thereof for the amount of the arrears of taxes thereon, it shall be lawful for such municipality to purchase the same. . . ."

There were 1,536 lots of land offered for sale on the 10th of April for most of which there were no bids, as there were apparently about 1,200 lots withdrawn from sale. Wm. F. Fleming, the city tax clerk, who was appointed auctioneer's clerk by Mr. Henderson, the auctioneer, said that where bids had been made on any parcel and it was withdrawn no record was kept of such bids.

The sale was adjourned by the treasurer to the 24th of April, when all the remaining lots were put up and sold, the city becoming purchaser of about 1,000 of the lots through Mr. R. J. Fleming, the assessment commissioner, who was on the 9th of April, 1901, authorized to purchase on behalf of the city on the recommendation contained in the following report of the board of control, adopted by the city council:

"Adjourned sale of lands for arrears of taxes.

"The board have received a communication from the city treasurer stating that the Assessment Act empowers municipalities to purchase lands offered for arrears of taxes when the price offered at the adjourned sale is less than the amount of arrears registered against such lands, provided the council of the municipality has signified its intention to do so at least one day before the sale, and, on the advice of the treasurer, recommend that such notice be given before the date of the adjourned sale on the 24th inst., and that an officer of the corporation, viz., the assessment commissioner, be authorized and instructed to purchase and acquire such lands for and on behalf of the corporation, as may be deemed advisable in the city's interest, the said lands so acquired to be again offered for sale within the time specified in the statutes, namely, seven years."

The plaintiff was an alderman of the city at the time the council adopted that report, and voted for its adoption. He did not by that act waive his right to have the sale set aside on the ground of its being invalid: *Blackwell on Tax Titles,* 5th ed., secs. 890, 891.

According to sub-sec. 3 of sec. 184, it is where the council of any local municipality in which is situate a lot which sub-sec. 2 refers (that is, has been put up for sale and withdrawn because no offer of the full amount of the arrears of taxes had been made), it shall be lawful for the municipality to become the purchaser for the amount of such arrears. It is, I consider, clear that the council must select the lot or lots which the municipality desires to purchase and has given notice in writing of its intention so to do, and that it could not delegate that discretionary power to the assessment commissioner authorizing him to purchase and acquire such lands as he might deem advisable in the city's interest: *Dillon on Municipal Corporations,* 4th ed., sec. 96.

The council, if it had selected and designated the lots of which it desired to become the purchaser, could have appointed an agent to attend the sale and purchase on its behalf. . . .

Mr. Fleming received no instructions as to what he was to purchase or refrain from purchasing. He had not examined any of the properties and was not aware of their values, and he purchased all the lots on which offers of the amount of the taxes in arrear had not been made. . . .

The defendant appealed.

GARROW J.A.: . . . I am, however, with deference, unable to agree with the second objection. It seems to me that the learned Judge has overlooked the fact that municipal councils have to do with two very distinct subject matters, one legislative, the other administrative. Their powers with respect to the former cannot be delegated, but not so with the latter, in which they may usually follow ordinary business methods in the absence of express statutory provisions, which of course when made must be observed. The collection of taxes is largely an administrative matter, and the sale for taxes and the buying in and selling again are all merely steps towards such collection. And I can see no objection to the council appointing an agent to attend the sale, giving him general instructions to buy in only such lots as he in his discretion may consider advisable. Circumstances might well arise at the sale itself requiring the immediate exercise of such a discretion —such, for instance, as a bid so near the amount of the arrears as to make it prudent to accept, rather than incur the trouble, risk and expense of the council buying in and re-selling. In this case the arrears are said to be $8,857.48. Surely it would have been a prudent thing to accept a bid if one had been made of say $8,857 rather than buy in, in the hope or realizing in the end the odd cents by re-selling.

But whether I am right or wrong in this view is really of little consequence in the result, because either of the other objections is sufficient to upset the sale unless cured by the validating Acts, which after all is the real question in the case. . . .

MEREDITH J.A.: I am far from thinking that the council must form and express a desire to purchase each particular lot separately. That would be practically impossible when hundreds, if not thousands, of lots of all sorts and kinds have to be dealt with. And what possible object could there be in requiring the council to so deal with each lot separately when hundreds may be exactly in the same position in all respects, and it would, of course, be useless in all cases in which the land realized the amount of the taxes from other bidders. It is the "municipality" which may buy if the "council" "desire" it; and so it is obvious that there must be some delegation of power.

IN RE BY-LAW 92, TOWN OF WINNIPEG BEACH. 1919. 30 Man. R. 192 (Manitoba. Court of Appeal). A public health by-law limited the number and size of tents that should be erected on town lots and required a permit. The by-law was passed under authority for "licensing and regulating or preventing and prohibiting or restricting" tents. A penalty provided for a fine of "$50 and costs, upon conviction before a magistrate, and in addition any permit issued hereunder may be cancelled and declared null and void by order of the Mayor". On a motion to quash, among other grounds, it was objected that the council had no authority to so delegate to the Mayor. The objection was upheld. DENNISTOUN J.A.:

"This by-law seriously interferes with the common-law rights of property owners and while it must be benevolently construed in so far as the health and the general welfare of the community are concerned, it must be strictly construed in so far as it derogates from private rights. The owner cannot place a temporary building or a tent upon his own land except by permit, which may be withdrawn by order of the mayor. Such drastic action may be clearly authorized by the Legislature. The absence from the statute of express power to cancel such a permit cannot be supplied by analogy from what may be done in other cases which are specifically provided for.

"The by-law entrusts the issuing of the license to the secretary-treasurer, but in a ministerial capacity only. On discharge of certain reasonable sanitary obligations by the owner of the land the license will issue apparently as a matter of right, and not of discretion. It is to be presumed that the secretary-treasurer will not act in an arbitrary manner and such delegation of authority to him is unobjectionable.

"But the power to cancel given to the mayor is of a different character. He may use his discretion and cancel or not as he sees fit, after conviction of the owner of a violation of the by-law, and thereby deprive him of the right to use his land in an unobjectionable manner. The opinion is therefore expressed that it was *ultra vires* of the council to make provision for the cancellation of permits regularly issued under the by-law.

"The fourth ground of objection is to the delegation of power to cancel permits to the mayor, and is a valid objection for the reasons given in respect to objection (3), and for further reason that even if power to cancel a permit under this by-law should be held to pertain to the council, that power could not be delegated without statutory authority. Powers which are given to a council constituted to act as one deliberative body to the end that the members may assist each other by their united wisdom and experience cannot even by vote be delegated to the mayor alone. . . ."

SIMON *v.* GASTONGUAY. 1931. 2 M.P.R. 470 (Nova Scotia. Supreme Court). The plaintiff objected to the removal of the ruins of his building, which had been destroyed by fire in 1919. The removal was undertaken by the city of Halifax pursuant to an order of the Committee on Works. The plaintiff contended that the Committee had no authority to issue the order, that it was exclusively within the jurisdiction of the city council, which could not delegate to the Committee on Works. Held, for the plaintiff. Ross J.: "The first question then is, can the power conferred on the Board of Control under the Act of 1915 be exercised by the Committee on Works.

"I quote the relevant sections from the Acts of Nova Scotia for the year 1919, ch. 80, part II.

" '15. In any case in which in the sections of the Charter of 1914 left in force, or in any enactment passed since the date of that charter any power is conferred upon the Board of Control of the City of Halifax, or any duty is specified to be discharged by that board, or anything may be done upon its recommendation, such power may be exercised or such duty discharged, or such recommendation made by the council of the city or by that committee, board or official of the city, by which or whom such power would have been exercised or such duty performed or such recommendation made under the provisions of the Charter of 1907.

" '16. Without derogating from the generality of the next preceding section henceforward the powers conferred and duties imposed upon the Board of Control by the Charter of 1914 shall in respect to city works and property be discharged by a committee on works, in respect to the police by a committee on police, in respect to finance, including the yearly estimates, by a committee on finance, and in respect to the fire department by a committee on firewards, all such committees to be constituted and appointed as is provided in the Charter of 1907.'

"I am of opinion that the power in this matter passed to the city council and that the defendants cannot justify their entry on plaintiff's property under the order made by the committee. This was certainly not a power that could have been exercised by any committee, board or official of the city, under the provisions of the Charter of 1907."

RE DUNDAS STREET BRIDGES. 1904. 8 O.L.R. 52 (Ontario. High Court) Early in the year 1889, Paul Shakespeare and a number of other persons, describing themselves as the owners of the real property upon certain portions of certain named streets in the city of Toronto, petitioned the city council asking for the construction of iron bridges over the Canadian Pacific and Grand Trunk Railway Companies' tracks where they crossed Dundas Street. The petitioners asked that the work should be carried out as a local improvement. They stated the cost approximately at $75,000; that the railway companies would pay $20,000 of the cost; and they proposed that the city should pay $30,000, and that the balance should be paid by the property immediately benefited by the work.

The city council some years before had passed a general by-law, as authorized by sec. 612 of the Municipal Act, applicable to all cases of local improvements, the cost of which was to be borne by the property benefited, and this general by-law was evidently considered as a sufficient authority for the carrying out of the objects of the petition. The petition was referred to the city engineer, whose report upon it came before the committee of the council on works, who ultimately, on July 15th, 1889, adopted, with an important amendment, the engineer's report as to the properties benefited. The details of the assessment then came before the court of revision and were confirmed by the county Judge. This assessment was intended to ascertain the properties which should be chargeable with the balance of the cost of the bridges over and above the $20,000 to be contributed by the railway companies and the $30,000 which it was assumed the city at large would provide.

After many years the land owners objected to pay the taxes on the property immediately benefited by the work. The real reason seems to have been that the price for the job was much greater than had been anticipated and although the railway companies had paid their shares and the city was ready to pay its general share, those specially benefited were not. Double the amount of the original price had to be paid for by someone. It was apparent that not a very good bargain had been struck. The court refused to shift the whole burden since no one was "blameable for the excess." It was then objected that in selecting the properties immediately benefited by the improvements the council had delegated its authority to the city engineer. The objection did not prevail. MEREDITH J.: "It is always to be borne in mind that these local improvement clauses are to be considered remedial legislation, and are to receive such large and liberal construction as will best attain the object of the enactment. They are to be worked out by that plain class of laymen which usually fills municipal office of township, town, and village, as well as of city. They are not to be the subject of expert hair splitting, nor to stand or fall upon very precise literary criticism, nor upon any Judge's or any court's notion of what is fair or unfair, beneficent or the opposite to the taxpayer. The Legislature may be well, and must, well or ill, be trusted to know what is best, and to know how to employ the proper language in which to express its will. . . .

"The first objection of this character is that the council did not act upon its own "opinion", in determining what lands were benefited by the improvements, and the proportion in which the cost thereof should be assessed against the lands so benefited, and otherwise in acting upon the petition, but delegated their powers and duties to the engineer of the corporation. This, of course, is, in one sense, a very substantial objection, but, in another sense, what may be called an objection of a technical character, for no one can now doubt the council's opinion, or that, if the objection prevailed, the duty which the Act requires them to perform would be speedily performed and nothing but delay and more costs be the result; and has there not been enough of one and the other?

"But the answer to the objection is that—so far as the first by-law is concerned—it is not supported by the facts. On the contrary, it appears that the council did form and express their opinion, first by resolution and afterwards by by-law, to the effect required by, and in the words of, the enactment. It is true that the engineer was deputed to make enquiry and report into and upon all the circumstances, but what better mode of procedure could be adopted? It can hardly be suggested that the council should go in a body and find for themselves all the data requisite for the formation and expression of their opinion, nor that each member should separately do so. They did that which was quite proper—required their most competent officer to investigate and to report—and then, upon the petition and report, their own knowledge, and all other information had, proceeded and expressed their opinion in accordance with their officer's report, except in one particular in which they differed from him, and changed the report accordingly before adopting it . . . "

RE KIELY

Ontario. Queen's Bench Division. 1887. 13 O.R. 451

A motion to quash By-law 1702 of the city of Toronto so far as it provided that "it shall be unlawful for any person or persons to establish or keep any livery, trading, [*sic*, boarding?] or sale stables, unless and until he shall have procured the consent in writing of a majority of the owners and lessees of the real property situate within an area of five hundred feet of the proposed site for such stable, and until he shall have obtained the consent of the Local Board of Health". The by-law also required "the approval of the Medical Health Officer of the city of the plans and drawings and other sanitary appliances connected therewith". It did not apply to "any livery or sale stable heretofore established".

The applicant had erected extensive livery stables on Charles Street, at a cost of $7,000, but was fined $5 for violating By-law 1702. Counsel could not agree whether the erection of the building had begun before the building was started, but Kiely's counsel contended that the by-law was passed to prevent Kiely from getting the benefit of his building. Counsel for the city contended that Charles Street was used almost wholly for private residences. He relied on *The Municipal Amendment Act, 1884*, S.O., c. 32, s. 13(6), which authorized council to pass by-laws "for preventing or regulating the keeping of cows, goats, pigs, and other animals, and defining limits within which the same may be kept".

WILSON C.J.: . . . The first question I shall consider is, whether the council had the power to pass the by-law, or whether the police commissioners are not the body to exercise that power. That depends upon the construction of the 49 Vic. ch. 37, sec. 9 (O.), amending the Municipal Act of 1883, sec. 437. The section enacts that the board of commissioners of police shall in cities regulate and license the owners of livery stables and of horses, cabs, &c., used for hire, and shall establish the rate of fare to be taken by the owners or drivers, &c., 3. And may provide for enforcing payment of such rates. 4. And for such purposes pass by-laws and enforce the same in the manner and to the extent in which any by-law to be passed under the authority of this Act may be enforced.

The city council has the power, as before stated, by 47 Vic. ch. 32, sec. 13, sub-sec. 6 (O.), to pass by-laws "for preventing or regulating the keeping of cows, goats, pigs, and other animals, and defining limits within which the same may be kept."

It must be noticed that horses are not named in that enactment. The enactment begins with cows, and then names goats and pigs, and generalises with the concluding provision as to *other animals*. The section would certainly include sheep, but I am of opinion it does not include horses, which may be said to be the worthier animal, and which would have been named the first in order if it had been intended to include them.

By the 29 & 30 Vic. ch. 51, the power was vested in the council to regulate and license the owners of livery stables, section 296, sub-sec. 31. By the 31 Vic. ch. 30, sec. 33, that power was expressly transferred to the board of commissioners of police in cities, and it has continued vested in that body to the present time. . . .

It appears to me the provision of the city by-law in question relates to matters which the commissioners of police could provide for by by-law of their own.

I am of opinion the board of police is the body which alone has the power to regulate and license livery stables, &c.; that the by-law of the city is one which assumes to regulate them, and cannot be supported. The power to *regulate* confers upon the commissioners the power to declare in what locality or localities such stables shall be allowed.

I am not so assured that the applicant for a license to have such a stable can be required to procure the consent of any number of the owners of property or of the residents within a certain distance of the proposed site of the livery, as a condition precedent to his obtaining his license, for that is a matter in the discretion of the commissioners, upon which they must be guided by their own judgment. . . . It appeared to me to be somewhat of a delegation to the persons whose consent is to be exercised by the commissioners.

It is as much a delegation to that number of persons as it would be to require the applicant to get the consent of the Municipal or Parliament representatives of that locality, or of any other person or body, as a condition to the commissioners acting. The commissioners could no doubt take an opinion from any one or from any body to enable them to decide whether the license should be granted or not, and exercise their judgment upon such information. I have referred to the cases which were cited on the argument.

The conclusion I come to is,

1. The by-law is *ultra vires*, because the right to pass it is expressly vested in the board of commissioners of police.

2. The by-law, if not *ultra vires*, is objectionable, because it requires, as a condition precedent to the granting of a license, that the applicant shall procure the consent of a number of persons in the neighbourhood, thus constituting these persons the judges of the right he asks, and divesting the commissioners of the power which they are required personally to exercise.

The subject of the by-law is, in the main, a police regulation, but it concerns and affects trade and an ordinary pursuit and business of life, and a necessity in such a city as this is, and it is not necessarily a nuisance. It may, however, by careless management become so. If so, it may be prosecuted and suppressed.

I am obliged to quash the by-law, and with costs.

REX EX REL. TAYLOR *v*. KEMP. [1943] O.W.N. 54 (Ontario. High Court). The accused was convicted of operating a motor car for hire within the town of Trenton without first obtaining a licence, contrary to a municipal by-law that provided: "All applications for license to operate motor cars for hire shall be made to the Chief of Police of the Town of Trenton, and the said Chief of Police shall have absolute discretion in regard to the granting or refusal of such application or license." GREEN J.: "Under subs. 4 of s. 271 of *The Municipal Act*, R.S.O. 1937, c. 266, the power conferred upon a council to grant or refuse a license of the nature here involved 'shall be in its discretion'. Para. 4 of the by-law shows clearly that the council did not exercise its discretion at all but attempted to delegate its discretionary power to the chief of police." The delegation was held to be "not what the Legislature intended."

REX EX REL. FLETCHER *v*. JOY OIL COMPANY LTD.
Ontario. Court of Appeal. [1951] 1 D.L.R. 632

The magistrate acquitted two defendants for keeping service stations open during prohibited hours on the ground that the by-law unlawfully delegated discretion to an advisory committee. Schroeder J. on a stated case affirmed the acquittals. He held that the authority committed to the Chief Constable "not only covers ministerial matters, but involves the devolution upon him of discretionary powers which were vested by statute in the Council and in no other person or persons."

LAIDLAW J.A. delivered the judgment of the Court: ... Section 82 (3) [am. 1939, c. 47, s. 19(2); 1942 c. 17 s. 5] of the *Factory, Shop and Office Building Act*, R.S.O. 1937, c. 194 empowers the council of a city, town or village to pass a by-law determining the hours of closing all or any class or classes of shops within the municipality. By 1948, c. 27, s. 2, the Act was amended by adding thereto the following section:

"82a. In addition to any matter authorized by section 82, any by-law thereunder applicable to retail gasoline service stations, gasoline pumps and outlets in the retail gasoline service industry as defined in *The Industrial Standards Act* may,—

(a) provide that the by-law shall apply only in the portion or portions of the municipality designated in the by-law;

(b) require that during the whole or any part or parts of the year such retail gasoline service stations, gasoline pumps and outlets be closed and remain closed at and during any time or hours between six of the clock in the afternoon of any day and seven of the clock in the forenoon of the next following day and between six of the clock in the afternoon of Saturday and seven of the clock in the forenoon of the next following Monday; and

(c) provide for the issuing of permits authorizing the retail gasoline service station, gasoline pump or outlet for which it is issued to be and remain open, notwithstanding the by-law, during the part or parts of the day or days specified in the permit."

Under date May 31, 1948, the Council of the Corporation of the City of Toronto passed By-law No. 17275 [which required service stations to remained closed during certain hours and which established a committee consisting of a representative of the Chief Constable and of the City Council and three service station employers and two employees to recommend to the Chief Constable the issuance of permits to allow specified stations to remain open when the others were closed pursuant to the by-law.] . . .

It is urged that the power to make exceptions from the by-law rests primarily with the council of a municipality and that power can not be vested by the council in any other subordinate authority or agency without power in the council of the municipality so to do, given to it either by the use of express language in a statute or by clear and necessary implication from an enactment of the Legislature. . . .

Counsel for the appellants argued that the learned Judge erred in interpreting the statute as if it had provided that the council itself was required or empowered to issue the permits. It was said by counsel for the appellant

Fletcher: "This duty was not delegated to the council by the statute." And: "The only duty that was delegated to the council by the statute was a duty to 'provide for the issue of permit'." Finally, counsel argued that the Chief Constable was not given by the by-law any legislative power, that his authority must be exercised within the limits provided by s. 6 of the by-law and is subject at any time to review or recall by the council itself. . . .

The answer to the question whether s. 6 of By-law 17275 is valid depends, obviously, upon the kind and extent of the power intended to be given to the council of a municipality by s. 82a (c) of the *Factory, Shop and Office Building Act*. If it was the intention of the Legislature to give to the council of a municipality, and to no other person or authority, the absolute discretion as to the persons and the times to be expected from the by-law requiring gasoline service stations, pumps and outlets to remain closed, such intention could and no doubt would have been made plain in a simple manner by the use of express language. In the absence of such language, I cannot conclude that the Legislature intended that every application for a permit to keep a gasoline station, pump or outlet open, notwithstanding a by-law requiring such places to remain closed, should be the subject of consideration and action by the council of a municipality. The inconvenience which would be caused to the council of a municipality, to the applicants for permits, and to the public generally by such a procedure and system would be known and appreciated by the legislators, and in my opinion they would regard such procedure and system as impractical.

It is my view that the intention of cl. (c) of s. 82a of the *Factory, Shop and Office Building Act* was to empower the council of a municipality to establish a system for the issuing of permits which would not require an application to be the subject of consideration and action by it but rather by some subordinate agency or authority subject to the regulations and control of the council. That is what has been done by ss. 5 and 6 of the by-law in question. The council of the municipality has not thereby divested itself of power to amend the by-law from time to time by way of making exceptions to it or otherwise. It has made regulations and imposed restrictions in respect of the issue of permits, and those regulations and restrictions are binding on the Advisory Committee and the Chief Constable as provided in the by-law. The council of the municipality retains control in the matter of the issuing of permits and may alter the present regulations and restrictions in such manner and to such extent as in its discretion it deems necessary or advisable. In my opinion, ss. 5 and 6 of the by-law in question fall within the power of the council of a municipality to "provide for the issuing of permits" as contained in s. 82a (c) of the *Factory, Shop and Office Building Act* and are in accordance with the intention of that enactment. Therefore, I hold that the by-law is valid. Accordingly, the decision of Schroeder J. and of Magistrate McKeown to the contrary should be reversed. The facts as they appear in the stated case show that if the Magistrate had not reached the conclusion that By-law 17275 was *ultra vires* of the Council of the City of Toronto, he would have found the respondent guilty in each case. My decision, therefore, is that the respondent is guilty in each case. The penalty should be a fine in the sum of $50 and costs in the Magistrate's Court for each offence.

The appeals by way of stated cases came before Schroeder J. and to this Court in separate proceedings and each appellant was represented by his own counsel. The appeals were argued together as a matter of convenience only and I can see no good reason to deprive either appellant of any costs to which he would be otherwise entitled. I would therefore allow each appellant his costs of the application to Schroeder J. and of his appeal to this Court.

QUESTIONS: Is the talk about "divesting itself of control" (i.e. "abdication") as distinct from "delegation" relevant? Can a body having powers conferred by statute ever "abdicate" its powers? Is there some general principle that a municipal council can delegate as long as it does not abdicate?

THE QUEEN *v.* SEPANARY
Ontario. Court of Appeal. 1961. 31 D.L.R. (2d) 91

ROACH J.A. delivered the judgment of the Court: This is an appeal by leave of this Court from the judgment of His Honour Judge McAndrew, District Court Judge of the District of Thunder Bay, delivered on September 8, 1961, dismissing an appeal from the local Magistrate against a conviction for breach of s. 2 of By-law 4686 of the City of Port Arthur, passed on April 24, 1951. The by-law was passed under ss. 78 and 79 of the *Factory, Shop and Office Building Act*, R.S.O. 1960, c. 130. By s. 2 of the by-law retail gasoline service stations are required to be closed on certain days within certain hours. Section 3 of the by-law provides that notwithstanding the closing provision contained therein it shall be lawful for any shop in the retail gasoline service industry to remain open during the hours otherwise forbidden "on the authority of a permit issued by the Inspector of Licenses in a form approved by the Council". Section 5 of the by-law provides that application for a permit authorized by this by-law shall be made in writing to the Inspector of Licences and countersigned by a duly authorized representative of the Fort William and Port Arthur Service Station and Garage Operators Association and the Inspector shall, when satisfied that there is no other valid permit in the area in which the applicant's shop is located, issue a permit, on the form of the general licence used by the City, upon payment of a fee of $10.

We are unanimous in the view that this by-law is invalid. The learned District Court Judge held that the provision therein which dealt with the countersignature of the Fort William and Port Arthur Service Station and Garage Operators Association, was invalid but he thought that it was severable from the rest of the by-law and that the remainder of the by-law was valid. In our opinion the learned County Court Judge erred both as to severability and the validity. It is impossible to say that the City Council would have passed the by-law if it did not include that provision. Obviously what the Council had in mind was this: that it was desirable that after the closing hours as otherwise provided in the by-law there should be some gasoline service stations open to serve those of the public who would find themselves in need of gasoline and other gasoline service station products and service and that it should be left to the members of the Association to decide among themselves who would or ought to be granted permits to stay open in the three districts into which the City was divided. The members of the Council may have thought that that was a very practical way of doing things but the fact remains that it was a delegation by the Council to this Association to decide in the first instance and subject to the later decision of the Inspector who, among all the service station proprietors in the City, would at different times be entitled to such a permit. Even if that particular provision was deleted from the by-law then the by-law would leave to the uncontrolled, unrestrained and ungoverned discretion of the Inspector of Licences the question as to who at any given time and in any one of these particular three areas would get a permit. The by-law does not set out the conditions upon which the permit shall issue other than the condition with respect to approval by the association or provide any guideposts for the exercise of the discretion vested in the Inspector. In *Bridge* v. *The Queen ex rel. Skalinski* (1953) the Supreme Court of Canada did not in terms state such a by-law would be invalid but it inferentially did so. The by-law there in question was held to be invalid because the Council had provided in the by-law with sufficient particularity the conditions for the issue of special permits to stay open and accordingly had not substituted the clerks' judgment and discretion for its own. There the clerks' duties were administrative only. Here the by-law purports to vest in the Inspector of Licences not administrative but legislative functions.

This case comes squarely within the more recent decision of this Court in *Musty's Service Stations Ltd.* v. *Ottawa* (1959), which held the by-law there in question to be invalid.

For these reasons the appeal is allowed with costs and the conviction vacated. The appellant should also have his costs on the appeal to the District County Court Judge.

THE PLANNING ACT
Ontario. Revised Statutes. 1960. Chapter 296

31. (1) By-laws may be passed by the councils of municipalities:

3. For authorizing the municipal architect or building inspector to permit, in special cases that in his judgment warrant it, such deviation as he may deem proper from the by-laws regulating the erection of buildings, except by-laws passed under section 30 or a predecessor of that section.

(*a*) This paragraph applies only to municipalities where the municipal architect or building inspector, as the case may be, is a member or licensee of the Ontario Association of Architects under *The Architects Act* or a member or licensee of the Association of Professional Engineers of the Province of Ontario under *The Professional Engineers Act.*

THE TOWN AND RURAL PLANNING ACT
Alberta. Revised Statutes. 1955. Chapter 337

80. (1) The council may pass a zoning by-law . . .

(4) The by-law may also state for each district

(a) the uses of lands and of buildings that shall be permitted only in the discretion of the council or in the discretion of an agent or servant of the municipality that is appointed in the by-law to exercise such discretion, and

(b) the uses of lands and of buildings that may be permitted for a limited time only and subject to such special conditions of use and occupancy as may be determined in each particular instance in a manner to be provided in the by-law.

(7) The by-law may prohibit the erection of a building on any site where it would otherwise be permitted under the by-law when, in the opinion of the council, or in the opinion of an agent or servant of the council authorized to act on its behalf, satisfactory arrangements have not been

made for the supply to such building of electric power, water, sewerage, street and other facilities, or any of them.

(10) The by-law may provide that when a person proposes a particular use that is not named or specified in the by-law, the matter shall be referred to the council or to an agent or servant of the council designated in the by-law for a decision as to whether the proposed use is sufficiently similar to a use permitted by the by-law to be considered a permitted use.

(11) For the purpose of securing flexibility in the requirements of the by-law, the by-law may provide that the council, or an agent or servant of the municipality designated by the by-law, in its discretion and in the particular circumstances set out in the by-law, may determine those conditions, regulations and requirements within the scope of subsection (6) that shall apply to a proposed use of land or a building.

[Section 80 was amended by S.A. 1957, c. 98, s. 13; 1959, c. 89, s. 10; 1960, c. 107, s. 20 and 1961, c. 79, s. 6.]

THE MUNICIPAL ACT
Manitoba. Revised Statutes. 1954. Chapter 173

895. (1) Any municipal corporation may pass by-laws, subject to the provisions of The Town Planning Act applicable thereto, . . .
(e) for controlling and regulating the advertising of any business conducted in any zone or district and for appointing an official to the approval of whom any such advertising must conform; . . .

5. Provincial Supervision

THE COMMUNITY PLANNING ACT, 1957
Saskatchewan. Statutes. 1957. Chapter 48

44. (3) The minister may refuse to approve a zoning bylaw where in his opinion the provisions therein contained are not in conformity with good community planning practice.

46. (3) The minister may refuse to approve a bylaw amending a zoning bylaw where in his opinion:
(a) the provisions contained therein are not in conformity with good community planning practices; or
(b) the character of the municipality has, since the passing of the zoning bylaw, altered to such an extent that the bylaw is no longer adequate; or
(c) it is expedient that the zoning bylaw and the amendments thereto be consolidated owing to the multiplicity of the amendments previously made to the bylaw or contained in the amending by-law.

QUESTION. What is "good community planning practice?" Should the answer to this question be left to a Court, the Minister or to an administrative tribunal?

THE MUNICIPAL ACT
Ontario. Revised Statutes. 1937. Chapter 266

406. (2) (b) No by-law passed under this section shall come into force or be repealed or amended without the approval of the municipal board; but such approval may be given, as to the whole or any part of an area or

highway affected, if it is shown to the satisfaction of the board that it is proper and expedient in view of:

(i) The purpose for which the original by-law was passed and the nature and class of occupancy and use of the land within the area or abutting on the highway at the time the by-law was passed;

(ii) Any change which may since have taken place affecting its suitability for such occupancy or use; and

(iii) The desirability of the proposed repeal or amendment in the interests of the owners of the land in the district affected and of the community as a whole.

NOTE. Section 406 (2) (b) was introduced by S.O., 1921, c. 63, s. 10 and remained intact until 1941 when chapter 35 of the statutes of that year repealed it. Since then the lawyer's only guide to Municipal Board action has been the reports of its decisions, which until a few years ago were virtually unavailable. They are now distributed to law libraries and appear sporadically in the Ontario Weekly Notes (now discontinued). *Municipal Board Decisions* (two volumes, 1958 and 1959) published by the Ontario Department of Municipal Affairs, and in Cornish (ed.) *Planning and Property Reports.*

CUMMING, "IS ZONING WAGGING THE DOG?" (1955)

. . . It is interesting to find that in the year 1922, immediately following the passage of the 1921 Act conferring upon the [Municipal Board] this new jurisdiction [to approve zoning by-laws] there were only 15 applications for approval of by-laws that were required to be heard—and ten of these were from the city of Toronto.

In contrast, the number of applications brought before the Board in the five year period from 1950 to 1954 inclusive, totalled 2,511. Of this number no fewer than 892 were new by-laws imposing zoning regulations and 1,619 were by-laws amending existing restrictions. In the same five-year period there were 2,455 days of public hearings devoted to this type of work . . .

A public hearing is required. Although the legislation does not specifically require it, it has been the practice of the Board from the beginning, to hear all applications for approval of zoning by-laws and amendments at a public hearing where those interested in approving or opposing the application are given ample opportunity to adduce evidence and argument, to examine any written submissions and exhibits, and to examine and re-examine witnesses.

Notice of the hearing is required to be given by the applicant in accordance with the directions of the Board, not only to the owners of the property affected but to the department of planning and development, to every planning board having jurisdiction in the area, and depending on the circumstances, to adjoining municipalities and various departments of the provincial government. Proof of the giving of notice in accordance with the Board's directions is required to be filed at the commencement of each hearing.

Although the Board is an administrative tribunal and therefore not bound to adhere to all the technical rules of evidence, it attempts to follow well recognized fundamental judicial principles in the conduct of the hearings and insists upon an orderly presentation of the case and proper dignity and decorum.

At the outset, the applicant must satisfy the Board as to the legality of the enactment having regard to the specific terms of the delegated power. As a result, it is not unusual for the Board to hear and determine questions of interpretation and other legal questions but, as has been pointed out, the Board's ruling on any such question is always subject to an appeal to the Court of Appeal of Ontario.

The Board has consistently taken the position that it is the duty of those supporting or objecting to the by-law to bring before the Board at the public hearing all relevant information that will enable it to come to a decision. It conceives that its function on these applications is to weigh the evidence and arguments presented rather than to undertake any independent investigation on its own account. In other words, it conceives that it is its duty to adjudicate and not to investigate. It does not pretend to be a body of experts on planning or zoning, or indeed, on any other subject.

As to the burden of proof, it is the view of the Board that the onus is always upon the applicant seeking approval of a by-law or an amendment. Zoning by-laws by their very nature must interfere with traditional private property rights, and they can be justified only if they can be shown to be necessary in the public interest. In the first instance, the responsibility for this decision rests upon the elected council that has adopted the by-law. When the matter comes before the Board it is considered that the council should be ready and willing to demonstrate the relationship of the by-law to the public interest in order to permit the Board to decide whether under all the circumstances the by-law is a reasonable and proper exercise of the delegated zoning power. Similarly, when the by-law or amendment proposes to give some individual or some property some special exemption from the operation of the by-law, it is conceived that it is his duty to show that under the special circumstances there will be no injury to the public or the community sufficient to outweigh his personal loss. The responsibility placed upon the Board in the adjudication of this basic issue constitutes the essential difference between the functions of the Board and the functions of the ordinary courts when by-laws of this type are under review. It is provided in Section 259 of the Ontario *Municipal Act* that a by-law passed by a council in the exercise of any of the powers conferred by and in accordance with the act, and in good faith, shall not be open to question or be quashed, set aside or declared invalid, either wholly or partly, on account of the unreasonableness of its provisions, or any of them. In all the United States jurisdictions, I understand the opposite situation is true, and local zoning by-laws are commonly challenged in the courts on the ground that they are alleged to be an unreasonable and improper exercise of the police power delegated to the local councils by the said legislature.

Some of the general principles which the Board seeks to apply in dealing with applications for approval of these by-laws have been recently stated in a written decision of the board (dated August 29th, 1955), in the city of Toronto apartment house case previously referred to. If time permits and if you will pardon a speaker quoting from his own previous pronouncements, I would like to read some extracts from that decision. The issue before the Board was whether approval should be granted to certain amending by-laws which drastically increased the restrictions applicable to the construction of apartment houses in certain zoning districts. The amendments were passed by the city council at the beginning of 1955 building season. They seriously affected a large number of apartment house building projects planned to conform with the existing by-law but for which building permits had not been issued when the amendments were passed. As a result, when the applications of the city for approval of the amending by-laws came on for hearing they were vigorously opposed, and some 35 lawyers appeared before the Board on one side or the other.

The objections most strongly urged throughout the hearing fell under three main headings:

"In the first place it was contended that the council had acted hastily and without proper investigation and consideration of the substantial issues involved and the rights and claims of those affected, and that, under all the circumstances, the by-laws were not passed in good faith and for that reason should not be approved.

"Secondly, it was urged that the proposed amendments were unsound in principle and could not be justified as being in the interest of the city generally from the point of view of good planning and good zoning.

"Finally it was contended that in any event the amendments constitute a drastic change of policy seriously affecting the legitimate plans and operations of many persons who, in good faith, had made substantial commitments on the basis of the existing regulations, and that in equity the by-laws should be amended to grant such persons complete or partial exemption from the new regulations."

In order to enable the Board to dispose of these objections, an exhaustive review of the origin and history of the general by-law and corresponding provisions of the official plan was necessary. It was also necessary to review in considerable detail the actions and procedure of the council at and prior to the meetings when the amendments were adopted. It upheld the power of the council to enact proper and necessary amendments to zoning by-laws in the following words:

"As to the contention that the final enactment of the existing by-law following a long period of discussion and revision was in effect a holding out to prospective builders and investors of a set of regulations which could reasonably be considered to be permanent and that the action of the council in adopting without previous warning more stringent restrictions was a breach of faith, it appears to the Board that this argument is based upon a misconception of the nature of the powers exercised by a municipal council in passing a zoning by-law. As pointed out in such cases as *Howard* vs. *Toronto* (61 O.L.R. 563), a municipal council is a legislative body and when acting within the limits of its delegated jurisdiction its power is plenary and absolute. No authority was cited in support of the suggestion that a municipal council is under any greater duty than any other legislature to act in what has been called a judicial manner when adopting or amending legislation within its powers. It may be very desirable that, wherever possible before adopting or amending by-laws such as those which by their very nature must interfere with private property rights, the council should guard against hasty and ill-considered changes, but, if it is assumed that the original by-law was passed to further what was sincerely considered to be the public interest, it would appear to be not only the right but the duty of the council to act promptly when it is convinced that the beneficial purpose and intent of the original bylaw is endangered by unsuspected errors or omissions in the enactment. The provincial legislature has imposed an important limitation upon the power of the council in requiring that by-laws such as these must be approved by this Board before they become effective, and on an application for such approval the Board should be satisfied after due inquiry into the circumstances that the council has in good faith decided to enact the by-law or amendment to protect or promote the public interest after considering all aspects of the situation including possible injury to private interests. It may also be true that the discretionary power of the board to withhold approval was intended to be much broader than the power of a court of law to set aside a municipal by-law for illegality or for want of good faith in the legal sense. Nevertheless, the Board does not consider that it should attempt to lay down arbitrary rules specifying the procedure to be adopted or the inquiries to be made by a council before it adopts or amends zoning or restricted area by-laws, nor can it accept the view that the enactment of such a by-law creates some sort of an equitable right which must be protected in subsequent amendments."

The second group of objections required the Board to delve into such expressions of basic planning policy as were available, and although in the course of this review the Board found that the amendments revealed serious deficiencies in the general by-law itself, it refused to withhold its approval for that reason, preferring to grant approval for a temporary period of one year in order to permit the council and the planning board to undertake the necessary investigations which should precede a revision.

The Board was then called upon to deal with the very considerable number of requests for special exemption, and the following quotation indicates the way this problem was approached:

"In the opinion of the Board, requests for exemption from the operation of newly adopted zoning by-law or amendments must be treated with extreme caution. In the enabling statute the Legislature has provided a considerable measure of protection where the plans for any building or structure had been approved by the municipal architect or building inspector prior to the date of the passing of the by-law (*The Municipal Act*, Section 390 (6)). In cases not covered by this subsection it has always been the opinion of the Board that each claim for exemption must be considered on its merits. While it is desirable that, wherever possible, undue or unnecessary hardship to individuals should be avoided, it is also necessary to keep in view the basic beneficial purpose of the by-law or amendment intended for the protection of the municipality as a whole. Bylaws of this type, if they are to be effective, must necessarily interfere with the rights of individuals and can be justified only if they are required in the public interest. Usually the nature and extent of the injury to an individual can be established in evidence without difficulty, but the possible damage to the immediate area and to the City as a whole, should the requested exemption be granted, is not so easily measured. The issue before the Board in each case is whether, under the special circumstances, the granting of the exemption will actually result in such public injury that the application must be denied.

"The matters to be considered in dealing with each of the applications now before the Board might well include the following:

(a) The nature and extent of the proposed variation.
(b) The actual character of the immediate neighbourhood and the propriety of its present zoning designation.
(c) Whether the character of the neighbourhood has already been changed by the erection or authorization of similar buildings.
(d) Whether the project appears likely to place an excessive strain on existing services.

(e) Whether there is serious local opposition from adjacent owners.
(f) Whether the design of the project can be altered to meet the most serious objections.
(g) The actual financial loss to be sustained by the applicant if relief is not granted.

"The above list is not intended to be exclusive, and the Board realizes that in any particular case other special circumstances may exist to justify some relief."

I am not suggesting, by any means, that the application just referred to is an average case. However, it may serve to illustrate the nature and importance of some of the issues commonly raised on these hearings and the differences between the approach of an administrative tribunal and that of a court of law. It was at no time suggested that the city council had exceeded its legal powers, but the Board was very definitely asked to find that the action of the council had been arbitrary and capricious and that it had acted without regard to its proper responsibilities. Another interesting aspect of the argument was the submission to the Board of conflicting opinions on planning and zoning policy and the willingness of both sides to debate this issue before an administrative tribunal appointed by the province. . . .

[The extract reproduced above is from a talk given by Mr. L. R. Cumming, Q.C., then Chairman of the Ontario Municipal Board, at the Montreal meeting of the American Society of Planning Officials in 1955. It is printed in full in *Planning 1955* at pages 112–123.]

RE TORONTO TOWNSHIP BY-LAW 1614
Ontario. Municipal Board. 1953. 1954

[The following passages are taken from edited excerpts prepared by the Secretary of the Toronto Township Planning Board from the typed transcript of the oral hearing. The page references are to the pages of the transcript.]

. . . . We appreciate your coming down here, and we know that these by-laws require the support of interested citizens of your type, and the Association, and we hope that that support will continue once the By-law is passed, and by the time it comes into force and is administered. I know the Township feels the same way. It is quite a step to them. In some ways a drastic restriction of private rights in the interests of the many, and if the officials and the Council are more or less left alone and not made to feel that they have the people behind them it very often happens that even a good by-law will not accomplish its desired result because of the lack of public support. [From p. 108]

. . . . The longer you wait the more difficult it becomes. It is far better to do something, even though it may be just the first feeble step, than to do nothing and let developers plan. [From p. 482]

. . . . Practically every zoning by-law takes away rights from the citizens, it has to. It says to the citizens what you may not do with your land and by restricting his freedom of the use of the land it takes away some rights, but it does so in the interest of the great majority of the interests in the whole district, of the municipality—what it considers to be their interest. [From p. 81]

. . . . Regardless of any private restrictions, there is nothing to stop the Township from zoning land any way it sees fit, providing or even though the private owner might have contemplated commercial uses the Township might refuse to permit it. [From p. 328]

.... People who buy property and hope to profit by the resale of it must assume a very considerable risk, both as to markets and as to legitimate regulation and by-laws that the municipality where the land exists may impose, and he may have made a foolish investment in buying that seventy-seven acres with the idea of future re-sale of it. But that isn't exactly our problem. Our problem is, is this a good zoning scheme? What is wrong with it on the whole? We know there will be hardships on various individuals. There have to be. [From p. 285]

.... The onus is on the attacker. You show us what is wrong with this zoning and you say that the municipality will show that again, and it is confined solely to the merits. I can easily understand from what I have heard today how council can be confused, because it is a big issue. No one has reduced this problem to an exact science, and there is very sincere difference of opinion. [From p. 152]

.... Should we, sitting here as a Board, in the absence of any protest from the owners, faced with an official plan and approved by the Department which seems to think this is sound zoning, should we interfere at this stage and say to the Council, you are wrong, you should have zoned that industrial. That is what concerns us. Or, on what type of evidence should we make such a decision. [From p. 413]

.... I sometimes wonder what planning doesn't embrace. It embraces not only land use policy, but financial policy. [From p. 283]

.... Council's last action is this by-law. We could spend a great deal of time hearing all the ramifications of the Council, even the debates and the meetings and all the rest of it, but so far as businessmen are concerned it is well known that even the Council's decision is by no means a last word on this particular subject. And what a Council or member of Council may or may not have promised, after all, means nothing to us. We want to know is this the proper zoning for this area or not. [From p. 552]

.... We won't argue about the evidence but I am saying this, and I think it is rather important because these by-laws involve a lot of expense and preparation and notice to the property owners of the particular by-law that is going to be brought before the Board. Everyone comes here today, and I think properly assuming that this by-law and this only is what the council wants us to approve, otherwise we would never be justified in granting an appointment for a hearing. [From p. 124]

.... Council are not always consistent. We know they are not. We know they may change their minds. I am sitting here as a Board. The only way they can change their minds is to bring in an amending by-law. [From p. 124]

.... Supposing Council meets a proposed subdivider and promises to him if he will buy such and such a piece of land that council will zone it in such and such a way and then the council changes its mind perhaps as a result of protest or whim with or without notice to the man. Now I am suggesting to you that in view of that fact well knowing that council can't zone a piece of land without the approval of the Board it means nothing, and anyone acting on the promise of council is relying on a stick of straw, and have no cause to complain if the council comes before the Board and seeks a different zoning than the one that it may have held out to the man, because the question is not what the council did or did not promise to do or what an owner perhaps in ignorance of the law went ahead and did on his own responsibility and though such and such a by-law would be passed and approved. The question is not how you promised to zone that land but what the arguments are not for or against the present zoning that they did zone. [From p. 122]

. . . . I have been on a good many of these things and I have heard such statements as the Council promises this and the Council promises that. I think the question of good or bad faith on the part of Council is not the point. I want to hear why you say this particular piece of land, no matter who owns it or no matter what its history is, why this particular piece of land should not be zoned R. 3 and should C. 1. . . . [From p. 120]

CUMMING Q.C. Chairman and YEATES Member [only the decision relating to Objection Number 8 and the Board's general conclusions are reproduced]: This objection arises from the proposed R-3 zoning of approximately 40 acres of land at the south-west corner of the Queen Elizabeth Way and the Dixie Road known as the "Hempstead" property and owned by Principal Investments Limited. The owner seeks a C-2 zoning to permit the establishment of what is called a "regional" shopping centre. The proposed amendment was vigorously opposed by G. S. Shipp and Sons Limited, the owners of a somewhat smaller C-2 area on the north side of the highway some distance west of the Dixie Road and also by Rome-Saracini Company Limited, the owners of a fairly large site on the south side of the highway to the east of the Dixie Road overpass, also zoned C-2. The evidence and argument with respect to this single objection continued through several days resulting in some 250 pages of transcript. The hearing of this particular controversy, in effect, became a contest between private interests with large investments at stake and at times the real issue before the Board was obscured in the efforts of the contending parties to advance their own plans for the development of their lands. The Board does not intend to review in any detail the background of the present proposals, or the negotiations said to have taken place between the various parties and the council prior to its final decision in favour of a residential zoning for this parcel. After reviewing the entire evidence the Board is forced to the conclusion that the decision of the council was not based upon any serious or objective consideration of the proper use of the land in question having regard to its strategic location immediately adjacent to the intersection of two major highways and an elaborate traffic interchange constructed by the Department of Highways. Counsel for the township frankly admitted that the by-law did not represent any final decisions of the council with respect to the zoning of future commercial areas anywhere in the township. The council had in most cases merely recognized certain existing commercial uses in the C-1 and C-2 areas which were shown on the zoning maps. The consultant for the Planning Board argued that any attempt to designate future commercial areas at the present stage of development of the township would be premature. He suggested that the township authorities should deal with such problems as they might arise from time to time in the consideration of private plans of subdivision. It seems to the Board, however, that this approach to the problem really amounts to a refusal on the part of the council to assume its plain duty to control the inevitable commercial developments which will accompany the expected residential growth of the municipality. In any event, it was quite apparent to the Board that in this particular case the only apparent policy of the township council was to favour the two companies which had been permitted certain commercial areas in their new residential subdivisions and with whom the Company had made an elaborate agreement with respect to the provision of sewer and other services. It was argued that the township was morally, if not legally, bound to resist any attempt by a competing company to establish a large commercial area in the immediate vicinity which would operate in competition with the two companies whose shopping areas had been approved. The Board is unable to see any merit in this argument, particularly when it is admitted that the council has not attempted to prove that the additional areas would be in excess of any future needs. The sole and only question before the Board in dealing with this objection is whether the lands in question should be restricted to single family residential development or whether, as claimed by the objecting company, the site is suitable for a major shopping area designed to serve a very large region. The weight of the opinion evidence heard by the Board favours the second of these alternatives. Moreover, the applicant company has had considerable experience, both in the Toronto area and elsewhere, in the design, construction and actual management of shopping centres of the type proposed and in this particular case it had secured the official approval of the council to the proposed re-zoning in the form of a resolution passed on June 5, 1953, before the purchase of the property was completed. It is true that the same council at a meeting two weeks later passed a second and contradictory resolution repealing the earlier approval and purporting to reestablish the residential zoning. It is significant that in both cases the council appears to have acted upon the *ex-parte* representations of one of the opposing interests in the absence of the other. The result is that the Board is forced to adjudicate the issue without the benefit of any impartial considered independent opinion from the elected representatives. For the above reasons the Board has come to the conclusion that the objection must be sustained and that the lands in question should be rezoned C-2 as requested.

Under the circumstances, however, the township is entitled to be protected by suitable provisions requiring the lands to be used only for the purposes of a planned regional shopping centre. A draft plan of development should be prepared by the owner and submitted to the Planning Board of the Township and to the Department of Highways of Ontario for approval before construction is commenced, and in the event of any dispute the owner or the Planning Board may apply to this Board for further directions. The Board is assuming that the applicant has a bona fide intention to proceed with the construction of a regional shopping centre within a reasonable time. The Board's approval of the proposed re-zoning of the lands in question will therefore be given for a temporary period only expiring on December 31, 1954 or such later date as may be fixed on application to the Board after notice to the Township Clerk and the Secretary of the Planning Board.

As it appears that the opinion of the Board is desired with respect to the proposed 27 acre shopping centre shown in the draft plan of the proposed extension to Applewood Acres located at the north-westerly corner of the Second Line and the service road, the Board is prepared to approve, without further hearing, any amendment which may be approved by the council which would permit the establishment of a shopping centre at this point. It is also prepared to approve without further hearing a change of the existing triangular C-2 area at the opposite corner of the same intersection to a C-1 classification if such change is approved by the council. . . .

The Board is well aware of the difficulties involved in the preparation and adoption of a general zoning by-law in a rapidly growing suburban municipality such as the Township of Toronto. These difficulties are greatly increased when as a result of its geographical position in close proximity to the expanding metropolitan area the township is faced with all the problems involved in a rapid transition from an agricultural to an urban and suburban community. It has been quite apparent to the Board as a result of the hearings on the present by-law and the former proposed by-law that the municipal council did not fully appreciate the necessity for careful planning and stringent zoning controls until they were much overdue. While making every possible allowance for the obvious deficiencies of the by-law under these circumstances, the Board nevertheless feels that it should not accept and approve the present by-law except for a temporary period. The proper zoning of an area such as this is not a simple matter and cannot be accomplished by an incomplete by-law hastily put together. However, such protection as is afforded by the present by-law should not be withheld pending the preparation of suitable amendments, and the Board is therefore prepared to grant its approval subject to the specific amendments listed in this decision and subject, of course, to the township being able to obtain the required approval of any corresponding amendments of its official plan. Such approval will be for a temporary period expiring on the 1st day of July, 1955, unless extended by subsequent order of the Board on the application of the council.

In addition to the amendments which will be required as a result of the Board's decision and which, if in proper form, can be approved without further hearing, there will undoubtedly be an accumulation of amendments proposed either by the council or individuals during the past year. The Board suggests that these should be all included in a single amending by-law and submitted to the Board as soon as possible as a public hearing will be required and directions must be given for notice thereof in the usual way. At the same time the council should without delay give the necessary instructions for the preparation of important and necessary amendments designed to improve the form of the by-law and to clarify its meaning.

In the opinion of the Board, however, the most urgent task to be undertaken during the period of temporary approval is the consideration and adoption of a comprehensive scheme for the zoning and regulation of commercial and industrial areas. In the present by-law there has been no real attempt to distinguish between desirable and undesirable commercial and industrial uses. For example, a stock car racing plant, a drive-in theatre or restaurant, a used car lot and a second-hand clothing store are commercial undertakings which could be established in any C-1 or C-2 district. Similarly, an undesirable industry of the nuisance type could be legally established in any M-1 or M-2 zone if conducted within an enclosed building or structure. It is true that certain types of dangerous uses can be controlled under Section 19(2) but many highly undesirable and obnoxious operations cannot be called dangerous. The situation is made more serious by the complete lack of any definition restricting the meaning of the words "commercial undertaking" in Section 49 or "manufacturing or industrial undertaking" in Section 55. In this connection the Board must again draw attention to a general objection already referred to, namely, the omission from Section 2 of many vitally important definitions of terms used in the by-law. It is elementary that a by-law such as this imposing restrictions upon the owners and occupants of property should be expressed in clear and definite terms. Otherwise, enforcement will be uncertain and difficult and the protection which the by-law is intended to provide will be found worthless.

The Board hopes that its suggestions in this respect will be given serious consideration and that before the period of temporary approval expires the township will find it possible to submit for final approval a general zoning by-law which has been greatly improved both in substance and in form.

In addition to the fee paid on the original application the municipality will be required to pay to the Board a further fee of $300, and the fees of the reporter for his attendance and transcript of the evidence, amounting to $597.60.

NOTE ON THE NEED FOR PROVINCIAL SUPERVISION. None of the statutes that require a zoning by-law to be approved by some provincial agency sets out the reason why the approval is considered necessary. The province of British Columbia, for example, does not require approval but does suggest in its statute some standard for the council to follow, and it does require the council to adopt the by-law only with a two-thirds vote. In Alberta the approval of the Provincial Planning Advisory Board is required at present, but the requirement was adopted by S.A., 1959, c. 89, s. 13, after a two year interval during which it was not required. Nothing in the Act, of course, indicates why the experiment with local autonomy was given up. The existence of provincial supervision is one bit of evidence of the myth of local autonomy, a dearly held notion which may be raised at any time in criticism of provincial interference of local government.

If the justification for provincial supervision is to be smoked out, some thought should be given to the existence of many particular powers of land use control that may be exercised by a local council without supervision. *Donald* v. *Whitby* is a good illustration. Paragraph 122 of section 379(1) of *The Municipal Act* in Ontario permits zoning and regulating of billboards without supervision, yet this particular power has been the subject of extensive and sometimes rather ridiculous litigation in the United States. Section 379(1) alone contains 134 paragraphs many of which authorize "zoning", that is, the "prohibiting" as well as "regulating" of an activity, frequently with an express power to prohibit in defined areas. See, for example, paragraphs 1, 2, 4, 12, 18, 29, 31, 32, 33, 84, 85, 110–125 and 129. See also section 377 paragraphs 9, 44 and 63. There are many powers, too numerous to mention, by the exercise of which the municipality may control the use of land, and, apart from prohibition, the power to regulate it is very extensive. In almost all of these cases, in Ontario, there is no requirement of provincial approval, but the power is usually stated in very precise and limited terms.

CHAPTER 12

ADMINISTRATIVE ADJUSTMENT OF ZONING

... unless great caution is used and variations are granted only in proper cases, the whole fabric of town- and city-wide zoning will be worn through in spots and raveled at the edges ...

BALDWIN J., *Heady* v. *Zoning Board* (1953)

Few jurisdictions today are lacking some kind of machinery of appeal to help smooth the rough edges of zoning by-laws. In this Chapter the functions of these agencies are examined. For those jurisdictions that have no power of delegation the adjustment agency is a kind of exception, and since it is usually authorized only to deal with single cases, it inevitably discriminates. The common charge against an agency is that it whittles away the zoning by-law until nothing is left but chaos. Is this a real danger? The belief that it is accounts in part for the confining form in which the adjusting agency's jurisdiction is usually set out, especially in Ontario. If the charge is valid are the legislative devices employed adequate to answer it and remove the danger? Are they excessive, so that the agency cannot do a proper job? How should the agency fit into a comprehensive planning programme? Are the interests of adjoining and probably affected landowners adequately protected? What are these interests and how are they to be recognized?

1. THE FUNCTION OF THE ADJUSTMENT AGENCY

MUNICIPAL ACT

British Columbia. Revised Statutes. 1960. Chapter 255

709. (1) The Zoning Board of Appeal shall hear and determine any appeal

(*a*) by a person who is aggrieved by a decision of any official charged with the enforcement of a zoning by-law or a by-law under subsection (5) of section 711 in so far as that decision relates to an interpretation of the by-law or by-laws or any portion thereof; and

(*b*) with respect to matters mentioned in subsection (4) of section 705; and

(*c*) by an applicant for a permit who alleges that enforcement of a zoning by-law with respect to siting, size, or shape of a building or of a structure would cause him undue hardship, in which case the Board may, to the extent necessary to give effect to its determination, exempt the applicant and subsequent owners of the building or structure from the applicable provisions of the zoning by-law; and

(d) with respect to matters mentioned in subsection (3) of section 705 and subsection (7) of section 711.

[Subsections (3) and (4) of section 705 are reproduced on pages 494–95 and subsection (5) of section 711 is reproduced on page 328. Subsection

(7) of section 711 provides that where land to be subdivided is zoned for agricultural, rural, or industrial use, the provisions of section 709(1) (*c*) apply to the enforcement of a by-law passed under section 711(5).]

THE TOWN AND RURAL PLANNING ACT
Alberta. Revised Statutes. 1955. Chapter 337

81. (1) A zoning by-law shall establish an appeal board . . .

(3) An appeal may be made by a person

(*a*) who claims that the strict enforcement of the requirements of a zoning by-law or of section 82 would cause him special and unnecessary hardship because of circumstances peculiar to his situation within the district,

(*b*) who is not satisfied with a decision made pursuant to the exercise of a discretionary authority, or

(*c*) when the by-law provides for an appeal.

(4) On an appeal made under clause (*a*) of subsection (3) the appeal board, having regard to the merits and circumstances of the particular case, and the general scope and intent of the by-law and in order to avoid unnecessary hardship, may

(*a*) confirm, reverse or vary a decision appealed from,

(*b*) impose such requirements or limitations as it deems to be desirable and proper in the circumstances, and

(*c*) Repealed. (1959, c. 89, s. 11)

(*d*) where the appeal concerns an existing use that is not permitted in a district under the zoning by-law, permit the continuance of the non-conforming use.

[Section 81 has been amended by S.A., 1957, c. 98, s. 13; 1959, c. 89, s. 11; 1960, c. 107, s. 21.]

THE COMMUNITY PLANNING ACT, 1957
Saskatchewan. Statutes. 1957. Chapter 48

52. (1) A zoning by-law may provide for an appeal in writing to the board of zoning appeals constituted under section 51, or to the Provincial Planning Appeals Board, constituted under section 126, by any person who:

(a) alleges that the council or any person acting for or on behalf of the council has misapplied the by-law in a particular case; or

(b) claims that there are practical difficulties or unnecessary hardships in the way of carrying out the by-law by reason of the exceptional narrowness, shortness, shape, topographic features or other unusual condition of a specified property.

(2) A person who appeals under clause (b) of subsection (1) shall not be entitled to have his appeal allowed if:

(a) the unusual condition is the result of his or the property owner's own actions;

(b) the adjustment requested would constitute a special privilege inconsistent with the restrictions on the neighbouring properties in the same district; or

(c) a relaxation of the provisions of the bylaw would be contrary to its purposes and intent and would injuriously affect the neighbouring properties.

(3) Where a zoning bylaw provides for an appeal to the board of zoning appeals the following rules apply: . . .

11. The board shall not grant any adjustment in respect of the use of property;

12. The board may affix such conditions to the granting of an adjustment as in its opinion will preserve the purposes and intent of the zoning by-law;

16. An adjustment granted by the board shall not become effective until the expiration of thirty days from the date on which the decision granting the adjustment is made or, if conditions are affixed pursuant to paragraph 12, until such time as the conditions have been complied with, whichever is the later; . . .

THE PLANNING ACT
Ontario. Revised Statutes. 1960. Chapter 296

32*b*. (1) The committee of adjustment, upon the application of the owner of any land, building or structure affected by any by-law that implements an official plan or is passed under section 30, or a predecessor of such section or any person authorized in writing by the owner, may, notwithstanding any other Act, authorize such minor variance from the provisions of the by-law, in respect of the land, building or structure or the use thereof, as in its opinion is desirable for the appropriate development or use of the land, building or structure, provided that in the opinion of the committee the general intent and purpose of the by-law and of the official plan, if any, are maintained.

(2) In addition to its powers under subsection 1, the committee, upon any such application,

(a) where any land, building or structure, on the day the by-law was passed, was used for a purpose prohibited by the by-law and such use has continued until the date of the application to the committee, may permit,

(i) the enlargement or extension of the building or structure, provided that the land, building or structure continues to be used in the same manner and for the same purpose as it was used on the day the by-law was passed, and provided that no permission may be given to enlarge or extend the building or structure beyond the limits of the land owned and used in connection therewith on the day the by-law was passed, or

(ii) the use of such land, building or structure for a purpose that, in the opinion of the committee, is similar to the purpose for which it was used on the day the by-law was passed or is more compatible with the uses permitted by the by-law than the purpose for which it was used on the day the by-law was passed, provided that the land, building or structure continues to be used in the same manner and for the same purpose as is authorized by the decision of the committee;

(b) where the land, building or structure adjoins any area in which the permitted uses differ from those permitted in the area in which it is situate, may permit the extension or enlargement, into the adjoining area, of the land, building or structure to such an extent as, in the opinion of the committee, is in keeping with the general intent and purpose of the by-law and of the official plan, if any; or

(c) where the uses of land, buildings or structures permitted in the by-law are defined in general terms, may permit the use of any land, building or structure, for any purpose that, in the opinion of the committee, conforms with the uses permitted in the by-law.

(9) Any authority or permission granted by the committee may be for such time and subject to such terms and conditions as the committee may deem advisable and as are set out in the decision.

[Section 32*b* is reproduced as enacted by S.O., 1961–62, c. 104, s. 8]

COMMITTEE OF ADJUSTMENT—AN INDISPENSABLE TOOL

Ontario. *Ontario Planning*. 1956. Vol. 3, No. 6

... *Principles to assist Committees of Adjustment*. The following comments are not intended as rigid rules for committee of adjustment action, but it is hoped that they may help to clarify the role of the committee of adjustment in the effective implementation of a sound planning programme.

1. As previously stated, the basic purpose of a committee of adjustment is to make minor adjustments in the strict application of the zoning by-law. This calls for a thorough knowledge of the official plan and zoning by-law, but above all an understanding of the intent and purpose of these documents, as the committee can only grant a variance when the intent and purpose is maintained. The responsibility is placed upon the committee to judge the extent of the variance so that the end result will still be within the intent and purpose of the official plan and zoning by-law.

2. The committee in carrying out its function must accept the official plan and zoning by-law as adopted by Council. It cannot use its powers to zone, or to permit uses that are not permitted, or to correct what it may consider and what may be defective planning or zoning, this being a matter for council as the elected body responsible for regulating land use by zoning by-law.

3. Normally, only an individual property should be considered. Groups of properties are a matter for an amendment to the zoning by-law.

4. The responsibility for showing necessity for the granting of a variance is upon the applicant, and in explaining that compliance with the by-law is unreasonable or impossible the applicant should provide reasons to the satisfaction of the committee.

5. The committee in analysing a case should satisfy itself:

(a) that there are practical difficulties which make the carrying out of the strict letter of the by-law unreasonable or impossible,

(b) that the circumstances which create the practical difficulties are peculiar to the property only and not common to the area,

(c) that by complying with the by-law, the applicant can make no reasonable use of the property,

(d) that the necessity for the variance is not one of convenience or monetary gain, where compliance with the by-law is possible and reasonable,

(e) that the necessity for the variance results only from the application of the by-law to the property and not from any other factor,

(f) that the applicant has not himself created the circumstances that prevent him from complying with the strict terms of the by-law,

(g) that the application has sufficient merits of its own not to create a precedent for similar requests from others.

6. In considering cases of non-conforming uses under 18(2) (a) of The Planning Act, 1955, the committee of adjustment:

(a) should bear in mind the intent of the by-law for the area,

(b) should ascertain that it is a lawful non-conforming use and that such use has continued until the date of application,

(c) should not grant an extension or enlargement of a building used for a non-conforming use except to prevent unreasonable hardship and where the depreciating effect on the area is no greater than the original building,

(d) should not grant a change of a non-conforming use, unless the new use is either similar to the old one or will be more compatible with the permitted uses for the area,

(e) should not permit the rejuvenation of a non-conforming use by the demolition of an old building and replacement by a new one for either the existing use or a new non-conforming use.

(f) should bear in mind that any extension or enlargement of a building used for a non-conforming use may extend the life of that use, whereas it is the hope that non-conforming uses will disappear to make way for conforming uses.

7. Under Section 18 (2) (b) of The Planning Act, 1955, the committee of adjustment should not grant any extension of land, building or structure into an adjoining zone except to enable the owner of that land, building or structure to utilize his property reasonably, and then only provided that the extension is in keeping with the intent and purpose of the official plan and zoning by-law and that the area into which the extension is to be made actually abuts the property that is to be extended. In effect, the purpose of the committee of adjustment in this instance is to permit minor adjustments in the zone boundaries where the existing zone boundary prevents the reasonable and logical development of the land, building or structure that is required to be extended.

8. A committee of adjustment should not use its powers to legalize contraventions of the by-law resulting from gross carelessness or indifference on the part of the applicant or from poor municipal administration.

To many, the powers of a committee of adjustment may appear to be wide, and as a result different interpretations of the authority granted to this body may be given. However in this regard it is emphasized that a committee of adjustment, although not elected by the people, is given discretionary powers. It would seem imperative that these powers be used and interpreted with considerable caution if the committee of adjustment is to serve its proper purpose in promoting the interests of the community as a whole and it is to gain the confidence of all concerned. An abuse of these powers may seriously reduce the effectiveness of the zoning by-law and cause conflict between the committee of adjustment and the municipal council through the former trying to usurp some of the powers of the latter.

A final word of warning: no council or planning board when preparing a zoning by-law should ignore the principles of good zoning or make insufficient studies and then expect the matter to be solved by the appointment of a committee of adjustment. This is not the function of a committee of adjustment. Many committees of adjustment are faced with poor zoning by-laws, which makes their task more difficult, and councils should not shirk their duty in this regard. As the title of this article suggests, a committee of adjustment is an indispensable tool performing an essential task in the implementation of planning through a zoning by-law. It is an agency intended to help zoning work more effectively, and to provide justice in removing some of the small inequities and frustrations that can arise in the zoning process, thus making this important implementing part of the planning process more acceptable.

RE LONDON BY-LAW, WESTERN TIRE AND AUTO SUPPLY LTD. AND WEINSTEIN

Ontario. Court of Appeal. 1960. 23 D.L.R. (2d) 175

MORDEN J.A. delivered the judgment of the Court: the respondents Medland are owners of lands in London known as 301 Talbot St. The Goodwill Rescue Mission is an association which conducts a hostel for derelict persons in London. This Mission, wishing to obtain larger quarters and to locate in the business district of London, has an option to purchase the Medland lands. These lands are situate in an area which is zoned by City of London By-law CP-98-133 as "Light Industrial" in which area the permitted uses are all those permitted in the "Single Family Residence," "Two Family Residence," "Multi-Family Residence," "Local Business" and "General Business" zones. In addition there are twenty-four other uses permitted in the "Light Industrial" zone. The only other zone mentioned in the by-law is the "Heavy Industrial" zone in which there are no enumerated permitted uses but certain specified ones are forbidden. The by-law, which specifies in some detail both permitted and forbidden uses, does not mention hostels or any use which would comprise the activities now carried on by the Goodwill Rescue Mission. The by-law, which implements the official plan for the City of London, was passed pursuant to s. 390 of the *Municipal Act*, R.S.O. 1950, c. 243 and, I assume, was duly approved by the Ontario Municipal Board.

In May or June 1959, certain persons on behalf of the Goodwill Rescue Mission asked the City Building Inspector whether a permit would be issued to permit the reconstruction of the building known as 301 Talbot St. for the purposes of the Mission. The Inspector was in doubt whether the work of the Mission was a use permitted by the by-law in the Light Industrial zone and refused to issue a permit without the instructions of the City Council. The Mission representatives then appeared before the Committee of Adjustment and obtained the opinion of that body that the proposed use was a permitted one as falling within the category of hotel or possibly rooming-house. This opinion was put in writing and sent to the City Architect. Relying upon that opinion, the City Council on July 6th authorized the City Architect "to issue a building permit to the Goodwill Rescue Mission to establish their Mission at 301 Talbot Street".

The appellant Weinstein is the owner of 304–310 Talbot St. and the respondent Western Tire & Auto Supply Ltd. occupies these premises under a lease ending in 1969 and giving that company an option to buy them. On July 13th the appellants learned that a permit would be issued and their solicitors then informed the City Clerk if this were done an action would be brought to restrain any one from proceeding to act under the permit. No permit was issued. The appellant company received on August 15th a notice of a public hearing to be held by the Committee of Adjustment to consider an application by the Medlands "for permission to establish a use on the premises for the purpose of the Goodwill Rescue

Mission". On August 24th, the solicitor for the appellants appeared before the Committee and objected to its jurisdiction to entertain the application upon the grounds that (a) the appellants would likely not receive a wholly impartial hearing from the Committee because it had previously expressed its opinion in June and (b) the proposed use involved more than a minor variation of a use permitted by the by-law. The Chairman then stated that the objection was noted but that matter was within the Committee's jurisdiction. The appellants' solicitor at this point withdrew, the hearing then proceeded, the application was granted. The decision of the Committee is in the following terms:

"We, the undersigned members of the Committee of Adjustment, London, Ontario, do hereby attest that the following was the decision reached by us at a meeting held on Monday, the 24th day of August, 1959, on the application of Earl and Mabel Medland, of 301 Talbot Street, London, Ontario, for permission to establish a use, under Zoning By-law C.P. 198–133, on the premises 301 Talbot Street; which are located in a Light Industrial Zone; for the purpose of the Goodwill Rescue Mission."

The Committee gave lengthy written reasons for its decision which concluded with the statement: "In summary, the Committee grants this application, being of the opinion that the variance applied for is desirable for the appropriate use of the subject property, and that the establishment of such use maintains the general intent and purpose of the By-law and the Official Plan."

Before appellants learned of the Committee's decision, they launched a motion for an order prohibiting the Committee from proceeding further with the Medlands' application upon the two grounds advanced by their solicitor at the hearing on August 24th and, in the event a decision had been made, for an order quashing it for the same reasons. As the decision had in fact been made, it was agreed by counsel on the return of the motion that it should be treated as a motion for an order of *certiorari* and for an order to quash the Committee's decision. The motion was heard on October 23, 1959 by Mr. Justice Barlow who dismissed it with costs upon the ground that *certiorari* did not lie to a committee of adjustment and alternatively that if it did the Committee had acted within its jurisdiction. The appellants now appeal from that order.

The first matter to be considered is whether the remedy of *certiorari* is available against a committee of adjustment established under the *Planning Act*, 1955 (Ont.), c. 61, and the amendments thereto. Mr. Laidlaw was frankly embarrassed by the number of decided cases upon this branch of the appeal he felt obliged to cite. It is no reflection upon the able arguments presented by both Mr. Laidlaw and Mr. Williston that I will refrain from reviewing or discussing them. The principle, approved and confirmed by many later decisions in both England and Ontario, is stated by Atkin L.J. in *R.* v. *Electricity Com'rs* (1924) in these words:

"The matter comes before us upon rules for writs of prohibition and certiorari which have been discharged by the Divisional Court. Both writs are of great antiquity, forming part of the process by which the King's Courts restrained courts of inferior jurisdiction from exceeding their powers. Prohibition restrains the tribunal from proceeding further in excess of jurisdiction; certiorari requires the record or the order of the court to be sent up to the King's Bench Division; to have its legality inquired into, and, if necessary, to have the order quashed. It is to be noted that both writs deal with questions of excessive jurisdiction, and doubtless in their origin dealt almost exclusively with the jurisdiction of what is described in ordinary parlance as a Court of Justice. But the operation of the writs has extended to control the proceedings of bodies which do not claim to be, and would not be recognized as, Courts of Justice. Wherever any body of persons having legal authority to determine questions affecting the rights of subjects, and having the duty to act judicially, act in excess of their legal authority they are subject to the controlling jurisdiction of the King's Bench Division in these writs."

There is no doubt in my mind that committees of adjustment are given the power to affect the rights of persons. Their decisions under s. 18 of the *Planning Act*, 1955, affect the rights of the owners and occupants of the lands which are the subject of applications before them and the rights given by s. 497 of the *Municipal Act* to ratepayers to take action to restrain the contravention of restrictive by-laws. The appellants did threaten such an action before the Committee entertained the application. If the Committee's decision stands, the appellants no longer have any right to restrain the proposed use of the lands in question by the Goodwill Rescue Mission. As the Committee has authority to affect the rights of others, it follows that it is under a duty to act judicially. . . . However, in the case at bar we do not need to draw the inference that Committee is bound to act judicially . . . such a duty is in plain terms imposed upon it by s. 17 (11), (12), (13) (as enacted in 1959 (Ont.), c. 71, s. 2) and by s. 18 (4), (6), (7), (8) [am. 1959 (Ont.), c. 71, s. 3] and (10) of the *Planning Act*, 1955 and by the Rules of Procedure of the London Committee which were approved by the Minister of Planning and Development. In my opinion, committees of adjustment are subject to orders of prohibition and *certiorari* and their decisions when made following proceedings which contravene the provisions of the Act and their Rules of Procedure or which exceed their statutory powers may be quashed by an order of the High Court.

I will now consider whether the London Committee did act in excess of its jurisdiction. Counsel for the appellants did not in this Court rely upon the danger of the Committee's partiality because of the opinion given by it to the City Architect; he did submit that s. 18(1) of the *Planning Act* limited the Committee to authorizing a minor variance and did not empower it to permit the establishment of uses not spelled out in the by-law and thereby to amend or supersede the by-law. . . .

Before dealing with this submission I must refer again to the Committee's decision—"to establish a use . . . for the purposes of the Goodwill Rescue Mission". Section 18(1) does not give the Committee any power to establish a use—it may authorize or permit a minor variance in respect of the use of land. That variance should be clearly and accurately described in the Committee's decision. We have obtained from the material a general idea of the proposed use and I assume the Committee received from the representations made to it a fairly clear appreciation of the proposed use but it is not set out in the decision. It is not sufficient, in my view, to define the use by reference to the purposes, all of which may not have been disclosed and which may change from time to time, of a named body. It is not a sufficient answer to this objection to say that the proposed use can be inferred from the name of the Mission. Another objection is that the permission might be construed as personal to the Goodwill Rescue Mission and not available to any successor in title to the lands; it does not appear from the written decision that the Committee was acting under s. 18(9). The decision which permits a new use affects the legal enjoyment of land and is a matter of public record. It should describe the use permitted with clarity. The Committee had jurisdiction to permit a use which would be a minor variance—but in this case the Committee has failed to express its decision with the clarity which, in my view the Act requires. To this extent, it has exceeded its jurisdiction and this error appears on the face of the record. Its decision can not stand and should be quashed upon this ground alone.

Mr. Williston argued that where an appeal lies, then the Court has a discretion whether or not to grant *certiorari* and based this submission upon the cases, recently decided, of *Ex p. Atikokan* (1959) and *Re Town of Weston Assessment* (1959). In those cases the error of law did not appear on the face of proceedings as it does in the instant case and they are therefore distinguishable.

I return now to Mr. Laidlaw's main contention that what the Committee purported to do was more than a "minor variance" and thus beyond the powers conferred upon it by s. 18(1). In my opinion, this matter cannot be decided upon the record as it now stands. For the reasons I have stated, it is not at all clear what particular uses the Committee intended to authorize and until that is clarified, it is impossible to say with any certainty whether the Committee acted in excess of its statutory powers. When one considers the great detail of uses enumerated in this by-law and in most zoning by-laws, one appreciates the need for a less cumbersome and more expeditious procedure than that required for the effective amendment of such by-laws to permit uses not mentioned and apparently not contemplated when the by-law was first enacted. The Committee is empowered to authorize "minor variances". It would be difficult to define the exact ambit of those words. For the purpose of this judgment I am not required to embark upon such a voyage. Numerous and diverse uses are permitted in the Light Industrial zone by the by-law. It may be that the proposed use by the Goodwill Rescue Mission when properly described and defined might fall within the term "minor variance". Although the decisions of committees of adjustment are subject to review by *certiorari* nevertheless whether a particular use is a minor variance and whether a committee arrived at the correct opinion upon the two other matters mentioned in s. 18(1), can not be satisfactorily reviewed upon an application for *certiorari*. Ample protection against an improper decision in a particular case is provided by an appeal by the applicant, the Minister or any other interested person, to the Ontario Municipal Board. That body is required by s. 18(14) to hold a public hearing and by s. 18(15) it "may dismiss the appeal, and may make any decision that the committee could have made on the original application". The Municipal Board rehears the application upon its merits and in so doing is governed by the provisions of s. 18(1). That body, having already approved the original by-law as provided by s. 390(8) of the *Municipal Act*, is much better fitted in my respectful opinion, to pass upon such questions than a Court of law upon *certiorari* proceedings. The Board would hear the evidence which would be transcribed and if a further appeal were taken to this Court upon a point of law we would have had the benefit of the Board's opinion together with the evidence. . . .

. . . In these circumstances I would . . . make an order . . . quashing the Committee's decision.

The question of costs has given me some concern. The Committee will now have an opportunity to cast its decision in proper form and it may be that its decision will be within its jurisdiction under s. 18(1). The appellants' success may turn out to be merely temporary. However, they have succeeded in having the present decision of the Committee quashed and they are entitled to their costs of the application and of the appeal to be paid by the respondents Medland. I would make no order with respect to the costs of the Committee of Adjustment.

QUESTIONS. Should the Court have entertained *certiorari* before the parties had exercised their statutory right of appeal to the Municipal Board? Might the Board not have stated the variance more precisely and saved the expense of this litigation? If *certiorari* is to lie at all, should it not lie to determine whether a particular variance is "minor"? Has the Municipal Board any competence to decide whether a variance is "minor"? Is it a fact that "[two members of] that body, having already approved the original by-law" make the Municipal Board "much better fitted . . . to pass upon such questions than a Court of law upon *certiorari* proceedings"? Is the Court at some disadvantage in *certiorari* proceedings that it is not when an appeal is taken from the Municipal Board? What would be "the benefit of the Board's opinion" to the Court of Appeal?

ONTARIO TEACHERS' FEDERATION *v.* DUNCAN

Ontario. Court of Appeal. 1958. 15 D.L.R. (2d) 358

AYLESWORTH J.A. delivered the judgment of the Court: This is an appeal by leave under s. 98 of the *Ontario Municipal Board Act*, R.S.O. 1950, c. 262, from a decision of the Ontario Municipal Board delivered on April 24, 1957 setting aside an order of the Committee of Adjustment of the City of Toronto dated October 31, 1956, which granted permission to the appellant to make certain additions to a building owned by it at 34 Prince Arthur Ave. in the City of Toronto. The appeal by the terms of the leave permitting it to be brought is limited to the following question: "Did the Ontario Municipal Board err in holding that the Committee of Adjustment of the City of Toronto had no jurisdiction in the matter?" . . .

The appellant some years ago acquired the residential property known as "34 Prince Arthur Avenue". Since 1945 appellant has used the building on this property as its executive head office; it now proposes to construct an addition or extension to that building at the rear thereof costing approximately $100,000. To that end and pursuant to s. 18 of the *Planning Act*, it duly made application to the Committee of Adjustment for the City of Toronto for exemption from the city's zoning By-law No. 18,642. The Committee granted the application for the following reason: "The Committee of Adjustment is of the opinion that the proposed addition is the extension or enlargement of an existing legal non-conforming use on to lands which were owned and used at time of passing of the by-law and will continue to be used in the same manner and for the same purpose." The Ontario Municipal Board allowed respondent's appeal and dismissed appellant's application to the Committee of Adjustment on the ground that By-law No. 8,834 of the City of Toronto as amended by By-law No. 16,347 was continued in effect by By-law No. 18,642 and "if the use being made of the building in question was permitted by By-law No. 8,834 so amended, then such use was not a use prohibited by By-law No. 18,642. If it was not a use so prohibited, then it does not qualify as a use that may be extended under the provisions of s. 18(2) (*a*) (i) of the Planning Act". Comment upon these various by-laws is essential to the determination of the appeal.

On September 26, 1921 By-law No. 8,834 was enacted, being a by-law to prohibit the use of land or the erection or use of buildings on property fronting or abutting on either side of Prince Arthur Ave. between Avenue Rd. and Huron St. for any other purpose than that of a detached private residence. On June 12, 1945 By-law No. 16,347 was enacted. . . . The by-law declares in terms that the provisions of By-law No. 8,834 "shall not apply to prevent the use of any building which, at the date of passing hereof, is located on any lands abutting on the north side of Prince Arthur Avenue, between Bedford Road and a point 300 feet east thereof, for the purpose of executive administrative quarters of any association of teachers engaged in publicly maintained schools, and the said By-law No. 8,834 is hereby repealed insofar as it prevents such use of such building". 34 Prince Arthur Ave. lies on the north side of the street "between Bedford Road and 300 feet east". It is to be observed that the combined effect of these two by-laws was to sanction what is the present use of the building on the premises known as 34 Prince Arthur Ave.; the rest of the premises apart from the building itself, and even the building save as to the existing use remained subject to the restrictions of By-law No. 8,834.

Before considering the present zoning by-law it is pertinent to turn to the provisions of s-s. 6 of s. 390 of the *Municipal Act*, R.S.O. 1950, c. 243. The relevant provisions of that subsection read as follows: "(6) No by-law passed under this section" (*i.e.* a by-law establishing a restricted area) "shall apply to any . . . building . . . which, on the day of the passing of the by-law, is used . . . for any purposes prohibited by the by-law, so long as it continues to be used for that purpose." The matter thus stood until the enactment of the City of Toronto Zoning By-law No. 18,642 pursuant to the provisions of s. 390 of the *Municipal Act*.

The city has duly availed itself of the provisions of the *Planning Act* by the adoption of an Official Plan and by the enactment of its By-law No. 18,642. The provisions of the by-law designate the area in which 34 Prince Arthur Ave. is situate as an R2V1 area and in consequence envisage new construction in that area only for purposes which do not include the purpose for which the enlargement or extension is now sought by the appellant. What then is the present legal situation with respect to the two former By-laws Nos. 8,834 and 16,347? In my view, so far as the immediate problem in the case at bar is concerned, these by-laws are still in full force and effect; in other words, I can find nothing in either the provisions of the *Planning Act* or of Zoning By-law No. 18,642 which expressly or by implication in any way purports to alter the effect of these by-laws so far as the *existing* building is concerned; indeed, s-s. (6) of s. 390 of the *Municipal Act* (pursuant to which section the zoning by-law was enacted) expressly prohibits any by-law enacted pursuant thereto from having any such effect. It is said that s-s. (2) of s. 18 of the zoning by-law affects that situation. I think not. That subsection reads in its relevant parts as follows: "wherever the use of . . . any building . . . is prohibited by any restrictive by-law heretofore passed by the council of the corporation and is permitted by this by-law, the provisions of this by-law shall prevail and such restrictive by-law shall to that extent be deemed to have been repealed but shall otherwise remain in full force and effect." I am not concerned particularly whether By-law No. 8,834 as amended by By-law No. 16,347 so far as *the existing building* is concerned is or is not a restrictive by-law as defined by another part of this subsection which I need not quote; the by-law as amended certainly does not "prohibit" the existing use of the building and if it does not, then the conditions wherein that by-law is "to that extent . . .

deemed to have been repealed", by s-s. (2) of s. 18 of By-law No. 18,642 are not met. It follows that at the time appellant's application was made to the Committee of Adjustment, By-law No. 8,834 as amended permitted the existing use of the existing building but no more; the contemplated use of the balance of the premises was, and would continue to be prohibited by the zoning by-law unless the Committee had power under the *Planning Act* to permit that contemplated use and did so. The Committee has purported to do so and there remains for consideration, the question of whether or not it had that power. . . . [Aylesworth J.A. reproduced what is now in substance section 32 *b* (1) and (2) modified in an irrelevant respect, and continued:]

The application made to the Committee by the appellant in my view must be brought within the provisions of s-s. (2) (*a*) (i) if authority is to be found anywhere for the permission granted to the appellant by the Committee. I have italicized significant passages in this subsection. I think this wording precisely fits the appellant's case. The existing use of the building is permitted by By-law No. 8,834 as amended but that existing use nevertheless is "for a purpose" which Zoning By-law No. 18,642 prohibits generally. I distinguish between the employment of the two words "use" and "purpose" and I think the Statute deliberately distinguishes between them; the "purpose" of using the building as executive offices in this particular area, classed as R2V1, is a purpose prohibited by the zoning by-law, the actual "use" of the existing building for that purpose was in terms approved by By-law No. 8,834 as amended. An illustration of a similar distinction between the employment of the words "use" and "purpose" is to be found in the provisions of s-s. (6) of s. 390 of the *Municipal Act*. Not only do I think that this distinction follows from the proper interpretation of the *Planning Act* but that the interpretation placed upon it by the Ontario Municipal Board is contrary to the whole scheme and intent of the Act as expressed therein.

This view of the matter makes it unnecessary for me to consider certain other submissions respectively put forward by counsel for the appellant and respondent. I conclude that the Ontario Municipal Board was in error and that the question addressed to this Court should be answered in the affirmative. The order of this Court will so certify to the Ontario Municipal Board and the proceedings accordingly will be remitted to the Board for rehearing and disposition under s-ss. (15) *et seq.* of s. 18 of the *Planning Act.* Respondent will pay the costs of this appeal, including the costs of the application to this Court for leave, to appellant. There will be no order as to the costs of the Attorney-General for Ontario.

[The italicised words in subsection (2)(a)(i) were: "the committee where any building was used for a purpose prohibited by the by-law and such use has continued until the date of the application to the committee, may permit (i) the enlargement or extension of the building or structure."]

2. Constitution: Personnel and Procedure

MUNICIPAL ACT

British Columbia. Revised Statutes. 1960. Chapter 255

708. (1) Where a Council has adopted a zoning by-law, there shall be established by by-law a Zoning Board of Appeal of three members, as follows:—

(*a*) One appointed by the Council, concerned; and

(*b*) One appointed by the Lieutenant-Governor in Council; and

(*c*) A Chairman, who shall be appointed by the other appointees.

(2) Each member appointed shall hold office for a term of three years or until his successor is appointed, but a person may be reappointed for a further term or terms.

(3) No person who is a member of the Advisory Planning Commission of the municipality or holds municipal office or municipal employment in the municipality is eligible to be appointed or to sit as a member of the Zoning Board of Appeal for the municipality.

(7) The appointee of a Council may be removed at any time by the Council concerned, and the appointee of the Lieutenant-Governor in Council may likewise be removed at any time by the Lieutenant-Governor in Council; the Chairman may be removed at any time by the Lieutenant-Governor in Council on the recommendation of the Council.

THE TOWN AND RURAL PLANNING ACT

Alberta. Revised Statutes. 1955. Chapter 337

81. (1) A zoning by-law shall establish an appeal board consisting of

(a) at least three persons, to be appointed annually by resolution of the council, none of whom shall be officials or servants of the council and a majority of whom shall consist of persons other than members of the council, or

(b) the Board,

except that when a zoning by-law applies to a part or parts of a municipality while the remainder of the municipality continues to be subject to interim development control, the zoning appeal board shall act as the interim development appeal board.

(2) A municipality other than a new town, an improvement district or a special area that is represented on a district planning commission or that employs a professional planning staff of one or more qualified persons, shall not establish the Board as the appeal board.

(5*a*) A decision of the zoning appeal board with respect to an appeal under subsection (3) is final and binding and there shall be no appeal therefrom.

THE PLANNING ACT

Ontario. Revised Statutes. 1960. Chapter 296

32*a*. (1) . . . the council . . . may by by-law constitute and appoint a committee of adjustment . . . composed of such persons, not less than three, as the council deems advisable.

(3) Every appointment to a committee of adjustment is subject to the approval of the Minister, but in no event is a member of the council of the municipality or an employee of the municipality or of a local board thereof eligible for appointment.

[A school teacher is eligible, ss. (2).]

(12) The committee shall adopt such rules of procedure as are approved by the Minister, and no committee shall hear or determine any matter unless such rules have heretofore been or are hereafter so adopted and approved, and such rules may be amended with the approval of the Minister.

(13) The Minister may require a committee to amend or revise its rules of procedure and, if the committee fails to comply with such require-

ment within the time limited by the Minister, it is without jurisdiction to hear or determine any matter until its rules are amended or revised and approved by the Minister.

32*b*. (7) . . . the decision of the committee, whether granting or refusing an application, shall be in writing and shall set out the reasons for the decision, and shall be signed by the members who concur in the decision. [Sections 32*a* and 32*b* were enacted by S.O., 1961–62, c. 104, s. 8.]

COMMITTEE RULES OF PROCEDURE

Ontario. Department of Planning and Development. 1962

Notice of Hearing

4. The Committee shall in the first instance consider each application and determine the persons to whom, and the manner in which, notice of the hearing of such application shall be given, and shall issue directions to the secretary-treasurer accordingly and in particular without limiting the foregoing may direct:

(a) at least one insertion be placed in the local press not less than seven days before the hearing; and

(b) that a notice be mailed to any interested public bodies such as railways or departments of the Federal, Provincial or Municipal government.

5. In addition to complying with any directions which may be issued under Rule 4, the secretary-treasurer shall send written notice of the hearing setting forth the time and place thereof and a summary of the relief applied for, not less than 10 days prior to the day of hearing to the applicant, the municipal clerk, the secretary-treasurer of the planning board, the building inspector, and each encumbrancer of the land concerned, and to all assessed owners within at least two hundred feet of the land concerned.

6. Such notice of hearing may be sent by regular mail to the assessed owners at the address shown on the latest revised assessment roll, but shall be sent by registered mail to the applicant and the owners of adjoining lands.

Hearing

7. Signed written submissions, will be received by the secretary-treasurer prior to the hearing, such written submissions to be available for inspection at the hearing by any interested person.

8. The Committee may request any municipal official to produce at the hearing, all papers and plans which in the opinion of the Committee may be of assistance on the hearing of the application, such papers and plans to be returned following the final disposition of the application and where the application is made in respect of a previous decision given by the official he may submit in writing a concise summary of his decision and the reasons therefor.

9. Where a hearing is adjourned and the Committee does not at the time of adjournment fix a time and place for the further hearing of the application and announce it to those in attendance, it should be the duty of the chairman of the Committee to announce to those in attendance that notice of the time and place for the further hearing will be sent to only those persons who leave their name and addess with the secretary-treasurer, and thereafter only such persons as do leave their name and address as provided should be entitled to notice of the further hearing.

[The rules above are taken from a current revision by the Minister of the rules he suggests to committees of adjustment and which he is prepared to approve under section 32*a* (12).]

COMMUNITY PLANNING ACT
New Brunswick. Statutes. 1960–61. Chapter 6

22(1) The zoning by-law shall establish a zoning appeal board for the municipality consisting of a chairman and four other members to be appointed by the council, but the members shall not be members of the council or the commission.

(3) The chairman of the zoning appeal board shall be a barrister of at least five years' standing unless, in the opinion of the council, this is impractical.

TOWN PLANNING ACT
Nova Scotia. Revised Statutes. 1954. Chapter 292.

20.(1) Appeal shall lie to the council in the following cases:

(a) by any person who is dissatisfied with the decision of any official charged with the enforcement of a zoning by-law;

(b) by any person desiring to obtain the benefit of any exception contained in a zoning by-law;

(c) by any person claiming that owing to special conditions the literal enforcement of a zoning by-law would result in unnecessary hardship;

(d) in any other cases where provision for appeal is made by a zoning by-law.

(2) No appeal shall be from the decision of the council.

THE URBAN AND RURAL PLANNING ACT, 1953
Newfoundland. Statutes. 1953. Number 27

31. When the Municipal Plan comes into effect the authorized Council shall develop fully a scheme for the control of the use of land in strict conformity with the Municipal Plan and shall prepare

(a) a map dividing the Municipal Area into use districts; and

(b) regulations prescribing

(i) the proposed use of land and buildings in the districts referred to in paragraph (a);

(ii) the conditions upon which a permit may be granted for the development of land, the subdivision of land, the erection of buildings or structures, or the change of the use of any land or building; and

(iii) provisions for appeal to the Advisory Board against any decision of the authorized Council relating to the use of land.

[Section 31 was amended by S.N., 1955, no. 19, s. 4.]

NOTE ON PROCEDURE. Notice. The Ontario Act leaves the matter of notice of an agency (committee) hearing to the discretion of the committee. In practice the committee probably only meets once a week, if that often, and the notices are probably sent out by the secretary-treasurer. Is this a valid delegation of the committee's duty to decide what notice should be sent? The secretary-treasurer probably asks the assessment department for the names and addresses of all ratepayers likely to be affected, or living within the prescribed range of 200 feet. Is this subdelegation? How else could the committee arrange to give notice? Is it practicable for the committee to examine each case on its merits and instruct the secretary-treasurer how to proceed? Is it fair to the applicant to force the delay this procedure requires? Could a decision based on a hearing at which notice was sent in the discretion of the secretary-treasurer or the assessment department be quashed? Would it be sufficient if in each case, at the hearing, the committee investigated the notice and ratified it if satisfied and postponed the hearing if further notice in its opinion is required?

The length of notice is also a matter for concern, particularly if the case is complex, and the committee, or the secretary-treasurer relies on the post office. In smaller places postal service may be very uncertain. Equally uncertain is advertising in the local newspaper. In larger cities this is an uneconomic method because the committee will be paying for distribution to thousands when the legitimate target is probably a dozen. Advertising in the local press in smaller centres is cheap enough, but the risk of not being read is even greater. Some committees "post the premises" by which is meant that a notice of the hearing is posted outside the applicant's premises for passersby to read. While this has some advantages it might be a mistake for the agency to rely upon it exclusively. Posting and notification by mail and advertising in the local (small town) press may be desirable in combination and they are frequently not too much to expect. On the other hand, there may be cases where no notice at all is necessary because the application is for some trifling variance and there are no very close neighbours. This is especially true in the case of early development in large subdivisions before any houses are sold and the only neighbour of the lot on the plan is the owner of the whole subdivision.

The matter of notice is probably the touchiest matter the committee deals with. More criticism will be directed toward the committee that notice was not received than that the decision is wrong on the merits. This is probably particularly true in Ontario where a right of appeal is provided for. Every care must be taken by an applicant to ensure that notice is adequate solely to protect himself in the event of a favourable decision. Is an applicant entitled to ask what notice has been given, to whom, and when?

Hearings. Hearings are presumably always public and the notice should have given a reasonable indication of the relief sought. At the hearing opportunity to present views should be given to all who ask for it, and in Ontario the chairman of the committee is authorized to administer oaths. This is the only suggestion of the formality of the hearing, which, because of the subject matter, can easily degenerate into an unorganized exchange of intemperate remarks between members of the public, particularly in a case where the variance is substantial or the applicant is a social outcast. Family quarrels have been known to seize upon this forum for outlet. This is one reason why an experienced lawyer (barrister, that is) is likely to be better able to conduct a hearing. Occasionally in Ontario an applicant, or sometimes a citizen opposing the application, will retain a lawyer. This may help the committee conduct an orderly meeting. It is possible for the committee to insist upon those who wish to speak waiting their turn, and to call upon them in some order.

Since the committee must hear the applicant there cannot be a hearing in the applicant's absence and the application must simply lie in abeyance.

Since the committee must hear "every other person who desires to be heard" it cannot refuse to hear a person who refuses to identify himself. Nor can it refuse to hear a person with no special interest beyond that of any citizen, whether resident in the municipality or not, who chooses to be heard.

A public hearing is presumably one in a place referred to in the notice and open to anyone who comes along. Could the hearing be held in a municipal office (mentioned in the notice) but otherwise behind closed doors?

Fact Finding. Under the Ontario Act the committee may or may not announce any determinations of fact. The Act is silent, although the committee must give written reasons for its decisions. Findings of fact are perhaps not necessary since the appeal to the Ontario Municipal Board is by way of trial *de novo.* Nevertheless the committee must find its jurisdictional facts before going further, and there will normally be both "adjudicative facts" and "legislative facts" to be determined. How far can the committee act "administratively" in finding its facts, or in collecting evidence? How free is it to inquire of other municipal departments before or after the public hearing? Can a committee examine any evidence received after the hearing? Can the committee call witnesses? Is there any right of cross-examination? Who are the adversaries? Is an applicant or any objecting neighbour entitled as of right to be represented by counsel?

The kind of facts the committee normally requires are suggested by the form of application. The investigation is usually into the neighbourhood, not only the applicant's property. Consequently drawings and maps, photographs, color slides, verbal descriptions are all helpful, if they show both the applicant's property and the area around it. Information about land use, the age of buildings, their size, set back, general condition, appearance, and the state of vegetation are often essential matters. Aerial or ground photographs or both, are helpful if the committee does not go to look at the property. Is a committee obliged to view the property? May it properly do so in the absence of the applicant? Of any objecting neighbour? What dangers are involved for the committee investigating the site on its own?

Reasons. The Ontario Act requires the committee to give its reasons in writing. Such a requirement is not made of a court and the courts have not insisted upon it in administrative tribunals generally. On an appeal to the Municipal Board, the Board, unlike the committee, does not have to give reasons. Requiring written reasons has a sound basis in intellectual discipline, for it forces the decider (or the author of the written reasons) to think out his problem more precisely than is likely if he can slough it off orally. This virtue may, in view of North American practice, enure to the benefit of the secretary-treasurer rather than the committee members. Properly written reasons also assure those participating in the hearing that their arguments were heard if not followed.

The writing of reasons might be thought to be impossible without a finding of facts, but the usual committee decision follows the requirements of the Act quite literally, and the statement of reasons stands by itself, detached from findings. A record of the finding is preserved usually in the minutes of the hearing, which the Act requires to be certified by the secretary-treasurer. The substance of the reasons depends upon the grounds provided for agency action, and for Ontario these grounds may be closely examined in the next section, where several decisions are reproduced.

Conditions. The committee under Ontario legislation may attach terms and conditions to its decisions. Free use is made of this power and experience may show that it is too freely used. Committees are sometimes asked to attach the condition that the applicant keep his premises in a neat orderly condition. This is particularly true in the case of extension of non-conforming uses, say, a service station, where the neighbours are prepared to withdraw their objections if the presently untidy station is cleaned up. Is the committee entitled to insist upon terms and conditions not required of conforming stations? If this is regarded as a legitimate price for the continued and expanded monopoly, is the committee entitled to insist upon conditions the by-law could not have imposed? Suppose a non-conforming service station is coupled with a run-down non-conforming motel business and the objecting neighbours ask that the motel shacks be torn down as part of the price of enlarging the service station? Suppose that the application is not to enlarge the service station but to commence a sand and gravel business at the rear of the lot consisting of say twenty acres, and the objectors insist that the shacks be removed. Is this a form of legalized blackmail?

In Ontario the committee, under s. 32*b* (2) (c) has a kind of interpretive power. Can it attach conditions when the only jurisdiction is under that clause? If the committee approves the application as a use for a purpose "which, in the opinion of the committee, conforms with the uses permitted in the by-law", but attaches conditions, could the applicant apply for mandamus to compel the issuance of a building permit without the conditions? Can a court attach conditions on a mandamus application?

Appeals and Review by the Provincial Authority. The system of administrative appeal set up in Ontario for committees of adjustment is an unusual system in common law jurisdictions. Other Canadian provinces have administrative appeals, to the provincial Minister in charge or to an administrative tribunal, but nothing is published and the procedure is not known to the editor, and not known to be as formal a procedure as in Ontario. Not only may any interested party appeal (even the municipal corporation?) but the Minister himself may appeal to the Board in Ontario. Formerly the Minister supervised the committees more directly, through exercise of an approving power, but his right to interfere is now limited to appeal. In this way, however, it is theoretically possible for the Minister still to supervise as closely as before, but the volume of work demands an extensive staff if appeals are to be intelligently processed. Since the Minister is rather remote from the land involved in the appeal, unless he has an investigator in the field his supervision is likely to suffer the weaknesses of absentee management. Lawyers sometimes struggle to get the committee to decide in their favour on the theory that if the Minister appeals, the Municipal Board will tend to support the local decision against attack on what are usually grounds of jurisdiction rather than the merits.

NOTE ON APPEALS IN ONTARIO. Section 32*b* (12) of *The Planning Act* permits the applicant, the Minister or any other person who has an interest in the matter to appeal to the Municipal Board. In an enlarged report of his talk at a Committee of Adjustment Conference in May of 1957. Mr. Cumming is reported [*Ontario Planning* (1957), Volume 4, No. 7] to have said that the appeal is a complete re-hearing, a trial *de novo*. "A practical consideration necessitating a re-hearing is the fact that there is no record before the Board of what was said at the Committee's hearing. Since the Board is not a court, it has no power to rule that the Committee exceeded its jurisdiction and that its decision was illegal. If the facts show that the Committee did act in excess of its powers, it would appear that the decision of the Committee is legally a nullity and an application might be made to a court to have it so declared. So far as the Board is concerned, the questions before it as an administrative tribunal are whether the Board itself has the power to grant the application and whether the application should be granted, either in the form originally applied for, or in some other form. If the Board happens to exceed its powers, there is provision in the *Ontario Municipal Board Act* for an appeal directly to the Ontario Court of Appeal."

Speaking of the committee's participation in the appeal process, Mr. Cumming said, "It's true their (the Committee's) decision is in writing . . . but I see nothing whatever wrong with the idea that a member of a Committeee of Adjustment, or for that matter, all the members of a Committee of Adjustment should appear before the Board on the hearing of an appeal and give any further information that is available . . . and defend their decision." Is it proper for a trial judge to sit in the public part of the court of appeal when that court is hearing an appeal from him? What objections might be taken? Should similar objections apply to a committee of adjustment member at a Municipal Board hearing?

NOTE AND QUESTIONS ON LEGISLATIVE POLICY. The variety of legislative policy shown above leaves open for reflection a number of questions about the constitution and function of administrative adjustment agencies. There is no unanimity of legislative opinion that the agency should be the council, a separate body but including a majority of council members, a separate body having a minority of council members or a separate body having no council members. Ontario used to straddle the fence nicely by giving the local council an option. If the council wished to have some voice it could persuade the planning board to declare itself to be the committee. Then if there were council members on the board (they cannot be a majority) they could sit as committee members. Planning boards adopted this course in some municipalities solely to ensure council membership on the committee. What are the advantages in keeping council members off, or allowing the council to act as the adjusting body? Compare *The Assessment Act*, R.S.O., 1960, c. 23, s. 64, which allows a council to name council members to the Court of Revision for assessment appeals.

Apart from negative qualifications the legislation is silent as to the kind of person who should be appointed. In Ontario if the planning board constituted itself as the committee the presumption was that the members would know something about planning, or at least be interested in planning, although the better the board's staff the less the board member need know. Is a knowledge of planning desirable in an agency member? Is the function of an adjusting agency a "planning" function or an "executing" function? Is the distinction a sensible one? Would a lawyer make a good member? Compare the backgrounds of Ontario Municipal Board members which include the law, municipal civil service including planning, Ontario land surveyers, and engineering. Why is the Minister's approval required of the appointment of a committee of adjustment member in Ontario?

Can a member become disqualified from interest? Suppose a committee member lives in the same area as the land that is the subject of the application. Must he retire from the hearing and decision? Would it be sufficient that he disclose his interest? Can a member be a member of a ratepayers' association? Would he be disqualified in a case where the ratepayers' association appeared at the hearing to support or resist an application?

In Ontario objection is sometimes heard, usually on the hustings, that planning board members should not be on the committee of adjustment. Is there any merit in this objection? Does the committee ever hear "appeals" from planning board decisions? Since the planning board recommended the official plan to the council and the "zoning" by-law must implement the plan, and the committee is asked to authorize a variance from the by-law, is the committee being asked to overrule a decision of the board? How closely does a plan have to coincide with the text of the by-law, or vice versa?

The Ontario Act authorizes the committee of adjustment to engage employees and consultants. Whether this happens depends upon the generosity of the appointing council. What qualifications should the secretary-treasurer have? Should he be a planner or an administrator? If the secretary-treasurer is an administrator should the committee also retain a planner on a part time or full time basis? Originally an Ontario committee could only be set up if there was an official plan in effect. There will almost certainly be a planning board if there is a plan. Should the committee refer applications to the board or to the board's staff? In some cases the secretary-treasurer of the committee of adjustment is the secretary-treasurer of the planning board. Is there any objection to this? In the Ontario "suggested" rules of procedure prepared by the Department, there is provision for consulting municipal employees. Is this a practicable suggestion? How can the committee discipline the employees who fail to reply to their requests for advice or information? If a committee asks for help from the assessment department, and it is overworked and understaffed (notwithstanding Parkinson's Law, a common enough condition) should the application be held up while the committee waits for a reply? The committee may make substantial use of a number of municipal departments: the building inspector and zoning administrator, the assessment commissioner, the engineer and the planning staff. Yet there may be a complete lack of liaison, despite the Minister's recommended rule of procedure. Should an applicant who thinks his position may be helped insist that a municipal official be consulted? Can a council request or demand that the committee use the council's staff and require its staff to cooperate?

Committee of adjustment decisions in Ontario are rarely published. It is not known to the editor that the decisions of agencies in other provinces are reported either. The decisions reproduced below have for the most part been obtained privately. The general practice throughout North America is said to be that the decision is made by the agency but is written by the secretary-treasurer. Is this a good practice? What is the value of writing a decision? Of giving reasons, as required by the Ontario Act? Will this division of responsibility produce unwise or hasty decisions wth reasons that are pure rationalizations, whereas they might be only partial rationalizations if written by the man who decides? Or will it result in the secretary-treasurer deciding the case in everything but name? Is this a Bad Thing?

3. Some Decisions For Discussion

The decisions below are not necessarily typical of decisions written by committees of adjustment in Ontario but it is hoped that they raise problems typical of those faced by committees and that the written reasons will give some help in understanding how the problems, which are both jurisdictional and substantive, can be solved. The form of these decisions is more elaborate than most. The decision of the city of Toronto Committee of

Adjustment reproduced in the *Ontario Teachers' Federation* case is typical of that Committee. There are no reasons given. Instead the Committee recites its belief that the application comes within its jurisdiction and this belief is stated after the words "reasons for decision." Other committees, around the province, write decisions varying between the sketchy "reason" given by Toronto and the perhaps too verbose decision of Toronto Township.

Whatever else the written reasons contain, for the sake of clarity they should state the findings necessary for jurisdiction; that the applicant is the owner of the land and the facts necessary to reach the conclusion that the variance is minor, that the use is a continuing non-conforming use, or as the case may be. There should also be a sufficient statement of the by-law requirements to make clear precisely what variance or concession is required. The reasons should be set out so that the applicant and those who were heard for and against can tell whether the committee understood their positions even if it disagrees with some of them. Whatever else the committee is expected by law to do, it has an important function in helping people to understand what zoning is about and how communities grow. One of its most important jobs is to give those who object to a variance the opportunity to "let off steam." A committee that herds applications and applicants through like cattle and looks rather tired and bored by the whole proceeding is hardly doing its job. Even hotly contested applications do not take over an hour or so to hear and the time is well spent, usually, in securing greater public understanding of the legal process and the character and growth of the community. Perhaps nowhere are the merits of "zoning" more severely tested than before the adjusting agency. Here, perhaps for the first time in the "planning process" the individual owner is heard on a specific land use dispute. Here, the roles of fiat and reason are clearly exposed and the agency has no easy task in deciding how far to support fiat.

(*a*) *Minor variances*

RE GEAR AND VERNON

Township of Toronto. Committee of Adjustment. 1956. Unreported

This is an application by Dr. J. Gear, Dr. Elizabeth Vernon and Dr. Howard Vernon, owners in equity of a lot having a frontage of 110 feet and a depth of 120 feet with an area of 13,200 square feet on the south side of Sayers Road, in Clarkson. On this lot, which is in an R3 Zone, the applicants propose to erect a one-storey building with an area of 3,000 square feet designed to be used as a four doctor medical clinic. By-law 1614, as amended, contains no provision expressly permitting medical clinics of the kind proposed; hence this application.

The Committee is confronted with two problems of unusual difficulty. The first relates to the jurisdiction of the Committee. We have to decide whether the departure from the permitted land uses in R3 zones comes within the meaning of "minor variance" in s. 18(1) of *The Planning Act, 1955,* which sets out the Committee's powers and jurisdiction. The second problem goes to the merits of the case. Can we properly hold the opinion the requested variance is "desirable for the appropriate development or use of the land, building or structure" and can we properly hold the opinion that "the general intent and purpose of the by-law and of the official plan" will be maintained. Although the solution to the first problem of jurisdiction would, if unfavourable to the applicants, eliminate the need to consider the second problem at all, we find it convenient even if more troublesome for us, to consider the merits of the application first, so that we may better appreciate the problem of jurisdiction.

The application was opposed by some fifteen residents in the neighbourhood who expressed themselves vigorously and with some emotion. The Committee could hardly be blamed if it conceded to this opposition without further consideration of the merits. But we believe that if we have the power to approve an application, we have a corresponding duty to deal responsibly with it. We cannot shirk that responsibility merely because of numerical opposition. Numbers alone ought not to carry much weight with a Committee of Adjustment. A committee is appointed to consider applications on their merits, and council members, who are elected by secret ballot, and who are expected to respond to majority will, regardless of its rational basis, are not permitted to sit on a Committee. We must look only at the rational arguments of those who oppose an application, and if the argument is convincing, then we must accept it, even if it is advanced by only one opponent to the applicant. But if, in a case such as this, we conclude as a responsible body of rational men, that what the applicants ask for ought to be considered "desirable for the appropriate development or use of the land" and that the "general intent and purpose of the by-law and of the official plan is maintained", we have no choice but to approve.

The consideration of the merits of this application requires us to examine into the existing land uses in the area affected, the permitted land uses under By-law 1614, as amended from time to time, the true character and effect the proposed use might have on existing uses and values, and throughout, the merits of the objections lodged with the Committee by letter and by oral submission at the public hearing.

First: *The Existing Land Uses.*

The applicants' lot fronts on Sayers Road, facing roughly north 168 feet east of the Clarkson Road. Sayers Road is a short road running easterly from the Clarkson Road 350 feet then turning a right angle north for a distance of about 350 feet until it joins Birchwood Drive, which runs easterly from the Clarkson Road parallel with the first part of Sayers Road. Birchwood Drive is the main entrance road to the Birchwood Subdivision, Plan 389. The applicants' lot is vacant land, containing a few fruit trees not apparently professionally cared for. West to the Clarkson Road is vacant land and along the line of the Clarkson Road is a line of evergreens. South of the lot is more vacant land, until one comes to a gully or small ravine. Across the ravine are a number of older houses on spacious grounds, fronting on the Clarkson Road. The second house has been recently built and has not yet been occupied. To the east of the lot is vacant land and what was described as a right of way, a projection of Sayers Road south. Along the right of way is a line of quite tall and thick evergreens. The right of way leads to the Pines Rest Home, a commercial establishment in spacious grounds almost hidden in the trees. Continuing east beyond the right of way is a 66 foot lot, itself presumably a once proposed right of way on which permission was sought from this Committee to build a house. The permission was refused (see Submission No. 50). North of this lot, which is still vacant is the property of Mr. Ernest Robinson, who has a relatively new residence built some years before By-law 1614 was passed. North of Mr. Robinson's lot lies a lot on Plan 389, which has a frontage of about 270 feet. This lot was, after By-law 1614 was passed, divided into two lots each with 135 feet frontage on Sayers Road. Neither lot of course conformed with the requirements of an R2 Zone, which requires 180 feet frontage when neither municipal water nor sewer is available. Both lots have, however, with the permission of this Committee, been built upon as a result of a previous submission. West of Sayers Road, opposite the recently divided lots just described, lies Lot 71 on Plan 389, which was also, with the permission of this Committee subdivided into two 135 foot lots fronting on Sayers Road.

On the north half of Lot 71 a new house has been erected, but the south half remains vacant although it too has several fruit trees, not professionally cared for. West of Lot 71 are three lots fronting on the Clarkson Road. North of the intersection of Sayers Road and the Clarkson Road on the first of these lots is the home of Doctors Howard and Elizabeth Vernon, two of the applicants in this case, who carry on a medical practice in full conformity with By-law 1614 and the restrictive covenants of Plan 389. The properties just described are, in the opinion of this Committee the properties immediately affected by this application. If we were to extend the affected area any further it would be only to take in the adjacent properties west of the Clarkson Road between the Hydro line on the north and the property opposite that adjoining the nursing home on the south. It perhaps should be noted that the affected area includes only a small portion of the area comprising Plan 389, which the Committee concedes to be one of the finest residential developments in the Township and due almost entirely to the foresight and wisdom of the subdivider, Mrs. A. L. Sayers. We say, without qualification, that if, in our opinion, to approve this application would have any serious effect on the residential development anywhere in Plan 389 we should not approve it. What may be called the internal area of Plan 389 is separated from the part just described by a fairly deep ravine and thick bush. The nearest houses are at least seven hundred feet away from the proposed clinic. We cannot agree that any internal lot could be adversely affected by this application.

It will be seen, then, that the existing land uses in the affected area are mostly residential, but there is one home where occupants, two of the applicants, operate a medical practice, and there is a nursing home. Neither "commercial" use seriously detracts from the residential character of the area, although various witnesses testified that as many as seven cars sometimes including trucks, were seen parked on Sayers Road near the doctors' office door in their house. No off-street parking is provided by the doctors.

Second, The Permitted Uses.

The affected area is all zoned for residential use, most of it being R2 or R3, the boundary being that part of Sayers Road running east and west, and east of the turn of Sayers Road, but somewhat south of it. Across the Clarkson Road the zoning is entirely R3. Plan 389 is zoned R2, internally and externally. It is not, however, to be supposed that the only permitted uses are houses of a minimum floor area (one storey) of 1,100 square feet (R2) or 900 square feet (R3). Several other land uses and buildings are permitted *anywhere* in these zones.

By-law 1614 in s. 36(b) permits a "physician, dentist, or drugless practitioner" to establish an office for consulting and emergency treatment in the one family dwelling used by him as his private residence. It is under this authority that the applicants, Drs. Vernon are conforming, although since they commenced their practice in their present home prior to the passing of By-law 1614, it could not adversely affect their right to continue their practice. It may be of interest to consider the implication of this use. Nothing in the by-law would prohibit the applicant Dr. Gear from acquiring a building lot on Sayers Road and erecting a large home there, part of which be devoted to his medical practice. A second lot might be similarly used by the as yet unnamed doctor who will be the fourth man in the proposed clinic. It is true, the last lot vacant on Sayers Road on the north side would probably not knowingly be sold to a doctor, since it is owned by Mrs. Sayers, who opposes the application, and the existing house east of the turn on Sayers Road, which is said to be for sale, would not be sold to a doctor, because the owner, Mr. Robinson, opposes the application (although his interest will be less once he has sold to anyone). But on the south side of Sayers Road there is vacant property which might well be sold for doctors' homes since the present owner, Miss Cain, not only supports the application but also has sold the land that is the subject of the application. If Dr. Gear and the fourth doctor were to purchase lots as we have suggested, Sayers Road would become a doctors' alley without adequate parking space or traffic controls. Sayers Road itself would then become a parking lot.

By-law 1752, passed June 28th, 1954, by s. 6 added clause (4) to s. 36 of By-law 1614 thus permitting *anywhere* in R1 to R4 zones the erection of 100 bed hospitals. Now it may be argued that this section has spent itself since the site of the South Peel Hospital has been selected. This may be an optimistic view since any private person, or a religious organization could decide to erect a hospital and provided it was a "general hospital of Group B or Group C class as defined in the regulations made under the Public Hospitals Act" it would be permitted. The definition of "Group B or Group C class" in the regulations seems to relate only to size and no other part of the regulations or the Act itself has been incorporated into the By-law.

By-law 1614, s. 36(d) permits the use of land or buildings for a religious or educational purpose other than the operation of a trade school (as defined in By-law 1752). Under this provision the South Peel School Board could acquire by expropriation and any private person by purchase, the land south of Sayers Road and erect a kindergarten school to accommodate 200 five year olds, almost all of whom would have to be brought by car or bus. The present by-law makes no attempt to regulate the conditions under which schools might be built. If this proposal seems to be improbable, it is well to remember that the Separate School Board is reported to the Committee to have recently acquired land for a school just south of the affected area, on the east side of the Clarkson Road, and the South Peel Board has land on the Lorne Park Road extending west, close to the north-easterly lots in Plan 389. We also had our attention drawn to the recent establishment of a lying-in home for unwed mothers on Meadow Wood Road, another residential area of the same kind as Plan 389. Not very long ago the United Church in Clarkson was looking for a new site and tentatively selected Lots 18 and 19 on Plan B-24 which is in the heart of what is now Plan 389. At the time many voices were raised in protest and the Church succeeded in acquiring a better site elsewhere.

By-law No. 1614, s. 36(c) also permits a public authority to establish a park, playground, recreational area or community centre *anywhere* in R1 to R4 Zones, and anyone may establish a public or private golf course.

It is quite clear then that the concept of residential zones under By-law

1614, as amended, is not one of pure residential use, but includes several community and professional services, in particular doctors' offices in homes and hospitals of at least 100 beds. No regulation of these two uses is set out, as to parking space, set backs or traffic control.

Third, The True Character and Effect of the Proposed Use.

It will be convenient here to comment on the particular proposal and the appropriate use class in which it ideally belongs, as well as the effect it would have in areas where other classes of use are permitted.

The proposal is for a one storey brick building with a flat overhanging roof and high small windows, with an attractive central entrance fronting diagonally on the lot so that it would face the home of the Doctors Vernon. This building would take up 3,000 square feet on the lot. Septic tank weepers would take another 1,000 square feet, 9,200 square feet remain for parking space and landscaping. The attached drawing illustrates the possible landscaping and arrangement of parking space which could be sunk a foot below the general grade level. The result of this arrangement would be to take the parking at the entrance to Sayers Road and put it behind suitable screening by landscaping. The whole layout is, of course, subject to the conditions stated in this decision. In this building the participating doctors plan to practise independently, but sharing accommodation and office staff, and co-operating to the extent that *a* doctor would, by agreement, always be available through a telephone answering service. On the other hand, the building would not be used as a hospital. There would be no beds for patients, nor would the building be used as a residence. There would be no night parties or bright lights, only four doctors carrying on general practice, but able, because of their co-operation, to give greater service to the public, and, as Mr. Vernon suggests, prolong their lives. [Mr. James Vernon, a builder and a brother of Dr. Vernon, represented him at the hearing.]

Many of those who objected did so on the ground that clinics of this sort belonged in a commercial zone and the objectors volunteered the information that there was plenty of land available for the clinic to go somewhere else.

It is by no means clear that a medical clinic necessarily belongs in a commercial zone. It is true that in years to come the Trusteel development of Fairfields to the north on the Clarkson Road may include a shopping centre. But as Mr. Vernon, who represented the applicant, pointed out a modern shopping centre is scarcely the sort of place a pregnant hysterical woman suffering from haemorrhage would care to go to see her doctor. Economically, a clinic in such an area would almost have to be on the second storey, an added handicap to the patient. We are forced to agree that it is by no means settled that forcing a medical clinic into a shopping centre would be "desirable for the appropriate development" of land. As for available land the only other commercial land in this area is at the intersection of the Clarkson Road and the Lakeshore Highway.

Part of the Commercial Zone there has recently been considered for development as a shopping centre. The rest of the zone is almost completely built up and the uses include five service stations, two banks, a fruit stand, a variety of shops, in short, precisely the same uses one might find in a shopping centre, but without the convenience of proper parking facilities. The resulting traffic congestion is severe. Near the railway station in Clarkson there is some land zoned for industry. There is also a good deal of rail siding there for the B.A. Oil Refinery. We find the suggestion that a group of doctors should be forced into such an area in the name of community planning rather ludicrous. As Mr. Vernon (at the public hearing) pointed out, the vibrations from frequent shunting and the movements of trains would be a serious handicap for any doctor who is dependent upon quiet (freedom from such vibrations) for much of his diagnostical work. We are told that Dr. Dunn in Lorne Park has a clinic in a commercial zone close to the same railway. The Committee is well aware of Dr. Dunn's clinic, having approved variances for him at the time it was established (see Submission No. 308). But it must be remembered that Dr. Dunn selected the site himself, he was not forced into it by the state, and it is no answer to the land use argument merely to refer to Dr. Dunn near a railway, and other doctors in shopping centres. We are satisfied that commercial and industrial zones near railways are not particularly suitable for medical clinics.

Some of those who objected suggested that other residential land is available. Mr. Vernon replies to this that the Trusteel Company, the biggest owner of residential land in the area refused to sell to the clinic, except in the shopping center, which is, of course, still far in the future. But we are unimpressed by the suggestion that other residential land is to be preferred to the site selected by the applicants. The clinic will have the same effect on its environment wherever it is, and there seems to be little justice in yielding to the objections of these particular landowners rather than another group.

Almost everyone who objected to this application was careful to say that he was not opposing a clinic as such. In fact the service to be supplied was generally accepted as desirable. The proposal was attacked chiefly because it was "the thin edge of the wedge" and ultimately the residential character of the affected area would deteriorate into a disorganized commercial zone. The "thin edge" argument is particularly attractive apparently, but is perhaps the least valid of all. First, the application must be considered as a single, isolated proposition. The Committee has no jurisdiction to rezone an area. It can only deal with the property of the applicant. Second, this Committee can only deal with a minor variance from existing by-laws. One witness hinted broadly that if this clinic is permitted, he knew a rich man who intended to build a drug store next door. There is, of course, no reason for assuming that because this Committee permits a clinic it will also permit a drug store. To assume this is to suggest that this Committee is not governed by reason at all, but decides arbitrarily; and to suggest that this Committee is usually sympathetic to rich men. We ignore the slight on our reason and integrity. If we can permit a clinic, it is because moving from doctors' offices in their homes to doctors' offices in a properly designed building with adequate off street parking is but a minor variance from the permitted use. There is no such commercial use as a drug store permitted in the zone which could act as a starting point for the variance. We are satisfied that sensible planning theory can justify a clinic in the area; we are equally satisfied that the same theory would not justify a drug store.

Far from regarding our approval as the thin edge of the wedge, we would consider something much more insidious as more dangerous. If one could imagine anyone who dishonestly and in defiance, both of section 2 (2) of By-law 1614 and clause 1 of the Schedule to conveyances of lots in Plan 389, were to erect a house with a self-contained basement apartment and to rent that apartment, this abuse would, in the course of time, create quite a different kind of residential area. Curiously enough, the chairman of the Committee received on the day of the hearing, a piece of sales advertising with the only address 1565 Spring Road, a house in the internal part of Plan 389. It is the quiet, almost unnoticed creeping in of undesirable uses that constitutes the thin edge, not the open consideration of the application of a very restricted statutory power by a responsible Committee.

We are convinced, upon the whole case, that the establishment of a four doctor clinic on the applicants' lot, coupled with a cessation of the home office practice of the applicants, is desirable for the appropriate development of the land. We are also satisfied that if appropriate conditions, as laid down in this decision, are followed by the applicants, the other properties in the affected area will not be adversely affected.

Fourth, The Question of Jurisdiction: Minor Variances

Most applicants before this Committee ask for, say, a reduction in a side yard where the building to be erected conforms with the use permitted in the By-law. That is to say, they ask for a variance of some regulation, rather than a variance of a use. On the other hand a careful reading of section 18 of *The Planning Act, 1955*, leads us to believe that we must regard a variance of use, so long as it is minor, as coming within our jurisdiction. We may authorize such minor variance from a provision of the by-law, "in respect of the land, building or structure *or the use thereof*", as in our opinion is desirable for the appropriate development or use of the land. Subsection (2) of s. 18 contains a further power: under that section we may extend uses permitted in one zone into another on contiguous land where the land is in one ownership. This power clearly permits us to introduce prohibited uses into a zone. Furthermore, if *The Planning Act, 1955*, were not intended to confer the power to vary a use it could easily have been so stated in the Act, as is in fact the case in one of the western provinces. We are, therefore, satisfied that the Committee has jurisdiction to vary a use, and has, therefore, in appropriate cases, the duty to vary the use. There remains, however, the question whether the variance requested is minor. Where a variance in use is asked for, there is little possibility of measuring the variances in terms of number, as there is where a regulation of side yards, for example, is to be varied. If we are asked to reduce a 40 foot front yard to a 2 foot front yard, we know that only the most extraordinary conditions would justify calling the variance minor, if indeed any conditions would. But here we are dealing with a relatively unmeasurable quality rather than a quantity. We feel, however, that we do have a guide, of sorts. We can envisage the extreme application of the permitted use in the by-law and compare the proposal with that extreme.

That is, we can envisage the situation described earlier in this decision where Sayers Road is resorted to by three or four more doctors as a place of residence or practice. If we permit the clinic, we will reduce the number of doctors in homes, because the applicants will not practice in both the clinic and their homes. Thus the amount of land and buildings actually used for doctoring and street parking may be reduced rather than increased by our approval.

In these circumstances we think the variance may well be regarded as "minor." We may note here, too, that although some discussion took place at the hearing about a six doctor clinic, the application has been amended and now asks for permission for a four doctor clinic only.

Fifth, The General Intent and Purpose.

Can we be satisfied that "the general intent and purpose of the By-law and the Official Plan is maintained"? Several of those who objected contended that the general intent would not be maintained, but unfortunately they did not say what that intent is. So far as the Official Plan is concerned, it merely designates this land for residential use. No further use classification is delineated. It cannot be said to have any intent in respect of this application. As for the By-law the intent there is that residential land be used for medical services, in a home or hospital, and that intent is certainly not lost by the approval of this application. The by-laws under which the Committee functions have no intent or purpose stated, and if one attempts to glean the intent from a reading of the by-law itself, the most interesting part of the by-law is the zoning map of Schedule A and B. For on that map it is apparent that the relatively small amount of commercial land is hard against, in many cases, R1 and R2 zones. No attempt seems to have been made to insulate the lower density zones from the commercial zones by any higher density zoning, or green belt, or park land, or any such device. In fact, as By-law 1614 now stands, it would be perfectly consistent for Council to amend it to permit any commercial use on the applicants' land. So much for the intent and purpose. Taking the most sympathetic view of the opposition to this application, we cannot see that the intent and purpose will be frustrated by approval of the applicants' proposal.

Sixth, Conditions of Approval.

Our powers in s. 18(9) to subject our decision to such terms and conditions as we deem advisable must not be overlooked. We may further safeguard the residential interests in the affected area with a number of conditions designed to secure the proper layout, to minimize traffic movements and parking, to obscure to some extent, the view of a large number of parked cars and to protect the area against a conversion of the building to another less compatible use at some time in the future.

We therefore approve this application subject to the following conditions:

Condition 1. The clinic shall be confined to the use of not more than four doctors with such nursing, technical and clerical assistance as may reasonably be necessary.

Condition 2. The clinic shall be confined to facilities for the general practice of medicine and emergency treatment, and no bed accommodation shall be provided for patients.

Condition 3. The applicants shall, upon the opening of the clinic, discontinue the practice of medicine in their homes, and take any necessary steps to restore the residential character of their homes and grounds.

Condition 4. The layout of the clinic and the clinic grounds shall as nearly as possible follow the sketch plan attached to this decision and forming part of it. In particular, there shall be a parking area of 4,000 square feet of compacted three-quarter inch crushed stone surface, dressed with three-eighth inch crushed stone on top, graded twelve inches lower than the finished established grade of the rest of the lot, and planted along the border with evergreens shown on the sketch plan. Except for the area occupied by the clinic the parking space and walks or driveways the lot shall be planted in lawn grass, shrubbery and shade trees, as shown on the sketch plan, and the whole maintained in a healthy growing state. In order to comply with this layout it will be necessary for the applicants to acquire ten feet frontage the full depth of the lot on the west side.

(The Committee wishes to acknowledge the valuable assistance of Mr. William Biggs of the Planning Board staff, who is a highly competent landscaping architect and who prepared the sketch plan in consultation with Mr. Vernon on behalf of the applicants.)

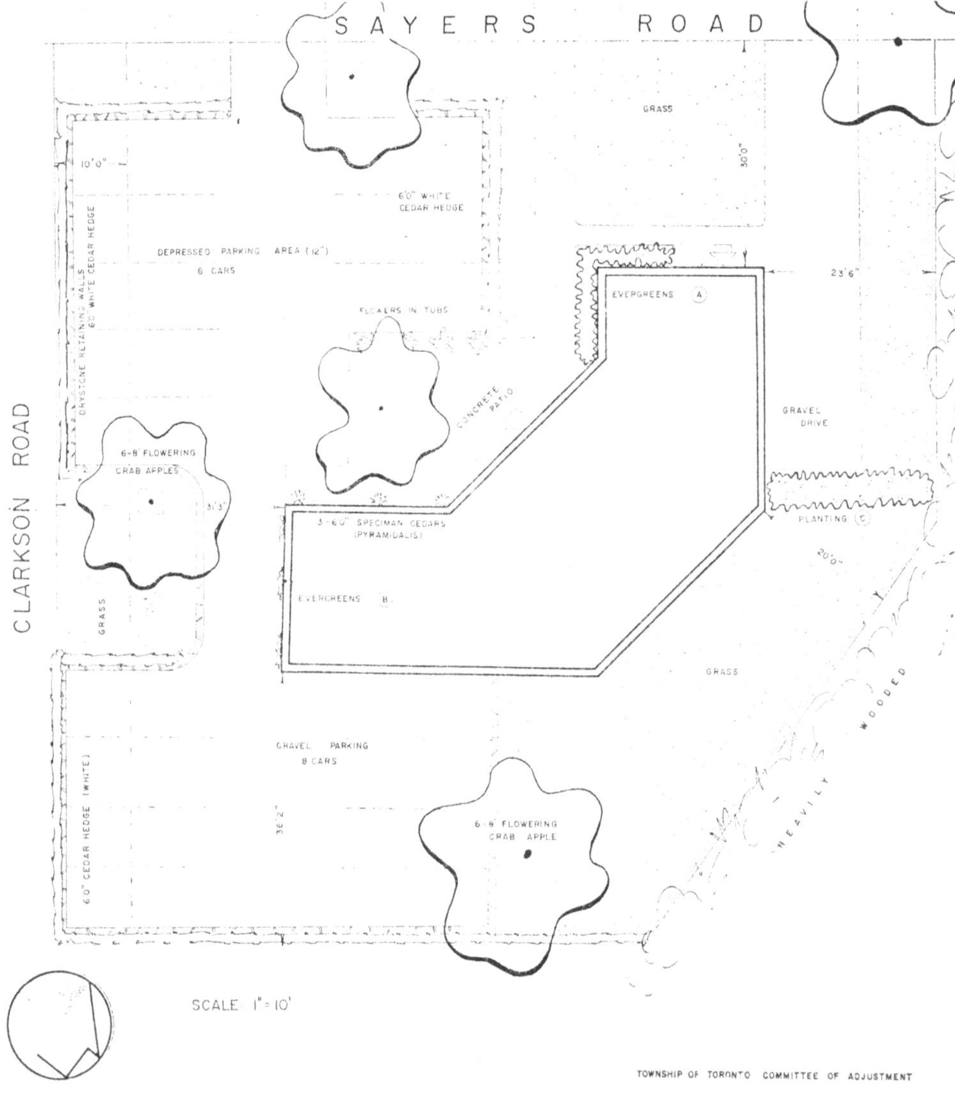

Medical Clinic Development Plan. In addition to prescribing horticultural particulars as to kinds and numbers of plants and the height of the hedge (6 feet), the plan required that the parking area be 12 inches below average grade with a drystone wall of Credit Valley stone.

Condition 5. The clinic shall be open to the public only during the customary hours of general physicians, save for emergency matters. Without attempting to fix the foregoing customary hours, we record that it is the present intention of the applicants to have clinic hours from one o'clock to three o'clock four days a week and from six o'clock to eight o'clock three evenings a week.

Condition 6. The clinic grounds shall be advertised to the public only by a sign not more than two feet square illuminated only by reflected light, and the parking area and the grounds generally shall be lighted only by shaded lights directed primarily to the ground and placed, as far as possible in the planted area of the lot.

Condition 7. The clinic shall be serviced with municipal water drawn from the main on the Clarkson Road. The area of the lot is well over the minimum of 10,000 square feet required for residential use in an R3 Zone, but it is under the minimum of 15,000 square feet required for R3 zones where municipal water is not available. It is understood that the applicants propose to use municipal water with permission of the Township authorities. The clinic may not be built on a 13,200 square foot lot if it is to be serviced by a well.

Condition 8. The clinic shall be constructed substantially in accordance with the plans lodged with the committee, which plans are available for inspection, at all reasonable times. The exterior surface shall be finished with a building brick of a colour and composition compatible with the surrounding buildings. In the event that any dispute arises over this condition a further application may be made to this committee.

Condition 9. When the clinic ceases to be used as a four doctor medical clinic this approval ceases and the land and building shall be used only for such purposes as may at that time and thereafter be permitted by By-law.

(The Committee wishes to emphasize here that this decision in no way establishes a precedent for a non-conforming use of *any* other sort.)

NOTE ON THE SUBSEQUENT HISTORY OF THE GEAR *CASE.* In due course the Minister of Planning and Development appealed the *Gear* case. The appropriate department official wrote,

"The subject submission of the Committee of Adjustment dated the 19th day of November, 1956, having been considered is now appealed by the Minister to The Ontario Municipal Board under Section 18(12) of The Planning Act, 1955.

"The decision of the Committee in this submission as now appealed to the Board, was to grant in part the application for a variance on the subject land owned by Drs. J. Gear, H. Vernon and E. Vernon, from certain provisions of By-law No. 1614.

"Appeal to the Board is made for the following reasons:

"1. Application is for permission to erect a medical clinic for four doctors in a R3 Zone, which as noted in the Agenda and at the end of the Decision of the Committee of Adjustment is a "non-conforming" use.

"2. It is submitted that under no circumstances can the creation of a non-conforming use be considered a minor variance under Section 18(1) of The Planning Act, 1955.

"3. The Committee, having stated that this is a non-conforming use, should not have granted the application as a minor variance."

An appeal was also taken by a group of property owners who lived on the adjoining lands, and a third appeal was taken by the Birchwood Property Owners Association, made up of residents on some of the lots on Registered Plan 389, both adjacent to the applicants' property and in the internal part of the subdivision.

The Municipal Board allowed the appeal but gave no written reasons. According to report the Board said that the proposed clinic building was an "office building" and that the Committee had exceeded its jurisdiction.

Is the Municipal Board competent to decide whether the Committee exceeded its powers? What powers has the Board on appeal?

What is an "office building"? Why did the Board refer to a general use of the building when it was not designed for general use and was subject to Condition 9 of the Committee's decision?

Why does the Minister object to the creation of a non-conforming use? If the proposed use conforms to the by-law use, why appeal to the Committee? Why can the creation of a non-conforming use under no circumstances be a "minor variance"? Does it not depend on whether the variance from the use restrictions of the by-law is minor? Is the variance in this case minor?

Within four years the Committee's suggestion of the possible development under the existing by-law had been proved justified in part at least. The doctors Vernon, who lived on the north east corner of the Clarkson Road and Sayers Road, had purchased the land on the south east corner and had erected a large house containing ample space and equipment for both of their practices. The house they vacated was immediately occupied by one of the other applicant doctors. At the beginning of 1963 the fourth applicant had not moved into the area. No particular provision for off street parking has been made.

[All the compass directions given in this case and the note are based on the parochial assumption that all the roads beginning at Lake Ontario run due north. As a matter of geography, the Clarkson Road runs almost due north west and Sayers Road almost due north east.]

RE TRENOUTH

Toronto Township. Committee of Adjustment. 1955. Unreported

This application arises from the concern of a mortgagee whose survey shows that a side yard in the applicant's lot is 2 inches under the minimum of 14 feet established by By-law 1614. The lot is situated on the north side of Gordon Drive. It has a frontage of 100 feet and the easterly side yard is 6 feet at front corner of the house and 6 feet 2 inches at the rear corner. The house is by that, 2 inches askew on the lot. This has resulted in the rear on the westerly side being the corresponding 2 inches closer to the west side line, 13 feet 10 inches instead of the required 14 feet, which it is at the front. We believe the siting error was unintentional and we approve the application for permission to build with an undersized side yard.

No person appeared to oppose this application, but the Committee received one letter from Mr. Albert Thorne who accused us of "splitting hairs." It is not, of course, the Committee, but the mortgagee who objects to the violation of the By-law, and since the violation could conceivably be regarded as a defect of title, the mortgagee might very well ask for the Committee's approval, although neither the municipal officials nor neighboring ratepayers would trouble themselves.

Application approved.

QUESTIONS. Would the maxim *de minimis non curat lex* apply to this situation if the township had prosecuted? What is the purpose of a side yard? Has that purpose been in any way defeated by this decision? Are the fears of the mortgagee's solicitor justified? Can contravention of the by-law affect title?

In this case the building was already up and the Committee was asked to get the owner "off the hook." Is this a proper function of a Committee of Adjustment?

In some municipalities in a case such as this the municipal clerk upon request will issue a "letter of tolerance" which amounts to no more than the council's assurance (not even by resolution or by-law in most cases) that it will not prosecute. Is this satisfactory? Would it prevent a neighbouring purist from seeking an injunction under s. 497 of the *Municipal Act*? Would the neighbour succeed in his action? Does the "letter of tolerance" amount to an amendment of the by-law? Is it "spot zoning"? Does it need the approval of the Municipal Board? Is it effective without?

RE CROMARTY AND BRUZZESE
Ontario. Municipal Board. 1962. N. 4439–62

GREENWOOD Member and ROBERTS Member: This appeal was heard at Welland on December 26, 1962 and decision was reserved.

The Committee of Adjustment approved a variance from the by-law to permit the reduction in the rear yard requirement to approximately 5 feet for a building which would in all other respects conform to the by-law. The situation with regard to the by-law requirement is not entirely clear but it is either 15 or 20 feet. The general zoning by-law 1,862 requires a 20 foot rear yard for the subject property. Bylaw 2,667 passed on October 21, 1958, reduces this requirement to 15 feet. For various reasons By-law 2,667 did not come on for hearing before this Board until May 1962, by which time it had been amended by several other by-laws. On June 4, 1962 the Board's decision approved the By-law subject to certain amendments and under date of November 27, 1962 the Board's formal order of approval issued. Seven parcels of land were by this order exempted from the approval but the property which is the subject of this hearing is not one or part of one of the seven.

The Committee of Adjustment sat on the 24th of October, 1962, i.e. about a month prior to the approval of By-law 2,667. It was argued by counsel for the appellants that under the circumstances existing in this case the Committee of Adjustment was without jurisdiction and from this it would follow that the Board also lacked jurisdiction. The Board reserved its decision on this point and proceeded to hear the evidence. In view of the decision arrived at on other grounds it is unnecessary to make a ruling on this point.

In the view of this Board a reduction in the rear yard to 5 feet from a requirement of either 15 feet or 20 feet can not here be regarded as a minor variation and the Board therefore finds that the Committee of Adjustment was without jurisdiction on that ground.

From the decision of City Council to exempt Peoples Stores Limited by By-law 3,156 from any rear yard requirement and from decisions of the Committee of Adjustment in granting other variances in this vicinity (which decisions were not appealed by the Council) it would appear that there is considerable doubt as to whether or not the rear yard requirement is a realistic one. In the view of this Board the whole block should be restudied and if in fact it is the intention of council to provide for a laneway as stated, more positive action should be taken to provide for it such as showing it on an official plan or acquiring the right of way so that reasonable provisions, if any, can be made for rear yards.

The appeal will therefore be allowed and the decision of the Committee of Adjustment set aside.

There will be no order as to costs other than that the city will refund to the appellants the hearing fee of $25.00 paid by them.

RE McCUTCHEON

Toronto Township. Committee of Adjustment 1955. Unreported

In this application the Committee is asked to approve the use of two undersized lots for single family dwellings. The lots were originally the whole of Lot 3 on Plan 443, which fronted on Halliday Avenue and was 134 feet 9 inches wide and had a depth of approximately 105 feet. The Planning Board has consented, in principle, to the proposed division provided this Committee agrees to the use of the lots. It is not our concern, of course, whether the division of the land is wise, but some of the factors that justified the Planning Board's actions also support the Committee in approving this application. The proposed division, is through the middle of the lot, making two lots each with a frontage of 67 feet 4½ inches. With depths of approximately 106 and 104 feet respectively, the areas will be 7,200 and and 7,000 square feet. The lots are in an R4 Zone, and the frontage requirement under By-law 1614 is only 50 feet, but the area is 7,500 square feet. One lot is therefore short by 300 square feet and the other by 500 square feet. Such a variance is, in our opinion, minor and we have merely to decide whether the proposed development is appropriate and the general intent and purpose of the Official Plan and By-law can be maintained.

These tests are easily answered when the surrounding development is examined, lots 1, 2, 4 and 5 in Plan 443 are narrower than the proposed lots in frontage: lots 1 and 2 are only 48 feet 2 inches. Lots 4 and 5 are 58 feet 5 inches. In area these lots are somewhat larger, 1 and 2 just reaching the required 7,500 square feet, and 4 and 5 approaching 9,000 square feet. As it stands lot 3 has an area of 14,000 square feet. The development of this outsized lot in the area is hardly desirable from an assessment point of view, the Planning Board agrees to the redivision, and the proposed size seems to this Committee to conform more closely to the neighbouring development than the existing lot does.

QUESTIONS. Does this case amount to an appeal from the Planning Board? Would it be improper for a member of the Committee to sit on this case if he were also a member of the Planning Board?

RE D. H. GATES LTD.

Ontario. Municipal Board. 1962. N. 3362–62

JAMIESON Member and MILBURN Member: This is an appeal by D. H. Gates Limited from a decision of the Committee of Adjustment of the Township of North York dated the 28th day of February, 1962, which dismissed its application for a variance from the provisions of the zoning by-law of the Township of North York.

The evidence in this matter indicated that the zoning by-law of the township was passed in the year 1952. Some years later the owner of Lot 48,

Registered Plan 3163, Township of North York, divided this lot into two parcels of land as shown on the plan which was filed as Exhibit 2 in this hearing. The owner now proposes to erect a house on each of these parcels of land and as there is a watercourse passing through the lot from the southeast corner to the northwest corner within the boundaries of the easement shown on the plan, there is a problem in connection with the siting of the two proposed dwellings. The Board, today, was concerned only with the westerly parcel as shown on Exhibit 2 on which, in green, is outlined the proposed location of a dwelling.

The Committee of Adjustment were requested to grant a minor variance from the terms of the by-law in two respects. Firstly to permit the construction of a dwelling on a lot having a frontage of 49.97 feet as opposed to the 50 foot minimum requirement contained in the by-law for an R4 district, and secondly to permit a variance from the minimum lot area requirements which the by-law gives as 6,000 square feet to the area of the parcel in question which is 5,321 square feet.

A number of owners of nearby properties appeared and opposed the granting of the variance and their objection was directed largely against the siting of the building which projected beyond the established building line on Basswood Road.

It is the opinion of the Board that the zoning by-law of the Township of North York does make provision for the use of lots which are smaller than the minimums described in the by-law and these regulations are found in section 7.2 et seq., and this refers to lots which existed at the time the by-law was passed. It would not appear that the by-law contemplates the creation of new lots, after the date of the passing of the by-law, which are smaller than the minimums set forth in the by-law. The Board is of the opinion that the Committee of Adjustment is without jurisdiction to grant a variance under these conditions and that this Board is also for this reason without jurisdiction. For these reasons the appeal is not allowed.

QUESTIONS. Suppose that neighbouring conforming lots with an area of just 6,000 square feet had one storey houses with areas of about 1,200 square feet, leaving about 4,800 square feet of open space on the lot. Suppose that on the lot in the *Gates* case, with an area of 5,321 square feet, the applicant proposed to erect a two and a half storey house with an area of 500 square feet on each of the first two storeys and 250 feet on the third (half) storey, or a total area of 1,250 square feet, and thus to leave about 4,821 square feet of open space. Would the committee have had jurisdiction, by setting such a condition, to permit the variance which would have meant a larger house with more open space about it than the conforming lots? How important is the area of the lot? Would it matter that the surrounding houses were all lower? Would it be possible for an architect to design a two and a half storey house for the lot, and for the adjoining lot, that fitted the sites and the neighbouring lots? Could the committee have required the architect's assistance as a condition? Should it?

RE SCHOOTS

Toronto Township. Committee of Adjustment. 1957. Unreported

The applicant is the owner of Lot 76, Plan D-23, at 902–9th Street, Lakeview, in an R-4 Zone. Lot 76 has a frontage of 40 feet and an area of 4000 square feet. Under s. 33 of By-law 1614, as amended by By-law 1760, because Lot 76 was registered prior to the date of the Municipal Board approval of By-law 1614, the minimum lot area applicable is 6000 square feet. Lot 76 is, therefore, 2000 square feet undersize. There is a house on Lot 76, erected prior to April 10th, 1953, the effective date of By-law 1614, but the front yard is only 21½ feet deep and one side yard is only 2 feet wide. By-law 1614 requires a 25 foot front yard and a 4 foot side yard. The applicant has been refused a building permit to erect an addition to the rear of his house for a bathroom and personal storage space. The main house is 23 feet wide and 26 feet long. The area of 598 sqare feet is 122 square feet under the minimum of 720 square feet required under the By-law. The area in which Lot 76 is situated is well established and built up at about the standard indicated by the applicant's house. Short of redevelopment, which is not widely predicted at the moment, there is little likelihood of the standard being raised. Meanwhile, the applicant wants to raise his own standards as much as he can afford.

This Committee is asked to approve a minor variance of 2000 square feet in area, 3½ feet in depth of front yard, 2 feet in depth of a side yard, and 2 sq. ft. (after the addition) in area of the house to permit 120 sq. ft. to be added to the house, pursuant to s. 18(1) of *The Planning Act, 1955*.

On the other hand, if the house, because it occupies space in what should be unoccupied and unobstructed open yard space, could be considered a non-conforming building, the application might be considered as one for an extension or enlargement of a non-conforming building under s. 18(2)(a)(i) of the Act. Clearly, the building is used for residential purposes and is thus not for a purpose prohibited by By-law No. 1614, but it is unquestionably in a place where any building or structure is prohibited. We cannot accept the argument that this application cannot be considered an enlargement of a non-conforming building. But we do not press the point as we are satisfied that the addition is an appropriate one and in the cirstances a minor variance and our approval will not jeopardize the general intent and purpose of the By-law and Official Plan. So far as any one can ascertain, the Official Plan has no general intent and purpose beyond the proposition that the area should be limited to residential use, but since the word "residential" is in no way defined, it represents only the loosest kind of guide to anyone. The addition of the extra living space on this lot can hardly affect the general intent of the By-law, even if it were possible to ascertain some general intent as distinct from the particular intent behind each section, which, so far as the words of the By-law are concerned, is the only intent indicated. We have no doubt that s. 18(1) of *The Planning Act, 1955* has some purpose in referring to the general intent of a Bylaw, but we must confess to considerable difficulty in finding any general intent in By-law 1614.

Application approved.

QUESTIONS. How do you determine the "general intent and purpose" of a specific provision in a by-law? Are you entitled to postulate any general proposition that could logically fit the minor premise and that makes sense of the problem?

(b) Enlargement or extension of non-conforming uses

RE CORMACK

Toronto Township. Committee of Adjustment. 1956. Unreported

This is an application to extend or enlarge an existing building in non-conforming use as a veterinary (small animal) establishment in an R-3 Zone coming within section 18(2)(a)(i) of *The Planning Act, 1955*. The building is on part of Lot 5, Con. 2, S.D.S. on the east side of the Dixie Road, south of the Queen Elizabeth Highway about 350 feet. The lot is irregularly shaped, having a 60 foot frontage on the Dixie Road and a depth of 140 feet. Along the south side of the lot there is a 12 foot driveway running back 240 feet where the 12 feet widens to a total of 102 feet, and the lot continues another 280 feet back. At the time By-law 1614 was passed, in 1953, the front part of the lot (measuring 60 feet by 140 feet) was occupied by a house, in the basement of which the applicant carried on a veterinary physician's practice: in two relatively small rooms and a "hallway" which he used as a waiting room, a small kennel room and his surgery with which he combined his examination room, X-ray department, drug shelf, basins and office. On the rear lot, measuring about 100 feet by 280 feet, which is joined by the 12 foot driveway extension, there was a kennel building surrounded by a white lattice fence enclosing runs for dogs. Behind the lattice fence there was a "rear yard" 100' deep not built on for any purpose. Around the back lot is a rapidly growing multiflora rose hedge, which in time will grow ten feet high at least.

When the applicant acquired the lot there was some semblance of subdivision control in the Township, and the applicant tells us, and we have no reason to disbelieve him, that he approached both the Council and the Planning Board and disclosed his plans. He wanted to locate his veterinary practice in what these two bodies considered a satisfactory place. Needless to say he was permitted to buy and build at this location. Unquestionably, he could have forced the hand of the community by court action, since no by-law or official plan was then in force, but he in fact received the "approval" of the Council and the Planning Board.

Shortly thereafter By-law 1614 was passed. The applicant did not oppose the By-law before the Municipal Board when it zoned his property R-3, and made his business a non-conforming use. He believed, as he says, that he had had the blessing of the planning authorities in the township and he supposed he would be allowed to continue his business.

The original form of By-law 1614 showed the property west of the Dixie Road as residential. This has since been rezoned commercial and a large shopping centre has been established there. Already part of the building is in use, and the area is flood lighted for long hours of darkness in the early winter evenings. Apart from the development as stated, the residential character of the area has been preserved and the only other change to the immediate neighborhood has been the erection of the Dixie Road overpass and the Queen Elizabeth Service road. East of the applicant's property the Rome-Saracini subdivision has been developed continuously and the rear of his lot adjoins the rear of lots in that subdivision. The land immediately around the applicant's property is vacant. The corner lot on the intersection of the service road and the Dixie Road may someday attract a service station, but at the moment the lot is zoned for residential use only. The lot fronting on the Dixie Road south of the driveway and west of the rear lot is now vacant. The next lot south is built upon.

It is in these circumstances that the applicant approaches the Committee for permission to erect a new clinic in front of the existing kennels on the back lot. The proposed building is a modernly designed veterinary clinic for small animals with a floor area of 2500 square feet. Into this building, which will be attached to the existing kennels and runs, the applicant proposes to move his examination-surgery-X-ray-pharmacy room, etc., from the basement of his house. The Committee has been shown a floor plan and a perspective drawing of the proposed building, which is of modern design and, so the applicant informs the Committee, represents the most modern ideas of clinic architecture.

It cannot be denied that if this application is approved, the applicant will have invested heavily in the perpetuation of a non-conforming use, and if it is the fond hope of Section 390 of the *Municipal Act* that non-conforming uses, like the communist state, will ultimately wither away, that result is admittedly less likely to result from this new investment.

With this thought before it, the Committee must decide whether to permit this extension and thus prolong the use; or refuse it in the hope that the use will shortly be discontinued. The Committee is agreed from the start that this is one of its most difficult cases.

Nine neighboring property owners were notified of this application by mail and on its first hearing no one appeared to support or protest it. When the Committee learned that the hearing had not been advertised in the local paper, consideration of the case was postponed for two weeks, and an advertisement placed in the Port Credit Weekly. At the subsequent public hearing no voice was heard. On neither occasion has any written communication been received supporting or protesting. In addition, the applicant spoke personally to his neighbors and he reports to the Committee that they had no objection.

The absence of objection, while it may comfort the Committee if it approves the application, offers no help whatever in coming to a decision on the merits.

On the merits two considerations seem to this Committee to predominate, and a third is subsidiary but of ranking importance. The first predominant consideration is the degree of compatibility of the land use. The second is the extent to which a Committee can and should permit the extension of a non-conforming use. The subsidiary consideration is the effect of the extended structure on the neighborhood design.

Land use: The Committee has been advised by its consultant, the Planning Board's Town Planner, that he would not object to the application on the ground of use. Under By-law 1614, veterinary clinics are expressly allowed in RR and RS zones (see s. 35 (a) (iv)) and perhaps by implication in Agricultural Zones, Open Space Zones and Greenbelt Zones. In Agricultural Zones the minimum lot is 25 acres, which is impractical for veterinary clinics. In Open Space and Greenbelt Zones, agricultural uses of land are permitted, but a study of the location and size of such zones in the Township will show that these zones are useless to the applicant. Commercially zoned land is scarce in the Township and it would hardly be considered that the two shopping centers nearby would be suitable.

We conclude that since the proposed clinic is of modern functional design it is well fitted to the surrounding land use as it would be to any location to which the applicant might reasonably be expected to turn, and on this consideration we hold in the applicant's favor.

The degree of extension: In order to determine the merits of this consideration it would be necessary to explore at some length the purposes of s. 390(6) of *The Municipal* Act as it stood in 1953. It then provided that a zoning by-law does not apply to land used on the day the by-law was passed for a purpose prohibited by the By-law. It is clear that the By-law was intended not to have retroactive effect. Had it been the legislature's intent wholly to discourage non-conforming uses, it would have stopped there, giving no further assistance to the non-conforming land. But by s. 390(16) Councils are given express powers to extend or enlarge not only a non-conforming building or structure, but also non-conforming *land*, with the approval of the Municipal Board. And the express authority of this Committee, in s. 18(2)(a) of *The Planning Act, 1955*, clearly contemplates that some non-conforming uses will not be allowed to wither, but may be enlarged or extended on the Committee's say so, without, necessarily, any approval by the Municipal Board. Clearly the Committee cannot escape its task on any general theory that non-conforming uses are to disappear. Nor can the Committee fall back on any excuse that the degree of enlargement of extension asked for here is beyond their jurisdiction. No such convenient phrase as "minor variance" is available in cases falling under subsection (2), unlike subsection (1) of s. 18. So far as the enabling legislation is concerned, the Committee has only one limitation. It cannot permit the extension beyond the limits of the land *owned and used* in connection with the non-conforming use on the day the by-law was passed. There being no limitation in the Act, how far may the Committee curb its generosity in the interests of planning? We conclude that we must determine those limits only by reference to the outside limits of planning principle. If an extension of 500 sq. ft. would be permissible, because it was a relatively reasonable land use, then any area within the limits of the land owned and used should be permissible, unless some planning principle becomes applicable because of the increase of size. Had the legislature intended to curb non-conforming uses, it might well have curbed committees of adjustment, but having curbed their power to vary, where the By-law applies, the legislature has left no substantial curb where the By-law does not apply. How the 1955 amendment to the Municipal Act affects the Committee's powers is uncertain, but that amendment presumably does not apply to By-laws passed prior to 1955. It is notable, however, that no concomitant curb was placed on Committees in 1955 consolidation of The Planning Act.

The Committee is, of course, free to restrict extensions of non-conforming uses in its own judgment, but if there is no statutory limit to the size of the extension, any Committee must necessarily feel responsible for protecting the interests of the owner or occupier of the non-conforming land so far as the law permits.

The design factor: It seems to this Committee that two general principles of planning may be invoked to help determine the limit of extension: (1) the compatibility of land use, which, however, goes primarily to determine whether to grant the extension at all, and (2) the design factor, where size, shape and location become very material. In this case, the Committee had the benefit of two advisers on this point.

The Town Planner advised the Committee that while he does not object to the use, he feels unhappy about the design of the building and its location. He does not object to the design by itself, it is bad because it is good, so good as to be so much better than the surrounding area that it will become the focal point in the area. Admittedly, the focal point of a residential area ought not to be a veterinarian clinic. It might be a church or a public building, or a large house. But in any case, if it is to be a focal point, the rest of the area should be correspondingly designed to promote the focus. Neither the appropriate building nor the general area design are to be found here. However, it is possible that if a house is built on the 90 foot lot south of the applicant's front lot on Dixie Road, the good design of the clinic may be obscured by the bad design of most modern housing. Even the applicant admits that his clinic is of much better design than his house. If a house would obscure the clinic, as we believe, then much of this objection fails, although we find it one of the most difficult ones to discard. We are aided in reaching our conclusion by the fact that the immediate area is still largely undeveloped and opportunity will arise for a good designer to minimize the effect of the new building. And we must also realize that an equally well designed house of very similar appearance could be built in the area on any available building lot and no one under existing township and provincial planning laws could prevent it.

Opposed to the planner's advice the Assessment Commissioner advises that he feels the building would "blend into the architecture of the neighborhood." Presumably the Assessment Commissioner is less sensitive to design than the Town Planner, and more aware of the effect the building will have on existing assessment values. Such values should follow the values of planning, that is, they should be mutually related: bad planning should reflect low assessment, good planning higher assessment. We have here, obviously, a borderline case, and in view of the past concern of the applicant to be assured by the Council and Planning Board of the appropriateness of his purchase of land for a disclosed purpose, we are reluctant to resolve the issue in favor of the institutions that may have, through lack of any plan, misled a citizen who tried to cooperate at the time when he was free to adjust his affairs to conform with the best institutional planning advice.

The application is approved, subject to the following two conditions, which were discussed at the first hearing and accepted by the applicant; (1) no signs of any kind are to be erected on or in connection with the new clinic. The Committee is aware of the sign the applicant presently has in front of his house, and that sign may be maintained or replaced with a new sign of the same area, so long as it is not illuminated. (2) The overall capacity of the new clinic is to be restricted to 75 small animals, i.e. cats, dogs, etc. The applicant stated to the Committee that he presently can handle 80 animals, but that he intends to reduce the number to 75.

Since the case is a borderline one reaching to outside limits of the Committee's discretion, the decision will be sent to everyone to whom written notice was sent, to make them aware of their right of appeal.

NOTE. Despite the fact that drawings and a site plan were submitted with this application the Committee came to a wrong result on the facts. The lot south of the applicant's house and west of the proposed clinic was not vacant, it already had a house on it.

In a sense this decision represents the application of "performance standards." The clinic to be erected was so designed that no barking could be heard outside the kennel and runs and no odours are perceptible. There is plenty of off street parking on the large lot and because of the hedges and the shape of the lot, it is not conspicuous.

RE CHARTERED TRUST COMPANY

Toronto Township. Committee of Adjustment. 1955. Unreported

This is an application of the Chartered Trust Company as owners and lessors of a lot being parts of lots 6 and 7, Plan 308, in an R-4 Zone, on the southeast corner of the new Queen Elizabeth Service Road and Northmount Avenue, on which the lessee, Flash Petroleum Co. Ltd. operates a non-conforming automobile service station. The service station until recently had access to the Queen Elizabeth Way, and when taken over in 1954 by the present lessee, who invested several thousands of dollars in it, sold about 7000 gallons a month. Since then the gallonage has almost doubled. Now the Department of Highways requires the front 50′ of the lot for the service road, and has demanded the removal of the service station pumps. The lessee requests permission from this Committee to relocate the station and pumps on what remains of the lot, which now measure about 132′ by 110′.

Two objections are taken to the application:

Firstly, the proposed continuation of the land use is said to be undesirable. Two studies, at least, have been made of the land in this area, one preceding the passage of By-law 1614 (admittedly an "amateur" study, by a local committee of the Planning Board, but supervised by the Board's Secretary and a reputable consultant, and the second in a more thorough and professional study made recently by township officials and the Planning Board. Both studies have resulted in the recommendation that the land in this area be kept exclusively for residential use. The Committee hardly feels competent, without further argument from interested parties, to go behind the Planning Board's technical advisers. We conclude, therefore, that it is not desirable to encourage the continuation of the commercial use of land in this zone.

Secondly, even if the Committee could accept the service station as a desirable use, it ought to test the suitability of this particular lot by the standards applicable to commercial lots under By-law 1614. Section 47 of the By-law establishes the standards the Committee should apply if it is to exercise its discretion in the applicant's favour. By-law 1614, s. 47, requires a 200 foot depth and the remnant of the lot in this case has a depth of only 110 ft. The pumps must be located 43 feet from the centre of the service road, which would require the pumps to be set 6 feet closer to the relocated station. The test of s. 47(a) would also apply.

The Committee discussed with both Mr. Armstrong for the Chartered Trust and Mrs. Murphy for the lessee, the implications of a refusal of the application. It seems clear that unless the Committee (or the Municipal Board on appeal) approves the applications, the effect of the Highways Department's expropriation will be to reduce the value of the property from a valuable commercial lot and business selling about 175,000 gallons a year to a not too desirable residential lot in an R-4 Zone.

Taking the foregoing factors into consideration the Committee concludes that the non-conforming use should now be terminated, and accordingly the applicant's request to be allowed to use the land in this lot for a similar use to the non-conforming use, pursuant to s. 18(2)(a)(ii) of *The Planning Act, 1955*, is refused.

NOTE. The decision of the Committee was appealed. On the appeal, which was allowed, no reasons were given. The Municipal Board's order follows: "Upon hearing an application made on the 25th day of November, 1955, unto this Board by Counsel for the appellants, Chartered Trust Company and Flash Petroleums Limited by way of an appeal from the decision of the Committee of Adjustment of the Township of Toronto, dated the 8th day of September, 1955, so as to permit the relocation and continuation of the operation of an automobile service station upon premises comprising the lands situated at the southeast corner of the new Queen Elizabeth

Service Road and Northmount Avenue and being all of lots 6 and 7 according to registered Plan 308 for the County of Peel, and it appearing that notice of the said hearing had been given to all parties in accordance with the direction of this Board, and upon hearing what was alleged by Counsel aforesaid and by Counsel appearing in answer to the said notice of hearing, and subsequently upon reading a certified copy of the resolution of the Council of the Corporation of the Township of Toronto passed on the 19th day of December, 1955, and filed on the 6th day of January, 1956, consenting to permission given to erect a new building;

"1. This board doth order that the decision of the Committee of Adjustment of the Township of Toronto, dated, Thursday, the 8th day of September, 1955, be and it is hereby set aside.

"2. And this Board doth further order that the appellants be and they are hereby permitted to relocate and operate the automobile service station building and pumps on the remainder of the lands owned by the appellants, and that the appellants be and they are hereby permitted to continue to use the lands and buildings to carry on the business as heretofore.

"3. And this Board doth further order that the appellants be and they are hereby permitted to erect on the remainder of the said lands and in compliance with the Building By-law of the said Township a new automobile service station building together with pumps and underground storage, in substitution for the old building herein permitted to be relocated, and that the appellants be and they are hereby permitted to continue to use the lands and new buildings to carry on the business as heretofore.

"4. And this Board doth not see fit to make any order as to the costs of this appeal."

The Municipal Board's order not only permits the relocation of the pumps as applied for to the Committee of Adjustment, but also permits the erection of an entirely new service station building. Where does the Board's jurisdiction to authorize something not asked of the Committee arise? Is an application to the Committee a condition precedent to the Board's jurisdiction under s. 32*b*(12) and (15)? Was proper notice given of an application for permission to erect a new building? Is there a difference in substance between the application as dealt with by the Committee and the application as dealt with by the Board?

RE CANADIAN OIL COMPANIES

Toronto Township. Committee of Adjustment. 1956. Unreported

The applicants are the owners of part of Lot 7, Range 1, S.D.S. the parcel being 189 feet 9 1/2 inches along the Dundas (No. 5) Highway, and 148 feet 6 inches along the west side of Carriage Road, in the Erindale area. At the present time the land is zoned R-1 but is in use for a service station and snack bar. The applicant's agent asks the Committee to permit the demolition of the present buildings and their replacement elsewhere on the lot, with a modern service station. We are invited to consider the application under s. 18(2)(a)(ii) of *The Planning Act, 1955*. We entertain some doubts about the extent of our jurisdiction under this clause, but we may first examine the merits of the case.

The Director of Planning for the Planning Board advises the Committee that the area has recently been studied by the Planning Board in consultation with Township officials, and the area east of the Carriage Road has been indicated on the Official Plan proposed amendment as commercial, and the recommended zoning is "established commercial." Were it not for the fact that the parcel now in non-conforming use is not deep enough to meet the standards of commercial lots either in By-law 1614 or the proposed amendment, the Planning Board would have recommended rezoning the applicant's land as well to "established commercial." In fact, the Planning Director suggests that the present use is not an unreasonable one and that we should approve the application, with one condition, that the new service station should be so sited as to attract the attention of east bound traffic on the Dundas Highway and to discourage west bound traffic from making a left hand turn. We agree that this would be a desirable feature of the new development, and we think the siting should be left to the approval of the building inspector, provided that he insist that the westerly front corner of the service station building be set back farther than the easterly corner. If the applicant or his agent cannot agree with the building inspector as to the siting, the matter may be referred to this committee for a decision.

Before deciding this application we must first consider further our jurisdiction to deal with what amounts to the establishment of a new non-conforming building under the powers conferred on Committees of Adjustment under *The Planning Act, 1955.*

. . . Now it is quite clear that we are not being asked to permit the use of "such . . . buildings or structure" for a similar purpose because it is intended to demolish all buildings or structures on the land the day the By-law was passed or on the date of the application. The question then, is whether, under an authority to permit a similar use of land we may permit the erection of new buildings. Is the erection of a building to be regarded as a "use" of "land" within the meaning of s. 18? On the one hand if s. 18 may be read with s. 390 of the Municipal Act, it will be noted that throughout land, buildings and structures are mentioned specifically and separately although in standard legal terminology "land" always includes buildings affixed to it unless some other meaning is clearly expressed. On this view, when the Committee is authorized to permit a similar use of land, it must mean a use of the land other than for the erection of buildings.

On the other hand, it is quite clear that in the jargon of town planners, land use refers broadly to any use of land, including its use as the foundation and support of a building or structure. It is difficult to conceive of land being reserved for residential use if the erection of houses was not permitted. We think it quite feasible to argue that in s. 18(2)(a)(ii) land has this broader meaning, and we accordingly assume jurisdiction and approve the application, subject to the conditional siting of the service station. We do recognize, however, that the Minister of Planning and Development may very well disagree with our interpretation of *The Planning Act, 1955*, in which case, no doubt he will appeal.

Our attention has been drawn to an earlier decision of this Committee, the application of the Chartered Trust Company and Flash Petroleums, Ltd. (Sub. No. 242). In that case the applicants wished to relocate a service station and pumps in non-conforming use on a lot that after the acquisition of land for the Queen Elizabeth south service road had only 110 feet of depth. In a letter to the Committee dated August 29, 1955, the Chartered Trust Company said: "We would prefer to erect a new building on the site, but in view of the time element and necessity of clearing the situation in advance of service road installation it would appear that our only alternative is to relocate the existing installations. Application is therefore submitted on this basis." This application, therefore, did not involve, as does the present one, the demolition of the existing buildings and the erection of new ones. Nevertheless, for the reasons given at the time, we refused the application. In their letter of October 5, 1955, the Department of Planning and Development concurred with our decision. The applicants appealed, and the Municipal Board allowed the appeal, apparently without giving reasons, but in their order dated January 23, 1956, they did "further order that the appellants be and they are hereby permitted to erect on the remainder of the said lands . . . a new automobile service station building together with pumps and underground storage in substitution for the old building . . . "

We conclude from this order that the Municipal Board takes the view that they could permit a similar use of land that included erecting new buildings where no buildings previously existed, although it is difficult to see how, in that case, they were competent to so order, since the case appealed from made no mention of erecting new buildings and no person was notified of such an application. Whatever may have been the jurisdiction of the Municipal Board in that instance, their interpretation of "similar use" is clear, and while the Municipal Board stands in no higher a position than this Committee in the interpretation of *The Planning Act, 1955*, particularly in a case where no reasons are given, it would seem desirable that uniformity of interpretation, right or wrong, should prevail until a proper court gives an interpretation or the legislature clarifies the position by an amendment.

Application approved, subject to the condition stated.

RE SUPERTEST PETROLEUM CORPORATION LTD.
Ontario. Municipal Board. 1957. Unreported

[The Supertest Company applied to the Committee of Adjustment in the city of London for permission to demolish a service station in non-conforming use and replace it with a more up-to-date building for the same purpose. The Committee refused the application and the Company appealed to the Municipal Board. On the question of jurisdiction the board said:]

Under Section 18(2)(a)(i) of "The Planning Act, 1955" the powers of a Committee of Adjustment are limited to permit an extension or enlargement of an existing building which is used for a non-conforming purpose provided that the same use is continued but do not include the removal of that building and the *substitution* of a new building with an increased life expectancy.

Under Section 18(2)(a)(ii) the Committee of Adjustment may permit a change from an existing non-conforming use of land, building or structure to a new non-conforming use that is either similar to or more compatible than the existing use but makes no reference to the enlargement of an existing building or the erection of a new building.

It is considered that as the word "land" is used together with the words "building" and "structure", the reference to "land" should apply only to land on which there are no buildings or structures. The rights of a non-conforming use of a building do not appear to be passed on to the land should that building be removed.

In short, the intent of the above-mentioned Section is to provide for non-conforming uses to a limited degree but does not appear to go as far as to permit the rejuvenation of a non-conforming use by the removal of a building and the substitution of a new building either for the same use or for a new non-conforming use.

The Committee of Adjustment decided that under the circumstances it was without jurisdiction. In this the Board concurs. On an appeal, the Board is governed by the same legislation and must therefore find that it has no jurisdiction. The appeal therefore is dismissed.

RE POULTON

Toronto Township, Committee of Adjustment. 1958. Unreported

The applicants are the owners of a parcel of land consisting of part of Lots 30 and 31, Con. 1, S.D.S. known as 2064 Fifth Line West, Clarkson, Ont., just north of the Queen Elizabeth Way in an M-1 Zone. The parcel contains a house and garage, and the house is so situated that a corner of it protrudes into the land taken by the Department of Highways in connection with the redesigning of the intersection of the Fifth Line and the Queen Elizabeth. The Highways Department have not expropriated the house and they have asked the applicants to remove it. The applicants propose to relocate the house on the same parcel, but somewhat to the north. Since the relocation is tantamount to erection under By-law 1614, and since a single family residence is forbidden in an M-1 Zone, the applicant has sought relief from this Committee.

The application is quite reasonable and there has been advanced no very serious objection to our approval. It is conceded that the immediate area, which is fairly fully developed in residential uses is unlikely to be converted to a conforming industrial use for some time. Meanwhile, the applicants are anxious to continue to live on land they own rather than try to sell it on a poor market and move the house elsewhere. It is understandable that reasons other than monetary ones might motivate their application, since the area has many pleasant features.

The problem for the Committee arises, not on the merits, but as a question of jurisdiction. If we regarded moving a house as erecting a house, and not "using" land, an argument that would appeal more to a badly trained lawyer than to a man with no training, but blessed with common sense, we should have to deny jurisdiction on the theory that s. 18(2)(a)(ii), in authorizing us to permit a similar use of the land, does not permit us to erect a new building. We have concluded, however, that we are not permitting a "new" building, but rather we are permitting a similar use of an old building, on a new site. We are thus concerned, not with the similar use of land, but with the similar use of the building or structure that is non-conforming. Had the applicants wished to tear down the present house and build a new one farther to the north of the lot, we should have had to refuse it, but since the application is to relocate the existing house, we have jurisdiction and we approve of the relocation on the merits.

(*c*) *Extension of permitted uses*

RE B.A. OIL COMPANY LIMITED

Committee of Adjustment (Toronto Township). 1955. Unreported

This is an application falling under s. 18(2)(b) of *The Planning Act, 1955*, to extend land in a C. 1 Zone into an adjoining residential area. The land in question is at the easterly boundary of Lot 5, Con. 1, N.D.S. on the north side of the Dundas (No. 5) Highway and east of the Dixie Road. This lot is 100 feet by 145 feet. Its zoning as C. 1 was evidently to legitimate the existing use as a service station. The zone coincides in area with the land owned by the Oil Company, the applicants today, at the time By-law 1614 was passed. The Official Plan of course shows a commercial use on this lot. The surrounding area is residential on the Plan, but it is only gradually being urbanized in fact, and on the south side of the Dundas Highway there is a structural steel storage yard and a wholesale warehouse.

The applicants have acquired a large parcel of land adjoining westerly along the Dundas and running north about 575 feet. On the Dundas frontage totalling 338 feet, and running north about 160 feet, the applicants propose to demolish the existing station and erect a modern station with better facilities. There is no doubt that the proposal will vastly improve the appearance of the area, and it is upon this fact that the applicants in substance rest their case. The applicants have, incidentally, acquired title to the land, but they admit they knew that it was zoned for residential use.

The application was opposed by Mr. Morris, who represented Mrs. Whistance Smith, owner of land in this area, whose application for a similar use was refused by this Committee (see Submission No. 71). The substance of Mr. Morris' objection was that his client had to wait until the area was rezoned, and he thought the applicant today should have to wait as well. He denied that his client's attitude was founded on spite or any similar ill motive. On the face of it, Mr. Morris' objection appears immaterial for there are significant differences between the two cases. The applicants today are carrying on a business permitted by the by-law and in conformity with the Official Plan. The intent of the Official Plan is frequently impossible to guess at, but it is not too unreasonable, we believe, to suggest that the land use determination in the Official Plan was an indication that a service station located at this point was considered desirable. If a small, rather worn out looking service station is desirable, a modern one on larger grounds, and more efficient, would be more desirable, within reasonable limits. On this analysis Mr. Morris' objection is met and the application appears to come squarely within the rationale of the Committee's jurisdiction under s. 18(2)(b).

But one aspect of Mr. Morris' objection remains: the known state of the revision of the Official Plan now being undertaken by the municipality. We are informed that the proposed land use to be designated on the revised Plan, if approved by the Minister, is industrial. Furthermore, it is notable that the present by-law originally permitted service stations in industrial zones, but at the request of the Planning Board this provision was repealed by Council, and it is not intended to restore this use in the implementation of the revised Official Plan.

The Committee must thus decide whether it should take into account the intent and purpose of an "Official Plan" not yet in existence. A court of law might well take the view that the race is to the swift–if a private developer of land moves faster than the community, he should be allowed to carry on with his activity; he should not be hampered by the discretionary remedies available to the courts. See the *Central Jewish Institute* case [1948] 2 D.L.R. 1. On the other hand, Spence J. has withheld mandamus when an Official Plan was still pending the Minister's approval. See *Re Marckity and Fort Erie* [1951] O.W.N. 836. With all respect it is difficult to see the justification for Spence J.'s view in the light of the Supreme Court of Canada's attitude, although in that case no Official Plan was in force. However, whatever may be the attitudes of the courts, we believe that a Committee of Adjustment is designed as a conscious instrument or agency of planning and the implementing of plans. If so, then we should be alert to see that our action does not hamper the running of the legal machinery if we can, at the same time, reasonably secure the interests of persons adversely affected.

The Committee takes the position that the applicant's interests today will be secured if we refuse this application, because he will be able to present his case to the Municipal Board when the By-law implementing the amendments to the Official Plan is submitted for approval. In the meantime it is also open to him to make representations to the Planning Board for revision of the Plan to include a commercial use on the southerly 160 feet of his lot. If advantage is taken of this procedure, and the proposed plan is revised, he will probably be able to secure the by-law amendment before the by-law goes to the Municipal Board. Application refused.

RE HUGH WHARTON

Toronto Township. Committee of Adjustment. 1958. Unreported

The applicant is the owner of Lots 11–17 on Plan 598 fronting on Mattawa Avenue and on the original plan of subdivision dropping back in the rear to the Etobicoke Creek. Subsequently the rear half of the lots was retained in the applicant's ownership as a proposed greenbelt area along the Etobicoke Creek. The new rear line of the lots, shown as a solid line on the sketch, runs more or less along the top of the bank, which drops from 382 feet 6 inches in elevation abruptly to 350 feet. North of the new rear lot lines, about 100 feet, (the broken line of the sketch) is the boundary of the Green Belt Zone and the CM1 Zone. Under By-law 1614, as amended, a CM1 Zone requires a front yard of 20 feet and, where the rear lot line is the boundary line of the CM1 Zone and the Green Belt Zone, a 35 feet rear yard is required. Here the lot line and the zone boundary do not coincide, but presumably for building purposes, the lots must be regarded as ending at the zone boundary, since commercial manufacturing uses are prohibited in a greenbelt zone.

So regarded the lots are considerably shallower than the plan shows. Lot 12, for example, is about 152 feet deep to the zone boundary, but 252 feet deep to the rear lot line, which, as we have stated, roughly follows the top of the bank. If the applicant is required to restrict his building to 20 feet short of the front line and 35 feet short of the zone boundary, he could only erect a 97 foot building on a lot containing 25,000 square feet in area, yet the 97 foot building, about 60 feet wide, will yield only a 5820 square foot building, which would require only 2910 square feet for parking, plus 7440 square feet for front, rear and side yards. Thus out of his 25,000 square feet, the owner can have a 5820 square foot building, together with all parking and yard space required, and still be using only about 4/5 of his lot. For this reason we are asked to permit larger buildings to be erected on the lots, and to permit some CM uses to creep into the Green Belt Zone. We could permit this intrusion under s. 18(2)(b) of *The Planning Act, 1955*, but only if we do not permit separate buildings to be erected in the Green Belt Zone. Our problem is to set suitable conditions under which this intrusion may be rendered acceptable.

It is to be kept foremost before all of us that the Green Belt serves a very specific purpose in this particular Zone. It is not there solely as a park, but because it is needed to conserve the bank slope and flood plain of the Etobicoke Creek. The critical line is the top of the bank. If erosion is to be prevented along the bank, it is essential that the bank be retained intact and the top so used that no increase in water flowing over the brim is encouraged. Provided the safety of the bank is assured, we think we may properly permit building to extend to the zone boundary, and even, if reasonably necessary for reasons of economy and efficiency in the permitted use of that part of the lot zoned CM1, extending the building into the Green Belt Zone a few feet. We could also permit parking in the Green Belt Zone, provided it was confined to the area away from the brink.

The applicant in effect asks us to permit any CM1 use to within 35 feet of the rear lot line, as if that were regarded as the zone boundary. We do not think we could properly go that far, and we gather from the applicant and his solicitor, Mr. Gerhart, that they do not really need that much extension.

We accordingly approve the application, subject to the following conditions, all of which are to be construed with the intention in mind of preserving, at all costs, the integrity of the Etobicoke Creek bank.

1. No building is to be erected or used within 50 feet of the rear lot line, which, for the purpose of these conditions, is regarded as the top of the bank.

2. No use except a permitted Green Belt Zone use is to be made of the rear 35 feet of the lots. Thus the effect of condition 1 and 2 is that if necessary, a building commenced in the CM1 Zone in any of Lots 11–17 may be extended into the Green Belt Zone up to within 50 feet of the top of the bank, and parking or similar non-constructional uses, may be continued to within 35 feet of the top.

3. Before building of any sort is commenced on any part of any of Lots 11 to 14 within the Green Belt Zone, the applicant, or the then owner of the lot concerned, shall furnish the Director of Planning of the Township Planning Board with a plot plan clearly showing all proposed land uses and relevant dimensions, with accurate contour lines at 2½ foot intervals clearly showing the area around the top of the bank, and no building shall be commenced until the Director has approved the plan and building thereafter shall be in accordance with the plan.

4. Before any use of any sort other than that permitted in Green Belt Zones is commenced in the Green Belt Zone on any of Lots 11–17 the applicant or the then owner shall satisfy the Director of Planning that (a) the area comprising the top of the bank back 35 feet into the lot is in a healthy state of vegetation, with no areas where there is bare soil, and if there are such areas of bare soil, the applicant or the then owner shall sod and peg the bare patches, and (b) neither he nor any person will throw on, or otherwise cause any dirt, fill, refuse, or other material to cover the natural vegetation of the slope of the bank.

5. The applicant or the owner for the time being shall maintain the Green Belt Zone area within 35 feet of the top of the bank in accordance with good conservation practice.

6. The applicant or the owner for the time being shall so grade any part of the lot in the Green Belt Zone that the drainage shall flow northerly into the storm drain on Mattawa Avenue, and shall not permit any drainage to flow down the bank of the Etobicoke Creek.

QUESTIONS. Is the Committee authorized to delegate such judgment to the Director of Planning? Can the Committee authorize the "extension" of a building not in existence into the next zone? What is being "extended"? Must the first part of the whole building be commenced in the zone where it is permitted?

NOTE. Re Wharton represents a stage in an interesting, if complicated, attempt to introduce a degree of flexibility into the control of land use in an area subject to flooding and erosion. It is intended, ultimately, to prepare a map, to be made a part of the Official Plan, on which will be shown a line representing the "critical line", or top of the bank of a river valley. The geographical theory is that anywhere between these critical lines on each side of a valley, there is danger of erosion and, in the "flood plain" of the river, of flooding. Neither the erodible bank nor the floodable plain is suitable for building, although other uses, mainly agricultural or recreational, are quite acceptable. Nevertheless, if proper care in design and execution is taken, houses can be built over the brink of the hill, and the so-called "split level" design is peculiarly apt. The uncontrolled building of "split-level" houses anywhere on the bank, and without proper attention to the restoration and maintenance of vegetation could be very dangerous. If sod or trees are removed and not replaced by buildings, other sod (properly pegged, if necessary) or other trees or both sod and trees, the bare earth is subject to acute erosion. It takes a very short time, depending, of course, on the extent of the bare area and on the weather conditions: rainfall, drying sun and wind, before large gullies are worn away.

The administrative theory being applied here is largely forced on the Township because it cannot lawfully delegate control over each individual building to the Building Commissioner. Nor according to the Court of Appeal, can it prohibit the removal of soil or trees under the s. 30 powers. Accordingly, the By-law will prohibit all building in the so-called Green Belt Zone, but the owner of land affected may apply to the Committee of Adjustment for permission to extend a building commenced within the R Zone into the G Zone, subject to conditions imposed by the Committee, which, if the Plan is properly prepared, could be taken by the Committee directly from the text of the Plan. If the Plan states its principles clearly enough, the zone boundary may be fixed precisely but arbitrarily, since the general intent of the Plan will contemplate crossing over it subject to Committee control.

The editor has been informed that this elaborate attempt has (1963) come to nothing.

Does s. 30 and s. 32*b*(2)(b) permit such a procedure? How could the Committee's decision be attacked? Does s. 32*b*(2)(b) authorize the Committee to permit a house to be built wholly within a G Zone where houses are prohibited by the By-law?

(*d*) *Uses described in general terms*

RE LORNE PARK COLLEGE

Toronto Township. Committee of Adjustment. 1957. Unreported

The applicants are the owners of an irregularly shaped parcel of land comprising part of Lot 13, Range 2, C.I.R. containing about 13 acres, situated east of the Lorne Park Road where it intersects the Queen Elizabeth Way. The parcel extends some 789 feet along the south side of the Queen Elizabeth Way. On this parcel there are several buildings, all at present in use in connection with the operation of a private school by the applicants. The largest building is the recently erected school building set back about 100 feet from the Lorne Park Road. One hundred feet from the Lorne Park Road, behind the school, is a two storey brick dwelling used as a girls' dormitory. Another 100 odd feet and one meets a line of tall evergreens on each side of a private lane. East of this lane, almost out of sight of the school building, are three frame dwellings, two one storey in height and one two storey. Each has a detached garage. These houses are used as residences for the faculty of the school. The proposal is now to move one of these houses 28 feet to the south, and to move two new houses on to the parcel, both in line, more or less, with the presently located houses. These houses are to serve as additional homes for faculty members, and in some instances senior boys, not more than two to a house, might be accommodated.

The general use of land for religious and educational purposes is permitted in residential zones by s. 36(d) of By-law 1614, but the building inspector queried whether s. 6 did not limit the number of houses per lot to one, thus preventing the introduction of more houses on the applicant's land. We were invited to consider the application under s. 18(2)(c) of *The Planning Act, 1955*. The uses permitted are unquestionably stated in general terms: "religious or educational purposes" (s. 36(d)) and "purpose incidental" (s. 6(4)), and we may permit the particular purpose sought by the applicant, if, in our opinion, it conforms with the uses permitted in the by-law. We are clearly of the opinion that By-law 1614 permits private schools in the normal or common practice, which we accept as including on the grounds a reasonable accommodation for classrooms, gymnasiums, sports fields, dormitories and houses for faculty members.

The application was opposed by two neighbouring ladies living on the west side of the Lorne Park Road opposite the school building and a little to the north of it. Their objection was to the possible disturbance of their view across the open fields of the applicant's land between the school and the Queen Elizabeth to the trees. When it became apparent that the houses were to be placed behind the trees, the opposition was greatly reduced. In any event, we cannot see that the opposition had any validity or merit. It must be remembered that the applicant's land is zoned R-2 and the applicant could, with the approval of the Minister of Planning and Development, put a plan of subdivision on this parcel of land with as many as 8 houses fronting on Lorne Park Road and completely blocking the view of the open space and trees now available.

It is perhaps not out of the way to remark that the neighbours are perhaps fortunate that by good luck alone this 12 acres of land is used for a purpose that probably ensures a pleasant prospect.

Under the circumstances we approve the application.

[Section 6(2)(c) provides that "where a lot is not described in and is not within a registered plan of subdivision and the area of the lot is more than five acres, no person shall erect more than one one-family detached dwelling on each parcel of land containing five acres within the lot and fronting on a street." Section 6(4) provides that "where this by-law provides that land may be used or a building or structure may be erected or used for a purpose that purpose includes any purpose incidental to the purpose."]

CHAPTER 13

DEVELOPMENT CONTROL

Law never *is*, but is always about to be.

CARDOZO

FULLER, "FREEDOM—A SUGGESTED ANALYSIS"*
Cambridge. 1955. 68 *Harvard Law Review* 1305

The Value of Choice in Context. My final observation is that, in arranging the forms of order through which individual choice is given social expression (or in taking steps to preserve the existing forms), we should bear in mind that choice is meaningless without understanding. A gambler at a roulette table has, in a sense, a wide range of choice, embracing, I am told, among other alternatives, thirty-seven different numbers. Yet no one, except a person simple-minded enough to believe in "systems" for beating the banker, would regard this as a truly significant choice. Indeed, when the player puts his chips on "17", he does not have the sense of choosing; rather, he has the titillation of subjecting himself to the risk of loss or gain without the responsibility of choice. If he has a sense of freedom, it is properly described as freedom from freedom.

When we speak of increasing freedom by expanding the range of choice open to the individual, we do not have in mind the roulette-table kind of freedom. We must intend choice in situations where the citizen knows, or can know, at least approximately the consequences of what he is doing.

How to bring about the understanding essential for meaningful choice is too big a subject to be exhausted here, except that I should like to recall in passing that Jeremy Bentham had definite, if somewhat fantastic, plans for educating the public into the meaning of the different legal forms by which economic ends are attained.

The point I wish to make here is that choice is most likely to be informed and intelligent when it is made, as it were, in context—when it relates not to tomorrow's need but to today's, when it compares not one hypothetical good with another but, let us say, two objects standing side by side on the same counter.

One great advantage of a well-functioning market is that it permits this kind of choice in context. One may contrast the choice a housewife now makes with her pocketbook in hand, and goods stretched out before her in the super market, with the choice imposed on the voter under Barbara Wootten's planned economy. Mrs. Wootton foresees a future in which political parties will campaign on essentially economic platforms. For example, she says, the Blue party may offer a 15 per cent increase in housebuilding, along with other economic benefits, while the Green party may concentrate on a 50 per cent speed-up in housing, postponing other economic benefits and tax reductions. The voter would cast his ballot in accordance with his preference between these two programs. I do not think I need expatiate on the fictitious character of the choice thus afforded the citizen.

The great advantage of systems of social order that are built up by the fitting together of many individual decisions is that those decisions have been reached with reference to specific situations of fact. The words of a language, for example, have come into existence because in some particular context people wanted to say something and needed a word to say it with. Words are not created by someone who thinks they might come in handy on some later occasion.

Even the unplanned path through the woodland may illustrate this point, though as one who suffers daily from the fact that our streets in Boston and Cambridge are laid out along ancient cow paths I should be the last to admit it. (It was not, of course, the fault of the cows. I am sure they made the right decisions for their purposes under the conditions then obtaining. The fault lies with those who took those bovine decisions out of context and applied them to purposes the cows did not have in mind.)

Imagine a newly settled rural community in which it is apparent that sooner or later a path will be worn through a particular woodland. Suppose the community decides to plan the path in advance. There would be definite advantages in this course. Experts could be brought in. A general view of the whole situation could be obtained that would not be available to any individual wayfarer. What would be lacking would be the contribution of countless small decisions by people actually using the path, the decision, for example, of those whose footprints pulled the path slightly to the east so that they might look at a field of daisies, or of those who detoured around a spot generally dry, but unaccountably wet in August.

I hope the figure of the path will not be taken with more seriousness than it is offered. Lest I be accused of romanticizing the problem, I should like to close by relating an actual incident that seems in point.

Through the foresight of the city fathers the Cambridge Common is provided with an elaborate network of paved sidewalks, carefully planned to serve the convenience of any person wishing to traverse the Common from any angle. It was found, however, that at certain points people perversely insisted on walking across the grass. The usual countermeasures were tried, but failed. Now the city is taking down its barriers and its "keep-off-the-grass" signs and is busily engaged in paving the paths cut by trespassing feet. Those who have had experience with the problem of designing forms for the life of the human animal will see here, I believe, a pattern of events that has repeated itself many, many times.

[The reference is to Wootton, *Freedom Under Planning* (1945).]

1. Unauthorised and Interim Development Control

KLINE *et al.* *v.* CITY OF HARRISBURG

Pennsylvania. Supreme Court. 1949. 68 A. 2d 182

Woodside J. in the Court of Common Pleas of Dauphin County: The plaintiffs here are seeking to restrain the City of Harrisburg and certain of its officials from enforcing the provisions of what is sometimes called an "interim" zoning ordinance, and to direct the proper city official to issue a building permit to the plaintiffs authorizing the construction of five apartment buildings in the city.

It is admitted by the defendants that the application, drawing and specifications and statement on the basis of which the building permit was requested conform in all respects to the requirements of the Building Code of the City of Harrisburg, and that the permit was refused by the defendants because of the aforesaid ordinance . . .

One of the plaintiffs who owns a four acre tract of land in the City of Harrisburg entered into an agreement with the other two plaintiffs whereby a business corporation is to be formed and five garden-type apartment buildings are to be erected on said tract and financed in the manner provided by the National Housing Act, 12 U.S.C.A. s. 1701 et seq.

The plaintiffs in order to make appropriate application for mortgage insurance under the provisions of said Act caused all necessary plans, drawings and specifications for the construction of said apartments to be prepared by a competent architect. The estimated cost of the construction of these buildings is $948,000. Pursuant to this agreement the plaintiffs, along with the Bryn Mawr Trust Company of Bryn Mawr, Pennsyvania, which has agreed to become mortgagee for the said project, made application on February 25, 1949, to the Federal Housing Administration for a loan. Two months later the plaintiffs were notified by the Trust Company that the Federal Housing Administrator had advised it that a rental housing commitment under Section 608 of the National Housing Act, 12 U.S.C.A. s. 1743, had been made available. It has been represented to us at argument that this commitment expires if not accepted prior to July 1 of this year, and that therefore a final determination is desirable by June 30.

On April 25, the plaintiffs applied to the Building Inspector of the City of Harrisburg, requesting the issuance of a building permit authorizing the construction of the apartment building, and as required by the Building Code, a fee of $1300 was tendered.

On May 6, 1949, Ordinance No. 153 Session of 1948–49 was read and placed before the Council of the City of Harrisburg and was passed finally on May 10 and, if valid, became effective May 20.

The following preamble is in the Ordinance:

"Whereas, the City Planning Commission of the City of Harrisburg, has for several years been studying the details of a comprehensive zoning ordinance for the City, and

"Whereas, the various zoning districts together with the regulations and restrictions to be imposed therein, have in a large part been reduced to writing, but the work has not matured to the point where public hearings can be had, and,

"Whereas, in the opinion of City Council it will take additional time to work out the details of a zoning plan, and, further, that it will be destructive of the plan if before the date of its final completion the status quo of the residential districts as contemplated by the plan should not be preserved, and,

"Whereas, it is the desire of City Council in order to promote the general welfare of the community to preserve the status quo of the residential districts of the City until the final zoning ordinance can be completed and adopted."

The Ordinance then provides: "that the erection or construction within the residential districts of the City of Harrisburg as hereinafter defined, of any building or premises which shall be used for, or designed for other than a single family detached dwelling, together with its usual accessories, or the alteration within the said residential districts of any existing single family detached dwelling for any other purpose be and the same is hereby prohibited."

Nothing else is contained in the Ordinance except the description of the two residential districts referred to above; a penalty clause for violation of the above and a general repeal clause.

The land on which the plaintiffs propose to erect the apartments lie wholly within one of the two residential areas described in Ordinance No. 153.

The City Planning Commission, which has been in existence since 1923, recommended the employment of a zoning specialist, who was employed by the City on about May 15, 1945.

On July 12, 1945 the City Planning Commission directed the office of the City Engineer to which the zoning specialist was assigned, to make a complete study of the problems arising in the preparation of a zoning ordinance and to present a zoning plan. Such plan was submitted to the City Planning Commission in 1946 and contained two residential areas known as "R-1" areas, which are the same areas as set forth in Ordinance No. 153. These areas accommodate in the main, single family detached dwellings. The final details of the comprehensive zoning plan and the regulations and restrictions to be imposed in the various districts have not as yet been approved by the said City Planning Commission.

It is agreed that in connection with the passage of Ordinance No. 153,

"(a) There were not recommended to the City Council of Harrisburg the boundaries of districts and appropriate regulations and restrictions to be imposed by the City Planning Commission of Harrisburg duly created and existing according to law, or a committee of the Council, or any other commission or committee created by City Council for said purpose;

(b) No tentative report was made and no public meetings thereon were held by the aforesaid City Planning Commission of Harrisburg, or a committee of Council of the City of Harrisburg, or any other commission or committee created by Council of the City of Harrisburg for said purpose;

(c) No final report was submitted to the City Council of Harrisburg by the aforesaid City Planning Commission of Harrisburg, or a committee of Council of the City of Harrisburg, or any other commission or committee created by Council of the City of Harrisburg for said purpose;

(d) No notice of hearing was published for ten consecutive days in a daily newspaper or newspapers of general circulation in the City of Harrisburg of a time and place at which the Council of the City of Harrisburg would afford persons affected an opportunity to be heard, and no such hearings were held; and

(e) Council did not appoint a board of appeals and did not provide that any Board of Appeals may, in appropriate cases and subject to the appropriate conditions and safeguards, make special exceptions to the terms of the Ordinance, its supplements and amendments, in harmony with its general purpose and intent and in accordance with general or specific rules." . . .

[The procedural deficiencies agreed to all relate to procedural requirements in the enabling legislation.]

The defendants admit that they did not comply with the above provisions of the statute, and cannot rely upon the expressed authority to zone contained therein, but contend "that such provisions carry with them the implied or inherent power to pass an interim ordinance to give effect to the power expressly granted in said sub-heading in order to prevent the defeat of the legislative intent of the expressed powers thus granted. And, furthermore, it is contended that the said Ordinance No. 153 was within the express grant of the police power as provided in Section 2403 of The Third Class City Law, 53 P.S. ss. 12198–2403."

Section 2403 of The Third Class City Law, supra, provides as follows:

"Specific powers. In addition to other powers granted by this act, the council of each city shall have power by ordinance: (then after 53 paragraphs)

54. Local Self-Government–In addition to the powers and authority vested in each city by the provisions of this act, to make and adopt all such ordinances, by-laws, rules and regulations, not inconsistent with or restrained by the Constitution and laws of this Commonwealth, as may be expedient or necessary for the proper management, care and control of the city and its trade, commerce and manufactures; and also all such ordinances, by-laws, rules and regulations as may be necessary in and to the exercise of the powers and authority of local self-government in all municipal affairs; and the said ordinances, by-laws, rules and regulations to alter, modify, and repeal at pleasure; and to enforce all ordinances inflicting penalties upon inhabitants or other persons for violations thereof, not exceeding three hundred dollars for any one offense, recoverable with cost, together with judgment of imprisonment, not exceeding ninety days, if the amount of said judgment and costs shall not be paid; Provided, however, That no ordinance, by-laws, rule or regulation shall be made or passed which contravenes or violates any of the provisions of the Constitution of the United States or of this Commonwealth, or of any act of Assembly heretofore or that may be hereafter passed and in force in said city." 53 P.S. 12198–2403.

We cannot agree that the above provision authorizes a city to enact a zoning ordinance without following the provisions of Article XLI of the same act which relate to zoning, nor that said zoning provisions carry with them the implied or inherent power to pass an interim zoning ordinance.

It is settled in Pennsylvania that in the absence of the granting of specific power from the Legislature municipalities do not have the authority to pass zoning ordinances.

Pennsylvania has had what today would be called "zoning" since the days of George Washington . . .

It is customary for zoning statutes to outline the procedure through which a zoning system may be adopted and the general rule is that a zoning ordinance is invalid where it is not passed as provided by the enabling statute. 58 American Jurisprudence, Page 944 and authorities there stated. See also "Zoning" by Edward M. Bassett, Page 31.

In Pennsylvania our highest court has said: "It is a fundamental principle that the authority of a municipal body is to be found in the statute which confers it, and must be exercised strictly in the manner therein provided." *Miners Savings Bank* v. *Duryea Borough* (1938).

Of course, it is well settled that zoning is a proper exercise of the police power and has a direct relation to the preservation of health, safety and general welfare. It is to be remembered, however, as was stated in *White's Appeal*, (1926) that "while (zoning) regulations may not physically take the property, they do so regulate its use as to deprive the owner of a substantial right therein without compensation." Powers with such serious consequence should be exercised only in the manner designated by the legislature.

It is contended by the defendants that without the power to enact such an interim ordinance as is here in question it would be possible for an owner of land to proceed with the erection of an undesirable building in a residential section immediately before the enactment of a zoning ordinance which would prohibit such building, and thus defeat what the city was attempting to establish after years of deliberation and study. There are two answers to this. In the first place, although the argument is not entirely without merit, it is one which must be directed to the legislature and not to the courts. If the legislature wishes to authorize the enactment of a "temporary" or "interim" ordinance to maintain the status quo it can so provide by legislation with proper safeguards. In the second place, apparently experience has not indicated that the failure to pass a "temporary" or "interim" ordinance has been any substantial menace to zoning. Not only cities but also boroughs and townships are authorized to pass zoning ordinances. Although there are scores and possibly hundreds of municipalities in Pennsylvania which have enacted zoning ordinances in accordance with the expressed provisions of the relevant statutes, all of which are similar in nature, there is no indication that we could find either by proposed legislation or by cases in any of the courts of this state that these municipalities have suffered from inability to maintain the status quo during the enactment of zoning ordinances.

"Interim" zoning ordinances, although never before known to the courts of this state, have been before the courts of other states.

In an annotation in 136 A.L.R. 850 it is stated: "Temporary zoning or 'stopgap' ordinances have, quite logically, it would seem, been held invalid where they were not enacted in compliance with constitutional or statutory provisions authorizing municipalities to enact zoning ordinances."

A few states have approved temporary zoning ordinances. Cases of each jurisdiction, of course, rest upon the constitution, statutes and decisions of the particular state, as well as the peculiar facts of the particular case, and are not satisfactory authority for our determination of the matter before us. We could thus dismiss further consideration of them, particularly since they are in conflict with each other, but since the argument of the defendant rests almost entirely upon the authority of a few such cases we shall refer to them. For the reason set forth above we shall discuss them only briefly. . . .

The defendants admit that the Ordinance before us could not "permanently" restrict the use or erection of the forbidden buildings in the described areas. Yet the Ordinance is drafted to do just that. There is nothing in it limiting the time when it shall be effective. In this respect it differs from the temporary ordinances referred to in the Kentucky and Oklahoma cases where the time the ordinance was to be effective was limited by the ordinance itself.

It is contended by the defendants that the Ordinance will remain in effect until the passage of another zoning ordinance, or for a "reasonable time." If there have been ordinances or statutes, which have been adopted without any provisions limiting their effective time; and which are admittedly illegal except for a "reasonable time," we have no recollection of ever having heard of such.

We have here the anomalous situation of an Ordinance providing an absolute prohibition without limit of time which the defendants admit cannot be valid for an unlimited time.

The record of the case indicates that the City has been in the process of preparing a zoning Ordinance since May 15, 1945, a period of over four years, and that "the work has not matured to the point where public hearings can be had" before the City Planning Commission. As a matter of fact a "final" zoning ordinance may never be enacted. There is no duty upon the Council to enact any zoning Ordinance. There is nothing contained in the so-called interim Ordinance by which the present Council even pledges itself to the enactment of a "final" Ordinance . . .

In summarizing we point out that we start in this case with the proposition that before specific legislative authority to zone was given municipalities, they did not have the authority under their general powers to enact zoning ordinances; that the legislature then gave them power to enact zoning ordinances but specifically set forth what they shall do before they impose any regulations or restrictions. It is our opinion that the municipalities must comply with the provision of the statute relating to zoning before they can enact any restrictions. The Ordinance before us containing restrictions was not enacted in accordance with the provisions of the statute relating to zoning and is therefore void, and the defendants must be restrained from enforcing it. As the building permit would be issued except for the Ordinance the building inspector must be directed to issue it . . .

[MAXEY C. J.: On this twenty-fifth day of June, 1949, it is Ordered that the decree of the court below in the above entitled case be affirmed on the opinion of Judge Robert E. Woodside. Each party will pay their own costs.]

NOTE. See 1 Yokley, *Zoning Law and Practice* (2nd ed., 1953), ss. 77–82, for a discussion of the American cases on "interim", "emergency", "temporary" or "stop gap" ordinances. The decisions divide fairly evenly, but the conclusion seems to be that the courts will uphold interim ordinances where the enabling legislation has been strictly followed and the ordinance is not too indefinite, contains no unlawful delegation, is not confiscatory, permits no unusual delays; in short, if it would have been valid as a zoning ordinance its interim character is not objectionable.

RE TORONTO TOWNSHIP BY-LAW 1614
Ontario. Municipal Board. 1954. Unreported

CUMMING Q.C. Chairman and MOORE Vice-Chairman: . . . Mr. S. G. Harmer, representing himself and a number of other owners of land affected having a total area of approximately 900 acres, objected to the proposed R-1 and RS zoning of a large area south of Dundas Street between the western boundary of the Township and the Fifth Line, extending southerly to the industrial strip along the north side of the Queen Elizabeth Way as shown on Schedule "A". They considered the R-1 zoning of this area unrealistic because of the proximity of the new industrial area referred to, and they contended that the residential section should be designed for homes for industrial workers. (Exhibit 14.) In their opinion the R-1 zoning should be changed to R-4 and the RS zoning to R-3. In answer counsel for the township informed the Board that the R-1 zoning was intended merely as a temporary measure to discourage large scale residential development in this area in advance of the actual location of the industries which the municipality hoped to have located in the adjacent industrial zone. Apparently the municipal council had in mind the possibility of a premature housing development in this area as an indirect result of the operation of the huge Ford industry in the adjoining township of Trafalgar approximately 1 1/2 miles to the west of the area, and the problem of supplying water and sewer services in an area which is a very considerable distance from the nearest existing services. Mr. Harmer's objection was developed with considerable skill and it undoubtedly reflects a serious conflict of opinion between the great majority of the owners concerned on the one hand and the Township Planning Board and Council on the other.

The real issue raised in this case is whether a highly restrictive interim zoning of lands considered suitable for future residential development is justified in order to provide temporary financial protection for the township. There is no doubt that no council can legally be forced to provide essential services of an urban type which are not economically feasible, notwithstanding the existence of a large resident population seeking such service. In an attempt to avoid such a situation the present zoning by-law is drawn so as to discourage the premature growth of such a population by the temporary expedient of insisting upon extremely large lots where water and sewer services are not available. If the present objection were sustained it is quite possible that a considerable number of owners would attempt to subdivide and sell lots having a minimum frontage of 100 feet only, with a minimum area of 15,000 square feet. This new population could then bring strong pressure on future councils to provide water and sewer services and the council might conceivably be compelled to provide services under *The Public Health Act*.

After giving the matter thorough consideration the Board has decided that, for the present at least, the R-1 and RS zoning of this area as proposed by the council should be approved. If and when the council is able to provide essential services to the proposed new industrial area similar services could then be provided at minimum expense for the area to the north. The by-law might then be quite reasonably amended on the application of either the council or the owners to permit the higher population density proposed by these objectors . . .

QUESTIONS. Do you agree with zoning on the principle adopted here? Have the owners of the land zoned R1 any "vested interest" in that zoning? If the zoning were to be changed would it be proper to take a poll of the neighbouring landowners? What significance should be attached to the result of the poll? How large an area should be polled? Should voting be by secret ballot?

EAST YORK TOWNSHIP BY-LAW 6,438 (1957)

Whereas the Municipal Council and Planning Board of the Corporation of the Township of East York have authorized the preparation of an official plan of the Township and a general zoning by-law respecting the use of land and premises and the erection, alteration and use of buildings therein pursuant to the statutory powers of the said bodies of either of them and such further statutory authority as may be hereafter granted.

And whereas the said bodies have jointly appointed Urban Planning Consultants Limited and have requested Urban Planning Consultants Limited to undertake the work of preparing the said official plan and the said general zoning by-law and to submit the same with their recommendations to the council with all possible speed.

And whereas it is estimated that a period of one year will be required for the proper preparation of a general zoning by-law for the entire Township and it is deemed expedient to provide for temporary zoning and building restrictions pending the preparation and adoption of the said general zoning by-law.

Therefore the Municipal Council of the Corporation of the Township of East York enacts as follows:

1. This by-law may be cited as "The Temporary Zoning By-law."

10. No person shall, on any lot, in any part of the Township of East York to which this by-law applies, erect, occupy or use any land, building, structure or premises, in whole or in part, for any purpose other than the type of use actually made at the date of the passing of this by-law. This paragraph shall not apply to prevent the use of any lands in a residential area for the purpose of multiple family dwellings provided, however, that such multiple family dwellings are adjoining and adjacent to already existing multiple family dwellings, fronting on the same street.

11. All buildings or structures hereafter erected in any part of the Township of East York to which this by-law applies shall be constructed and located so as to conform to any restricted area by-laws now in force and where there is no restricted area by-law then such buildings or structures shall conform to the present prevailing established standards of the street upon which it fronts, determined in the manner set forth in paragraph 10 in respect of each of the following matters:

Maximum basic height: Minimum front yard depth: Minimum side yard width:

Minimum lot frontage: Minimum lot area: Minimum lot coverage: Minimum ground floor area.

15. No person shall change the existing use of any land, building or structure to a different class or kind of use unless and until he shall have first obtained from the Building Inspector a permit certifying that the new use is in accordance with the provisions of this by-law.

18. This by-law shall continue in force for a period of one year from and after the date of the formal order of the Ontario Municipal Board granting approval, and for such further period or periods as may be requested from time to time by resolution of the Municipal Council and the said Board may approve.

NOTES AND QUESTIONS. The by-law was approved by the Municipal Board for one year.

In section 11, to what do the words "paragraph 10" refer? Does the unnumbered second sentence of section 10 permit new construction of multiple family dwellings or merely the conversion of an existing building? Note the careful distinction between the use of land and the erection and use of a building or structure in section 30(1) paragraphs 1 and 2, of *The Planning Act.*

Would a by-law that restricted the whole municipality to single family dwellings be a more satisfactory scheme than that adopted in East York? Would a by-law that prohibited all land use and the erection or use of any building or structure within the municipality be a more satisfactory scheme? In view of section 30 of *The Planning Act* would the effect be the same? What uses are permitted by the first sentence of section 10? What is meant by the words "type of use" in that sentence? Is this a primitive form of "use classes"?

Does section 30 of *The Planning Act* contemplate the creation of "zones" or "restricted areas"? What is the zone or restricted area in the East York by-law?

RE BERNARDO-HOFFMAN LTD.

Ontario. Municipal Board. 1962. N. 2656–61

J. A. KENNEDY Chairman and LUDGATE Member: This application is the last stage so far in a saga as bizarre as it is unusual. The appellant seeks an order to compel the council of the City of London to pass a by-law in substantially the same terms as one which city council passed on February 20, 1961, but repealed before it had been approved by this Board.

The lands in question are in an area annexed from the Township of London to the city by order of this Board effective January 1, 1961. The block which is especially in issue is known as Block "A", rectangular in shape, with a north-south depth of 249 feet and a length of 807 feet, so that it contains about 4.6 acres. The parcel abuts at the north the rear limit of a row of lots fronting on the south side of Huron Street and at the west the rear limit of a row of lots fronting on the east side of Taylor Street.

The lots on Huron and Taylor are developed with single family residences and most of the houses are still in that use. The surrounding development which has occurred has left this block as something of an orphan from the standpoint of geography and hardly suitable for economic development as single family or even duplex building lots. The surrounding development occurred while the land was still in the Township of London. Why the former owner stood by and allowed inattention to his land to produce this situation has not been explained. Indeed the chain of title was not traced from this standpoint.

The appellant purchased the land in 1959 and set about plans and negotiations for subdivision and development. A plan based on cul-de-sac streets was proposed and proceeded apace until the township engineer opposed the blind streets as a hindrance in servicing, ploughing, etc. This brought about a proposal for row housing which is quite different in density and appearance from the surrounding development. A by-law to permit this development was passed by the council of the Township of London December 6, 1960, and forwarded to this Board for approval. For some reason yet unexplained no one, developer, planning board or council, thought it necessary to consult resident owners in the area before bringing about such a serious change in the permitted use of these lands.

Application for approval did not come to the attention of this Board until after annexation had become effective and the Board ruled the by-law could not be processed for approval unless enacted by the council of the city. City council considered this ruling and enacted the by-law on February 20, 1961, as reported by the city (Exhibit 15) "on the assurance from the township members that the whole matter had been considered by the Township of London council and was satisfactory".

Neither the London and Suburban Planning Board nor the London Planning Board had considered the matter or the plans attached to the by-law.

The first knowledge the resident owners had of the by-law appears to have been when they received notice of the hearing before this Board. After a hearing the Board decided to refer the by-law back to the city council for amendment. By this time it seems city council had been made aware of the protest of the resident owners and decided to repeal the by-law.

Words cannot point up too strongly the folly of attempting to change the designated or permitted use of land without notice to owners of adjacent and surrounding land who will certainly be interested in such a change. It might not be just to place all the blame on any one person or group but this failure to notify those interested before the by-law was passed must rank as the main cause of the confusion which has resulted.

As noted above, surrounding development makes it next to impossible to subdivide this block for single family or duplex dwelling lots. Some more dense type of multiple dwelling seems to be the only solution but the density proposed seems much too high to introduce into this area as at present developed. Greater setbacks at front and rear and more open space among the buildings can be achieved by a substantial reduction in the number of dwelling units proposed. There is no reason to believe that by proceeding along this line the appellant will not be able to develop this parcel to economic advantage.

Fifty-nine dwelling units are proposed. The Board hesitates to suggest a number but does find that the reduction ought to be more than ten as suggested. It might be kept in mind as a guide that in suburban development about four single family dwellings per gross acre is what may be expected. It is true that returns from multiple development are less per unit but against this the present owner cannot expect to be permitted too high a density since the resident owners now complaining are in no way responsible for the fact that the block in question presents problems of subdivision and development.

This appeal should be dismissed but the planning board and council should endeavour to work out a development with lower density, greater setbacks and more open space so that a reasonable use may be made of this land.

There will be no order as to costs.

CITY OF TORONTO *v.* MANDELBAUM
Ontario. High Court. [1932] O.R. 552

WRIGHT J.: In this action the plaintiff corporation claims an injunction restraining the defendant from establishing or proceeding to establish a lumber yard or woodyard at the north-west corner of Dufferin Street and Geary Avenue in the City of Toronto, in alleged contravention of By-law No. 9868 of the City of Toronto without having obtained the permit required by said by-law . . .

The defendant for some years carried on the business of wrecking buildings under the firm name and style of the Ontario Wrecking Co., and maintained a yard at 1348 Dufferin Street in the City of Toronto where he stored the wreckage from the various buildings purchased by him in the course of his business.

The defendant was a tenant of the said premises. The City of Toronto acquired the lands upon which the plaintiff's yard was located and gave him notice to vacate. He secured a new location on the north-west corner of Dufferin Street and Geary Avenue and proceeded to move his stock of lumber from his former premises and to establish his place of business at the new premises, after having applied for a permit to establish and operate a lumber yard at the latter, which was refused by the city authorities. Thereupon the plaintiff corporation applied for and obtained an interim injunction which was subsequently continued to the trial of this action.

The defendant resold such of the wreckage as was saleable at his premises, and evidence was given that on September 18th, 1931, a police constable purchased a second-hand tap at the store of the defendant at 1348 Dufferin Street. This was the day on which this action was commenced.

The first mentioned By-law No. 9868 was passed by the City of Toronto under the provisions of the former *Municipal Act,* corresponding to sec. 399, sub-sec. 25 of the present Act which provides that councils of urban municipalities may pass by-laws for prohibiting or regulating the carrying on of manufactures or trades which may be deemed dangerous in causing or spreading fire.

Evidence was given at the trial that a lumber yard such as that operated by the defendant where both new and second-hand lumber were stored, was deemed dangerous in causing or spreading fires, and I have no hesitation in holding that the City Council had jurisdiction to pass a by-law for prohibiting or regulating the carrying on of a lumber yard.

Cap. 30, sec. 1 of By-law 9868 provides as follows:

"1. Establishment of yards.

"No lumber yard, wood yard or planing mill shall be established in any place within the city unless a permit therefor is first obtained from the Committee on Property, said permit to be approved by the City Council before being issued."

Section 2 provides for the location and size of the piles of lumber, which may be placed on the said lands, and also makes provision for roadways between the piles, etc.

I shall proceed to deal with that branch of the case which concerns the establishment of the lumber yard. The defendant contends, *inter alia*, that this by-law is invalid in that the provision requiring a permit is enacted without authority, and is, therefore, *ultra vires* of the Council of the plaintiff municipality.

It will be noted that sec. 399, sub-sec. 25 of the *Municipal Act* empowers a Municipal Council to pass by-laws for prohibiting or regulating the carrying on of dangerous trades, etc., but nowhere in the section is there any provision authorizing a municipal corporation to require a permit or license to be obtained by any person in order to carry on any of the dangerous trades covered by this enactment. On this ground alone the by-law is invalid, so far as it requires a permit to be obtained.

By-law 9868 does provide that no lumber yard, wood yard or planing mill shall be established in any place within the City, and if it contained no other provisions then it would be competent for the Municipal Council so to enact as it would then be a prohibitory by-law within the meaning of the Municipal Act, but the by-law extends much further and contains the words "unless a permit therefor is first obtained from the Committee on Property, such permit to be approved by the City Council before being issued."

In effect, this section of the by-law enacts that no lumber yard, etc. shall be established in any place within the City unless with the approval of the City Council, and the question is now presented for solution as to whether the Municipal Council had power to impose such a condition.

In considering this by-law, I think the rule of construction laid down by Mr. Justice Osler in *Merrit* v. *City of Toronto* (1895), should be followed and applied. This rule has been approved by several later authorities and I think it well to quote it here.

"Municipal Corporations in the exercise of the statutory powers conferred upon them to make by-laws should be confined strictly within the limits of their authority and all attempts on their part to exceed it should be firmly repelled by the Courts. *A fortiori* should this be so where their by-laws are directed against the common law right and the liberty and freedom of every subject to employ himself in any lawful trade or calling he pleases." . . .

In my view, however, the fatal objection to the by-law is that it is discriminatory in its nature, is open to favouritism and tends to create a monopoly.

The Municipal Council under the provisions of the by-law virtually vote on every application for a permit and thus would be in a position to grant to one person only and refuse all others, which would contravene the provisions of sec. 263, sub-sec. 1 of the *Municipal Act*, R.S.O. 1927, ch. 233.

A by-law very similar in its terms was dealt with in *Re Nash and McCracken* (1874). The by-law in that case provided:

"No person shall keep a slaughter house within the City without the special resolution of the Council."

In quashing a conviction under this by-law, Mr. Justice Wilson, in delivering the judgment of the Court, held that while the by-law was not prohibitory altogether it gave the power to the council to make it prohibitory as to one person and permissive as to another, and that in effect it conferred the power upon the council of saying who shall not follow a particular trade within the city. . . .

When the Legislature confers upon a municipal corporation the power to pass by-laws prohibiting a particular trade or business, it is not intended that the municipal council shall deal with each case individually, but that its legislation shall be so framed as to be of general application, and that all persons shall receive like treatment.

As already stated, this by-law reserves to the municipal council the right to say whether or not a particular person should be allowed to operate a lumber yard in the city, and therefore invalid under the principle enunciated in the decision in *Re Nash and McCracken*. This branch of the plaintiff's claim therefore fails.

It was contended by counsel for the plaintiff that the by-law in question was intended to regulate the conduct of a lumber yard. This matter is dealt with by Mr. Justice Middleton in *Forst* v. *City of Toronto* (1923). At the bottom of page 278 that learned Judge is reported as follows:

"When the municipality is given the right to regulate, I think that all it can do is to pass general regulations affecting all who come within the ambit of the municipal legislation. It cannot itself discriminate, and give permission to one and refuse it to another; and, *a fortiori*, it cannot give municipal officers the right, which it does not possess, to exercise a discretion and ascertain whether as a matter of policy permission should be granted in one case and refused in another."

This dicta is particularly applicable to the present case. The by-law in question does contain regulations as to the manner in which the lumber yard should be conducted, and so far the by-law would be valid as being in exercise of the regulatory powers, but when it purports to say that a permit may be issued at the discretion of the council, it at once becomes discriminatory in its operation, and therefore invalid. As stated in the judgment of the Judicial Committee in *Toronto* v. *Virgo* (1896) regulation implies the continued existence of that which is regulated.

It would be the logical conclusion of this principle that regulation follows and does not precede the establishment of that which is to be required, and that requiring something as a condition precedent is not a regulation.

In my view the provision as to requiring a permit cannot be supported as an exercise of the power to regulate. . . .

[Part of the judgment dealing with a by-law regulating second hand sales, on which ground as well the City failed, is omitted.]

THE MUNICIPAL ACT
Ontario. Revised Statutes. 1960. Chapter 249

248.(1) Subject to section 249, and to section 6 of *The Ferries Act* and to section 100 of *The Telephone Act*, a council shall not confer on any person the exclusive right of exercising, within the municipality, any trade, calling or business, or impose a special tax on any person exercising it, or require a licence to be taken for exercising it, unless authorized or required by this or any other Act so to do; but the council may require a fee, not exceeding $1, to be paid to the proper officer for a certificate of compliance with any regulations in regard to the trade, calling or business. [Section 248(1) is in substantially the language of section 263(1) of R.S.O. 1927, c. 233.]

379. (1) By-laws may be passed by the councils of local municipalities:

129. For limiting the number of public garages and automobile service stations where gasoline is stored or kept for sale.

CITY OF TORONTO ZONING BY-LAW NO. 20,623 (1959)

6. (3) No person shall, within any R.1 district (1) erect any *church* until the plans and elevations thereof have been considered by the Committee on Buildings and Development and City Council after receiving reports thereon from a committee consisting of the Commissioners of Buildings and City Planning and at least two members of the Toronto Chapter of the Ontario Association of Architects and from the Toronto City Planning Board; . . .

QUESTIONS. The effect of section 6(3) appears to be a possible delay of indefinite duration. Is there anything in section 30 of *The Planning Act* in Ontario that authorizes an indefinite (or any) delay? If the principle is sound, should there be any procedural safeguards? Should the applicant be entitled to appear before the Committee on Buildings? Before the committee of architects, the Planning Board and the Commissioners? Should there be a time limit? Should there be any appeal? To whom? Why?

CONSOLIDATED TORONTO DEVELOPMENT CORPORATION LIMITED ("VENDOR") and ETOBICOKE TOWNSHIP, AGREEMENT (1962)

1. The Vendor agrees contemporaneously with the signing of this agreement, to deliver to the Township a conveyance of the lands described in Schedule "1" and in such conveyance or by separate agreement as may be satisfactory to the Township, impose upon the lands described in Schedule "2" the restrictions attached in Schedule "B" and "C" in favour of the lands described in Schedule "1" and the Vendor agrees to affix to any agreement of purchase and sale entered into by the Vendor with respect to any part of the lands described in Schedule "2" attached hereto, for the

erection of multiple-family dwellings the Schedule attached hereto and marked "B" and to obtain a covenant from a purchaser to comply with the terms and conditions therein contained.

2. The Vendor further agrees to affix to any agreement of purchase and sale entered into by the Vendor with respect to any part of the lands described in Schedule "2" attached hereto, for the erection of buildings for commercial use the Schedule attached hereto and marked "C" and to obtain a covenant from a purchaser to comply with the terms and conditions therein contained.

3. The covenants by such purchasers and of the Vendor (which is hereby given) to comply with the provisions of Schedule "B" and "C" are herein called the "restrictions." The Vendor agrees to transfer to the Township the lands described in Schedule "1" being in proximity to the lands described in Schedule "2" to which latter lands the Restrictions shall attach and it is agreed that the benefit of the covenant of the Restrictions shall pass to the Township and the owners from time to time of the lands described in Schedule "1" provided that the said Restrictions and the construction of any and all buildings on the said lands shall be supervised and controlled by the Design Approval Committee as hereinafter provided. In the event of any breach of the Restrictions and after the said Committee has given notice to the purchaser of a breach of the Restrictions and its recommendations for compliance, the said Township at the request of the said Committee shall have the authority to enforce compliance of the Restrictions against the said purchaser.

4. There shall be constituted a Committee to be known as "DESIGN APPROVAL COMMITTEE" to be composed of a nominee of the Vendor and a nominee of the Township for the purpose of examining and approving in writing, plans submitted by any purchaser or any amendments or variances thereto and to consider any alleged breach of the Restrictions and to ascertain whether a breach has or has not occurred and the method or manner of correcting the same. The parties hereto shall have the right to appoint one or more alternate nominees who may act in the event of the failure to act of the other nominee. The parties hereto agree to forthwith appoint and to advise the other party of their respective nominees to such Committee. Any party may revoke the appointment of its nominee at any time and may nominate in his place and stead in its absolute discretion a successor and so on from time to time and upon any such nominations being made by any party hereto and the notice delivered to the other party, the person so nominated shall forthwith and without further requirement or approval become a member of the said Committee with all the powers and subject to all the duties set forth in Schedule "B" and "C" hereto and as provided in this agreement. In the event that either party hereto shall not appoint a nominee within twenty (20) days of a request in writing so to do by the other party, or in the event of the nominee of either party ceasing to act for any reason, and such party failing to nominate any nominee within five (5) days of a demand in writing from the other party so to do, then the nominee of the party not being in default shall be deemed to be the Design Approval Committee for all purposes of this agreement.

5. In considering applications for approval and in all other matters the Design Approval Committee shall be bound by the following rules:—

(1) The Committee shall have ten (10) days within which to either approve or reject the application of a Purchaser.

(2) If the application of a purchaser is not approved or rejected with-

in the ten (10) days period then the Purchaser may within three (3) days thereafter, request the Committee in writing to appoint a third party acceptable to the Committee and being a registered architect in the Province of Ontario to become a member of the Committee for the purpose of considering his application. The Committee as increased shall have a further period of seven (7) days within which to either approve or reject the application of the Purchaser and the decision of a majority of the Committee as constituted, shall be final and binding upon the Purchaser with respect to any such application without prejudice to the right of the purchaser to submit such further and other applications as he sees fit.

(3) If the Committee are unable to agree as to:

(a) whether or not there has been a breach of the Restrictions; or,

(b) the method or manner of correcting a breach of the restrictions

within a period of seven (7) days of its becoming aware of the condition which is the subject of disagreement, then the Committee shall, within a period of three (3) days thereafter, appoint a third party acceptable to the Committee and being a registered architect in the Province of Ontario to become a member of the Committee for the purpose of considering the condition which is the subject to disagreement. The Committee as increased shall have a further period of seven (7) days within which to determine whether or not there has been a breach of the restrictions or the method or manner of correcting a breach of the restrictions and the decision of a majority of a Committee conveyed to the Purchaser in writing shall be final and binding on a Purchaser.

(4) A Purchaser shall have the period of seven (7) days from receipt of the decision of the Committee in writing that he has breached the restriction in which to take steps to remedy such breach, and upon his failure to do so the Committee shall report the matter to the Township to take whatever action it sees fit.

(5) In the event that the Committee are unable to agree upon a third party to become a member of the Committee for the purpose of these rules, then the Committee shall apply to the Ontario Association of Architects to appoint a registered architect to act on the Committee.

(6) Approvals of such plans are to be consistent with the Building By-laws and the Restricted Area By-laws of the Township of Etobicoke and the restrictions attached hereto.

6. This agreement shall be binding upon and enure to the benefit of the parties hereto and their successors and assigns, and the said restrictions in Schedule B and C shall be binding upon the Vendor while it is the owner of lands in Schedule 2 or any part thereof.

SCHEDULE "B"

This Schedule is to apply to lands used for and is to be annexed to any offer to purchase, agreement for sale, conveyance or transfer of land for the erection of multi-family dwellings, and contains the Restrictions referred to in the annexed document.

2. No building shall be erected without first obtaining the approval in

writing of the Design Approval Committee to the plans and location of any building to be erected and no building shall be erected except in conformity with the plans and location so approved but the Design Approval Committee may at any time amend or vary the plans and location of any building being erected or erected on the lands.

3. An application shall be made by the Vendor to the Design Approval Committee or if the lands have been sold by the Vendor then by the Purchaser to the Vendor for presentation to the said Design Approval Committee, to include the following information:—
   (a) Location of proposed buildings.
   (b) Height of proposed buildings.
   (c) Location of entrances and exits.
   (d) Area and location of lands to be used for off-street parking.
   (e) Use of lands not covered or to be covered by buildings.
   (f) The number and dimensions of each dwelling unit and location of same in the building.
   (g) Architectural elevations of the proposed buildings.

7. In the event that construction has not commenced within one year from the date of the approval of the Design Approval Committee, the application must be resubmitted containing the information outlined in Paragraph 3 hereof for approval by the Design Approval Committee.

8. The Design Approval Committee may amend or vary any of the above Restrictions herein contained.

[Clauses 1, 4, 5 and 6 of Schedule "B" have been omitted.]

NOTE. The Consolidated Toronto Development Corporation Ltd. agreement is a rather special one in Etobicoke, in that it puts the ultimate approval in the hands of an independent committee. Is this desirable? What are the advantages and disadvantages? Another form of agreement in use in Etobicoke reserves the final approval to Township authorities. Is this a "better" arrangement? Why?

THE TOWN AND RURAL PLANNING ACT
Alberta. Revised Statutes. 1955. Chapter 337

68. (1) The council, on passing a resolution authorizing the preparation of a general plan, shall forthwith make application to the Minister for authority to exercise control over development that takes place in the municipality or part thereof prior
   (*a*) to the completion and adoption of the general plan, and
   (*b*) to the passage of a zoning by-law prepared in accordance with the general plan.

(2) Control shall be exercised over the development within the municipality by the council on the basis of the merits of each individual application for permission to develop, having regard to the proposed development conforming with the general plan being prepared.

69. The council, in making an application under section 68, shall submit to the Minister
   (*a*) a certified copy of the resolution authorizing the preparation of the general plan,
   (*b*) a description of the area over which interim development control is to be exercised, and

(*c*) a statement of the arrangements that the council has made for
(i) the preparation of the general plan, and
(ii) the administration of interim development control.

70. The Minister, upon receipt of an application for authority to exercise interim development control, and upon being satisfied that the arrangements made for the preparation of the general plan and for administration of the interim development control are satisfactory, may make an order to be known as an interim development order, which shall

(*a*) suspend the operation of any existing zoning by-law in the municipality within the described area over which the interim development control is to be exercised, and

(*b*) authorize the council, upon the coming into effect of a by-law adopting the Minister's interim development order, to exercise interim development control over the described area.

70*a*. For the purpose of removing doubt it is hereby declared that an interim development order made by the Minister pursuant to section 70 is not a regulation within the meaning of *The Regulations Act*.

71. An interim development order shall prescribe

(*a*) the date upon which the suspension of the operation of any existing zoning by-law comes into effect, and

(*b*) the manner in which the council, its agents or servants may exercise interim development control and the matters to be subject to such control, and

(*c*) the appointment by the council of an interim development board or an interim development officer to assist the council in the administration of interim development control.

71*a*. (1) Subject to subsection (2*a*), all applications in respect of matters arising out of the exercise of interim development control shall be considered and determined by the council.

(2) The interim development by-law shall provide for the appointment of either an interim development board, or an interim development officer and shall authorize the council to delegate to such board or officer authority to act pursuant to subsection (2*b*).

(2*a*) At any time during the exercise of interim development control, a council may by resolution bring into operation,

(*a*) any part or parts of the general plan before the completion of the full general plan,

(*b*) rules specifying types of development in all or any part of a municipality.

(2*b*) Such resolution may authorize the interim development board or the interim development officer to consider and decide on behalf of the council, any application with respect to development that is subject to the terms of such resolution.

(2*c*) The technical planning board, the planning advisory commission, the interim development board, or the interim development officer of a municipality may recommend to the council that a resolution be passed under subsection (2*a*) with respect to any matter that may be dealt with under that subsection.

(2*d*) No resolution passed under subsection (2*a*) has any force or effect until it has been approved by the Board.

(2*e*) When a resolution is submitted to the Board for its approval under subsection (2*d*), it shall be accompanied by a report in writing from the planning officer or planning consultant appointed under clause (*a*) of section 64 indicating the nature of the planning considerations on which the resolution is based.

(3) A person affected by the decision of an interim development board or an interim development officer may appeal

(*a*) to an appeal board established pursuant to subsection (4), or

(*b*) where no appeal board is established, to the council.

(4) A council may by by-law establish an appeal board consisting of at least three persons to be appointed annually by resolution of the council, none of whom shall be officials or servants of the council or members of the interim development board and at least one of whom shall be a member of the council.

(5) The appeal board shall hear an appeal from a decision of the interim development board or the interim development officer and shall recommend a decision to the council, giving reasons for the recommendation.

(6) After considering the recommendation of the appeal board the council shall give a decision in the appeal.

(7) A person affected by a decision of a council under this section may appeal the decision to the Board.

(8) The Board may confirm, reverse or vary the decision appealed from as the Board deems desirable and necessary.

(8*a*) In determining an appeal the Board shall have regard to the general scope and intent of the order and the by-law and the general plan that is being prepared but the Board is not bound thereby.

(9) An appeal under subsection (3) or subsection (7) shall be made in the manner and within the period stated in the order.

72. (1) Interim development control becomes effective within a municipality when, pursuant to the interim development order and in accordance with section 83, the interim development by-law is passed and approved.

(2) Where an interim development order is in effect in a municipality other than an improvement district or special area, the council shall make an annual report to the Board on the progress made in the preparation of the general plan, and on the operation of interim development control.

(3) The Minister upon the recommendation of the Board may rescind an interim development order if he is not satisfied with the progress being made in the preparation of the general plan or with the manner in which interim development control is being administered.

(4) Where the Minister amends, rescinds or replaces an interim development order, the council shall forthwith amend, rescind or replace its interim development by-law accordingly.

72*a*. With respect to the control of development in a special area or an improvement district, the Minister may delegate to such person as he may appoint any or all of the functions required of the Minister by section 71*a*.

73. (1) At any time after the adoption of a general plan, or while interim development control is being exercised, the council may prepare and adopt a development scheme for the purpose

(*a*) of ensuring that any proposal contained in the general plan will be carried out, or will be carried out in a particular way, or

(*b*) of amplifying as to its details any such proposal.

(2) Without limiting the generality of subsection (1), the council by a development scheme

(*a*) may make available any land for agricultural, residential, commercial, industrial or other purposes of any class at any particular time, and provide for the acquisition, assembly, consolidation, subdivision and sale or lease by the municipality of such land and buildings as are necessary to carry out the development scheme, or

(*b*) may reserve land for future acquisition as the site or location of any road, service, public building, school, park or other open space, and impose such building and other restrictions on the use of the land and make such agreements with the owners of the land as are necessary to carry out the development scheme, or

(*c*) may specify the manner in which any particular area of land is to be subdivided and prohibit buildings and works that would interfere with the carrying out of the development scheme.

74. A development scheme shall describe and set out

(*a*) the manner in which the scheme is intended to implement a proposal or part of a proposal contained or to be contained in the general plan,

(*b*) the land affected by the scheme, and the names and addresses of owners of such land, and

(*c*) the details

(i) of the development to be carried out,

(ii) of the land to be reserved and the manner in which the reservation is to be exercised, or

(iii) of the manner in which land affected by the scheme is to be subdivided.

75. A development scheme does not come into force until it has been adopted by by-law in accordance with section 83.

[R.S.A. 1955, c. 337, s. 75; 1957, c. 98, s. 12]

76. When a development scheme comes into force, the council may acquire by expropriation or otherwise any lands or buildings the acquisition of which is essential to the carrying out of the scheme, together with lands

(*a*) that are the remnants of parcels, portions of which are necessary for carrying out the scheme, or

(*b*) that may be injuriously affected by the scheme.

77. (1) When any land is acquired under the authority of section 76, the owner of the land has the same right to compensation therefor as he would have if the land were land being acquired for public purposes by the municipality under the provisions of the municipal Act by which it is governed.

78. The council, for the purpose of carrying out a development scheme, may dispose of any lands acquired for the purposes of the development scheme without the approval of the proprietary electors, subject to such building or other restrictions as may be set out in the development scheme.

79. An expense incurred by the council in acquiring lands or in imposing building or other restrictions for the purposes of the development scheme shall be met as part of the cost of the scheme, and the proceeds of any sale or other disposition of the lands so acquired shall be applied against the cost of the development scheme.

[The sections above have been reproduced as amended by S.A., 1957, c. 98; 1958, c. 86; 1959, c. 89; 1960, c. 107; 1961, c. 79 and c. 30, Schedule Two.]

BILL 57
Alberta. 14th Legislature. 5th Session. 1963

104. (1) A development control by-law shall, subject to this section, provide for the control of development by means of a system of permits.

(2) The by-law may provide that where a development permit is refused, an application for the same development may not be submitted by the same or any other person until at least six months, or such longer period (not exceeding two years) as may be fixed by the by-law, after the refusal.

(3) A council may issue a development permit on conditions as to the construction of public roadways required to give access to the development and the installation of utilities that are necessitated by the development.

(4) If the development authorized by a permit is not commenced within twelve months from the date of its issue the permit ceases to be valid.

107. (1) A land use classification guide and a schedule of permitted land uses may be prepared and adopted by a resolution of a council under section 105 for the purposes of development control, but such a guide or schedule is not part of the development control by-law.

(2) Where the owner or prospective owner of land wishes to develop the land for a use for which the land is not classified in the guide, he may apply to the council for provisional approval of the use desired and the council may grant a provisional approval of that use.

(3) A provisional approval granted under subsection (2) is effective for twelve months from the date thereof and within that time an application may be made for a specific development of the land in conformity with the approved use and if a development permit is granted the land use classification guide shall be so amended.

109. A development control by-law may provide for the establishment of a development appeal board, which shall consist of at least three persons to be appointed annually by resolution of the council, none of whom shall be officials or servants of the council or members of the municipal planning commission, and at least one of whom shall be a member of the council and a majority shall be persons other than members of the council.

110. (1) A person affected by a decision of a municipal planning commission or a development control officer made pursuant to section 105 may appeal

(a) to the development appeal board, or

(b) where no development appeal board is established, to the council.

[Section 105 is similar to section 71*a* in the present Act.]

NOTE. Somewhat similar legislation in Saskatchewan (S.S., 1957, c. 48, ss. 35ff, as amended by S.S., 1959, c. 107, s. 5) limits "interim" control to three years from the date of approval of the Minister or from such later date as he may specify. Newfoundland also authorizes "interim" control for two years (S.N., 1953, No. 27, s. 11(1).)

RE GIANNONE'S APPEAL
Alberta. Supreme Court. 1961. 35 W.W.R. (N.S.) 320

MILVAIN J.: . . . Mr. Giannone, exercising the right conferred upon him by sec. 71*a* of *The Town and Rural Planning Act* (added 1957, ch. 98, sec. 9; substituted 1959, ch. 89, sec. 8; and amended 1960, ch. 107, sec. 17), appealed from the decision of council to the provincial planning advisory board, and that board caused hearings to be held on June 15 and November 7, 1960, and finally handed down its decision on December 9, 1960, from which decision the appeal has been carried to me. From that decision of the board I quote as follows:

"The Board Finds That:

"1. The development proposed by the appellant entails a service station, shopping centre and an hotel on a parcel of land situated between 135th and 137th Avenues and 97th and 101st Streets, comprising approximately 4.4 acres in area.

"The City of Edmonton Council varied the conditional recommendation for approval made to it by the Interim Development Appeal Board by eliminating approval of the hotel from the proposed development. By its decision therefore, Council has approved the development of a service station and shopping centre, occupying in the proposal the south part of the parcel, but has refused the development of an hotel proposed to be situated at the north part of the parcel.

"Preliminary layout plans for the proposed development were prepared on the basis of the size and shape of parcel which would evolve after completion of a replotting scheme, which among other things provides for the acquisition by the City of sufficient lands to undertake its major intersection proposals at 137th Avenue and 97th Street. As the consent of the appellant to the scheme was conditional on his receiving a development permit for his proposal and as such permit was not obtained it is assumed that the scheme has, as yet, not followed to completion with the registration of a plan.

"The north portion of the parcel, by virtue of the replotting scheme, evolves as a triangularly shaped piece and it is on this piece that the hotel building is proposed to be located.

"The major portion of the approximately 325 car parking spaces provided is in the area of the parcel proposed for shopping centre development. It is the intention that the parking area will be used jointly by the hotel and shopping centre. Access to the site is proposed to be gained from both 97th Street and 135th Avenue.

"2. Protesting parties centred their arguments on one or more of the following salient points:

"(a) There was no need for an hotel in the general area;

"(b) The proposal was too near planned and established residential area and also institutions such as the Beulah Home, a home for retarded children and a proposed, but as yet undeveloped, convent.

"(c) An hotel should not be located on a main traffic artery and parking should not be jointly utilized by an hotel and other uses as a hazard would result, with increase in erratic driving.

"(d) That the prime reason for the proposal was to make a profit through the sale of spirituous liquor and

"(e) On general moral and pseudo-religious grounds.

"3. Main arguments submitted in support of the appeal centred on the following salient points:

"(a) The present site was chosen in preference to a site approved for hotel development, also on 97th Street but on 132nd Avenue to remove the development as far distant as possible from established institutional uses. It was felt that this was necessary in order to obtain the necessary approval of the Alberta Liquor Control Board. For the same reason it was considered that it would be desirable to locate the hotel at the extreme north portion of the parcel in the present application.

"(b) The site is suitable for its intended purposes and will fulfill a need of the travelling public.

"(c) Conditional approval of the development and location has been obtained from the Alberta Liquor Control Board.

"(d) Council varied the recommendation of the Interim Development Appeal Board and of the Interim Development Officer on other than planning grounds and

"(e) The proposed use of the site for hotel purposes has long been indicated on tentative plans of the City prior to the land being obtained by the present owners.

"4. A previously approved hotel development fronting onto 97th Street in the vicinity of 129th Avenue, proposed by other interests, has not been proceeded with. The development permit has lapsed and the approval of hotel construction has been withdrawn by the Alberta Liquor Control Board.

"The Board after due consideration is of the opinion that:

"1. The appeal should be determined solely on technical or planning grounds. In particular the use of the subject site for business purposes should be thoroughly examined, notwithstanding that by its decision Council has permitted the development of a commercial nature on part of the site but has adjudged the hotel on another part unacceptable.

"2. Both 97th Street and 137th Avenue are main arterial roadways, the latter at present, being the northern limits of the City. The major construction proposed for the intersection of the two main arteries together with the recently completed underpass at the C.N.R. trackage south of 127th Avenue establishes the great importance of 97th Street (Highway No. 28). Level crossing exists at present of the main line at 127th Street to the west and 82nd Street to the east. It is possible that another crossing will in the future be established between 97th Street and 127th Street. With the completion of development of only the four neighbourhood units immediately adjacent to it 97th Street will increase in importance. The establishment of commercial development along 97th Street should therefore be carefully controlled so as not to reduce the capabilities of the important thoroughfare. Particularly commercial development should be discouraged in close proximity to major intersections with due regard to access problems and additional generation of traffic.

"3. Apparently it was the original intention to limit commercial development south of 132nd Avenue and west of 97th Street but it has been stated that design and land assembly problems made this proposal impractical.

"4. Prospective developers also exerted pressure to enable their location along 97th Street. To date little actual development of retail facilities has occurred north of 132nd Avenue with the exception of service stations. Apparently though Council has approved several large sites by way of reclassification for commercial use principally for large food concerns. These though, in the main, are still located either south of 132nd Avenue or immediately north of the Avenue. Complete lineal development therefore of the street has not yet occurred. It has been submitted that some 25 acres is available for commercial development in the area, considerably more than is needed.

"5. Notwithstanding, the City's argument that design problems are unsolvable, an opinion not shared by the Board, the Board cannot condone the lineal 'ribbon' spread of commercial development along the arterial roadway and must therefore oppose the proposed development on this ground.

"The Board has therefore decided that:

"The appeal should be refused on the ground that further lineal development along the major thoroughfare is wholly undesirable."

In my view the city council and the provincial planning advisory board, in considering the whole matter, lost sight of the most important provision of *The Town and Rural Planning Act* from which both the council and the board derive their authority. Sec. 2*a* of the Act (added 1959, ch. 89, sec. 2) reads as follows:

"The purpose of this Act is to provide means whereby municipalities, either singly or jointly, may plan for orderly and economical development without infringing on the rights of land owners except to the extent that is necessary, for the greater public interest, to obtain orderly development and use of land in the province."

Sec. 2*a* above quoted makes it clear that the owner of land is not to have his rights infringed upon except to the extent that it is necessary to do so in order to carry out orderly development. There can be no doubt but that at common law the owner of land may do anything with it that he desires to do and that right is not to be infringed except to the extent that a statute in clear terms permits. In my view the city council and the provincial planning advisory board have made it clear that it is not necessary to interfere with Mr. Giannone's common-law rights with regard to the commercial development of his property. The city council and the provincial planning advisory board in permitting a shopping centre and a service station indicate very clearly that it is not necessary to prevent commercial development in the public interest for orderly development or any other reason.

Commercial development of the property by creation thereon of a shopping centre and service station is a development, in my view comparable in character to the erection of a hotel. All projects envision the coming on to the property of considerable numbers of the public. The hotel cannot be said to be more noisome or undesirable than the activity of a shopping centre or service station. In fact the desirability of the licensing of a hotel as an outlet for spirituous beverages is governed by an entirely different Act and by a different board under the provisions of *The Liquor Licensing Act*, 1958, ch. 38.

In my view the city council and the provincial planning advisory board once they gave countenance to a commercial development in the way of a shopping centre and service station, usurped a jurisdiction not given by the Act in discriminating against a hotel as part of the development. In my view the appeal should be allowed, and the recommendation of the Edmonton interim development appeal board should be implemented on the basis that the conditions imposed by the interim development appeal board be added to with a provision requiring an adequate fence between the hotel and the Beulah Home, as has been discussed and I understand agreed upon between Mr. Giannone and the Beulah Home.

As it was the provincial planning advisory board which took the most active interest in opposing the appeal before me, I direct that it shall pay to the appellant the costs of this appeal, which I fix at the sum of $250 and disbursements.

RE EDMONTON DEVELOPMENT PERMIT

Alberta. Supreme Court. 1962. 38 W.W.R. (N.S.) 267

KIRBY J.: . . . On September 25, 1961, Rheinhold Kapchinsky, one of the registered owners of lots 1, 3 and 16, block 62, Bronx subdivision, in the city of Edmonton, applied to the city of Edmonton, office of the interim development officer, city planning department, for a development permit for the purpose of erecting a self-service dry-cleaning plant on the aforesaid lands. The lands form part of a shopping centre. The application was endorsed with the unconditional approval of W. B. Weir on September 28, 1961.

Pyrch & Co., the applicants [for an order of *certiorari* to quash the development permit] were the owners of the property situate across the land to the north of the aforesaid lots, on which was located a bowling alley, the entrance to which faces south to the area on which the said dry-cleaning plant was to be erected. This area has been used for car parking.

On October 21, 1961, the applicants, by letter addressed to the city planning department, objected to the location of the proposed development, claiming that the view to the main entrance of the bowling alley was blocked off completely by the proposed dry-cleaning plant, and that the entrance to the bowling alley would look into the rear of the dry-cleaning plant. This letter came before city council and was referred to the city commissioners for consideration.

On November 22, 1961, the applicants and Kapchinsky, represented by their solicitors, attended a meeting of the city commissioners, at which this matter was discussed.

On November 27, 1961, the city council concurred with the opinion of the commissioners that the issuance of the development permit was in order; that since no objection to the proposed development was received within the statutory period of 10 days from the date of the decision of the officer, the development should be allowed to proceed. . . .

In my view . . . the issuing of a development permit pursuant to the authority derived from *The Town and Rural Planning Act* through the interim development order No. 2 and by-law No. 1988, is not an act which can be regarded as simply ministerial. Assuming the conditions of authority to be complied with, the interim development officer has the "right or duty to decide" whether to issue a permit, with or without conditions, to refer the proposed development to the city council, or to refuse the application with reasons. These are the powers which likewise may be exercised by the city council on appeal. I am therefore of the opinion that the approving of the development permit by the interim development officer is a matter properly brought into this court by *certiorari* proceedings.

I now pass on to consider the grounds for objection to the granting of the permit raised by the applicants. . . .

The interim development control commenced with the enactment of interim development by-law No. 2 on September 1, 1959, and did not expire until the council adopted a general plan and enacted a new zoning by-law, or when the interim development order was rescinded. The new zoning by-law was not enacted until November 28, 1961, and as there is no evidence that the order had been rescinded, such interim development control remained in effect until that date. . . .

The fourth ground of objection was that if the zoning by-law was usable it does not give the power to the interim development officer here used. It is pointed out that in the zoning by-law referred to above, the proposed development is in a C-1 area, in which, under sec. 25 of the zoning by-law the only use which could be approved relative to dry-cleaning is "Dry Cleaners' Distributing Stations." Sec. 68 (2) of the Act provides:

68. (2) Control shall be exercised over the development within the

municipality by the council on the basis of the merits of each individual application for permission to develop, having regard to the proposed development conforming with the general plan being prepared."

This section gives wide discretion in the exercise of control over development. I do not see any justification for interfering with the manner in which that discretion has been exercised in this case.

To sum up: I am of the opinion that the development permit signed by W. B. Weir on September 28, 1961, was properly and legally approved in accordance with the provisions of the Act, interim development order No. 2, and interim development by-law No. 2. . . .

2. British Development Control

TOWN AND COUNTRY PLANNING ACT, 1947
England. Statutes. 1947. Chapter 51

12. (1) Subject to the provisions of this section and to the following provisions of this Act, permission shall be required under this Part of this Act in respect of any development of land which is carried out after the appointed day.

(2) In this Act, except where the context otherwise requires, the expression "development" means the carrying out of building, engineering, mining or other operations in, on, over or under land, or the making of any material change in the use of any buildings or other land;

Provided that the following operations or uses of land shall not be deemed for the purposes of this Act to involve development of the land, that is to say:

(a) the carrying out of works for the maintenance, improvement or other alteration of any building, being works which affect only the interior of the building or which do not materially affect the external appearance of the building;

(b) the carrying out by a local highway authority of any works required for the maintenance or improvement of a road, being works carried out on land within the boundaries of the road;

(c) the carrying out by any local authority or statutory undertakers of any works for the purpose of inspecting, repairing or renewing any sewers, mains, pipes, cables or other apparatus, including the breaking open of any street or other land for that purpose;

(d) the use of any buildings or other land within the curtilage of a dwellinghouse for any purpose incidental to the enjoyment of the dwellinghouse as such;

(e) the use of any land for the purposes of agriculture or forestry (including afforestation), and the use for any of those purposes of any building occupied together with land so used;

(f) in the case of buildings or other land which are used for a purpose of any class specified in an order made by the Minister under this section, the use thereof for any other purpose of the same class.

(3) For the avoidance of doubt it is hereby declared that for the purposes of this section—

(a) the use as two or more separate dwellinghouses of any building previously used as a single dwellinghouse involves a material change in the use of the building and of each part thereof which is so used;

(b) the deposit of refuse or waste materials on land involves a material change in the use thereof, notwithstanding that the land is comprised in a site already used for that purpose, if the superficial area or the height of the deposit is thereby extended.

Provided that nothing in paragraph (b) of this subsection shall be deemed to require permission in respect of the deposit of refuse or waste materials on a site already used for that purpose if the height of the deposit does not exceed the level of the land adjoining such site, and the superficial area of the deposit is not thereby extended.

(4) Without prejudice to the provisions of any regulations made under the provisions of this Act relating to the control of advertisements, the use for the display of advertisements of any external part of a building which is not normally used for that purpose shall be treated for the purposes of this section as involving a material change in the use of that part of the building.

(5) Notwithstanding anything in this section, permission shall not be required under this Part of this Act—

(a) in the case of land which, on the appointed day, is being used temporarily for a purpose other than the purpose for which it is normally used, in respect of the resumption of the use of the land for the last-mentioned purpose;

(b) in the case of land which, on the appointed day, is normally used for one purpose and is also used on occasions, whether at regular intervals or not, for any other purpose, in respect of the use of the land for that other purpose on similar occasions after the appointed day;

(c) in the case of land which on the appointed day is unoccupied, in respect of the use of the land for the purpose for which it was last used:

Provided that—

(i) in determining for the purposes of paragraph (a) of this subsection the purposes for which land was normally used and in determining for the purposes of paragraph (c) of this subsection the purposes for which land was last used no account shall be taken of any use of the land begun in contravention of previous planning control within the meaning of section seventy-five of this Act:

(ii) paragraph (c) of this subsection shall not apply to land which was unoccupied on the seventh day of January, nineteen hundred and thirty-seven and has not been occupied since that date.

["Use", in relation to land, does not include the use of land by the carrying out of any building or other operations thereon; (s. 119 (1).]

120. (2) This Act shall come into force on the appointed day . . .

["appointed day" means such day as the Minister may by order appoint. (s. 119(1)). The Minister appointed July 1, 1948. The Act received Royal Assent on August 6, 1947.]

19. (1) Where permission to develop any land is refused, whether by the local planning authority or by the Minister, on an application in that behalf made under this Part of this Act, or is granted by that authority or by the Minister subject to conditions, then if any owner of the lands claims—

(a) that the land has become incapable of reasonably beneficial use in its existing state; and

(b) in a case where permission to develop the land was granted as aforesaid subject to conditions, that the land cannot be rendered capable of reasonably beneficial use by the carrying out of the permitted development in accordance with those conditions;

(c) in any case, that the land cannot be rendered capable of reasonably beneficial use by the carrying out of any other development for which permission has been or is deemed to be granted under this Part of this Act, or for which the local planning authority or the Minister have undertaken to grant such permission,

he may, within the time and in the manner prescribed by regulations made under this Act, serve on the council of the county, borough or county district in which the land is situated a notice (hereinafter referred to as a "purchase notice") requiring that council to purchase his interest in the land in accordance with the provisions of this section.

(2) Where a purchase notice is served on any council under this section, that council shall forthwith transmit a copy of the notice to the Minister, and subject to the following provisions of this section the Minister shall, if he is satisfied that the conditions specified in paragraphs (a) to (c) of the foregoing subsection are fulfilled, confirm the notice, and thereupon the council shall be deemed to be authorised to acquire the interest of the owner compulsorily in accordance with the provisions of Part IV of this Act, and to have served a notice to treat in respect thereof on such date as the Minister may direct:

Provided that—

(a) if it appears to the Minister to be expedient so to do, he may, in lieu of confirming the purchase notice, grant permission for the development in respect of which the application was made or, where permission for that development was granted subject to conditions, revoke or amend those conditions so far as appears to him to be required in order to enable the land to be rendered capable of reasonably beneficial use by the carrying out of that development;

(b) if it appears to the Minister, that the land, or any part of the land, could be rendered capable of reasonably beneficial use within a reasonable time by the carrying out of any other development for which permission ought to be granted, he may, in lieu of confirming the notice, or in lieu of confirming it so far as it relates to that part of the land, as the case may be, direct that such permission shall be so granted in the event of an application being made in that behalf;

(c) if it appears to the Minister, having regard to the probable ultimate use of the land, that it is expedient so to do, he may, if he confirms the notice, modify it, either in relation to the whole or in relation to any part of the land to which it relates, by substituting any other local authority for the council on whom the notice is served, and in any such case the foregoing provisions of this subsection shall have effect accordingly.

(3) If within the period of six months from the date on which a purchase notice is served under this section the Minister has neither confirmed the notice nor taken any such other action as is mentioned in paragraph (a) or paragraph (b) of the last foregoing subsection, nor notified the owner by whom the notice was served that he does not propose to confirm the notice, the notice shall be deemed to be confirmed at the expiration of that period, and the council on whom the notice was served shall be deemed to be authorised to acquire the interest of the owner compulsorily in accordance with

the provisions of Part IV of this Act, and to have served notice to treat in respect thereof at the expiration of the said period.

TOWN AND COUNTRY PLANNING (USE CLASSES) ORDER, 1950
England. 1950. S. I. No. 1131

[The *Town and Country Planning Act, 1947*, by s. 12 contemplated a freezing of land use in England and Wales as of the appointed day, July 1, 1948, but it also contemplated that "planning permission" would be granted by the county or county borough council, subject to appeal to the Minister. Inevitably many cases would arise where as a matter of course planning permission would be granted, and to reduce what is sometimes called "red tape", the Minister made two orders. One was the *Town and Country Planning (Use Classes) Order, 1950*, and the schedule is set out below in full as an illustration of the technique used in England today. The other was the *Town and Country Planning (General Development) Order*. 1950 S.I. No. 728. Its provisions are only briefly sampled.]

3. (1) Where a building or other land is used for a purpose of any class specified in the Schedule to this Order, the use of such building or other land for any other purpose of the same class shall not be deemed for the purposes of the Act to involve development of the land.

(2) Where a group of contiguous or adjacent buildings used as parts of a single undertaking includes industrial buildings used for purposes falling within two or more of the classes specified in the Schedule to this Order as Classes III to IX inclusive, those particular two or more classes may, in relation to that group of buildings, and so long as the area occupied in that group by either general or special industrial buildings is not substantially increased thereby, be treated as a single class for the purposes of this Order.

(3) A use which is ordinarily incidental to and included in any use specified in the Schedule to this Order is not excluded from that use as an incident thereto merely by reason of its specification in the said Schedule as a separate use.

SCHEDULE

Class 1. Use as a shop for any purpose except as:
- (i) a fried fish shop;
- (ii) a tripe shop;
- (iii) a shop for the sale of pet animals or birds;
- (iv) a cats-meat shop

Class II. Use as an office for any purpose.
Class III. Use as a light industrial building for any purpose.
Class IV. Use as a general industrial building for any purpose.
Class V. Use for any work which is registerable under the Alkali, etc. Works Regulation Act, 1906(d), as extended by the Alkali, etc. Work Orders, 1928 to 1950(e), except a process ancillary to the getting, dressing or treatment of minerals, carried on in or adjacent to a quarry or mine.

Use for any of the following processes, except as aforesaid, so far as not registerable under the above Act:
- (i) smelting, calcining, sintering or other reduction of ores or minerals;
- (ii) converting, re-heating, annealing, hardening or carburising, forging or casting, of iron or other metals;
- (iii) galvanising;
- (iv) recovering of metal from scrap;
- (v) pickling or treatment of metal in acid;

(vi) chromium plating.

(Special Industrial Group A.)

Class VI. Use for any of the following processes so far as not included in Class V and except a process ancillary to the getting, dressing or treatment of minerals, carried on in or adjacent to a quarry or mine:

(i) burning of building bricks;
(ii) lime and dolomite burning;
(iii) carbonisation of coal in coke ovens;
(iv) production of calcium carbide, lampblack or zinc oxide;
(v) crushing or screening of stone or slag.

(Special Industrial Group B.)

Class VII. Use for any of the following purposes so far as not included in Class V:

The production or employment of
(i) cyanogen or its compounds;
(ii) liquid or gaseous sulphur dioxide;
(iii) sulphur chlorides.

Salt glazing.

Sintering of sulphur bearing materials.

The manufacture of glass, where the sodium sulphate used exceeds 1.5 per cent of the total weight of the melt.

The production of ultramarine or zinc chloride.

(Special Industrial Group C.)

Class VIII. Use for any of the following purposes so far as not included in Class V:

The distilling, refining or blending of oils, the production or employment of cellulose lacquers (except their employment in garages in connection with minor repairs), hot pitch or bitumen, or pyridine; the stoving of enamelled ware; the production of amyl acetate, aromatic esters, butyric acid, caramel, hexamine, iodoform, B-naphthol, resin produces (except synthetic resins, plastic moulding or extrusion compositions and plastic sheets, rods, tubes, filaments, fibres or optical components produced by casting, calendering, moulding, shaping or extrusion), salicylic acid, or sulphonated organic compounds; paint and varnish manufacture (excluding mixing, milling and grinding); the production of rubber from scrap; or the manufacture of acetylene from calcium carbide, for sale or for use in a further chemical process.

(Special Industrial Group D.)

Class IX. Use for carrying on any of the following industries, businesses or trades so far as not included in Class V:

Animal charcoal manufacturer. Blood albumen maker. Blood boiler. Bone boiler or steamer. Bone burner. Bone grinder. Breeder of maggots from putrescible animal matter. Candle maker. Catgut manufacturer. Chitterling or nettlings boiler.

Dealer in rags or bones (including receiving, storing, sorting or manipulating rags in or likely to become in an offensive condition, or any bones, rabbit skins, fat or putrescrible animal products of a like nature).

Fat melter or fat extractor. Fellmonger. Fish curer. Fish oil manufacturer. Fish skin dresser or scraper. Glue maker. Gut scraper or gun cleaner. Leather dresser.

Maker of meal for feeding poultry, dogs, cattle or other animals from any fish, blood, bone, fat or animal offal, either in an offensive condition or subjected to any process causing noxious or injurious effluvia.

Manufacturer of manure from bones, fish, fish offal, blood, spent hops, beans or other putrescible animal or vegetable matter.

Parchment maker. Size maker. Skin drier. Soap boiler. Tallow melter or refiner. Tanner. Tripe boiler or cleaner.

(*Special Industrial Group E.*)

Class X. Use as a wholesale warehouse or repository for any purpose.

Class XI. Use as a boarding or guest house, a residential club, or a hotel providing sleeping accommodation.

Class XII. Use as a residential or boarding or a residential college.

Class XIII. Use as a building for public worship or religious instruction or for the social or recreational activities of the religious body using the building.

Class XIV. Use as a home or institution providing for the boarding, care and maintenance of children, old people or persons under disability, a convalescent home, a nursing home, a sanatorium or a hospital (other than a hospital, home, hostel or institution included in Class XVI).

Class XV. Use (other than residentially) as a health centre, a school treatment centre, a clinic, a creche, a day nursery or a dispensary, or use as a consulting room or surgery unattached to the residence of the consultant or practitioner.

Class XVI. Use as a hospital, home or institution for persons of unsound mind, mental defectives, or epileptic persons, or a home, hostel or institution in which persons may be detained by order of a court or which is approved by one of His Majesty's Principal Secretaries of State for persons required to reside there as a condition of a probation or a supervision order.

Class XVII. Use as an art gallery (other than for business purposes), a museum, a public library or reading room, a public hall, a concert hall, an exhibition hall, a social centre, a community centre or a non-residential club.

Class XVIII. Use as a theatre, a cinema, a music hall, a dance hall, a skating rink, a swimming bath, a Turkish or other vapour or foam bath or a gymnasium, or for indoor games.

TOWN AND COUNTRY (GENERAL DEVELOPMENT) ORDER, 1950

England. 1950. S.I. No. 728

[The *Town and Country Planning* (*General Development*) *Order, 1950* set out in the First Schedule twenty-two classes of development which were permitted subject to conditions stated in the schedule without planning permission. Only Class I is reproduced in full, and the remaining twenty-one are listed as an indication of the scope of "decontrol" involved, in what was sometimes referred to in the newspapers as "Dr. Dalton's experiment with freedom."]

3. (1) Subject to the subsequent provisions of this Order, development of any class specified in the First Schedule to this Order is permitted by this Order and may be undertaken upon land to which this Order applies, without the permission of the local planning authority or the Minister:

Provided that the permission granted by this Order in respect of any such class of development shall be subject to any condition or limitation imposed in the said First Schedule in relation to that class.

(2) Nothing in this Article or in the First Schedule to this Order shall operate so as to permit any development contrary to a condition imposed in any permission granted or deemed to be granted under Part III of the Act otherwise than by this Order.

(3) Any development of Class XII authorized by an Act or order subject to the grant of any consent or approval shall not be deemed for the purposes of this Order to be so authorized unless and until that consent or approval is obtained; and in relation to any development of Class XII authorized by any Act passed or order made after the first day of July, 1948, the foregoing provisions of this Article shall have effect subject to any provision to the contrary contained in the Act or order.

FIRST SCHEDULE

Part I

The following development is permitted under Article 3 of this Order subject to the conditions set out opposite the description of that development in column (2). The references in that column to standard conditions are to the conditions numbered and set out in Part II of this Schedule.

Description of Development:	*Conditions*
Class I. Development within the curtilage of a dwelling-house.	
1. The enlargement, improvement or other alteration of a dwelling-house so long as the cubic content of the original dwelling-house (as ascertained by external measurement) is not exceeded by more than 1,750 cubic feet or one-tenth whichever is the greater, subject to a maximum of 4,000 cubic feet; provided that the erection of a garage, stable, loose-box, or coach-house within the curtilage of the dwellinghouse shall be treated as the enlargement of the dwelling-house for the purposes of this permission.	(1) The height of such building shall not exceed the height of the original dwelling-house. (2) No part of such building shall project beyond the forwardmost part of the front of the original dwelling-house. (3) Standard conditions 1 and 2.
2. The erection, construction or placing, and the maintenance, improvement or other alteration, within the curtilage of a dwelling-house, or any building or enclosure (other than a dwelling, garage, stable, loosebox or coach-house) required for a purpose incidental to the enjoyment of a dwelling-house as such, including the keeping of poultry, bees, pet animals, birds or other livestock for the domestic needs or personal enjoyment of the occupants of the dwelling-house.	(1) The height shall not exceed, in the case of a building with a ridged roof, 12 feet, or in any other case, 10 feet. (2) Standard conditions 1 and 2.

Class II. Sundry Minor Operations.
Class III. Changes of use.
Class IV. Temporary buildings and uses.
Class V. Uses by members of recreational organisations.
Class VI. Agricultural buildings, works and uses.
Class VII. Forestry buildings and works.

Class VIII. Development for industrial purposes.
Class IX. Repairs to unadopted streets and private ways.
Class X. Repairs to services.
Class XI. War Damaged buildings, works and plant.
Class XII. Development under local or private Acts, or Orders.
Class XIII. Development by Local Authorities.
Class XIV. Development by Local Highway Authorities or the London County Council.
Class XV. Development by River Boards or Drainage Authorities.
Class XVI. Development by Sewerage Authorities.
Class XVII. Development by Educational Authorities.
Class XVIII. Development by Statutory Undertakers.
A. Railway or Light Railway Undertakings.
B. Dock, Pier, Harbour, Water Transport, Canal or Inland Navigation Undertakings.
C. Water or Hydraulic Power Undertakings.
D. Gas Undertakings.
E. Electricity Undertakings.
F. Tramway or Road Transport Undertakings.
G. Lighthouse Undertakings.
Class XIX. Development by Mineral Undertakers.
Class XX. Development by National Coal Board.
Class XXI. Development previously sanctioned by a Government Department.
Class XXII. Uses of aerodrome buildings.

Part II.
Standard Conditions

1. This permission shall not authorize any development which involves the formation, laying out or material widening of a means of access to a trunk or classified road.

2. No development shall be carried out which creates an obstruction to the view of persons using any road used by vehicular traffic at or near any bend, corner, junction or intersection so as to be likely to cause danger to such persons.

[Both orders superseded earlier versions.]

MINISTER OF HOUSING AND LOCAL GOVERNMENT, REPORT 1959
England. 1960. Cmnd. 1027

Analysis of Planning Applications and Decisions. During 1959 the Department carried out a survey of development control by 29 local planning authorities in Yorkshire and the East Midlands for the years 1956 to 1958. The authorities readily co-operated in this survey and their help was greatly appreciated.

In the area covered by the survey the total number of planning applications appears to have risen during the period by about 13 per cent, at a higher rate in the counties than in the county boroughs. The number of appeals received, apart from advertisement appeals, increased over the three years by 12 per cent.

In the counties easily the largest class of application (41 per cent) was for residential development, usually for a single house. Housing applications increased in the counties over the period by 22 per cent. The rate of refusal was 13.4 per cent (in the county boroughs 5.6 per cent). Industrial development had a low rate of refusal in the counties and boroughs alike, about 7 per cent against 10 per cent for all decisions. The largest class of applications in county boroughs (32 per cent) was for garages of one kind or another. This class showed an appreciable increase (about 20 per cent) in the number of both applications and refusals. The upward trend was even more marked in applications for changes of use in the county boroughs, with refusals showing a greater increase than applications. Judging by the high rate of refusal (24.4 per cent) proposals for change of use were the most contentious type of application in the county boroughs.

The information obtained from the Department's survey was not representative of the south of England and the West Midlands where rates of development are generally greater. It has been supplemented with information provided by the County Planning Officers' Society for all the administrative counties of England and Wales for the twelve months ended 31st March, 1958. This has made it possible to set out the table below and draw some tentative conclusions.

England and Wales

Year ended 31st March 1958

Population	44,425,000	(mid 1957)
Planning applications including advertisements	400,000	estimated
Permissions, with or without conditions	360,000	estimated
Refusals	40,000	estimated
Planning appeals including advertisements	9,068	
Planning appeals excluding advertisements	7,192	
English and Welsh administrative counties		
Population	31,274,000	
Planning applications including advertisements	269,353	
Planning appeals including advertisements	6,087	
English and Welsh county boroughs		
Population	13,151,000	
Planning applications including advertisements	130,000	estimated
Planning appeals including advertisements	2,981	

About 90 per cent of the applications were permitted (52 per cent without conditions) and about 10 per cent refused. The rate of refusal in the counties (1 in 3) was higher than in the county boroughs (1 in 13). Appeals, whether against refusals or against conditional permissions, appear to have been about 2.2 per cent of all applications. Excluding advertisement appeals, the figure was about 1.8 per cent.

The rate of planning applications in relation to population was generally much higher in southern England and in the Midlands than in the North and Wales and their incidence showed a close correspondence with recent population increases and private housebuilding. In the year ended 31st March 1958 applications in all the administrative counties of England and Wales averaged 8.6 per 1,000 population. But whereas in the north-east of England and Yorkshire the average was only 6.7 (no county in the North showed more than 10), it was generally between 10 and 20 in the southern counties (London and Middlesex being notable exceptions with very low rates). The rate of appeals also showed a similar increase southward

Advertisement applications amounted to about 40,000 in 1958, approximately 10 per cent of all applications for planning permission. It seems that in recent years there has been a considerable rise in the number of applications in the counties and a small rise in the county boroughs. Of the total applications some 33/34,000 (about 84 per cent) received consent. The rate of refusal therefore appears to be about 16 per cent higher than the general rate of refusal for other applications. The rate of advertisement appeals, whether reckoned as a proportion of applications or of refusals, is higher than the rate of other appeals, so that in England and Wales in 1958 advertisement appeals amounted to 21 per cent of all planning appeals.

Planning Appeals. Apart from advertisement appeals, which are dealt with later in the chapter, the number of appeals made to the Minister during the year was 8,857, much the highest total so far. It compared with 7,499 in 1958. The figures have risen each year since 1952 and in the course of the last six years the intake has doubled. During 1959, 5,673 appeals were decided and 2,533 were withdrawn; the comparable figures for the previous year were 4,930 and 2,238 respectively. Figures for the years 1956 to 1959 inclusive are given in table C in appendix XIV. The percentage of appeals allowed during the year was 30.6 compared with 32.2 in 1958.

Figures for some of the more common types of proposal giving rise to appeals are given in table D of appendix XIV. Proposals for single houses in rural areas, which had risen steadily from 216 in 1951 to a peak of 1,442 in 1957, and fallen to 1,209 in 1958, continued their decline to 1,100 in 1959. They were still the largest single group of appeals. The number of appeals relating to housing estates rose sharply from 540 in 1958 to 1,000 in 1959.

The number of occasions on which the Minister's decision differed from the Inspector's recommendation remained at about 5 per cent of the total number of decided appeals, the same percentage as in 1958. (This percentage indeed held good for all types of planning inquiries.)

A few of the appeals dealt with in 1959, chosen for their general interest, are described below. The publication "Selected Planning Appeals," gives particulars of a number of representive cases intended to illustrate the Minister's policy and to serve as a guide to local planning authorities and to developers. An issue was published in June, and another will be published in 1960.

High Buildings. Developments during the year confirmed that the appearance of London and some other large cities was likely to be changed by the erection of more high buildings.

It is the Minister's policy that each proposal for a high building should be considered on its own merits, including not only the design proposed for the building itself but the characteristics of the area in which it stands, including any other high buildings which exist or have been approved near by; and that the standards applied to buildings in general shall apply to high buildings in the same way. Thus the same car parking and day-lighting tests are applied and the plot-ratio (that is the ratio of the aggregate floor area to the net site area) is to be the same as in lower buildings. In other words, the bulk of a high building will be distributed differently but will not be greater than that of a differently shaped building constructed for the same purpose in the same place.

The London County Council have worked out a set of questions which they apply to a high building project and the Minister is in general agreement with this approach. The questions are:—

(1) Would it disrupt the pattern of existing development or obtrude on the skyline to the detriment of existing architectural groups?
(2) Would it have a positive visual or civic significance?
(3) Would the site be large enough to permit a base of lower buildings or open space?
(4) Would it overshadow adjoining areas and stifle good development there?
(5) Would it be better than a lower building and relate satisfactorily to other buildings nearby?
(6) Would its design and materials be of high quality?
(7) Would it relate satisfactorily to open spaces and the River Thames?
(8) Would its illumination at night detract from London's night scene?

Special considerations naturally arise in particular cases. In some cases the problems posed can be satisfactorily resolved only if comprehensive development of the area is decided upon.

In the Report for 1958 reference was made to the Minister's decision to refuse permission for an hotel in Park Lane, Westminister, which would have been 390 feet high. The design was revised and permission was granted by the London County Council for a building 311 feet high, with 27 storeys. By the end of 1959 the Shell building on the south bank of the Thames near Waterloo Station was nearing completion. Permission had been granted for a number of other high buildings, including buildings at Millbank and on Euston Road. The London County Council themselves were building high blocks of flats in Tidey Street, Stepney, and at the Elephant and Castle. Models of some of these schemes were displayed at an exhibition held in the County Hall during December.

LCC FIVE POINT GUIDE. July, 1962. *London Daily Telegraph*. "Plans to strengthen the principles that guide the London County Council when dealing with applications to erect high buildings will be considered at the council's meeting next Tuesday. The Town Planning Committee proposes that the onus of demonstrating that a high building is necessary shall be placed 'clearly on the applicant.'

"In a report the committee states: 'Developers may have been led to believe that, provided the eight questions formulated in 1956 were answered satisfactorily, consent for a high building would be automatically forthcoming.

" 'It has always been the intention that the developer must make out a convincing case for a high building before it can be approved.'

"The 1956 questions included references to the quality of building and design and their effect on existing buildings and landscapes.

"The committee states five points on which the council must be satisfied. They are:

"1. That a development conforming with the general height level of surrounding buildings would have serious disadvantages and that substantial advantages to the public interest would be gained by a high building.

"2. That the building, from wherever it is seen, will not seriously mar the skyline nor spoil traditional, pleasing, and well loved views, such as those of the Palace of Westminster and of London squares or views from the royal parks and the River Thames.

"3. That the proposed high building would look well with its immediate surroundings, both existing and proposed.

"4. That the amenities of surrounding sites will not be harmed nor their development possibilities unreasonably affected.

"5. That, in view of the prominence of high buildings, developers have been successful in securing the highest quality of architectural and external finishes for their high buildings.

"The committee adds that because high buildings attract public attention over a wide area, the council must be satisfied that such development will will make 'a worthy contribution to London's townscape.' "

[See also the House of Lords debate on high buildings, partly reproduced above at page 82.]

BIBLIOGRAPHY. In addition to the impressionistic account of the operation of development control under the English legislation given by the extract from the Ministry's annual report, an excellent report of a year's close study of the legislation in operation is available in Mandelker, *Green Belts and Urban Growth* (1962), a study by an American law professor. *Green Belts and Urban Growth* is a valuable supplement to Haar, *Land Planning Law in a Free Society* (1952) coming as it does a decade after Professor Haar's pioneer effort. Despite its title it is a searching inquiry into the actual administration of the 1947 Act as it appeared to the author during 1959–60. Professor Mandelker supplies a good bibliography including periodical literature, plans and plan reports and governmental materials. See also, the *Journal of Planning and Property Law* which reprints Ministry decisions on planning appeals gleaned by contributing local authorities.

3. Redevelopment

(*a*) *Replotting*

MUNICIPAL ACT
British Columbia. Revised Statutes. 1960. Chapter 255

824. The Council may, by by-law adopted by an affirmative vote of at least two-thirds of all the members thereof, define any part of the municipality as a district for the purpose of replotting, and authorize the preparation of a scheme, including incidental preliminary surveys, for the replotting of the district.

825. A replotting scheme shall indicate the proposed relocation and exchange of parcels of real property in which the Crown or the municipality has no estate or interest, and whether compensation is to be proposed to the respective owners and the amount of such compensation, and the value of any surplus real property, and where any building, structure, erection, or utility is to be moved shall indicate its new location, and may set out an apportionment of the net cost of the scheme between the municipality and the said owners, consideration being given to the saving which the scheme may effect in the expenditure of the municipality for highways and municipal utilities and the increased taxation which may be derived by the municipality from the increased value of the real property in the district, and this apportionment may or may not be as provided by section 849.

826. (1) For the purpose of the replotting, all the parcels and highways and all other real property in the district at the initiation of the scheme shall be thrown together and shall form one parcel of real property, hereinafter referred to as the "common mass."

(2) From the common mass is to be taken the real property necessary for highways, parks, or public squares, and such real property shall

stand in the stead of and compensate the Crown, the municipality, and the public for the surrender of all former highways, parks or public squares.

(3) The remainder of the common mass shall be divided into parcels for allotment to the owners in a fair and equitable manner, so that as far as possible the value of new parcels allotted to them shall be equal to the value of their former parcels.

827. (1) Endeavour shall be made to allot to owners new parcels in approximately the same location as their former parcels. Parcels with buildings, structures, erections, or utilities erected thereon shall, subject to the necessary adjustment of boundaries, be returned to their former owners wherever practicable.

(2) The allotment of new parcels in exchange for former parcels shall be carried out as far as practicable with the consent of the respective owners.

(3) Failing such consent, there may be allotted to him a new parcel or new parcels of value equal as nearly as possible to the value of his former parcel or parcels, or compensation in money may be made to him in lieu of an allotment of real property.

(4) Unavoidable differences of value between former parcels and new parcels may be equalized by granting money compensation, or with the consent of or by agreement with an owner a new parcel may be allotted to him of greater value than his former parcel for a cash payment or on terms, in which latter case a mortgage, with interest thereon as may be agreed, may be taken by the municipality from the owner for payment of the difference in value.

(5) Any real property not allotted as above provided may be allotted to any owner at an agreed price, the amount of which shall be paid to the municipality.

(6) The whole of the real property remaining unallotted shall be allotted to the municipality and is herein referred to as "surplus real property."

828. The municipality may, subject to making compensation therefor, acquire any charge against a former parcel and hold it as a charge against a new parcel allotted to the owner of the former parcel and take all necessary proceedings for the collection of the amount due under and by virtue of such charge or for the sale, transfer, or realization of the security created thereby.

829. Before initiating a replotting scheme, the Council shall cause notice of the scheme to be published in a newspaper published or circulating in the municipality, and shall also cause to be sent to each owner of a parcel within the district, in the same manner as prescribed for the giving of a notice by section 401,

(*a*) A plan showing the real property within the district as presently subdivided and a plan showing the real property within the district as if replotted under the proposed scheme. Both plans shall have marked on them the dimensions of the boundaries of each parcel shown and the scale of the plan, which scale shall be the same for both plans and shall not be smaller than one hundred feet to the inch;

(*b*) a statement showing

(i) an estimate of the total cost of the scheme;

(ii) an estimate of the cost of the scheme to be borne by the municipality;

(iii) an estimate of the total cost of the scheme to be borne by all the owners other than the municipality;

(iv) an estimate of the portion of the cost of the scheme in respect of each new parcel;

(v) the number of instalments by which such owner's share of the cost may be paid, and at what interval after the completion of the scheme a first instalment shall be due and at what intervals thereafter any remaining instalments shall be due;

(vi) the proposed allotment of new parcels in exchange for former parcels;

(*c*) a form of consent to the replotting set forth in the scheme as it affects the real property of such owner and setting forth the details of compensation (if any) proposed to be paid by the municipality in respect of such real property or the details of any sums requested to be paid to the municipality in respect of such real property as a result of the execution of the scheme, which consent may be signed by such owner and returned to the Clerk;

(*d*) in a space provided on the form of consent, the owner who consents under clause (c) shall set out the market or true value of the real property and the amount or proportion thereof which he considers to be the value of his interest.

830. (1) If the owners of parcels of real property, the assessed land value of which constitutes at least seventy per centum of the total assessed value of all the land in the district according to the last authenticated real-property assessment roll, consent in writing in the form referred to in clause (*c*) of section 829 to the replotting set forth in the scheme, the Council may by resolution authorize the undertaking and completion of the scheme without any further consent of any other owners in the district.

832. Alterations may be made in the scheme before its completion, unless they affect the owners who have consented as herein provided, in which event the consent of all such affected owners is again required.

834. (1) Within four months after the initiation of the scheme, the Council shall by resolution either

(*a*) discontinue the undertaking; or

(*b*) authorize the completion of the scheme and the putting into effect of the scheme of replotting.

(3) If the Council resolves to authorize the completion of the scheme ... the municipality shall make application [to the Registrar of Titles] ... to have title to the common mass registered in fee-simple in trust for the owners of the new parcels. The application shall be accompanied by

(*a*) a reference plan defining the common mass ...

(*c*) a subdivision plan defining the new parcels ...

(5) The deposit of the reference plan as aforesaid vests in the municipality, in trust as aforesaid, in fee-simple, the common mass, and extinguishes all highways, parks, or public squares within the common mass, and this provision binds Her Majesty. The said vesting of title in trust in fee-simple is free from all charges registered against the former parcels. . . .

(6) The Registrar of Titles shall thereupon deposit the sub-division plan ...

(7) ... the deposit of the subdivision plan as aforesaid vests title to the respective new parcels on the persons named ...

835. Upon the completion of the scheme,

(*a*) except as otherwise dealt with pursuant to the provisions of this Division, all rights, obligations, and incidents of ownership of the owner of a former parcel or of an interest therein, and all public and private legal relationships whatsoever with respect to a former parcel, shall to all intents and purposes be deemed to be transferred to and exist with respect to the new parcel allotted to the owner of such former parcel to the same extent and in the same manner as they existed with regard to the former parcel;

(*b*) all conveyances, agreements, mortgages, and other instruments, including grants of letters probate or letters of administration, in respect of parcels of real property described therein by a description appropriate to a former parcel and in respect of which registration of title had not been applied for prior to the completion of the undertaking shall be construed as if the estate or interest passing or created or vested thereby was in respect of the new parcel;

(*c*) the new parcels and the respective owners thereof are subject to and liable for all municipal charges, rates, taxes, and assessment levied against their former respective parcels, and are subject to all proceedings taken and to be taken for the collection of municipal charges, rates, taxes, and assessments in any manner provided for by law.

836. Upon the completion of the replotting scheme, the allotments of real property pursuant thereto are absolutely binding to all intents and purposes upon all the owners in the district, subject only to the right of the non-consenting owners to complain as to the adequacy of compensation proposed or the failure to propose compensation.

838. Each non-consenting owner who gives notice of his complaint as provided in section 842 has the right to compensation in money

(*a*) for the loss of value of the former parcel in so far as adequate compensation is not afforded by the new parcel allotted;

(*b*) for the loss of or damage to or the cost of moving buildings or improvements upon the former parcel;

(*c*) for the loss of income from the use of buildings or the special condition or use of the former parcel caused by the undertaking.

839. (1) In determining the amount of compensation,

(*a*) a former parcel shall be valued at its market value at the time of the initiation of the undertaking, but any increase in the value thereof caused by the anticipation or initiation of the undertaking shall not be taken into consideration; and

(*b*) a new parcel shall be valued at its market value upon the completion of the undertaking.

(2) No person is entitled to compensation for

(*a*) any costs, expenses, loss, damage, or inconvenience incurred or sustained in investigating the replotting proceedings or in presenting any complaint or making any appeal, or caused by the initiation of or delay in or discontinuance of the undertaking;

(*b*) any actual or anticipated loss or inconvenience of access to new parcels or of use of any municipal or public utility or service due to the new highways not being open for traffic;

(*c*) any actual or anticipated loss, damage, or inconvenience suffered in common with all or with the major part of other owners;

(*d*) any building or structure constructed, erected, placed, or altered, or any improvement made to land subsequent to the initiation of the undertaking or any actual or anticipated loss, damage, or expense incidental thereto, or incidental to the removal of such building or structure;

(*e*) any reduction in or loss of value due to reduction in area within the limits of a right to take land for highway purposes contained in the Crown grant of or Statute applying to the land.

840. (1) Within one month after the completion of the undertaking, the Council shall apply to the Supreme Court ex parte by petition for the appointment of a Commissioner to hold a public hearing of and to decide any complaints . . .

(*b*) *Redevelopment and renewal*

THE PLANNING ACT
Ontario. Revised Statutes. 1960. Chapter 296

20.—(1) In this section,

(*a*) "redevelopment" means the planning or replanning, design or redesign, resubdivision, clearance, development, reconstruction and rehabilitation, or any of them, of a redevelopment area, and the provision of such residential, commercial, industrial, public, recreational, institutional, religious, charitable or other uses, buildings, works, improvements or facilities, or spaces therefor, as may be appropriate or necessary;

(*b*) "redevelopment area" means an area within a municipality, the redevelopment of which in the opinion of the council is desirable because of age, dilapidation, over-crowding, faulty arrangement, unsuitability of buildings or for any other reason;

(*c*) "redevelopment plan" means a general scheme, including supporting maps and texts, approved by the Municipal Board for the redevelopment of a redevelopment area.

(2) The council of a municipality that has an official plan may, with the approval of the Minister, by by-law designate an area within the municipality as a redevelopment area and the redevelopment area shall not be altered or dissolved without the approval of the Minister.

(3) When a by-law has been passed and approved under subsection 2, the municipality, with the approval of the Minister, may,

(*a*) acquire land within the redevelopment area;

(*b*) hold land acquired before or after the passing of the by-law within the redevelopment area; and

(*c*) clear, grade or otherwise prepare the land for redevelopment.

(4) If, at any time before a redevelopment plan for the redevelopment area has been approved by the Municipal Board, the Minister is not satisfied with the progress made by the municipality in acquiring land within the redevelopment area or in preparing a redevelopment plan, he may withdraw his approvals under subsections 2 and 3 and thereupon the by-law designating the redevelopment area ceases to have effect and the redevelopment area ceases to exist.

(5) When a by-law has been passed and approved under subsection 2, the council, with the approval of the Municipal Board, may by by-law adopt a redevelopment plan for the redevelopment area.

(6) No redevelopment plan shall be approved by the Municipal Board unless it conforms with the official plan.

(7) A redevelopment plan adopted and approved under subsection 5 may be amended by by-law with the approval of the Municipal Board.

(8) For the purpose of carrying out the redevelopment plan, the municipality, with the approval of the Minister, may,

(*a*) construct, repair, rehabilitate or improve buildings on land acquired or held by it in the redevelopment area in conformity with the redevelopment plan, and sell, lease or otherwise dispose of any such buildings and the land appurtenant thereto;

(*b*) sell, lease or otherwise dispose of any land acquired or held by it in the redevelopment area to any person or governmental authority for use in conformity with the redevelopment plan.

(9) Until a by-law or amending by-law passed under section 30 after the adoption of the redevelopment plan is in force in the redevelopment area, no land acquired, and no building constructed, by the municipality in the redevelopment area shall be sold, leased or otherwise disposed of unless the person or authority to whom it is disposed of agrees with the municipality that he will keep and maintain the land and building and the use thereof in conformity with the redevelopment plan until such a by-law or amending by-law is in force; but the municipality may, with the approval of the Minister, during the period of the development of the plan, lease any land or any building or part thereof in the area for any purpose, whether or not in conformity with the redevelopment plan, for a term of not more than three years at any one time.

(10) Notwithstanding subsection 1 of section 282 of *The Municipal Act,* debentures issued by the municipality for the purpose of this section may be for such term of years as the debenture by-law, with the approval of the Municipal Board, provides.

RE TOWNSHIP OF SANDWICH WEST BY-LAW NO. 2061
Ontario. High Court. 1960. 25 D.L.R. (2d) 534

SPENCE J. (oral): This is an application to quash By-law No. 2061 of the municipal corporation of the Township of Sandwich West on the ground of the invalidity of the said by-law alleging it is *ultra vires* of the township. The by-law purports to be enacted for the purpose of carrying out a redevelopment scheme or proposal which has been the subject of an agreement between the municipal corporation and Morris Construction (Windsor) Ltd. The by-law in short terms approves the entering into of the agreement which is annexed thereto. This agreement is dated March 15, 1960. The agreement, and therefore the by-law authorizing its execution by the corporation, has been the subject of attack on four different grounds: 1st,—It is said that the municipality cannot enter into such an agreement until there is, firstly, a by-law creating a redevelopment area and, secondly, a by-law creating a redevelopment plan, and in the present case neither one exists or did exist at the time the agreement was executed, *i.e.*, March 15, 1960. 2nd,—It is alleged that the agreement contains covenants to pass by-laws in the future, that is, it is an attempt by the municipality to abdicate its powers and its duties under the provisions of the municipal legislation, and it is therefore for that reason *ultra vires.* 3rd,—That the agreement, and the by-law which empowers its execution, is in effect the borrowing of money by the municipality, and that that borrowing is contrary to the provisions of s. 300(1) of the *Municipal Act*, R.S.O. 1950, c. 243, as re-enacted 1959, c. 62, s. 10(1). 4th,—That the proposed plan does not comply with the official plan of the municipality, and therefore under the provisions of s.

20(6) of the *Planning Act*, 1955 (Ont.), c. 61, the proposed redevelopment plan cannot be approved by the Municipal Board.

Under the provisions of the *Planning Act* there is brought within the jurisdiction of the municipality the power to enter into redevelopment schemes in certain designated redevelopment areas. That power is set out particularly in s. 20 of the *Planning Act*, which I have cited. I think it is a necessary result of the granting of that power to the municipality that the municipality possesses all power incidental, and properly incidental, to the carrying out of such redevelopment schemes. The agreement which is the subject-matter of By-law No. 2061 is in its essence an agreement for the purpose of determining (a) what area should be a redevelopment area, and (b) whether the redevelopment can be economically carried out....

The covenants in the agreement which are subject to attack are particularly those contained in the following sections: Part I, s. 1—A covenant to pass a by-law designating an area as a redevelopment area. The actual area is set out in a schedule to the agreement. The consideration of the agreement and the passing of a by-law would entail a consideration of the actual area, and therefore the municipality instead of abdicating its power to pass by-laws, or to refuse to pass them, in the future has actually exercised that power in dealing with the by-law included in the agreement, that is, By-law No. 2061 in question here. The second covenant objected to is that in s. 2, that is, that the township shall, subject to the approval of the Minister of Planning and Development, pass the requisite by-law pursuant to s-s. (3) of s. 20 of the *Planning Act*, 1955, for the acquisition of the land described in the schedule. As I have said, the actual lands are already set out in the schedule of the agreement, which have already been debated upon the enactment of By-law No. 2061. Moreover, the township has already passed two readings of a redevelopment area by-law, which is numbered 2080—See the affidavit of Lawrence Brunet, the Reeve of the respondent municipality, para. 10. That by-law is now ready for the approval of the Minister under the provisions of s. 20(2), of the *Planning Act*, and of course the applicant, as any other ratepayer of a municipality, has a right to make such representation as he sees fit to the Minister.

Section 4 of Part I is also objected to on the ground that discretion is allowed to the company as to whether it will proceed with the redevelopment plan upon determining the cost of the land. That, of course, carries out the whole purpose of the agreement, and it is only when the company can determine the cost of the acquisition of the land, and therefore whether the scheme of development may be economically carried out, that either it or the municipality could determine whether redevelopment should proceed. I find no objection and nothing *ultra vires* in permitting the company, that is, Morris Construction (Windsor) Ltd., to determine whether or not it will continue with the redevelopment and do so before lands are actually acquired.

The same answer, in my opinion, covers all the objections to the various sections where it is said the municipality has exceeded its power in that it has undertaken to pass by-laws. The by-laws which it has definitely undertaken to pass are by-laws which by the provisions of the *Planning Act* it is empowered to pass, and the policy of enacting such by-laws has already been considered when this by-law, No. 2061, was considered and enacted. That agreement was of course itself a subject of approval in the by-law under attack, and the enactment of that by-law is, in my opinion, not an abdication of the municipal corporation's power but its exercise. It should be remembered that, although the by-law fixing a planning area had not been enacted, the respondent corporation has proceeded so far as it is able to do so. It has given the by-law two readings and it has submitted it to the Minister for approval. This would appear to be the course indicated as the proper one by the Supreme Court of Canada in *Scarborough Tp.* v. *Bondi*. It should also be remembered that the planning development by-law, that is, the by-law contemplated by the provisions of the *Planning Act*, s. 20(5), has also not been enacted. And it is the argument of counsel for the applicant that that by-law must be enacted prior to any such step as was taken by the enactment of By-law No. 2061—the one under attack. I am of the opinion that the provisions of the agreement which have been authorized by the said By-law No. 2061 do not require the municipality to enact the development planning by-law.

On the other hand, the agreement would seem to give the municipality a discretion therein. In Part II, s. 1, of the agreement it is provided that upon the acquisition of the said lands the township and the company, at the expense of the company, shall prepare a redevelopment plan as set forth in s. 20 of the *Planning Act*. That section, in my view, requires an agreement —a meeting of minds between the municipal corporation and the company —and leaves to the municipal council a discretion in the approving of the plan; and unless the plan is prepared in accordance with their wishes, they simply have not prepared a plan, and the whole matter would stop at that point. Now, therefore, at that time the municipal council will be subject of course to the influence of the ratepayers, and will have to take into consideration the views of the ratepayers in determining what redevelopment plan they will settle on, and the applicant, with other ratepayers, may make such representation as it deems fit. Such a redevelopment plan must be approved by the Municipal Board under the provisions of the said s. 20(5), and again on such approval there will no doubt be hearings and again the ratepayers may make such representations as they deem fit. For these reasons, I am of the opinion that this by-law is not subject to attack on the ground that the municipality has covenanted to pass by-laws in the future and has therefore abdicated its function in this matter.

The attack upon the by-law as being an illegal money by-law contrary to s. 300(1) of the *Municipal Act* depends upon the provisions of the agreement—in Part I, s. 4, of it—which provides that in the event that the said lands may be purchased at an amount that allows the area to be economically developed, in the opinion of the company, as hereinafter set forth then the company shall deliver to the township the requisite funds to complete the purchase of the said lands including all legal and other expenses. Counsel for the applicant puts it that under s. 300(1), of the *Municipal Act* the corporation shall not incur any debt the payment of which is not provided for in the estimates of the current year, unless a by-law of the township authorizing it has been passed with the assent of the electors; and of course the amount which the company will be called upon to pay to the municipal corporation, so the municipal corporation may in turn pay the owners of the lots, has neither appeared in the annual estimates nor been the subject of a by-law approved by the electors. I am of the opinion that the simple answer is that given by counsel for the respondent that these are not debts at all, these are merely deposits made by the company to the municipal corporation who for this purpose is its agent or trustee in acquiring the lands and in conveying the lands to the company.

The fourth objection is that the proposed development plan does not comply with the official plan. It is admitted substantially in the affidavit of Mr. Brunet that such is the fact, but it is said that the municipal council are agreed on the necessary amendments of the official plan, and such official plan will be amended, but of course it need not be amended unless and until this redevelopment scheme is adopted by the company and the municipality. Procedure in such an orderly fashion would seem to be efficient. When the area designating by-law is already in effect, the redevelopment plan will be submitted to the Municipal Board for its approval, and at the same time there will be submitted the necessary amendments of the official plan. I find no objection to this procedure.

For these reasons the application will be dismissed with costs.

RE TOWNSHIP OF SANDWICH WEST
Ontario. Municipal Board. 1961. P.F.N. 1309–61

JAMIESON Member and MILBURN Member: This is an application for approval of the proposed redevelopment plan and of By-law 2204 to adopt the said re-development plan.

The evidence in this matter showed that the subject lands had remained undeveloped while the surrounding lands were developed and most of them built upon. The subject lands did not develop as part of this was an old subdivision containing very small lots laid out in the early 1920's and these are now held by estates and non-residents.

The municipality has acquired through tax arrears about 12% of the area. Because of the many ownerships it was felt the only way to develop this area, which can now be serviced, was to seek approval of a redevelopment plan. The municipality does not wish to extend services past this area to service properties to the south because of the increased cost, and further, they are anxious to avoid having a large undeveloped area in the centre of a built-up area.

Those who opposed the application did so on several grounds, one being that the commercial area which is proposed for the intersection of the Third Concession Road and Partington Avenue is wrongly located and would create a movement of shoppers away from the established commercial area which lies to the south of the subject redevelopment area.

A second objection was raised on behalf of The Canada Trust Company, and this was that there was adequate land in other areas for development which they felt should be proceeded with before that of the subject lands. Also, Mr. Gignac stated that his clients own 25% of the subject lands and do not want them taken away from them.

There was evidence from the consulting engineer for the Township as to servicing, and the Board is satisfied that municipal services could be supplied to the subject property and that the proposed development for this land is reasonable at the present time.

After considering all of the evidence submitted, the Board does not consider that it has been shown that the Municipal Council has acted in an unreasonable way in proceeding with the preparation of this plan as a whole; however, the provision of the commercial area, as referred to earlier in this decision, appears to be in conflict with the official use plan of the municipality and for that reason the area shown on the plan which was filed as Exhibit 4 in this hearing as Block "B" will not be approved at this time, and in this connection, the Board requires the municipality to keep them advised of the status of any amendment to their official use plan affecting this commercial block. The Board also feels that it is not reasonable to include lands which are a part of an existing dwelling as in the case of Newmans and Martell, and the plan will be approved when it is amended to delete the holdings of these parties. Other than this, the plan is approved as submitted.

NATIONAL HOUSING ACT, 1954
Canada. Statutes. 1953–54. Chapter 23

[The long title of this Act is "An Act to Promote the Construction of new Houses, the Repair and Modernization of existing Houses, and the Improvement of Housing and Living Conditions".]

23. (1) In order to assist in the clearance, replanning, rehabilitation and modernization of blighted or substandard areas in any municipality, the Minister, with the approval of the Governor in Council, may enter into an agreement with the municipality providing for the payment to the municipality of contributions in respect of the cost to the municipality of acquiring and clearing, whether by condemnation proceedings or otherwise, an area of land in the municipality.

(2) The contributions paid to a municipality under this section shall not exceed one-half of the cost to the municipality or the municipality and the province jointly, of acquisition and clearance, including costs of condemnation proceedings, as agreed between the Minister and the municipality.

(3) No contributions shall be paid to a municipality under this section unless

(a) the government of the province in which the area is situated has approved the acquisition and clearance therof by the municipality;

(b) the costs of acquisition and clearance, including the cost of condemnation proceedings, less the amount of the contributions made under this section in respect thereof, are borne by the municipality or jointly by the municipality and the province;

(c) the families to be dispossessed by the acquisition and clearance of the area are offered at the time of their dispossession housing accommodation in a housing project constructed under section 16, 19 or 36, at rentals that, in the opinion of the municipality and the Minister, are fair and reasonable, having regard to the family incomes of the families to be dispossessed, except where the municipality can establish to the satisfaction of the Minister that decent, safe and sanitary housing accommodation is available to the families to be dispossessed at rentals that, in the opinion of the Minister and the municipality, are fair and reasonable, having regard to the family incomes of the families to be dispossessed; and

(d) a substantial part of the area at the time of acquisition was, or after redevelopment will be, used for residential purposes.

(4) An agreement entered into under subsection (1) shall provide

(a) an estimate of the costs of the acquisition and clearance of the area;

(b) that the municipality will acquire and clear the area;

(c) that the area will be developed in accordance or in harmony with an official community plan satisfactory to the Minister;
(d) for the manner, terms and conditions of sale, lease, retention, exchange or other disposition of the area or any part thereof;
(e) for the times at which the Minister's contributions will be paid to the municipality;
(f) for payment to the [Central Mortgage and Housing] Corporation of a share of the revenue from the project or the proceeds of sale or other dispostion thereof proportionate to the contributions made under subsection (2);
(g) for the examination, inspection and audit of the accounts of the municipality maintained in respect of the project; and
(h) for such other things as may be deemed necessary, including the security that may be taken by the Minister by way of joint title or otherwise to safeguard the Minister's rights of recovery out of the project.

(5) The Corporation shall on behalf of the Minister carry out any agreement entered into by the Minister under subsection (1).

(6) Where a project is undertaken under section 36 in a blighted or substandard area, for the purpose of calculating the Corporation's share of the capital cost of the project, the cost of acquisition of the land for the project shall be an amount that, in the opinion of the Minister, represents a fair and reasonable price for the land, not including any amount in respect of the cost of clearing the land.

[This part of s. 23 is reproduced as re-enacted by S.C., 1956, c. 9, s. 7, as Part III, Urban Redevelopment.]

36. (1) The Corporation may, pursuant to agreements made between the Government of Canada and the government of any province, undertake jointly with the government of the province or any agency thereof projects for

(a) the acquisition and development of land for housing purposes;
(b) the construction of housing projects for sale or for rent; and
(c) the acquisition, improvement and conversion for housing purposes of existing buildings situated in an area specified in an agreement between the province, a municipality in that province and the Corporation as an urban renewal area.

(2) An agreement referred to in subsection (1) shall provide that the capital cost of the project and the profits or losses thereon shall be shared seventy-five per cent by the Corporation and twenty-five per cent by the government of the province or any agency thereof and shall contain such other provisions as are considered necessary or advisable to give effect to the purposes and provisions of this section, and notwithstanding section 18 of the *Central Mortgage and Housing Corporation Act*, shall be executed on behalf of the Government of Canada by the Minister with the approval of the Governor in Council.

(6) The Governor in Council may make regulations with respect to the projects that may be undertaken by the Corporation under this section prescribing

(a) the type of land that may be acquired for housing purposes and the maximum purchase price that may be paid for such land;

(b) the type, maximum costs and rentals of housing units that may be constructed;
(c) the number of housing units for which commitments may be given;
(d) the rates of interest and amortization that may be charged against the capital costs of a project undertaken under this section;
(e) the conditions under which family housing units may be sold or leased; and
(f) any other matters deemed necessary or advisable to carry out the purposes or provisions of this section.

[Section 36 is reproduced as amended by S.C., 1960–61, c. 1, s. 6.]

NOTE ON THE "WRITE DOWN" POLICY. Redevelopment of our cities receives a good deal of publicity and it seems likely that in the near future money will be found, either with federal or provincial, or both federal and provincial, assistance, or by the cities themselves. Once money is available the city may acquire large tracts of land by expropriation if necessary. If the city government is inclined politically, it could redevelop the area itself, as proprietor or landlord. This is a common British reaction. In Canada, while it is possible that a city might enter into a ninety-nine year ground lease, it is more likely to sell the land to a private developer who puts forth an acceptable proposal. It may happen, however, that the developer will be reluctant to invest his money if the price of the land is, in his opinion, such as to make his investment unattractive. Land in downtown Toronto, for example, is likely to be expropriated at not less than $300,000 an acre. Is the city justified in selling the land to a developer (on condition that he develop it according to his approved proposal) for less than the expropriation price? Such a practice is sometimes described as a "write down" to the developer. It is, of course, a way in which the ratepayers of the city may pay for getting the land use they think is desirable. Should the city so subsidize private residential development of, say, high density apartments near the city centre? Should it contribute in this way to private development of commercial buildings? What are the objections? The advantages?

BIBLIOGRAPHY. Redevelopment and renewal are sometimes distinguished by the extent of demolition involved. If an area is razed and new buildings put up in place of old, one might say that that area has been developed again, whether for the same kinds of uses, or for different ones, or for the same ones to a greater density. For a critical study of the redevelopment of a residential area where the density increased slightly, from about 95 to 125 persons per acre, see Rose, *Regent Park* (1960). Regent Park is a small area in downtown Toronto. Its "redevelopment" greatly increased the amount of open space. Redevelopment usually takes place on a grander scale, or at least it is planned to do so. Two excellent redevelopment studies may be mentioned, Stephenson, *A Redevelopment Study of Halifax, Nova Scotia* (1957) and Stephenson and Muirhead, *A Redevelopment Study of Kingston, Ontario* (1960). General texts include Colean, *Renewing Our Cities* (1953), Marsh, *Rebuilding A Neighbourhood* (1950) and Woodbury (ed.), *The Future of Cities and Urban Redevelopment* (1953), and *Urban Redevelopment: Problems and Practices* (1953).

Urban renewal, if limited to systematic conservation of existing buildings by a programme of repair and selected demolition and rebuilding, involves rather different techniques. For a discussion of the problems involved in state promotion of house maintenance, see *A Better Place to Live* (1962), a study on minimum standards of occupancy and maintenance of dwellings jointly sponsored by Central Mortgage and Housing Corporation and the Ontario Department of Municipal Affairs.

(c) *A problem in relocation*

STEPHENSON, A REDEVELOPMENT STUDY OF HALIFAX, NOVA SCOTIA (1957)

There is a little frequented part of the City, overlooking Bedford Basin, which presents an unusual problem for any community to face. In what may be described as an encampment, or shack town, there live about seventy negro families. They are descendants of early settlers, and it is probable that Africville originated with a few shacks well over a century ago. Title to some of the land will be difficult to ascertain. Some of the hutted homes are on railway land, some on City land, some on private land. There will be families with squatters rights, and others with clear title to land which is now appreciating considerably in value.

The citizens of Africville live a life apart. On a sunny, summer day, the small children roam at will in a spacious area and swim in what amounts to their private lagoon. In winter, life is far from idyllic. In terms of the physical condition of buildings and sanitation, the story is deplorable. Shallow wells and cesspools, in close proximity, are scattered about the slopes between the shacks.

There are no accurate records of conditions in Africville. There are only two things to be said. The families will have to be rehoused in the near future. The land which they now occupy will be required for the further development of the City.

A solution which is satisfactory, socially as well as economically, will be difficult to achieve. Africville stands as an indicment of society and not of its inhabitants. They are old Canadians who have never had the opportunities enjoyed by their more fortunate fellows.

NOTE. The relocation of dispossessed persons is a serious problem in any programme of urban redevelopment. Very often a programme for financially assisted repair and maintenance will prove more sensible than redevelopment. Social groups will be far less disrupted and greater social harmony retained. The difficulties of relocation are increased if, as is usually the case, the inhabitants of the area are poor and, in rare cases in Canada, but commonly in the United States, coloured. The Halifax/Africville situation presents both of these added difficulties on a scale so small that almost every human problem can be studied in detail and perhaps properly understood.

Africville had, according to a staff report of the City's Development Department dated July 23, 1962, a population of about 370, made up of about eighty families. Some were regularly employed with the C.N.R., the Dockyards, and the City Corporation. Some worked at seasonal jobs and as domestic help. Some had no apparent employment. While the population has been fairly mobile, the community has been in existence for a century and some families have been there for forty years. The community has no "legal" boundaries, water or sewer services, the roads are unsurfaced, and if current health standards were applied, probably few houses are "fit for human habitation". If the land were to be expropriated, difficulties in proving even a prescriptive title might deprive many residents of compensation. The expense of proving title might be greater than "due compensation". The programme of redevelopment is said to be justified on the ground that the houses could not be "salvaged" if the residents are to be helped to obtain housing meeting a desired public health standard, and the land is intended ultimately for industrial or commercial use. The City also proposes a Shore Drive routed through the area.

The Development Department's report suggested three possible courses of action: "(1) The City can do nothing about the problem—this has been the basic approach for over 100 years. (2) The City can make full use of its statutory powers to remove blight. It can limit compensation and assistance to the absolute minimum required by Law. (3) The City can use its statutory powers to remove the blight, and, at the same time, temper justice with compassion in matters of compensation and assistance to families affected." The report recommended the third alternative as the most acceptable approach. It considered that "the offer of alternative housing must be an integral part of the programme for Africville". The report goes on to say:

"It seems to be the general opinion that most families in the Africville area would like to remain in that general location. Some of the conditions which influence the desire of families to remain in the area will disappear as more attention is focused on the area. The City must determine whether it is prepared to provide housing in the location or whether alternative housing in other locations would serve to satisfy any moral obligations to the families displaced. Despite the wishes of many of the residents, it would seem desirable on social grounds to offer alternative housing in other locations within the City. The City is a comprehensive urban community and it is not right that any particular segment of the community should continue to exist in isolation.

"The City is now studying a major subsidized rental public housing project in the Uniacke Square Area. This project is intended to create approximately 1100 family housing units. These housing units are designed to assist all those families from all of the City who are unable to provide themselves with decent accommodation. This project, when started, could easily provide the alternative housing for the 80 families now living in the Africville Area.

"Aside from the apparent social necessity to integrate the Africville community with the City as a whole, there appear to be sound financial reasons why this should be done. A separate housing project for the Africville community would necessitate the construction of a project which might well cost $800,000. This project might be built with assistance under Section 36 of the *National Housing Act* but such assistance might be somewhat difficult to obtain. Section 36 projects are not normally built for a particular segment of the community. In addition, family incomes from the Africville area would probably not be sufficient to produce the average shelter rental required from such projects. In other words, the Africville community might not by itself be able to create the average rental required for a Section 36 project whereas, if it were integrated with the community at large, incomes would not likely create a major problem in relation to the required average rental."

In a letter from the City Development Officer dated November 21, 1962, addressed to a representative of the Africville residents, the rental arrangements for the Uniacke Square subsidized programme were described as follows:

"1. Rentals are based upon the total income of the family. This total income is considered to be the income of the head of the house, a working wife, resident children over 25, and up to $75 per month of resident children 25 or under who are working. Shelter rentals approximate 20%–21% of the gross family income. The cost of heat, hot water, etc., if supplied, is additional.

"2. The subsidized rental projects are constructed in partnership with the Provincial and Federal Governments and are amortized over a period of up to 50 years. The average rental required to be obtained on each unit in the average project in order to meet the costs of operation and to write off the costs of investment is between $85-$90 per month. This does not include the cost of heat, hot water, etc., if these are provided.

"3. The Partnership of the Federal-Provincial-Municipal Government is prepared to subsidize each rental housing unit to an average of $25–$30 per unit per month. The apartments or housing units within the project must, therefore, be rented in such a manner as to attain an average rental return of about $55–$60 per month. This means that for every low income family admitted to the project, a family of higher income must be admitted.

"In order to establish a subsidized rental project for the residents of Africville in the area of Africville, it would be necessary to prove that the incomes of those who wished admission to the project were such as to provide an average rental return, excluding services, of $55–$60 a month. It would seem that such a rent level might be difficult to attain. On the other hand, the lower income people from the Africville area could go into one of the existing or contemplated subsidized rental projects without affecting the rent levels. If these families were unable to meet the average required rental, this average could still be attained by admitting higher income groups from other areas."

BIBLIOGRAPHY. The Institute of Public Affairs at Dalhousie University in Halifax has recently been conducting a programme of research concerning the Negroes of Nova Scotia. Two reports have been published by the Institue: Shand, *Adult Education Among the Negroes of Nova Scotia* (1961) and Henson (Director) *The Condition of the Negroes of Halifax City, Nova Scotia* (1962).

INDEX

This is a broad subject-matter index only, but the names of authors whose work is reproduced in part are also listed. It is not a word index.

www.ingramcontent.com/pod-product-compliance
Lightning Source LLC
LaVergne TN
LVHW010445080826
844660LV00027B/1220

* 9 7 8 1 4 8 7 5 7 8 8 6 2 *